Routledge History of World Philosophies
Volume 1

Routledge History of World Philosophies

Since the publication of the first volumes in 1993, the prestigious *Routledge History of Philosophy*, edited by G.H.R. Parkinson and S.G. Shanker, has established itself as the most comprehensive chronological survey of Western philosophy available. It discusses all the most important philosophical movements from the sixth century B.C. up to the present day. All the major figures in Western philosophy are covered in detail in these volumes. These philosophers are clearly situated within the cultural and scientific context of this time.

Within the main corpus of the *Routledge History of Philosophy*, the Jewish and Islamic traditions are discussed in the context of Western philosophy, with which they are inextricably linked. *The History of Islamic Philosophy* and *The History of Jewish Philosophy* are designed to supplement the core volumes by dealing specifically with these two philosophical traditions; they provide extensive analysis of all the most significant thinkers and concepts. In keeping with the rest of the series, each additional volume has a comprehensive index and bibliography, and includes chapters by some of the most influential scholars in the field. They will form the first volumes of a new series, Routledge History of World Philosophies.

Routledge History of World Philosophies
Volume I

History of Islamic Philosophy

Part I

EDITED BY

Seyyed Hossein Nasr
and Oliver Leaman

ROUTLEDGE

London and New York

First published 1996
by Routledge
11 New Fetter Lane, London EC4P 4EE

Simultaneously published in the USA and Canada
by Routledge
29 West 35th Street, New York, NY 10001

Reprinted 1997 and 1999

Typeset in Garamond by Florencetype Ltd,
Stoodleigh, Devon

Printed and bound in Great Britain by
T. J. International Ltd., Padstow, Cornwall

British Library Cataloguing in Publication Data
A catalogue record for this book is available from
the British Library

Library of Congress Cataloguing in Publication Data
A catalogue record for this book has been requested

ISBN 0–415–13159–6 (Part I)
0–415–13160–X (Part II)
0–415–05667–5 (Set)

Contents

Part II

VII Philosophy and its parts

X Interpretation of Islamic philosophy in the West

XI Bibliography

Notes on contributors

M. Abdel Haleem studied in Cairo and Cambridge, and teaches Arabic and Islamic studies at the School of Oriental and African Studies, University of London, and has written on Qur'ānic, Arabic and Islamic topics.

Shukri B. Abed studied at Tel Aviv and Harvard, and is currently at the Center for International Development and Conflict Management at the University of Maryland, College Park. He has written on Islamic and Arabic culture.

Ibrahim M. Abu-Rabi' studied at Bir Zeit, Cincinnati and Temple Universities, and is currently at the Hartford Seminary, USA. He has written on the modern Arab world.

Shabbir Akhtar studied in Cambridge and Alberta, and is currently at the International Islamic University, Malaysia. He is the author of several books on Islam, Christianity, current affairs and poetry.

Branko Aleksić studied in Belgrade and Paris, and is currently at the Université Européenne de la Recherche, Paris, where he works on the links between philosophy and poetry. He has written poetry and works on the relationship between poetry and philosophy.

Mehdi Aminrazavi was educated at Temple University and the University of Washington, and is currently at Mary Washington College, USA. His main area of specialization is non-Western philosophical and religious traditions.

Mehmet Aydin studied at Ankara and Edinburgh, and is now at Dokuz Eylul University, Turkey. He has written widely on philosophical topics.

Osman Bakar studied in London and Temple Universities, and is now at the University of Malaya, Kuala Lumpur, where he teaches philosophy of science. He has written on the history and philosophy of Islamic science.

Deborah L. Black is at the Pontifical Institute of Mediaeval Studies in the University of Toronto. She is the author of several works on medieval Latin and Arabic philosophy, mainly on psychology, epistemology and logic.

Alexander Broadie was educated at Edinburgh and Oxford, and is now at Glasgow University. His chief areas of research are medieval logic and philosophy, Maimonides and Duns Scotus.

Norman Calder was educated at Oxford and SOAS, and teaches Arabic and Islamic studies in the University of Manchester. He has published in the fields of Islamic law and early Islamic history.

Massimo Campanini studied and teaches Islamic philosophy at Milan University and has written widely on both medieval and modern Islamic thought.

William C. Chittick studied at Tehran University and teaches religious studies at the State University of New York, Stony Brook. He has written extensively on Sufism.

John Cooper studied at Oxford and in Iran, and now teaches Persian at Cambridge.

Hamid Dabashi studied at the University of Pennsylvania and teaches Persian Studies at Columbia University and has written on political and theological topics in Islamic thought.

Hans Daiber studied at Saarbrücken and Heidelberg, taught at the Free University, Amsterdam and is now at the University of Frankfurt am Main. He has published on Greek–Arabic thought, Islamic philosophy and theology, history of science in Islam, and the cataloguing of Arabic manuscripts.

Paul B. Fenton studied at the Sorbonne, and is now at the University of Strasbourg, where he teaches post-Biblical Jewish literature. He has published widely on Jewish culture in Muslim countries, and in particular on the interaction of Jewish and Islamic mysticism.

Daniel H. Frank studied at the Universities of California, Cambridge and Pittsburgh, and now teaches at the University of Kentucky. He has published in the areas of Greek philosophy and medieval Islamic and Jewish philosophy.

Gad Freudenthal studied at the Hebrew University and the Sorbonne, and is at the Centre National de la Recherche Scientifique, Paris. His main research interests are in the history of theories of matter before the seventeenth century and the history of science in the medieval Jewish communities.

Charles Genequand was educated at the Universities of Geneva and Oxford, and teaches at the University of Geneva. His main areas of research and publication are in the Aristotelian tradition in Islam, Islamic gnosticism, and the *Alexander Romance* in Arabic literature.

Hafiz A. Ghaffar Khan was educated at Peshawar and Temple Universities, and is now at the Atlanta Dar al-Ulum, Atlanta, USA. He writes on Islamic philosophy and theology.

Lenn E. Goodman teaches at Vanderbilt University, and was educated at Harvard and Oxford. He has written widely on philosophy, including books on Ibn Ṭufayl, Ibn Sīnā and Saadiah Gaon.

Syed Nomanul Haq was educated at Hull, London and Harvard Universities, and now teaches at Brown University. He has written on Islamic alchemy, particularly Jābir ibn Ḥayyān, as well as on Islamic intellectual history and religion.

Arthur Hyman was educated at Harvard University and teaches at Yeshiva University. His research and publications are in medieval Jewish and Islamic philosophy with a special interest in the thought of Maimonides and Averroes.

Shams Inati studied at the American University of Beirut and the State University of New York at Buffalo, and teaches at Villanova University, specializing in Islamic philosophy, and in particular in the thought of Ibn Sīnā.

Rahimuddin Kemal was educated at Glasgow University and is interested in Sufism, Persian poetry and Islamic studies. He has published on constitutional law in Islam.

Salim Kemal was educated at Cambridge, taught at Penn State University and is now at Dundee University. He has published on Islamic and Kantian aesthetics.

Mahmud Erol Kiliç teaches Islamic gnosis at Marmara University, Istanbul. He is mainly interested in Akbarian thought and the Ottoman Sufi tradition.

Felix Klein-Franke teaches at the Hebrew University in Jerusalem. His specialities are the history of the religion of Islam, the history of philosophy, science and medicine in Islam, and traditional Chinese medicine and history.

Alexander Knysh was educated in Leningrad and now teaches at Ann Arbor, Michigan. He has published widely in Islamic studies, and in particular on Ibn ʿArabī.

Barry Kogan was educated at UCLA, Hebrew Union College and University of Toronto, and teaches philosophy at Hebrew Union College–Jewish Institute of Religion, Cincinnati. He is the author of books on Averroes and articles on medieval Jewish and Islamic philosophy.

Abderrahmane Lakhsassi was educated at the American University of Beirut, the Sorbonne and Manchester University. He has published articles on Islamic thought and on the Berber oral tradition in Morocco.

Irene Lancaster studied at the Beruria Academy, Jerusalem, and teaches Hebrew and Judaism at Liverpool University. She writes on medieval Jews in Spain, Jewish philosophy and mysticism.

Oliver Leaman was educated at Oxford and Cambridge, and has taught at the University of Khartoum. He is now at Liverpool John Moores University, and his main interests are in medieval Islamic philosophy.

Pierre Lory teaches Islamic philosophy at the Ecole Pratique des Hautes Etudes, Sorbonne, with a particular specialization in esoteric thought. He has written on Islamic alchemy, Sufism, magic and the occult sciences in Islamic culture.

John Marenbon was educated at Trinity College, Cambridge, where he is now a Fellow. He has written extensively on medieval philosophy.

Zailan Moris was educated at Carleton University, Canada and the American University, Washington DC, and now teaches in the Department of Philosophy in University Sains Malaysia. Her main interests are Islamic philosophy, comparative religion and Sufism.

Abbas Muhajirani was educated in Hamadan, Qom and Tehran, and has written on Islamic theology and literature.

Azim Nanji was educated in Kenya, at Makerere University, Uganda, and McGill University, Canada. He teaches at the University of Florida, and has written on Islam, Ismā'ilism, religion and culture.

Seyyed Hossein Nasr was educated in Tehran, at Massachusetts Institute of Technology and at Harvard University. He has taught at a number of universities in the USA and the Middle East, and is now at the George Washington University. He has written extensively on Islam and philosophy.

Ian Richard Netton studied at SOAS and Exeter, taught at the University of Exeter and is now at Leeds University. He has written on al-Fārābī, the Ikhwān al-Ṣafā' and on Islamic philosophy in general, as well as on other issues in Islamic civilization.

Sari Nuseibeh was educated at Oxford and Harvard, and has taught at Bir

Zeit, the Hebrew University and al-Najah University. He has written on contemporary political issues in the Middle East and on Islamic philosophy.

Elsayed Omran was educated at Ain Shams, Cardiff, Newcastle and Georgetown Universities. His main interests are in Arab and Islamic culture and civilization, and Arabic linguistics.

James Pavlin is currently at New York University and specializes in Islamic theology.

F. E. Peters is at New York University and has taught both Greek and Islamic philosophy. He has written on the influence of Aristotle on Islamic philosophy, and on the Platonic and Hellenic traditions in Islam.

Everett K. Rowson studied at Princeton and Yale, is at the University of Pennsylvania, and has written on Islamic philosophy and Arabic literature, and especially on al-ʿĀmirī.

Yegane Shayegan studied at Geneva and Harvard Universities, and is now researching the Aristotelian commentators at University College London.

Abu'l-Wafa al-Taftazani was educated at the Sorbonne and Cairo. He taught Islamic philosophy at Cairo University, and published generally in the area, and on Sufism. He died in 1994.

M. Suheyl Umar was educated at Lahore and is now at the Iqbal Academy, Pakistan. He specializes in Sufism as well as in the thought of Iqbal and in the intellectual history of the Indian subcontinent from Shah Walīullāh to Iqbal. He also teaches at ISTAC, Kuala Lumpur, Malaysia.

Dominique Urvoy was educated in Bordeaux and Damascus, and is now at the University of Toulouse. He has written on Islamic thought in Spain, and on Lull.

Catherine Wilson studied at Yale, Oxford and Princeton, teaches at the University of Alberta and has written on Leibniz and on early modern science, as well as on philosophy in general.

Hossein Ziai studied at Yale and Harvard, and is now at the University of California, Los Angeles. He has published on Illuminationist philosophy and post-Avicennan philosophy.

Preface

There are a variety of possible approaches to the question of what a history of Islamic philosophy should be. Until now, the most common approach has been to treat leading individual thinkers and at best put them within the context of their own times. There are advantages to this approach in that it makes leading intellectual figures well known and helps relate Islamic philosophy to other aspects of the culture of the period in question. This approach tends often, however, to concentrate more on individual thinkers than on philosophical ideas, and there is the danger of treating Islamic philosophy as a constituent of the history of ideas rather than as part of the history of philosophy.

As editors of these volumes we very much view Islamic philosophy as a living philosophical tradition while, of course, accepting its relation to other intellectual developments of Islamic civilization. Islamic philosophy in fact deals with conceptual issues which are not tied to a particular author or period, and which have universal import. We have, therefore, sought to deal as much with philosophical ideas as individual thinkers, and to deal with the subject as a whole but not necessarily cover everyone who might be described as an Islamic philosopher. There are other general reference books with entries for most Islamic intellectual figures and we do not wish to compete with them. We have had to select from among the vast body of thought which constitutes Islamic philosophy particular thinkers, ideas and intellectual movements which we regard as the most significant.

The sections of the *History* are written by different authors who have been selected to represent the various approaches to the subject, and we should not be taken to share their views. We hope that this work reflects the different tendencies and methods prevalent in the field of the study of Islamic philosophy today. We have not sought to impose uniformity on the different ways in which the authors of these volumes have treated their topics. We want to represent the diversity existing within the contemporary study of Islamic philosophy, with all the controversy and disagreement that such diversity entails. Our task has been to safeguard the scholarly content of these volumes. It is for the reader to decide what attitude to Islamic philosophy is most successful and will be most fruitful in the future.

There are a number of people whom we should like to thank for their help in bringing this project to completion. We have first of all to thank the contributors for their efforts and for having found time to write their chapters. Our editor at Routledge, Richard Stoneman, has been a steadfast supporter of the project, and Heather McCallum and Vicky Peters have been hugely efficient and helpful voices at the end of the telephone when things seemed to be going wrong. Harry Gilonis created the index, and Joanne Snooks saw the whole project through the printing stage. Finally, the editors would like to thank each other for what we hope the reader will find to be a fruitful collaboration.

OL
SHN
June 1995

Transliteration and style

Transliteration has normally been carried out in accordance with the schedule set out here. This has not always been done, though, especially for terms very frequently used, and it seemed more natural to allow authors slight differences in transliteration, particularly in the sections on Jewish philosophy. The original attempt to apply the transliteration schedule strictly proved unsatisfactory, since it resulted in a text which often looked rather strange. Authors have followed their own preferences in some respects for spelling and capitalization of key terms. Some additional bibliographical material has been supplied by the editors.

ARABIC CHARACTERS

ء	'	غ	gh
ب	b	ف	f
ت	t	ق	q
ث	th	ك	k
ج	j	ل	l
ح	ḥ	م	m
خ	kh	ن	n
د	d	ه	h
ذ	dh	و	w
ر	r	ي	y
ز	z	ة	ah; at (construct state)
س	s	ال	(article) al- and 'l- (even before the anteropalatals)
ش	sh		
ص	ṣ		
ض	ḍ		long vowels
ط	ṭ	اى	ā
ظ	ẓ	و	ū
ع	'	ي	ī

short vowels

......َ	a
......ُ	u
......ِ	i

diphthongs

و......َ	aw
ي......َ	ai (ay)
ـيّـ	īy (final form ī)
ـوّ	uww (final form ū)

Persian letters added to the Arabic alphabet

پ	p
چ	ch
ژ	zh
گ	g

Introduction

Oliver Leaman

The obvious question which arises for anyone looking at these volumes is why the thinkers who are discussed here are classified under the description of Islamic philosophy. Some of these thinkers are not Muslims, and some of them are not philosophers in a straightforward sense. What is Islamic philosophy? This has been a controversial question for a long time, and it is indeed difficult to find a label which is entirely satisfactory for such thinkers and systems of thought. To label such philosophy as Arabic does indeed make appropriate reference to the language in which the Qur'ān was originally transmitted, but it is hardly appropriate as a description of the philosophy we have in mind here. Many of our thinkers did not write in Arabic, and many of them were not Arabs. It is true that an important strand in Islamic philosophy developed in the Arabic language, and in Arabic translations of Greek texts, but this is only a strand, however important it may have been. A vast proportion of Islamic philosophy was written in languages other than Arabic, especially Persian, and by non-Arabs, and that continues to be the case today. Whatever is meant by Arabic philosophy cannot hope to be comprehensive enough to encompass the whole of Islamic philosophy.

Islamic philosophy might be thought to be the sort of philosophy produced by Muslims, but this would be too narrow also. A good deal of philosophy which we have included was produced by non-Muslims, and some of it has no direct religious relevance anyway as the term religion is understood in the West today, so that the religious provenance we might seek to apply to it is misleading. Many Christian and Jewish philosophers worked within the style and tradition of Islamic philosophy, and it would be invidious to exclude them merely on account of their religious beliefs. Also, we do include some philosophical work here which has no direct reference to any religious topic at all but which is just philosophy, a formal enquiry into the structure of the most general concepts available. Work on logic and grammar, for example, has this character. It is possible to derive some religious implications from such work, of course, if one tries very hard, but not usually very fruitfully. So the Islamic credentials of some of this kind of philosophical work seem to be rather slim, and it might appear problematic to include such work in a book on Islamic philosophy.

There are discussions in these volumes which clearly are Islamic, but which are certainly not clearly philosophy. For example, we thought it was important to have an account of different kinds of theology, since theology played such a large part in the development of Islamic philosophy, often as something which that philosophy could react against. It is important to understand the context within which ideas are produced, not just as an essay in the history of ideas but in order to understand those ideas more clearly. Despite the best efforts of some of the philosophers we shall consider, it is not always easy to distinguish philosophy from theology, or even from law or grammar, the traditional Islamic sciences. Many of the questions which arise within these contexts have direct philosophical relevance, and the shape of that philosophy was powerfully affected by the disciplines which produced the issues. It is important to realize that we have here a dynamic relationship between the Islamic sciences and philosophy, with a constant interplay of arguments and suggestions, so that it is important to include a discussion of those sciences in such a way that one can see how they have both affected and been affected by philosophy.

It would be tempting to argue that what makes Islamic philosophy an appropriate general concept is that it encompasses a feature of that philosophy which is shared by all its instances. For example, if there is an agenda which is implicit or explicit in all such philosophy, then it would be easy to argue that it should all go under the same general name. Many commentators have argued that indeed there is such an agenda. A very influential school of interpretation originating with Leo Strauss is convinced that the basis of all work in Islamic philosophy is the opposition between religion and reason, between faith and philosophy, and between Islam and Greek thought. Sometimes this is phrased as representing the clash between Jerusalem and Athens. Followers of this approach claim that it is possible to interpret any aspect of Islamic philosophy in line with this central problem, since this problem runs through all such writing. If it is not obvious that it does, then there are ways to find appropriate clues beneath the surface of the text which will show that the central problem lurks there somewhere, and in fact represents the deep structure of the argument of the text. A different but not unrelated view has it that the whole of Islamic philosophy represents an attempt to accommodate Islam with rationality, so that the central issue is to carry out such a reconciliation. This was the leading motive of the philosophers themselves, and when we assess their work we have to bear this in mind if we are to understand what the texts they produced actually mean. Unless we grasp the central idea which is the basis to the philosophical writings, we are in danger of misunderstanding those writings, and the assumption is made that there is just such a common theme to those writings. After all, calling philosophy "Islamic" implies, or might seem to imply, that the religious character of what is discussed is crucial, and, since it is linked with philosophy, the apparent conflict between two different approaches to the same issue might seem to be highlighted.

We should resist this temptation. Although there are many discussions in Islamic philosophy of religion and reason, it is entirely mistaken to see this dichotomy as lying at the heart of that philosophy. It might be that that dichotomy lies at the heart of medieval Jewish and Christian philosophy, or at least of much of it, but there is no reason to import such a dichotomy as a leading principle in Islamic philosophy. The attempt to reduce a vast variety of philosophical endeavour to just one such slogan is simplistic and should be avoided. It runs the danger of trying to fit the whole of Islamic philosophy into a conceptual straitjacket which will inevitably restrict its scope and interest. The intention has been to present in these volumes as much of the variety of Islamic philosophy as possible, and to represent it as a continuing and living tradition of philosophical work, not a dead and completed doctrine from the Middle Ages. Even the work produced in the Middle Ages is too varied in form and content to be subsumed under a simple concept, and forms very much of a dialogue which continues to have resonance today.

Is there, then, no philosophical agenda which Islamic philosophy has and which uniquely characterizes it? There is such an agenda, but it is more various than is commonly realized. Quite obviously, a society which is Islamic will produce thinkers who will frame their philosophical questions in terms of that society. Sometimes these are just Islamic versions of entirely universal philosophical issues. For example, the question of how it is possible to know God will take a particular form within an Islamic context, given the emphasis on the unity of God. Knowing God will involve knowing a being from which all anthropomorphic description is removed. Yet this is not a uniquely Islamic issue, since many religious philosophies will have an account of how it is possible to know a God who cannot be described in terms which apply to His creation. What is philosophical about the discussion is its use of very abstract concepts to make sense of the idea of such knowledge. What is Islamic about the discussion is its conception of God and His Qualities. This need not be a uniquely Islamic idea, but it will be framed within the language of Islam and will reflect on the way in which that conception of divinity has been refined and developed within Islam. It is not a huge step from discussing the relationship between God and His properties, which is after all an important aspect of what it is to know God, to wondering what the relationship is between a subject and its properties in general. This latter enquiry has no direct reference to the religious context out of which it originally arose, and yet it is still part of a way of doing philosophy which starts with a religious problem.

What justification is there in calling such a logical problem a part of Islamic philosophy? The problem itself is clearly not only an Islamic problem, nor is it a problem with any direct relevance to religion as such, albeit the way in which it is answered will have an impact upon the way in which one answers questions about God and His properties. It certainly would be mistaken to think that the philosophers whom we are considering would have in the forefront of their minds the religious implications of their work on logic while they were engaged upon such work. They need not have been thinking about those implications, and it would not be far-fetched to suggest that they may not ever have considered those implications. It certainly would be dangerous, then, to refer to an Islamic logic, but not to the inclusion of logic within Islamic philosophy. Such an inclusion makes appropriate reference to the context within which a piece of intellectual work was produced, within the cultural context of Islamic society. We can usefully employ a concept from the Islamic sciences here, that of a chain of transmission. The relevant question is how far the particular philosophical idea or theory can be connected with predominantly Islamic ideas along a chain of transmission or influence. This leaves us with a series of issues and topics which range very widely across traditional philosophical concerns, and that is how it should be. Islamic philosophy is first of all philosophy, and its content is going to resemble the content of philosophy in general. Yet there will remain a connection with ideas or thinkers who worked within the context of Islamic culture at some stage.

Of course, there is a limit to how far one can trace the chain of transmission, and some writers are wildly over-ambitious in claiming to discover a link between aspects of Islamic philosophy and subsequent developments in Western philosophy. On the other hand, there are interesting links, and these have been to a degree described here, but not as part of the commonplace attitude that such a link would establish the significance of Islamic philosophy. The latter has a significance which is entirely *sui generis*, as readers of these volumes will surely realize, but what makes it significant is the excellence of the philosophy itself, and the wealth of ideas which were produced. It is patronizing to suggest that one has to stress the impact of Islamic philosophy on the West, and beyond, for it to be taken seriously. None the less, that impact has to be acknowledged and assessed. The emphasis here is not on transmission either into or out of Islamic philosophy but is rather on the ideas of that philosophy itself, since it is the ideas which ultimately demand our attention and deserve our respect. It is not always easy for Islamic philosophers to pursue those ideas and hold on to the version of Islam with which they started, and the tension which often exists as a result is a very fruitful feature of the intellectual creativity which results.

So when we talk about Islamic philosophy we have in mind a very general concept of an Islamic culture out of which that philosophy grew, and it is consequently important to understand aspects of that culture if the philosophy is to be properly understood. This does not mean that we should fall into the danger of treating Islamic philosophy as though it were only a part of the history of ideas. The history of ideas is far too limiting to encompass the scope of Islamic philosophy. Yet there has often been an over-concentration on the pursuit of Islamic philosophy as an historical task, which has led to what are really philosophical problems about validity being misrepresented as historical problems about attribution and context. While these historical questions are no doubt interesting and difficult to answer, so that it is an intriguing intellectual task to resolve them, they are of an entirely different order from philosophical questions. The time has come to put Islamic philosophy within its appropriate context, that of philosophy, so that it can be recognized as a dynamic and living tradition which speaks to philosophers today just as it did in the past.

Although we have stressed here the role of Islamic philosophy as a vibrant and important philosophical activity, it cannot be doubted that much of the discussion of this type of philosophy is carried out in terms of exploring its roots in other areas. That is, commentators will examine how the non-philosophical aspects of Islam affect the development of the philosophy which appeared in the Islamic world, and also how different cultural factors influenced Islamic philosophy. In particular, a whole range of that sort of philosophy was quite clearly influenced by Greek thought, and the peripatetic tradition in Islamic philosophy is obviously based upon an originally non-Islamic source. It is important to emphasize that this is but one type of Islamic philosophy, and a type which has been criticized by some Islamic philosophers for its very distance from religion. They have argued on occasion that what we have here is the mere replication of Greek ideas in Arabic dress, without any real attempt at showing how those ideas link up with specifically Islamic issues. It will be fairly clear to any reader of the sections in this book which look at this sort of philosophy that such a criticism is misplaced. There was a genuine attempt at seeing how the conceptual machinery of Greek thought could be applied to Islamic issues, and in this contact between two cultural movements a great deal of interesting and perceptive work resulted.

Yet we should be very careful in what we say about such cultural contact. It is all too easy to link discussions in Islamic philosophy with earlier Greek discussions, and to think as a result that what is going on is quite different from what is really going on. Let us take as an example the sorts of discussions which often went on in Islamic philosophy concerning political thought. We are immediately obliged to confront a difficulty here, a difficulty concerning translation. There was a tendency for Greek terms like *nomos* (law) to be translated not as *nāmūs*, the new Arabic term coined to convey the same meaning as the Greek term, but as *Sharī'ah*, the term for law in Arabic. Now, the latter is a term with religious connotations, which is absent from the Greek notion of law. What the philosophers like al-Fārābī meant by this is that the Arabic term can be used to illustrate the sort of point which the Greek thinkers wished to make, and he tried to show this in terms of the language which would strike a resonance with his Muslim compatriots. After all, he did not only wish to convey the nature of the argument to the Islamic community, he wished also to naturalize the argument, to show that this is an argument which is both relevant and interesting to his contemporaries.

This approach is likely to lead to a difficulty in interpretation, though. Many readers will observe al-Fārābī using religious terminology to express a point from Greek philosophy, and they will argue that what he is doing is arguing that the latter form of thought is compatible with Islam. That is, they will see the task of reconciling reason with religion as the leading theme of Islamic philosophy, whereas all that an Islamic philosopher may be doing is representing an originally Greek argument in a manner which would make sense to his audience, in this case using Islamic language. Of course, it might be said that it would be far more accurate to construct a new term, a term which wears its Greek heart on its sleeve, as it were, to convey the original argument. To do otherwise is to run the risk of misleading one's audience, since it appears to be a matter of representing what was an originally secular argument as in fact a religious argument. Perhaps al-Fārābī was deliberately trying to pass off Greek thought as being far more religious, or at least Islamic, than it really was. Perhaps he was using Islamic language to describe Greek arguments in order to take a short cut along the path of reconciling Islam with Greek philosophy. After all, once the key terms of Plato's *Republic* have been translated into Islamic language, it seems to be an easy matter to argue that Plato's argument is perfectly compatible with Islam itself.

This is not an inevitable conclusion. The *falāsifah* tended to use the language which came most naturally to them, and this obviously meant that they would be using the sort of language which was most familiar with their peers. In any case, they wanted to show that the kinds of issues which arose within the Greek world had interesting and important implications for contemporary problems in the Islamic world, and the best way to present this view is by using the ordinary language of the community for which they were writing. Neologisms were then kept to a minimum. Those thinkers who were directly concerned with the nature of religion and religious experience did not wish to distinguish precisely between the Greek use of philosophical terminology and its Islamic version, since they went on to try to show how relevant the conceptual distinctions in question are to the living experience of faith. It has to be acknowledged also that the philosophers were interested in campaigning for not only the acceptability, but also the inevitability of what they were doing. They wanted to show that the Islamic sciences which were part of the traditional canon of doing things and sorting out problems needed to be supplemented by the ancient sciences, and especially by philosophy, and this could only be done if the same sort of language is used in both cases.

If all that the philosophers were doing was to use what were originally Greek ideas and applying them to Islamic problems, one might think that there is not much originality or creativity at issue here. All that was going on would have been highly derivative, and at the most we would be able to observe an interesting arrangement of material which actually was developed elsewhere. In fact, much of the work which goes on in Islamic philosophy is of this nature, it looks for the roots of the discussion elsewhere and implies that the interest of the discussion within the Islamic world is secondary to its original manifestation in the Greek original context. Islamic philosophy then gets relegated to the history of ideas, and is regarded as an interesting aspect of cultural contact, as compared with the systems of philosophy which created the conceptual materials of the debate in the first place. To this situation is added the observation that the Islamic philosophers did not have access to the Greek thinkers in their original language or even in many cases in very accurate translations, and they misidentified some of the authors anyway. Their interpretation of Greek philosophy was highly mediated by Hellenistic and Neoplatonic traditions, and failed to represent clearly what the original debate was.

What this version of Islamic philosophy does not capture adequately is the fact that cultural contact is a far more complicated notion than many understand. It is far too simple to suggest that a term moves from the context of Greek culture to a new Islamic home and then takes up the same form of existence in its new surroundings. The whole semantic structure of the Greek term has not moved into the Islamic world; on the contrary, the new term will incorporate aspects of the original term but will also be very different. We have seen how this applies to terms like *nomos* and *Sharīʿah*, but they are far from unique in this respect. That is, it is possible to use the new term to make many of the same points made by the old term, yet this should not conceal from us that the new term is different from the old term. The system of concepts and practices in which the old term was embedded are now absent, or at least different, and the way in which the new term will have to be related to such a system is distinct.

This is very relevant to the accusation that Islamic philosophy is derivative and so not of the first calibre in so far as philosophical thought goes. It is not the case that the Islamic philosophers took Greek (and indeed other) concepts and then used them in their attempts to make sense of the Islamic world. Concepts are not like clothes which one can just pick up and put on. But they are like clothes to the extent that, if they have to go on a different frame, then they will only fit if they are adapted to the new body. It is very difficult to adapt a concept which was appropriate within a particular context to a very different state of affairs, and it is on this that the significance of much Islamic philosophy rests. It was capable of taking some of the key philosophical concepts from earlier cultures and using them to answer problems which arose within their own culture, and of adapting the concepts so that they could carry out such a task. The combination of abstract philosophical thought on the one hand with problems which arose within Islam on the other is a potent and unstable mixture responsible for the richness and diversity of Islamic philosophy itself.

It might be accepted that Islamic philosophy is interesting, and yet its dependence on a system of thought coming originally from without the Islamic world has led to the development of a tendency to study it from an historical rather than a philosophical perspective. After all, if one is interested primarily in the philosophical issues, one might be tempted to study them within the context of their original Greek expression rather than via the accretions which occurred during their passage through the Islamic world. But the Islamic philosophers should not be seen as being primarily concerned with *ersatz* philosophical notions derived originally from non-Islamic cultures. These thinkers certainly did use the notions which came to them through the rich intellectual background which was available to them, and they transformed them in the ways in which they used them. This was a matter not just of choice but really of necessity. The philosophical issues which arose in the Greek world could not always be simply replicated in the Islamic world but have to be adapted to make sense, since the terms themselves when moved from one context to another have a different range of meanings.

This is not to suggest that some of the traditional philosophical issues and controversies which arise within every developed culture did not arise within the Islamic world in much the same way as everywhere else. Some problems, especially the most abstract metaphysical ones, appear to be common to a whole range of cultures. It is just that the nature of a particular culture puts the emphasis upon a different aspect of the problem depending upon the nature of that culture. For example, in discussions of the creation of the world it is important to note that the Islamic world wanted to mark the fact that according to the Qur'ān the world had a beginning and will have an end. This is not to say that Islamic philosophers could therefore abandon Aristotelian accounts of the creation of the world which seem to point to its being eternal because it went against the scriptural truth. Many Islamic philosophers produced modifications of the Aristotelian theory which made it compatible, or apparently compatible, with their understanding of the Qur'ān, while others criticized the certainty which philosophers applied to Aristotle's theory. They could not just say that Aristotle was wrong because he seemed to go against scripture – this would be very poor philosophy or indeed theology indeed. They could not just say that Aristotle was right and the Qur'ān was wrong, since this would also be to refuse to examine the interesting conceptual links which exist between two apparently distinct and contrary descriptions of creation. It is in the tension between different accounts of the same phenomenon that philosophy really gets to work, presenting a solution which satisfies the need for a rational explanation of the apparent aporia or difficulty. Some of these philosophical expositions are more interesting and well-constructed than others, of course, but the important point to make is that they are all philosophical arguments, and are to be assessed from the perspective of philosophy.

How creative were the Islamic philosophers? I think it will be clear to anyone who reads many of the chapters in these volumes that many of them were very creative. They certainly did not have a *tabula rasa* on which to write, but, given the concepts and ideas which they had available to them, they used these to their fullest extent. They did not just accept the concepts which were handed down to them, but adapted them and constructed new concepts to make sense of the nature of the problem as they saw it. There is a tendency for us to identify creativity with an entirely new way of tackling an issue, and we live in a period of great artistic creativity in this respect. Artists use a vast variety of often novel forms of expression, some so novel that we are unsure how to assess them. Yet there is good reason to call creative those works by earlier artists which were constructed within the constraints of a particular system of representation, and in some ways it is easier to say that something is creative if we can judge it within the context of an artistic tradition. We can then see precisely how the new contribution to the aesthetic area borrows from what has preceded it and extends the previous understanding of what was possible to do something new. A similar point can be made about Islamic philosophy. We can grasp the context within which it worked, and we can often see how influenced it was by the competing pressures of a variety of cultural traditions, but it does not follow that it cannot be creative because it is dependent upon previously existing intellectual traditions. On the contrary, we can see how on the basis of those traditions it represents a new direction of thought, or, at the very least, is capable of stepping out in a new direction. Much Islamic philosophy, like much philosophy of any kind, is just the accretion of new technical representations of existing issues, but some of it is capable of establishing entirely new ways of going on which in turn establish new traditions of thinking about problems and resolving difficult conceptual issues.

Islamic philosophy is primarily philosophy, and the appropriate techniques to use in order to understand it are going to be philosophical. There is certainly no one philosophical approach present in Islamic philosophy, but a large variety of different techniques which depend upon the particular point of view of the thinkers themselves. The very diversity of approach might lead one to query yet again the notion of philosophy being "Islamic" at all, since we might expect that label to represent a common view or a consensus as to how to do philosophy. If that expectation was justified, then the philosophy which resulted would be of far less interest, since it would be comparatively narrow and represent something of a party line on how to operate. The breadth of Islamic philosophy represents the diversity of cultures in which Islam has featured, and in these volumes we have attempted to celebrate both.

Introduction

Seyyed Hossein Nasr

Although of course a single reality in itself, Islamic philosophy nevertheless has had and continues to have several historical "embodiments" which are also reflected in how the subject is studied in both East and West. There is first of all the living and continuous tradition of Islamic philosophy in Persia and certain adjacent areas from Iraq to India. When one sits at the feet of a master of this discipline in Isfahan, Tehran or Qom one experiences a living tradition and an organic bond to figures such as Ibn Sīnā (the Latin Avicenna) and al-Fārābī who lived, visited or taught in those very cities or in cities nearby over a millennium ago. In this "embodiment" Islamic philosophy has had a continuous history going back to the earliest Islamic centuries and based not only on written texts but also on an oral tradition transmitted from master to disciple over numerous generations. Moreover, in this ambience Islamic philosophy, called *falsafah* and later *ḥikmah*, is an *Islamic* intellectual discipline in contention, debate, accord or opposition with other intellectual disciplines but in any case it was and remains a part and parcel of Islamic intellectual life despite the opposition of many jurists. One need only look at the number of students studying Islamic philosophy today in Qom in Iran, that is, in the premier centre of religious studies in that land, to realize how true is this assertion and how significant is Islamic philosophy even in comparison with jurisprudence, not to speak of *kalām* or theology which it overshadows in those intellectual circles in many ways.

Then there is the tradition of Islamic philosophy in the Arab part of the Islamic world. Although often called "Arabic philosophy" in the West because of the predominant but not exclusive use of Arabic as its language of discourse, strangely enough in the Arab world, with the exception of Iraq and to some extent Yemen, this philosophy was to have a shorter life as an independent intellectual perspective than in Persia, being consumed in lands west of Iraq after the seventh/thirteenth century by *kalām* on the one hand and doctorial Sufism (*al-ma'rifah* or *al-'irfān*) on the other. In this world *falsafah* as a separate discipline came to be marginalized in the centres of Islamic learning, replaced by *kalām* and *uṣūl al-fiqh* and often considered as a foreign intrusion. In fact it was not until the last century that Islamic philosophy was revived in Egypt by Jamāl al-Dīn al-Afghānī (Astrābādī) who had been a student of the school of Mullā Ṣadrā in Persia before migrating to Cairo. But in any case, despite the appearance of a number of well-known scholars of Islamic philosophy in Egypt, Syria and Lebanon since Jamāl al-Dīn's days, the relation between *falsafah* and the Islamic sciences in most parts of the Arab world has been different from what one finds in such places as Iran and certain centres of Islamic learning in the Indo-Pakistani subcontinent. Nor has there been the continuous oral tradition in the domain of philosophy in the Arab world that one finds in Iran and adjacent areas. To some extent this situation also holds true for Turkey although the tradition of Islamic philosophy survived in a continuous manner there longer than it did in Egypt, the Arab Near East and North Africa.

There is also an Islamic philosophy seen by the West as part of its own intellectual tradition and usually referred to as Arabic philosophy. This view saw Islamic philosophy as having stopped abruptly with Ibn Rushd (the Latin Averroes), when the influence of Islamic philosophy upon the West diminished and gradually died out. For over seven centuries in such places as Paris, Louvain, Padua and Bologna this version of Islamic philosophy has been taught as part and parcel of Western intellectual history. Moreover, this Eurocentric view of Islamic philosophy has been taken in the West for Islamic philosophy itself, a view that has been confirmed during this century by much of the scholarship from the Arab world, some of whose well-known figures have found in the European identification of Islamic philosophy with Arabic philosophy a solid theoretical support for the suppositions of Arab nationalism. In any case this understanding of Islamic philosophy, held mostly in Catholic circles and by those interested in medieval European philosophy and theology, has produced a number of great scholars who, however, until quite recently have preferred to remain impervious to the eight centuries of Islamic philosophy after Averroes and the fact that Islamic philosophy is not only "medieval" but also contemporary if not modern.

Parallel with this view is that of Jewish philosophy which developed in a remarkably similar fashion to Islamic philosophy and which also used to a large extent the same language and vocabulary as Islamic philosophical Arabic at least until the destruction of Islamic rule in Spain after which Western Jewish philosophy parted ways from Islamic modes of thought. But in any case there is such a thing as the Jewish understanding of Islamic philosophy and a close rapport between the two from at least the third/ninth to the seventh/thirteenth centuries, a link which is reflected not only in the development of schools of Jewish thought closely parallel to those of Islam but also in the contribution of a number of Jewish scholars in the late thirteen/nineteenth and early fourteenth/twentieth centuries to the early modern studies of Islamic philosophy in Europe and America.

Also, from the middle of the thirteenth/nineteenth century onwards, with the rise of the discipline of the "history of philosophy" in Germany and then other European countries, combined with the development of Oriental studies, the attention of a number of Western scholars turned to Islamic philosophy, which they sought to study "scientifically". This Orientalistic view of Islamic philosophy, while contributing much to the editions of texts and historical data, was primarily philological and historical rather than philosophical, the appearance of a figure such as Henry Corbin being quite exceptional. At best this view has dealt with Islamic philosophy in the context of cultural history or the history of ideas but hardly ever as philosophy. The fact that in the West the study of Islamic philosophy continues to be largely confined to departments of Oriental, Middle Eastern or Islamic studies, and is rarely treated in philosophy departments, is not only due to the narrow confines of much of modern philosophy, which has reduced philosophy to logic and linguistics. It is also due to a large extent to the way in which Islamic philosophy has been studied and presented by Orientalists for over a century.

To make matters even more complicated it is necessary to point also to the understanding of Islamic philosophy by three generations of Muslim scholars themselves, scholars who, while Muslim, have learned their Islamic philosophy from Western sources and still look upon their own intellectual identity through the eyes of others. The latter group have produced a number of works in Arabic, Turkish, Urdu and English – and much less so in Persian – which seem to deal with Islamic philosophy from the Islamic point of view but in reality reflect works of Western scholars which they then try to accommodate to their own situation. One needs only to look at the number of universities in Pakistan and India, the land of such figures as Shah Walīullāh of Delhi, where the *History* of De Boer is still taught, a work according to which Islamic philosophy came to an end six hundred years before Shah Walīullāh.

All these "embodiments" of the Islamic philosophical tradition have received treatments in various histories of Islamic philosophy which have appeared in both Islamic and Western languages during the past few decades although most available works still reflect the Western views of Islamic philosophy, whether it be the older school going back to the medieval period or modern Orientalism which shares one major feature with the earlier school in that it also considers Islamic philosophy to have come to an end with Ibn Rushd or soon thereafter.

It was precisely to avoid such a limitation of historical perspective, and also the refusal by many to take Islamic philosophy seriously as philosophy, that when invited by Routledge to edit these volumes on Islamic philosophy with Oliver Leaman, I accepted the task despite full knowledge of the impossibility of doing full justice to the subject with our present knowledge of the various aspects and periods of Islamic philosophy. Having had long training in the study of Islamic philosophy in Persia with traditional masters as well as in the West and also being acquainted with the Arab world, I thought that my co-operation with Oliver Leaman would make possible the presentation of Islamic philosophy not only in its Western but also in some of its other "embodiments", especially the one identified with this tradition as it has been viewed from within.

Our choice of topics and authors was dictated precisely with these points in mind. In the work that follows we have sought to study Islamic philosophy both morphologically and historically, in relation to the Islamic revelation and other intellectual disciplines within Islamic civilization and in itself, as an independent philosophical tradition and in its relation to earlier schools of thought, especially the Greek, as well as its influence upon later Western thought. We have also drawn our authors from both the diverse regions of the Islamic world and the West, from Muslims trained in traditional schools and those who have studied in modern universities, from Western scholars well versed in Jewish and Christian thought and those whose interest in philosophy is more secular. There is no unanimity of opinion among the authors of these volumes but they do represent as a whole the various perspectives, methods and approaches to the study of Islamic philosophy prevalent today in the Islamic world and the West taken together.

There are among the authors those whose interests are primarily in cultural history, history of ideas or philology. But we have sought to combine such interests with the philosophical in such a way as to emphasize that Islamic philosophy is philosophy, a point with which Oliver Leaman and I are in full agreement whatever differences we may entertain in the understanding of various aspects of the subject. There are of course among the authors also differences of a philosophical nature. There are those who follow Thomism or traditional schools of Jewish philosophy and others who espouse the views of phenomenology or historical or logical positivism. And then there are those who take Islamic philosophy seriously and identify with it. We have not sought to exclude various philosophical suppositions as long as the subject has been treated in a scholarly fashion. The net result reflects naturally the tension which actually exists today between various understandings of Islamic philosophy not only between the Islamic world and the West but also within each of those worlds.

The current state of knowledge of Islamic philosophy has of course dictated both the plan and content of these volumes. At present there is a dearth of critical editions of Islamic philosophical texts, and in fact there is not a single Islamic philosopher all of whose works have been critically edited. Then there are whole periods of Islamic philosophy, such as that ranging from the seventh/thirteenth to the tenth/sixteenth centuries in Persia, the Ottoman period, or the whole tradition of Islamic philosophy in the Subcontinent, which have not been carefully studied and whose history cannot therefore be as yet written in any detail. There are also important figures of Islamic philosophy from Bahmanyār, Muḥammad al-Shahrazūrī, Athīr al-Dīn al-Abharī, Quṭb al-Dīn al-Rāzī and Manṣūr Dashtakī in Persia to Ibn Sab'īn in Spain and many others especially in India and Turkey about whom much more monographic study needs to be carried out in order to clarify whole areas and periods of Islamic philosophy.

There is also the question of the interaction between Islamic philosophy and other disciplines ranging from jurisprudence to the natural sciences. This work has tried to take this important domain into consideration but the present state of research leaves much to be desired in such fields as the philosophy of mathematics, the philosophy of medicine and the vast domain of the philosophy of art. Lack of available knowledge and scholars who could treat such subjects in a work of this nature are reflected indirectly in the contents of the chapters which follow. It is obvious that we as editors could avail ourselves only of scholars capable and willing to participate in such a venture but it is necessary to add that the fact that certain important questions have not been treated in the present work does not mean that they were not of concern in the Islamic intellectual universe. Even today there is a vast body of knowledge especially in such domains as the philosophy of art, including both architecture and music, which remains oral and is transmitted only personally by traditional masters many of whom refuse to present their knowledge in written form.

As a result of those and other factors related to the present state of the art as far as the study of Islamic philosophy is concerned, the present work cannot and does not claim to be complete and exhaustive. What it has sought to do, however, is to cast its net as widely as possible to deal with all the periods of Islamic philosophy up to the present day as opposed to the supposed termination of this philosophical tradition with Ibn Rushd, bridging the artificial gap created by Western and some modern Muslim scholars between Islamic philosophy, which it classifies as being medieval, and so-called modern Islamic thought, which is often studied in a vacuum as if it had suddenly sprung up in a civilization without any significant previous intellectual history. We have also sought to deal as much as possible with other disciplines with which Islamic philosophy has reacted in one way or another over the ages, including law, science and mysticism. We have sought also to situate Islamic philosophy globally by studying the pre-Islamic schools of thought which nurtured it and other philosophical traditions such as the Jewish and Christian which it influenced deeply and with which it interacted in many ways. Finally, we have tried to bring out the relation of Islamic philosophy to the Islamic revelation itself and also to point out its rapport with other religious and theological discourses and disciplines which grew over the ages as branches of that tree of knowledge which has its roots in the Qur'ānic revelation and whose many branches include Islamic philosophy itself.

I wish to terminate this introduction with a subject which in a sense should have come at the beginning of this discussion, but, having already been treated in another way by Oliver Leaman, is perhaps more suited as the concluding comment of my introduction. That subject is why we have called Islamic philosophy Islamic philosophy. My co-editor has provided his own reasons to which I wish to add mine. First of all, the tradition of Islamic philosophy is deeply rooted in the world view of the Qur'ānic revelation and functions within a cosmos in which prophecy or revelation is accepted as a blinding reality that is the source not only of ethics but also of knowledge. It is therefore what Henry Corbin quite rightly called *la philosophie prophétique*. Secondly, while being philosophy in the fullest sense of the term, its very conception of *al-ʿaql* (reason/intellect) was transformed by the intellectual and spiritual universe within which it functioned in the same way that reason as transformed by the rationalism of the Age of Enlightenment began to function differently from the *ratio* and *intellectus* of a St Thomas. This fact is an undeniable truth for anyone who has studied Islamic philosophy from within the tradition and it remains an essential reality to consider despite the attempt of a number of not only Western but also Westernized Muslim scholars who, having surrendered to the rationalism of modern philosophy, now wish to read this understanding of reason back into Islamic philosophy. Thirdly, the Islamic philosophers were Muslim and nearly all of them devout in their following of the *Sharīʿah*. It should never be forgotten that the paragon of rationalistic philosophy in Islam, Ibn Rushd, long considered in the robe of Averroes as the epitome of rationalism in the West, was the chief religious authority of Cordova (modern Spanish Córdoba) and that Mullā Ṣadrā, one of the greatest of Islamic metaphysicians, journeyed seven times on foot to Mecca (Makkah) and died during the seventh pilgrimage. There are also other reasons which it is not possible to discuss here but which are mentioned in several of the essays that follow.

All these factors converge to point to the Islamic nature of Islamic philosophy in the same way that Christian philosophy is Christian and Jewish philosophy is Jewish. It is strange that no one protests against the use of the term Jewish philosophy because a number of Talmudic scholars over the centuries have opposed it, and the same holds true *mutatis mutandis* for Christianity. In the case of Islam, however, most Western scholars of the subject have chosen to identify other schools of Islamic thought such as *kalām* as Islamic and Islamic philosophy as "foreign", appealing to those very voices within the Islamic world which, like the Talmudic scholars in Judaism, have opposed Islamic philosophy.

Furthermore, this Western view has been adopted by a number of Muslim scholars trained in the rationalistic and sceptical modes of Western thought and impervious to the still living tradition of Islamic philosophy within the Islamic world and the possibility of gaining certitude (*al-yaqīn*) intellectually. Certainly, Islamic philosophy has had its opponents in Islamic circles but it has also had its defenders in not only the Shi'ite world but also in certain areas and schools of the Sunni world, although, as already mentioned, *falsafah* became more or less wed to either *kalām* or *ma'rifah* in later centuries in much of Sunnism at least in the Arab world. In any case Islamic philosophy has remained a major intellectual activity and a living intellectual tradition within the citadel of Islam to this day while continuing to be fully philosophy if this term is not limited to its recent caricature in the Anglo-Saxon world which would deny the title of philosopher to even Plato and Aristotle.

Islamic philosophy is not Arabic philosophy for several reasons, although this term has a respectable history in the West while having no historical precedence in the Islamic world itself before the fourteenth/twentieth century. First of all, although most works of Islamic philosophy were written in Arabic, much was also written in Persian going back to Ibn Sīnā himself. Secondly, while many of the Islamic philosophers were Arabs, such as al-Kindī or Ibn Rushd, many and in fact most were Persian while some were from Turkish or Indian ethnic backgrounds. Moreover, Persia has remained the main centre of Islamic philosophy during most of Islamic history.

And then there are arguments from the other side. Much of Jewish philosophy was written in Arabic but is not called Arabic philosophy and there is a whole Christian Arabic literature of a philosophical nature which is of some significance in the early history of Islamic philosophy but which belongs to a distinct philosophical tradition. If one puts modern nationalistic and chauvinistic ideas aside and looks upon the whole of the Islamic philosophical tradition, one cannot but call it Islamic philosophy for both intellectual and historical reasons, and if the term Arabic philosophy is still used in European languages it must be understood strictly in its medieval sense and not transposed into the modern understanding of this term. Islamic philosophy was created by Muslims who were Arabs, Persians and later Turks, Indians, Malays etc. on the basis of translations often made by Christians and influenced to some extent by Christian and

Jewish interactions with Greek philosophy. And yet, Islamic philosophy functioned in a universe dominated by the Qur'ānic revelation and the manifestation of the nature of the Divine Principle as *the One*. In such a world, a philosophical tradition was created which acted as catalyst for the rise of medieval Jewish philosophy and had a profound impact upon both philosophy and theology in the Christian West. It also exercised an influence upon Hindu India with which the present volumes have not been greatly concerned although some allusions have been made to this important chapter in the interaction of Islamic philosophy with intellectual traditions of other civilizations. The Islamic philosophical tradition reacted in numerous ways with other schools of Islamic thought and, on the basis of much of the wisdom of antiquity, created one of the richest intellectual traditions in the world, one which has survived as a living reality to this day. It is our hope that the present volumes will reveal some of the riches of this tradition as well as clarify its history and role for Islamic civilization as well as for European intellectual history in which it played a crucial role at an important stage of the development of Western thought.

wa'Llāhu ā'lam

I

Religious, intellectual and cultural context

CHAPTER 1

The meaning and concept of philosophy in Islam

Seyyed Hossein Nasr

In the light of the Qur'ān and *Ḥadīth* in both of which the term *ḥikmah* has been used,[1] Muslim authorities belonging to different schools of thought have sought over the ages to define the meaning of *ḥikmah* as well as *falsafah*, a term which entered Arabic through the Greek translations of the second/eighth and third/ninth centuries. On the one hand what is called philosophy in English must be sought in the context of Islamic civilization not only in the various schools of Islamic philosophy but also in schools bearing other names, especially *kalām*, *ma'rifah*, *uṣūl al-fiqh* as well as the *awā'il* sciences, not to speak of such subjects as grammar and history which developed particular branches of philosophy. On the other hand each school of thought sought to define what is meant by *ḥikmah* or *falsafah* according to its own perspective and this question has remained an important concern of various schools of Islamic thought especially as far as the schools of Islamic philosophy are concerned.

During Islamic history, the terms used for Islamic philosophy as well as the debates between the philosophers, the theologians and sometimes the Sufis as to the meaning of these terms varied to some extent from one period to another but not completely. *Ḥikmah* and *falsafah* continued to be used while such terms as *al-ḥikmat al-ilāhiyyah* and *al-ḥikmat al-muta'āliyah* gained new meaning and usage in later centuries of Islamic history, especially in the school of Mullā Ṣadrā. The term over which there was the greatest debate was *ḥikmah*, which was claimed by the Sufis and *mutakallimūn* as well as the philosophers, all appealing to such *Ḥadīth* as "The acquisition of *ḥikmah* is incumbent upon you and the good resides in *ḥikmah*."[2] Some Sufis such as Tirmidhī were called *ḥakīm* and Ibn 'Arabī refers to the wisdom which has been unveiled through each manifestation of the *logos* as *ḥikmah* as seen in the very title of his masterpiece *Fuṣūṣ al-ḥikam*,[3] while many *mutakallimūn* such as Fakhr al-Dīn al-Rāzī claimed that *kalām* and not *falsafah* was *ḥikmah*,[4] Ibn Khaldūn confirming this view in calling the later *kalām* (*kalām al-muta'akhkhirīn*) philosophy or *ḥikmah*.[5]

Our discussion in this chapter is concerned, however, primarily with the Islamic philosophers' understanding of the definition and meaning of the concept of philosophy and the terms *ḥikmah* and *falsafah*.[6] This understanding includes of course what the Greeks had comprehended by the term *philosophia* and many of the definitions from Greek sources which were to find their way into Arabic sometimes with only slight modifications. Some of the definitions of Greek origin most common among Islamic philosophers are as follows:[7]

1 Philosophy (*al-falsafah*) is the knowledge of all existing things *qua* existents (*ashyā' al-mawjūdah bi mā hiya mawjūdah*).[8]
2 Philosophy is knowledge of divine and human matters.
3 Philosophy is taking refuge in death, that is, love of death.
4 Philosophy is becoming God-like to the extent of human ability.
5 It [philosophy] is the art (*ṣinā'ah*) of arts and the science (*'ilm*) of sciences.
6 Philosophy is predilection for *ḥikmah*.

The Islamic philosophers meditated upon these definitions of *falsafah* which they inherited from ancient sources and which they identified with the Qur'ānic term *ḥikmah* believing the origin of *ḥikmah* to be divine. The first of the Islamic philosophers, Abū Ya'qūb al-Kindī wrote in his *On First Philosophy*, "Philosophy is the knowledge of the reality of things within people's possibility, because the philosopher's end in theoretical knowledge is to gain truth and in practical knowledge to behave in accordance with truth."[9] Al-Fārābī, while accepting this definition, added the distinction between philosophy based on certainty (*al-yaqīniyyah*) hence demonstration and philosophy based on opinion (*al-maẓnūnah*),[10] hence dialectic and sophistry, and insisted that philosophy was the mother of the sciences and dealt with everything that exists.[11]

Ibn Sīnā again accepted these earlier definitions while making certain precisions of his own. In his *'Uyūn al-ḥikmah* he says "*Al-ḥikmah* [which he uses as being the same as philosophy] is the perfection of the human soul through conceptualization [*taṣawwur*] of things and judgment [*taṣdīq*] of theoretical and practical realities to the measure of human ability."[12] But he went further in later life to distinguish between Peripatetic philosophy and what he called "Oriental philosophy" (*al-ḥikmat al-mashriqiyyah*) which was not based on ratiocination alone but included realized knowledge and which set the stage for the *ḥikmat al-ishrāq* of Suhrawardī.[13] Ibn Sīnā's foremost student Bahmanyār meanwhile identified *falsafah* closely with the study of existents as Ibn Sīnā had done in his Peripatetic works such as the *Shifā'*, repeating the Aristotelian dictum that philosophy is the study of existents *qua* existents. Bahmanyār wrote in the introduction to his *Taḥṣīl*, "The aim of the philosophical sciences is knowledge of existents."[14]

Ismā'īlī and Hermetico-Pythagorean thought, which paralleled in development the better-known Peripatetic philosophy but with a different philosophical perspective, nevertheless gave definitions of philosophy not far removed from those of the Peripatetics, emphasizing perhaps even more the relation between the theoretical aspect of philosophy and its practical dimension, between thinking philosophically and leading a virtuous life. This nexus, which is to be seen in all schools of earlier Islamic philosophy, became even more evident from Suhrawardī onward and the *ḥakīm* came to be seen throughout Islamic society not as someone who could only discuss mental concepts in a clever manner but as one who also lived according to the wisdom which he knew theoretically. The modern Western idea of the philosopher never developed in the Islamic world and the ideal stated by the Ikhwān al-Ṣafā' who lived in the fourth/tenth century and who were contemporary with Ibn Sīnā was to echo ever more loudly over the ages wherever Islamic philosophy was cultivated. The Ikhwān wrote, "The beginning of philosophy (*falsafah*) is the love of the sciences, its middle knowledge of the realities of existents to the measure of human ability and its end words and deeds in accordance with knowledge."[15]

With Suhrawardī we enter not only a new period but also another realm of Islamic philosophy. The founder of a new intellectual perspective in Islam, Suhrawardī used the term *ḥikmat al-ishrāq* rather than *falsafat al-ishrāq* for both the title of his philosophical masterpiece and the school which he inaugurated. The ardent student of Suhrawardī and the translator of *Ḥikmat al-ishrāq* into French, Henry Corbin, employed the term *theosophie* rather than philosophy to translate into French the term *ḥikmah* as understood by Suhrawardī and later sages such as Mullā Ṣadrā, and we have also rendered *al-ḥikmat al-muta'āliyah* of Mullā Ṣadrā into English as "transcendent theosophy"[16] and have sympathy for Corbin's translation of the term. There is of course the partly justified argument that in recent times the term "theosophy" has gained pejorative connotations in European languages, especially English, and has become associated with occultism and pseudo-esoterism. And yet the term *philosophy* also suffers from limitations imposed upon it by those who have practised it during the past few centuries. If Hobbes, Hume and Ayer are philosophers, then those whom Suhrawardī calls *ḥukamā'* are not philosophers and vice versa. The narrowing of the meaning of philosophy, the divorce between philosophy and spiritual practice in the West and especially the reduction of philosophy to either rationalism or empiricism necessitate making a distinction between the meaning given to *ḥikmah* by a Suhrawardī or Mullā Ṣadrā and the purely mental activity called philosophy in certain circles in the West today. The use of the term *theosophy* to render this later understanding of the term *ḥikmah* is based on the older and time-honoured meaning of this term in European intellectual history as associated with such figures as Jakob Böhme and not as the term became used in the late thirteenth/nineteenth century by some British occultists. Be that as it may, it is important to emphasize the understanding that Suhrawardī and all later Islamic philosophers have of *ḥikmah* as primarily *al-ḥikmat al-ilāhiyyah* (literally divine wisdom or *theosophia*) which must be realized within one's whole being and not only mentally. Suhrawardī saw this *ḥikmah* as being present also in ancient Greece before the advent of Aristotelian rationalism and identifies *ḥikmah* with coming out of one's body and ascending to the world of lights, as did Plato.[17] Similar ideas are to be found throughout his works, and he insisted that the highest level of *ḥikmah* requires both the perfection of the theoretical faculty and the purification of the soul.[18]

With Mullā Ṣadrā, one finds not only a synthesis of various earlier schools of Islamic thought but also a synthesis of the earlier views concerning the meaning of the term and concept philosophy. At the beginning of the *Asfār* he writes, repeating verbatim and summarizing some of the earlier definitions, "*falsafah* is the perfecting of the human soul to the extent of human ability through the knowledge of the essential reality of things as they are in themselves and through judgment concerning their existence established upon demonstration and not derived from opinion or through imitation".[19] And in *al-Shawāhid al-rubūbiyyah* he adds, "[through *ḥikmah*] man becomes an intelligible world resembling the objective world and similar to the order of universal existence".[20]

In the first book of the *Asfār* dealing with being, Mullā Ṣadrā discusses extensively the various definitions of *ḥikmah*, emphasizing not only theoretical knowledge and "becoming an intelligible world reflecting the objective intelligible world" but also detachment from passions and purification of the soul from its material defilements or what the Islamic philosophers call *tajarrud* or catharsis.[21] Mullā Ṣadrā accepts the meaning of *ḥikmah* as understood by Suhrawardī and then expands the meaning of *falsafah* to include the dimension of illumination and realization implied by the *ishrāqī* and also Sufi understanding of the term. For him as for his contemporaries, as well as most of his successors, *falsafah* or philosophy was seen as the supreme science of ultimately divine origin, derived from "the niche of prophecy" and the *ḥukamā'* as the most perfect of human beings standing in rank only below the prophets and Imāms.[22]

This conception of philosophy as dealing with the discovering of the truth concerning the nature of things and combining mental knowledge with the purification and perfection of one's being has lasted to this day wherever the tradition of Islamic philosophy has continued and is in fact embodied in the very being of the most eminent representatives of the Islamic philosophical tradition to this day. Such fourteenth/twentieth-century masters as Mīrzā Aḥmad Āshtiyānī, the author of *Nāma-yi rahbarān-i āmūzish-i kitāb-i takwīn* ("Treatise of the Guides to the Teaching of the Book of Creation"); Sayyid Muḥammad Kāẓim 'Aṣṣār, author of many treatises including *Waḥdat al-wujūd* ("The Transcendent Unity of Being"); Mahdī Ilāhī Qumsha'ī, author of *Ḥikmat-i ilāhī khwāṣṣ wa 'āmm* ("Philosophy/Theosophy – General and Particular") and 'Allāmah Sayyid Muḥammad Ḥusayn Ṭabāṭabā'ī, author of numerous treatises especially *Uṣūl-i falsafa-yi ri'ālizm* ("Principles of the Philosophy of Realism") all wrote of the definition of philosophy along lines mentioned above and lived accordingly. Both their works and their lives were testimony not only to over a millennium of concern by Islamic philosophers as to the meaning of the concept and the term philosophy but also to the significance of the Islamic definition of philosophy as that reality which transforms both the mind and the soul and which is ultimately never separated from spiritual purity and ultimately sanctity that the very term *ḥikmah* implies in the Islamic context.

NOTES

1 For the use of *ḥikmah* in the Qur'ān and *Ḥadīth* see S. H. Nasr, "The Qur'ān and *Ḥadīth* as Source and Inspiration of Islamic Philosophy", Chapter 2 below.

2 *'Alayka bi'l-ḥikmah fa inna'l-khayr fi'l-ḥikmah.*

3 See Muḥyī al-Dīn Ibn 'Arabī, *The Wisdom of the Prophets*, trans. T. Burckhardt, trans. from French A. Culme-Seymour (Salisbury, 1975), pp. 1–3 of Burckhardt's introduction; and M. Chodkiewicz, *Seal of the Saints – Prophethood and Sainthood in the Doctrine of Ibn 'Arabī*, trans. S. L. Sherrard (Cambridge, 1993): 47–8.

4 See S. H. Nasr, "Fakhr al-Dīn Rāzī", in M. M. Sharif (ed.), *A History of Muslim Philosophy*, 1 (Wiesbaden, 1963): 645–8.

5 'Abd al-Razzāq Lāhījī, the eleventh/seventeenth-century student of Mullā Ṣadrā who was however more of a theologian than a philosopher, writes in his *kalāmī* text *Gawhar-murād*, "Since it has become known that in acquiring the divine sciences and other intellectual matters the intellect has complete independence, and does not need to rely in these matters upon the *Sharī'ah* and the proof of certain principles concerning the essence of beings in such a way as to be in accord with the objective world through intellectual demonstrations and reasoning . . . the path of the *ḥukamā'*, the science acquired through this means is called in the vocabulary of scholars *ḥikmah*. And of necessity it will be in accord with the true *Sharī'ah* for the truth of the *Sharī'ah* is realized objectively through intellectual demonstration" (*Gawhar-murād* (Tehran, 1377): 17–18). Although speaking as a theologian, Lāhījī is admitting in this text that *ḥikmah* should be used for the intellectual activity of the philosophers and not the *mutakallimūn*, demonstrating the shift in position in the understanding of this term since the time of Fakhr al-Dīn al-Rāzī.

6 There is considerable secondary material on this subject in Arabic as well as in European languages. See 'Abd al-Ḥalīm Maḥmūd, *al-Tafkīr al-falsafī fi'l-islām* (Cairo, 1964): 163–71; Muṣṭafā 'Abd al-Rāziq, *Tamhīd li-ta'rīkh al-falsafat al-islāmiyyah* (Cairo, 1959), chapter 3: 48ff.; G. C. Anawati, "Philosophie médiévale en terre d'Islam", *Mélanges de l'Institut Dominicain d'Etudes Orientales du Caire*, 5 (1958): 175–236; and S. H. Nasr, "The Meaning and Role of 'Philosophy' in Islam", *Studia Islamica*, 37 (1973): 57–80.

7 See Christel Hein, *Definition und Einleitung der Philosophie – Von der spätantiken Einleitungsliteratur zur arabischen Enzyklopädie* (Bern and New York, 1985): 86.

8 This is repeated with only a small alteration by al-Fārābī in his *al-Jam' bayn ra'ay al-ḥakīmayn*. According to Ibn Abī Uṣaybi'ah, al-Fārābī even wrote a treatise entitled *Concerning the Word 'Philosophy'* (*Kalām fī ism al-falsafah*) although some have doubted that this was an independent work. See S. Strouma, "Al-Fārābī and Maimonides on the Christian Philosophical Tradition", *Der Islam*, 68(2) (1991): 264; and *Aristoteles – Werk und Wirkung*, 2, ed. J. Weisner (Berlin, 1987).

9 Quoted in Ahmed Fouad El-Ehwany, "Al-Kindī", in M. M. Sharif (ed.), *A History of Muslim Philosophy*, 1 (1963): 424.

10 *Kitāb al-Ḥurūf*, ed. M. Mahdi (Beirut, 1969): 153–7.

11 *Kitāb Jam' bayn ra'ay al-ḥakīmayn* (Hyderabad, 1968): 36–7.

12 *Fontes sapientiae ('Uyūn al-ḥikmah)*, ed. 'Abdurraḥman Badawī (Cairo, 1954): 16.

13 On Ibn Sīnā's "Oriental philosophy" see Chapter 17 below.

14 *Kitāb al-Taḥṣīl*, ed. M. Mutahharī (Tehran, 1970): 3.

15 *Rasā'il*, 1 (Cairo, 1928): 23.

16 See S. H. Nasr, *The Transcendent Theosophy of Ṣadr al-Dīn Shīrāzī* (Tehran, 1977).

17 See his *Talwīḥāt*, in H. Corbin (ed.) *Oeuvres philosophiques et mystiques*, 1 (Tehran, 1976): 112–13.

18 See S. H. Nasr, *Three Muslim Sages* (Delmar, 1975): 63–4.

19 *Al-Asfār al-arba'ah*, ed. 'Allāmah Ṭabāṭabā'ī (Tehran, 1967): 20.

20 Mullā Ṣadrā, *al-Shawāhid al-rubūbiyyah*, ed. S. J. Āshtiyānī (Mashhad, 1967).

21 See the Introduction of the *Asfār*.

22 Muḥammad Khwājawī, *Lawami' al-'ārifīn* (Tehran, 1987): 18ff., where many quotations from the different works of Mullā Ṣadrā on the relation between authentic *ḥikmah* and revelation and the spiritual power and sanctity of the Imāms (*walāyah*) are cited.

CHAPTER 2

The Qur'ān and *Ḥadīth* as source and inspiration of Islamic philosophy

Seyyed Hossein Nasr

Viewed from the point of view of the Western intellectual tradition, Islamic philosophy appears as simply Graeco-Alexandrian philosophy in Arabic dress, a philosophy whose sole role was to transmit certain important elements of the heritage of antiquity to the medieval West. If seen, however, from its own perspective and in the light of the whole of the Islamic philosophical tradition which has had a twelve-century-long continuous history and is still alive today, it becomes abundantly clear that Islamic philosophy, like everything else Islamic, is deeply rooted in the Qur'ān and *Ḥadīth*. Islamic philosophy is Islamic not only by virtue of the fact that it was cultivated in the Islamic world and by Muslims but because it derives its principles, inspiration and many of the questions with which it has been concerned from the sources of Islamic revelation despite the claims of its opponents to the contrary.[1]

All Islamic philosophers from al-Kindī to those of our own day such as 'Allāmah Ṭabāṭabā'ī have lived and breathed in a universe dominated by the reality of the Qur'ān and the *Sunnah* of the Prophet of Islam. Nearly all of them have lived according to Islamic Law or the *Sharī'ah* and have prayed in the direction of Makkah every day of their adult life. The most famous among them, such as Ibn Sīnā (Avicenna) and Ibn Rushd (Averroes), were conscious in asserting their active attachment to Islam and reacted strongly to any attacks against their faith without their being simply fideists. Ibn Sīnā would go to a mosque and pray when confronted with a difficult problem,[2] and Ibn Rushd was the chief *qāḍī* or judge of Cordova (Spanish Cordoba) which means that he was himself the embodiment of the authority of Islamic Law even if he were to be seen later by many in Europe as the arch-rationalist and the very symbol of the rebellion of reason against faith. The very presence of the Qur'ān and the advent of its revelation was to transform radically the universe in which and about which Islamic philosophers were to philosophize, leading to a specific kind of philosophy which can be justly called "prophetic philosophy".[3]

The very reality of the Qur'ān, and the revelation which made it accessible to a human community, had to be central to the concerns of anyone who sought to philosophize in the Islamic world and led to a type of philosophy in which a revealed book is accepted as the supreme source of knowledge not only of religious law but of the very nature of existence and beyond existence of the very source of existence. The prophetic consciousness which is the recipient of revelation (*al-waḥy*) had to remain of the utmost significance for those who sought to know the nature of things. How were the ordinary human means of knowing related to such an extraordinary manner of knowing? How was human reason related to that intellect which is illuminated by the light of revelation? To understand the pertinence of such issues, it is enough to cast even a cursory glance at the works of the Islamic philosophers who almost unanimously accepted revelation as a source of ultimate knowledge.[4] Such questions as the hermeneutics of the Sacred Text and theories of the intellect which usually include the reality of prophetic consciousness remain, therefore, central to over a millennium of Islamic philosophical thought.

One might say that the reality of the Islamic revelation and participation in this reality transformed the very instrument of philosophizing in the Islamic world. The theoretical intellect (*al-'aql al-naẓarī*) of the Islamic philosophers is no longer that of Aristotle although his very terminology is translated into Arabic. The theoretical intellect, which is the epistemological instrument of all philosophical activity, is Islamicized in a subtle way that is not always detectable through only the analysis of the technical vocabulary involved. The Islamicized understanding of the intellect, however, becomes evident when one reads the discussion of the meaning of *'aql* or intellect in a major philosopher such as Mullā Ṣadrā when he is commenting upon certain verses of the Qur'ān containing this term or upon the section on *'aql* from the collection of Shi'ite *Ḥadīth* of al-Kulaynī entitled *Uṣūl al-kāfī*. The subtle change that took place from the Greek idea of the "intellect" (*nous*) to the Islamic view of the intellect (*al-'aql*) can also be seen much earlier in the works of even the Islamic Peripatetics such as Ibn Sīnā where the Active Intellect (*al-'aql al-fa''āl*) is equated with the Holy Spirit (*al-rūḥ al-qudus*).

As is well known to students of the Islamic tradition, according to certain *ḥadīth* and also the oral tradition which has been transmitted over the centuries, the Qur'ān and all aspects of the Islamic tradition which are rooted in it have both an outward (*ẓāhir*) and an inward (*bāṭin*) dimension. Moreover, certain verses of the Qur'ān themselves allude to the inner and symbolic significance of the revealed Book and its message. As for the *Ḥadīth*, a body of this collection relates directly to the inner or esoteric dimension of the Islamic revelation and certain sayings of the Prophet refer directly to the esoteric levels of meaning of the Qur'ān.

Islamic philosophy is related to both the external dimension of the Qur'ānic revelation or the *Sharī'ah* and the inner truth or *Ḥaqīqah* which is the heart of all that is Islamic. Many of the doctors of the Divine Law or *Sharī'ah* have stood opposed to Islamic philosophy while others have accepted it. In fact some of the outstanding Islamic philosophers such as Ibn Rushd, Mīr Dāmād and Shah Walīullāh of Delhi have also been authorities in the domain of the Sacred Law. The *Sharī'ah* has, however, provided mostly the social and human conditions for the philosophical activity of the Islamic philosophers. It is to the *Ḥaqīqah* that one has to turn for the inspiration and source of knowledge for Islamic philosophy.

The very term *al-ḥaqīqah* is of the greatest significance for the understanding of the relation between Islamic philosophy and the sources of the Islamic revelation.[5] *Al-ḥaqīqah* means both truth and reality. It is related to God Himself, one of whose names is al-*Ḥaqq* or the Truth, and is that whose discovery is the goal of all Islamic philosophy. At the same time *al-ḥaqīqah* constitutes the inner reality of the Qur'ān and can be reached through a hermeneutic penetration of the meaning of the Sacred Text. Throughout history, many an Islamic philosopher has identified *falsafah* or *ḥikmah*, the two main terms used with somewhat different meaning for Islamic philosophy, with the *Ḥaqīqah* lying at the heart of the Qur'ān. Much of Islamic philosophy is in fact a hermeneutic unveiling of the two grand books of revelation, the Qur'ān and the cosmos, and in the Islamic intellectual universe Islamic philosophy belongs, despite some differences, to the same family as that of *ma'rifah* or gnosis which issues directly from the inner teachings of Islam and which became crystallized in both Sufism and certain dimensions of Shi'ism. Without this affinity there would not have been a Suhrawardī or Mullā Ṣadrā in Persia or an Ibn Sab'īn in Andalusia.

Philosophers living as far apart as Nāṣir-i Khusraw (fifth/eleventh century) and Mullā Ṣadrā (tenth/sixteenth century) have identified *falsafah* or *ḥikmah* explicitly with the *Ḥaqīqah* lying at the heart of the Qur'ān whose comprehension implies the spiritual hermeneutics (*ta'wīl*) of the Sacred Text. The thirteenth/nineteenth-century Persian philosopher Ja'far Kāshifī goes even further and identifies the various methods for the interpretation of the Qur'ān with the different schools of philosophy, correlating *tafsīr* (the literal interpretation of the Qur'ān) with the Peripatetic (*mashshā'ī*) school, *ta'wīl* (its symbolic interpretation) with the Stoic (*riwāqī*),[6] and *tafhīm* (in-depth comprehension of the Sacred Text) with the Illuminationist (*ishrāqī*).[7] For the main tradition of Islamic philosophy, especially as it developed in later centuries, philosophical activity was inseparable from interiorization of oneself and penetration into the inner meaning of the Qur'ān and *Ḥadīth* which those philosophers who were of a Shi'ite bent considered to be made possible through the power issuing from the cycle of initiation (*dā'irat al-walāyah*) that follows the closing of the cycle of prophecy (*dā'irat al-nubuwwah*) with the death of the Prophet of Islam.

The close nexus between the Qur'ān and *Ḥadīth*, on the one hand, and Islamic philosophy, on the other, is to be seen in the understanding of the history of philosophy. The Muslims identified Hermes, whose personality they elaborated into the "three Hermes", also well known to the West from Islamic sources, with Idrīs or Enoch, the ancient prophet who belongs to the chain of prophecy confirmed by the Qur'ān and *Ḥadīth*.[8] And they considered Idrīs as the origin of philosophy, bestowing upon him the title of Abu'l-Ḥukamā' (the father of philosophers). Like Philo and certain later Greek philosophers before them and also many Renaissance philosophers in Europe, Muslims considered prophecy to be the origin of philosophy, confirming in an Islamic form the dictum of Oriental Neoplatonism that "Plato was Moses in Attic Greek". The famous Arabic saying "philosophy issues from the niche of prophecy" (*yanba'u'l-ḥikmah min mishkāt al-nubuwwah*) has echoed through the annals of Islamic history and indicates clearly how Islamic philosophers themselves envisaged the relation between philosophy and revelation.

It must be remembered that al-*Ḥakīm* (the Wise, from the same root as *ḥikmah*) is a Name of God and also one of the names of the Qur'ān. More specifically many Islamic philosophers consider Chapter 31 of the Qur'ān, entitled *Luqmān*, after the Prophet known proverbially as a *ḥakīm*, to have been revealed to exalt the value of *ḥikmah*, which Islamic philosophers identify with true philosophy.

This chapter begins with the symbolic letters *alif*, *lām*, *mīm* followed immediately by the verse, "These are revelations of the wise scripture [*al-kitāb al-ḥakīm*]" (Pickthall translation), mentioning directly the term *ḥakīm*. Then in verse 12 of the same chapter it is revealed, "And verily We gave Luqmān wisdom [*al-ḥikmah*], saying: Give thanks unto Allah; and whosoever giveth thanks, he giveth thanks for [the good of] his soul. And whosoever refuseth – Lo! Allah is Absolute, Owner of Praise." Clearly in this verse the gift of *ḥikmah* is considered a blessing for which one should be grateful, and this truth is further confirmed by the famous verse, "He giveth wisdom [*ḥikmah*] unto whom He will, and he unto whom wisdom is given, he truly hath received abundant good" (2: 269).

There are certain *Ḥadīth* which point to God having offered prophecy and philosophy or *ḥikmah*, and Luqmān chose *ḥikmah* which must not be confused simply with medicine or other branches of traditional *ḥikmah* but refers to pure philosophy itself dealing with God and the ultimate causes of things. These traditional authorities also point to such Qur'ānic verses as "And He will teach him the Book [*al-kitāb*] and Wisdom [*al-ḥikmah*]" (3: 48) and "Behold that which I have given you of the Book and Wisdom" (3: 81): there are several where *kitāb* and *ḥikmah* are mentioned together. They believe that this conjunction confirms the fact that what God has revealed through revelation He had also made available through *ḥikmah*, which is reached through *'aql*, itself a microcosmic reflection of the macrocosmic reality which is the instrument of revelation.[9] On the basis of this doctrine later Islamic philosophers such as Mullā Ṣadrā developed an elaborate doctrine of the intellect in its relation to the prophetic intellect and the descent of the Divine Word, or the Qur'ān, basing themselves to some extent on earlier theories going back to Ibn Sīnā and other Muslim Peripatetics. All of this indicates how closely traditional Islamic philosophy identified itself with revelation in general and the Qur'ān in particular.

Islamic philosophers meditated upon the content of the Qur'ān as a whole as well as on particular verses. It was the verses of a polysemic nature or those with "unclear outward meaning" (*mutashābihāt*) to which they paid special attention. Also certain well-known verses were cited or commented upon more often than others, such as the "Light Verse" (*āyat al-nūr*) (24: 35) commented upon already by Ibn Sīnā in his *Ishārāt* and also by many later figures. Mullā Ṣadrā was in fact to devote one of the most important philosophical commentaries ever written upon the Qur'ān, entitled *Tafsīr āyat al-nūr*, to this verse.[10]

Western studies of Islamic philosophy, which have usually regarded it as simply an extension of Greek philosophy,[11] have for this very reason neglected for the most part the commentaries of Islamic philosophers upon the Qur'ān, whereas philosophical commentaries occupy an important category along with the juridical, philological, theological (*kalām*) and Sufi commentaries. The first major Islamic philosopher to have written Qur'ānic commentaries is Ibn Sīnā, many of whose commentaries have survived.[12] Later Suhrawardī was to comment upon diverse passages of the Sacred Text, as were a number of later philosophers such as Ibn Turkah al-Iṣfahānī.

The most important philosophical commentaries upon the Qur'ān were, however, written by Mullā Ṣadrā, whose *Asrār al-āyāt* and *Mafātīḥ al-ghayb*[13] are among the most imposing edifices of the Islamic intellectual tradition, although hardly studied in the West until now. Mullā Ṣadrā also devoted one of his major works to commenting upon the *Uṣūl al-kāfī* of Kulaynī, one of the major Shi'ite texts of *Ḥadīth* containing the sayings of the Prophet as well as the Imāms. These works taken together constitute the most imposing philosophical commentaries upon the Qur'ān and *Ḥadīth* in Islamic history, but such works are far from having terminated with him. The most extensive Qur'ānic commentary written during the past decades, *al-Mīzān*, was from the pen of 'Allāmah Ṭabāṭabā'ī, who was the reviver of the teaching of Islamic philosophy in Qom in Persia after the Second World War and a leading Islamic philosopher of this century whose philosophical works are now gradually becoming known to the outside world.

Certain Qur'ānic themes have dominated Islamic philosophy throughout its long history and especially during the later period when this philosophy becomes a veritable theosophy in the original and not deviant meaning of the term, *theosophia* corresponding exactly to the Arabic term *al-ḥikmat al-ilāhiyyah* (or *ḥikmat-i ilāhī* in Persian). The first and foremost is of course the unity of the Divine Principle and ultimately Reality as such or *al-tawḥīd* which lies at the heart of the Islamic message. The Islamic philosophers were all *muwaḥḥid* or followers of *tawḥīd* and saw authentic philosophy in this light. They called Pythagoras and Plato, who had confirmed the unity of the Ultimate Principle, *muwaḥḥid* while showing singular lack of interest in later forms of Greek and Roman philosophy which were sceptical or agnostic.

How Islamic philosophers interpreted the doctrine of Unity lies at the heart of Islamic philosophy. There continued to exist a tension between the Qur'ānic description of Unity and what the Muslims had learned from Greek sources, a tension which was turned into a synthesis of the highest intellectual order by such later philosophers as Suhrawardī and Mullā Ṣadrā.[14] But in all treatments of this subject from al-Kindī to Mullā 'Alī Zunūzī and Ḥājjī Mullā Hādī Sabziwārī during the thirteenth/nineteenth century and even later, the Qur'ānic doctrine of Unity, so central to Islam, has remained dominant and in a sense has determined the agenda of the Islamic philosophers.

Complementing the Qur'ānic doctrine of Unity is the explicit assertion in the Qur'ān that Allah bestows being and it is this act which instantiates all that exists, as one finds for example in the verse, "But His command, when He intendeth a thing, is only that he saith unto it: Be! and it is [*kun fa-yakūn*]" (36: 81). The concern of Islamic philosophers with ontology is directly related to the Qur'ānic doctrine, as is the very terminology of Islamic philosophy in this domain where it understands by *wujūd* more the verb or act of existence (*esto*) than the noun or state of existence (*esse*). If Ibn Sīnā has been called first and foremost a "philosopher of being",[15] and he developed the ontology which came to dominate much of medieval philosophy, this is not because he was simply thinking of Aristotelian theses in Arabic and Persian, but because of the Qur'ānic doctrine of the One in relation to the act of existence. It was as a result of meditation upon the Qur'ān in conjunction with Greek thought that

Islamic philosophers developed the doctrine of Pure Being which stands above the chain of being and is discontinuous with it, while certain other philosophers such as a number of Ismāʿīlīs considered God to be beyond Being and identified His act or the Qur'ānic *kun* with Being, which is then considered as the principle of the universe.

It is also the Qur'ānic doctrine of the creating God and *creatio ex nihilo*, with all the different levels of meaning which *nihilo* possesses,[16] that led Islamic philosophers to distinguish sharply between God as Pure Being and the existence of the universe, destroying that "block without fissure" which constituted Aristotelian ontology. In Islam the universe is always contingent (*mumkin al-wujūd*) while God is necessary (*wājib al-wujūd*), to use the well-known distinction of Ibn Sīnā.[17] No Islamic philosopher has ever posited an existential continuity between the existence of creatures and the Being of God, and this radical revolution in the understanding of Aristotelian ontology has its source in the Islamic doctrine of God and creation as asserted in the Qur'ān and *Ḥadīth*.[18] Moreover, this influence is paramount not only in the case of those who asserted the doctrine of *creatio ex nihilo* in its ordinary theological sense, but also for those such as al-Fārābī and Ibn Sīnā who were in favour of the theory of emanation but who none the less never negated the fundamental distinction between the *wujūd* (existence) of the world and that of God.

As for the whole question of "newness" or "eternity" of the world, or *ḥudūth* and *qidam*, which has occupied Islamic thinkers for the past twelve centuries and which is related to the question of the contingency of the world *vis-à-vis* the Divine Principle, it is inconceivable without the teachings of the Qur'ān and *Ḥadīth*. It is of course a fact that before the rise of Islam Christian theologians and philosophers such as John Philoponus had written on this issue and that Muslims had known some of these writings, especially the treatise of Philoponus against the thesis of the eternity of the world. But had it not been for the Qur'ānic teachings concerning creation, such Christian writings would have played an altogether different role in Islamic thought. Muslims were interested in the arguments of a Philoponus precisely because of their own concern with the question of *ḥudūth* and *qidam*, created by the tension between the teachings of the Qur'ān and the *Ḥadīth*, on the one hand, and the Greek notion of the non-temporal relation between the world and its Divine Origin, on the other.

Another issue of great concern to Islamic philosophers from al-Kindī to Mullā Ṣadrā, and those who followed him, is God's knowledge of the world. The major Islamic philosophers, such as al-Fārābī, Ibn Sīnā, Suhrawardī, Ibn Rushd and Mullā Ṣadrā, have presented different views on the subject while, as with the question of *ḥudūth* and *qidam*, they have been constantly criticized and attacked by the *mutakallimūn*, especially over the question of God's knowledge of particulars.[19] Now, such an issue entered Islamic philosophy directly from the Qur'ānic emphasis upon God's knowledge of all things as asserted in numerous verses such as, "And not an atom's weight in the earth or the sky escapeth your Lord, nor what is less than that or greater than that, but it is written in a clear Book" (10: 62). It was precisely this Islamic insistence upon Divine Omniscience that placed the issue of God's knowledge of the world at the centre of the concern of Islamic philosophers and caused Islamic philosophy, like its Jewish and Christian counterparts, to develop extensive philosophical theories totally absent from the philosophical perspective of Graeco-Alexandrian antiquity. In this context the Islamic doctrine of "divine science" (*al-'ilm al-ladunī*) is of central significance for both *falsafah* and theoretical Sufism or *al-ma'rifah*.

This issue is also closely allied to the philosophical significance of revelation (*al-waḥy*) itself. Earlier Islamic philosophers such as Ibn Sīnā sought to develop a theory by drawing to some extent, but not exclusively, on Greek theories of the intellect and the faculties of the soul.[20] Later Islamic philosophers continued their concern for this issue and sought to explain in a philosophical manner the possibility of the descent of the truth and access to the truth by knowledge based on certitude but derived from sources other than the senses, reason and even the inner intellect. They, however, pointed to the correspondence between the inner intellect and that objective manifestation of the Universal Intellect or *Logos* which is revelation. While still using certain concepts of Greek origin, the later Islamic philosophers such as Mullā Ṣadrā drew heavily from the Qur'ān and *Ḥadīth* on this issue.

Turning to the field of cosmology, again one can detect the constant presence of Qur'ānic themes and certain *Ḥadīth*. It is enough to meditate upon the commentaries made upon the "Light Verse" and "Throne Verse" and the use of such explicitly Qur'ānic symbols and images as the Throne (*al-'arsh*), the Pedestal (*al-kursī*), the light of the heavens and earth (*nūr al-samāwāt wa'l-arḍ*), the niche (*mishkāt*) and so many other Qur'ānic terms to realize the significance of the Qur'ān and *Ḥadīth* in the formulation of cosmology as dealt with in the Islamic philosophical tradition.[21] Nor must one forget the cosmological significance of the nocturnal ascent of the Prophet (*al-mi'rāj*) which so many Islamic philosophers have treated directly, starting with Ibn Sīnā. This central episode in the life of the Prophet, with its numerous levels of meaning, was not only of great interest to the Sufis but also drew the attention of numerous philosophers to its description as contained in certain verses of the Qur'ān and *Ḥadīth*. Some philosophers also turned their attention to other episodes with a cosmological significance in the life of the Prophet such as the "cleaving of the moon" (*shaqq al-qamar*) about which the ninth/fifteenth-century Persian philosopher Ibn Turkah Iṣfahanī wrote a separate treatise.[22]

In no branch of Islamic philosophy, however, is the influence of the Qur'ān and *Ḥadīth* more evident than in eschatology, the very understanding of which in the Abrahamic universe was alien to the philosophical world of antiquity. Such concepts as divine intervention to mark the end of history, bodily resurrection, the various eschatological events, the Final Judgment, and the posthumous states as understood by Islam or for that matter Christianity were alien to ancient philosophy whereas they are described explicitly in the Qur'ān and *Ḥadīth* as well as of course in the Bible and other Jewish and Christian religious sources.

The Islamic philosophers were fully aware of these crucial ideas in their philosophizing, but the earlier ones were unable to provide philosophical proofs for Islamic doctrines which many confessed to accept on the basis of faith but could not demonstrate within the context of Peripatetic philosophy. We see such a situation in the case of Ibn Sīnā who in several works, including the *Shifā'*, confesses that he cannot prove bodily resurrection but accepts it on faith. This question was in fact one of the three main points, along with the acceptance of *qidam* and the inability of the philosophers to demonstrate God's knowledge of particulars, for which al-Ghazzālī took Ibn Sīnā to task and accused him of *kufr* or infidelity. It remained for Mullā Ṣadrā several centuries later to demonstrate the reality of bodily resurrection through the principles of the "transcendent theosophy" (*al-ḥikmat al-muta'āliyah*) and to take both Ibn Sīnā and al-Ghazzālī to task for the inadequacy of their treatment of the subject.[23] The most extensive philosophical treatment of eschatology (*al-ma'ād*) in all its dimensions is in fact to be found in the *Asfār* of Mullā Ṣadrā.

It is sufficient to examine this work or his other treatises on the subject such as his *al-Mabda' wa'l-ma'ād* or *al-Ḥikmat al-'arshiyyah* to realize the complete reliance of the author upon the Qur'ān and *Ḥadīth*. His development of the philosophical meaning of *ma'ād* is in reality basically a hermeneutics of Islamic religious sources, primary among them the Qur'ān and *Ḥadīth*. Nor is this fact true only of Mullā Ṣadrā. One can see the same relation between philosophy and the Islamic revelation in the writings of Mullā Muḥsin Fayḍ Kāshānī, Shah Walīullāh of Delhi, Mullā 'Abd Allāh Zunūzī, Ḥājjī Mullā Hādī Sabziwārī and many later Islamic philosophers writing on various aspects of *al-ma'ād*. Again, although as far as the question of eschatology is concerned, the reliance on the Qur'ān and *Ḥadīth* is greater during the later period, as is to be seen already in Ibn Sīnā who dealt with it in both his encyclopedic works and in individual treatises dealing directly with the subject, such as his own *al-Mabda' wa'l-ma'ād*. It is noteworthy in this context that he entitled one of his most famous treatises on eschatology *al-Risālat al-aḍḥawiyyah*, drawing from the Islamic religious term for the Day of Judgment.

In meditating upon the history of Islamic philosophy in its relation to the Islamic revelation, one detects a movement toward ever closer association of philosophy with the Qur'ān and *Ḥadīth* as *falsafah* became transformed into *al-ḥikmat al-ilāhiyyah*. Al-Fārābī and Ibn Sīnā, although drawing so many themes from Qur'ānic sources, hardly ever quoted the Qur'ān directly in their philosophical works. By the time we come to Suhrawardī in the sixth/twelfth century, there are present within his purely philosophical works citations of the Qur'ān and *Ḥadīth*. Four centuries later the Safavid philosophers wrote philosophical works in the form of commentaries on the text of the Qur'ān or on certain of the *Ḥadīth*. This trend continued in later centuries not only in Persia but also in India and the Ottoman world including Iraq.

As far as Persia is concerned, as philosophy became integrated into the Shi'ite intellectual world from the seventh/thirteenth century onwards, the sayings of the Shi'ite Imāms began to play an ever greater role, complementing the Prophetic *Ḥadīth*. This is especially true of the sayings of Imāms Muḥammad al-Bāqir, Ja'far al-Ṣādiq and Mūsā al-Kāẓim, the fifth, sixth and seventh Imāms of Twelve-Imām Shi'ism, whose sayings are at the origin of many of the issues discussed by later Islamic philosophers.[24] It is sufficient to study the monumental but uncompleted *Sharḥ Uṣūl al-kāfī* of Mullā Ṣadrā to realize the philosophical fecundity of many of the sayings of the Imāms and their role in later philosophical meditation and deliberation.

The Qur'ān and *Ḥadīth*, along with the sayings of the Imāms, which are in a sense the extension of *Ḥadīth* in the Shi'ite world, have provided over the centuries the framework and matrix for Islamic philosophy and created the intellectual and social climate within which Islamic philosophers have philosophized. Moreoever, they have presented a knowledge of the origin, the nature of things, humanity and its final ends and history upon which the Islamic philosophers have meditated and from which they have drawn over the ages. They have also provided a language of discourse which Islamic philosophers have shared with the rest of the Islamic community.[25] Without the Qur'ānic revelation, there would of course have been no Islamic civilization, but it is important to realize that there would also have been no Islamic philosophy. Philosophical activity in the Islamic world is not simply a regurgitation of Graeco-Alexandrian philosophy in Arabic, as claimed by many Western scholars along with some of their Islamic followers, a philosophy which grew despite the presence of the Qur'ān and *Ḥadīth*. On the contrary, Islamic philosophy is what it is precisely because it flowered in a universe whose contours are determined by the Qur'ānic revelation.

As asserted at the beginning of this chapter, Islamic philosophy is essentially "prophetic philosophy" based on the hermeneutics of a Sacred Text which is the result of a revelation that is inalienably linked to the microcosmic intellect and which alone is able to actualize the dormant possibilities of the intellect within us. Islamic philosophy, as understood from within that tradition, is also an unveiling of the inner meaning of the Sacred Text, a means of access to that *Ḥaqīqah* which lies hidden within the inner dimension of the Qur'ān. Islamic philosophy deals with the One or Pure Being, and universal existence and all the grades of the universal hierarchy. It deals with man and his entelechy, with the cosmos and the final return of all things to God. This interpretation of existence is none other than penetration into the inner meaning of the Qur'ān which "is" existence itself, the Book whose meditation provides the key for the understanding of those objective and subjective orders of existence with which the Islamic philosopher has been concerned over the ages.

A deeper study of Islamic philosophy over its twelve-hundred-year history will reveal the role of the Qur'ān and *Ḥadīth* in the formulation, exposition and problematics of this major philosophical tradition. In the same way that all of the Islamic philosophers from al-Kindī onwards knew the Qur'ān and *Ḥadīth* and lived with them, Islamic philosophy has manifested over the centuries its inner link with the revealed sources of Islam, a link which has become even more manifest as the centuries have unfolded, for Islamic philosophy is essentially a philosophical hermeneutics of the Sacred Text while making use of the rich philosophical heritage of antiquity. That is why, far from being a transitory and foreign phase in the history of Islamic thought, Islamic philosophy has remained over the centuries and to this day one of the major intellectual perspectives in Islamic civilization with its roots sunk deeply, like everything else Islamic, in the Qur'ān and *Ḥadīth*.

NOTES

1 Within the Islamic world itself scholars of *kalām* and certain others who have opposed Islamic philosophy over the ages have claimed that it was merely Greek philosophy to which they opposed philosophy or wisdom derived from faith (*al-ḥikmat al-yūnāniyyah* versus *al-ḥikmat al-īmāniyyah*). Some contemporary Muslim scholars, writing in English, oppose Muslim to Islamic, considering Muslim to mean whatever is practised or created by Muslims and Islamic that which is derived directly from the Islamic revelation. Many such scholars, who hail mostly from Pakistan and India, insist on calling Islamic philosophy Muslim philosophy, as can be seen in the title of the well-known work edited by M. M. Sharif, *A History of Muslim Philosophy*. If one looks more deeply into the nature of Islamic philosophy from the traditional Islamic point of view and takes into consideration its whole history, however, one will see that this philosophy is at once Muslim and Islamic according to the above-given definitions of these terms.

2 When accused on a certain occasion of infidelity, Ibn Sīnā responded in a famous Persian quatrain: "It is not so easy and trifling to call me a heretic; / No faith in religion is firmer than mine. / I am a unique person in the whole world and if I am a heretic; / Then there is not a single Muslim anywhere in the world." Trans. by S. H. Barani in his "Ibn Sina and Alberuni", in *Avicenna Commemoration Volume* (Calcutta, 1956): 8 (with certain modifications by S. H. Nasr).

3 This term was first used by H. Corbin and myself and appears in Corbin, with the collaboration of S. H. Nasr and O. Yahya, *Histoire de la philosophie islamique* (Paris, 1964).

4 We say "almost" because there are one or two figures such as Muḥammad ibn Zakariyyā' al-Rāzī who rejected the necessity of prophecy. Even in his case, however, there is a rejection of the necessity of revelation in order to gain ultimate knowledge and not the negation of the existence of revelation.

5 See Corbin, *op. cit.*: 26ff.

6 The term *riwāqī* used by later Islamic philosophers must not, however, be confused with the Roman Stoics, although it means literally stoic (*riwāq* in Arabic coming from Pahlavi and meaning *stoa*).

7 Corbin, *op. cit.*: 24.

8 On the Islamic figure of Hermes and Hermetic writings in the Islamic world see L. Massignon, "Inventaire de la littérature hermétique arabe", appendix 3 in A. J. Festugière and A. D. Nock, *La Révélation d'Hermès Trismégiste*, 4 vols (Paris, 1954–60); S. H. Nasr, *Islamic Life and Thought* (Albany, 1981): 102–19; F. Sezgin, *Geschichte der arabischen Schrifttums*, 4 (Leiden, 1971).

9 See for example the introduction by one of the leading contemporary traditional philosophers of Persia, Abu'l-Ḥasan Sha'rānī, to Sabziwārī, *Asrār al-ḥikam* (Tehran, 1960): 3.

10 Edited with introduction and Persian translation by M. Khwājawī (Tehran, 1983).

11 The writings of H. Corbin are a notable exception.

12 See M. Abdul Haq, "Ibn Sīnā's Interpretation of the Qur'ān", *The Islamic Quarterly*, 32(1) (1988): 46–56.

13 This monumental work has been edited in Arabic and also translated into Persian by M. Khwājawī who has printed all of Mullā Ṣadrā's Qur'ānic commentaries in recent years. It is interesting to note that the Persian translation entitled *Tarjuma-yi mafātīḥ al-ghayb* (Tehran, 1979) includes a long study on the rise of philosophy and its various schools by Ayatullah 'Ābidī Shāhrūdī, who discusses the rapport between Islamic philosophy and the Qur'ān in the context of traditional Islamic thought.

14 See I. Netton, *Allah Transcendent* (London, 1989), which deals with this tension but mixes his account with certain categories of modern European philosophy not suitable for the subject.

15 See E. Gilson, *Avicenne et le point de départ de Duns Scot, Extrait des archives d'histoire doctrinale et littéraire du Moyen Age* (Paris, 1927); and A. M. Goichon, "L'Unité de la pensée avicennienne", *Archives Internationale d'Histoire des Sciences*, 20–1 (1952): 290ff.

16 See D. Burrell and B. McGinn (eds), *God and Creation* (Notre Dame, 1990): 246ff. For the more esoteric meaning of *ex nihilo* in Islam see L. Schaya, *La*

Création en Dieu (Paris, 1983), especially chapter 6: 90ff.

17 This has been treated more amply in Chapter 16 below on Ibn Sīnā. See also Nasr, *An Introduction to Islamic Cosmological Doctrines* (Albany, 1993), chapter 12.

18 See T. Izutsu, *The Concept and Reality of Existence* (Tokyo, 1971).

19 The criticisms by al-Ghazzālī and Imām Fakhr al-Dīn al-Rāzī of this issue, as that of *ḥudūth* and *qidam*, are well known and are treated below. Less is known, however, of the criticism of other theologians who kept criticizing the philosophers for their denial of the possibility of God knowing particulars rather than just universals.

20 See F. Rahman, *Prophecy in Islam, Philosophy and Orthodoxy* (London, 1958), where some of these theories are described and analysed clearly, but with an over-emphasis on the Greek factor and downplaying of the role of the Islamic view of revelation itself.

21 On this issue see Nasr, *An Introduction to Islamic Cosmological Doctrines*; and Nasr, "Islamic Cosmology", in *Islamic Civilization*, 4, ed. A. Y. al-Hassan *et al.* (Paris, forthcoming).

22 See H. Corbin, *En Islam iranien*, 3 (Paris, 1971): 233ff.

23 Mullā Ṣadrā dealt with this debate in several of his works especially in his *Glosses upon the Theosophy of the Orient of Light* (of Suhrawardī) *(Ḥāshiyah 'alā ḥikmat al-ishrāq)*. See H. Corbin, "Le thème de la résurrection chez Mollā Ṣadrā Shīrāzī (1050/1640) commentateur de Sohrawardī (587/1191)", in *Studies in Mysticism and Religion – Presented to Gershom G. Scholem* (Jerusalem, 1967): 71–118.

24 The late 'Allāmah Ṭabāṭabā'ī, one of the leading traditional philosophers of contemporary Persia, once made a study of the number of philosophical problems dealt with by early and later Islamic philosophers. He once told us that, according to his study, there were over two hundred philosophical issues treated by the early Islamic philosophers and over six hundred by Mullā Ṣadrā and his followers. Although he admitted that this approach was somewhat excessively quantitative, it was an indication of the extent of expansion of the fields of interest of Islamic philosophy, an expansion which he attributed almost completely to the influence of the metaphysical and philosophical utterances of the Shi'ite Imāms which became of ever greater concern to many Islamic philosophers, both Shi'ite and Sunni, from the time of Naṣīr al-Dīn al-Ṭūsī onwards.

25 The Qur'ān and *Ḥadīth* have also influenced directly and deeply the formation of the Islamic philosophical vocabulary in Arabic, an issue with which we have not been able to deal in this chapter.

CHAPTER 3

The Greek and Syriac background

F. E. Peters

The Islamic philosopher, the *faylasūf*, was engaged in an enquiry that was numbered, together with the study of medicine, mathematics, astronomy and physics, among what were called the "foreign sciences". The categorization was neat and altogether commonplace in Islamic circles, this setting of the "foreign sciences" over against the traditional "Islamic sciences", and, while it represents a judgment about the origins of the two bodies of knowledge, it also suggests that we might here be in the presence of an academic distinction, two curricula, perhaps, representing two schools, or, on the model of a medieval European university, even two different faculties of the same institution of higher learning.

The historical judgment is, in fact, correct. The *faylasūf*, like the physician and scientist, was caught up in an intellectual enterprise whose foreign and, more precisely, Hellenic origins are as transparent as the name. The *faylasūf* was a *philosophos*, the heir to an intellectual tradition that had originated among the Greeks and, after a long career in that milieu, had passed, without break or diminution, into the possession of Islam. That was the received wisdom of the ninth and tenth century A.D. Muslims, and it is not very far from the fact. Much farther from the fact is the suggestion that the "foreign" or Hellenic sciences constituted part of an academic curriculum or faculty in the official *madrasahs*. They did represent a kind of idealized school curriculum, but in an academic setting that few Sunni savants had ever seen or could likely have even imagined, although *falsafah* has been taught in traditional *madrasahs* in the Shīʿī world.

The Islamic view, or, better, the view of the relatively few Muslims who engaged in the "foreign sciences", was that they were the heirs of Plato and Aristotle. Indeed they were, though their inheritance was mediated through the long and highly creative file of philosophers who stretched between the ancient paradigms and themselves, thinkers the Muslims knew about, but whose position and role in the history of later Greek philosophy they but ill understood. We are somewhat better informed on the subject, to be sure, at least for the first three or four centuries of the Christian era; but our knowledge too grows somewhat faint as we approach the fifth, sixth and seventh century A.D. stages of the Platonic and Aristotelian traditions, the very ones to which the Muslims were more precisely heirs. Many of the texts we have; so too did the Muslims, though not a great number are preserved. Where we differ is on what to make of them, how to trace the passage, and the subsequent transformations, of Plato and Aristotle at the hands of their commentators, all of them professors in the universities of the Eastern Roman Empire.

To understand *falsafah* it is not enough to acknowledge what the Muslims knew of Plato and Aristotle, to note which works of the masters were translated, how and by whom and when; some measure must be taken of the quality of their inherited Platonism and Aristotelianism, which turn out to be very different from that of their eponyms. And to do that we turn first to the Muslims' own best and most complete account, that provided by Ibn al-Nadīm, and attempt to reconstruct, with the aid of his witness, the complex philosophical tradition of late antiquity.

In 377/987 or 988 the Baghdad bookseller Abu'l-Faraj Muḥammad ibn al-Nadīm completed his *Fihrist* or *Catalogue*. The work may have begun simply as a bookseller's handlist, but the author's own learning and curiosity and the bracing intellectual climate of Būyid Baghdad eventually produced something more ambitious: the *Catalogue* is nothing less than a tenth-century A.D. encyclopedia of the literary arts and sciences of Islam. From calligraphy to alchemy, Ibn al-Nadīm noted down, with biographical and historical comments, the sum of the books of Islam. But it is something more as well. The *Catalogue* paid particular attention to the Muslims' translation activity, and so it is one of our better guides to their understanding of the philosophical and scientific landscape of the Islamic world in late antiquity. With the *Catalogue* in hand it is possible to describe in some detail how much and what kind was the "foreign" heritage available to the Muslims, and to make some surmises why it was such.

Two extraordinary elements of the Hellenism inherited – or, perhaps better, expropriated – by Islam spring immediately to eye from the pages of Ibn al-Nadīm. The complex of literary, political and philosophical values we call Hellenism had met and in varying degrees transformed other cultures, even religious cultures, before, but normally through a native intelligentsia that had already learned Greek. This encounter of Hellenism with Islam was, however, remarkable: the Muslim accepted neither the language nor the humanistic values nor, he thought, the religion of the Greeks; his borrowings came exclusively through translation and, more, were severely limited to a technical and scientific Hellenism. The few professional translators apart, the Muslims knew Greek philosophy but no Greek; read Plato and Aristotle, Euclid, Galen and Ptolemy, but never so much as glimpsed a page of Homer, Sophocles or Thucydides.

This latter omission was not the Muslims' own choice. In the centuries before the Muslims came in contact with that culture, the humane values of the Hellenic legacy were absorbed, transformed or discarded by Christianity. As a result, the rich hoard of scientific learning that the *Catalogue* reveals was transmitted almost intact to the Muslims, accompanied by a few random ethical *gnomai* but with little real understanding of Greek *paideia*, the cultural and humane ideals of Hellenism. This easy separation of the head from the trunk reflects ominously on the educational practices of late antiquity, when higher education must have been so severely professional in tone and content that it was possible to pass to others the curricula of the natural sciences, medicine and philosophy without any intimation that they were once part of an *enkyklios paideia*, a general education that included grammar and rhetoric.

As we read the evidence, rhetoric was the chief vehicle for the professional study of humane letters in late antiquity. It was a popular subject even among the Christian intelligentsia, and there were endowed municipal chairs in rhetoric scattered over the provinces of the Eastern Roman Empire. But there was one venue in late antiquity that was, despite its high professional standards in medicine, philosophy and the mathematical sciences, notoriously uninterested in rhetoric. Egypt, with its great intellectual centre of Alexandria, conforms very precisely to a hypothesized source for the Muslims' scientific but decidedly illiberal version of Hellenism. The university there, which was still very much alive in the seventh century A.D., had a curriculum that was strongly developed in philosophy and the sciences (particularly medicine and mathematics) and weak in rhetoric – the humanities and law.

We are not very well informed on the higher schools of the early Byzantine Empire. Something is known, however, of the teaching of philosophy at Athens and Alexandria in the fifth and early sixth centuries A.D., and what is plain in the evidence is that, whatever the homage rendered to Aristotle, it was one or another variety of Platonism/Neoplatonism that dominated the few places where philosophy was formally taught. The Muslims were confused on this matter. Most of them were transparently Neoplatonists and yet were so oblivious of the true nature of their Platonism that they could not identify its author. The lecturers at Athens and Alexandria knew whence they had come, however. Truth lies in Platonic orthodoxy, Plotinus had taught, and his

Greek successors did not forget the lesson. But the Muslims, who had as much claim to be heirs of Plato as the Hellenized Damascius or Olympiodorus, did not recognize their affiliations and read Plotinus as a *pseudepigraphon*: an abridgement of books 4–6 of the *Enneads* circulated in Islam under the title of the *Theology of Aristotle*.

Ibn al-Nadīm knew nothing of the actual Plotinus. Even his treatment of Plato in the *Catalogue* is foggy and unenlightening: a jumble of epitomes, a scattering of commentaries that had been turned into Arabic, and not much more; the entry represents, we assume, the little about the Platonic school tradition or its practitioners that was known to Ibn al-Nadīm or his sources. Following upon his unenlightening and almost tabular treatment of Plato, however, is Ibn al-Nadīm's presentation of the biography of Aristotle and his informed history of the Aristotelian translations. This emphasis was not a peculiarity of the *Catalogue*; whatever the actual content of their philosophical heritage, Aristotle was regarded by the Muslims as the chief of the file of Hellenic sages, and al-Fārābī, the most considerable Muslim Platonist, was being measured not against Plato but against Aristotle when he was flatteringly called "the Second Master".

The *Catalogue*'s review of the post-Aristotelian philosophers reveals the same perspective. The list includes Theophrastus, Proclus "the Platonist", Alexander of Aphrodisias, Porphyry, Ammonius (Hermieu), Themistius, Nicolaus, Plutarch (of Chaeronea), Olympiodorus, Hippocrates, Epaphroditus, "another Plutarch", John Philoponus, and a final hodge-podge of names drawn from some other source which includes Gregory of Nyssa and Theon of Smyrna, "whose periods and order of sequence are not known". In the entire group only Proclus and Theon are identified as Platonists; the rest are seen almost exclusively through the focus of an Aristotelian exegetical tradition.

When and where did this dissimulation arise? In talking about the late antique scholastic tradition we mean nothing more than the history of the Platonic schools. At the beginning of the third Christian century the actual schools of Epicurus, Zeno and Aristotle were moribund, if not dead; after A.D. 200 there existed among the Greeks of the Empire only the Platonic academies at Alexandria and Athens and their lesser reflections at Apamea and Pergamum. And, four hundred years later, on the eve of the Muslim invasion, there remained only Alexandria. The final masters at Alexandria, and their solitary and non-teaching Platonic contemporary at Athens, were, however, deeply invested in the study of Aristotle.

Somewhere within this paradox lies the explanation of the Muslims' confusion about their own philosophical identity. The Athenian Academy traced its mixed Platonism of the second and third centuries A.D. from the insights first of Plotinus (d. 270), and then of Porphyry (d. *c.* 306),

Iamblichus (d. 325) and Proclus (d. 485), men whose penchant for magic and the occult proved dangerous and finally deadly to Athenian Platonism. The pains of this transformation from Platonists to somewhat disingenuous syncretizers, from philosophers to theosophists, were lost on the Muslims, though they had perhaps inherited, without fully understanding it, the same dissimulations that enabled the Alexandrian Platonists to outlive their Athenian colleagues.

One of Proclus' fellow students at Athens under the brief tenure of Syrianus as scholarch there (A.D. 432–7?) was Hermias, and it was from him that the last Alexandrians descended. At Athens itself Proclus' immediate successors, Isidore and Zenodotus, were not distinguished. We are aware of them solely from Damascius' *Life of Isidore*, an important historical source denied to the Muslims; no trace of their own work survives. There were, in addition, growing difficulties with the Christian authorities. Even Proclus, who could be prudent when need be on the subject of his paganism, was forced to go into exile for a year. His successors in the Academy were apparently less careful in a world that had reached the limits of its tolerance of the old heathen cults, and in A.D. 529 the Emperor Justinian closed down the Athenian school for good and confiscated its properties.

There followed the curious and interesting sojourn of the seven Athenian philosophers, including the current Platonic "successor" Damascius with his student Simplicius, at the court of the Sassanian Shah Khusraw I at Ctesiphon. Their stay there was exceedingly brief, less than a year perhaps, before their return to Byzantine territory under terms of the peace treaty of 532, and so it is probably unwise to draw many conclusions from the episode. When it was all over what was left can be described only as a chastened Platonic paganism. Such was certainly the posture of Simplicius who, upon his return to Athens after 533, devoted his researches exclusively to the study not of Plato but of Aristotle. On his return from Persia Damascius was well into his seventies, but Simplicius still had an active career before him. But not as a teacher. Lecturing had ceased for ever in the Athenian Academy, and so Simplicius became of necessity a library scholar, a philosopher whose chief monuments are his learned commentaries on Aristotle. Of these the Muslims appear to have known only those on the *Categories* and *On the Soul*. They did not possess his extensive commentaries on the *Physics* or *On the Heavens*, though they were well instructed on the controversies with the Christian philosopher John Philoponus that unfolded there.

How Philoponus and Simplicius, both students at Alexandria of Ammonius, who had in turn matriculated with Proclus at Athens, came to be debating Aristotle and not Plato in the first half of the sixth Christian century carries us back to Ammonius himself. Like his father Hermias, Ammonius had gone to Athens for his philosophical education. Both men, father and son, eventually returned to Alexandria to teach and write, Hermias on Plato and Ammonius chiefly on Aristotle. The interest in Aristotle is not strange in someone trained in a Platonic tradition that had been studying Peripatetic works at least since the days of Plotinus and Porphyry, but the publication of almost exclusively Aristotelian material is curious and abrupt. And among its results was the fact that the Muslims, who had limited literary access to late antiquity, regarded Ammonius and his successors almost exclusively as Aristotelian commentators.

Ammonius' students dominated at both Athens and Alexandria during the next generation; the Athenian "successor" Damascius, who was unknown to the Muslims, and his student Simplicius; Olympiodorus, Asclepius and John Philoponus at Alexandria. Olympiodorus, who was almost certainly not a Christian, appears to have moved none the less to a more accommodating posture *vis-à-vis* Christianity, but there is no mention of a Christian in the *Catalogue* until the next of Ibn al-Nadīm's entries, that on John Philoponus, "a bishop over some of the churches of Egypt, upholding the Christian sect of the Jacobites".

John "the grammarian", as the Muslims called him and as he styled himself (*grammatikos*) in his own works, was a well-known figure in Islam as an Aristotelian commentator, a medical writer and historian, and, considerably more obscurely, as a Christian theologian. Over the years John's work apparently turned away from his earlier scholastic work under Ammonius. His redaction of his professor's notes on the *Physics* dates from A.D. 517, but by 529, the same year that Justinian closed the Academy for its flagrant paganism, Philoponus was working in a far more Christian vein. In that year appeared his *On the Eternity of the World against Proclus*, followed shortly by the complementary *Against Aristotle*, a twofold attack on the current Neoplatonic position on the eternity of the cosmos. The Muslims, who naturally shared Philoponus' view of creation in time, were highly interested in the controversy and could follow it closely through the Arabic versions of the *Timaeus* (albeit in an epitome), Aristotle's *On the Heavens* and *Physics*, Proclus' *Arguments* and commentary on the *Timaeus*, and, finally, Philoponus' refutation. But they knew or cared nothing about the rest of Philoponus' career after A.D. 530, his progressive involvement with Christian theology and his final bout with tritheism.

In the Muslims' version of the history of philosophy, Olympiodorus' Christian students at Alexandria, Elias and David, have no place, nor do the Christian Platonists of Gaza: Aeneas, Zacharias the bishop of Mytilene, and his brother Procopius. The last known scholarch at Alexandria, Stephen, was summoned to Constantinople some time about A.D. 616 to assume a teaching post there. His portrait among the Muslims is thin but congruent with Greek sources. Stephen's commentaries on the

Categories and *On Interpretation* were extant in Arabic, as well as some medical writings.

This is the end of the Greek philosophical tradition in late antiquity. Stephen, who served Heraclius, touches the chronological limits of Islam. The Muslims who followed pieced together their knowledge of that tradition from the philosophical texts available to them and from a far less easily identified set of historical perspectives. Both, however, betray their origins in a clear way: clustered around the works of Aristotle are the names of the great commentators from the Platonic school tradition at Alexandria from Ammonius in the fifth century A.D. to Stephen in the seventh. From there it is possible for us, though not for Ibn al-Nadīm and his contemporaries, to trace the connection back to Porphyry in the fourth century, the man who introduced the textual exegesis of Aristotle in the curriculum of the Platonic schools.

On the witness of Porphyry's biography of his teacher, Aristotle was already carefully and critically studied by Plotinus. Porphyry himself did the same, and in a somewhat more systematic manner than Plotinus, whose approach to philosophy had been formed in his own teacher's notoriously informal seminars. There may have been some sense of a school curriculum in the Platonic school tradition before Plotinus, a notion that was ignored by Plotinus but reasserted by Porphyry. And it is clear from Porphyry's own work that Aristotle was part of that curriculum. Porphyry was the first Platonist to produce formal commentaries on the treatises of Aristotle, a fact that guaranteed in the sequel that Aristotle would be studied in the Platonic schools.

According to the view that emerged in the post-Porphyrian school tradition, there were two major branches of philosophy, that which had to do with the various manifestations of physical reality, the study known generally as physics, and that which devoted itself to the contemplation of supra-sensible reality, that is, theology, or, to use the word favoured by later Platonic pietists, "mystical viewing" (*epopteia*). Whatever role ethics may have played in the scheme, it was severed from its original connection with politics and reduced to the status of a cathartic preliminary to the study of philosophy proper.

The position of logic was paradoxical. On the original Aristotelian view, logic was a method, or an instrument (*organon*), and not a part of philosophy. This was a departure from Plato's teaching, which united dialectic and metaphysics, philosophy and philosophizing, in an intimate and inviolable union. The later Platonists continued to pay lip service to the Platonic ideal, but in reality they were dogmatists and not dialecticians. Whatever they may have said about dialectic, they used logic as a tool, and in the manner set down by Aristotle. Porphyry installed the logical *Organon* at the starting point of the curriculum, and it remained there during the rest of the history of the school.

From the *Organon* the Platonist proceeded to the study of the Aristotelian philosophy proper, particularly the physical and psychological treatises. When Proclus was doing his studies at Athens in the fifth century A.D., the Aristotelian part of the curriculum took two years. At its completion the student was ready for natural theology, a theology that was, of course, Platonic and centred upon the exegesis of the *Timaeus* and the *Parmenides*. Beyond that lay the sacred theology of the *Chaldean Oracles*, the touchstone of late Platonic occultism.

This was, we are certain, the standard curriculum in the only surviving philosophical school in late antiquity, the Platonic. It was not, however, what was passed on to the Muslims. What they knew of a curriculum came from translated examples of a standard "introduction to Aristotle" and not from what was actually being taught in the schools of Athens or Alexandria. The laying-out of the Aristotelian treatises from the *Categories* to the *Metaphysics*, the arrangement found in Ibn al-Nadīm's *Catalogue*, and the one that determined the structure of most Muslim encyclopedias of the "foreign sciences", was not a curriculum at all. Rather, it was an academic "division of the sciences". The simple fact is that neither we nor the Muslims have much information about the actual curriculum of any Aristotelian school.

The Muslim celebration of Aristotle, to which Ibn al-Nadīm bears such detailed witness, was a novel event in the Near East. During the preceding five centuries all who studied the philosopher did so from a far more limited pragmatism than that which the Muslims brought to the task. The Neoplatonists had granted him a place in their curriculum, but it was a subordinate one. And the Christians too, when they discovered their own need of Aristotle, were even more severe in their restrictions on his use.

The Christian use of Aristotle was, in the end, more important than the restrictions placed upon it. The works of the great eastern Neoplatonists appeared in no other language but their original Greek until the coming of Islam; Christianity and its theologians leaped cultural frontiers, including that which separated the Hellenes from the Semites of the Aramaic-speaking East. Before there was an Arabic Aristotle there was a Syriac Aristotle, who served, in this limited capacity, the cause of Christian theology.

Though Syriac literature was properly a creation of Christian times, the Aramaic-speaking peoples of the Near East had been living within a Hellenized milieu since the time of Alexander's conquests. And if at Edessa the contact between Aramean and Hellene produced a literature that was overwhelmingly Christian in its sentiments and interests, the same contact at nearby Harran brought forth a far different cultural mix: pagan, scientific and occult, rather than meditative, ascetic, musical and primarily Christian. Harran produced no literature until the days of the Muslim conquest, but what was otherwise revealed there shows that Greek learning had been at work in some of the Semitic centres of the Near East for a considerable length of time, and that not all of its offspring were impeccably Hellenic.

The Christian embrace of scholastic Platonism of the type prevalent in the schools from Porphyry to Proclus was hesitant and, in the end, indirect. The Neoplatonists were among the severest intellectual critics of Christianity, and neither the polemics of Porphyry, the attempts at a Neoplatonic revival by Julian nor the theurgic pieties of Proclus reassured the Christian intellectual that there was some common ground between Jerusalem and Athens. The revival of the doctrines of Origen on the pre-existence of the soul and the controversies they provoked in the sixth century A.D. made the Christian theologians even more cautious on the subject of Plato – and that, paradoxically, when a major piece of Neoplatonic metaphysics was beginning to circulate in the East under the name of Dionysius the Areopagite.

Origenism was, however, a theological diversion in the sixth century. The central issue continued to be the Christological debate begun in the previous decades and inflamed, not settled, by the decisions of the two councils at Ephesus in A.D. 431 and 449 and that at Chalcedon in 451. The fathers assembled at Chalcedon had condemned Monophysitism, but by the mid sixth century both Egypt and Syria were largely Monophysitic in their sympathies and conviction. The great ideologue of the sect was Severus of Antioch (d. 538), but their great strength lay in the labours of missionaries, not theologians, men like Jacob Baradai (d. 578), who, through the friendly influence of the Empress Theodora, was consecrated bishop of Edessa and, in the years that followed, almost singlehandedly reconstituted the sore-pressed Monophysite hierarchy in the East.

Severus was a theologian of some subtlety, and the Christological controversy itself was intricately interwoven with semantic considerations. The Chalcedonians, Monophysites and Nestorians were engaged, as none of their predecessors, in a *bellum lexicographicum* fought over the meanings of substance, nature, person and *hypostasis*. The terms had arisen gradually into view since Nicea, but by A.D. 500 none could follow the turnings of the polemic without considerable instruction in what had unexpectedly come to be the handbook to the theological warfare, the *Organon* of Aristotle.

The theologians of Antioch may have been the first to lay their hands on the new weapons, and because they were primarily exegetes rather than metaphysicians in the Alexandrian style, they found the logical Aristotle of more use than the theologian Plato. The primary exegete of the Antiochene school, "the Interpreter" par excellence, was Theodore of Mopsuestia (d. A.D. 428). His approach to Scripture was carefully literal and historical, and his exegetical instruments were dialectical in the manner of Aristotle rather than allegorical in the style of Plato and the later Platonists.

Whatever the judgments about Theodore's own orthodoxy, he held for the East Syrians the same position that he held at Antioch, that of the authoritative exegete of the Christian Scriptures. We do not know a great deal about theological instruction at Antioch, but it seems highly likely that during Theodore's lifetime, or in the century following, the training in Christian exegesis was preceded by some kind of instruction in Aristotelian logic, since the introduction of Theodore's works and methods into the Syriac-speaking school at Edessa was marked by the simultaneous appearance of the *Organon* in the curriculum there.

The school at Edessa, founded during the life-time of the famous Ephraim the Syrian (d. A.D. 373), was the centre for higher theological studies among the Aramaic Christians of the East, both those within the borders of the Roman Empire and those farther east under the rule of the Sassanian shahs. During the first half of the fifth century A.D. instruction at Edessa was closely tied to the theology of Antioch, and it was during that period that the works of Theodore were translated into Syriac and made the basis of the programme of studies. It was then too that Proba, one of Theodore's translators, turned his hand to the Aristotelian logic. Parts of his Syriac translations of Porphyry's *Eisagoge* and Aristotle's *On Interpretation* and *Prior Analytics* have been preserved, and the *Categories* too must have come into Syriac at that time.

In A.D. 431 the Council of Ephesus condemned the Christology of Theodore's student Nestorius. The notorious connection of the Edessan faculty both with Nestorius and with Antioch began to create problems with the ecclesiastical authorities in Syria at this time, and particularly when Hiba, the great champion of Theodore of Mopsuestia, was promoted to the bishopric of Edessa in A.D. 435. Hiba's power and prestige protected the school until his death in 457, but thereafter the faculty at Edessa, still faithful to the Antiochene tradition, was discomforted by the rising tide of Monophysitism, until in 489 the Emperor Zeno ordered the school to be closed for good.

Even before the final closure, some of the faculty at Edessa had begun to migrate to the friendlier atmosphere of the Shah's territories to the east. They included Narsai, who had been the director at Edessa for twenty years, and who, some time after 471, crossed the frontier to Nisibis and opened there a new school, or rather a continuation of the old school in a new location. In the genuine Antiochene and Edessan tradition, the scholarch was also "the Interpreter". But if exegesis was the principal concern of the school, it was undergirded by instruction in the elements of writing, including the copying of manuscripts, and in reading the Scriptures of Syriac-speaking Christianity.

It is difficult to draw many conclusions about the substance of the curriculum at Nisibis except that it was, on the face of it, resolutely theological. There are, however, some occasional illuminations. One is the work of a Syrian called "Paul the Persian" in the Byzantine sources. This Paul debated with a Manichaean in Constantinople in A.D. 527, and later wrote for Junilius, the Quaestor of the Sacred Palace, a Greek version of the hermeneutical textbook used at Nisibis. This *Parts of the Divine Law* shows the now close relationship between the Antioch–Edessa–Nisibis exegetical tradition on one hand and the Aristotelian logic on the other. The first part is quite simply the adaptation of a Porphyrian–Aristotelian "how to approach the study of a book" to the reading of the Bible; the terminology is lifted directly from the early Syriac translation of *On Interpretation*.

The second section of the *Parts of the Divine Laws* lays down in a didactic manner the theological principles underlying the study of Scripture: God, His essence and power; the Divine Names; creation and providence; the present world, its creation and governance; an analysis of free will and its works; and, finally, the world to come. Again, the method is scholastic and Aristotelian, and the resemblance to what Muslim theologians would be discussing in the eighth century A.D. is no less striking.

In the sixth century A.D. the school of Nisibis fell upon hard days. In 540 one of its teaching staff, Mar Aba (d. 557), was named Nestorian Catholicos or patriarch at the Sassanian capital of Seleucia-Ctesiphon, but the promise of the event came to nothing when Khusraw Anūshīrvān closed down the school and shortly afterwards sent the new Catholicos into exile. What occurred instead is that Christian physicians began appearing in Sassanian court circles, and when Nisibis was eventually reopened it boasted a new medical faculty.

The last great director at Nisibis was Henana, who after a stormy thirty-year career as "the Interpreter", led the bulk of his students and faculty out of Nisibis and into a form of self-imposed exile. This occurred about A.D. 600, and the school never recovered. The immediate cause of the dispute was Henana's attempts at replacing Theodore of Mopsuestia and the Antiochene exegetical tradition with something palpably more Alexandrian and Platonic, a position that struck many of his Nestorian contemporaries as tantamount to betraying their Christology to the Monophysites.

By Henana's day Aristotelian logic was thoroughly domesticated in Syriac and was a hallmark of the education shared by the Christian exegetes and theologians who constituted the east Syrian intelligentsia. The study of medicine was likewise flourishing. The Alexandrian medical school curriculum was translated into Syriac at the beginning of the sixth century by the west Syrians and must already have been in use at what was emerging as the Nestorians' chief medical centre at Jundishapur in

Khuzistan in Persia. The material was Hellenic and Hellenistic, but its study did not necessarily imply a knowledge of Greek. The only east Syrian churchman of the sixth century who is credited with a knowledge of Greek is Mar Aba, who was educated at Nisibis but had to return to Byzantine Edessa to learn Greek.

SELECT BIBLIOGRAPHY

Baumstark, A. (1900) *Aristoteles bei den Syrern von V–VIII Jahrhundert* (Leipzig).
Bergsträsser, G. (1913) *Ḥunain ibn Ishaq und seine Schule* (Leiden).
Endress, G. (1973) *Proclus arabus* (Beirut).
Galen (1951) *Compendium Timaei Platonis aliorumque dialogorum synopsis quae extant fragmenta*, ed. P. Kraus and R. Walzer (London).
Gätje, H. (1971) *Studien zu Überlieferung der aristotelischen Psychologie im Islam* (Heidelberg).
Georr, K. (ed.) (1984) *Les Catégories d'Aristote dans leurs versions syro-arabes* (Beirut).
Greene, T. (1992) *The City of the Moon God* (Leiden).
Gutas, D. (1975) *Greek Wisdom Literature in Arabic Translation* (New Haven).
Horovitz, S. (1903) "Über den Einfluss des Stoizismus auf die Entwicklung der Philosophie bei den Arabern", *Zeitschrift der deutschen morgenländischen Gesellschaft*, 57: 177–96.
Kraus, P. (1941) "Plotin chez les arabes", *Bulletin de l'Institut d'Egypte*, 22: 263–95.
Makdour, I. (1934) *L'Organon d'Aristote dans le monde arabe, ses traductions, son étude et ses applications* (Paris).
Meyerhof, M. (1930) *Von Alexandrien nach Bagdad: ein Beitrag zur Geschichte des philosophischen und medizinischen Unterrichts bei den Arabern* (Berlin).
Peters, F. (1968) *Aristotle and the Arabs: the Aristotelian Tradition in Islam* (Albany).
—— (1979) "The Origins of Islamic Platonism: The School Tradition", in P. Morewedge (ed.), *Islamic Philosophical Theology* (Albany): 14–45.
—— (1990) "Hermes and Harran: The Roots of Arabic–Islamic Occultism", in M. Mazzaoui and V. Moreen (eds) *Intellectual Studies on Islam* (Salt Lake City): 185–218.
Pines, S. (1986) *Studies in the Arabic Version of Greek Texts and in Mediaeval Science* (Jerusalem).
Rosenthal, F. (1992) *The Classical Heritage in Islam* (London).
Schacht, J. (1936) "Über den Hellenismus in Bagdad und Cairo im 11. Jahrhundert", *Zeitschrift der deutschen morgenländischen Gesellschaft*, 90: 526–45.
Steinschneider, M. (1960) *Die arabischen Übersetzungen aus dem Griechischen* (Graz).
Walzer, R. (ed.) (1952) *Plato arabus* (London).
—— (1962) *Greek into Arabic: Essays on Islamic Philosophy* (Oxford).

CHAPTER 4

The Indian and Persian background

Syed Nomanul Haq

The phenomenon of the transmission of Indian and Persian ideas into the world of Islam and their influence upon Islamic thought constitutes an immensely complicated problem for the historian. To begin with, an exchange of ideas had existed between India and Persia long before the rise of Islam.[1] Among other things, this process consisted in a doctrinal blending and therefore much modification, even transformation, of the ideas of the one by the local traditions of the other. Then, both India and Persia had come variously under Hellenistic influence. And this meant that many ultimately Greek notions and systems had reached India and Persia not from the Near Eastern centres of Hellenistic learning but indirectly from each other after having undergone local treatments. But at the same time, to make the situation even more intractable, both India and Persia had also received Greek ideas directly, by means of translations of authentic Greek texts.[2] All this gave rise to a highly intricate intellectual complex of what may be called the pre-Islamic Perso-Indian ethos, and it is this complex which was subsequently inherited by Islam.

Again, in the formative phases of Islam's own philosophical and scientific tradition ideas were flowing into it from a multiplicity of sources, and here the complications of the situation were further compounded. When Alexandria fell in 21/641, the Arab conquest of the Near East was virtually complete, and with this came the legacy of many Hellenized academies that had variously flourished during the first six centuries of the Christian era. Among them were the powerful seats of Syriac learning that had existed in Edessa (al-Ruhā', modern Urfa east of the upper Euphrates),[3] Nisibis (near the upper Tigris, north-west of Mosul),[4] Resain (Ra's al-'Ayn, Theodosiopolis),[5] Kinnesrin (Qinnasrīn),[6] Homs and Baalbek (Heliopolis). Also gained by Muslims was the important centre of Ḥarrān (Classical Carrhae), which lay a short distance south of Edessa. Ḥarrān was primarily a locality of star worshippers which perpetuated an indigenous religion and influences from far in the East – these influences, it is important to note, included also those received from India.[7]

But this represents only part of what the Muslims inherited. In 651 the last Sassanian shah died and Persia came completely into the expanding fold of Islam. Some fifteen years later, Muslim armies crossed the river Oxus, and by 95/713 Sind and Transoxiana were being ruled by Damascus. These cultural areas now contributed additional elements to a developing intellectual matrix of Islam. One of the most important elements from our point of view was that provided by the academy at Jundishapur in southern Persia which reached its zenith around the middle of the sixth century A.D. during the reign of Anūshīrvān. Continuing to flourish long after the Islamic conquest, Jundishapur had become a cradle of intellectual activity when in A.D. 489 Emperor Zeno closed the academy of Edessa and some fleeing Nestorian scholars found in the Persian ruler a hospitable and enthusiastic host. Settling first at Nisibis, some of these Hellenized scholars later joined Jundishapur. Then, in 529 the Neoplatonic school at Athens too was closed by a decree of Emperor Justinian and, again, sacked scholars took refuge in Persia. Thus, with its elaborate hospital and enormous academic resources, Jundishapur came to function as the hub of exchange for the learning of Persia, Greece, Rome, Syria and, significantly, that of India. Indeed, reports have it that it actually housed a number of Indian sages.[8]

Given this complex multiplicity of channels through which foreign ideas were travelling into the early world of Islam, and given the intellectual exchanges that had taken place within these channels whereby many indigenous ideas had been modified, integrated and transformed, it seems hardly possible to provide a simple and neat account of the role of Indian and Persian ideas in the development of Islamic thought. In fact, the problem is rendered even more difficult by the fact that Arabic translations of Sanskrit, Pahlavi and Syriac texts were carried out during the earliest phase of Islamic intellectual history, a phase at the end of which translators had directed their attention almost wholly to Greek works. These earliest translations have barely survived; likewise only fragments of some of the writings of the earliest Muslim thinkers have come down to us. Moreover, much of what has survived still lies unstudied in manuscripts in various libraries of the world. It seems, then, that the best one can accomplish at this stage of modern scholarship is a tentative and somewhat disjointed exposition based largely on later Arabic sources and secondary accounts, an exposition making no pretensions to a definitive grand picture.

Contemporary scholars have for some time been speaking about Indian influences upon the cosmological doctrines of *kalām*, the non-

Aristotelian atomistic philosophical tradition of Islam, often somewhat misleadingly dubbed Islamic scholastic theology. Having been introduced into modern scholarship by Schmölders in the 1840s,[9] the question of Indian influence upon *kalām* has received many scholarly treatments since. In fact some fifty years after Schmölders, the French historian Mabilleau could feel so confident as to declare that the entire doctrine of *kalām* atomism had come from India.[10] And, in an atmosphere where Goldziher was receiving tributes for seeing the whole Sufi tradition as a shadow of Buddhism,[11] Horten "tried to paste Indian labels on all kinds of *kalām* views"[12] – something that elicited the censure of Massignon, who remarked that Horton was making sweeping claims on the basis merely of "isolated coincidences".[13]

But a somewhat narrower and qualified view was expressed in 1928 by Macdonald, who claimed only that *some* aspects of *kalām* atomism show Indian influences.[14] He pointed out that the Indian Buddhist school of Sautrāntikas (originated in the first or second century B.C.) held a doctrine of time atomism, namely that time is not infinitely divisible but rather consisted ultimately of discrete atomic moments which cannot be further divided.[15] Macdonald placed against this doctrine the report of the *faylasūf* Maimonides (d. 601/1204) that the *mutakallimūn* (espousers of *kalām*, sing. *mutakallim*) believed that "time consists of moments (*ānāt*); this means that time consists of a great many 'times' which cannot be further divided".[16] Given that a developed theory of time atomism was not to be found in the Greek tradition, argued Macdonald, the *mutakallimūn* must have borrowed their doctrine from the Buddhists. Indeed, a learned support for this conclusion came in 1936 from Pines, who spoke also of the influences on *kalām* of the Indian atomistic cosmology of Jainism (originated *c.* sixth century B.C.) as well as that of the Brahmanic Nyāya-Vaiśeṣka (originated *c.* third century B.C.).[17]

But, in view of the problem's intricacies which we have already noted, it is hardly surprising that later scholarship found reasons to disagree with these conclusions.[18] First, there is no clear evidence that Indian philosophical texts expounding atomistic doctrines were available to early *mutakallimūn*. What was, then, the channel of transmission? No doubt one does find in *kalām* writings references to an Indian philosophical fraternity "Samaniyyah", but there still seems to be no agreement among historians as to who these Samaniyyah were.[19] References are found also to "Brāhimah"; again, scholars have hesitated to identify these Brāhimah simplistically with the Indian Brahmans.[20] Besides, in neither case is the context of these references atomistic. More important, however, is the recent discovery of some primary *kalām* texts which were unknown to earlier historians such as Pines.[21] Warranting a revision of many earlier views which were based perforce on secondary Arabic sources, these discovered texts provide no direct evidence that the early *mutakallimūn* did believe in time atomism.[22] Indeed, Maimonides himself had only *inferred* logically on the basis of an Aristotelian analysis of motion that the *mutakallimūn* must have "of necessity" believed in time atomism.[23] Similarly, significant differences have now been shown to exist between the specific features of *kalām* atomism and that of both Greek and Indian atomism;[24] therefore, this whole problem needs to be examined afresh. At this juncture now rests the question of a direct Indian influence on the *mutakallimūn*.

It should be pointed out, however, that there does exist unmistakable evidence of some knowledge of Indian philosophical thought on the part of early Arabic writers. For example, in the *Kitāb Sirr al-khalīqah* attributed to Balīnās (pseudo-Apollonius of Tyana, the Neopythagorean sage of the first century A.D.),[25] an early source that has played a fundamental role in much of Islam's alchemical tradition, one finds a refutation of the views of the "Brahman" concerning the attributes of God. Thus the author of the *Sirr* tells us that

> the Brahman[s] say: "the Creator [*al-Khāliq*] is Light [*Nūr*], unlike the lights [*anwār*] seen by the eye; for He is Light, and He is All-Knowing [*'Alīm*], All-Hearing [*Samī'*], All-Seeing [*Baṣīr*], All-Powerful [*Qadīr*]." They say to us: "You, the people of Byzantine, worship only a name, for you know not what this name means!"[26]

These views are then vehemently dismissed, and in this dismissal a favourable rhetorical reference is made to the Buddha (al-Budd).[27] Evidently, it is not easy to identify these "Brahmans" in a definitive manner, and yet it seems plausible that the reported views were derived from the doctrines of classical Vedic philosophy. We recall that the *Upaniṣads*, a corpus of metaphysical dialogues written as commentaries on the *Vedas* (*Vedāntas*), go beyond the idea of anthropomorphic deities and speak of one All-Transcending principle from which all else proceeds, something that led to the doctrine of non-duality in Indian philosophy.[28] Therefore to say that God is Light which is unlike the lights of the corporeal world is to remain consistent with the metaphysical thrust of the *Upaniṣads*.

Similarly in the *Book of Treasures* of al-Ma'mūn's physician Job of Edessa (Ayyūb al-Ruhāwī, *fl. c.* 203/817)[29] there are references to unnamed Indian sages and their medical and cosmological ideas. But in this case some of these sages have indeed been clearly identified with historical Indian figures, such as the great medical authority Caraka of Kashmir (second century A.D.), and the famous physician of an earlier period, Suśruta.[30] References to these and other Indian medical authorities are found also in the *Firdaws al-ḥikmah* of Ibn Sahl Rabban al-Ṭabarī (d. *c.* 247/861) who in addition speaks of an interesting Indian cosmological theory of elements.[31] Yet, from the point of view of the discipline of philosophy, and notwithstanding the familiarity of the Muslims with Sanskrit medical texts, the Indian cosmological ideas referred to by these two authors cannot clearly be demonstrated to have played any direct role in determining the character of Islamic cosmological theories.[32]

What is clear, however, is the role of Persian dualism in the formation of certain fundamental cosmological and theological doctrines of *kalām*. To be sure, there exists overwhelming evidence of an early contact between the *mutakallimūn* and the Manichaean dualists of Persia, something that generated much polemical *kalām* literature against dualist ideas. Thus we read in the *Kitāb al-Aghānī* of Abu'l-Faraj al-Iṣfahānī (d. 357/957) that some students of the grand patriarch of *kalām*, al-Ḥasan al-Baṣrī (d. 110/728), held discussions with those who were accused of espousing Manichaeism[33] – evidence that an active contact with the dualists was established already during the earliest formative period of *kalām*. Indeed, many *kalām* accounts of dualist cosmology are recorded by, among others, the *mutakallimūn* 'Abd al-Jabbār (d. 415/1025)[34] and al-Māturīdī (d. 331/942),[35] the bio-bibliographer Ibn al-Nadīm (d. 385/995),[36] and the heresiographer al-Shahrastānī (d. 548/1153).[37] At the same time, Muslim historians and bibliographers have consistently told us of Arabic translations of Manichaean tracts, and these included, they report, the books of Mānī himself.[38]

The interest of the *mutakallimūn* in dualism and their contacts with Persian dualists should hardly surprise us. Historically, this situation seems inevitable since Muslim conquerers had inherited a sizeable Manichaean population within their expanding borders. And, philosophically, it makes much sense given the *mutakallimūn*'s intense preoccupation with the problem of causality. The Manichaean doctrine that light and darkness were both active and alive principles, that both had a will and were capable of causing real phenomena, and that both had a nature which restricted the former from producing evil and the latter from producing good – all this stood in fundamental conflict with certain essential premisses of *kalām* doctrines.

Indeed, the *mutakallimūn* had in general rejected the notion of natural causation,[39] namely that things have "natures" which cause them necessarily to be, or to behave, always in a certain way. For the *mutakallimūn* the characteristics of corporeal bodies did not arise out of any "nature" or inalienable permanent qualities; rather, these characteristics were both logically and physically reducible to atoms and accidents created by God, the only Active Agent (*'Āmil, Fa''āl*).[40] Indeed, the sole Regulator, Sustainer and the Cause of the cosmos was God, not the principle of light or darkness, nor any other entity. Evidently, dualism had threatened the very foundation of *kalām*; therefore it is small wonder that there arose an enormous body of Arabic philosophical literature aimed at refuting the doctrines of Persian Manichaeans. In fact the term *jawhar* which the *mutakallimūn* frequently used for their atom was itself an Arabicization of the Persian word *gawhar*.

But it was not only for the sake of defending their own views that the *mutakallimūn* subjected dualism to such feverish critical examination. To be sure, there existed also a positive aspect to their enterprise, namely an active search for a coherent doctrine of primary constituents of things, a doctrine that would comprehensively explain the qualitative and quantitative characteristics of the corporeal world, including the phenomenon of motion and change.[41] Much relevant material was provided to this search by the dualist cosmological literature; and this included not only Manichaean writings but also those derived from the teachings of the Aramaic philosopher Bardaiṣan (d. A.D. 222)[42] and the Christian heretic Marcion (*fl. c.* A.D. 140).[43] This material seems to have played a fundamentally important role in the articulation and crystallization of *kalām* cosmology.

There is in addition a theological aspect to the *mutakallimūn*'s preoccupation with Manichaeism. It is known that many dualist texts written within the early Islamic empire had attacked some of the basic tenets of Islam such as prophecy and revelation; effectively, this constituted an attack both on the Prophet and on the Qur'ān.[44] What was shocking to the sensibilities of Islamic piety was the fact that some authors of these texts were professed Muslims. Among them was the well-known Persian convert to Islam, 'Abd Allāh ibn al-Muqaffa'[45] – the writer of model Arabic prose to whom we owe, besides much else, the ever-fresh Arabic translation from Pahlavi of the tales of the Indian sage Bidpai, *Kalīlah wa Dimnah*. Ibn al-Muqaffa''s life came to an abrupt and tragic end when, like numerous others who were considered to have concealed old Persian religious ideas under the veil of Islam, he was put to death in 139/776 on the charge of this specific kind of "heresy" called *zandaqah*.[46] The works of the *zanādiqah* (sing. *zindīq*, the one who commits *zandaqah*) were certainly known to early *mutakallimūn*, who wrote powerful refutations in response.[47] In fact, the *mutakallimūn*'s involvement in the issue was so well recognized that the first 'Abbāsid caliphs actually recruited some of them in the official crusade launched in the second/eighth century against these *zanādiqah*.[48] It is highly probable, then, that much of the early *kalām* literature on reason and revelation, on God's creation *ex nihilo*, on His justice and His attributes, were all shaped by Manichaean attacks on these fundamental theological notions of Islam.

Attacks on the notion of prophecy and revelation came also from some freethinking individuals of the early period of Islam's intellectual history. Among them is the outstanding Persian alchemist and physician from Rayy, Abū Bakr al-Rāzī (d. 313/925), the celebrated Rhazes of the Latin West.[49] Rāzī's dismissal of the necessity of prophecy, however, was not directed specifically against Islam; rather it was a general rejection of the necessity of all prophets who professed revealed knowledge. Thus in his *Tricks of the Prophets* he rejects the necessity of not only the prophets of the three monotheistic religions but also the dualist Mānī.[50] Rāzī's religious nonconformism is further manifested by his belief in the transmigration of the soul. But he was a philosophical nonconformist too, a non-Aristotelian in his belief in an atomic constitution of matter; and in his doctrine of absolute space which he thought of as pure extension, and of absolute time which he called eternity (*dahr*).[51] Again, as opposed to Aristotelians, Rāzī believed in the temporal creation of the world and posited in his cosmogony five pre-eternal principles: Creator (*al-Bārī'*), Soul (*al-nafs*), Matter (*al-hayūlā'*), Time (*al-dahr*) and Space (*al-makān*).[52]

What was the source of Rāzī's daring ideas? Scholars generally claim that he drew much of his philosophy from the non-Islamic Perso-Indian ethos. This is a plausible claim, particularly in view of the fact that the greatest Muslim authority on India, al-Bīrūnī (d. 440/1048), had a great deal of interest in this freethinker, painstakingly preparing an extensive bibliography of his writings.[53] Al-Bīrūnī speaks also of one Abu'l-'Abbas al-Īrānshahrī, a Persian, whom he considers practically the only scholar of the Islamic world to give an objective account of the religious beliefs of the Indians.[54] While no writings of this Īrānshahrī have come down to us, he is mentioned by one other source, the Persian Ismā'īlī author Nāṣir-i Khusraw (d. 481/1088), who quotes Īrānshahrī and reports that Rāzī was associated with him and that it was Īrānshahrī from whom Rāzī took his idea of matter, space and time.[55] Indeed, concerning Rāzī's familiarity with Manichaeism there is no doubt since he explicitly cites the writings of Mānī. As for his knowledge of Indian philosophy, it has been pointed out that both his atomism and his concept of the five pre-eternal principles show a striking resemblance to the system of Nyāya-Vaiśeṣka[56] – and this may have been the result of his learning from Īrānshahrī.

But this claim can be only tentative, since we have no direct evidence at hand, and since Rāzī's own perception of himself was that he was a disciple of Plato.[57] Further, one cannot here rule out the possibility of a heavy dependence upon Harranian sources, for in his historical work *Kitāb al-shawāhid* ("Book of Testimonies") the authority most quoted by Rāzī is one Sālim al-Ḥarrānī.[58] And as for the resemblance between certain features of Rāzī's ideas and those found in the Nyāya-Vaiśeṣka system, a resemblance there evidently is, but the two still remain profoundly dissimilar in their fundamental drift. Thus one wonders if this resemblance between certain elements of the two is not an isolated phenomenon. The most important thing, however, is to note that the philosophical views of the great Persian physician do *not* represent a trend or a tradition in Islamic thought: he was an individual free spirit, a solitary figure who "had to pay the classic price for his intellectual boldness: the consignment of most of his literary output to oblivion".[59]

Concerning the rich and enduring *falsafah* tradition of Islam, something that has typically been considered by Western scholarship virtually to be the sole expression of Islamic philosophy, it is a tradition which postdates *kalām*. In fact the dates of the first representative of this tradition, "the Philosopher of the Arabs" al-Kindī (b. mid third/ninth century), practically coincide with those of the aggressive and highly systematic translation activity in the Bayt al-Ḥikmah – and at this centre the interests of prolific translators had quickly and systematically shifted almost exclusively to Greek texts. The *falsafah* tradition, to which some towering giants belonged, received its fundamental inspiration from the translated Greek works, remained committed to Aristotelian logic, operated in the framework of Neoplatonic metaphysics, and held the *mutakallimūn* in intellectual contempt. If these Hellenized personages such as al-Kindī, al-Fārābī (d. 339/950) and Ibn Sīnā (d. 429/1037) – known in the Islamic tradition as the *falāsifah* (sing. *faylasūf*) – are the only representatives of Islamic speculative philosophy, then the pre-Islamic Perso-Indian tradition would appear not to have played an important role in the intellectual history of Islam although even here Indian sources have been posited by some scholars for some of Ibn Sīnā's visionary recitals, and Suhrawardī's *ishrāqī* doctrines draw heavily from ancient Persian sources.

If we now finally move from the discipline of philosophy to that of the natural sciences, medicine and mathematics, the picture becomes much clearer and definitive, thanks to the critical researches of some recent scholars.[60] Here, particularly in the case of astronomy, we are now in a position to trace the myriad historical channels through which the Perso-Indian tradition had reached early Islam; equally, we are now able to demonstrate the role which this tradition played as one of the essential elements determining the very course of the Islamic exact sciences. But here we are outside the domain of philosophy proper, and therefore only a summary account is warranted. An account must be given none the less, since the two disciplines of science and speculative philosophy were frequently integrated in the mind of one and the same individual, and since one discipline had implications for the other.

One can identify in the Islamic astronomical tradition, to take one of the best studied areas first,[61] three distinct elements which determined the course of its development. The first, and chronologically the earliest, element was provided by Arabic translations and adaptations in the second/eighth century of Sanskrit and Pahlavi texts. This introduced into the world of Islam some concepts of Greek mathematical astronomy, concepts which were largely non-Ptolemaic altered in one way or another by the local traditions of Persia and India. The Greco-Syrian and Byzantine astronomical traditions, the former being partially Ptolemaic and the latter entirely Ptolemaic, constitute the second element reaching Islam in the late second/early ninth century. But these two traditions, we pause to note, were themselves not altogether independent of India and Persia. Finally, the third element came from the general availability in Arabic renderings of the works of Ptolemy himself whose *Almagest* was first translated, presumably from a Syriac version, under the patronage of the Persian Barmak family during the reign of Hārūn al-Rashīd (170/786–194/809). "This led to the development in Islam," we learn from Pingree, "of a mathematical astronomy that was essentially Ptolemaic, but in which new parameters were introduced and new solutions to problems in spherical trigonometry derived from India tended to replace those of the *Almagest*."[62]

A word ought be said in elaboration, since here we have a case that illustrates the process of a curious blending of ideas, something of which we spoke in the beginning of this chapter. Long before the rise of Islam, Persians had become familiar not only with the *Almagest* but also with Greek and Indian astrological texts through translations sponsored by the earliest Sassanian rulers Ardashīr I (A.D. 226–41) and Shāpūr I (A.D. 241–72). Around the middle of the fifth century A.D., a set of royal astronomical tables, the fateful *Zīk-i shahryārān*, were composed. This *zīk* (astronomical tables; Arabic *zīj*) incorporated some parameters of the Indian Brāhmapakṣa school which had come into being in the fifth century, and which had itself integrated some Greek material. A century later, the Sassanian Shah Anūshīrvān ordered a comparison of the *Almagest* with an Indian text called in Arabic *Zīj al-arkand* (*arkand* being an Arabic corruption of Sanskrit *ahargaṇa*) belonging to the partially Hellenized Ārdharātrikapakṣa school of the fifth century. This resulted in a new redaction of the *Zīk-i shahryārān*, and this was known to Arabic writers. Finally, during the reign of the last Sassanian monarch Yazdigird another version of *Zīk-i shahryārān* was made, once again combining Persian, Greek and Indian elements; again, this too was known in the Islamic world.[63]

It is clear that Indian texts constituted the proximate source of the earliest Islamic astronomical works. Thus we have the *Zīj al-arkand* written in 117/735 in Sind essentially on the basis of the *Khaṇḍakhādyaka* composed by Brahmagupta in 665. Not long after, two other sets of tables were composed – the *Zīj al-jāmiʿ* and *Zīj al-hazūr*, both deriving from the *Arkand*. Then, in 125/742 we got the *Zīj al-harqan*, again combining Persian and Indian material including that found in the *Āryabhaṭīya* of Āryabhaṭa (b. 476).[64] Then, during the reigns of al-Manṣūr (137/754–159/775) and Hārūn al-Rashīd more Indian material was infused, and this was accompanied by Arabic translations of the *Zīk-i shahryārān* (*Zīj al-shāh*) and of the works of Ptolemy. The Indian material was provided by the translation of a Sanskrit text related to the Brāhmapakṣa school, apparently bearing the title *Mahāsiddhānta* and dependent on the

Brāhmasphuṭasiddhānta of Brahmagupta written in 628. Thus came into being the *Zīj al-sindhind al-kabīr*, a text that combines various Indian elements with those derived from Ptolemy as well as from *Zīj al-shāh* and other Persian sources; and this introduced a distinct *Sindhind* tradition in early Islamic astronomy.[65]

It would appear, then, that the role of the Perso-Indian tradition in the development of Islamic astronomy looms large. Indeed, a very large number of early astronomers of Islam were Persians – al-Nawbakht al-Fārisī, Ibn al-Farrukhān al-Ṭabarī, Māshā' Allāh, all of whom were associated with the court of al-Manṣūr; and Yaḥyā ibn Abī Manṣūr and Ibn Mūsā al-Khwārazmī, the astronomers working under al-Ma'mūn (198/813–218/833); these are only some of the significant Persian figures of the period. As for the Indians who actually worked in the Islamic world, Ibn al-Nadīm names Manka (or Kanka),[66] Ibn Dahn,[67] Jūdar,[68] Ṣanjahil,[69] and Naq[70] – none of these is reported to be a speculative philosopher; rather, we are told that they were translators of Sanskrit astronomical, astrological and medical works. In fact Manka is generally recognized as a member of the Indian embassy which brought the *Mahāsiddhānta* to al-Manṣūr.[71]

The role of India and Persia in the field of medicine and mathematics is, again, clear and significant. Ibn al-Nadīm and other Muslim sources list early Arabic translations of the works of a large number of Indian medical authorities including Suśruta, Caraka and Vagbhaṭa (a Buddhist of no later than the third/ninth century);[72] added in these lists are also several Indian medical texts of unnamed authors, for example, *Sundastāq*; the *Book of Rūsā*; *Book of Indian Drugs*;[73] etc. In fact, the translation of one Indian medical texts is actually preserved, namely, *Kitāb Shānāq fī sumūm wa'l-tariyāq* ("Book of Chānakya [third century B.C.] on Poisons and Antidotes").[74] But it seems that most of these works were translated from Pahlavi versions – and here the contribution of Jundishapur is paramount.

From the beginning Jundishapur provided the Muslim caliphs with loyal and able physicians,[75] such as the Nestorian family of Bukhtishū', whose earliest representative at the court of al-Manṣūr, Georgius ibn Jibra'īl, was the head of the medical school at Jundishapur and was instrumental in the establishment of the first hospital in Baghdad.[76] Indeed, it is said that the very first translator of Syriac medical texts into Arabic was none other than a Persian from Jundishapur, the physician Māsarjawayh (*fl. c.* first half of second/eighth century).[77] Representing the character of his school, Māsarjawayh's own Arabic medical works expressly blend Greek, Indian and Persian material.[78] But contacts with Jundishapur seem to have been established as early as the birth of Islamic society itself, for the medical historian Ibn Abī Uṣaybi'ah (d. 669/1270) reports in detail the activities in that school of al-Ḥārith ibn Kaladah, an elder contemporary of the Prophet.[79] Finally, we recall another venerable physician from Jundishapur, Yuḥannā ibn Māsawayah (d. 243/857), the first head of the celebrated Bayt al-Ḥikmah during the reign of al-Ma'mūn, and the teacher of the greatest translator of Islam, the Nestorian Christian Ḥunayn ibn Isḥāq (d. 264/877).[80]

The contribution of Indian quantitative techniques in the development of the mathematical tradition of Islam is a relatively well-known phenomenon. Indeed, this is effectively recognized by everyone who speaks of "Arabic numerals" – the numerals 1 to 9 and 0 functioning in a decimal place-value system. These are, in fact, *Indian* numerals systematically introduced to the world of science by a Persian: the outstanding mathematician and astronomer Muḥammad ibn Mūsā al-Khwārazmī (d. *c.* 233/847), a Muslim of Zoroastrian ancestry to whose Latinized name we owe the living term "algorism" (these days spelt "algorithm"). While it is certainly possible that al-Khwārazmī was not the first Muslim writer to have become familiar with the Indian place-value decimals, he does remain the first scientific figure to expound them systematically. Needless to say, his work was of seminal importance for the whole field of exact sciences; and here we ought to recognize an ultimate debt to India, even though al-Khwārazmī's proximate sources may well have been Pahlavi or Syriac.[81]

A brief word might be added concerning trigonometry. This subject, one can safely claim, is essentially a creation of the Islamic world[82] – but, once again, it is a creation in which the Indian background has played a fundamental role. The pre-Islamic proto-trigonometry, to give a highly simplified account, was based on a single function, the chord of an arbitrary circular arc. The Indians transformed the chord functions into varieties of the sine, and this marks a crucial stage in the birth of trigonometry. By the third/ninth century the mathematicians of the Islamic world had taken the sine function from India; then, for the next six centuries the new sine function and the old shadow functions (tangent, secant, etc.) were elaborately tabulated by them as sexagesimals. At the same time, Muslim mathematicians preoccupied themselves with enunciating a large number of theorems which freed their subject from dependence upon the complete quadrilateral, a feature of the Hellenistic proto-trigonometry due to the application of the theorem of Menelaus (*c.* first century A.D.).[83] "With this development," writes an expert, "the first real trigonometry emerged, in the sense that only then did the object of study become the spherical or plane *triangle*, its sides and angles."[84] It seems, then, that the Arabic knowledge of the Indian sine function (Sanskrit *ardhajya* (half chord) → Arabic *jyb* (*jayb*, pocket) → Latin *sinus* → English "sine") marks the turning point in the history of trigonometry.

But whatever Islam received from the Indian and Persian background, it was all transformed and assimilated into a new matrix that was characteristically Islamic. Transmitted ideas and systems functioned in this matrix in novel ways as integral elements of a distinct intellectual synthesis: it is this synthesis wherein lies the originality of Islamic thought. By the time Islamic philosophy crystallized into a fully developed and independent tradition, Persia had been totally absorbed into the framework of Islam. And while Sind was achieving its political and administrative freedom from the central caliphal authority, India once again became a mysterious, remote outpost. Al-Bīrūnī came too late to make a difference: "I find it very hard to work in the subject [of India]," he lamented, "although I have a great liking for it – but in this respect I stand quite alone in my time!"[85]

NOTES

1 The well-known fourth/tenth-century bio-bibliographer Ibn al-Nadīm, for example, tells us that the founder of the Sassanian dynasty Ardashīr I "sent to India and China for books in those directions . . . Shāpūr, his son, followed his example so that there were transcribed into Persian all of those books, such as those of . . . Ptolemy and Farmāsib the Indian" (Dodge, trans. (1970): 574). Indeed, the reliability of such accounts is borne out by overwhelming independent evidence. Cf. Ṭabarī (1879–90), 1: 1052–3, 10; Meyerhof (1937); Nasr (1975); Pingree (1973).

2 An illustrative example of this tangled web of transmission channels is to be found in Pingree's studies of the history of Islamic astronomy. See particularly Pingree (1973).

3 One recalls Caliph al-Mahdī's (158/775–169/785) chief astrologer Thawfil al-Rūmī (Theophilus of Edessa, d. 169/785) who not only knew Greek, Syriac and Arabic but was familiar also with Indian sources. Ayyūb al-Ruhāwī (Job of Edessa) was another important personage from this city; he too knew Indian sources (see below).

4 This was the home town of the famous bishop Severus Sebokht (*fl.* mid seventh century A.D.). He is said to have known Indian ("Arabic") numerals. See Pingree (1973): 35.

5 To this place belonged the great scholar Sergius (d. 536 A.D.) who translated Galen into Syriac (cf. Brunet and Mieli (1935): 880). It is believed that Sergius was responsible also for the Syriac version of Ptolemy's *Almagest*, and this was probably the version used by al-Ḥajjāj ibn Yūsuf (*fl.* 170/786–218/833) for his Arabic translation. See Pingree (1973): 34.

6 Severus Sebokht had settled here (see n. 4 above).

7 Ḥarrān is considered to have been the major agency for the transmission to Islam not only of Neopythagorean, Hermetic and Gnostic doctrines but also of indigenous Chaldaean notions and certain characteristically Chinese ideas. Ḥarrānians had styled themselves "Sabaeans" (Ṣābi'ūn) in the third/ninth century in the time of al-Ma'mūn to enjoy the privileges of the "People of the Book" (*Ahl-al-kitāb*), proclaiming themselves to be the Ṣābi'ūn mentioned in the Qur'ān (5: 72–3). Indian influences on Harrān are clearly evident from the accounts

found in pseudo-Majrīṭī's *Ghāyat al-ḥakīm* (composed 340s/950s; German trans. Ritter and Plessner 1962): there were similarities between the Ḥarrānian and Indian worship of planets, and the Sanskrit names of planets were known at Ḥarrān. See the classic study of Chwolson (1856); cf. Kraus (1942–3): 305ff.

8 See Meyerhof (1937): 22. For the history of Jundishapur see Yāqūt (1966–70), 2: 130; Campbell (1926), 2: 46; "Djundai-Sābūr," *Encyclopaedia of Islam*, new ed. (Leiden, 1960), 1: 1064.

9 Schmölders (1942).

10 Mabilleau (1895): 328ff.

11 See, e.g., Duka (1904).

12 Wolfson's remark (1976: 68) on Horten (1912).

13 Massignon (1912): 408.

14 Macdonald (1928).

15 Macdonald cited Jacobi (1910) as his authority. For the atomism of Sautrāntikas see Keith (1921); Pines (1936): 104–6.

16 In his *Guide of the Perplexed* (Pines, trans. (1963)), Maimonides gives a list of twelve fundamental propositions of the atomistic position of *kalām*. Macdonald (p. 10) quotes from the third proposition; I have only slightly changed his translation.

17 Pines (1936): 102–23. Cf. Radhakrishnan, ed. (1953): 139–51; 219–30.

18 For example, Wolfson was not sympathetic to Pines's views (see Wolfson (1976): 473ff.).

19 Thus Lang tells us that Classical Greek sources had adapted the Prakrit term *samaṇa*, "an ascetic", to refer to Buddhists as "Samanians"; and that this term excluded Brahmans (Lang (1957): 24). Concerning Arabic writers, he says: "Adapting, like the classical writers before them, the Indian term *samana*, usually used to designate a Buddhist ascetic, some of the Arabic authorities refer to the Buddha as the prophet of *samaniyya*" (*ibid*: 30; emphasis added). Lang does not cite any Arabic sources here; rather, he makes the statement on the authority of two of his colleagues (1957: 30; n. 1). Sachau in his introduction to al-Bīrūnī's *India* vocalizes the term as "Shamaniyya" which, he says, not only derived from the Indian term, but also from the Arabic *al-Muḥammarah*, i.e. the red-robed people (= *raktapaṭa*); this referred to the red-brown cloaks of the Buddhist monks (Sachau, trans. (1888): 261).

On the other hand, Dodge informs us that "*Shamanīya* [were] idolators of *Central Asia* who became *somewhat* influenced by Buddhism" (Dodge, trans. (1970), 2: 923; emphasis added). He cites Monier-Williams as his authority (Monier-Williams (1891): 75, 261–3). Schmölders traced the Samaniyyah to Chārvākas in India (Schmölders (1842): 114). Dhanani says only that the Samaniyyah were "an Indian group which espoused skepticism and therefore denied the possibility of any knowledge beyond that derived from the senses" (Dhanani (1991): 47; cf. Vajda (1937)). Finally, it is interesting to note that the historian Ḥamzah al-Iṣfahānī (d. 356/957) mentions the view that in the most ancient times humanity was of one kind but distinguished by the name *Samāniyyūn* in the East and *Kaldāniyyūn* in the West (Gottwaldt, ed. and trans. (1844–8): 5).

20 Paul Kraus was of the opinion that it was the renegade *mutakallim* Ibn al-Rāwandī's (d. mid third/ninth century) *Kitāb al-Zumurrud* which served as the

source for the Arabic writers' view that the "Brāhimah" reject prophecy on account of the supremacy and sufficiency of the human intellect; and that "Brāhimah" was a mere invention of Ibn al-Rāwandī meant to disguise views which were his own (Kraus 1933, 1934). A recent scholar, Stroumsa, however, disagrees with Kraus, arguing that the views attributed to "Brāhimah" are genuinely Indian and were known to early *mutakallimūn* (Stroumsa 1985).

21 A recent study of *kalām* atomism is Dhanani (1991) which takes into account these newly discovered texts. I draw heavily upon this study.

22 Dhanani (1991): 259.

23 In his third proposition Maimonides says (see n. 16 above): "This premise is . . . necessary for them because of the first premise [namely, that all corporeal bodies are made up of atoms]. That is to say, they must have seen Aristotle's demonstration in which he had demonstrated that distance, time and motion are all three of them equivalent with respect to existence. I mean that the relationship of each of them to the other is the same and that when one is divided so is the other in the same proportion. Hence, they knew necessarily that if time were continuous and capable of infinite division, then it follows that the part which they considered indivisible must likewise be capable of infinite division . . . For this reason they presumed that . . . time reaches a limit, namely the moments, beyond which further division is impossible . . ." (Pines, trans. (1963), 1: 196; quoted by Dhanani (1991): 259). In his comments, Dhanani writes: "Maimonides does not have direct evidence for time-atoms in *kalām*, but he insists on the basis of Aristotle's analysis that such a doctrine must, of necessity, be held by any kind of atomism" (Dhanani (1991): 260).

24 See Dhanani (1991): 182–330.

25 This text is available in Weisser's 1979 critical edition.

26 Weisser, ed. (1979): 63.

27 Weisser, ed. (1979).

28 See Radhakrishnan (1924); Schweitzer (1951).

29 Mingana, ed. and trans. (1935).

30 *Ibid.*: xxv. See n. 32 below.

31 Siddiqi, ed. (1938). The parts relevant to Indian knowledge have been translated in Siggel (1950).

32 The renegade *mutakallim* Abū ʿĪsā al-Warrāq (d. 247/861) says in his account of the *dahriyyah* (natural philosophers who believed in the eternity of the world) that "one group [of the *dahriyyah*] claims that the world is constituted out of five things, which like it are eternal: hot, cold, dry and moist. The fifth is pneuma (*rūḥ*) . . .". (This account is preserved in the *Muʿtamad fī uṣūl al-dīn* of the *mutakallim* Rukn al-Dīn al-Malāḥmī (d. 536/1141); the section on the *dahriyyah* has been edited and translated in McDermott (1984). I have taken the selection from Dhanani's citation (1991: 88), making minor changes in the translation.) Dhanani places against this account the report of Ibn Sahl Rabban al-Ṭabarī on an Indian theory of five elements (*mahābūt*): "The term *mahābūt* means the elements (*ṭabāʾiʿ*) which they take to be five by [the addition of] wind [*rīḥ*]" (*Firdaws al-ḥikma*, Siddiqi, ed. (1938): 557; I quote Dhanani's citation (1991): 93). A similar account of the Indian theory is to be found in the *Book of Treasures* of Job of Edessa: "Some Indians . . . believe in the existence of five elements, four of which we ourselves believe in, while the fifth is the

wind" (Mingana, trans. (1935): 221). Dhanani's conclusion, however, is that the source of the *dahriyyah* view was not Indian but Stoic (1991: 94).

33 Quoted by Vajda (1937): 193, n. 6; Dhanani (1991): 47, n. 1.

34 *Al-Mughnī*, Cairo ed. (1960–5).

35 *Al-Tawḥīd*, Kholeif, ed. (1970).

36 *Fihrist*, Flügel, ed. (1871); Dodge, trans. (1970).

37 *Al-Milal wa al-niḥal*, Badrān, ed. (1956); Haarbrüker, ed. and trans. (1850).

38 See, e.g., the *Murūj al-dhahab* of the historian al-Mas'ūdī (d. 345/956), Pellat, ed. (1966–79), 5: 212.

39 There are possible exceptions: see Wolfson (1976): 559–78.

40 An extensive discussion of the *kalām* doctrines of causality is to be found in Wolfson (1976): 518–600. See also Dhanani (1991): 53ff.

41 Cf. Dhanani (1991): 46ff.

42 Embracing Christianity in 179 A.D., this Aramaic philosopher had blended gnosticism with dualism. See Shahrastānī, Haarbrüker, ed. and trans. (1850), 1: 293; "Ibn Daiṣān", *Encyclopaedia of Islam*, 2: 370; Ibn al-Nadīm, Dodge, trans. 1970): 776, 805–6; Drijvers (1966).

43 Probably a Christian shipmaster in Pontus. Around A.D. 140 he went to Rome and founded a heretical sect. See Ibn al-Nadīm, Dodge, trans. (1970): 775–6, 806–7; Shahrastānī, Haarbrüker, ed. and trans. (1850), 1: 295.

44 See Mas'ūdī, Pellat, ed. (1966–79), 5: 212; Vajda (1937).

45 Among them were also al-Warrāq and Ibn al-Rāwandī whom we have met above.

46 See Ibn Khallikān, de Slane, trans. (1843–7), 1: 431; Ibn al-Nadīm, Dodge, trans. (1970): 24, 99, 259, 275–6, 366, 581, 598, 599, 715; "Ibn al-Muḳaffa'", *Encyclopaedia of Islam*, 3: 883. Fragments of Ibn al-Muqaffa''s Manichaean tract are preserved in a refutation by the Zaydī Imām al-Rassī (d. 246/860), *al-Radd 'alā al-Zindīq al-La'īn Ibn al-Muqaffa'*, Guidi, ed. and trans. (1927). Cf. Dhanani (1991): 50ff. On the phenomenon of *zandaqah* an important study is Vajda (1937); see also Nicholson (1969): 372–5.

47 Dhanani (1991): 50ff.; Vajda (1937).

48 This is reported, e.g., by Mas'ūdī, Pellat, ed., 5: 212.

49 A good account of Rāzī is the article of Pines, *s.v., Dictionary of Scientific Biography*. Cf. Pines (1936); 34–93; Kraus, ed. (1939); Fakhry (1983): 94–106.

50 Pines, *Dictionary of Scientific Biography*, 11: 323.

51 Pines (1936); Pines, *Dictionary of Scientific Biography*, 11: 324.

52 Pines, *ibid.*: 326; Fakhry (1983): 94–106.

53 This has been edited by Kraus (1936).

54 *India*, Sachau, trans. (1888): 4; al-Īrānshahrī is mentioned also in al-Bīrūnī's *al-Āthār al-bāqiya*, Sachau, ed. (1878): 222, 225. Cf. Pines (1936): 34.

55 *Zād al-musāfirīn*, Belin, ed. (1341), quoted by Pines (1936): 34ff.

56 Pines (1936): 34ff.

57 Pines, *Dictionary of Scientific Biography*, 11: 324.

58 Stapleton, Azo and Ḥusain (1927): 340–2; Stapleton and Azo (1910): 68, 72.

59 Fakhry (1983): 33.

60 Thanks, particularly, to the painstaking works of David Pingree, E. S. Kennedy and David King.

61 My account of the history of Islamic astronomy draws rather heavily upon

Pingree (1973); in fact what I give below is practically a paraphrase of this important study.

62 Pingree (1973): 32.

63 *Ibid.*: 36.

64 *Ibid.*: 37. Around the end of second/beginning of ninth century another version of *Āryābhaṭīya* was circulating among Muslim astronomers (Pingree, "'Ilm al-Hay'a", *Encyclopaedia of Islam*, 4: 1136). The Indian text has been studied by Clark (1930).

65 Pingree (1973): 38.

66 Dodge, trans. (1970): 589, 644, 710. This personage is mentioned by other sources too, such as Qifṭī, Lippert, ed. (1903): 265.

67 Dodge, trans. (1970): 590, 710. He looked after the *bīmāristān* (hospital) under the Persian Barmak family. Cf. Flügel (1857).

68 Dodge, trans. (1970): 645. See Ibn Abī Uṣaybi'ah, Müller, ed. (1884), 2: 33.

69 Dodge, trans. (1970): 645. Cf. Ibn Abī Uṣaybi'ah, 2: 32.

70 Dodge, trans. (1970).

71 *Ibid.*: 1027.

72 *Ibid.*: 710. All three of them are mentioned also by Ibn Sahl Rabban al-Ṭabarī, Siggel, trans. (1950).

73 These titles appear in Ibn al-Nadīm, Dodge, trans. (1970).

74 Chānakya was Chandragupta's minister the fragment of whose book on statecraft is preserved in Kautiliya's (third century A.D.) *Arthaśāstra*. But the Arabic text also draws material from Suśruta and Caraka. See the critical study of the *Shānāq* by Strauss (1934).

75 That physicians from the Persian academy were held in high esteem is illustrated in a delightful manner by the famous literary and philosophical figure al-Jāḥiẓ (d. 255/868) in his *Kitāb al-bukhalā'* ("Book of the Misers"): "Once, when his [an Arab physician Asad's] practice of medicine was not much in demand, somebody asked him: . . . 'How is it that your practice is so little in demand?' He gave this answer: 'First, . . . I am a Muslim; and with the patients the belief is deep rooted . . . that Muslims are not good for medicine. Then, my name is Asad, but it should have been Ṣalība, Marā'il, Yūḥannā or Bīrā: moreover my *kunya* is Abu'l Ḥārith, but it should have been Abū 'Isā, Abū Zakariyyā or Abū Ibrāhim. I wear an upper garment made of cotton, but it should have been made of black silk. Finally, my way of speaking is Arabic, but it should be that of the people from Jundīshāpūr!'" (quoted by Meyerhof (1930): 402).

76 See Ibn al-Nadīm, Dodge, trans. (1970): 697; Ibn Abī Uṣaybi'ah, Müller, ed. (1884), 1: 138; Qifṭī, Lippert, ed. (1903): 102.

77 See Ibn Nadīm, Dodge, trans. (1970): 698; Ibn Abī Uṣaybi'ah, *op. cit.*, 1: 163, 204; Qifṭī, *op. cit.*: 324.

78 Meyerhof (1937): 22.

79 See *ibid.*: 23.

80 See Ibn Nadīm, Dodge, trans. (1970): 584, 695–6, 742; Ibn Abī Uṣaybi'ah, *op. cit.*: 175; Qifṭī, *op. cit.*: 380.

81 A comprehensive account of al-Khwārazmī is given by Toomer, *s.v.*, *Dictionary of Scientific Biography*: 358–65. Arabic sources include Ibn al-Nadīm, Dodge, trans. (1970): 652, 662, 665, 668; Qifṭī, *op. cit.*: 286.

82 The authority on this subject is Kennedy. See, e.g., Kennedy (1969): 333ff.; (1970): 337ff.

83 The theorem asserts a metric relation between six segments on any complete quadrilateral, plane or spherical. Kennedy (1970): 337 points out that it had been possible in the pre-Islamic mathematics to compute the magnitudes of any solvable plane or, in principle, spherical figure by use of the table of chords and Menelaus' theorem. But that application of the theorem to spherical problems was, however, very difficult in practice.

84 Kennedy (1969): 334.

85 *India*, Sachau, ed. (1888), 1: 24.

REFERENCES

'Abd al-Jabbār al-Hamadhānī (1960–5) *al-Mughnī fī abwāb al-tawḥīd wa'l-'adl*, Cairo edition, 16 vols (Cairo).

(pseudo) Apollonius of Tyana (1979) *Kitāb Sirr al-khalīqah wa ṣan'at al-ṭabī'ah*, ed. U. Weisser (Aleppo).

al-Bīrūnī, Abū Rayḥān (1878) *al-Āthār al-bāqiyah*, ed. E. C. Sachau (Leipzig).

—— (1888) *India*, trans. E. C. Sachau (London).

—— (1936) *Risālah fī fihrist kutūb Muḥammad ibn Zakariyyā al-Rāzī*, ed. P. Kraus (Paris).

Brunet, P. and Mieli, A. (1935) *L'histoire des sciences (antiquité)* (Paris).

Campbell, D. (1926) *Arabian Medicine and its Influence in the Middle Ages*, 2 vols (London).

Chwolson, D. (1856) *Die Ssabier und der Ssabismus*, 2 vols (St Petersburg).

Clark, W. E. (1930) *The Āryabhaṭīa of Āryabhaṭa* (Chicago).

Dictionary of Scientific Biography (1970–6), ed. C. D. Gillispie (New York).

Dhanani, Alnoor (1991) *Kalām and Hellenistic Cosmology* (doctoral diss., Harvard University).

Drijvers, H. (1966) *Bardaiṣan of Edessa* (Groningen).

Duka, T. (1904) "The Influence of Buddhism upon Islam", *Journal of the Royal Asiatic Society of Great Britain and Ireland* (January): 125–41.

The Encyclopaedia of Islam (New Edition) (1954) ed. H. A. R. Gibb *et al.* (Leiden).

Fakhry, M. (1983) *A History of Islamic Philosophy* (New York).

Flügel, G. (1857) "Zur Frage über die ältesten Übersetzungen indischer und persischer medicinischer werke ins Arabische", *Zeitschrift der morganländischen Gesellschaft* (11): 148–53, 325–7.

Ḥamza al-Iṣfahānī (1844) *Ta'rīkh sinī mulūk al-arḍ wa'l-anbiyā'*, ed. and trans. J. M. E. Gottwaldt (Leipzig).

Horten, M. (1912) *Die philosophischen Systeme des spekulativen Theologen im Islam* (Bonn) (rev. L. Massignon, *Der Islam* (1912) 3: 408).

Ibn Abī Uṣaybi'ah, Abu'l-'Abbās (1884) *'Uyūn al-anbā' fī ṭabaqāt al-aṭibbā'*, ed. A. Müller (Königsberg).

Ibn Khallikān, Aḥmad (1843–71) *Biographical Dictionary*, trans. M. de Slane, 4 vols (London).

Ibn al-Nadīm, Abu'l-Faraj (1871) *Kitāb al-Fihrist*, ed. G. Flügel (Leipzig). *The Fihrist of Ibn al-Nadīm*, trans. B. Dodge (New York and London, 1970).

Jacobi, H. (1910) "Atomic Theory (Indian)", *Encyclopaedia of Religion and Ethics*, ed. J. Hastings (New York).

Job of Edessa (1935) *The Book of Treasures*, ed. and trans. A. Mingana (Cambridge).

Keith, A. B. (1921) *Indian Logic and Atomism* (London).

Kennedy, E. S. (1969) "The History of Trigonometry", *31st Yearbook*, National Council of Teachers of Mathematics (Washington DC).

—— (1970) "The Arabic Heritage in the Exact Sciences", *al-Abḥath*, 23: 327–44.

Kraus, P. (1933; 1934) "Beiträge zur islamischen Ketzergeschichte, das *Kitāb al-Zumurrud* des Ibn Rāwandī", *Rivista degli Studi Orientali*, 14: (1933) 93–129, (1934) 220–3.

—— (1942–3) *Jābir ibn Ḥayyān*, 2 vols (Cairo).

Lang, D. M. (1957) *The Wisdom of Balahvar* (London).

Mabilleau, L. (1895) *Histoire de la philosophie atomistique*, (Paris).

McDermott, M. (1984) "Abū ʿĪsā al-Warrāq on the *Dahriyya*", *Mélanges de l'Université Saint-Joseph*, 50: 387–402.

Macdonald, D. B. (1928) "Continuous Re-creation and Atomic Time in Moslem Scholastic Theology", *Moslem World*, 17(1): 6–28.

Maimonides, *see* Mūsā ibn Maymūn.

(pseudo) al-Majrīṭī, Maslama (1962) *Ghāyat al-ḥakīm*, trans. H. Ritter and M. Plessner (London).

al-Masʿūdī, ʿAlī ibn al-Ḥusayn (1966–79) *Murūj al-dhahab wa maʿādin al-jawhar*, ed. C. Pellat, 7 vols (Beirut).

al-Māturīdī, Abū Manṣūr (1970) *Kitāb al-Tawḥīd*, ed. F. Kholeif (Beirut).

Meyerhof, M. (1930) "Von Alexandrien nach Baghdad", *Sitzungsberichte der preussischen Akademie der Wissenschaften*, 23: 389–429.

—— (1937) "On the Transmission of Greek and Indian Science to the Arabs", *Islamic Culture* (January): 18–29.

Monier-Williams, M. (1891) *Brahmanism and Hinduism* (London).

Mūsā ibn Maymūn (1963) *Dalālat al-ḥāʾirīn* ("Guide to the Perplexed"), trans. S. Pines (Chicago and London).

Nāṣir-i Khusraw (1922) *Zād al-musafirīn* (Berlin).

Nasr, S. H. (1975) "Life Sciences, Alchemy and Medicine", *Cambridge History of Iran*, ed. R. N. Frye, 4: 396–418 (Cambridge).

Nicholson, R. A. (1969) *A Literary History of the Arabs* (Cambridge).

Pines, S. (1936) *Beiträge zur islamischen Atomenlehre* (Berlin).

Pingree, D. (1973) "The Greek Influence on Early Islamic Mathematical Astronomy", *Journal of the American Oriental Society*, 93(1): 32–43.

al-Qifṭī; Jamāl al-Dīn (1903) *Taʾrīkh al-ḥukamāʾ*, ed. J. Lippert (Leipzig).

Radhakrishnan, S. (1924) *The Philosophy of Upaniṣads* (London).

—— (ed.) (1953) *History of Philosophy Eastern and Western* (London).

al-Rassī, al-Qāsim ibn Ibrāhīm (1927) *al-Radd ʿalā al-Zindīq al-Laʿīn Ibn al-Muqaffaʿ*, ed. and trans. M. Guidi (Rome).

al-Rāzī, Abū Bakr Muḥammad ibn Zakariyyāʾ (1939) *Rasāʾil falsafiyyah*, ed. P. Kraus (Cairo).

Schmölders, A. (1842) *Essai sur les écoles philosophiques chez Arabes, et notamment sur la doctrine l'Algazzali* (Paris).

Schweitzer, A. (1950) *Indian Thought and its Development* (London).

al-Shahrastānī, Ibn ʿAbd al-Karīm (1956) *Kitāb milal waʾl-niḥal*, ed. M. Badrān,

2 vols (Cairo).
Siggel, A. (1950) *Die indinischen Bücher aus dem "Paradies d. Weisheit über d. Medizin" des 'Alī ibn Sahl Rabban al-Ṭabarī*. (Wiesbaden).
Stapleton, H. E. and Azo, R. F. (1910) "An Alchemical Compilation of the 13th Century", *Memoirs of the Asiatic Society of Bengal*, 3: 57.
Stapleton, H. E., Azo, R. F. and Ḥusain, M. H. (1927) "Chemistry in Iraq and Persia in the 10th Century", *Memoirs of the Asiatic Society of Bengal*, 8: 315–417.
Strauss, B. (1934) "Das Giftbuch des Shānāq; eine literaturgeschichtliche Untersuchung", *Quellen u. Studien z. Gesch. d. Naturwiss. u. d. Medizin*, 4: 89–152.
Stroumsa, S. (1985) "The Brāhima in Early Kalām", *Jerusalem Studies in Arabic and Islam*, 6: 229–41.
al-Ṭabarī, 'Alī ibn Sahl Rabban (1938) *Firdaws al-ḥikma*, ed. M. Siddiqi (Berlin).
al-Ṭabarī, ibn Jarīr (1879–90) *Ta'rīkh al-rusul wa'l-mulūk*, ed. M. J. de Goeje, 14 vols (Leiden).
Vajda, G. (1937) "Les Zindīqs en pays d'Islam au début de la période abbaside", *Rivista degli Studi Orientali*, 17: 173–229.
Wolfson, H. A. (1976) *The Philosophy of the Kalām* (Cambridge, Mass.).
Yāqūt, Shihāb al-Dīn (1966–70) *Mu'jam al-buldān*, ed. F. Wüstenfeld, 6 vols (Leipzig).

CHAPTER 5

Early *kalām*

M. Abdel Haleem

Kalām, or *'ilm al-kalām* (the science of *kalām*), is a title of that branch of knowledge in Islam that is usually translated as "speculative theology". Literally, *kalām* means "speech", "talk" or "words"; *yatakallam fī* means to talk about or discuss a matter or topic. In an early usage of the word *kalām* in this sense, the Prophet is reported to have come out and found a group of Muslims *yatakallamūna*[1] *fi'l-qadar* i.e. talking about, or discussing, predestination.[2] The opposite of *takallama fī* is *sakata 'an* – to keep silent about – such a matter or topic. The word occurred in other traditions and continued to be used in the same sense even when discussions on theological matters had become more extensive and specialized. A statement by Mālik (d. 179/795) explains the connection between such discussions and the word *kalām* in its lexical meaning. He said: "Beware of innovations . . .; those who talk about [*yatakallamūn fī*] the names and attributes of God, His Word, His Knowledge and Power, and do not keep silent [*yaskutūn*] about things about which the Companions of the Prophet and their followers have kept silence."[3] As a jurist, he also stated: "I do not like *kalām* except in what involves *'amal* (action), but as for *kalām* about God, silence is better than it."[4]

Kalām here means discussion on theological matters. As M. 'Abd al-Rāziq has rightly observed, such discussions were called *kalām* before the science of *kalām* became independent and recorded in writing, and people who engaged in such discussions were also called *mutakallimūn*. When books were written about these issues, the science which was written down was given the title that had been applied earlier to such discussions.[5] In Islamic sources a number of reasons were offered for giving such a title to the science of *kalām*. Taftāzānī (d. 793/1390)[6] put together such reasons as follows:

1 Traditionally the title that was given to the discussions of any separate issue, was *al-kalām fī kathā wa kathā* (an exposition of/a chapter or section on).
2 The question of *kalām Allāh* (the speech of God) was the most famous question and the one that gave rise to the most disputes.
3 The science of *kalām* generates in one the power to talk about or discuss religious matters and impress one's arguments on one's rivals as logic does in the field of philosophy.

As regards the first reason, it is true that chapters in such early books as *al-Ibānah* of al-Ash'arī (d. 324/935) and *al-Mughnī* of 'Abd al-Jabbār (d. 415/1024) bear such titles but these works appeared much later than the name of *kalām* as a science. The same can be said of the second reason, since the title was well known before the discussions on *kalām Allāh* (the createdness or otherwise of the Qur'ān). Similarly, the third suggestion refers to the stage when logic and Greek philosophy became well known and influential in the Islamic cultural milieu in the third/ninth century, after the title of *kalām* had become well established. Other suggestions were put forward[7] which can be explained away as post-dating the appearance of *'ilm al-kalām* as an established science in the second/eighth century. Western scholars, on the other hand, argue for a non-Islamic origin of the term *kalām* as being derived from the Greek *dialexis* used by the Church Fathers, or *logos*, directly or via Syriac,[8] but none of the arguments for such views appears to be conclusive. The term in Islamic culture predates any presumed contact with Christian, Greek or Syriac sources and in any case *kalām,* as will be explained below, is not the only term used by Muslims for this science: six other terms were used. The most plausible explanation for the appearance of this term remains the original lexical meaning as used in the above-mentioned prophetic traditions.

J. van Ess considers that not every discussion on any religious question can be considered part of *kalām*; rather *kalām* requires a specific way of treating religious issues: it is a treatment where it is necessary to have an adversary in the discussion. *Kalām* "means a procedure" where you have a discussion about a topic that usually occurs according to a certain structure by question and response, frequently built up in the form of dilemmas.[9] Van Ess cites a *risālah,* ascribed to al-Ḥasan ibn Muḥammad ibn al-Ḥanafiyyah, an anti-Qadarite *risālah,* which he dates at 73/692, to exemplify *kalām* in this sense as a dialectic formula which begins by posing a question, in the form of a disjunction: whichever choice the adversary makes, he loses, and is trapped in a position which is either manifestly untenable or identical with that of the questioner.

As to the question of dates, Michael Cook has convincingly argued that the ascription rests on the sole authority of the Zaydī Imām al-Hādī

(d. 298/910), that many of the arguments advanced by van Ess are questionable and the result could not be said to constitute proof, suggesting that it would be difficult to sustain a date later than the first half of the second/eighth century.[10] The persistence in using the dialectical formula for such a lengthy *risālah* and the fact that the style of the text is so clearly different from the style of al-Ḥasan in his other *Risālat al-irjā'* make it more difficult to accept the ascription to al-Ḥasan on the sole authority of al-Hādī.

On the basis of this *risālah*, van Ess argues that the form was borrowed from Greek sources, while Cook, on the basis of a Syriac text, similar in form to that of the *risālah*, argues that the origin for the *risālah* was Syriac.

Without going here into the question of any relationship of Islamic culture to either Greek or Syriac, it is difficult to agree that Muslim writers had necessarily to resort to either source to become acquainted with such a formula, or that it did not exist in their culture. In fact we have a piece of argument dated much earlier than the dates suggested by either van Ess or Cook: that is the dialogue between Ibn 'Abbās and some Khārijites who rebelled against 'Alī.

> On being sent by the Caliph 'Alī to argue with them, Ibn 'Abbās asked: "What do you have against 'Alī?" They answered "Three things: one, he set men as judges *fī amr Allāh*, while judgment is only for Allāh; two, he fought but did not take captives or booty. If his enemies were believers it would not have been lawful for him to fight them, and if they had been unbelievers, he had the right to kill and take them captive. Three, he abdicated his position as *Amīr al-mu'minīn*. If he was not *Amīr al-mu'minīn* he must be *Amīr al-kāfirīn*."
>
> Ibn 'Abbās asked: "If I cite from the Qur'ān and *Sunnah* what refutes your argument, would you come back to him?" They replied "Why not?" To the first question he cited Qur'ān 6: 95 and 4: 35 in which it is enjoined that arbiters be set up to decide on the price of a hare killed in the *ḥaram* and in marital disputes, and put to them: "Do you consider giving men authority to decide in matters of the blood of Muslims and reconciliation better, or to decide on the price of a hare or a matter involving whether it is lawful for a man to have intercourse with his wife?" They conceded the point. As to the second point that 'Alī fought without taking captives or booty, Ibn 'Abbās asked the Khārijites "Would you take your mother[11] 'Ā'ishah captive? If you say she is not our 'mother' you would be unbelievers, so you see that you are cornered between two unlawful things. Have I answered your arguments over this?"

> They said yes. "As to your objection that he abdicated the position of *Amīr al-mu'minīn*, I can cite what the Prophet did at Ḥudaybiyah when the representative of the Quraysh did not accept 'Alī writing 'This is what has been agreed between the Messenger of Allah and . . .' to which Abū Ṣufyān and Suhayl objected 'If we had known you were a messenger of Allāh we would not have fought you', at which the Prophet said to 'Alī, 'Wipe that out and write "This is what has been agreed between Muḥammad, son of 'Abdallāh and Abū Ṣufyān and Suhayl."'"
> At this point, two thousand of the Khārijites changed their position and did not fight 'Alī.[12]

In this dialogue both the Khārijites and Ibn 'Abbās use the disjunction formula, at a time much earlier than that of the *risālah* van Ess and Cook cite to suggest a non-Muslim origin for the formula.

Van Ess' view that *kalām* must involve such dialectical structure does not agree with the Islamic view of *kalām*. The dialectical situation and disjunction formula are of course part of *kalām* but are not the only form it takes. Throughout the history of *kalām* theological writings with different characteristics have also been accepted as part of *kalām*.

As mentioned, *kalām* has not been the only title given to this science as an independent subject. As many as seven names in Arabic have been used for it, which is perhaps unknown in any other science, and may suggest that the reservation regarding *kalām* shown by such scholars as Mālik continued afterwards.

1. One of the oldest titles was given by Abū Ḥanīfah (d. 150/767), in the second/eighth century, who named it *'ilm al-fiqh al-akbar*. *Fiqh* is a Qur'ānic word (9: 122) and this shows the relationship between *kalām* and *fiqh*. The adjective *al-akbar* shows the superiority of matters related to the principles of the faith over practical aspects of the *Sharī'ah*.
2. *'ilm al-kalām*: this is also one of the oldest names. Ja'far al-Ṣādiq (d. 148/765), Abū Ḥanīfah (d. 150/767), Mālik (d. 179/795) and Shāfi'ī (d. 204/819) are said to have given their opinions on *kalām* and the *mutakallimūn*.[13] This title seems to have been the most common and enduring.
3. *'ilm uṣūl al-dīn*: another early title which is based on the division of religious knowledge into *uṣūl* and *furū'* (roots and branches). This title was used by Ash'arī (d. 324/935) in his *al-Ibānah 'an uṣūl al-diyānah* and by al-Baghdādī (d. 429/1037) in his *Uṣūl al-dīn*. The faculties of theology in Al-Azhar University, for instance, are called *kulliyyāt uṣūl al-dīn*.
4. *'ilm al-'aqā'id*: a later title, dating perhaps from the fourth/tenth century. This name appears in the works of such writers as al-Ṭaḥāwī

(d. 331/942), al-Ghazzālī (d. 505/1111), al-Ṭūsī (d. 671/1272) and al-Ījī (d. 756/1355).

5 *ʿilm al-naẓar wa'l-istidlāl*: this was mentioned by Taftāzānī in his introduction to *Sharḥ al-ʿaqā'id al-nasafiyyah*. The title used to be given in early *kalām* books to the first introductory chapter, which discusses proofs and the methodology of *ʿilm al-kalām*. This can be seen in the *Uṣūl al-dīn* of al-Baghdādī (d. 429/1037) and *al-Mughnī* of ʿAbd al-Jabbār (d. 415/1024). Perhaps because of the importance of the methodology of *kalām*, the title was applied to the whole science.

6 *ʿilm al-tawḥīd wa'l-ṣifāt*: so called probably because of the importance of the Unity and other Attributes of God. This appears in the introduction to *Sharḥ al-ʿaqā'id al-nasafiyyah* by Taftāzānī.

7 *ʿilm al-tawḥīd*: this being the most important article of faith in Islam. This title was used by Muḥammad ʿAbduh (d. 1323/1905) in his *Risālat al-tawḥīd*, and became more common amongst modern theologians.

As *ʿilm al-kalām* became an independent science, various definitions of this term were introduced; the following definitions, given at different times in the history of *kalām*, are often quoted. Amongst the earliest is that by Abū Ḥanīfah (d. 150/767), who gave it the name *al-fiqh al-akbar* and stated: "*fiqh* in *uṣūl al-dīn* is better than *fiqh* in *furūʿ al-aḥkām*. *Fiqh* is knowledge of the beliefs and practices which are permitted and which are obligatory in both. What relates to beliefs is called *al-fiqh al-akbar* and what relates to practices is simply *al-fiqh*."[14] Such distinctions influenced later Ḥanafī theologians such as al-Nasafī (d. 537/1142),[15] and the knowledge involved in both types of *fiqh* is that which is based on traditional (*naqlī*) or rational (*ʿaqlī*) proofs.

Al-Fārābī (d. 339/950) makes the distinction between *kalām* and *fiqh* and defines *kalām* in his *Iḥṣā' al-ʿulūm* as: "a science which enables a person to support specific beliefs and actions laid down by the Legislators of the religion and to refute all opinions contradicting them".[16] Al-Bayḍāwī (d. 680/1281) and al-Ījī (d. 756/1355) give the definition of *kalām* as: "a science which enables one to establish religious beliefs, by adducing arguments/proofs and banishing doubts". Ibn Khaldūn (d. 807/1404) defines *kalām* as: "the science that involves arguing with rational proofs in defence of the articles of faith and refuting innovators who deviate from the beliefs of early Muslims and Muslim orthodoxy".[17] In the modern era, Muḥammad ʿAbduh (d. 1323/1905) gives the following definition:

> The science that studies the Being and Attributes of God, the essential and the possible affirmations about Him, as well as the negations that are necessary to make relating to Him. It deals also with the apostles and the authenticity of their message and

> treats of their essential and appropriate qualities and what is incompatibly associated with them.[18]

The earliest stage of *kalām* in Islam is surely to be found in the Qur'ān itself. *Kalām* in its technical sense involves providing rational proofs to establish the articles of faith. This is, in fact, an essential feature of the way the Qur'ān treats theological subjects. In the first verses that were revealed, we read: "Recite, in the name of your Lord, who created, Created man from clots of blood . . ." (96: 1–5). This shows the power that takes creation from one stage to another; later on the various stages of embryonic development are shown, from the germinal fluids, through the embryo, to the foetus and the infant, adult, degeneration by old age and death, to show that He who can do this can also take a person through the further stage of resurrection after death (22: 5–7, 23: 12–16).

Resurrection is dealt with on many occasions in the Qur'ān. The following example has been discussed by the two Muslim philosophers, al-Kindī and Ibn Rushd who analysed the rational basis of the Qur'ānic arguments for ressurrection in these verses:

> Is man not aware that We created him from a little germ? Yet he is flagrantly contentious. He answers back with arguments, and forgets his own creation. He asks: "Who will give life to rotten bones?"
>
> Say: "He who first brought them into being will give them life again: He has knowledge of every creation; He who gives you from the green tree a fire when you light your own fires with it."
>
> Has He who created the heavens and the earth no power to create their like? That He surely has. He is the all-knowing Creator. When He decrees a thing, He has only to say: "Be," and it is. (36: 77–82)[19]

Without being a book of theology that provides a systematic analysis, the Qur'ān dealt with all the issues that were discussed in *kalām* as fully developed later. Thus al-Qushayrī (d. 465/1072) says, "One is surprised by those who say there is no *'ilm al-kalām* in the Qur'ān when the verses dealing with *al-aḥkam al-shar'iyyah* are limited, while those that draw attention to principles of the faith far exceed them."[20] Similarly, al-Rāzī (d. 606/1209), a pre-eminent commentator on the Qur'ān and *mutakallim*, points out that discussion is widespread in the Qur'ān on *tawḥīd*, prophethood and the hereafter. This is because the Prophet had to contend

> with all manners of unbelievers, atheists, or those who deny the power and predetermination of God, and those who attributed a partner to God, be it from the celestial spheres, like the stars, or the lower spheres, like the Christians and the pagans, and those who denied prophethood altogether or those who disputed

> the prophethood of Muḥammad, like the Jews and the Christians, together with those who denied resurrection and so on. The Qur'ān discussed the views of such groups, refuted and answered their claims.[21]

Accordingly he states:

> Qur'ānic verses dealing with *al-aḥkām al-shar'iyyah* are fewer than six hundred, while the rest explain questions of the unity of God, prophethood and refutation of idol-worshippers and various other types of polytheists. . . . If you examine *'ilm al-kalām* you will find nothing in it other than discussions of these questions and refutations of doubts and counter-arguments.[22]

Likewise, Ibn Taymiyyah (d. 728/1327) states that: "The Qur'ān has established the principles of the faith, and also their arguments and proofs."[23] Ibn Rushd, a philosopher who wrote on the Qur'ānic methods of proving the beliefs of the Islamic faith, states: "The whole Qur'ān is an invitation to reflect and draw lessons and directs attention to the methods of reflection."[24]

Discussion on religious matters began very early in Islam. We have seen earlier reference to the Prophet coming out and finding a group of Muslims discussing *qadar*. In fact the polytheists themselves relied on *qadar* to justify their stand and the Qur'ān directed the Prophet to answer them (6: 148; 16: 35), and although the Prophet did not encourage disputation over such matters as predestination, he answered all questions that were directed to him, unless they went beyond human knowledge, like the time of the Hour of Judgment.[25] On such matters he would direct the questioner to what is more useful. When he was asked by a Companion, "When is the hour of judgment?" he replied, "What have you prepared for it?"

He himself conducted theological discussions with non-Muslims. An example of this is the one he had with the delegation from Najrān, headed by their chiefs, al-'Āqib and al-Sayyid. When he requested them to become Muslims and they refused, he commented:

> "What prevents you from becoming Muslims is your claim that God had a son and your worship of the cross and eating the flesh of swine." They asked, "If Jesus was not the son of God, whose son is he then?" and they all argued with him about Jesus. He said, "Don't you know that there is no son who does not resemble his father?" They agreed. He asked them, "Don't you know that our Lord is living and does not die, while Jesus' life has come to an end?" They said, "Yes." He said, "Don't you know that our Lord is guardian over everything and protects and sustains living things?" They said, "Yes." "Does Jesus have power

> over any of this?" They said, "No." He said, "Our Lord has formed Jesus in the womb as He wished, and our Lord does not eat, drink, or excrete." They said "Yes." He said, "Don't you know that Jesus was borne by his mother as a woman bears a child, and she gave birth to him as any woman gives birth to a child. He was fed like a child and he used to feed, drink and excrete?" They said "Yes." So he said, "How could he then be as you claim?" to which they could not give an answer.[26]

Discussions on such matters as *qadar*, the Attributes of God, the nature of belief and unbelief, eschatology and the fate of sinners, continued during the times of the *ṣaḥābah* (Companions of the Prophet) and the *tābiʿūn* (those who followed them), laying the foundations for the later issues of *ʿilm al-kalām*. What they refrained from was not the discussion of such issues but from going deep into them or forcing the issues.[27]

In order to have a clear picture of the nature of theological discussions in the era of early *kalām* it would be useful to show it in relation to subsequent eras. We find it suitable to adopt the following scheme in five stages.[28]

1 the beginning, which covers the first and the very early years of the second/eighth century;
2 recording and the emergence of various schools and sects of *kalām*. This occupies four centuries, approximately from the early years of the second to the end of the fifth/eleventh century;
3 evolution and mingling with philosophy, which lasts from the sixth/twelfth to the ninth/fifteenth century;
4 decadence and imitation, from the tenth/sixteenth to the end of the twelfth/eighteenth century,
5 the modern period, covering the last two centuries.

In the first stage, discussions dealt only with separate issues of *kalām* where differences of opinion showed themselves as tendencies that did not develop into "schools" until later. It was during the second stage that the various *kalām* schools emerged with their distinctive features, where all aspects of the science of *kalām* were discussed and written down.

During the early years of Islam, theological discussions revolved around a number of separate issues. We have seen that discussion of the question of *qadar* appeared at the time of the Prophet. When the Prophet died, the problem of *khilāfah* (succession) arose and the *fitnah* (dissent) at the time of ʿUthmān and ʿAlī witnessed the beginning of *firaq* (sects) with the appearance of the Shīʿah, Khārijites and Murjiʾites. The discussions of the last two arose primarily as a result of their understanding of the texts. Some chose to adhere to the literal meaning of texts while others were inclined to *taʾwīl* (interpretation) or taking a middle course.

The influence of the Qur'ān on *kalām* discussions was due to a number of factors. Firstly, it had discussed all the issues relating to belief in God, prophethood and eschatology, which were to become the main issues of *kalām*, supporting its statements with rational arguments. Secondly, it discussed the beliefs and thoughts of other religions such as first paganism, and then Judaism and Christianity. Thirdly, it also called for *naẓar* and *tafkīr* (reflection and thought), making these an obligation in Islam.[29] Fourthly, the Qur'ān contains verses known as *muḥkamāt* (in precise language), and these the Qur'ān calls "the essence of the Book", and others known as *mutashābihāt* (ambiguous). The *ta'wīl* (interpretation) of this latter category – taken in isolation or understood in the light of the former – was one of the distinguishing factors between sects and schools. *Kalām* thus originated completely in the Islamic environment and foreign elements came only later as a result of mixing with other nations and also as a result of the translation of Greek texts into Arabic.

The emergence of the Khārijites gave rise to an early major issue of *kalām*, namely the status and fate of *murtakib al-kabīrah*: whether committing a grave sin makes a person a *kāfir* (infidel, to be condemned to Hell fire for ever) or not. Here we find that the Khārijites take the extreme view of considering such a person as an infidel, interpreting in their own way Qur'ānic verses that do not agree with this stand. At the opposite extreme, there were the Murji'ites who considered that sinners are still believers and that action is not part of the faith, to the extent that no sins would harm anyone who is a believer and no good deed would benefit an infidel. Again they based their view on Qur'ānic verses that promise a good future for the believers and interpreted other verses that contain warnings and threats to suit this stand. Scholars of the *ṣaḥābah* and *tābi'ūn* stood up to both the sects basing their views on combining the two sets of Qur'ānic verses, showing that a sinning believer remains a Muslim, and that his or her destiny is left with God, who may pardon him or her or give the deserved punishment, but not eternally in Hell.[30]

As mentioned earlier, during the Prophet's time the question of *qadar* gave rise to much discussion as to whether people have free will or are under compulsion. This gave rise to two groups. The Qadarites held that people had *qudrāh* (power) over their actions: some went to the extent of denying the pre-existent knowledge of God in order to remove any compulsion, saying that people perform all their actions without divine assistance. These are the early Qadarites, who should not be confused with the Mu'tazilites who recognized the pre-existent divine knowledge, even though they affirmed people's freedom and responsibility for their actions. The former group includes Ma'bad al-Juhanī (d. 80/699) and Ghaylān of Damascus (d. 150/767). At the opposite extreme of this argument there were the Jabriyyah, who affirmed the divine power and held that one is under compulsion to the extent that God creates one's actions, good or bad, and one is like a feather in the breeze without any power of one's own. Amongst this group al-Jahm ibn Ṣafwān (d. 128/745) is the most important representative. Some argued that the Umayyads encouraged the Jabriyyah for their own political reasons, but such conjecture is not borne out by the fact that Jahm, as well as Maʿbad, the leader of the Qadarites, rebelled against the Umayyads and were killed by them.

Both the upholders of *jabr* (compulsion) and *tafwīḍ* (delegation of action and responsibility to man) relied on certain verses in the Qur'ān explaining away others. Scholars of the *ṣaḥābah* and the *tābiʿūn* argued against both groups, confirming the pre-existent knowledge of God and negating compulsion at the same time, attributing to man power, will and actions with an attitude which takes the middle course between absolute *jabr* and absolute *tafwīḍ*. Such an explanation was given by Imām ʿAlī, Ibn ʿUmar and al-Ḥasan ibn ʿAlī.[31]

Another issue which has resulted from the beginning in much discussion is the question of the Imāmate which gave rise in particular to Shiʿism. In the early stage Shiʿism in general meant affection for, and loyalty to, the *ahl al-bayt*. This was enhanced by the catastrophe they met at the hands of the Umayyad authorities and particularly at the battle of Karbala, in which al-Ḥusayn, the grandson of the Prophet, was killed, along with other members of the family (61/680). As a result of such events, we find armed rebellions by some and the beginning of such doctrines as the *ʿiṣmah* (infallibility) of the Imāms, *ghaybah* (occultation), *rajʿah* (return), the *mahdiyyah* (belief in the coming of the Mahdī as saviour of humanity), and the knowledge of the unseen and esoteric interpretation. Some members of the family of the Prophet preferred engaging in the pursuit of knowledge and the education of followers rather than in politics, such as ʿAlī Zayn al-ʿĀbidīn (d. 114/732), Muḥammad ibn ʿAlī (Ibn al-Ḥanafiyyah) (d. 81/700), al-Bāqir (d. 114/732) and Jaʿfar al-Ṣādiq (d. 148/765). These figures held a position of spiritual and intellectual *imāmah*, combining the function of spiritual guide and *faqīh mujtahid*. The only exception was Zayd who rebelled against the Umayyads and was killed in 125/742. Extreme views grew at the beginning of the second/eighth century, and were opposed by members of *ahl al-bayt* themselves such as al-Bāqir and al-Ṣādiq.

In addition to the previously mentioned theological questions, by the time of the early ʿAbbāsids, other questions came to the fore such as the createdness or uncreatedness of the Qur'ān, the Divine Attributes of the Word and other Attributes in general as regards their existence and connection with the Divine Essence and its Unity. In fact, by this time, all essential themes which were to constitute *ʿilm al-kalām* had arisen.

As *ʿilm al-kalām* grew and the different sects and schools appeared, and some *mutakallimūn* began to adopt methods of argument that are different in style from those of the Qur'ān, some began to question whether it was lawful to engage in *kalām* discussions. When Abū Ḥanīfah forbade his son to engage in debates on *kalām*, he said to him, "Why do you forbid for me what you engaged in yourself?" To which he replied, "When we engaged in that, we all fell silent, fearing that a speaker might err, whereas you engaged in these discussions, each one of you wishing his companion to slip and fall into disbelief. Whoever wishes this falls into the same trap."[32]

Some considered it unlawful in view of some *ḥadīth* that disapproved of it or because of such negative characteristics as the neglect of traditional proofs or the fact that some *mutakallimūn* questioned the faith of opponents or because of the employment of Greek logic. This is seen in the reported disapproval of *kalām* by the leaders of Sunni schools of law as well as traditionists, such as Ibn Qutaybah and some reservations even by scholars of *kalām* such as al-Ghazzālī in his *al-Jām' al-'awāmm 'an 'ilm al-kalām*, and then Suyūṭī in his *Ṣawn al-manṭiq wa'l-kalām 'an fannay al-manṭiq wa'l-kalām*.

On the other hand, there were supporters of *kalām*, some of whom went to the extent of making it an obligation on Muslims, relying on the fact that it supports the creed and stands against doubters and opponents. Al-Ash'arī wrote his treatise entitled *Istiḥsān al-khawḍ fī 'ilm al-kalām*, in which he refuted the opposite views and defended his own. Support came also from many other scholars, including al-'Āmirī, al-Ghazzālī, al-Subkī, Ibn 'Asākir and al-Bayāḍī,[33] who argued that the Prophet's objection was to discussions on the Essence of God and those that involve debating with the wrong motives or without knowledge or which would lead to acrimony, since the Qur'ān itself is full of verses that deal with theological issues and produce rational arguments for them. The debate was finally resolved by the fact that numerous scholars, throughout the Islamic era, of various schools, came to engage in theological discussion and created this very important science in Islam for which theological colleges are now well established in the main Sunni and Shi'i centres of learning.

In discussing the various stages and schools of *kalām* it is important to consider the type of arguments employed and the attitude of the *mutakallimūn* to such arguments. In early *kalām* both traditional and rational arguments were given due weight. We find at first people like al-Ḥasan al-Baṣrī, Ja'far al-Ṣādiq, Abū Ḥanīfah and al-Thawrī relying on both, even though the traditional proof comes first for them. When the Mu'tazilites came, they raised the status of *'aql* (reason) almost making it equal to *naql* (tradition), as can be seen from statements of Wāṣil, who said: "Truth can be known from four sources: the Qur'ān, agreed *Ḥadīth*, rational argument, and *ijmā'*." The rational tendency grew gradually until it gave *'aql* a status which is above *naql*, even if they continued to use them both, limiting the field in which *naql* can be used. This tendency reached its peak with Naẓẓām, but some moderation followed, at least theoretically, especially as witnessed in the works of 'Abd al-Jabbār and his followers who tried to go back to accepting the four sources as did Wāṣil. However, this equilibrium was practically neutralized by the concept of *dawr* (circularity in argument): since *'aql* is our first means of establishing the truthfulness of the Prophet and the Qur'ān, if one later puts *naql* above *'aql*, one is undermining the very means which led to the acceptance of *naql*.

But this argument would have made better sense if the Qur'ān had consisted only of a sacred text to be followed without questioning. However, the verses of the Qur'ān are not merely sacred texts but can also be viewed as propositions which come with their rational proofs. Why should we not rely on the rational proofs that occur in the Qur'ān, even when they are seen to be more convincing, closer to the hearts of men, and less inclined to convolution and polemics, than the traditional arguments of *kalām*? Ibn Rushd, for instance, who was above all a philosopher, examined the Qur'ānic methods, compared them to those of the *mutakallimūn* and found them to be better, for both scholars and the general masses at the same time.[34] Ibn Taymiyyah also observed that religion consists of issues and proofs, as did Ghazzālī and al-Juwaynī.[35]

The Ash'arites began by taking a balanced view between *naql* and *'aql* in the days of Ash'arī and Bāqillānī, when they stated that there were five ways to knowledge: *'aql*, Qur'ān, *Sunnah*, *ijmā'* and *qiyās*. Al-Māturīdī again recognized two sources, *sam'* (Qur'ān and *Sunnah*) and *'aql*, but the scale tended to favour *'aql*, when the concept of *dawr* infiltrated into Ash'arī *kalām*, from al-Juwaynī onwards until it reached its peak with Rāzī. Al-Āmidī tried to return to some balance, as did 'Abd al-Jabbār, but the concept of *dawr* had been too deeply rooted.[36] It was such developments that led Ibn Taymiyyah to write his book, *al-Muwāfaqah* ("harmony") or *Dar ta'āruḍ al-'aql wa'l-naql* ("Rejection of the conflict between *'aql* and *naql*") in which be criticized the methods of al-Rāzī, al-Āmidī and others who put *'aql* before *naql*.

As already mentioned, the earliest *kalām* is to be found in the Qur'ān itself which treated theological issues supported by rational proofs. It was chiefly their ways of understanding the Qur'ān and the way their views related to the Qur'ānic position that differentiated theological sects and schools. The early *kalām* was closest to the Qur'ānic position which was generally adopted in the discussions of the *'ulamā'* of the *ṣaḥābah* (Companions of the Prophet); the *tābi'ūn* (those who followed them), and their followers in the first three centuries, the Sunni schools as well as the Imāms of *ahl al-bayt*, and whoever followed their lead without neglect or excess.

Table 1 was devised by H. M. al-Shāfi'ī,[37] who is a leading authority of our time on *kalām* in the Arab world. It shows at a glance how the

Table 1

al-ʿaql / *al-tanzīh*	The Qurʾānic position	*al-naql* / *al-ithbāt*
Ismāʿīlīs	*Ṣaḥābah*	Māturīdīs
Muʿtazilites	*Tābiʿūn*	Ashʿarites
Ithnāʿasharites	Imāms of *madhāhib*	Ẓāhirites
Khārijites	Imāms of *ahl al-bayt*	Ḥanbalīs
Zaydīs		Ḥashwiyyah

Qur'ānic middle position compares to other positions. Shāfi'ī selected ten schools which have their own distinctive features and together expressed various types of thoughts and methods within *kalām*, which still survive for the most part to influence the intellectual and religious life of the Muslims up to the present.

The Qur'ānic viewpoint, which could be called *salafī*, is placed in the middle, since it is the origin of all the schools of thought and is taken as the criterion against which each is measured. The basis of this horizontal arrangement is twofold: (1) the predominance of *ithbāt* (taking the text at face value) or *tashbīh* (anthropomorphism) on the right hand, and the predominance of tendency to *ta'wīl* (interpretation) and *tanzīh* (transcendence) on the left hand; (2) tendency to adhere to *naql* (proof from tradition) on the right hand and that of adhering to *'aql* (rational proof) on the left hand. The diagram thus shows horizontally the extent of nearness or distance from the Qur'ānic viewpoint which combines *'aql* and *naql* and also *ithbāt* and *tanzīh*. The length of the vertical lines shows the variations between these vertical groups in their adherence to each of *naql*, *ithbāt* or *'aql* and *tanzīh*. For instance the Zaydīs are the nearest to *salaf* amongst the groups that tend towards *'aql* and *tanzīh*, and the least in going deep in that direction, whereas the Ismā'īlīs are the most committed to *'aql* and most deeply devoted to philosophy to the extent of *ta'ṭīl* (stripping of all attributes) even though they give this the form of *bāṭin* (esotericism) and *ta'wīl*.

On the right hand side, the Māturīdīs are nearest to this Qur'ānic middle position, followed by others up to the Ḥashwiyyah, who are at the same time the most committed to *naql* and *ithbāt*.

The Qur'ānic median position is characterized by the following features:

1 It takes the middle course between *'aql* and *naql*, giving the highest authority to revelation, but this does not mean neglect of *'aql* since the text of the revelation itself includes rational arguments which conform with it.
2 Lack of excessive *ta'wīl*, which is done only in accordance with the rules of the language and the usage of *Sharī'ah*, negating, at the same time, meanings that involve anthropomorphism, thus achieving *ithbāt* without *tashbīh* and *tanzīh* without *ta'ṭīl*.
3 Accepting sound traditional *dalīl* (proofs), beginning with those from the Qur'ān, followed by those from *ijmā'* then the *mutawātir ḥadīth*, then accepting *aḥād ḥadīth* whether *saḥīḥ* or *ḥasan* and rejecting the weak and forged *ḥadīth*.
4 Adherence to the *Sharī'ah* in its totality without raising practical *furū'* to the status of the principles of the faith.

The development of theological terms also reflects the various stages of development of *'ilm al-kalām*. Again, early *kalām* was closest in Qur'ānic terms. In a study on early Islamic theological and juristic terminology[38] I discussed *Kitāb al-ḥudūd fi'l-uṣūl* by Abu'l-Ḥasan ibn Fūrak (d. 404/1015),[39] and a number of other works including *al-Mubīn fī sharḥ ma'ni alfūẓ al-ḥukamā' wa'l-mutakallimūn* by Sayf al-Dīn al-Āmidī (d. 631/1233), which give some indication of the development of *kalām* terminology in their period. By *uṣūl* Ibn Fūrak clearly means *uṣūl al-dīn* (theology) and *uṣūl al-fiqh* (jurisprudence). The relationship between the two types of *uṣūl* was strong from the beginning. Abū Ḥanīfah's book *al-Fiqh al-akbar* is on *kalām*. The term *uṣūliyyūn* was, moreover, used for scholars of both subjects. A continued tradition of combining the terminology of both subjects was observed even after *kalām* became strongly connected to philosophy,[40] and Ibn Fūrak's book is significant for combining the terms of *kalām* and *uṣūl al-fiqh*. This was an early phase of *kalām* (*al-kalām al-qadīm*) before it became connected with philosophy (*al-kalām al-jadīd*). Early scholars such as Ibn Fūrak and other authors who followed his approach, such as Ibn Taymiyyah, seem to have wished to relate *uṣūl al-dīn* to *uṣūl al-fiqh*, keeping away from the approach of Greek logic (Ibn Taymiyyah writing a refutation of the latter), unlike other authors such as al-Ghazzālī, al-Rāzī and Naṣīr al-Dīn al-Ṭūsī.

The fact that *al-Ḥudūd* is an example of the early *kalām* is confirmed by the introductory terms which deal with *al-'ilm* and *al-naẓar* etc. These are also to be seen in the works of such early authors on *kalām* as al-Bāqillānī and 'Abd al-Qāhir al-Baghdādī, whereas later works usually begin with more philosophical terms like *al-wujūd wa'l-'adam* or *al-ashkāl al-arba'ah*, as we see in Ṭūsī's *al-Tajrīd*, or mix the earlier terms of *'ilm*, *naẓar*, etc. with philosophical ones, as did al-Rāzī in his *Muḥaṣṣal afkār al-mutaqaddimīn wa'l-muta'akhkhirīn*. It is, moreover, noticeable that most of the terms Ibn Fūrak defined are of Qur'ānic origin, e.g. *'ilm* (1), *naẓar* (6), *kasb* (19), *ibtidā'* and *irādah* (35, 36), rather than from Greek philosophy. From number 58 to number 100, for instance, (i.e. forty-three terms) there are only four terms that can be said to be non-Qur'ānic words (70, 73, 77, 90). Thus Qur'ānic words are not less than ninety per cent of the whole. This contrasts sharply with *al-Mubīn* by al-Āmidī where the percentage is clearly much lower. A comparison between *al-Ḥudūd* of Ibn Fūrak and *al-Mubīn* of al-Āmidī (which is on philosophical and *kalām* terms) is interesting: the former has 133 definitions, 98 of which are *kalām*; the latter has 223 definitions. Out of the 98 on *kalām* in *al-Ḥudūd* only 26 (twenty per cent) can be found in *al-Mubīn*. Al-Āmidī died 230 years after Ibn Fūrak, and both men were Sunni authors. Our comparison here may serve as an indication of how far "the new *kalām*" moved towards adopting philosophical terminology.

NOTES

1 In another version *yakhtaṣīmūn fī* – disputing over *qadar*.
2 He also said, "*Man takallama fī al-dīn bi ra'yihi fa qad ittahamah*", meaning, "Whoever discusses religion, relying [solely] on his own opinion, has doubted it."
3 Y. H. Farghal, *Nash'at al-ārā' wa'l-madhāhib wa'l-firaq al-kalāmiyyah*, 1 (Cairo, 1972): 36, 65; M. 'Abd al-Rāziq, *Tamhīd li tārikh al-falsafah al-islāmiyyah* (Cairo, 1966): 266.
4 'Abd al-Rāziq, *op. cit.*: 266–7; Shāfi'ī, *al-Madkhal ilā dirāsat 'ilm al-kalām*, (Cairo, 1991): 28–9.
5 *Op. cit.*: 265.
6 *Sharḥ al-'aqā'id al-nasafiyyah*, ed. Nūr Muḥammad (Karachi, n.d.): 5.
7 See Shāfi'ī, *op. cit.*: 28.
8 M. Cook has summed up these positions in "The Origins of *Kalām*", *Bulletin of the School of Oriental and African Studies*, 43 (1980): 42–3.
9 See *Anfänge Muslimischer Theologie* (Beirut, 1977): 55–6 (Arabic summary); *The Cultural Context of Medieval Learning*, ed. J. M. Murdoch and E. Dudley Sylla (Boston, 1975): 89, 105.
10 *Op. cit.*: 32.
11 As a wife of the Prophet, she is a "Mother of the Faithful".
12 Ibn 'Abd al-Barī, *Jāmi' bayān al-'ilm wa faḍluh* (Cairo, n.d.): 376–7.
13 See Shāfi'ī: 26.
14 K. A. al-Bayāḍī, *Ishārāt al-marām min 'ibārāt al-imām* (Cairo, 1949): 28–9.
15 See Taftāzānī, *op. cit.*: 4ff; Shāfi'ī, *op. cit.*: 15.
16 *Fī Iḥṣā' al-'ulūm*, ed. 'Uthman Amīn (Cairo, 1968): 69–70.
17 *Op. cit.*: 458.
18 *The Theology of Unity*, trans. I. Musa'ad and K. Cragg (London, 1960): 29.
19 See A. Mahmoud, *The Creed of Islam*, "V. The Resurrection" (London, 1976): 71–2 quoting *Rasā'il al-Kindī al-falsafiyyah*, ed. M. A. Abū Rīdah; *Manāhij al-adillah fī 'aqā'id al-millah*, ed. M. Qāsim (Cairo, 1969): 244–5.
20 Al-Bayāḍī, *op. cit.*: 36.
21 *Al-Tafsīr al-kabīr*, 15 vols, 2.1 (Beirut, 3rd ed., n.d.): 90.
22 *Op. cit.*: 88ff.
23 Muṣṭafā 'Abd al-Rāziq, *op. cit.*: 280–1.
24 *Op. cit.*: 149.
25 See Farghal, *op. cit.*: 37–43.
26 Ibn Kathīr, *Tafsīr al-qur'ān al-'aẓīm*, 1 (Cairo, n.d.): 368; Farghal, *op. cit.*: 33.
27 Al-Bayāḍī, *op. cit*: 33.
28 Shāfi'ī, *op. cit.*: 53–4.
29 A. M. al-'Aqqād dedicated a volume to this theme, entitled *al-Tafkīr farīdah islāmiyyah* (Cairo, many editions).
30 A. S. Nashshār, *Nash'at al-fikr al-falsafī fi'l-islām*, 1 (Cairo, 1965): 243–6.
31 Shāfi'ī, *op. cit.*: 65.
32 See Farghal, *op. cit.*: 79–87.
33 Shāfi'ī, *op. cit.*: 38.
34 See M. Qāsim in his introduction to *Manāhij al-adillah fī 'aqā'id al-millah*.
35 *Op. cit.*:148.

36 Shāfi'ī, *op. cit.*: 137–61.
37 *Op. cit.*: 72–5.
38 M. Abdel Haleem, *Bulletin of the School of Oriental and African Studies*, 65(1) (1991): 5–41.
39 The first book on *uṣūl* terminology to be written by a Sunni author. The first known work on *kalām* terminology was by Abū Ḥātim Aḥmad ibn Ḥamdān al-Rāzī, an Ismā'īlī Shi'i author who died in 322/933, but it is different in that it is not on *ḥudūd per se*, like Ibn Fūrak's work, which is still the first of its kind in this respect (*op. cit.*: 6).
40 Ibn Fūrak, *op. cit.*: 9.

BIBLIOGRAPHY

For an excellent bibliography see the section in Daiber, H. (1975) *Das theologisch–philosophische System des Mu'ammar ibn 'Abbād as-Sulamī* (Beirut).

Allard, M. (1965) *Le Problème des attributs divins dans d'al-Ash'ari et de ses premiers grands disciples* (Beirut).
Al-Ash'arī, Abū 'l-Ḥasan (1967) *The Elucidation of Islam*, trans. W. Ivanow (New York).
Beelo, I. (1989) *The Medieval Islamic Controversy between Philosophy and Orthodoxy* (Leiden).
Bernard, M. (1980) "La critique de la notion de nature (Ṭab') par le kalām", *Studia Islamica*, 51: 59–106.
Brunschvig, R. (1964) "Devoir et pouvoir: histoire d'un problème de théologie musulmane", *Studia Islamica*, 20: 5–46.
Campanini, M. (1986) *La Surah della Caverna: meditazione filosofica sull'unicità di Dio* (Florence).
Chehata, C. (1965) "Etudes de philosophie musulmane du droit", *Studia Islamica*, 23: 5–25.
Cook, M. (1980) "The Origins of *Kalām*", *Bulletin of the School of Oriental and African Studies*, 43: 32–43.
Frank, R. (1966) *The Metaphysics of Created Being according to Abū l'Hudhayl al-'Allāf: a Philosophical Study of the Earliest "Kalām"* (Istanbul).
—— (1978) "Reason and Revealed Law: a Sample of Parallels and Divergences in *Kalām* and *falsafa*", *Recherches d'Islamologie, recueil d'articles offert à Georges C. Anawati et Louis Gardet*, Bibliothèque Philosophique de Louvain: 107–21.
—— (1983) "Moral Obligation in Classical Muslim Theology", *Journal of Religious Ethics*, 11: 204–23.
—— (1989) "Knowledge and *Taqlīd*: the Foundations of Religious Belief in Classical Ash'arism", *Journal of the American Oriental Society*, 109(1): 37–62.
—— (1991) "Elements in the Development of the Teaching of al-Ash'arī", *Le Muséon*, 104(1–2): 141–90.
Gardet, L. (1966) "La notion de prophétie en théologie musulmane", *Revue Thomiste* (July–September): 353–409.
Gardet, L. and Anawati, M. (1948) *Introduction à la théologie musulmane: essai de théologie comparée* (Paris).

Gimaret, D. (1980) *Théories de l'acte humain en théologie musulmane* (Paris).
Goldziher, I. (1931) *Introduction to Islamic Theology and Law*, trans. A. and R. Hamori (Princeton).
Grunebaum, G. (1970) "Observations on the Muslim Concept of Evil", *Studia Islamica*, 31: 117–34.
Hallaq, W. (1987) "The Development of Logical Structure", *Der Islam*, 64(1): 42–67.
Horovitz, S. (1909) *Über den Einfluss der griechischen Philosophie auf die Entwicklung des Kalām* (Berlin).
Hourani, G. (1971) *Islamic Rationalism: the Ethics of 'Abd al-Jabbār* (Oxford).
—— (1985) *Reason and Tradition in Islamic Ethics* (Cambridge).
Ivry, A. (1976) "Al-Kindī and the Mu'tazila: a Philosophical and Political Reevaluation", *Oriens*, 25–6: 69–85.
Al-Juwaynī (1938) *El-Irchad, par Imām al-Ḥaramayn*, trans. J. Luciani (Paris).
McCarthy, R. (1953) *The Theology of the Arabic Texts of al-Ash'arī's Kitāb al-Lumā' and Risālāt al-khawḍ fī 'ilm al-kalām* (Beirut).
McDonald, D. (1965) *Development of Muslim Theology* (New York).
Martin, R. (1980) "The Role of the Basrah Mu'tazilah in Formulating the Doctrine of the Apologetic Miracle", *Journal of Near Eastern Studies*, 39(3): 175–89.
Nader, A. (1956) *Le Système philosophique des Mutazélite penseurs de l'Islam* (Beirut).
Pretzl, O. (1940) *Die frühislamische Attributenlehre* (Munich).
Reinhart, A. (1995) *Before Revelation: the Boundaries of Muslim Moral Thought* (Albany).
Robinson, N. (1991) *Christ in Islam and Christianity* (London).
Rosenthal, F. (1960) *The Muslim Concept of Freedom prior to the Nineteenth Century* (Leiden).
Van Ess, J. (1972) *Frühe mu'tazilitische Häresiographie* (Beirut).
—— (1975) *Zwischen Hadith und Theologie: Studien prädestinatianischer Überlieferung* (Berlin).
Watt, W. (1948) *Free Will and Predestination in Early Islam* (London).
Wensinck, A. (1932) *The Muslim Creed* (Cambridge).

CHAPTER 6

The transmission of Greek philosophy to the Islamic world

Yegane Shayegan

The question of the transmission of Greek philosophy and science to the Islamic world covers an extremely vast area: the last centuries of the Hellenistic world, the Sassanian Empire and its specific Christian church, and the Islamic period. In order to understand the question of transmission we cannot avoid referring to the first two cultures which constitute the backbone and the playground of this historical development. We will be concerned with the underlying forces which brought about changes in each period and opened the path for the actual transmission.

The subject of transmission is related to a great number of different academic fields: philosophy, history of philosophy, history of science, Classics, history of the Christian church, both Western and Eastern, Iranian, Syriac and Arabic studies – and the list can go on. The traditional culture which we call late Hellenism was a combination of many elements, especially many contradictory elements, and in order to understand its transmission we first have to understand it. The comprehension of such a complicated period requires the collaboration of a variety of specialists such as Classicists, Arabists, church historians and researchers on gnosticism, etc. It is a task that can be undertaken only through joint work.

Scholars from different fields are already paying attention to each other's researches. The article of M. Tardieu (1986), a historian of gnosticism, is taken up in detail by I. Hadot (1990: 275–303), a Classicist. After a century and a half of research and studies in various fields many obscure matters still remain in the dark owing to scarcity of sources; for example we are still at odds as to the whereabouts of the last Athenian Neoplatonist philosophers after Justinian's edict of A.D. 529 whereby the

Academy at Athens was closed and its property was confiscated. It is difficult to imagine how philosophers could work in such a situation.

Greek philosophical and scientific thought was pushed eastwards, and the thesis of its transfer from Alexandria to Baghdad held by some medieval Islamic writers is perfectly plausible. However, their thesis should be accepted in general terms and not in detail, since a great number of their statements were based on hearsay transmitted to them in the form of an oral tradition from Nestorians and Jacobites. Oral tradition is not usually chronological and the very fact that information was exchanged in a non-chronological order is indicative of the existence of an oral tradition which E. G. Browne (1921: 114) refers to as "a living tradition".

I see the movement of Greek thought eastwards as based on two underlying forces: the Christianization of the Roman Empire, and the internationalization of the Sassanian Empire.

THE CHRISTIANIZATION OF THE ROMAN EMPIRE

The question to be asked is the following: what do we mean by Christianization of the Roman Empire? The Hellenistic world was Christianized at a very slow pace, the process taking more than two hundred years. The Emperor Constantine granted formal toleration in 313 to the Christian religion and in 325 he summoned the first general Council at Nicaea. This latter's duty was to bring about discipline in the disputed Christian doctrine; it was in fact, the first attempt to canonize the Christian church, and many other councils were to follow in order to consolidate a unified doctrine. The pressure always came from the state. However, Christianity was not declared a state religion until the last quarter of the fourth century by the edict of the Emperor Gratian. The transformation of pagan into Christian culture continued well into the sixth century and was more or less ended with the edict of Justinian in 529.

This change, even though gradual, was a qualitative change, one that I shall call *epistemic* in the sense of change occurring in the general consciousness, and it struck at the very heart of the Western world view. This fundamental change brought about a linear and historical interpretation of time and replaced the cyclical view which had prevailed during the Hellenistic period. I cannot elaborate this point further here but can point out that Philoponus in his *Physics* (456.17ff.) rejects the cyclical view and accepts the linear view of time. This change has been underestimated by historians of ideas who emphasize the epistemic change occurring in the seventeenth century with the advent of modern science.

What actually did occur in the change from the Hellenistic to the Christian world view was that all apocryphal interpretations of texts were banned, and this ban was not limited to the Scriptures; it also extended to gnostic texts; and Neoplatonist interpreters of Platonic dialogues did not escape the ban. It was in fact a ban on symbols and myths in exchange for the acceptance of the official dogma. This state of affairs led eventually to the divorce between creative imagination and rational thought which had also been developed by Neoplatonists. This is what I mean by an epistemic change. What could emperors who wished to establish law and order do other than attack disorder? The latter, having been created with the appearance of Christianity, was becoming unacceptable to the state authorities.

Constantine opted for Christianity out of political motives, but the real problem was that Christianity, as E. R. Hayes (1930: 35) suggests, was "in a certain sense a reformed Judaism". When separated from Judaic law it had no legal authority for dealing with regulations as in the case of Judaism and Islam which have the *Halakhah* and the *Sharī'ah* respectively. Christianity claimed a Jewish origin as it came for the "salvation of the Jews" (St John, 4: 22). This very fact was a blessing in disguise for the future development of the Western world, but it certainly did not appear so during the first four centuries of Christianity. Emperors were confronted with great difficulties since the new creed, which had no legal base, led to a great number of free interpretations. These latter problems did not just concern the gnostics but were within the church itself. There was anarchy and a constant struggle between a great number of sects such as Monophysites, Dyophysites, Tritheists and many others. In Alexandria the followers of three different patriarchs fought one another at the same time. The Western part of the Empire did not escape what came to be referred to as heresies. The majority of the bishops in fourth-century Spain were Priscillianists and emphasized the symbolic interpretation of the Trinity.

To resolve this disparity of doctrinal interpretations, the Bible was translated from Greek into Latin by St Jerome in the fourth century A.D. and Roman law was imposed by the state in order to replace the lack of Christian legal authority. Thus, Latin was replacing Greek which had represented early Christianity. As E. Stein (1949: 411) and A. Cameron (1967: 663) remark, Justinian's edict of A.D. 529 gave the monopoly of the study of law to three centres – Rome, Constantinople and Beirut – and banned it from Caesarea, Athens and Alexandria. These two latter were the most important centres for rhetoric. If Roman law was to bridge the gap resulting from the Christian lack of legality, it also had to replace Greek rhetoric, which had played the part of law in Greek pagan culture. In fact it was through rhetoric that people were trained for the bar in Greek culture. Greek rhetoric as a legal discipline received its first blow at the end of the fourth century A.D. and with the gradual decline of Greek rhetoric the legitimacy of the Greek world was shaken. Since it is law that binds society together, a change in basic legality can affect the very structure of a society. It is an irony of history, since this very Roman law that was now promulgated in a Christian world had penalized Christianity as a crime deserving death under Emperor Trajan (Lactantius, *Instit.*, 5.11, 12).

The fate of philosophers as well as their works followed that of rhetoric. Even before the closure of the Academy of Athens, troubles were already looming on the intellectual horizon of Alexandria. In A.D. 391 an edict was issued by Theodosius I forbidding pagan sacrifices. Groups of monks attacked and destroyed pagan temples in Alexandria. Many pagan scholarchs left Alexandria; among them were Olympius, a philosopher and a priest of the God Serapis, and Helladius and Ammonius, both grammarians and priests, the former of Zeus and the latter of the ape-god. Many had their salaries withdrawn and some were not allowed to teach. A tragic episode was the death of Hypatia, the pagan philosopher, who was lynched by a group of monks in 415 (Cameron (1967): 667–9). In the last quarter of the fifth century A.D., Ammonius (d. *c.* 517) was the head of the Alexandrian school of Neoplatonism, but there was a great deal of pressure on him exerted by the Christian authorities with respect to his pagan philosophical teachings. In fact he was attacked by two Christian scholarchs, Zacharias Scholasticus and Aeneas of Gaza, because of his doctrine of the eternity of the world.

The Alexandrian school underwent extreme transformations. According to a papyrus of the fifth century A.D. (Maspero (1914): 165–71), there was a Christian association called the Philiponoi whose main occupation was to organize fights against the pagan teachers and students and attack pagan temples. Severus, the future patriarch of Antioch, was a member of this association. This fact demonstrates that the academic atmosphere was extremely tense. Under these circumstances, it is normal for a man like Ammonius to be forced to sign an agreement with Athanasius II in the 490s. This incident was reported by Damascius (d. *c.* 538) (*Vita Isidori*, fr. 316: 251, ed. Zintzen) who is rather harsh on Ammonius and charges him with financial motives. The result of the deal was no doubt financial, for otherwise Ammonius could not have taught since his salary depended on the municipal authorities.

Nevertheless Ammonius had to make some concessions in exchange. What were these concessions? This question was extremely important for it had far-reaching and determining effects on the future of philosophy. Ammonius turned away from Platonic commentaries and concentrated on Aristotle, not just on Aristotle's *Organon* but also on his *Metaphysics*. This is a clear indication that Ammonius did in fact make some concessions in exchange for financial gain in the deal with the Patriarch

Athanasius II. It is difficult to imagine how he could have acted otherwise under those circumstances. No commentaries on Plato by Ammonius have reached us, and it is possible that he never wrote any Platonic commentary. None the less, it was strange to have studied under Proclus and to have remained unaffected by the master's zeal for speculative metaphysics. Olympiodorus (b. *c.* A.D. 495/505, *in Gorg.*, 198.8) reports that Ammonius lectured on the *Gorgias*, but no mention is made of the dialogues about which Neoplatonists were so keen on writing commentaries such as the *Republic*, *Timaeus* and *Parmenides*.

Ammonius had no other choice but to turn away from Platonic dialogues, which were controversial in their Proclean interpretations and were identified with pagan polytheism (cf. Mahdi, (1967): 234 n. 2 and Saffrey (1954): 400–1). The best possible action was to turn to Aristotle and Neoplatonize Aristotle. A twofold process took place in the Ammonian interpretation of Aristotle. As K. Verrycken (1990: 230) rightly remarks, "the Neoplatonisation of Aristotle's metaphysics is met by a corresponding *Aristotelianisation* of the Neoplatonic system". The legacy of Ammonius was the harmonization of Plato and Aristotle, a legacy that al-Fārābī (d. 339/950) inherited from Ammonius. Simplicius (*in Phys.*, 1360.28–31) refers to Ammonius' aim as that of harmonizing Aristotle with Plato. It is in this Ammonian form that Alexandrian philosophy was transmitted to the Islamic world in general and to al-Fārābī in particular.

In order to understand the Alexandrian dilemma the following questions should be asked: what do we mean (1) by the Neoplatonization of Aristotle's metaphysics and (2) by the Aristotelianization of the Neoplatonic system? The former concerns a metaphysical question related to cosmology, and the latter refers to the ontological levels of being. According to Simplicius (*in Phys.*, 1360.24–1363.24, *in Cael.*, 271. 13–21), Ammonius ascribed to the Aristotelian God not only final causality but also efficient causality. Aristotle's unmoved Mover is the final cause, it is the intelligible (*noēton*) which moves the intellect (*noūs*) without being moved (Arist., *in Metaph.*, 12.7.1072a26–7, 30–1). There is an ontological problem in Aristotle's explanation. If the unmoved Mover moves, then who bestows existence? For surely, if there *is* nothing, neither can there be motion. To *be* must be prior to *to be in motion.* Simplicius (*in Phys.*, 1361.31–4) reports that Alexander recognized an efficient causality with respect to heavenly motion but denied it to heavenly substance (*in Phys.*, 1362.11–15). Simplicius (*in Phys.*, 1363.9–10) defends Ammonius by arguing that if something receives its motion from outside it should also receive its existence from outside. This argument seems right out of Avicenna's misunderstood doctrine of the exteriority of existence. Final causality as the principle of motion (Arist., *in Phys.*, 2.6.198a3) alone seems to be ontologically insufficient to Simplicius, Ammonius and Avicenna (Ibn Sīnā). In their view efficient causality must also be the principle that brings substance (*ousia*) into existence (Simplicius, *in Phys.*, 1363.2–8). We find an identical criticism of Aristotle and his commentators by Avicenna (1947: 23.21–24.4) in his commentary on book *Lambda* of Aristotle's *Metaphysics* (1072a23–6; Booth (1983): 109). Avicenna argues:

> it is absurd to reach the first reality through motion and through the fact that it is a principle of motion and also require it to act as the principle of essences. These people offered nothing other than the proof that it is a mover not that it is a principle of being. I should be [hopelessly] incompetent [were I to admit] that motion should be the means of proving the first reality which is itself the principle of all being. Their turning the first principle into a principle for the motion of the heavenly sphere does not necessarily make it [also] a principle for the substance of the heavenly sphere.

The Avicennan argument, which is similar to that of Simplicius (*in Phys.*, 1363.2–8), is at the very centre of his metaphysics, and his ontology originates from this very question. This demonstrates what transmission is all about and how ideas are taken up and further developed. Transmission cannot be explained only through geography.

It should be added that the idea of coming to be through efficient causality in Ammonius had no connection with the Christian doctrine of creation *ex nihilo*. Neoplatonists, like their counterparts the Islamic philosophers, believed in the "eternity" of the world. The harmony of efficient and final causalities or the immanent and the transcendent were probably part of a genuine theory which also served to shield and preserve philosophy from ecclesiastical wrath.

As for the question of the Aristotelianization of the Neoplatonic system, the tripartite division of being was replaced by a gradual and hierarchical chain of being, each level containing both matter and form (Ammonius, *in Cat.*, 35.18–36.4; Verrycken (1990b): 230). It was again in this form that the Aristotelian logico-ontology was transmitted to the Islamic world where it underwent still greater developments in the hands of al-Fārābī, Avicenna and other Peripatetics who perpetuated the school's tradition. With Ammonius began a school whose philosophical theories, even though provoked by the persecution of a state-run religion, became very elaborate. In a sense one could say that the revival of Aristotelian exegesis in Islamic philosophy is indirectly indebted to the severity of the state Orthodox church.

After Ammonius the Alexandrian School went through a gradual process of Christianization. In A.D. 529, the very year of the closure of the Athenian Academy, Philoponus (d. *c.* 570) wrote his well-known treatise *De aeternitate mundi contra Proclum*, and a little later his

De aeternitate mundi contra Aristotelem which is preserved only in the Arabic version and is reported in *De caelo* of Simplicius. Philoponus used the occasion of Christian–pagan controversy in order to distance himself from the Neoplatonist doctrine of the eternity of the world. He then wrote theological works in which he held the Monophysite position, such as the *Diaetētēs* (Arbiter) in 552, despite the fact that the Council of Chalcedon in 451 had rejected this doctrine according to which Christ had one nature not two (divine and human, as in the case of Dyophysites or Nestorians). Towards the end of his life in 567 he wrote *De trinitate*, in which he held a Tritheist view of Christology whereby Father, Son and Spirit were three substances consubstantial in nature. This led to a further split among the anti-Chalcedonians. Philoponus was charged with heresy and was anathematized in A.D. 680, that is, more than a hundred years after his death. As Sorabji (1987: 1) rightly remarks: "This had the ironical result that his ideas were first taken up in the Islamic world, not in Christendom".

Philoponus was greatly appreciated among the Jacobite–Monophysite community of Persia; Ammonius, on the other hand, was preferred among the Nestorians–Dyophysites. The philosophical as well as theological works of Philoponus were translated into Syriac, for example his *Arbiter*, a Monophysite treatise, was translated into Syriac, and edited by A. Sanda in 1930. But his Tritheist views had no echo in the Eastern world. The case of Philoponus is a clear example that even Christians were not immune from persecution in a state-run religion, that is, when their views were nonconformist or conflicted with the widely held exegesis. This religious state of affairs affected another area, the scientific, and the Western world was deprived of Philoponus' scientific legacy. His dynamics was taken up by Avicenna, who developed it to such an extent that later it could serve as the foundation and ground for the seventeenth century Scientific Revolution. It passed into the Latin West through the eleventh-century A.D. translations and was carried through and further developed by John Buridan and others (Zimmerman (1987): 121–9; Shayegan (1986): 30–3).

As for his doctrine of the creation of the world, it was taken up by the Islamic theologians who for centuries fought against the philosophers on this issue. Later, their arguments returned to the Western Christian Scholastics. Philoponus should also be held responsible for the important change from the cyclical to the linear world view of time. As Chadwick (1987: 87) points out, "Philoponus dismisses the myth of eternal return and the cycle of unending time (cf. *in Phys.*, 456.17ff.). The material cosmos is in continual change. No individual once perished can ever come to live again." This is a crucial point regarding another aspect of the transmission which was taken up by Islamic theologians and produced some interest among the philosophers.

Philoponus was succeeded by Olympiodorus who probably was a pagan, but in order to guard himself against eventual Christian attacks and out of caution declared himself a monotheist (*in Gorgiam*, 32–3; cf. Westerink (1990): 331).

He was followed by three Christians: Elias, David and Stephanus. Alexandria somehow managed to survive by gradually shedding its pagan features and losing its philosophical vital force.

The fate of Athens, the cradle of Greek philosophy, was not different from that of Alexandria; however, being a private institution it suddenly came to an abrupt end in A.D. 529 by royal decree and its philosophers fled to the Persian Sassanian Empire. In the Western Empire, Boethius could translate only the Aristotelian *Organon* before his premature death in *c.* 524. His Orthodox–Catholic exegesis of Christology against Monophysites and Nestorians in *Liber contra Eutychen et Nestorium* (512) probably did not please the Ostrogoth King Theodoric, who was an Arian (Arianism had affinities with the Monophysite doctrine). The motives for his condemnation can be interpreted as politico-religious, as a Catholic martyr being persecuted by an Arian king (Sharples (1990): 35).

The Christian doctrinal disagreement and confusions over Christology were not just restricted to the Eastern Empire. These historical elements seem rather confusing, but in reality contributed to the shaping of the destiny of people in the West by mixing the profane with the sacred, the state with religion. They did not have to obey and pay unconditional allegiance to the static, unchanging religious law as did their counterparts in the Islamic world.

The Islamic world inherited Greek thought and science with all its problems. The pagan–Christian controversy was discussed by philosophers and scientists alike such as al-Bīrūnī (d. *c.* 449/1050), Avicenna (Nasr and Mohaghegh (1973): 13, 51ff.) and al-Fārābī in his lost treatise *The Beginnings of Greek Philosophy*, reported by Ibn Abī Uṣaybīʿah in his *History of Physicians* (cf. Meyerhof (1933): 114). This demonstrates that the recipients were aware of the transmission with all its sociopolitical implications. Al-Fārābī, for example, perhaps out of caution and in order not to undergo the fate of the Athenian and Alexandrian scholarchs, added a section of Islamic law, *al-Sharīʿah*, to his commentary on the *Laws* of Plato.

THE INTERNATIONALIZATION OF THE SASSANIAN EMPIRE

We now turn to the part played by the Persian Empire in anticipating and preparing the way for the reception of Greek thought in the Islamic world.

In A.D. 529, when Justinian closed the Academy in Athens and confiscated its properties, seven pagan philosophers fled to Persia, to the court of the Sassanian King Chosroes Anūshīrvān (d. 578). This must have been in *c.* 531. According to the historian Agathias, these philosophers were the following: "Damascius the Syrian, Simplicius the Cicilian, Eulamius the Phrygian, Priscianus the Lydian, Hermeias and Diogenes both from Phoenicia, Isidore of Gaza" (cf. Hadot (1990): 278 n. 15). They stayed between one and two years in Persia and settled most probably in Harran. They could not have returned to Athens as recent scholarship has suggested (Tardieu (1986): 1–44; (1987): 40–57; Frantz (1975): 29–38; Sorabji (1983): 199–200).

During their period of stay in Persia they could have envisaged the possibilities of teaching in Persian academies, whether secular and scientific as Jundishapur, Rayshahr or Shiz or Christian like Nisibis, Marv and Ctesiphon. Their decision must have depended on the language employed in these academies for educational purposes. The main language used for instruction was Syriac, even though Greek and Pahlavi were also used for translation of texts, and Persian in scientific centres (*Dēnkard* (1911), 1: 412.17ff.). A Pahlavi post-Sassanian text declares that a great number of scientific and philosophical texts of Greek and Indian origin were incorporated into the *Avesta* during the reign of Shāpūr I (A.D. 241–72) (Zaehner (1955): 8). Syriac was the liturgical language of the Persian church later referred to as Nestorian after Nestorius, the patriarch of Constantinople, and also many Zoroastrian Persians who were converted to Christianity used Syriac for religious purposes.

Already during the Achaemenian Empire (558–330 B.C.) Aramaic was used throughout the multilingual territories as the *lingua franca* of the Empire from the Nile to the Indus. This tradition continued with Syriac during the Sassanian Empire (Panoussi (1968): 244 n. 24). Ḥājjī Khalīfah (1833–58, 1: 69–70) says that the languages used in Persian academies were "Pehlevica . . ., Persica . . ., Syriaca" (cf. Chabot (1934): 9). We cannot refer to those who used the Syriac language as Syrians only. They were Assyrians, Chaldeo–Babylonians and Persians as well as Syrians who previously had used Aramaic as their means of communications and were now using Syriac as their liturgical Christian language. Aramaic is used in some parts of the Old Testament, portions of Ezra (4: 8–6, 18) and Daniel (2: 4b–7, 28) and had two main dialects, the Eastern and the Western. The former spread into the Persian Empire and became *Suraye*, the name given by Eastern Aramaic writers to their language, which has produced both a pre-Christian and a Christian literature; the latter survived in the mountains of the present Lebanon and only fragments of its literature have been discovered. The Aramaic alphabet was even used for Pahlavi inscriptions of the Parthian Empire (248 B.C.–A.D. 226) and for Sassanian (226–632) inscriptions on rocks.

The transmission of Greek philosophical and scientific thought is more complex than just the coming together of Greek–Islamic civilizations via Nestorians. The Persian element was crucial for the flourishing of such a transmission; as Peters (1968: 42) rightly points out,

> the flowering of Greek studies in Islam was something more complex than the mere encounter of the Arabs, newly thrusting from the desert, with Byzantine guardians of the Hellenic legacy. Nor is the question, how did Greek learning pass into Islam? The answer is, simply, through the Nestorians. On all sides there is evidence of an Iranian cultural synthesis which was, in the final analysis, to provide the soil from which Greek sciences were to bloom.

The synthesis of Greco-Persian culture does not only go back to the Seleucid period, but the interaction of these two cultures can be dated from the sixth century before Christ. This issue cannot be discussed here, and I shall limit myself to the statement that relations between the two cultures were close since the Achaemenian period (558 B.C.). It is obvious that after Alexander this mutual influence was felt at all levels of the populations from 330 to 248 B.C. and beyond.

It is generally accepted that the Sassanian monarchs were quite tolerant towards foreign ideas. The questions to be asked are the following: (1) Why were they tolerant to Greek paganism? (2) Why did they show tolerance towards Christianity? These two issues are completely separate and cannot be treated as proceeding from one single background, even though the outcome of both turned out to be the same: that is, tolerance on the religious level facilitated the development of Greek thought on Persian soil. One point, however, should be borne in mind, that Persian religious tolerance and intolerance were both grounded in politics. The persecution of natives such as Māni and Mazdak was a perfect example.

Concerning the first question, as mentioned above, the interaction between the two cultures was a millennium old. We have evidence of a letter of Tansar to the king of Tabaristan published in Persian by Darmesteter (1894: 185–250). Tansar was a *herpātān herpāt*, that is, a high Zoroastrian priest who wrote this letter at the request of Ardeshīr (d. 248), the first Sassanian king, to the king of Tabaristan in the north of Persia, inviting him to join the newly united Empire. This letter was originally translated from Pahlavi by Ibn Muqaffa' (102/720–140/756) into Arabic and from Arabic into Persian in 607/1210 by Muḥammad ibn al-Isfandyār. Al-Mas'ūdī (d. 345/956) in his *Murūj al-dhahab* (1865, 2: 161) mentions this Mobed Tansar and refers to him as belonging to the Platonic sect; he repeats his claim in his *al-Tanbīh wa'l-ishrāf* (1894: 90–100). This seems a good example of Hellenized Magians and it demonstrates that Neoplatonic influence had already existed in Persia; otherwise it could not be the common concern of the high priesthood. Events in the Seleucid period (330–248 B.C.) must have played a determining part in it, but this must not undermine the fact that Persia was not a cultural desert into which Seleucid kings brought fertility. Alexander burned all the books in Persia; so the Parthians and Sassanians had a hard time reconstructing even the Avestic tradition.

During the Parthian period coins were in the Greek alphabet, but the Parthian kings were concerned with their past; so they started searching for traditional texts which according to Pahlavi writings Alexander had destroyed. The second thorough search came during the reign of the Sassanian King Shāpūr I (A.D. 241–72). We have the evidence of *Dēnkard* (1911, 1: 412.17–21; cf. Chaumont (1988): 85) according to which Shāpūr I collected religious and scientific texts from other nations, from countries like India and the Byzantine Empire. There was an international atmosphere of learning which was both genuine and politically inclined. It was genuine, since one cannot underestimate the inclinations of a monarch such as Chosroes I for learning. In one of his edicts Chosroes recognizes the rational value of Aristotelian logic as a means of theological investigation, a phenomenon that can also be observed in Philoponus' theological writings and those of Syriac and Islamic theologians. Chosroes declares: "Those who say that it is possible to understand being through the revelation of Religion and also by analogy are to be deemed searchers (after truth)" (Zaehner (1955): 9). Procopius (*Anecdote*, 18.29) confirms the philosophico-theological interest of Chosroes I. Agathias (*Hist.*, 2.2) describes him as possessing knowledge of Plato and Aristotle. Concerning Plato he seems to have known the *Timaeus*, *Phaedo* and *Gorgias*.

As to Aristotle, apart from Agathias' report, we have the evidence of a Syriac manuscript (British Museum, MS 14660) studied by Renan (1852: 311–18) whose title reads: *Discourse Composed by Paul the Persian on Aristotle, the Philosopher's Logical Works Addressed to the King Chosroes.* Reinaud, working on Syriac philosophical manuscripts in the British Museum in the days of Queen Victoria, wrote that the court of Chosroes was "L'asile de la philosophie grecque expirante" (Renan (1852): 311). He added that both philosophers expelled from Greece by the edict of Justinian and Nestorians persecuted by the Orthodox church found refuge in Persia and brought about a great movement of Hellenistic ideas during the sixth century. He further remarked: "C'est assurémment un singulier phenomène que celui d'un perse écrivant en syriaque un traité de philosophie grecque à l'usage d'un roi barbare".

To answer the second question, that is, the reason for the tolerance of the Sassanians towards Christianity, the answer should be sought in politics. Religious tolerance had always been the *modus operandi* of Sassanian politics and was already apparent before them in the Achaemenian tradition of Cyrus (558–530 B.C.) when he conquered Babylonia. In the Babylonian inscriptions it is written that Cyrus regarded the God Marduk and his son Nabi as other names for Ahura Mazda and his son Atarsh (the sacred fire). But the theory is hardly tenable and it is evident that his position is not that of a religious leader but rather that of a wise politician. By liberating the Jews of Babylonia and by obtaining the name of "Shepherd of Jahweh" he further proves his sheer sense of imperial politics (Gray (1908): 70). This policy was followed by his son Cambyses (contrary to the claims of Herodotus, 3.16 and according to an Egyptian text on an anaophoric statue in the Vatican; Petrie, *History of Egypt*, 3: 361–2) and Darius I, and became the established policy for the preservation and domination of the diversity of creeds within the Empire.

The Sassanian kings were no exception. Ardeshīr, the first king of the Sassanian dynasty, followed the footsteps of Cyrus by perpetuating the perennial assimilation and transformation of myths and symbols of different cultures and religions. In a legendary historical Pahlavi novel, *Karnāmagh-e Ardeshīr-e Pābhaghān*, Ardeshīr pursues the legend of Cyrus. He kills the dragon, Haftanbokht, as the Babylonian God Marduk had killed the monster Tiamat (Christensen (1944): 58. n. 5, 96). Cyrus had started this policy of using myths for political domination, and his legitimate heirs, the Sassanians, emulated him seven centuries later. The idea of having an international empire was the central policy of the Achaemenians, and of the Parthians to a lesser degree.

The Sassanians assimilated what they thought appropriate of Greek culture. The first two Sassanian kings, Ardeshīr and Shāpur I in the third century A.D., wrote their two first inscriptions on the rocks in Sassanian Pahlavi, Parthian Pahlavi and Greek. This was not entirely due to the availability of cheap Greek labour, as has been suggested, but was done in order to make a political point. However, the Sassanians had acted differently with the Nestorians and Monophysites, since these groups have myths which could not be replaced by those of the Zoroastrians. By refusing to accept the Orthodox doctrine and the laws it implied, Nestorians and Monophysites were left in a precarious legal position. The Sassanian king could only influence the legal aspect of Christianity in order to make it acceptable to the High Zoroastrian priests and to Persian society at large.

Nestorians and Monophysites were successively losing their support from Constantinople through consecutive synods. The Nestorians lost state legitimacy after the second Synod of Ephesus in A.D. 449. This synod, which was called the Latrocinium or the "Synod of Brigands" by Pope Leo, ended the Cyril of Alexandria and Nestorian controversy which had begun in 428 and resulted in the extirpation of Nestorians. As for

Monophysites, their days were also numbered, and the important Council of Chalcedon in 451 was directed against them as well. Chalcedon marks an important time in Roman church history since the state officially opted for the Orthodox body of the church. The law was implemented in 489 when the Emperor Zeno finally closed the School of Edessa which was called the School of Persians. The Nestorian bishops and their students were expelled and migrated to Persia where they were joined by Barsauma, the patriarch of Nisibis who played a crucial part in the Persian church with the blessing of King Pīrūz. This event brought a split in Christianity by geographically determining two different Christologies. The Byzantine Empire became the homeland of the Orthodox church while the Sassanian Empire officially recognized Nestorianism.

Barsauma's acute sense of diplomacy was combined with the political shrewdness of Pīrūz, and the result was a Persianized church whose canons were not issued in Constantinople or Alexandria any more but in Beit Laput (Jundishapur), Ctesiphon and Nisibis. In these councils the vow of celibacy was limited to hermits, and marriage of Catholicoi, bishops and priests was formally legalized. The legal aspect of Christianity was entrusted to royal decree and Catholicoi were appointed by Sassanian kings. This situation was satisfactory for the Sassanian dynasty, whose fundamental aim was the political integrity of their multinational empire. Modern church historians such as Labourt (1904: 43–7) acknowledge that the persecution of Christians had political causes especially after the establishment of Christianity as a state religion in the fourth-century Byzantine Empire when Persian Christians were not unjustly suspected of high treason.

The post-Chalcedonian era marked a new cultural flourishing in Persia with the closure of the School of Edessa. In addition to theology, the School of Edessa was well known for its Greek learning even by the second century A.D. In fact, it was the first Hellenistic and Syriac centre in the East (Georr (1948): 6). At the beginning the school's interest in Aristotelian logic was purely theological, for it had to explain and defend the Nestorian doctrine (Tkatsch (1928–32), 1: 58a). Edessa was also important for breaking the two churches (the Nestorian and the Orthodox) apart; it is owing to this very fact that Nestorians could freely indulge in Aristotelian translations and commentaries.

The School of Edessa was itself indebted to the School of Caesarea, whose philosophical tradition, however, was not long-lasting. From A.D. 363 in the School of Edessa Aristotle's works and Alexander of Aphrodisias' commentaries were studied. In the fifth century the Ammonian theory concerning harmony between Aristotle and Plato had already reached the shores of Edessa. The translators and commentators of Greek philosophy began working when Hiba became the head of the school in 435. He had three collaborators: Probus, Mani and Cumi.

When the Emperor Zeno closed the School of Edessa in 489 and the Persian school returned to Persia, it added a new vitality to existing Greek philosophy and science in Persia itself. Nisibis being more restricted to theology, Greek philosophy and science found their way into other Syriac schools such as Marv and Jundishapur. This latter was created by Shāpūr I (d. *c.* 272) with the deportation of Roman, Greek and Syrian soldiers after Valerian's defeat. The deportation phenomenon was also a conscious policy of Shāpūr I for creating a multicultural society (Chaumont (1988): 56–89). All these events contributed to the later development of Greek science and philosophy inherited by the Islamic world.

The conclusion to be drawn is that political conflicts between two ambitious empires played a central role in the decline and resurrection of Greek pagan thought.

BIBLIOGRAPHY

Avicenna (1947) "Scholia on Aristotle's Metaphysics XII", in 'A. Badawī (ed.), *Arisṭū 'ind al-'arab*, 23, 21–24, 4 (Cairo).

Bailey, H. M. (1943) *Zoroastrian Problems in the Ninth-century Books* (London).

Baumstark, A. (1922) *Geschichte der syrischen Literatur* (Bonn).

Booth, E. G. T. (1983), *Aristotelian Aporetic Ontology in Islamic and Christian Thinkers* (Cambridge).

Browne, E. G. (1921) *Arabian Medicine* (Cambridge).

Cameron, A. (1967) "The End of the Ancient Universities", *Cahiers d'Histoire Mondiale*, 10(3): 653–73.

Chabot, J. B. (1896) "L'Ecole de Nisibis", *Journal asiatique*: 1–93.

—— (1934) *Littérature syriaque* (Boucard).

Chadwick, H. (1987) "Philoponus the Christian Theologian", in R. Sorabji (ed.), *Philoponus and the Rejection of Aristotelian Science* (London): 42–56.

Chaumont, M. L. (1988) *La Christianisation de l'Empire iranien*, Corpus Scriptorum Christianorum Orientalium, 499 (Louvain).

Christensen, A. (1944) *L'Iran sous les Sassanides* (Copenhagen).

Darmesteter, M. (1894) "Lettre de Tansar au roi de Tabaristan", *Journal asiatique*: 185–250.

Dēnkard (1911), ed. D. M. Madan (Bombay).

Duval, R. (1892) *Histoire d'Edesse* (Paris).

—— (1907) *Littérature syriaque* (Paris).

Frantz, A. (1975) "Pagan Philosophers in Christian Athens", *Proceedings of the American Philosophical Society*, 119: 29–38.

Furlani, G. (1919) "L'anatema di Giovanni d'Alessandria contro Giovanni Filopono", *Atti della Academia delle Scienze di Torino*, 55: 188–94.

—— (1920) "Una lettera di Giovanni Filopono all'imperatore Giustiniano", *Atti dell'Instituto Veneto di Scienze, Lettere ed Arti*, 79: 1247–65.

Georr, Kh. (1948) *Les Catégories d'Aristote dans leurs versions syro-arabes* (Beirut).

Gray, L. (1908) "Achaemenians", *Encyclopaedia of Religion & Ethics* (Edinburgh), 1: 67–73.

Hadot, I. (1990) "The Life and Work of Simplicius in Greek and Arabic Sources", in R. Sorabji (ed.) *Aristotle Transformed* (London): 275–303.

Ḥājjī Khalīfah (1835–58) *Lexicon bibliograficum* ..., ed. and trans. G. Fluegel (London).

Hayes, E. R. (1930) *L'Ecole d'Edesse* (Paris).

Kraemer, J. L. (1965) "A Lost Passage from Philoponus' contra Aristotelem in Arabic Translations", *Journal of the American Oriental Society*, 85: 318–27.

Kremer, K. (1961) *Der Metaphysikbegriff in den Aristoteles Kommentaren der Ammonius-Schule*, (Beiträge zur Geschichte der Philosophie und Theologie des Mittelalters, 39(1)) (Münster).

Labourt, J. (1904) *Le Christianisme dans l'Empire perse, sous la dynastie sassanide (224–632)* (Paris).

Mahdi, M. (1967) "Alfarabi against Philoponus", *Journal of Near Eastern Studies*, 26: 233–60.

Maspero, J. (1914) "Horopollon et la fin du paganisme", *Bulletin d'Institut français d'Archéologie Orientale du Caire*, 12: 165–71.

—— (1923) *Histoire des patriarches d'Alexandrie* (518–616) (Paris).

Mas'ūdī (1865) *Murūj al-dhahab wa ma'ādin al-jawhar*, ed. C. Barbier de Meynard (Paris).

—— (1894) *Kitāb al-tanbīh wa'l-ishrāf*, ed. J. de Goeje, in *Bibliotheca Geographorum Arabicorum*, 7 (Leiden).

—— (1896), *Le livre de l'avertissement et de la révision*, trans. Baron Carra de Vaux (Paris).

Meyerhof, M. (1930) "Von Alexandrien nach Baghdad", *Sitzungsberichte der preussischen Akademie der Wissenschaften*, 23: 389–429.

—— (1933) "La fin de l'Ecole d'Alexandrie d'après quelques auteurs arabes", *Bulletin de l'Institut d'Egypte*, 15: 109–23.

Nasr, S. H. (1960) "A Comparative Study of the Cosmologies of Aristotle and Ibn Sīnā and their place in the Islamic Tradition", *Pakistan Philosophical Journal*, 3(3): 13–28.

Nasr, S. H. and Mohaghegh, M. (eds) (1973) *Al-Bīrūnī and Ibn Sīnā: al-as'ilah wa'l-ajwibah* (Tehran).

O'Leary, De L. (1948) *How Greek Science Passed to the Arabs* (London).

Panoussi, E. (1968) "La Théosophie iranienne source d'Avicenne", *Revue philosophique de Louvain*, 66: 239–66.

Peters, F. E. (1968) *Aristotle and the Arabs* (New York).

Petrie, W. (1894–1905) *A History of Egypt* (London).

Pines, S. (1938) "Les Précurseurs musulmans de la théorie de l'impétus", *Archeion*, 21: 298–306.

Renan, E. (1852) "Lettre à Reinaud", *Journal Asiatique*, 19: 293–333.

Saffrey, H. D. (1954) "Le Chrétien Jean Philopon et la survivance de L'Ecole d'Alexandrie au VII siècle", *Revue des Etudes Grecques*, 67: 396–410.

Sanda, A. (1930) *Johannes Philoponi opuscula Monophysitica que ex mss. vaticano et britannica syr. edi. et lat. vert* (Beirut).

Sharples, R. W. (1991) *Cicero, on fate (de fato); Boethius: The Consolation of Philosophy* (Warminster).

Shayegan, Y. (1986) *Avicenna on Time* (unpublished Ph.D., Harvard University).

Sheppard, A. (1987) "Proclus' Philosophical Method of Exegesis, the Use of Aristotle and the Stoics in the Commentary on the Cratylus", in J. Pepin and P. Saffrey (eds), *Proclus, lecteur et interpreteur des anciens* (Paris): 137–51.

Sorabji, R. (1983) *Time, Creation and the Continuum* (London).

—— (1987) "John Philoponus", in R. Sorabji (ed.), *Philoponus and the Rejection of Aristotelian Science* (London): 1–40.

Stein, E. (1949) *Histoire du Bas Empire*, 2 (Paris).

Tannery, P. (1896) "Sur la période finale de la philosophie grecque", *Revue philosophique*, 42: 226–87.

Tardieu, M. (1986) "Ṣabiens coraniques et Ṣabiens de Ḥarrān", *Journal Asiatique*: 1–44.

—— (1987) "Les Calendriers en usage à Ḥarrān d'après les sources arabes et le commentaire de Simplicius à la *Physique* d'Aristote", in I. Hadot (ed.), *Simplicius, sa vie, son oeuvre, sa survie*, Actes du colloque international de Paris (Berlin).

Tkatsch, J. (1928–32) *Die arabische Uebersetzung der Poetik des Aristoteles*, 2 vols (Vienna and Leipzig).

Verrycken, K. (1990a) "The Development of Philoponus' Thought and its Chronology", in R. Sorabji (ed.), *Aristotle Transformed* (London): 233–74.

—— (1990b) "The Metaphysics of Ammonius Son of Hermeias", in R. Sorabji (ed.), *Aristotle Transformed* (London): 199–231.

Westerink, L. G. (1990) "The Alexandrian Commentators and the Introdution to their Commentaries", in R. Sorabji (ed.), *Aristotle Transformed* (London): 325–48.

Wilberg, C. (1987) "Prolegomena to the Study of Philoponus' *contra Aristotelem*", in R. Sorabji (ed.), *Philoponus and the Rejection of Aristotelian Science* (London): 197–209.

Wolff, M. (1987) "Philoponus and the Rise of Preclassical Dynamics", in R. Sorabji (ed.), *Philoponus and the Rejection of Aristotelian Science* (London): 84–120.

Zaehner, R. C. (1955) *Zurvan, a Zoroastrian Dilemma* (Oxford).

Zimmermann, F. (1987) "Philoponus' Impetus Theory in the Arabic Tradition", in R. Sorabji (ed.), *Philoponus and the Rejection of Aristotelian Science* (London): 121–9.

CHAPTER 7

Sunni *kalām* and theological controversies

James Pavlin

The issue of *kalām* is extensive and encompasses many subject matters. Accordingly, the orthodox reaction to *kalām* is complex and varied. In order to focus on the heart of the orthodox reaction, its methodology and goals, we need to focus on some of the major theological controversies in Islam. In general, these revolve around the nature of God and His Attributes. This topic includes concepts such as God's Speech, which relates to the belief in the uncreatedness of the Qur'ān, and God's Will, which relates to the belief in the createdness of the world. An intricate part of these controversies is the methodology used to explain the nature of God. The *mutakallimūn* believe that the verses of the Qur'ān related to God's Attributes need to be interpreted through argument based on logical proofs. This view takes the form of upholding the denial of a reality for the Attributes, as in the case of the Mu'tazilah, or of defending a restricted meaning of them, as in the case of the Ash'ariyyah. The traditionalists, on the other hand, attempt to discredit the use of *kalām* and to refute many of the conclusions of the Mu'tazilah and the Ash'ariyyah. In this chapter we shall trace the differing beliefs connected to the Attributes of God in order to understand some of the various issues concerning the opposition to *kalām* in certain schools of orthodox Islamic thought.

The orthodox scholars of Islam, starting with the Companions of the Prophet, have maintained a belief in the clarity of the Qur'ān based on the seventh verse of the third *sūrah*. This verse states that the Qur'ān contains clear verses of legislation, which the believers follow, and obscure or allegorical verses, which the believers accept without questioning. The verse further states that only those who have deviation in their hearts and desire controversy attempt to interpret these allegorical verses. When we look at the statements of the earliest orthodox scholars, we see that all information in the Qur'ān and in the authentic *ḥadīth* referring to the Attributes of God fall under the category of obscure or allegorical verses. This belief concerning the Attributes of God was clarified by a statement of Imām Mālik ibn Anas (d. 179/795) when he responded to a question concerning how God rises above the Throne. He said that God's rising above the Throne is well known but how it occurs is not understandable, and the belief in it is obligatory, and asking questions about it is innovation (al-Saqā 1988).[1] Although Imām Mālik was talking about God being above the Throne, his statement is valid for all of God's Attributes such as Speech, Knowledge, Mercy, Love, Seeing, Hearing or any others mentioned in the Qur'ān and *Ḥadīth*.

Some of the earliest theological controversies in Islam, which form a basis for the development of *kalām*, revolve around the interpretations of God's Attributes. The Muslim sources trace these controversies back to Ja'd ibn Dirham and his student, Jahm ibn Ṣafwān (d. 127/745), and to Wāṣil ibn 'Aṭā' (d. 130/748). In the orthodox literature, it is Jahm ibn Ṣafwān who is seen as the actual founder of *kalām*, and the vague term *Jahmiyyah* is used to refer to all groups which use *kalām*. These early arguments included diverse issues such as God's speaking to Moses and the status of 'Alī, Mu'āwiyah, and their followers, after the arbitration at the battle of Ṣiffīn. Eventually, these arguments developed into theological controversies concerning the meaning of *tawḥīd* (the oneness of God) and the nature of His Attributes, as well as the meaning of *īmān* (faith) and the definition of a believer. Although the reasons are not perfectly clear, the terms *kalām* and *mutakallimūn* came to refer to those who engaged in any form of speculation concerning the Attributes of God.

A major impetus for the use of *kalām* came as the influence of Greek philosophy and logic made its way into Muslim thinking. As the use of *kalām* gained momentum during the reign of the 'Abbasid Caliph al-Ma'mūn (d. 220/833), who openly supported the Mu'tazilah, a strong reaction arose amongst the traditional scholars against both the methods of *kalām* and many of the conclusions reached by the *mutakallimūn*.

In the forefront of this reaction to the interpretation of these allegorical verses, which the orthodox scholars view as a denial of God's Attributes, were the *Ḥadīth* scholars or traditionalists such as Imām Aḥmad ibn Ḥanbal (d. 245/855) and Muḥammad ibn Ismā'īl al-Bukhārī (d. 256/870). Ibn Ḥanbal led the attack against the claim of the Mu'tazilah that the Qur'ān was created and not the eternal Attribute of God. Ibn Ḥanbal relied on the belief that God has an eternal Attribute of Speech and that the Qur'ān was a part of this. His evidence is the verses in the Qur'ān which state that God spoke to Moses. His particular argument was that the words of the Qur'ān which people utter or write are not eternal, but that the Qur'ān is part of God's eternal Attribute of Speech. This traditionalist attack against the *mutakallimūn* was continued by Imām Aḥmad's student, al-Bukhārī, who put together what came to be regarded as the most authentic collection of *Ḥadīth* in Islam.

In his commentary on the final book of al-Bukhārī's collection, known as *Kitāb al-tawḥīd*, Ibn Ḥajar al-'Asqalānī (d. 852/1456) tells us that one of the main purposes of the book is to refute the claims of the Mu'tazilah by collecting the authentic statements of the Prophet concerning the Attributes of God (al-Bukhārī, (n.d.); Ibn Ḥajar (n.d.)).[2] Thus using verses of the Qur'ān and authentic *Ḥadīth*, the traditional scholars maintained the reality of God's Names and Attributes without questioning how they exist in Him. In this way, a complete picture of the nature of God was formulated. For example, it is confirmed that God has an Essence (*Dhāt*) and a Self (*Nafs*), that He has ninety-nine beautiful Names, that He interacts with His creation through actions and words, that He knows all things and wills all things into existence, and that He is beyond comprehension and is only known by the descriptions He has revealed. For the traditionalists, this was accepted based on the prohibition of asking how God's Attributes exist. However, the *mutakallimūn* and the Muslim philosophers continued to speculate about the nature of God's Attributes. To varying degrees, Muslim scholars rose up to defend orthodoxy, and in the process many borrowed arguments from *kalām* and philosophy to uphold the reality of the Divine Attributes.

One of the main arguments concerning *kalām* revolves around the value of logic as a means of attaining truth. This is exemplified by a celebrated debate, which is reported to have taken place in Baghdad in the early fourth/tenth century, between the Christian logician Abū Bishr Mattā bin Yunus (d. 328/940) and the Muslim philologist Abū Sa'īd al-Sīrāfī (d. 368/979). The heart of the controversy deals with the question of whether logic is a universal tool of expression or an instrument limited to the Greek language (Chejne (1984); Margoliouth (1905)).[3] Many of the traditional scholars maintain that logic is a product of the Greek language and has no place in Arabic nor any value to Islam. This attitude is carried to the extreme conclusion that logic leads to disbelief. This is expressed as whoever practises logic practises heresy (*man tamanṭaqa tazandaqa*). On the other hand, a belief was forming that logic is an important instrument or craft which supplies rules for right thinking and could be used in the attainment of truth. One such scholar who sought to use logic as a means to defend orthodox beliefs was Ibn Ḥazm al-Andalūsī (d. 456/1064). Although regarded as a Ẓāhirī and thus severely criticized by other Sunni scholars, Ibn Ḥazm's views concerning the evolution of sects were quoted by many traditional scholars. For example, Ibn Ḥajar refers to Ibn Ḥazm's famous *al-Fiṣāl fi'l milāl wa'l-aḥwā' wa'l-niḥāl* in his introduction to al-Bukhārī's *Kitāb al-tawḥīd*. Of particular importance to our discussion is the fact that Ibn Ḥazm advocated the need for logic but maintained a subservient role for it in relation to revelation.

Firstly, Ibn Ḥazm claims that the "first sources of all human knowledge are the soundly used senses and the intuitions of reason, combined with a correct understanding of a language" (Hourani 1979).[4] Only when a student is capable of knowing what is a sound proof as opposed to false argumentation can he or she achieve "the reality of things, and . . . discern falsehood without a shred of doubt" (Chejne 1984).[5] Now the student can proceed to defend the statements in the Qur'ān without reverting to a circular argument. Ibn Ḥazm argues that one must believe in the revelation but be prepared to make a defence of it based on demonstrative proofs and sound argumentation. But in order to uphold this methodology, Ibn Ḥazm had to refute the opponents of logic. When confronted with the argument that the earliest generations of the Muslims neither dealt with nor had any need of logic, Ibn Ḥazm responds by stating that they had direct access to revelation and that their belief was not corrupted by false doctrines. He compares the use of logic with the need of books on grammar and lexicography. When the Arabic language began to be corrupted, the scholars produced books to maintain the purity of Arabic. Likewise, the later Muslims need logic to maintain a proper understanding of God's revelation to the Prophet. Thus for Ibn Ḥazm logic becomes a tool of revelation.

Ibn Ḥazm's main task was to refute what he saw as the extremes of the philosophers and the *mutakallimūn*. In this case he had to show that logic could not replace revelation as the means to attaining truth, it could be used only to defend what God has revealed. He does this by maintaining the unique and incomparable nature of God and by rejecting any attempt to assign to God conclusions reached through logic about the perceivable world. For example, if one defines the relation between cause and effect as necessary based on observations in this world, one cannot project this relation on God. To say such things destroys the idea of *tawḥīd* because it establishes a necessary relation between God as Creator and His creation. It also infringes on God's absolute autonomy, on His Will to do what He wants, when He wants. For Ibn Ḥazm there is an unbridgeable gap between what exists in time as God's creation and the eternality of God. Ibn Ḥazm refutes the accepted metaphysics of Aristotle as expressed by the Muslim philosophers. God is absolutely incomparable to any created thing. Therefore, one cannot speculate about God nor contradict the truths that He revealed in the Qur'ān.

Another controversy which relates to the Attributes of God is the issue of free will. Here Ibn Ḥazm once again uses logic in defence of traditional positions. He argues against the Mu'tazilite claim that moral and ethical decisions must be based on reason, even at the expense of statements in the Qur'ān. That is, if reason dictates that a particular act is good or bad, then that determination must be valid absolutely, even if it restricts God's actions. But according to Ibn Ḥazm, the categories of good and bad, reward and punishment, are not necessary and do not confine God's actions. He argues that if God so wills, He could reward evil and punish good. Also, Ibn Ḥazm claims that left to its own devices, the human emotional soul (*nafs*) would counsel towards evil, and that there is no salvation through reason alone without the aid of revelation. Thus, in opposition to Mu'tazilite claims, Ibn Ḥazm holds that humanity is completely in need of God's favour to attain good behaviour and reward, and reason alone will leave us in doubt. Ibn Ḥazm does not hesitate to state that all things, i.e., each person's destiny, is dependent on God's Mercy. He rejects the Mu'tazilite doctrine of free will based on their interpretation of the Qur'ānic verse that good comes from God and evil from humanity (6: 81). Ibn Ḥazm points out that God first states that all things come from Him. Thus any evil that befalls us comes from God, for "we deserve punishment for the moral evil that appears to proceed from us as its subject" (Hourani 1979).[6] God's actions are based on His Wisdom and Justice which we are simply incapable of understanding. Concerning the nature of good and evil, Ibn Ḥazm maintains the complete autonomy of God and His Will and Power over all things.

Ibn Ḥazm attempted to describe and define the human condition in relation to what God has revealed and what humanity has thought. For him, it had to occur through the medium of Islam and logic. His stress on the interdependence of all knowledge indicates his belief in the unity of all things under God's Will and Guidance. The revelation of the Qur'ān and the Prophetic *Sunnah* supplies the guiding principles for belief and moral behaviour. God tells us who He is, what our purpose is, and what path we need to follow to return to Him. Philosophy, that is, the study of the natural world and the study of logical thinking, supplies us with an understanding of God's creation and the rational faculties for benefiting from what God has created. However, Ibn Ḥazm had an antagonistic approach towards all of the major religious and philosophical factions of his time, which led to his isolation in the community of believers. The strict observance of the Mālikī school in Andalusia, combined with the fact that Ibn Ḥazm did not travel outside of Andalusia, facilitated the censuring of his writings and beliefs. Thus the kind of synthesis towards which he strove was not realized until al-Ghazzālī (d. 505/1111) formulated similar ideas within the acceptable limits of Sunni Islam. Yet Ibn Ḥazm's full contribution to this intellectual movement is little appreciated and deserves far more attention.

In contrast to Ibn Ḥazm, who was confined to the western Islamic lands, al-Ghazzālī was an orthodox scholar who operated in the political and intellectual heart of the Islamic world. After a long spiritual and intellectual voyage through philosophy and mysticism, al-Ghazzālī eventually came to accept and defend orthodoxy as understood by the mainstream Ash'arīs. Although not as fundamental in their interpretations of God's Attributes as the traditionalists, the Ash'arīs defend the reality of the Divine Attributes partly through philosophical argumentation. Thus in order to defend orthodoxy, al-Ghazzālī had to refute the Muslim philosophers who had developed a Neoplatonic concept of God as First Cause from which the universe emanates.

Similar to Aristotle's Unmoved Mover, the First Cause or the Uncaused Cause of the Muslim philosophers is seen as the only logical explanation to avoid an infinite regression of causes. Consistent with the idea of a perfect, absolute One which is the cause of all that exists, the Muslim philosophers developed a description of God which coincided with rigid philosophical definitions of what that One must be. This definition of the One began with al-Kindī (d. 259/873) who uses the term the True One (*al-wāḥid al-ḥaqq*) in reference to God. Al-Kindī claims that the True One could bear no multiplicity of any kind in its being and thus is devoid of any attributes. The One's existence is necessary and its perfect oneness is the cause of all that exists in this world. Al-Kindī maintains that the world is temporal and that all motion and time is caused by the True One (al-Kindī (1953); Ivry (1974)).[7] This attitude towards the temporality of the world was changed by the arguments of al-Fārābī (d. 338/950), whose main contribution is the theory of emanation (*fayḍ*) (al-Fārābī 1985).[8] This step can be considered as a more complete absorption of Neoplatonic thought by the Muslim philosophers. Al-Fārābī refers to God as the First Existent (*al-mawjūd al-awwal*) whose existence is necessary and devoid of any deficiency or multiplicity. He adopts an emanative scheme in which the First Existent causes the existence of an incorporeal Second which then begins to think about its essence and about the First. This produces a Third which continues the process until the existence of the sublunary world comes into being. Al-Fārābī is very careful to state that the emanation of the Second and all that follows does not add anything to the First nor detract from it. Finally, Ibn Sīnā further specifies the philosophers' ideas concerning God by referring to God as the Necessity of Being (*wājib al-wujūd*) (Ibn Sīnā (1981); Hourani (1972)).[9] Ibn Sīnā contrasts the necessity of existence with the possibility of existence (*mumkin al-wujūd*) to show that the necessity of existence must be uncaused in order to avoid an infinite regression. Besides the now standard belief that the One has no multiplicity of any kind, Ibn Sīna further refines the description of God by saying that "his quiddity is his individual nature" (Hourani 1972).[10] He argues that if God's existence were not His only true essence, then His existence would be an accident added to His reality. This contradicts the necessity of His existence because any accident added to His reality would need a cause. Ibn Sīnā then developed a theory of emanation based on his concept of the necessity of existence.

Al-Ghazzālī needed to criticize and refute these conclusions drawn by the philosophers. In his *Tahāfut al-falāsifah*, he seeks to defend the more orthodox views of Ash'arism by proving through philosophical demonstration that the beliefs of the philosophers were not necessary and in fact often contradictory (Kamali (1963); al-Ghazzālī, (1965)).[11] In his very lengthy first chapter on the question of the eternity or temporality of the world, al-Ghazzālī offers many examples and arguments to support the view that the creation of the world in time is logical and reasonable. He argues that, by establishing the criteria which one must use for the terms and definitions concerning the discussion about the nature of God, philosophers are able to prove their opponents wrong because they are not working within the limits of accepted premises and axioms. This becomes clear when we look at one of al-Ghazzālī's refutations of Ibn Sīnā concerning the creation of the world in time.

Al-Ghazzālī accepted the necessity of God as the First Cause because an infinite regression is logically impossible. However, he claims that the necessity of God's existence as First Cause does not mean that His function as First Cause is necessarily eternal. Instead, he proposes that God possesses a Divine Will that is identical to His Essence. By means of this Will He was able to initiate the creation whenever He chose. The philosophers argue that a will and its object must necessarily exist together and that a separation between the willer and the existence of its object necessitates a new determinant to the willer which enables him or her to bring the object into existence at that specified time. In reference to God, this meant that He is not perfect in His Will but needs a new Attribute to achieve what He wills. This, of course, is intrinsically impossible. Al-Ghazzālī points out that the philosophers are inconsistent in their use of definitions and terms concerning the nature of God and adds that they are equating God's Divine Will with human will. Their arguments apply only to human will, for God cannot be compared to anything else, according to their own statements. As proof he points to their discussions about Divine Knowledge. They claim that God knows the universals without the existence of any plurality in His Knowledge. Yet, if one compares God's Knowledge with human knowledge, then one must say that plurality exists in God as it does in humans. The philosophers avoid this analogy by saying Divine Knowledge cannot be conceived in terms of temporal knowledge. Al-Ghazzālī maintains that if God's Knowledge is unique then so must be His Will (Kamali 1963).[12] Thus, by changing the focus of the debate, al-Ghazzālī is able to show the inconsistencies in the arguments of the philosophers.

Al-Ghazzālī continues with this form of argumentation concerning God's knowledge of particulars. The philosophers reject the idea that God knows every individual thing for two reasons. Firstly, to know an individual thing means perceiving its specific qualities through sense perception. Since these attributes are not part of God's Essence, He could not perceive individuals. Secondly, the process of the knower knowing the known indicates multiplicity in actions and in the number of things known. Again, it could only be said that God is the One in which there is no plurality. Any hint of God acquiring something to His being through a dependent relation with what is other than Him has to be rejected. Thus Ibn Sīnā's theory of God's knowledge of particulars poses some difficult problems in that he seems to attempt a compromise between the philosophical and theological viewpoints on this topic. Perhaps in an attempt to placate the orthodox theologians, Ibn Sīnā uses a verse from the Qur'ān to show that God knows all things, even the weight of an atom (Ibn Sīnā (1960); Marmura (1962)).[13] However, he qualifies this by saying that God knows the particulars in a universal way. He expresses this with two phrases: God knows the particulars "in as much as they are universal" or "in a universal way" (Marmura 1962).[14] His explanation of these two phrases is based on the assumption that God is pure intellect. Thus the epistemological process which occurs in humans not only does not apply to God but is in fact completely reversed in Him.

Before he begins his criticism of Ibn Sīnā's theory, al-Ghazzālī summarizes the orthodox view concerning the nature of God. He states that the Muslims consider the world to be temporal, only God and His Attributes are eternal and everything other than Him was created by Him through His Will. Thus everything is necessarily known to Him because the object of the will must be known to the willer. Once it is confirmed that He is the knowing Willer, then it must be accepted that He is necessarily living, for every living being knows other than itself. Thus in this way the Muslims know that God knows the universe because He created it through His Will (al-Ghazzālī (1965); Kamali (1963)).[15] But the philosophers can have no such certainty because of their belief in the eternity of the world. Thus al-Ghazzālī challenges them to prove that God can know other than Himself while remaining consistent with their assumptions.

In his criticism of Ibn Sīnā, al-Ghazzālī focuses on the issue of God's Will and Knowledge. He claims that if Ibn Sīnā remains faithful to his belief that God has no will and that emanation is a necessary act, then he would have to accept that God has no knowledge of the other. Al-Ghazzālī bases his claim on the argument that knowledge of an action is necessary only in the case of voluntary actions (al-Ghazzālī (1965); Kamali (1963)).[16] So if one claims that the universe necessarily emanates from God without His Will or Choice, as light comes from the sun, then it requires no knowledge on the part of God. Al-Ghazzālī similarly rejects the claim that because God's Knowledge is His Essence it is the cause of all that exists, thus indicating that God knows the effects of which He is the cause. Again he states that Ibn Sīnā is being inconsistent with the beliefs of other philosophers and with what he himself claims about the emanation of the universe. Even if it is granted that God knows what He is the cause of, all philosophers agree that His Act is one and from Him comes only one, i.e., the First Intelligence. All else flows from the First Intelligence and only indirectly comes from God through intermediaries. It is not necessary that God knows other than the First Intelligence. If the emanation is a necessary act, then knowledge of the effects is not required by God (al-Ghazzālī (1965), Kamali (1963)).[17] Even for a voluntary act knowledge is needed only for the first movement, not for the indirect effects. According to al-Ghazzālī, all of the demonstrations and proofs presented by the philosophers are based on unprovable premisses. A general theory must first be adopted, and then one can present proofs. However, all the terms must be clearly defined in order for the demonstrations to work. The internal logic of a system is not in itself proof of the correctness of that system. Muslim philosophers adopted the theories and definitions from the Greek philosophers and then attempted to mould Islamic beliefs into a Greek philosophical framework. Al-Ghazzālī accepted the basic tenets of orthodox Islamic beliefs and then showed that these beliefs cannot be disproved philosophically.

Ibn Ḥazm and al-Ghazzālī made conscious attempts to use logical argumentation to defend orthodox beliefs. In the process, however, they drifted away from the traditionalist approach towards discussing the Attributes of God. For the *Ḥadīth* scholars, the issue was far more fundamental: Revelation is supreme, and reason must be subjugated to it. In opposition to the arguments of al-Ghazzālī and others, traditionalists continued to argue for the complete acceptence of God's revelation without resorting to any form of *kalām*. However, even the traditionalists were developing more sophisticated arguments to support their basic belief in the attributes without questioning how they exist. Two scholars of the later classical period of Islam deserve our attention for their rigorous defence of traditionalism. They are Muwaffaq al-Dīn ibn Qudāmah (d. 620/1223) and Taqī al-Dīn ibn Taymiyyah (d. 728/1328). Although each approached the topic of *kalām* and the Attributes of God from a common Ḥanbalite backround, we shall focus on specific aspects of each to form an overall view of the traditionalists' beliefs.

In his famous refutation of *kalām, Taḥrīm al-nāẓar fī kutūb ahl al-kalām* (translated as the *Censure of Speculative Theology*), Ibn Qudāmah lists nine points why *kalām* must be avoided (Ibn Qudāmah 1962).[18] Firstly, he starts with the seventh verse of the third *sūrah* and states that

God links the follower of allegorical interpretation (*ta'wīl*) with those who seek trouble and go astray. Thus God has made such interpretations unlawful. Ibn Qudāmah takes this to be a prohibition against *kalām*, for he relates *kalām* to *ta'wīl*. His second point continues in this line of prohibition by stating that if allegorical interpretation were allowable, then the Prophet would have prescribed it. But it is well known that the Prophet never engaged in it, and if it were of benefit to the Muslims he would have mentioned it. The prohibition continues in his third point in which ibn Qudāmah states that the pious predecessors of the Muslim *ummah* regarded these Qur'ānic verses without allegorical interpretation and without divesting God of His Attributes. This refers to the fact that, if *ta'wīl* were of any benefit, the Companions of the Prophet would have surely spoken of it. Skipping to his fifth point, which fits in with the general prohibitions, we must mention that Ibn Qudāmah states that *kalām* is an innovation (*bid'ah*) and is thus opposed to the *Sunnah* of the Prophet. Here he quotes some well-known *ḥadīth* about remaining faithful to the Prophet's *Sunnah*. In the remaining points, Ibn Qudāmah attempts to give reasons for this prohibition based on other verses of the Qur'ān and examples from the *Sunnah*.

Ibn Qudāmah's fourth point states that *kalām* is tantamount to passing judgment on God in matters that the interpreter does not know. The *mutakallimūn* cannot possibly know what God intends by these verses. Even if the language admits of one meaning, it does not necessarily limit it to that meaning alone. Thus the interpreter might choose a meaning which God does not intend and would thus be speaking of God out of ignorance, which God has forbidden in *sūrah* 7: 33. His sixth point is that allegorical interpretation is mere foolishness and meddlesomeness that has no practical results. According to him, a Muslim has no need to know the true meaning of God's Attributes for no course of action or rule of law is dependent on them. God has enjoined belief in His angels, His books and His prophets, but the details of these matters are not known. Thus we should simply believe in what has been revealed (2: 136) and not be immoderate and meddlesome (38: 86). Ibn Qudāmah's seventh point is similar in that he says it is mere arrogance to permit oneself to speak falsely of God. He explains that if allegorical interpretation were obligatory, it would be so for every Muslim even if one does not understand the proofs for it. Thus people would have to speak out of ignorance on the topic of God's Attributes, which we know is forbidden. By insisting on the use of *kalām*, the *mutakallimūn* would have people speaking out of ignorance. His eighth point is that *kalām* is the use of *ijtihād* (private opinion) concerning the unknown matters in the Qur'ān and *Sunnah*; and this is not allowable even if one happens to be correct. Ibn Qudāmah states that Abū Bakr even refused to comment on the term *abba* (herbage) in *sūrah* 80: 31 because he did not want to say something about the Book of God which he did not know. And finally in his ninth point, Ibn Qudāmah states that the *mutakallimūn* are guilty of attributing to God what He has not attributed to Himself and denying Him what He has attributed to Himself. This they do when they say that one Attribute actually means something else. For example, they say that *istawā* does not mean "raised above" (the Throne) but that it means *istawlā* ("gained mastery over").

In this review of Ibn Qudāmah's arguments against *kalām*, we see a fairly well developed summary of the traditionalist opposition to the *mutakallimūn*. It can be classified as a negative argument because it focuses on the outright prohibition against *kalām* without speaking directly about the Attributes of God. In the case of Ibn Taymiyyah, we shall see how he approaches the discussion of God's Attributes in a positive argument. He explains how they are properly understood within the boundaries of the Arabic language and within the guidelines of the Qur'ān and *Sunnah*.

Ibn Taymiyyah starts with the basic points established by Ibn Qudāmah but views them as complete and sufficient to explain the nature of God's Attributes. That is, he understands the Qur'ān and *Sunnah* to contain all that one needs to know about God and to explain His Attributes plainly and clearly without resorting to any type of philosophical argument. He does not view the issue of the Attributes of God as a separate theological problem but rather includes it in his overall approach to understanding the Qur'ān. Thus he deals with this issue in a treatise entitled *Muqaddimat al-tafsīr* ("Introduction to Qur'ānic Explanation") as a problem of applying the proper methodology of understanding the Qur'ān (Ibn Taymiyyah 1966).[19] The basis of Ibn Taymiyyah's approach to the *tafsīr* (explanation) of any verse in the Qur'ān is to refer to other verses and to authentic *ḥadīth*. Using *sūrah* 16: 44, in which God states that the Prophet was sent to explain clearly (*tubayyin*) what was revealed to people, Ibn Taymiyyah asserts that the Prophet explained the meanings of the Qur'ān and its terms. That is, in order to fulfil his mission as prophet and messenger, the Prophet had to clarify all the proper and allowable meanings of the Qur'ān and not hold back any information. Thus there is no secret or hidden knowledge for an elite group such as the philosophers. In order to explain God's Attributes, one has to turn to the Qur'ān and understand its language.

According to Ibn Taymiyyah, the first thing one should know is that God makes use of synonyms to explain one thing by applying various names to it. This is how one must understand the beautiful Names of God mentioned in the Qur'ān. Just as there are various names for the Prophet and for the Qur'ān, there are various Names for God. Ibn Taymiyyah states that if one supplicates by use of one of God's Names this is not in opposition to a supplication through another of His Names. As proof he quotes *sūrah* 17: 110 which states: "Say! Invoke God or invoke the Most-Merciful [*al-Raḥmān*], whichever you invoke, it is He who has the most beautiful names." From this Ibn Taymiyyah concludes that each Name of God indicates one and the same Essence. That is, whichever name God uses in the Qur'ān refers to Him. Then he states that each Name indicates an Attribute included in that Name. Thus, for example, the Name All-Knowing refers to Essence and Knowledge, All-Powerful refers to Essence and Power, and All-Merciful refers to Essence and Mercy. In this way Ibn Taymiyyah links all of God's Names and their respective Attributes to one and the same essence. As a counter-argument he points out the inherent contradiction of those who deny that His Names are an indication of His Attributes. He quotes as an example those who say that God is not living and He is not without life. Now resorting to logic, Ibn Taymiyyah states that they are negating both terms of a contradiction. Thus, he claims, it is a matter of necessity that each name refers to God's Essence and to one of His Attributes.

To prove this point, Ibn Taymiyyah uses other examples to show that one essence can have various names and attributes. The first example is based on *sūrah* 20: 123: "whoever turns away from My remembrance [*man a'raḍ 'an dhikrī*]". He states that remembrance (*dhikr*) could refer either to what God has revealed or to what a worshipper does by way of prayer and supplication. Taken in the context of the whole verse, *dhikr* becomes a synonym for God's guidance and revelation. Thus the essence is all that God revealed and the names and attributes are remembrance and guidance. In other words, the Essence of what God has revealed can be referred to as God's remembrance, His guidance, His book or His word; each term referring to one and the same Essence.

Returning to the immediate issue of God's Attributes, Ibn Taymiyyah states that whoever is questioning a particular Attribute in a Name should realize that it corresponds to a denotation of the specifically named thing; that is, Names of God such as the Holy One, Peace and the Upholder of Faith, are synonyms for God. They are Names referring to God's one Essence and to Attributes of that Essence. As for probing into the meaning of the nature of a particular Attribute, Ibn Taymiyyah relies on the methods of the traditionalists. Referring to the Companions of the Prophet and the earlier generations of Muslims, he states that none of them explained an Attribute by indicating the Essence of it, even if it is an Attribute unlike any other. Thus the Holy One is the Forgiving One and the Merciful One, i.e., they are one and the same thing.

In his discussion of God's Attributes, Ibn Taymiyyah attempts to give greater depth of explanation to the traditionalist view of the nature of God. His main tool for this is the Arabic language. He sees Arabic as the unique vehicle of revelation, and thus all of its nuances must be understand properly and clearly. In addition to the Arabic language itself, one must read and understand the verses of the Qur'ān within their natural setting, i.e., the Qur'ān must be interpreted by the Qur'ān. The examples, parables and linguistic usages of the Qur'ān must be analysed for their rules and principles, which in turn must be applied in a consistent and uniform manner. In this way, Ibn Taymiyyah does not reject the rational faculties of the mind (*'aql*), but uses them in submission to revelation in order to explain revelation.

NOTES

1 Aḥmad Ḥijāzī al-Saqā, in his introduction to Ibn Taymiyyah *Ṣiḥḥah uṣūl madhhab ahl al-madīnah* (Cairo, 1988).
2 Al-Bukhārī (n.d.); Ibn Ḥajar (n.d.).
3 Chejne (1984): 60. A translation of the debate appears in Margoliouth (1905).
4 Hourani (1979): 143.
5 Chejne (1984): 62.
6 Hourani (1979): 150.
7 Ya'qūb ibn Isḥāq al-Kindī, "Fī al-falsafat al-ūlā", in *Rasā'il al-Kindī al-falsafiyyah*, ed. M. A. Abū Rīdah (Cairo, 1953): 98–126; Ivry (1974).
8 Al-Fārābī (1985): 89.
9 Ibn Sīnā (1981): 16; Hourani (1972): 77.
10 Hourani (1972): 78.
11 Kamali (1963); Al-Ghazzālī (1965).
12 Kamali (1963): 19–20.
13 Ibn Sīnā (1960): 359; Marmura (1962): 304; Qur'ān, 10: 61; 34: 3.
14 Marmura (1962): 300.
15 *Tahāfut al-falāsifah*, p. 198; Kamali (1963): 143.
16 *Tahāfut al-falāsifah*, p. 200; Kamali (1963): 146.
17 *Tahāfut al-falāsifah*, p. 201; Kamali (1963): 147.
18 Ibn Qudāmah (1962): 20–3.
19 Ibn Taymiyyah (1966): 329–76.

BIBLIOGRAPHY

al-Bukhārī (n.d.) *Ṣaḥīḥ al-Bukhārī*, Arabic–English, 9, trans. Muḥammad Muḥsin Khān (Medina).
Chejne, A. G. (1984) "Ibn Hazm of Cordova on Logic", *Journal of the American Oriental Society* 104(1) (January–March): 57–72.
al-Fārābī (1985) *Al-Fārābī on the Perfect State*, trans. Richard Walzer (Oxford).
al-Ghazzālī, A. H. (1965) *Tahāfut al-falāsifah*, ed. Sulaymān Dunyā (Cairo).
Hallaq, W. B. (1993) *Ibn Taymiyya against the Greek Logicians* (Oxford).
Hourani, G. F. (1972) "Ibn Sīnā on Necessary and Possible Existence", *The Philosophical Forum*, 4: 74–85.
—— (1979) "Reason and Revelation in Ibn Hazm's Ethical Thought", in *Islamic Philosophical Theology*, ed. Parviz Morewedge (Albany).
Ibn Ḥajar (n.d.) *Fatḥ al-bārī*, 13 (Beirut).

Ibn Qudāmah (1962) *Taḥrīm al-naẓar fī kutūb ahl al-kalām*, trans. George Makdisi, *Censure of Speculative Theology* (London).
Ibn Sīnā (1380/1960) *al-Shifā': Ilāhiyyāt* (2), ed. Ibrāhīm Madkur (Cairo).
—— (1981) *al-Risālah al-'arshiyyah*, ed. Ibrāhīm Ḥilāl (Cairo).
Ibn Taymiyyah, (1386/1966) "Muqaddimat al-tafsīr", in *Majmū' fatāwā Ibn Taymiyyah*, 13 (Riyadh).
Ivry, A. (1974) *Al-Kindi's Metaphysics: a translation of Yaqub ibn Ishaq al-Kindi's treatise on First Philosophy* (Albany).
Kamali, S. A. (1963) *Tahāfut al-Falāsifah: The Incoherence of the Philosophers* (Lahore).
al-Kindī, Y. I. (1953) "Fī al-falsafat al-ūlā", in *Rasā'il al-Kindī al-falsafiyyah*, ed. M. A. Abū Rīdah (Cairo).
Marmura, M. (1962) "Some Aspects of Avicenna's Theory of God's Knowledge of Particulars", *Journal of the American Oriental Society*, 82(3): 299–312.
Margoliouth, D. S. (1905) "The Discussion between Abu Bishr Matta and Abu Sa'id al-Sirafi on the Merits of Logic and Grammar", *Journal of the Royal Asiatic Society*, n.s., 37: 79–129.
al-Saqā, A. Ḥ. (1988), in his introduction to: Ibn Taymiyyah, *Ṣiḥḥah uṣūl madhhab ahl al-madīnah* (Cairo).

CHAPTER 8

Twelve-Imām Shi'ite theological and philosophical thought

Abbas Muhajirani

TWELVE-IMĀM SHĪ'AH MUSLIMS

The term *shī'ah* is not an invented or a new one. It has been mentioned in the Qur'ān in four places. Two of them (28: 15; 37: 83) are:

> so he found therein two men fighting, one being of his party [*shī'ah*] and the other of his foes, and he who was of his party cried out to him for help against him who was of his enemies.

> of his persuasion verily was Abraham.

According to the dictionary, the word *shī'ah* in its plural form means: followers, partisans, a group of people showing unanimity over an issue or a faith which they support and defend. Soon, however, the term became synonymous with the followers of Imām 'Alī ibn Abī Ṭālib. "This word has taken the connotation of the partisans of the Commander of the Faithful ('Alī) by way of following and belief in his Imāmate after the Messenger without separation, and non-recognition of his predecessors who assumed the office of caliphate (vice-gerency and successorship)" (Shaykh al-Mufīd, 1993a). In his *Muqāddimah*, Ibn Khaldūn gives this definition:

> According to jurists and speculative theologians, both contemporary and past, *shī'ah* is a term that describes the followers of 'Alī, his sons (May Allāh be pleased with them) and their school of thought [*madhhab*]. They [followers of Imām 'Alī] are unanimous in this regard that the Imāmate is not a public office which can

> be left to the discretion of the *ummah* [Muslim community], i.e., it is not a matter for them to choose who will become Imām. It is the pillar of religion and the foundation of Islam. It is not within the prerogative of an Apostle to neglect it or delegate [the responsibility] of choosing the Imām to the *ummah*. It is a must that he [the Prophet] appoint the Imām, who should be infallible and morally perfect.
>
> (1958: 196)

Quoting from *al-Zīnah*, a work by Abū Ḥātim Sahl ibn Muḥammad al-Sijistānī (d. 206/820), Ḥājjī Khalīfah, in his book *Kashf al-ẓunūn*, has written the following:

> During the lifetime of the Messenger of God, the term "*shī'ah*" was the title of four of the Companions: Salmān al-Fārsī, Abū Dharr al-Ghifārī, al-Miqdād ibn 'Amr, and 'Ammār ibn Yāsir. After the Prophet Muḥammad's death, a number of distinguished Companions rallied around 'Alī ibn Abī Ṭālib and were identified with him. [Also,] a group of *muhājirūn* (Meccans) and *anṣār* (Madanites) from among the Companions did not come forward to pledge allegiance to Abū Bakr. They sided with 'Alī ibn Abī Ṭālib. Among them were: al-'Abbās ibn 'Abd al-Muṭṭalib, al-Faḍl ibn al-'Abbās, al-Zubayr ibn al 'Awwām, Khālid ibn Sa'īd, al-Miqdād ibn 'Amr, Salmān al-Fārsī, and Abū Dharr al-Ghifārī.
>
> (al-Ya'qūbī, *Ta'rīkh*, 2: 124)

Those Companions and others who followed in their footsteps believed that the Imāmate was an extension of prophethood, and that 'Alī was the most knowledgeable authority, among the Companions, concerning the Qur'ān and the ways of righteousness. Thus, they resorted to 'Alī for guidance in matters of religion which needed a ruling or interpretation. They heard the Prophet say in favour of 'Alī: "I am the city of knowledge, and 'Alī is its gate. And I am the house of wisdom and 'Alī is its door (on the authority of al-Ḥākim in *al-Mustadrak*, al-Ṭabarānī in *al-Kabīr*, and Abū Nu'aym in *al-Ḥilyah*)."

ISLAMIC PHILOSOPHICAL MOVEMENTS

It was expected that Muslims would take to philosophical and intellectual reasoning during the lifetime of Prophet Muḥammad (s.a.w.a.s.)[1], for the seed of philosophical reasoning in the universal sense of the term was sown in the Noble Qur'ān and nurtured by the Blessed Prophet through his sayings and general guidance. In the Qur'ān there is a plethora of verses dealing with and urging human beings to ponder the creation of humanity, the universe, the heavens and the earth, and view the phenomena of existence with a critical mind and understanding in order to reach satisfaction as to the wisdom of the Almighty. (See for example verses 16: 164; 3: 190; and 4: 53.) Also, in other verses the command is not to follow doubt in matters of faith, urging people to pursue knowledge and that which will make them firm in belief (17: 36.) On the authority of exegetes, it has been related that when the last ten verses of chapter 3, *al-'Imrān*, were revealed, the Prophet recited them and said, "Lo! to him who read them and did not ponder them."

As a consequence of the encouragement of intellection and reasoning, and the pursuit of knowledge in matters relating to faith and the universe, there have sprung up many denominations, sects and schools of thought in Islam. This is so not only in matters of faith but also in religious rituals and norms of worship. However, there have not been great differences in rulings on prayer, fasting, pilgrimage and other ritual practices of the faith. This is clearly manifested in the way Muslims, irrespective of their persuasions, and despite the lapse of fourteen centuries since the advent of Islam, go about all these acts of worship and devotion in almost the same way.

It is worth noting that, during his lifetime, Muḥammad (s.a.w.a.s) told his Companions on more than one occasion that differences among his followers were inevitable. His famous reference to the Muslims dividing into more than seventy groups will suffice in this respect. He said, "My *ummah* [Muslim community] will divide into seventy-three denominations."

Right from the outset of intellectual and juridical dispute, the Shī'ah sided with 'Alī and after him with his sons. In their opinion, the evidence for favouring 'Alī is overwhelming, not least because of the numerous prophetic traditions urging the following of 'Alī. Of the many *ḥadīth*, the following one is unequivocal: "The parallel of my household is that of the Ark of Noah. He who got on board was delivered and he who lagged behind was drowned." Many of the leaders and those who dabble in religion have done so without knowledge, but rather through speculation and doubt. In order to attain firm belief and conclusive conviction, therefore, it is imperative to resort to those who have acquired knowledge in religion and the ways of spiritual prosperity. Once when Imām Muḥammad al-Bāqir was asked about the meaning of the verse, "Then let man look to his food" (80: 24), he said, "It is his knowledge and where he acquired it from" (al-Kulyanī (n.d.), 1:5).

SHI'ITE INTELLECTUAL PROWESS

The intellectual and gnostic aspects of the personality of Imām 'Alī had a great impact on the formation of Shi'ite intellectual and philosophical thought and their openness to intellectual discourse. As evidence of this unique quality of the Imām, one needs not go further than the collections of his sermons, letters and sayings which were compiled by al-Sharīf al-Raḍī (d. 406/1015) entitled *Nahj al-balāghah* ("Path of Eloquence"). The book has been commented on and annotated by many writers and *'ulamā'* both of bygone generations and contemporary ones. Shaykh Muḥammad 'Abduh (d. 1905), the former Rector of al-Azhar and a towering figure of reform and modernity in Islam, was one of those textual editors and critics who wrote a commentary on it. Describing his state of mind when he was reading it, he wrote in his introduction (*Nahj al-balāghah*: 4),

> Sometimes I used to see that a luminous intellect, unlike human bodily creation, was detached from the Divine . . . and supplanted in the human spirit. Thus, the darkness of nature was plucked off and it was raised to the realm of the aura of the Most Brilliant Light.

The influence of 'Alī and his philosophical heritage was vouchsafed only to be manifested in the Imāms of his descent, especially at the hands of three of them, namely: Imām Muḥammad al-Bāqir (d. 115/732), Imām Ja'far al-Ṣādiq (d. 148/765) and Imām 'Alī al-Riḍā (d. 203/818), who taught their disciples free philosophical debate, polemics, wisdom and goodly exhortation. However, the ruling establishments, which were anti-Shī'ah in the main, did their best to conceal Shi'ite philosophical and scientific achievements for centuries.

IMĀMITE FUNDAMENTALS OF RELIGION

The basis of religion is that part of belief which deals with the doctrinal aspects of the tenets of Islam. Discernment and proof are central parts of reaching a firm belief, and it is not acceptable to emulate others, without a proof, in this matter. It is incumbent on every Muslim to seek knowledge leading to a firm conviction, albeit through a simple proof. Al-Shahrastānī (1975, 1: 51) has said:

> Religion is divided into two categories: knowledge and obedience. Knowledge is the origin and obedience is the branch. Origins or fundamentals are the subject of *kalām* science (speculative theology.) The branches are the domain of jurisprudence. Some

> scholars have said: Everything that is logical (or rational) and can be proven to be so through pondering and deduction is of the fundamentals. And everything that is opined through analogy and theological legal judgement is of the branches.

According to Imāmite Shi'ite Muslims, the fundamentals of religion are five: Oneness of God, Justice, Prophethood, Imāmate and Day of Judgment. These five fundamentals are of a philosophical and speculative or theological nature.

As for the theologians, the Ash'arites do not consider Justice and Imāmate as part of the fundamentals of religion. The Mu'tazilites do not recognize the Imāmate as one of the fundamentals. It is in fact grossly inaccurate to equate the Imāmī Shī'ah and the Mu'tazilites as one denomination. More than one of the *'ulamā'* has discussed the differences between the two, among them being Shaykh al-Mufīd (d. 1022/1614) in his book *Awā'il al-maqāl.* According to the Mu'tazilites, the fundamentals of religion are Oneness of God, Justice, Reward and Punishment, the station between the two stations and enjoining good and forbidding evil.

PROMISE AND THREAT AND THE POSITION BETWEEN THE TWO STATIONS

It is worth pondering these two phrases in order to know what they really mean. In his book *al-Intiṣār*, Abu'l-Ḥasan al-Khayyāt says: "No one can warrant to be called a Mu'tazilite unless he believes in the five fundamentals: Oneness of God, Divine Justice, Promise and Threat, the Position between the Two Stations, and Enjoining Good and Forbidding Evil." The Ash'arites say:

> No one from among those setting their face towards Mecca [i.e. Muslims] can be rendered an unbeliever for a sin he committed even though it be a cardinal one such as fornication/adultery. Neither is a sinner of this sort condemned to fire, nor is an obedient monotheist sent to paradise. It is up to Allāh to send them wherever He likes. If He wills it, He may chastise or forgive them. As the reports from the Messenger of God have it, Allah will extricate a group of monotheists from hell fire. We have no right to maintain that it is incumbent on Allah to reward the pious and punish the transgressor. Rather it is all in His Hands. If He so wishes, He will have mercy on them and enter them into paradise or condemn them to hell fire.
>
> (Al-Ash'arī (1980): 279)

However, the Mu'tazilites maintain:

> Threats shall definitely be carried out. The transgressor will be punished. No one will be exempt; that is in compliance with the reports from the Creator. For when the source of reports is Allah, and especially when they are of a general nature such as, "And most surely the wicked are in burning fire (82: 14), so he who has done an atom's weight of good shall see it. And he who has done an atom's weight of evil shall see it (7: 99)." It is inconceivable not to treat such reports as applicable to all who fall within such a category.
>
> (Al-Ash'arī (1980): 279)

The meaning, therefore, of promise and threat is the duty of rewarding the pious as Allah has promised and the necessity of punishing the transgressors as Allah has threatened.

As for "the position between the two stations", the first to espouse it was Wāṣil ibn 'Aṭā'. He maintained that one who has committed a major sin is neither a believer nor an unbeliever; rather in the middle ground between faith and unbelief:

> Those who say prayers [the faithful] and commit major sins are labelled as such by a number of people [proponents of schools of thought]. The Khārijites used to charge them with unbelief and polytheism. The Murji'ites hold that they are believers. The followers of al-Ḥasan [al-Baṣrī – the Ash'arites] level the charge of hypocrisy against them. Wāṣil, however, holds that they are godless [i.e.] neither believers, nor unbelievers or hypocrites.
>
> (Al-Sharīf al-Murtaḍā 1: 114)

The Shī'ah tried to take up a position in the middle, between the Mu'tazilites and the Ash'arites. God ought to carry out His promises, but He is not forced to do so. He should carry out His promises because this is in accordance with justice and fairness, and to go against such principles would be repugnant. Yet He does not have to act in accordance with those principles, in the sense that he is obliged in more than a moral sense to do so.

ONENESS OF GOD (AL-TAWḤĪD)

Monotheism or unity of God is the foundation of Islam. The Noble Qur'ān has dealt with this subject in hundreds of verses. It covers all facts of referring to Allah as the One and only God – He has no peers, no match and no partners, He is Eternal and none is like Him. He is the only One worthy of worship and He is second to none. Muslims are unanimous in their agreement on this matter of faith.

ONENESS OF THE ESSENCE AND THE ATTRIBUTES

Oneness (*tawḥīd*) is of two kinds. Firstly, Allāh the Exalted, is One in His Essence and in the necessity of His Existence. He is Self-existing. He is beyond all matter and potentially not composed of anything. He does not branch out into other beings, be it in existence, notionally, or realistically. Secondly, Allah's Attributes are of the same nature as His Essence. Scholars of speculative theology and rational philosophy say that the Attributes of Allah are of two types, positive and negative. Some of the positive Attributes are Everlasting Life, Omniscience, Omnipotence and Eternity. So it is said that Allah is Ever-living, Omniscient, Omnipotent, and Eternal, Just, All-hearing, All-knowing.

As for the negative Attributes, they assert that Allah is far above all limitations. These Attributes are also called the Attributes of Majesty or Dignity which negate the possibility of Him being created, i.e. they prove He is Self-existing, far above things like composition, corporeality, occupying a place, poverty, incarnation. So it is said, Allah has no body, no form, and no imperfection. He is not composed of anything. He cannot be described as incarnate. In summary, He is far above any of the attributes of any contingent being. The Shi'ite belief in *tawḥīd* is of the purest form. It deems Allah to be far above any anthropomorphic elements of the concept of Deity which may encroach upon His Lofty Divinity such as polytheism and corporeality. His Divine Will is free from oppression and monstrosity; and there are no partners with Him in His Eternal Being.

THE IMĀMITE SHI'ITE VIEW

Shī'ah Muslims believe that Allah's Attributes are identical to His Essence. It is impossible for God to have any Attribute which is additional to His Being in any way.

The discussion of His Attributes has also entered the domain of Islamic philosophy. Shi'ite philosophers have discussed it extensively. The philosopher Ṣadr al-Dīn Shīrāzī (1964: 54) has said:

> His Attributes are verily His Essence (i.e. inseparable), not as the followers of Abu'l-Ḥasan al-Ash'arī maintain in that their numerousness in existence calls for a corresponding number of

> eternals, and not as the Mu'tazilites maintain by rejecting their origin but accepting their vestiges, and render the Essence as proxy, but through those firm in knowledge who maintain that His Existence is His very Essence, which is the confirmation of His Attributes of Perfection [*kamāliyyah*] and the manifestation of those Attributes of Beauty [*jamāliyyah*] and Majesty [*jalāliyyah*].

Shi'ite and Mu'tazilite speculative theologians benefited a great deal from the views of Imām 'Alī on *tawḥīd*. This is what he said in the first sermon of his *Nahj al-balāghah*:

> The foremost act in religion is the acknowledgement of Him. The perfection of acknowledging Him is believing in Him; the perfection of believing in Him is acknowledging His oneness; the perfection of acknowledging His oneness is pledging loyalty to Him and the perfection of pledging loyalty to Him is denying [in the human sense] Attributes pertaining to Him, because of the qualities of His creation that could be attributed to humans. Every one of them is a proof that it is different from that to which it is attributed and everything to which something is attributed is different from the attribute. Thus, whoever assigns attributes to Allah recognizes His like, and who recognizes His like regards Him as dual, and who recognizes Him as dual recognizes parts of Him, and who recognizes parts of Him has mistaken Him.

ALLAH IS IMMATERIAL

The Imāmites and Mu'tazilites agree that Allah's Essence is above corporeality. Accordingly, He cannot be confined to space or time. However, Ḥanbalites, Ash'arites, and Karamites are of the view that Allah can be limited to the station of His loftiness which is adjacent to the uppermost part of the Throne. They based this belief on the esoteric meaning of certain verses such as: "The Beneficent God is firm in power" (20: 5) and "Nay, both His hands are spread out" (5: 64). Consequently, in his *Maqālāt al-islāmiyyīn*, al-Ash'arī said, "Allah is on His Throne. He has two hands but not as property; He has eyes but not as manner; and has a face as He said, 'And there will endure forever the Face of thy Lord, the Lord of glory and honour' (60: 27)" (1980: 295).

'Alī ibn Abī Ṭālib, the exemplar for Shī'ah Muslims, made a glaring statement which refuted the view of corporeality of Allah and puts Him above those qualities that could be attributed to His creation:

> Those who claim to be equitable to Thee did not do Thee justice when they equated Thee with their idols, falsely assigned to Thee that which could befit Thy creation, and abstractly assumed that Thou art composed of parts in the same way as material things.
> (*Nahj al balāghah*: 144)

HISHĀM IBN AL-ḤAKAM

Some authors of books dealing with denominations, sects and schools of thought accused Hishām ibn al-Ḥakam (d. 198/812), who is considered one of the great speculative theologians, a towering figure of his time and the most famous of Imām Ja'far al-Ṣādiq's disciples, of upholding the view of the corporeality of God. Al-Jāḥiẓ, al-Naẓẓām and al-Ash'arī went to extremes in attributing this idea to him, quoting him as saying, "Allah is a body like other material beings".

However, research has proved that such an accusation does not hold. It was precipitated by envy; his opponents, who could not put up with the veracity and strength of his arguments, wanted to tarnish his reputation, especially the Mu'tazilites, whose claims he refuted in his polemics against their teachings. In Hishām's biography in *Mu'jam rijāl al-ḥadīth* ("Biographies of Transmitters of Traditions"), Imām Abu'l-Qāsim al-Khoei (d. 1992) referred to the stories about Hishām (vol. 18) and concluded:

> I believe that the stories accusing Hishām of holding the view on corporeality [of God] are all concocted. This has stemmed from envy as evidenced by the statement of [Imām] Abu'l-Ḥasan al-Riḍā who said in his favour "May Allah have mercy on Hishām for he was a good person, to whom justice was not done by his people out of envy."

His opponents allege that Hishām described the Lord, the Most High, as of seven *ashbār* (a measure equivalent to the expanse of an open hand between the tips of the little finger and the thumb). This is not worthy of anyone who is even of mediocre knowledge and experience, let alone Hishām, of whose character and knowledge his teacher and Imām Ja'far ibn Muḥammad al-Ṣādiq said, "O Hishām! You are still supported by the Holy Spirit."

Despite Hishām's young age, Imām al-Ṣādiq used to give him precedence over all his companions. Moreover, if Hishām had uttered such words, it does not follow that his doctrine was corporeality. The alleged words are akin to those said by philosophers and speculative theologians in the context of their treatises and debates, that Allah is "a thing [*shay'*] like other things".

Also, the quotation is taken out of context. The passage which is claimed to have been reproduced from Hishām's work does not prove that he believed in the corporeality of God, for what is said by way of argument or counter-argument in a debate and as a simile does not necessarily represent real belief or the views of the person advancing the argument. Hishām's debate was with al-'Allāf; he said, "You say that the Creator knows everything through His knowledge, and that His knowledge is unlike the knowledge of all other scholars (His creation). Then why do you similarly not say that He is a body unlike the bodies of His creation?" (al-Musawi (1986): 482).

In conclusion, Imāmite Shī'ah Muslims put Allah above all that which may befit and/or constrain material things such as corporeality, space or time and composition. They interpret verses such as 10: 48 and 5: 20 whose outer meaning belies their inner one giving the impression that Allah has a face, a hand, or moves from one place to the other into meanings which are in harmony with sound reason; paramount in all this is the preservation of the integrity of the Sovereign Lord from any shortcomings worthy of likeness and potentiality. In reference to this same quotation, Ṣadr al-Dīn Shīrāzī, the famous philosopher, wrote a treatise on the ambiguous verses of the Qur'ān and how the different Sunni, the Imāmite schools of thought, as well as gnostics and mystics have dealt with such verses.

VISION AND PERCEPTION

Is it possible that one can see Allāh, the Exalted, with one's naked eyes in this world or the hereafter? In their belief that it is possible to see God, the Ash'arites relied on the patent meaning of some verses of the Noble Qur'ān. Ash'arī states, "Allah, the Most High, can be seen with eyesight on the Day of Judgment as the full moon can be seen. The believers can see Him but not the unbelievers because they will be denied the privilege of seeing Him" (1980: 292).

There is a general consensus among the Imāmites, however, that it is impossible to see Allāh either in this world or in the next. It is impossible to perceive God for it is against logic: what is not a body, or incarnate, or occupying a space or time, a counterpart or perceived as such cannot be seen. It is equally implausible to see the Creator through eyesight. Reason bears witness to this fact and the Qur'ān attests to it, as do the traditions which have reached us through an unbroken chain from the Imāms of Guidance of the Progeny of the Prophet. The generality of Imāmites and the majority of their speculative theologians hold this view. In his monumental book, *al-Kāfī*, al-Kulaynī has recorded twelve traditions from the Imāms in which they have stated unequivocally the impossibility of seeing Allah here or in the Hereafter. The philosopher Ṣadr al-Dīn Shīrāzī expounded these narrations exquisitely and eloquently, concluding that perfect intellects separated from matter can see Allah through intellectual perception not through physical eyesight. He vigorously refuted the views of al-Ghazzālī who, in his book *al-Iqtiṣād fi'l-i'tiqād*, holds that it is possible to see God (al-Kulaynī (n.d.): 258).

Pivotal to the Ash'arites' proof of the possibility of seeing God is this deduction: Allah is self-existent, and since this is the case then any existing being can be seen, for what confirms seeing is existence. It has been related that the believers can see Him in the Hereafter (al-Shahrastānī (1975): 131). "The Imāmites' and 'Adlites' proofs of the impossibility of seeing God revolve around the fact that the permissibility of seeing the Creator should necessitate that He be a body or physical entity occupying a space and can be identified. It then implies that He be limited and with a limit" (al-Kulaynī).

DIVINE WISDOM

Wisdom is one of the Attributes of God. The Lord has described Himself as Wise, one of His Names being "The Wise" which is mentioned in some one hundred verses in the Noble Qur'ān. One of these verses is, "*Alif Lām Rā*, [this is] a book, whose verses are made decisive, then are they made plain, from the Wise, All-Aware" (11: 1). Wisdom is the quality of the knowledge of God of all things, and the perfect creation thereof. "And you see the mountains, you think them to be solid, yet they pass away as the passing away of the cloud, the handiwork of Allah Who has made everything thoroughly; surely He is Aware of what you do" (27: 88).

Allah's possession of wisdom necessarily means that His actions are not in vain, that anything which may be characterized as repugnant cannot emanate from Him, and that whatever He does or acts upon is absolutely good and proper. Scholastic and philosophical writings on this subject and that of Allah's Justice abound. These can be found under the topic "Right and Wrong – matters of common sense". From this branched out another enquiry into Divine Justice which in turn gave rise to the discussion about reward and punishment according to action, and our worship of Allāh, and also the topic of decree and destiny. These philosophical questions are all interrelated.

THE IMĀMITES' VIEW

Since the Imāmites believe in the independence of the intellect in perceiving what is good and what is evil, it follows that one can be absolutely certain that what Allah has ordained is good and what He has forbidden is repugnant. To give an example, the intellect has judged lying as a vile trait; and also that Allah does not commit that which is improper. The Mu'tazilites are of the same view as the Imāmites. The contention that the intellect has jurisdiction over what it perceives as good or evil necessitates knowing Allah, putting Him above irresponsibility, the obligation of sending Apostles, inappropriateness of punishment without justification, and humanity having free will in actions.

DIVINE JUSTICE

Justice is one of the Attributes of God and one of His Sublime Names. He is neither tyrannical nor is He prone to whim which may precipitate Him to be unjust in judgment. He has made it clear in more than one passage of the Noble Qur'ān that He is devoid of oppression: "Surely Allah does not do injustice to the weight of an atom" (4: 40); "Surely Allah does not do injustice to men" (10: 44); "and your Lord does not deal unjustly with anyone" (18: 49).

As a consequence to the dictum that Allah is Just, a number of serious questions arise as we have mentioned earlier, among which is human free will and the fact that Allah is incapable of injustice. Shaykh al-Mufīd, an outstanding Imāmite theologian, has said (1993: 57):

> Allah is Just, gracious. He created men to worship Him and forbade them to disobey Him. He did not charge anyone with any obligation beyond their ability. His creation is far from frivolity and His action is free from impropriety. He has remained above sharing his servants' actions and rose above coercing them to do any deed. He does not chastise anyone except when they have sinned and does not chide any bondsman or bondswoman except when they do a horrid deed. He does not do injustice, not even an atom's weight.

'Allāmah al-Ḥillī argued that the following principles are prerequisites to Allah's Wisdom and Justice.

1 He does not commit evil deeds.
2 He acts with purpose and wisdom and all His actions are proper.
3 He cherishes devotion and hates transgression.

4 He does not commission anyone with that which is beyond his ability.
5 He does not judge only that which is just, but all actions. Accordingly, His bondsmen should accept His judgment, bitter or sweet as the case may be.

As for the Ash'arites, they contend that there is no creator save Allah. The misdeeds of people are created by Allah. The intellect has no power over things, in that it does not need to differentiate between what is good and what is evil. He does not make His servants suffer aimlessly and without purpose. He does whatever He wants and judges as He pleases. If He wishes to leave His bondsmen in hell fire for eternity, He is the One to be obeyed as He is the Sovereign. Rebellion has no effect on His actions. Rather, He is the absolute Creator (al-Ash'arī (1980); al-Shahrastānī (1975)).

PREDESTINATION

The question of human actions and how they emanate is one of the oldest philosophical issues which has reached its peak in Islamic philosophical thought. Muslim scholars and followers of various Islamic schools of thought have multifarious views on the subject.

There is not much difference between the view of the Najjarites, Ḍarūrites and Ash'arites, on the one hand and the theory of the Jahmites, although the Ash'arites tried to distance themselves from being followers of predestination. They maintain that their belief in the doctrine of human predestination is as follows: "There is no creator except Allah and human deeds and misdeeds are God-given. People are therefore, incapable of effecting any one of them" (al-Ash'arī (1963), 1: 291). Imām Fakhr al-Dīn al-Rāzī, an Ash'arite theologian, said, "Man's actions are commissioned according to Allah's decree and destiny, over which men have no choice, and there is not in existence anything other than predestination" (1924, 2: 517). In defence of the unity of creation and demonstration of the principle that "there is no creator in existence except Allah", the Ash'arites believed in predestination.

The Mu'tazilites, however, who are called the exponents of Justice and Oneness, say that we are capable of acting freely. We are the creators of our actions be they good or evil, and, according to the course of action taken, we deserve reward or punishment in the next world.

What led the Mu'tazilites to hold the view that we are independent and have power over and free will in our actions is their belief in the principle of justice. However, the claim that our actions are created by Allah goes against the grain of justice, for if Allah creates our misdeeds, and then He punishes us for them, this amounts to injustice, and Allah is not unjust. "Whoever does good, it is for his own soul; and whoever does evil, it is against it; and your Lord is not in the least unjust to men" (41: 46).

THE IMĀMITES' VIEW ON COMMISSIONING ACTIONS

In the discussion of fundamentals of religion, we have already said that monotheism is the cornerstone of Islam and the most important of the fundamentals of belief by all Muslim schools. Believing in the oneness of God consists of believing in the Essence of the Creator in that He is one, none is like Him and He has neither partner nor peer. And He is only One (*aḥad*) in that He is not composed of parts whether outwardly or inwardly and that He is above any corporeality.

Belief in the unity of the Attributes of Allah means that His Attributes such as Everlasting Life, Omniscience and Omnipotence are the same as His Essence. He is Everlasting in Essence, Omniscient in Essence, and Omnipotent in Essence. Believing in the unity of creation and actions means that there is no creator in the domain of existence apart from Allah, and that all things in the universe are His creation. Among those is humanity, which is Allah's creation, not only its being but its actions also in a precise philosophical sense.

The verses which pronounce that there is no creator save Allah are many. Here is one of them: "That is Allah, your Lord, there is no god but He; the Creator of all things" (6: 102). (See also 13: 16, 35: 3 and 40: 62.)

Out of their belief in the doctrine of unity of actions, *al-tawḥīd al-af'ālī*, the Ash'arites say there is no creator in existence save Allah. Human beings and what actions may emanate from them are a creation of God, and they have neither choice in nor power over their actions. Justice is one of the Attributes of Allah. Thus, He is Wise in what He does and He is not capable of evil deeds and injustice. It is not befitting for Him to chastise us for actions in which we have no choice.

Believing in Divine Justice, the Mu'tazilites resorted to the doctrine of delegation of authority or empowerment (*tafwīḍ*) and said that Allah created us and imbued us with power and intellect and entrusted us with all our affairs. We are therefore completely independent in what we do, and Allah has no influence on our actions. This claim warrants the denial of the unity of creation, i.e. *tawḥīd* based on reason and tradition, *al-'aql wa'l-naql*, and entrusts us with the commissioning of actions.

Between the Ash'arites' predestination and the Mu'tazilites' delegation, the Imāmite Shī'ah hold the middle between the two extremes. Theirs is called "the position between the two positions", *al-amr bayn al-amrayn.* Reports indicate that the person who coined this phrase was Imām Ja'far ibn Muḥammad al-Ṣādiq (d. 148/765), who said, "It is neither predestination nor delegation but a position between the two positions" (al-Kulaynī (n.d.), Decree and Destiny section, *ḥadīth* no. 13).

The following conversation between Imām al-Ṣādiq and a man has been related:

> "May I be made your ransom! Has Allah coerced his bondsmen to sin?" Imām al-Ṣādiq replied, "Allah is more just than to make them commit misdeeds then chastise them for what they have done." The man asked, "Has he empowered them with their actions?" The Imām said, "If He had delegated it to them, He would have not confined them to enjoining good and forbidding evil." The man further asked, "Is there a station or a position between the two?" The Imām said, "Yes, wider than [the space] between the heaven and the earth."
>
> (al-Kulaynī (n.d.), Determinism and Destiny section, *ḥadīth* no. 11)

What is gleaned from the reports related from the Imāmite Shi'ite Imāms, on which the Shī'ah have a consensus, is that our actions are of our own making after Allah has infused in us the ability to commit or avoid the act. Good and evil are done by our free will, i.e., we have a choice in doing either of them or forsaking the same. Allah, the Most High, urges His servants to do good deeds and to refrain from misdeeds. Imāmite philosophical and theological activity in the matters of justice, predestination, delegation, and free will was so prolific that Shi'ite thinkers wrote hundreds of books and treatises on these subjects. Among those who compiled well-known books dealing with these issues are al-Shaykh al-Mufīd, 'Allāmah al-Ḥillī, Naṣīr al-Dīn al-Ṭūsī and Ṣadr al-Dīn Shīrāzī. The last wrote a tractate on the subject of predestination in action. He says in the introduction: "He, may He be exalted, is far removed from doing any evil deeds and goes about His Kingdom at will." In this statement, he referred to "the station between the two stations". He then discussed the views of the Mu'tazilites and the Ash'arites and added:

> Their claim that there are partners with Allah in the creation [of action] is unsustainable for there is no doubt that it is more preposterous than rendering idols as intercessors with Allah. Furthermore, what makes their contention untenable is the fact

> that what the King of kings willed to be in His Kingdom is not available in it, but what He is averse to can be found in it. This is an absurd shortcoming in rulership and sovereignty. He is far above that.

In his refutation of the Ash'arites' theory on this matter, he had this to say:

> There is no doubt that this contention debars one from practising wisdom . . . , detaches the intellect from discharging its duties, does not lend credence to the Creator, and shuts off the gateways of reasoning. Also, in what they maintained is the admissibility of the Creator being unjust so that it is quite rationally permissible that He may chastise the prophets, honour the unbelievers in the Hereafter, take a wife, a son, a partner, and so forth of scandalous deeds which stem from invalidation of wisdom and reason; and consequent to the invalidation of the latter is the incapacitation of the reports or traditions, for their authentication is done through reason. "Glory be to the Creator and exalted be He in high exaltation above what the unjust say."

He then discusses his philosophical and theological viewpoint in great detail and precision, substantiating it with a statement by Imām 'Alī, the summary of which is:

> There is no affair but His. By the same token there is no action save His. There is no rule but Allah's. There is neither strength nor power except in Allah, the Sublime, the Great. It means every power comes from His Exaltedness and Greatness. He moves between the different stations and acts accordingly. Also, despite His uniqueness and glorification above that of all beings, neither the earth nor the heavens are devoid of Him. As the Imām of believers in unity, 'Alī, said, "He is with everything but without drawing a parallel, not like anything without cessation." Since this is the case, it then follows that attributing the realization of action to man is correct in the same way that existence is attributed to him.

It follows that people are the agents of all actions emanating from them in a real sense, not metaphorically. Nevertheless, their actions are also actions of God without any deficiency (Mullā Ṣadrā (n.d.): 371).

Thus, the question of justice as espoused by Imāmites has remained untainted, respected, original and without a blemish on the doctrine of unity of creation. Our actions have two dimensions. The first is commissioning the action of our own volition. The second is the creation of that action by Allah's Will with which He imbued us, giving us the power to commission the action. Imāmite Shī'ah Muslims adhere to all these matters. They, therefore, have made Divine Justice one of the five fundamentals of religion.

ALLAH'S SPEECH

Among the questions on which Islamic schools differ is the issue of "Allah's Speech". Among the positive Attributes of God is "Speech". Accordingly, it is said that the Torah, the Gospels and the Qur'ān are the Word of Allah. The dispute between the Mu'tazilites, Sunni jurists, and the Ash'arites erupted over this question as to whether His Speech is created or eternal. The Ash'arites hold that "Speaking is a positive Attribute. Allah's Speech is spiritual unlike love and hate. The Qur'ān is the Word of God and it is not created. He who alleges that it is created is an unbeliever condemned to hell fire" (al-Ash'arī 1980).

THE IMĀMITES' VIEW OF GOD'S SPEECH

The Imāmite Shī'ah are agreed that God's Speech is created like other creations. He is a speaker in the sense that He creates speech in some organism or body such as Allah's speech to Moses through the tree.

The Mu'tazilites too maintain that God's Speech is created and novel. On the other hand, the Imāmite Shī'ah study Divine Speech in a wider context which embraces the entire universe – earth and heaven, the manifest and the hidden. The Imāmite philosopher Ṣadr al-Dīn Shīrāzī (1964: the fourth *mash'ar*) states:

> His speech, be He exalted, is not like the Ash'arites' claim "as a spiritual Attribute which is independent of His Essence". Nor is it an expression of sounds and words that convey a meaning. Otherwise, every speech could be God's speech. It is merely a creation of consummate words, and the revelation of perfect signs in the form of expressions and utterances. Allah says, ". . . and His Word which He communicated to Mariam (Mary)". In a tradition [*ḥadīth*] it is related thus: "I seek refuge in all the perfect Words of Allah from the evil deeds of His creation."

Everything that purports a meaning of the speaker is His Words. The entire existential world is His Speech. He spoke through creating and composing it. In the following lines of Imām 'Alī, one can detect a reference to this meaning: "Exalted is He, His Speech is of His own creation, the like of which did not exist before. Had it been eternal it would have meant there were a second god" (*Nahj al-balāghah*, sermon no. 228).

DECREE AND DESTINY

The philosophical revival, care accorded to the study of philosophy and resorting to it have been more characteristic of Shi'ite circles than of the adherents of other Islamic schools of thought. This comes as no surprise, for their Imām, 'Alī ibn Abī Ṭālib, was the first in Islam to speak in philosophical terms. He discussed matters pertaining to the universe in a philosophical and discursive manner. Ibn Abi'l-Ḥadīd has said:

> As for theosophy and dealing with matters of divinity, it was not an Arab art. Nothing of the sort had been circulated among their distinguished figures or those of lower ranks. This art was the exclusive preserve of Greece whose sages were its only expounders. The first one among Arabs to deal with it was 'Alī. That is why you find exquisite discussions on unity and justice related from him scattered among his sermons and axioms. You cannot find among the words of the Companions or the second generation of Muslims [*tābi'ūn*] a single word of this kind; they neither thought of it, nor did they understand it even if they were to be taught.
>
> (*Nahj al-balāghah*, 2: 128)

DECREE

The first philosophical discussion in Islam which could be traced back to the lifetime of the Prophet is that of decree (*qadar*) which reached serious proportions in the first half of the first century of the *hijrah*.

In a number of passages, the Qur'ān announced that Allāh has decreed certain things of His servants that are made absolute. The Prophet confirmed the question of decree and destiny in his sayings. Among his most famous words on "decree" is: "The Pen has gone dry as of the creation. Your Lord has finished with men as to who will go to paradise and who will go to hell fire" (al-Jazarī n.d.). Since the Companions of the Prophet were not at ease in understanding the issue of decree, he said:

> There is not a single soul without it being decreed by Allah for a place in either heaven or hell, and decreed to be either happy or

> unhappy. A man then retorted, "O Messenger of Allah! Are not we better off if we were to stick to our lot and forsake our work?" The Messenger of God replied, "Nay, work. Everything is made easy. As for the happy ones, their course of action shall be facilitated towards the people of happiness. As regards the unhappy ones, their actions shall be within easy reach in the direction of wretchedness."

Imām 'Alī was the first to answer questions of a philosophical and theological nature which were lingering in the minds of the people. He used to urge people to ask him. One day, he addressed the people thus: "O Men! Ask me before you miss me. I am more conversant with the gateways of heaven than those of earth" (*Nahj al-balāghah*, 3: 215). None among the Companions or the *'ulamā'* dared to make such a statement except 'Alī ibn Abī Ṭālib, who in the sermon quoted above said, "Our affair is difficult and perceived as such. No one can shoulder it save men whose hearts Allah has tried with resilience in faith. Our talk can be comprehended only by those with truthful intentions and sedate reflective minds."

'Alī is the first to prove human choice in actions, through the belief in decree and destiny. Historians have recorded that when 'Alī returned from the Battle of Ṣiffīn, an elderly man asked him, "Tell us about our expedition in Sham [Syria]. Was it according to Allah's decree and destiny?" 'Alī replied, "We do not set a foot nor do we descend on a valley [*wādī*] except with Allah's decree and destiny." The elderly man commented, "I trust in Allah for my toil. I do not contemplate any reward." 'Alī said,

> Woe to you! You take it as a final and unavoidable destiny [according to which we are bound to act]. If it were so there would have been no question of reward and punishment and there would have been no sense in Allah's promises and warnings. [On the other hand] Allah, the Glorified, has ordered His servants to act by free will and has cautioned them against [evil-doing]. He has placed easy obligations on them, not heavy ones. He gives them much [reward] in return for little [action]. He is disobeyed not because He is overpowered. He is obeyed but not under duress. He did not send prophets just for pleasure.
> (*Nahj al-balāghah*: 78)

Imāmite Shi'ite philosophers have shown great interest in the question of decree and destiny and examined it thoroughly. They have no rivals amongst the *'ulamā'* of other Islamic schools of thought. It would suffice to mention the valuable works of the philosopher Ṣadr al-Dīn Shīrāzī in his commentary on *Uṣūl al-kāfī*, his treatise on decree and destiny, and his monumental work, *al-Asfār*. We should also allude to a number of theologians, exegetes and philosophers who excelled in these disciplines during the eleventh/seventeenth to the fourteenth/twentieth century such as Mullā Muḥsin Fayḍ Kāshānī (d. 1093/1680) and 'Abd Allāh Zunūzī, and among contemporaries the philosopher and exegete 'Allāmah Sayyid Muḥammad Ḥusayn Ṭabāṭabā'ī in his Qur'ānic commentary *al-Mīzān* and his philosophical work *Nihāyat al-ḥikmah*.

PROPHETHOOD AND PROPHETS

The philosophers of Islam, whose leader is Ibn Sīnā (Avicenna), argue that the necessity of sending prophets hinges upon Divine Providence. Ibn Sīnā (1960, section 6) defines Divine Providence thus:

> It must be known that Providence is the reality through which the Originator is aware of his person and of the state of existence in the system of goodness, and the causation of his person in goodness and perfection in so far as it is possible. He is satisfied with it in the same manner. The system of goodness must be understood in the most effective way possible. There emanates from it a comprehensible system and goodness in the most effective way possible which overflows into a perfect manageable system according to the circumstance. This is the meaning of Providence.

According to this premise, since human beings, in their dealings with their fellow human beings, need a code of practice and justice, and there has to be an equitable legislator from among them sent by Allah, the most Exalted, the need for such a person is more pressing than the need for the growing of hair on the eyebrows. "It is inconceivable that Divine Providence necessitates those benefits and does not necessitate the latter ones which are its foundation" (*al-Shifā', Ilāhiyyāt*). Imām al-Rāzī, Khwājah Naṣīr al-Dīn al-Ṭūsī and the author of *al-Asfār* are of the same opinion.

However, theologians stuck to the principle of graciousness (*luṭf*) saying that we cannot understand what may benefit us and be detrimental to us in our conduct towards our Lord and His Supreme Perfect Being. Since this is the case, it was incumbent on Allah, out of His mercy and benevolence, to send a Messenger to guide us as a harbinger and warner. Being gracious to us is a quality of Allah's Absolute Perfection. He is the Kind, the Knowing and the Generous, not miserly with His creatures. On the other hand, the theologians espoused, as a proof of the prophethood of the messengers, their performance of miracles whereby they challenged the people to whom they were sent.

INFALLIBILITY OF THE PROPHETS

The Imāmites hold that the Lord is above polytheism, injustice and is incapable of evil deeds and creating sins, then punishing us for committing them. By the same measure, they consider prophets above committing disobedience, lying, meanness of character and baseness of conduct both outwardly and inwardly. They believe in the impeccability (*'iṣmah*) of prophets throughout their lifetime:

> All apostles of God were inerrant concerning wrong deeds prior to prophethood and after it, and all misdemeanours which the doer may take lightly. And Muḥammad is a prophet who did not infringe upon the command of Allāh, the Most High, from his birth until his death. He did not sin either on purpose or through forgetfulness. This has been proclaimed in the Qur'ān and attested by successive reports from members of the Household of Muḥammad. It is the belief of the generality of Imāmites. All the Mu'tazilites, however, are diametrically opposed to this view.
>
> (al-Mufīd 1993a)

THE IMĀMATE

The Imāmate was the first issue on which the Islamic *ummah* (community) differed after the death of the Prophet Muḥammad (s.a.w.a.s.) and, because of this dispute, bloody wars between Muslims ensued. In any case, the Imāmite Shī'ah Muslims believe:

> The Imāmate is a divine position, for the spiritual and temporal leadership of Muslims. It is a grace from Allah bestowed on His bondsmen, making it second to prophethood. The Imām is appointed by Allah through the prophet. He must be inerrant with respect to grave wrongdoings and petty misdemeanours. There must be, at all times, an impeccable Imām who is the proof of Allah to mankind. His presence is the safeguard of complete religious interests. He must be knowledgeable in all religious sciences. The appointment of the Imām by Allah is an act of grace from Him towards His bondsmen. And the graciousness of sending the prophet and appointing the Imām are incumbent upon Allah. The Imāmites are of the view that the inerrant Imāms are the best among their contemporaries of different times and in all fields, in knowledge and intellectual capacity. They do not know the unseen, but they know the intentions of people through a process of inspiration imbued by Allah.
>
> (al-Mufīd 1993a)

Commenting on *al-Baqarah*, chapter 2, verse 124, 'Allāmah Ṭabāṭabā'ī in his Qur'ānic commentary, *al-Mīzān*, has deduced seven fundamental points which may throw light on the issue of Imāmate. These are:

1 The Imāmate is Allah's prerogative.
2 The Imām must be immune against sin and error by Divine Providence.
3 As long as there are people on the earth, it will not be without a true Imām.
4 The Imām must be supported by Allah, the Exalted.
5 The actions of people are not veiled from the Imām.
6 The Imām must be knowledgeable in all that the people need in their daily life as well as the provision for the hereafter.
7 It is impossible that anyone could surpass him in sublime qualities.

Imāmite theologians and philosophers have presented documented evidence, as well as rational proof, on the need of people for a competent authority (*ḥujjah*), and that the earth shall never be void of such an authority, be it an apostle and messenger or an infallible Imām.

Al-Kulaynī, in his compendium of the *Ḥadīth*, *al-Kāfī*, collected all traditions related from the Prophet and his pure progeny on the subject of the Imāmate and the need for a competent authority. Also, the great philosopher Ṣadr al-Dīn Shīrāzī, in his philosophical exposition of *Uṣūl al-kāfī*, discussed the rational arguments for the necessity of the existence of the Imām at all times.

The function of the Imām is not confined to him being a teacher, interpreter and ultimate guide in religion. It transcends those areas into esoteric practices resulting in benefits to people, although these may not be tangible. He has unseen spiritual proximity to humanity. The Imām is, therefore, at one and the same time, a master and a friend in the journey of the spirit, guiding and initiating us into the inner truth of religion. His similitude, when unseen, is that of the sun which, though hidden behind the clouds, yet has effects which are felt. The Imām is the most perfect person, both in knowledge and in practice, whether he is seen or unseen.

THE IMĀMS OF TWELVER SHĪ'AH MUSLIMS

The Imāmites have agreed that Imāmate after Muḥammad (s.a.w.a.s.) is the exclusive preserve of the "Banū Hāshim". 'Alī ibn Abī Ṭālib is the first Imām, then his son al-Ḥasan ibn 'Alī, then his second son al-Ḥusayn ibn 'Alī, the sons of al-Ḥasan being excluded, then 'Alī ibn al-Ḥusayn, then Muḥammad ibn 'Alī al-Bāqir, then Ja'far ibn Muḥammad al-Ṣādiq, then Mūsā ibn Ja'far al-Kāẓim, then 'Alī ibn Mūsā al-Riḍā, then

Muḥammad ibn 'Alī al-Jawād, then 'Alī ibn Muḥammad al-Naqī, then al-Ḥasan ibn 'Alī al-'Askarī. Then the Imāmate was vouchsafed to Muḥammad ibn al-Ḥasan al-Mahdī, who is in occultation (*al-ghaybah*).

The Imāmites believe that the Prophet made 'Alī his deputy during his lifetime and designated him to be the Imām after him. The Imāmate of al-Ḥasan, al-Ḥusayn and 'Alī ibn al-Ḥusayn was also designated by the Prophet. And after that, every Imām designated the Imām who followed him up to the twelfth Imām (may Allah hasten his reappearance). All these Imāms are inerrant and of impeccable character, innate probity and endowed with filial piety.

RESURRECTION

Resurrection is one of the five fundamentals of religion in which the Imāmites believe. It is one of the philosophical and theological issues dealing with the "feasibility or otherwise of bringing back to life that which had perished". The question also deals with the issue of whether or not "the human soul is immortal". The discussion which stems from this subject, therefore, concerns the truth about the human body – what is it? Or, what does it consist of?

The Imāmite Shī'ah Muslims believe in what the Noble Qur'ān spelt out regarding resurrection in that it will be a bodily one and in a new (form of) creation and that resurrection will be of both body and soul: "Paradise will be the abode of perpetual comfort. Those who reside in it will face neither hardship nor fatigue. They will enjoy food, drink, scenery and marriage. Hell will be the abode of those who disregard Allah. No one is going to stay in it for good except the unbelievers" (al-Mufīd, *Taṣḥīḥ al-i'tiqād*).

As for the philosophers, they differed over the question of resurrection as to whether it will be in body and soul or in the soul alone. The Shaykh (master) of Islamic philosophers, Ibn Sīnā, who was of a Shi'ite persuasion, believed in bodily resurrection by way of traditional evidence and religious dictates, although he could not demonstrate it rationally. In two books, *al-Shifā'* and *al-Ishārāt*, he tried to prove that reward and punishment would be meted out to both the body and soul. He wrote an epistle on resurrection and conditions of the soul. In the seventh section of chapter 9 of his book *al-Shifā'*, he wrote:

> It must be known that proof of resurrection can be derived from religious knowledge. However, there is no other way to proving its occurrence than that of the *Sharī'ah* and the acknowledgment of Prophetic tradition; it is that of bodily resurrection. Good and evil aspects of the body are well known; they do not need to be

delved into, in that the true *Sharī'ah*, brought to us by our Prophet and master, Muḥammad (s.a.w.a.s.), explained both the states of the body – happiness and wretchedness. As for happiness or wretchedness of the soul, it is proved both rationally and through logical deduction and traditional evidence as acknowledged by prophethood.

The philosopher Ṣadr al-Dīn Shīrāzī discussed the argument for bodily resurrection in his two books *al-Asfār* and *al-Mabda' wa'l-ma'ād*. He also discussed the subject in his book *Sharḥ al-hidāyah*, with a slight variation in argument. However, he too eventually resorted to acknowledging traditional evidence produced by the Islamic religion. To this effect he wrote, "The truth upheld by us is that the crux of the matter pertaining to the acknowledgment of and belief in the question of resurrection is that which has been proved by the Holy Book, and the *Sunnah*, and all that which is reached at in the body of religious teaching. It is true in the full sense of the literal meaning" (1976: 407).

It is noteworthy that, while acknowledging the veracity of bodily resurrection as reported by the *Sharī'ah*, Shīrāzī maintained that this did not require interpretation and inferring meanings from utterances other than their literal meaning. Thus he wrote (1976), "It is a matter of fact that bodies in the hereafter shall be bereft of many of their necessary manifestations. The body in the hereafter shall be a shadow of the soul, a reflection and an image of it". The Imāmite Shī'ah Muslims have other views and tenets relating to *badā'* (revocation of a decree), the truth about belief and Islam, *raj'ah* (return) and intercession. These are extensively discussed in their theological and philosophical books, but are outside the scope of this chapter.

Translated by N. al-Khafaji
and Oliver Leaman

NOTE

1 An acronym of "*Ṣallallāhu 'alayhī wa'alā ālihī wa sallam*", meaning "May Allāh's blessings be upon him and his Household."

BIBLIOGRAPHY

al-Ash'arī, Abū'l Ḥasan (1980) *Maqalāt al-islāmiyyīn*, ed. H. Ritter (Wiesbaden).

Ibn Sīnā (1960) *Kitāb al-shifā': al-ilāhiyyāt*, 1, ed. G. Anawati, M. Mūsā, S. Dunyā and S. Zāyid (Cairo).

al-Jazarī, Ibn al-Athīr (n.d.) *Jāmi' al-uṣūl* (Damascus).

Ibn Khaldūn (1958) *The Muqāddimah: an Introduction to History*, trans. F. Rosenthal (New York).

al-Khu'ī (Khoei), Abu'l Qāsim (n.d.) *Mu'jam rijāl al-ḥadīth* (Najaf).
al-Kulaynī, Muḥammad ibn Ya'qūb (n.d.) *al-Kāfī* (Beirut).
al-Mufīd, Muḥammad ibn al-Nu'mān (1951) *Taṣḥīḥ al-i'tiqād* (Tabriz).
—— (1981) *al-Irshād (The Book of Guidance into the Lives of the Twelve Imams)*, trans. I. Howard (London).
—— (1993a) *Awā'il al-maqalāt* (Tehran).
—— (1993b) *al-Ḥikāyah* (Tehran).
—— (1993c) *al-Nukat fī muqaddimat al-uṣūl* (Tehran).
al-Murtaḍā, 'Alī ibn Ḥusayn al-Shārīf (1990) *al-Amālī* (Tehran).
al-Musawi, A. H. S. (1986) *The Right Path* (London).
Nahj al-balāghah, compilation of Imām 'Alī's sermons, letters and sayings by al-Sharīf al-Raḍī (Cairo).
al-Rāzī, Fakhr al-Dīn (1924) *al-Mabāḥith al-mashriqiyyah* (Hyderabad, India).
al-Shahrastānī, Muḥammad ibn 'Abd al-Karīm (1975) *al-Milal wa'l-niḥal* (Beirut).
al-Shīrāzī, Mullā Ṣadrā (1964) *al-Mashā'ir*, ed. H. Corbin (Tehran).
—— (1966) *al-Asfār al-arb'ah*, ed. S. Ṭabāṭabā'ī (Qom).
—— (1976) *al-Mabda' wa'l-ma'ād*, ed. S. J. Āshtiyānī (Tehran).
—— (n.d.) *al-Rasā'il al-falsafiyyah* (Qom).
al-Ya'qūbī (1883) *Ta'rikh*, ed. M. Houtsma (Leiden).

Additional bibliography is available in:

Amir-Moezzi, M. (1994) *The Divine Guide in Early Shi'ism* (Albany).
Chittick, W. (ed.) (1980) *A Shi'ite Anthology* (Albany).
Halm, H. (1991) *Shi'ism* (Edinburgh).
Kohlberg, E. (1991) *Belief and Law in Imami Shi'ism* (Aldershot).
McDermott, M. (1978) *The Theology of al-Shaikh al-Mufid* (Beirut).
Ṭabāṭabā'ī, S. (1975) *Shi'ite Islam* (Albany).
—— (1987) *The Qur'ān in Islam* (London).

CHAPTER 9

Ismā'īlī philosophy

Azim Nanji

Ismā'īlism belongs to the Shī'ah branch of Islam, and, in common with various Muslim interpretive communities, has been concerned with developing an intellectual discourse to elucidate foundational Qur'ānic and Islamic beliefs and principles. Ismā'īlī philosophy grew out of an attempt at discursive reflection aimed at an explanation of the *ḥaqā'iq* or truths grounded in revelation but intelligible to human reason, which was regarded as a gift of God. The appropriate use of the intellect in the service of exegesis was thus regarded as both necessary and legitimate.[1]

One of the terms of self-description used in the Qur'ān is *Umm al-kitāb*.[2] Literally, the "Mother of the Book", the concept is also by extension the archetypal ground of all knowledge and revelation. Shi'i and Ismā'īlī intellectual self-expression have thus sought throughout history to represent themselves as the quest for truth in a continuing conversation with this transcendent text, the source of all revelation.

This conversation was further enhanced by the additional interaction with other intellectual traditions encountered by Muslims in the course of the expansion and growth of the world of Islam. In addition to Jews and Christians, there were Zoroastrians, Hindus and others, some of whom were accorded the status of "People of the Book", and who also included in their heritage residual philosophical traditions of classical antiquity in the Near East. The access to tools of inquiry afforded particularly by the philosophical heritage of works in Greek and Syriac was adopted willingly by many Muslims. The reflective process engendered by the interaction of the two allowed Ismā'īlīs to articulate a distinctive philosophical stance. During this early period one finds, therefore, among Muslims a shared intellectual climate, a commonality of issues and a plurality of discourses. This "exchange" took place also within a common linguistic framework, namely Arabic and, later, Persian.

It would, however, be misleading to label Ismāʿīlī and other Muslim philosophical stances, as has been done by some scholars in the past, simplistically as manifestations of "Ismāʿīlī/Muslim Neoplatonism", "Ismāʿīlī/Muslim gnosticism", etc. While elements of these philosophical and spiritual schools were certainly appropriated, and common features may be evident in the expression and development of Ismāʿīlī as well as other ideas, it must be noted that they were applied within very different historical and intellectual contexts and that such ideas came to be quite dramatically transformed in their meaning, purpose and significance in Islamic philosophy.[3]

In view of the bias towards Ismāʿīlism that developed among certain schools of Islamic thought, it has been designated by several pejorative names in the past. By those who were hostile to it or opposed its philosophical and intellectual stance, the Ismāʿīlīs were regarded as heretical, legends were fabricated about them and their teachings and it was implied that they had strayed from the true path. Such a dogmatic posture, adopted primarily by some heresiographers and polemicists, tended to marginalize Ismāʿīlī and in general, the Shiʿi contribution to intellectual life in Islam. Unfortunately, early Western scholarship on Islamic philosophy inherited some of these biases and tended to project a negative image of Ismāʿīlism, perceiving its philosophical contribution as having been derived from sources and tendencies "alien" to Islam. Recent scholarship, based on a more judicious analysis of primary sources, provides a balanced perspective. Indeed, scholars of Islamic thought, such as Muhsin Mahdi, Seyyed Hossein Nasr, Wilferd Madelung, Henry Corbin, M. Hodgson, W. Ivanow and S. Stern have tried to show how Ismāʿīlī thought has been in constant interaction with and to a certain extent influenced well-known currents of Islamic philosophy and theology.[4] Their views represent a consensus that it is inappropriate to treat Ismāʿīlism as a marginal school of Islamic thought; rather it constitutes a significant philosophical branch, among others, in Islamic philosophy.

Early Ismāʿīlī philosophical works dating back to the Fāṭimid period (fourth/tenth to sixth/twelfth century) are in Arabic; Nāṣir-i Khusraw (d. 471/1078) was the only Ismāʿīlī writer of the period to write in Persian. The Arabic tradition was continued in Yemen and India by the Mustʿalīs and in Syria by the Nizārīs. In Persia and in Central Asia, the tradition was preserved and elaborated in Persian. Elsewhere among the Ismāʿīlīs, local oral languages and literatures played an important part, though no strictly philosophical writings were developed in these languages.[5]

There has, as a result, been considerable diversity of thought and intellectual development in Ismāʿīlism throughout history. While more of the Arabic and Persian literature of the past has become available, much still remains to be properly edited – let alone carefully studied. The following exposition of main trends in Ismāʿīlī philosophy is meant to outline the general features that represent a shared tradition and common thematic concerns.

LANGUAGE AND MEANING: THE STANCE OF ISMĀʿĪLĪ PHILOSOPHY

Among the tools of interpretation of Scripture that are associated particularly with Shiʿi and Ismāʿīlī philosophy is that of *ta'wīl*. The application of this Qur'ānic term, which connotes "going back to the first/the beginning", marks the effort in Ismāʿīlī thought of creating a philosophical and hermeneutical discourse that establishes the intellectual discipline for approaching revelation and creates a bridge between philosophy and religion. Its meaning in the Shiʿi context must not therefore be confused with its usage in Sunni *kalām*.

As set forth in Ismāʿīlī writings, the purpose and goal of *ta'wīl* is to arrive at an "original" understanding of Scripture by going beyond the formal, literal meaning of the text, not limiting the total significance nor rejecting entirely the validity of such a formal reading, but affirming that the ultimate significance and totality of meaning of any text could only be grasped by the application of *ta'wīl*. Such hermeneutics, in their view, complemented *tafsīr*, the mode of formal interpretation in Islamic thought, and did not reflect a dichotomized way of viewing Scripture. Rather, it attested to the divine use of language in multiple ways, particularly as exemplified in the Qur'ānic verses that employ symbolic and figurative language. Philosophy as conceived in Ismāʿīlī thought thus seeks to extend the meaning of religion and revelation to identify the visible and the apparent (*ẓāhir*) and also to penetrate to the roots, to retrieve and disclose that which is interior or hidden (*bāṭin*). Ultimately, this discovery engages both the intellect (*ʿaql*) and the spirit (*rūḥ*), functioning in an integral manner to illuminate and disclose truths (*ḥaqā'iq*).[6]

In his works *al-Risālat al-durriyah* and *Rāḥat al-ʿaql* the Fāṭimid philosopher Ḥamīd al-Dīn al-Kirmānī (d. *c.* 412/1021) juxtaposes a discussion of speech and language to his exposition of the concept of God and *tawḥīd*.[7] He argues that languages grow out of words which are composed of letters which allow words to signify specific meanings. But words as well as languages are contingent and relative. Since God is not contingent but absolute, language, by its very nature, cannot appropriately define Him in a non-contingent way and take account of that which makes God different from all that is contingent. Thus language in itself fails to define God as befitting His glory. Language, however, is a beginning, because it is the foremost tool for signifying and representing the possibility of what God is. The fact of being human and possessed of an intellect compels one to speak of and inquire about the agent from whom existentiation (or origination) comes forth. Thus when one speaks of God, one does not necessarily describe Him as He is, but one has affirmed that He is indeed the originator of all that we employ to understand and describe His creation.

The appropriate mode of language which serves us best in this task is, according to al-Kirmānī, symbolic language. Such language, which employs analogy, metaphor and symbols, allows one to make distinctions and to establish differences in ways that a literal reading of language does not permit. *Taʾwīl*, additionally understood as a hermeneutic and symbolic process, has the capacity to relate meaning to its beginnings – for that not only is the root sense of the word *taʾwīl* itself but also expresses the religious purpose for which such a process is to be employed – as an intellectual and spiritual journey to understanding God and His creation. This understanding starts as the deciphering of words used in the Qurʾān, where God is indeed referred to as the "Sublime Symbol" (30: 27), thus legitimating the use of symbolic language. Such language employs a special system of signs, the ultimate meaning of which can be "unveiled" by the proper application of *taʾwīl*.

ARTICULATING TRANSCENDENCE: THE CONCEPT OF UNITY

Early Muslim reflection on *tawḥīd*, the Qurʾānic concept of the oneness and unity of God, sought to clarify the distinction between a transcendental Creator and a contingent, created and pluralistic universe.

This process of conceptual clarification among various Muslim groups was related to the presence of other monotheistic traditions such as Judaism and Christianity as well as a developing awareness of the philosophical understanding of a divine reality available in the Hellenistic influences on these monotheistic traditions. The creation of a philosophical vocabulary to understand divinity took place concurrently with the rise of legal and traditionalist modes of interpretation among Muslims who were seeking to articulate the relevance of monotheistic faith to Muslim lives in more immediate terms as affecting *praxis*. Some of them perceived the quest for what they saw as a theoretical understanding of God as having dubious values in the practice of the truth. It is against this background that Ismāʿīlī thinkers began their intellectual formulations of the uniqueness of God.

Among al-Kirmānī's predecessors, one of the best-known thinkers of the Faṭimid period is Abū Yaʿqūb al-Sijistānī (d. *c.* 361/971).[8] His works, building on previous writings, enable us to see the formulation of a position in the context of the larger debate in the fourth/tenth century among Muslim theologians and philosophers. While discounting those outside the pale of monotheistic faith, whose beliefs, according to him, are polytheistic or anthropomorphic, he classifies others under several broad categories – those who ascribe to God the attributes He ascribes to Himself in the Book, but who do not wish to speculate unduly about these attributes; and those who argue in favour of speculation and wish to negate the attribution of human-like qualities to God and therefore maintain that God can neither be defined, described, characterized, nor seen, nor be anywhere. He concludes that none of these positions allows one to accord to God the correct worship due to Him, nor do they allow for the articulation of transcendence in an appropriate manner. He states: "Whoever removes from his Creator descriptions, definitions and characteristics falls into a hidden anthropomorphism, just as one who describes Him and characterizes Him falls into overt anthropomorphism."[9]

In particular, he seeks to refute those who follow the Muʿtazilite position by pushing it to what he regards as its logical conclusion. Like al-Ashʿarī, he points to the problem of separating essential and descriptive attributes and argues that the ascribing of essential attributes, by perpetuating a duality between essence and attribute, would also lead to a plurality of eternal attributes. He argues further that the negation of specific attributes (knowledge, power, life, etc.) cannot be maintained, since human beings also have a share in such attributes. If these were to be denied, the negation would be incomplete, since the denial takes account only of characteristics of material creations (*makhlūqāt*) and not of spiritual entities. If one is to adopt the path of negation, he argues, then it must be a complete negation, denying that God has either material attributes or spiritual ones, thereby rendering Him beyond existence (*ays*) and non-existence (*lays*).

In formulating such a sweeping concept of *tawḥīd*, Sijistānī assumes three possible relations between God and His Creation: God can resemble His Creation entirely, in part, or not at all. In order to affirm the total distinction implied in *tawḥīd*, the third relation is the most appropriate, involving a total distinction from all forms of creation. Basing himself on a Qur'ānic verse, "To Him belong the Creation [*al-khalq*] and the Command [*al-amr*]" (7: 54), he divides all originated beings into (1) those that can be located in time and space, i.e., those that are formed (*makhlūqāt*), and (2) those that were originated through the act of command, all at once (*dafʿatan wāḥidatan*), and which are beyond time and space and are created (*mubdaʿāt*). The former possess attributes, while the latter are entirely self-subsistent. The establishing and articulation of true transcendence (*tanzīh*) must therefore deny both:

> There does not exist a *tanzīh* more brilliant and more noble than the one by which we establish the *tanzīh* of our Mubdiʿ

> [Originator] by using these words in which two negations, negation and a negation of negation [*nafyun wa-nafyu nafyin*], oppose each other.[10]

Thus, the first negation disassociates God from all that can possess attributes, and the second from all who are "attributeless". He is careful to avoid suggesting that even that which is without attributes, defined and non-defined, is God – in his schema God is beyond both, rendering Him absolutely unknowable and without any predicates.

Such a concept of *tawḥīd* immediately presents two problems for a Muslim: the first concerns how one might worship such a God; and the second, if He indeed so transcends His creation, how is it that it comes into existence? The "grammar of divinity" affirming distinction now leads in Ismā'īlī thought to the "ladder of meaning" by which transcendence manifested through creation becomes "knowable".

MANIFESTING TRANSCENDENCE: KNOWLEDGE OF THE COSMOS

Among the most serious charges laid against a doctrine of "creationism" – i.e., the assumption of a Creator as the ultimate cause, through a special act of creation – is that it assumes in the form of a complex deity the very thing that one wishes to explain, organized complexity. It is this relationship between Creator and creation, and the transformation that is implied in the former by the very occurrence of change, that constitutes the greatest intellectual knot that a religious philosophy must tackle.

It has been argued that Ismā'īlī cosmology, particularly as expressed in the work of al-Sijistānī, integrates a manifestational cosmology (analogous to some aspects of Stoic thought) within an adapted Neoplatonic framework to create an alternative synthesis. The starting point of such a synthesis is the doctrine of *ibdā'* (derived from Qur'ān 2: 117). In its verbal form it is taken to mean "eternal existentiation" to explain the notion in the Qur'ān of God's timeless command (*Kun*: "Be!"). *Ibdā'* therefore connotes not a specific act of creation but the dialogical mode through which a relationship between God and His creation can be affirmed – it articulates the process of beginning and sets the stage for developing a philosophy of the manifestation of transcendence in creation. By making creation emerge as a result of a process of origination, Sijistānī hopes to maintain his distinction between God and creation by making *amr*, God's eternal expression of His Will, the ultimate point of origin. In this sense, to quote Corbin: "la philosophie première de l'ismaélisme n'est une métaphysique ni de l'*ens*, ni de l'*esse*, mais de l'*esto*".[11] It can be said to express the distinction between God and creation even more sharply than the schema of emanationism associated with Plotinus, and, as with other Muslim ontological formulations, does not confuse the act of being with the state of being.

Al-Kirmānī attempts to distance the Ismāʿīlī view from a purely emanationist outlook and to resolve what he regards as the ambiguities in Sijistānī's formulation by arguing that the process of emanation and its source cannot, strictly speaking, be differentiated. He cites as an analogy the light emanating from the sun, which, issuing from the fountain of the sun, partakes of the essence out of which it emanates, since at the point of emanation it is no different from the essence of the sun, its source. They are thus linked, though not identical, by being together in existence; and they could not logically be conceived of, one without the other. Such mutuality cannot be associated with God, for to conceive of existence as emanating from Him necessitates multiplicity in its source, which is its very essence. For al-Kirmānī, then, the only absolute way in which creation and *tawḥīd* can be distinguished is through a much sharper definition of that which is originated through *ibdāʿ*, namely the First Existent or the First Intellect. He states: "It did not exist, then it came into existence via *ibdāʿ* and *ikhtirāʿ*, neither from a thing, nor upon a thing, nor in a thing, nor by a thing, nor for a thing and nor with a thing."[12]

Like the number one, it contains all other numbers, which depend on it for their existence. Yet it is independent and separate from them, and it is the source and the cause of all plurality. In order to establish the singularity of the First Intellect, he refers to what the ancient sages (*ḥukamāʾ*) have said: "From the First Existent, which is the First Cause, nothing comes into existence but a single existence . . . or the Prime Mover moves only one, even though by it many are moved."[13]

Having used the arguments of the ancients for the purpose of validating his point, al-Kirmānī is nevertheless quick to separate himself from the view that all these attributes can then be applied to God, for that would compromise his insistence on absolute transcendence. They can only apply to the First Intellect, which in his scheme now becomes the Source, that which is inherently the synthesis of the One and many (*jāmiʿ li'l-waḥdah wa'l-kathrah*). At this stage, anterior to time and space, the two qualities were in the First Intellect, but they comprise the dual dimension that relates the First Intellect to *tawḥīd*, as well as to the role by which its generative capacity can be manifested. With respect to God, the First Intellect exists to sanctify Him. Such sanctification (*taqdīs*) on the part of the First Intellect reflects the nobler aspect of its dual dimension, where it is an affirmation of its own createdness and distinction from God. On the other hand, the sanctification generates a state of happiness and contentment within it, which produces actual and potential intellects, which in turn become the causes for the creation of the subsequent spiritual and material realms. Al-Kirmānī distinguishes in the First Intellect between multiplicity and diversity. Though the forms within the Intellect can be said to be multiple, they do not yet possess this aspect, since no diversity or differentiation exists within the Intellect. His analogy for the actual intellect is the Qur'ānic symbol of the "Pen", and of the potential intellect, the "Tablet", which represent *form* and *matter*, respectively.

In attempting to resolve the problem of explaining the First Intellect's dual capacity for form and multiplicity, Sijistānī argues for a distinction between the concepts of multiplicity (*kathrah*) and diversity (*tafāwut*). Extending the analogy of the Pen, which contains all the subsequent forms of expression in writing – letters, words and names – before they appear in this differentiated form, he tries to argue that they are all one within the Pen. Also, this singularity does not resemble any of the expressed forms as they appear subsequently in written form. Thus, each letter, prior to its manifestation, cannot be distinguished from the rest of the letters "pre-existing" inside the Pen.

More interestingly, as Mohamed Alibhai shows in his analysis of Sijistānī's epistemology,[14] he illustrates the role of the intellect by using the analogy of a seed, out of which the cosmos, in its spiritual as well as material form, develops. This metaphor, drawn from biology, suggests a process where the intellect is manifested in the natural domain and participates in time. Such a view of creation seems to imply that the process of generation and development involves the Intellect's participation as a "vital" principle in the cosmos progressively manifesting itself in both material and spiritual forms. The process by which this generation takes place is called *inbiʿāth*. Al-Kirmānī, for example, employs two similes to illustrate this process, one from the natural order, one relating to human relations: the reflection of the sun in a mirror, and the blush on the cheek of the lover at the sight of the beloved. *Inbiʿāth*, manifestation, thus is contrasted with *fayḍ*, or emanation. The former, like the image of the sun in a mirror or a pool of water, is mere representation; it is from something and being figurative can permit one to retrace it to the original. Such symbolism is particularly suited to evoking the sense of religiosity so central to the Islamic affirmation of the distinction between God and creation. The rest of the intellects are manifested, one from the other, leading to the creation of the spheres, stars and the material world, including human beings.

In sum the process of creation can be said to take place at several levels. *Ibdāʿ* represents the initial level, *inbiʿāth*, the secondary level – one transcends history, the other creates it. The spiritual and material realms are not dichotomous, since in the Ismāʿīlī formulation matter and spirit are united under a higher genus and each realm possesses its own hierarchy. Though they require linguistic and rational categories for definition, they represent elements of a whole, and a true understanding of God must also take account of His creation. Such a synthesis is crucial to how the human intellect eventually relates to creation and how it ultimately becomes the instrument for penetrating through history the mystery of the unknowable God implied in the formulation of *tawḥīd.*

At the philosophical level, for al-Kirmānī, an understanding of *tawḥīd* requires the believers to recognize that they must in some way "deconstruct" the First Intellect, divesting it of divinity. *Ibdāʿ* and then *inbiʿāth* reflect the "descending" arc of a circle, where God's command creates the First Intellect, which is then manifested through successive existents down to the human intellect. The action of the believers can be seen to be the ascending arc, where each unit leading up to the First Intellect is divested of divinity until the process is completed on reaching the One itself. It is in this particular context that he cites a tradition of the Prophet: "The believer is the *muwāḥḥid* [literally, maker of the One] and God is *muwāḥḥid*"[15] – the believer, because he or she divests the First Intellect of divinity, and God, because He originated the First Intellect as the symbol of the One. It is possible for the human intellect to comprehend this because God provides assistance to the human intellect through His "dual" messengers, making accessible the tools formalized in religious language and ritual, which go hand in hand with the intellectual and spiritual capacity for reflection and knowledge.

When al-Mu'ayyad fi'l-Dīn al-Shīrāzī (d. 470/1077) interprets the Qur'ānic verse "God created the heavens and earth in six days" (7: 54), he is concerned to show that the "days" stand figuratively for the six major cycles of prophecy, each of which represents a journey to God.[16] Their existence in time is not a function of priority or primacy; they merely succeed each other, like day and night. The believers in each of these cycles of prophecy are recipients of knowledge which assists in understanding *tawḥīd.* In Sijistānī there is an elaboration of the two types of prophecy. The first relates to the human intellect, the second to human history embodied in the messages communicated through the various prophets. These messengers come to confirm that which the human intellect already knows, and human beings appropriately, by the acceptance of the message, corroborate the validity of each historical messenger. The actual intellect thus corroborates that which the potential intellect brings to it.

Human history, as conceived in Ismāʿīlism, operates cyclically. According to this typological view, the epoch of the great prophets mirrors the cosmological paradigm, unfolding to recover the equilibrium and harmony inherent in the divine pattern of creation. Prophets and, after them, their appointed successors, the Imāms, have as their collective goal the establishment of a just society. The essence of governing in such a society is not mere juridical order but rather an integrated vision of equilibrium where individuals mature intellectually and spiritually, through right action and knowledge. The function of the Prophet is to initiate the cycle for human society and of the Imām to complement and interpret the teaching to sustain the just order at the social and individual levels. The metaphors of Ismāʿīlī thought evoke a *qiyāmah* (from the Qur'ān)[17] not simply as the ultimate day of judgment or resurrection but also as the constantly recurring moment in history, which connects the cosmic, natural order with the social world and with the individual's pursuit of personal salvation.

As Nāṣir-i-Khusraw, the best known of the Ismāʿīlī writers in Persian, states in a passage paraphrased by Corbin:

> Time is eternity measured by the movements of the heavens, whose name is day, night, month, year. Eternity is Time not measured, having neither beginning nor end. . . . The cause of Time is the Soul of the World . . . ; it is not in time, for time is in the horizon of the soul as its instrument, as the duration of the living mortal who is "the shadow of the soul", while eternity is the duration of the living immortal – that is to say of the Intelligence and of the Soul.[18]

This synthesis of time as cycle and time as arrow, to borrow a phrase from the scientist Stephen Jay Gould, lies at the heart of an Ismāʿīlī philosophy of active engagement in the world.

NOTES

1 This chapter synthesizes material from some of my previously published works, in particular, "Transcendence and Distinction: Metaphoric Process in Ismāʿīlī Muslim Thought", in *God and Creation*, ed. David B. Burrell and Bernard McGinn (Notre Dame, 1990): 304–15; "Ismāʿīlism" in *Islamic Spirituality: Foundations*, ed. S. H. Nasr (New York, 1987): 179–98, and "Toward a Hermeneutic of Qur'ānic and Other Narratives in Ismāʿīlī Thought", in *Approaches to Islam and Religious Studies*, ed. R. C. Martin (Tucson, 1985): 164–73. I am grateful to Professor Seyyed Hossein Nasr and Dr Aziz Esmail for their valuable comments and suggestions.

2 The title *Umm al-kitāb* is also used for a work that is attributed to the early period of Shiʿism in its Persian form. It has been an important esoteric text among Ismāʿīlīs of Central Asia. See Pio Fillipani-Ronconi, *Umm al-kitāb, Introduzione, traduzione e note* (Naples, 1966).

3 Muhsin Mahdi makes the point generally, in a recent review article devoted to Richard Walzer's study of al-Fārābī, "Al-Fārābī's Imperfect State", *Journal of the American Oriental Society*, 110(4): 691–726.

4 The most important reference source for Ismāʿīlī literature and of secondary studies of modern scholarship is Ismail Poonawala, *Biobibliography of Ismāʿīlī*

Literature (Malibu, 1977). For the historical development of Western Studies, see Farhad Daftary, *The Ismā'īlīs* (Cambridge, 1990): 1–132, who also refers to the efforts of modern Ismā'īlī scholars.

5 Daftary: 232–49.

6 Nanji, "Ismā'īlism": 184–6.

7 This section on Kirmānī's thought based on his writings is drawn from Faquirmohamed Hunzai, *The Concept of Tawḥīd in the Thought of Ḥamīd al-Dīn al-Kirmānī* (Ph.D. dissertation, McGill University, 1986).

8 For al-Sijistānī, see Paul Walker, *Early Philosophical Shiism: the Ismaili Neoplatonism of Abū Ya'qūb al-Sijistānī* (Cambridge and New York, 1993) and Mohamed Alibhai, *Abū Ya'qūb al-Sijistānī and "Kitāb Sullam al-Najāt": a Study in Islamic Neoplatonism* (Ph.D. dissertation, Harvard University, 1983). For a broader view of the relationship between Neoplatonic and Muslim thought, see *Neoplatonism and Islamic Thought*, ed. Parviz Morewedge (Albany, 1992).

9 Sijistānī, *al-Maqālid*, trans. Hunzai, in *The Concept of Tawḥīd*: 69.

10 *Ibid.*: 70.

11 Henry Corbin, *Nāṣir-e-Khosraw: Kitāb jāmi' al-ḥikmatayn* (Paris, 1983): "Etude Preliminaire", 45.

12 Kirmānī, *Rāhat al-'aql*, trans. Hunzai: 165.

13 *Ibid.*: 166.

14 I am grateful to Mohamed A. Alibhai for sharing with me his paper "The Transformation of Spiritual Substance into Bodily Substance in Ismaili Neoplatonism", in *Neoplatonism and Islamic Thought*, ed. Parviz Morewedge (Albany, 1992): 167–77.

15 Hunzai, *Kirmānī*: 151.

16 For a further discussion, see Nanji, "Toward a Hermeneutic": 167–8.

17 For a discussion of the *ta'wīl* of the Qur'ānic concept of Resurrection, see Naṣīr al-Din Ṭūsī, *Taṣawwurāt*, ed. and trans. W. Ivanow (Leiden, 1950): 66–71.

18 Corbin, *Cyclical Time and Ismā'īlī Gnosis*, trans. R. Mannheim and J. Morris (London, 1983): 33.

CHAPTER 10

Islamic humanism in the fourth/tenth century

Oliver Leaman

A group of thinkers who lead up to Ibn Miskawayh are frequently called "Islamic humanists", a list which generally includes Abū Ḥayyān al-Tawḥīdī (d. 399/1009), his teacher Abū Sulaymān al-Sijistānī (d. 371/981) and many other minor characters of the period. The reason why this label is applied has much to do with the character of the thought produced by these thinkers, which appears to be far more audacious and frank than much of the work of their predecessors or successors. They seem to downgrade the importance of religion, even Islam, without denying its significance, and perceive their task as consisting in the analysis of human being *qua* human being, as opposed to *qua* Muslim. There is much in their work which suggests that they give a significance to pure reason which is not found in many of the *falāsifah*. These thinkers worked at a time of immense self-confidence in the culture of the Islamic world, with Baghdad as the effective centre of a vast civilization comprising a variety of courts with their attendant officials and patrons of learning. The latter half of the fourth/tenth century under the control of the Būyid (Buwayhid) dynasty was perhaps the high point of what might be called "humanism", since then there was an impressive mingling of a large variety of scholars sharing an interest in the "ancient sciences" and a common language in which to discuss it, despite the diversity of their backgrounds and religious allegiances. Some commentators on this period such as Netton (1992) have described the leading school of philosophy as "Fārābist", and the influence of al-Fārābī is clearly of enormous significance here. He surely set the agenda of the period, and it is interesting to note the chain of transmission (one might even say *isnād*) which links him with the period being analysed here.

Al-Fārābī's distinguished pupil, the Jacobite Christian Abū Zakariyyā' Yaḥyā ibn 'Adī (d. 374/984), did much to institute the process of commentary, translation and enquiry which came to dominate philosophical life. It is worth recalling that al-Fārābī himself was the pupil of the Nestorian Yuḥannā ibn Ḥaylān and was dependent for his work on Plato and Aristotle on the Syriac-speaking Christians whose most famous representative was the Nestorian Mattā ibn Yūnus. Ibn 'Adī was followed by the Nestorian Abu'l-Khayr al-Ḥasan ibn Suwār ibn al-Khammār, the Jacobite Abū 'Alī 'Īsā ibn Isḥāq ibn Zur'ah and many distinguished Muslims, especially Muḥammad ibn Isḥāq al-Warrāq (Ibn al-Nadīm), 'Isā ibn 'Alī, al-Sijistānī and al-Tawḥīdī. Ibn Miskawayh is perhaps the most distinguished product of this school barring al-Fārābī himself, but what is to be noted here is how cosmopolitan the cultural atmosphere of the time came to be. That atmosphere consisted of the thought of Muslims, Christians, Jews and pagans, and, perhaps even more significantly, of those within a religious group regardless of doctrinal differences. The leading point of agreement was that the "ancient sciences" (*al-'ulūm al-awā'il*) are the property of all humanity, and no particular religious or cultural group can claim exclusive ownership of them. Hence the description of this group of thinkers as "humanists", and of those of them who were Muslims as "Islamic humanists".

One might wonder how accurate this description is, though. As Kraemer (1986a) shows, a very wide gamut of theoretical ideas is compatible with "humanism", and there seem to be marked differences on occasion between the Greek idea of what human beings are and that current among the *falāsifah*. There are certainly important differences between the notions of the universality of unaided reason and the role of religion in the Classical and Islamic cultural milieu, but also sometimes interesting resemblances. Perhaps the closest they come is on the topic of education. The Arabic *adab* is certainly equivalent to the Greek *paideia*, and represents what is necessary to produce an elegant, courteous, refined and cultured individual. In fact, the sort of individual who would fit in well with court life of the time, when the vast bureaucracy of the empire required a host of civil servants, secretaries, scribes and courtiers. One might wonder what scope for religion survives in this description of education. One might expect that *Islamic* "humanists" would stress the importance of religion in the upbringing of the cultured individual, and they do, of course, but often with less whole-hearted enthusiasm for the religion of Islam than the class of *'ulamā'*. Islam seems to come into the picture because it is the religion of the time. Although some commentators on this period such as Netton (1992) will go a long way to emphasize the common adherence of the philosophers in a theory of salvation which stems from al-Fārābī but which is at the very least compatible with Islam, it is difficult to argue that the specifics of Islam play much part in their work. As good Aristotelians they divide up the sciences into practical and theoretical, and into the former category go activities such as jurisprudence (*fiqh*) and theology (*kalām*), which strengthens the impression that the form of education at issue is hardly different at all from its Greek model apart from the nature of the religious commitment which is represented within it and the literary tradition upon which it is based.

We have to look here not just at particular doctrines as they were propounded by the "humanists" in the Islamic world but also at the sort of literature they produced. One of the characteristic literary forms of this period was the construction of wisdom literature. This consists of a selection of aphorisms, arguments, anecdotes, biographical comments and comments on natural phenomena which generally have a firm basis in ancient Greece. The form is often to represent a series of sayings by scholars and savants from the earliest days of Greek and Persian culture and extending up to relatively contemporary thinkers. One of the points of such literature was to display the nature of life as an *adīb* (*phronimos*) by showing what sort of lifestyle and thoughts such an individual might be expected to acquire. How better to represent this form of life than through often vivid and witty illustrations of those in the past who enjoyed it? We do not know now precisely how these texts were used, but there is a good deal of evidence that they were popular across a wide gamut of the social structure and much quoted by those who regarded themselves as educated (Gutas 1975). One assumes that the more serious treatment of these texts involved analysing and explaining the meanings of the quotations and showing how relevant they are to contemporary life and thought. No doubt they were also found to be attractive to those just looking for a pithy saying or inspiring expression. The important aspect to note about this form of writing is that it linked contemporary life in the Islamic world with Classical civilization as an apparently seamless web based on the idea of a perennial wisdom, one of the books of Ibn Miskawayh bearing the title *Jāwidān khirād* (literally *philosophia perennis*). The description "humanist" then seems to be highly appropriate.

We should distinguish between this form of "humanism" and the very radical approach of thinkers such as Ibn al-Rāwandī (d. *c.* 245/910) and Abū Bakr al-Rāzī (d. 313/925). The latter in particular did not try to show that contemporary thought followed on quite naturally from classical thought, but on the contrary that the former was inferior to the latter. Al-Rāzī seems to regard religion as a malign influence, which can be challenged only by the use of reason, and the unbridled use of reason at that. Religion is not just a way of explaining truths to those incapable of understanding them theoretically, as with most of the *falāsifah*, but is actually an institution which can communicate falsehoods, and some of its leading figures are on a par with magicians and imposters. Some have argued that what we are presented with here is a form of "humanism" which differs in degree rather than in kind from that most commonly found in Islamic philosophy, or that al-Rāzī is a franker author than are most of his peers. Arguing thus is to misunderstand the difference between al-Rāzī and the more moderate Islamic philosophers. While the latter produced work which is certainly far from a simple repetition and acknowledgment of the truth of Islam as formulated by legal authorities, they had a good argument for their position, namely that it is not the role of philosophers to establish religious truths. Those truths have to be established by other means and then they can be examined from a rational point of view. In the case of Islam, it can be seen that religious doctrines are entirely reconcilable with philosophy, after one has learnt to understand those doctrines in the right sort of way, or so the *falāsifah* argued. Whether this was their real view we cannot tell, but have to rely on their writings and the consistency of their arguments. Al-Rāzī is clearly arguing in a different way, that reason and religion are irreconcilable, and that the latter is of less value in understanding the world and ourselves than is the former.

This does little to resolve the issue of whether it is right to call this group of thinkers stemming from al-Fārābī and Yaḥyā ibn 'Adī "Islamic humanists", where this label is applied to the Muslim thinkers ending up with Miskawayh. One way of tackling the question is to wonder what difference the religion of Islam makes to their actual arguments. What we need here are some examples of arguments which would not work within a different religious context, where the form of the argument as compared with the matter is irretrievably tied up with the principles of a particular religion. We do not find such examples in their writings, though, and it would be surprising if we could. Since the tradition of philosophy following on from al-Fārābī emphasizes the subordinate role of religion with respect to philosophy from a theoretical point of view, the nature of a particular religion cannot really be expected to shape the nature of a particular philosophy. What distinguishes the Muslim *adīb* from the Greek *phronimos* does not appear to be great. Although Von Grunebaum claims that "the basic difference between the Greek *paideia* and the Islamic educational ideal is that the Greek is ever aware of the state, the Muslim of the service of God" (1964: 86), one might be sceptical of the significance of the contrast. Muslims' religious obligations draw them nearer to the community of which they are a part. Their religious practices define their activity within that community and express their relationships with others, and within such a society it is clear that religion has a significant role to play. In different kinds of society religion might be less important, or even of no importance whatsoever. Again, in societies with different religions it would be important to carry out the obligations as specified by those religions if one were to fit in smoothly and be able to carry out the normal civil functions which are so helpful to a peaceful existence. Not only is one's life likely to be more comfortable if one carries out one's conventional duties, it will also make possible the elevation of one's thought to higher levels of abstraction. Like Aristotle, the *falāsifah* seemed to think that the secondary and social virtues are a necessary step on the route to the primary and intellectual virtues, although it is always unclear what the precise nature of the relationship between the different sorts of virtues is taken to be.

What are these higher levels of abstraction? They are often given a religious description and related to salvation or coming closer to God. As our thinking becomes more and more purified of those issues which arise in the world of generation and corruption we are able to think in ways which approach the Divine. Given the sort of Neoplatonic scheme of emanation so popular with all al-Fārābī's followers, it is easy to think of thought as capable of moving up a scale of different levels until it becomes identical with the most abstract level of which we as human beings are capable. Now, it is beyond doubt that this model of the perfectibility of thought is far from primarily a religious idea, but arose within a philosophical context which had as its aim the reconciliation of particular Platonic with Aristotelian ideas. Neoplatonism is actually perfectly suited to religious employment, since it provides an account of the link between this world and its creator which can be made to fit quite nicely into a whole variety of religious contexts.

Neoplatonism also suggests an account of how we might through our own efforts ascend along the scale of reality until we manage to perfect ourselves in so far as we are capable. This sort of intellectual development is surely in principle available to all humanity, although it might also be argued that Muslims are more likely to avail themselves of it given the excellence of their particular religion. The latter is often held to be the best expression of philosophical truths in language which anyone can follow, and al-Fārābī and his followers could argue that Muslims had an advantage over non-Muslims in that their religion is the most skilfully organized from a political point of view. What the Islamic "humanists" would have to accept, though, is that Classical thinkers were capable of perfecting their thinking along the appropriate lines even without the assistance of the revelation of God in a directly Islamic sort of way although they believed that the origin of philosophy itself was divine and came from earlier revelations. What has changed over the many centuries since ancient Greece is that religions have arisen which are capable of making more perspicuous the route to perfection, especially for the sections of the community who are only able to follow this route part of the way, but the essential nature of that theoretical perfection has remained unchanged.

This is even clearer when we examine the many ethical treatises which the Islamic "humanists" produced. These works take the Aristotelian notion of practical reasoning to its logical conclusion, and they are largely practical in their suggestions and prescriptions. They present a moral psychology and methodology which is intended to assist individuals to carry out their duties in the most efficient and productive manner, while permitting them the intellectual space to perfect their theoretical capacities. Much advice is proffered, and that advice is in line with the particular lifestyle which the individual author is recommending. Here we find a mixture of influences from Arabic, Persian, Islamic and Classical cultures and particularly Sufism presented in such a way as to enable readers to develop in themselves the appropriate dispositions to follow an ethics of virtue. At first sight these treatises appear to be rather banal, historically interesting perhaps as the reflection of a particular model of perfection within a certain historical context, but disappointing in their lack of philosophical sophistication and excess of syncretistic reasoning. What we have here is an illustration of how one ought to live if one adheres to a set of philosophical principles largely stemming from a wide variety of Greek and ancient Persian thought. We find here a loose combination of Platonic, Aristotelian, Pythagorean and Stoic ideas, not to mention the important influence of Galen and a wide variety of Presocratic thinkers along with pre-Islamic Persian thought, with more contemporary writers in Arabic appearing as well. It seems to be a mixture of ideas and arguments, a list of other people's observations, and sometimes rather unexciting advice as to how one should conduct oneself. Sometimes the language is rather poetic, and at other times it is prosaic and dull, but the focus of the argument is firmly on the practice of the reader, on showing readers how they should behave and think if they are to fit into the role of educated participants in the community.

Since today in the West this sort of writing is not classified as philosophical, it is tempting to reject it as real philosophy and classify it with literature as a mainly literary form of production with little if any philosophical interest. This would be a shame, though, since these ethical treatises do contain an attempt at presenting in practical form a theoretical position. The latter may be made up of a large variety of philosophical ingredients, but they do on the whole make up a reasonable thesis with sensible implications for practical life. Readers are then able to think about how they might set about changing their lives in order to take account of the sort of end which they themselves can attain, a long and tortuous process, no doubt, but one which is surely aided by philosophical reflection on the processes involved. In this respect we should remember how close the Islamic philosophers were to their Greek forebears in both time and inclination. We tend not to spend much time on the practical illustrations which the Greek philosophers spent so much effort on elaborating, preferring to concentrate upon the entirely conceptual issues which they produced. Yet there is surely some mileage to be extracted from explaining clearly what the practical implications of following a certain end might be, and the Islamic "humanists" put a great deal of effort in this direction. It is this emphasis upon practice and example that contributed to the popularity of their writings, which without doubt outstripped in readership the main works of the major *falāsifah* many times over. It has been suggested that it is acceptable to call them "Islamic" in the sense that they were operating within the conditions and presuppositions of Islamic culture, but it should not be inferred from this that they allowed their religion to intrude frequently into their arguments. In fact, they tend to use examples from Islam to illustrate points which they had already described using examples from Greek writings. Islam is then treated as yet another piece of the jigsaw which is useful in contributing to the whole pattern, but it is far from being the key to the pattern itself, while providing the general matrix for such types of "humanistic" writing.

BIBLIOGRAPHY

Gutas, D. (1975) *Greek Wisdom Literature in Arabic Translation: a Study of the Graeco-Arabic Gnomologia* (New Haven).

Kraemer, J. (1986a) *Humanism in the Renaissance of Islam: the Cultural Revival during the Būyid Age* (Leiden).

—— (1986b) *Philosophy in the Renaissance of Islam: Abū Sulaymān and his Circle* (Leiden).

Netton, I. (1992) *Al-Fārābī and his School* (London).

al-Sijistānī (1979) *The Muntakhab Ṣiwān al-Ḥikma of Abū Sulaymān as-Sijistānī*, ed. D. M. Dunlop (The Hague).

Takriti, N. (1978) *Yaḥyā Ibn 'Adī: a Critical Edition and Study of his Tahdhīb al-Akhlaq* (Beirut).

Tawḥīdī (1953) *Kitāb al-imtā' wa'l-mu'ānasah*, ed. A. Amīn and A. al-Zayn (Beirut).

Von Grunebaum, G. (1964) *Modern Islam: the Search for Cultural Identity* (New York).

II

Early Islamic philosophers in the East

CHAPTER 11

Al-Kindī

Felix Klein-Franke

Abū Yūsuf Ya'qūb ibn Isḥāq al-Kindī[1] is generally held to have been the first Muslim philosopher. This does not mean, however, that the Muslims prior to al-Kindī had no cognizance at all of Greek philosophical ideas. On the contrary, some philosophical knowledge, though fragmentary, can be attributed to the early Mu'tazilī *kalām*. Some of their main representatives – Abu'l-Hudhayl al-'Allāf[2] and al-Naẓẓām[3] – developed a theology built on certain Greek philosophical elements. Thus the theologian Abu'l-Ḥasan al-Ash'arī[4] named Aristotle as the source of some of Abu'l-Hudhayl's doctrines,[5] and al-Baghdādī[6] blamed al-Naẓẓām for having borrowed from Greek philosophers the idea of matter being infinitely divisible.[7] The impact of Greek philosophy upon early Mu'tazilī *kalām* is evident and has been stated also by early Muslim theologians and heresiographers. But this impact remained rather marginal; for none of the early Mu'tazilī theologians ever elaborated an encyclopedic system of Greek philosophy as this was out of the range of their interests. It was al-Kindī who pursued this aim and who may therefore rightly be called the first Muslim philosopher, whereas the representatives of Mu'tazilī *kalām* were theologians and no philosophers. This fact alone puts al-Kindī in some opposition to the Mu'tazilah with whom he should not be identified.[8]

Ibn al-Nadīm[9] listed some 260 titles of al-Kindī's, an enormous scientific bibliography, even if many of the works may have been of small extent. Al-Kindī's treatises encompass the whole Classical encyclopedia of sciences: philosophy, logic, arithmetic, spherics, music, astronomy, geometry, cosmology, medicine, astrology, etc., according to Ibn al-Nadīm's arrangement. Ibn al-Nadīm's bibliographical list reveals al-Kindī's predilection for natural science. Only few manuscripts, approximately ten per cent of all his literary output, have come to light and been edited up to now. It seems that the vast majority of the manuscripts have been lost.

It is hardly surprising that later Muslim philosophers rarely quote from any of al-Kindī's philosophical treatises. Both facts – the loss of the bulk of his manuscripts and the lack of reference to him by later authors – need an explanation. Some books may have been lost already during the reign of the caliph al-Mutawakkil[10] who fought vehemently against the rationalizing tendencies of his time and confiscated for a while al-Kindī's library. The famous eighth/fourteenth-century historian Ibn Khaldūn[11] adds further proof to the lack of manuscripts when he says: "We have not found any information concerning [al-Kindī's] book [called *al-Jafr*], and we have not seen anyone who has seen it. Perhaps it was lost with those books which Hulagu, the ruler of the Tatars threw into the Tigris when the Tatars took possession of Baghdad and killed the last caliph, al-Musta'ṣim."[12] The obscurity of al-Kindī's language, due to the lack of an Arabic philosophical terminology, rendered his writings hard of access and made them obsolete while al-Fārābī's philosophical œuvre eventually overshadowed them. Abū Sulaymān al-Sijistānī al-Manṭiqī[13] recorded the ruler of Sijistan, Ja'far ibn Bābūyah, as having criticized al-Kindī because of his bad language.[14]

It is, nevertheless, the merit of al-Kindī to have made access to Greek philosophy and science possible and to have established from rare and obscure sources the foundation of philosophy in Islam, partly continued and enlarged later on by al-Fārābī.[15]

Al-Kindī enjoyed the confidence and support of the seventh and eighth 'Abbasid caliphs, al-Ma'mūn[16] and his brother and successor. To al-Mu'taṣim[17] he dedicated his *On First Philosophy*, and some other treatises to the caliph's son Aḥmad with whose education he was entrusted. Unlike his contemporary Ḥunayn ibn Isḥāq,[18] al-Kindī knew neither Greek nor Syriac. He therefore commissioned or adopted translations, e.g. those made by Ibn Nā'ima, Eustathius (Asṭāt) and Ibn al-Biṭrīq.[19] The old translations, commissioned or used by al-Kindī, still lack the high philological standards set later on by Ḥunayn ibn Isḥāq. But it was al-Kindī who broke new ground in a fertile soil and introduced into the Arab-speaking world the first translations of Greek philosophy. He was above all interested in gathering and translating works of Plato and Aristotle, both of whom he mentioned by name. But under the cover of these two philosophers other pseudepigraphic works became known, e.g. Porphyry's paraphrase of part of Plotinus' *Enneads* known as Aristotle's *Theology*. Al-Kindī, however, had a good grasp of the genuine works of Aristotle. He commissioned a translation of Aristotle's *Metaphysics* and commented upon some of Aristotle's logical writings, such as *Categoriae, De interpretatione, Analytica posteriora* and *Analytica priora* – and also on *De caelo*, as we are informed by Ibn al-Nadīm. He had before him even the otherwise lost Aristotelian dialogue *Eudemus*, a fragment of which he transmitted.[20]

Al-Kindī was eager to introduce Greek philosophy and science to his Arabic-speaking "co-linguists" (*ahl lisāninā*), as he often stressed,[21] and opposed the orthodox *mutakallimūn* who rejected foreign knowledge.[22] As long as he enjoyed the caliphs' protection he was free to do so and did not feel compelled to defend his philosophical stand as was the case with so many later scientists who came under pressure at the hand of the orthodox legalists. As long as al-Kindī clung to tenets held by late Greek Neoplatonists, mostly Christians, who believed in one God who had created the world out of nothing, he was in apparent harmony with the divine law of Islam. But as soon as he adopted pagan philosophical doctrines, especially those of Aristotle, he openly deviated from the revealed truth of Islam. His view adduced in the name of Aristotle – that one should gratefully accept any contribution to truth, wherever it comes from, even from Greek philosophy[23] – is incompatible with the exclusive postulate of Islam as the sole mediator of truth.

Al-Kindī's own philosophical stand reflects the doctrines he found in Greek Classical and, above all, Neoplatonic sources. His treatise *On Definitions and Descriptions of Things*[24] may be accepted on the whole as the base of his own views. He supposedly extracted the definitions from Greek literature with the intention of giving a summary of Greek philosophy in definitions. As I have shown elsewhere,[25] many of these definitions are literal borrowings from Aristotle. Al-Kindī's diligence in collecting definitions from Aristotelian works and his predilection for Aristotle cannot be ignored even where he extracted from spurious sources which were at the time attributed to Aristotle. The lemmata and their arrangement correspond to a Neoplatonic source. God is referred to in the first definition as the "First Cause", similar to Plotinus' "First Agent", an expression al-Kindī has likewise made use of,[26] or to his "the One is the cause of the cause".[27] The subsequent definitions in al-Kindī's treatise are arranged in an order that distinguishes between the upper world and the lower world. The former is marked by the definitions of Intellect, Nature and Soul, followed by definitions that mark the lower world beginning with the definitions of Body (*jirm*), Creation (*ibdā'*), Matter (*hayūlā'*), Form (*ṣūrah*), etc. Thus al-Kindī conceived an upper world of uncreated spiritual beings and a lower world of created corporeal beings. The Soul is an uncreated, spiritual being, whereas Matter, Time and Place are finite, created and corporeal. Creation (*ibdā'*) in this Muslim context is Creation from nothing in time.[28] Both worlds, the upper and the lower one, go finally back to one and the same source which is the common cause of everything. From this final source which is the Godhead everything proceeds subsequently by hypostases.

In his treatise *On Definitions and Descriptions of Things* al-Kindī explained the world through emanation, a system that later was adopted and enlarged also by al-Fārābī.[29] The Muslim orthodox, however, were on the whole irritated by the attempt to explain creation as an incessant outflow from the ultimate source, an argument that could not be upheld by scriptural evidence. They were especially offended by extolling Intellect to immediate proximity to God as His first hypostasis. Emanating from the Uppermost Cause, everything passes through, and develops from, the reflexion of the first intellect. Thus the intellect was to replace the angels as the mediator of divine truth. Al-Fārābī took the sharp edge off the doctrine of emanation by equating the Active Intellect with the Angel Gabriel and by explaining prophecy as the result of the Soul's faculty of imagination. Nevertheless, emanation could not explain the divine act of creation in a way acceptable to the orthodox community of the faithful. "It should be known," said Ibn Khaldūn, "that the [opinion] the [philosophers] hold is wrong in all its aspects. They refer all existentia to the first intellect and are satisfied with [the theory of the first intellect] in their progress toward the Necessary One [the Deity]. This means that they disregard all the degrees of divine creation beyond the [first intellect]."[30]

Al-Kindī did not intend to explain the "progress toward the Necessary One", i.e. the way of attaining knowledge of God, as an intellectual progress. On the contrary, towards the end of his *On First Philosophy* he made it clear beyond all doubt that God cannot be comprehended by intellect.[31] According to al-Kindī the philosopher is unable to make any positive statement concerning God. All he is able to state is in the negative: that "He is no element, no genus, no species, no individual person, no part (of something), no attribute, no contingent accident".[32] Thus al-Kindī's philosophy leads to a negative theology, i.e. where God is described only in negative terms. In this he followed Plotinus[33] who taught: "We state, what is not; what is, we do not state."[34] If the intellect is unable to lead people to knowledge of God in positive terms, philosophy is not superior to theology. On its "progress towards the Necessary One" philosophy reaches up to the intellect, but does not go "beyond the intellect", to use again Ibn Khaldūn's words.[35]

What is "beyond the intellect"? For the Muslim faithful it is the world of the angels. They are God's messengers and are the mediators between humans and God. It is the Angel Gabriel, as the Muslim faithful say – and not the intellect, as the philosophers have it – who conveyed the divine revelation to the Prophet. The angelic essence is of "pure perception and absolute intellection".[36] Al-Kindī does not speak of angels. According to him the intellect is in immediate proximity with God.

The longest text of al-Kindī's treatises that have come down to our time is his *On First Philosophy* (only the first part of this treatise has been preserved). This is another name for metaphysics. Aristotle had called metaphysics the "first philosophy".[37] Al-Kindī, adopting this name, explained its meaning in the following way:

> Knowledge of the first cause has truthfully been called "First Philosophy", since all the rest of philosophy is contained in its knowledge. The first cause is, therefore, the first in nobility, the first in genus, the first in rank with respect to that knowledge which is most certain; and the first in time, since it is the cause of time.[38]

The first cause is, therefore, explorable and it is the intellect that transmits "most certain knowledge" of it. The aim of writing this treatise was to establish "the proof of His Divinity and the explanation of His Unity", as al-Kindī declared in the introduction.[39] In spite of the intellectual certainty which can be attained of the Deity, al-Kindī admits at the end of his treatise that the intellect is able to describe God only in negative terms.

God's unity stood at the very centre of the Muʿtazilī doctrine so that the Muʿtazilah were called accordingly "the people [who made] the confession of [God's] unity [the basis of their creed]" (*ahl al-tawḥīd*). Supported by the evidence of Muʿtazilī themes like God's unity in al-Kindī's philosophical writings, al-Kindī was held to be "the philosopher of the Muʿtazilite theology".[40] Later research, however, made it evident that this statement, linking al-Kindī peremptorily with the Muʿtazilah, could not be upheld. Against some sporadic similarities, significant philosophical differences between al-Kindī and the Muʿtazilah were brought to light by further research.[41] One point of dissent was the structure of matter. Most of the Muʿtazilah were of the opinion that matter consisted of small and indivisible particles, i.e. atoms. They were led to this opinion by supposing that everything created is finite in spatial and temporal extension. Hence they concluded that the divisibility of matter must also be finite. So they assumed the existence of atoms. Al-Kindī, however, denied the atomistic structure of matter, a topic he elaborated in his treatise *On the Falsity of the Statement of Whoever Thinks that a Body Exists that is Indivisible*.[42] He adopted Aristotle's view of the continuous structure of matter. This difference of opinion had a great impact on many parts of the physical sciences. The Muʿtazilah accepted the discontinuity of matter and believed in the existence of a vacuum, denied by Aristotle. Contrary to the Muʿtazilah, however, al-Kindī conceived matter as being continuous and of unintermittent structure, but not of infinite extension. The universe is a finite body, a statement that al-Kindī expounded in a separate treatise.[43] By its finiteness the universe is separated from the immaterial, upper world of the spiritual beings.

Right after the introduction of his treatise *On Allāh's Unity and the Finiteness of the Body of the Universe*[44] al-Kindī stated six primary propositions which can rationally be comprehended "without mediation" (*ghayr mutawassiṭ*). Al-Kindī referred obviously to those propositions "that cannot be proved syllogistically by means of a middle term".[45] Propositions of this kind convey knowledge that cannot be proved (*anapódeiktos*), i.e. that is achieved *a priori* (*'ilm awwal, 'ilm badīhī*). As an example of a proposition that conveys primary knowledge al-Kindī stated that, if one joins two finite bodies one with the other, the new body is again finite. It is, however, impossible to disjoin a certain, finite part from a body which is held to be infinite. This is to prove that the corporeal world is finite. In the same way al-Kindī proved that time is finite. For you cannot pass a certain amount of time and suppose that the rest of time is infinite and eternal.[46] Likewise al-Kindī proved that the world cannot be eternal and that it is created in time (*muḥdath*).[47]

Al-Kindī's arguments go ultimately back to the late School of Alexandria. John Philoponus (Arabic Yaḥyā al-Naḥwī) used them in his refutation *On the Eternity of the World against Proclus*.[48] He wrote his book in the year 529 against the Neoplatonic philosopher Proclus.[49] Philoponus' refutation *On the Eternity of the World against Proclus* was translated into Arabic[50] and furnished al-Kindī with some philosophical arguments which were current among Christian philosophers in late Hellenistic Alexandria. This has been attested by a recently found text of John Philoponus in an early Arabic translation.[51] Al-Kindī has been influenced to a great extent also by Proclus. Traces of his *Institutio theologica*, almost literally the same, have been identified in al-Kindī's *On First Philosophy*.[52] They attest to al-Kindī's efforts at harmonizing the Aristotelian and the Neoplatonic systems of philosophy within the religious climate of Islam.

Al-Kindī's predilection for Aristotle's philosophy, witnessed already in his treatise *On Definitions and Descriptions of Things*, is most strikingly felt also in his *On First Philosophy*. In writing this treatise al-Kindī lavishly quoted from Aristotle's *Metaphysics*.[53] But it seems that the subject matter used by al-Kindī differed from the text now generally accepted. Book *Alpha elatton* allegedly written by Pasicles of Rhodes, a nephew of Eudemus, was apparently missing, but appears in 'Abd al-Laṭīf ibn Yūsuf al-Baghdādī's[54] paraphrase of Aristotle's *Metaphysics*, although in a reversed order, i.e. preceding book *Alpha*.[55] Although al-Kindī elaborated many of the ideas that go back to Aristotle's *Metaphysics*, his *On First Philosophy* is not a mere paraphrase of this book. For he relied extensively also upon other books of Aristotle. Thus many of al-Kindī's conceptions reflect ideas expressed by Aristotle in his *Physics*, *De anima* and *Categoriae*, to name only those books most quoted.[56] As well as giving a summary of Aristotle's *Metaphysics* he supplemented his *On First Philosophy* by drawing upon other writings of Aristotle.

The knowledge of the true nature of things, the foremost aim of philosophy, was not confined to the world of senses. For al-Kindī philosophy included also knowledge of the divinity.[57] This led to the merging of physics and metaphysics, science and theology. For later

Muslim generations this amalgamation became offensive. The faithful accused the philosophers of valuing intellectual speculation higher than the revered tradition and establishing the articles of faith as correct through reasoning and not through tradition.[58] Thus al-Kindī's philosophy, and especially his natural theology, contained already the seeds of the later conflicts between the orthodox and the intellectuals in Islam. Only as long as he was protected by the caliph al-Muʿtaṣim was he safe to engage in philosophy.

Al-Kindī did not conceal his indebtedness to earlier and alien philosophers by acquiring the truth "wherever it comes from".[59] For him the truth of the philosopher cannot differ from the truth of the Muslim faithful. Philosophy and theology served one end: the knowledge of the True One, of God. Acclimatizing philosophy in an Islamic society was made easier through the medium of texts of late Greek philosophy. From among these texts it was the so-called *Theology* in which al-Kindī took an interest. Falsely attributed to Aristotle, the *Theology* was in the nineteenth century identified as Porphyry's paraphrase of Plotinus' *Enneads*, 4–6.[60] With all these texts at his disposal al-Kindī elaborated a philosophy that was an able instrument to support by rational arguments the Muslim belief founded upon revelation and tradition, thus creating harmony between speculation and revelation.

In spite of this apparent harmony al-Kindī's language is distinct from that of the Qur'ān. Instead of "Allah", which is the common name of God in the Qur'ān and even in *kalām* literature, al-Kindī used "*al-bāri'*" (Creator) or "*al-ʿillat al-ūlā*" (the First Cause). The former name is recorded only once in the Qur'ān;[61] the latter is of course completely missing from the Qur'ān and the Holy Scriptures, for the faithful reject as polytheism the idea that God Almighty is the first of a series of causes that emanate from Him. God is for the faithful the only cause, the Creator of all. Al-Kindī referred to creation out of nothing by the word *ibdāʿ* which replaced the Qur'ānic *khalq*, *jirm* was chosen instead of *jism*, etc. This choice of language gives the impression that al-Kindī deliberately avoided the corresponding Qur'ānic expressions, holding aloof the language of speculation from the inimitable language of the Qur'ān.

"First Philosophy" means the knowledge of the True One. Whereas every thing is the effect of what precedes and the cause of what follows, the True One is the only cause. The world, emanating ultimately from the first cause, is thus dependent on, and connected with, the True One, but is separated from Him by being finite in time and space. The oneness of the first cause is contrasted with the plurality of the created world: every thing has five predicables: genus, species, difference, property and accident. The modes of existence are explained by the categories. Al-Kindī is in full harmony with Islam in stating that the world has been created out of nothing and is created in time, having come into existence after not having existed. This is not only his religious credo but also his conviction as philosopher.

Al-Kindī was, apart from metaphysics, also interested in mathematics and natural sciences. His efforts to study the whole encyclopedic range of sciences proved him to be a true follower of Aristotle. With regard to his strong inclination towards mathematics he even surpassed Aristotle. He wrote a treatise entitled *That Philosophy Cannot be Acquired except with a Knowledge of Mathematics*.[62] His predilection for mathematics is emphasized also in his treatise *On Definitions and Descriptions of Things*. Many of the definitions are expressed in a double way: physically (*min jihat al-ṭab'*) and mathematically (*min jihat al-ta'līm*).[63] It was also in the field of mathematical computation that he exerted his greatest authority as teacher. His two famous pupils, Ja'far ibn Muḥammad ibn 'Umar al-Balkhī (Albumasar in medieval Latin literature)[64] and Abu'l-'Abbās Aḥmad ibn al-Ṭayyib as-Sarakhsī,[65] continued and enlarged the mathematical research of their teacher.[66] Al-Kindī's strong inclination for mathematics probably influenced also the so-called Brethren of Purity in the late fourth/tenth century. Favouring practical application of science, al-Kindī elaborated a system of calculating the efficacy of medical drugs. This became necessary since the physicians moved over from simple to compound drugs. The first physician recorded as having used compound drugs was Abu'l-Ḥakam from Damascus.[67] In order to achieve the intended efficacy the pharmacist had to calculate the right proportion of the ingredients of the drug. Al-Kindī undertook to divide the medical ingredients into grades according to the strength of their curative properties.[68] He was also the author of many treatises and handbooks of medical and pharmaceutical concern.[69]

In one of these medical treatises, recently found, al-Kindī again connected medicine with mathematics by giving the rule for calculating in advance the critical days of a developing disease.[70] Being the quickest planet in the firmament, the moon was held to influence acute diseases. On certain days of the lunar monthly revolution the diseases were held to change for the better or the worse. This theory, already expounded by Galen, was further elaborated by al-Kindī.

Al-Kindī's mathematical curiosity did not halt even before the Holy Scripture. He wrote a treatise *On the Duration of the Reign of the Arabs*,[71] and based his calculation upon the letters at the head of twenty-nine chapters of the Qur'ān. They form fourteen enigmatic words that contain fourteen different letters out of the twenty-eight letters of the Arabic alphabet. By adding the numerical value of each of these letters, counting only once those letters which are repeated several times, one receives the approximate number of years of Arab rule until the Mongols in 656/1258 conquered Baghdad and "Arab hegemony was lost for ever".[72]

It is generally held that al-Kindī's philosophy is in harmony with the Muslim creed. This is supported for example by the argument that al-Kindī speaks of creation out of nothing. It should be kept in mind, however, that in his treatise *On Definitions and Descriptions of Things* al-Kindī speaks of the existence of an upper world that is above the world of creation. This is incompatible with the Muslim faith. The same is true with regard to the theory of emanation, which opposed the article of faith that the world was created in one instant by God's command.

It is difficult, if not impossible, to give a conclusive judgment of an author whose literary work has been preserved only to a very small extent. Nevertheless, the treatises that have come down to us and Ibn al-Nadīm's bibliographical list that contains the titles of al-Kindī's writings allow us to express an approximate evaluation of al-Kindī as philosopher and scientist. Such an evaluation has to take into account that al-Kindī could not have recourse to any of his "co-linguists". There were, it is true, also learned men besides al-Kindī who commissioned scientific translations or translated themselves, like the sons of Mūsā ibn Shākir, Ḥunayn ibn Isḥaq, Thābit ibn Qurrah and 'Umar ibn al-Farrukhān, as we are told by Abū Ma'shar.[73] But al-Kindī was the first to transfer Greek philosophy systematically from foreign literary sources and to channel it into his Islamic environment where philosophy was received with coldness and even with hostility. At some time in his life he enjoyed the support of the caliph. But, like most of the later philosophers, he had no authority as an academic teacher because there was no official philosophy teaching. He kept himself aloof through his choice of language from colliding with the orthodox faithful or the *mutakallimūn*. Apart from metaphysics he engaged in research on almost all the natural and mathematical sciences.

Through Latin translations al-Kindī influenced medieval European philosophers. They became acquainted with works from the whole spectrum of his literary output, especially with those that dealt with natural sciences and mathematics.[74] Gerard of Cremona[75] and Avendauth[76] translated several of al-Kindī's scientific works, among them *On Optics* (*De aspectibus*) which Roger Bacon,[77] dealing with the speed of light, used.[78] Also translated by Gerard of Cremona were *On Degrees* [*of Compound Medicines*], *On Sleep and Vision*, and *On the Five Essences* (*De quinque essentiis*)[79] cited also by Roger Bacon in his *Nature and Multiplication of Light or Species*.[80] *De quinque essentiis* was one of the main sources for the knowledge of al-Kindī the philosopher until Abū Rīdah edited in 1950 a collection of fourteen treatises mostly on philosophical subjects. Besides these works only fragments of other works were known from medieval secondary sources. Thus for example the historian al-Mas'ūdī[81] cited from a treatise of al-Kindī in his *Murūj al-dhahab*,[82] where he denied the possibility of artificially producing gold and silver. Abū Bakr Muḥammad ibn Zakariyyā' al-Rāzī[83] wrote a refutation of this treatise.[84]

NOTES

1 *c.* 185/801–252/866.
2 Died *c.* 235/849.
3 Died between 220/835 and 230/845.
4 260/873–324/935.
5 Ritter (1929–39): 486.
6 Died 429/1037.
7 Laoust (1965): 103.
8 Corbin (1964): 219; Ivry (1974): 22ff.
9 Died 380/990.
10 232/847–247/861.
11 732/1332–808/1406.
12 Ibn Khaldūn (1958), 2: 219.
13 Died *c.* 375/985.
14 Wiedemann (1970), 2: 562f.
15 Died 339/950.
16 Died 218/833.
17 Died 227/842.
18 192/808–260/873.
19 Asṭāt/Eustatius translated Aristotle's *Metaphysics*; 'Abd al-Masīḥ ibn Nā'imah translated Porphyry's interpretation of Plotinus' *Enneads*, 4–6, known as Aristotle's *Theology* (cf. Brockelmann (1937), Suppl. 1: 364) and Yaḥyā ibn al-Biṭrīq translated Aristotle's *De caelo, De anima*, Plato's *Timaeus*, possibly also writings of Proclus, e.g. the summary of his *Institutio theologica* (cf. Endress (1973) *passim*).
20 Walzer (1963): 14.
21 Cf. e.g. Abū Rīdah (1950): 260.8; Rosenthal (1956), 2: 445.
22 Walzer (1945), 29: 20f.; Ess (1966): 235.
23 Abū Rīdah (1950): 103; cf. Gutas (1975): 196, Nr 69.
24 *Fī ḥudūd al-ashyā' wu-rusūmihā*, in Abū Rīdah (1950): 165–80.
25 Klein-Franke (1982b): 191–216.
26 E.g. Abū Rīdah (1950): 207, l. 11; cf. Rosenthal (1952): 474; Plotinus (1959): 275; (1955): 184.
27 Plotinus (1963): 8.18.
28 Walzer (1963): 189; Endress (1973): 231.
29 Died 313/925.
30 Ibn Khaldūn (1958), 3: 250.
31 Abū Rīdah (1950): 160, l. 6; Walzer (1963): 188.
32 Abū Rīdah, *op. cit.*
33 *Ibid.*: 205–70.
34 Plotinus (1959): 324 = *Enn.*, 5.3[49], 14.6: 'kaì légomen hó mé estin, hó dé estin où légomen'.
35 Supra ann. 11; cf. Zintzen (1983): 312–28, esp. 314.

36 Ibn Khaldūn (1958), 1: 195.
37 Cf. the Neoplatonic philosopher Simplicius [first half of sixth century] commenting on Aristotle's *De caelo* 277b10, in Simplicius (1894): 269.31.
38 Ivry (1974): 56, l. 6.
39 *Ibid.*: 59, l. 3.
40 Walzer (1950): 9.
41 Ivry (1974): 27ff.
42 Ibn al-Nadīm (1871): 259, l. 19.
43 Abū Rīdah (1950): 201–7.
44 *Ibid.*: 202, l. 4.
45 Aristotle (1831): *Analytica Priora* 72b19: *ámesos* = *ghayr mutawassiṭ*; cf. Böhm (1967): 67.
46 Abū Rīdah (1950): 205 penult.
47 *Ibid.*: 207, l. 1.
48 Philoponus (1899).
49 412–85. This year was remarkable also because of two other events: the Roman Emperor Justinian closed the school of philosophers in Athens (cf. Gibbon, chapter 40) and St Benedict founded the religious order named after him.
50 Ibn Abī Uṣaybiʿah (d. 668/1270) (1882/4), 1: 105, l. 5.
51 Pines (1972): 320–52.
52 Especially with reference to prop. 1–3 and prop. 5; Endress (1973): 242ff.
53 Ivry (1974): 205–7.
54 557/1162–629/1231.
55 Neuwirth (1977–8): 84–100.
56 Ivry (1974): 205–7.
57 Abū Rīdah (1950): 104, l. 5.
58 Ibn Khaldūn (1958), 3: 347.
59 Abū Rīdah (1950): 103, l. 4. This reminds one of Pliny, who admitted: "We are swept by the puffs of the clever brains of Greece"; Pliny (1963), 8: 188f.
60 Steinschneider (1960): 77.
61 *Sūrah* 59 [*al-Ḥashr*]: 24.
62 Ibn al-Nadīm (1871): 255 ult.
63 Klein-Franke (1982b): 194.
64 Died 272/886.
65 Died 286/899.
66 Rosenthal (1943): 17.
67 *Fl.* second half of the first/seventh century; cf. Klein-Franke (1982a): 35.
68 Harig (1974): 148 and 200.
69 Sezgin (1970): 244–7.
70 Klein-Franke (1975): 161–88.
71 Loth (1875): 261–309.
72 Hitti (1958): 484; Rosenthal (1949): 122; Plessner (1962): 184f.; Nöldeke (1919), part 2: 68–78.
73 Ibn Abī Uṣaybiʿah (1882/4), 1: 207; Wiedemann (1970), 2: 551.
74 Thorndike and Kibre (1963), col. 1731 *et passim*.
75 *c.* 1114–87.
76 First half of the sixth/twelfth century; cf. Alverny (1954), 1: 19–43.
77 *c.* 1214 to soon after 1292.

78 Grant (1974): 396.
79 *Ibid.*, 494.
80 Nagy (1897).
81 Died 345/956.
82 al-Masʿūdī (1974), 5: 159f.
83 Died 313/915.
84 Ibn Abī Uṣaybiʿah (1882/4), 1: 316, l. 12; Ranking (1913): 249, Nr 40: "Responsio ad Philosophum el-Kendi eo quod artem al-Chymiae in impossibili posuerit"; Wiedemann (1970), 1: 51ff.

BIBLIOGRAPHY

Abū Rīdah, M. A. (1950) *Rasāʾil al-Kindī al-falsafiyyah* (Cairo).
Alverny, M. T. d' (1954) "Avendauth", in *Homenaje a Millás-Vallicrosa* (Barcelona).
Aristotle (1831): *Aristotelis Opera*, ed. I. Bekker (Berlin).
Atiyeh, G. (1985) *Al-Kindī: the Philosopher of the Arabs* (Islamabad).
Böhm, W. (1967) *Johannes Philoponos Grammatikos von Alexandrien* (Munich).
Brockelmann, C. (1937–49) *Geschichte der arabischen Litteratur* (Leiden).
Corbin, H. (1964) *Histoire de la philosophie islamique* (Paris).
Endress, G. (1973) *Proclus Arabus: Zwanzig Abschnitte aus der Institutio Theologica in arabischer Übersetzung* (Beirut).
Ess, J. van (1966) *Die Erkenntnislehre des Aduddin al-Ici: Übersetzung und Kommentar des ersten Buches seiner Mawaqif* (Wiesbaden).
Gibbon, E. (1890) *The Decline and Fall of the Roman Empire* (London).
Grant, E. (1974) *A Source Book on Mediaeval Science* (Cambridge, Mass.).
Gutas, D. (1975) *Greek Wisdom Literature in Arabic Translation: a Study of the Graeco-Arabic Gnomologia* (New Haven).
Harig, G. (1974) *Bestimmung der Intensität im medizinischen System Galens* (Berlin).
Hitti, Ph. K. (1958) *History of the Arabs* (London).
Ibn Abī Uṣaybiʿah (1882/4) *ʿUyun al-anbāʾ fī tabaqāt al-aṭibbāʾ*, ed. A. Müller (Cairo and Königsberg).
Ibn Khaldūn (1958) *The Muqaddimah: an Introduction to History*, trans. F. Rosenthal, 3 vols (New York).
Ibn al-Nadīm (1871) *Kitāb al-fihrist*, ed. G. Flügel (Leipzig).
Ivry, A. L. (1974) *Al-Kindī's Metaphysics: a Translation of Yaʿqūb al-Kindī's Treatise "On First Philosophy" (fī al-Falsafah al-Ūlā) with Introduction and Commentary* (Albany).
Klein-Franke, F. (1975) *Die Ursachen der Krisen bei akuten Krankheiten: Eine wiederentdeckte Schrift al-Kindī's*, Israel Oriental Studies (Tel Aviv).
—— (1982a) *Vorlesungen über die Medizin im Islam*, Sudhoffs Archiv: *Zeitschrift für Wissenschaftsgeschichte*, Beiheft 23 (Wiesbaden).
—— (1982b) "al-Kindī's *On Definitions and Descriptions of Things*", *Le Muséon: Revue des Etudes Orientales*, **95**.
Laoust, H. (1965) *Les Schismes dans l'Islam* (Paris).
Loth, O. (1875) "al-Kindī als Astrolog", in *Morgenländische Forschungen: Festschrift für H. L. Fleischer* (Leipzig) (repr. 1981).
al-Masʿūdī (1974) *Les Prairies d'Or*, ed. B. de Meynard and P. de Courteille, revue

et corrigée par C. Pellat, Publications de l'Université Libanaise: Section des Etudes Historiques XI (Beirut).

Nagy, A. (1897) "Die philosophischen Abhandlungen des Ja'qūb Ben Isḥāq Al-Kindī", *Beiträge zur Geschichte der Philosophie des Mittelalters*, 2(5) (Münster).

Neuwirth, A. (1977/8) "Neue Materialien zur arabischen Tradition der beiden ersten Metaphysik-Bücher", *Die Welt des Islams*, n.s., 17.

Nöldeke, Th. (1919) *Geschichte des Qorans* (Leipzig).

Philoponus (1899) *De aeternitate mundi contra Proclum*, ed. H. Rabe (Leipzig).

Pines, S. (1972) "An Arabic Summary of a Lost Work of John Philoponos", *Israel Oriental Studies*, 2.

Plessner, M. (1962) *"Picatrix": Das Ziel des Weisen von Pseudo-Magriti* (London).

Pliny (1963) *Natural History*, with English trans., 10 vols, vol. 8 by W. H. S. Jones (Cambridge, Mass.).

Plotinus (1955) *Plotinus apud Arabes: Theologia Aristotelis et fragmenta quae supersunt*, ed. 'A. Badawī (Cairo).

—— (1959) *Opera*, 2, *Enneades 4–6*, ed. P. Henry and H.-R. Schwyzer (Paris).

—— (1963), *Ennéades 6*, ed. and trans. E. Bréhier (Paris).

Ranking, S. A. (1913) "The Life and Works of Rhazes", *Acts of the XVII. International Congress of Medicine* (London).

Ritter, H. (1929–39) *Die dogmatischen Lehren der Anhänger des Islam von Abū 'l-Ḥasan 'Alī ibn Ismā'īl al Ash'arī* (Leipzig).

Rosenthal, F. (1943) *Aḥmad B. Aṭ-Ṭayyib As-Sarahsī* (New Haven).

—— (1952) "Aš-Šaiḫ al-Yūnānī and the Arabic Plotinus Source", *Orientalia, Commentarii Periodici Pontificii Instituti Biblici*, 21.

—— (1956) "al-Kindī and Ptolemy", in *Studi orientalistici in onore di Gorgio Levi della Vida*, 2 vols (Rome).

Sezgin, F. (1970) *Geschichte des arabischen Schrifttums*, 3 (Leiden).

Simplicius (1894) *De caelo*, ed. I. L. Heiberg, in *Commentaria in Aristotelem Graeca*, 7 (Berlin).

Steinschneider, M. (1960) *Die arabischen Übersetzungen aus dem Griechischen* (Graz) (repr.) [*Beihefte zum Centralblatt für Bibliothekswesen*, 12, 1893].

Thorndike, L. and Kibre P. (1963) *A Catalogue of Incipits of Mediaeval Scientific Writings in Latin* (London).

Walzer, R. (1945) *Bulletin of the John Rylands Library*, 29: 160–83.

—— (1950) "The Rise of Islamic Philosophy", *Oriens*, 3.

—— (1963) *Greek into Arabic* (Oxford).

Wiedemann, E. (1970) *Aufsätze zur arabischen Wissenschaftsgeschichte*, 2 vols (reprint) (Hildesheim).

Zintzen, C. (1983) "Bemerkungen zum Aufstieg der Seele in Jamblichs De Mysteriis", in *Platonismus und Christentum: Festschrift für Heinrich Dörrie*, ed. H. D. Blume and F. Mann [*Jahrbuch für Antike und Christentum*, Suppl. 10] (Münster).

CHAPTER 12

Al-Fārābī

Deborah L. Black

LIFE AND WORKS

What little information there is about the life of Abū Naṣr al-Fārābī comes mostly from medieval Arabic biographers whose writings date from the fourth/tenth to the seventh/thirteenth centuries. The earliest account in Ibn al-Nadīm's (d. 380/990) *Kitāb al-fihrist* gives only minimal information about al-Fārābī's life; later accounts add to these bare bones extensive lists of his writings, information about his teachers and pupils and a few anecdotes of dubious reliability.[1] Al-Fārābī was probably of Turkish origin, born around 257/870 in Fārāb in Turkestan. Although the details of his early education are murky, he is reported to have studied logic in Baghdad under the Christian scholars Yuḥannā ibn Ḥaylān (d. 910) and Abū Bishr Mattā (d. 940), one of the translators of Aristotle's works into Arabic. Since the School of Baghdad was the principal heir in the Arabic world to the philosophical and medical tradition of Alexandria, al-Fārābī's connection with these teachers forged one of the earliest links between Greek philosophy and the Islamic world.[2] Al-Fārābī himself is listed as the teacher of Yaḥyā ibn 'Adī (d. 974), another of the important Christian translators and a noted logician in his own right. Al-Fārābī is also reported to have taught logic to the grammarian Ibn al-Sarrāj, who in turn instructed al-Fārābī in the science of Arabic grammar (Ibn Abī Uṣaybi'ah (1965): 606; Zimmermann, Introduction to al-Fārābī (1981a): cxviii–cxxii). Although there are numerous anecdotes told about al-Fārābī's subsequent life and death by the later biographers, their historical accuracy is suspect.[3] Al-Fārābī appears to have left Baghdad for Syria in 330/942, travelling to Aleppo and Damascus, and perhaps also to Egypt, between 330/942 and 337/948. He then returned to Damascus, where he died in 339/950.

From the lists of writings provided by the medieval biographers, al-Fārābī's philosophical output appears to have been enormous, with over one hundred works being credited to him (Walzer (1965): 780). If these lists are accurate, only a small portion of al-Fārābī's writings has survived. Many of these have only recently become available in modern editions, so the interpretation of al-Fārābī's work is continually being revised. By far the largest part of al-Fārābī's writings is dedicated to logic and the philosophy of language. Indeed, al-Fārābī's logical acumen is mentioned as the basis of his great renown by a number of the medieval biographers, and the philosopher and historian Ibn Khaldūn (732/1332–808/1406) claimed that it was principally because of his logical achievements that al-Fārābī was dubbed the "second teacher" (*al-mu'allim al-thānī*), second, that is, only to Aristotle himself (Nasr (1985): 359–60). Apart from his logical writings, which include both independent treatises and commentaries on Aristotle, al-Fārābī also wrote extensively on political philosophy and the philosophy of religion, which he treated as a branch of political philosophy, on metaphysics and on psychology and natural philosophy.[4]

LOGIC, PHILOSOPHY OF LANGUAGE AND EPISTEMOLOGY

Al-Fārābī's writings on logic and the philosophy of language include both loose commentaries on the Aristotelian *Organon* and independent treatises. In the former category al-Fārābī produced a full set of epitomes of the *Organon*, including, as had been the custom since the days of the Alexandrian commentators, Porphyry's *Isagoge* and Aristotle's *Rhetoric* and *Poetics* (al-Fārābī 1959; 1971a; 1986–7). He also wrote a great commentary (*sharḥ*) on the *De interpretatione* (al-Fārābī 1960a; 1981a). His epitomes are not detailed efforts at exegesis of the Aristotelian texts, nor mere summaries of them, but take their overall organization and inspiration from Aristotle while developing personal interpretations of Aristotelian logic and the school tradition that had developed from it. Of his more personal writings, the *Kitāb al-ḥurūf* ("Book of Letters", al-Fārābī 1969b) and *Kitāb al-alfāẓ al-musta'malah fi'l-manṭiq* ("Book of Utterances Employed in Logic", al-Fārābī 1968a) are also devoted in large part to logical and linguistic topics, emphasizing the need to understand the relationship of philosophical terminology to ordinary language and grammar.[5]

One of the overriding concerns of al-Fārābī's logical writings is to delineate precisely the relationship between philosophical logic and the grammar of ordinary language. The historical reality of the importation of philosophy into Arabic from a foreign language and culture, that of ancient Greece, and the attendant difficulties created by the need to invent a philosophical vocabulary in Arabic, had made this issue of paramount importance for the earliest Arabic philosophers, including al-Fārābī's own teachers and pupils. In addition to this, the linguistic focus of much of Aristotelian logic produced territorial disputes with the practitioners of the indigenous science of Arabic grammar, who were concerned that the philosophers' interest in Greek logic was nothing but an attempt to substitute the grammar of Greek for the grammar of Arabic. Al-Fārābī's logical and linguistic writings represented one of the most systematic efforts to harmonize these competing approaches to the study of language.

Throughout his linguistic writings, al-Fārābī upholds a conception of logic as a sort of universal grammar that provides those rules that must be followed in order to reason correctly in any language whatsoever. Grammar, on the other hand, is always confined to providing the rules established by convention for the use of the particular language of a particular culture. As al-Fārābī puts it in a well-known passage from his *Iḥṣā' al-'ulūm* ("Catalogue of the Sciences"), "this art [of logic] is analogous to the art of grammar, in that the relation of the art of logic to the intellect and the intelligibles is like the relation of the art of grammar to language and expressions. That is, to every rule for expressions which the science of grammar provides us, there is a corresponding [rule] for intelligibles which the science of logic provides us" (al-Fārābī (1968b): 68).

By arguing in this way that logic and grammar are two distinct, rule-based sciences, each with its own proper domain and subject matter, al-Fārābī strives to establish logic as an autonomous philosophical study of language that complements, rather than conflicts with, traditional grammatical science. But though logic and grammar remain distinct and autonomous sciences, al-Fārābī also holds that the logician and the philosopher are dependent upon the grammarian for their ability to articulate their doctrines in the idiom of a particular nation. Hence "the art of grammar must be indispensable for making known and alerting us to the principles of the art [of logic]" (al-Fārābī (1987): 83; Black (1992): 48–56). Al-Fārābī's *Kitāb al-alfāẓ* is one attempt to implement this co-operation of logic with grammar. It illustrates, however, the extent of independence from conventional grammatical constraints that the logician still retains in al-Fārābī's scheme. For while the text opens with a declaration of the need to classify Arabic particles along logically perspicuous lines, it goes on to make the bold assertion that the classification of particles offered by the Arabic grammarians themselves is inadequate for this purpose, thereby forcing al-Fārābī to borrow the underlying grammatical theory from the works of Greek grammarians, a declaration hardly likely to appease the champions of Arabic grammatical theory (al-Fārābī (1968a): 48; Black (1992): 77–83).

The *Kitāb al-ḥurūf* shows another facet of al-Fārābī's approach to the philosophy of language.[6] It opens with an extended classification of Arabic particles in relation to the Aristotelian categories. The discussions of individual particles in turn explore the relations between popular uses of these terms in non-philosophical Arabic and the modifications they undergo when they are transformed into technical philosophical terms (al-Fārābī (1969b): 61–130; see Druart (1987b) for a study of al-Fārābī's treatment of *jawhar* ("substance"). The second part of the text presents a discussion of the origins of language, the history of philosophy, and the relations between philosophy and religion. One of its purposes is to situate the more abstract linguistic discussions into an historical and anthropological context, explaining how language itself originates and branches out into popular and technical forms. The theme of the relations between philosophy and religion is also cast in linguistic terms. Religion is viewed as the expression of philosophical truth in popular language, using the tools provided by the logical arts of rhetoric and poetics. There is also a normative side to this discussion, in so far as it lays out the ideal scenario for the development of a philosophical vocabulary from ordinary language, and for the establishment of a religion suitable for translating the fruits of that philosophy back into popular terms. In passages that are meant to evoke the historical reality of Islam's encounter with Greek philosophy, al-Fārābī also identifies and ranks a variety of possible deviations from the ideal developmental pattern, in which neither the philosophy nor the religion of a nation springs from its indigenous linguistic and logical development; they are instead imported from another culture (*ibid.*: 131–61). In the third and final part of the *Kitāb al-ḥurūf* al-Fārābī returns to the theme of philosophical terminology, offering an elaborate classification of interrogative particles, their uses in different types of philosophical inquiry and their relation to the types of explanations offered by Aristotle's four causes (*ibid.*: 162–226).

Although a large proportion of al-Fārābī's logical output is dedicated to linguistic topics, he also made important contributions to the more formal aspects of logic, such as syllogistics, the theory of demonstration and related epistemological issues. A predominant strand in al-Fārābī's logic and epistemology is the adoption of a hierarchical interpretation of the syllogistic arts (including rhetoric and poetics), in which demonstration is identified as the proper method of philosophy, and all the other methods are relegated to the status of tools for non-philosophical communication. This strand is most evident in those writings where al-Fārābī is echoing the logical theory of the Alexandrian commentators, although it is also closely linked to al-Fārābī's personal teaching that religion is a popular imitation of philosophy whose tools are the non-demonstrative arts (Black (1990): 1–19, 31–51, 63–71, 78–94). An excellent summary of this hierarchical approach is given in the following statement found in the logic chapter of al-Fārābī's *Iḥṣā' al-'ulūm:*

> The fourth [part of logic] contains the rules by which demonstrative statements are tested, the rules which pertain to those things from which philosophy is welded together, and everything by which its activity becomes most complete, most excellent, and most perfect. . . . And the fourth part is the most vigorous of them, pre-eminent in dignity and authority. Logic seeks its principal intention only in this fourth part, the remainder of its parts having been invented only for its sake.
>
> (al-Fārābī (1968b): 87–9)

Al-Fārābī goes on to identify two principal roles for these non-demonstrative arts: to act as tools to sustain the fourth part in its proper function, and to provide safeguards that keep the demonstrator from error.

It would be misleading, however, to take the attitude expressed by this text as an accurate reflection of al-Fārābī's overall approach to either demonstration or the remaining arts of dialectic, rhetoric and poetics. When al-Fārābī discusses each of these arts in its own right, his views emerge as far more complex, and seem to allow the non-demonstrative arts to play an integral rather than a peripheral role within philosophy. In the opening discussions of his *Kitāb al-jadal* ("Book of Dialectic"), for example, al-Fārābī tries to show how dialectic functions to serve and support philosophy by identifying five ways in which it contributes to the attainment of demonstrative knowledge: (1) by offering training in the skills of argumentation; (2) by providing an initial exposure to the principles of the individual demonstrative sciences; (3) by awakening awareness of the innate self-evident principles of demonstration, in particular for the physical sciences; (4) by developing the skills useful for communicating with the masses; and (5) for refuting sophistry (al-Fārābī (1986–7), 3: 29–38). While all of these uses continue to reflect the general conception of dialectic as a pedagogical and ancillary art, the breadth of the contributions that are outlined by this list, and the inclusion of the second and third uses in particular, seems to elevate dialectic from the status of a mere handmaiden to a *de facto* partner with demonstration in philosophical pursuits.

Al-Fārābī's rhetorical and poetical theories display a similar appreciation of the autonomy of these arts. In the case of his poetics, al-Fārābī is one of the first Islamic authors to identify for poetical discourse a unique epistemological aim which is distinct from the aims of all the other logical arts, *takhyīl,* the evocation of an imaginative depiction of an object (al-Fārābī (1968b): 83–5; (1959): 92–5). This theory of imaginative evocation was to become the cornerstone of subsequent Islamic interpretations of poetic imitation, and through its psychological underpinnings, which are outlined in the next section, it became the means whereby the emotive and cognitive appeal of poetry and poetic discourse could be explained, and its role in prophecy and religion established.[7] In his discussions of rhetoric al-Fārābī makes a similar effort to explain the unique epistemic character of rhetorical persuasion as dependent upon what al-Fārābī calls assent to propositions "widely accepted at first glance" (*fī bādi' al-ra'y*), basing his explanation upon a detailed analysis of the role of social consensus and inchoate rational intuitions in everyday human beliefs. Al-Fārābī even extends this analysis to the formal aspects of rhetoric, offering an explanation of how the truncated form of rhetorical enthymemes and example-arguments reflects the peculiar epistemic goals of rhetoric, and contributes to its utility in communicating with the masses, whose formal logical skills are merely inchoate (al-Fārābī (1971a); for studies of al-Fārābī's rhetoric see Aouad (1992), Black (1990): 103–79, Butterworth (1984): 111–19).

Finally, in considering the role of the non-demonstrative arts within philosophical pursuits, we would do well to note al-Fārābī's assertion in his *Taḥṣīl al-sa'ādah* ("Attainment of Happiness"): "To be a truly perfect philosopher one has to possess both the theoretical sciences and the faculty for exploiting them for the benefit of all others according to their capacity" (al-Fārābī (1981b): 89; (1969a): 43). Al-Fārābī, following Plato, holds that all true philosophers are charged with the task of attempting to communicate their philosophy to others, and that this task is essential to the fulfilment of the philosophical ideal. From this it follows that the arts of rhetoric, poetics and dialectic, in so far as they represent the principal means of communication with the mass of humanity, are an integral part of philosophy and a necessary complement to demonstrative science.

Al-Fārābī's theory of demonstration itself centres on an analysis of the conditions that must be satisfied for the acquisition of science or knowledge (*'ilm* = Greek *epistēmē*). Like the other Islamic Aristotelians who were to follow him, al-Fārābī bases this analysis upon a distinction between two fundamental cognitive acts, conceptualization (*taṣawwur*) and assent (*taṣdīq*). The former act is that whereby we apprehend simple concepts, and when it is complete or perfect, it enables us to extract the essence of the object conceived. The latter act of assent issues in a judgment of truth or falsehood, and when it is perfect or complete, it yields certain knowledge. These two cognitive acts are in turn identified as the respective goals sought by definitions and demonstrative syllogisms, the two principal topics treated in Aristotle's *Posterior Analytics*, so that the analysis of the conditions for complete conceptualization and assent becomes the keynote of al-Fārābī's ensuing interpretation of Aristotle's theory of demonstration (*Kitāb al-burhān*, in al-Fārābī (1986–7), 4: 19–22, 45).

One important facet of this interpretation is al-Fārābī's analysis of the certitude that characterizes perfect assent. Al-Fārābī defines absolute certitude in terms of what we would now call second-order knowledge, arguing that certitude comprises both (1) a belief that the truth to which we have assented cannot be otherwise; and (2) a belief, in addition to this, that no other belief than the one held is possible. (Al-Fārābī adds that this process can in fact go on *ad infinitum*.) Certitude, in short, requires not merely our knowing that something is the case but also our knowing that we know it (al-Fārābī (1986–7), 4: 20). Having defined certitude in this way, al-Fārābī is able to free it from its traditional modal interpretation, thereby allowing for the existence of both necessary certitude, in which what one believes to be the case cannot be otherwise at any time; and non-necessary certitude, which is certitude "only at some [particular] time". Necessary certitude requires an object which exists necessarily and immutably; non-necessary certitude does not: "Necessary certitude and necessary existence are convertible in entailment, for what is verified as necessarily certain is necessarily existent" (*ibid*.: 22).[8]

Despite this broadening of the notion of certitude, al-Fārābī holds with Aristotle that demonstration in the strictest sense pertains only to matters that can be known with necessary certitude. But al-Fārābī has none the less added a new dimension to the theory of demonstration that takes account of the subjective element within certitude – one's awareness of and knowledge that one knows – as well as the more traditional objective element rooted in the necessity and immutability of the object known.[9]

PSYCHOLOGY AND PHILOSOPHY OF MIND

With the exception of his *Risālah fi'l-'aql* ("Treatise on the Intellect"), al-Fārābī left no independent treatises on philosophical psychology and the philosophy of mind. His views on these topics are contained in his metaphysical and political writings. The most detailed presentation of his views on the human soul occurs in the *Mabādi' ārā' ahl al-madīnah al-fāḍilah* ("Principles of the Opinions of the People of the Virtuous City"), where al-Fārābī adopts an Aristotelian approach to psychology. The soul's principal faculties are identified as the nutritive, sensitive, imaginative and rational; they are ordered hierarchically to one another, and within each there are "ruling" and "subordinate" elements. Al-Fārābī does not separate the common sense off as a distinct faculty, but treats it simply as the ruling faculty within the sensible soul "in which everything that is apprehended by [the five senses] is collected" (al-Fārābī (1985): 166–9). Nor does al-Fārābī have any doctrine of "internal senses" to unify his treatment of the common sense, imaginative and memorative faculties, and he does not mention anything like the faculty that Ibn Sīnā (Avicenna) will later call "estimation" (*wahm*).[10] Like Aristotle, he locates the physiological seat of the common sense and the imagination in the heart, a tradition that later internal sense philosophers will modify in the light of Galenic physiology, placing the organs of these faculties in the brain. As for the appetitive activities of the soul, al-Fārābī views them as intimately tied to the activities of the corresponding cognitive powers which give rise to them. Thus, for every cognitive faculty – sensation, imagination and reason – an appetition towards the objects perceived naturally supervenes upon their acts of apprehension. Al-Fārābī does isolate an appetitive faculty as the origin of all sensible and rational voluntary acts, but it does not serve to explain the actual arousal of desire. Rather, it functions principally as the motive power through which the soul controls the body, enabling it to seek what the soul perceives as desirable, and to flee what it perceives as harmful.

Al-Fārābī's view of the imaginative faculty deserves special attention because of the role assigned to imagination in prophecy and divination. According to al-Fārābī, imagination (*takhayyul*, equivalent to Aristotle's *phantasia*) is a retentive and a judgmental faculty, responsible both for the retention of the images of sensible things after they have absented themselves from the senses and for exercising control over them by composing and dividing them to form new images (*ibid.*: 168–9). To these two functions al-Fārābī also adds a third function, that of imitation (*muḥākāh*), using the Arabic term equivalent to *mimēsis* as it had been used in Aristotle's *Poetics*. By means of this ability, the imaginative faculty is able to represent objects with the images of other objects, and thereby to extend its representative ability beyond the depiction of sensible qualities to encompass the imitation of bodily temperaments, emotions and desires, and even immaterial realities (*ibid.*: 211–19). This mimetic ability of the imagination provides the psychological underpinnings of al-Fārābī's claim in his logical writings that the art of poetics has as its goal the evocation of acts of imagination, *takhyīl*. In the context of psychology, al-Fārābī also employs it to explain prophecy and divination. To understand this explanation, however, one must first understand al-Fārābī's conception of the rational faculty and the process of intellectual cognition.

Al-Fārābī's account of the faculties and stages which characterize intellectual cognition belongs to a tradition of interpreting Aristotle's *De anima* that goes back to the Greek commentators. Within this tradition, Aristotle's rather loose descriptions in *De anima*, 3.4 and 5 of an intellect which "becomes all things" and an intellect "which makes all things" are given the standard labels "potential" and "agent" intellect.[11] The potential intellect is identified as a faculty within the individual human soul;

the agent intellect, however, is treated as an immaterial, eternal substance that functions as the efficient, moving cause of human intellection, enabling universal concepts to be abstracted from sensible images.

In addition to the potential and agent intellects, this tradition also identified a variety of distinct stages between potency and actualization within the human intellect and affixed them with their own labels. In al-Fārābī's psychology, this development yields four different meanings for the term "intellect" (*'aql*):[12] (1) the potential intellect (*al-'aql bi'l-quwwah*); (2) the actual intellect (*al-'aql bi'l-fi'l*); (3) the acquired intellect (*al-'aql al-mustafād*); and (4) the agent intellect (*al-'aql al-fa''āl*). Following Alexander of Aphrodisias, al-Fārābī identifies the potential intellect as a pure disposition for abstracting the forms or quiddities of the object to be known from their corresponding sensible images. As this potential intellect comes to acquire intelligible concepts, it passes from pure potency into actuality, and thus becomes the second type of intellect, an actual intellect. The process of actualizing intelligibles is of course a gradual one, which has as its goal the acquisition of all the intelligibles and all the sciences available to human knowledge. When eventually the intellect reaches this goal (which probably only a few individuals can achieve), it loses all remaining tinges of potency, and thus is rendered pure form and pure actuality. Since on Aristotelian principles anything is intelligible to the degree that it is form and actuality, only at this point does the intellect realize its full capacity for self-contemplation. This, then, marks the attainment of the third stage of intellect, the acquired intellect. At this stage, by virtue of having become fully actualized, the individual human intellect attains a rank akin to that of the other immaterial intellects, including the agent intellect, and becomes one or similar in species with them. As a consequence, it is now able to contemplate not only itself and the intelligibles it has acquired from material things, but also the agent intellect and the other separate, immaterial substances (al-Fārābī (1985): 196–207, 240–5; (1948): 12–32 and (1973): 215–20; see also Davidson (1972): 134–54; Jolivet (1977)).

This last consequence of the doctrine of the acquired intellect is upheld, with only minor variations, in all of Fārābī's extant discussions of intellectual cognition, and it is implied by the eschatological theories of his political philosophy (discussed under "Practical Philosophy" below). But mention must be made of the conflicting evidence provided by later philosophers such as Ibn Ṭufayl, Ibn Bājjah, and Ibn Rushd (Averroes), who tell us that in a commentary on Aristotle's *Nicomachean Ethics* al-Fārābī repudiated the possibility of a direct cognitional union or "conjunction" (*ittiṣāl*) with the agent intellect (see Pines (1972)). More precisely, according to Averroes al-Fārābī rejected the ontological transformation that the doctrine appeared to require, that is, its assertion that, through intellectual development, a generable and corruptible mortal human being could become an eternal and incorruptible separate intellect (Ibn Rushd (1953): 433, 481, 485). How al-Fārābī would have reconciled this claim with the doctrines expressed in his surviving works, and whether it represents al-Fārābī's mature and considered view on the matter, must remain an open question, however, given the lamentable loss of the *Nicomachean Ethics* commentary itself.

Against the backdrop of al-Fārābī's teachings on the acquired and agent intellects, and on the imaginative faculty, the psychological aspects of his theory of prophecy can now be outlined. According to al-Fārābī, prophecy in its various manifestations is the result of an interaction between the intellect and the mimetic capacities of the imaginative faculty. What makes prophetic knowledge unique is not its intellectual content *per se*, for that belongs equally to the philosopher and the prophet: true prophecy, like the true religion based upon it, is a symbolization and imitation of the selfsame truths known demonstratively and intellectually in philosophy. But all prophets possess, in addition to their intellectual capacities, the gift of an especially keen imaginative faculty. This gift allows their imaginations to receive an influx or emanation of intelligibles from the agent intellect, an emanation that is normally reserved for the intellectual faculty alone. Since by its nature the imagination cannot, however, receive abstract intelligibles as abstract, the prophet exploits the mimetic abilities of the imagination to represent these intelligibles in concrete, symbolic form. In this way, what is normally available only to the select few who can attain the level of the acquired intellect can be communicated by the prophet, under the guise of sensory images, to a much wider, non-philosophical public (al-Fārābī (1985): 210–27, 240–7; see also Rahman (1958), Walzer (1962), Macy (1986), Daiber (1986b).

METAPHYSICS

Al-Fārābī's metaphysical teachings have posed certain interpretive difficulties to modern scholars, not only because of the attribution to him of the works mentioned above which are now generally believed to reflect Avicennian teaching but also because of the ambiguity of the attitude he takes in his authentic writings towards Aristotelian and Neoplatonic metaphysics. Recent scholarship has shown that al-Fārābī very carefully avoids mentioning Neoplatonic emanational metaphysics in his accounts of Aristotelian philosophy, and that, with the exception of the *Kitāb al-jam'* ("Harmonization of the Opinions of Plato and Aristotle", al-Fārābī (1960b)), he never treats the spurious *Theology of Aristotle* as an authentic work. The most plausible interpretation of al-Fārābī's metaphysics in the light of these observations is that recently proposed by Druart, arguing that al-Fārābī personally upheld the emanational cosmology central to

Neoplatonism, even while he recognized that it was not Aristotelian. Emanation was, in short, adopted to fill in the lacuna that al-Fārābī felt had been left by Aristotle's failure to complete his account of the part of metaphysics that comprises theology or divine science, in which the causal relations between divine and natural beings is set forth (Druart 1987a).

Viewed from this perspective, al-Fārābī's emanational theories form an integral part of his contribution to the discussion within Islamic philosophy of the nature and scope of metaphysics and its relation to natural philosophy. Al-Fārābī's influence on subsequent developments in this area is attested to in a well-known episode from Avicenna's autobiography, in which Avicenna relates how he had read Aristotle's *Metaphysics* forty times and yet still remained confused as to its purpose. Only after chancing upon a copy of al-Fārābī's opusculum *Fī aghrād al-Ḥakīm fī kitāb al-ḥurūf* ("On the Aims of Aristotle's *Metaphysics*") was his perplexity finally dissolved. Although Avicenna does not make explicit exactly how al-Fārābī's exceedingly short treatise resolved his mental impasse, it appears that Avicenna was impressed by al-Fārābī's remarks regarding the relationship between Aristotle's *Metaphysics* and the science of theology or "divine science" (*al-'ilm al-ilāhī*). For al-Fārābī opens his treatise by noting that while Aristotelian metaphysics is often described as "divine science", the text is in fact dedicated to the study of being and its principles and properties, not to the study of divine, separate substances. Al-Fārābī observes that many readers have been confused by this point, expecting the entire text to be about God, the soul and the intellect, and finding that these topics are all but missing, save from book *Lambda* (Gutas (1988): 238–42). Al-Fārābī then proceeds to outline a conception of metaphysics as the universal science which studies the common properties of being *qua* being. He affirms that theology is indeed a part of this science, not as its primary subject but rather only to the extent that "God is a principle of absolute being" (*al-wujūd al-muṭlaq*) (al-Fārābī (1890): 34–7, trans. in Gutas (1988): 240–2).

In these corrections of what he takes to be the previous misreadings of Aristotle's *Metaphysics*, al-Fārābī affirms that divine science is indeed an important part of metaphysics, while acknowledging that only a very small portion of Aristotle's text – a single book – is devoted to the topic. Perhaps this is why al-Fārābī declares at the end of his *Falsafah Arisṭūṭālīs* ("Philosophy of Aristotle") that "we do not possess metaphysical science" ((1961a): 133; (1969a): 130; cf. Druart (1987a): 35). But the major doctrine of Neoplatonic metaphysics known to al-Fārābī, the theory of emanation, has as its focal point divine beings and their causal links to the sublunar world. And it is this doctrine that provides the metaphysical foundations for al-Fārābī's two most important personal works, *al-Madīnah al-fāḍilah* and *al-Siyāsah al-madaniyyah* ("The Political

Regime"), also known as the *Mabādi' al-mawjūdāt* ("Principles of Beings") in virtue of its metaphysical parts.

The theory of emanation espoused by al-Fārābī in these works rests upon the twin pillars of Ptolemaic geocentric cosmology and the metaphysics of the divine. The framework of emanation is provided by cosmology. The universe is viewed as a series of concentric spheres: the outermost sphere, called the first heaven; the sphere of the fixed stars; and the spheres of Saturn, Jupiter, Mars, the Sun, Venus, Mercury, and finally, the Moon. The mechanics of emanation as a theory explaining the generation of the universe from God draws upon a variety of sources. In its basic premise it represents a radical departure from Aristotle, for whom God was not an efficient cause of the very existence (*wujūd*) of all other beings, but only the first cause of motion in the universe. Many of the properties of al-Fārābī's emanational God are Aristotelian, however: God is one, immaterial, eternal, and acts of necessity. Most importantly, however, God is characterized by al-Fārābī as an intellect whose principal activity is self-understanding, echoing Aristotle's conception of God's activity as a "thinking of thinking" (*nōesis noēseos*). It is God's intellectual activity which, in al-Fārābī's scheme, underlies God's role as the creator of the universe. As a result of his self-contemplation, there is an overflow or emanation (*fayḍ*) from God of a second intellect. This second intellect, like God, is characterized by the activity of self-contemplation; but it must, in addition to this, contemplate God himself. By virtue of its thinking of God, it generates yet a third intellect; and by virtue of its self-contemplation, it generates the celestial sphere that corresponds to it, the first heaven. Al-Fārābī then repeats this dyadic pattern of emanation for each sphere in the cosmology and its corresponding intellect, arriving at a total of ten intellects other than God.[13] The terminus of the emanational process is our own sublunar world, whose corresponding intellect is none other than the agent intellect familiar from Aristotle's *De anima* (al-Fārābī (1985): 88–107; (1964): 47–8, 52–3).

Through its culmination in the agent intellect, al-Fārābī's adoption of the Neoplatonic metaphysics of emanation provides the means whereby Aristotelian philosophy can be placed in a more systematic framework than the Stagirite's own writings allow. For in Aristotelian terms, natural philosophy includes the study of psychology: hence one and the same being, the agent intellect, represents the upper terminus of physics and the lower terminus of metaphysics. In this way, emanation allows al-Fārābī not only to fill in the gap between the theological and ontological elements within metaphysics but also to forge a link between the theoretical sciences of metaphysics and physics that is not clearly articulated by Aristotle himself.

PRACTICAL PHILOSOPHY

The unity that al-Fārābī forges between the theoretical sciences of metaphysics and psychology is also mirrored in al-Fārābī's political philosophy which, along with logic, represents the major focus of his philosophical writings. While the rest of al-Fārābī's philosophy is generally Aristotelian in character, supplemented by the Neoplatonic elements that have already been noted, al-Fārābī's political philosophy is Platonic, and reflects Plato's ideal of basing political philosophy upon metaphysical foundations. Thus, al-Fārābī's two principal works on political philosophy – the *Siyāsah madaniyyah* and the *Madīnah fāḍilah* – also contain the fullest expression of his metaphysical views. Although al-Fārābī does devote some attention in these and other works of practical philosophy to ethical issues such as the nature of practical wisdom, the moral virtues and deliberation, most of al-Fārābī's interest is on political theory, in particular the requirements of the ideal state and its ruler, and the question of the relationship between philosophy and religion within such a state.[14]

In his work the *Taḥṣīl al-sa'ādah* ("Attainment of Happiness"), al-Fārābī argues for the real and conceptual identity of the notions of philosopher, legislator and Imām, and claims that the diversity of religious and philosophical labels reflects nothing more than different emphases on distinct aspects of a single reality. This means, in good Platonic fashion, that those who do not attempt to apply their theoretical perfection to practical and political pursuits cannot claim to be true philosophers: such people remain what al-Fārābī calls "vain" or futile philosophers. Given the need to communicate this philosophy to the general populace, such a philosopher must presumably also have rhetorical, poetic and imaginative abilities, and thus fulfil as well the conditions of prophecy outlined in the psychological portions of al-Fārābī's political works (al-Fārābī (1981b): 89–97, (1969a): 43–9; cf. Mahdi (1972a): 188–92).

Of course, al-Fārābī recognizes that the ideal combination of prophecy and philosophy, religious and political leadership, and moral and intellectual virtue in a single ruler is something that is seldom if ever realized in political practice.[15] As a result, the harmony between philosophical and religious beliefs that is theoretically possible, but which requires a very specific historical development and fulfilment of these ideal conditions, is not easy, and perhaps even impossible, to realize in practice (al-Fārābī (1969b): 152–7). Thus both of al-Fārābī's major political treatises also outline the varieties of departures from the ideal state that may occur, following the model of Plato's discussion of virtuous and vicious political regimes in the *Republic*. Al-Fārābī classifies the corruptions of the ideal political union into three general categories: ignorant, wicked and errant cities, each of which has several different types within it. The ignorant cities all have in common their failure to comprehend the true nature of humanity, its place in the cosmos and, hence, its natural end. In their ignorance of human teleology, they substitute some other false goal for the true end discerned by philosophy. Al-Fārābī isolates the following varieties of ignorant cities: (1) indispensable cities, which seek mere subsistence as their goal; (2) vile cities, which seek only to accumulate wealth; (3) base cities, which exist solely for the sake of sensual gratification; (4) timocratic cities, whose goal is honour and fame; (5) tyrannical cities, in which power and domination of others is the principal goal; and (6) democratic cities, in which there is no single motivating end, but each citizen is left to seek whatever he or she deems best.

The wicked and errant states are those which possess now or once possessed some sort of knowledge of the true human end, but fail none the less to follow that knowledge. Wicked cities are those in which the virtuous end is deliberately abandoned for another one, whereas errant cities are those in which the leader personally has true knowledge of the proper end that his city should follow, but deceives the citizens by presenting them with false images and representations of that end. Finally, al-Fārābī also gives some attention to those whom he calls "the weeds" in the virtuous cities, people who, for lack of ability or other baser motives, inhabit the virtuous city and conform to its laws, while failing to participate personally in its goals (al-Fārābī (1964): 74–108, Mahdi and Lerner (1963): 35–56; (1985): 228–59).[16]

Although one purpose of the foregoing classification of corrupt states is clearly to educate philosophers so as to enable them to become virtuous leaders of virtuous regimes, al-Fārābī's focus upon the proper discernment of the true human end as the defining characteristic of the virtuous city reminds us that the ultimate motivation of his political philosophy is to ensure that the conditions for happiness are met by all people as far as possible. For this reason, al-Fārābī concludes his classification of cities and citizens with a consideration of human happiness in eschatological terms, in which reward and punishment in the afterlife is interpreted in accordance with al-Fārābī's belief that human happiness ultimately consists in the assimilation with the agent intellect that is achieved when one reaches the stage of acquired intellect.[17] Only the citizens of the virtuous city will be able to achieve this goal and thereby survive after death when their actualized intellectual souls separate from their bodies. Al-Fārābī implies that this immortality is not personal, however, since the body, the principle of numerical diversity within the human species, is no longer present, and hence "the differences of the souls are equally indeterminable in number" (1985: 264–5). Those who lived in ignorant cities will suffer no punishment in the afterlife, since their ignorance was not culpable: they will simply be annihilated as a natural consequence of their failure to actualize their intellectual powers, which is the condition for the soul's survival after death. The same is true for the citizens who have been misled by their leaders in the errant cities. Punishment in the afterlife is reserved for the citizens of the wicked cities and the rulers of the errant cities, who possessed knowledge of the true end but deliberately rejected it to pursue other ends. Their punishment consists in the simple continuance of their corrupt desires after death, desires which, because of their bodily roots, can no longer be fulfilled and so eternally torment their possessors (al-Fārābī (1985): 258–77).

AL-FĀRĀBĪ'S SUBSEQUENT INFLUENCE

The picture that emerges from the variety of al-Fārābī's writings is an impressive one. Al-Fārābī's logical and epistemological achievements, which have only recently come to light, have a very modern ring to them: his interest in careful linguistic analysis as an essential tool for philosophical precision, and his broadening and sharpening of the standards by which knowledge is measured and evaluated, have a strong affinity with recent trends in philosophy, in particular within the Anglo-American world. But in al-Fārābī these interests were as much a result of the peculiar historical circumstances in which he practised philosophy as were his political and metaphysical teachings. They reflected the need to address seriously the sometimes competing claims between philosophy and religion, and to find a niche for philosophy and its discourse in an Arabic and Islamic milieu. Al-Fārābī's interest in types of rationality, in modes of discourse and argumentation, and in the relations between ordinary and philosophical language, are an integral part of his answer to this historical challenge, although they remain philosophically important in their own right.

The linguistic sensitivity that al-Fārābī displays, his concern to communicate philosophy to a wide variety of audiences and his careful efforts to assimilate the Greek philosophical tradition into an Islamic context are all hallmarks of al-Fārābī's writings that help to explain the high esteem in which he was held by subsequent philosophers in the Islamic, Jewish, and to a lesser extent Christian, traditions. We have seen the debt that Avicenna openly acknowledged to al-Fārābī in metaphysics; Averroes and his fellow Andalusian philosophers also held al-Fārābī up as a key authority, especially in logic, psychology and political philosophy. In the Jewish philosophical tradition, Moses Maimonides gave al-Fārābī the highest praise among all his predecessors, once again in the area of logic in particular: "As for works on logic, one should only study the writings of Abū Naṣr al-Fārābī. All his writings are faultlessly excellent. One ought to study and understand them. For he is a great man"

(Introduction to Moses Maimonides (1963): lx). In the Latin West, although al-Fārābī's writings were less extensively translated than those of Avicenna and Averroes, works like his *Iḥṣā' al-'ulūm* and *Risālah fi'l-'aql* were of central importance in the early transmission of Aristotelian thought, and gave Christian thinkers their first glimpse of the wealth of new philosophical material that was to follow.

NOTES

1 Al-Fārābī's full name was Abū Naṣr Muḥammad ibn Muḥammad ibn Ṭarkhān ibn Awzalugh (or Ūzlugh) al-Fārābī. The principal medieval biographies from which information on his life derive are: Ibn al-Nadīm (d. 380/990) (1970): 599–602, 629–31; al-Mas'ūdī (d. 345/956) (1960): 39–41; Ṣā'id ibn Aḥmad ibn Ṣā'id al-Taghlibī (d. 463/1070) (1985): 137–40; Ibn Abī Uṣaybi'ah (d. 668/1269/70) (1965): 92–4, 318, 604–9; Ibn Khallikān (d. 680/1282) (1969–71), 5: 154–7; al-Bayhaqī (d. 565/1170) (1946): 30–5; Ibn al-Qifṭī (d. 646/1248) (1903): 277–9. For convenient summaries of this data see Walzer (1965): 778–9, as well as Walzer's Introduction to al-Fārābī (1985): 2–5; Fakhry (1983): 107–9; and Madkour (1963): 450–2.

2 On the School of Baghdad see Meyerhoff (1930).

3 See Walzer, Introduction to al-Fārābī (1985): 2–5 for a summary of these tales; convincing arguments against their historicity are given in Mahdi (1990): 693–4, 705–7, 712–13.

4 Scholarly interpretations of al-Fārābī's metaphysical and psychological views written before the mid twentieth century must be approached with caution because of the attribution to al-Fārābī of a number of treatises now believed to have been written by Avicenna or one of his later followers. These treatises include the *Fuṣūṣ al-ḥikām* (in al-Fārābī (1890); see Georr (1941–6) and Pines (1951)); the *Ta'liqāt fi'l-ḥikmah* (in al-Fārābī (1927); see Michot (1982)); the *Zinūn al-kabīr al-yūnānī* (in al-Fārābī (1927); see Druart (1987a): 25 n. 9); and *Ithbāt al-mufāriqāt* (in al-Fārābī (1927); see Madkour (1963): 452). The *'Uyūn al-masā'il* and the related *Da'āwī qalbiyyah* are also of doubtful authenticity (see Cruz Hernández (1950–1); Rahman (1958): 21–2), although recently Lameer has argued for restoring the *'Uyūn* as genuinely Fārābīan (Lameer (1994): 24–30). Rahman's arguments against this text remain compelling, however. Marmura (1985): 347 and Lameer (1994): 33–43 have questioned as well the authenticity of the *Kitāb al-jam' bayna ra'yay al-ḥakīmayn Aflāṭūn al-ilāhī wa-Arisṭūṭālīs* (al-Fārābī 1960b), a work in which the traditional Neoplatonic theme of the identity of Aristotle's and Plato's teachings is upheld, and the sole text in which al-Fārābī treats the spurious *Theology of Aristotle* (based on Plotinus, *Enneads*, 4–6) as a genuinely Aristotelian text.

5 For general discussions of al-Fārābī's logic in its historical context see Abed (1991), Elamrani-Jamal (1983), Eskanasy (1988), Gätje (1971), Hasnawi (1985), Langhade (1981) and Zimmermann in al-Fārābī (1981a).

6 The title of the work is usually translated as *Book of Letters*, although *Book of Particles* is equally possible. For studies of this text see Arnaldez (1977), Vajda

(1970), Mahdi (1972b).

7 For further consideration of al-Fārābī's poetics, see Black (1989 and 1990), Galston (1988), Heinrichs (1978) and Kemal (1991).

8 In addition to the discussion in the *Kitāb al-burhān*, al-Fārābī also wrote a short independent work on this topic, called the *Sharā'iṭ al-yaqīn* ("Conditions of Certitude", in al-Fārābī (1986–7) 4: 97–104).

9 For a discussion of other aspects of al-Fārābī's treatment of Aristotelian demonstration, see Galston (1981).

10 The only appearances of this term occur in the spurious *'Uyūn al-masā'il* and *Fuṣūṣ al-ḥikam.*

11 Often these are rendered as "possible" and "active". In the *Madīnah fāḍilah*, al-Fārābī also uses the Alexandrian term "material intellect" as a synonym for the potential intellect.

12 These are the subdivisions of the meanings of "intellect" *within* psychology, which is itself only one of six meanings of the term identified in the *Risālah fi'l-'aql.*

13 The use of a dyadic model separates al-Fārābī from earlier Neoplatonic thinkers and from the later Avicenna, who use triadic models to account for the emanation of a distinct rational soul for each celestial body. Al-Fārābī does not distinguish the soul as mover of the sphere from its intellect. See, for example, al-Fārābī (1964): 34–5; 53.

14 There are numerous studies of al-Fārābī's practical philosophy, including Butterworth (1983): 226–30, Daiber (1986a), Mahdi (1975a and 1975b) and Strauss (1945 and 1957). The most comprehensive is Galston (1990).

15 Al-Fārābī also allows a plurality of rulers to pool their diverse talents if no one person can be found to combine all of the qualities needed by the virtuous ruler (al-Fārābī (1985): 253–4).

16 Al-Fārābī also outlines in some detail the nature of the false religious beliefs that underlie the ignorant and errant views of the human end in al-Fārābī (1985): 286–329.

17 Of course, the reports about al-Fārābī's views in his lost *Nicomachean Ethics* commentary have made the interpretation of these passages problematic.

BIBLIOGRAPHY

Primary sources

Al-Bayhaqī, Abū al-Ḥasan 'Alī ibn Zayd (1946) *Tarīkh ḥukamā' al-Islām*, ed. M. Kurd 'Alī (Damascus).

Al-Fārābī (1890) *Alfarabi's philosophische Abhandlungen*, ed. F. Dieterici (Leiden).

—— (1927) *Rasā'il al-Fārābī* (Hyderabad).

—— (1948) *Risālah fi'l-'aql*, ed. Maurice Bouyges (Beirut).

—— (1959) "*Kitāb al-shi'r li-Abī Naṣr al-Fārābī*", ed. Mushin Mahdi, *Shi'r*, 3: 91–6.

—— (1960a) *Sharḥ al-Fārābī li-Kitāb Arisṭūṭālīs fī al-'ibārah*, ed. W. Kutsch and S. Marrow (Beirut).

—— (1960b) *Kitāb al-jam' bayn ra'yay al-ḥakīmayn Aflāṭūn al-ilāhī wa-Arisṭūṭālīs*, ed. Albert Nader (Beirut).

—— (1961a) *Falsafah Arisṭūṭālīs*, ed. M. Mahdi (Beirut).
—— (1964) *Alfarabi's Political Regime: Al-Siyāsah al-Madanīyah also Known as The Treatise on the Principles of Being*, ed. F. M. Najjar (Beirut).
—— (1968a) *Kitāb al-alfāẓ al-musta'malah fi'l-manṭiq*, ed. Muhsin Mahdi (Beirut).
—— (1968b) *Iḥṣā' al-'ulūm*, ed. Uthman Amin, 3rd ed. (Cairo).
—— (1969a) *Alfarabi's Philosophy of Plato and Aristotle*, trans. M. Mahdi (Ithaca).
—— (1969b) *Al-Farabi's Book of Letters (Kitāb al-Ḥurūf): Commentary on Aristotle's "Metaphysics"*, ed. Muhsin Mahdi (Beirut).
—— (1971a) *Al-Farabi: Deux ouvrages inédits sur la rhétorique*, ed. and trans. Jacques Langhade and Mario Grignaschi (Beirut).
—— (1973) "The Letter Concerning the Intellect", trans. A. Hyman, in A. Hyman and J. J. Walsh (eds) *Medieval Philosophy: the Christian, Islamic, and Jewish Traditions*, 2nd ed. (Indianapolis): 215–21.
—— (1981a) *Al-Farabi's Commentary and Short Treatise on Aristotle's "De interpretatione"*, ed. and trans. F. W. Zimmermann (Oxford).
—— (1981b) *Taḥṣīl al-sa'ādah*, ed. Jafar Al Yasin (Beirut).
—— (1985) *Al-Farabi on the Perfect State: Abū Naṣr al-Fārābī's Mabādi' Arā' Ahl al-Madīnah al-Faḍilah*, ed. and trans. Richard Walzer (Oxford).
—— (1986–7) *Al-Manṭiq 'ind al-Fārābī*, ed. Rafiq al-'Ajam and Majid Fakhry, 4 vols (Beirut).
—— (1987) *Kitāb al-tanbīh 'alā sabīl al-sa'ādah*, ed. Jafar Al Yasin (Beirut).
Ibn Abī Uṣaybi'ah (1965) *'Uyūn al-anbā' fī ṭabaqāt al-aṭibbā'*, ed. N. Rida (Beirut).
Ibn Khallikān (1969–71) *Wafayāt al-a'yān*, ed. I. Abbas, 7 vols (Beirut).
Ibn al-Nadīm (1970) *The Fihrist of al-Nadīm*, trans. B. Dodge, 2 vols (New York).
Ibn al-Qifṭī (1903) *Tarīkh al-Ḥukamā'*, ed. J. Lippert (Leipzig).
Ibn Rushd (Averroes) (1953) *Commentarium magnum in Aristotelis De anima libros*, ed. F. S. Crawford (Cambridge, Mass.).
Ibn Ṣā'id al-Taghlibī, Ṣā'id ibn Aḥmad (1985) *Ṭabaqāt al-umam*, ed. Ḥ. Bū'alwān, (Beirut).
Al-Mas'ūdī (1960) *Al-Tanbīh wa'l-ishrāf*, trans. S. M. Stern, "Al-Mas'ūdī and the Philosopher al-Fārābī", in S. M. Ahmad and A. Rahman (eds) *Al-Mas'ūdī Millenary Commemoration Volume* (Aligarh): 28–41.
Moses Maimonides (1963) *The Guide for the Perplexed*, trans. S. Pines (Chicago and London).

Secondary sources

Abed, S. B. (1991) *Aristotelian Logic and the Arabic Language in Alfarabi* (Albany).
Aouad, M. (1992) "Les Fondements de la *Rhétorique* d'Aristote reconsidérés par Fārābī, ou le concept de point de vue immédiat et commun", *Arabic Sciences and Philosophy*, 2: 133–80.
Arnaldez, R. (1977) "Pensée et langage dans la philosophie de Farabi (à propos du *Kitab al-huruf*)", *Studia Islamica*, 45: 57–65.
Black, D. L. (1989) "The 'Imaginative Syllogism'" in Arabic Philosophy: a Medieval Contribution to the Philosophical Study of Metaphor", *Mediaeval Studies*, 51: 242–67.

—— (1990) *Logic and Aristotle's "Rhetoric" and "Poetics" in Medieval Arabic Philosophy* (Leiden).

—— (1992) "Aristotle's *Peri hermeneias* in medieval Latin and Arabic philosophy: logic and the linguistic arts", in R. Bosley and M. Tweedale (eds), *Aristotle and His Medieval Interpreters, Canadian Journal of Philosophy*, suppl. vol. 17: 25–83.

Butterworth, C. E. (1983) "Ethics in Medieval Islamic Philosophy", *Journal of Religious Ethics*, 11: 224–39.

—— (1984) "The Rhetorician and his Relationship to the Community: Three Accounts of Aristotle's *Rhetoric*", in Michael Marmura (ed.), *Islamic Theology and Philosophy: Studies in Honor of George F. Hourani* (Albany): 111–36.

Cruz Hernandez, M. (1950–1) "El 'Fontes quaestionum' (*'Uyūn al-masā'il*) de Abū Naṣr al-Fārābī", *Archives d'Histoire Doctrinale et Littéraire du Moyen Age*, 25–6: 303–23.

Daiber, Hans (1986a) *The Ruler as Philosopher: a New Interpretation of al-Farabi's View* (Amsterdam and New York).

—— (1986b) "Prophetie und Ethik bei Fārābī (Gest. 339/950)", in Ch. Wenin (ed.) *L'Homme et son univers au moyen âge*, vol. 2 (Louvain): 729–53.

Davidson, H. A. (1972) "Alfarabi and Avicenna on the active intellect", *Viator*, 3: 109–78.

Druart, Th.-A. (1987a) "Al-Farabi and Emanationism", in John F. Wippel (ed.) *Studies in Medieval Philosophy* (Washington DC): 23–43.

—— (1987b) "Substance in Arabic Philosophy: al-Farabi's Discussion", *Proceedings of the American Catholic Philosophical Association*, 61: 88–97.

Elamrani-Jamal, A. (1983) *Logique aristotélicienne et grammaire arabe (étude et documents)* (Paris).

Eskenasy, P. E. (1988) "Al-Fārābī's Classification of the Parts of Speech", *Jerusalem Studies in Arabic and Islam*, 11: 55–82.

Fakhry, M. (1983) *A History of Islamic Philosophy*, 2nd ed. (London and New York).

Galston, M. (1981) "Al-Fārābī on Aristotle's Theory of Demonstration", in P. Morewedge (ed.) *Islamic Philosophy and Mysticism* (Delmar): 23–34.

—— (1988) "Al-Farabi et la logique aristotélicienne dans la philosophie islamique", in M. A. Sinaceur (ed.) *Aristote aujourd'hui* (Toulouse): 192–217.

—— (1990) *Politics and Excellence: The Political Philosophy of Alfarabi*, (Princeton).

Gätje, H. (1971) "Die Gliederung der sprachlichen Zeichen nach al-Fārābī", *Der Islam*, 47: 1–24.

Georr, K. (1941–6) "Fārābī est-il l'auteur de *Fuçuç al-hikam*?", *Revue des Etudes Islamiques*, 15: 31–9.

Gutas, D. (1988) *Avicenna and the Aristotelian Tradition: Introduction to Reading Avicenna's Philosophical Works* (Leiden).

Hasnawi, A. (1985) "Fārābī et la pratique de l'exégèse philosophique (remarques sur son *Commentaire au De interpretatione* d'Aristote)", *Revue de Synthèse*, 3rd ser., 117: 27–59.

Heinrichs, W. (1978) "Die antike Verknüpfung von Phantasia und Dichtung bei den Arabern", *Zeitschrift der deutschen morganländischen Gesellschaft*, 128: 252–98.

Jolivet, J. (1977) "L'Intellect selon al-Farabi: quelques remarques", *Bulletin d'Etudes Orientales*, 29: 251–9.

Kemal, Salim (1991) *The Poetics of Alfarabi and Avicenna* (Leiden).
Lameer, J. (1994) *Al-Fārābī and Aristotelian Syllogistics: Greek Theory and Islamic Practice* (Leiden).
Langhade, J. (1981) "Grammaire, logique, études linguistiques chez al-Fārābī", *Historiographia Linguistica*, 8: 365–77.
Macy, J. (1986) "Prophecy in al-Farabi and Maimonides: the Imaginative and Rational Faculties", in S. Pines and Y. Yovel (eds) *Maimonides and Philosophy* (Dordrecht): 185–201.
Madkour, I. (1963) "Al-Fārābi", in M. M. Sharif (ed.) *A History of Muslim Philosophy*, 2 (Wiesbaden): 450–68.
Mahdi, M. (1972a) "Alfarabi", in L. Strauss and J. Cropsey (eds) *History of Political Philosophy* (Chicago): 182–202.
—— (1972b) "Alfarabi on Philosophy and Religion", *Philosophical Forum*, 4: 5–25.
—— (1975a) "Remarks on Alfarabi's *Attainment of Happiness*", in G. F. Hourani (ed.) *Essays on Islamic Philosophy and Science* (Albany): 47–66.
—— (1975b) "Science, Philosophy, and Religion in Alfarabi's *Enumeration of the Sciences*", in J. E. Murdoch and E. D. Sylla (eds) *The Cultural Context of Medieval Learning* (Dordrecht): 113–47.
—— (1990) "Al-Fārābī's Imperfect State", *Journal of the American Oriental Society*, 110: 691–726.
Mahdi, M. and Lerner, R. (eds) (1963) *Medieval Political Philosophy: A Sourcebook* (Ithaca).
Marmura, M. E. (1985) "Die islamische Philosophie des Mittelalters", in M. E. Marmura and W. M. Watt, *Der Islam II: Politische Entwicklungen und theologische Konzepte* (Stuttgart): 320–92.
Meyerhoff, M. (1930) "Von Alexandrien nach Baghdad", *Stizungsberichte der Preussischen Akademie der Wissenschaften*, 23: 389–429.
Michot, J. (1982) "Tables de correspondance des *Ta'liqat* d'al-Farabi, de *Ta'liqat* d'Avicenne et du *Liber Aphorismorum* d'Andrea Alpago", *Mélanges de l'Institut Dominicain d'Etudes Orientales du Caire*, 15: 231–50.
Nasr, S. H. (1985) "Why was Al-Fārābī Called the Second Teacher?", *Islamic Culture*, 59: 357–64.
Netton, I. (1992) *Al-Fārābī and his School* (London).
Pines, S. (1951) "Ibn Sina et l'auteur de la *Risalat al-fusus fi'l hikma*: quelques donnés du problème", *Revue des Etudes Islamiques*, 19: 121–4.
—— (1972) "The Limitations of Human Knowledge According to al-Farabi, ibn Bajja, and Maimonides", in I. Twersky (ed.), *Studies in Medieval Jewish History and Literature* (Cambridge, Mass.): 82–109.
Rahman, F. (1958) *Prophecy in Islam: Philosophy and Orthodoxy* (Chicago).
Strauss, L. (1945) "Farabi's Plato", in *Louis Ginsberg Jubilee Volume* (New York): 357–93.
—— (1957) "How Fārābī read Plato's *Laws*", in *Mélanges Louis Massignon*, 3 (Damascus): 319–44.
Vajda, G. (1970) "Langage, philosophie, politique et religion, d'après un traité d'al-Farabi", *Journal asiatique*, 258: 247–60.
Walzer, R. (1962) "Al-Fārābī's Theory of Prophecy and Divination", in R. Walzer (ed.) *Greek into Arabic: Essays on Islamic Philosophy* (Oxford): 206–19.
—— (1965) "Al-Fārābī", *Encyclopaedia of Islam*, 2nd ed. (Leiden), 2: 778–81.

CHAPTER 13

Muḥammad ibn Zakariyyā' al-Rāzī

Lenn E. Goodman

Physician, philosopher, chemist and freethinker, al-Rāzī (*c.* 250/864–313/925 or 320/932), known to the Latins as Rhazes, was born, as his name suggests, in Rayy, near present-day Tehran. Well versed, according to tradition, in musical theory and practice, he is said to have been an alchemist before his formal training in medicine. He headed hospitals in Rayy and later in Baghdad, returning often to Rayy, where he died. His great houses in Rayy and elsewhere in the south Caspian district of Jibal attested his wealth. The author of some two hundred works, he is said to have taught the Jacobite Christian philosopher/translator Yaḥyā ibn 'Adī (893–974) and was called "the unsurpassed physician of Islam".[1] But later thinkers generally rejected his philosophical ideas, typically with repugnance, although influenced by him even in rebuttal.

Dedicated to the Sāmānid governor of Rayy, al-Manṣūr ibn Isḥāq (d. 313/925), al-Rāzī's *Manṣūrī* was said by 'Alī ibn al-'Abbās (d. 385/994) to omit nothing essential to medical practice, although offering few explanations of its dicta. Its twelfth-century Latin translation by Gerard of Cremona, the *Liber Almansoris*, became a mainstay of medical education; *Liber nonus*, its ninth book, was still used in late sixteenth-century Europe. Al-Rāzī's *Mulūkī*, or *Regius*, was dedicated to 'Alī ibn Wēh-Sūdhān of Tabaristan. But what is perhaps al-Rāzī's best-known work was not meant for publication. Often confused with his *magnum opus* the *Kitāb al-jāmi' al-kabīr* ("Great Medical Compendium"), the *Continens* (*Kitāb al-ḥāwī fi'l-ṭibb*) was al-Rāzī's private medical journal and notebook.[2] 'Ubaydallāh ibn Jibrīl, a fifth/eleventh-century scion of the famous Bukhtīshū' medical family, tells how it was preserved at the instance of the warrior scholar/statesman Ibn al-'Amīd (appointed in 327/939 vizier to Rukn al-Dawlah, d. 349/960), who bought the pages from al-Rāzī's sister and commissioned al-Rāzī's students to edit the text. Filling some twenty-five volumes, the *Ḥāwī* was the most voluminous of Arabic medical texts; its Latin translation for King Charles of Anjou, completed in 1279 by the Jewish physician Faraj ibn Salem ("Farraguth"), absorbed much of the translator's life.[3] Arranged anatomically, "from top to toe", it collated al-Rāzī's learning and observations on all aspects of pathology, hygiene and therapeutics, using Greek, Byzantine, Syriac and sometimes Indian sources, especially in the tradition from Hippocrates to Isḥāq ibn Ḥunayn (d. 298/910). It included al-Rāzī's records of his self-treatment when ill. Opinions are noted dispassionately; but the sections regularly end with al-Rāzī's own views and clinical observations, under the heading *lī*, my own. Al-Rāzī kept up the file system of the *Ḥāwī* throughout his life and quarried it in writing his books. Besides the published works identifiable in draft, three nearly finished books are embedded here in embryo: *On Urine, On Fevers* and *On Crises and Critical Days*.[4]

Al-Rāzī's medical writings included works on diet and treatment; paralysis, arthritis, diabetes, colic and gout; anatomies of the liver, eye, testes, ear and heart; a study on the dilation of the pupil, an abridgment of Galen's (129–*c.* 199) *De pulsibus*, and a warning against premature purging of fever patients. Among his most famous works were *Gallstones, Kidney and Bladder* and *Smallpox and Measles*, the first work devoted to smallpox, translated over a dozen times into Latin and other European languages. Its lack of dogmatism and Hippocratic reliance on clinical observation typify al-Rāzī's medical approach.[5] His irreverent spirit peeps out more puckishly from the titles of some of his books on the medical profession: *On the Reasons for People's Preference of Inferior Physicians, To Whoever is Unattended by a Physician, A Mistaken View of the Function of the Physician, On Why Some People Leave a Physician if he is Intelligent, That an Intelligent Physician Cannot Heal all Diseases, Since that is not Possible* and *Why Ignorant Physicians, Common Folk, and Women in the Cities are more Successful than Scientists in Treating Certain Diseases – and the Physician's Excuse for This.*

Al-Rāzī heeded the counsel of Galen's work, *That the Outstanding Physician must also be a Philosopher.* Al-Bīrūnī (362/973–*c.* 442/1050) lists some eighty philosophical titles in his al-Rāzī bibliography, and al-Nadīm lists dozens of his works on logic, cosmology, theology, mathematics and alchemy.[6] Among his writings are a commentary on Plato's *Timaeus*, perhaps based on the epitome of Galen,[7] a rebuttal of Iamblichus' response to Porphyry's *Letter to Anebos*,[8] an appraisal of the Qur'ān, a critique of Mu'tazilism, another on the infallible Imām of the Ismā'īlīs, a work on how to measure intelligence, an introduction to and vindication of algebra,[9] a defence of the soul's incorporeality, a debate with a Manichaean, and an explanation of the difficulty people have in accepting the sphericity of the earth when they are not trained in rigorous demonstration.

Al-Rāzī wrote works on *eros*, coitus, nudity and clothing, the fatal effects of the Simoom on animal life, the seasons of autumn and spring, the wisdom of the Creator, and the reason for the creation of wild beasts and reptiles. One work defends the proposition that God does not interfere with the actions of other agents. Another rebuts the claim that the earth revolves. Al-Rāzī discussed the innate or intrinsic character of motion, a sore point between Democritean and Aristotelian physics; he wrote several treatments of the nature of matter, and one on the unseen causes of motion. His exposé of the risks of ignoring the axioms of geometry may aim at *kalām* defenders of dimensionless atoms; and his book on the diagonal of the square may have defended his own atomism against the ancient charge, first levelled at Pythagoreanism, that atomism excludes the demonstrated incommensurability of a square's side with its diagonal – a charge disarmed by al-Rāzī's acceptance of the void and rejection of Aristotle's doctrine of the relativity of space. For al-Rāzī's absolute space is a Euclidean continuum and need not, like his matter, be composed of discrete, indivisible quanta.

Only a few short works, fragments and essays[10] survive of al-Rāzī's philosophical writings, but the record of his conversation shows that he regarded philosophy not merely as an adjunct to medical work but as an end in itself. His *Ṭibb al-rūḥānī*, written for al-Manṣūr as a companion to the *Manṣūrī,* follows al-Kindī's precedent in treating ethics as a kind of psychic medicine or clinical psychology, an approach later used by Ibn Gabirol and Maimonides.[11] Hence the title, *Spiritual Physick*, as quaintly archaized by Arberry, that is, Spiritual or Psychological Medicine.[12] In an *apologia pro vita sua*, *The Philosophical Way of Life* (*Kitāb al-sīrat 'l-falsafiyyah*) al-Rāzī describes his lifestyle, defensively but revealingly, in some dudgeon with unnamed critics, who apparently took issue with his philosophical hedonism:

> In a practical regard, I can say that with God's help and support I have never gone beyond the upper and lower limits [of indulgence and self-denial] I have defined. No act of mine has ever revealed any but a philosophic way of life. I consorted with the ruler not as a man at arms or an officer of state but as a physician and a friend, serving in illness to treat him and improve his body or in health as a companion and adviser. My sole ambition, so help me, was his well-being and that of his subjects. No one has ever seen me avidly pursuing wealth, spending extravagantly, or being disputatious, quarrelsome or unfair. Everyone knows that I am just the opposite, even to the point of often neglecting my own rights [*ḥuqūqī*].
>
> In food, drink and entertainment, those who have spent much time with me know that I am not prone to excess.

> The same is true in other respects, as those who know me can attest – whether in dress, riding animals, attendants and maids. But in love of learning and dedication to knowledge, those who have spent time with me and know me personally know that from my youth until today my commitment has been unabating. So much so, that I have never come across a book I had not read or a man I had not met without dropping everything – even at significant harm to my interests – and getting into that book or taking the measure of that man's thinking. My perseverance and dedication reached such extremes that in a single year I wrote over twenty thousand pages in a hand like an amulet maker's. I have kept at work on my big compendium [the *Jāmiʿ*] for fifteen years, night and day, until my eyes grew weak and my hand muscles deteriorated, so that now I can no longer read or write. But even so, I have not given up reading or writing in such fashion as I can. For I constantly employ someone to read and write for me.[13]

A contemporary who did know al-Rāzī enlarges this self-portrait, describing him as an old man "with a large head shaped like a sack":

> He used to sit in his reception room [*majlis*] with his students around him, surrounded by *their* students, and then still other students. A patient would enter and describe his symptoms to the one he first met. If they did not know what was wrong, he would progress to the next group. If they did not know, al-Rāzī himself would discuss the case. He was generous, dignified and honest with the people – so compassionate with the poor and sick that he would supply ample food for them and provide them with nursing care . . . He was never to be seen not taking notes or transcribing information, and I never went in to see him without finding him writing out either a draft or a revision . . . He went blind at the end of his life.[14]

Al-Rāzī was enough of a Galenist that he wrote a bibliography of works by Galen unlisted in Galen's own catalogue or that of the great translator Ḥunayn ibn Isḥāq.[15] But his empiric bent made him chary of authority. His *Doubts about Galen*[16] rejects Galen's claims as to the superiority of the Greek language and criticizes many of his cosmological and medical views. It claims medicine for philosophy and argues that sound practice depends on independent thinking. Al-Rāzī's own clinical records, he reports, diverged more often than they confirmed Galen's descriptions of the course of a fever. One urinary disease, which Galen had seen only twice, perhaps because it was "rare in his country", al-Rāzī had seen over a hundred times. Beyond these matters of sheer experience, al-Rāzī rejects the notion, central to the theory of humours, that the body is warmed or cooled only by warmer or cooler bodies, since a warm drink may heat the body to a degree much hotter than its own. Tugging at the edges of the classic tangle we now differentiate under the rubrics of physical and chemical change, he reasons that the drink must trigger a response rather than simply communicating warmth or coldness.

Like Aristotle, al-Rāzī was impatient with mathematics. He blamed the inadequacies of Galen's theory of vision on an excessive reliance on mathematics, which Galen had imbibed from his mathematician father. Al-Rāzī's own account was more Aristotelian, tracing visual images from the object to the eye and the optic nerve. And, like Aristotle, al-Rāzī treated the soul as a substance. The brain was its instrument, like any other organ.

But although al-Rāzī upheld the substantial, incorporeal soul, and creation, in his own fashion, he was the least orthodox and most iconoclastic of the major philosophers of Islam. To be a philosopher, he had to explain, does not mean belonging to a sect or school, modelling one's actions and ideas on those of a master. One learns from one's predecessors but can also hope to surpass them. Al-Rāzī knew that he would never be a Socrates, and he cautioned against anyone's expecting in short order to rival Socrates, Plato, Aristotle, Theophrastus, Eudemus, Chrysippus, Themistius or Alexander of Aphrodisias.[17] But he denied the view, widely held in his time and gaining ground once again in our own, that human beings are trapped within the teachings of the great founders of traditions: he told a hostile contemporary, who reports his words incredulously,

> You must understand that every later philosopher who commits himself creatively [*ijtahada*], diligently and persistently to philosophical inquiry where subtle difficulties have led his predecessors to disagree will understand what they understood and retain it, having a quick mind and much experience of thought and inquiry in other areas. Rapidly mastering what his predecessors knew and grasping the lessons they afford, he readily surpasses them. For inquiry, thought and originality make progress and improvement inevitable.[18]

Al-Rāzī's interlocutor[19] counters that, without intellectual authorities, men would rapidly succumb to hopeless confusions and contradictions. Like critics of philosophy before and since, he sees philosophical disagreements not as seedbeds of intellectual possibilities but as scandals of intellectual irresponsibility. But al-Rāzī values independent thinking above consensus. Indeed, he sees it as the key to the liberation of the soul, even if one's thoughts remain inconclusive. All people, he argues, can think for themselves. They do not need a leader or guide to show them how to live or what to think. Asked how philosophy comports with faith in a revealed religion, he replies: "How can anyone think philosophically while committed to those old wives' tales, founded on contradictions, obdurate ignorance, and dogmatism?"[20] Special prophecy, he insists, is an imposture, a bone of needless contention: "How can you imply that God would prefer one people as the standard bearers of mankind, making all the rest dependent on them? How can you reconcile with the wisdom of the Allwise God's singling out one people in this way, setting mankind at one another's throats, fomenting bloodshed, warfare and conflict!"[21] Turning the tables on the favourite Muʿtazilite argument, Stoic in origin, that God morally must give guidance to humankind, al-Rāzī argues that divine benevolence precludes special revelation. Prophetic experience is the work of dead souls too ignorant and evil to make a clean break with physicality. Such demonic spirits linger in the world, bound to physicality by sensuous appetites and passions. Finding some vile body as a vehicle, they appear in the guise of angels to deceive and mislead us, so as to cause bloodshed, dissension and destruction among humankind.[22]

What God's goodness demands, al-Rāzī insists, is guidance for all. This *is* provided, through the universal gift of intelligence. In the democratic tradition of Epicurean epistemology, heightened by his antagonism to the Ismāʿīlī mystique of the infallible Imām, al-Rāzī insists that no one is wiser than another:

> I have no special claim to philosophy over anyone else. I have simply pursued it where others neglected it. They are deprived only by their restiveness with theory, not by any inner deficiency. The proof is people understand things relevant to their trade and livelihood and handle them perfectly well, applying their ingenuity to devise things that would be much too subtle for many of us. That is because they are interested. If they applied their interest where I have applied mine and pursued what I have sought, they would grasp what I have.[23]

Part of what al-Rāzī had grasped was that creation would be indefensible against "the eternalists", unless one could posit five eternal beings whose interactions framed the world we know: God, Soul, time, space and matter. In the beginning these five coexisted. God and Soul were beyond time and space. Matter was extended in them, but not throughout them, leaving some room for the void. Matter was not yet in motion. But Soul, passionately desirous of embodiment, confounded herself in matter, setting the world into a confused and disordered motion. God intervened by imparting knowledge to the Soul and order to the movements of nature,[24] averting a cataclysm, and enabling Soul to recognize that the world her motions enlivened was not her true home. God had permitted her fall, although He did not cause it, because He knew that souls learn only through experience. Now her task, throughout the course of history, is to return to the spiritual world, where all souls are one. Soul falls by a spontaneous motion, neither compelled by nature nor chosen by intelligence. She returns, through God's grace, the intelligence vouchsafed to her.

Nāṣir-i-Khusraw[25] summarizes the dilemma that al-Rāzī's use of the gnostic/Neoplatonic myth of the fall of the soul seems intended to dissolve: if God created the world by an act of will, we must ask why now rather than earlier or later? Did God change His mind or His essence, becoming a Creator after eons, perhaps, of exercising no such intention?[26] But if the origin of the world is a natural event, God is enmeshed in temporality along with the very events His act should ground, and we embark on a spurious search for the cause of the Cause of causes. The only solution, al-Rāzī reasons, is to find a third alternative to natural and volitional events. This, despite the ridicule of his Ismāʿīlī detractor, he finds in Aristotle's occasional mention of spontaneity, a theme well developed in the Epicurean thesis of the *clinamen*, or spontaneous swerve of the atoms – a kind of motion readily ascribed to Soul, but not to God.

Eternal matter, space and time sidestep the paradoxes Aristotle had raised against an origin of the world, by admitting that there never was a time before which there was no time or a substrate for the coming to be of matter, the universal substrate of all change. But al-Rāzī draws the line at change itself: motion *is* originated. The potential for it in matter requires soul to actualize it; and mind (soul rendered intelligent), to give it order. Creation, then, becomes *formatio mundi*; time and space will be absolute, rather than relative as in Aristotle; and al-Rāzī will adopt and adapt to his own purposes the atomism of Epicurus, accepting the void (absolute space) and the seeming paradox of the reality of nothingness as the price of his cosmogony. Critics of Avicenna's (Ibn Sīnā's) eternalism little appreciate that in embracing Plotinian emanation and treating the cosmos as a whole as contingent, although eternal, Avicenna is overcoming what monotheists found most objectionable in the creationism of al-Rāzī. For Avicenna, as a Neoplatonist, includes matter among the things whose existence depends (eternally) on the act of God. Al-Rāzī, by contrast, treats matter, time, space and even Soul, as eternal, hence self-subsistent beings.[27]

The atomism of al-Rāzī, like that of Epicurus before him and Gassendi after him, but unlike that of the more radical *mutakallimūn*, assigned sizes to the ultimate constituents of things, making them physically, not geometrically, indivisible. And for al-Rāzī, unlike the *kalām* atomists, atomism was an explanatory theory, not a religious doctrine or metaphysical dogma. He takes Galen to task for excluding all other views but that of the atomists. And, unlike Democritus and Epicurus, he does not attempt to explain *everything* atomistically, since he is not a materialist. God and the Soul are not atomic phenomena.

Al-Rāzī's curious doctrine that the void exerts an attractive force[28] may arise from the need to explain the uncaused Epicurean swerve, the *clinamen*, which al-Rāzī seems to exploit as a model of the spontaneous motion of the Soul. For al-Rāzī connects the attractive force of the void with his theory of appetite and thus with his central idea that (kinetic) pleasures are the sensation of repletion. Appetites would result from the progressive distension of the relevant organs, presumably, from rarefaction. Sensuous desire would be the conscious correlate of a literal, physical, lack. And what is free in choice would correspond to the spontaneous movement of the organism to fill some specific void.

Epicurus had counted on the *clinamen* for exceptions to the rigid determinism of Democritus. If atoms are absolutely solid, the absolute positivity of their impacts would leave no room for chance or freedom – were it not for the absolute emptiness of the void. If asked what would *cause* the purported spontaneous swerve that allows both chance and freedom in his world, Epicurus could answer in all candour and consistency: What would prevent it? Al-Rāzī may have filled in the gap left by such a *reductio ad ignorantiam*, with a force of attraction (ancestral to the notorious idea of "suction"). Such a force, exerted by the already hypostatic void,[29] would match the "repulsion" (mutual exclusion) of solid atoms, laying down atomic foundations for the two primitive motives of classical physiology, "attraction" and "repulsion", the volitional grounds of pursuit and avoidance.

Al-Rāzī's chemistry departs from the hermetic style and spiritualizing aims of Jābir ibn Ḥayyān and his Greek alchemical predecessors and Arabic successors. The *Fihrist* of al-Nadīm ascribes to him the transcription of a key work of Jābir's into verse, but modern scholars find in al-Rāzī's writings little trace of what is distinctive in Jābir's thinking. As Peters points out, al-Rāzī would have no more use for the dogmatic authority of a Hermes Trismegistus than for that of a Muḥammad.[30] The mercury he uses comes from Persian cinnabar, a red sulphide of the metal; his sal ammoniac (ammonium chloride), a substance unknown to the Greeks, but called "the eagle" by al-Rāzī, because of its volatility, "was perhaps obtained from the burning coal deposits of Central Asia". Other substances come from the marketplace, the kitchen, the mine and petroleum well, the laboratory and the artisan's crucible.[31] For al-Rāzī was plainly not averse to watching traders and craftspeople work, as his remark about their ingenuity reveals.

His alchemy, with its Persian nomenclature and updated stock room, comes closer to chemistry than anything found in the Hellenistic sources. Although he uses blood, urine and various sorts of plant matter in his preparations, there is nothing here of the "eye of newt and toe of frog" variety – reagents whose power seeps from their symbolism. But in alchemy, as in medicine and philosophy, al-Rāzī does not reinvent the wheel. Even his God does not create *ex nihilo*. Rather, the philosopher's aim is a thorough revision of the tradition. He defends alchemy, in Islamic legal terminology, as "Closer to the Obligatory than to the Prohibited"; he also defends it against the criticisms of the philosopher al-Kindī. Defending the "work" of transmutation, he rejects the idea of "potions". His alchemical practice is (Neoplatonically) naturalistic in assumptions, but empirical in method. Like his successors al-Ghazzālī and Maimonides (who also relied on Neoplatonic hylomorphism), al-Rāzī allies his empiricism to a mistrust of established theory, the theory that arrogates to itself the title of rationality. Like the Greek Peripatetics, he collects anomalous observations, refusing to reject what is perceived merely because it is not explained, and arguing that those who hasten to deny what they cannot prove are inconsistent in accepting, say, magnetism (on which he wrote a treatise). For clearly they cannot explain it.[32] Thus al-Rāzī prefers the methods to the conclusions of Aristotle.

Al-Bīrūnī ascribes some twenty-one works on alchemy to him, the greatest of them being the *Kitāb sirr al-asrār* or *Secretum secretorum*. In keeping with al-Rāzī's very unhermetic spirit, the secrets here are not mystical arcana but trade secrets of the alchemist, which al-Rāzī freely reveals in discussions of the materials, apparatus and methods of the art. The aim is to traverse the boundaries dividing one type of substance from another, using a powerful substance that will permeate and transform the substrate, by adding or removing specific properties, transforming base metals into gold or stones into gems. But al-Rāzī will also use some of his preparations in his medical practice; and his methods as an alchemist smack more of the surgery than of the occult.

His materials, grouped under six rubrics, include four "spirits" (sulphur, arsenic sulphides, mercury and sal ammoniac), seven "bodies" (gold, silver, iron, copper, tin, lead and zinc), thirteen stones (mainly gems, but also glass), five vitriols (plus alum as a sixth), six boraxes and eleven salts. The theory is fairly crude, and not helped much by its overlay upon the familiar Aristotelian/Empedoclean scheme of fire, water, earth and air, and their four fundamental qualities, hot and cold, wet and dry. But experience in the laboratory has by now deformed the symmetry of the Aristotelian scheme, demanding new primary qualities like salinity and inflammability – the latter ascribed to "oiliness" and "sulphuriousness". Mercury is said to remove moisture; ammonium chloride, earthiness. Sulphur produces whiteness and removes oiliness; calcination dissociates bodies and removes their sulphur or oil; and so forth. Al-Rāzī's recipes are hard for modern chemists to follow, and his experimentalism is rudimentary, held in check by inadequate theory, just as theory itself is held in check by insufficient experience. But what is striking is the effort to move from a qualitative scheme of essences in unformed matter to a level of explanation that will treat observed qualitative changes in terms of quantitative relations. Thus all the properties of the five Aristotelian elements – fire, water, earth, air and the celestial substance – heaviness and lightness, opacity and transparency, and the like, are reduced to density and rarity of particles: iron makes sparks when struck on stone, by cleaving the air, rarefying it into fire. The properties of the elements themselves result from the proportions in them "of absolute matter and the substance of the void".[33] All changes of properties in the substances of nature are explained by "pairing" and "parting" – the combining and separating of Empedocles, now understood not as a blending and tempering of opposed qualities, but quantitatively and reactively, in terms of the rearrangement of particles and parts.[34]

Al-Rāzī's ethics, like his cosmology, profits from Epicurean elements.[35] Like an Epicurean, he is a naturalist and an empiricist in ethics, reaching a mildly ascetic hedonism via a familiar Epicurean route.[36] For he argues that a proper understanding of pleasure does not lead us to seek ever more intense sensations or to mass up pleasurable experiences, as though they could be hoarded, but to the recognition that peace of mind and the surest life, from the standpoint of maximizing human happiness, is the life of prudence, in which modest desires, tailored to the demands of nature, are easily satisfied by modest means. The sybaritic life is a trap which leads not to enhanced but to ever diminished enjoyment:

> You need to know that those who consistently give precedence to their appetites, feeding and fostering them, reach a point, as a result, where they are no longer able to enjoy them, or to give them up. Thus those who are addicted to orgasms with women, or to drinking wine, or listening to music, do not enjoy these things – although they are some of the most powerful and instinctual pleasures of our nature – as do those who are not addicted to them. For to those who are dependent on them they become mere states of mind like any other, matters of familiarity and habit. Yet those who are so inured to them are not readily able to shake them off. For they have become, as it were, necessities for them, rather than niceties or refinements.[37]

Al-Rāzī wrote a separate work on pleasure, defining it as a form of repose.[38] All (kinetic) pleasures are the sensed return of the body to its natural state, from which it has been removed, either suddenly and sensibly, or gradually and insensibly. Thus all pleasures presuppose a prior pain (more properly: a dislocation, since the "pain" need not be felt).[39] The doctrine may be guided by Plato's *Timaeus*. But the model, and the confinement of the issue to hedonic concerns, is paradigmatically

Epicurean – fed, in part, by the early Sceptic ideal of the good life. For Ibn al-Qifṭī and others rightly see here a connection with Pyrrho's doctrine of repose. Perhaps al-Rāzī, in his naturalism, simply rederives the physiology of pleasure as a return to the resting state from Plato's analysis of desire, much as Epicurus did.[40] For al-Rāzī plainly relies on Plato's argument that the greater the appetite the harder it is to fill, making a life devoted to satisfying the appetites (which grow in response to their satiation) about as sensible as trying to carry water in a sieve.[41] But al-Rāzī also seems to use an Epicurean model when he argues that all pleasures and pains are transitory in so far as they are dislocations from and sensed returns to the natural state.[42]

Like an Epicurean, al-Rāzī finds the optimum of pleasure not in a seesaw of sensations but in a moderate life, meeting the needs of nature, not straying far from the physical norm of natural adjustment to our milieu. In place of Aristotle's sophisticated and intellectualist anatomy of the virtues, he offers an anatomy and catalogue of human vices: excess in food or drink, sexual activity, or even music, is unhealthy, he argues, trading on his medical authority. But, in an argument echoed by both Saadiah and Maimonides, he holds that denial too can be unwholesome.[43] We must seek the middle ground, understood not simply as an Aristotelian mean of appropriateness to be located by reason but largely physiologically, in terms of the requirements of nature. For these alone, al-Rāzī argues, show us the need to rein in our passions. Anger in excess defeats its biological purpose of self-preservation and becomes self-destructive, like the anger of Galen's mother, who, in her frustration, once tried to bite off a padlock. Social climbing and ambition for rank and office are similarly self-defeating.[44] Lying is rejected not on the (deontic) grounds that it is intrinsically wrong but on the prudential, Epicurean grounds that the liar will never be trusted and can never enjoy peace of mind. The Ismā'īlī author Ḥamīd al-Dīn al-Kirmānī (d. 411/1020) criticized al-Rāzī on this score: Had al-Rāzī known how ruinous lying is to the soul, he argues, adopting the perspective of virtue ethics pioneered in Islam by Ibn Miskawayh, he would never (as he does, following Plato) have made an exception to the prohibition of lying, for the sake of saving a human life.[45]

Like Epicurus, al-Rāzī deems it a moral error to base ethical judgments on any considerations beyond personal pleasure in the sense of *ataraxia*. His entire ethics is focused on the appeal to reason to control passion (*al-hawā*). And, as Mohaghegh remarks, "Rāzī uses the word *hawā* more than any other Muslim moral philosopher", speaking of the need to combat, suppress, restrain and rein it in.[46] He analyses all virtues and vices by way of the resultant prudential standard. Thus, stinginess results from a miscalculation about one's real desires, and so can be refuted (and cured!) by an appeal to reason. Here the Socratic tendency of the soul becomes a kind of moral therapy of the sort that Aristotle sometimes practised. Al-Rāzī tells, for example, of treating a stingy man by calling his attention to his true desires and then prevailing upon him to practise spending modest sums. Rational psychiatry does its moral work by placing reason in the service of our own wholesome hedonic intentions, aiding us to the good life – first by clarifying the true nature of pleasure and then by reminding us (against the unreason of the passions) of the effectual means to our (rationally edited) ends.

Maimonides, who excoriates al-Rāzī's Epicurean view that evils outweigh goods in this life,[47] none the less follows his example in ethics – not to the extent of abandoning virtue ethics and eudaimonism or treating pleasures as the only good (the false assumption he exposes at the heart of the Epicurean dilemma), but to the extent that his important ethical work, the *Eight Chapters*, includes not only an anatomy of the soul but also chapters on its illnesses and their cure, and a prescription for moral weaknesses modified unabashedly from al-Rāzī's model:

> if a man appears to have developed the trait of depriving himself of anything good (because of niggardliness) . . . and we wish to cure him of this illness, we must not order him merely to be more liberal. That would be like treating a man who had a high fever with some mild dose that would not break his fever. No, what we must do is have him spend extravagantly, over and over again, so many times that his propensity to be stingy disappears and he is nearly a spendthrift. But we do not let him become one; we order him to keep up his generous actions but guard against both excess and deficiency.[48]

Where Maimonides sees some therapeutic value in temporary excess, al-Rāzī had prescribed only modest spending, lest one feed the passions that are peculiarly drawn to excess. In context, Maimonides is explaining the relative and temporary value of ascetic exercises, although rejecting asceticism as a way of life. His therapeutic model, couched in a disagreement with al-Rāzī, is entirely Rāzīan.

Al-Rāzī's ethics is consistently prudential. Even the excessive intellectualism that he seems to diagnose in himself, following the advice of Galen, that we may discover our own vices by heeding the criticisms of our enemies,[49] is recognized as a vice by its destructiveness to our health and peace of mind, and by the inevitable frustration met by too lofty an intellectual ambition. Thus, as I argued years ago, "pleasure" for al-Rāzī here "becomes the judge of reason, not reason of pleasure".[50] Excessive or impatient eagerness to learn is a vice because it makes one prone "to delusion and melancholia".[51] The analysis is no different from that al-Rāzī provides of those who are addicted to romance – or power[52] – or to the case of the ophthalmic child who compulsively rubs his eyes, eats dates and can't be kept from playing in the sun,[53] or the grown man who seems to be unable to stop playing with his beard.[54] Granted al-Rāzī does, in the case of romantic love[55] (a special bugbear of Epicureans[56]), lapse into almost pietistic language about the need to keep the soul, and not just the body, clean.[57] His central theme is clear when he classifies the affliction of the lover, etiologically, along with that of the alcoholic, as a form of dependency, or, to use his word, addiction.[58]

Like Epicurus, al-Rāzī has an interest in the pathological side of religion and hopes that reason can dispel certain religious compulsions, in the interest of mental health, or moral sanity. Ritual (*madhhab*) he argues, pertains to the passions, not the mind: "Cleanliness and purity must be judged solely by the senses, not by deduction, and treated in accordance with perception, not presumption."[59] It is compulsive to demand levels of purity that are warranted neither by the demands of religion (!) nor even by the responses of squeamishness. For, al-Rāzī argues, neither religion nor sensibility can respond rationally to impurities that cannot be sensed. Al-Rāzī's rejection of excessive fastidiousness as a vice is in keeping with his psychiatric understanding, particularly of melancholia, that is, depression.[60] It betrays him into a stance whose hygienic dangers will remain unseen until the times of Semmelweiss and Pasteur. But it reveals both the depth and the target of his naturalism. For his point is that purity should be a physical not a notional matter, and his remark that neither religion nor revulsion *can* respond to what remains unseen has a normative rather than a descriptive force. For religions in general and the Ismā'īlī Islam al-Rāzī confronted in particular make quite an issue of unseen, symbolic purity and impurity. That is what al-Rāzī insists is a matter of passion, not of reason. In religion, as in life in general, passion (*hawā*) is the enemy.

Part of the profit of his physiological understanding of pleasure, al-Rāzī argues, is that it frees one from the fear of death. Escaping that fear is of moment to al-Rāzī not only for the specific and immediate mental peace it brings, but for longer range moral reasons as well. For all vices, he argues, following the lead of Epicurus, result from obsessive desires, which are themselves products of the fear of death: "As long as the fear of death persists, one will incline away from reason and towards passion (*hawā*)."[61] Immortality for al-Rāzī is an object of desire and to be pursued as such, by Socratic, Platonic, Aristotelian means. Its pursuit, which Epicureanism eschewed, is justified on prudential grounds – partly because it is understood here (as it was not in Epicureanism) as a *prima facie* good – and partly on the grounds that the hope of immortality serves the Epicurean end of freeing us from the fear of death. For monotheism has banished the terror of a pagan, diabolical afterlife; and Islam, at least for al-Rāzī, has failed to restore it. But for those who cannot accept the reality of immortality, because they believe that the soul dissolves with the body, a more characteristically Epicurean consolation remains: "For pain is a sensation, and sensation is a property only of the living being."[62]

Al-Rāzī tries hard to apply al-Kindī's prescription for banishing anxiety and sorrow – considering one's loved ones as already lost, for example, and recognizing that death only removes one to a higher place.[63] But he admits that this is hard: the fear of death "can never be banished altogether from the soul, unless one is certain that after death it shifts to a better state" – a conclusion al-Rāzī acknowledges to be fraught with difficulties: "For this rubric would require very lengthy argumentation, if one sought proof rather than just allegations [*khabar*]. There really is no method whatever for argument to adopt on this topic, least of all in this book. For the subject is too elevated and too broad as well as too long, as I have said. It would require examination of all faiths and rites that hold or imply beliefs about an afterlife and a verdict as to which are true and which are false" – a task al-Rāzī has no intention of attempting. He excuses himself by adopting the committed but mildly, and appropriately, agnostic lead of Socrates,[64] treating immortality and dissolution disjunctively: For those who are certain of a better state in the hereafter, death should hold no fear.[65] Yet the Epicurean idea that death "is nothing to us" can still join hands with the Biblical idea (Job 3: 13) of death as surcease. Putting aside the vexed (*yaḍṭarru*) and problematic thesis of an afterlife, al-Rāzī argues, we can satisfy those who are convinced that the soul perishes with the body, by showing them that even without immortality "death is more salutary for man than life", since in death there is no pain; whereas in life pain is the inevitable concomitant of pleasure.[66]

NOTES

1 The encomium is from Ṣā'id's *Ṭabaqāt al-umam* (Beirut, 1912): 52–3.

2 The *Ḥāwī* was published at Hyderabad in Arabic in 1955. Before his death, al-Rāzī published four medical books under the title *Kitāb al-ḥāwī*. But he can hardly be blamed for using the same title (literally, "The Collection") as was later chosen by his students for the posthumous compilation of his files.

3 Ibn Abī Uṣaybi'ah, *'Uyūn al-anbā' fī ṭabaqāt al-aṭibbā'* (Cairo, 1882), 1: 314; see M. Meyerhof, "Thirty-three Clinical Observations by Rhazes", *Isis*, 23 (1935): 321–56. The Latin *Continens* was printed at Brescia in 1489 and repeatedly in the next century.

4 See Albert Z. Iskandar, "The Medical Bibliography of al-Rāzī", in G. Hourani (ed.), *Essays on Islamic Philosophy and Science* (Albany, 1975): 41–6.

5 See W. A. Greenhill, trans., *A Treatise on the Smallpox and Measles* (London, 1847); P. de Koning, trans., *Traité sur le calcul, les reins et la vessie* (Leiden, 1896).

6 Al-Bīrūnī, *Risālah fī Fihrist kutub M. b. Zakariyā' al-Rāzī* (Paris, 1936); ed. with Persian trans., M. Mohaghegh (Tehran, 1984/5); al-Nadīm, *Fihrist*, trans. B. Dodge (New York, 1970): 82, 377, 435, 599, 701–9.

7 *Galeni compendium Timaei Platonis*, 14, ed. P. Kraus and R. Walzer in *Plato Arabus* (London, 1951): 19, 65–6. But al-Bīrūnī ascribes translations as well as abridgments to al-Rāzī, and even mentions a poem of his, "in the Greek language". Al-Rāzī knew Plutarch's *On the Production of the Soul in the Timaeus*, as Frank Peters points out. Peters writes: "No Arabic version of a Platonic dialogue has been preserved. And yet Ibn al-Nadīm, writing in the late tenth century at the height of Islam's reception of Hellenism, knew . . . of translations of the *Republic*, the *Laws*, the *Sophist*, the *Timaeus*, and finally the *Letters*. But as soon as we approach more closely to the works themselves, we find ourselves in the presence of epitomes rather than translations" (*Allah's Commonwealth* (New York, 1973): 287–8).

8 Peters writes: "Iamblichus the author of *On the Mysteries of the Egyptians* is transformed into the mysterious Anebo ('Anabun'), the priest to whom Porphyry directed the original letter. . . . We do not, of course, possess the Greek of Porphyry's *Letter to Anebo*, though the Arabs certainly did, at least in part" (*Allah's Commonwealth*: 291). Iamblichus answers Porphyry in his *De mysteriis*, trans. Thomas Taylor as *On the Mysteries of the Egyptians, Chaldeans and Assyrians* (London, 1968 [1821]). Although the name Iamblichus vanishes, al-Rāzī would side with Porphyry's critical questioning, counter to Iamblichus' work, which is couched as *The Answer of the Preceptor Abammon to the Epistle of Porphyry to Anebo*.

9 Although it has earlier roots, algebra was established in Arabic mathematics in 236/850, by al-Khwarazmī's use of two methods for reducing specific problems to canonical form, in his *Kitāb al-mukhtaṣar fī ḥisāb al-jabr wa'l-muqābalah*; see *Encyclopaedia of Islam*, 2nd ed. (Leiden), *s.v. "al-djabr"*.

10 The term is used by al-Rāzī himself, as al-Nadīm notes. The essay form grew from the epistolary style in early Arabic prose and so bore the name *risālah*, originally, a letter.

11 See Ibn Gabirol, *Tikkun middot ha-nefesh*, trans. Stephen S. Wise, as *On the Improvement of the Moral Qualities* (New York, 1902); Maimonides, *Shemonah Perakim*, trans. Joseph I. Gorfinkle, as *The Eight Chapters of Maimonides on Ethics* (New York, 1912); both works were reprinted in New York by AMS in 1966.

12 *The Spiritual Physick of Rhazes* (London, 1950); and see M. Mohaghegh, "Notes on the 'Spiritual Physick' of al-Rāzī", *Studia Islamica*, 26 (1967): 5–22.

13 In Paul Kraus, *Abi Mohammadi filii Zachariae Raghensis (Razis) opera philosophica fragmentaque quae supersunt* (Cairo, 1939; Pars Prior, all that was published; repr. Beirut, 1973): 109–10.

14 M. ibn al-Ḥasan al-Warrāq, quoting an elderly contemporary who knew al-Rāzī, ap. Ibn al-Nadīm, *Fihrist*, trans. Dodge: 701–2. Al-Rāzī's blindness was apparently caused by a cataract, developed not long before his death. He refused surgery, saying that he had seen enough of the world.

15 See L. E. Goodman, "The Translation of Greek Materials into Arabic", *Cambridge History of Arabic Literature: Religion, Learning and Science in the 'Abbasid Period* (Cambridge, 1990): 487–91.

16 See S. Pines, "Razi Critique de Galien", *Actes du Septième Congrès International d'Histoire des Sciences* (Jerusalem, 1953): 480–7.

17 *The Philosophical Life*, trans. A. J. Arberry: 704; *Spiritual Physick*, trans. Arberry: 67.

18 *Munāẓarāt bayn al-rāziyayn*, in Kraus: 301: "*idh kāna'l-baḥth wa'l-naẓar wa'l-ijtihād yūjibu'l-ziyādah wa'l-faḍl*".

19 Al-Rāzī's interlocutor was Abū Ḥātim al-Rāzī (d. 322/933), chief lieutenant to the Ismā'īlī *dā'ī* of Rayy, and later *dā'ī* himself. He is credited with winning over Aḥmad ibn 'Alī, the governor of Rayy, to Ismā'īlism. He reports his debates with our al-Rāzī in *A'lām al-nubuwwah*, ed. Salah al-Sawy with an English introduction by S. H. Nasr (Tehran, 1977); extracts are translated by F. Brion, *Bulletin de Philosophie Médiévale*, 28 (1986): 134–62.

20 *Munāẓarāt*: 303: "*muqayyam 'alā al-ikhtilāfāt, muṣirr 'alā al-jahl wa'l-taqlīd.*"

21 *Munāẓarāt*, ed. Kraus: 295. Al-Rāzī's *The Tricks of the Prophets* or *Ruses of the Self-Styled Prophets*, cited in al-Bīrūnī: 17 (cf. Muṭahhar al-Maqdisī's *Kitāb al-Bad' wa'l-ta'rīkh*, ed. C. Huart, 4: 113), seems to have inspired later thinkers and fed the enlightenment interest in the theme of the Three Imposters. Al-Rāzī's contemporary, the heretical Shi'ite and quondam Mu'tazilite Ibn al-Rāwandī (d. *c.* 910) made an even broader attack on revealed religion, cloaking his critiques of prophetic miracles and even the inimitable style of the Qur'ān, under the thin veil of an ascription to the "Brahmins" – whose rejection of special prophecy was a staple of Islamic dogmatics.

22 Nāṣir-i Khusraw, in Kraus: 177; Arabic: 178. Al-Rāzī's realism about apparitions, his assumption that the something in fact is seen by prophets, echoes the Epicurean claim that the gods must be real, since men have seen them; *To Menoeceus*, in Diogenes Laertius, *Lives of the Eminent Philosophers*, 10.123–24; Cicero, *De natura deorum*, 1.46; for the veracity of the senses cannot be questioned (*Kyriae Doxai*, 24). But the claim that wicked spirits linger in the world, trapped by sensuality, is Platonic.

23 *Munāẓarāt*: 296. Restiveness here is *iḍṭirāb*; cf. the Epicurean idea of trouble or disturbance. Al-Rāzī brings his "democratic" or sensualist epistemology to the defence of absolute space, arguing from the untutored intuitions of the common man against the sophisticated sophisms of Aristotle on the relativity of space, as Pines points out in the *Dictionary of Scientific Biography*, *s.v.* al-Rāzī.

24 Cf. Najm al-Dīn al-Qazwīnī on Fakhr al-Dīn al-Rāzī's *Kitāb muḥaṣṣal afkār al-mutaqaddimīn wa'l-muta'akhirīn min al-'ulamā' wa'l-ḥukamā' al-mutakallimīn*, in Kraus: 203, where it is explained that for al-Rāzī matter is eternal but form is temporal and imparted.

25 Kraus: 282–3; see M. Mohaghegh, "Razī's *Kitāb al-'ilm al-ilāhī* and the Five Eternals", *Abr-Nahrain*, 13 (1973): 16–23; L. E. Goodman, "Rāzī's Myth of the Fall of the Soul: Its Function in his Philosophy", in G. Hourani (ed.), *Essays on Islamic Philosophy and Science* (Albany, 1975): 25–40.

26 This argument runs back to Parmenides and was used by Proclus (A.D. 410–85) in his eighteen arguments for the eternity of the world. Al-Rāzī had written a book against Proclus, clearly not satisfied with the responses of John Philoponus (sixth century), which had proved so welcome to al-Kindī and would be used by al-Ghazzālī and Maimonides, although rebutted by al-Fārābī.

27 See L. E. Goodman, *Avicenna* (London, 1992): 63, 79.

28 See Kraus: 265.

29 Al-Rāzī bit the bullet as to the substantiality of "space", sharply distinguishing space or the void from the Aristotelian "place", the outer boundary of a body: "Clearly time and space are not accidents but substances. For the void does not

subsist 'in' a body, since, if it did, it would be destroyed when that body was destroyed, as growth is destroyed with the destruction of that which grows" (Kraus: 198, ll. 20–1; cf. al-Rāzī's further arguments on p. 199).

30 *Allah's Commonwealth*: 371.

31 J. R. Partington, "The Chemistry of Rāzī", *Ambix*, 1 (1938): 193. Sal ammoniac is known to the Chinese sources from the second century C.E.

32 Cf. Cicero, *De divinatione*, 1.39.86: "You ask why everything happens. You have a perfect right to ask, but that is not the point at issue now. The question is, Does it happen, or does it not? For example, if I were to say that the magnet attracted iron and drew it to itself, and I could not tell you why, then I suppose you would utterly deny that the magnet had any such power. At least that is the course you pursue in regard to the existence of the power of divination, although it is established by our own experience and that of our forefathers."

33 Nāṣir-i-Khusraw, in Kraus: 172.

34 *Fihrist*, trans. Dodge: 703, 707–8.

35 See L. E. Goodman, "The Epicurean Ethic of Muḥammad b. Zakariyā' al-Rāzī", *Studia Islamica*, 34 (1971): 5–26.

36 Al-Rāzī's approach was not without its influence on far more traditional figures. Ibn al-Jawzī, for example, borrowed both the title and the organization of his own ascetically inclined *Ṭibb al-rūḥānī* from al-Rāzī.

37 *Spiritual Physick*, ed. Kraus: 22–3; cf. Arberry's rendering: 25. See Vatican Fragments 21, 25, 33, 35, 58–9, 67–9.

38 See Ibn Abī Uṣaybi'ah; Kraus: 139; cf. *ataraxia* in *Kyriae Doxai*, 3, and Saadiah on rest in the *Book of Critically Selected Beliefs and Convictions*, 10.16. For al-Rāzī's theory of pleasure, see L. E. Goodman, "Rāzī's Psychology", *Philosophical Forum*, 4 (1972): 26–48.

39 *Spiritual Physick*, chapter 5, trans Arberry: 39.

40 See Plato, *Phaedo*, 60a, *Phaedrus*, 258e, *Republic*, 9.583d; cf. *Philebus*, 42–3, 51–2; and the resolution at *Laws*, 1.644c; Epicurus, *Kyriae Doxai*, 3: "The magnitude of pleasure reaches its limit in the removal of all pain"; cf. Vatican Fragments, 14.

41 Plato, *Gorgias*, 492–3.

42 See Kraus: 143; Epicurus, *Kyriae Doxai*, 4.

43 Cf. Epicurus, Vatican Fragments, 63: "There is a limit even to simplicity, and one who ignores it is as much in error as one who goes too far."

44 Mehdi Mohaghegh, *Fīlsūf-i Rayy* (Tehran, 1970): 22, traces al-Rāzī's disparagement of the quest for rank to Galen's *On the Passions and Errors of the Soul* (Columbus, 1963), a work that al-Rāzī seems to have followed on a number of points. The rejection of a political life and the argument that the quest for rank finds no natural or inherent limit are both Epicurean, and this work may provide a key link between al-Rāzī's ethical calculus and that of Epicurus.

45 See Mohaghegh: 19.

46 Mohaghegh: 11 notes with amusement that Ibn al-Jawzī misread (or played upon?) *zamm*, "reining in", as *dhamm*, "censure or blame" and went on to use the phrase as the title of his well-known *Dhamm al-hawā* ("The Censure of Passion").

47 See *Guide*, 3.12, citing al-Rāzī's *Theology*; see *Rambam* (New York, 1976), 287; Saadiah had absorbed the Rāzīan line of argument.

48 *Eight Chapters*, 4, trans. L. E. Goodman, *Rambam*, 227.

49 Al-Rāzī cites and summarizes Galen's *Good Men Profit by their Enemies* and *How a Man may Discover his own Vices* in *Spiritual Physick*, chapter 4; Kraus: 35. As Walzer pointed out (*Encyclopaedia of Islam* (Leiden), *s.v. akhlāq*) the two Galenic titles represent parts of Galen's *On Moral Character*; but they circulated as independent works in Arabic and were used by Ibn Miskawayh as well as al-Rāzī; see Mohaghegh: 13–14.

50 See L. E. Goodman, "The Epicurean Ethic of al-Rāzī": 17.

51 *Spiritual Physick*, chapter 11, trans. Arberry: 67.

52 *Spiritual Physick*, chapter 5, trans. Arberry: 38.

53 *Spiritual Physick*, chapter 2, trans. Arberry: 24.

54 *Spiritual Physick*, chapter 6, trans. Arberry: 85.

55 Al-Rāzī, like most Arabic writers, including Saadiah after him, clearly distinguishes the erotic dalliances of romantic love from coitus *per se*; see L. E. Goodman, "Saadya's Ethical Pluralism", *Journal of the American Oriental Society*, 100 (1980): 407–19, "The Sacred and the Secular: Rival Themes in Arabic Literature", in M. Mir (ed.) *The Literary Heritage of Islam: Studies in Honor of James Bellamy* (Princeton, 1993): 287–330.

56 "The pleasures of love never did anyone any good, and one is lucky if they do him no harm" (Epicurus, Vatican Fragments, 51; cf. Lucretius, *De rerum natura*, 4.1056–191).

57 *Spiritual Physick*, chapter 5, trans. Arberry: 48; similarly with gluttony in chapter 13, trans. Arberry: 76–7.

58 *Spiritual Physick*, chapter 14; al-Rāzī's word for an addict is *mudmin*, Kraus: 23, ll. 1, 2.

59 *Spiritual Physick*, chapter 16, ed. Kraus: 79; trans. Arberry: 86.

60 See al-Rāzī's extracts from Rufus of Ephesus, in F. Rosenthal, *The Classical Heritage in Islam* (London, 1965): 198–200.

61 *Spiritual Physick*, ed. Kraus: 93, trans. Arberry: 103; cf. *Kyriae Doxai*, 11–12, 30.

62 *Spiritual Physick*, ed. Kraus: 93, trans. Arberry: 103; cf. Epicurus, *Kyriae Doxai*, 2.

63 Al-Kindī "Essay on How to Banish Sorrow", ed. with Italian trans. by H. Ritter and R. Walzer, in *Uno scritto morale inedito di al-Kindī* (Rome, 1938); cf. *Spiritual Physick*, chapters 11–12. Note al-Rāzī's use of al-Kindī's term *daf'*, banishing or repelling, in the titles of these chapters.

64 *Apology*, 42: "Now it is time that we were going. I to die and you to live, but which of us has the happier prospect is unknown to anyone but God."

65 Indeed al-Rāzī relies on transmigration for the only acceptable justification of the slaughter of domestic animals. For, consistent with his hedonism, he regards the pain of brutes as morally decisive – justifiable only for the alleviation or prevention of greater pain. Thus hunting is acceptable only if directed against carnivores, whose nature leads them to cause more pain than they will suffer; abuse or overwork of domestic animals, only, for some greater good, as, for example, when a horse is spurred on to save a human life, preferably that of a learned, good or useful human being; but slaughter of domestic animals for meat, only because it facilitates the deliverance of their souls to a higher stage.

66 *Spiritual Physick*, chapter 20, ed. Kraus: 92–4; trans. Arberry: 103–5.

CHAPTER 14

Al-ʿĀmirī

Everett K. Rowson

In its methodological sophistication, its metaphysical elaboration and its distinctive approach to the problem of revealed religion, the thought of al-Fārābī represents not only an advance on that of al-Kindī but a break with it. The cumulative achievements of the Baghdad translators, and in particular the intellectual discipline of the Baghdad philosophical school led by al-Fārābī's teacher Mattā ibn Yūnus, would seem to relegate the earlier al-Kindī to the role of a primitive initiator, enjoying some historical importance but little if any abiding philosophical influence. That such was not the case, however, is clear from the works of his most prominent epigone, the Khurasanian philosopher Abu'l-Ḥasan Muḥammad ibn Yūsuf al-ʿĀmirī (d. 381/992).

Of al-Kindī's immediate pupils we know relatively little, and only two of them can be said to be more than shadows. Aḥmad ibn al-Ṭayyib al-Sarakhsī (d. 286/899) was a prolific author of philosophical, scientific and literary works who enjoyed the patronage of the caliph al-Muʿtaḍid but was subsequently imprisoned and then executed for political offences; none of his works appears to be extant, and we have no direct evidence for any of his students.[1] Somewhat better known is the Khurasanian Abū Zayd al-Balkhī (d. 322/934), who, after studying for some years with al-Kindī in Iraq, returned to his native Balkh, where he wrote extensively in many fields, including philosophy, science and literary topics, as well as religion and theology.[2] Modern scholars have been chiefly aware of al-Balkhī's influential geographical work, but a treatise on medicine and ethics, entitled *Sustenance for Body and Soul*, has also been preserved.[3] The legacy of al-Kindī was carried on in the following generation by two known pupils of al-Balkhī, the obscure Ibn Farīghūn,[4] author of a *Compendium of the Sciences*,[5] and al-ʿĀmirī.

Like al-Balkhī, al-ʿĀmirī was a native of eastern Iran, and spent most of his life there. As he died only in 381/992, he must have been a very young man when he studied with his aged master, and it was only some two decades after the latter's death that he set out for the West, spending some five years in Rayy, at the court of the Būyid vizier Ibn al-ʿAmīd (d. 360/970), a patron of philosophers who also employed Ibn Miskawayh (d. 421/1030) as his librarian. From Rayy al-ʿĀmirī made at least two visits to Baghdad, where he came into contact with the philosophers of the local school, now led by the Christian Yaḥyā ibn ʿAdī (d. 364/974); but according to al-Tawḥīdī (d. 414/1023), the brilliant and sardonic chronicler of intellectual life in the city at this time, al-ʿĀmirī was not well received by his Baghdad colleagues, who treated him as an unsophisticated provincial, and he soon retreated to the more congenial society of the East. In his later years al-ʿĀmirī enjoyed the favour of prominent figures in the Sāmānid realm of Khurasan and Transoxania, and resided both in the dynasty's capital, Bukhara, and its leading city, Nishapur, where he died in 381/992.[6]

The titles of some twenty-five of al-ʿĀmirī's works are known, and of these six (or seven, depending on a contested attribution) are extant and have been published.[7] With the possible exception of Ibn Miskawayh, then, al-ʿĀmirī is the best-documented Muslim philosopher from the half century between al-Fārābī and Ibn Sīnā. That he perceived himself as continuing a Kindī "school" is clear not only from his own explicit statements – he praises al-Kindī and al-Balkhī, contrasting their thought with the "ravings" of Abū Bakr al-Rāzī (d. 313/925) and avoiding any mention of al-Fārābī or other Baghdad philosophers[8] – but also from both the range and content of his oeuvre. We have fragmentary evidence for his commentaries on parts, at least, of the Aristotelian *Organon*, and some titles which suggest direct treatment of topics in Aristotelian and Neoplatonic physics and metaphysics, as well as other titles concerned – like many of al-Kindī's and al-Balkhī's works – with such non-philosophical subjects as medicine, horticulture and good manners. But it is striking that in his extant works al-ʿĀmirī is concerned above all to show how philosophy can be applied to questions of a theological nature, and how philosophy and Islam can be not only reconciled but treated as complementary avenues to truth. It is in this approach, and in his relatively conservative treatment of Islam itself, that al-ʿĀmirī shows himself to be a true Kindian.

Perhaps the most eloquent testimony to al-ʿĀmirī's views on reason and revelation is his best-known work, *An Exposition on the Merits of Islam.*[9] Addressing himself to a lay audience, he argues in this work for a rational investigation of religious belief and praxis, and, on the basis of his claim that the ultimate purpose of knowledge is virtuous action, attempts in a programmatic comparison of Islam with other religions to show how Islam is more successful than its rivals at achieving this goal. In his introductory chapters, al-ʿĀmirī reviews the utility of both the secular sciences – represented by the quadrivium – and the religious sciences – Tradition, Law and Theology – and defends the value of each of these two kinds of knowledge against attacks from adherents of the other; he further insists on the equal validity of each of the religious sciences, supporting the study of Law against conservative traditionists, of Theology against conservative jurisprudents and of Tradition against rationalizing jurisprudents and theologians. Singled out by him for particular criticism are certain philosophers, pseudo-sophisticates and "esoterists" (by which he means certain Ismāʿīlī circles) who claim that the sufficiently enlightened can dispense with observance of religious duties. In general, al-ʿĀmirī maintains the superiority of the religious to the secular sciences; while reason can testify to the validity of revelatory knowledge, prophets are superior to sages. He then devotes individual chapters of this book to showing Islam's superiority to Christianity, Judaism, Magianism and Manichaeism with respect to belief, ritual, political organization, social structure and intellectual endeavour, and in an appendix defends Islam against attacks on its purported approval of violence, its factionalism, the ambiguity of its Scripture and its problematic claim to having been prefigured in Jewish and Christian Scripture.

There is an apparent reference to this work in an account by al-Tawḥīdī of a celebrated altercation between al-Maqdisī, a member of the Brethren of Purity (Ikhwān al-Ṣafāʾ, see next chapter), and the religious conservative al-Jarīrī, in which the latter's arguments point up the basic difference in attitude towards the revealed religion between members of the Kindī school and the Baghdad philosophers.[10] Attacking the Brethren for their attempt to harmonize philosophy with the religious law, al-Jarīrī refers to previous attempts to do something of a similar nature, giving three specific examples: Abū Zayd al-Balkhī, who compared philosophy and the *Sharīʿah* to a mother and a wet-nurse, Abū Tammām al-Nīsābūrī, an obscure philosopher with Ismāʿīlī ties, and al-ʿĀmirī, whom al-Jarīrī describes as persecuted for his godless views, forced to seek sanctuary with Ibn al-ʿAmīd, and attempting to gain favour with the masses by writing books in support of Islam. In this same passage, al-Tawḥīdī depicts his master, Abū Sulaymān al-Sijistānī of the Baghdad school of philosophy, as equally opposed to the kind of harmonization envisaged by the Brethren, albeit for reasons very different from those of al-Jarīrī: in contradistinction to such philosophers as al-Balkhī and al-ʿĀmirī, the interconfessional Baghdad school found it in their interest to keep their philosophical discussions as far away from the domain of revealed religion as possible.

Besides his general defence of Islam, al-ʿĀmirī also applied philosophical arguments to specific theological questions, as can be seen most clearly from his discussion of the fate of the individual soul after death in his book *On the Afterlife*.[11] Relying heavily on a lost Neoplatonic commentary on Plato's *Phaedo*, al-ʿĀmirī reproduces in this work a series of standard arguments for the immortality of the soul, accompanied by a survey of Aristotelian psychology as modified in the Alexandrian Neoplatonic tradition. Granting that the pagan Greek philosophers did not acknowledge the resurrection of the body, although they accepted both the immortality of the soul and its reward and punishment in the afterlife, al-ʿĀmirī presents the Qur'ānic revelation concerning the Garden and the Fire as a necessary supplement to philosophical analysis, providing crucial information inaccessible to the unaided human intellect, but retains a prudent agnosticism about the exact form of bodily resurrection. In the introductory chapters of this work he offers a survey of early Greek philosophy, summarizing the lives and opinions of Empedocles, Pythagoras, Socrates, Plato and Aristotle, and asserting historical connections between the prophetic and philosophical traditions; these chapters proved to be the single most influential piece of all of al-ʿĀmirī's work, reappearing in some form in most of the major doxographies of the following centuries.

In another pair of works, al-ʿĀmirī applies Aristotelian and Neoplatonic concepts to the fraught question of free will and predestination. *The Deliverance of Mankind from the Problem of Predestination and Free Will*,[12] the earlier of the two, focuses on this question as formulated by Islamic theologians, but attempts to resolve it through an analysis of Aristotelian causation; the conclusion is presented as a "middle path" between the two extremes, and identified with a celebrated pronouncement by Abū Ḥanīfah denying both divine compulsion (*jabr*) and unrestricted human delegation of power (*tafwīḍ*). Here, as elsewhere in al-ʿĀmirī's writings, his theological affiliation seems to be essentially Māturīdite; the Muʿtazilites are occasionally attacked by name, the Ashʿarites more obliquely by doctrine but anonymously. In this work al-ʿĀmirī also explicitly reiterates a fundamental doctrine of al-Kindī, identifying God's act of creation *ex nihilo* (*ibdāʿ*) as a unique form of causation, distinct from and superior to the four Aristotelian causes. In his later *Determination of the Various Aspects of Predestination*[13] he repeats many of these arguments, but treats the entire question in a more purely philosophical way, relying particularly on Aristotle's discussion of chance in the *Physics*.

An ostensibly more technical work, *Vision and the Visible*,[14] is primarily devoted to reviewing various Greek theories in optics and the physiology of vision; yet here again al-ʿĀmirī shows his concern with theological questions, launching into a spirited attack on theological occasionalism, and framing the entire discussion with two laments on the anti-intellectualism of the present day.

While various aspects of al-ʿĀmirī's philosophical tenets emerge in all these works, the only extant example of something approximating an exposition of a philosophical system is his *Chapters on Metaphysical Topics*,[15] which consists primarily of a paraphrase of the celebrated *Liber de causis*, itself a reworking of Proclus' *Elements of Theology*. While recognizing, like al-Kindī, the basic hypostases of Plotinian Neoplatonism, al-ʿĀmirī's system lacks both the complexities of Proclean *henads* and the cascading intellects associated with the celestial spheres which are found in al-Fārābī and Ibn Sīnā. His concentration on the hypostasis of Soul, its intermediary position in the universe and the ethical consequences of this position, is most comparable to what we find in the ethical works of his contemporary Ibn Miskawayh, with whom he undoubtedly shared some basic sources.

Although he rarely cites Greek philosophers or their works by name, al-ʿĀmirī clearly had access to a wide range of translated Greek materials, particularly pseudonymous ones. Besides the *De causis*, he quotes passages from the *Theology of Aristotle*, the *Liber de pomo*, and the bizarre doxography of pseudo-Ammonius, and the influence of other, unidentifiable works is detectable throughout his *œuvre*. The span of Greek sources at his command would be increased even more if we could be sure of his authorship of the work entitled *On Happiness and its Creation in Human Life*,[16] a major doxography of ethical and political thought in which extensive citations from Plato and Aristotle, as well as various pre-Socratics and later Greek philosophers, are juxtaposed with others from Sassanian wisdom literature and from the Qur'ān and *Ḥadīth*, major Islamic religious figures and Arabic poets, to form a coherent disquisition on happiness in both the individual and the polity.

Al-ʿĀmirī's interpretation of Greek philosophy as a whole, and his particular brand of Neoplatonism, can be widely paralleled in works by his contemporaries, in particular Ibn Miskawayh and, with reservations, the Brethren of Purity; but, in his particular concern to convince the religiously committed of the acceptability and utility of this philosophy, he appears to be the last representative of a trend initiated by al-Kindī. To the extent a reconciliation between philosophy and Islam of enduring influence was to be achieved, it was on a very different basis, that of the thought of another Khurasanian philosopher from the next generation, Ibn Sīnā. Ibn Sīnā had little use for any of his predecessors, with the exception of al-Fārābī, and he attacked the Kindians in general as well as al-ʿĀmirī by name;[17] whether, and in what ways, al-ʿĀmirī's thought may nevertheless have contributed to Ibn Sīnā's new synthesis is a question in need of further investigation.

NOTES

1 See Franz Rosenthal, *Aḥmad b. aṭ-Ṭayyib as-Sarasẖsī* (New Haven, 1943).
2 See *Encyclopaedia of Islam*, new edition (Leiden and London, 1954), *s.v.* "al-Balkhī, Abū Zayd"; E. K. Rowson, "The Philosopher as Littérateur: al-Tawḥīdī and His Predecessors", *Zeitschrift für Geschichte der Arabisch-Islamischen Wissenschaften*, 6 (1990): 50–92.
3 *Maṣāliḥ al-abdān wa'l-anfus*, facsimile edition (Frankfurt am Main, 1984).
4 See *Encyclopaedia of Islam*, new edition, Supplement, *s.v.* "Ibn Farīghūn".
5 Ibn Farī'ūn, *Jawāmi' al-'ulūm*, facsimile edition (Frankfurt am Main, 1985).
6 For al-'Āmirī's biography, see Everett K. Rowson, *A Muslim Philosopher on the Soul and Its Fate: al-'Āmirī's Kitāb al-Amad 'alā l-abad* (New Haven, 1988): 3–7, and Joel L. Kraemer, *Humanism in the Renaissance of Islam: The Cultural Revival during the Būyid Age* (Leiden, 1986): 233–41.
7 Al-'Āmirī's works are surveyed in Rowson, *A Muslim Philosopher*: 7–17, and M. Minovi, "Az Khazā'in-i Turkīyya", *Majalla-yi Dānishkāda-yi Adabiyyāt, Dānishgāh-i Tehrān*, 4, 2 (1954): 75.
8 Rowson, *A Muslim Philosopher*: 76–7.
9 *Al-I'lām bi-manāqib al-Islām*, ed. A. Ghorab (Cairo, 1967).
10 Al-Tawḥīdī, *al-Imtā' wa'l-mu'ānasah*, ed. A. Amīn and A. al-Zayn (Cairo, 1953), 2: 13–23; see Joel L. Kraemer, *Philosophy in the Renaissance of Islam: Abū Sulaymān al-Sijistānī and His Circle* (Leiden, 1986): 230–43; *Humanism*: 168–74, 237f.; Rowson, *A Muslim Philosopher*: 22–4.
11 *Al-Amad 'ala'l-abad*, in E. K. Rowson, *A Muslim Philosopher*.
12 *Inqādh al-bashar min al-jabr wa'l-qadar*, ed. S. Khalīfāt, *Rasā'il Abī'l-Ḥasan al-'Āmirī wa-shadharātuhu'l-falsafiyyah* (Amman, 1988): 247–71.
13 *Al-Taqrīr li-awjuh al-taqdīr*, ed. S. Khalīfāt, *op. cit.*: 301–41.
14 *Al-Qawl fi'l-ibṣār wa'l-mubṣar*, ed. S. Khalīfāt, *op. cit.*: 409–31.
15 *Fuṣūl fi'l-ma'ālim al-ilāhiyyah*, ed. S. Khalīfāt, *op. cit.*: 361–79; see also E. K. Rowson, "An Unpublished Work by al-'Āmirī and the Date of the Arabic *De causis*", *Journal of the American Oriental Society*, 104 (1984): 193–9.
16 *Al-Sa'ādah wa'l-is'ād*, facsimile of copy by M. Minovi (Wiesbaden, 1957–8); for the problem of attribution, see Rowson, *A Muslim Philosopher*: 15–17.
17 See Dimitri Gutas, *Avicenna and the Aristotelian Tradition* (Leiden, 1988): 292.

CHAPTER 15

The Brethren of Purity (Ikhwān al-Ṣafā')

Ian Richard Netton

INTRODUCTION: THE CAULDRON OF SYNCRETISM

The Brethren of Purity, or Ikhwān al-Ṣafā' as they are called in Arabic, hold a certain place in the affections and interests of those who have studied the intellectual development of Arabic and Islamic thought. They are particularly beloved by the Ismā'īlīs who claim them as their own (see Netton (1982): 95–104). They continue to intrigue because of the synthetic quality of their thought and the mystery of their identity and place of origin. This chapter will concentrate principally on the former and only briefly refer to the latter. Their thought is indeed worthy of more than superficial study, for the Brethren are as famed in the Middle East as Hegel, Kant and Voltaire in the West. Their self-designation as "Sleepers in the cave of our father Adam" (*R*, 4: 18), clearly deriving from the Qur'ān and the Seven Sleepers of Ephesus legend, certainly reflects the mystery of their identity. And while there are some things that do remain unclear about their thought – for example, were they, or were they not, Ismā'īlīs? – there is much that may be said with satisfaction and positive conviction about that thought. In particular, while it would be unfair and unjust to characterize it as a total syncretism, there is no doubting the impact of the ideas of Plato, Aristotle, and especially Plotinus, on the philosophy of the Brethren of Purity. Such elements will be surveyed in this chapter.

A useful starting point in any analysis of this philosophy is the City of Basrah in southern Iraq. Like that philosophy it was – and is – open to much outside contact and influence. In the forefront of the news in recent times because of the 1980s Iran–Iraq War and the 1991 Persian

Gulf War, it was famed in the Middle Ages as a cradle of Arabic philology. It was home to a huge variety of immigrants from areas as diverse as Sind, India and Malaya. Its commercial and financial acumen made it the medieval equivalent of London or Tokyo today with all the cosmopolitan overtones which mention of such cities implies. And we start with reference to the city of Basrah because most scholars believe that this was the Brethren's home. "The rest", as I have put it elsewhere, "must be conjecture. Arabic sources differ over their individual names and perhaps it is a successful measure of the secrecy which they sought for themselves in their age that we know so little about their lives in our own. Like the deserted camp of the beloved in early Arabic poetry, the traces of their passage have become faint and shadowy" (Netton (1982): 1).

We will not, therefore, agonize here over the precise identities of these philosophers, nor their Age beyond situating them loosely in the tenth or eleventh century A.D. We may, however, with some certainty, reject from the start the extraordinary idea that the real author of the writings of the Brethren of Purity, their *Epistles* (*Rasā'il*), was the fourth Islamic Caliph 'Alī ibn Abī Ṭālib (d. 40/661), or the sixth Imām Ja'far al-Ṣādiq (d. 148/765).

The Brethren of Purity produced as their *magnum opus* what was gathered into a veritable encyclopedia, a corpus of fifty-two *Epistles* of varying length and quality which survey a huge range of subjects ranging from music to magic. They are heavily didactic in tone and highly eclectic in content, providing both a pedagogical and a cultural mirror of their Age and its diverse philosophies and creeds. The *Epistles* themselves neatly divide into four main parts: fourteen focus on the mathematical sciences, seventeen deal with the natural sciences, ten with the psychological and intellectual sciences, and eleven conclude the latest four-volume Arabic edition by concentrating on what are called metaphysics or the theological sciences. A key aspect of the *Epistles* is its central section featuring a long debate between humans and delegates from the animal kingdom; this fills much of the twenty-second *Epistle* which goes by the name of *On How the Animals and their Kinds are Formed* (Netton (1982): 2). It has been magisterially surveyed, analysed and translated by L. E. Goodman (1978).

Seyyed Hossein Nasr (1978: 39) has warned that "the sources of the Ikhwān should not, however, be considered solely as historical texts". He translates part of a passage (*R*, 4: 42), in which "they themselves inform the reader of the universality of their sources, which include Revelation and Nature in addition to written texts", as follows:

> We have drawn our knowledge from four books. The first is composed of the mathematical and natural sciences established by the sages and philosophers. The second consists of the revealed

> books of the Torah, the Gospels and the Qur'ān and the other Tablets brought by the prophets through angelic Revelation. The third is the books of Nature which are the ideas [*ṣuwar*] in the Platonic sense of the forms [*ashkāl*] of creatures actually existing, from the composition of the celestial spheres, the division of the Zodiac, the movement of the stars, and so on . . . to the transformation of the elements, the production of the members of the mineral, plant and animal kingdoms and the rich variety of human industry . . . The fourth consists of the Divine books which touch only the purified men and which are the angels who are in intimacy with the chosen beings, the noble and the purified souls . . .

We should not, therefore, lose sight of the sheer diversity of source material drawn upon by the Brethren of Purity, even though in this chapter we will restrict ourselves to the more "philosophical" elements of those sources. Moreover, all that follows presupposes a background or, to put it another way, a cauldron of syncretism, a Middle Eastern milieu familiar with the thought of both Aristotle and Plotinus which it absorbs but dresses in its own forms, not without some change, from much (but by no means all) of the translated Aristotelian corpus. We note, finally, the existence in the background of pseudo-Aristotelian texts, like the notorious *Theologia Aristotelis*, which had far more in common with the philosophy of Plotinus than that of the Stagirite (see Netton (1989): 12–13). With all this, it is small wonder that the *Epistles* of the Brethren of Purity have been characterized as syncretic.

PYTHAGORAS: PHILOSOPHY AND NUMBER

Even the most cursory reading of the *Epistles* highlights the Brethren's devotion to number. It is good that one study mathematics and number before other (higher) branches of knowledge like physics, logic and divinity (*R*, 1: 49). The Brethren held "the Pythagorean belief that the nature of created things accords with the nature of number" and stated: "This is the school of thought [*madhhab*] of our Ikhwān" (Netton (1982): 10). They also followed the Pythagoreans in their devotion to *certain* numbers: in particular the Brethren manifested a particular reverence for the number four, a reverence which transcended the sphere of pure mathematics: they drew attention, for example, to the four seasons, four winds, four directions and four Empedoclean elements. There were four natures and four humours. The lute had four strings and even matter was divisible into four types. The reasoning behind such veneration for this particular number is not hard to find: God created "most things in groups of four and . . . natural matters are arranged in fours principally to correspond to, or harmonise with, the four spiritual principles which rank above them, consisting of the Creator, the Universal Intellect, the Universal Soul and Prime Matter" (Netton (1982): 11).

For the Brethren one could learn about God's unity by knowing something of number and they stated that Pythagoras held that the second led to the first (*R*, 3: 200). Yet with all their devotion to number the Brethren managed to avoid the prime Pythagorean error, noted by Aristotle, in which a number and the thing(s) numbered were confused. They also rejected Pythagorean notions of transmigration, holding rather that purification achieved in a single life on earth gained humans admission to Paradise (Netton (1982): 12–14).

PLATO: PHILOSOPHY AND THE HERO

Despite some references there is no deep discussion of, or involvement with, the Platonic Forms or "Ideas" (*ideai*) in the *Epistles* of the Brethren of Purity. These *Epistles* can in no way be described as Platonic. What the Brethren do stress very powerfully, however, is their conception of the Platonic philosopher as hero. In passages which show some familiarity with at least the outlines of the *Phaedo* and *Crito* dialogues, Socrates is held up for admiration and respect as a great philosopher who knows how to die bravely. It is also interesting that the Brethren orient their description of Socrates' death scene towards their own doctrines. Terminology is put into Socrates' mouth which is heavily reminiscent of the Brethren's own chosen hierarchy (Netton (1982): 16–19). Plato's own view that the body was an impediment to the achieving of spiritual perfection was also shared by the Brethren of Purity, but the latter rejected Plato's epistemology with its suspicion of sensory perception. The Brethren "explain carefully that the method of instruction should be through the senses, then by the intellect and finally by logical deduction; but without the senses one can know nothing" (*R*, 3: 424). The contrast between this view and that of Plato could not be more apparent (Netton (1982): 17–18).

ARISTOTLE: PHILOSOPHY, DEFINITION AND STRUCTURE

Loosely speaking, from a philosophical point of view, we can say that the *Epistles* of the Brethren of Purity rest on twin foundations: Aristotelianism and Neoplatonism. What must be enunciated and stressed right at the beginning however, in any coverage of either the Aristotelianism or the Neoplatonism of the Brethren is that they used the doctrines of Aristotle and Plotinus and shaped them in accordance with their own beliefs, not always producing a hybrid which either Aristotle or Plotinus would have recognized.

That the Brethren respected Aristotle is not hard to prove. Quite apart from the influence of the Stagirite on the content and terminology of their *Epistles*, the Brethren produced "a story about Muḥammad in which the Prophet claims that, had Aristotle lived to know the Islamic message brought by him, the Greek philosopher would have undoubtedly been converted to Islam" (*R*, 4: 179; Netton (1982): 19).

Apart from direct references to, and *Epistles* based upon, several of Aristotle's major treatises (see especially Netton (1982): 115 n. 79), the primary contribution of Aristotle to the writings of the Brethren was in the field of metaphysical terminology, an area frequently invaded by the terminology of Neoplatonism. Thus we find substance and accident, matter and form, potentiality and actuality, and many other Aristotelian terms being peddled throughout the text of the Brethren. Two examples must suffice here of the way in which the basic terms of Aristotle were Neoplatonized: the first relates to Aristotle's Classical four causes:

> Of the four causes of plants, two are recognizably Aristotelian: the material cause of plants is the . . . four elements while the final cause is the provision of nourishment for animals; but the efficient cause is the powers of the Universal Soul and the formal cause is linked with astral reasons involving a lengthy explanation.
>
> (*R*, 2: 155; Netton (1982): 25)

My second example illustrates what the Brethren did with Aristotle's categories. If hierarchy, division and emanation may be said to be the key features of Neoplatonism, then the first two at least are apparent in full measure in the following:

> substance divided first into its corporeal [*jusmānī*] and spiritual [*rūḥānī*] aspects. Corporeal substance then further divided into that which pertained to the celestial sphere [*falakī*] and the natural sphere [*ṭabīʿī*], and so on outwards until a final division into animals born from the womb, those born from an egg, and those born from decayed matter, was reached. Quantity [*kamm*] was similarly divided into the separate [*munfaṣil*] and the linked [*muttaṣil*].
>
> (*R*, 1: 408–9; Netton (1982): 37)

Most extraordinary perhaps of the metamorphoses which overtake Aristotle's terms is the following, in which form is described in terms of substance:

> The Ikhwān wrote: Know that form [*al-ṣūrah*] is of two kinds: constituting [*muqawwimah*] and completing [*mutammimah*]. The scholars called constituting forms substances [*jawāhir*] and completing forms accidents [*a'rāḍ*].
>
> (*R*, 1: 401; Netton (1982): 45)

PLOTINUS: PHILOSOPHY, EMANATION AND HIERARCHY

The principal focal point in any study of the *Rasā'il* or *Epistles* of the Brethren of Purity must be their Neoplatonism which pervades the entire text. A survey of the Brethren's use of the main features of this doctrine will therefore here conclude this chapter.

Both emanation and hierarchy, those key features of classical Neoplatonism, figure prominently in the thought of the Brethren of Purity. Making use of a sun simile, which has analogies with an earlier comparison employed by Plotinus, the Brethren tell

> how the generosity and virtues which were in God emanated [*afāḍah*] from Him "by the necessity of wisdom [*bi-wājib al-ḥikmah*]" in the same fashion that light and brightness emanated from the eye of the sun. The first product of this unbroken emanation [*fayḍ*] was called the Active Intellect, from which emanated, in turn, the Passive Intellect [*al-'Aql al-munfa'il*] or Universal Soul; from the latter emanated Prime Matter.
>
> (Netton (1982): 35)

However, a major difference between Plotinus and the Brethren of Purity is instantly perceptible in the latter's hierarchy of being. Plotinus postulated a relatively "simple" structure, at least in its composition if not in its theological elaboration, of One, Intellect and Soul. The Brethren enlarged this hierarchy of being into a ninefold emanationist structure comprising:

The Creator

↓

The Intellect

↓

The Soul

↓

Prime Matter

↓

Nature

↓

The Absolute Body

↓

The Sphere

↓

The Four Elements

↓

The Beings of this World
(mineral, plant & animal)

(*R*, 1: 54, *R*, 3: 56, 181)

It seems that in such complexity and multiplication of hypostases, the spirits of the later Neoplatonic masters like Iamblichus (*c*. A.D. 250–*c*. 326) and Proclus (A.D. 412–85) are abroad. And it is clear from the briefest study of the *Epistles* of the Brethren of Purity that the concepts of emanation and hierarchy dominate the entire text in a profound and penetrating fashion, even invading and "Neoplatonizing" Aristotle's own categories (see Netton (1982): 36–7). As for their view of God, it is obvious that the Brethren perceived Him in two different and unharmonized ways: on the one hand, God takes on many of the classical Neoplatonic characteristics like unknowableness; on the other, elsewhere in the text, He is the traditional Qur'ānic Deity, acting in a recognizable Islamic fashion. No specific attempt is made by the Brethren to reconcile what are often opposing or contradictory views of Divinity (see Netton (1982): 39–42).

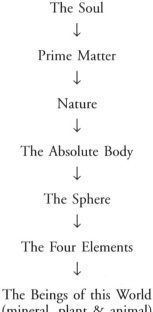

The Neoplatonism of the *Epistles* produced by the Brethren of Purity cannot be overemphasized. Its permeation of these writings, together with the Aristotelian and other elements, makes their corpus one of the most syncretic known in the history of the intellectual development of Islamic thought. That said however, we must not leave their writings giving the impression that they constitute a total unoriginal syncretism and nothing else. The *Epistles* are not simply a sum total of influences and no more. The reality is much more subtle, as I hope will be apparent from the concluding paragraphs. The syncretism probably explains some of the contradictions in their text; but their intention highlights their true originality.

What the Brethren of Purity were really intent upon, and the goal towards which they employed every Islamic and un-Islamic doctrine which they could muster, was salvation to be achieved by purification in this life. As I have summarized it elsewhere:

> They were Neoplatonic teachers intent on, and infatuated with, the propagation of a doctrine of purity, achieved through asceticism, self-denial and righteous living, as a passport for entry to the Islamic Heaven. The pillars of this doctrine were tolerance, mutual help [*taʿāwun*] and a philosophy of eclecticism *which utilised any text* which might bolster their own teaching.
>
> (my italics: Netton (1982): 108)

Were the Brethren of Purity really Muslims? The point can be argued both ways and must depend on how exclusivist or inclusivist an image one has of the Islamic religion anyway (see Netton (1982): 106). Perhaps a neat way of characterizing them, or summing them up, is to describe the Brethren as "Wisdom Muslims" (Netton (1981): 67). They had an immense veneration for knowledge and wisdom. Revering the intellect they often despised the body in a truly ascetic and Platonic fashion (*ibid.*: 66). Their desire for thoroughness in thought, and support for their ideas, led them to a thorough eclecticism which sometimes embraced the Christian and the Indian as well as the further reaches of mathematics. Were they really philosophers or mere intellectual magpies without a system? If one defines a philosopher according to the actual etymological sense of that word, then the answer must be a resounding "yes". They may not have produced a single "tidy" system but neither did Wittgenstein! Their text may appear sometimes to be shot through with contradictions but there is no doubting that it is underpinned by a genuine philosophical and theological stance, that of salvation via asceticism and wisdom.

REFERENCES

Goodman, Lenn Evan (1978) *The Case of the Animals versus Man Before the King of the Jinn: a Tenth-century Ecological Fable of the Pure Brethren of Basra* (Boston).

Nasr, Seyyed Hossein (1978) *An Introduction to Islamic Cosmological Doctrines*, rev. ed. (London).

Netton, Ian Richard (1981) "Foreign Influences and Recurring Ismā'īlī Motifs in the *Rasā'il* of the Brethren of Purity", in Alessandro Bausani (ed.) *Convegno sugli Ikhwān Aṣ-Ṣafā' (Roma, 25–26 Ottobre 1979)* (Rome): 49–67.

—— (1982) *Muslim Neoplatonists: an Introduction to the Thought of the Brethren of Purity (Ikhwān al-Ṣafā')* (London); paperback edition: Edinburgh, 1991 (Islamic Surveys no. 19).

—— (1989) *Allāh Transcendent: Studies in the Structure and Semiotics of Islamic Philosophy, Theology and Cosmology* (London).

R (1957) *Rasā'il Ikhwān al-Ṣafā'* ["Epistles of the Brethren of Purity"], 4 vols (Beirut).

CHAPTER 16

Ibn Sīnā

Shams Inati

LIFE AND WORKS

Ibn Sīnā, Avicenna (370/980–429/1037),[1] also known as al-Shaykh al-Ra'īs ("Master and Head"), is among the very few medieval Muslim thinkers to have written an autobiography, which was completed by his student Abū 'Ubayd al-Jūzjānī.[2] This autobiography/biography was later transmitted by a number of biographers, including al-Bayhaqī (d. 565/1170), al-Qifṭī (d. 646/1248), Ibn Abī Uṣaybi'ah (d. 669/1270) and Ibn Khallikān (d. 680/1282).[3]

Ibn Sīnā was born in Afshanah (a small village neighbouring Bukhara, the capital of the Sāmānid dynasty), where his father 'Abd Allāh, originally from Balkh, met and married Sitārah. They had three sons, 'Alī, al-Ḥusayn (Ibn Sīnā) and Maḥmūd. When Ibn Sīnā was about five years of age, the family moved to Bukhara. There the father was appointed governor of Kharmayathnah, a village in the suburbs of Bukhara.

The rest of the story of Ibn Sīnā's life, education and career is well known, and there is no need to recount it here in detail. Suffice it to say that the most striking features of this story, as he and al-Jūzjānī tell it, are (1) his completing the study of the Qur'ān and Islamic literature by the age of ten and the rest of the sciences, including Islamic law, astronomy, medicine, logic and philosophy, by the age of eighteen, and (2) his enormous productivity in spite of the unstable political conditions under which he lived that forced him at times to flee from one territory to another, to move in disguise and even to be imprisoned. His great achievement in the various branches of learning seems to have resulted from a rare memory that enabled him to retain by heart, for example, the Qur'ān and Aristotle's *Metaphysics*; a high intellectual curiosity that helped him consider and solve difficult problems even in his sleep;[4] and an inner determination that generated extraordinary physical and intellectual energy. The number of works he wrote (estimated to be between 100 and 250),[5] the quality of his work and his other involvement in medical practice, teaching and politics all reveal an unusual level of competence.

At a very early age, Ibn Sīnā was introduced to various religious, philosophical and scientific teachings. For example, he was introduced to the *Epistles* of the Brethren of Purity and Ismāʿīlism by his father, who was a member of this sect. He was also exposed to the Sunni doctrine, as his *fiqh* teacher, Ismāʿīl al-Zāhid, was a Sunni, and to Twelve-Imām Shiʿism. In addition, he was given some background in logic, geometry and astronomy by his other teacher, al-Nātilī. He exercised his independence of thought very quickly, however. First, he dispensed with teachers, continuing his education on his own; and second, he did not adhere to any of the doctrines to which he was exposed. Rather, he drew on various sources, selecting only what he considered convincing. Thus, we see in his system traces of Platonism, Aristotelianism, Neoplatonism, Galenism, Fārābīanism and other Greek and Islamic ideas. His system is unique, however, and cannot be said to follow any of the above schools. Even *al-Shifā'*, which reflects a strong Aristotelian tendency, is not purely Aristotelian, as it is usually considered. The theory of creation, for example, which is basically Neoplatonic, and that of prophecy, which is Islamic in essence, are but two examples of its many non-Aristotelian teachings. Al-Jūzjānī confirms the uniqueness of this work and asserts that it is nothing but the product of Ibn Sīnā's own thought.[6] Ibn Sīnā himself makes a similar point, stressing his originality in this work, especially, in the *Logic* and *Physics*.[7]

The most important of Ibn Sīnā's books are *al-Qānūn fi'l-ṭibb* ("The Canon of Medicine"), *al-Shifā'* ("Healing"), *al-Najāh* ("Deliverance"), *'Uyūn al-ḥikmah* ("Sources of Wisdom"), *Dānishnāma-yi 'alā'ī* ("The Book of Science Dedicated to 'Alā' al-Dawlah") and *al-Ishārāt wa'l-tanbīhāt* ("Remarks and Admonitions"). *Al-Qānūn fi'l-ṭibb* consists of five parts. Translated into Latin a number of times, it was considered the most important medical source both in the East and in the West for about five centuries (i.e., until the beginning of the eleventh/seventeenth century) and continues to be the primary source of Islamic medicine wherever it is practised to this day, such as the Indo-Pakistani subcontinent. The enormous amount of material in *al-Shifā'*, which is the most detailed philosophical work of Ibn Sīnā, is grouped under four main topics: *Logic*, *Physics*, *Mathematics* and *Metaphysics*. *Logic* is divided into nine parts, *Physics* into eight, and *Mathematics* into four. *Physics* (with the exception of the two parts dealing with animals and plants, which were completed after *Mathematics*) was the first to be written, followed by *Metaphysics*, then *Logic*, and finally *Mathematics*. *Al-Najāh*, which is a summary of *al-Shifā'*, also consists of four parts. The *Logic*, *Physics* and *Metaphysics* of this work were prepared by Ibn Sīnā, and the *Mathematics* by al-Jūzjānī. *'Uyūn al-ḥikmah*, known also as *al-Mūjaz* ("Epitome"), seems to have been intended for class instruction in logic, physics and metaphysics. This is evident from the simplicity, clarity and brevity with which the work is presented. *Dānishnāma yi 'alā'ī* also consists of four parts and is particularly significant in that it is the first work of Islamic Peripatetic philosophy in the Persian language. *Al-Ishārāt wa'l-tanbīhāt*, which is the most mature and most comprehensive philosophical work of Ibn Sīnā, also consists of *Logic*, *Physics* and *Metaphysics*. It closes with a treatment of mysticism, a treatment that may be classified more properly under ethics considered in its Sufi sense than metaphysics. In addition, Ibn Sīnā left a number of essays and poems. Some of his most important essays are *Ḥayy ibn Yaqẓān* ("The Living Son of the Vigilant"), *Risālat al-ṭayr* ("The Epistle of the Bird"), *Risālah fī sirr al-qadar* ("Essay on the Secret of Destiny"), *Risālah fi'l-'ishq* ("Essay on Love") and *Taḥṣīl al-sa'ādah* ("Attainment of Happiness"). His most important poems are *al-Urjūzah fi'l-ṭibb* (an iambic poem on medicine),[8] *al-Qaṣīdat al-muzdawijah* (an ode in couplets),[9] and *al-Qaṣīdat al-'ayniyyah* (an ode whose verses end with the letter ').[10] He also wrote a number of Persian poems.

DIVISION OF THE SCIENCES

Ibn Sīnā understands "the purpose of philosophy to be the determination of the realities of all things, inasmuch as that is possible for a human being".[11] There are two types of philosophy, theoretical and practical. The former seeks knowledge of the truth; the latter of the good.[12] The purpose of theoretical philosophy is to perfect the soul through knowledge alone. The purpose of practical philosophy is to perfect the soul through knowledge of what must be done, so that the soul acts in accordance with this knowledge.[13] Theoretical philosophy is knowledge of things that exist not owing to our choice and action. Practical philosophy is knowledge of things that exist on account of our choice and action.

The individual subjects of theoretical knowledge are of two main types: those to which movement can be attached, such as humanity, squareness and unity; and those to which movement cannot be attached, such as God and the intellect. The former are again divided into those that cannot exist unless movement is attached to them, such as humanity and squareness; and those that can exist without any movement being attached to them, such as unity and multiplicity. The former of the last two types is either such that it cannot be free from movement either in reality or in thought (e.g., humanity and horseness), or such that it can be free from movement in thought but not in reality (e.g., squareness).[14] There are, therefore, three branches of theoretical philosophy: that which deals with things inasmuch as movement is attached to them both in reality and in thought; that which deals with things inasmuch as movement is attached to them in reality but not in thought; and that which deals with things inasmuch as movement is attached to them neither in reality nor in thought, regardless of whether movement can be attached to them, as in the case of unity, or cannot be attached to them, as in the case of God. The first is physics, the second is pure mathematics and the third is metaphysics.[15]

Practical philosophy, on the other hand, is concerned with learning one of the following: (1) the principles on which public sharing among people is based, (2) the principles on which personal sharing among people is based, or (3) the principles on which the affairs of the individual are based. The first is the management of the city, referred to as political science; the second is home management;[16] and the third is management of the individual, referred to as ethics.[17] The principles of practical philosophy are derived from the divine *Sharīʿah*, and its complete definitions are made clear by the divine *Sharīʿah*.[18] The benefit of the science of management of the city is to make known the manner in which sharing among people occurs for the purpose of the well-being of the human body and of the preservation of humanity. The benefit of the science of home management is to make known the type of sharing that must take place among the members of the same home in order to ensure their well-being. Such sharing occurs between husband and wife, parent and child, and master and slave. The science of management of the individual yields a twofold benefit – to make known the virtues and the manner of acquiring them in order to refine the soul, and to make known the vices and the manner of avoiding them in order to purify the soul.[19]

Only an outline of the most important aspects of Ibn Sīnā's philosophy can be provided here. The most essential elements of his logic, which he considers the introductory part to philosophy,[20] are discussed in Chapter 48 below. Only a sketch of his general logical scheme will be given in this chapter.

LOGIC

Ibn Sīnā considers logic as the key to philosophy, whose pursuit (knowledge) is the key to human happiness. Logic performs this function by helping to derive unknown concepts and judgments from known ones, thus increasing our degree of knowledge (concepts are mental objects with no affirmation or negation; judgments are mental objects with affirmation or negation). Logic does this by acting as a set of rules for distinguishing the valid from the invalid explanatory phrases, which embody concepts and are the instruments for moving from known concepts to unknown ones, and proofs, which embody judgments and are the instruments for moving from known judgments to unknown ones. Since the valid leads to certitude and the invalid to falsehood, knowledge is attained only through the use of logic, except when, on rare occasions, God provides this knowledge without any human effort.[21]

While the logician's function is to open the way for the knowledge of the natures of things, he or she is not concerned with such natures in themselves or as they exist externally or in the mind, but only with concepts, representing these natures under the aspect of being subject or predicate, individual or universal, essential or particular.[22] Only when the concepts of the natures of things are considered inasmuch as they have certain states and a certain relationship to each other can they help to move thought from the known to the unknown. Even though the primary concern of the logician is concepts inasmuch as they are arranged in a certain manner, the logician must deal with expressions, as they are the only way to reason about or to communicate concepts.[23] With this in mind, Ibn Sīnā opens his logical treatises with a discussion of expressions, beginning with single expressions, the smallest elements of the explanatory phrase and proof.

As the ultimate goal of the logician is to pave the way for knowledge of the natures of things, universal expressions that mirror universal concepts, which in turn mirror these natures, must be his or her concern. That is why most of the discussion of the single expression focuses on the study of universal terms (the five predicables): genus, species, difference, property and common accident. The main types of the explanatory phrase, definition and description, are then introduced. The former, which consists of a genus and a difference or differences, is said to be the most reliable form of the explanatory phrase.

The proof, which utilizes explanatory phrases as its parts – these are the propositions or premisses – is of three types: syllogism, induction and analogy. The most reliable form of proof is the syllogism, which is also of three types: the conjunctive, the conditional and the exceptive. The propositions that form the premisses of the various types of the syllogism fall into nine categories. Each of these categories derives its assent or judgment from a different source, which will be indicated here in parentheses following the name of the category of propositions: sensible (from the external senses only); experiential or observational (from memory of repeated sense experience); based on unanimous traditions (from multiple testimonies); received (from scholars or respected religious leaders); estimative (from the estimative power); widespread (from being widely known); presumed (from the realization that the opposite is possible); imagined (from resemblance to propositions involving assent); primary (from the clarity of reason).[24] Demonstration is the most reliable form of the syllogism; composed of propositions characterized by certainty, it leads to a conclusion with certainty. Such propositions are either primary, experiential, sensible or widely known. A demonstration requires three elements: those principles with which the demonstration is made (the premisses), those issues that are the object of demonstration (the problems), and those subjects in which demonstration is made. Ibn Sīnā usually closes his logical discussions with a study of ambiguities, whether in expression or in meaning.

PHYSICS

Physics is concerned with the study of certain principles and of the things that are attached to natural bodies. These principles are mainly three: matter, form and the agent intellect.[25] This intellect is considered a natural principle inasmuch as it is the cause of holding matter and form together and, as such, is the cause of the existence of natural bodies. Only inasmuch as it has this relation to the physical realm is the agent intellect discussed in physics, and not inasmuch as it has such and such a nature or such and such a relation to separate principles or intelligibles. The things that are attached to natural bodies include motion, rest, time, place, void, the finite and so forth.

For example, every natural body is said to have a natural place and a natural shape. All natural motions lead to a creative, circular motion that is not subject to generation and corruption. This circular motion belongs to the heavenly bodies, which are followed by the bodies that are subject to generation and corruption. The first of the latter type of bodies in existence is the four elements: water, air, fire and earth. These elements are subject to the celestial influences.[26] When the four elements come together, their mixtures vary in temperament owing to the influence of the celestial powers. This variation in temperament results in the composition of these elements: minerals, plants and animals (the last and highest of whom are human beings). The closer their temperament is to equilibrium, the higher the form of the natural body. For this reason, there is a gradation in being from minerals to plants to animals, as well as a gradation of the various kinds subsumed under every level of these three types of being. The closest temperament to equilibrium causes the existence of human bodies, which have the highest form in the terrestrial sphere – this form being the human soul. This kind of soul is defined as "a primary perfection of an organic, natural body to which it belongs to perform acts of life".[27] Primary perfection is what gives actuality to the species of a thing, as shape gives actuality to the sword. This is to be contrasted with secondary perfection, which is what gives actuality to the actions and reactions that follow upon the species, as does cutting for the sword.[28]

The discussion of the soul takes up a large portion of Ibn Sīnā's *Physics*. We are told that if the function of the soul is limited to nutrition, growth and reproduction, it is a mere plant soul.[29] If sensation and movement are added to these, then it is a mere animal soul.[30] The soul of a human being includes these, but has an additional part, namely the human or rational, which divides into the practical and the theoretical faculties or intellects.[31] When this rational part occurs to a being, that being becomes a human being.[32] Through conjunction with the agent intellect that contains the intelligibles, the theoretical part of the rational soul receives its proper perfection, the perfection that makes it what it is. This perfection is the best thing a human being can achieve, as it is the best thing for any being to achieve its proper perfection, which completes its nature.

A brief discussion of the animal and rational souls is now in order, given the important role that they play in achieving this perfection. As mentioned, the animal soul has sensation and movement. The sensitive part consists of the external and the internal senses. The external senses are, in order of necessity for animals, touch, taste, smell, hearing and sight. The internal ones are common sense, representational faculty, imagination, estimative faculty and memory. The common sense is the faculty in which external sensations or forms of external objects collect. It is the faculty that enables us to judge, for example, that honey is sweet when we perceive honey visually, without the gustatory sensation that it is sweet. The reason is that the faculty of common sense simultaneously receives from the different external senses the different sensations of the one external object, which we call *honey*. This makes it possible for us to distinguish between the yellow colour and the sweet taste of honey, while realizing at the same time that they belong to the same object. The representational faculty retains the forms that the common sense receives from the outside. The objects of this faculty are present even in the absence of external objects. In contrast, the objects of the common sense are present only when the external objects are there – except in rare cases when they are poured into the common sense from the internal senses, which either manufacture them or receive them from the divine world.[33] The estimative faculty is said to grasp sense notions that are different from the sense forms grasped by the common sense. These notions are exemplified by the lamb's fear of the wolf. The memory retains the notions of the estimative faculty, as the representational faculty retains the sense forms. Finally, the imagination combines some objects of the representational faculty and of memory with each other, while separating the rest from each other. It must be mentioned that this faculty is called *imagination*, but only if employed by the estimative faculty. If it is employed by the intellect, it is called *cognition*.[34]

The locomotive part of the soul is responsible for the motion of the organs by means of the nerves and muscles due to the will. This motion is assisted by primary and secondary instruments. The primary ones, which concern us here, are either the imagination or the rational soul. These cause inclination either in the direction of or away from a perceived object. Inclination in the direction of an object is for an object that is imagined or presumed to be useful. When a power expresses such an inclination, it is called *appetitive*, while the inclination itself is called *appetition*. Inclination away from an object is for an object that is imagined or presumed harmful. When a power expresses such an inclination, it is called *irascible*, while the inclination itself is called *anger*. Both intellection and motion are affected by the condition of their instruments. If, for example, the instrument of sight is diseased or has aged, then sight declines or disintegrates totally.[35]

The human or rational soul performs either bodily actions and reactions, or purely intellective actions. The former do not belong to it and proceed from it and the body, whereas the latter belong to it and proceed from its essence. The actions that the rational soul performs in conjunction with the body are exemplified by consideration of the particular matters that must be done or avoided voluntarily, including the practical crafts such as carpentry, farming and animal husbandry. Reactions, on the other hand, are states consequent upon the preparations of the body and the rational soul, such as the preparation for crying or shyness. The purely intellective acts, which are performed by the rational soul, consist of grasping the quiddities or natures of things as universal concepts, such as "humanity" and "horseness". Such concepts cannot be grasped by any of the external or internal powers, for these powers belong to the animal world and thus whatever they grasp must be to some degree material and particular.[36] Contrary to the animal powers, the rational soul can grasp the quiddities or natures of things apart from matter and particularity. From such universal concepts, it composes judgments possessing certainty.

As mentioned, the rational soul has two parts, one with a capacity for action and the other with a capacity for knowledge. The former, called the *practical intellect*, is directed towards the body. With it, one can distinguish between what must and what must not be done, as well as between good and bad particular things. This intellect is perfected through habits and experiences. The latter, called the *theoretical intellect*, is directed towards the divine world and enables one to receive the intelligibles.[37]

The theoretical intellect passes through four stages. Firstly, it is in potentiality and has not yet formed any concepts or grasped any intelligibles. This is the *potential* or *material intellect* (*al-ʿaql al-hayūlānī*). This intellect is called *material*, not because it is material in nature but because it has the capacity for receiving intelligible forms as matter has the capacity for receiving material forms. Secondly, it is this potentiality actualized by the occurring of primary intelligibles in it. This is the *habitual intellect* (*al-'aql bi'l-malakah*). Thirdly, it is the acquisition of the intelligibles made constant. This is the *actual intellect* (*al-'aql bi'l-fi'l*). Fourthly, it is these intelligibles themselves. This is the *acquired intellect* (*al-'aql al-mustafād*).[38]

For a thing to move from potentiality to actuality, another thing, which is already in actuality, must give it the form that actualizes it. What moves the theoretical intellect from potentiality to actuality cannot be a body, because it must already possess the intelligible forms, which are non-material and which it gives to our theoretical intellect. Therefore it must be an intellect – this intellect being the agent intellect. The agent intellect sheds its light on the objects of our imagination, which have been received originally from the external world, thus making them visible to our theoretical intellect, as the sun sheds its light on the external things, thus making them visible to our sight. When the light of the agent intellect reaches the objects of the imagination, it renders them intelligible to our theoretical intellect by abstracting them from matter.[39]

Since the rational soul can receive the intelligible forms, it must be in its substance of the nature of these forms. If what receives the intelligible forms were a body or a power in a body, these forms would be divisible, and a simple form could not be intelligible. Arguments are advanced to show that the idea that the rational soul is either a body or a power in a body is false. The conclusion is drawn that, like the agent intellect and the intelligible forms, the rational soul is immaterial.[40] It follows that the rational soul is simple, for multiplicity lies in materiality. Because it is simple, it is indestructible. Contrary to Alexander of Aphrodisias and al-Fārābī, who believe that the only human soul assured of indestructibility is that which knows at least some realities – that which is completely deficient in such knowledge is eventually destroyed – Ibn Sīnā considers all human or rational souls to be indestructible. To him, knowledge of the realities of things is necessary only for happiness but not for existence after death.

METAPHYSICS

Metaphysics[41] is the science that provides knowledge of the principles of theoretical philosophy. This it does by demonstrating through the intellect the complete acquisition of these principles.[42] Metaphysics deals with the existent inasmuch as it exists, that is, with the general or absolute existent and what is attached to it. In other words, the subject of metaphysics is the existent, not inasmuch as it applies to some things and inasmuch as something particular is attached to it, as in physics and mathematics (such as quantity and quality, action and reaction, which are attached to the objects of physics) but inasmuch as it applies to the principle of existence and inasmuch as something universal is attached to it (such as unity and multiplicity, potentiality and actuality, eternity and coming into being, cause and effect, universality and particularity, completeness and incompleteness, necessity and possibility).[43] These qualities are *essential* accidents of the existent inasmuch as it exists, as well as being *non-essential* accidents of the particular existent. Metaphysics seeks to study the general existent and its essential accidents. We understand from Ibn Sīnā's logic that an essential accident is one that does not constitute or enter into the essence of a thing, yet necessarily accompanies it, as "laughter" for "human being". A non-essential accident neither constitutes the essence of a thing nor necessarily accompanies it; however, it resides in it, as "white" may reside in "human being".

The existent is either substance or accident. A substance is anything that is not in a subject, whether or not it is in matter. Thus, substance is of two main types: (1) that which is in matter, and (2) that which is not in matter. The latter category is broken down into three types: (2a) matter, (2b) that which is accompanied by matter, and (2c) that which is neither matter nor accompanied by matter. This scheme means that substance is of four types: (1) form in matter, as the soul is in the body; (2a) matter with no form – this is absolute matter, which has no existence in actuality but only in conception; (2b) the composite of form and matter, as the human being is a composite of soul and body; (2c) form separate from matter, as God or any intellect is neither matter nor in contact with matter.[44] Accident, on the other hand, is in a subject and is divided into nine types: quality, quantity, relation, time, place, position, condition, action and reaction.

The existence of a thing is either necessary or possible (contingent). Necessary existence is such that if the thing to which it belongs is assumed to be non-existent, an impossibility arises. Possible existence is such that if the thing to which it belongs is assumed to be non-existent or existent, no impossibility arises.[45] Ibn Sīnā mentions that in other contexts "possible existence" could also be used in the sense of "being in potentiality".[46] Necessary existence is either that which always belongs to a thing through that thing itself, or that which always belongs to it through another. For example, the existence of burning is necessary, not because of the burning itself, but because of the meeting of two things, one naturally capable of burning and the other naturally capable of being burnt.[47] What is necessary through itself cannot be necessary through another and conversely. For example, if the existence of A is necessary through A itself, this existence cannot be necessary through B. Similarly, if it is necessary through B, it cannot be necessary through A itself. This is to say that if, in the second case, one considers A in itself, one finds its existence non-necessary, or possible in itself. If this is not the case, its existence would be either necessary in itself, but this has been denied, or impossible, which cannot be, for its existence has been affirmed. Therefore, its existence is possible in itself, necessary through another, and impossible without another. Its existence through another is other than its existence without another. By the former, it is necessary; by the latter, it is possible.[48]

The existence of a being necessary in itself is determined on the basis of two principles: first, the chain of possible beings at any time cannot be infinite and, second, this chain cannot be necessary since it consists of possible units. Thus, it must lead to a necessary cause external to this chain – this cause being the Necessary Existent or Being, otherwise known as God.[49]

Being eternally prior in existence to everything and the source of the existence of everything, this Existent is said to be the first cause.[50] It is free from matter, one and simple in all respects.[51] Thus it has no genus or difference, the two necessary elements of a definition. Therefore there is no definition of it, but only a name. Being immaterial, it is purely good, for only in matter, the source of privation, does evil lie.[52] Owing to its immateriality, it is also an intellect, and, owing to its simplicity, the intellect and the intelligible in it are one.[53] In itself, it is the Beloved and the Lover, the pleasurable and the pleased. It is the Beloved because it is the highest Beauty. It is the highest Beauty because there is no higher beauty than that of being a pure intellect, above all manner of deficiency, and one in all respects. Suitable and apprehended beauty or goodness is desired and beloved. The more the apprehension grasps the essence, and the more the essence of the apprehended is beautiful, the more the power of apprehension loves it and finds pleasure in it.[54]

> Thus the Necessary Being, who is most beautiful, perfect, and best, who apprehends itself at this ultimate beauty and goodness and in the most complete manner of apprehension, and who apprehends the apprehender and the apprehended as one in reality is in essence and by its essence, the greatest lover and beloved and the greatest thing pleased and pleasurable.[55]

From this Necessary Being, the rest of the existing things overflow through the process of emanation. The first things that emanate are the celestial intellects, followed by the celestial souls, the celestial bodies and finally terrestrial beings. All these things emanate from It in eternity; otherwise, a state would arise in It that was not there before. But this is impossible in a being whose existence is necessary in all respects.[56] This emanation is a necessary outcome of God's Essence and cannot be linked to any intention external to His Essence. Firstly, there is nothing in Him external to His Essence – He is a total simplicity, but He can be considered from different points of view. It is only by virtue of such consideration that one can speak of His Attributes. Secondly, even if it were possible for Him to have Attributes external to His Essence, it would not be possible for Him to have among such Attributes any intention relating to the world. "The reason is that every intention is for the sake of the intended and is less in existence than the intended. This is because if a thing is for the sake of another, that other is more complete in existence than it."[57] This is to say that whatever is more complete in existence than another cannot intend that other. God, therefore, cannot intend the world or anything in the world, since He is more complete in existence than the world.

Even though neither God nor any other cause can be perfected essentially by its effects and therefore cannot intend its effects or anything for them, still it may lead accidentally to beneficial effects and, if it is divine, know and be pleased with these effects. Health, for example, is such "in substance and essence, not to benefit the sick; but it results in benefiting the sick".[58] Similar to health, superior causes are what they are in themselves, not to benefit anything else; but they do benefit other things accidentally. They differ from health, though, in that they know the things that exist and the order and goodness according to which such things exist.[59] Still, providence is attributed to God, the first cause of all things. Providence must be understood, however, not in the sense of divine guidance of the world or concern about it. Rather, providence is defined as God's knowledge of the order of existence and the manner of its goodness, His knowledge that He is the source of the emanation of this order inasmuch as that is possible, and His being pleased with it.[60]

Ibn Sīnā's thought had a clear and strong impact on the East and on the West, in science, literature and philosophy. The impact of his philosophical thought, which concerns us here, was exhibited in a large number of commentaries on his works and in other forms of writings on his various ideas, reflecting the spirit of his thought or rejecting it. The best known of such commentaries are those of Ibn Kammūnah, Fakhr al-Dīn al-Rāzī and Naṣīr al-Dīn al-Ṭūsī on *al-Ishārāt*, and Ṣadr al-Dīn al-Shīrāzī on parts of *al-Shifā'*. Among the most prominent Eastern thinkers whose thought reflects that of Ibn Sīnā are al-Ṭūsī, Suhrawardī, Quṭb al-Dīn al-Shīrāzī, Mīr Dāmād, Ṣadr al-Dīn al-Shīrāzī (Mullā Ṣadrā) and the Syriac Christian Ibn al-'Ibrī. Suhrawardī's and al-Shīrāzī's theories of illumination, for example, stem from Ibn Sīnā's "Oriental philosophy". Also, their discussions of being and essence were generated by Ibn Sīnā's view on this subject. Ibn al-'Ibrī too adheres closely to Ibn Sīnā's analysis of God's relationship to the world, the presence of evil, and the nature and unity of the human soul as well as the impossibility of the soul's pre-existence and transmigration.[61]

But, as mentioned, not all those who felt the effect of Ibn Sīnā's thought responded to it positively. Ibn Sīnā had his strong critics, such as al-Ghazzālī and al-Shahrastānī in the East, and William of Auvergne and Thomas Aquinas in the West. These critics rejected primarily his ideas concerning God's nature, knowledge of particulars and relationship to the world, as well as the eternity of the universe. Even Mullā Ṣadrā, a follower of Ibn Sīnā, rejected strongly the eternity of the universe and the denial of the resurrection of the body. Also, Ibn Rushd, who in his major work, *The Incoherence of Incoherence*, seeks to defend philosophy as embodied primarily in Ibn Sīnā's works, charges that Ibn Sīnā misunderstood and distorted Aristotle at times.

Such opposition to Ibn Sīnā's ideas, however, did not prevent even these critics from borrowing heavily from him. Al-Ghazzālī's logic and philosophical terminology, to give but two examples, are, for the most part, those of Ibn Sīnā. Also, the distinction Ibn Sīnā introduced in his theodicy, for example, between evil in itself and evil for another was borrowed by Aquinas, and from him by Suarez. Because Ibn Sīnā's works are not sufficiently known in the West, however, the credit for this distinction is given in the West to Aquinas. Furthermore, two of Aquinas's well-known proofs of God's existence, that from efficiency and that from contingency, as well as his distinction between essence and existence, were also borrowed from Ibn Sīnā. The numerous references Aquinas gives to Ibn Sīnā in *Being and Essence* and elsewhere are sufficient to show the influence Ibn Sīnā had on this prominent Christian philosopher and theologian whose ideas dominated Western thought for so long. Gundissalinus, Albert the Great and Roger Bacon are also among the Western thinkers whose work reflected elements of Ibn Sīnā's thought, especially with regard to the nature of the human soul. No doubt the following factors facilitated Ibn Sīnā's influence on Latin philosophical circles: first, the translation into Latin, and fast circulation in universities, of the most essential parts of *al-Shifā'* as early as the twelfth and thirteenth Christian centuries; and, second, Ibn Sīnā's efforts to synthesize Greek and Islamic thought, an attempt in which the West found the seed for a synthesis between Greek philosophy and Christianity.

NOTES

1 His full name is Abū 'Alī al-Ḥusayn ibn 'Abd Allāh ibn 'Alī ibn Sīnā – Abū 'Alī being his nickname. Perhaps his titles, Master and Head, refer respectively to his prominent rank in learning and his high political position as a vizier (A. F. al-Ahwānī, *Ibn Sīnā* (Cairo, 1958): 18). This would correspond to his

other title, al-Ḥakīm al-Wazīr (Wise Man and Vizier). He was also known as Ḥujjat al-Ḥaqq (Proof of the Truth).

2 He was one of Ibn Sīnā's closest students, who accompanied him during most of his later life. For a translation of his bibliography see W. E. Gohlman, *The Life of Ibn Sīnā* (Albany, 1974).

3 See Ẓ. D. al-Bayhaqī, *Tārīkh ḥukamā' al-islām*, ed. M. K. 'Alī (Damascus, 1976): 52–72; A. H. al-Qifṭī, *Tārīkh al-ḥukamā'*, ed. J. Lippert (Leipzig, 1903): 413–26; I. A. Uṣaybi'ah, *'Uyūn al-anbā' fī ṭabaqāt al-aṭibbā', Part Three*, ed. Samīḥ al-Zayn (Beirut, 1987): 2–28; I. Khallikān, *Wafayāt al-a'yān wa anbā' abnā' al-zamān, Part Two*, ed. Iḥsān 'Abbās (Beirut, 1978): 157–62.

4 See Ibn Abī Uṣaybi'ah, *'Uyūn al-anbā'*: 5.

5 For a list of Ibn Sīnā's works, see G. C. Qanawātī (Anawātī), *Mu'allafāt Ibn Sīnā* (Cairo, 1955) and Y. Mahdavi, *Fihrist-i muṣannafāt-i Ibn Sīnā* (Tehran, 1954).

6 Ibn Sīnā, *al-Shifā', al-Manṭiq, al-Madkhal* (hereafter *al-Madkhal*), ed. G. C. Anawātī, M. al-Khuḍayrī and A. F. al-Ahwānī (Cairo, 1952): 2–4. Unless otherwise specified, all works referred to in the rest of this chapter are by Ibn Sīnā.

7 *Ibid*: 10.

8 This is Ibn Sīnā's longest poem, consisting of around one thousand verses.

9 In this ode, which was written for al-Suhaylī, Ibn Sīnā summarizes the study of logic in a poetic form so that his brother 'Alī could remember it easily.

10 This poem on the soul is Ibn Sīnā's best known.

11 *Al-Madkhal*: 12. *Falsafah* (philosophy) and *ḥikmah* (wisdom) are used by Ibn Sīnā interchangeably.

12 *Al-Madkhal*: 14.

13 *Ibid.*: 12.

14 *Ibid.*: 12–13.

15 *Ibid.*: 14. For the division of the sciences, see also *al-Shifā', al-Ilāhiyyāt* (hereafter *al-Ilāhiyyāt*), 1, ed. M. Y. Mūsā, S. Dunyā and S. Zāyid (Cairo, 1960): 3–4; *Manṭiq al-mashriqiyyīn* (Cairo, 1910): 6–7; and *'Uyūn al-ḥikmah*, ed. A. R. Badawī (Cairo, 1954): 17.

16 No specific name is given to the science of home management, but it may be referred to as *social science*; it corresponded to the Greek understanding of "economics".

17 *Al-Madkhal*: 14.

18 *'Uyūn al-ḥikmah*: 16.

19 *Ibid.* For the division of the sciences, see also *Tis' rasā'il*, ed. Ḥasan 'Āṣī (Beirut, 1986): 83–5.

20 For a study of the relation of logic to philosophy, see Shams Inati, *Remarks and Admonitions, Part One* (Toronto, 1984): 9–11.

21 *Al-Madkhal:* 19.

22 *Remarks and Admonitions, Part One*: 11.

23 *Ibid.*: 12.

24 Ibn Sīnā, *al-Najāh*, ed. M. Fakhrī (Beirut, 1985): 97–101; *Remarks and Admonitions, Part One*: 28–9 and 118–28.

25 The agent or active intellect (*al-'aql al-fa''āl*) is, according to Islamic philosophy, the intelligence governing the Moon. This term seems to have been coined by al-Fārābī, as al-Kindī before him seems unfamiliar with it. Al-Kindī calls this

intellect instead the first intellect. In any case, according to Ibn Sīnā, this intelligence is caused by intellectual emanation proceeding from God and ending with the human rational soul. The agent intellect is the last divine intelligence and is responsible for administering the sublunary world. Its primary function is to give corporeal form to matter and intellectual form to the rational soul, hence its name the giver of forms (*wahib al-ṣuwar*). For a summary of Ibn Sīnā's cosmology and natural philosophy see S. H. Nasr, *An Introduction to Islamic Cosmological Doctrines* (Albany, 1993): 215ff.

26 *'Uyūn al-ḥikmah*: 33.

27 *Al-Shifā', al-Ṭabī'iyyāt, al-Nafs* (hereafter *al-Nafs*), ed. F. Rahman (London, 1959): 11. See also *Tis' rasā'il*: 69, where the definition of the soul is given, but there the perfection is not described as primary, and the body is described as having "life in potentiality".

28 *Al-Nafs*: 11. For the distinction between primary and secondary perfections, compare with Aristotle, *De anima*, 2.412A.

29 *Tis' rasā'il*: 55 and *'Uyūn al-ḥikmah*: 35.

30 *Tis' rasā'il*: 55–6 and *'Uyūn al-ḥikmah*: 35–7.

31 *Al-Nafs*: 45.

32 *Tis' rasā'il*: 51.

33 *Ibid.*: 59.

34 *Al-Ishārāt wa'l-tanbīhāt, Part Two* (published with *Part Three* and *Part Four*), ed. S. Dunyā (Cairo, 1958): 382 and *Tis' rasā'il*: 57. For a list of the faculties of the three parts of the soul, see *al-Nafs*: 39ff. and *al-Ishārāt wa'l-tanbīhāt, Part Two*: 373–86. See also *al-Nafs*: 39ff. for an elaboration of the faculties of the plant soul; 58ff. for an elaboration of the external senses; and 152–4 and 159ff. for an elaboration of the internal senses. For a brief account of the internal senses, see *'Uyūn al-ḥikmah*: 38–9.

35 *Ibid.*: 39–40.

36 *Tis' rasā'il*: 57–8.

37 *Ibid.*: 68.

38 *Ibid.*: 68–9. For a discussion of the rational soul, see *'Uyūn al-ḥikmah*: 42–3.

39 For the relation of the agent intellect to us, see *Tis' rasā'il*: 69 and *'Uyūn al-ḥikmah*: 43.

40 For the immateriality of the rational soul, see *ibid.*: 44–46.

41 Ibn Sīnā also refers to this branch of philosophy as *first philosophy, divine science* or *wisdom in an absolute sense (al-Ilāhiyyāt*, 1: 5).

42 *Ibid*: 17.

43 *Al-Najāh*: 235–6 and *'Uyūn al-ḥikmah*: 47.

44 See *al-Najāh*: 237; *al-Ilāhiyyāt*, 1: 93; and *'Uyūn al-ḥikmah*: 48.

45 *Al-Najāh*: 261.

46 *Ibid.*

47 *Ibid.*

48 *Ibid.*: 262 and *'Uyūn al-ḥikmah*: 55.

49 *Al-Najāh*: 271–2.

50 *Al-Ilāhiyyāt*, 2: 342–3.

51 *Al-Najāh*: 264–5.

52 For a detailed discussion of God's Attributes, see *al-Ilāhiyyāt*, 1: 344–69.

53 *Al-Najāh*: 280.

54 *Al-Ishārāt wa'l-tanbīhāt, Part Four*: 782.
55 *Al-Najāt*: 282.
56 *Ibid.*: 265.
57 *Ibid.*: 305.
58 *Ibid.*: 307.
59 *Ibid.*
60 *Al-Ilāhiyyāt*, 2: 415.
61 See al-Ab Būlus Bahnām, "Fi'l-Ādāb al-Siryāniyyah", in *Majallat al-kitāb*, 11 (Cairo, 1952): 514–28.

SELECT BIBLIOGRAPHY

For bibliographical material see:

Janssens, J. (1991) *An Annotated Bibliography on Ibn Sina* (Leuven)

and the references in:

Black, D. (1990) *Logic and Aristotle's Rhetoric and Poetics in Medieval Arabic Philosophy* (Leiden)
Goodman, L. (1992) *Avicenna* (London).

CHAPTER 17

Ibn Sīnā's "Oriental philosophy"

Seyyed Hossein Nasr

One cannot discuss the thought of Ibn Sīnā seriously, especially as it has influenced Islamic philosophy during the past millennium, without delving into the meaning of his "Oriental philosophy" (*al-ḥikmat al-mashriqiyyah*) which has drawn the attention of many Western scholars from L. Massignon, C. A. Nallino and S. Pines to H. Corbin, who has provided the most extensive plausible reconstruction of it.[1] Although this dimension of Ibn Sīnā's thought did not influence the West and has not been taken seriously by contemporary Western scholars save for Corbin and some of his students,[2] it remains an important link in the uninterrupted tradition of Islamic philosophy marking a notable stepping stone from the synthesis of Ibn Sīnā to the Illuminationist doctrines of Suhrawardī, who in his *Qiṣṣat al-ghurbat al-gharbiyyah* ("The Story of the Occidental Exile") refers explicitly to the *Ḥayy ibn Yaqẓān* of Ibn Sīnā[3] and considers his work to be the achievement of what Ibn Sīnā had set out to accomplish without reaching the ultimate goal, implying that the "Oriental philosophy" was a prelude for *Ḥikmat al-ishrāq*, or theosophy of the Orient of Light formulated a century and a half later by Suhrawardī. Far from being a "harmless" and rational formulation of the well-known *mashshā'ī* philosophy by Ibn Sīnā, as claimed by C. A. Nallino, Ibn Sīnā's "Oriental philosophy" belongs to the same world as that of Suhrawardī's *ishrāq* and was seen as belonging to the same universe by such later figures as Mullā Ṣadrā and Sabziwārī. In this tradition, which must be taken seriously by anyone who is interested in Islamic philosophy as a distinct and integral intellectual tradition and not simply as a chapter of Western philosophy, *mashriqī* and *ishrāqī* can hardly be considered to be so distinct as to be unrelated. As Corbin has asserted, "Suhrawardī's representation of Ishrāq moves in a circle. *Illuminative wisdom* (*ishrāqī*) is neither in any opposition to Oriental wisdom (*mashriqī*) nor even distinguished from it: such a divine wisdom or *theosophia* is illuminative *because* Oriental, and Oriental because illuminative."[4] In any case one cannot deal fully with Ibn Sīnā in the context of the later Islamic philosophical tradition without paying serious attention to what he calls *al-ḥikmat al-mashriqiyyah*.

At the beginning of his short work *Manṭiq al-mashriqiyyīn* ("Logic of the Orientals"), of which what remains extant is devoted almost solely to logic and where Ibn Sīnā expresses certain logical views different from those of Aristotle,[5] he distances himself explicitly from his Peripatetic works and states that what is to follow, that is the *mashriqī* philosophy, contains his real views concerning philosophy:

> We have been inspired to bring together writings upon the subject matter which has been the source of difference among people disposed to argumentation and not to study it with the eye of fanaticism, desire, habit or attachment. We have no fear if we find differences with what the people instructed in Greek books have become familiar with through their own negligence and shortness of understanding. And we have no fear if we reveal to the philosophers something other than what we have written for the common people – the common people who have become enamored of the Peripatetic philosophers and who think that God has not guided anyone but them or that no one has reached Divine Mercy except them.
>
> Although we admit the wisdom of the most learned predecessor of these philosophers [that is, Aristotle], and we know that in discovering what his teachers and companions did not know, in distinguishing between various sciences, in arranging the sciences in a better manner than before, in discovering the truth of many subjects . . . he was superior to those who came before him, the men who came after him should have brought to order whatever confusion had existed in his thought, mended whatever cracks they found in his structure, and expanded his principles. But those who came after him could not transcend what they had inherited from him. Bigotry over whatever he had not found out became a shield, so that they remained bound to the past and found no opportunity to make use of their own intellects. If such an opportunity did arise, they did not find it admissible to use it in increasing, correcting and examining the works of their predecessors.
>
> When we turned our attention to their works, however, from the beginning the comprehension of these works became easy for us. *And often we gained knowledge from non-Greek sources*. When we began on this project, it was the beginning of our youth, and God shortened the time necessary for us to learn the works of our

> predecessors. Then we compared everything word for word with the science which the Greeks called logic, and it is not improbable that the Orientals had another name for it. Whatever was contrary by this means of comparison we rejected. We sought the reason for everything until the Truth became separate from error.
>
> Since those who were the people of learning were strongly in favor of the Greek Peripatetics, we did not find it appropriate to separate ourselves and speak differently from everyone else. So, we took their side, and with those philosophers who were more fanatical than any of the Greek sects, we too became fanatical. Whatever they sought but had not found and their wisdom had not penetrated, we completed. We overlooked their faults and provided a leader and tutor for them while we were aware of their errors. If we revealed some opposition it was only in matters in which no patience was possible. But in most cases we neglected and overlooked their faults ... We were forced to associate with people devoid of understanding who considered the depth of thought as innovation [*bid'ah*] and the opposition to common opinion as sin ...
>
> Under these conditions, we longed to write a book containing the important aspects of real knowledge. Only the person who has thought much, has meditated deeply, and is not devoid of the excellence of intellectual intuition can make deductions from it ...
>
> We have composed this book only for ourselves, that is, those who are like ourselves. As for the commoners who have to do with philosophy, we have provided in the *Kitāb al-shifā'* more than they need. Soon in the supplements we shall present whatever is suitable for them beyond that which they have seen up to this time. And in all conditions we seek the assistance of the Unique God.[6]

It is of great significance that this revealing passage should appear in a book entitled *Manṭiq al-mashriqiyyīn* which was most likely the first part of Ibn Sīnā's work *al-Ḥikmat al-mashriqiyyah* that for the moment is lost. We must therefore seek to reconstruct his "Oriental philosophy" from his non-Aristotelian works, remembering not only that Ibn Sīnā wrote the *summa* of Peripatetic philosophy in Islam, the *Kitāb al-shifā'* ("The Book of Healing") but that he also composed the last chapters of the *Ishārāt* dealing with the exposition and defence of Sufism and gnosis (*'irfān*), wrote commentaries upon the Qur'ān, composed treatises on visiting the tombs of saints and on eschatology and wrote the first complete cycle of visionary recitals in the history of Islamic philosophy. This cycle, consisting of *Ḥayy ibn Yaqẓān* ("The Living Son of the Awake"), *Risālat al-ṭayr* ("The Treatise of the Bird") and *Salāmān wa Absāl* ("Salāmān and Absāl") and forming together an initiatic trilogy as demonstrated by Corbin, was to serve as a model for Suhrawardī's recitals and contains the outlines of the universe of the "Oriental philosophy" even if we do not possess all the details of that universe.

In Ibn Sīnā's "Oriental philosophy' it is not so much that the Aristotelian cosmos is repudiated as it is transformed. The outline and content of the universe remain the same; and yet, there is a profound transformation. Reason becomes wedded to the Intellect, the external cosmos becomes interiorized, facts become symbols and philosophy becomes a veritable *sophia* inseparable from the gnosis which Ibn Sīnā defended so vigorously in the ninth chapter of his *Ishārāt* entitled *Fī maqāmāt al-'ārifīn* ("On the Stations of the Gnostics"). The goal of philosophy becomes not only the theoretical knowledge of the substances and accidents of the cosmos but the experience of their very presence and actualization in such a manner as to enable the soul to free itself from the confines of the cosmos considered as a crypt.[7] "Hence the cosmos is no longer the external object, the distant model, of descriptions, of theoretical inventions, of deductive explanations: it is experienced and shown as a succession of the stages of a more or less perilous exodus upon which one is able to enter or which one has essayed."[8]

The "Oriental philosophy" of Ibn Sīnā, far from being an unimportant appendix to his *mashshā'ī* philosophy, marks a step in the direction of that intellectual universe dominated by Illumination and gnosis which was to characterize most of later Islamic philosophy. In that universe of discourse where such figures as Suhrawardī, Ibn 'Arabī, Ibn Turkah Iṣfahānī and later Mīr Dāmād and Mullā Ṣadrā dominated the scene, Ibn Sīnā continued to be read and studied avidly not only as a Peripatetic exponent of rational (*baḥthī*) philosophy but also as a gnostic. His "Oriental philosophy" was seen as the intermediary step between his *mashshā'ī* works and the doctrines of *ishrāq* and thereby helped in the integration of Ibn Sīnā's philosophy into a vast schema which began with the study of logic and terminated with wonder (*al-ḥayrah*) in the contemplation of the Divine Mysteries. One cannot therefore understand the full significance of Ibn Sīnā in the Islamic philosophical tradition without paying some attention to his "Oriental philosophy" and what can be reconstructed from his extant works concerning that philosophy whose full and complete exposition from the pen of the master of the Peripatetics has never reached us.

NOTES

1 Corbin has summarized the views of various recent and contemporary scholars concerning the meaning of the "Oriental philosophy" in his *Avicenna and the Visionary Recital*, trans. W. R. Trask (Irving, 1980), "Postscript": 271–8. See also S. H. Nasr, *An Introduction to Islamic Cosmological Doctrines* (Albany, 1993): 187ff.

2 One of Corbin's students, Christian Jambet, has in fact written a book entitled *La Logique des Orientaux* (Paris, 1983), named after Ibn Sīnā's *Manṭiq al-mashriqiyyīn*, in which he speaks of his *al-ḥikmat al-mashriqiyyah*.

3 Suhrawardī writes after mentioning the last part of *Ḥayy ibn Yaqẓān* there is an allusion to the secret known only to the Sufis and "people of unveiling" and also "I decided to mention something [of that secret] for some of our respected brothers in the form of a story and I entitled it *Qiṣṣat al-ghurbat al-gharbiyyah*". Sohravardi, *Oeuvres philosophiques et mystiques*, 2, ed. H. Corbin (Tehran, 1977): 275–6.

See also H. Corbin (trans.), Sohravardī Shaykh al-Ishrāq, *L'Archange empourpré* (Paris, 1976): 273.

4 Corbin, *Avicenna and the Visionary Recital*: 38.

5 See the edition of Shukrī Najjār (Beirut, 1982). In the introduction the editor deals with Ibn Sīnā's innovations upon the logic of Aristotle.

6 Nasr, *An Introduction to Islamic Cosmological Doctrines*: 186–7.

7 See *ibid.*, chapter 15, "Nature and the Visionary Recitals": 263ff.

8 Corbin, *Avicenna . . .*: 33.

CHAPTER 18

Ibn Miskawayh

Oliver Leaman

Aḥmad ibn Miskawayh (d. 421/1030) was a member of a distinguished group of thinkers who combined political careers with philosophical activity. As treasurer of the Buwayhid ruler 'Aḍud al-Dawlah, he was very much part of the practical side of his society, while as a member of the group of intellectuals including al-Tawḥīdī and al-Sijistānī he contributed a great deal to theoretical debate at the time. Although many of his contemporaries were rather disparaging about his work, not to mention his person, he is an interesting thinker who displays much of the style of the times. Miskawayh wrote on a wide number of topics, as did so many of his contemporaries, and although there can be no question but that his work is less distinguished than that of Ibn Sīnā, what we know of it today provides evidence of some very interesting contributions to the development of philosophical thought. Within philosophy itself Miskawayh's main claim for attention lies in his well-constructed system of ethics, with which we shall largely be concerned here.

Before we look at the ethics, however, it is important to get a grasp of Miskawayh's general philosophical position. Since he covered so many distinct areas, ranging from history to psychology and chemistry, it would be tempting to look for a central philosophical principle which unites all his contributions to knowledge, but none is readily available. It must of course be admitted, though, that many of his works are no longer extant, and so it is difficult to form an impression of his entire body of thought with any likelihood of accuracy. In his *Fawz al-aṣghar* ("The Lesser Victory") he presents a rather unusual account of the nature of Neoplatonism, in which he claims that the ancient (i.e. Greek) philosophers were in no doubt over the existence and unity of God, so that there is no problem in reconciling their thought with Islam. He even claims that Aristotle's identification of the Creator with an unmoved mover is a powerful argument in favour of a creator acceptable to religion, since the very distinct nature of such a creature prevents our normal categories of description from getting a grip. The only way in which such a creator can be described is in terms of negative concepts, an interesting prefigurement of the notion of the *via negativa* in philosophy. Miskawayh concludes that since there is no rational route to understanding the Deity, we should follow the indications of religion and the general views of the religious community. He is so intent on reconciling philosophical with religious views of the nature of the world that he finds no problem in bringing together the view that God created the world out of nothing with the Neoplatonic notion of constant emanation. Many *falāsifah* argued that there is a problem here, of course, but Miskawayh does not seem to see the problem. Perhaps he was helped here by his rather unusual model of emanation, whereby the Deity produces the Active Intellect, the soul and the heavens straight off. Within the tradition of Islamic Neoplatonism these results of divine emanation generally appear some way down the scale of being, which suggests that Miskawayh has difficulties understanding the real basis to the distinction between creation and emanation. There are good grounds for accusing Miskawayh of not so much seeking to combine the various metaphysical theses which he uses into a satisfactory argument but rather combining them in arbitrary ways to produce a conclusion that fails to recognize the important issues which they raise.

Miskawayh's ethical work is very different, though, and shows evidence of a real understanding of conceptual difficulties in the area. There are a number of important works here, the *Ṭahārat al-a'rāq* ("Purity of Dispositions") better known as *Tahdhīb al-akhlāq* ("Cultivation of Morals"), but not to be confused with the work of the same name, but of much less interest, by Yaḥyā ibn 'Adī. Miskawayh's work sets out to show how we might acquire the right dispositions to perform morally correct actions in an organized and systematic manner. The basis of his argument is his account of the nature of the soul, which he takes quite readily from Plato to be a self-subsisting entity or substance, in marked contrast with the Aristotelian notion of the soul. The soul can be seen to be distinct from the body, he argues, for a variety of reasons. The soul distinguishes us from animals, it distinguishes us from other human beings, it uses the body and its parts and it seeks to come into contact with more spiritual and higher realms of being. The soul cannot be an accident because it has the power itself to distinguish between accidents and essential concepts, and is not limited to awareness of accidental things by the senses but can apprehend a great variety of immaterial and abstract entities. If the soul were only an accident, it could do none of these things but would be limited in its scope as are the other physical aspects of the body. Not only is the soul not an accident, but when we want to concentrate upon abstract issues the body with its accidents is actually an obstruction which we should avoid if we are to make contact with intelligible reality. The soul is then an independent substance which controls the body, and must be immortal. The essence of the soul is opposite to the essence of the body, and so the former cannot die, and it is involved in an eternal and circular motion, replicated by the structure of the heavens. There are two directions which this motion can take, though, either upwards towards reason and the Active Intellect, or downwards towards matter. Our happiness arises through the former, and our misfortunes through the latter.

When Miskawayh comes to discuss the nature of virtue he combines Aristotelian with Platonic ideas while his theory also has much affinity with Sufism. Virtue comes out as the perfection of that aspect of the soul which represents the essence of humanity, namely, our reason, and distinguishes it from lower forms of existence. Our virtue increases in so far as we develop and extend the ability we have to deliberate and apply reason to our lives. The ways in which we do this should be in accordance with the mean, the most distant point from two extremes, and justice arises when we manage to bring this off. He develops a set of virtues relating to wisdom, courage, temperance and justice which outline the range of moral development at which we should aim. He combines the Platonic division of virtues with an Aristotelian understanding of what virtue actually is, and adds to this the idea that the more these virtues can be treated as a unity the better. This is because he identifies unity with perfection, and multiplicity with the meaningless plurality of physical objects. Such a Pythagorean notion has more than aesthetic charm in its favour. Miskawayh can argue plausibly for the idea that the notion of divine or perfect justice is a simple idea, dealing as it does with eternal and immaterial principles. Human justice, by contrast, is variable and depends upon the character of particular communities and their inhabitants. The divine law specifies what should be done everywhere and at every time, while the law of the state takes account of the changeable and contingent customs of the time.

Miskawayh spends a lot of time discussing the variants of friendship which brings out nicely the distinction between relationships which are essentially transitory and variable (especially those based upon pleasure) and those based upon the intellect, which are also pleasurable but not in a physical way. Our souls are capable of recognizing similar perfected souls, and the effect of such recognition is intense intellectual delight. This is very different from the ordinary way in which people form relationships with each other because they want to get something out of the relationship. Miskawayh differentiates between a wide category of types of friendship, but he does not conclude that only the highest and most intellectual form is important. On the contrary, even those capable of this ultimate level of friendship have to live in society, and so must assume the other types of friendship if they are to be able to attain perfection. We find ourselves firmly on Aristotelian ground here again, with the claim that perfection of the virtues and satisfaction of our more mundane demands go hand in hand. Yet Miskawayh also argues that the highest form of happiness exists when we manage to abandon the requirements of this world and can receive the emanations flowing from above which will perfect our intellects and permit us to be illuminated by Divine Light. There seems here to be an even higher level of happiness which is something like mystical awareness of God, where we throw off all the trappings of our corporeal existence and allow our souls to partake of entirely spiritual aims.

Miskawayh spends much time describing the joys of this mystical relationship between the enfranchised soul and divine reality, and it obviously is for him an even higher form of happiness than that available to us through intellectual perfection. One of the intriguing features of his work, though, is that he combines the ability to discuss both what is supposed to happen at the highest level of human perfection with practical advice on how to develop our ordinary capacity for virtue. He regards the cultivation of our moral health in a very Aristotelian way as akin to the cultivation of physical health, necessitating measures to preserve our moral equilibrium. We should try to keep our emotions in check, and carry out practices which help both to restrain us on particular occasions and to develop personality traits which will maintain that restraint throughout our lives. To try to eradicate faults, we have to investigate the ultimate cause of the faults, and then seek to replace them with their virtuous alternatives. It is interesting to observe how this approach copes with particularly difficult problems, like the fear of death. This fear Miskawayh regards as without basis, and it is intriguing to see why. The soul itself cannot die, and so there is no problem in wondering what happens after death. We all have to die, and it is indeed part of our very nature to perish eventually, and to accept both that we are contingent and yet that we should not die is to contradict oneself. If we fear the pain consequent of dying, then the object of our fear is not death but the pain. Once we have died there will be no more pain, which suggests that death is rather to be welcomed than rejected. What is important in this treatment is not the strength of the arguments themselves which Miskawayh produces but the way in which he argues. He suggests, along with al-Kindī and the Cynics and Stoics who wrote on this issue, that to reconcile ourselves to reality we have to understand what the real nature of our emotions is. That is, we have to come to understand their character, and we can do this by using reason. Reason will help us to understand dispassionately that the only important things we have are those things which cannot be taken away, like reason itself, the soul and morality. Once reason shows us what is important, we know how to behave and think, and without the ability to carry out this type of exercise we are at the mercy of our feelings and the influence of others.

This belief in the capacity of human reason to help us determine what we should do and what our role in the world is has led the most distinguished recent commentator on Miskawayh, Mohammed Arkoun, to call him a humanist, a part of the general humanist movement of his time involving al-Tawḥīdī and al-Sijistānī. In some ways this description is very apposite, since it does mark the importance in Miskawayh's thought of reason and what reason can tell us, by contrast with religion and the teachings of religion. This is not to say that he did not think the teachings of Islam are important. There is no reason to believe that he was not entirely sincere in his adherence to Islam. Yet, it is philosophy that is his central concern and even when he considers religious practices he sometimes gives them an instrumental rationale.

Al-Ghazzālī came to be infuriated by Miskawayh's suggestion that the point of communal prayer is to base religion upon the natural gregariousness of human beings in society. It seemed to al-Ghazzālī that, if this was the point of the practice, then it would be seen as not having the importance it should have as one of the basic rituals of religion. The significance of such communal rituals, according to al-Ghazzālī, is that they are specified by the religion, and for no other reason. Their reason is that they are not only reasonable; God points to the vast gap between us and Himself by setting us unpleasant and difficult tasks. For Miskawayh the reason for the ritual is that it has a part to play in helping us adapt to religious life using the dispositions which are natural to us, so that the rules of religion are essentially reasonable. Miskawayh quotes from the Qur'ān, Aristotle, Plato, al-Kindī and his contemporaries in his writings without emphasizing the position of the Qur'ān above that of the other authorities. The teachings of Islam have a part to play in informing us how to live and what is real, but so also do other more theoretical approaches, and in any case the greatest respect seems to be accorded to the Greek authorities.

This might suggest the question as to how original Miskawayh's thought is. It clearly was influential, and both during his life and after his death in 421/1030 it was much quoted and copied. The style of some of his works, combining abstract thought with practical suggestions, is a compelling one, capable of attracting a whole range of different audiences, and was popular long after he died. Yet Miskawayh does seem to have presented a mixture of ideas and theories which were not properly integrated, and which consisted of a ragbag rather than a synthesis. Commentators do frequently comment upon the complex nature of his sources, some of which we can only conjecture about today, as though his main contribution is to try to weave all these different authors into a particular text. It is true that some of his writings are just lists of "wisdom" from a range of cultures and religions (the *Jāwīdān khirad* or "Perennial Philosophy", for example). Some of his practical comments upon moral problems seem rather better suited to the *Reader's Digest* than to analytical philosophy. Yet it is worth acknowledging that at its best his philosophy is highly analytical and maintains high standards of consistency and coherence. The fact that he mixes together Plato, Aristotle, Neoplatonism, Pythagoras, and so on is not an indication so much of his collecting different theories, but rather of a creative attempt at using these different approaches to cast light upon important issues. There is nothing basically wrong with being an Aristotelian and yet going off into Platonic or Pythagorean directions. Miskawayh shows how possible it is to combine a Platonic conception of the soul with an Aristotelian account of moral development. The notion of a yet higher realm of being at which the soul comes into contact with divine reality is a perfectly possible addition to the account which he gives of social and intellectual life. His arguments throw up many problems of their own, but they are noticeable as arguments, and there is no attempt at importing revelation to resolve theoretical difficulties. It is perhaps the combination in Miskawayh of elegance of style, practical relevance and philosophical toughness which prolonged his influence in the Islamic world.

REFERENCES

Miskawayh, Aḥmad (1901) *Al-Fawz al-aṣghar* (Beirut).
—— (1964) *Fī māhiyyat al-'adl*, ed. M. S. Khan (Leiden).
—— (1951) *Al-Ḥawāmil wa'l-shawāmil*, ed. A. Amin (Cairo).
—— (1952) *Al-Ḥikmah al-khālidah* (*Jāwīdān khirad*), ed. A. Badawī (Cairo).
—— (1928) *Kitāb al-sa'ādah* (Cairo).
—— (1966) *Tahdhīb al-akhlāq*, ed. C. Zurayk (Beirut), trans. by him as *The Refinement of Character* (Beirut, 1968).

The two outstanding contemporary commentators on Miskawayh are Mohammed Arkoun and Majid Fakhry. Their most relevant works are:

Arkoun, M. (1961) "Deux épîtres de Miskawayh", *Bulletin d'Etudes Orientales*, 17: 7–74.
—— (1963) "Texts inédits de Miskawayh", *Annales Islamalogiques*, 5: 181–205.
—— (1970) *Contribution à l'étude de l'humanisme arabe au IVe/Xe siècle: Miskawayh (320/325–421) = (932/936–1030)* (Paris).
Fakhry, M. (1973) "The Platonism of Miskawayh and its Implication for his Ethics", *Studia Islamica*, 42: 39–57.
—— (1983) *A History of Islamic Philosophy*, 2nd ed. (New York).
—— (1991) *Ethical Theories in Islam* (Leiden).

CHAPTER 19

Al-Ghazzālī

Massimo Campanini

If we wish to place al-Ghazzālī within a history of Islamic philosophy we must make some preliminary remarks. The most obvious starting point is that al-Ghazzālī did not consider himself a philosopher, nor liked to be considered as such. Yet it is interesting that the Christian thinkers of the Middle Ages, reading his book *Maqāṣid al-falāsifah* ("The Aims of Philosophers"), a reasoned and objective exposition of the main philosophical topics of his time, looked on him as a *faylasūf* like Ibn Sīnā or Ibn Rushd. It not only means that al-Ghazzālī studied and assimilated philosophy deeply, being aware of its theoretical glamour and its structural strength, but also it leads us to believe that philosophy must have had at least an indirect influence even on his mystical thought. Moreover, although al-Ghazzālī, who was essentially a theologian, a mystic and a jurist, fought sharply against philosophy, trying to demonstrate its contradictions, it would be misleading not to recognize that his mysticism and theology are not simply practical and religious doctrines but have a noticeable theoretical depth.

A second important issue arises regarding the strictly philosophical question of the relation between truth and certainty, an issue al-Ghazzālī viewed as a vital problem for the scholar. He argued that philosophy cannot assure the truth because it does not produce certainty; and brought against philosophy the same charge Ibn Rushd brought against theology, namely of yielding to huge compromises about the logical coherence of its arguments. In the *Munqidh min al-ḍalāl*, al-Ghazzālī wrote:

> They [the philosophers who apply logic] draw up a list of the conditions to be fulfilled by demonstration which are known without fail to produce certainty. When, however, they come at length to treat of religious questions, not merely are they unable

to satisfy these conditions, but they admit an extreme degree of relaxation.

(al-Ghazzālī (1967a): 36)

Actually, in al-Ghazzālī's opinion, the relation of necessity which exists between the premisses and the conclusions of a syllogism is not able to persuade both the mind and the *heart*. True knowledge is the consequence of illumination (*ilhām*), of a divine inspiration. Al-Ghazzālī says that "when God takes care of the heart . . ., the breast lightens and the mystery of the spiritual realm [*malakūt*] is revealed, and the veil of error vanishes and the reality of divine things shines in the heart" (al-Ghazzālī (1985), 3: 21). Once the heart becomes owner of truth, the mind then obtains certainty: "the necessary truths of the intellect became once more accepted, as I regained confidence in their certainty and trustworthy character. This did not come about by systematic demonstration or marshalled argument, but by a light which God most high cast into my breast" (al-Ghazzālī (1967a): 25).

It does not mean that al-Ghazzālī denied, for instance, the compulsory nature of reasoning (Marmura 1965), especially mathematical and logical reasoning;[1] but it is important to point out that he considered theoretical certainty as an effect of the highest kind of knowledge, a knowledge which attains its top level by mystical experience and taste (*dhawq*). Here, notwithstanding that his starting point was philosophical, al-Ghazzālī arrives at conclusions very far from ordinarily philosophical.

Abū Ḥāmid Muḥammad ibn Muḥammad al-Ghazzālī was born at Ṭus, a city in Khurasan, in Persia, in 450/1058. He received a good traditional education first at Jurjan and then Nishapur, the provincial capital, where he attended the lessons of the most distinguished theologian of his time, the Ash'arite Imām al-Ḥarāmayn Abu'l-Ma'ālī al-Juwaynī. Under his guide, al-Ghazzālī adopted the main principles of the Ash'arite *kalām*, to which he remained faithful until the end of his life.[2]

Principles like the Unity of God (*Tawḥīd*) and the reality of Divine Attributes, which must be distinguished from the very Essence of God, together with other characteristic topics of al-Ash'arī's theology are held by al-Ghazzālī too: the belief in the eternity of the Qur'ān; the acceptance of the Qur'ānic apparently anthropomorphic descriptions of God, who is said to have sight, hearing and a body even though we cannot know how;[3] the conviction that all the blessed will see the Face of God in Paradise like "a moon in a bright night"; the repeated assertion that the only way to know God is revelation, because human reason is too weak to grasp such sublime realities; and the acknowledgment that the succession of the four righteous caliphs (*al-rāshidūn*) is legitimate according to the order of morality.

All these utterances are clearly opposed to the Mu'tazilite doctrines and can be judged "orthodox", although it is notoriously difficult to understand the real meaning of orthodoxy in Islam. Some scholars deny that Ash'arism must be considered the chief orthodox school in the Islamic world (see Makdisi (1963) and (1983)) and even maintain, in relation to al-Ghazzālī, the impossibility of identifying Ash'arism with Shāfi'ite *madhhab* (Makdisi in UNESCO (1987)). The solution of this problem does not matter here. The essential point is that al-Ghazzālī turned Ash'arite *kalām* into the dialectical basis of his religious revival, making of it the actual framework of his philosophical and to some extent mystical reflection.

In 478/1085 al-Ghazzālī joined the court of Niẓām al-Mulk, omnipotent vizier of the Seljūq Sultan Malikshāh, and became a close friend of the vizier. Niẓām al-Mulk appointed him teacher of Shāfi'ite jurisprudence in the Madrasah Niẓāmiyyah of Baghdad (484/1091), and soon al-Ghazzālī collected around himself a great number of students. After a few years, al-Ghazzālī was an intellectual of the court, if not a courtier. Occupying this position, he appreciated the corruption and immorality of power, the compromises of orthodox *fuqahā'* and *'ulamā'* with depraved kings and emirs, and his political ideas matured (see Laoust (1970) and Watt (1963)).

Al-Ghazzālī professed a sincere loyalty to the caliphate, recognizing the legitimacy of 'Abbasid rule. Anyway, he argued that caliphs and sultans had to co-operate to bring peace and safety to the Muslim empire. The caliphs, who were given complete religious authority, had to receive the oath of allegiance from the sultans, on whom supreme political authority rested. The sultan had not only the duty to defend the caliphate but also to repress any possible revolutionary tendency (see Binder (1955) and the papers collected in Lambton (1980)). Above all, al-Ghazzālī's political attitude was inspired by a sort of quietism, because he stigmatized any revolt, even against an oppressive and evil monarch (Laoust (1970): 368ff.). This attitude is induced by a particular meaning of the relation between the outward and inner world. In fact, political quietism is functional to the renaissance of religious sciences. Nobody – and surely not a scholar or a mystic – can look after his or her conscience if the outside world is troubled by wars and injustice. The reform of the heart needs social peace and harmony, even though this silence has to be paid for with an autocratic power. The wise person may, however, close the windows of the world to open the door of soul.

Obviously, it can be argued that this quietism was justified by fear and dislike of Ismā'īlī Shi'ism which, at the end of the fifth/eleventh century, seemed still very strong in Fāṭimid Cairo and indeed was vigorously spreading throughout the Middle East after Ḥasan Ṣabbāḥ founded at Alamut a Bāṭinī state of warrior monks improperly known as "Assassins". The same Niẓām al-Mulk was finally killed by an Assassin in 485/1092. Farid Jabre interpreted the development of almost all al-Ghazzālī's thought in the light of his anti-Bāṭinite polemic (Jabre 1958). This thesis is undoubtedly too simple, but it is true that al-Ghazzālī viewed Ismā'īlism as a real danger for orthodox Islam, both politically and dogmatically. So he devoted many works to the confutation of Ismā'īlism, perhaps the most important of which is the *Faḍā'iḥ al-bāṭiniyyah wa faḍā'il al-mustaẓhiriyyah* or *al-Mustaẓhirī* ("The Infamies of the Bāṭinites and the Excellences of the Mustaẓhirites"), composed in 487–8/1094 and dedicated to the new caliph al-Mustaẓhir.

The core of al-Ghazzālī's anti-Bāṭinite criticism consists in underlining the absurdities and the heretical innovations which follow the blind submission (*taqlīd*) the Bāṭinites show to the authoritarian teaching (*ta'līm*) of their Imāms. Really, the only living guide for the Muslims must be the Prophet Muḥammad, whose acts and utterances compound the body of *Ḥadīth* and *Sunnah* and are necessary and sufficient to rule the life of the Islamic community. An orthodox Muslim, al-Ghazzālī says,

> claims knowledge of only two questions: one of them is the existence of the Maker, the necessary existent, in no need of maker and manager; and the second is the veracity of the Apostle. And regarding the remaining questions, it suffices us to learn them by blind acceptance from the Apostle.
>
> (al-Ghazzālī (1980a): 250)

Even though al-Ghazzālī seems here to be substituting a blind submission to another authority, it is also worth pointing out that he charges the Bāṭinites with being bad theologians, making a poor use of logic and arbitrarily altering the meaning of the holy texts. Al-Ghazzālī thinks that it is deceptive and contradictory to try to invalidate intellectual reasoning by an apodeictic proof exalting the infallibility of the Imāms (al-Ghazzālī (1980a): 218). Indeed, if we pay unconditional approval to the Imām's utterances, how can we build our doctrine on reasoning? The *ta'līm* is in opposition to intellect (al-Ghazzālī (1980a): 249).

This is quite an intriguing point. Although al-Ghazzālī continues to speak against the gnoseological legitimacy of reasoning, he does not cease to emphasize the greater rationality of his own position. The same attitude al-Ghazzālī shows in the *Tahāfut al-falāsifah* ("The Incoherence of the Philosophers"), the famous work directed properly against philosophy. Dogmatically, philosophy is as dangerous as Ismā'īlism, and in the *Tahāfut* al-Ghazzālī intends to demonstrate that philosophers are unable to prove, from a theoretical point of view, the religious truths. Anyway, he does not fight philosophers with the weapons of authority and divine revelation, but with the same techniques philosophy uses (see Leaman (1985): chapters 1–3; and Bello (1989): chapters 6–8). In this sense, al-Ghazzālī takes perhaps an even more rationalistic position than Ibn Rushd, who, in his *Faṣl al-maqāl* and *Tahāfut at-tahāfut*, tried to transform philosophy into a doctrine which, if not close to religious law, at least does not contrast with it, rather than describing theology as a rationalist discipline (see Campanini (1989): Introduction). On the contrary, al-Ghazzālī keeps religion and philosophy well separated, being aware of the essential irreducibility of the two positions.

In the *Tahāfut al-falāsifah* he argues that philosophers cannot demonstrate the creation of the world by God, nor the spiritual substance of the human soul. In particular, he argues that philosophers become infidels on three questions: the eternity of the world (a thesis peculiar to Aristotle); the impossibility of God's knowledge of particulars (a thesis strongly held by Ibn Sīnā), and the denial of bodily resurrection and mortality of the individual souls, a naturalistic theory which is not exclusively Aristotelian. These three subjects are enough to transform the philosophical message into a potentially corrupting theory. After all, even if the greatest philosophers cannot in general be charged with infidelity (al-Ghazzālī (1928): 6–7), their doctrines lead many people "to refuse the details of religions and creeds, and to believe that they are human constructed laws and artifices" (al-Ghazzālī (1928): 5).

A correct and orthodox starting point must begin by considering God as the highest Being and as the unique actually acting Will. On the one hand,

> in God there is an Essence [*ḥaqiqah*] and a quiddity [*māhiyyah*], and this Essence is equivalent to his Existence, namely that God is free from non-being and privation. However, His Existence is not additional to Essence . . . No agent has produced the existence of a God who does not come to an end and is eternal without any determining cause.
>
> (al-Ghazzālī (1928): 196)

On the other hand, "The First Principle is all-knowing, all-powerful and all-willing. He acts as He wants and decides as He wants; He creates all the creatures and natures as He wants and in the shape He wants" (al-Ghazzālī (1928): 131)

Al-Ghazzālī stresses vigorously the Will of God, a quality which transforms itself in the potentiality (and actuality) of action. Considering these premisses, is there a place in al-Ghazzālī's system for natural causes or *causae secundae*? The problem of causality is perhaps the most discussed in the historiographical literature on our thinker. Even in recent times, several scholars have faced this issue (see Goodman (1978); Alon (1980); Abrahamov (1988)).

It is wrong to think that al-Ghazzālī absolutely denied the existence of natural causality. To deny that fire burns cotton would be foolish.

What al-Ghazzālī denies is the existence of a necessary connection between the cause and the caused independently of the Will of God who creates the fact of burning. If the contingent world is also the world of all-possibility, al-Ghazzālī claims that this possibility is just the field of God's free action. The difficulty does not lie in the objective existence of things which are concrete just because God created them. The epistemological problem resides in the impossibility of connecting directly an effect to a cause. The causes can be always hypothetical, and the only certainty we have is that they are consequences of God's Will.

It is well known that al-Ghazzālī precedes David Hume in his theory that the nexus of causality is only apparent and is the effect of the human custom of linking together two occurrences which are happening uniformly in nature: "The continuity of custom [*'ādah*] regarding them [i.e. the things which seem necessary but are only possible], time after time, implants in our mind so strong [an impression of] flow [*jarayān*] in accordance with past habits that [the continuity] cannot be separated from the things" (al-Ghazzālī (1928): 285).

Al-Ghazzālī expresses the same concept in other places in the *Tahāfut* (al-Ghazzālī (1928): 277–8), but he always stresses the fact that it is God who creates the linkage among the phenomena: "As to what appears outwardly of the connection . . . it depends on the determining action [*taqdīr*] of God – praise be to Him! – who creates [the appearances] in a sequence [*'alā'l-tasāwuq*]."

God is able to overturn the rules of natural eventualities and submit the functioning of nature to completely new laws. But this does not mean that God really behaves in such a manner or that He does not give the fire or the water the natural properties to burn and to extinguish. So it is worth moderating the sceptical value of some of al-Ghazzālī's statements such as the following: "I proceeded therefore with extreme earnestness to reflect on sense-perception and on necessary truths, to see whether I could make myself doubt them. The outcome of this protracted effort to induce doubt was that I could no longer trust sense-perception either" (al-Ghazzālī (1967a): 23).

Even though al-Ghazzālī sometimes seems attached to a vaguely Cartesian methodical doubt, it does not imply an authentic denial of religious truths nor a refusal of the objective world's reality. Rather, doubt has a prevailing epistemological meaning, and it is addressed to the trustworthiness of the human sciences.

In 488/1095, owing to a spiritual and psychological crisis whose veracity cannot be questioned (Poggi 1967),[4] al-Ghazzālī left Baghdad and for two or three years he lived in Syria and Palestine and made the pilgrimage to Mecca. He came back to Persia before 493/1099, and he carried on his concealment till the summer of 499/1106 when Fakhr al-Mulk, vizier of the Seljūq Sultan Sanjār, persuaded him to resume his juridical teaching in the Madrasah Niẓāmiyyah of Nishapur. Al-Ghazzālī's return to public life lasted only a little more than two years, because in 503/1109 he retired finally to Tus, where he died in 505/1111.

The long period of concealment witnessed a deep transformation of al-Ghazzālī's speculative interests and even of his *Weltanschauung*. He did not attend any more to philosophy and applied himself totally to Sufism and to the renewal of orthodox religion. In the *Munqidh*, the spiritual autobiography composed approximately between 501/1107 and 503/1109, he reveals an almost messianic feeling of being aware that "God Most High has promised to revive His religion at the beginning of each century" (al-Ghazzālī (1967a): 75). Al-Ghazzālī had the conviction that he was the person designated to carry out this task for his epoch, and pursued his reforming aim by composing a great work, whose title is significantly *The Revivification of the Sciences of Religion* (*Iḥyā' 'ulūm al-dīn*), and an exhaustive abridgement of the major work, that is the *Book of the Forty Principles of Religion* (*Kitāb al-arba'īn fī uṣūl al-dīn*), as well as its Persian summary *Kīmiyā-yi sa'ādat* ("The Alchemy of Happiness").

Many scholars argued that al-Ghazzālī achieved the reconciliation of Sufism and orthodoxy (among the last Glassen (1981)). A fact is that, at the end of his life, he considered Sufism as the best doctrine in comparison with philosophy or theology, because, while the human sciences are abstract and superficial, Sufism leads the learned to a positive knowledge of God and nature:

> I apprehended clearly that the mystics are men who had real experiences, not men of words, and that I had already progressed as far as possible by way of intellectual apprehension. What remained for me was not to be attained by oral instruction and study, but only by immediate experience and by walking in the mystic way.
>
> (al-Ghazzālī (1967a): 55)

The path to God throughout Sufism is a living experience and like an ascending parabola whose starting point is "science". In the *Arba'īn* al-Ghazzālī interprets "science" as the knowledge of God and His Attributes and of the religious duties like prayer, pilgrimage and the alms tax (al-Ghazzālī (1970): 12–51). But this kind of science, although necessary, is just propaedeutic to an evaluation of a set of subsequent preparatory stages.

There is, first of all, the necessity of avoiding unlawful and blameworthy behaviour, like wrath, avarice, love of worldly goods, etc., which can remove the faithful and the novice (*murīd*) from the right path. In opposition to these reprehensible attitudes, al-Ghazzālī suggests commendable conduct, among which of great importance are repentance, asceticism and fear of God.

Repentance is "the way of reverting from the remoteness to the proximity of God" (al-Ghazzālī (1970): 197; al-Ghazzālī (1985), 4: 11–12). Asceticism is "the dislike of the soul for materiality", a dislike whose roots (*aṣl*) are the science and the light, that is the mystical knowledge and illumination shining in the heart (al-Ghazzālī (1970): 211). Fear of God is "pain in the heart and its burning because of the expectation of future adversities" (al-Ghazzālī (1970): 205), and the best fruit of this feeling is the opening of the soul's inner doors to a quiet hope (al-Ghazzālī (1985), 4: 135ff.). In the end, the correct behaviour of a mystic implies a silent satisfaction with God's decrees. Both in the *Iḥyā'* and in the *Arba'īn* al-Ghazzālī concludes his exposition by the *riḍā' bi'l-qaḍā'* which is coupled with a sincere thanksgiving for all the benefits (and also all the sufferings) God decides to bring to humankind.

After having attained the best possible disposition, the *murīd* is ready to begin the proper approach to God (Campanini 1991). The first step is the frank intention of worship (*nīyyah*); but the two main moments are the *dhikr* and the *tawakkul*. The *dhikr* is the continuous remembrance of God's Name (Gardet and Anawati (1961): the fourth part) and it leads the mystic to immersion and annihilation (*fanā'*) in God. Anyway, the *fanā'* or ecstatic grasp is only a short and transient instant (al-Ghazzālī (1970): 62) and does not concern any kind of *ḥulūl*, or descent and incarnation of God in the mystic. Al-Ghazzālī strongly rejects every immoderate claim of some Sufis, such as the theophatic utterances by al-Ḥallāj or al-Basṭāmī, because they are dangerous and can lead through incomprehension to heresy and polytheism (*shirk*).

Rather, al-Ghazzālī underlines the importance of love (*maḥabbah*) (Siauve 1986) and this represents surely an element of distinctness from some of the other Islamic Sufis. In the *Arba'īn* al-Ghazzālī writes that "a true learned man loves only God Most High; and if he loves somebody who is not God, he loves him for God, the Almighty and Sublime" (al-Ghazzālī (1970): 257). The highest degree of love involves a full confidence in God: this is the meaning of *tawakkul*, such a complete trust in the Creator that the believer gives himself up to Him "like a dead man in the hands of a corpse-washer" (al-Ghazzālī (1970): 249; al-Ghazzālī (1985), 4: 242–3).

Some scholars however denied that al-Ghazzālī's mysticism was a real ecstatic experience, stressing on the contrary the technical and practical aspects of his theory (Jabre 1958), although all Sufis themselves consider him to be one of the most outstanding among them. It is difficult to reach a balanced answer to this problem from the outside. An important issue is to point out that the Sufi way did not imply for al-Ghazzālī the neglect of the orthodox practices of worship and the careful fulfilment of the *Sunnah* (al-Ghazzālī (1967a): 71–2). Al-Ghazzālī is persuaded that exteriority leads to interiority (al-Ghazzālī (1970):

102ff.), so that Makdisi is right when he says, drawing a comparison between al-Ghazzālī and Ibn Taymiyyah on Sufism, that both criticized sharply the exaggerations of some Sufis because Sufism often sides against the religious law and devalues the external (and social) meanings of that law (Makdisi (1983): 55).

Finally, Sufism is not for al-Ghazzālī simply an individual path to reach perfection but a whole conception of life including ethics and morality, behaviour and belief, cosmology and metaphysics. In this sense, it is perhaps true that al-Ghazzālī's mysticism is not *only* a lived experience but also a rational construction by which the learned person can taste the beatitude of ecstasy without relinquishing the satisfaction of theoretical inquiry.

Already the *Mīzān al-'amal*, composed in the last year of al-Ghazzālī's period in Baghdad, shows a tendency to an intellectual reading of the mystical way of life. Commenting on this book, Laoust writes that in it "al-Ghazzālī is associating the method of the Sufis with the method of speculative theologians, and in particular of the Ash'arites" (Laoust (1970): 73). So we can realize that there is not a complete break in al-Ghazzālī's conception of ethics before and after the crisis of 488/1095. Reason and mysticism have never been separated in al-Ghazzālī's mind.

Even in works devoted primarily to religious reform like *Iḥyā'* and *Arba'īn*, we find a well articulated image of God who "in his Essence is unique, individual, without companions and there is nothing which looks like Him . . . He is everlasting, continuous in His existence" (al-Ghazzālī (1970): 13). The concrete reality of God seems absolutely stated, but

> He is not a body with a shape, nor a measured or definite substance. Nothing looks like Him, either regarding measurability or regarding divisibility in parts. God is not a substance, nor can substances define Him; He is not an accident nor can accidents define Him. No existent being looks like Him and "nothing can be compared with Him" (Qur'ān, 42: 11). God does not look like things. Quantity cannot limit Him; no region can enclose Him; no side can surround Him.
>
> (al-Ghazzālī (1970): 14)

This description of God, as far as His transcendence is concerned, is very close to the Mu'tazilite negative theology described by al-Ash'arī in his *Maqālāt* (al-Ash'arī (1969), 1: 235), and signifies the irreducibility of God to the natural world and his transcendence (Shehadi (1964); Burrell (1987)). This kind of negative theology removes God from nature and grants his untouchability by any deficiencies or limitations, death or dissolution.

But a danger is implicit in the Mu'tazilite position, namely the *ta'ṭīl*, the denial of those Divine Attributes, apparently anthropomorphic, which, none the less, are explicitly declared in the Qur'ān. Al-Ghazzālī wants to avoid such a risk. For him, the Divine Attributes are positive realities, and they are separated from the Essence of God:

> God Most High knows science, lives life, is powerful through power, willing through will, speaking with a word, hearing by a capacity to hear, seeing by a capacity to see. He has these qualifications in virtue of the eternal attributes. If someone [a Mu'tazilite] says that God knows without science, he would say that it is possible to be rich without richness or that there is a science without a scientist or a knowing without an object of knowledge.
>
> (al-Ghazzālī (1985), 1: 102–3)

The idea of God al-Ghazzālī sketches is strongly Islamic. God is a person living and willing. He decides the destiny of people and animals and can make people suffer without granting them any reward (al-Ghazzālī (1985), 1: 104). Anyway, as we have already pointed out, this arbitrary power does not mean irrational subjectivity in choices. Rather, there are a few places where al-Ghazzālī seems to approach Leibniz's concept of "the best of all possible worlds" (see Ormsby (1984)). In the *Iḥyā'*, we read:

> Everything which God apportions to man . . . is . . . pure right, with no wrong in it. Indeed, it is according to the necessarily right order, in accord with what must be and as it must be and in the measure in which it must be; and there is not potentially anything whatever more excellent and more complete than it.
>
> (al-Ghazzālī (1985), 4: 229–30)

And in the *Arba'īn*:

> There are different ways for grasping, with perfect awareness, the perfection of God's generosity and wisdom. One of these ways is the reflection on the manner in which God organized [*tartīb*] the causes determining the caused. One may regard the knowledge of the decree [*qaḍā'*] by which God produced everything in the twinkling of an eye, and of the predestination [*qadar*] which is the clear cause [*sabab*] of the decree's details. They are the most perfect and the best possible [decisions] and there is no way to act better and more adequately.
>
> (al-Ghazzālī (1970): 202)

Obviously, al-Ghazzālī does not argue that our world is the best world God was able to create, but simply that the omnipotence of God has established for *this* universe the most perfect possible rules of functioning, even if He would have been able to produce infinitely different worlds. Al-Ghazzālī's theory of God's omnipotence is perhaps comparable to the Western medieval distinction between *potentia absoluta et ordinata Dei*,[5] a question faced by the most important Christian thinkers such as Duns Scot, Thomas Aquinas and William of Ockham. In al-Ghazzālī's view, God can act *extra legem*, but actually He does not, because He provides for the world after having created it. Furthermore, al-Ghazzālī thinks that the two *potentiae* are not two dissimilar divinely acting ways but the result of only one determining disposition.

The rationality of God's creation is clearly expressed also in the *Maqṣad al-asnā fī sharḥ asmā' Allāh al-ḥusnā* ("The Highest Aim in the Commentary of the Beautiful Names of God"), a book composed approximately at the same time as *Iḥyā'* and a text which can be placed in a long tradition of Islamic studies about the metaphysical, religious and even cosmological meaning of God's ninety-nine beautiful Names (Gimaret 1988). So in the *Maqṣad* we read that "what comes out from non-existence to existence needs, first of all, a measure (*taqdīr*); secondly, to exist in accordance with this measure; and thirdly, to obtain a right shape" (al-Ghazzālī (1987): 75).

These operative functions are signified by three of God's Names: *al-Khāliq*, or "who gives the things their measure", *al-Bāri'*, or "who brings out the things from nothing to being" and *al-Muṣawwir*, or "who creates the things in accordance with the measure" (al-Ghazzālī (1987): 76). In reference to the Name *al-Muṣawwir*, al-Ghazzālī specifies that "God disposes the things in the best possible arrangement" (al-Ghazzālī (1987): 77), so that it is really difficult not to infer a perfect disposition of the universe.

From a mystic cosmological point of view, this universe is double-faced: there is a natural world which is subdued to God's compulsory Will and is called by al-Ghazzālī *mulk*; and there is a heavenly world which is called *malakūt* (Wensinck (1940): 79ff.). Now, the *mulk* is only the shadow of the true world. In the *Arba'īn* al-Ghazzālī uses quite Neoplatonic terms to maintain that

> the corporeal world has no real existence [*wujūd ḥaqīqī*], but it is, in relation to the world of Order [*'ālam al-amr*], like the shadow of a body; the shadow of a man is not the real substance [*ḥaqīqah*] of that man, and so the individual being is not really existent but it is a shadow of the real substance.
>
> (al-Ghazzālī (1970): 62)

Even though deprived of metaphysical independence, the world is not a mere phantasm. Otherwise, we would not be able to understand the following statement: "All the beings of this world are the effects of God's omnipotence and lights of His Essence. There is no darkness more obscure than non-existence and there is no light more bright than existence. The existence of all things is a light of the Essence of God Most High" (al-Ghazzālī (1985), 4: 398).

All the beings in the world receive their contingent illumination from God who is absolute Being and absolute Light. Indeed, God is completely manifest in the world, but the divine Light is so blinding that it conceals its original source (al-Ghazzālī (1987): 136–7, in reference to the beautiful Names *al-ẓāhir* and *al-bāṭin*). Analogically, the light of the sun, which is shining over the world, cannot be perceived by an observer who is looking only at the objects and does not turn his or her eyes up to the sky. There is a mystical idea beneath this symbol: that is, all worldly things are nothing in front of the Creator according to the famous Qur'ānic verse: "All who live on earth perish, but the Face of your Lord will abide for ever" (55: 26–7).

The path we have hitherto followed may suggest that al-Ghazzālī's thought is noticeably homogeneous. Perhaps this is quite correct if we consider the metaphysical problems, but the perspective is different if we consider the epistemological problems. We have already acknowledged al-Ghazzālī's trust in reasoning, but in the "Introduction" or *muqaddimah* to the *Tahāfut al-falāsifah* he argues that natural sciences and physical utterances cannot be judged by theological or scriptural counterarguments. Al-Ghazzālī even suggests that whoever tries to contest the mathematical proofs by a literal interpretation of the *Ḥadīth* and *Sunnah* damages religion, because the methods of religion are different from the methods of natural inquiry (al-Ghazzālī (1928): 7–8). Here, al-Ghazzālī seems to partake of the same epistemological positions Galileo maintained in his famous letter dated 21 December 1613 to Benedetto Castelli, that the Holy Scriptures are not suitable for scientific questions.[6] Anyway, the Muslim thinker immediately adds: "The theoretical value of natural questions, in relation to research about God, is like asking how many layers an onion or how many seeds a pomegranate has. The only really important thing to point out is that they are acts of God" (al-Ghazzālī (1928): 8).

In the *Iḥyā'*, written after the psychological crisis which led to al-Ghazzālī's conversion to Sufism, natural sciences are said to be potentially dangerous for religion, save those practices, like medicine, useful for caring for human life (al-Ghazzālī (1985), 1: 27). Al-Ghazzālī speaks about the intellect as the noblest human attribute, but the context shows that he regards intellect (*'aql*) as the privileged tool for receiving divine illumination and for grasping the mystic science of *dévoilement* (*mukāshafah*), the science of opening the heart to the ecstatic knowledge of God (al-Ghazzālī (1985), 1: 19 and 25).

Some hesitations are manifest, and the beginning of concealment after 488/1095 denotes a deep mental transformation. So a final judgment on al-Ghazzālī's attitude towards knowledge and science must be very tenuous. There is at least one thing for sure: the only important and true knowledge is the knowledge of God and His Acts, because the world is valuable only as an effect of God's Will. Moreover, even though a deep insight into the mystery of reality can be granted exclusively by an illumination coming from God, it would be silly to obliterate demonstrative reasoning. First of all, there is the necessity to defend religion against all its enemies, many of whom are dangerously skilled in persuasive demonstration. As we have already seen, philosophy can be used against philosophy, supposing that the apologetic aim is prevalent. As to the indispensability of science, from al-Ghazzālī's point of view, knowledge of the world and its laws are worthwhile but, employing a strictly juridical vocabulary, supererogatory.

Learned men cannot but know God and appreciate his omnipotence and providence. But this learning is not fitted for the masses. There are many passages where al-Ghazzālī argues against the desirability of the widespread divulging of esoteric knowledge among ordinary people (al-Ghazzālī (1970): 31; al-Ghazzālī (1967a): 39ff.).[7] A deep insight into the mysteries of faith and theology does not help in obtaining eternal salvation. Al-Ghazzālī wrote his very last work, the *Iljām al-'awāmm 'an 'ilm al-kalām* ("Restraint of the Common People from the Science of *kalām*") to show how many and how great are the hazards of propagating science among people not prepared to receive it. Although Ibn Rushd charged al-Ghazzālī with the intention of divulging knowledge to the unlearned, al-Ghazzālī's perplexity in regard to an uncontrolled circulation of science is at least equal to the reluctance of his great adversary from Cordova.

The mystical conversation with God is undoubtedly for al-Ghazzālī essentially a *soliloquium*: the mystic finds in himself all the answers and certainties his soul needs. But the existence of other people and the necessity to relate to them cannot be ruled out. Al-Ghazzālī is much too good a jurist to deny any of the pillars of Islamic behaviour and tradition, for instance the common prayer on Friday or the assertion that the Islamic community cannot agree on a mistake. In this sense, the knowledge shared by the *'ulamā'* and *fuqahā'* possesses an obvious social value determined by legal presuppositions. The statements of *ahl al-sunnah wa'l-jamā'ah*, namely the orthodox community, are binding for everyone. For Ibn Rushd too the pillars of faith are outstanding references for everyone, philosophers and common people equally. It is characteristic that al-Ghazzālī often provides for the orthodox a "middle way" between opposite extremities (al-Ghazzālī (1970): 16–27), a *medietas* which is coherent with the teachings of the Prophet.

The significance of al-Ghazzālī's position is that he blames both the person who is blindly subjugated to the principle of authority, and the person who exceeds in trusting reason. Both depart from obeying the law and the juridical prescriptions of religion which are important because they have the task of determining social relations.

Al-Ghazzālī is universally known as "the proof of Islam" (*ḥujjat al-islām*) and this qualification is meaningful only if we admit that his work is a conscious synthesis of three main aspects of the Islamic conception of rationality: theoretical and philosophical inquiry, juridical legislation and mystical practice. Perhaps this kind of rationality appears quite distant from Western rationality. Yet, the breadth of al-Ghazzālī's thought means that he can be viewed as the prototype of the Muslim intellectual (Watt 1963).[8]

NOTES

1 There are many passages (for instance al-Ghazzālī (1967a): 33, or al-Ghāzzalī (1928): 11–12) where he defends the authority of mathematical sciences; moreover he composed treatises such as *Mi'yār al-'ilm* ("The Standard of Science") to demonstrate the usefulness of logic for distinguishing true propositions from the erroneous and for establishing the inherent strength of a discourse.

2 It is important to remember that al-Ghazzālī wrote only one treatise properly concerning *kalām*, namely *al-Iqtiṣād fi'l-i'tiqād*, composed the last time he stayed in Baghdad as a professor in the Madrasah Niẓāmiyyah.

3 It is the famous question of the *balkafah* or *bilā kayfah*, especially characteristic of the Ash'arites (see Gardet and Anawati (1981): 52ff.; Caspar (1987): 174ff.).

4 It is likely (as Jabre argued) that the concealment of al-Ghazzālī was provoked *also*, but not exclusively, by political reasons, for instance the fear of the Bāṭinite threat or the hostility of the Sultan Berkiyārūq who succeeded his father Malikshāh in 488/1094. But it would be misleading to undervalue the deeper religious motives.

5 About this problem in Western medieval philosophy, see T. Rudavsky (ed.), *Divine Omniscience and Omnipotence in Medieval Philosophy* (Dordrecht and Boston, 1985); W. Courtenay, *Covenant and Causality in Medieval Thought* (London, 1984); M. T. Fumagalli Beonio-Brocchieri (ed.), *Sopra la volta del mondo: onnipotenza e potenza assoluta di dio tra medioevo e età moderna* (Bergamo, 1986).

6 See G. Galilei, *Opere*, ed. by F. Flora (Milan and Naples, 1953): 988–9. Galileo's firm position in favour of the independence of science from religion scandalized the Church and the official authorities. On the contrary, it is noticeworthy that this – perhaps – accidental statement by al-Ghazzālī has been neglected by the scholars who studied his thought.

7 In the *Mīzān al-'amal* (al-Ghazzālī (1945): 35) we read that the majority of people need action (namely, obedience to legal and religious rules) more than reasoning. What is important is the Truth, because "doctrine" is always changing (al-Ghazzālī (1945): 148).

8 The necessity of considering al-Ghazzālī as a prototype of a Muslim intellectual and thinker is underlined also by Veccia Vaglieri (1970), and it is important

for a correct understanding of al-Ghazzālī's position, so that his Sufi creed does not obliterate the meaning of human legal acts and the historical value of Islam.

BIBLIOGRAPHY

Abrahamov, B. (1988) "al-Ghazālī's Theory of Causality", *Studia Islamica*, 67: 75–98.

Abu'l-Qasem, M. (1978) *The Ethics of al-Ghazālī* (New York).

Alon, I. (1980) "al-Ghazālī on Causality", *Journal of the American Oriental Society*, 100: 397–405.

Arkoun, M. (170) "Révélation, vérité et histoire d'après l'oeuvre de Ghazālī", *Studia Islamica*, 31: 53–69.

Al-Ash'arī, A. (1969) *Maqālāt al-islāmiyyīn wa ikhtilāf al muṣalliyyīn*, ed. M. Muḥyī al-Dīn 'Abd al-Ḥamīd (Cairo, 2 vols).

Asín Palacios, M. (1934–41) *La espiritualidad de Algazel y su sentido cristiano* (Madrid and Granada).

Badawī, 'A. (1961) *Mu'allafāt al-Ghazzālī* (Cairo).

Bakar, O. (1986) "Meaning and Significance of Doubt in al-Ghazālī's Philosophy", *Islamic Quarterly*, 30: 31–44.

de Beaurecueil Laugier, S. and Anawati, G. (1959) "La Preuve de l'existence de Dieu chez Ghazālī", *Mélanges de l'Institut Dominicain d'Etudes Orientales du Caire*, 3: 207–58.

Bello, I. A. (1989) *The Medieval Islamic Controversy between Philosophy and Orthodoxy: Ijmā' and Ta'wīl in the Conflict between al-Ghazālī and Ibn Rushd* (Leiden).

Binder, L. (1955) "al-Ghazālī's Theory of Islamic Government", *Muslim World*, 45: 229–41.

Bouyges, M. (1959) *Essai de chronologie des oeuvres de al-Ghazālī* (Beirut).

Burrell, D. (1987) "The Unknowability of God in al-Ghazālī", *Religious Studies*, 23: 171–82.

Campanini, M. (1989) *L'intelligenza della fede: filosofia e religione in Averroè e nell'Averroismo* (Bergamo).

—— (1991) "Una via a Dio nel pensiero mistico di al-Ghazālī", *Rivista di Storia della Filosofia*, 46: 463–79.

Caspar, R. (1987) *Traité de theologie musulmane* (Rome).

Frank, R. (1994) *Al-Ghazālī and the Ash'arite School* (Durham, N.C.).

Gardet, L. and Anawati, G. (1961) *Mystique musulmane: aspects et tendances, expériences et techniques* (Paris).

—— (1981) *Introduction à la théologie musulmane* (Paris).

Al-Ghazzālī, Abū Ḥāmid (1891–2) *Iljām al-'awāmm 'an 'ilm al-kalām* (Cairo).

—— (1928) *Tahāfut al-falāsifah*, ed. M. Bouyges (Beirut).

—— (1929) *El justo medio en la creencia*, trans. M. Asín Palacios (Madrid).

—— (1937) *al-Mustaṣfā min 'ilm al-uṣūl* (Cairo).

—— (1945) *Mīzān al-'amal*, trans. H. Hachem (Paris).

—— (1961) *Maqāṣid al-falāsifah*, ed. S. Dunya (Cairo).

—— (1962) *al-Iqtiṣād fi'l-i'tiqād*, ed. H. Atay and I. A. Cubukçu (Ankara).

—— (1964a) *Jawāhir al-qur'ān*, ed. M. Muṣṭafā Abu'l-'Alā (Cairo).

—— (1964b) *Naṣīḥat al-mulūk*, trans. F. Bagley (London).
—— (1964c) *Mi'yār al-'ilm fī'l-manṭiq* (Beirut).
—— (1967a) *al-Munqidh min al-ḍalāl*, trans. W. M. Watt, *The Faith and Practice of al-Ghazālī* (London).
—— (1967b) *Bidāyat al-hidāyah*, trans. W. M. Watt, *The Faith and Practice of al-Ghazālī* (London).
—— (1970) *Kitāb al-arba'īn fī uṣūl al-dīn*, ed. M. Muṣṭafā Abu'l-'Alā (Cairo).
—— (1972) *Tahāfut al-falāsifah*, ed. S. Dunya (Cairo).
—— (1973) *Mīzān al-'amal*, ed. M. Muṣṭafā Abu'l-'Alā (Cairo).
—— (1980a) *Fadā'iḥ al-bāṭiniyyah wa faḍā'il al-mustaẓhiriyyah*, trans. R. J. McCarthy, *Freedom and Fulfillment* (Boston).
—— (1980b) *Munqidh min al-ḍalāl*, trans. R. J. McCarthy, *Freedom and Fulfillment* (Boston).
—— (1980c) *Fayṣal al-tafriqah bayn al-Islām wa'l-zandaqah*, trans. R. J. McCarthy, *Freedom and Fulfillment* (Boston).
—— (1980d) *al-Qisṭās al-mustaqīm*, trans. R. J. McCarthy, *Freedom and Fulfillment* (Boston).
—— (1985) *Iḥyā' 'ulūm al-dīn*, ed. A. 'Izz al-Dīn al-Sīrwān (Beirut).
—— (1986) *Mishkāt al-anwār*, ed. A. 'Izz al-Dīn al-Sīrwān (Beirut).
—— (1987) *al-Maqṣad al-asnā fī sharḥ asmā' Allāh al-ḥusnā*, ed. B. 'Abd al-Wahhāb al-Jābī (Limassol).
—— (1989) *The Remembrance of Death and the Afterlife*, trans. and int. T. Winter (Cambridge).
—— (1992) *The Ninety-Nine Beautiful Names of God*, trans. and int. D. Burrell and N. Daher (Cambridge).
Gimaret, D. (1988) *Les Noms divins en Islam* (Paris).
Glassen, E. (1981) *Der mittlere Weg: Studien zur Religionspolitik und Religiosität der späteren Abbasiden Zeit* (Wiesbaden).
Goodman, L. (1971) "Ghazālī's Argument for Creation", *International Journal of Middle Eastern Studies*, 2: 67–85; 168–88.
—— (1978) "Did al-Ghazālī deny Causality?", *Studia Islamica*, 47: 83–120.
Hourani, G. (1958a) "The Chronology of al-Ghazālī's Writings", *Journal of the American Oriental Society*, 79: 225–33.
—— (1958b) "The Dialogue between al-Ghazālī and the Philosophers on the Origin of the World", *Muslim World*, 48: 183–91; 308–14.
—— (1984) "A Revised Chronology of al-Ghazālī's Writings", *Journal of the American Oriental Society*, 105: 289–302.
Jabre, F. (1954) "La Biographie et l'oeuvre de Ghazālī réconsidérées à la lumière des *Ṭabaqāt* de Sobkī", *Mélanges de l'Institut Domenicain d'Etudes Orientales du Caire*, 1: 73–102.
—— (1956) "L'Extase de Plotin et le *Fanā'* de Ghazālī", *Studia Islamica*, 6: 101–24.
—— (1958) *La Notion de certitude selon Ghazālī dans ses origines psychologiques et historiques* (Paris).
Lambton, A. (1980) *Theory and Practice of Medieval Persian Government* (London).
Laoust, H. (1970) *La Politique d'al-Ghazālī* (Paris).
—— (1983) *Les Schismes dans l'Islam* (Paris).
Lazarus-Yafeh, H. (1975) *Studies in al-Ghazālī* (Jerusalem).
Leaman, O. (1985) *An Introduction to Medieval Islamic Philosophy* (Cambridge).

Makdisi, G. (1962) "Al-Ash'arī and the Ash'arites in Islamic Religious History", *Studia Islamica*, 17: 37–80 (part one).
—— (1963) "Al-Ash'arī and the Ash'arites in Islamic Religious History", *Studia Islamica*, 18: 19–39 (part two).
—— (1983) *L'Islam hanbalisant* (Paris).
Marmura, M. E. (1965) "al-Ghazālī and Demonstrative Science", *Journal of the History of Philosophy*, 3: 183–204.
—— (1975) "Ghazālī's Attitude to the Secular Sciences and Logic", in G. Hourani (ed.), *Essays on Islamic Philosophy* (Albany).
—— (1988) "Ghazālī and the Avicennian Proof from Personal Identity for an Immaterial Self", in R. Link Salinger (ed.) *A Straight Path: Studies in Medieval Philosophy and Culture* (Washington DC).
Morabia, A. (1993) *La Notion de Ǧihād dans l'Islam médiéval des origines à al-Ghazālī* (Paris).
Nakamura, K. (1973) *Ghazali on Prayer* (Tokyo).
Obermann, J. (1921) *Der philosophische und religiöse Subjektivismus Ghazālīs* (Vienna).
Ormsby, E. (1984) *Theodicy in Islamic Thought* (Princeton).
Poggi, V. (1967) *Un classico della spiritualità musulmana: Saggio sul Munqidh di al-Ghazālī* (Rome).
Qumayr, Y. (1969) *Ibn Rushd wa'l-Ghazālī: Tahāfutān* (Beirut).
Sawwaf, A. (1962) *al-Ghazzālī: Etude sur la réforme ghazzalienne dans l'histoire de son développement* (Fribourg).
Shalhut, V. (1957) "al-Qisṭās al-mustaqīm wa'l-ma'rifat al-'aqlīyyah 'ind al-Ghazālī", *al-Mashriq*, 51: 551–81.
Shehadi, F. (1964) *Ghazali's Unique and Unknowable God* (Leiden).
Sherif, M. A. (1975) *al-Ghazālī's Theory of Virtue* (Albany).
Siauve, M. L. (1986) *L'Amour de Dieu chez al-Ghazālī* (Paris).
Stern, M. S. (1979) "Notes on the Theology of al-Ghazālī's Concept of Repentance", *Islamic Quarterly*, 23(2): 82–98.
UNESCO (1987) *al-Ghazālī: la raison et le miracle* (Paris).
Van den Bergh, S. (1957) "Ghazālī's Gratitude towards God and its Greek Sources", *Studia Islamica*, 7: 77–98.
Van Leeuwen, A. T. (1958) "Essai de bibliographie d'al-Ghazālī", *Institut des Belles Lettres d'Algiers*, 2: 221–7.
Veccia Vaglieri, L. and Rubinacci, R. (1970) "Introduzione" to *Scritti scelti di al-Ghazālī* (Turin).
Watt, W. M. (1952) "The Authenticity of the Works Attributed to al-Ghazālī", *Journal of the Royal Asiatic Society*: 24–45.
—— (1961) "The Study of al-Ghazālī", *Oriens*, 13–14: 121–31.
—— (1962) *Islamic Philosophy and Theology* (Edinburgh).
—— (1963) *Muslim Intellectual: a Study of al-Ghazālī* (Edinburgh).
Wensinck, A. J. (1940) *La Pensée de Ghazzālī* (Paris).

III

Islamic philosophers in the Western lands of Islam

CHAPTER 20

Ibn Masarrah

Lenn E. Goodman

Muḥammad ibn ʿAbd Allāh ibn al-Masarrah was born in Cordova (Cordoba) in 269/883. His father, an ascetically inclined theologian, had journeyed to Basrah nearly thirty years before with a much older merchant son of his, reportedly to study the ideas of the Muʿtazilah. The school, then in its heyday, was soon to be widely condemned, with the ascendancy of its traditionalist rivals. For it ascribed human acts to human choices rather than to God's inscrutable power, and it held God responsible for doing justice to humankind and requiting unmerited sufferings, if not in this world then in the next. Ruddy-skinned and fair-haired, ʿAbd Allāh might have passed for a Norman or a Slav in Iraq. But he was a Spanish Muslim, client, by the fortunes of history, to a Berber from Fez. His close friend Khalīl, branded by the orthodox with the sobriquet Khalīl al-Ghaflah, "the intimate of indifference", had also travelled to Iraq and was, we are told, cross-examined on his return by an erudite of Islamic tradition: "What do you say of the balance in which God will weigh man's deeds?" His answer, defiant of the literalism that was now growing strident: "I say it is God's justice. So it is a balance that has no pans." "What do you say about the narrow path that souls must walk to reach paradise?" "I say it is the straight way, the religion of Islam." Another slap at literalism, although couched in conciliation of the still ill-fitting faith. "What do you say of the Qur'ān?" Here, the hostile sources tell us, Khalīl could only babble, "The Qur'ān, the Qur'ān", but it was clear from his silence that he held to the hated Muʿtazilite doctrine that the Qur'ān was created, not eternal. "And what do you say of destiny and the determination of human acts?" "I say that the good acts come from God, but the bad from man." This alone, the master seethed, would be grounds enough to denounce you as an infidel and make you pay with blood for all your impieties. In fact the young scholar was merely driven away and banned from his master's classes.

But at his death a mob of jurists ransacked his house and burned all but his law books.

The story of Khalīl's questioning bears the marks of an apology for his acceptance by a revered master. But it vividly conveys the growing intolerance of the later ninth century C.E. In that atmosphere 'Abd Allāh wisely kept his Mu'tazilite leanings to himself, entrusting them only to his son and imparting not a whiff even to his closest disciples. But the father was forced by debts to leave the West and settle in Mecca, where he died in 286/899, when Ibn Masarrah was only seventeen. The sources tell us nothing of the boy's maturation, but by the early fourth/tenth century he was the leader of a Sufi retreat in the hills above Cordova, with a band of disciples trusted to keep his teachings to themselves. Rumour had it that the "mountain man" (*al-jabalī*) favoured Mu'tazilism and denied the torments of Hell. Later it was said that he taught an atheism founded on the philosophy of Empedocles. In time the suspicions would grow to formal charges, but, long before they did, Ibn Masarrah's teachings were denounced in a short book by the learned jurist al-Ḥabbāb.

The Umayyad caliph was in no position to take such denunciations lightly. For mystics of suspect orthodoxy often heard the schemes and voiced the grievances of dissidents and rival princes. Not waiting for the other shoe to fall, Ibn Masarrah judiciously left Cordova, accompanied by two close disciples, with the traditional pretext of a pilgrimage to Mecca. Visiting many masters of law and theology as he journeyed across North Africa, he sat as a simple student, we are told, at the feet of the successor of the great Saḥnūn in Kairouan, revealing his own greatness only in the dignity and sobriety of his answers to questions asked. He deepened his acquaintance with Mu'tazilite teachings at their source in Iraq. At Mecca he may well have met Abū Sa'īd, a traditionalist disciple of the great monistic mystic al-Junayd.[1] Abū Sa'īd's teachings made *Ḥadīth* a vehicle of mystic speculation and allusion. Yet, like al-Junayd, he skirted the most extreme extensions of monism. In defence of his own repute, he later wrote a book condemning Ibn Masarrah's pantheistic tendencies.

Visiting the sacred sites of Arabia, Ibn Masarrah meditated in Medina on the Prophet's bench on the rooftop of the tiny cottage of the concubine Māriyah, mother of Muḥammad's legendary lost son. His disciples saw him measure with his handspans the rooms of the little house, and he explained that he planned to model his new retreat in the Sierra de Cordova exactly on the plans of this sacred space. The accession of 'Abd al-Raḥmān III (ruled 299/912–350/961) made a prophecy of this hopeful, votive gesture. For the new caliph promulgated a policy of tolerance, to ease the sufferings of his subjects from the near inquisition of the Malikite jurists, laying claim to a generosity of spirit that had grown unfamiliar among his rivals in Baghdad. Returning to Cordova, Ibn Masarrah, still guarded about his inner teachings, used a subtle and suggestive imagery to avoid overt affront to orthodoxy, relying on paradox and allegory to convey his ideas by indirection. Much of what passes for mystery in mysticism, we must observe, much of the touted ineffability of mystic experience, stems not from any inner paradox but from the unacceptability of the construction put upon the experience by adepts and detractors alike, the holism or monism often taken to be its portent.

Secure under the new caliph, Ibn Masarrah taught, wrote and guided his ascetics. His *ṭarīqah*, or Sufi path, modelled on those of the great Sufis Dhu'l-Nūn al-Miṣrī (d. 245/860) and the Meccan al-Nahrajūrī (d. 330/941), followed the pietist contemplative theme of constant examinations of one's own conscience.[2] Despite his devout conduct and his circumspection, the publication of his books led to his denunciation by traditionists in the East. Of his writings, only the titles survive from two of them: *The Book of Letters*, a title also used by al-Fārābī; and *The Book of Enlightenment*, a title that resonated with the usage of al-Jāḥiẓ. But his books were apparently never burnt while he lived; and, unlike the monistic mystic al-Ḥallāj, crucified at Baghdad in 309/922 for his ecstatic cry, "I am the Truth!", Ibn Masarrah died peacefully at his mountain retreat in October 319/931.[3]

The gist of his teachings was reconstructed by the Spanish Arabist Miguel Asín Palacios,[4] relying on the criticisms lodged against him and on testimonies from the mystic virtuoso Ibn 'Arabī, the doxographers Ibn Ḥazm of Cordova, Ṣā'id of Toledo, al-Shahrastānī and al-Shahrazūrī, and the biographical encyclopedists Ibn Abī Uṣaybi'ah and Ibn al-Qifṭī. The picture Asín drew from these sources represents Ibn Masarrah's thought as a confluence of pseudo-Empedoclean teaching and Mu'tazilism. But my teacher Samuel Stern[5] showed that Asín's linking of Ibn Masarrah's views to those of pseudo-Empedocles rested on a passage in Ṣā'id of Toledo's *Ṭabaqāt al-umam*[6] that was vague, polemical and, Stern believed, conjectural. What clinched the matter for Stern was his discovery of Ṣā'id's source in the philosopher al-'Āmirī (d 381/992),[7] where Ibn Masarrah is not mentioned, but the influence of "Empedocles" is ascribed generically to "Bāṭinīs" – a term that meant Ismā'īlīs in the East, but tended to be used as a broad term of abuse in the Islamic West for heretical-seeming Sufis. Ṣā'id may have arbitrarily grafted the name of Ibn Masarrah to al-'Āmirī's notions of Empedoclean thinking.

Influenced by Stern's work, Dominique Urvoy drew the conclusion that Ibn Masarrah was primarily an ascetic, somewhat anti-clerical figure, whose two lost works consisted essentially of imagery that did not bespeak an ordered line of argument. But Stern thought that apart from its reliance on the questionable pseudo-Empedoclean remark, Asín's account, based on the reports of Ibn Ḥazm and Ibn 'Arabī, was "of lasting value". So Urvoy may go a bit too far. For Sufis, like Kabbalists, often clothe or conceal a tacit line of argument in their imagery. But to say this is not to impeach Urvoy's broader conclusion: "Il faudra attendre Ibn Gabirol (1020–1057) pour qu'apparaisse le premier 'système philosophique' andalou."[8] For surely the highly disciplined, original and indeed deeply pseudo-Empedoclean Neoplatonism of Ibn Gabirol's *Fons vitae* sets a standard of systematic philosophy that Ibn Masarrah never pretended to meet.

What was the tenor of Ibn Masarrah's thought? The question is worth asking, since he represents a period at which Andalusian philosophy was in its infancy or, perhaps even more interesting, in an embryonic stage. Stern was an orientalist, one of the greatest of his generation, but, by his own confession, rather innocent of philosophy. His premature death from asthma prevented him from laying out his case about Ibn Masarrah in full, but he did write: "I can only say that I can discover in Ibn Masarrah's doctrines as reproduced in later authors no trace of pseudo-Empedoclean doctrines, and think that no one would have discovered such traces without the prompting of Ṣā'id's statement." In what follows, I may be able to show where later writers could have seen "Empedoclean" affinities in Ibn Masarrah. But I certainly cannot claim that the evidence would have thrust such notions before our eyes without Asín's prompting.

The Mu'tazilites were radical monotheists, describing themselves, somewhat combatively, as the advocates of monotheism and theodicy (*Ahl al-tawḥīd wa'l-ta'dīl*). The early *kalām* polemics against Zoroastrian dualists and Christian trinitarians had honed their sense of the absoluteness of God's unity. To concede that God's Attributes of Will or Wisdom might be distinct from His Identity was, in effect, to admit the reality of hypostases too readily transformed into persons of the Trinity. Similarly, an eternal Qur'ān would be the eternal Word and Wisdom of God – all too easily, the second person of the Trinity. Later critics of the Mu'tazilah, for whom trinitarianism was in a very raw sense no longer a live option, cared little for the old dialectic and had not much use for negative theology. To them the eternity of the Qur'ān would become a dogma, not combating but absorbing Christian and Jewish notions of God's eternal Word, by which the Transcendent was linked with this world, through creation, governance, revelation and judgment. But, to the philosophically inclined, negative theology and monistic monotheism preserved an appeal beyond the immediate inter-confessional stimulus that had aroused them. The absolute simplicity of God seemed to mirror and indeed to argue God's ontic absoluteness as well. For surely what was simple and without opposite was also indestructible and uncreated, a suitable counterpart to the temporality of creation and a fitting correlative to the mystic's ecstatic sense of unity and power.

The Empedocles of al-'Āmirī was a sage and nobleman of Agrigentum, a subtle philosopher and devoted ascetic who had studied with King Solomon and his legendary contemporary the Arab sage Luqmān (Qur'ān 31: 12–19).[9] Writings in the name of this ascetic Empedocles were known to al-Shahrastānī and al-Shahrazūrī, as well as al-'Āmirī. He had, we are told, sought to explain the world's creation to his fellow Greeks but was rejected by most of them, because his theories implied denial of an afterlife. A treatise of his denying the resurrection was seen by Ibn al-Qifṭī in the library at Jerusalem. Despite his horror at what he saw, Ibn al-Qifṭī's account shows how the writings ascribed to a pre-Socratic philosopher might be deemed relevant to the concerns of a Mu'tazilite mystic. Ibn al-Qifṭī writes of Empedocles, "He was the first to grasp the unity of the meanings of the Attributes of God: All reduce to a single Identity."[10]

From the fragmentary appraisals in which our sources carefully preserved the record of what they took to be the writings of the ancient sage, we learn that "Empedocles" opened his text with praise of philosophy, the science with which ordinary people are least concerned. He argued that philosophy proves its worth through its luminous self-evidence and inspires us, as in Plato's *Phaedrus* myth, to flee this world for a higher one. Like Plato, the shadowy author addresses the would-be philosopher as though his goal were to become a mystical adept. He advises those who aspire to knowledge of higher things to begin not with the ultimate reality, which will no doubt elude them, nor with lower, physical beings, which will enmesh them in their coarseness, but with the intermediate, the human soul. From an adequate understanding of the self one may make one's way to both higher and lower realities. Such a path of self-exploration, based on the idea that the soul mediates between the material and the spiritual worlds, is the perennial course of pietists from Baḥyā to Pascal. Indeed, the idea that self-knowledge is the key to wisdom is the methodological basis of philosophy from Socrates to Descartes and Sartre.[11]

The soul, pseudo-Empedocles lays down, is a simple substance, not like fire, which has only the relative simplicity of the corporeal, but like light. The truth about the self reflects and reveals the truth about the simplicity of God. If we consider this, we will grasp what it implies but does not state: the attributes of the human psyche are what we are; they are not a thing apart. We are (in a sense well examined by the Mu'tazilite moralists, who held that our fortunes and destiny are the product of our own acts and choices) what we make ourselves – although in a far lesser sense than is comprehended in the idea of God's self-necessity. Here we see a basis for the mystic quest for unity in God and with God, and a basis as well, perhaps, for linking mystic praxis with the search for immortality, through the Platonizing idea that it is only by the inner unification of the self, morally, intellectually and spiritually, that one can be folded into the Unity that is God.

God, whose absolute simplicity is approached by contemplation of the lesser simplicity of a perfect or perfected human consciousness, is His own pure being: He is his own knowledge, will, bounty, power, justice and truth.[12] As al-ʿĀmirī writes:

> The doctrine of Empedocles as to the Attributes of the Creator is that he is described in terms of knowledge, existence, will and power; but there are no distinct notions in him identifiable by these diverse names. For just as we say that every being in the world is known by Him, is under His power, and is an emanation of His bounty without affirming thereby any plurality of notions in it, so too do we describe Him who gives them being in terms of knowledge, existence, will and power, even though He is one and indivisible.
>
> And, just as His existence is unlike that of anything that exists in the world – for all worldly things realize a contingent existence, dependent on their creation, whereas His Godhead is necessarily existent and not dependent on creation – so is His unity unlike that of any existent in the world. For the unity of all worldly things is subject to division, by partition, by conceptual analysis, or by having some counterpart. But His Identity transcends all multiplicity.[13]

"Empedocles", Abu'l-Faraj explains in his *History*, "was the first to deny that the essence of the Creator had Attributes, saying: 'The Essence of the Creator is His existence' and vice versa. His life and knowledge are two relative ideas that do not necessarily imply diversity in His Identity."[14]

Thus the "Empedoclean" theory of God's attributes sustains the Muʿtazilite doctrine of God's absolute unity: just as God has no parts but is uncompounded and indestructible, so His unity is indivisible even conceptually. For if there were attributes in God genuinely distinct from one another, it would be possible to ask whether God might have had a different nature than He has; it would be conceivable that this nature might have been differently compounded or composed, and the very existence of God would become contingent. For what can be broken down into its elements needs a cause to explain their combination. Any synthesis (any synthetic judgment!) is contingent. Further, if God had counterparts, as all natural particulars do, then God would have a plurality of genuinely distinct characteristics, some in common with others of His putative kind and others that differentiate Him from them. This too would make God contingent, no longer a necessary being, an effect rather than the ultimate cause, and so not God. Clearly, if God is necessary, He is absolutely simplex, not only in having no parts as an extended body has, but also in the sense of unanalysability, having no attributes distinct from His Identity or Godhead (*Dhāt*), no nature or Essence distinct from His existence. He belongs to no kind but is unique and therefore undefinable. As pseudo-Empedocles argues, in the true spirit of rational mysticism, "Understanding is simple, but language is compound."[15]

In the work of "Empedocles" a Muʿtazilite could find conceptual roots and a historical pedigree, then, for the celebrated *kalām* formulae that God was wise but not by wisdom (as though God's wisdom were something separate from Himself), powerful but not by power. Here too is rooted the idea that in a necessary being there is no differentiation of essence from existence. And beyond that we discern the goal of the mystic quest to share in God's unity and seek dissolution in it of the all too vulnerable, all too durable self. One can readily see how theological critics of Ibn Masarrah might link the Platonizing "Empedocles" with the charge that Ibn Masarrah denied the afterlife. For to such critics Platonic immortality would seem little more than spiritual dissolution in the divine; the Neoplatonic flight of the alone to the Alone would hardly be an acceptable substitute for physical resurrection, judgment and requital, as al-Ghazzālī's scornful rejection of the purely spiritual immortality of the Philosophers makes very clear.[16] If Khalīl thought that God's scales need no pans and that God's judgment marks no visible but a moral and spiritual path, was it not clear that Ibn Masarrah understood the resurrection as his contemporary al-Fārābī and other philosophers did, as the pictorial symbol of a spiritual truth? Such affirmations would be hard to discriminate from denials.[17]

Similarly with creation, the accounts we have of pseudo-Empedocles link up with our sketchy knowledge of Ibn Masarrah's views and the charges made against him. The most striking doctrine of pseudo-Empedocles was his account of emanation based on the idea of intellectual matter.[18] The problem that readers of pseudo-Empedocles identified as that of creation was the emergence of a physical and multifarious world from God's absolute simplicity and incorporeality. In Neoplatonic terms, how did the many arise from the One?[19] The problem parallels the mind–body problem acute in modern philosophy since Descartes. As with all questions of theophany, the issue was the interaction of the physical with a reality that is never adequately described in mechanistic terms. Creation was just a special case.[20]

It was the relevance of the mind–body interaction that led pseudo-Empedocles to recommend that one begins the philosophic quest from the examination of the self. For, in pseudo-Empedocles, mind is to body not simply as kick is to leg, nor even as pilot to ship, but in many ways as God is to the world:

> God is the absolute originator. He did not create from something else. Nor was anything coeternal with Him. Rather, He created

> the simple thing which is the first simple Idea, the primal matter or element [*'unṣur*]. Then a number of simple things proliferated from that single, first, simple kind [*naw'*]. Then composite things developed from the simples. Thus He is the Creator of every thing and non-thing – intellectual, notional or supposed. Which is to say, the Creator of all opposites and contraries known to the intellect, the imagination and the senses.[21]

This passage requires a bit of glossing, as Shahrastānī himself, who is our source, is the first to recognize, for the last sentence is his gloss of "Empedocles'" obscure words. But once we see what the philosopher is driving at, we will recognize a seminal thesis, the affirmation that the first reality to emanate from God is Intellectual Matter. The idea was soon to be rejected by many of the best medieval Neoplatonists, but it was never quite expelled from the core of Neoplatonic thinking. We know how irritated al-Fārābī was by would-be philosophers who could not keep it straight what was matter (*hyle*) and what was element (*'unṣur*),[22] but here we see some of the source of al-Fārābī's irritation. Pseudo-Empedocles was relying on the Neoplatonic view that prime matter is a direct emanation from the One[23] and combining it with the view that the first moment of differentiation from divine simplicity is a hypostasis that Plato calls the Indefinite dyad, identified with the form of the Great and Small, and equated here with matter.[24]

In a bold appropriation of the historic Empedocles' reliance upon Love and Strife as the principles promoting combination and separation among the elements, fire, water, earth and air, pseudo-Empedocles assimilated these two quasi-naturalistic, quasi-mythic principles to the Platonic forms of the Great and the Small, setting them above the four elements and suggesting a dialectic of complementarity rather than mere opposition between them, by renaming them Love and Domination (*al-maḥabbah wa'l-ghalabah*). As Shahrastānī reports:

> The first Element [*'unṣur*] is simple in relation to the Intellect, which is below it, but it is not simple in an absolute sense, i.e., not sheerly simple *vis-à-vis* its Cause. For any effect must be composite conceptually or perceptually, and the Element is compounded of Love and Domination. From these stem the spiritual substances that are simple and the physical substances that are compound.[25]

Opposition of some kind, we may reason, is necessary to differentiate the first effect from its Cause. But, in keeping with the spirit of monotheism, the otherness that differentiates Intellectual Matter from God is not called hate or strife, but dominance, an aggressive or outgoing self-assertion. The yearning by which what has been separated looks back upon its Source is still called love, but now assimilated to the love that is the motive force of the Aristotelian cosmos and to the Platonic and Neoplatonic yearning for return. The two forces are now opposing aspects of the same one relationship, just as Aristotle's criticism of the historic Empedocles had implied they should be. These two moments become the explanations of the "still" movement, by which neo-Empedoclean counterparts of Aristotle's unmoved movers impart motion to all things – not merely physical movement but the prior movement of outflow and return that animates all Neoplatonic hypostases.[26] The same two principles, we can reason, will explain the differentiation of the Neoplatonic Intellects from one another and the yearning of the lower for the Higher in all things. Dominance will be a principle of rule and so of providence, never a Gnostic or Zoroastrian recalcitrance. These cosmic or metaphysical principles will function rather like the Kabbalistic divine attributes (*middot*) of Mercy and Justice; and the spirit of Domination, like the Rabbinic "evil impulse", will not be an ultimate force for evil but a necessary component in the self-assertion of all finite beings, to the extent that they are at all differentiated from the absolute unity of God.

Plato equated God or the One with the form of Sameness or Equality, and matter with the principle of otherness or difference. Matter in itself, of course, does not exist in any positive sense, since reality is actual only to the extent of its realization by form. So there is no absolute matter but only the final darkness beyond which the light of emanation does not reach. Matter is always relative, and the highest phase of matter, pseudo-Empedocles inferred, is the pure emanation of the first simple hypostasis to emerge from God, a pure Idea, in fact, but one that can be called first matter, inasmuch as it is the first phase of otherness, differentiated from the absoluteness of God's perfect unity only by the relative partiality of its consciousness. From this "element" God produces the universal Mind, and, from these two, the universal Soul. All of these are simple, but by their mediation it is possible for God to produce composites: Universal Nature and secondary (i.e., physical) matter. Thus the complex emerges from the simple by the Neoplatonic expedient of mediation, the less simple providing a ground, a "material" basis, for the emergence of what shows still lesser unity or simplicity.

An account of this kind was exactly the sort of thing that al-Fārābī and Ibn Sīnā found sloppy and repugnant and sought to replace with a more disciplined procession of disembodied intellects and celestial spheres. They eliminated the mythicism of Love and Domination. Clearly they objected to the unclarity as to how the Second and the rest emerge from the First. This emergence, they insisted, is a result of thought. They objected too to the manifest softness of the pseudo-Empedoclean account to the temporality of creation. It was against such softness and sloppiness, and not against rigorous Peripatetics, that Ibn Sīnā launched his critique of the philosophy of "the Westerners".[27] To both al-Fārābī and Ibn Sīnā it was clear from the arguments of such Neoplatonists as Proclus and from those of Aristotle himself that temporal creation was an incoherent notion that impiously dragged divine eternity down into the mud of temporality and irrationally compromised the timeless immutability of causal necessity. In reality, scriptural accounts of creation were simply the myths or noble lies that Plato had commended as means of mediating philosophic insights to those who still dwelt within the darkness and flickering torchlight of the cave.

Despite their distaste for all things even associated with the *kalām*, and in part because of it, al-Fārābī and Ibn Sīnā refined on and did not merely reject the emanative continuum of pseudo-Empedocles. For by insisting that matter in general was not, somehow, a thing apart, but merely the lower end of a continuum that began with God, that began, one might say, *within* God and in a sense never really left Him, followers of "Empedocles" could resolve at a stroke the problems of God's responsibility for nature, bridging the chasm that seemed to loom between the physical and the spiritual.

Like the historic Empedocles, pseudo-Empedocles is concerned with purifications (*katharmoi*),[28] as shown in an elaborate and rather gnostic exegesis of the historic Empedocles' notion that the body is a mere shell or husk (*epikalumma*). In the pre-Socratic philosopher there is a gnomic hint, a fragmentary phrase speaking of "Earth that envelops mortals" (Frg. 148). In pseudo-Empedocles, this hint has become an elaborate system designed to explain the alienation of humanity from its Source, and to show how such distance (*bu'd*), which is never absolute, can and will be overcome. The effect, "Empedocles" argues, is always subordinate and subsequent to its cause. This Neoplatonizing axiom alone shows both that the individual is never fully removed from the divine and that it is never self-sufficient or co-equal with its cause. The diminished simplicity of the effect, as an effect, entails its lesser reality, signalled by the differentiation of lower beings in the procession of their advancing embodiment. The universal power of the One thus generates multiplicity without partaking of it, and each lesser hypostasis yields a still lower one, until we reach the heart of man (*lubb*), the spiritual heart that is the cynosure of all pietist attentions, encased in its bodily husk. The Aristotelian "vegetative" soul, concerned with growth and reproduction, is the husk of the "animal" soul, which gives us motility and sensibility. The animal soul is the husk of the discursive or dialectical soul (cf. Plato, *Republic*, 6.511b), which is in turn the husk (vehicle, sanctuary and prison) of the mind, the intellectual soul.

The core or heart at each level is the rind or husk of the next; for, like matter and form, the ideas of husk and heart are applied relatively, reflecting the ontic hierarchy, which is (if we look upward) a hierarchy of progressive stages of realization. In any Neoplatonic scheme the degrees of reality are degrees of intellectuality, spirituality, remoteness from physicality. Thus the practical value of austerities and meditations like Ibn Masarrah's. Every "core" or heart precipitates from that above it. When these cores, which are Platonic essences, reach particularity, and their universality can differentiate no further, they give form to bodies. The Universal Intellect knows these, because it discerns the core within them. That is, by virtue of its affinity to what is spiritual/intellectual, it recognizes the form that gives being to each body. In the human case its very glance diffuses the beauty of an individual soul upon that body. This soul never loses its connection to the Universal Soul and so is the rightful and capable ruler of the body and can rescue and redeem all that is spiritual or intellectual, all the forms trapped in physicality. Where human minds are led astray by the fractious animal and vegetative souls, they are redeemed by the superior rational soul of a prophet, again sent down by the Universal Soul, but subtler and purer than other souls. In every revolution of the Sphere the highest manifestations of the spiritual world on earth are distilled, as it were, in a single individual, charged with the salvation of the rest. But although the prophet and all souls and minds come from above, each human being must work out his or her own salvation and has the God-given means to do so. Salvation is by grace, but not by arbitrary election; and it is actively to be sought, not passively awaited.

From the doxography of Ibn Ḥazm (d. 454/1064), the brilliant, radically conservative theologian, jurist and belle-lettrist,[29] we learn of two scandalous doctrines of Ibn Masarrah. Firstly, the Muʿtazilite mystic discriminated an eternal and a created knowledge and power of God, lest God's omniscience and omnipotence exclude the free acts of humankind. As a proof-text for his shocking view, Ibn Masarrah called to witness Qur'ān 6: 73, 13: 9 and 32: 6, where God is said to know all things hidden and perceived (*ʿālim al-ghayb wa'l-shahādah*). The plain sense of the text, Ibn Ḥazm insists, is that God knows human actions even if we seek to conceal them – past, present and future. But Ibn Masarrah glossed *ghayb*, the unseen, as a reference to the Platonic universals, which are beyond sense perception. These God knows by an eternal knowledge. But the realm of particulars, which we know by way of experience (*shahādah*), God knows temporally. He knows nothing about the contingent facts of Zayd's decision to believe or disbelieve in the mission of Muḥammad, until Zayd's decision is actually made. For without this (rather Socinian) doctrine, human freedom, our power to do otherwise than we will, might seem able to contradict God's perfect knowledge. To avoid such an outcome Ibn Masarrah distanced one part of God's knowledge from His Identity, making it a created and indeed temporal effect.

Corresponding to his bifurcation of God's knowledge, we learn from Ibn Ḥazm that for Ibn Masarrah God's power or sovereignty, the actual authority that rules the world, is His throne. Part of what Ibn Masarrah meant was undoubtedly that the scriptural throne of God (Qur'ān 7: 54, 9: 129, 10: 3, 11: 7, 17: 42, 20: 5, 21: 22, 23: 86, 27: 26, etc.) is a symbol of God's power. Al-Makkī (d. 386/996), an important source for al-Ghazzālī, would write similarly that the throne of God was his will, a primal hypostasis in the differentiation of the many from the One, as Ibn Gabirol, for one, plainly understood. For, as al-Ghazzālī and many others would argue, no mere procession of simplex emanations devoid of volition could ever account for the differentiation of divine simplicity. But the thrust of Ibn Masarrah's equation of God's power with His Throne cannot be understood without reference to his teaching that God's knowledge too was distinguishable from His Godhead.

The apparent separation of God's power and knowledge from His Identity may seem to consort poorly with the monistic thrust of Ibn Masarrah's theory of the attributes. But if we bear in mind Ibn Ḥazm's hostility we may perhaps glimpse what motivated Ibn Masarrah and find some measure of coherence here. As explained by Ibn al-Ru'aynī, the disciple who reported Ibn Masarrah's doctrine to Ibn Ḥazm, "God is too great to ascribe to Him" the mere governance of the world. Or as Ibn Ḥazm put it, under the curtain of oblique discourse and with marked antipathy for Mu'tazilite essays at a theology of transcendence: "God is too great to attribute to Him the act of actually doing anything."

Al-Ghazzālī himself would one day avail himself of the Neoplatonic notion that the transcendence of the Absolute is mediated by a lesser hypostasis, just as he set the husk/heart distinction at the core of his spiritual encyclopedia, the *Revival of the Religious Sciences*. The same idea, of a lesser hypostasis, to mediate between the Infinite and creation, would be a mainstay of the Kabbalah, under the name of the *sefirot*, the mystic numbers that are the archetypes of all things; the husks of pseudo-Empedocles would survive too in Kabbalah, as the *klippot*, vessels of alienation which the redemption of the cosmos must shatter. But, despite al-Ghazzālī's reliance on a mediating hypostasis, and despite the survival of other pseudo-Empedoclean ideas within and around Neoplatonism, in the early days, when such methods were new and exotic among scriptural monotheists, Ibn Masarrah's approach would carry a certain shock value.

What aroused Ibn 'Arabī in Ibn Masarrah's teachings was their potential for visionary applications. As a visionary Ibn Masarrah would seem drab by an Ibn 'Arabī's standards. But his capacity to link visionary expressions (especially architectural images) to concepts and theories already grounded in argument was exciting. For if philosophy was a mystic quest, the adept would want a map of the terrain to be traversed conceptually and experientially. And if the goal was to take up lodging in the house of God, one would need to know the layout and the furniture of the place. The traditional repertoire of philosophy might supply navigational principles, but only the visionary imagination could supply the map.

Rather than explaining simply that the Throne is a symbol of God's power or governance, as an al-Fārābī might do, Ibn Masarrah *uses* the symbolism, much as the Rabbis of the Midrash uninhibitedly enter into the scriptural conceit of God as king. Indeed, the affinity between Midrash and mysticism here, in method and matter, is no accident. Mysticism relies on poetry to clothe the Transcendent in the notional trappings of Glory, without commitment to the dangerous realm of direct, conceptual discourse. Midrash, more specifically, uses pictorial symbols that are "deniable" in their literal application, always preceded by an explicit or understood "as it were". Such disclaimers allow images to communicate with a precision that properly conceptual descriptions and attributions cannot attain by pretending faithfully to represent the Transcendent, for all but the narrowest laser beam of an analogy is excluded.

"It has been reported to us," Ibn 'Arabī writes, "as coming from Ibn Masarrah, one of the greatest masters of the mystic way in knowledge, ecstatic states, and inspiration, that the Throne which is carried is in fact God's sovereignty."[30] Ibn 'Arabī goes on to develop the image in an analysis of the powers by which God rules the temporal and the eternal worlds, embroidering his conceit upon the scriptural affirmation that on the day when God's sovereignty is most fully manifested "eight shall bear the throne of thy Lord" (Qur'ān 69: 17), rather than the four who bear it in this life. The bearers of the Throne, according to Ibn 'Arabī, are in effect carrying the universe. The sense Ibn Masarrah gives the image, in the gloss that Ibn 'Arabī expands, is clearer if we hold in mind that philosophers of Peripatetic stamp identified the Throne with the outermost sphere of the heavens, at which are felt the first impulses attributable to the attractive force of the Prime Mover. Like all Neoplatonists, Ibn Masarrah is seeking to explicate the nexus between this world and Eternity, but he is doing so in visionary language.

The bearers, according to Ibn 'Arabī's testimony, are Adam and Isrāfīl, who carry all bodily forms; Muḥammad and Gabriel, who bear all spirits; Abraham and Michael, who bear provender; and Mālik and Riḍwān, who bear the promise and the threat, that is, our requital of recompense and retribution. Each pair but the last, the two angels who preside over Heaven and Hell, comprises a mortal and an angel, representing the outer (or phenomenal) and the inner (or timeless) dimension of human existence in its phases of creation, sustenance (i.e., providence), revelation, and (with the final pair) judgment. All eight are present only on the Judgment Day, when temporality and Eternity intersect.

In a related teaching, again reported and expanded by Ibn 'Arabī, Ibn Masarrah gives visual content to the unitive intuition of the mystic:

> You must know that this ecstatic state, although its essential content is the intuition of God's absolute unity and transcendence, is at the same time manifested in the illumination of the soul by a concrete form. It appears in the guise of a house supported by five columns, covered by a raised roof that surmounts the walls, in which there is no open door, so that no one of those who contemplate it can penetrate it. But outside this house stands another column, fastened to the outer wall. This column the *illuminati* may touch, just as they kiss and touch the black stone which God placed outside the sacred House.[31]

Syncretism with Kabbalistic imagery comes to the surface here when the Ka'bah at Mecca is denominated by the phrase "sacred House", as though it were the Temple in Jerusalem. In the Kabbalistic *Heikhalot* literature, which Gershom Scholem traces at least to the second century, Jewish mystics contemplated God's chariot and throne, the mansions of His house, and even the graphically envisioned parts of the divine "body". The kabbalistic theme of divine self-contraction (*ẓimẓum*) took its rise in speculations about the theophanic condescension of the Infinite in occupying the circumscribed space of the Sanctuary, designated in Scripture as God's dwelling-place. That act of self-contraction becomes a paradigm for the finite manifestation of the Infinite, whether in the primal act of creation or in providence, revelation, judgment or any other theophany – all labelled, in accordance with rabbinic usage, under the problematic of Ezekiel's all too graphic "account of the Chariot".

Voiced in such terms, these speculations and the meditations surrounding them met and mingled with pagan ideas like Porphyry's about the consecration of idols, in which the god is invested in what would otherwise be inanimate matter. It would take us far afield to explore the full range of such theories and meditations, from the initiation rites of the pagan mysteries to the transubstantiation of the host, the charisma of the Shi'ite Imām, the perpetuum mobile of the alchemists (which moves by a spirit thaumaturgically inducted into it), the Kabbalistic tradition of the golem, and the alchemical *magnum opus* of the homunculus. Suffice it to say that such paradigms of theophany are rarely without philosophic counterparts. For they spring not from unmediated mystical contemplation but from efforts to wrestle conceptually with the Infinite in the here and now. Asín speculates that the outer column might be the Imām, and if the Imām is as charismatic as Shi'ism would suggest, actually bringing to earth something or more than merely something of the divine afflatus, that gloss seems more than credible. Similarly, in the Kabbalistic idea of *ẓimẓum*, we see provision not just for the specification of the Divine Law out of God's infiniteness, but also for human freedom, a central preoccupation of the Mu'tazilites. Shi'ism is often a vehicle of Mu'tazilite ideas, and clearly was so in the case of Ibn Masarrah. But the Neoplatonic portent of his imagined mandala is visible as well. For the conjunction of the outer column with the walls it abuts signifies the absence of any absolute division between the impenetrable mystery of the Infinite and its manifestation through the Active Intellect or mediating hypostasis, which may touch the mind of the devotee. The image, like that of the Greek mystic poet St Simeon, of sunlight shining on the grass, light mingling with matter in "union without confusion" voices the possibility of the mind's contact (*ittiṣāl*; cf. Plotinus, *aphe*) with the divine.

NOTES

1 See Ali Hassan Abdel-Kader, *The Life, Personality and Writings of al-Junayd* (London, 1962).

2 As we learn from the work of Baḥyā Ibn Paqudah, such self-scrutiny could have both moral and philosophical significance. See L. E. Goodman, "Baḥyā on the Antinomy of Free Will and Predestination", *Journal of the History of Ideas*, 44 (1983): 115–30, esp. 122–4. For the Christian and Muslim parallels, see Asín Palacios (note 4): 89.

3 Closer to home, a religious preacher who claimed to be a faithful son of Islam was crucified under orders from 'Abd al-Raḥmān II after proclaiming himself a prophet in 237/851; Asín: 22–3.

4 M. Asín Palacios, *The Mystical Philosophy of Ibn Masarrah and his Followers*, trans. E. H. Douglas and H. W. Yoder (Leiden, 1972; first published in Spanish, Madrid, 1914).

5 S. Stern, "Ibn Masarrah, Follower of Pseudo-Empedocles – an Illusion", *Fourth Congress of Arabic and Islamic Studies* (Lisbon, 1968): 325–37.

6 Ed. L. Cheiko, p. 21 = R. Blachère's French translation, p. 59.

7 Al-'Āmirī's work on immortality has now been published: Abu'l-Ḥasan al-'Āmirī, *Kitāb al-amad 'ala'l-abad*, ed. and trans. Everett K. Rowson, in *A Muslim Philosopher on the Soul and its Fate* (New Haven, 1988).

8 D. Urvoy, "Sur les débuts de la pensée spéculative en Andalus", *Mélanges de l'Université Saint-Joseph*, 50(2) (1984): 707–17.

9 For Luqmān, see *Encyclopaedia of Islam*, 2nd ed. (Leiden, 1965), 5: 811–14; for pseudo-Empedocles, Al-'Āmirī, ed. Rowson: 70–1, 78–81.

10 Ibn al-Qifṭī, *Tārikh al-ḥukamā'*, ed. Müller-Lippert: 16.

11 See Alexander Altmann, "The Delphic Maxim in Medieval Islam and Judaism", in his *Studies in Religious Philosophy and Mysticism* (Ithaca, 1969) and L. E. Goodman, "Crosspollinations: Philosophically Fruitful Interactions between Jewish and Islamic Thought", in Jacob Lassner (ed.) *The Jews of Islamic Lands* (Detroit, forthcoming).

12 Al-Shahrazūrī, quoted in Asín: 47–9.

13 Al-'Āmirī, ed. Rowson: 78; the translation here is my own.

14 Abu'l-Faraj, *Historia dynastiarum*, ed. Pococke (Oxford, 1663): 50, quoted in Asín: 49.

15 Shahrastānī, *Kitāb al-milal wa'l-niḥal*, ed. Cureton (London, 1842–6), 2: 261, l. 3; cf. Maimonides on God's ineffability, *Guide*, 1.50–60. It is perhaps because of its impact on the theory of God's attributes that al-Ghazzālī calls divine unity a vast and shoreless sea.

16 See al-Ghazzālī, *Tahāfut al-falāsifah*, 18–20.

17 Not only did Neoplatonists confine immortality to the spiritual and tend, by their arguments, towards the Platonic view that the immortal soul, being disembodied (and only so being transtemporal), lost its individuality and merged with the Universal Soul. They also allegorized the torments of Hell, as the alienation of the worldly from the bliss of spiritual union. See Ibn Ṭufayl's *Ḥayy ibn Yaqẓān*, trans. L. E. Goodman (Los Angeles, 1984): 153–4; cf. Asín: 57, and his account of the hybrid view of al-Jāḥiẓ: 150.

18 Asín: 87–8, notes that Ibn 'Arabī ascribes the (pseudo-Empedoclean) doctrine of a primal, intellectual matter to Sahl al-Tustarī, a disciple of the Sufi Dhu'l-Nūn, "from whose lips Ibn Masarrah could very well have learned it during his stay in Mecca".

19 See Arthur Hyman, in L. E. Goodman, *Neoplatonism and Jewish Thought* (Albany, 1992): 111–35; cf. Dillon, McGinn, Goodman, Novak and Popkin in the same volume.

20 See L. E. Goodman, *Rambam: Readings in the Philosophy of Moses Maimonides* (New York, 1976), Introduction: 18–27, and parts one and four.

21 Shahrastānī, ed. Cureton, 2: 260, ll. 11–15.

22 See al-Fārābī, *Kitāb al-ḥurūf*, ed. M. Mahdi (Beirut, 1969): 159; cf. Asín: 66.

23 Proclus, *Elements of Theology*, prop. 72, corollary, ed. E. R. Dodds (Oxford, 1964; 1st ed. 1933): 68, l. 24.

24 For intellectual matter in Plotinus, see *Enneads*, 2.4.1–5. As Asín notes, Plotinus stops short of objectifying spiritual matter as a hypostasis, as pseudo-Empedocles and Ibn Gabirol do. Maimonides sagely stays with Plotinus, as signified by his insistence that "the *saṭan*", the principle of otherness and alienation, is not one of the "sons of God" (i.e., not a real "principle") but a concomitant of finite creation ("because he is in the throng of the 'sons of God'"); see *Guide*, 3.22.

25 Shahrastānī, ed. Cureton, 2: 261; the idea that the effect must be composite smacks of Proclus, see *Elements of Theology*, 2.4–5, ed. Dodds: 3–7.

26 See Shahrastānī, ed. Cureton: 261, l. 3; cf. Asín: 50.

27 Dimitri Gutas, in *Avicenna and the Aristotelian Tradition* (Leiden, 1988): 249–52, finds a paradigm of Avicenna's targets in al-'Āmirī, who was a follower of the philosophy of al-Kindī. Al-Kindī had defended temporal creation and added the production of something out of nothing to the four kinds of change acknowledged by Aristotle. Ibn Masarrah may also typify Ibn Sīnā's targets in his aborted work on eastern philosophy: a true Westerner, whose works, published in al-Fārābī's time, did not escape censure from the orthodox as far east as Ahwaz; see Asín: 41 n. 24. Ṣā'id al-Andalusī, himself a Westerner, is, as Gutas shows (212–14), a prime continuator of the traditions we find in al-'Āmirī about "Empedocles". If Avicenna read Aristotle's *Metaphysics* forty times, as he reports, he certainly knew that the Empedocles we meet in Ṣā'id al-Andalusī and al-'Āmirī, who would have been the Empedocles of Ibn Masarrah, was not the

Empedocles of Aristotle. Thus, perhaps, Avicenna's vagueness in naming of his targets: Western sources, clearly, and philosophers, but not exponents of the historical Empedocles.

28 Asín: 55–6.

29 See A. G. Chejne, *Ibn Ḥazm* (Chicago, 1982).

30 Asín: 78–80.

31 Asín: 74–5. Maimonides does not fail to profit, in his parable of the palace, from Ibn Masarrah's type of approach; see *Guide*, 3.51; M. Kellner, *Maimonides on Human Perfection* (Atlanta, 1990): 14–31.

BIBLIOGRAPHY

Addas, C. (1992) "Andalusi Mysticism and the Rise of Ibn 'Arabi", in *The Legacy of Muslim Spain*, ed. S. K. Jayyusi (Leiden).

Asín Palacios, M. (1972) *The Mystical Philosophy of Ibn Masarrah and his Followers*, trans. E. Douglas and H. W. Yoder (Leiden).

Ibn Masarrah (1982) *Min al-turāth al-falsafī li-ibn Masarrah: 1. Risālat al-i'tibār, 2. Khawāṣṣ al-ḥurūf*, ed. M. Ja'far (Cairo).

Stern, S. (1983) "Ibn Masara, Follower of Pseudo-Empedocles – an Illusion", in *Medieval Arabic and Hebrew Thought* (London).

Ternero, E. (1993) "Noticia sobre la publicación de obras inéditas de ibn Masarrah", *al-Qantara*, 14: 47–64.

CHAPTER 21

Ibn Bājjah

Lenn E. Goodman

The Islamic West – that is, Andalusia (Muslim Iberia) and the Maghrib (western North Africa) – felt a cultural lag familiar to regions remote from the notional centres of economic and social influence. Umayyad dynasts, escaping the 'Abbāsid onslaught that destroyed their house in the East in the mid second/eighth century, flourished in Spain until the fifth/eleventh. Translation of Greek scientific works into Arabic, which had preceded the birth of Islamic philosophy in Baghdad in the third/ninth century, continued in Cordova, with the rendering, for example, of a brilliantly illustrated Greek manuscript of Dioscorides' *Materia medica* in 340/951. The original was a gift from the Byzantine Emperor Constantine VII to the Umayyad Caliph 'Abd al-Raḥmān III (fourth/tenth century), whose Jewish vizier Ḥasday ibn Shaprūṭ (905–75), a scholar, linguist and physician as well as a statesman, personally oversaw translation and other learned activity under the auspices of the court. 'Abd al-Raḥmān's son al-Ḥakam II (ruled 350/961–366/976) founded seven schools in Cordova endowed with stipends for indigent scholars and amassed a library of some 400,000 volumes. But most of the books were gathered by his agents in the East; and many, especially in logic and astronomy, were burnt by order of the Caliph Hishām (ruled 366/976–399/1009), during a popular reaction against "the ancient learning".

The philosophical tradition depended on the writings of Eastern figures: al-Fārābī and Ibn Sīnā (Avicenna). Ibn Ṭufayl, a key exponent of Andalusian philosophy, wrote: "Before the spread of philosophy and formal logic to the West, all native Andalusians of any ability devoted their lives to mathematics. They achieved a high level in that field but could do no more. The next generation surpassed them in that they knew a little logic. But study logic as they might, they could not find in it the way to fulfilment."[1] Many of these mathematicians were physicians; their astronomy laid the foundation for the "Andalusian revolt" against the Ptolemaic system.[2] 'Abd al-Raḥmān ibn Ismā'īl "the Euclidean" travelled east in search of learned books. The Cordovan astronomer al-Majrīṭī (d. 398/1007), whose name marks his origins in Madrid, was trained by the geometer 'Abd al-Ghāfir. He too travelled to the East and adapted the astronomical tables of al-Khwarazmī, an eastern Persian, to the meridian of Cordova. He wrote a small book on the astrolabe and another on commercial arithmetic, applying computation, geometry and algebra to problems of sales, valuations and taxation. He apparently tried to break out of the mathematical mould, for he introduced the popular Neoplatonism of the Ikhwān al-Ṣafā', or Brethren of Purity of Basrah,[3] to Andalusia. His disciple, al-Kirmānī, brought it to Saragossa, the birthplace of Ibn Bājjah.

The scientism rife among the mathematicians, along with a certain gingerly and prudent diffidence in speculative matters, fostered a near positivism, still palpable in the verses Ibn Ṭufayl quotes from one writer, who lamented the polarity between the tantalizing wisdom of metaphysics and the trivial immediacy of mathematics:

> How can it be that life's so small.
> Two sciences we have – that's all.
> One is truth beyond attaining.
> The other vain and not worth gaining.[4]

Yet metaphysics was prized here; it was mathematics that seemed vain. Philosophy took hold strongly in the next generation. The best of its exponents, Ibn Ṭufayl writes, was Ibn Bājjah (Avempace, born in the late fifth/eleventh century, d. 533/1139). He was a creative and iconoclastic thinker, an instigator of the "Andalusian revolt", who operated an observatory of his own[5] and made original contributions to physical theory, with his account of projectile motion. He equated the velocity of a projectile with the difference between its "motive force" and the resistance it encountered – where Aristotle had made velocity directly proportional to motive force and inversely proportional to "resistance". Defended by Aquinas and Scotus, the view was rejected by Averroes (Ibn Rushd) and Albertus Magnus. But Galileo used it in his early critique of the Aristotelian view.[6] A true Neoplatonist, Ibn Bājjah treated gravity as a spiritual force. "He thereby removed the barrier between the heavens and the sublunary world", as Nasr remarks, not by terrestrializing the celestial, as Galileo was to do, but by finding spiritual influences in all natural events, an approach that commended itself to Ibn Ṭufayl, Maimonides and others.[7]

Of Jewish ancestry, according to the redoubtable tenth/sixteenth-century physician and traveller Leo Africanus, Ibn Bājjah grew up in Saragossa. He was a physician, musician, writer of popular songs and poet with "a real lyrical gift".[8] In 504/1110, Saragossa fell to the Almoravids,

Muslim revivalists from North Africa. Ibn Bājjah stayed in the city and, still in his twenties, emerged as vizier to the Berber governor Ibn Tīfalwīṭ, brother-in-law of the Almoravid Prince 'Alī. Sent on an embassy to the still independent former ruler, he was imprisoned, presumably for throwing in his lot with the conquerors. Released after several months, he travelled to Valencia, where he learned of the death of Ibn Tīfalwīṭ in 510/1117 and of the conquest of Saragossa in 512/1118 by Alphonso I of Aragon. Making his way to Seville, he supported himself as a physician, moving on to Granada, where his learning soon made him well known. Travelling through Játiva, he was imprisoned again, now by the Almoravid ruler Ibrāhīm ibn Yūsuf ibn Tāshfīn, reportedly for heresy. He gained his release only by the intervention of the *qāḍī*, father or grandfather of the philosopher Ibn Rushd (Averroes), who knew well what he was about when he tried to draw a clear and firm line of demarcation between the claims of the faith and the aims of the philosopher.[9]

At Fez, Ibn Bājjah entered the court of the governor, Abū Bakr ibn Tāshfīn and again became vizier, this time for some twenty years, circulating among the cities of Granada, Seville and Oran. His friend and disciple Abū'l-Ḥasan ibn al-Imām was also to become a vizier, and is saluted as such in one of Ibn Bājjah's works. Noted for his generosity (he reportedly donated over a quarter of his wealth to a destitute countryman), Ibn al-Imām paid tribute to his mentor as the first to give life to the philosophic manuscripts al-Ḥakam had collected.[10] Indeed, Ibn Bājjah's writings show a keen and living responsiveness to the philosophic problematics of Plato, Aristotle and Galen. Recognizing in his teacher the first creative philosopher of the Islamic West, Ibn al-Imām took care to copy his writings while serving as the chief fiscal officer of Seville, using the autograph of his teacher and under his supervision; his copy was copied in turn in the manuscript now preserved at Oxford.[11]

Among the logicians of Andalusia was Mālik ibn Wuhayb, famed for his learning in many sciences, including astronomy and (judicial) astrology and known in his day as the Philosopher of the West. His name earns no mention by Ibn Ṭufayl, since his only philosophical writings were brief expositions of the rules of thought.[12] Yet he was celebrated for his brilliance and summoned from Seville to the Almoravid capital to confront the Almohad leader Ibn Tūmart, whose movement would soon destroy the Almoravid regime. Long after, he was remembered as the only man in the West to see through Ibn Tūmart's imperial designs when the Berber rebel debated with the clerics of Marrakesh in 515/1121 or 516/1122. He was mentor and patron to Ibn Bājjah at the Almoravid court and defended him when the philosopher was denounced as a heretic (*zindīq*), although Mālik himself had turned his talents to divinity and given up open discussions of philosophy, as Ibn al-Imām reports, "because of the attempts on his life to which he was subject on their account, and on account of his contentiousness in all discussions of scientific matters".[13] Ibn Bājjah died at Fez, still in his prime, reportedly poisoned at the instance of the man who had called for his execution, the rival physician and courtier Ibn Zuhr (d. 525/1130), who seems earlier to have denounced Mālik, and who was the father of the famous Avenzoar (d. 557/1161), a friend, fellow student and collaborator of Ibn Rushd's.

Ibn Khaldūn, the great Arab social theorist, names al-Fārābī and Ibn Sīnā as the chief philosophers of Islam in the East; Ibn Bājjah and Ibn Rushd in the West. Maimonides too admires Ibn Bājjah, citing his commentary on Aristotle's *Physics*, following his lead in astronomy, epistemology and the metaphysics of the soul. In a famous letter to the Hebrew translator of his Arabic *Guide of the Perplexed*, he calls Ibn Bājjah a great philosopher and ranks all his writings first rate.[14] But Ibn Ṭufayl complains of the disordered and incomplete state of Ibn Bājjah's works, surmising, since he never met the man personally, that worldly occupations left him little leisure for philosophy, "as he himself says, he was pressed for time with the trouble of getting down to Oran . . . he was so preoccupied with material success that death carried him off before his intellectual storehouses could be cleared and all his hidden wisdom made known".[15] Ibn Ṭufayl also complains of Ibn Bājjah's critique of mysticism. Yet his oeuvre ranged from *The Art of Healing* to commentaries on Aristotle, to the critique of Ptolemy's astronomy and Aristotle's physics, to a work on plants, and even one on hunting. Some thirty brief works, many indeed in unfinished state, survive in manuscript. They include commentaries on al-Fārābī's logic, and essays on the aim of human life, the Active Intellect, *The Regimen of the Solitary*, and a valedictory *Epistle of Farewell* to Ibn al-Imām. He contributes at least three philosophical themes to the repertoire of his successors – Ibn Ṭufayl, Averroes and Maimonides: his theory of *ittiṣāl*, intellectual contact with the Divine; his subtle approach to the doctrine of monopsychism, and his ideal of the governance of the solitary.

THEORY OF *ITTIṢĀL*

Like al-Fārābī and Ibn Sīnā, Ibn Bājjah believes that knowledge is not acquired by the senses alone. Universal and necessary judgments, the predictive and explanatory meat of science and the foundation of all apodeictic reasoning about nature, are reached only with the aid of the Active Intellect, the governing intelligence of nature.[16] Casual readers of Aristotle might suppose that he intended no more than a remark about individual cognition when he spoke (in *De anima*, 3.5) of an active intelligence that moves our potential for thinking to actuality. But the Hellenistic Peripatetic Alexander of Aphrodisias (*fl.* 200) surely knew that in the *Eudemian Ethics* (1248a) Aristotle argued that thought cannot simply start itself up by thinking but, like any process, requires a prime mover, which is indeed divine. So Alexander identified the Active Intellect with Aristotle's God, *nous*, untroubled by the quite Aristotelian thought that the Divine works immanently, within us, and unwilling to commit Aristotle to the absurd claim that the passivity in us that needs something to start it up might be said to actualize itself. Later Greek thinkers like Marinus (fifth century), the disciple and biographer of Proclus, preserving the transcendence of the Highest God, demoted the Active Intellect to a quasi-deity, *daimonion*. Al-Fārābī and Ibn Sīnā, for similar reasons, treat the Active Intellect as the disembodied intelligence that governs the terrestrial sphere.[17]

Its functions are manifold. Not only does it impart the forms which order nature and those which permit the mind to follow the hints of sensory images and construct concepts on the basis of experience, but it also sheds upon specially prepared minds that comprehensive and abiding flow of ideas which is the intellectual source of prophecy. Thus the Active Intellect of the *falāsifah*, or philosophers of Islam, is the reality answering to the symbolism of the Angel Gabriel, the vector of revelation. Al-Fārābī argues that a prophet differs from a philosopher only in clothing the concepts received from the Active Intellect in symbols and rhetoric: it is the work of the imagination that transforms pure ideas into myths, rituals, laws and institutions. Avicenna calls a prophet a "sacred intellect", in whom all the ideas springing from the Active Intellect come together to light up a mind capable of internalizing those ideas sufficiently to become, as it were, a secondary source of light. Al-Fārābī, the Ikhwān al-Ṣafā'[18] and Ibn Sīnā all offer the same intellectualist model for mystical experience, philosophic discovery and prophetic revelation.

Avicenna is wary of the potential for pantheism latent or (among "drunken Sufis") sometimes patent, in mysticism. He is careful, in importing ideas from the repertoire of Plotinus (205–70), to choose the idea of "contact" (Greek *aphe*, Arabic *ittiṣāl*) rather than "union" (*ittiḥād*) with the divine. He rejects the Plotinian notion of the divinity of the soul and inveighs against Porphyry, Plotinus' disciple (*c.* A.D. 232–*c.* 305), for holding that the soul unites with the Active Intellect. If that were so, Avicenna argues, then either the Active Intellect would be divisible or the individual mind that knows anything would know everything.[19] In developing al-Fārābī's intellectualist account of enlightenment, Ibn Bājjah stands forthrightly with Ibn Sīnā, for *ittiṣāl*, communion, over and against *ittiḥād*, union.

In his note on "Recognition of the Active Intellect",[20] Ibn Bājjah sketches four arguments for the reality of this hypostasis:

Firstly, from the relationship of means to ends. Means are typically necessary to ends in nature; but in the realm of ideas, ends come first.

And ideas are naturally prior to bodies, or there would be no constancy surmounting (and directing) the otherwise ungoverned play of genesis and corruption.[21]

Secondly, from the processes of change. Things become what they are not; they do not become their causes but rather become *like* the causes that produce change in them. Thus change is governed by universal forms. Effects are produced not by a unique particular but by any cause of an appropriate nature. (So receptivities to change, dispositions in things, are formal and universal, not material and idiosyncratic.) "For example, if this clump of grass catches fire from some other fire, it takes nothing of the fieriness of *that* fire, which is the cause; nor does it catch fire from some particular fire only. Rather, it turns *like* the fire that started it, which might be any fire that comes along."[22]

Thirdly, from the faculty of imagination that guides the instincts of animals. Animals seek not some particular drink of water or morsel of food, as friend seeks friend, or parents offspring, but *any* food or water answering to their natures. But beasts have no universal concepts. The ideas manifest in their behaviour must be present implicitly and objectively rather than explicitly and subjectively. Ibn Bājjah chides Galen (129–*c.* 199) here for treating imagination, which animals have, as though it were rationality (*al-'aql*), which they have not. No one, he argues, can claim that the crane, dove or sandgrouse truly grasps universal ideas. Yet such social creatures, indeed all that do not live in isolation, seek their own kind.[23] Without the discourse of reason (by which alone, as the work of Socrates shows) abstract concepts are discovered, how can the images that direct beasts to their needs aim true at specific classes? The only viable answer, Ibn Bājjah thinks, is that the relevant images are projected by the Active Intellect, much as it projects the forms that make our minds aware of universal concepts, and exactly as it projects the forms that impart natures to things, stabilizing their characters and rendering them intelligible.

Fourthly, from the work of the mind itself. We judge that we perceive a substance only in so far as we can ascribe predicates to it; without the predicates we know nothing of it and cannot say that we apprehend it at all. But predicates are necessarily universal, although their subject may be a particular. (Thus, without universals, perception of things would be impossible; radical empiricism would never get off the blocks.) Predicates are always signified by some noun or analogous expression, such as a definition that stands in for a noun.[24] These terms signify an idea in so far as they apply to a class. (So language too is impossible without universals.)[25] But how do we reach universals? A definition would normally be predicated of some subject. Suppose we start with bodies. These are the primary sort of objects of apprehension, and the means by which they are apprehended is sense perception. But bodies, although they are objects of apprehension, cannot be subjects of it. Now sense perceptions in turn are apprehended as images in the imagination. This (as Avicenna proved) is again something physical. But, for that very reason, images are not self-conscious. Indeed, given the passivity of matter, we must conclude that no physical organ or faculty can apprehend itself. But reason or intelligence does apprehend both its proper objects and its own act of apprehension by the same faculty or power. So plainly it is not anything physical.

This last argument, if sound, proves that human reason is not reducible to physicality or to any sensory function. From here Ibn Bājjah evidently thinks it an easy step to the hypostatic Active Intellect, as the source and support of human rationality. He mentions that there are various difficulties with the idea. But, perhaps typically, the surviving note does not list them. His first argument seems to parallel the Stoic sort of design argument, offering a spiritual immanence of the kind favoured by Peripatetics and Neoplatonists as an alternative to the physicalist immanence favoured by the Stoics in explaining the ordering of means to ends in nature. The second and third arguments similarly take issue with some form of nominalist reduction. They aim to establish the Active Intellect as the only credible solution to problems that materialism is unable to resolve.[26] Modern theists might cut to the chase, imputing design and governance in nature to God, rather than to some intermediary. But the Active Intellect, like Philo's *logos* or the angels of scriptural discourse, does protect God's transcendence, which remains as important a theological value to Ibn Bājjah as it was to his Neoplatonic predecessors.

The epistemology of the Active Intellect commits Ibn Bājjah to a Platonic realism, although, like other Neoplatonists, he houses the forms not in a realm of their own (risking Aristotelian arguments against the self-sufficiency of the Ideas) but in the Active Intellect, which the Ideas *constitute*, as a Peripatetic might have expected, since Aristotle himself had argued that, in the act of consciousness, thought, thinker and the act of thinking are one and the same. Drawing on Plato's Myth of the Cave, as an allegory of the condition of the masses, whose only contact with ideas comes by way of sensory surrogates and whose inexperience of light, uncoloured by shadows, leads them to deny the very existence of light itself, that is, the pure disembodied light of intelligence, Ibn Bājjah lays out a clear defence of realism about the ideas:

> The forms that Plato posits and Aristotle denies are as I shall describe them: They are ideas devoid of matter and apprehended by the mind [*dhihn*], just as the senses apprehend the forms of sensory things. Thus the mind is like a faculty of perception for ideas; and [perception is] like reason in apprehending patterns [*al-mutakhayyalāt*].[27] It follows that the thought concepts of these

> forms are simpler than the forms themselves. [For these thoughts are higher order abstractions, cutting away from the particularities of form in the particular just as the senses cut away from the matter of an object of perception.] So there are three items to be concerned with: sensory notions, forms and the ideas of forms. And the [Aristotelian] refutations of the forms apply only in this regard: that Plato gave the forms the name of the thing and assigned them its definition.[28] But we say that the spiritual form of a man, for example, is the form of Man, or the form of Fire. We do not refer to them as a "realm". And so we can say that our idea of fire has no fire in it, and we do not say of that idea that it is fire. For if it were fire, it would burn. Socrates said of the form he posited that it was the Good and the Beautiful, and of the form of Man, that it was man. That was what implicated him in all the absurdities Aristotle mentions in the *Metaphysics* (e.g., 1.9, 13.4, 8).[29]

Working in the tradition of al-Fārābī and Ibn Sīnā, Ibn Bājjah is able to provide a rationale for the possibility of prophetic revelation and for the special knowledge of the intimates of God, that is the saints (*awliyā'*), among whom he counts the associates (*ṣaḥābah*) of the Prophet. Through a special intercourse between reason and imagination such persons acquire from the angels, which is to say, in the language of the Philosophers, they acquire from the disembodied Intelligences that rule the spheres, an "insight of the heart", as Ibn Bājjah calls it, echoing the Socratic phrase about an inner eye. The resultant knowledge, he reasons, is abstracted from the temporal conditionedness of events, enabling these individuals not only to make moral and practical judgments but to anticipate the future and apprehend the unknown, to receive, as it were, the very intentionalities by which the spheres are directed to execute God's will in nature.[30] The key intermediary, of course, is the Active Intellect. But its primary role, as in al-Fārābī, is not in inspiring prophets or instructing seers but in informing nature and the minds of the intelligent.

Some writers find Ibn Bājjah's account of human contact with the Active Intellect rather intellectual, as contrasted with the moral or spiritual ideals of, say, traditional mystical writers. They may relate this to Ibn Bājjah's criticism of mystics, sensing a rejection of the religious significance of *ittiṣāl*. But we must bear in mind both the roots and the goals of Ibn Bājjah's project if we want to understand it aright. Like Aristotle, he thinks that the best way to attain the goal of knowing God is to know as God does, understanding all things through their universal ideas. Like al-Fārābī and Ibn Sīnā, he sees in the mystic quest no rival to the sciences but their culmination and fruition.

Scientific knowledge is constitutive of the comprehensive inflow of the forms that is the true goal of the adept. Further, science for Ibn Bājjah is not the value-free or value-neutral enterprise we may associate with the term. To understand a thing in the Platonic and Aristotelian context of a philosophy like Ibn Bājjah's, is to see its value and its perfection, its goodness, not just to us but in itself. For in that goodness it manifests God's goodness. Comprehensive knowledge here does not exclude moral and spiritual truths. They are, in fact, explications of our own nature and role and of our destiny among the intelligences that transcend the merely physical.

Ibn Bājjah does not, like many Sufis, merge mystic gnosis with a regime of pietist conventions. But the main reason, as we shall see, is that he has his own idea of a fitting regimen for the wise. Where he does take aim at mystic theory and practice is in regard to the blurring of identities between the aspirant and the Divine. He complements Avicenna's epistemic critique of monistic or unitive mysticism with a psychological analysis of what the enthusiasts of union actually attain: resolution of the data supplied by memory, imagination and the *sensus communis* (whose normal function is integration of the reports of the senses). Such resolution is in fact the work of the Active Intellect, which can bring divergent sense-based data into registry, projecting spiritual forms "as though they were a sensory image". The effect is startling, and the Sufis, who fall short of the pure ideas, put these "spiritual forms" in their place and suppose the integrative experience they undergo to be "man's ultimate goal", and "highest felicity", speaking of it as "union" and even praying for such union for one another:

> When these faculties converge they can produce strange shapes and potentially frightening apparitions, creatures far fairer than those that actually exist. So these folk suppose them to be the highest objects of apprehension. That is why al-Ghazzālī said that he apprehended spiritual objects and beheld spiritual substances, resorting to the words of the poet to represent the enormity of what he experienced: "It was; what it was don't ask me to say."[31]

The same line of verse about the ineffability of the mystic experience is quoted from al-Ghazzālī by Ibn Ṭufayl with more welcoming intent. Ibn Bājjah, he contends, should not have blamed the Sufis for pursuit of fruits he had not tasted. Perhaps, he reflects, Ibn Bājjah's remarks carry a savour of sour grapes: he must have seen the incompatibility of the Sufi life with his own "encouragement of amassing wealth and the use of various artful dodges to acquire it".[32] But Ibn Bājjah does not hesitate to commend the fruits of (rational) mysticism. His discomfort is with the sensuousness he detects in Sufi practice. His concern is not that the object of the mystic's quest is illusory but that in seeking unity Sufis, with al-Ghazzālī's apparent encouragement, may have substituted a phenomenal surrogate of suspect origin for the legitimate object of their quest.

MONOPSYCHISM

With still visible excitement, Ibn Bājjah reports on his discovery of a new line of argument about the soul:

> Conscious as I am of how hard it is for us to meet at this time, I thought I should come right to the point and set out the theory whose proof I have found . . . A technical exposition would be too long, too explicit, too convoluted, and too costly in premises. I have been diverted from taking that approach by time constraints and a steady stream of other business. If I do get the leisure to lay out a formal proof, I shall directly send it to you. But I wanted to waste no time in communicating what I have now, for fear of losing it, given that it is as big and as unusual as it is.[33]

Ibn Bājjah goes on to describe the unity of the rational soul, as the principle of individual identity – and, the life principle in general, as the "prime mover" of all animals (and in a lesser sense, even of plants).

> A child's teeth may fall out and new ones come in; he is still the same child. And the same would be true if he could grow new hands or feet in place of those that he'd lost: he'd still be the same person. Just as a carpenter who loses his adze or rule and gets another is still the same carpenter, so if it were possible for one to have other organs in place of these he would still be one and the same person.[34]
>
> It is clear from this argument that the prime mover remains the same whether he loses some instrument and finds no replacement, like the toothless old man, or does find one, like the youngster whose adult teeth are coming in. Once certain students of natural science understand this, it leads them to the theory of metempsychosis. This has been shown elsewhere to be absurd and untenable. But those who voiced this theory were reaching for a different idea but fell short of it. They took the prime mover of man to be an undifferentiated whole and treated as arithmetically one what is not one.[35]

Like Ibn Sīnā, Ibn Bājjah means to preserve the identity of the individual human soul, even when it no longer has any matter to individuate it. Sundered from the body, the rational soul, which Ibn Sīnā had argued would preserve its identity by virtue of its prior history of temporality, retains its individual consciousness, according to Ibn Bājjah, and "becomes one of those lights that gives glory to God. Singing his praise it joins the ranks of the prophets and saints, the martyrs and the blessed."[36] But although this soul remains unique and individual even without a body, it is (as we might put it) at one with all other souls, by virtue of its contact (*ittiṣāl*) with the Active Intellect. Likewise, it is at one with the Active Intellect itself. It is not identical with other souls, or with the Active Intellect. But it is not separate from them. For, Ibn Bājjah argues,

> What is connected is said to be one as long as it remains connected; once it is divided it becomes multiple. Things that cohere are spoken of in the same way as things that are connected. Things that are linked are treated the same as those that cohere; and things that are tied together, like those that are linked. A collectivity whose parts are organized to serve a definite purpose is also called one, as Ṭabarī's *History* [with its many volumes] is called one composition, and the present discussion [with its multiple words] is also called one. Even a mixture is called one, as oxymel is, which is composed of vinegar and honey.

This point seems to be the breakthrough that excites Ibn Bājjah: not the unity of all souls, which was, as he perceived, the teaching of Plato, a corollary of the argument of the *Phaedo* that the soul would be immortal to the extent that it was like an idea (and therefore had shed not only materiality and temporality but individuality, becoming, as it were, a universal). Rather, the excitement is about the possibility of a unity among spiritual beings that retain their individuality. Ibn Bājjah senses a breakthrough here, because the approach he takes, based on the idea of an organic unity which preserves diversity, makes possible retention of Plato's intellectualist argument for immortality without discarding individual accountability, crucial in the Qur'ān – and in Plato himself.[37] Plato had wrestled with the implications of the intellectualism of the *Phaedo* in the *Republic* (609–17). He had clearly sought to establish the credibility of reward and retribution for individual human souls, relying on the argument that, if virtue is a strength, virtuous souls would be the ones to enjoy immortality: the experience and propensities of choice which together had formed their lives would set the stage for their condition in each new phase of their existence. But if souls were immortal, Plato reasoned (611), their number would never change, none would ever be created or destroyed. It was here that Ibn Bājjah saw transmigration as the apparent outcome of the Platonic line of reasoning: if each soul acquired an individual fate based on its own individual choice of destiny, would not immortality make individuality insurmountable? What seemed to follow was the "absurd and untenable" view that souls would flit from body to body, even occupying the bodies of animals. Plato had enunciated such a view, but the truth that he and others were reaching for when they spoke in that vein, Ibn Bājjah urges, was not captured in the myth of metempsychosis. Rather, Ibn Bājjah caught sight of a solution in the Neoplatonic idea that the "prime mover" in each of us is the rational soul, groping for the highest good. This is what is one and undifferentiated, although present in a variety of embodiments and soul-settings:

> The mind is a rational faculty, but "rational faculty" refers in the first instance to a spiritual form that is *receptive* to intelligence and so is called active or actual intelligence. It was of this that al-Fārābī raised the question whether it was present in an infant but altered [and so made ineffectual] by the moistness [of a youthful temperament], or whether it arises later.

Ibn Bājjah answers al-Fārābī's question by arguing[38] that a human being is like a plant while in the womb, growing and taking nourishment. At birth, beginning to move about and use one's senses, one is like an animal. One is only potentially human (rational) in infancy. This account of the realization of the potential for intelligence (and analogously, of the life principle in all things) applies an Aristotelian, developmental conception to the resolution of what is at bottom a Platonic question, that is, a question about innate ideas. At the same time Ibn Bājjah's reply avoids the suggestion that human intelligence is some sort of indestructible matter poured out and interchanged among individuals or even spilling across the boundaries of diverse species. The unity of rational beings, like the larger unity of beings in general, is functional, organic, not merely qualitative, but not such as to negate the individuality of the diverse members of the over-arching whole:

> If this mind is arithmetically one in every man, then clearly, from what has been sketched thus far, the people who exist and come and go would all be one arithmetically, although that might seem bizarre and perhaps absurd. But if they are not arithmetically identical, this Intellect is not one. And in short, if this Intellect is one arithmetically, then all the individual persons that have such an intellect are one arithmetically – as if you held a magnet, swathed it in wax and moved now this iron and now that, and then swathed it in pitch and it moved the iron the same way, and then swathed it in other bodies: all these moving bodies

> would be arithmetically one, as with the master of a ship – except that bodies cannot be in several places at one and the same time, as these ideas can. That is what the transmigrationists believed, although they fell short of it.[39]

Strange as it might seem, then, all persons who share in the distinctive characteristic of humanity, a rational soul or intelligence, are identical – not just in kind but arithmetically.[40] They are the same individual. But this does not imply that they are the same person, nor that "soul stuff" is simply partitioned off from a single source of supply and distributed among individuals, as imagined by those who take literally the image of transmigration. For rationality is shared not by partitioning but by the realization of potential, the activation or actualization of matter, or in the present case, the "informing" of the animal spirit that here plays the role of matter. Individuals do not lose their identity in the spiritual unity that underlies intelligence, since unity has been qualified from the outset as an organic or functional uniting of diversity. Diversity is maintained when each rational soul "becomes one of those lights that gives glory to God". Ibn Ṭufayl captured Ibn Bājjah's sense perfectly when he elaborated the same Islamic recension of Plato's vision:

> Here too was an essence free of matter . . . Only this being had seventy thousand faces. In every face were seventy thousand mouths; in every mouth, seventy thousand tongues, with which it ceaselessly praised, glorified, and sanctified the being of the One who is the Truth . . . It was as though the form of the sun were shining in rippling water from the last mirror in the sequence, reflected down the series from the first, which faced directly into the sun.[41]

If the forms of all things are their reality, then in a sense all reality is one individual, as the idea of a macrocosm, so widely held among medieval philosophers, suggests. But what makes all beings one, Ibn Bājjah argues, is not that plants, animals and persons are indistinguishable or interchangeable or even that all are "parts" of a larger whole but that all (in their different ways) share a common source of life and movement; all are animated in that way, despite their diversity, by a common end – the Good Itself, as a Platonic philosopher would put it. Rationality in human beings, body heat or animal spirit in animals, and in the case of plants (as Ibn Ṭufayl writes), "whatever they have to fill the role of body-heat in animals"[42] is a principle of unity. Ibn Bājjah had closely studied the characters that plants have in common,[43] and what he found is again summed up by Ibn Ṭufayl: all things, even inanimate objects (as Ibn Bājjah's theories of motion and gravity reveal), "must have some special thing to make them behave in their own peculiar way, and give them their particular qualities to the senses and their ways of moving. This is the form, or as philosophers call it, the nature of the thing."[44] Philosophers before Ibn Bājjah had held that all forms flow from above, and some had held that the unity of human beings, resultant from their partaking of rationality, made all humans (at least potentially) one individual, identical with one another, with the Active Intellect, and thus, for some, with God. But the distinction of Ibn Bājjah was to have shown how the unity of forms in general and of rational minds in particular left room for the differentiation of individual identities, as particulars united in a common movement towards the good.[45] Without such a possibility of differentiation, creation and emanation would have been impossible, and immortality would have been valueless.

THE GOVERNANCE OF THE SOLITARY

Ibn Bājjah was a close reader of Plato's *Republic*, of Aristotle's *Nicomachaean Ethics* and of al-Fārābī's syntheses of the metaphysics of Neoplatonism with an Islamicized version of Platonic politics and Aristotelian ethics. He knows that the human being is a social, indeed a civil being by nature (*zoon politikon*) and that happiness is the life in accordance with the virtues. He also knows that the virtues are socially and civilly instilled, and that the mediation of imagination is crucial in the implementation of social policies by which moral virtues are inculcated and intellectual virtues fostered. Yet, like Plato and Aristotle, Ibn Bājjah is rather alienated from the society in which he lives. He is hardly prepared to be its apologist. Like al-Fārābī, Ibn Bājjah knows that a state might not always be fortunate enough to find and adequately empower its true philosophical ruler. There is an irony here, of course, like that of the Stoic Emperor Marcus Aurelius, who also felt powerless. For Ibn Bājjah was a vizier, as Aristotle was the tutor of Alexander and closest friend of Antipater, Alexander's regent; and Plato was born into the highest ruling circles of Athens. Yet it is characteristic of politics, in Machiavelli's and not in Plato's ideal sense, that even those who are placed structurally in the seats of authority may lack authority to alter the structures in which they sit. Clearly Ibn Bājjah was in no position to implement the rule of philosophy, which he, like Plato, saw as the ideal. And, while al-Fārābī could rationalize the myths and rituals, laws and institutions of the Prophet and his followers as symbols mediating the way to realities best known by the philosophers, it would take a special gift of insensitivity for a philosopher at the seat of power to identify a regime like that of the Almoravids, or their Almohad successors, among whom Ibn Ṭufayl served, as a faithful expression of the Platonic ideal rather than an unhappy recurrence of all that was ugliest in, say, Plato's Syracusan disaster. Ibn

Ṭufayl clearly identified Islamic religiosity and law – and culture in general – as both more and less than symbolic entryways to philosophy. They were necessary evils, condescensions to the inadequacies of *homo vulgaris*. Law could draw a line around the worst of human viciousness, but only at the cost of making a minimal requirement seem somehow a standard of moral adequacy. And public piety raised up a symbol system that could point the way for the rare few who were almost capable of finding the truth for themselves, but at the cost of most people's taking the symbols for the reality, allowing, or even insisting that they search no further. Religion, then, the core of culture, pointedly including Islam, was, for Ibn Ṭufayl, a vehicle, yes, but also an obstacle to moral, spiritual and intellectual growth.[46] He confides his criticism to fiction, masked, as he puts it, only with the sheerest of veils;[47] but Ibn Bājjah pours his doubts into a reflective meditation, *The Regimen of the Solitary*.[48]

A person may live well in the world, he writes, managing his affairs, staying healthy and maintaining homes and property, but "none of these things amounts to greatness or nobility, and we cannot convince ourselves that such things are the consummation of any sort of admirable life . . . they are simply the goals of a contentious soul . . . common to the irrational animals and thus bestial".[49] Summing up a line of reasoning found in Aristotle, Plato and Socrates, and later in Spinoza and Kant, he argues that it is only when we act rationally that we are free.[50] Our proper aim is spiritual knowledge, contact with the Active Intellect and thus, with the Divine. But the proper application of such knowledge is in rule, assigning priorities among competing values, especially when matters of dignity, nobility or honour are at stake.[51] In a just society, like that of the *Republic*, the wise are rulers; all human affairs are wisely regulated; no physicians or jurists are needed, since all individuals are governed by wisdom, their relations ruled by love. But, in a lesser state, the wise are "weeds" – "The name is borrowed from the plants that spring up of themselves among a sown crop"[52] – for they are deemed a blot on the landscape in the rare event that among a benighted polity someone does stumble upon the truth or recognizes the falsity of the conventional impostures. In the perfect society, of course, there are no weeds – just as there are no jurists or physicians – for there are no false views to be rejected. But in the kind of state and city that we live in, and that Ibn Bājjah himself feels powerless to alter in this regard, we find all three of these classes, their presence, a symptom of dysfunctionality:

> And it seems that if happy persons can exist in such states, their happiness must be solely private [*mufrad*], and the right sort of rule in such a case would be private, whether the party concerned was an individual or a group – unless the state or the nation as a whole shared their views. Such people are the ones that the Sufis

call strangers. For they are aliens in their outlook even in their own homelands, among their own comrades and neighbours. They have travelled, in their thoughts, to other planes. And these, in effect, are their homelands.[53]

NOTES

* Warm thanks to Majid Fakhry for his helpful suggestions.

1 Ibn Ṭufayl, *Ḥayy ibn Yaqẓān*, trans. L. E. Goodman (New York, 1972; repr. Los Angeles, 1990): 99.

2 See A. I. Sabra, "The Andalusian Revolt against Ptolemaic Astronomy: Averroes and al-Biṭrūjī", in Everett Mendelsohn (ed.) *Transformation and Tradition in the Sciences* (Cambridge, 1984). Other figures in the revolt were Ibn al-Haytham (d. *c.* 432/1040), Ibn Bājjah and Maimonides.

3 See Ian Netton, *Muslim Neoplatonists* (London, 1982); L. E. Goodman, trans., *The Case of the Animals vs. Man before the King of the Jinn* (Boston, 1978; reissued, Los Angeles, 1984).

4 *Ḥayy ibn Yaqẓān*, trans. Goodman: 99.

5 Al-Biṭrūjī, a key critic of Ptolemy, names Ibn Ṭufayl as his inspiration; Maimonides (*Guide of the Perplexed*, 2.24) cites Ibn Bājjah. Seyyed Hossein Nasr writes, "Avempace, under the influence of Aristotelian cosmology, which was then becoming dominant in Andalusia [as a counterforce to Ptolemy], proposed a system based solely on eccentric circles; Ibn Ṭufayl is regarded as the author of a theory [now lost] which was more fully developed by his student, the seventh/thirteenth-century al-Biṭrūjī (Alpetragius). This was an elaborate system of homocentric spheres, which has also been called the 'theory of spiral motion,' because in its view the planets appear to perform a kind of 'spiral' movement." *Science and Civilization in Islam* (Cambridge, Mass., 1968): 72; for Ibn Bājjah's observatory, p. 80. Ibn Ṭufayl specifies an understanding of the retrogradation of the planets as a benchmark of knowledge in the ideal inquirer of *Ḥayy ibn Yaqẓān*, trans. Goodman: 130.

6 See Ernest Moody, "Galileo and Avempace: the Dynamics of the Leaning Tower Experiment", *Journal of the History of Ideas*, 12 (1951): 163–93, 375–422.

7 See Nasr: 315–16, and my "Maimonidean Naturalism", in L. E. Goodman (ed.) *Neoplatonism and Jewish Thought* (Albany, 1992): esp. 157.

8 D. M. Dunlop, "Ibn Bādjdja", *Encyclopaedia of Islam*, 2nd ed., 3: 728.

9 See Averroes, *Kitāb faṣl al-maqāl wa-taqrīr mā bayna'l-sharī'ah wa'l-ḥikmah min al-ittiṣāl* ("The Book Clearly Distinguishing the Discourse and Demarcating the Nexus between Religion and Philosophy"), ed. George Hourani (Leiden, 1959); trans. in Hourani's *Averroes on the Harmony of Religion and Philosophy* (London, 1967).

10 See D. M. Dunlop, "Philosophical Predecessors and Contemporaries of Ibn Bājjah", *Islamic Quarterly*, 2 (1955): 100–16; M. S. H. al-Ma'sumi, "Ibn al-Imām, the Disciple of Ibn Bājjah", *Islamic Quarterly*, 5 (1959): 102–8.

11 Bodleian, Pococke 206. Other MSS survived in Egypt and in the Escurial. But

the Berlin MS used by some modern scholars was apparently destroyed during the Second World War.

12 Ibn Ṭufayl also slights Ibn Ḥazm, the ultra-conservative jurist, theologian and exponent of courtly love, an Andalusian whose learning was vast and whose radical opposition to rationalism and mysticism fired his highly original thinking but placed him outside the lineage to which Ibn Ṭufayl laid claim, that of al-Fārābī, Ibn Sīnā, al-Ghazzālī and indeed Ibn Bājjah.

13 See Dunlop, "Philosophical Predecessors": 100.

14 See S. Pines, translator's introduction to *The Guide of the Perplexed* (Chicago, 1969): lx.

15 *Ḥayy ibn Yaqẓān*, trans. Goodman: 98–9.

16 See L. E. Goodman, *Avicenna* (London, 1992): 123–49.

17 See L. E. Goodman, "Knowledge in Islamic Philosophy", in Indira Mahalingam and Brian Carr (eds) *Encyclopedia of Asian Philosophy* (London, forthcoming).

18 See L. E. Goodman, "Jewish and Islamic Philosophies of Language", in *Sprachphilosophie* (Berlin, 1992): sec. 1.2.1.

19 See Goodman, *Avicenna*: 164–72.

20 *Al-Wuqūf 'ala'l-'aql al-fa''āl*, ed. M. Fakhry in *Ibn Bājjah (Avempace): Opera Metaphysica* (Beirut, 1968): 107–9. In the manuscript the item is labelled: "Also among his discussions of the factors through which one can recognize the Active Intellect." It is discussed and very roughly translated by M. S. H. al-Ma'sumi in *The Journal of the Asiatic Society of Pakistan*, 5 (1960): 34.

21 See Aristotle, *Metaphysics*, 3.6, 4.4, 5 esp. 11–12, 9.8, 12.5–7.

22 *Al-Wuqūf*, ed. Fakhry, *Opera*: 108.

23 Ibn Bājjah's argument illuminates Saadiah's unusual gloss of Job 39: 13–18, *The Book of Theodicy*, trans. L. E. Goodman (New Haven, 1988): 392–4; it also illuminates Ibn Ṭufayl's interest in showing that Ḥayy ibn Yaqẓān is capable of searching for and recognizing his own kind – among the disembodied intelligences.

24 Arabic semantics does not sharply distinguish nouns from adjectives, characteristically treating the same terms both attributively and substantively.

25 Maimonides uses this thought when he argues in the *Guide of the Perplexed* that human language can never signify what God is, since its terms are universal and God is unique.

26 Galen's discussion, with which Ibn Bājjah takes issue, has a Stoic tang, reminiscent of the Stoic claim that one can see animals using the undemonstrated syllogism (or schema) *Either the first or the second; not the first, therefore the second*, when a dog coursing a hare comes to a fork in the road and sniffs only one path before racing down the other. Ibn Bājjah reacts against the materialism latent in the Stoic idea that even dogs have a logic in their behaviour. The Stoics' intentions parallel those of the Neoplatonists: not that dogs reason but that an implicit surrogate of reasoning guides them. For Ibn Bājjah this marks the work of the Active Intellect. For the Stoics the logos will be immanent, but physical. Hence Ibn Bājjah's complaint against Galen – essentially for muddling a spiritual cause with its physical effect. A conversation with Julia Annas helped keep me fair to the Stoic intentions here.

27 I read with Asín here: M. Asín Palacios, "Tratado de Avempace sobre la unión del intellecto con el hombre", *Al-Andalus*, 7 (1942): 1–47, see p. 20, para. 18, l. 4.

28 This is what modern philosophers call the problem of self-predication, which Vlastos, for one, has also identified as the core issue in Plato's realism.
29 *Ittiṣāl*, ed. Fakhry, *Opera*: 169.
30 Pococke 206, fol. 120b–121b; see M. S. H. al-Ma'sumi, "Ibn Bājjah on Prophecy", *Sind University Research Journal*, Arts Series, 1 (1961): 22–9.
31 *Tadbīr al mutawaḥḥid* ("The Governance of the Solitary"), ed. Fakhry, *Opera*: 55. Al-Ghazzālī uses the verse in his spiritual autobiography, *Al-Munqidh min al-Ḍalāl* ("Deliverance from Error"), trans. W. Montgomery Watt in *The Faith and Practice of al-Ghazālī* (London, 1963). Ibn Bājjah alludes to al-Ghazzālī's references to the mystic's vision of the Pen and other furniture of the heavenly pleroma.
32 *Ḥayy ibn Yaqẓān*, trans. Goodman: 98.
33 *Ittiṣāl al-'aql bi'l-insān* ("Man's Contact with the Intellect"), ed. Fakhry, *Opera*: 155. For the audience of Ibn Bājjah's presentation, see the MS note, ***ibid.***
34 Cf. Ibn Sīnā's Floating Man argument and my discussion in *Avicenna*: 155–8.
35 *Ittiṣāl*, ed. Fakhry, *Opera*: 157–8.
36 *Ibid.*: 162.
37 Ibn Bājjah seems to echo Plato's excitement about the unity of the virtues as diverse but interdependent strengths. But the unity of the virtues is chiefly that of species in a genus. What Ibn Bājjah posits here is an organic unity, service to a common end. Ibn Bājjah adapts the characteristically biological means by which Aristotle had united the diverse human goods by reasoning that all rational intellects are, in effect, pursuing the same goal. Maimonides follows Aristotle (and traces the structure of Ibn Bājjah's argument) when he unifies the seemingly disparate ends of human activity under a single goal in "Eight Chapters", 5; see L. E. Goodman, "Maimonides' Philosophy of Law", *Jewish Law Annual*, 1 (1978): 72–107 and "Saadya's Ethical Pluralism", *Journal of the American Oriental Society*, 100 (1980): 407–19.
38 Fakhry, *Opera*: 159–60.
39 *Ittiṣāl*, ed. Fakhry, *Opera*: 161–2.
40 *Ibid.*: 156, 162.
41 *Ḥayy ibn Yaqẓān*, trans. Goodman; 153.
42 *Ibid.*: 123.
43 See M. Asín Palacios, "Avempace Botánico", *Al-Andalus*, 5 (1940): 255–99.
44 *Ḥayy ibn Yaqẓān*, trans. Goodman: 123.
45 One can see the sense here of Spinoza's insistence that modes *are* differentiations of Substance, but not partitively.
46 *Ḥayy ibn Yaqẓān*, trans. Goodman: 161–5.
47 *Ibid.*: 166.
48 See D. M. Dunlop, trans. in "Ibn Bājjah's *Tadbīru'l-Mutawaḥḥid*", *Journal of the Royal Asiatic Society* (1945): 61–81 and the discussions in E. I. J. Rosenthal, *Political Thought in Medieval Islam* (Cambridge, 1968); Oliver Leaman, "Ibn Bājja on Society and Philosophy", *Islam*, 57 (1980): 109–19.
49 Ibn Bājjah, "*Fi'l-ghāyati'l-insāniyyah* ("On the Human Goal"), ed. Fakhry, *Opera*: 102.
50 *Tadbīr*, trans. Dunlop: 79.
51 *Tadbīr*, ed. Fakhry, *Opera*: 37–40.
52 *Tadbīr*, ed. Fakhry, *Opera*: 42; I translate after Dunlop, p. 77. For the term "weeds", see al-Fārābī, *Siyāsat al-madaniyyah*, ed. F. Najjar as al-Fārābī's *The*

Political Regime (Beirut, 1964): 87, 104.
53 *Tadbīr*, ed. Fakhry, *Opera*: 43.

SELECT BIBLIOGRAPHY

Al-'Alawī, J. (1983) *Mu'allafāt ibn Bājjah* (Beirut).
Ibn Bājjah (1973) *Sharḥ al-samā' al-ṭabī'ī*, ed. M. Fakhry (Beirut).
— (1992) *Rasā'il ibn Bājjah al-ilāhiyyah*, ed. M. Fakhry (Beirut).
— (1994) *Ta'ālīq 'alā manṭiq al-Fārābī*, ed. M. Fakhry (Beirut).
Lettinck, P. (1994) *Aristotle's Physics and its Perception in the Arabic world* (Leiden).
Zainaty, G. (1979) *La Morale d'Avempace* (Paris).

CHAPTER 22

Ibn Ṭufayl

Lenn E. Goodman

Born in the first decade of the sixth/twelfth century at Wādī Āsh (Cadiz), north-east of Granada, Ibn Ṭufayl (d. 581/1185–6) was trained in medicine, perhaps at Seville or Cordova (Cordoba), and studied philosophy, including the work of Ibn Bājjah, although he never met this founding figure of Andalusian philosophy. Practising as a physician, he moved in court circles and became secretary to the governor of Granada and then to the governor of Ceuta and Tangier, a son of 'Abd al-Mu'min, the military lieutenant and successor of the charismatic Ibn Tūmart (*c.* 473/1080–524/1130), who founded the Almohad dynasty in Spain and North Africa. Ibn Ṭufayl served as court physician to the Almohad caliph Abū Ya'qūb Yūsuf (ruled 558/1163–580/1184) and possibly as a *qāḍī* in his regime. He is even named in one source, improbably, as a vizier. The ruler genuinely enjoyed his company, spending hours, sometimes days, in conversation with him. For Abū Ya'qūb loved learning and books and took pride in assembling at his court more scholars and thinkers than any previous monarch in the Muslim West. A contemporary source describes Ibn Ṭufayl lining up for his pay, "with all the regular employees – medics, engineers, secretaries, poets, archers, soldiers, etc.", and joking with them about the eclectic interests of the crown: "If they're in the market for musical theory, I can supply it."

Ibn Ṭufayl acted as a kind of culture minister, seeking out and bringing to court many men of erudition and science, including the young Ibn Rushd (Averroes), whom he presented to Abū Ya'qūb around 564/1169. The historian al-Marrākushī has the story on the authority of Bundūd ibn Yaḥyā of Cordova, a disciple of Ibn Rushd's, who reported in Averroes' words how Ibn Ṭufayl sang his praises before the Commander of the Faithful, and how the caliph asked him about the views of the philosophers on the burning issue of the world's eternity or creation. Ibn Rushd was hard pressed to respond, since the Almohad regime was known for its doctrinal stringency, and the philosophers of Islam were committed, to the extent of their Aristotelian rigour, to the eternity of the universe. Most treated scriptural accounts of creation as allegories of the eternal emanation of the cosmos from its divine source, condescensions to vulgar imagination, and surrogates for the subtler truth: that God timelessly caused the world's ordered but eternal motion. Al-Ghazzālī, whom legend made the teacher of Ibn Tūmart, had declared the philosophers of Islam atheists for holding that view, since an eternal world, as he reasoned in his polemic, *The Incoherence of the Philosophers*, would have no need of God.[1]

The young Averroes feigned ignorance at the caliph's questioning, but was soon put at ease by hearing Ibn Ṭufayl and the monarch discuss the issue between themselves with learning and sophistication. He joined the conversation and was sent home with a robe of honour and a splendid new mount. This interview, we are told, was the first official notice taken of Ibn Rushd's talents. Later, at Ibn Ṭufayl's instance, he was commissioned to write the commentaries which eclipsed the fame of his sponsor and his patron alike. When Ibn Ṭufayl retired as court physician in 577/1182, he was succeeded by Ibn Rushd. But he continued to enjoy the favour of the caliph, and of his son, when Abū Ya'qūb died in 579–580/1184, of wounds received at the siege of Santarem in Portugal. Ibn Ṭufayl died at Marrakesh the following year. But long afterwards, when Bundūd had become a respected professor, he still repeated the story of Averroes' commission in the master's words:

> Abū Bakr ibn Ṭufayl summoned me one day and told me that he had heard the Commander of the Faithful complaining about the disjointedness of Aristotle's mode of expression – or that of the translators – and the resultant obscurity of his intentions. He said that if someone took on these books who could summarize them and clarify their aims, after first thoroughly understanding them himself, people would have an easier time comprehending them. "If you have the energy," Ibn Ṭufayl told me, "you do it. I'm confident you can, because I know what a good mind and devoted character you have, and how dedicated you are to the art. You understand that only my great age, the cares of my office – and my commitment to another task that I think even more vital – keep me from doing it myself."[2]

The intellectual work Ibn Ṭufayl cited in excusing himself from the project that would become Averroes' monumental three-tiered commentary on the Aristotelian corpus, was his effort to reconcile scriptural religion with philosophy. He approached the task from a solid grounding in the natural sciences, which were integral to the philosophic method and outlook. Beyond his work as a physician and authorship of two medical treatises and a correspondence with Averroes about the latter's medical *Kulliyyāt*, Ibn Ṭufayl was a key figure in the "Andalusian Revolt" against Ptolemaic astronomy, a critical movement which was continued by his friend and disciple al-Biṭrūjī.[3] He wrote several works on natural philosophy no longer extant, including a philosophical treatment of the soul, which al-Marrākushī saw in Ibn Ṭufayl's own hand. But the key to the task of reconciliation was his philosophical fable *Ḥayy ibn Yaqẓān*, the story of a self-taught philosopher of perfect intelligence, growing up on an equatorial island without parents, language or culture, who discovers for himself all phases of knowledge, from the technical and physical to the spiritual truths underlying scriptural religions. Tracing the inquiries and discoveries of such a mind, unguided, but also unblinkered by tradition, Ibn Ṭufayl believed, could elucidate the truths of philosophy and mysticism and help compose the now century-old quarrel between religion and philosophy in Muslim lands.

As his talk with Abū Ya'qūb the day of Ibn Rushd's "discovery" made clear, Ibn Ṭufayl knew well the issues that divided al-Ghazzālī from the Neoplatonizing Aristotelians al-Fārābī and Ibn Sīnā. In *Ḥayy ibn Yaqẓān* he sought a synthesis of their themes with al-Ghazzālī's Sufi-influenced recasting of Islamic mysticism and pietism. For all these pathways, he believed, sought the same goals. Al-Ghazzālī himself had drunk deep of Neoplatonic emanation theory and Aristotelian virtue ethics.[4] And the Muslim philosophers, as al-Ghazzālī had acknowledged, were, at least in their intentions, theists, *muḥaqqiqūn*, thinkers dedicated to the Truth.

Ḥayy ibn Yaqẓān, like any fiction, is a thought experiment. It builds on the famous Floating Man thought experiment of Avicenna. The title is taken from one of the allegories Ibn Sīnā wrote while imprisoned in the castle of Fardajan near Hamadhan and refers to the living human intelligence, aroused by the ever-wakeful Active Intellect, the hypostasis by which God communicates His truth to the human mind, and indeed imparts all order and intelligibility to nature. In the Floating Man argument, recurrently used in Avicenna's non-allegorical writings, the philosopher demonstrates the substantiality of the human soul, that is, its independence or self-sufficiency, by calling on his readers to conceive themselves suspended in the air, isolated from all sensations, even from all sensory contact with their own bodies. One would still, he argued, have self-consciousness. Since one conceives of one's own awareness without positing the body or any bodily sensation, the idea of the self is not logically dependent on that of any physical thing; the soul, then, is not to be thought of in merely relative terms but as a primary given, a substance.[5] The argument was refined and simplified when Descartes recast it in epistemic terms: I can abstract from the supposition of all external things, but not from the supposition of my own consciousness.

Ibn Ṭufayl gave the argument a social twist, transposing the fictive situation of the mind from sensory deprivation to cultural isolation. It was not uppermost among his intentions to speculate about the empirics of the "wild boy" phenomenon – although his narrative does draw on the Romulus and Remus sort of motif, proposing a fallow doe as the nurse of the castaway or neophyte Ḥayy ibn Yaqẓān. His central purpose was to show what human intelligence can discover with no help beyond a divinely imparted insightfulness – the human receptivity to ideas and active penchant for inquiry that al-Ghazzālī had claimed for himself and that Aristotle had set down as a premiss when he opened the *Metaphysics* with the words, "All men by nature desire to know."

The finding of Ibn Ṭufayl's thought experiment is that language, culture, religion and tradition are not necessary for the development of a perfect mind but may well impede its progress. This outcome voices a sharp reproof against existing social structures in general and institutional Islam in particular. The social critique, which complements Ibn Ṭufayl's irenic message, is not left implicit. It is spelled out in passages describing the encounters between the perfected Ḥayy ibn Yaqẓān and the members of a society governed under a prophetically revealed religion that is (in Ibn Ṭufayl's phrase) a "thinly veiled" generic counterpart of Islam.

Ibn Ṭufayl begins the story of Ḥayy ibn Yaqẓān by relating two rival accounts of his origin, suggestive of the rival scientific and religious accounts of the nature and origin of humankind. The scientific account ascribes Ḥayy's origin to spontaneous generation, relying heavily on the precise characteristics of the matter in which the new organism would take shape. The alternative account resorts to fable, positing a human society and a human drama in which a royal infant is conceived but cast away, like Moses in the bulrushes, to be borne by a providential current, after moving prayers by his tearful mother, to an uninhabited island, where he is cast up on a shore the tide would not reach for another year. In both accounts, chance plays a role. But in the naturalistic version chance becomes the opportunity of nature; in the fabular version, which repeatedly echoes Qur'ānic language, chance becomes the plaything of providence, anthropomorphically addressed.

Ibn Ṭufayl is careful to avoid saying that the two stories contradict each other. Those who tell the one story do deny the other. Yet neither account can exclude reference to the imparting of life, spirit and intelligence, "the spirit which is God's" (Qur'ān 15: 28–9, 32: 6–9, 38: 71–2), and which is indissoluble from the body, not only in the purview of the senses, but also for the mind.[6] Clearly both stories are meant to be adequate and insufficient in complementary ways; those who affirm the one and deny the other are only depriving themselves of a portion of the truth which can never be fully expressed in human language, regardless of its sanctity.

Ḥayy ibn Yaqẓān, like Aristotle's ideal of all men, has an innate desire to know. Nursed and nurtured by his doe foster mother, he learns to rely on her and trust in her care. His desires and aversions come into focus much in the manner of the Stoic developmental psychology of moral consciousness;[7] and he learns shame, jealousy, emulation and covetousness – conditions of childhood in Ibn Ṭufayl's thinking. By adolescence Ḥayy has reached the age of practical reason, making clothes and weapons, tired of waiting for horns to sprout on his head and weary of fighting losing battles with the animals. As his foster mother weakens with age, he learns to care for her and discovers the active side of the love which had been mere passive dependency in childhood. When she dies, he tries to restore her, but then realizes that the vital spirit has fled, and that the body which remains is a mere putrid mass without its ruling principle.

Ontogeny recapitulates phylogeny as Ḥayy discovers fire and uses it for light and cooking, associating its power with the missing life principle of his doe mother, becoming infatuated and ready to worship the flame. He dissects the bodies of animals and uncovers the workings of their anatomy and physiology, but increasingly his interests are spiritual, and at twenty-one he begins to think seriously about metaphysics. Ḥayy discovers the organic form and unity of the cosmos, the distinction between matter and substantial forms, and the ultimate Cause of all that he observes, working immanently, through the natures of things, as is figured forth in the language of the Qur'ān (8: 17), where God informs his prophet of the unseen dimensions of a battle: "When you shot it was not you who shot but God." Advancing independently in the same path as the philosophers, Ḥayy discovers for himself proof of the world's finite size: if there were an infinite magnitude, then removing a finite part of it would either make it finite or leave it infinite; if the former, then two finite quantities combined would form an infinite; if the latter, then one infinity exceeds another, which is impossible (p. 129).

The argument, rooted in Aristotle, is used by Spinoza to prove not that the world is finite but that the world, being infinite, cannot really be divided into parts. If the universe had isolable parts, Spinoza argues, the dilemma would be inescapable: one would be forced either to admit that a whole is not equal to the sum of its parts or to regard one infinity as greater than another. (And then one would need to know by how much.) Ibn Ṭufayl's argument is rejected in modern mathematics only as a result of Georg Cantor's showing in 1874 that coherent sense can (and must) be made of the notion that one infinity does exceed another. And that argument, in turn, rests in part on a Spinozistic reconstruction of the continuum – and, in a way, even on Ibn Bājjah's[8] idea of a continuity among distinguishable identities. For the undenumerable infinity of Cantor is mapped by the "irrational" numbers, the glue, as it were, connecting the discrete milestones of the set of all rational numbers. But, for Ibn Ṭufayl, Ḥayy's reasoning about the finitude of the cosmos represents the pinnacle of the attainments of pure reason – beyond which Ibn Ṭufayl believes the human mind still has some way to travel, its progress always guided by the reason that has carried it to this point, and the meaning of its discoveries left to the interpretation of reason, guided by divine grace and the virtue of humility.

The classic standoff between Aristotelian eternalism and scriptural creationism is recapitulated as an antinomy (it would become the first of Kant's four antinomies) in the reasonings of Ḥayy ibn Yaqẓān: if the world is eternal, its age would be infinite, subject to the same paradoxes that beset a world of infinite size – was it less than eternal a year ago? But if the world began, then (recapitulating the reasoning of Aristotle) there was a time before which there was no time. And the very notion of *before which* implies that this too was a time and that the notion of time's first moment is incoherent.

> For some years Ḥayy pondered over this problem, but the arguments always seemed to cancel each other. Baffled and exhausted by the dilemma, he began to wonder what each of the beliefs entailed. Perhaps the implications were the same! For he saw that if he assumed that the universe had come to be in time, *ex nihilo*, the necessary consequence would be that it could not have come into existence by itself, but must have had a Maker to give it being . . . Alternatively, he saw that if he assumed the eternity of the world, that is, that it has always been as it is now and never emerged from non-being, this would imply that its motion too is eternal and had no beginning, never started up from rest. Now every motion requires a mover. This mover can be either a force distributed through some body – self-moving or externally moved – or a force which is not distributable or diffusible in physical bodies . . . it has already been proved that every material body must be finite. Should we discover a force engaged in an infinite task, that force cannot belong to a physical thing. But we have found the motion of the heavens to be ceaseless and eternal, for *ex hypothesi* it has gone on for ever and had no beginning. *Ergo* the force that moves them must be neither in their own physical structure nor in any external physical being. It can only belong to some Being independent of all material things and indescribable by any predicate applicable to them.[9]

On either account then, that of the philosophers, who prided themselves on their science (for eternalism left no room for exceptions to the eternal rule of causal laws), or that of scriptural monotheists (who sustained God's free governance of the universe with the idea that God chose to create, with no prior condition or constraint), natural theology would still flourish: a scriptural appeal to the world's dependence on the act and choice of God, or an Aristotelian appeal to the Prime Mover – either would lead to a God who is incorporeal and unimaginable yet governs the world, as its creator or as the emanative Source of the forms and dispositions that distinguish and energize all that is.

The resolution is a sharp rebuke to al-Ghazzālī's claim not only that the two accounts were irreconcilable but that the eternalism of the philosophers was incompatible with their would-be theism and that it made them atheists in spite of themselves. For al-Ghazzālī had held, in opposing the teachings of al-Fārābī and Avicenna, that no meaning could be found for the idea of the world's contingency and God's authorship of nature unless there was a time before which the world did not exist.

Ibn Ṭufayl's truce did not hold, even in the Islamic West. Averroes sought a line of demarcation between the claims of the philosophers and the aims of mass religion. But, within the territory still held by philosophy, he resolutely maintained the eternity of the cosmos, arguing in *The Incoherence of the Incoherence*, his riposte to al-Ghazzālī, that it was not the eternalism of the philosophers but the sophistries of the theologians that were incoherent. But Ibn Ṭufayl's resolution did appeal to Maimonides, who ascribed much of the heat and confusion on the issue to the efforts of philosophers and *mutakallimūn* to prove creation or eternity *a priori*. The eternalism of the philosophers, he argued, resulted in an unwanted and untenable determinism, which, if taken at face value, would render change as well as choice impossible. The radical contingency of the *mutakallimūn* led to an equally untenable occasionalism, which left every event to the immediate agency and arbitrary discretion of God. One must confront the fact, he argued, taking his cue from Ibn Ṭufayl, that we cannot prove the point demonstratively one way or the other. But that does not leave us without reasons to guide us: creation is preferable to eternity and more probable; more probable, because strict emanation, unguided by the sort of will or grace that we humans can grasp only in volitional terms, does not seem capable of differentiating divine simplicity into the multiplicity we observe; theologically preferable, because it makes more sense to speak of an Author of the world if the world is something that need not have existed, that once did not exist, but now does exist and has the nature it has because of the act of God.

The reasons are al-Ghazzālī's, but the moderation is Ibn Ṭufayl's: the philosophers are not atheists; their arguments do work, although the eternity of the world is a postulate of theirs more problematic than they may care to acknowledge, not an axiom, and still less the conclusion of an apodeictic demonstration. But the alternative too is problematic, since creation posits a volitional side to God, which strict monotheists know to be undifferentiable in reality from divine wisdom. Radical monotheists, those who follow through on the logic and dynamic of the idea of the Divine in all its absoluteness, know, as al-Ghazzālī knew when he described a form of monism as the logical outcome of monotheism, that the distinction of divine will from wisdom, which theistic voluntarists fought so hard to shield within the doxological bastion of the idea of creation, must in the end be absorbed in the transcendent unity of an absolutely simplex Being. Maimonides in fact treats all differentiation of God's attributes as an artifact of human subjectivity and finitude.[10] But this too is a strategy he shares with Ibn Ṭufayl, who argues at the climax of *Ḥayy ibn Yaqẓān* that the very notions of unity and diversity are compromised by the rootedness of our modes of thought in the physical world.[11]

Thomas follows Maimonides in holding that resolution of the dispute between creation and eternity lies beyond unaided reason. And Kant follows too, when he assigns a name and a cause to the antinomy, ascribing it, as Maimonides had done, to the overreaching of pure reason. What mattered, in Ibn Ṭufayl's view, was the integrated cosmos, "one organism whose parts are joined organically together" (p. 128), all clearly the work of the one God, the "eternally existing Being, Whose existence is uncaused, but Who is the cause of all existence" (p. 135), whose transcendence both the idea of creation and the idea of eternity endeavour to protect.

The discovery of God, as Ibn Ṭufayl's fiction shows, is the discovery of human vocation, salvation and felicity. It is also the discovery of the meaning of perdition:

> If there is a Being Whose perfection is infinite, Whose splendour and goodness know no bounds, Who is beyond perfection, goodness, and beauty, a Being such that there is no perfection, no goodness, no beauty, and no splendour that does not flow from Him, then to lose hold of such a Being and having known Him to be unable to find Him must mean infinite torture, as long as He is not found. Likewise, to preserve constant awareness of Him is to know joy without lapse, unending bliss, infinite rapture and delight. (p. 137)

The project of the Sufis and the Neoplatonic philosophers is the same: pursuit of gnosis; and the perdition and paradise of Qur'ānic poetry are but images by which mystic contemplation and its loss are figured forth as bliss or torment, to an audience not yet initiated into such intimate experience of the Divine, and perhaps not capable of it.

Ḥayy ibn Yaqẓān discovers his own vocation before he knows what people in general are or what societies are like. He promptly sets about to pursue it, recognizing in such spiritual felicity the sole avenue and content of immortality. He devises his own, natural Sufi discipline –

ascetic, to minimize the distractions of the body that would call him away from concentration on God's unity. And he emulates the rhythmic circling of the heavenly bodies, whose luminous clarity and diaphanous substance seem to him clear evidence that they too, of all the beings in his world, are aware of the perfection of the Perfect Being and offer recognition to it.

For Ḥayy ibn Yaqẓān knowledge is obligation, and to know what manner of being he is and where he is situated in the cosmos is to know how he must live:

> Seeing that what made him different from all other animals made him like the heavenly bodies, Ḥayy judged that this implied an obligation on his part to take them as his pattern, imitate their action and do all he could to be like them. By the same token, he saw that his nobler part, by which he knew the Necessarily Existent, bore some resemblance to Him as well. For, like Him, it transcended the physical. Thus another obligation was to endeavour, in whatever way possible, to attain His attributes, to imitate His ways, and remould his character to His, diligently execute His will, surrender all to Him, accept in his heart His every judgment, outwardly and inwardly . . . rejoice in His rule. (p. 142)

Here the resignation and submission entailed by the very word Islam become the *homoiosis theoi* of Plato and the *imitatio Dei* of monotheism in general. But obligations stem not simply from resemblances. There is a definite directionality to the scheme, and that directionality is clearly Platonic. For there are some resemblances that Ḥayy must minimize. It is the spiritual that he, and the human beings whose situation he models, must maximize:

> He recognized, however, that he was like the lesser animals in his lower half, the body, for it belonged to the world of generation and decay. It was dull and dark and demanded sensory things of him – food, drink, intercourse. Still he knew that this body had not been created for him idly . . . He must care for it and preserve it, even though in doing so he would do no more than any animal.
>
> His duties, then, seemed to fall under three heads, those in which he would resemble an inarticulate animal, those in which he would resemble a celestial body, and those in which he would resemble the Necessarily Existent Being: he had to act like an animal to the extent that he had a dull, sublunary body with differentiated parts and conflicting powers and drives. He had an obligation to imitate the stars in virtue of the vital spirit in his

> heart, which was the command point for the rest of his body and its powers. It was his obligation to become like the Necessarily Existent because he was (and to the extent that he was) himself, that is, to the extent of his identity with that self which brought him his awareness of the Necessarily Existent. (pp. 142–3)

Eating, drinking, and other bodily functions were distractions, but necessary to the maintenance of the vital spirit, which in turn enabled Ḥayy to emulate the celestial bodies. This meant three things. Firstly, to be like the stars he must adopt a role of stewardship over nature: he must not only minimize the demands of his body and interfere to the least degree possible with the fulfilment of every natural project set forth for living beings by God, but he must actively care for all natural kinds, to emulate the governance and benevolent influence of the stars, "never allowing himself to see any plant or animal hurt or sick, encumbered or in need without helping it if he could".

Secondly, "Ḥayy made sure always to be clean, washing frequently with water, getting all the dirt and grime off his body, cleaning his teeth, nails, and every nook and cranny of his body – even scenting it as best he could with plant fragrances and various pleasant smelling oils. He took great care to see that his clothes were always clean and fragrant, and soon he did begin to sparkle with vitality, cleanliness, and beauty" (p. 146). Here Ibn Ṭufayl appeals to the emulation of the stars to assimilate the toilet of Ḥayy ibn Yaqẓān not only to the ablutions of Islam but further, to the courtly sparkle ascribed to philosophers like Avicenna, and prescribed by the courtly ethical philosopher Ibn Miskawayh, whose emphasis on dressing well, as a component of the virtue of personableness, al-Ghazzālī had rejected in favour of a Sufi–Pietist asceticism of simple dress and an ideal of minimal attention to such externals.[12]

Finally, Ḥayy must emulate the motions of the heavens, whose perfection visibly manifests their adoration of God's absolute perfection, as Aristotle had argued. Ḥayy does this by spinning in place and circling his island – in effect, recreating the rituals in which Muslims circumambulate the Ka'bah in the rites of pilgrimage and Sufi devotees spin to reach the ecstasy of vertigo in the practice of the *dhikr*, the whirling invocation of the name and thought of God, aimed at focusing consciousness on God alone by blotting out all sensory things and all promptings of imagination.

But it was in pure meditation, "submersion", obliterating the externality and otherness of the personality itself, leaving only "the One, True Identity" of the Necessarily Existent, that Ḥayy found his highest and most perfect emulation, the end to which all his other activities must be means. Even the whirling of the *dhikr* must here be left behind, as a vestige of physicality, and stewardship itself becomes a distraction from the perfect ecstasy the self-taught philosopher now seeks, as Muḥammad had done, in a cave.

Practice of the discipline that his three forms of mimesis enjoined allows Ḥayy to become a mystic adept, capable of sustaining his gnostic contact with the Divine. With great labour the goal is achieved: "From memory and mind all disappeared . . . And with the rest vanished the identity that was himself" (p. 149), and Ḥayy ibn Yaqẓān experiences the beatific vision.

His return to self confuses the mind and leads him to confound his own identity with the higher object of his knowledge, a pantheistic notion that Islam had battled among extremist Sufis and that Avicenna had battled among philosophers, blaming Porphyry, for example, for taking the mind's "contact" with the divine hypostasis known as the Active Intellect to entail the identity of the two.[13]

> This specious thinking might well have taken root in his soul, had not God in His mercy caught hold of him and guided him back to the truth. He then realized that he never would have fallen prey to such a delusion unless some shadows of the physical or taint of sensory things still lurked within him. For "many", "few" and "one"; "singularity" and "plurality"; "union" and "discreteness", are all predicates applicable only to physical things. (p. 150)

Ibn Ṭufayl here relies on a Plotinian line of argument in order to show that the very categories of unity and difference themselves pertain exclusively to the sensory world, that in the spiritual or intellectual world, the question of the identity or difference of the perfected human soul with the divine simply does not arise.

Ibn Ṭufayl mounts Aristotle's argument that matter is the principle of individuation and that intellectual entities like Plato's forms therefore have a problematic arithmetic as a kind of canon for use against the Aristotelian fusion of thought, thinker and object of thought. True, he agrees, the mind is what it knows. But with intellectual things, there is no identity or difference. Similarly, Ibn Ṭufayl deploys Plotinus' idea that the intellectual realm (*nous*) is a "one/many" against Plotinus' own quest for the divinization of the soul, preferring Plato's more modest goal of *homoiosis theoi*, "to the extent that this is possible", echoing the very qualification Plato himself had used. And he relies on Ibn Bājjah's reconciliation of the individual immortality of Avicenna (and al-Ghazzālī) with the loss of individuality in the disembodied or ecstatic soul, seemingly demanded by Plato's intellectualist arguments for immortality and by the Sufi theme of *fanā'*, dying unto self. True again, he holds, the ecstatic transcends mere selfhood. But in so doing, what he leaves behind are the limitations of the ego, not the consciousness of individuality.

What Ibn Ṭufayl takes from Ibn Bājjah here is the idea of contact among the souls that have managed to detach themselves from matter, a contact that does not negate their individuality. All such souls are members of a continuous whole, but that fact does not merge them with Divinity and annihilate the very awareness in which their bliss is consummated.[14] What Ibn Ṭufayl contributes to Ibn Bājjah's theme and argument is the image of the community of immortal souls, which here becomes part of Ḥayy ibn Yaqẓān's ecstatic vision, his first direct encounter with other beings that are not merely like him, as are the celestial bodies, but of his own kind:

> Passing through a deep trance to the complete death-of-self and real contact with the divine, he saw a being corresponding to the highest sphere . . . neither identical with the Truth and the One nor with the sphere itself, nor distinct from either . . . at the pinnacle of joy, delight and rapture, in blissful vision of the being of the Truth, glorious be His majesty.
>
> Just below this, at the sphere of the fixed stars, Ḥayy saw another . . . like the form of the sun appearing in one mirror, reflected from a second . . . Thus for each sphere he witnessed a transcendent immaterial subject, neither identical with nor distinct from those above, like the form of the sun reflected from mirror to mirror with the descending order of the spheres . . . until finally he reached the world of generation and decay, the bowels of the sphere of the moon.
>
> Here too was an essence free of matter, not one with those he had seen – but none other. Only this being had seventy thousand faces. In every face were seventy thousand mouths; in every mouth, seventy thousand tongues, with which it ceaselessly praised, glorified, and sanctified the being of the One who is the Truth. (pp. 152–3)

Functionally, as Ibn Bājjah would argue, we have unity here. But the individualities remain distinct, each enjoying the reward of its own quest, in communion with the Highest, and in community with one another. Reflection from mirror to mirror both preserves and differentiates the intellectual reality that is imparted from above or beheld from below. At the level of individual creatures and created species, refraction might be a more fitting metaphor than reflection. But, in keeping with Ibn Bājjah's argument, the unity of all disembodied souls does not compromise their Avicennan individuality. And their Platonic inviolability does not render them identical with – nor yet different from – the Divine. For, in the Plotinian terms that Ibn Ṭufayl adopts as the framework of his metaphysic, all being is by participation in the reality, unity and goodness of the Divine.

To lose contact with God absolutely would be to be annihilated. But even the souls of the damned do not undergo quite that fate. Rather, they are preserved in being, but distanced from the light that might have given meaning and fulfilment to their being. As Ḥayy's vision images the fact:

> From this height he saw other selves like his own . . . more like tarnished mirrors covered with rust, their faces averted and their backs to the brilliant mirrors in which shone the image of the sun. They were ugly, defective, and deformed beyond his imagining. In unending throes of torture and ineradicable agony, imprisoned in a pavilion of torment, scorched by the flaming partition . . . (p. 153)

The partition here is alienation, and the torments of Hell so vividly detailed in the Qur'ān now belong to the imagery of separation, which can never be absolute while anything endures of creaturely existence.

It is only as a mature and practising mystic that Ḥayy ibn Yaqẓān first encounters another living human being, in the person of the anchorite Absāl, a philosophical refugee from an inhabited island long ruled under the laws of a scriptural religion. There are elements of pathos and parody when the two men first meet. Absāl is sure that Ḥayy is another anchorite like himself. Ḥayy is curious about Absāl's long black Sufi coat of wool, which he takes to be this creature's natural coat. He approaches for a closer look. But Absāl, anxious not to distract the other from his devotions, runs away and must be caught and calmed by the powerful Ḥayy ibn Yaqẓān.

Absāl, like the theologian of Voltaire's *Philosophical Dictionary*, has studied many tongues, in his quest for subtlety and sophistication in the exegesis of scripture. When he realizes that Ḥayy has no language at all, "the fears he had felt of harm to his faith" from contact with this exotic person are relieved: "he became eager to teach him to speak, hoping to impart knowledge and religion to him, and by so doing earn God's favour and a greater reward" (p. 160). But what he learns, of course, is that Ḥayy already knows the truth, of which his own religion bears the mere symbols. Reward, to mention the case nearest to hand, is not a sort of salary for winning hearts and souls to the one true faith, but the inner consequence of insight and spiritual advancement. Ḥayy, for his part, readily recognizes the true intentions behind the symbolic representations used by the prophet of Absāl's faith. He willingly "accepts" it, fulfilling the formal conditions so welcome to the Islamic ideal of proselytization. But in fact, as their acquaintance deepens, it is clear that Absāl is the convert and disciple, and Ḥayy the teacher.

As Absāl tells his friend about his own culture, religion and society, Ḥayy finds two things incomprehensible. Firstly, "why did this prophet rely for the most part on symbols to portray the divine world, allowing mankind to fall into the grave error of conceiving the Truth corporeally", imagining God Himself in physical terms, and supposing that reward and punishment are meted out in sensory pleasures and chastisements? And secondly, in laying out the obligations of humanity, "why did he confine himself to these particular rituals and duties" – which Ḥayy accepted gladly – "and allow the amassing of wealth and overindulgence in eating, leaving men idle to busy themselves with inane pastimes and neglect the Truth?" – when property meant nothing to Ḥayy, and, as he believed, "no one should eat the least bit more than would keep him on the brink of survival".

> When he saw all the provisions of the Law to do with money, such as the regulations regarding the collection and distribution of welfare or those regulating sales and interest, with all their statutory and discretionary penalties, he was dumbfounded. All this seemed superfluous. If people understood things as they really are, Ḥayy said, they would forget these inanities and seek the Truth. (pp. 161–2)

Moved by compassion for humanity, so far removed from the truth that they must rely on surrogates and so undisciplined and blind that they become an easy prey to temptations and distractions, Ḥayy determines to accompany Absāl to his own island, hoping "that it might be through him" that these people will be saved. The irony of Ibn Ṭufayl's allowing his hero to expect to "save" a populace already in receipt of a religion indistinguishable from Islam would not have been lost on a Muslim audience.

On the arrival of the two men in Absāl's land, there is great interest, of course, in Ḥayy's novelty and great excitement at his story. But when the neophyte philosopher settles down to teach the people, "the moment he rose the slightest bit above the literal or began to portray things against which they were prejudiced, they recoiled in horror from his ideas and closed their minds" (p. 163). In the end, class by class, Ḥayy "saw 'every faction delighted with its own' (Qur'ān 23: 55, 30: 31)" and realized that their appetites and passions made them incapable of following in his footsteps, let alone seeing what he had seen. Reluctantly, he reaches the conclusion that symbols and restrictive laws, rather than the unvarnished truth and the discipline of self-perfection, are the best that the mass of men are capable of receiving. Admittedly, symbols can be mistaken for the truth itself and the minimal restrictions of a civil and criminal code are readily taken as the substance of righteousness and fulfilment of God's will. But such confusions are a necessary evil. For without the prophet's wise condescension to the moral and intellectual inadequacies of humanity and the weaknesses of human culture, even worse confusions of spirit and depravities of character than the Candide-like Ḥayy had observed would take hold, and they would grow far more widespread than the moral and intellectual vices and spiritual weaknesses that he had detected in the recipients of civilization. Ḥayy and Absāl return to their isolated island and continue their devotions: "Ḥayy searched for his ecstasy as he had before, until once again it came. Absāl imitated him until he approached the same heights, or nearly so. Thus they served God on the island until man's certain fate overtook them" (p. 165).

Ibn Ṭufayl's indictment of religious culture and tradition in general and of Islam in particular is mild and oblique, compared to the severe and pessimistic evaluation of human nature at large from which it springs. But, like Ibn Bājjah, Ibn Ṭufayl places great faith in "weeds", those social and intellectual "misfits" who seek the truth for themselves, outside the bonds of established tradition, the confines of language and the imagery that invariably compromises and betrays the truth. Like Matthew Arnold, Ibn Ṭufayl believes that

> moral rules, apprehended as ideas first, and then rigorously followed as laws, are and must be for the sage only. The mass of humankind have neither force of intellect enough to apprehend them clearly as ideas, nor force of character enough to follow them strictly as laws. The mass of humankind can be carried along a course full of hardship for the natural man, can be borne over the thousand impediments of the narrow way, only by the tide of a joyful and bounding emotion.[15]

The requisite emotion, for Ḥayy ibn Yaqẓān, springs naturally from his God-given interest, curiosity, concern and eagerness for perfection. But in the mass of humankind, Ibn Ṭufayl believes, such natural springs of interest are crusted over with the accretions of spiritual laziness and moral complacency. Humanity in general, with the exception of a few rare "weeds", to use Ibn Bājjah's term, are "engulfed in ignorance. Their hearts are corroded by their possessions" (p. 163).

Yet even in the midst of this melancholy appraisal, which is as much a backhanded rationale for the inadequacies of religion as it is an expression of disappointment with the human spirit in general, we must recall that Ibn Ṭufayl, unlike Ḥayy ibn Yaqẓān and Absāl, did not abandon society but continued to live in it, if not wholly of it. And his work voices a clear, if indirect, invitation to any like-minded spirit, to pursue the higher spiritual path and the supererogatory moral path, which the Prophet of Islam wisely saw were beyond the reach of most men.

For Ibn Ṭufayl argues from the very triviality of human pursuits and the revulsion that wholesome spirits might feel towards them, for a higher pursuit, into heights that are surmounted by no summit. Unlike Ibn Bājjah, he does not call such men weeds, perhaps because he takes to heart the example of his persona, Ḥayy ibn Yaqẓān, who made such a point of disentangling one plant from another, and transplanting those specimens that had been seeded by the wind in rocky or infertile soil into an environment where, like Ibn Rushd, they might flourish.

But the generality of the invitation should not be overlooked, even in the setting of the Arabic *risālah* form, the intimate essay in the guise of a letter to a disciple, in which the narrative of *Ḥayy ibn Yaqẓān* is couched. Breaking out of his narrative at the point where Ḥayy realizes that most men are trapped by their own passions and that in that sense, even while they were still living, "the torture pavilion already encircled them", Ibn Ṭufayl writes:

> What weariness is heavier, what misery more overburdening than recounting all you do, from the time you get up to the time you go to bed without finding a single action that does not amount to seeking one of these vile, sensory aims: money making, pleasure seeking, satisfying some lust, venting rage, saving face, performing religious rites for the sake of honour, or just to save your neck! All these are only "cloud upon cloud over a deep sea" (Qur'ān 24: 40).

Here, much in the spirit of Plotinus, alienation itself becomes an invitation to transcendence. Drawing upon a Qur'ānic image that goes back to Hellenistic and New Testament times and was a favourite of Origen, the image of a marathon race, where every finisher is in some sense a winner, yet there is real merit and virtue in running hardest and fastest, Ibn Ṭufayl contrasts the ordinary human condition with the rare attainment of individuals who rise above the mass: "*But* 'those who run in the forefront, those who run in the forefront, *they* will be brought near' (Qur'ān 56: 10–11)."[16]

NOTES

1 See *Tahāfut al-falāsifah*, 3, 4, 9, ed. M. Bouyges (Beirut, 2nd ed., 1962): 89, 110, 154.

2 See R. Dozy, ed. (in Arabic), 'Abdu'l-Waḥid al-Marrākushī, *The History of the Almohades* (Amsterdam, 1968): 174–5.

3 See Chapter 21 above on Ibn Bājjah. Al-Biṭrūjī's *Kitāb fi'l-hayah* was translated into Latin by Michael the Scot, whose version was published with critical comparison with the Arabic original by Carmody (Berkeley, 1952). A Hebrew version by Moses Ibn Tibbon (1259) was translated into Latin by Kalonymus ben David (Venice, 1531).

4 See L. E. Goodman, "Ghazālī's Argument from Creation", *International Journal of Middle East Studies*, 2 (1971): 67–85, 168–88; "Did al-Ghazālī Deny Causality?", *Studia Islamica*, 47 (1978): 83–120; "Morals and Society in Islamic

Philosophy", in I. Mahalingam and B. Carr, *Encyclopedia of Asian Philosophy* (London, forthcoming).

5 See L. E. Goodman, *Avicenna* (London, 1992): 149–63.

6 Ibn Ṭufayl's *Ḥayy ibn Yaqẓān*, trans. L. E. Goodman (New York, 1972): 106–7. This translation is cited parenthetically in the text that follows. It contains cross-references to the Arabic edition of Léon Gauthier.

7 See Cicero, *De finibus*, 3.5–8.

8 See Chapter 21 above on Ibn Bājjah.

9 Trans. Goodman: 131–2.

10 See L. E. Goodman, "Matter and Form as Attributes of God in Maimonides' Philosophy", in *A Straight Path: Studies . . . in Honor of Arthur Hyman*, ed. R. Link-Salinger (Washington DC, 1988): 86–97.

11 Trans. Goodman: 150–6.

12 See my discussion of Miskawayh and al-Ghazzālī on this point in Mahalingam and Carr (eds) "Islamic Ethics and Social Philosophy", in *The Encyclopedia of Asian Philosophy.*

13 See L. E. Goodman, *Avicenna*: 163–72.

14 See Chapter 21 above on Ibn Bājjah.

15 Matthew Arnold, "Marcus Aurelius", in *Essays in Criticism* (first series, 1865), ed., Sister T. M. Hocter (Chicago, 1964; 1958): 205.

16 Trans. Goodman: 165; cf. Origen, *De principiis* (3.6.6, trans. G. W. Butterworth as Origen, *On First Principles* (New York, 1966; 1936): 251–2. Cf. Philo's athletic imagery, *Som.*, ll. 130, 152, 165, where God is pictured as the *Agonothete*, the President of the games, who sets out an athletic challenge; and see David Winston, *Logos and Mystical Theology in Philo of Alexandria* (Cincinnati, 1985): 12.

SELECT BIBLIOGRAPHY

Hourani, G. (1956) "The Principal Subject of Ibn Ṭufayl's Ḥayy Ibn Yaqẓān", *Journal of Near Eastern Studies*, 15(1): 40–6.

Hawi, S. (1973) "Ibn Ṭufayl's Ḥayy Ibn Yaqẓān, its Structure, Literary Aspects and Methods", *Islamic Culture*, 47: 191–211.

—— (1974) "Beyond Naturalism: a Brief Study of Ibn Ṭufayl's Ḥayy Ibn Yaqẓān", *Journal of the Pakistan Historical Society*, 22: 249–67.

Ibn Ṭufayl (1936) *Ḥayy ibn Yaqẓān* ed. L. Gauthier (Beirut); trans. L. E. Goodman (1972) as *Ibn Ṭufayl's Ḥayy Ibn Yaqẓān, a Philosophical Tale* (New York, repr. Los Angeles 1984).

CHAPTER 23

Ibn Rushd

Dominique Urvoy

Through his attachment to Greek thought and his scientific practice – especially in medical matters – Ibn Rushd (Averroes for the West) places himself in the line of the *falāsifah* (Islamic philosophers). But he distinguishes himself from them through his participation in public life, not as an adviser of princes but as a lawyer in contact with daily realities. His family background led him to this position. His namesake Abu'l-Walīd Muḥammad *al-jadd* ("the grandfather") had been the leading *qāḍī* (judge) of Cordoba and had played an important role in the opposition of his city to Almoravid power to which it later submitted. He left some notable legal judgments on the permissibility of the leading dynasty's customs, on the Mozarabs, and so on, indicating his interest in public matters. His theoretical works demonstrate that he was an eminent specialist in legal methodology (*uṣūl al-fiqh*) and in the study of the various solutions offered by the great legal schools (*ikhtilāf*). This connects him with a reform of Malikite law which advocated the integration of analogical reasoning. Although he did not leave comparable work, his son Abu'l-Qāsim Aḥmad was also connected to public life since he occupied the same position in 532/1137 and lost it only when Spain was occupied by the Almohads in 541/1145–6.

Abu'l-Walīd Muḥammad ibn Aḥmad ibn Rushd *al-ḥafīd* ("the grandson") was born in Cordoba in 520/1126, the year of his grandfather's death. He followed the Muslim curriculum, learning *ḥadīth* with his father. A chain of transmissions (*isnād*) shows that both were esteemed in that area. Biographical reports mention him more as a jurist than as a scholar and philosopher, but it is said that in the former role he preferred the science of law (*dirāyah*) to the science of traditions (*riwāyah*). He was well known also in the science of legal controversies (*khilāf*), where he frequently refers to his grandfather (*jaddī*). By contrast his training in scientific and philosophical areas, on which his fame in the West rests, was very little known. The only indication is given by an Eastern historian of medicine, Ibn Abī Uṣaybiʿah, in the biography of one of his masters in the subject, Abū Jaʿfar ibn Hārūn of Trujillo. The latter had been very knowledgeable in philosophy and well read in the works of Aristotle and other philosophers of antiquity. No other contact is discernible with the philosophical circles of his time, and it is only on the topic of medicine that Ibn Rushd was in contact, at first by letter, with Ibn Ṭufayl.

The chief factor which specifically brought about the connection between law on the one hand and science and philosophy on the other is adherence to the Almohad movement. The Almohad reform was started by a Berber from south Morocco, Ibn Tūmart (*c.* 471–4/1078–81 – 524/1130). The Sus, his home area, had been Islamicized by Kharijism, where the fundamental elements of his doctrine can be found. These are insistence upon "the divine promise and threat", which connect human activity and revelation, the reduction of the attributes of God to simple qualities, and the internal necessity of divine action. He had been a pupil for a time in Cordoba of Ibn Ḥamdīn who was the leading light in the opposition to the growing influence of al-Ghazzālī. He had also studied in the East but one cannot precisely say what his influences there had been. A story that he was a disciple and defender of al-Ghazzālī clashes with the absolute opposition between their respective doctrines, Eastern mysticism versus Maghrebi rationalism.

In effect his doctrine rests on two aspects which are apparently antagonistic but in fact are complementary, an entirely positive system of law and a rational theology, the latter justifying the authority of the divine decree and at the same time the positive character of *fiqh* (jurisprudence). The legal activity of Ibn Tūmart showed itself in his initiation of the practice of the "order of good and the ban on evil", recalling the exact prescriptions of the *Sharīʿah*. Thus he extended the action of the Almoravids, but in place of looking for the norm in the authority of former jurists, Ibn Tūmart looks for it in revelation itself. His contemporaries also qualified the Almohad "doctrine of thought" (*madhhab al-fikr*). His text on the "profession of faith" (*ʿaqīdah*) is very short but philosophically very dense. It was restricted to the intellectual elite, the rest of the population having to content itself with "spiritual guides" (*murshidāt*) which summarize the essential dogmas. Later, the celebrated Eastern traditionalist Ibn Taymiyyah detected a deep affinity between the conception of the divine essence of *falsafah* and that of Almohadism. Departing from the sole requirement of purity of intention, Ibn Tūmart goes back to a God established only by the demands of reason, according to a chain of reasons where "divine promise and threat" play a pivotal role in the articulation of a rational Islamic theology. So Almohadism is the fusion of a theology relying on the analysis of the problem of inference and positing Absolute Being, and a practical philosophy which quite naturally takes the form of Islamic law, and which is entirely dependent upon divine transcendence.

Despite his family ties with the Almoravids, Ibn Rushd clearly opted for the Almohads. The intellectual perspective of his grandfather prepared him for this decision. One cannot talk about opportunism here since the new regime was not well accepted in Spain, and to present oneself as an adherent while staying in Andalus itself, unlike Ibn Ṭufayl who was based in the Maghreb, was a courageous act. But it was only indirectly, through the intervention of Ibn Ṭufayl, and also perhaps of his medical teacher, Ibn Hārūn, who was the doctor of the governor of Seville and future caliph, that Ibn Rushd came into contact with the government. The chronicler al-Marrākushī gives, following Abū Bakr Bundūd (who conveys the words of the persons concerned), an important report of the first interview. Ibn Ṭufayl praised his young friend and the sultan, after having asked about the latter's family, asked him point blank, "What is the opinion of the philosophers on the heavens? Is it an eternal substance or did it begin?" Agitated, Ibn Rushd kept quiet, but the sultan and Ibn Ṭufayl started to discuss in front of him this topic in a very erudite way, and led him gradually to become part of the discussion. Another time Ibn Ṭufayl – or perhaps Ibn Hārūn – confided in him that the "prince of believers" had urged, "Let it please God that he meets someone who wished to comment on [the] books [of Aristotle] and clearly explain them in order to make their meaning accessible to men!", and, feeling himself to be too old and too busy for this work, passed it on to him. These apparently simple reports are difficult to interpret. It is reasonable to place the latter around 554/1159, at the court of the governor of Seville, Abū Ya'qūb, who was later to become caliph. The presentation described in the first account would have been made to the same person, in the same place, some years before. One imagines that Ibn Ṭufayl, concerned more with Illuminationist philosophy than with the technical explication of Aristotle, had refused the task proposed by the ruling Almohad, but the enthusiastic support of Ibn Rushd suggests a particularly deep harmony with the latter's point of view.

Still, it was first as a jurist that Ibn Rushd acted. In 565/1169 he was appointed *qāḍī* of Seville, which had become the capital of Andalus. He returned to Cordoba ten years later as *qāḍī*, continuing to make frequent trips to Seville and Marrakesh. Appointed a second time to Seville in 575/1179, he became chief *qāḍī* of Cordoba three years later. Some months earlier he had succeeded Ibn Ṭufayl as the sultan's doctor, and, after the accession to the throne of Abū Yūsuf, the brother of the preceding sovereign, in 580/1184, he lived near him and became an intimate. During a ceremony he was placed symbolically at the level of the highest sectors of the Almohad hierarchy. These promotions were due to his important writings, as much on law as on medicine, which he pursued together with his philosophical commentaries throughout his life. In law, for example, he added in 584/1188–9 a long chapter on pilgrimage to his great treatise. He also maintained contacts with the literary disciplines, which was useful for his commentary on Aristotle's *Poetics*, and there are many works by him on the Arabic language, which he especially used in his *Faṣl al-maqāl* by resolving many philosophical problems through linguistic analysis.

A short time before his death, however, he fell into disgrace. The chroniclers give many confused details on this subject. In fact, when confronted by an external threat, the government sacrificed to the mob many eminent people engaged in intellectual pursuits. Moreover, with one exception, the later biographies suggest that this disgrace was unjustified. Ibn Rushd had in spite of everything to submit to a humiliating exile in Lucena, a small town to the south of Cordoba, inhabited largely by Jews. He none the less continued his work, knowing that his case was defended by the important people of Seville. At the end of two or three years, the sultan summoned him to Marrakesh, where they died within a few months of each other. The most probable date of Ibn Rushd's death is Thursday 9 Ṣafar 595/10 December 1198. Some sources speak of his death taking place in a house of detention, which signifies an ultimate disgrace. First of all buried there, his remains were returned to Corboba on a mule paid for by his philosophical writings. Among his sons many continued the family tradition and became *qāḍīs*. One of them was the sultan's physician.

If his contemporaries speak little of his philosophical work, they all emphasize his human qualities and his disinterestedness. He wore frayed clothes and was never suspected of corruption. He carried out zealously his duties as a judge, remaining always courteous, generous and humble, as relaxed with the people as with the sultan. He liked also to give sermons in the mosque. The first Maghrebi to judge him philosophically is Ibn Sab'īn, who severely criticizes his apparent servility towards Aristotle, but adds "he was always an excellent man, discreet, fair and conscious of his weakness" (p. 143). These qualities of modesty, exceptional in a Muslim intellectual, explain his attachment more than anything else to his work as a commentator, more than to law or science, or even to philosophy itself.

The legal work of Ibn Rushd is really far from being negligible, and embodies a philosophical point of view. Besides many occasional pieces of work, he left, in his major work *Bidāyat al-mujtahid wa nihāyat al-muqtaṣid* ("Beginning for Whoever Makes a Personal Effort and an End for Whoever is Contented") of which the greater part dates from around 564/1168, a monument of logical explication of Muslim law. It is a treatise of *ikhtilāf* (the science of comparing different schools of legal interpretation) considering at each point solutions proposed by small schools or significant individuals and not only by the major schools of interpretation. One could point out (Yate (1991): 21) that although *ikhtilāf* is most often polemical, for Ibn Rushd it is a method in itself, a matter of bringing to light the principles which engender differences. It is the idea which one finds again in medicine in the *Kulliyyāt*. In law, the principal consequence is that the doctrinal leanings of the author do not intrude. Each doctrine is given in its own terms, and it can even happen that one school is approved in terms of another school of interpretation.

Laws have been transmitted to people by the Prophet through the Qur'ān and the *Sunnah*. Both give three types of expression of a rule: through a word, through an act or through tacit approbation. To this should be added the way of analogy (*qiyās*), for topics which had not been considered by the Prophet. Analogy is the most important, since the prophetic discussion is limited and the number of problems immense. Furthermore even the prophetic discussion needs *qiyās* in order to be usable in human societies. Against the use of analogy is the fact that it leads to the outbreak of divergences, limited only to the extent that there is consensus (*ijmā'*), but once such differences have been posited they are kept in existence by the spirit of imitation (*taqlīd*). Also, from the start of the work, Ibn Rushd claims that he deals only with questions raised between the period of the Companions of the Prophet and that of the appearance of *taqlīd*, without being precise about the latter.

The goal of the *Bidāyah* is to show what all jurists would have to see if they had not been blinded by allegiance to a particular school. This is exactly the Almohad approach, extended through the application of an Aristotelian formula. True jurists are conspicuous not because of what they know about facts but through their capacity to apply them to each concrete situation. The contents of the *Bidāyah* ought to suffice to give them this capacity.

Ibn Rushd is a sincere believer, persuaded that the law in itself cannot be deficient. If there is a point of inconsistency, it must be due to differences of interpretation of the sources. The *Bidāyah* is a commentary on the law which is supposed to deal with each point in an ideal order – in fact very rarely realized in the text – as Yate (1991: 34–5) has organized in this way:

1 Quick indication of common ground.
2 General indication of controversial territory.
3 The views of the individual jurists which have led to controversies are eventually pointed out.
4 An examination of the reasons for the differences.

5 The proposing of ways to understand these differences rationally, and also to harmonize them or at least to class them in order of admissibility.
6 An examination of the authenticity of *ḥadīth.*
7 An examination of the impact of the text (for example: is it literal or metaphorical?) for each jurist.
8 An examination of texts and their use according to each jurist (general sense or specific).
9 The question of eventual abrogation.
10 The relative force of a text (for example, obligation or simple recommendation).
11 A consideration of the intellectual preferences (*dhawq 'aqlī*) of each jurist.
12 The occasional rejection of an opinion as devoid of meaning.
13 On some rare occasions, the declaration of his own opinion.

So the *Bidāyah* takes place as part of an evolution of bringing a methodology to a system of universal claims. This wish to be logical goes very far since Ibn Rushd eventually suggests proofs for some solutions whose justification he ignores or which he finds feeble. Now, going by the number of his pupils and the audience he acquired, he appears in the biographies as a teacher of importance, if not of the first rank, but at least very appreciable status. If his philosophical work properly speaking did not have a large effect, the impact of his intellectual project remains considerable. It is advisable to return further to the detail of this project. The first point to raise is that even if the particular nature of the legal material imposes on Ibn Rushd the same method of reasoning as in later additions, in the scientific and philosophical domain by contrast he will follow a clear progression.

Some Spanish Arabists half a century ago sketched out a chronology of the works of Ibn Rushd (Alonso (1947): 51–98), which has recently been completed and verified by the Moroccan academic J. D. al-'Alawī, working on all the texts preserved in Arabic. The latter distinguishes between seven phases in the succession of the writings as well as three levels of reading – philosophical/scientific, Aristotelian and Islamic or more precisely theological (*kalām*). But he thinks it is possible to synthesize these differences by schematizing the global evolution of the Cordoban in only two main stages, one where Ibn Rushd, still young, "aims only at reaching what is necessary in scientific knowledge for human perfection" (al-'Alawī (1986): 205), and the other where, more mature, he wants "to really reach philosophy, that of Aristotle, and his triumph lay in defending it against the attacks as much of the ancients as of his contemporaries" (p. 214). This classification, however, does not take sufficient account of the theological works, which are to be sure very much in the minority in volume and which concern a very short period but which are still specific and major; it is in them only that Ibn Rushd used his own name. This leads us to suggest a tripartite chronology.

Firstly, Ibn Rushd concentrated on the small commentaries (*jāmiʿ*) up to 567/1171, then on the middle commentaries (*talkhīṣ*), from 564/1168 to 571/1175. The former are introductory works, with a general presentation of logic and physics, psychology, science and so on rather than the real Aristotelian teaching. They make possible access to the scientific work which Ibn Rushd elaborates elsewhere. First comes a consistent and impersonal commentary on the medical poem of Ibn Sīnā. Then there is the large medical synthesis of the *Kulliyyāt*, and the treatise on the theriac (antidotes against poisons), where he adopts an original position on therapy. Physics, cosmology, psychology and the natural sciences are added and presented through the work of Aristotle. In effect, in his middle commentaries Ibn Rushd sets himself to follow the order of the text, by contrast with al-Fārābī and Ibn Sīnā, or with himself in his short commentaries. But he does it in his own way, imposing his own structure and hierarchy on the issues.

Secondly, following 573/1177 his work took an aggressive doctrinal shape. It was the time when the religious authorities of the Almoravid era gave way to the new generation (Urvoy (1978): 177–81). The philosopher of law went off in another direction from that of the practical philosophers, writing a middle commentary on the *Nicomachean Ethics*. We do not know why this direction is abandoned leading up to 591/1194, the date of the last middle commentary, dedicated to the *Republic* of Plato. In the meantime Ibn Rushd had made a trip to Marrakesh (574/1178) and then to Seville where he produced his three most independent works, dealing with religious issues – *Faṣl al-maqāl, Kashf ʿan manāhij al-adillah* and *Tahāfut al-tahāfut*. This was also the time of original philosophical writings, discussions of the intellect, reconsidering and correcting the problematic of Ibn Bājjah and the *De substantia orbis*.

Thirdly, once he was confirmed as the sultan's physician and the grand *qāḍī* of Cordoba, Ibn Rushd essentially concentrated on the great commentaries (*tafsīr*). The first, on the *Posterior Analytics*, seems to have been taken up in 576/1180. The last, on the soul, was composed in 586/1190 and extended in a special tract, the *De animae beatitudine*. In what can strictly be called the commentaries he set about doing nothing else but explaining the text of Aristotle. If, on rare occasions, Ibn Rushd differs in opinion from him, or advances a view of his own on a question which the Stagirite had not settled, he points clearly to it. At the end of his career he takes up again some "questions" (*masāʾil*), notably from logic, and one can raise the hypothesis that he thought in this way to start a fourth phase of his approach to Aristotle. He also completed his medical and political work.

One can say that after a logical and scientific preparation, our thinker elaborated a purely "Rushdian" thought for a brief period in order to draw out the ultimate consequences of trying to give the most complete picture possible of the universe of reason, through a deep analysis of what seemed to him to be the most excellent philosophy Aristotelianism.

Ibn Rushd's scientific work is notable in two areas, astronomy/cosmology and medicine. In the first area he made some observations in his youth, but he is especially interested in dealing with the consequences of an Aristotelian critique of the Ptolemaic system, a critique started already by Ibn Bājjah and Ibn Ṭufayl. In his commentaries he hardened the demonstrative side of the Aristotelian text, but he ended up only with a general hypothesis. This is that all the heavenly phenomena, notably the apparent variations in the speed of the planets, ought to be able to be explained by movement "along a helix" (*lawlabī*) or "along a screw" (*ḥalazūnī*), which Aristotle talks about many times. Since the Greek thinker has been far from explicit on this subject, Ibn Rushd suggests that it is a matter of the movement of the pole of a heavenly sphere on the axis of the poles of another sphere. It was only with al-Biṭrūjī (Alpetragius) that the mathematical model for this was suggested, still in an *a priori* way, which did not find an audience until the tenth/sixteenth century.

The medical work, stemming from professional practice, is much more continuous. It consists of commentaries on Galen and Ibn Sīnā, and in a great synthesis, the "General Points" (*Kulliyyāt*). These were written under the direction of the Almohad caliph, in order to examine minutely by rational analysis all the formulated opinions and to collect all those which are useful. Departing from the Aristotelian idea that real science is knowledge of the universal, Ibn Rushd insists that in medicine the general is to be found beyond observation, in the linking of phenomena to causes. With the exception of the purely empirical anatomy, the model to follow is the *Physics* of the Stagirite, and that presupposes in the reader a knowledge of logic. Ibn Rushd knows how to integrate a large part of medical teaching which has been established through experience, but his criterion of selection remains rational analysis.

A curious paradox of this ideology which rejects the empirical in the name of the necessary is that it wishes to give a material substrate to the latter. The intellectual faculties have, as in Aristotle, their seat in the heart, but, not being proper organs, their "places" are in the brain where they appear. The heart makes possible the activity of the brain by passing heat to it, and the rational faculty, which is external to the individual and only occasionally instantiated, is embodied as a memory in society or in humanity. The order is thus "embodied", and that has two consequences. From a metaphysical point of view, the approach of the divine is made through observation of a scientific nature. From a moral point of view, humanity and nature are based upon a similar teleological structure established by God.

A list of Ibn Rushd's works preserved in manuscript in the Escurial suggests that he composed a commentary on the Almohad profession of faith (Renan (1861): 73, 464). According to the biography of al-Anṣārī, he also composed a work on Ibn Tūmart himself (Yate (1991): 16, 62–3). Both are lost, but one can find in the *Kashf 'an manāhij al-adillah* ("Discovery of the Methods of the Proofs") almost all the Almohad theses, without explicit reference to Ibn Tūmart however, and following a quite different order, sometimes for doctrinal but mostly for pedagogical reasons (Urvoy (1991): 71–7).

The existence of God is established through a double experience. The life of beings presupposes providence, and contingency presupposes a creator. But the proof is purged of anything which is not analytical. Ibn Rushd reintroduced here his scientific perspective, claiming that in order to know exactly that God exists one has to relate His existence to that of the substance of things. There are among others two types of understanding of these proofs, that appropriate for the masses who understand them only in accordance with their sense experience, and that appropriate for the intellectual elite who know how to see apodeictic proofs in them. The *mutakallimūn*, by contrast, have a method which is inaccessible to the masses, without at the same time being able to reach a real demonstration. All the same, Ibn Rushd thinks that whoever tries to resolve the possible ambiguities of revelation through allegorical interpretation will succeed only in confusing personal opinion (*rā'y*), already condemned by Ibn Tūmart. The wise and the masses will not find any ambiguity there, but the former regard it in a reflective manner and appreciate it thus as in perfect harmony with philosophy. In general, Ibn Rushd makes every effort, like Ibn Tūmart, to preserve the letter of the revealed text together with the conclusions of rational meditation. He throws up a bridge between the two by borrowing from revelation expressions such as "God is light", which can be understood equally well literally as from an intellectual point of view, and by rejecting the false logical implications of the *kalām* which only serve to trouble the spirit. Al-Ghazzālī is expressly labelled as the heir of all these *agents provocateurs*, as much theologians creating false problems as Sufis creating false solutions.

The *Faṣl al-maqāl* ("Decisive Chapter") is an introduction to the methodology of this philosophical and religious reflection. It states that it is the Qur'ān itself (59: 2; 17: 184) which recommends rational study. For this Ibn Rushd reintroduces allegorical interpretation, but within strictly defined limits in order to avoid arbitrary speculation. The methodological connection between the *Faṣl* and the *Bidāyah* is obvious and Ibn Rushd does not hesitate to defend philosophy against the accusation of impiety through a legal form of argument.

The conciliation of faith and reason is found in the Almohad perspective of a gradation of types of adherence, according to the intellectual level of each individual, from the simple "spiritual guide" to the elaborate "profession of faith". Ordinary religion is enough for the masses, but philosophy is necessary to satisfy the cultivated person. There are two languages, symbolic for the masses, and demonstrative for the philosopher, which do not oppose each other but which are no longer in touch with each other.

The *Tahāfut al-tahāfut* ("Incoherence of the Incoherence") extends these two texts by refuting point by point the objections of al-Ghazzālī. It is more flexible than the *Faṣl* in affirming the superiority of a religion based on revelation as opposed to reason linked to a purely rational religion. But it is also faithful to the *Faṣl*, which saw in the Prophet a man who had received the active intellect at the time in the form of rational representations, like philosophers, and who changed them through the use of the imagination into symbols appropriate for the masses. The religious rationalism of Ibn Rushd is thus not reductionist. It is, like all Almohadism, the belief in the possibility of reconstituting *a posteriori* the chain of reasons.

But Ibn Tūmart is also useful to Ibn Rushd in order to resolve particular technical objections. On the question of the creation, the *mahdī* had introduced the idea that it was the rupture between an unqualified state, pure potentiality, and a state qualified by beings. Ibn Rushd can in turn bring up the question of the appearance of time at the level of the action of an actual being on a potential being, that is to say on the level of the action of higher spheres on particular beings. Moreover, as he challenged emanationism, he is entirely within the Almohad perspective where the act of creation is based on this absolute transcendence of God towards what He produces. Thus one can speak of the free will, or the knowledge, of God only metaphorically. In addition, God creates the metaphysical compound from matter and from form on which the secondary causes act in order to instantiate what was only potential, or in order to annihilate it. Nothingness appears to be secondary in relation to existence, and there is no real creation *ex nihilo*. Thus this priority of existence leads to refuting the Avicennan distinction between necessary being and possible being, and in establishing the negation of the independent reality of divine attributes on the basis of concrete being. God is the necessary being by comparison with beings in the world, but we cannot make statements about His essence. It is only from His actions *ad extra* that thought can relatively distinguish attributes, and by recognizing that the logic of those attributes is not, like ours, conditioned by the multiplicity of concrete objects. God thus does not behave through abstraction, and if He has a knowledge of particulars, it is not through a particular knowledge, but in so far as He is a creator who possesses entirely in Himself all that He creates. The authority of Aristotle on the opinion of Ibn Rushd can thus be seen. It is not absolute, but the Stagirite is for him the paradigm of human knowledge, and his task is only to complete, to systematize or even to correct some details. The thought of Aristotle is not only for him what is given to us in the texts but everything which is coherent with them, even if it appears in religious guise. None the less it is necessary to restore correctly and cleanse the texts of Aristotle from all Neoplatonic additions. It is this idea which allowed Ibn Rushd to discover the fundamental axiom of the method of internal criticism, to know that a particular author "could" or "could not" make a certain point. His intuitions in the matter are admirable, for he worked on translations which were often defective, and he knew how to make corrections from among the different translations, how to fill in the gaps and even how to restore the authentic text by looking at the meaning.

Renan saw absolutely no originality in Ibn Rushd in connection with Aristotle. We, on the contrary, now stress the differences. But it is not easy to co-ordinate the points of detail which are isolated in this way. If one can speak of "Rushdian thought" in order to describe the unity of the three philosophical/theological texts, *Faṣl*, *Kashf* and *Tahāfut*, which express a specific synthesis of Almohad Islam and Aristotelianism, it is above all on the commentaries on Aristotle that the Latin Middle Ages relied to speak of "Averroism". Why this word when the other commentators have not given their name to a school?

One might consider as characteristic five propositions:

1 The world is eternal.
2 God does not know particulars and there is no providence.
3 There is no free will.
4 The potential intellect is numerically one, as is the active intellect. It follows that there is no individual immortality or moral responsibility of the individual.
5 Philosophy and theology are contradictory, and the supernatural ought to be rejected.

This latter point, or the "theory of double truth", is a poor understanding of the hierarchical conception of our author. The rejection of the supernatural, and some of his other theses, rests only on the commentaries. Ibd Rushd's own thought has been indicated above and it is necessary to add here that his position on free will is mixed but remains flexible since he is clearly opposed to the predestinarianism of Ibn Tūmart, from whom, as from others, he borrows so much.

There remains the fourth point, which St Thomas Aquinas has described as "the most shameful error". It is true that the synthesis of Ibn Rushd concerning this topic is different from the investigation undertaken by Aristotle. The latter is a naturalist who follows in each area (the mechanisms of consciousness, the causation of beings) the logic of observation. Ibn Rushd is more systematic and unifies the noetic, the metaphysics of causality and astronomy. It seems that the reason for this unification ought to be sought in the necessity of moving from a non-creationist philosophy to a universe created by a mind. Aristotle, in effect, does not answer the crucial question, "Where does the form originate which receives the matter prepared to receive it?" Ibn Rushd challenges the Platonic vision of Themistius which returns to a soul of the world separated from matter. An immaterial being can act on matter and provide it with a form only through the intermediation of unchanging material beings, the heavenly bodies. But then it is necessary to avoid the objection of al-Ghazzālī to Ibn Sīnā that the first mover for the philosophers ought to be a body (the Sun, the highest Heaven or something else). Now Ibn Tūmart had insisted on the action of divine Wisdom in order to bring about a perfectly organized world, and that only according to its own necessity, without an exterior model. So it is possible to conceive of the first mover in terms of intellect, for here philosophy and theology agree:

> The philosophers . . . understand . . . by the differentiating principle only that which is determined by the wisdom in the product itself, namely the final cause, for according to them there is no quantity or quality in any being that has not an end based on wisdom, an end which must either be a necessity in the nature of the act of this being or exist in it, based on the principle of superiority.
>
> (Van Den Bergh (1969): 248–9)

Divine wisdom establishes an organized world by permitting the potential forms to affect the act, and in this way they gather together the concrete individuals in terms of genus and species. Conversely the human spirit can, through the act of abstraction, bring about the separate existence of these forms. It is at once the most characteristic human act and what links us with the divine. This is not Neoplatonism, but it arises from the core of the Rushdian problematic. Only the concrete is real, and the intelligible being of the forms ought to correspond to a level on the hierarchic structure of the existent where they can have a purely intellectual status. Ibn Rushd finds it in the separate intellects, moving the heavenly bodies as the lover is moved by the one who is loved, and with a universal and continuous movement without individual character which can come only from the senses and the imagination.

The status of the intellect thus rests on the scientific idea of the hierarchic structure of the universe. To understand is to conceptualize the real, that is to say to transcend the intelligible until we reach the organizing wisdom of everything. The doctrine of the unity of the intellect unifies the themes of providence, of the hierarchic structure of the universe and of the role of the human intellect turning like a hinge around the idea of the eternity of the intelligible. The latter takes root in the struggle of Aristotle against the Megarians and against Plato, for he had demanded a repetition of contact with the concrete in order to justify the attribution of a concept by a single mind, just as Ibn Rushd requires us to go beyond individual experience so that the intelligible may always be thought. The material intellect, called thus because it can be turned into anything by primary matter, thinks always in the activity of the human species, assumed to be eternal, and through it the intelligible is eternal. The individual person loses contact only through the removal of the forms of the imagination which are corruptible.

Wisdom is then transcendent to the individual. The wise find their happiness in being the subject in which wisdom actualizes itself on occasion. Philosophy is the business of all humanity and what is personal in the thought of the individual is taken from the imagination and so is perishable. This sort of approach is quite naturally extended into political philosophy. Besides a commentary which is entirely theoretical on the *Nicomachean Ethics*, Ibn Rushd left us another commentary on Plato's *Republic* which contains frequent references to current affairs. The choice of the Platonic dialogue is explained by the fact that Ibn Rushd did not know any translation of the *Politics* of Aristotle, and he deals with those parts of the text which contain only demonstrative arguments, leaving alone what he sees as dialectical or mythological, and rounding it off with psychological and epistemological themes from Peripatetic philosophy. That is remarkable since, in the rest of philosophy, Ibn Rushd is aware of divergences between Plato and Aristotle and does not try to make them agree, as did al-Fārābī. He follows the latter in the way in which he treats the agreements between political philosophy and religious law, but being a *faqīh* he emphasizes the supremacy of the latter. He accepts the essential conclusions of Plato's politics, corrected nevertheless by Aristotle, and even claims they are applicable, except that for Plato the required conditions were unrealizable unless there were enlightened rulers. He adapts the description of the degradation of political regimes to the recent history of his country. He sees in the continuing war a condition for the exercise of virtue by the city. He even prefers the most radical choices of Plato, not only with respect to Aristotle but also for Muslim tradition, and strongly condemns, for example, the forced uselessness of women in his period.

Political reflection is also the means of bringing together the analyses made before in the area of logic and rhetoric (which the Middle Ages made part of the *Organon*). Conforming to the Almohad way of forming a hierarchy, Ibn Rushd, who rejects for philosophy what is not convincing, retains for the masses most of the rhetorical arguments in order to help them stick to good beliefs and so bring about good actions. The citizen summoned to responsibility ought then to struggle against the persuasive arguments which initially trained him or her in order to rise up to demonstrative arguments. It is an opportunity once again to attack the methods of the *kalām*. For example, the theory of punishment ought to be interpreted carefully because, according to Ibn Rushd, if it is taken literally it is opposed to the stability of good and evil as it moves to action only if the reward appears to be sufficient or the fear dissuasive enough.

The Platonic assertion of the necessity of stable knowledge in order to safeguard a common language and so a social community is clearly at the basis of the Rushdian reflection, from the treatise on law to the commentary on the *Republic*. That includes not only the logical works but also the scientific work. Like Plato, Ibn Rushd compares the political ruler to the doctor, and the latter (according to the *Kulliyyāt*) acts according to each case, while regarding the order of nature, in order to provide both with an approach regulated by the laws for the discovery of the truth. It all culminates in the affirmation of the unity of the intellect which "embodies" in humanity this stability of thought.

This synthesis remains none the less paradoxical. Paradoxical in itself, for it is public as well as elitist. Paradoxical in its expression, since Ibn Rushd himself succeeded in leading philosophy out of the ghetto in which it was confined, showing that he was a notably important teacher by the number of his disciples, but not succeeding in fitting in with the system of education and remaining isolated despite his fame (Urvoy (1978): 178–9). Even his disciples did not spread his philosophy, and the logician Ibn Ṭumlūs, who seems to have been one of them, did not quote him and claimed to be a pupil of al-Fārābī, or even of the combination of Almohadism and the teaching of al-Ghazzālī. Ibn Sab'īn pretends that he was ready to accept anything from Aristotle. Ibn 'Arabī for his part tells us a story in which he had in his youth beaten the old philosopher by ascribing to him words in contradiction with all his work. It was only in the thirteenth/nineteenth century that the Arabs became interested again in Ibn Rushd, and in a polemical climate which for a long time distorted the meaning of this rediscovery. His fortune is only due to his reception outside the Muslim world, notably among Jewish writers, who contributed to transmitting him to the Latin West, which eventually was to betray him but which none the less knew how to accord him the respect to which he was due.

REFERENCES

Al-'Alawī, J. D. (1986) *Al-matn al-rushdī* (Casablanca).
Alonso, M. (1947) *Teología de Averroes* (Madrid and Granada).

Arnaldez, R. (1957–9) "La Pensée religieuse d'Averroès", *Studia Islamica*, 7: 99–114; 8: 15–28; 10: 23–41.
Bello, I. A. (1989) *The Medieval Islamic Controversy between Philosophy and Theology: Ijmā' and ta'wīl in the Conflict between al-Ghazālī and Ibn Rushd* (Leiden).
Genequand, C. (1986) *Ibn Rushd's Metaphysics, book lām* (Leiden).
Hourani, G. F. (1959) *Ibn Rushd (Averroes) Kitāb Faṣl al-maqāl* (Leiden).
Hyman, A. (1986) *Averroes' De substantia orbis* (Cambridge, Mass.).
Ibn Rushd (1935) *Bidāyat al-mujtahid* (Cairo).
—— (1938–48) *Tafsīr mā ba'd al-ṭabī'ah*, ed. G. Bouyges (Beirut).
—— (1964) *Kashf 'an manāhij al-adillah*, ed. M. Qāsim (Cairo).
—— (1987) *Kitāb al-kulliyyāt fi'l-ṭibb*, ed. J. M. Forneas-Besteiro (Madrid and Granada).
Ibn Sab'īn (1978) *Budd al-'ārif*, ed. J. Kattūra (Beirut).
Jolivet, J. (1982) "Divergences entre les métaphysiques d'Ibn Rushd et d'Aristote", *Arabica*, 29: 225–45.
Kogan, B. S. (1985) *Averroes and the Metaphysics of Causation* (Albany).
Leaman, O. (1988) *Averroes and his Philosophy* (Oxford).
Lerner, L. (1974) *Averroes on Plato's Republic* (Ithaca).
Luciani, D. (1903) *Le Livre de Mohammed Ibn Toumert, Mahdi des Almohades* (Algiers).
Martin, A. (1987) *Averroès: grand commentaire de la Métaphysique d'Aristote, livre lām-lambda* (Paris).
Renan, E. (1861) *Averroès et l'Averroïsme* (Paris).
Urvoy, D. (1978) *Le Monde des ulémas andalous* (Geneva).
—— (1991) *Ibn Rushd (Averroes)* (London).
Van Den Bergh, S. (1969) *Averroes' Tahāfut al-tahāfut (The Incoherence of the Incoherence)*, 2 vols (London).
Yate, A. (1991) *Ibn Rushd as Jurist* (unpublished Ph.D. dissertation, University of Cambridge).

(Translated by Oliver Leaman with the assistance of Yegane Shayegan.)

SELECTED WORKS OF IBN RUSHD (AVERROES)

Averroes (1562–74; repr. 1962) *Aristotelis opera . . . cum Averrois Cordubensis variis in eosdem commentariis* (Venice; Frankfurt am Main).
—— (1953) *Averroes Cordubensis commentarium magnum in Aristotelis De anima libros*, ed. F. Crawford (Cambridge, Mass.).
—— (1954; repr. 1969 and 1978) *Averroes' Tahāfut al-tahāfut (The Incoherence of the Incoherence)*, trans. and int. S. Van Den Bergh (London).
—— (1956; repr. 1966 and 1969) *Averroes' Commentary on Plato's "Republic"*, ed., trans. and int. E. Rosenthal (Cambridge).
—— (1958) *Averroes on Aristotle's De generatione et corruptione Middle Commentary and Epitome*, trans. and int. S. Kurland (Cambridge, Mass.).
—— (1961a) *Averroes' Epitome of Aristotle's Parva Naturalia*, trans. and int. H. Blumberg (Cambridge, Mass.).

—— (1961b; repr. 1967 and 1976) *Averroes on the Harmony of Religion and Philosophy*, trans. and int. G. Hourani (London).
—— (1969) *Middle Commentary on Porphyry's Isagoge and on Aristotle's Categoriae*, trans. and int. H. Davidson (Cambridge, Mass.).
—— (1974) *Averroes on Plato's "Republic"*, trans. and int. R. Lerner (Ithaca).
—— (1977a) *Averroes' Three Short Commentaries on Aristotle's "Topics", "Rhetoric" and "Poetics"*, ed., trans. and int. C. Butterworth (Albany).
—— (1977b) *Jihād in Medieval and Modern Islam*, trans. R. Peters (Leiden).
—— (1983) *Averroes' Middle Commentaries on Aristotle's Categories and De Interpretatione*, ed., trans. and int. C. Butterworth (Princeton).
—— (1984) *Ibn Rushd's Metaphysics*, trans. and int. C. Genequand (Leiden).

Details of Arabic editions, and relevant books and articles, may be found in the bibliographical sections of:

Hayoun, M.-R. and De Libera, A. (1991) *Averroès et l'Averroïsme* (Paris).
Leaman, O. (1988) *Averroes and his Philosophy* (Oxford).
Urvoy, D. (1991) *Ibn Rushd*, trans. O. Stewart (London).

CHAPTER 24

Ibn Sab'īn

Abu'l-Wafa al-Taftazani and Oliver Leaman

'Abd al-Ḥaqq ibn Ibrāhīm Muḥammad ibn Naṣr was a Sufi philosopher of Andalusia, known in Christian Europe for his replies to questions sent to him by Frederick II, ruler of Sicily. He is commonly called Ibn Sab'īn, and sometimes Quṭb al-Dīn (the pole of religion) or Abū Muḥammad. Ibn Sab'īn was of Arab extraction and came from a distinguished background. He was born in 614/1217 in Valle de Ricote, Murcia. There he studied Arabic language and literature, Islamic theology, Mālikī jurisprudence, logic and philosophy. He became a Sufi and won many followers.

In 640/1242 he emigrated to North Africa with some of his disciples, settling in Ceuta. It was during his stay there that he received Frederick's four philosophical queries concerning Aristotelianism. He later travelled to Egypt around 646/1250. North African jurists had forewarned Egyptian jurists about what they considered to be his heretical belief in pantheism, which led to a hostile reception by thinkers in Egypt such as Quṭb al-Dīn al-Kastalānī. Ibn Sab'īn went on to Mecca, and kept a low profile. He had been accused of Shi'ism, and Egypt since Saladin's reign had become predominantly Sunni.

Ibn Sab'īn's tranquil life in Mecca gave him the leisure to accomplish some of his writings. It was there that he drafted the Meccan community's declaration of allegiance to the ruler of Africa, Sultan Zakariyyā' ibn Abu Ḥafṣ. He also corresponded with Ibn 'Arabī's disciple, Najm al-Dīn ibn Isrā'īl. He was on good terms with the Yemeni ruler al-Muẓaffar Shams al-Dīn Yūsuf, but his relationship with his vizier, who was an anthropomorphist, was naturally rather strained. During the last two years of his life he came under such strong attack from the jurists in Mecca that he thought of moving to India. He died in Mecca in 669/1270. Some have suggested that he committed suicide while others think that he was poisoned by the vizier.

Ibn Sab'īn produced forty-one works, most of which are not extant. His greatest work is the *Budd al-'ārif* ("Escape of the Gnostic"). His *Rasā'il* ("Epistles") and his replies to Frederick II tell us a lot about his philosophical views. His style is highly esoteric and his reading was obviously very broad, covering Greek philosophy, ancient oriental philosophies such as hermeticism, Zoroastrianism and Hinduism. He was well read in the works of al-Fārābī and Ibn Sīnā, from the east of the Islamic world, and among Andalusian thinkers he was familiar with Ibn Bājjah, Ibn Ṭufayl and Ibn Rushd. He was familiar with the *Rasā'il* ("Epistles") of the Brethren of Purity and was well grounded in both the Islamic sciences and Sufi thought.

Ibn Sab'īn was a follower of the Shūzī Sufi way founded by al-Shūzī of Seville. This was a continuation of the school founded by Ibn Masarrah (269/882–319/931), which was especially influential among those Sufis in Andalusia who had a philosophical tendency. Still, in his references to Ibn Masarrah and his followers, Ibn Sab'īn was highly critical, as he was of Ibn 'Arabī, whose thought he described as "corrupted". Ibn Sab'īn founded a Sufi group which came to be known as the Sab'iniyyun. They followed an eclectic path which combined Greek, Islamic and ancient oriental elements. This form of Sufism survived up to the time of Ibn Taymiyyah (d. 728/1328), who attacked its followers in Alexandria when he visited the city. His work *The Book of the Alexandrian Issues* in reply to the Sab'īnite pantheist heretic is directed at this form of Sufism. A follower of the Sab'īnite path was Abu'l-Ḥasan al-Shūshtārī, who developed a distinct but related path of his own.

The pantheism of Ibn Sab'īn is based on the concept of *waḥdat al-wujūd*, the idea that only God really exists. There is no real basis to the distinction between the existence of God and of everything else. The existence of God is not a quality added to his essence, but existence is rather an essentially permanent single reality. This form of pantheism is distinct from other Sufi views on the unity of being in that Ibn 'Arabī, for example, admits the existence of contingent things. Ibn Sab'īn designates his view as pure *waḥdat al-wujūd*, or comprehensiveness, by which the notion of union with God and God himself is deprived of all description and names. The absolute existence of God is the source of all that he was, is and will be. Material existence is equivalent to absolute spiritual existence. Being is spiritual rather than material. He sometimes compares existence with a circle, with a periphery that is absolute existence and controlled or limited existence which is within the circle. In fact there is no real distinction between the two modes of existence, since their essences are the same. The absolute can be seen in the relative and the union of the two is complete. He sometimes considers the absolute existence of God and contingent beings as the relation between form and matter. Ibn Sab'īn seeks support for his views in certain Qur'ānic verses such as "He is the First and the Last, and the Outward and the Inner" (57: 3), and "Everything will perish except his Face" (28: 88).

Ibn Sab'īn's pantheism is the basis of his concept of the genuine gnostic. This concept is quite similar to that of other Sufis such as Ibn 'Arabī and Ibn al-Fārid when writing of the Muḥammadan Reality (*al-Ḥaqīqat al-muḥamadiyyah*) or the Pole (*al-Quṭb*), and 'Abd al-Karīm al-Jīlī when discussing the perfect individual (*al-insān al-kāmil*). Genuine gnostics are the most perfect of human individuals. They have achieved genuine oneness and are distinct when compared with all who have preceded them. They combine the perfections of the jurist, the theologian, the philosopher and the Sufi. They are greater than them in that they possess their own special knowledge, real gnosis, which is the gateway to the Prophet from whom everything derives. Ibn Sab'īn is in little doubt that he himself enjoys the condition of genuine gnosis. In his *The Escape of the Gnostic* he seeks to undermine Aristotelian logic and replace it with a new "illuminative" logic. The logic of the gnostic is achieved not through reasoning but through intuition, and avoids the multiplicity of Aristotelianism. This logic leads to the conclusion that logical forms are innate, and that the six logical terms (genus, species, difference, property, accident and person) which give the impression of multiplicity are indeed illusory, as are the ten categories. Although these may be various, they really refer to the absolute unity of existence. He takes issue here with Ibn Rushd, who shares Aristotle's view that the categories cannot be identified as belonging to just one genus.

Ibn Sab'īn extends his pantheism to other areas of Sufi philosophical thought. For example, he argues that the soul and our rationality cannot have real existence as independent phenomena. Their existence derives from the One, and the One cannot be multiplied. Good and evil are the same from the point of view of existence. Since existence is One and is absolute Good, how can evil come about? Furthermore, the real gnostic cannot be described as happy or good or perfect since he or she is Happiness itself, Goodness itself and Perfection itself. Ibn Sab'īn's main criticism of other thinkers is that they do not sufficiently emphasize the unity of everything which is implied in the *waḥdat al-wujūd* principle, since, if this principle is understood as he thinks it ought to be, the sorts of divisions and distinctions which we customarily make are merely indications of a greater and entirely unified reality. We can see this quite clearly when we look at the ways in which he analyses the concept of knowledge, which leads him to be highly critical of the approach of the *falāsifah*. They suggest that the mind, and especially the intellect, is really just a means for the acquisition of knowledge. We can progressively purify our mind and gradually acquire more and more knowledge, eventually leading to contact with the active intellect, which represents the highest level of knowledge which the *falāsifah* think can be realized.

Ibn Sab'īn is contemptuous of this theory. He bases his argument upon the *ḥadīth* "The first thing that God created was the intellect, and God then told it to approach, which it did, and then he told it to withdraw, which it also did". What he takes this to show is that the intellect is nothing more than a divine creation, and so should have no problems in actually uniting and knowing that which created it. There is no need to think of knowledge as consisting of the piecemeal process which the *falāsifah* describe which may result in a gradual progress towards, but never actually to, God. Since we are divine creations, it is natural to expect that it would be possible for us to understand the deity, albeit obviously not in an unrestricted manner. In the Qur'ān it says that God has taught Adam all names (2: 29) and has sent him to earth as a vice-regent, in possession of information about the world and about God's intentions with respect to it. Clearly, then, we are in possession of divine properties, and if we wish to come closer to God, we need to engage in the process of trying to understand the secret which he has given us.

[Professor Taftazani died before he could finish his chapter, and it has been completed by Oliver Leaman.]

BIBLIOGRAPHY

Selected works by Ibn Sab'īn

Rasā'il Ibn Sab'īn (Letters of Ibn Sab'īn), ed. A. R. Badawī (Cairo, 1965).
Budd al-'ārif ("Escape of the Gnostic"), ed. G. Kattora (Beirut, 1978).
Asrār al-ḥikmat al-mashriqiyyah ("Mysteries of Oriental Wisdom") (unpublished).
Correspondance philosophique avec l'Empereur Frédéric II de Hohenstaufen (Al-kalām 'ala'l-masā'il al-ṣiqliyyah), ed. S. Yaltkaya (Paris, 1943).

Secondary literature

Ibn Taymiyyah (1930) *Rasā'il wa'l-masā'il* ("Letters and Issues") (Cairo).
Kattora, G. (1977) *Das mystische und philosophische System des Ibn Sab'in* (Tübingen).
Lator, E. (1944) "Ibn Sab'in de Murcia y su Budd al-'Ārif", *Al-Andalús*, 9(2): 371–417.
Taftazani, A. (1973) *Ibn Sab'īn and his Philosophical Sufism* (Beirut).

CHAPTER 25

Ibn Khaldūn

Abderrahmane Lakhsassi

LIFE AND WORK

Life

Abū Zayd ʿAbd al-Raḥmān ibn Khaldūn al-Ḥadramī[1] was born in Tunis in 732/1332 and died in Cairo in 808/1406 after having, five years earlier, met Tīmūr (Tamerlane) outside the walls of Damascus. A contemporary of the Merinids in Morocco, the Banū ʿAbd al-Wādid in the central Maghreb (Algeria), the Ḥafṣids in Ifriqiya (Tunisia), the Naṣirids in Granada and the Mamluks in Egypt, he was acquainted with all these regimes and lived in their respective courts. His different jobs within the sphere of these political powers gave him a valuable asset: they allowed him to experience the political game in the Muslim West and have direct contact with the tribal world in north-western Africa. From these two sets of experiences he drew theoretical consequences of tremendous importance broadly outlined in his *Muqaddimah* ("Prolegomena"). His whole life can be broadly divided into two main phases: the period in the Muslim West and the Egyptian phase. Two predominant events affected his life during the first period: the Black Death (748–9/1348–9) which had taken most of his teachers and particularly his own parents; and the assassination of his friend and competitor Lisān al-Dīn ibn al-Khaṭīb in 774/1374.

The young Ibn Khaldūn was educated in a milieu strongly influenced by traditional culture. His grandfather was a minister at the Ḥafṣid court in Tunis, and his father, without being a scholar, understood the times. Although he studied with his parents, his real intellectual education started with scholars brought to his birthplace from Fez and Tlemcen by the Merinid Sultan Abū ʿInān. Later on, in 755/1354, he joined the Sultan's court in Morocco as a member of his council of scholars (*ʿulamā*ʾ)

and ended up by being appointed one of his secretaries. There he spent eight years between serving the Sultan and learning from various scholars – mostly from Qarawiyīn, Granada and Tlemcen – attracted by the Merinid court. The young and ambitious Ibn Khaldūn did not miss the opportunity of taking advantage in Fez of the rich galaxy of *'ulamā'* considered at the time to be among the most prestigious ones in the Muslim West. Three years earlier, he already occupied the post of chamberlain (*ḥājib*) in Bougie (Algeria). Thus started Ibn Khaldūn's diplomatic and political adventures in the Muslim West. If, in terms of his scholarly education, his stay in the Merinid court had been so crucial in acquiring a solid intellectual basis in juridico-religious, historical, literary and philosophical sciences, the following two years in Granada could be considered as ending his intellectual formation.

In 764/1362, Ibn Khaldūn left for the first time for his ancestors' country, Muslim Spain. There he became the ambassador of the Sultan of Granada, Muḥammad V, to Pedro the Cruel, king of Castile. During his sojourn in the Merinid capital, he was acquainted with Muḥammad V as well as with his distinguished vizier, Ibn al-Khaṭīb. Two years later, however, he left for Bougie after feeling that his two friends no longer had warm feelings for him.

The following seven years (766/1365–774/1372) were spent between Bougie, Biskra and Tlemcen, before he returned to Fez for a second sojourn of only two years. Ibn Khaldūn's period in the central Maghreb is probably the most unstable in terms of his political career and his experience with rulers and political adventurers. If this experience was for him the worst politically, it was not necessarily so in terms of his intellectual development. What he gained from these seven years is rather a direct knowledge of the tribal milieu. As a *ḥājib* in Bougie he was charged with collecting taxes by whatever means from the tribes.

Initially, it was after his diplomatic failure in the Central Maghreb that Ibn Khaldūn decided first to go to Morocco and then to Andalusia, only to find himself in the central Maghreb again after three years of absence. During the time preceding his final retreat to north-western Africa, he was once more responsible for the office of chamberlain in the court of Bougie. Concurrently, in 776/1374, Ibn al-Khaṭīb was strangled in his prison and, one year later, if not less, Ibn Khaldūn went on his intellectual retreat.

When the Banū 'Ārif tribe gave him protection and welcomed him in their fort, Qal'at ibn Salamah, south of Bougie between Tlemcen and Biskra, Ibn Khaldūn was forty-five years old. There he started reflecting on history and the Berber states and engaged in writing his *Kitāb al-'ibār* ("The Book about Events which Constitute a Lesson"), i.e. the *Muqaddimah* and the history of the Berbers. After four years, from 776/1374 to 780/1378, Ibn Khaldūn completed his initial plan. He then went to Tunis which he had left while still in his early twenties. But even in his home town he did not find the rest he was now longing for. Thus he went on pilgrimage and left for Egypt.[2]

For more than a quarter of a century, Ibn Khaldūn was directly involved in the political turmoil the Muslim West was going through in the eighth/fourteenth century. He experienced court intrigues, prison, power and authority with glory and prestige as well as countryside and desert life with different tribes. His flight from his own world to the Arab East became vital. Two important events can be considered to have affected his life in Egypt: the loss near the Alexandrian coast of his family, who came to join him two years after his arrival there, and his encounter with the Tatar ruler in Syria.

Apparently Ibn Khaldūn was already known to the Egyptians through his *Muqaddimah* before he arrived.[3] After being introduced to the sultan al-Ẓāhir Barqūq the following year, and before accomplishing his pilgrimage in 789/1387, he was appointed professor in Qamḥiyyah Madrasah and Grand Mālikī judge in Cairo. But his way of conceiving and settling juridical matters was soon criticized by the Egyptians, and after one year he was replaced in his juridical post. In the newly founded Ẓāhirīyyah school he was then nominated Professor of Mālikī jurisprudence.

After his return from Mecca, Ibn Khaldūn was appointed Professor of *Ḥadīth* in Sarghatmash Madrasah, and before meeting Tīmūr he was designated in 791/1389 Shaykh to the Baybar Sufi Institute and relieved of this post in the same year. Once more, he was nominated Mālikī judge and dismissed from his job after little more than a year. Between the time of his encounter with the Tatar ruler for negotiations in 803/1401 and his death, he retrieved his position as a Mālikī judge four more times and lost it on three occasions.

During his life in Egypt, Ibn Khaldūn continued to reflect on the state and was continuously in contact with the Muslim West. After writing for Tīmūr a detailed descriptive report on the north-western dynasties, he took care to inform the Sultan of Fez about the Tatar ruler and his hordes, in a long letter. He even worked for the betterment of political relations between Egypt and the Maghrebi regimes. Besides his lectures – mainly on *Ḥadīth* and Mālikī *fiqh* – he also continued to study and carry on research. As a matter of fact, Ibn Khaldūn never stopped to add to, correct and polish his "exhaustive history of the world" (*Q*, 1: 7; *R*, 1: 12) and particularly what came to be seen and known as the *Muqaddimah* and his autobiography were worked on up to only a few months before his death in 808/1406.

Works

During the Muslim West period of his life, apart from his diplomatic and political jobs, Ibn Khaldūn spent his time studying, teaching and writing. Generally speaking, we can say that he incessantly tried to satisfy two basic needs: one for political action and the other for scientific knowledge (Nassar (1967): 25–6). Whereas he failed to achieve the first goal to his satisfaction, he did succeed in attaining the second – but only relatively late in life, at Qalʿat ibn Salamah. Before 776/1375, however, he had written many treatises, though of minor importance. The majority of his work then dealt with theologico-philosophical questions.[4]

The first book, *Lubāb al-muḥaṣṣal* ("The Gist of the Compendium"), was finished under the supervision of his favourite teacher, al-Ābilī, when Ibn Khaldūn was only nineteen years old and still in Tunis. The last one, a commentary on a *rajaz* poem on the principles of jurisprudence (*uṣūl al-fiqh*) by Ibn al-Khaṭīb, was done probably in Granada, around 765/1363, when he was already thirty-two. The rest must have been done between these two dates, during his first stay in Fez.

There is still one more work before the *Kitāb al-ʿibār*, that is *Shifāʾ al-sāʾil* ("The Healing of the Seekers"), written during his second sojourn in Fez around 775/1373 (Pérez (1991): 17–20). He did not breathe a word about this text (which is a real contribution to Islamic mysticism) in his autobiography. Both those who are surprised at his silence about these works as well as those who deny his authorship for the same reason often forget that an autobiography is necessarily subjective, and is not a biography. Whereas the latter tries to be objective, the former looks mainly to the self as the author would like others to perceive him.[5] Ibn Khaldūn probably wanted to be known only for his work on history, and, for him, nothing more is worth mentioning in his autobiography which, as a matter of fact, is deliberately linked, in the form of an appendix, to the *Kitāb al-ʿibār*.

Be this as it may, in his retreat from the political chaos of the Muslim West, the now cynical and ambitious politician spent nearly four years reflecting and writing. The result, *Kitāb al-ʿibār*, is a monumental work on medieval world history centred on the Muslim powers and preceded by a long introduction (*muqaddimah*). This independent book constitutes the first of seven volumes. The six remaining volumes can be seen as forming two significant sets: book two (volumes two to five) deals with universal history up to the author's era, and book three (volumes six and seven) concerns the history of the Western Muslim world.[6]

What can be said about *Kitāb al-ʿibār* is that Ibn Khaldūn's initial plan is to write the history of north-western Africa (book three) of which – as he himself says – he has a direct knowledge (*R*, 1: 65; *Q*, 1: 52). Later on, during his first and only return to Tunis, and particularly while in Egypt, he added to his text the history of the Muslim East (book two). No historian of the Maghreb since and particularly of the Berbers can do without his historical contribution.

Philosophy of history and social theory

Even more original is Ibn Khaldūn's book one, the *Muqaddimah*. In this methodological work "he has conceived and formulated a philosophy of history which is undoubtedly the greatest work of its kind that has ever yet been created by any mind in any time or place" (Toynbee (1935): 322). One sometimes wonders if Toynbee's judgment still holds true today. But the fact that remains is that the author of the *Muqaddimah* explicitly claims to be the founder of a new science of history with "its own peculiar object – that is, human civilization and social organization. It also has its own peculiar problems – that is, explaining the conditions that attach themselves to the essence of civilization one after the other" (*Q*, 1: 61; *R*, 1: 77). Particular attention was given to the interaction between natural and non-physical factors underlining human culture which, in turn, presupposes political and social organization centred on a power-state. In the *Muqaddimah* he also investigated human phenomena and social institutions which culminate in crafts, sciences and their transmission. The driving force behind the historical process is, in his mind, to be found in *'aṣabiyyah*. This "social group feeling" gives rise to political action leading to the seizure of the state apparatus.

The general structure of Ibn Khaldūn's historical theory spinning around that of the state – where religion plays a crucial role – is concisely schematized by Gellner who calls it "the theory of the tribal circulation of elites" as three concentric circles:

> In the inner circle, the tribes of government, those tribes connected by kin links or otherwise with the ruling dynasty, exempt from taxation and employed as a kind of taxation-enforcing army against other tribes. The middle circle consisting of those tribes who have taxes extracted from them, and finally the outer circle of those who do not allow taxes to be extracted from them. Urban life generally exists only within the inner two circles, and the towns are protected not by their own effort but by the governmental, central tribes.
>
> (Gellner (1986): 10)

These central tribes, further pictured as sheepdogs, were once wolves of the outer circle absorbed in antagonism and local feuds. But once united under the leadership of a group having an *'aṣabiyyah* with a religious message (*da'wah*), they are able to assault the central government. Thus the death of the state is imminent and a new dynasty takes over. Later on, the wolves, now turning themselves into sheepdogs, move to the middle circle (Gellner (1968): 13). The sheep occupy only the inner space. In Ibn Khaldūn's mind, it takes three generations of forty years each for the wolves to become sheepdogs and guard sheep.

These three stages correspond to the "natural" age of the state. Each generation is marked by certain features. The first is characterized by the naturally necessary (*ḍarūrī* and *ṭabī'ī*) related to some psychological aspects pertaining to the nomadic life while the second generation is marked by the humanly necessary. Simultaneously, its most positive aspects such as the militant spirit of the nomadic personality are weakened. As to the third generation, it is characterized by conveniences and luxuries (*kamālī*) which go with the complete loss of that spirit of cohesion intrinsic to *'aṣabiyyah*. As can be remarked, these respective characteristics of the three generations are in fact the same as those pertaining to the human soul in Greek thought. They are in turn related to its three principles as ascribed to it by Plato and Aristotle: the concupiscent, the irascible and the speculative. Indeed Ibn Khaldūn's theory of human organization (*'umrān*), revolving around the state, takes the concept of the soul as its core pattern.

Though Ibn Khaldūn analyses various natural, social and human factors in predicting the death of the state and human culture, he does take into account a basic extraterrestrial element. His philosophy of human history and civilization constantly has in the background what he terms *mashiyyat Allāh* (God's plan for the world). God creates conditions for social and historical change. As he put it, even "prophets in their religious propaganda depended on groups and families, though they were the ones who could have been supported by God with anything in existence, if He had wished, but in His wisdom He permitted matters to take their customary course" (*Q*, 1: 287; *R*, 1: 324). However, terrestrial and celestial determinisms do not come into conflict for the simple reason that the divine will is always the definitive and inevitable factor (Fakhry (1970): 369). The *faqīh* in Ibn Khaldūn never loses sight of the philosopher of history to whom it can never occur to step outside the predestined decree of Allah.

As to his social theories, the following passage can help us appreciate the vastness of their framework as well as their comprehensiveness.

> Civilization may be either desert (Bedouin) civilization as found in outlying regions and mountains, in hamlets (near suitable) pastures in waste regions, and on the fringes of sandy deserts. Or it may be sedentary civilization as found in cities, villages, towns, and small communities that serve the purpose of protection and fortification by means of walls. In all these different conditions,

there are things that affect civilization essentially in as far as it is social organization.

(*Q*, 1: 67; *R*, 1: 84–5)

In comparison with other living beings, Ibn Khaldūn characterizes humankind with certain basic qualities peculiar to it: (1) human efforts in acquiring the means of life; (2) the need for a restraining authority; and (3) the sciences, crafts and arts, i.e. civilization. As can be noticed, these qualities actually correspond to the three basic dimensions (the economic, the political and the cultural) found in any human organization, once more related to the three principles pertaining to the human soul mentioned above. What is unique in Ibn Khaldūn's social theory is its large view concerning human society and particularly the interrelationship between these three levels.

PHILOSOPHICAL IDEAS AND CONTRIBUTION

Before considering Ibn Khaldūn's philosophical ideas in the *Muqaddimah*, we should first see his contribution to Islamic thought in the two minor works written before that masterpiece. Though he showed in *Lubāb al-muḥaṣṣal fī uṣūl al-dīn* a great mastery of theological as well as philosophical knowledge, he admittedly added to it "little from his own". His personal efforts consisted in summarizing and uprooting all unnecessary elements for its comprehension, adding corresponding answers to its questions by using Naṣr al-Dīn al-Ṭūsī's ideas and objections. Even al-Rāzī's original outline is kept untouched (*L*: 3).

In *Shifā' al-sā'il*, however, his achievement is more substantial.[7] Ibn Khaldūn's point of departure was an open public question posed by his Sufi contemporaries in Granada: whether or not it was possible to attain mystical knowledge without the help of a Sufi master leading the novice in the difficult Path. The issue requires a legal opinion (*fatwā*) but Ibn Khaldūn, in addition to his religious opinion on the matter, developed a whole treatise on Islamic mysticism. His main efforts can be seen as being in the line of al-Ghazzālī pushed to its ultimate conclusion. Like al-Ghazzālī in his often quoted *Iḥyā' 'ulūm al-dīn*, he involves Sufism in theology and distinguishes the science of practical behaviour, considered to be lawful, from that of revelation, believed to be illicit. But unlike the author of *Iḥyā'* who speaks of the science of *bāṭin* versus the science of *ẓāhir*, Ibn Khaldūn prefers to talk about *fiqh* (jurisprudence) in his *bāṭinī/ẓāhirī* distinction, thus absolutely enclosing Sufism within the juridical category. By the same token, he openly opposes al-Ghazzālī in separating the domain of the jurisprudent (*faqīh*) from that of the Sufi. For the author of *Shifā' al-sā'il*, it is possible for the jurisprudent to possess both the exoteric and the esoteric *fiqh* (*Sh*: 13).

Moreover, Ibn Khaldūn classifies the three types of *mujāhadāt* (spiritual struggles) under the science of practical behaviour. From *taṣawwuf* he excludes the revelation of the so-called modern Sufis which he relates rather to the science of the secrets of letters (*Sh*: 70). He writes that Sufism is

> a particular path different from the general path of the *Sharī'ah* found by the righteous people who followed it for the sake of higher degrees [of satisfaction]. They learned – after having experienced through spiritual taste its realities and discovered by intimate experience its perceptions – how the five legal qualifications apply to this particular path.
>
> (*Sh*: 95)

His conception of the Sufi Shaykh itself is rather close to that of the theologian being the legal heir of the prophets (*Sh*: 99 and 102).

There is no question that Ibn Khaldūn's view of the Islamic philosophical enterprise is more theological than philosophical. As Fakhry concisely noted, "the fourteenth century may be called the century of Neo-Ḥanbalism" (p. 359). And Ibn Khaldūn, whatever his genius and interesting contribution to modern human thought, falls within this cultural framework. We can even go further and maintain that – apart from his personality – it is probably the fact of standing on such purely theological ground that helped him to avoid the now sterile question that preoccupied medieval philosophers, whether Jewish, Christian or Muslim: how to reconcile faith with reason. Such avoidance led him in opening a hitherto unknown and completely new field in human knowledge and thus in founding the science of *'umrān*.

In Ibn Khaldūn's attack on the philosophical sciences we can discern two basic targets: formal logic and Neoplatonism. As a matter of fact, his classification of the sciences follows two criteria: that of their sources according to which he separates positive (religious) from intellectual (rational) disciplines and that of their *raison d'être* according to which he distinguishes instrumental and preparatory sciences from sciences studied for themselves. Formal logic, studied by the "moderns", is criticized for transgressing the second criterion. The first criterion allowed him to assign to each category of sciences a separate realm. On that basis, philosophy, as a rational discipline, went beyond its domain and claims to surpass the possibilities of reason as a means of cognition. Here can be recalled Ibn Khaldūn's conception of human reason, which he compares to a balance meant for gold but sometimes misused for weighing mountains.[8]

> The intellect, indeed, is a correct scale. Its indications are completely certain and in no way wrong. However, the intellect should not be used to weigh such matters as the oneness of God, the other world, the truth of prophecy, the real character of the divine attributes, or anything else that lies beyond the level of the intellect. That would mean to desire the impossible. . . . [The fact that this is impossible] does not prove that the indications of the scale are not true [when it is used for its proper purpose].
>
> (*Q*, 3: 30; *R*, 3: 38)

In his chapter entitled "A Refutation of Philosophy and the Corruption of its Students", Ibn Khaldūn selects the Neoplatonic thesis according to which there is a hierarchy of being, from the sensible (particulars) to the supra-sensible culminating in the First Intellect identified with the Necessary One (God) and the idea that the human mind is capable of arriving at knowledge without the aid of revelation. Moreover, to the knower, knowledge produces happiness.

On the one hand, for Ibn Khaldūn all metaphysical reasoning rests upon "second intelligibles". Even the conformity we find between primary *intelligibilia* (particulars) and the individual *existentia* (propositions describing them) is not logically necessary but only empirically attested. Referring to Plato against the pseudo-Aristotle of *Theologia*, he says that in this realm we can only obtain conjectures.[9] Additionally, in claiming to expose and reveal the divine nature, Neoplatonic theories have pernicious effects on political entities since they can dislocate religion from its proper function which is necessary not only for the state but also for social organization. Indeed, as Gellner (1968: 6) noted, "Islam appears to be a cement of empires, and not an acid corroding them." The social theorist of the eighth/fourteenth century is fully aware of this particular fact and is not ready to accept the tremendous and dangerous consequences of damaging the glue.

On the other hand, philosophers claim that "happiness consists in coming to perceive *existentia* as they are". Such conjunction (*ittiṣāl*) between the knower and the active intellect – reached solely by means of logical arguments – produces felicity, "identical with the promised happiness" (*Q*, 3: 121, 215, 218; *R*, 3: 152, 253, 255). For Ibn Khaldūn, this claim wrongly supposes "that anybody who has perception comprises (the whole) of existence in his perceptions". But for him, neither existence, which is too vast for human intellect, nor the promised happiness can be encompassed.

> When [pseudo] Aristotle and his colleagues [al-Fārābī and Ibn Sīnā] speak about union and perception in this way, they mean the perception of the soul that comes to it from its own essence

> and without an intermediary, but such [perception] is attained only by the removal of the veil of sensual perception.
>
> (*Q*, 3: 217; *R*, 3: 255)

If we are to summarize Ibn Khaldūn's attitude to philosophy in general, we would say that, for him, although this discipline is natural to people and useful to the historian, it is none the less dangerous to faith. Moreover, it is inadequate in achieving its goal which it sees to be the perception of reality *per se*.

Another point where Ibn Khaldūn criticizes Muslim philosophers is their political theories. He dismisses the Ideal City of al-Fārābī as a simple hypothesis not worth discussing.[10] The rational government (*siyāsah 'aqliyyah*) is based on a law consisting of a mixture of the divinely revealed Prophetic Law and of the ordinances of the ruler.

To be sure, this firm opposition to the political philosophy of the *falāsifah* can be expected from such an empiricist who is more interested in political reality as it was and as it is than in what it ought to be ideally or in the future. Theoretically however, the religious government (*siyāsah shar'īyyah*) is far more comprehensive than both rational politics and political utopianism (*siyāsah madaniyyah*) "because the lawgiver knows the ultimate interest of the people and is concerned with the salvation of man in the other world" (*Q*, 2: 127; *R*, 2: 138). But the fact that such regimes based on principles derived from the divinely revealed Law were supposed to have gone with the Prophet and his guided caliphs means they were the lost ideals which were as non-existent for him as the Virtuous City of the philosophers. Thus Ibn Khaldūn's political philosophy is more concerned with what he calls the second type of rational politics (since the first type had gone with the pre-Islamic Persians) where public interest is secondary to the ruler's concern and is practised by both Muslims and non-Muslims, except that the Muslim regimes mix it with religious laws "as much as they are able to" (*Q*, 2: 128; *R*, 2: 139).

At this stage one may legitimately inquire about Ibn Khaldūn's position in Islamic thought in general. If we take for instance the al-Ghazzālī/Ibn Rushd controversy on philosophy as our starting point, there is no doubt that Ibn Khaldūn sided with the first against the second. For one thing the author of the *Muqaddimah* did not even mention the fact that Ibn Rushd responded to the author of *Tahāfut al-falāsifah* when he speaks about al-Ghazzālī's book (*Q*, 3: 121; *R*, 3: 153). Be this as it may, there are some basic common points between al-Ghazzālī and Ibn Khaldūn worth mentioning. Both accept reason to be a just balance when used within its limits, and logic as a valid instrument of thought. Both reject secondary causality for being incompatible with some Qur'ānic verses, and dismiss the Neoplatonists' pretensions for being religiously ruinous for humanity and its organization (Fakhry (1970): 365).

Since Ibn Khaldūn assigns to reason and revelation respectively a separate and different domain, there would be no possible conflict between the two. Whereas Ibn Rushd, following the Aristotelian line, tried to merge the two means of cognition, Ibn Khaldūn did his best to clarify once more the resulting confused situation. His attack on both "modern" dialectical theologians and the extreme Sufis for mixing up their respective disciplines with metaphysical propositions falls within this preoccupation (*Q*, 3: 122; *R*, 3: 153).

There is, however, a basic difference between their respective assaults on philosophy. Al-Ghazzālī's goal is religion itself as an answer to his thirst for certitude (*yaqīn*), while Ibn Khaldūn's reflection has the state as its centre and his attack on Neoplatonism is intended mainly to protect the function religion holds in society. The fall of religion means for Ibn Khaldūn that of the state.

Additionally, Ibn Khaldūn is more influenced by Ibn Sīnā than by Ibn Rushd in the sense of having reacted against the first and almost ignoring the second. But the link between the two is not necessarily always direct. It is often through Fakhr al-Dīn al-Rāzī who responded to Avicenna's philosophy before him that Ibn Khaldūn indirectly espoused many an idea of the latter.[11] On this point, it is worth remarking that his refutation of Ibn Sīnā's theory of emanation and his rejection of the Avicennan doctrine that God does not know particulars are also al-Rāzī's (Fakhry (1970): 357). Even the Khaldūnic refutation of the Platonic view of knowledge as reminiscence can be traced back to al-Rāzī.[12] However, if he moves closely in the latter's wake while assaulting Islamic Neoplatonism and particularly Avicennan philosophy, Ibn Khaldūn does not fail to criticize the author of *Mabāḥith al-mashriqiyyah* ("Oriental Disputations") himself or the "modern" theologians when they amalgamated rational with religious knowledge.

Ibn Khaldūn's way of thinking can be characterized as that of orthodox theology which started to take the upper hand in the eighth/fourteenth century, that "century of Neo-Ḥanbalism". Notwithstanding Ibn Rushd's reaction to al-Ghazzālī's attack, philosophy lost the final battle in the Islamic milieu to both the dynamic orthodox *fiqh* and theosophy. What is particular to Ibn Khaldūn's way of reasoning within this victorious ultra-orthodoxy is that it tries to extend juridical thought to embrace domains other than the traditional space hitherto reserved for Islamic jurisprudence. This is what we have seen him already doing in *Shifā' al-sā'il*. In the *Muqaddimah* he warns students of the harmful and ruinous aspects of philosophy, putting as a prerequisite condition for its study the mastery of religious sciences and particularly *tafsīr* (Qur'ānic exegesis) and *fiqh* (jurisprudence) (*Q*, 3: 220; *R*, 3: 257). Furthermore, in the last chapter of the *Muqaddimah*, like al-Ghazzālī before him, he clearly evaluates the Islamic sciences and their classification from a purely theological angle, leaving aside – surprisingly enough – his theory of knowledge developed at the beginning of his masterpiece.[13]

One should admit by now that a man of genius such as Ibn Khaldūn can easily combine diverse and "contradictory" trends in such a complex and multifarious civilization as the Islamic one. He was amazingly conscious of the crucial period of his culture which was going through a "general change of conditions . . . as if the entire creation had changed and the whole world been altered" (*Q*, 1: 52; *R*, 1: 65). In that sense all the conflicting aspects of the era were reflected in him. The man occupies a critical point in the history of Muslim thinking which ended a big phase and started another and totally new one – lasting until the thirteenth/nineteenth century if not until today. In terms of philosophical history we can say that Ibn Rushd majestically closed the first period and Ibn Khaldūn had the opportunity to outdistance it and could contemplate that phase with ease and from a panoramic position. At the same time, from his retreat in Qal'at Ibn Salamah, he foretold future trends with equal lucidity.

NOTES

1 Before Arab nationalism took solid roots in northern Africa in the late 1930s, Egyptian scholars such as Taha Hussein (*Etude analytique et critique de la philosophie sociale d'Ibn Khaldoun* (Paris, 1917)) and 'Abdallāh 'Inān (*Ibn Khaldūn, ḥayātuhu waturāthuru al-fikrī* (Cairo, 1353), translated into English as *Ibn Khaldūn, His Life and Works* (New Delhi, 1984)) doubted Ibn Khaldūn's Arab descent. They both think that, at a certain point, Ibn Khaldūn himself suspects the authenticity of his own genealogical tree based on Ibn Ḥazm's (d. 457/1065) work. "This doubt is strengthened by our knowledge of the circumstances of antagonism and rivalry between the Arabs and the Berbers in Andalusia" ('Inān (1984): 3–4). Indeed, we are told that Ibn Ḥazm's family suffered a great deal from the Berbers' rebellion against the Umayyads in 403/1013 and was himself "expelled from Cordova and his property was confiscated" (Fakhry (1970): 348). However, in 1943, one of the ideologues of Arab nationalism, Sāṭi' al-Ḥuṣrī, considered the issue so crucial that he tried to refute, point by point, these claims of Ibn Khaldūn's father's Berber descent; see *Dirāsāt 'an muqaddimat ibn Khaldūn* (Cairo and Beirut, 3rd ed., 1967): 552–60.

2 Ibn Khaldūn's life in Egypt is well documented. Here we have many Egyptian biographers, students and contemporaries to check the discourse of his autobiography. See W. J. Fischel's two studies, "Ibn Khaldūn's Activities in Mamluk Egypt (1382–1406)", in *Semitic and Oriental Studies Presented to William Popper* (Berkeley and Los Angeles, 1951): 103–24, and *Ibn Khaldūn and Tamerlane* (Berkeley and Los Angeles, 1952). But his proper work like *Shifā'* and particularly the *Muqaddimah* is much more helpful in representing his way of thinking.

3 In a letter addressed to Ibn Khaldūn in 769/1368, Ibn al-Khaṭīb says that he has sent his book *al-Iḥāṭah fī akhbār Gharnāṭah* ("History of Granada") – where a biography of Ibn Khaldūn is given – to Egypt. See his autobiography (*T*) translated into French by A. Cheddadi as *Le Voyage d'occident et d'orient* (Paris, 1980): 107. This explains his post as a lecturer in al-Azhar immediately after his arrival.

4 These are: (1) *Lubāb al-muḥaṣṣal,* (2) a commentary on *Burdah,* (3) commentaries on Ibn Rushd, (4) a summary book on logic, (5) a book on logic and arithmetic, and (6) a commentary on a *rajaz* poem on jurisprudence by Ibn al-Khaṭīb. On these works listed by Ibn al-Khaṭīb (*History of Granada,* quoted by al-Maqqarī, *Nafḥ al-Ṭib* (Cairo, 1886–7), 4: 11), we have only the first. We also ignore the question of which of Ibn Rushd's books, theological or philosophical, Ibn Khaldūn commented on. For Ibn al-Khaṭīb's translated text see Rosenthal's Introduction to the *Muqaddimah* in *R,* 1: xliv and also xxx, note 3.

5 See T. Kroeber (*Ishi, le testament du dernier indien sauvage* (Paris, 1968): 453) quoted by J. Poirier, S. Clapier-Valladon and P. Raybaut, *Les Récits de vie* (Paris, 1983): 116.

6 In his own foreword to the *Muqaddimah,* Ibn Khaldūn writes: "I divided the work into an introduction and three books: the Introduction deals with the great merit of historiography, (offers) an appreciation of its various methods, and cites errors of the historians. The First Book deals with civilization and its essential characteristics, mainly, royal authority, government, gainful occupations, ways of making a living, crafts and sciences, as well as with the causes and thereof. The Second Book deals with the history, races and dynasties of the Arabs, from the beginning of creation down to this time. This will include references to such famous nations and dynasties contemporaneous with them, as the Nabataeans, the Syrians, the Persians, the Israelites, the Copts, the Greeks, the Byzantines and the Turks. The Third Book deals with the history of the Berbers and of the Zanatah who are part of them; with their origins and races; and, in particular, with the royal authority and dynasties in the Maghreb" (*Q,* 1: 6; *R,* 1: 11–12).

7 After a long introduction composed of four preliminary discussions on the human soul, its natural inclination to mystical knowledge, the Islamic aspects of such legitimate aspirations and the happiness derived from Sufi revelation, Ibn Khaldūn distinguishes three stages in the Sufi path. Each stage is a spiritual struggle called a *mujāhadah* (*al-taqwā, al-istiqāmah* and *al-kashf*). From this tripartite division, his answer to the initial question is clear: in order to attain the first two stages there is no need for a Shaykh. Books on Sufism, such as al-Ghazzālī's, al-Muḥāsibī's and al-Qushayrī's, are enough. As to the last stage, a Shaykh is necessary.

8 As rightly remarked by Nassar (p. 90 n. 1) and others, Ibn Khaldūn, like the majority of his predecessors, does not always distinguish between reason, intellect and thought.

9 As to his attitude towards physics, Ibn Khaldūn uses his criteria of conformity (*muṭābaqah*) existing between primary (but not secondary) *intelligibilia,* defined as abstractions derived from the *sensibilia* (*Q,* 3: 211; *R,* 3: 247) and the individual *existentia* and concedes to philosophers their claims in this respect. He

admits that "judgment becomes unequivocal, comparable to judgment in the case of *sensibilia*, since the primary *intelligibilia* are more likely to agree with the outside world, because they conform perfectly (by definition, to the individual manifestations of the *existentia*)" (*Q*, 3: 214; *R*, 3: 251).

10 The fact that he did not include politics among the practical sciences is a much more complicated issue. In fact history is not included either in his classification of the sciences. On this last point see A. Lakhsassi, "Ibn Khaldūn and the Classification of the Science[s]", *The Maghreb Review*, 4(1) (1979): 21–5.

11 Ibn Khaldūn knew of al-Rāzī not only *al-Muḥaṣṣal* but also *al-Maḥsūl* – of which he says that it is an abridgement of four books on *kalām* (*Q*, 3: 22; *R*, 3: 28–9) – and particularly *al-Mabāḥith al-mashriqiyyah* (*Q*, 3: 122; *R*, 3: 153). Al-Rāzī's encyclopedic knowledge is mastered by Ibn Khaldūn under his highly praised teacher, al-Ābilī with whom he has studied logic, principles of jurisprudence and *kalām* (*manṭiq wa-aslayn*). In his introduction to *Lubāb al-muḥaṣṣal*, he calls him "*Fakhr al-dunyā wa'l-dīn, ḥujjat al-islām wa'l-muslimīn*".

12 See A. Lakhsassi, *The Epistemological Foundations of the Sciences in Ibn Khaldūn's Muqaddimah*, unpublished thesis, University of Manchester, 1982: 49–53.

13 This point has been fully developed in my thesis, *op. cit.*

BIBLIOGRAPHY

Abbreviations of Ibn Khaldūn's works

B *Kitāb al-'ibār wa-dīwān al-mubtada' wa'l-khabar fī ayyām al-'arab wa'l-'ajam wa'l-barbar wa-man 'āṣarahum min dhawī al-sulṭān al-akbar,* ed. Naṣr al-Ḥūrīnī, 7 vols (Cairo, 1867).

L *Lubāb al-muḥaṣṣal fī uṣūl al-dīn*, ed. L. Rubio (Tetouan, 1952).

Q *Muqaddimat Ibn Khaldūn (*Les Prolégomènes d'Ebn Khaldoun), ed. E. M. Quatremère, 3 vols (Paris, 1858).

R *The Muqaddimah*, trans. F. Rosenthal, 3 vols (Princeton, 1958, 2nd ed., 1967).

Sh *Shifā' al-sā'il li-tahdīb al-masā'il*, ed. Muḥammad ibn Tāwīt al-Ṭanjī (Istanbul, 1957).

T *al-Ta'rīf bi-ibn Khaldūn wa-riḥlatuhu gharban wa-sharqan,* ed. Muḥammad ibn Tāwīt al-Ṭanjī (Cairo, 1951).

Secondary works

The most recent, by far the most comprehensive (854 titles) and certainly most usable bibliography on Ibn Khaldūn – since it is topically classified (ten thematic sections) with an author index – is given by A. al-Azmeh at the end of his *Ibn Khaldūn in Modern Scholarship, a Study in Orientalism* (London, 1981): 229–324.

Fakhry, M. (1970) *A History of Islamic Philosophy* (New York and London).

Gellner, E. (1968) "A Pendulum Swing Theory of Islam", *Annales Marocaines de Sociologie* (Rabat): 5–14.

Johnson, S. (1991) "The 'Umranic Nature of Ibn Khaldun's Classification of the Sciences", *The Muslim World*, 81: 254–61.

Nassar, N. (1967) *La Pensée réaliste d'Ibn Khaldūn* (Paris).

Pérez, R. (1991) Introduction to *La Voie et la Loi ou le maître et le juriste*, French trans. of Ibn Khaldūn's *Shifā' al-sā'il* (Paris).

Toynbee, A. J. (1935) "The Relativity of Ibn Khaldūn's Historical Thought", in *A Study of History*, 3, 2nd ed. (London).

IV

Philosophy and the mystical tradition

CHAPTER 26

Introduction to the mystical tradition

Seyyed Hossein Nasr

In order to speak of the mystical tradition of Islam, it is first of all necessary to understand the meaning of mysticism in the Islamic context, especially considering the nebulous nature of the meaning of this term in English today. We can speak of Islamic mysticism only if we understand by this term its original meaning as that which deals with the Divine Mysteries. One must recall that silence or the closing of one's lips is the root meaning of the Greek verb *muo* from which the word *mysterion* and mysticism derive. As such, one might relate it in the Islamic context to such terms as *asrār* (mysteries) or *bāṭin* (the inward or esoteric), remembering that the Sufis refer often to themselves as the people who are the guardians of the Divine Mysteries or *asrār*. In the Islamic context mysticism means the esoteric dimension of Islam identified for the most part with Sufism but also with Shi'ite esoterism, both Twelve-Imām and Ismā'īlī.[1]

Moreover, Islamic mysticism understood in this sense is primarily a path of knowledge (*al-ma'rifah*, *'irfān*) to which the element of love is attached in accordance with the structure of the Islamic revelation, but it is very rarely the sentimental and individualistic mysticism found in many circles in the Christian climate since the Renaissance. That is precisely why Islamic mysticism has had a close rapport with Islamic philosophy over the ages; and one might say that despite the criticism made by many Sufis against Islamic philosophers, particularly from the sixth/twelfth to the ninth/fifteenth centuries, the Islamic philosophers, especially those of the later period, belong to the same spiritual family as the Sufis, both being concerned with the attainment of ultimate knowledge.[2] It did not take too long before the intellect (*al-'aql*) of the Islamic philosophers became identified with the *rūḥ al-qudus*, the Holy Spirit, and the angels of the religious universe with the intelligences of the philosophers. Nor must one forget that some Sufis were given the title of Ibn Aflāṭūn, literally the son of Plato.

What is most essential to emphasize is that Islamic esoterism and especially Sufism have remained alive and vibrant over the centuries, providing practical means for the realization of the Real and the activation of the potentialities of the noetic faculty within human beings. They have continued to provide the possibility for the attainment of a realized knowledge, a sapience or gnosis, which the Islamic philosophers could hardly ignore. In fact, in the same way that from the Scientific Revolution onwards Western philosophy became more and more the handmaid of a science based on the empirical data drawn from the outward senses, Islamic philosophy became wedded even more closely to the fruits of that other way of knowing which is based on the inner senses and the opening of the "eye of the heart" (*'ayn al-qalb* in Arabic and *chishm-i dil* in Persian) which can "see" the invisible world hidden to the outward eye.

The first notable Islamic philosopher in whom one observes direct interest in Sufism is al-Fārābī, who was in fact a practising Sufi. The influence of Sufism on his writings is, however, not evident except in the *Fuṣūṣ al-ḥikmah* ("Bezels of Wisdom"), which some have attributed to Ibn Sīnā. The presence of Sufism is to be seen mostly in the personal life of al-Fārābī, which needless to say must have influenced his thought, and also in his musical compositions. Few realize that some of these compositions are sung and played in Sufi orders to this day in both Turkey and the Indo-Pakistan subcontinent.

The rapport with Sufism is more evident in al-Fārābī's chief successor in the Peripatetic (*mashshā'ī*) school, Ibn Sīnā. Although the account of his meeting with Abū Sa'īd Abi'l-Khayr, the celebrated Sufi of Khurasan, is considered by most contemporary scholars to be apocryphal, there is little doubt that Ibn Sīnā was greatly interested in Sufism,[3] and his "Oriental philosophy" (*al-ḥikmat al-mashriqiyyah*) is impregnated with mystical ideas.[4] Moreover, in the ninth book (*namaṭ*) of his last masterpiece, *al-Ishārāt wa'l-tanbīhāt* ("Directives and Remarks"), entitled *Fī maqāmāt al-'ārifīn* ("Concerning the Stations of the Gnostics") he provided the most powerful defence made of Sufism by any of the Islamic philosophers. There he admits openly the attainment by gnostics or intellectually inclined Sufis of knowledge of the spiritual world and the possibility of discovering its hidden mysteries.[5] This chapter of Ibn Sīnā's enduring work which has been taught for the past millennium in Persia and elsewhere is not only a testament of the influence of Sufism upon Islamic philosophy but has been itself influential in furthering this influence.

In the same period as the advent of early Peripatetic philosophy and the rise of such men as al-Fārābī and Ibn Sīnā, one observes the rise of

Ismāʿīlī philosophy, which reached its peak in the fourth/tenth and fifth/eleventh centuries with such figures as Ḥamīd al-Dīn al-Kirmānī and Nāṣir-i Khusraw. This whole school identifies philosophy with the esoteric dimension of Islam.[6] Such basic doctrines of Ismāʿīlī philosophy or theosophy as hermeneutic interpretation (*ta'wīl*), the rapport between the *imām* and the human intellect, initiation, cycles of prophecy and imamology as well as cosmogony and anthropology bear witness to its close rapport with a certain dimension of Islamic esoterism. Moreover, such Greco-Alexandrian mystical teachings as those of the Pythagoreans and Hermeticists found an echo in Ismāʿīlī philosophy, as we see in the *Rasā'il* ("Epistles") of the Ikhwān al-Ṣafā' (Brethren of Purity) with their great emphasis upon the mystical significance of numbers.

While Peripatetic philosophy was being criticized by both Ashʿarite theologians and Sufis such as al-Ghazzālī and Sanā'ī in the Eastern lands of Islam, the flourishing of Islamic philosophy in the Western lands of Islam was again marked by its close affiliation with Sufism. In fact the whole phenomenon of Islamic philosophy in Spain was to bear the early imprint of Sufism upon philosophical thought given by Ibn Masarrah. Nearly all the notable Islamic philosophers of Spain, with the exception of Ibn Rushd (Averroes), had a strong mystical dimension which is clearly reflected in their writings. One needs only to recall the mystical love of Ibn Ḥazm, the mathematical mysticism of Ibn al-Sīd of Badajoz, the doctrine of intellectual contemplation of Ibn Bājjah and the role of the Active Intellect in Ibn Ṭufayl to confirm this assertion. But it is most of all in the last of the great Andalusian philosophers, Ibn Sabʿīn, that one can observe the clearest manifestation of the rapport between Sufism and philosophy. At once a Sufi and philosopher, Ibn Sabʿīn created one of the major syntheses between Sufi doctrine and philosophy in the history of Islamic thought.

In the sixth/twelfth century it was back in the Eastern lands of Islam and especially Persia that the most significant and influential synthesis of mysticism and philosophy was to take place in the hands of Shihāb al-Dīn Suhrawardī, the founder of the School of Illumination (*al-ishrāq*). A Sufi in his youth who also mastered the philosophy of Ibn Sīnā, Suhrawardī created a new philosophical perspective which is based on knowledge through illumination and the wedding between the training of the rational mind and the purification of one's inner being. Suhrawardī was himself fully aware of the centrality of this synthesis between rational knowledge and mystical experience and included the Sufis along with the Peripatetic philosophers as constituting the categories and stages leading to that of the "theosopher" (*ḥakīm muta'allih*) who is the ideal of *ishrāqī* doctrine.[7] Through Suhrawardī, Islamic philosophy became inextricably bound to spiritual realization and inner purification associated with the mystical life during nearly all later periods of Islamic history. Subsequent *ishrāqī* philosophers such as his major commentators Muḥammad Shahrazūrī and Quṭb al-Dīn Shīrāzī as well as major later representatives of his doctrines such as Ibn Turkah Iṣfahānī were at once philosophers and mystics.

The close nexus between philosophy and mysticism characterizes in fact nearly all later Islamic philosophy. The reviver of Ibn Sīnā's Peripatetic philosophy in the seventh/thirteenth century, Naṣīr al-Dīn al-Ṭūsī, who was at the same time one of the great mathematicians and astronomers of history, also wrote *Awṣāf al-ashrāf* ("Descriptions of the Nobles") on Sufi virtues. His contemporary Afḍal al-Dīn Kāshānī, at once philosopher and poet, was a Sufi whose tomb is visited by pilgrims to this day as that of a saint, and Jalāl al-Dīn Dawānī, at once philosopher and theologian, was also seriously interested in *ishrāqī* and esoteric doctrines and even commented upon Suhrawardī.

In the Safavid period with the establishment of the School of Isfahan in the tenth/sixteenth century, the relation between philosophy and mysticism came to be taken nearly for granted by most philosophers and the experience of the Real through practice and intellection became almost inseparable from the philosophical discussion of the Real; hence the importance in the Islamic metaphysics of this period of the relation between *ḥaqīqat al-wujūd* (the reality of being) and *mafhūm al-wujūd* (the concept of being).[8] The founder of the School of Isfahan, Mīr Dāmād, one of the most rigorously rational philosophers, also wrote mystical poetry under the pen-name *Ishrāq* and composed a treatise on ecstatic mystical experience.[9]

The major figure of this school, Mullā Ṣadrā, underwent a long period of inner purification along with formal learning and considered illumination and revelation as vital sources of knowledge along with ratiocination. The new intellectual perspective established by him and called "the transcendent theosophy" (*al-ḥikmat al-muta'āliyah*) is based on the three foundations of revelation, inner illumination and ratiocination, and many of the most basic doctrines mentioned in his works are considered by him to have been unveiled to him by God. Therefore, he refers to them by such terms as *ḥikmah 'arshiyyah* (wisdom descended from the Divine Throne).[10] Some of the works of Mullā Ṣadrā, such as *al-Shawāhid al-rubūbiyyah* ("Divine Witness"), have a strong *'irfānī* or gnostic colour, and the author was a strong defender of the great Sufis of old such as Ibn 'Arabī whom he quoted extensively in his *magnum opus*, *al-Asfār al-arba'ah* ("The Four Journeys"). Mullā Ṣadrā also wrote a biographical work, the *Si aṣl* ("The Three Principles"), and *Kasr al-aṣnām al-jāhiliyyah* ("The Breaking of the Idols of the Age of Ignorance") in which, while attacking some of the deviant, popular forms of Sufism, he defends strongly the authentic Sufis and their doctrines. In fact Ṣadrian philosophy or theosophy cannot be understood without the immense influence of

Ibn ʿArabian doctrines and other Sufi teachings including those of al-Ghazzālī upon Mullā Ṣadrā.

Islamic philosophy was to continue this close relationship to mysticism especially as far as later proponents of Mullā Ṣadrā's school were concerned. His immediate students, ʿAbd al-Razzāq Lāhījī and Mullā Muḥsin Fayḍ Kāshānī, distanced themselves somewhat from Mullā Ṣadrā because of the political climate of the day and devoted themselves mostly to the religious sciences and theology. But they did write some works inspired by their teacher and both composed mystical poetry. Kāshānī also wrote a number of important mystical prose treatises such as *Kalimāt-i maknūnah* ("The Hidden Words"). Their student Qāḍī Saʿīd Qummī also composed important mystical treatises and must be considered a notable mystical philosopher.[11] Likewise, the Qajar philosophers who revived Mullā Ṣadrā's teachings were at the same time mystics and philosophers, notable among them being Ḥājjī Mullā Hādī Sabziwārī, who composed, in addition to logical and philosophical texts, mystical ones in both prose and poetry. He must in fact be called a philosopher-saint, being considered by his contemporaries and later generations as at once a towering philosophical figure and a mystic saint.[12]

This trend was to continue into the fourteenth/twentieth century. Many of the most emiment Islamic philosophers of Persia of the past century such as Mīrzā Mahdī Āshtiyānī, Sayyid Muḥammad Kāẓim ʿAṣṣār, ʿAllāmah Ṭabāṭabāʾī and Mahdī Ilāhī Qumshaʾī were at once philosophers and mystics, many following rigorously a spiritual path. There are thus witnesses in this period of an age-old rapport and later wedding between philosophy and mysticism going back to Ibn Sīnā, Suhrawardī and Mullā Ṣadrā.

Nor is this situation confined to Persia. In India where Islamic philosophy began to flourish, especially during the Mogul period, the same close relation between mysticism and philosophy is to be observed among many of the major figures, chief among them Shah Walīullāh of Delhi, perhaps the greatest Islamic thinker of the subcontinent. In reading his works, it is difficult to decide whether he is a theologian, philosopher or Sufi. The truth is that he was all three at once, a thinker who created yet another synthesis of these disciplines. One can likewise observe figures of this type in the Ottoman Empire and also in the Arab world in modern times. One of the most important religious figures of Egypt during the fourteenth/twentieth century, ʿAbd al-Ḥalīm Muḥmūd, who was also Shaykh al-Azhar, was at once a Sufi and an Islamic philosopher and wrote important works on both subjects.

In modern times the influence of Western thought has drawn many people in the Islamic world away from both Sufism and traditional Islamic philosophy. But to the extent that this philosophy, grounded in a twelve-hundred-year-old tradition, survives, the nexus between mysticism and philosophical thought continues. In any case the nature of Islamic philosophy as it has developed over the century cannot be fully understood without grasping the significance of that reality which can be called Islamic mysticism and its influence upon many of the leading figures of Islamic philosophy from al-Fārābī and Ibn Sīnā to those of the contemporary period.

NOTES

1 See M. Lings, *What is Sufism?* (Cambridge, 1993); T. Burckhardt, *An Introduction to Sufism*, trans. D. M. Matheson (Wellingborough, 1990); see also S. H. Nasr, *Ideals and Realities of Islam* (London, 1994).

2 On the relation between Sufism and Islamic philosophy in the context of Persian culture, see S. H. Nasr, "The Relation between Sufism and Philosophy in Persian Culture" (trans. H. Dabashi), in S. H. Nasr, *The Islamic Intellectual Tradition in Persia*, ed. M. Aminrazavi (London, 1995).

See also the important study of F. Schuon, *Sufism – Veil and Quintessence*, trans. W. Stoddart (Bloomington, 1981), chapter 5, "Tracing the Notion of Philosophy": 115–28.

3 See Nasr, *An Introduction to Islamic Cosmological Doctrines* (Albany, 1993): 191ff.; and B. Forouzanfar, "Abū 'Alī Sīnā wa taṣawwuf", in Dh. Ṣafā (ed.), *Le Livre du millénaire d'Avicenne*, 2 (Tehran, 1953): 188ff.

4 See H. Corbin, *Avicenna and the Visionary Recital*, trans. W. Trask (Irving, 1980).

5 See Ibn Sīnā, *al-Ishārāt wa'l-tanbīhāt*, ed. Maḥmūd Shahābī (Tehran, 1960): 151. The last chapters of this work dedicated to Sufism and related subjects have been translated into English by Shams Inati and are to appear soon. See also the French translation of this work by A.-M. Goichon, *Le Livre des directives et remarques* (Paris, 1951): 467ff.; and A. F. von Mehren, *Traités mystiques . . . d'Avicenne* (Leiden, 1889–91).

6 The works of Corbin deal extensively with this subject. See especially his *L'Homme et son ange* (Paris, 1983); Corbin (with S. H. Nasr and O. Yahya), *A History of Islamic Philosophy*, trans. L. Sherrard (London, 1993); also his *Cyclic Time and Isma'ili Gnosis* (London, 1983).

7 See "Suhrawardī", in Nasr, *The Islamic Intellectual Tradition in Persia*; Nasr, *Three Muslim Sages* (Delmar, 1975), chapter 2: 52ff.; H. Corbin, *En Islam iranien*, 2 (Paris, 1971); I. R. Netton, "The Neoplatonic Substrate of Suhrawardī's Philosophy of Illumination: *Falsafa* as *Taṣawwuf*", in L. Lewisohn (ed.), *The Legacy of Mediaeval Persian Sufism* (London, 1992): 247–60.

8 See T. Izutsu, *The Concept and Reality of Existence* (Tokyo, 1971).

9 See H. Corbin, "Confession extatique de Mīr Dāmād", in his *En Islam iranien*, 4 (Paris, 1972): 9ff.

10 See J. Morris (trans.), *Mullā Ṣadrā's Wisdom of the Throne* (Princeton, 1981); and Nasr, *Ṣadr al-Dīn Shīrāzī and His Transcendent Theosophy* (Tehran, 1977), especially chapters 4 and 5: 69ff.

11 On these figures see H. Corbin, *La Philosophie iranienne islamique aux XVIIe et XVIIIe siècles* (Paris, 1981): 96–115; 179–87; and 245–91. Corbin has also

devoted a major separate study to Qummī's work on the symbolism of the Ka'bah. See his *Temple and Contemplation*, trans. P. Sherrard (London, 1986): 183–262.

12 See "Sabziwārī", in Nasr, *The Islamic Intellectual Tradition in Persia*; and M. Mohaghegh and T. Izutsu (trans.), *The Metaphysics of Sabzavarī* (Delmar, 1977).

CHAPTER 27

ʿAyn al-Quḍāt Hamadānī and the intellectual climate of his times

Hamid Dabashi

At the commencement of his recuperative reading of Thomas Aquinas' *Aesthetics*, Umberto Eco took strong exception to Benedetto Croce's hasty dismissal of Aquinas as a serious philosopher and aesthetician, accusing the medieval theologian "not [of] false, but extremely general" ideas. Croce had decreed that "The essential thing is that the problems of aesthetics were not the object of any genuine interest, either to the Middle Ages in general, or to St. Thomas in particular." Opposing this judgment, Eco produced a sustained, highly relevant and brilliantly enabling reading of Aquinas' theory of aesthetics based on the preliminary assumption that "It is true that these theories were entangled in their theology as well as in their philosophy, but to disentangle them all one has to do is to read their theology in a philosophical light. This way of reading them is quite in keeping with their own intentions."[1] Suspending Eco's own unexamined, logocentric, privileging of "philosophy" for a moment, much of what he says about the disentangling of medieval theories from their surrounding theology remains thoroughly valid, and not just for Christian theology. But whereas, in his innately Christian hermeneutics, Eco can visualize only "philosophy" in binary opposition with "theology", in the intellectual context to the east of the Mediterranean basin a much richer and intellectually more complex picture exists which requires an even more careful distinguishing of theories expounded by a medieval Persian from their fabric of historical presence. At a time by one century younger than that of Aquinas, ʿAyn al-Quḍāt Hamadānī's theoretical concerns, his theory of aesthetics included, were delivered in a narrative context much richer than a mere dichotomy between "theology" and "philosophy". But Eco's corrective should remain constant in any attempt to disentangle 'Ayn al-Quḍāt's theoretical concerns from an innately theocentric narrative.

In this exposition of 'Ayn al-Quḍāt's theories on a range of issues, I shall first give an account of the political and intellectual forces operative in his time and then place him and his modes of writing in that context. The disentangling will then fall into place.

LIFE AND TIMES

'Ayn al-Quḍāt Hamadānī was one of the most remarkable figures in Islamic intellectual history whose life and thought has been seen mostly only within the "mystical" tradition while less attention has been paid to him as part of the Islamic philosophic tradition.[2] He was born in 492/1098 in the city of Hamadan, then under the rule of the Seljūq Prince Maḥmūd, and was executed in the same city at the prime age of thirty-three in the year 525/1131. Scores of treatises and "letters" have been attributed to him, not all of which are from his pen. Scores of other texts, of which we have no trace, are reported to have been written by 'Ayn al-Quḍāt.

Not much is known about 'Ayn al-Quḍāt's life and circumstances in Hamadan.[3] In comparison to a number of scattered references in sources close to him, from which a schematic biography may be sketched out, there is an avalanche of hagiographical sources which, feeding on each other, are of no biographical use but of considerable significance in charting out the narrative and institutional appropriations of 'Ayn al-Quḍāt into the "Persian mystical tradition".[4] By far the most reliable sources of information about 'Ayn al-Quḍāt are his own writings. In chronological order, 'Ayn al-Quḍāt's writings which with a degree of certainty can be safely attributed to him are *Zubdah al-ḥaqā'iq* (516/1122), *Maktūbāt* (between 517/1123 and 525/1131), *Tamhīdāt* (521/1127) and *Shakwā' al-gharīb* (525/1131). Four other extant treatises have been attributed to 'Ayn al-Quḍāt, but almost certainly are not his: *Sharḥ-i kalamāt-i Bābā Ṭāhir*, *Risālah-yi yazdān-shinākht*, *Ghāyah al-imkān fī dirāyah al-makān* and *Risālah-yi lawāyiḥ*.

'Ayn al-Quḍāt was born during a tumultuous and exciting period in Iranian social and intellectual history. The year of his birth, 492/1098, coincides with the height of the Seljūq rule (429/1038–590/1194) over much of the Iranian territory and beyond. The Seljūqs controlled much of the eastern Islamic Empire, from Transoxania to Mesopotamia. Originally from the Qïnïq clan of Oghuz Turkish people, the Seljūqs came into the Iranian plateau as slaves and mercenaries from the steppes north of the Caspian and Aral Seas. Their first principal warlord, Toghrïl I (ruled 429/1038–455/1063), took a considerable chunk of Ghaznavid (ruled

366/977–582/1186) territory, from Khwarazm to Azarbaijan and Baghdad, and established the initial territory of the Seljūq Empire.[5] At the birth of 'Ayn al-Quḍāt in 492/1098, the Seljūq Empire was more than half a century old. Two major warlords who before and in the wake of 'Ayn al-Quḍāt's birth would expand the territories of the Seljūqs from the Mediterranean to Transoxania were Malikshāh I (ruled465/1072–485/1092) and Sanjar (ruled 511/1118–552/1157). The warlord under whose immediate reign 'Ayn al-Quḍāt was born was Rukn al-Dīn Barkiyāruq (ruled 487/1094–498/1105) who spent much of his reign fighting against his brother Muḥammad I (ruled 498/1105–511/1118). But 'Ayn al-Quḍāt's early youth and education in Hamadan was under the direct rule of Mughīth al-Dīn Maḥmūd II (ruled 511/1118–525/1131) who succeeded his father Muḥammad I with a claim over the entire Seljūq Empire, and yet his aspirations were thwarted by his uncle Sanjar who as the most senior member of the Seljūq clan, with a long history of ruling over the easternmost part of the empire, punished Maḥmūd and sat supremely at the throne of the Seljūq Empire for a long time.[6]

Despite their massive and almost unbridled power, these Seljūq warlords were not the sole custodians of power in the realm. At least two other, court-affiliated, centres of power ought to be identified if we are to have a full grasp of the political circumstances under which 'Ayn al-Quḍāt was born and raised. The Persian vizierate, in a long tradition of institutional authority that preceded and succeeded the Seljūqs, was a principal source of power, rivalled very closely by what may be termed Turkish "Khātunate", or the unending power of Seljūq queens and princesses. The principal vizier who served the Seljūqs with remarkable statesmanship was the legendary Niẓām al-Mulk (d. 485/1092), perhaps the most brilliant political mind of medieval Persia. Niẓām al-Mulk was instrumental in organizing the structural foundation, the operative bureaucracy, as well as the political ideology of the Seljūqs. He was equally instrumental in keeping the chief menace of the Seljūq realm, the Ismā'īlī movement, at bay. Niẓām al-Mulk served Alp-Arsalān (ruled 455/1063–465/1072) and his son Malikshāh I (ruled 465/1072–485/1092) with remarkable tenacity. Among his principal achievements, at the service of the Seljūqs' political/religious legitimacy, was the establishment of the multi-campus Niẓāmiyyah colleges, in the Baghdad campus at which Abū Ḥāmid al-Ghazzālī (d. 505/1111) taught, whose writings 'Ayn al-Quḍāt read voraciously and whose younger brother Aḥmad al-Ghazzālī (d. 520/1126) he befriended half-way through his (i.e., 'Ayn al-Quḍāt's) tragically short life.

Before his brutal murder at the hand of Abū Ṭāhir, an Ismā'īlī assassin, Khwājah Niẓām al-Mulk was outwitted and outmanoeuvred by Malikshāh's shrewd and ambitious Queen Tarkān Khātūn, the daughter of Tamqhāj Khān ibn Bughrā Khān. This Tarkān Khātūn was by far the best and most distinguished representative of the institution of "Khātūnate" (and I submit that the power of these queens was crucial and considerable enough to merit the coinage of a term for them). As the end of Malikshāh's life and reign was in sight, and having lost two of her sons as heir-apparent to her husband and king, Tarkān Khātūn campaigned gallantly for her third son Maḥmūd. In the meantime, Niẓām al-Mulk and many of Malikshāh's generals had their eyes on Barkiyāruq (ruled 487/1094–498/1105), Malikshāh's older son from a different marriage. Tarkān Khātūn's campaign against Niẓām al-Mulk was successful and resulted in Malikshāh's dismissing the old Persian vizier from his post and replacing him with Tāj al-Mulk Abu'l-Ghanā'im al-Qummī, the private secretary of Tarkān Khātūn.[7]

When 'Ayn al-Quḍāt was twenty, Muḥammad I (ruled 498/1105–511/1118) died and his son Mughīth al-Dīn Maḥmūd succeeded him in the western part of the Seljūq Empire, under the supreme rule of his uncle Sanjar. Two high-ranking officials at Maḥmūd's court in Hamadan were closely connected to 'Ayn al-Quḍāt, albeit with two diametrically opposed attitudes. Maḥmūd's treasurer, 'Azīz al-Dīn al-Mustawfī (d. 525/1131), was a close friend and confidante of 'Ayn al-Quḍāt, while Abu'l-Qāsim al-Daragazīnī (d. 525/1131) was a sworn enemy of al-Mustawfī and then, by extension and the logic of "the friend of my enemy is my enemy", a staunch enemy of 'Ayn al-Quḍāt. The animosity between Daragazīnī and Mustawfī was rooted not only in the usual rivalries among high-ranking Seljūq officials but also in an endemic financial crisis. The details of this financial crisis apparently have to do with a substantial dowry that Sultan Sanjar gave to his daughter Mahmalik Khātūn when as part of a political settlement with his nephew Sultan Maḥmūd he gave her in marriage to him. After giving Maḥmūd a son, Mahmalik Khātūn died at a very young age. Sultan Sanjar sent another of his daughters as a political bride to Maḥmūd but asked him to return to his court in Khurasan the substantial dowry he had given the first bride. Maḥmūd accepted the second cousin as his bride but, having entirely spent it, was unable to return the dowry to his king and uncle Sanjar. As the treasurer of Maḥmūd, Mustawfī was of course the chief person who knew that the dowry had been wasted. At this point, Daragazīnī intervened and turned these unfortunate events into his advantage and against the treasurer. Mustawfī was immediately arrested and imprisoned, an event which had dire consequences for 'Ayn al-Quḍāt, as I shall explain.[8]

The Seljūqs' political power was of course executed under the supreme, however ceremonial, authority of the 'Abbasid caliphs who continued to preside nominally over the "Islamic Empire" and dispensed salvation and benediction in the form of titles to Seljūq warlords. As new converts, the Turkish Seljūqs were extremely conscious of their religious legitimacy at the court of the ʿAbbasid caliphate. Although their own court and administrative apparatus was very much modelled on pre-Islamic Persian monarchy, the ideological legitimacy of their role was in effect an extension of the central authority of the ʿAbbasid caliphate. The result of this political necessity was an inordinate amount of attention paid by Seljūq warlords, their viziers and their queens to matters of religious legitimacy. The Seljūq warlords, and their court, were Ḥanafī Muslims and as such gave full political support to Ḥanafī law in their domain. As a result, the nomocentric doctrinaires of the faith then had their heyday under the Seljūqs. As Ḥanafī Sunnis, the Seljūqs fully recognized the authority of the central caliphate and in return received their legitimizing blessings. The Seljūqs, as indeed the Ghaznavids before and contemporaneous with them, reciprocated by brutally suppressing sectarian movements, particularly the Ismāʿīlīs. The political necessity of sustaining the ʿAbbasid caliphate in power by the Seljūq warlords resulted in a symbiotic relationship between the two political apparatuses: the Seljūqs necessitated and legitimated the ʿAbbasids by the power of their swords, and the ʿAbbasids responded by bestowing their blessings and legitimizing authority on the Seljūqs. By defending the ʿAbbasids against the onslaught of the Crusaders, the Seljūqs in effect extended their authority beyond the Islamic lands and on to the boundaries of Christendom. The father of Ṣalāḥ al-Dīn al-ʿAyyūbī, the legendary general who fought against Richard the Lionheart, was a prison guard in Tikrit where ʿAzīz al-Dīn al-Mustawfī, the chief political supporter of ʿAyn al-Quḍāt, was imprisoned.[9]

The triumphant ascendancy of nomocentrism (the primacy of law) in the Islamic religious tradition is evident in the final consolidation of the four major schools of law in this period. Although the legal schools of the Ḥanafīs, the Shāfiʿīs, the Malikīs and the Ḥanbalīs were all present and active in the Seljūq realm, the Ḥanafīs and the Shāfiʿīs were in the majority and principally located in the easternmost part of the empire. There were pockets of Shīʿī communities in the West, and the Ismāʿīlīs were of course aggressively active throughout the realm. The two prominent Seljūq viziers, ʿAmīd al-Mulk Abū Naṣr al-Kundurī (d. 456/1063) and Niẓām al-Mulk, were Ḥanafī and Shāfiʿī, respectively. The result was that the law schools that the Seljūqs and their viziers established, the multi-campus Niẓāmiyyah system chief among them, were principally devoted to Ḥanafī and Shāfiʿī law. The three principal centres of power under the Seljūqs – i.e., the sultanate, the vizierate and the khātūnate – competed with each other in establishing and funding law schools devoted to Ḥanafī and Shāfiʿī jurisprudence.

In these schools, a variety of subjects and disciplines was studied, all giving momentous institutional and epistemic power to the nomocentricity of Islamic thought. *ʿilm al-qirāʾah* ("The Science of the Reading of the Qur'ān"), *'ilm al-tafsīr* ("Qur'ānic Hermeneutics"), *'ilm al-fiqh* ("Jurisprudence"), *'ilm al-kalām* ("Theology") all produced prominent scholars in their respective fields. Abu'l-Qāsim Maḥmūd ibn 'Umar al-Zamakhsharī al-Khwārazmī (d. 538/1143) wrote an influential Qur'ānic commentary, known as *al-Kashshāf*, and in it propagated the theological positions of the Mu'tazilites. Among the Sufis, Abū 'Abd al-Raḥmān Muḥammad ibn Ḥusayn al-Sulamī (d. 412/1021) and Abu'l-Qāsim 'Abd al-Karīm al-Qushayrī al-Nīshāpūrī (d. 465/1072) wrote influential commentaries on the Qur'ān from their respective points of view. In 520/1126 al-Maybudī joined his Sufi brethren and wrote a monumental commentary on the Qur'ān in beautiful Persian prose. Among the Shī'īs, Shaykh al-Ṭā'ifah Abū Ja'far Muḥammad ibn Ḥasan al-Ṭūsī (d. 460/1067) singlehandedly established the principal textual foundations of Shī'ī law. Another luminary Shī'ī authority, Abū 'Alī Faḍl ibn Ḥasan ibn Faḍl al-Ṭabarsī (d. 548/1153), wrote his monumental Qur'ānic commentary, *Majma' al-bayān*, in this period.

The most influential of all theologians and jurists of this period, a man whom 'Ayn al-Quḍāt read voraciously, was Abū Ḥāmid Muḥammad al-Ghazzālī (d. 505/1111) whose treatises on law and theology were principal texts of study throughout the Seljūq realms and beyond. In such seminal works as *al-Iqtisād fi'l-i'tiqād* and *al-Jāmi' al-'awāmm 'an 'ilm al-kalām*, al-Ghazzālī summarized the principal theological position of the Ash'arite school. Al-Ghazzālī wrote also copiously against the Ismā'īlīs. *Faḍā'iḥ al-bāṭiniyyah* is his famous treatise against the position of the Ismā'īlīs.[10] Another major theologian and historian of religion at this time, someone that 'Ayn al-Quḍāt undoubtedly knew and read, was Abu'l-Fatḥ Muḥammad ibn Abu'l-Qāsim 'Abd al-Karīm al-Shahrastānī (d. 548/1153). His *al-Milal wa'l-niḥal* is an encyclopedic compendium of world religions in this period. Shahrastānī was an Ash'arite theologian, and a Shāfi'ī in his legal predisposition. He entered the services of Sultan Sanjar in Khurasan and there he wrote *al-Muṣāri'ah* on Ash'arite theology. The production of a text like *al-Milal wa'l-niḥal* and the comprehensive universality of Shahrastānī's vision should not be interpreted as a sign of tolerance under the Seljūqs. The same period witnessed the appearance of Abu'l-Faraj ibn al-Jawzī's (*c.* 508/1114–597/1200) *Talbīs iblīs*, a visceral condemnation of all "heterodox" tendencies, including attractions to philosophy and a pervasive phenomenon generally dismissed as "Sufism". Be that as it may, the ultimate sign of the success of nomocentrism in 'Ayn al-Quḍāt's time was the attraction of such eminent philosophers as Imām Fakhr al-Dīn al-Rāzī (d. 606/1209) to theology.

As all other periods in the history of Islamic metaphysics, during the time of 'Ayn al-Quḍāt philosophy received the brunt of the legalistic attack against logocentrism. Shaykh Shahāb al-Dīn 'Umar Suhrawardī (d. 632/1234), a prominent Sufi, was also opposed to the philosophers and wrote *Rashf al-naṣā'iḥ al-īmāniyyah wa kashf al-faḍā'iḥ al-yūnāniyyah* in which, as the title suggests, he juxtaposed "the guidance of faith" against "the travesties of the Greeks". Almost a century before him, Abū Ḥāmid al-Ghazzālī (d. 505/1111) had issued the most damning condemnation of the philosophers in *Tahāfut al-falāsifah*.[11] The impact of al-Ghazzālī's views was so strong that even such indirect students of Ibn Sīnā as Imām Farīd al-Dīn 'Umar ibn Ghaylān al-Balkhī, who had himself studied philosophy with Abu'l-'Abbās al-Lūkarī, a student of Bahmanyār, who was an immediate student of Ibn Sīnā, joined the chorus of condemnation of philosophy. Outside the Seljūq realm, the greatest and most enduring defence of philosophy came in the eloquent voice of Ibn Rushd (520/1126–595/1198) who was born five years before 'Ayn al-Quḍāt's death. Closer to Ibn Sīnā and 'Ayn al-Quḍāt's homeland, 'Abd al-Karīm al-Shahrastānī (d. 548/1153), whose generosity of spirit had made him write a thorough chapter on philosophy in his *al-Milal wa'l-niḥal*, singled out Ibn Sīnā for an exclusive attack.[12] Anti-philosophical sentiments in 'Ayn al-Quḍāt's time extended to poetry. Sanā'ī and Khāqānī, two prominent poets of this period, among scores of others, composed heartfelt poems against the Greeks, their philosophies and the primacy of reason. They placed unconditional faith in the Prophet and his religion at the top of a hierarchy that included all that was necessary for happiness in this world and salvation in the next.

Such visceral condemnation of logocentrism in favour of a nomocentricism that had lawful answers for everything drawn from the Qur'ānic master narrative does not mean that prominent philosophers with strong political connections did not exist at the time of 'Ayn al-Quḍāt in the Seljūq period. One of the most distinguished philosophers of this period in the eastern part of the empire was Abu'l-'Abbās Faḍl ibn Muḥammad al-Lūkarī al-Marwazī who as a student of a student (Bahmanyār) of Ibn Sīnā became a major proponent of Shaykh al-Ra'īs' philosophy. Lūkarī trained a whole new generation of Peripatetic philosophers who read Ibn Sīnā closely and commented on his works extensively. In the western part of the empire, closer to 'Ayn al-Quḍāt's homeland, Abu'l-Barakāt al-Baghdādī (d. 547/1152) wrote extensively on Peripatetic philosophy, some of whose tenets he criticized. He was Jewish but converted to Islam when captured by Sultan Mas'ūd in a battle he waged against al-Mustarshid, the 'Abbasid caliph.[13] One generation after 'Ayn al-Quḍāt, Shaykh Shihāb al-Dīn Yaḥyā Suhrawardī (549/1154–587/1191) initiated a major shift in Ibn Sīnā's metaphysics and through a radical re-reading of ancient Persian sources in conjunction with Neoplatonic and Hermetic ideas founded the school of *Ishrāq* or Illumination. His radically daring expositions, and the hybrid nature of his metaphysics angered and antagonized the clerical establishment in Aleppo, and the great Ṣalāḥ al-Dīn al-Ayyūbī, anxious to secure the help of the clerics in his battles against the Crusades, had Suhrawardī executed.[14] In the same generation of Suhrawardī, but with a radically more critical mind, was another prominent philosophical theologian, Imām Fakhr al-Dīn al-Rāzī (543/1148–606/1208) who made a reputation by taking no one less than Ibn Sīnā to task and raising serious issues with his philosophical positions. A generation later, Khwājah Naṣīr al-Dīn al-Ṭūsī, while at the services of the Ismā'īlīs, in Alamut, wrote a commentary on this commentary and defended Ibn Sīnā's position, calling Rāzī's text a "diatribe" rather than a "commentary".

Philosophy was of course not the only version of the dominant logocentrism operative in this period. An array of distinguished mathematicians, biologists, physicians, astronomers and physicists carried on the work and research which had started generations earlier. Among the distinguished scientists of this period was Bahā' al-Dīn Abū Bakr Muḥammad ibn Aḥmad ibn Abī Bashar al-Kharaqī al-Marwazī (d. after 536/1141) from the Kharaq village of Marv. He wrote extensively on mathematics and theoretical astronomy. His major work in astronomy is *Muntahī al-idrāk fī taqsīm al-aflāk*. His other text on the same subject is *al-Tabṣirah fī 'ilm al-hay'ah*. Another major mathematician–astronomer of this period, at the service of Niẓām al-Mulk and the Seljūq court, was Omar Khayyām, whose just reputation as a poet supersedes his equally just reputation as a scientist and philosopher. Another major scientist of this time was Abu'l-Ḥasan 'Alī ibn Zayd al-Bayhaqī (d. 565/1164), who was known primarily as a mathematician but had a wide range of interests. He wrote a history of science and philosophy, *Tatimmah ṣiwān al-ḥikmah* as an addendum to the *Ṣiwān al-ḥikmah* of Abū Sulayman al-Manṭiqī al-Sijistānī. He wrote a three-volume textbook on astronomy in Persian, *Jawāmi' aḥkām al-nujūm*. Among his interests were history and biography. His *Tārīkh-i Bayhaq* is a compendium of historical, biographical, literary and scientific information about Bayhaqī's birthplace.

Against the grain of both logocentrism and nomocentricism of 'Ayn al-Quḍāt's time stood Sufism, which opposed and negated the reign of reason with almost the same tenacity that it challenged the exclusively legalistic interpretation of Islam. Against the logocentrism of philosophers, Sufism launched its anti-rationalist rhetoric, and against the jurists' nomocentrism it launched its critical approach. For both it proposed a theo-erotic doctrine in which "love" (*'ishq* or *maḥabbat*), "ecstasy" (*shawq*), "light" (*nūr*), "fire" (*nār*), and "unity" (*waḥdah*) are set against the categories of rational philosophy and jurisprudence. Being, in this theo-erotic vision, was of an undifferentiated unity interrupted by material creation which resulted in the separation of humanity (as lover) from God (as Beloved). The purpose of creation was the realization of this amorous urge in being. Through ascetic and ecstatic exercise (fasting, invocation, Sufi dancing, singing, poetry, etc.) human-as-lover has to emulate the moment of unison with God-as-Beloved, until such time that the final union shall occur.[15] Manṣūr al-Ḥallāj and Bāyazīd al-Bisṭāmī, the former in particular, continued to be the chief champions of generations of Sufis who propagated these ideas. Among the most prominent Sufi masters of this period were Shaykh Abū Sa'īd Abi'l-Khayr (d. 440/1048), Shaykh Abu'l-Qāsim al-Qushayrī (d. 465/1072), Khwājah Quṭb al-Dīn Mawdūd al-Chishtī (d. 527/1132), and Khwājah 'Abd Allāh Anṣārī (d. 481/1088). They wrote treatises and hagiographies, and some formed powerful orders. The power, prestige and some of the outlandish behaviour of the Sufis created much anger, anxiety and hostility among the nomocentric jurists in particular. Abu'l-Faraj ibn al-Jawzī al-Baghdādī (d. 597/1200) devoted a good portion of his *Talbīs iblīs* to condemning the Sufis and their, in his judgment, blasphemous behaviour.

Beyond the philosophers, the jurists and the Sufis, 'Ayn al-Quḍāt's intellectual world was also filled with the literary humanism of poets and literati who were principally affiliated with the various Seljūq courts. Seljūq warlords, princes, viziers and courtiers not only patronized such prominent poets as Anwarī and Sanā'ī, but themselves were occasionally first-rate poets. Poets were chief among the instruments of political legitimation. In the words of one historian of Persian literature:

> The princes of this period were eager to have prominent poets in their court. This was particularly due to the fact that poets and their powerful panegyrics were the instruments of the monarch's fame and reputation. The presence of poets, men of knowledge, and the literati was considered among the apparatus of leadership. Thus even local leaders and members of the gentry were attentive to the presence of poets at their court. Occasionally the insistence on this matter [even] led to competition among the princes.[16]

Naturally panegyrics was the most prevalent form of poetry in these, as in the previous, times. Mu'izzī (d. *c.* 521/1127), Anwarī (d. 583/1187), Ẓahīr Fāryābī (d. 598/1201), Mujīr (d. *c.* 586/1190), Athīr Akhsīkatī (d. *c.* 570/1174) and 'Imādī (d. *c.* 582/1186) were among the most prominent panegyrists of this period. The necessary complement of panegyrics was satire: the Seljūq warlords loved themselves praised almost as much as they liked their enemies and adversaries mocked, and the poets were the best instrument of this mode of effective propaganda war. Sūzanī Samarqandī (d. *c.* 562/1166) and Anwarī were prominent satirists of this period. More pious poets like Sanā'ī began to give institutional definition and authority to a mode of didactic poetry delivered for the proper edification of their royal or regular audience. Persian lyrical poetry began to take momentum from such earlier lyricists as Rūdakī and Shahīd-i Balkhī. Sanā'ī and Mu'izzī were two of the most masterful lyricists of the Seljūq period. By the middle of the sixth/twelfth century, Persian literature benefited much from the beautiful imagination of Anwarī, Ẓahīr Fāryābī, Khāqānī, Niẓamī, and Jamal al-Dīn 'Abd al-Razzāq, and the road was thus paved for the master practitioners of the genre – Sa'dī, Rūmī and Ḥāfiẓ – to crown it in the seventh/thirteenth and eighth/fourteenth centuries. Persian lyricism very soon attracted Persian Sufism and such poets as Sanā'ī, and later 'Aṭṭār, used amorous expression of "The Lover", "the Beloved", "Separation" and "Union" to construct a vision of togetherness–separation–togetherness for what they thought was a false extreme separation between God and humanity, opting for the moment in pre-eternity when God–human was not yet separated.

But perhaps the most powerful genre of Persian poetry in this period, with a wide appeal to a diverse group of readers/listeners and with an equally powerful command over the creative imagination of its composers and propagators, was narrative poetry with an irresistible urge to tell a story. Drawing from pre-Islamic Persian, Indian, Chinese, Greek and Arabic sources, a remarkable array of stories were set into an unbelievably beautiful and engaging poetry. Early in the fifth/eleventh century, 'Unṣurī rendered *Wāmiq wa 'Adhrā*, a beautiful love story, into poetry. These stories were not just the idle pastime of the courtiers. Such prominent men of science as Abū Rayḥān al-Bīrunī found them important enough to translate quite a number of them from Persian to Arabic.

One of the most beautiful pre-Islamic Iranian love stories, *Wīs wa Rāmīn* (composed in 446/1053), was translated and rendered into a hauntingly beautiful poetry by Fakhr al-Dīn As'ad Gurgānī.[17] Even the Qur'ān was not immune to poetic renditions. A singularly romantic story in the Qur'ān, *Yūsuf wa Zulaykhā*, was rendered into a full poetic narrative at the court of Shams al-Dawlah Abu'l-Fawāris Tughānshāh ibn Alb Arsalān and erroneously attributed to Firdawsī. Persian narrative poetry went through a significant period of maturation in 'Ayn al-Quḍāt's century, coming to a magnificent conclusion in the poetry of Niẓāmī, in whom were gathered Homer's taste for the epic with Shakespeare's penchant for drama. The epic poetry proper was in full swing under the Seljūqs. Under the long shadow of Firdawsī's *Shāh-nāmah*, epic poems of lesser significance but of nevertheless equal narrative attraction were composed in this period, among them *Garshāsp-nāmah* of Asadī Ṭūsī (d. 465/1072), *Bahman-nāmah* of Īranshāh ibn Abi'l-Khayr, and *Bānū gushasp-nāmah*. The last one was an imaginative story about Bānū-Gushasp, the daughter of Rustam, the chief protagonists of Firdawsī's *Shāh-nāmah*.

PHILOSOPHICAL STYLE

'Ayn al-Quḍāt was a creature of this age, full of power and energy from its inner possibilities and impediments. He was empowered to think and write in the context of a full participation in the politics of his time. He mastered philosophy and then rejected its rationalism. He mastered and practised law and then denounced its exclusive legalistic interpretation. He enjoined the Sufi sentiments and practices of his time and took full advantage of its "theo-erotic" doctrines to challenge the power-based production of merely rational or juridical knowledge. But his transformative urges, working through an ironic mode, went beyond all these diverse discourses and reached for the very act of narrativity, the mysterious urge of "Truth-telling" which he exposed and de-narrated via a deliberate, potent, and masterfully ironic mode of "writing" which is exclusively his.

Even a fuller picture of 'Ayn al-Quḍāt's time would draw a sharper image of his narrative presence in the midst of issues and anxieties that engaged him and his contemporaries. In the absence, or rather scarcity, of contemporary material about 'Ayn al-Quḍāt, we should have a rather complete picture of his time in order to be able to place him in the social and intellectual currents of his time. It is not until well into the ninth/fifteenth century, i.e., some three hundred years after the death of 'Ayn al-Quḍāt, that hagiographical material began to appear about him. The principal function of these Sufi hagiographies is to assimilate and appropriate 'Ayn al-Quḍāt into the pacific pantheon of "Persian Sufism".[18]

As already mentioned, by far the most reliable source of information about 'Ayn al-Quḍāt is the collection of his own writings. *Zubdat al-ḥaqā'iq* ("The Best of Truths") is the first text which contains considerable information about his life and writings. Not much information exists about 'Ayn al-Quḍāt between 492/1098 and 516/1122. These twenty-four years were obviously the time of prodigious learning and reflection for the young 'Ayn al-Quḍāt. There are scattered references to the titles of his writings before *Zubdah*, both in 'Ayn al-Quḍāt's own texts and in other sources. Neither the authenticity of these texts nor their content can be ascertained by these scattered references. What *is* evident, however, is that most probably 'Ayn al-Quḍāt was a prodigious and precocious child who came to scholastic fruition very early in life. He appears to have had a wide range of interests and was deeply involved in the dominant intellectual issues of his time. Again from his later writings, especially from the *Shakwā' al-gharīb* ("The Complaint of the Exile" or the *Apologia* which he wrote in his own defence while incarcerated in a prison in Baghdad), it is quite evident that he had an early, and perhaps lasting, fascination with "writing" as such. "Writing" constituted a reality *sui generis* for him. In *Shakwā'* he claims that at the writing of that *Apologia* he was beyond his youthful preoccupation with stylistic prose and masterful writing. But there are enough indications in his later writing, even, or perhaps particularly, in *Shakwā*, which indicate that he continued to be concerned with the sheer reality of writing, with the act of literary being.[19] That is why *Shakwā'*, a document which is supposed to defend him against the dangerous accusations he was charged with, begins, continues and ends with unmistakable rhetorical tropes, almost every other paragraph of the text studded with poetry. The titles of three treatises among 'Ayn al-Quḍāt's early writings point to a considerable attention to literary issues: *Risālah amālī al-ishtiāq fī layālī al-firāq* ("Dictations of Longing in the Nights of Separation"), *Nuzhat al-'ushshāq wa nahzat al-mushtāq* ("The Pleasure of Lovers and Opportunity of the Passionate") and *al-Madkhal ila'l-'arabiyyah wa riyāḍat 'ulūmuha'l-adabiyyah* ("An Introduction to Arabic and the Practice of Its Literary Sciences"). 'Ayn al-Quḍāt himself informs us, at the conclusion of *Shakwā,* that he had intended this last book to be expanded into a ten-volume introductory text on *adab*. We have no extant trace of this text, or indication of its actual accomplishment. But if it was what its title suggests, then it is a strong indication of 'Ayn al-Quḍāt's interest in the humanist institution of *adab*, which included a paramount attention to poetry, rhetoric and other aesthetic and literary devices.

Erotic lyricism was particularly attractive to 'Ayn al-Quḍāt. He informs his readers at the conclusion of *Shakwā*, where he gives a rhetorical list of his writings:

> Amongst the offspring of my thoughts are a thousand erotic verses which I was inspired to compose in ten days; these are collected together in a sheet known as *Nuzhat al-'ushshāq wa nahzat al-mushtāq* ["The Pleasures of Lovers and Opportunity of the Passionate"]. The following lines occur there:
>
> Ah, and the maiden of Ma'add descent
> On either side, the best of ancestry,
> Guarded by warriors powerful as lions
> Who raid the foe on noble, short-haired steeds,
> Furnished with tempered swords of polished steel
> And each with slender lances, true and long!
> She came, whilst my companions slept a-bed,
> Escorted by her modest maids of Sa'd;
> They trod the heights of hillocks and the vales
> To visit a generous and mighty man;
> Clad in the robes of glory and renown,
> They passed the night in soft, delightful ease,
> And I right cheerful, Hind being by my side,
> Kissing her, mantled in sweet perfumery,
> And culling with my lips the rose of her cheeks.[20]

The second extensive project that 'Ayn al-Quḍāt had in mind but was not able to complete reveals his interest, very broadly speaking, in the religious dimensions of his primarily epistemic concerns with all narrative acts of "Truth-telling". "[The] Interpretation of the Real Truths of the Qur'ān"[21] is the title that 'Ayn al-Quḍāt gives to this book. There is no extant trace of this text. But by this reference one might estimate the range of 'Ayn al-Quḍāt's concerns with all hermeneutic acts that try to break through the word to "realities" thus represented. As evidenced in his other, extant, writing, 'Ayn al-Quḍāt was particularly fascinated by the nature of revelation as the master-narrative. His interest in revelation, as evidenced in his concern with Qur'ānic hermeneutics, is matched by an equal interest in the related issue of prophethood, or, put very simply, what does it mean that someone is "chosen" (*ba'th*) to be a messenger of God to humanity and thus speak via revelation? On this latter issue, he informs the readers of *Shakwā* that in his youth he wrote a treatise on *Ghāyat al-baḥth 'an ma'nī al-ba'th* ("The Last Word on the Meaning of [Prophetic] Mission").[22] Judging from such rhetorical titles as "The Last Word" (*Ghāyat al-baḥth*) and "The Real Truths of the Qur'ān" (*Haqā'īq al-qur'ān*) one can deduce that 'Ayn al-Quḍāt had certain unconventional opinions about the issues of revelation and prophethood. The two related issues of revelation (*waḥy*) and prophethood (*ba'th*) narrowed in on 'Ayn al-Quḍāt's concern with the nature and authority of God's spoken Word (*Kalām*) as the most important issue of Islamic theology. *Kalām* is essentially a problem of language as the Qur'ānic (revelatory) instrument of "Truth-telling". God, according to the Qur'ān, "spoke" and "wrote". He taught humanity all the names of things. He taught with "the Pen". He in fact swore by "the Pen". Reading/writing/speaking/listening constitute the very narrative principles of the Qur'ān (literally *the* Recitation) as revelation. Throughout his writings, 'Ayn al-Quḍāt never lost sight of this irreducible narrativity of the revelatory nature of faith, of believing in One Unseen God, of recognizing Muḥammad as his chosen messenger, of knowing for certain that there will be a final day of judgment when this story of truth, this act of "Truth-telling", will come to an end.

Although the first extant book of 'Ayn al-Quḍāt is *Zubdah al-ḥaqā'iq*, which he wrote in 516/1122, from his introduction to this text and other references we may reconstruct the issues addressed in at least two of his pre-*Zubdah* treatises of which we have no manuscript.

We have 'Ayn al-Quḍāt's own reference in his introduction to *Zubdah al-ḥaqā'iq* that some time before or in 513/1119 he wrote a treatise he calls *al-Risālat al-'alā'iyyah*. The reason that we can narrow in on or about 512/1118 is that 'Ayn al-Quḍāt wrote *Zubdah* in 516/1122, when he was twenty-four years old and he says he wrote *Ghāyat al-baḥth* three years earlier, when he was twenty-one.[23] This puts the date of *Ghāyah* in 513/1119, and since he refers to *al-'Alā'iyyah* in an earlier part of the introduction (p. 1 of the critical edition) than the section he writes about *Ghāyah* (p. 3 of the critical edition), we *may* conclude that *al-'Alā'iyyah* was written slightly earlier than *Ghāyah*. Another, perhaps more convincing, reason that *al-'Alā'iyyah* was written shortly before *Ghāyah* is that on the very first page of *Zubdah*, immediately after the conventional salutations and prayers, he says:

> And then, this [i.e., *Zubdah*] is a spark of fire called *Zubdat al-ḥaqā'iq* which consists of the unveiling of the hidden [*Kashf al-ghiṭā'*] from the three principles which the entirety of people believe in and obey. I have divided it into one hundred chapters, each adorned with subtle points on every one of these principles. And these should be sufficient substance for those who seek the [meaning and significance of] the [three] principles of the faith, and ample material for the seekers to reach their objectives, from a [mere] knowledge of certainty to the very essence of certainty. I have already covered in "The *al-'Alā'iyyah* Treatise" which I wrote in the manner of [blessed] ancestors – May God be Pleased with them and with those who follow their path – what is necessary for the general belief of the populace in these [three] principles. But that which is exclusive to the selected few I have covered in the following chapters.[24]

We may thus tentatively conclude that both *'Alā'iyyah* (512/1118) and *Ghāyah* (513/1119) preceded by about three years the writing of *Zubdah* (516/1122).

Although we do not have any extant copy of *Ghāyah*, in his introduction to *Zubdat al-ḥaqā'iq* 'Ayn al-Quḍāt gives a synopsis of the content of this treatise. Putting for the moment aside the conventional expression of "A group of my friends, may God grant me the ability to deserve their friendship and companionship and make me succeed in performing my duties towards them as friends, were diligent in their insistence to dictate a few chapters to . . .", there are very specific references in 'Ayn al-Quḍāt's introduction to his *Zubdat al-ḥaqā'iq* to the content of his previous book. Indeed, this part of the introduction reads like an intellectual autobiography in which 'Ayn al-Quḍāt reports of his circle of friends, questions and issues with which they were concerned, and the fundamental changes that occurred in his thinking on these issues. It is also evident from 'Ayn al-Quḍāt's introduction that *Ghāyah* had introduced certain issues which are then picked up and discussed further in *Zubdat al-ḥaqā'iq*.

What are the issues that concerned 'Ayn al-Quḍāt and his contemporaries? First and foremost, a rational understanding of the nature and essence of God (*mā yantahī ilayhī naẓar al-'uqūl fi'l-'ilm bi-dhāt Allāh 'azza wa jalla*)[25] is at the centre of 'Ayn al-Quḍāt's concern, and that of his contemporaries. The expression *dhāt Allāh* must be understood as "the Essence" or "the Nature" of God, or very simply "what" God is. The formulation of the question is rather pre-emptive, which is to say it does not postulate the question of the "isness" of God for a problematic consideration, but puts forward the "howness" of that *a priori* supposition of "isness". Nevertheless the mere proposition of what "the Essence of God" is has always been a dangerous question that could be posed only with considerable risk to the questioner. Constitutional to this theoretical inquiry is 'Ayn al-Quḍāt's concern with God's "Attributes" (*Ṣifāt*), i.e., a thematic expansion of the pre-emptive question of the "howness" of God's Being. A prophetology and soteriology extend from this theology, which is to say, after the question of the "howness" of God's Being, arise the questions of His ways of communicating His Will to His created beings in a way that corresponds to His primary Attribute of Mercy (*al-Raḥmān, al-Raḥīm*) and yet does not violate His Attribute of Oneness (*waḥdah*). This constitutes the necessary intermediary status of prophethood, *al-nubuwwah*, which 'Ayn al-Quḍāt says he addressed in his *Ghāyah*. The issue of soteriology also emerges from His Attributes of Justice, i.e., the punishment of those who have disobeyed His commands and reward for those who have been obedient.

'Ayn al-Quḍāt is quite jubilant about the eloquence with which he addressed these theological and other related issues in *Ghāyah*. He also reports that there was a period of delay, perhaps even procrastination, on his part in producing *Ghāyah*, until, "I saw them [i.e., his friends] in dire need of it [i.e., of a book addressing these issues], especially in the belief in the truth of prophethood, and the truth of the Attributes with which the Creator of the heavens and earth is characterized, and I realized that attending to this matter was a rather urgent necessity."[26] 'Ayn al-Quḍāt reports that he dealt exclusively with the issue of "prophethood" in *Ghāyah*.

This is as much general information as we can deduce from 'Ayn al-Quḍāt's introduction to *Zubdat al-ḥaqā'iq* as to the content of *Ghāyah*. From the subtext of 'Ayn al-Quḍāt's narrative it is quite evident that the age-old theological question of the Essence and Attributes of God had continued well into the sixth/twelfth century and that the leading intellectuals of Hamadan, Baghdad and Isfahan (the three intellectual metropolises of the time which 'Ayn al-Quḍāt frequented) were deeply engaged with these issues. And this is not surprising, because 'Ayn al-Quḍāt wrote *Ghāyah* when he was twenty-one years old,[27] i.e., in 513/1119, which was not more than eight years after the death of the great Abū Ḥāmid al-Ghazzālī (d. 505/1111). Although al-Ghazzālī produced most of his works in the fifth/eleventh century, his monumental intellectual presence began to exert itself in the sixth/twelfth century, as indeed 'Ayn al-Quḍāt himself, as a representative intellectual of his age, testifies that he read al-Ghazzālī voraciously.[28]

MAIN WORKS

'Ayn al-Quḍāt gives the exact date of the writing of his full-length book that has reached us, *Zubdah* (516/1122), and says, and here is the irony, that it is the last book he wrote: "and the book I entitled *Zubdat al-ḥaqā'iq*," he concludes his defence in *Shakwā'*, "was the last book I composed, being then twenty-four years of age".[29] Of his writings between *Zubdat al-ḥaqā'iq* and *Shakwā' al-gharīb* I shall write momentarily. But this statement puts the date of the *Zubdah* at precisely 516/1122 when 'Ayn al-Quḍāt was twenty-four.

In his introduction to *Zubdah*, after giving a synopsis of his dealing with the question of prophethood in the *Ghāyah*, 'Ayn al-Quḍāt proceeds to give a preparatory description of why he is now writing what is in effect a sequel to that text and to the *'Alā'iyyah* treatise which he had (probably) written even earlier than the *Ghāyah*. There are many indications in this introduction that point to some major transformations in 'Ayn al-Quḍāt's epistemic assumptions and operations between the writing of the *'Alā'iyyah* treatise in (or about) 512/1118, of the composition of the *Ghāyah* in 513/1119, and the writing of *Zubdah* in 516/1122. He says that he had written the *'Alā'iyyah* treatise in the traditional manner of "the blessed ancestors", which is a code-name for the law-based narrative of Muslim jurists, which is to say, in that treatise he had addressed the three principal (doctrinal) issues of theology, or *kalām*, which centres on the principle of *tawḥīd* or the Oneness of God, prophetology (or *nubuwwah*, which is the second dogma in Islamic faith), and soteriology (or *qiyāmah*, which is the third principle of the Muslim creed) in the dominant juridical discourse. His principal occupation with these credal foundations of Islam continue from the *'Alā'iyyah* treatise to *Ghāyah*, where he specifically concentrates on the issue of prophetology but, more important, he shifts his epistemic operation from a law-based, juridical narrative to a reason-based, philosophical narrative. The key reference here, again from the introduction to *Zubdah*, is that 'Ayn al-Quḍāt's friends were asking him to address the theological question of "the knowledge of the Essence of God" in a "rational" manner (*naẓar al-'uqūl*).[30]

Zubdat al-ḥaqā'iq thus comes in fact at the conclusion of a narrative *tour de force* that has led 'Ayn al-Quḍāt from a dominant juridical discourse in the *'Alā'iyyah* treatise to the often questioned philosophical discourse in *Ghāyah* and now finally to the "theo-erotic" discourse of Sufism in the *Zubdah*. There are quite a number of indications in the introduction to *Zubdah* that support this supposition of an epistemic move away from both the juridical and rationally based approaches. Firstly, having identified the three principal doctrinal beliefs of Islam (*tawḥīd*, *nubuwwah*, *qiyāmah*), 'Ayn al-Quḍāt writes in the introduction to *Zubdah* that he has already dealt with these issues in the dominant juridical manner of "our blessed ancestors" in his *'Alā'iyyah* treatise but that now he is going to write for a selected few (*qalīl al-khawāṣṣ*), who need to be led from a mere "knowledge of certainty" (*'ilm al-yaqīn*) to the superior position of "the [very] essence of certainty" (*'ayn al-yaqīn*). Secondly, he writes that in his *Ghāyah* he was asked to address precisely the same issues from a "rational perspective" (*naẓar al-'uqūl*), but that that sort of explanation can satisfy only those who are concerned with "proofs" (*al-barāhīn*) and the "knowledge of certainty" (*'ilm al-yaqīn*). Thirdly, he writes that gaining knowledge about such issues as the Essence of God, or the nature of prophethood, or the reality of bodily resurrection through mandatory norms, laws and proofs is just like gaining an appreciation for poetry without any genuine taste (*dhawq*) for poetry. He writes.

> Indeed the confirmation [*taṣdīq*] of belief in the truth of prophethood as it is deduced from rational understanding [*al-mustafād min al-'ilm*] is similar to a kind of confirmation obtained by someone who has no taste [*dhawq*] in poetry. And of course the person who is not blessed with a taste for poetry can indeed gain [only] a belief [*'i'tiqād*] in what the tasteful person actually possesses. But that *belief* is vastly different from the specific truth which is exclusively that of a person with taste.[31]

Fourthly, 'Ayn al-Quḍāt confesses to a major intellectual transformation in his mind and spirit between 512/1118 and 513/1119, i.e., when he composed the *'Alā'iyyah* treatise and *Ghāyah*, respectively, and 516/1122, when he began to compose the *Zubdah*. He writes in 516/1122 that for quite some time, i.e., since the writing of his previous two texts, his friends (*ikhwān*, which can also mean "followers" or "admirers") had been pressing him to write a treatise for them on the principles of doctrinal beliefs more convincing than his previous ones, delivered, as they were, in the juridical and philosophical narratives, respectively. He confesses that he was unable to do as his friends demanded because he himself was deeply involved in his own studies (*idh kuntu mushtaghilan bi-taḥṣīl al-'ilm wa istifādatuhu*).[32] His nights and days, he reports, were consumed in studies. His friends gradually lost hope that he would ever fulfil their wishes. But he says he was so preoccupied with his own thoughts and feelings on these matters that he could not think of composing a treatise, or writing a book. "My heart was in a tumultuous sea with no shores, drowned in it were all the beginnings and all the ends";[33] which could very well mean a major crisis of belief in these doctrinal principles on his own part. But finally he ran into a particularly dear friend of his, or at least so goes his recollection of these events or his preferred rhetorical narrative in staging *Zubdah*, who reminded him that they had no hope other than him and that he must write a treatise for them. He finally conceded, and, having consulted the Qur'ān for a good omen (*'istikhārah*), he set out to write the *Zubdah*.[34]

He further reports that the three years between 513/1119 (the writing of the *Ghāyah*) and 516/1122 (the writing of the *Zubdah*) have been particularly revealing for him:

> When I was writing that treatise [*Ghāyah*] I was twenty-one years old, and right now I am twenty-four years old. By the grace of the Everlasting I have been blessed during these three years by a variety of hidden learnings and many precious discoveries which I am incapable of describing or explaining. Much of these, however, are impossible to render into the world of speech with letters and sounds. I shall do my best to describe in subtle expressions and proper phrases some of those [discoveries] in the following chapters.[35]

At this point 'Ayn al-Quḍāt gives an account of the reasons why he has proceeded to try to communicate his ideas despite the fact that he has to use expressions that may cause confusion among his readers:

> But the truth of the matter is that many of the expressions used in this book are extremely vague [*mutashābih*]. Thus, if you see in this book an expression which does not exactly correspond to the meaning [ordinarily] intended for it, do not launch your criticism against me because I have two obvious reasons in doing so. First, I made these references to meanings in a condition devoid of any attention to [proper] expressions and thus I did not utter them in the best possible way. Moreover, conveying such meanings in expressions which are devoid of vagueness is almost, nay indeed definitely and positively, impossible. And second, I indeed wrote these chapters for those whose concern for the ambiguity of expressions does not prevent them from grasping the truth of meanings, and because of the frequency of their dealings with rational truths they have reached a point where the ways of affinity with the sublime are not closed to them by virtue of their presence in the material world.[36]

'Ayn al-Quḍāt then proceeds to give an account of how he has now reached a point of comprehension beyond rational discourse. Given the autobiographical significance of this passage, I translate a rather larger passage from it. He begins with his preoccupation with rational discourse:

> Thus I proceeded on this path and looked at both the strengths and weaknesses of rational thought [*al-'ilm*], and wreaked both its benefits and harms until I attained what I had intended in my

> endeavour . . . But knowledge is great and life is so short that wasting it on what is of no benefit is sheer stupidity.
> My excuse in trying all the possibilities that rational thought could offer is perfectly clear: A person who is drowning reaches for anything that could possibly save his life. And only God could save me with His grace and magnanimity from falling into a hole of fire. The reason for that [state of confusion] was that I kept reading books of theology [*kutūb al-kalām*] hoping to move out of the nadir of emulation and reach the zenith of understanding. But I did not succeed in reaching my objective with those books. I became [conversely] totally confused about the principles of the faith until I doubted [my way into] the depth of such pits I cannot recount them here in this short treatise. Also, there is no benefit for the general public to hear them, because they cause great damage to small minds and weak hearts. I was totally baffled in my affair, a bafflement which utterly darkened my days until the Guide of the confused led me to the [Right] Path and His Grace helped me with subsistence and success. In short, I was not saved from falling [from grace] except, after the grace of God Almighty, by reading the books of al-Shaykh al-Imām Ḥujjat al-Islām Abū Ḥāmid Muḥammad ibn Muḥammad ibn Muḥammad al-Ghazzālī, may God be pleased with him and please him. I read him closely for almost four years and during this time of preoccupation with learning I witnessed such strange things which saved me from the path of blasphemy and misguidedness, confusion and doubt. It is not necessary to go into the details of these, because they are much too extensive and ultimately there is no use in [recounting] them.[37]

This intellectual transformation leads 'Ayn al-Quḍāt from a rational and juridical succession of discourses towards the discovery of a "theo-eroticism" as the narrative urge of his new discourse. He credits Abū Ḥāmid al-Ghazzālī's brother, Aḥmad al-Ghazzālī, as principally responsible for this transformation:

> The very essence of perception began to open little by little. I was halted in the midst of this by some major barriers which prevented me from reaching what is beyond knowledge. I remained in that condition for about a year. Later, I could not completely grasp the gravity of what had befallen me in that year until fate brought my master and my lord, al-Shaykh al-Imām al-Ajal, Ṣultān al-Ṭarīqah, Tarjumān al-Ḥaqīqah, Abu'l-Futūḥ, Aḥmad ibn Muḥammad ibn Muḥammad ibn al-Ghazzālī – may God grace the Muslims with His continued presence and grant

> him my utmost gratitude – to Hamadan which is my home town. While I was in his service, he unveiled for me in a matter of twenty days, much to my astonishment, the true meaning of that incident. And in that condition, I recognized the true meaning of what had occurred. Then something dawned on me whereby there remained nothing from me or my objective except what God willed. And now for two years I do nothing but wish for annihilation in that matter. And [only] God is He who helps in completing that of which I only saw a small portion. And if I live to be Noah's age and be annihilated in this quest, it would not be much to offer.[38]

The rhetorical phrasing of this crucial passage leaves no doubt that 'Ayn al-Quḍāt's reading of Abū Ḥāmid al-Ghazzālī was instrumental in saving him from complete and absolute blasphemy, and that his encounter with Aḥmad Ghazzālī was instrumental in converting him from a rational narrative of the philosophers to a "theo-erotic" narrative of the Sufis. The process and progression of the dominant discourses is rather normal. It was normal for 'Ayn al-Quḍāt's generation to begin their religious pre-occupations and concerns with a "traditional", law-and-order-based juridical perspective. Beyond the juridical approach stood the attractive possibilities of reason. "Reason" was the most widely celebrated alternative to the juridical approach of dogmatic learning. But beyond rational thought, when reason failed to assure and ascertain, haunting moments of doubt, unbelief and blasphemies would naturally ensue. The "theo-erotic" language of Sufism, with its comprehensivity of the oneness of Being, a unifying vision of existence that embraced and celebrated all the otherwise inexplicable tensions and anxieties of being, offered a way out of this impasse.

Two major conclusions can be made from this tentative reconstruction of the content of the *'Alā'iyyah* and the *Ghāyah*, the two pre-*Zubdah* treatises of 'Ayn al-Quḍāt which have not reached us: first, that the principal problems with which 'Ayn al-Quḍāt was concerned were the three doctrinal foundations of Islam: belief in One Omnipotent God (*tawḥīd*), the necessary intervention of a prophetic mission to communicate God's will to humanity (*nubuwwah*), and the absolute conviction in a Day of Judgment when humanity will face the Creator and be accountable for worldly actions (*ma'ād*); and, second, that the *Zubdah*, chronologically the first extant text of 'Ayn al-Quḍāt, is in fact the last "book" that he wrote in a cycle of narrative engagements with the principal doctrines of Islam which took him from a juridical account in the *'Alā'iyyah* treatise to a rational rendition in the *Ghāyah*, and finally to a "theo-erotic" version in the *Zubdah*.

It is also evident from this introduction that 'Ayn al-Quḍāt went through a major intellectual crisis, or more accurately a crisis of faith, very similar to that of Abū Ḥāmid al-Ghazzālī (as recorded in his *al-Munqidh min al-ḍalāl*), and that is probably the reason that he found the writing of al-Ghazzālī helpful in guiding him in that period of crisis. Since he uses a version of the word *al-munqidh* in his description of his being saved from that crisis of faith, one may conclude that whether consciously or subconsciously he had al-Ghazzālī's *al-Munqidh min al-ḍalāl* in mind when writing this sentence. *Al-Munqidh min al-ḍalāl* ("Deliverance from Misguidedness") is al-Ghazzālī's autobiographical account of his crisis of faith.[39] Because of this rather tumultuous period of crisis, 'Ayn al-Quḍāt had a rather difficult time bringing himself to writing a sustained treatise. The *Zubdah* is in fact the last such sustained treatise that he wrote. 'Ayn al-Quḍāt's writings after the *Zubdah* are characteristically of a non-book type, principally in the rhetorical tropes of "personal letters". Both *Maktūbāt,* his collection of "letters", and the *Tamhīdāt,* a collection of letter-like "prefaces" or "preparations", are quite deliberately non-books. *Shakwā' al-gharīb,* his last writing, is in fact the text of a defence he delivered to clear himself against charges that the clerics had brought against him, and thus it is not a "book" [*al-kitāb*] or a "treatise" [*al-risālah*] in the ordinary sense of the term.

The *Zubdah* is the culmination of 'Ayn al-Quḍāt's metaphysical concern with the principal doctrines of the Islamic faith – *tawḥīd, nubuwwah* and *ma'ād* – delivered in a "theo-erotic" language of love that effectively substitutes the rhetorics of love, devotion and annihilation in the God-Beloved for both the rigid nomocentricism of law and the futile misplacedness of reason in a logocentricism which is faith-bound. In the one hundred short chapters (*faṣl*) of the *Zubdah,* 'Ayn al-Quḍāt experiments with the limits of such metarational categories as *kashf* ("revelation" or "discovery") and *dhawq* ("taste" or "disposition") in order to reach for an "understanding" of the principal doctrines of the faith beyond what reason and the law can offer. In his judgment, the principal point of contention in every "revealed" religion is precisely the nature of that "revelation", or, very simply, how can one believe that a "prophet" or a "messenger" can come up with a "revelation"? What does it mean that some ordinary people have been given this "message" by "God" to convey to others? 'Ayn al-Quḍāt divides people into four categories in relation to the central problem of "revelation". Firstly, there is a group of people who do not need to rely on the confirmation of the possibility of "revelation" by rational argumentation; secondly, those who do rely on such arguments but in doing so they simply follow the lead of the established authorities in different schools of thought; thirdly, those who do need such rational argumentations but need to draw them themselves; and finally, fourthly, those who equally pursue theoretical knowledge (*al-'ilm al-naẓarī*) in believing in such doctrines as "revelation" and yet they look forward to realities beyond "knowledge" (*al-'ilm*) and "reason" (*al-'aql*), as in "discovery" (*kashf*) or "taste" (*dhawq*) for example, in reaching that certainty.[40] 'Ayn al-Quḍāt's preference is obviously for the last category, and indeed the *Zubdah* is a sustained assimilation of the two subjective categories of "taste" and "discovery" into a systematic theology that tries to account for "revelation". The word *'ārif* signifies for 'Ayn al-Quḍāt the personification of "taste" and "discovery" as two supra-rational instruments of understanding. He postulates the existence of God (*wujūd Allāh*) as the ontological origin of everything that there is. But the ontic reality of God is beyond the reach of human grasp. This postulation is then the epistemic assumption (or more accurately a sustained problematic) upon which 'Ayn al-Quḍāt begins to construct his own ontology. There is nothing particularly revolutionary about 'Ayn al-Quḍāt's ontology. It remains essentially Ibn Sīnan in such basic categories as *al-qadīm* (the pre-eternal), *al-ḥādith* (the-created-in-time), *al-kāmil* (the perfect), *al-nāqis* (the imperfect), *al-wāḥid* (the unified), *al-kathīr* (the diversified), etc. God's Names (*Asmā'*) and Attributes (*Ṣifāt*) are the primary categories of His definition. 'Ayn al-Quḍāt is cautious not to make God's existence, however, contingent upon His Names and Attributes.

The ontic reality of God is not by virtue of a Name, *Allāh*, or an Attribute, *al-Raḥīm*, referring to and signifying His reality:

> The nominal Name is constructed in order to lead to that Pearl [*al-durrah*] [of the Unity of God], not because of its relationship to existent beings which have [themselves] emanated from it, but by virtue of its very essence [*dhatuhā'*], by virtue of seeing it as existent. And if somebody calls that Pearl "pre-eternal" [*qadīmah*], then he calls it so by virtue of seeing it as different from other beings which are in need of a cause to bring them into being. And the same is true if you consider the Names al-Ḥayy ["The Living"] and al-Ḥaqq ["The Truth"], you realize that one has created these [expressions] with an eye towards the "death" of the other and its "un-truthfulness".[41]

The deduction of such binary oppositions, e.g. between "The Living" and "The Dead", is a typical 'Ayn al-Quḍāt trope whereby he de-signifies the words from their ordinary assumptions. The Name *al-Ḥaqq* ("The Truth") thus has nothing quintessentially representative about it. It has significance only to the degree that it stands in opposition to "un-truthfulness".

'Ayn al-Quḍāt is quite anxious in his *Zubdah* to "prove" such credal doctrines of Islamic theology as God's knowledge of the specifics,[42] and the non-contingent nature of that knowledge, i.e. that, like the sun's rays, it is irrelevant whether or not the earth is capable of receiving all of it. It is and it shines.[43] But this "proving" is always through a mode of narrative constitutionally different from the dominant metaphysics of Reason and/or law. Beyond "discovery" (*kashf*) and "taste" (*dhawq*), 'Ayn al-Quḍāt postulates *baṣīrah* ("perception") as yet another metarational agency of grasping the nature of God. *Al-Baṣīrah* begins to operate when *al-'aql* ("reason") cannot any more. There are theoretical intricacies (*ghawāmiz al-naẓariyyah*) that "reason" cannot grasp but "perception" can.[44] 'Ayn al-Quḍāt argues that *al-baṣīrah* is in fact something like the rational faculty itself, or the ability to see or the taste for poetry. Those who do not have them do not know how they work. The difference between a "philosopher" (*al-'ālim*) and a "knower" (*'ārif*) is that a philosopher can partake of truth only as something which is "known" (*ma'lūm*), whereas the *'ārif* partakes in "the beauty of truth" (*jamāl al-ḥaqq*), and by virtue of this pleasure/understanding he has an overwhelming ecstasy (*shawq 'aẓīm*) towards God.[45]

Uns is yet another virtue, or force in 'Ayn al-Quḍāt's counter-metaphysics, by which he identifies the nature of the *'ārif*'s grasp of truth. *Uns*, rather difficult to translate, has a range of meanings pointing to a comfortable and intimate, habitual and frequent, relationship between two persons or a person and an object. To have *uns* with someone means to have grown to like the cosy companionship of that person. 'Ayn al-Quḍāt suggests that the *'ārif*, as opposed to the philosopher, or the person who operates through reason, gets used to (*uns*) beholding the beauty of the Divine Presence. Then whatever increases human *uns* with heavenly concerns subverts one's *uns* with the material world.[46] *Kashf* (discovery), *dhawq* (taste), *baṣīrah* (perception), *uns* (companionship) are thus modes of subtle counter-thoughts, or counter-intelligibilities, which define an *'ārif* and distinguish him from a rationalistic philosopher.

This leads 'Ayn al-Quḍāt to three hierarchically ordered epistemic positions *vis-à-vis* the knowledge of the existence of God or *īmān*: firstly, *al-ma'rifah*, which means "knowing" in the most intimate sense of the term and ought to be distinguished from *'ilm* or "knowledge", which is not even in the hierarchy; secondly, *al-walāyah*, which means "friendship" or "companionship", and which is a higher form of "knowing" God; and, thirdly, *al-nubuwwah*, which means "prophethood" and which constitutes the most intimate "knowing" of God with certainty.[47]

Kashf, *dhawq*, *baṣīrah*, *uns* and a number of other, related, terms constitute the principal vocabularies of 'Ayn al-Quḍāt's soft metaphysics, deliberately postulated against the hard metaphysics of law and reason which determined the narrative tropes of Islamic jurisprudence and Islamic philosophy, respectively.[48] The soft counter-metaphysics of 'Ayn al-Quḍāt is formulated deliberately and consciously against the hard metaphysics of logocentrism that particularly with the advance of Greek philosophy cross-countered Islamic nomocentrism and created a binary opposition between reason and law in the two opposing/apposing faces of Islamic metaphysics. The tripartite theocentric epistemology that ʿAyn al-Quḍāt postulates – *al-maʿrifah*, *al-walāyah* and *al-nubuwwah* – is construed with reference to such counter-intelligibilities as *baṣīrah*, *ʿirfān* and *uns*, all replacing the hard metaphysics of reason and law with the soft metaphysics of a "theo-erotic" nature. Love (*al-ʿishq*) is in fact the defining/dividing factor that separates *baṣīrah* from *ʿaql*. Only *baṣīrah* can grasp the conditions (*aḥwāl*) of love (*ʿishq*), whereas reason (*al-ʿaql*) cannot understand anything but forms of knowledge (*al-ʿulūm*).[49] In ʿAyn al-Quḍāt's "theo-erotic" opposition to the metaphysics of reason and law, "love" is the supreme defining factor that constitutes the relationship between person-as-lover and God-as-Beloved.[50] ʿAyn al-Quḍāt is determined that there is a mode (*ṭawr*) of understanding (*idrāk*) which is beyond reason:

> Whoever has been blessed with the pleasure of this mode, his reason is rendered blind by virtue of its disability to grasp the truth of the First and comprehend the truth of His Attributes. The last universe from the rationally understood universes is the recognition of reason that there are many things that it does not understand. This inability is the vanguard of what lies beyond in that mode which is beyond reason. The final frontiers of the mode of reason are linked to the first frontiers of the mode which is beyond it. As for [example] the last frontiers of the recognition of good from evil [*al-tamyīz*] is connected to the first frontiers of reason. Among the characteristics of a person of rational knowledge [*al-ʿālim*] is that when he or she has reached perfection in knowledge [*ʿilm*] he or she knows for certain that it is impossible to grasp the Everlasting Truth [*al-Ḥaqīqat al-azaliyyah*].[51]

In order to postulate a mode of understanding beyond reason, ʿAyn al-Quḍāt always "reasons" by referring to a state below reason, as for example in the passage I just quoted where he says that the last frontiers of *al-tamyīz*, a simple recognition of good from evil, refers to the first frontiers of reason. Elsewhere, he postulates *al-wahm* ("fantasy" or "the estimative faculty") as a state beneath reason. He suggests that as *al-wahm* cannot grasp its real inability to grasp rational intelligibilities, so does reason not truly understand that it cannot comprehend "the truth of the Truth" and "the truth of His Attributes".

From this anti-rationalistic, "counter-metaphysics" of "theo-eroticism", ʿAyn al-Quḍāt proceeds to address such seminal theological problems as the pre-eternity or createdness of the world,[52] or the contingent reality of all created beings.[53] In one of the most compelling narrative strategies of the *Zubdah*, 'Ayn al-Quḍāt constructs the image of a mirror wherein external objects are reflected. As the image in the mirror, *ipso facto*, points to a pre-existing reality *a priori* to it, this (material) world should be considered as a mere mirror image of a supernal reality beyond itself.[54] Another typical example of how 'Ayn al-Quḍāt subverts the reigning rationality-based discourse of his time is his suggestion that the priority of God over existent beings is not a "temporal priority" (*qabliyyah zamāniyyah*) but a priority in "essence" (*al-dhāt*) and "nobility" (*al-sharaf*). In a passage remarkably reminiscent of Plato's *Phaedo*, 'Ayn al-Quḍāt argues for the immortality of the human soul, that it has existed before entering the body, that it has then entered the body and that it will survive after its separation from the body.

> You ought to know that the human mind does not grasp the true nature of the soul, except such aspects of it which are evident in the body and its attributes, such as the fact that it understands and that it prompts action. In these two attributes, all animal species are identical. But it [i.e., the human intellect] does not understand its continuity [i.e., the continuity of the soul] after its departure from the body, while it may be grasped through theoretical observation in a rational way. Because the soul is the locus of all knowledge and knowledge is not divisible, and thus the division of its locus is unimaginable. And whatever is like that cannot disintegrate. And as for the supposition that it exists before [entering] the body, no one has been able to provide a convincing proof which is beyond suspicion and doubt. The problem with the rational people in that respect goes back to their lack of proper expressions to convey that meaning. And as for their supposition that it is found in the body, and that the body is a pre-condition, a causal factor, for its existence, that is [entirely] wrong. That it changes its condition when entering the body is perfectly evident. The fact of the matter is that the soul exists before entering the body. That is perfectly clear to me. But I cannot explain this in such a way that aborts all possibilities of doubt and reversal. And my guess is that whoever understands this is equally at pains to explain what he understands. This opinion of mine, I have not reached in its entirety by virtue of any observations of rational proof and logical argumentation. Except for the fact that rational observations, as elaborated in logical observations of theoretical sources, have considerably helped me [in this respect]. To the degree that it is possible to elaborate in this short treatise, [I might say] that the reason for the existence of the soul [before entering the body] is due to its supreme causality which is in existence before it enters the body,

> and that the cause and the caused are [both] in it. Certainly, its operation in the body is contingent upon the existence of certain specific conditions, and it does not come-into-being (*yūjad*) except after the existence of such conditions.[55]

The *Zubdah* is thus a remarkably condensed text, culminating in 'Ayn al-Quḍāt's brilliant formulation of a "theo-erotic" epistemics deliberately and in detail postulated against the reigning rational tendency of philosophy. As the last book written on the principal doctrinal beliefs of Islam, the *Zubdah* is an historical testimony to the creative imagination and the theoretical prowess of its author. The *Zubdah* testifies not only to his brilliant command of the whole juridical and philosophical traditions developed by his time, but, more important, to his rare analytical capabilities to formulate theoretical positions. The *Zubdah* is indeed a revolutionary manifesto for a radically different epistemics that introduces a whole new spectrum of phenomenological sensibilities in "understanding". That that epistemic revolution remains constitutionally theocentric, that it is put whole-heartedly at the service of "proving" the Islamic credal doctrines via a phenomenological hermeneutics radically different from, and subversive to, the reigning rational approaches of his time, does not, in any significant way, detract anything from the serious viability of its major propositions. One must, as Eco argued about Aquinas, be able to disentangle 'Ayn al-Quḍāt's theoretical formulations, particularly his epistemology, from his theocentric mode of narrative in the *Zubdah*. Soon after the *Zubdah*, as I shall demonstrate presently, he will surpass that theocentricity, and the twin problematics of knowing-and-telling become paramount in his writings. Operating within the general doctrinal mandates of his faith, in the *Zubdah* 'Ayn al-Quḍāt transcends both the legalistic approach of the juridical tradition and the rational one of the philosophical, and yet ultimately remains in the *Zubdah* within the theocentric confinements of his ancestral faith. The introduction to the *Zubdah* leaves no doubt that both the nomocentrism of law and the logocentrism of philosophy had left 'Ayn al-Quḍāt totally dissatisfied and indeed abandoned him desperately in a critical state of doubt and confusion. In the *Zubdah* he found and formulated a mode (*al-ṭawr*) of thought-as-being beyond that of reason.[56] As perhaps the most theoretically consistent and sustained text produced on the defining terms of his revolutionary epistemic mode, the *Zubdah* was the zenith of what could still be called "Islamic" imagination. This he achieved when he was twenty-four. Still he had a long and productive life ahead of him. That long and productive life was cut brutally short by the political circumstances of his life. But before that tragic end he still managed to go beyond this zenith of Islamic sacred imagination, he still managed to explore "modes" of thought-as-being beyond what he had done in the *Zubdah*. The conclusion of the *Zubdah* in 516/1122 coincided with the commencement of his extensive writings in the form, or "mode", of "letters", and it is to his "letters" that I now would like to turn our attention.

THE LETTERS

Both in the *Zubdah* (516/1122) and in the *Shakwā'* (525/1131), 'Ayn al-Quḍāt himself asserts that the *Zubdah* is the last book he ever wrote. Three scholars, A. J. Arberry, A. 'Usayrān and A. Zarrīnkūb, have actually accused 'Ayn al-Quḍāt of "approximating the truth" (i.e., lying) in this respect in the *Shakwā'* in particular for fear of his life.[57] They suggest that 'Ayn al-Quḍāt deliberately did not refer to his *Maktūbāt* and *Tamhīdāt* in his "apologia" in order not to add more ammunition at the disposal of his enemies. An alternative reading of these two passages in the *Zubdah* and the *Shakwā'* is that 'Ayn al-Quḍāt in fact means what he says, that after the *Zubdah* he did not write any "book" in the ordinary sense of the term. While it may be supposed that in the *Shakwā'*, written in 525/1131 in a prison in Baghdad, 'Ayn al-Quḍāt suppressed the existence of his *Maktūbāt* and *Tamhīdāt* for fear of adding to his problems, that supposition is seriously challenged by the fact that as he was defending himself in the *Shakwā'*, 'Ayn al-Quḍāt does not for once conceal his utter contempt for his accusers. It is possible to take 'Ayn al-Quḍāt's remarks at their face value and assume that he did not consider either his "letters" or his "preparations" as "books" in the ordinary sense of the term. The chief characteristics of 'Ayn al-Quḍāt's *Maktūbāt* and the *Tamhīdāt* is that (1) they are identical in their narrative, i.e., the "chapters" of the *Tamhīdāt* read almost exactly like "the letters" of the *Maktūbāt*; (2) they are not in "book" form, i.e., each individual "letter" or "chapter" can be read almost independently (and there are as many cross-references among the "chapters" of the *Tamhīdāt* as there are among "the letters" of the *Maktūbāt*); and (3) they both break radically loose from all the dominant metanarratives of Islamic metaphysical Truth-telling and relentlessly search for an autonomous, individual, irreducibly self-conscious narrativity. The assumption that the *Tamhīdāt* "is in a sense the same as the *Zubdah* in a different expression – more expanded and more poetic"[58] is utterly incorrect. In their basic narrative strategies, both the *Tamhīdāt* and the *Maktūbāt* break radically from the *Zubdah*. One of the political strategies of subsequent "mystical" readings of 'Ayn al-Quḍāt has been to whitewash all the crucial internal developments in 'Ayn al-Quḍāt's thinking and writing tropes. It is imperative to date his writings and carefully distinguish between one text and another. Otherwise, not only 'Ayn al-Quḍāt's diversified modes of writing but some fourteen hundred years of vigorous intellectual debates and developments are packed together and appropriated as "Persian Sufism".

Between 517/1123 and 525/1130 'Ayn al-Quḍāt wrote a substantial but unknown number of "letters". These "letters" constitute a remarkable narrative strategy radically different from 'Ayn al-Quḍāt's other writings, and in their rhetorical tropes entirely their own. While these "letters" contain some insightful references to 'Ayn al-Quḍāt's personal and public life, they are essentially a series of short treatises on thematic issues. He selects a subject, e.g. "intentionality", and writes a series of "letters", not just one, on it. There are references to actual, historical persons in these "letters", such as Kāmil al-Dawlah or 'Azīz al-Mustawfī, two of his most devoted and influential friends. But that is not an indication that these historical persons were the sole addressees of these letters. In fact, 'Ayn al-Quḍāt himself is quite emphatic in one of his "letters" that he has a larger audience in mind, extended into the future, for these "letters", and indeed the extant manuscripts of 'Ayn al-Quḍāt's "letters" indicate that subsequent generations reproduced them with a liberal attitude as to their number and/or content. There is no way to ascertain the number of 'Ayn al-Quḍāt's "letters". At one point in the *Tamhīdāt* he says that he wrote "volumes" of letters to his friends and acquaintances.[59] One anthology of his letters in Istanbul contains 127 "letters", another 67.[60] Quite a number of these anthologies have no date of preparation, which is a typical way of dehistoricizing these texts and collectively assimilating them into a grand mystical metanarrative. The few extant dated anthologies of manuscripts of these "letters", however, do indicate that from the fourth decade of the seventh/thirteenth century onwards a growing number of texts were produced that contained samples of 'Ayn al-Quḍāt's "letters". In the Sipahsalār Library in Tehran there is an anthology, dated 638/1240, which is the oldest extant manuscript found so far. This anthology contains only six letters of 'Ayn al-Quḍāt. The most recent dated manuscript is in the Bibliothèque Nationale in Paris; it was prepared in 1025/1616 and contains ninety-eight "letters". The editors of a critical edition of these letters believe that this manuscript was copied from an undated anthology now kept in the National Library in Tehran.[61] If we disregard all the extant but undated manuscripts and consider the two oldest and most recent dated collections, we see that, starting from the seventh/thirteenth century, there is an increased interest in 'Ayn al-Quḍāt's "letters", an "interest" which indicates a persistent appropriation of 'Ayn al-Quḍāt by active Sufis. The seventh/thirteenth century, with the presence of Jalal al-Dīn Rūmī (d. 672/1273) and Ibn 'Arabī (d. 638/1240) and his Persian followers, was in fact the height of mystical imagination. After Rūmī, there appears to be an increased interest in 'Ayn al-Quḍāt's "letters" among the Turkish Sufis.

The presence of Rūmī, and later his legacy, among the Turkish-speaking Sufi communities in Asia Minor probably acted as a catalyst in assimilation of 'Ayn al-Quḍāt, and particularly his "letters", into the mystical tradition. In 668/1269 a collection of 'Ayn al-Quḍāt's "letters" was prepared in what is identified as "Turkish *naskh*"[62] and by someone "who did not know Persian quite well".[63] This scribe also ventured to summarize some of 'Ayn al-Quḍāt's "letters". This trend continued until the middle of the eighth/fourteenth century, when another scribe, who identifies himself as Yūnus ibn Shādī ibn Walī al-Dīn Mawlawī (obviously a Mevlevi Sufi), prepared an anthology of sixty-four "letters" of 'Ayn al-Quḍāt between Jumādā II, 733/February–March 1333, and Shawwāl 762/August–September 1361. This scribe also produced a verbatim, interlineal, Turkish translation of fourteen of the sixty-four "letters", presumably intended for some young Turkish novices who did not know Persian. The beautiful calligraphy and the red ink used for Qur'ānic and *Ḥadīth* passages may indicate the interest of a wealthy and/or powerful patron in the production of this anthology. The inclusion of Aḥmad al-Ghazzālī's letters to 'Ayn al-Quḍāt in some manuscripts, such as in the one produced in 853/1449 and now kept in the Mullā Murād Library in Istanbul, testifies to the textual institutionalization of a sustained dialogue between the two and symbolic configuration of a pantheon of "Persian Sufis".[64]

Despite this massive appropriation of these "letters" into a monolithic "Sufi tradition", a closer reading of them reveals a rather different picture. In their very narrative strategy, 'Ayn al-Quḍāt's "letters" are implicit (and thus effective), rhetorical subversions of "book" (*al-kitāb*) and "treatise" (*al-risālah*) as the dominant metaphysical forms of Truth-telling. It is almost impossible to attend to "the content" of these "letters" without a simultaneous attention to their preferred narrative strategy: a simultaneous attention which must inevitably lead to the final destruction of the presumed binary opposition between "content" and "form". Developed over a relatively extended period of time, i.e., between 517/1123 and 525/1130, these "letters" are the last and final choice of 'Ayn al-Quḍāt for his preferred narrative. *Zubdat al-ḥaqā'iq*, with qualifications which I identified in the preceding passages, was the last "book" that 'Ayn al-Quḍāt wrote as the culmination of his relentless engagement with, for him, the "classical" mode of addressing the supreme metaphysics of Truth-telling.

'Ayn al-Quḍāt achieves a narrative voice in his "letters" unlike anything else in the long, rich and diversified history of intellectual activities to which as a Muslim of extraordinary learning he had access. The first and foremost narrative feature of these "letters" is precisely their preferred rhetorical choice of "personal letters", that they are written in a specific context, that they defy and subvert the metaphysics of anonymity which informs and authorizes the entire spectrum of "knowledge" he had inherited. 'Ayn al-Quḍāt is quite emphatic in pointing out that "it was Monday, the seventeenth of Muḥarram. I wrote a short passage to my student", or "this letter, I wrote on the eve of Saturday [i.e., on Friday evening], after the evening prayer [just to inform you] of [my] good health and fortune. Yesterday, which was the first of Muḥarram, I received a letter from that dear brother, may God increase his days."[65] This insistence on temporality gives 'Ayn al-Quḍāt's "letters" a peculiar kind of temporal "authenticity" absent in the dominant modes of Truth-telling in most of the established (nomocentric, logocentric or even theo-erotic) discourses. As in most traditions of power-basing narratives, the effacement of temporality is one of the principal modes of universalizing an otherwise perfectly particular vision of reality.

Writing "letters" was of course nothing new in the Persian or Islamic intellectual traditions. The most distinguished intellectual of 'Ayn al-Quḍāt's generation, Abū Ḥāmid al-Ghazzālī's brother, Aḥmad, whom 'Ayn al-Quḍāt had met, admired and corresponded with, in fact wrote letters to 'Ayn al-Quḍāt. There is indeed a whole genre of *Makātīb al-'urafā'* with which 'Ayn al-Quḍāt's letters are identified. Abū Ḥāmid al-Ghazzālī himself wrote quite a number of "letters" to Seljūq warlords, advising them on matters of politics and statecraft. But there is something peculiar to 'Ayn al-Quḍāt's "letters" which is absent in others, and that is the gradual but persistent vibration of a personal voice fully conscious, self-conscious even, of the subjectivity, temporality and, most significant of all, narrativity of his voice. 'Ayn al-Quḍāt is self-consciously present in his narratives as no one else is willing to face or admit that central presence.

Central to the temporality of 'Ayn al-Quḍāt's self-conscious narrative in his "letters" is a full and rare unresoluteness about its movements that precisely in its unresoluteness discloses the constructability of all narrative acts. Through his narrative disclosure of the temporality of his own act of "telling", 'Ayn al-Quḍāt discloses the temporal reality of *all* acts of "telling", and, *a fortiori*, all temporal acts of Truth-telling that hide behind a metaphysics of atemporality. But even more important, through this narrative disclosure of the physical temporality of "telling", 'Ayn al-Quḍāt reveals the irreducible temporality of all cognitions of *being*, if they were only not subverted, distorted and concealed behind the reigning demands of the metaphysics of atemporality. Thus, through the transparent temporality of 'Ayn al-Quḍāt's narrative, not only all metaphysical acts of Truth-telling, but with them that metaphysics itself and ultimately the "Being" which is postulated by it are all transformed. Here is a good example:

> You ought to know, my dear friend, may God increase your days and by His grace grant you what you wish, that that statement

> which I wrote to you in addition to this one on the subject of the endowment that [our mutual friend] Kāmil [al-Dawlah] has made, is an unbelievable piece of writing. Since yesterday that I wrote that piece, a number of times it has occurred to me to tear it into pieces, for reasons which I am not at liberty to mention. Today I consulted [the Holy Text], whether or not to send it, both on Fatḥah's grave and on Ṭāhir's. I thought perhaps to write you something else, less subject to misinterpretation. It is thus that I write you this letter. I hope that from [my] pen shall come [only] what is best for you and me, and for all Muslims.[66]

Such rhetorical suppositions as "I would have", "if I could have", or "only if I could I would have" are conditional phrases with which 'Ayn al-Quḍāt both constitutes and at the same time subverts his own subjectivity. Central to the subjectivity of 'Ayn al-Quḍāt's narrative is his consistent self-consciousness of the existential individuality of his perceptions. 'Ayn al-Quḍāt in effect takes the overwhelming temporality of his narrative and works it through a conscious recognition of the existential nature of all acts of "telling", including the supreme act of Truth-telling before it has taken refuge, for fear of being recognized as yet another act of "telling", behind the metaphysics of primordiality, atemporality. That metaphysics that informs everything in the "Islamic" intellectual traditions, from the logocentricism of "Islamic philosophy" to the nomocentricism of "Islamic law", the theo-eroticism of "Islamic mysticism", and I even dare say the humanism of Persian and Arabic traditions of *adab*, is what is radically suspended in this self-conscious subjectivity of 'Ayn al-Quḍāt's preferred rhetoric of "letter-writing".

Equally central to the very self-conscious narrativity of 'Ayn al-Quḍāt's preferred mode of writing, the fact that he is alert to the "telling" nature (whether written or vocal) of all claims to "Truth", is a prose that moves by a dialectic energy generated by the active divestment of its own highly alert rhetoric. 'Ayn al-Quḍāt is the master practitioner of making his own writing actively alert to its written-ness. The result of this prose, highly alert to its temporality, subjectivity and narrativity, is the generation and sustenance of an almost audible "voice" that in its potent poeticity "shatters", to use Heidegger's expression, the thick walls of the presiding metaphysics of Truth-telling.

The subjectivity of 'Ayn al-Quḍāt's narrative in his letter-writing is thoroughly contingent on his insistence to place his letters in time, space, occasions, frames of very specific reference:

> In the Name of God, the Merciful, the Compassionate. Praise be to God, the Giver of Reason and Life, so excellent is His giving. Yesterday, Thursday, the eleventh of Rabīʿ al-Awal, I wrote a letter to that dear brother, may God lengthen his life and may

> He show him the path of salvation, on the issue concerning certain questions that you had raised, about which I have remained silent. Concerning that issue, there is much to be said. But yesterday, when I received your letter, I felt really depressed, so I wrote very briefly. Today, somebody kindly asked me for a letter. So I thought of writing something for him. Since I had already started the letter, I thought to finish it. Of course I do not know what I will end up writing![67]

This pre-emptive suspension of intentionality in writing gives writing a reality *sui generis* quite independent of the will of the author. There are innumerable occasions in his "letters" where 'Ayn al-Quḍāt writes that he is not completely in charge of his writings, that writing itself is a reality *sui generis*.

Equally constitutional to that radical subjectivity is 'Ayn al-Quḍāt's penchant for using the act of writing itself, from the letters of the alphabet to sentence structures, as the verisimilitudes of being:

> If someone wants to learn the Qur'ān, they must necessarily be taught the letters of the alphabet. Their learning [the Qur'ān] is contingent upon learning these letters. The teacher will teach them A, B, C [etc.]. It is perfectly evident that if the letter "A" is not [taught] first, it does not make any difference. The objective shall nevertheless be reached. It is perfectly possible to start with the letters "T", "U" or "K", to the end, in whatever way that they are presented. It is possible to start [the teaching of the alphabet] with any letter. It does not make any difference what "letter" a child is taught first. What *is* important is to teach the alphabet. But it is not necessary to start with "A" or "T", "N"or "U". You can do it in a reverse order. There is a point here that if you search the whole world you will not hear it from anybody [else].[68]

He then takes this example and applies it to the very heart of Islamic juridical laws concerning prayers, fasting, etc., with a full intention of exposing the decidability of such juridical mandates.

'Ayn al-Quḍāt's ultimate objective in such deliberate breakdowns of habitual conformities is to alert his readers to the artificiality of all binary oppositions:

> My dear! Suppose someone is in his entire being in love with knowledge; spending his days and nights doing nothing but seeking knowledge. If he loves pens, paper, ink and ink-case, you cannot say that he is not entirely in love with knowledge. Quite to the contrary! The Beloved cannot necessarily be but one. There is nothing wrong with loving other things so far as they

> are loved by virtue of [their relatedness to] the beloved. If man loves God, he necessarily loves His messenger, and loves his own guide [*pīr*], and loves his own life and health, and loves eating and drinking, because they sustain his life, and he loves [his] wealth, by means of which he attains his daily sustenance. He also necessarily loves the cold and the warm weather, the snow, the rain, the sky and the earth. Because were it not for the earth, the wheat will not grow. So he loves the farmer too. This is so far as the philosophers [*'uqalā'*] see it. Put in other terms, someone who is in love, loves the place where his beloved lives; and the whole world is His House; and he loves the handwriting, the artefact and the written compositions of the person he loves, and the whole world is His handwriting and his written composition. Indeed everything is just Him. Let me put it even more bluntly. Once there was an army going on an expedition against the infidels. Abu'l-'Abbās al-Qaṣṣāb turned to them and said, "O, if I could only sacrifice my life for that infidel whom you are going to kill for Him!" If the wishes of the beloved are to burn a letter that she has written to her lover, then the lover must necessarily burn that letter. And here no one can say that a disrespect has been demonstrated against the letter of the beloved, because [the lover] has done as the beloved has wished. And this is a great calamity! If the Chosen One, peace be upon him, and Abū Bakr eliminated the infidels who were against Him, they simply obeyed His commands. They meant to make Him happy with themselves. Otherwise a lover has no business interfering in the rule of the beloved. And that indeed is a long story. Peace and salutations [upon you]. Praise be to God, the Lord of both worlds, and peace and benedictions be upon His best creation, Muḥammad, and all his relatives![69]

The burning of the letter or message of the beloved here could not have been lost to critical readers of 'Ayn al-Quḍāt, as to what exact message, letter or book he specifically had in mind.

Even when 'Ayn al-Quḍāt engages in familiar theoretical debates he does so in his own radically transformative way, in a constantly moving epistemic roller-coaster that does not yield to any narrative authority. In one of his long letters, for example, he engages in the vexed problem of theodicy. He addresses his reader and refers to a previous letter in which he had said that the theological position of the Qadarites (those who believe in free will as opposed to predestination) has been distorted, that originally their position was perfectly correct and that gradually the successive generations of interpreters have distorted their original position. The current, i.e., 'Ayn al-Quḍāt's time, Qadarite position is that

God cannot be the cause of evil. 'Ayn al-Quḍāt says this is blasphemy because it necessitates another God, "which is the religion of the Zoroastrians ['Ayn al-Quḍāt uses the derogatory term of *gabr* for Zoroastrians], who believe in Yazdān and Ahrīman". And the Qadarites are the Zoroastrians among my followers, "[a presumed prophetic statement] refers to this [fact]".[70]

Through a reconstruction of what he considers to be the "original" position of the Qadarites, 'Ayn al-Quḍāt postulates six principles by which the problem of theodicy may be resolved. The first principle by which 'Ayn al-Quḍāt commences his "letter" concerning the problem of theodicy is, typically, a linguistic proposition. When a word or an expression or a signifier refers to more than one signified, and one of those signified is a wrong proposition, then one can very easily be confused. The expression "to bring to life a dead person", 'Ayn al-Quḍāt suggests,[71] has a literal meaning, that is to say, what the expression "literally means, and [then] it has a symbolic meaning, which is to say when God turns an ignorant person into a person of knowledge". There are variations and modifications on how a signifier can be "multi-significatory" (*mushtarik al-dilālah*) which does not concern 'Ayn al-Quḍāt here. Usually, 'Ayn al-Quḍāt insists, it is from the context of the signifier that the exact signified is understood. Nevertheless when we receive an expression which is multi-significatory, and one of its signifieds is a fallacious proposition, we are bound to be confused.

The second principle is that whatever we receive from the intermediary sources (*wāṣilān*) concerning doctrinal positions is by definition multi-significatory, and it cannot be otherwise.[72] The principal reason for this is that the signifiers are finite and yet the signifieds are infinite, "and since the signifieds [*ma'ānī*] are hundreds of times more than the signifiers [*alfāẓ*], then necessarily multi-signification (*ishtirāk-i dar alfāẓ*) is inevitable".[73] But what is more important is 'Ayn al-Quḍāt's assertion that:

> Every constructed signifier is made to refer to tangible signifieds (*ma'ānī-i ẓāhir*). Such signifieds that the multitude do not see and know have no constructed signifiers. Since in the material world the signifiers are verified only through the external eye, then they have constructed expression, such as "the sky", "the earth", "the mountain", "the land", "the sea", "honey", "man", etc. While heavenly [= *malakūt*, by which he means "non-material"] intelligibles have no constructed signifiers, because not everyone can observe them. Thus when someone wants to talk about such [non-material] expressions, they have to borrow [*isti'ārah*] from those signifiers constructed [for the material signifieds].[74]

ʿAyn al-Quḍāt further elaborates on this principle, that as various branches of knowledge have developed in Arabic then specific expressions have been "borrowed" from tangible signifiers in order to construct technical vocabularies. Thus jurists, theologians, grammarians, prosodists, etc. have all constructed their respective technical vocabularies by borrowing words and expressions that do not refer to their original signifieds any more.[75] The same is true about all other-worldly references in the Qur'ān, wherein worldly expressions have been used to refer to other-worldly realities still beyond human comprehension. Of course, there cannot be any absolute correspondence between other-worldly realities and worldly expressions, and thus as the Qur'ān says one must "believe in the unseen". Expressions such as "Heaven" and "Hell" are thus closer to realities that are unseen and other-worldly than such expressions as "bread, meat, and honey".[76] At this point ʿAyn al-Quḍāt introduces his reading of such non-meaningful Qur'ānic expressions as *Khyʿṣ*, *Ḥmʿsq*, *Almṣ*, *Ṭsm*, *Ṭh* and *Ys*. These are signifiers, ʿAyn al-Quḍāt contends, to other-worldly realities for which there are no worldly comparisons. There is a pattern to these signifiers. Occasionally, they are only one letter, such as *Q* (as in 50: 1), *Ṣ* (as in 38: 1) or *N* (as in 68: 1). Sometimes they are two, such as *Ṭh* (as in 20: 1) or *Ys* (as in 36: 1) or *Ḥm* (as in 40: 1). They might be three, such as *Alr* (as in 10: 1), *Ṭsm* (as in 26: 1), *Alm* (as in 2: 1). There are combinations of four, such as *Almṣ* (as in 7: 1), *Almr* (as in 13: 1). And finally, they might be a combination of five letters, such as *Khyʿṣ* (as in 19: 1) or *Ḥmʿsq* (as in 42: 1). ʿAyn al-Quḍāt contends that all these differences have a significance. There is a reason that some are only one letter, others two, three, four or five. There is also a reason why there are not more than five. But all these combinations of letters are scattered signifiers that point to signifieds beyond the common comprehension of people in their material frame of reference. When grammarians say "subject", "object" or "predicate", they have borrowed these terms from their common uses and given them technical meaning. There are such uses of common expressions for non-common realities in the Qur'ān too. But there are also Qur'ānic constructions, such as *Alm*, which are not borrowed from the material world because they signify realities utterly alien to the material form of ordinary linguistic references. Not only the significance of these letters but the whole mystery of other letters concerns ʿAyn al-Quḍāt. He says that there must be a significance as to their numbers, shapes, correspondences to realities. ʿAyn al-Quḍāt is quite boastful of his observations in this respect.

> Do not think for a moment that as long as Islam has existed anyone has had the [intellectual] power to say what I have said concerning these broken letters. Everyone has simply followed
> Ibn ʿAbbās [an early Qur'ānic commentator] in this respect,

> maintaining that [for example] "A" refers to "Allāh", "L" to "Jibra'il", and "M" to "Muḥammad". And even this much not everyone knows what it exactly means. It is a long way before one recognizes what the "A" of "Allāh" signifies, or the "L" of "Jibra'il", or the "M" of "Muḥammad". Simply to know what Ibn 'Abbās said is one thing, but to learn [why] something is something [else] is an entirely different thing. It is not such an accomplishment to know that Ibn 'Abbās maintained that "A" refers to "Allāh". As if for example, someone learned that "the world is created". This is not knowledge, unless one knows why the world is created.[77]

The third principle that 'Ayn al-Quḍāt proposes, in this apparently theological but effectively hermeneutic theory, is that one can compose an expression that on the one hand reads like the Qadarite position that "God does not create evil", which is not acceptable, because it then necessitates a second god who can cause evil, just like the Zoroastrian belief, and on the other corresponds to a meaning which is acceptable. In the second, 'Ayn al-Quḍāt's preferred reading is that God cannot cause evil, but that proposition is to be understood only in the grand scheme of things. There are things that "appear" as evil to us but in an absolute sense they are not. When a child is given a medicine which is bitter, the child considers it an evil act, but in reality it is good. If the child had the wisdom of his parents it would know that taking the medicine was a good not an evil act. With the same logic, there are things which in God's grand wisdom are good, but in our limited perceptions, always limited to our specific realities, they appear as evil. The reason, 'Ayn al-Quḍāt says, that the Prophet has prohibited discussions of theodicy is that whoever engages in it will inevitably go astray.[78] Whoever believes in the existence of such evil acts as "blasphemy, adultery, sodomy and theft"[79] either has to attribute them to God, which is blasphemy, or to some other source, which is equally blasphemous. An alternative view would be to hold that there is no evil, which is more acceptable but still it posits certain problems such as appearing not to consider "blasphemy, adultery, sodomy, theft, robbery and murder"[80] as evil acts. Three positions thus become evident in the matter of theodicy: two are blasphemous, one acceptable. It is blasphemous to believe that evil exists and that God has created it; it is equally blasphemous to believe that there is evil but God did not cause it. The acceptable position is that "there is evil but it is like a kind of therapy and medicine which is evil-in-appearance but good-in-truth".[81]

The fourth principle is that all, or most, (theological) positions were correct in their original formulations but that they were distorted by misguided transmitters. This should become evident, 'Ayn al-Quḍāt points out, only by observing one's own age. Every age, he maintains, is just like others, consisting of four major groups: the dogmaticians (*'ulamā'*), the philosophers (*'uqalā'*), the ignorant (*juhhāl*) and the insane (*majānīn*). If someone today starts an utterly insane idea, such as that nothing exists at all, and there are enough people believing in it, before long there would be a school of thought to that effect; as indeed the Sophists had a similar position and for a long time they had their followers.[82] 'Ayn al-Quḍāt then turns the question around and suggests that such an utterly inane position could not have been that of the Sophists, that undoubtedly their positions have been altered ever time. 'Ayn al-Quḍāt's example, again as usual, is a linguistic one: "We read in the Qur'ān," he says, "that Pharaoh's followers said, 'And over them we shall be victorious' [Qur'ān 7: 127]. And we know that by 'over them' a 'victory' is intended. Now, imagine someone were to translate this to Persian or Turkish, and the equivalent of 'victorious' is [inadvertently] dropped. Then the story of Moses and Pharaoh will be misunderstood, and some people may think that [the phrase] 'over them we . . .' means that we are sitting over their head, and this is wrong and fallacious."[83] 'Ayn al-Quḍāt does the same hermeneutic explications of the expression "come down" in the statement attributed to Prophet Muḥammad that "Every night God comes down from the heavens to the earth", and to the word "wisdom" (*ḥikmah*) in the Qur'ānic passage "And to whomever He gives wisdom, He has indeed given a great blessing."[84] Very naturally, substitutions of words and meanings can gradually distort the original intentions of a phrase. On this premise, 'Ayn al-Quḍāt makes the radical proposition that such religions as Christianity or Zoroastrianism that now Muslims consider misguided were originally of a different nature which has not come down to us, "as indeed Islam [itself] which little by little is being discarded, these religions too have been little by little discarded".[85] Did the Prophet himself not say, "There shall be a time when people will gather in mosques and pray and not a single Muslim shall be among them"?[86] When during the immediate generation after the Prophet, Ḥasan al-Baṣrī complained that no trace of Islam were to be found, what was to be understood of the state of "Islam" in 'Ayn al-Quḍāt's time, he retorted, some five centuries after the initial Muḥammadan message? The same is true about Zoroastrianism which has been around "for four or five thousand years".[87] How could we know what exactly was the nature of this faith when it started? "I have a friend from Badakhshan," 'Ayn al-Quḍāt further elaborates, "who once told me that in his native land is a place where people consider themselves to be Muslims. They considered their leader to be a person who could read the Qur'ān; and yet they had no one who could understand the meaning of the Qur'ān. They do not pray, and they have no idea that in Islam praying is mandatory. They know that they have to perform their *ḥajj* pilgrimage, and yet they do not know that they have to fast during the month of Ramaḍān."[88]

The fifth principle is that there are varieties of distortions (*taḥrīf*) which cannot be counted or enumerated. 'Ayn al-Quḍāt distinguishes, for example, between the spoken words and the written statements. He is deliberately conscious of the fact that the spoken words have certain intonations which are utterly missing in the written statements. A person might say to his slave, 'Ayn al-Quḍāt says, "go do whatever you want" in a state of anger and frustration; and the same person might say "go do whatever you want" to his son in a state of parental love and care. When they are spoken, they have different intonations and "meanings", but when they are written, they are identical, "because one cannot write the difference between the condition of anger and that of contentment, since it pertains to the shape of the person". There is the added element of the addressee, of which 'Ayn al-Quḍāt is equally aware: "When you are present, I engage in a dialogue with you in correspondence to your knowledge. While if a child or an adult of limited rational faculties were present, they would not be able to understand me, and should they report what I had said on a [different] occasion, they would misrepresent it [inevitably]."[89]

The sixth principle is that someone who seeks the truth must never dwell on any religion or school of thought, should only get to know them and then go beyond them. Using the image of a pilgrimage, 'Ayn al-Quḍāt says that to reach Kufah from Hamadan, one must first reach Baghdad. But Baghdad is not the ultimate destination. It is only a stage to get to Kufah, and then Kufah itself is not the end; one only goes there to go to reach the Ka'bah in Mecca.

HERMENEUTICS

It is impossible to exaggerate the radical implications of 'Ayn al-Quḍāt's historical hermeneutics as expounded in this letter, which he wrote to his close friend and confidante 'Azīz al-Dīn al-Mustawfī.[90] In six successive moves he transforms the entire edifice of "Islamic" epistemic assumptions as institutionalized in not only the juridical and philosophical but any other hegemonic reading. While he engages in the rather common problem of theodicy through a reading of the Qadarite position, he pursues a much more serious line of hermeneutic argument. The fact of the multi-significality of all acts of signification is 'Ayn al-Quḍāt's path to a remarkably radical hermeneutics with monumental implications for the historical veracity of any ahistorical notion of "Truth".

The six principles through which 'Ayn al-Quḍāt develops his re-reading of the Qadarite theological position correspond to the primary features of his historical hermeneutics, or his theory of reading such historical events as the rise of a religion. The first and foremost feature of this hermeneutics is the principality of language in any act of understanding. He maintains that "since the discourse (*sukhan*) of the intermediary sources (*wāṣilan*) is multi-significatory (*mushtarik al-dilālah*) to two or three signifieds, only one of which is right and the others wrong, then whoever does not know this will fall into a fallacy".[91] This revolutionary observation in the whole spectrum of "Islamic" intellectual history renders all acts of the production and reception of knowledge contingent upon language. This is not a casual observation, or in any way limited to the theological position of the Qadarites. 'Ayn al-Quḍāt insists in the second principle that "the discourse of the intermediary sources cannot but be multi-significatory, and it is impossible for it not to be so".[92] As a hermeneutic principle, all received statements are, *ipso facto*, multi-significatory. They signify more than one signified. This is so not as a matter of theological or philosophical position or preference, but as a matter of a hermeneutic principle, as a governing theory of reading. The term *wāṣilān* means the intermediary sources between the origin of a hermeneutic event (as the original "message" of a religion) and its subsequent interpreters. By recognizing the historical instrumentality of these intermediary interpreting sources, 'Ayn al-Quḍāt constitutes the subjective individuality of the human agency as the primary vehicle of linguistic transformation of any "original message". Language is spoken by people, and as a linguistic proposition, people can and do make "mistakes" in translating a message from one generation to the next. 'Ayn al-Quḍāt repeatedly uses examples of how such words as *ḥikmah* (wisdom) or *nazala* (to come down) can have a range of meanings associated with them in one age and then be totally transformed in another. Language thus constitutes the principal problematic in any hermeneutic act, a problematic which is particularly aggravated by the human agency which is at the centre of any linguistic transference of any "original message".

Emerging immediately from the linguistic problematic at the core of any hermeneutic act is the phenomenon of multi-signification at the very core of that event. The essential problem with this multi-significatory aspect of language is that from a presumed "original message" point of view only one signification is "correct", 'Ayn al-Quḍāt says, and the rest are wrong. But no one knows exactly which reading is correct and which are wrong. ('Ayn al-Quḍāt of course in his typical self-confident way exempts himself from this hermeneutic principle and says that he can tell the difference. But that boastful rhetoric is a different matter in the general scheme of his hermeneutics to which I shall turn momentarily.) This complex of multiple readings makes of the hermeneutic event a pregnant occasion, precisely in the illusion or recognition that only one reading is correct. But which one is it? Thus 'Ayn al-Quḍāt makes "mis"-understanding a principal component of his hermeneutics. Since the intermediary sources (*wāṣilān*) cannot speak or write except through a multi-signifying language, and since all readers operate under the assumption that only one reading is correct and the rest are wrong, then "mis"-readings are constitutional to all acts of hermeneutics.

But who is to decide which is a correct reading of an original message? Here, 'Ayn al-Quḍāt is patently conscious of the agency of power, political or intellectual, in deciding the "correct" reading from a network of multi-significatory possibilities. Notice that in his third principle he observes that "there is an expression which in one reading verifies the position of the Qadarites, and in another it is [perfectly] correct".[93] He further elaborates that one can say, for example in the theological position now under scrutiny, that "Yes, there is evil in the world", and from it one can conclude that the Qadarites are right. But, 'Ayn al-Quḍāt stipulates, this reading of the statement is not acceptable because it creates two principal conclusions, each of which is blasphemous. Namely, either evil exists and God did not create it, "thus the creator of evil is someone else and this is blasphemy because [the person] has constituted two gods", or else evil exists and God created it, which is equally blasphemous because "He [i.e., God] has willed evil, which is to say, absolute evil in which there is no good, and a person [*sic*] like that is not proper to be considered magnanimous and benevolent, and it follows from this position that God Almighty is not benevolent, because if He can avoid doing evil, and yet He commits it, then it is impossible for Him to be benevolent, and this position is blasphemous because it requires denying God Almighty perfect Attributes."[94] But there is an alternative reading of the statement "Yes, there is evil in the world" which, 'Ayn al-Quḍāt proposes, is correct and that reading maintains that "there is evil but it is like medical therapy and taking of medicine which is evil-in-appearance but good-in-reality".[95] But that reading is "correct" either by virtue of the power of 'Ayn al-Quḍāt's argument or by virtue of the political necessity of maintaining the absolute theological monotheism of the Qur'ānic revelation. In fact the two religious adversaries with which 'Ayn al-Quḍāt compares the Islamic monotheism are Zoroastrian dualism ("fire-worshipping") and Christian trinitarianism ("cross-worshipping"), one of which Islam defeated and eradicated in 'Ayn al-Quḍāt's homeland, and the other Muslim armies faced continually, but particularly during 'Ayn al-Quḍāt's time which coincided with the advent of the Crusades. The triumphant reading of "there is evil but it is like medical therapy and taking of medicine which is evil-in-appearance but good-in-reality" is made possible only under the supreme metaphysical power of Islamic monotheism at the service of which is 'Ayn al-Quḍāt's intellectual power. Lest we might think that this is just an implicit aspect of 'Ayn al-Quḍāt's hermeneutics, we should note that he recognizes very explicitly the power of the crowd and history in producing legitimacy for a particular reading of a religion or a school of thought. During his observations about the Sophists he points out that if today someone were to propose that nothing exists in or outside this world, nobody would believe him, and yet "if [only] one person were to believe in it and turn it into a religion [or school of thought = *madhhab*], and then a multitude of people were to join this religion, then it would remain in this world for thousands of years".[96] Or elsewhere he says,

> We hear that in previous times there existed a group of people who maintained that nothing exists, so much so that they said "you do not exist, I do not exist, and the sky and the earth do not exist." Now, we know that in our time there is not anybody who would even entertain such a possibility, let alone daring to express it without a fear of being laughed at by the people. Now, suppose someone made such a proposition, you are sure that nobody would believe him. [You think that] people will surely laugh at him. It would be indeed strange if one or two people from all over the world were to believe him. And yet if a few thousand people were to follow the person [who made such a proposition], they would then make a religion [or school of thought = *madhhab*] from this nonsense.[97]

This is as close and as accurate a description of the constitutional force of political power as one can get in the historical formation of any school of thought, religions included. Again, it is impossible to exaggerate the interpretative implications of such a direct and immediate recognition of the instrumentality of power in the working of a religion out of a primary proposition, and thus understandably this aspect of 'Ayn al-Quḍāt's hermeneutics must have remained rather tacit and implicit in his exposition.

What is not tacit and implicit, and in fact perfectly explicit in 'Ayn al-Quḍāt's hermeneutics, is his belief in the historicity of understanding which, as 'Ayn al-Quḍāt himself rightly boasts, is remarkably new and revolutionary, totally unprecedented in the history of Islamic dogmatics. 'Ayn al-Quḍāt's rhetorical proposition in this respect is that "all religions [or schools of thought = *madhāhib*], or most of them, were true in their origin and [then] in the passage of time they have been "distorted".[98] Dwelling within this rhetoric is the crucial proposition that "the passage of time" can change and modify "the truth" or "original message" of a religion or school of thought. "To become distorted over a long period of time"[99] is 'Ayn al-Quḍāt's expression for recognizing the instrumentality of history in re-shaping and re-defining the nature of an "original message". While he continues to elaborate this hermeneutic principle of the instrumentality of history in understanding through an account of the Sophists' position, he does not hesitate for a moment to apply it to "Islam" in history. "You should know, my friend [he addresses 'Azīz al-Dīn al-Mustawfī], that if you seriously consider the conditions of your own age and the people of your own age, you would certainly see [the truth of] this [proposition], because in every age people are exactly as they are now."[100] The historical nature of understanding is as much applicable to the history of Zoroastrianism and Christianity as it is to Islam. As for Zoroastrians, "for years they have been worshipping the fire. But we know that the origin of this has been something else which has not reached us. As indeed Islam [literally 'being-a-Muslim' = *musalmānī*] is piece by piece being eroded, these religions too have piece by piece been eroded. Now all that remains is idol-worshipping [Buddhism], cross-worshipping [Christianity] and fire-worshipping [Zoroastrianism]."[101] Looking at himself at a "present" of an "Islamic history", he observed, "when Islam existed during the time of the immediate generation after the Prophet (*tābi'iyān*), Ḥasan al-Baṣrī used to say, "[Islam] is eroded. What do you think has remained from it now? How do we know what will it be like in a thousand years? What do we know about what the evil followers and misguided transmitters have done to fire-worshipping which has been around for four to five thousand years?"[102]

Extended from the principality of history in understanding is the next hermeneutic principle which gives full recognition to the communal (or sociological) definition of what constitutes "the Truth". Here, 'Ayn al-Quḍāt's report of a friend of his from Badakhshan that there a group of people who considered themselves Muslims and yet they knew no Arabic, read the Qur'ān but did not understand what it meant, did not ever pray or fast during the month of Ramaḍān and yet performed their *ḥajj* pilgrimage is a case in point. 'Ayn al-Quḍāt reports this without any judgment, and adds to his report the phrase "And in this report there is a lesson [to be learnt] by someone who seeks the right path and a clue for those who seek it."[103] The Badakhshānī community of Muslims here was the primary agency in defining what constitutes being a Muslim and what are its principal requirements. Elsewhere, 'Ayn al-Quḍāt elaborates that some time in the future there could be a community of Muslims who would radically modify their prayer rituals, commencing without the opening chapter of the Qur'ān for example, or without ablution.[104] For this possibility he also resorts to a prophetic tradition according to which "There will come a time that people will gather in mosques and pray, and there will not be a single Muslim among them."[105] From the perspective of this prophetic prediction, that community will not be "Muslim", but so far as that community itself is concerned, they are. These examples elaborate 'Ayn al-Quḍāt's awareness of the principality of communal definitions of what constitutes "Truth", i.e., how *they* read "the original message" of, in this case, "Islam".

Embracing 'Ayn al-Quḍāt's hermeneutics is a solid grasp of the irreducible subjectivity of all acts of understanding. In his fifth principle, 'Ayn al-Quḍāt observes that "there is a variety of distortions and it is impossible to enumerate them".[106] The reason for this, 'Ayn al-Quḍāt observes, is that the instrumentalities (*asbāb*) of distortion are many and no one can have a complete account of them. Here he makes a further distinction between the spoken and the written words. He does not give the primacy to the spoken words. He simply suggests that there are emotive conditionings of verbal expressions, such as when a man talks in anger to his slave (that is the example that he gives) as opposed to when he talks to his son. There are differences in the mode of address that are evident in the shape and face of the speaker, qualities that cannot be represented in the written words. This phenomenon aggravates the possibilities of (mis)interpretations beyond measure. He also adds the element of dialogue to this list of forces conducive to (mis)understanding. This is how he is conscious of the force of dialogue as a determining factor:

> In addition [to other factors that he has indicated as instrumental in conditions of (mis)understanding], the [nature] of address differs in relation to the addressee. For example, when you [he means 'Azīz al-Dīn al-Mustawfī] are present, I engage in a dialogue with you in correspondence to your level of knowledge. While if a child or a man of limited rational faculties were present, they would not be able to understand me, and should they report what I had said in a [different] occasion, they would misrepresent it.[107]

As a matter of practical example, 'Ayn al-Quḍāt refers to a state of confusion in the prophetic traditions, where many discrepancies existed in the correct form, and even the actual number of *Ḥadīth*. This is the case, 'Ayn al-Quḍāt emphasizes, "While Islam is still young, there will be a time when this would be much more so, and no one will be able to solve [this problem]. Thus how could you tell what does fire-worshipping really mean? Or what does the fire [in the story] of Moses, peace be upon him, mean?"[108] The multiple instrumentalities of human agencies, added to the transgenerational problem of those who transmit the accounts of various claims to truth, added to the constitutionally multi-significatory nature of language, added to the primacies of community, dialogue and power in establishing a reading as true over others, all lead to the existential subjectivity of all acts of understanding, with no particular way to account for even the numbers of such possible (mis)readings.

Perhaps the most revolutionary proposition in 'Ayn al-Quḍāt's hermeneutics is that because of this phenomenal subjectivity of all acts of understanding and of historical transmissions of "Truth-telling", anyone who wants to know the truth should not dwell in, nor believe in the absolute veracity of, any single claim to truth. A person in search of truth, 'Ayn al-Quḍāt observes in his sixth and final hermeneutic principle, "must go over these religions [or schools of thought = *madhāhib*]".[109] The expression he uses here is *ḍarūrat ast kah bar in madhāhib gudhar kunad*, which means that it is obligatory for the person to get to know and then surpass all such claims to absolute truth. All religions or schools of thought are "way-stations" (*manāzil*) towards the ultimate recognition of God, 'Ayn al-Quḍāt observes in his inevitably theocentric language. But some have erroneously made of these way-stations an ultimate destination. This is an absolutely remarkable and daring observation. Because what in effect he is saying is that Islam, and Christianity, Zoroastrianism, Buddhism, etc., are all historical versions of the ultimate and transcendent truth. One has to know and then surpass them in order to reach an understanding which is the sum total of all and totally present in none. 'Ayn al-Quḍāt himself is absolutely aware of the radically revolutionary and unprecedented nature of his observation here. At the conclusion of this "letter" he assures Mustawfī that:

> Whatever I have written in this letter and in my other letters I have written them exclusively from my own *dhawq* [which is an extremely difficult word to translate into any language. It means, as 'Ayn al-Quḍāt uses it here, something like an irreducibly individual perception of things based on taste and penchant rather than rational calculations, logical conclusions, etc.]. Except for a few expressions which I have read or heard there is not anything [taken or quoted from others] in my letters. Had it not been that I had discovered these things through my own *dhawq*, how else could I have come up with something like [the recognition that] fire-worshipping, idol-worshipping, cross-worshipping and the Qadarite [theological] school are in their own respect true [or correct]?[110]

Finally, 'Ayn al-Quḍāt's hermeneutics is a solid, counter-systemic celebration of the individual as the ultimate locus of any hermeneutic encounter. What drives 'Ayn al-Quḍāt's narrative throughout his writings, but particularly in these "letters", is his relentless individuality, and even more significant, his awareness of this individuality. The consciousness of this individuality is in fact a tacit, and thus forceful, factor in 'Ayn al-Quḍāt's hermeneutics. At the end of the last passage I just quoted in which he self-confidently boasts of the instrumentality of his own *dhawq* in developing his theory of understanding, he makes a rather remarkable reference to his uncontrollable passion for writing. These references to his passion for writing are endemic to 'Ayn al-Quḍāt's works, particularly in his "letters", and they read as sudden existential outbursts of what ultimately drives any act of writing. Referring to his theory of the broken letters of the Qur'ān, that they represent other-worldly realities for which there is no common linguistic expression he concludes:

> [Had I not discovered these things through my own *dhawq*,] how would I dare to write so much on interpreting the broken letters [of the Qur'ān] like *Ṭh*, *Ys*, *Ḥm* and *Almṣ* so much so that whenever I write something, this [issue] comes forth and forces me to write. It is so that even if I want not to write, I cannot. And may God Almighty protect the readers of this from such a disease [*wabālan*]. You cannot imagine what dangers lie in writing about such issues. But
>
> They threw him into the sea, with his hands tied up and
> [yet] they told him:
> Be careful! be careful! Do not get wet![111]

On another occasion, having just presented his theory of the same "broken letters" of the Qur'ān, he exclaims: "Don't you think for a moment that as long as Islam has been around anyone has had the power to say these things about the broken letters."[112] After presenting his theory of the necessarily historical distortions of all claims to truth, he assures Mustawfī: "This is as a matter of teaching [you these principles], otherwise, it is perfectly clear to me what exactly is the origin of fire-worshipping, and how it was distorted. And all these issues have become clear to me on my own. Because I have never heard anything remotely like them from anybody, nor have I read them in any book."[113]

The principal working of this rather boastful individuality becomes the subjective locus, the *modus operandi*, of 'Ayn al-Quḍāt's hermeneutics. That the hermeneutical experience is an intrinsically linguistic proposition, that all acts of signification are irreducibly multi-significatory, that relations of power have a decidedly political impact on the hermeneutic outcome, that the hermeneutical encounter is an effectively historical proposition, that the hermeneutical event always occurs in a communal set-up and in the context of a dialogical exchange, that all acts of hermeneutics are quintessentially subjective in the wide and open-ended possibility of readings that they propose, and finally that all versions of the historically mediated claims to truth ought to be learnt and mastered and then abandoned for the next, are all specific features of a theory of understanding which in 'Ayn al-Quḍāt's own narrative ultimately rests on the irreducibly individual encounter with the supreme metaphysics of Truth-telling: a metaphysics which he effectively transforms via his own hermeneutics of counter-narrativity.

METAPHYSICAL PRINCIPLES

As "non-books", the *Maktūbāt* and the *Tamhīdāt* are textual culminations of 'Ayn al-Quḍāt's active experimentations with a counter-narrativity that tests the limits of Islamic metaphysics. Through them is produced a highly personal and soft "voice" in which is collapsed the serious metaphysics of "Truth-telling" and all its surrogate agencies operative in the nomocentricity of the Islamic Law, the logocentricity of the Islamic philosophy, and here I insist against a whole history of mystifying 'Ayn al-Quḍāt, the theo-eroticism of Islamic mysticism. Language as the inaugurating moment of all acts of narrativity assumes, or rather regains, a unique access to the shattering of the poetic word and, as it ceases to be representational, begins to generate and sustain worlds independent of all claims to reality, sacred or secular, theocentric or anthropocentric. 'Ayn al-Quḍāt achieved this revolutionary language by first mastering and then surpassing all the metaphysical surrogates of Islamic onto-theology in Islamic law, philosophy and Sufism. Neither as a legal theorist nor as a philosopher in the ordinary sense of the term nor certainly a Sufi, 'Ayn al-Quḍāt can be understood only through the deliberate rhetoricity of his language, his conscious and deliberate attempt to shatter and break loose from the absolutist metaphysics of representation and Truth-telling.

Towards precisely that direction, the *Tamhīdāt* (521/1127) continues with the same soft counter-metaphysics which is evident in the *Maktūbāt* (517/1123–525/1131). 'Ayn al-Quḍāt begins his *Tamhīdāt*, which he divides into ten *tamhīds* ("preface" or "preparation"), which read very much like his "letters", with a rhetorical and evocative voice, with a counter-epistemological distinction between a form of knowledge which is "acquired" (*muktasib*) and one which is *ladunī* (perhaps the best translation for this is "innate" or "God-given"). This distinction is crucial for 'Ayn al-Quḍāt's subsequent formulation of his own counter-version of a theo-ontology which is actively aimed at the nomocentric proclivities of Islamic law and the logocentrism of the Islamic theological (or theocentric) philosophy. In his second *tamhīd*, 'Ayn al-Quḍāt turns to the individual person as the primary point of reflection for any existential understanding (of "faith" for example). This remarkable shift from the dominant nomocentric–logocentric epistemics to a subjective, "innate" or "God-given" intelligibility and then a major existential move to "the individual" as the main point of any legitimate theology are the principal characteristics of 'Ayn al-Quḍāt's revolutionary "counter-metaphysics". The *sālik*, or the individual seeker of Truth, becomes the primary point of reference in 'Ayn al-Quḍāt's "counter-metaphysics". He elaborates on the nature of humanity in the third *tamhīd*, examines the borderlines of what constitutes humanity, or what it means to be a "human" (*ādam*), and charts the venues of those who reach the upper limits of their humanity in their recognition of a "Truth" which is hermeneutically facilitated.[114]

For 'Ayn al-Quḍāt there is a direct line between his anthropology and his theology. "Know thyself in order to know God",[115] the content of the fourth *tamhīd*, is more than a motto. It is the existential connection between the human reality and the possibility of one's grasp of a signifying truth beyond that of the human condition. From the irreducible individuality of this perspective, 'Ayn al-Quḍāt then proceeds to discuss the meaning and significance of the five pillars of Islam: *shahādah* means a confession of faith identical to that of the Prophet;[116] *namāz* means a prayer which is a distraction from the world and a concentration on God;[117] *zakāh* means giving alms but not from one's wealth, from one's knowledge of certainty;[118] *ṣawm* does not mean fasting, it means feasting, but feasting with God, eating His food, drinking His drink;[119] and *ḥajj* does not mean travelling left or right, north or south, east or west, it means a journey to the heart.[120] As evident in this 'Ayn al-Quḍātian redefinition of the five pillars of Islam, he is a master rhetorician, always putting the external meaning of every principle of faith on its head by reaching for its inner meaning: *ṣawm* is not fasting but feasting; *ḥajj* is not going out but going in, etc. This, if anything, is the trademark, the unmistakable trait, of 'Ayn al-Quḍāt's mode of rhetorical writing, the syntax and morphology of his technique of subversion.

"The Truth and Conditions of Love" is the subject of the sixth *tamhīd*. Up to this point in the text, 'Ayn al-Quḍāt has constructed an effective (soft) narrative which postulates a counter-nomocentric/logocentric metaphysics, constitutes "the individual" as the starting point of any understanding (of God for example), charts the human capabilities of that individual, makes theology contingent upon the anthropology of that individual, and then re-reads the principal doctrinal creeds of the individual's faith from the vantage point of this existential, individual-based, "counter-metaphysics". Now, in the second half of the *Tamhīdāt*, beginning with the sixth *tamhīd*, the principality of "Love" comes to shift this entire "counter-metaphysics" to a new, theo-erotic, direction. The theo-eroticism of 'Ayn al-Quḍāt's "counter-metaphysics" casts a long and sustained shadow over his theo-ontology. The leading phrase of 'Ayn al-Quḍāt's theo-eroticism is actually a statement of the Prophet Muḥammad: "Whoever falls in love and yet conceals it until his death, he has died a martyr."[121] Love, in 'Ayn al-Quḍāt's theo-eroticism, is the very constitutional foundations of creation, of being, of living and of dying. The "inferior" (*ṣaghīr*) love is the love of man for God; the "superior" (*kabīr*) love is the love of God for man; and there is a middle (*mīyānah*) love, of which 'Ayn al-Quḍāt says he cannot talk except surreptitiously and with tact.[122] In the heat of his adulation for "love" as the principal motive and motion of being, 'Ayn al-Quḍāt refuses all measures of prudence. He takes the famous piety of "you should have the faith of old women" and does this with it: "'You should have the faith of old women!' Indeed, how splendidly he put it! Whoever wants to be in Paradise, they call him stupid. A whole world wants to go to Paradise. Not a single person seeks Love! Because Paradise is the bounty of the [carnal] soul [*nafs*] and of the heart [*dil*], while Love is the reward of the soul [*jān*] and of Truth [*Ḥaqīqat*]."[123]

'Ayn al-Quḍāt's postulation of "Love" as the principal *modus operandi* of being then functions as the premiss of a further elaboration of his "counter-metaphysics". *Rūḥ* (soul) and *dil* (heart) now emerge as the subjects of the seventh *tamhīd*, as the defining "faculties" of a counter-intelligibility conducive to 'Ayn al-Quḍāt's preferred conceptions of "understanding". In the context of this "understanding", which 'Ayn al-Quḍāt's "counter-metaphysics" makes possible, he then links, in an extremely unusual but highly imaginative move, the purpose of the creation of humanity to his Qur'ānic hermeneutics. In his Qur'ānic hermeneutics, 'Ayn al-Quḍāt separates words or signifiers (*lafẓ*) from their intended referentialities or signifieds (*dilālah*). The Qur'ān, he says, will not be understood unless and until people have reached their divinely bestowed attributes. The enemies of the Prophet, for example, could hear the Arabic of the Qur'ān but could not understand its significance.[124] The revelation of the Qur'ān is the supreme sign of God's Mercy, so that people can recognize themselves. People are made constitutionally free to choose between good and evil, which in a radical departure from much of Islamic theology, 'Ayn al-Quḍāt attributes both to God.[125] All binary oppositions are *made* in order for people to choose.

By the ninth *tamhīd*, 'Ayn al-Quḍāt is ready to redefine entirely the meaning of belief (*īmān*) and disbelief (*kufr*). There is a kind of (supreme) faith which 'Ayn al-Quḍāt identifies with madness, and through madness with disbelief. In the same category are the drunk: "Another group is the drunkard, those who have hung the cross upon themselves, they speak intoxicated words. Some of them were killed, and some were afflicted by His calamity, as it will happen to me! I do not know when! It is too soon now!"[126] These words 'Ayn al-Quḍāt wrote in 521/1127, some four years before his execution. He here postulates a complete suspension of worldly, i.e., hegemonic, definitions of things as doctrinally established by the juridical custodians of the Faith: "Unless you disregard the *khalq* [the created beings], you will never reach the Khāliq [the creator of beings]."[127] That suspension of the familiar is always dangerous, and 'Ayn al-Quḍāt is aware of this danger, vividly!

> As I said, disbelief is of different kinds. Now, listen: There is the apparent disbelief, there is the-disbelief-of-the-soul, and there is

> the-disbelief-of-the-heart. The disbelief-of-the-soul is related to Satan; while the-disbelief-of-the-heart is related to Muḥammad. As for the-disbelief-of-the-Truth, that is related to God. After all this, then there is faith. O that I may be saved from my own deeds [lit., my own hands], daring as I do to utter these words, for which there is no room in this or in the world to come. But I utter them anyway! Come what may![128]

Thus the entire ninth *tamhīd* is launched against a radical re-definition of what ordinarily is defined and constituted as "belief" and "disbelief" by the long historical authority of the clerical establishment. Through a radically transformative reading of such letters as *ī* in *Rūḥī* (which means "my" in God's phrase "*my* soul" in the Qur'ān) or *k* in *'alayk* (which means "you" in the phrase "Peace be upon *you*, O Prophet, and so be God's bounty and benedictions"), 'Ayn al-Quḍāt postulates for himself a position from which to author a whole new reading of the faith. That postulation of course entails a supposition of extraordinary sensibilities.

> Alas! I was kept in this sacred paradise, to which I referred, for a month. So much so that people thought me dead. Then much to my regret they sent me to a place wherein I was for some time. In this second place, I committed a sin, for which transgression you shall soon see me killed. What do you say?! Do you see what befalls a person who prevents a lover from reaching his beloved? In this matter, I have been so afflicted by Him that I think I shall never recover. Have you ever seen a man who loves two different persons, and yet he has to behave himself, because if he spent time with one of them, the other wants to shed his blood, and if with the other, so would the other? Alas! Have you never been in love with God and Muḥammad, and then, in the midst of all this, has Satan not tempted you?[129]

These are moments of self-authorization, when 'Ayn al-Quḍāt presides over a radical redefinition of his faith. In such moments, time contracts, space dissolves, sheer narrativity subsumes both the sacred and the non-sacred, and thus 'Ayn al-Quḍāt writes and speaks with a language irreducibly his, and yet with a universal certitude echoing throughout all its resonances:

> Shaykh Siyāwash told me: I saw the Chosen One [Prophet Muḥammad] in a dream tonight. He came in and said, "Tell our 'Ayn al-Quḍāt that we are not yet the residents of the Divine abode. You wait for a while! Be patient! Until we are all close together, and separation is all over. Then we shall all have unity, with no separation." When he told me of this dream, my

> patience ran over. I became completely drowned in these verses. As I looked up, I saw the Chosen One who came in and said, "What I had told Shaykh Siyāwash, he could not have taken it when awake." From the light of the Chosen One a flame came out, and from that a spark hit him and he was instantly burnt out. And then the people think this is all magic and illusion.[130]

The tenth and final chapter of the *Tamhīdāt* is the culmination of 'Ayn al-Quḍāt's "counter-metaphysics", where he combines "the light of Muḥammad, peace be upon him, and that of Satan".[131] This is the ultimate, the most radically transformative, deconstruction of the two binary oppositions between good and evil, a binary opposition at the very root of Islamic theology as it has been historically institutionalized. This *tamhīd* begins with a long and sustained commentary on the Qur'ānic passage "God is the Light of the heavens and the earth" (24: 35). "God", 'Ayn al-Quḍāt maintains, is the substance (*jawhar*) and "the light" is the accident (*'araḍ*) of that essence. From the accidental light then the lights of heaven and earth emerge, the heaven standing for the Muḥammadan light, the earth for the light of Satan.[132] By thus tracing the whole phenomenological reality of the heavens and earth to the supreme and inaugurating Divine Light, but through the intermediary, symbolic lights of Muḥammad and Iblīs, 'Ayn al-Quḍāt reaches for a final re-unification of all existence. He does a similar reading of the prophetic tradition, "The first thing God created was my light",[133] and ultimately concludes with a poem which he puts down in the last chapter after considerable hesitation:

> The heart is a step for The True in this dungeon,
> Only for a while it is a guest in the material world.
>
> The heart is a bird of Truth in the abode of The True,
> Indeed, it is a falcon, adoring The King.
>
> The heart is alive in soul, and the soul is alive in The True,
> Sometimes the soul is in the heart, and sometimes the heart in the soul.
>
> From the light of God, the soul came about,
> Have you not read "light upon light" in the Qur'ān?
>
> That dark light is from the source of anger and wrath,
> The fountainhead of disbelief, the abode of Satan.
>
> This is the secret of The True which I just explained,
> None of this is known among the religious doctors.
>
> His intention in creating this and the other world
> Was only one thing, which is all the necessary proof:

It was to see Himself in the mirror of the soul,
So He can fall in love with Himself, so perfect that He is.

We too see ourselves in Him,
Thus the Beholder and the Beheld are one and the same.

Thus the Lover and the Beloved sit next to each other,
Because one is the soul, and the other the soul of the soul.

Thus Love is the meeting of one another and talking.
And thus His eating and drinking is also by us.

Thus the soul shall be everlasting in the Living World,
What's the point of saying this, of course it shall always be.[134]

Such overwhelming reversals of Islamic metaphysics were too much for its doctrinal custodians to grasp or tolerate, or for the political establishment that was legitimated by it to tolerate or permit. 'Ayn al-Quḍāt paid dearly for his daring experimentations with the transformative reversals of the very metaphysics of "Truth-telling". His writings angered two powerful institutions in the Western Seljūq Empire: the religious and the political, and the two conspired to eliminate him. Abu'l-Qāsim al-Daragazīnī, the powerful vizier to the Seljūq warlord Mughīth al-Dīn Maḥmūd, had a *fatwā* (a religious edict) issued against 'Ayn al-Quḍāt by the leading clerical establishment in Hamadan. Daragazīnī's immediate cause of hostility against 'Ayn al-Quḍāt was his friendship with 'Azīz al-Dīn al-Mustawfī, the treasurer to Maḥmūd, whom the vizier disliked in the context of a court rivalry and intrigue which also involved a lucrative dowry that the great Seljūq king Sultan Sanjar had given to his daughter Māhmalak when he married her to Maḥmūd as part of a political settlement.[135]

'Ayn al-Quḍāt was captured in Hamadan in 525/1130, charged with blasphemy and sent to a prison in Baghdad. In prison he wrote his famous "defence" or "apologia", which he called *Shakwā' al-gharīb*. The *Shakwā'* is a remarkable document[136] in which 'Ayn al-Quḍāt engages his enemies in a sustained debate, the outcome of which is (or must have been) rather evident to him.

The *Shakwā'* reads like a long, arduous and heart-wrenching confession of a young man matured painfully beyond the limits of his elders. In it he tries to defend himself against the charges of blasphemy that the senior doctors of law had levelled against him, and yet he can hardly conceal his utter contempt for their mediocrity of intelligence and spirit.

The first charge against which he feels compelled to defend himself is that he has postulated a "mode" (*ṭawr*) of understanding beyond reason in order to grasp the nature of messengership.[137] The reference here is most probably to the *Zubdah* which he had written ten years earlier in 516/1122, not twenty as recorded in various manuscripts. 'Ayn al-Quḍāt reiterates his position here, that in his epistemological hierarchy there is a "mode" of knowing beyond reason which he identifies with the state of *wilāyah*, or being among the saintly few, and then there is another "mode" of knowing even beyond *wilāyah*, which he identifies with the state of prophethood or *nubuwwah*. He contends that:

> Contemporary theologians have disapproved of me on this account amongst others, thinking that to claim there is a stage beyond the stage of reason is to bar the way to the common people to faith in prophethood, inasmuch as it is reason that proves the veracity of the prophets. Whereas I do not claim that faith in prophethood is contingent upon the attainment of a mode [of knowing] beyond the mode of reason. What I claim is rather that the truth of prophethood constitutes a mode [of knowing] beyond the mode of sainthood [*wilāyah*], and that sainthood constitutes another mode [of knowing] beyond that of reason.[138]

'Ayn al-Quḍāt refers to many instances in early Islamic history when the Companions of the Prophet, i.e., those in the *wilāyah* category, knew of things that reason could not have had access to, such as 'Uthmān telling one of his companions that on his way to visit the third Rightly-Guided Caliph he had looked at a woman, attributing his clairvoyance not to "revelation", which of course had ended with the Prophet, but to his "intuition".

But more than just 'Ayn al-Quḍāt's prophetology was objectionable to his contemporary doctors of law. They asked him why he referred to God as "The Source and Origin of Being", or as "The Real Being". To which he answers: "All these expressions occur in many places in the *Iḥyā' 'ulūm al-dīn*, the *Mishkāt al-anwār wa misfāt al-asrār* and the *al-Munqidh min al-dalāl wa al-mufṣiḥ 'an al-aḥwāl*, all of which are works of al-Ghazzālī, God have mercy on him."[139]

Beyond his theology and prophetology, his Imamology is equally unpalatable to the Sunni doctors of law. They accuse him of Shī'ī, particularly Ismā'īlī, tendencies when he has argued for the necessity of an Imām, or leader or guide, in matters of religious certainty and practice. 'Ayn al-Quḍāt denies any Ismā'īlī tendencies, and points out:

> My adversary, however, had chosen to interpret my words as being in line with the doctrine of the Ismā'īlīs, understanding me to subscribe to the belief in the infallible Imām. Yet how could he arrive at such a vexatious misconstruction, seeing that the

> second chapter of my treatise is devoted to demonstrating the existence of Almighty God by way of rational demonstration and incontrovertible proof? It is well known that the Ismāʿīlīs reject rational speculation, asserting that the way to knowledge of Almighty God is the prophet, or the infallible Imām.[140]

Thus ʿAyn al-Quḍāt goes through all the principal charges that were brought against him and point by point answers them via references to the Qur'ānic and *Ḥadīth* passages, the statements of famous philosophers, poets, historians and Sufis. But in a peculiar way ʿAyn al-Quḍāt's "defence" is full of extremely powerful rhetorical passages in which with a remarkably proud self-confidence he dismisses his opponents as jealous mediocrities:

> Why should I consider it so curious that the theologians of the present age should disapprove of me, seeing that the greatest scholars of every age have always been the object of envy, and have been the targets of every kind of persecution? . . . It is no wonder that I am envied, seeing that I composed as a mere youth, sucking the udders of little more than twenty years, books which baffle men of fifty and sixty to understand, much less to compile and compose.
>
> I do not blame them if they envy me,
> Before my time,
> And for no crime,
> Savants have felt the lash of jealousy.[141]

The content of *Shakwā'* could not but have further frustrated and angered ʿAyn al-Quḍāt's enemies. He was brought back from Baghdad to Hamadan and on Tuesday evening 6 Jumādā II 525/5 May 1131 executed in front of the school in which he taught, according to generations of hagiographers who kept a vigilant gaze on ʿAyn al-Quḍāt's legacy.

NOTES

1 See Eco (1988): 1–2.
2 Secondary literature on ʿAyn al-Quḍāt is sparse. The first serious study of ʿAyn al-Quḍāt was by Mohammed ben Abd al-Jalil who in 1930 prepared a critical edition of *Shakwā'* and translated it into French with a long introduction and elaborate notes. The next person to work extensively on ʿAyn al-Quḍāt was ʿAfīf ʿUṣayrān who in 1961–2 published the complete critical edition of all of ʿAyn al-Quḍāt's works except his letters. We owe the critical editions of *Zubdah*, *Tamhīdāt*, and a new edition of *Shakwā'* to ʿUṣayrān. To ʿUṣayrān we also owe a sustained philosophical reading of ʿAyn al-Quḍāt against a massive history of mystification of his ideas. ʿAlī Naqī Munzawī, collaborated with

'Afīf 'Uṣayrān in preparing a two-volume critical edition of 'Ayn al-Quḍāt's letters, *Maktūbāt*, in 1969. Another Iranian scholar with a long-term interest in 'Ayn al-Quḍāt is Raḥīm Farmanish, who in 1959 wrote a comprehensive book on his life and ideas. Farmanish also edited *Risālah-yi lawāyiḥ* under the impression that this treatise belonged to 'Ayn al-Quḍāt. Since then, 'Uṣayrān has established that *Lawāyiḥ* is not actually 'Ayn al-Quḍāt's. Another treatise falsely attributed to 'Ayn al-Quḍāt, *Risālah-yi yazdānshinākht*, was edited by Bahman Karīmī in 1948. A third treatise falsely attributed to 'Ayn al-Quḍāt, *Sharḥ-i kalāmāt-i Bābā Ṭāhir*, was edited by Jawād Maqsūdlū in 1975 with a long introduction on the life and ideas of 'Ayn al-Quḍāt. The Iranian historian of ideas 'Abd al-Husayn Zarrīnkūb wrote a brilliant essay on 'Ayn al-Quḍāt in his *Justujū dar taṣawwuf-i Īrān*. Nasrullāh Pourjavādī prepared a critical edition of the "correspondence" between 'Ayn al-Quḍāt and Shaykh Aḥmad Ghazzālī. Not too much serious attention has been paid to 'Ayn al-Quḍāt by Orientalists. Arberry translated *Shakwā'* into English, wrote a brief introduction, and added some useful notes in 1969. Christiane Tortel translated *Tamhīdāt* into French in 1992. Bertels (1971) has a generally useful chapter on 'Ayn al-Quḍāt. The *Maktūbāt* and the *Zubdah* are not translated into any European language. There is no comprehensive study of 'Ayn al-Quḍāt's corpus in any language. Lewisohn (1993) is a typically mystical, but brilliantly executed, reading of *Tamhīdāt*. Landolt (1978) is in the same vein, but with a more comparative glance at 'Ayn al-Quḍāt and Suhrawardī. Awn (1983) and Ernst (1985) have useful references to 'Ayn al-Quḍāt's "ecstatic words" and his references to Satan, respectively.

3 For a useful compilation of data on 'Ayn al-Quḍāt, see Farmanish (1959).

4 As an example, see Jāmī (1957): 414–16.

5 On the rule of Seljūqs in Persia, see Bosworth (1968).

6 For a good primary account, see Mustawfī (1985): 448–54.

7 For further details, see Bosworth (1968): 76–7; Mustawfī (1985): 437–8.

8 The series of events which I have just narrated in the above coherent account is actually scattered throughout our sources. Perhaps the most crucial piece of evidence is to be found in al-Qummī (1984): 20–2. Al-Qummī's account of the rivalries between Daragazīnī and al-Mustawfī, which he recorded in 584/1188, is corroborated by Kirmānī (1959): 74–7, who wrote his account in 725/1324. Both these accounts are also compatible with al-Iṣfahānī (1900): 109–15, who was actually a cousin of al-Mustawfī and practically an eyewitness to these rivalries.

9 See al-Iṣfahānī (1900): 139 for further details.

10 On the Ismā'īlīs, see Daftary (1990); on al-Ghazzālī, see Humā'ī (1938).

11 Ibn Rushd is known for having given an effective answer to al-Ghazzālī's criticism of philosophy. For the most recent discussion of this debate, see Urvoy (1991): 80–1.

12 See Ṣafā (1977), 2: 253f. for further details.

13 For further details, see Ṣafā (1977), 2: 295.

14 The most comprehensive account of Suhrawardī's "Illuminationist" philosophy is to be found in his *Ḥikmah al-ishrāq*. See Suhrawardī (1982).

15 The active cultivation of this "theo-erotic" vocabulary continued and comes to full fruition in the seventh/thirteenth century. Shaykh Maḥmūd Shabistarī's

(687/1288–720/1320) *Gulshan-i rāz* comes at the crucial culminating point of this theo-erotic language. In it Shabistarī provides, in a hauntingly simple and beautiful poetry, a glossary of amorous words – "eyes", "lips", "face", "hair", "mole", "candle", "beloved", "idol", "the Christian boy", etc. – and their symbolic significance. See Shabistarī (1982): 71–94.

16 Ṣafā (1977), 2: 346.

17 For the critical edition and a comprehensive introduction by the editor, see Gurgānī (1959).

18 A good example of such hagiographies is to be found in Jāmī (1957): 414–16.

19 After a rather long, elaborate, poetry-studded prologomena (five pages in the critical edition) in his "defence", 'Ayn al-Quḍāt refers to literature and writes "Yes indeed; but this branch of learning, though it is more appealing to human nature and is lighter on the ears, yet I have bidden it farewell and departed from it ever since I approached puberty and manhood. I have gone forth in quest of the religious sciences, and have busied myself with treading the path of the Sufis; and how foul it is for a Sufi to turn away from a thing and then to return to it, and apply himself to it with all his heart." *Shakwā*: 6, *Apologia*: 29.

20 *Shakwā'*: 40–1; *Apologia*: 71.

21 *Shakwā'*: 41; *Apologia*: 72.

22 *Shakwā'*: 40; *Apologia*: 70; *Zubdah*: 3.

23 *Zubdah*: 4.

24 *Ibid.*: 1.

25 *Ibid.*: 3.

26 *Ibid.*: 3.

27 *Ibid.*: 4.

28 *Ibid.*: 6.

29 *Shakwā'*: 40; *Apologia*: 71.

30 *Zubdah*: 3.

31 *Ibid.*: 4.

32 *Ibid.*: 2.

33 *Ibid.*: 2.

34 *Ibid.*: 2.

35 *Ibid.*: 4.

36 *Ibid.*: 4.

37 *Ibid.*: 6.

38 *Ibid.*: 7.

39 "From my early youth," writes al-Ghazzālī in *al-Munqidh*, "before I was twenty years old and as I neared the age of puberty, up until now, when I am fifty years old, I have plunged deep into this shoreless ocean, like courageous ones, not like the coward. I swim through its hidden depth, and step into the darkness of every mystery. I attack every problem, and fearlessly step into every danger. I question the beliefs of every sect. I discover the secrets of the religion of every community, so that I can distinguish between their right and wrong, their traditions and their conventions" (al-Ghazzālī (1983): 24). There are passages like this that must have fascinated 'Ayn al-Quḍāt.

40 *Zubdah*: 9–10.

41 *Ibid.*: 17.

42 *Ibid.*: 22.
43 *Ibid.*: 23.
44 *Ibid.*: 27.
45 *Ibid.*: 29.
46 *Ibid.*: 30.
47 *Ibid.*: 31.
48 By soft as opposed to hard metaphysics, I wish to designate a mode of epistemic operation for 'Ayn al-Quḍāt's thinking in *Zubdah* which is true to his detection of a series of non-rational intelligibilities, such as "taste" and "perception" which are not reason-based and logocentric. I believe that it is exactly the same mode of epistemic operation that the contemporary Italian philosopher Gianni Vattimo calls *il pensiero debole*, which has been translated as "weak or post-foundational thought". "All the categories of metaphysics," Vattimo asserts, "are violent categories: Being and its attributes, the 'first' cause, man as 'responsible', and even the will to power, if that is read metaphysically as affirmation or as the assumption of power over the world. They must be 'weakened' or relieved of their excess power" (Vattimo (1993): 5–6). I believe that 'Ayn al-Quḍāt's active postulation of such terms as *dhawq*, *baṣīrah*, etc., and indeed his entire anti-nomocentric, anti-logocentric counter-metaphysics is geared towards a mode of *il pensiero debole*.
49 *Zubdah*: 33.
50 *Ibid.*: 34.
51 *Ibid.*: 35.
52 *Ibid.*: 43.
53 *Ibid.*: 47.
54 *Ibid.*: 48–51.
55 *Ibid.*: 80.
56 It is crucial to keep in mind that precisely this point is one of the charges which were brought against 'Ayn al-Quḍāt when the clerical establishment in Hamadan issued an edict (*fatwā*) against him. See *Shakwā'*: 7, *Apologia*: 30. 'Ayn al-Quḍāt's reference here to "a treatise which I composed twenty years ago" is almost certainly a mistake which is left uncorrected in both the critical editions of 'Uṣayrān and Abd el-Jalil and in Arberry's translation. 'Abd al-Jalil notes the discrepancy in his introduction, *La Šakwā* 7 n. 2, but leaves the "twenty years" in the text. *Shakwā* was composed in 525/1131. Twenty years before would be 505/1111 (the year of al-Ghazzālī's death) when 'Ayn al-Quḍāt was thirteen and to the best of our knowledge author of no significant text. But ten years before 525/1131 is 516/1122 and coincides with the date of the *Zubdah*; and thus most probably 'Ayn al-Quḍāt is referring to this text, and in fact to this very passage. Arberry's appendix A to *Apologia*: 94–6 is an excellent, point-by-point, verification of the fact that in the *Shakwā* almost all of 'Ayn al-Quḍāt's references to his youthful *Risālah* are in fact to the *Zubdah*.
57 Arberry on p. 15 of his Introduction and appendix C to *Apologia*: 99–101 and Zarrīnkūb in his chapter on Bābā Ṭāhir and 'Ayn al-Quḍāt in Zarrīnkūb (1978): 197.
58 Zarrīnkūb (1978): 197.
59 *Tamhīdāt*: 15.

60 For details, see 'Uṣayrān's introduction to *Tamhīdāt*: 9.
61 See 'Alī Naqī Munzawī and 'Afīf 'Uṣayrān's Introduction to their critical edition of 'Ayn al-Quḍāt's "letters" in *Maktūbāt*: 5.
62 Introduction to the *Tamhīdāt*: 6.
63 *Ibid.*
64 For further details on these manuscripts see the editors' Introduction to *Maktūbāt*: 3–15.
65 From a letter quoted in 'Uṣayrān's Introduction to *Tamhīdāt*: 12.
66 *Maktūbāt*, 1: 433.
67 *Ibid.*, 2: 1.
68 *Ibid.*, 2: 17–18.
69 *Ibid.*, 3: 34.
70 *Ibid.*, 2: 281.
71 *Ibid.*, 2: 283.
72 *Ibid.*, 2: 286.
73 *Ibid.*, 2: 286.
74 *Ibid.*, 2: 286–7.
75 *Ibid.*, 2: 287.
76 *Ibid.*, 2: 288.
77 *Ibid.*, 2: 291.
78 *Ibid.*, 2: 293.
79 *Ibid.*, 2: 293.
80 *Ibid.*, 2: 294.
81 *Ibid.*, 2: 294–5.
82 *Ibid.*, 2: 297–8.
83 *Ibid.*, 2: 299.
84 Qur'ān 2: 269.
85 *Maktūbāt*, 2: 301–2.
86 *Ibid.*, 2: 302.
87 *Ibid.*, 2: 302–3.
88 *Ibid.*, 2: 303.
89 As this careful account of 'Ayn al-Quḍāt's historical hermeneutics unfolds, occasionally he interjects a few words that reveal his remarkable, rather arrogant, self-confidence. Right at this point, for example, he writes, "[I elaborate this] for the sake of explication, otherwise I know perfectly well, what the origin of the fire-worship was, and how it was distorted. I have known these all by myself. I have never heard anything remotely resembling this from anybody, nor have I read it in any book" (*Maktūbāt*, 2: 304–5).
90 As evident in his remark on the penultimate page of the letter, where he says, "When somebody, for example, reaches your status of the treasurer, then he must have gone through the stages that you have" (*Maktūbāt*, 2: 307).
91 *Maktūbāt*, 2: 282.
92 *Ibid.*
93 *Ibid.*
94 *Ibid.*, 2: 293.
95 *Ibid.*, 2: 295.
96 *Ibid.*, 2: 297.
97 *Ibid.*, 2: 298.

98 *Ibid.*, 2: 282.
99 *Ibid.*, 2: 298.
100 *Ibid.*, 2: 297.
101 *Ibid.*, 2: 301–2.
102 *Ibid.*, 2: 302–3.
103 *Ibid.*, 2: 303.
104 *Ibid.*, 2: 302.
105 *Ibid.*, 2: 302.
106 *Ibid.*, 2: 282.
107 *Ibid.*, 2: 304.
108 *Ibid.*, 2: 304.
109 *Ibid.*, 2: 282.
110 *Ibid.*, 2: 308.
111 *Ibid.*, 2: 308.
112 *Ibid.*, 2: 391.
113 *Ibid.*, 2: 305.
114 *Tamhīdāt*: 39–43.
115 *Ibid.*: 56.
116 *Ibid.*: 66–78.
117 *Ibid.*: 78–88.
118 *Ibid.*: 88–91.
119 *Ibid.*: 91–2.
120 *Ibid.*: 92–6.
121 *Ibid.*: 96.
122 *Ibid.*: 100.
123 *Ibid.*: 111.
124 *Ibid.*: 170.
125 *Ibid.*: 186–9.
126 *Tamhīdāt*: 209.
127 *Ibid.*: 207.
128 *Ibid.*: 209.
129 *Ibid.*: 232.
130 *Ibid.*: 234.
131 *Ibid.*: 254.
132 *Ibid.*: 258.
133 *Ibid.*: 765.
134 *Ibid.*: 270.
135 The details of this are reported in various historical sources of the period. See, for example, al-Iṣfahānī (1900): 109–24; al-Qummī (1984): 1–26; Kirmānī (1959): 74–7; Mustawfī (1985): 453–5; and al-Rāwandī (1985): 203–8.
136 I have read *Shakwā'* closely in an earlier article on him to outline the principal charges which were brought against 'Ayn al-Quḍāt. See Dabashi (1993).
137 *Shakwā'*: 7–8; *Apologia*: 30.
138 *Shakwā'*: 9; *Apologia*: 32, with some modification of Arberry's translation.
139 *Shakwā'*: 10; *Apologia*: 33.
140 *Shakwā'*: 11; *Apologia*: 34–5, with slight modification of Arberry's translation.
141 *Shakwā'*: 39; *Apologia*: 69–70.

BIBLIOGRAPHY

Abbreviations used for ʿAyn al-Quḍāt's writings

Apologia. *A Sufi Martyr: The Apologia of ʿAyn al-Quḍāt al-Hamadhānī*, trans. with intro. and notes by A. J. Arberry (London, 1969).
Maktūbāt. *Nāmah-hā-yi ʿAyn al-Quḍāt Hamadānī*, ed. ʿAli Naqī Munzawī and ʿAfīf ʿUṣayrān (Tehran, 1969).
La Šakwā. *Šakwā-l-Ğarīb ʿan l-ʾAwtān ʾilā ʿulamāʾ-l-Buldān*, ed. and trans., with intro. and notes, by Mohammed Ben Abd el-Jalīl, *Journal asiatique* (Janvier–Mars 1930): 1–76; (Avril–Juin 1930): 193–291.
Shakwā. *Risālah Shakwāʾl-gharīb*, ed. with intro. by ʿAfīf ʿUṣayrān (Tehran, 1962).
Tamhīdāt. *Tamhīdāt*, ed. with intro. by ʿAfīf ʿUṣayrān (Tehran, 1962).
Zubdah. *Zubdah al-ḥaqāʾiq*, ed. with intro. by ʿAfīf ʿUṣayrān (Tehran, 1961).

Other References

Awn, Peter (1983) *Satan's Tragedy and Redemption: Iblīs in Sufi Psychology* (Leiden).
Bertels, Y. E. (1971) *Taṣawwuf wa adabiyyāt-i taṣawwuf*, trans. from Russian into Persian by Sīrūs Īzadī (Tehran).
Bosworth, C. E. (1968) "The Political and Dynastic History of the Iranian World (A.D. 1000–1217", in J. A. Boyle (ed.) *The Cambridge History of Iran*, 5, *The Saljuq and Mongol Periods* (Cambridge): 1–202.
Dabashi, Hamid (1993) "ʿAyn al-Quḍāt Hamadhānī wa Risāla-yi shakwāʾl-gharīb", *Īrān Nāmah*, 11(1): 57–74.
Daftary, Farhad (1990) *The Ismāʿīlīs: Their History and Doctrines* (Cambridge).
Eco, Umberto (1988) *The Aesthetics of Thomas Aquinas* (Cambridge, Mass.).
Ernst, Carl (1985) *Words of Ecstasy in Sufism* (Albany).
Farmanish, Raḥīm (1959) *Sharḥ-i aḥwāl wa āthār-i ʿAyn al-Quḍāt al-Miyānjī al-Hamadānī* (Tehran).
al-Ghazzālī, Abū Ḥāmid (1983) *al-Munqidh min al-ḍalāl* (Tehran).
Gurgānī, Fakhr al-Dīn Asʿad (1959) *Wīs wa Rāmīn*, ed., annotated with intro. by Muḥammad Jaʿfar Maḥjūb (Tehran).
Humāʾī, Jalāl al-Dīn (1938) *Ghazzālī-nāmah* (Tehran).
al-Iṣfahānī, ʿImād al-Dīn Muḥammad (1900) *Kitāb taʾrīkh dawlat āl Saljūq*, abridged by Muḥammad al-Bundārī al-Iṣfahānī (Cairo).
Jāmī, Mawlānā ʿAbd al-Raḥmān ibn Aḥmad (1957) *Nafaḥāt al-uns* ed. Mahdī Tawḥīdī-Pūr (Tehran).
Kirmānī, Nāṣir al-Dīn Munshī (1959) *Nasāʾim al-ashʿār min laṭāʾim al-akhbār: Dar taʾrīkh-i wuzarāʾ*, ed. Mīr Jalāl al-Dīn Ḥusaynī Urmawī (Muḥaddith) (Tehran).
Landolt, Hermann (1978) "Two Types of Mystical Thought in Muslim Iran: an Essay on Suhrawardī *Shaykh al-Ishrāq* and ʿAynulquzāt-i Hamadānī", *The Muslim World*, 68.
Lewisohn, Leonard (1993) "In Quest of Annihilation: Imaginalization and Mystical Death in the *Tamhīdāt* of ʿAyn al-Quḍāt Hamadānī", in Leonard Lewisohn (ed.), *Classical Persian Sufism: From Its Origins to Rumi* (London and New York).

Maqsūdlū, Jawād (1975) *Sharḥ-i aḥwāl wa āthār wa du-bayti-hā-yi Bābā Ṭāhir 'Uryān* . . . (Tehran).
Mustawfī, Ḥamd Allāh (1985) *Tārīkh-i Guzīdah*, ed. 'Abd al-Ḥusayn Nawā'ī (Tehran).
al-Qummī, Najm al-Dīn Abū al-Rajā' (1984) *Tā'rīkh al-wuzarā'*, ed. Muḥammad Taqī Dānishpazhūh (Tehran).
al-Rāwandī, Muḥammad ibn 'Alī ibn Sulaymān (1985) *Rāḥat al-ṣudūr wa āyat al-surūr dar tā'rīkh āl-i Saljūq*, ed. Muḥammad Iqbāl, with additional notes by Mujtabā Mīnuwī (Tehran).
Ṣafā, Dhabiḥullah (1977) *Tārīkh-i adabīyat dar Īrān*, 2 (Tehran).
Shabistarī, Shaykh Maḥmūd (1982) *Gulshan-i rāz*, ed. Ṣābir-i Kirmānī (Tehran).
Suhrawardī, Shaykh-i Shahīd Shahāb al-Dīn Yaḥyā (1982) *Ḥikmah al-ishrāq*, trans. Sayyid Ja'far Sajjādī (Tehran).
Urvoy, Dominique (1991) *Ibn Rushd (Averroes)* (London).
Vattimo, Gianni (1993) *The Adventure of Difference: Philosophy after Nietzsche and Heidegger* (Baltimore).
Zarrīnkūb, 'Abd al-Ḥusayn (1978) *Justijū dar taṣawwuf-i Īrān* (Tehran).

CHAPTER 28

Shihāb al-Dīn Suhrawardī: founder of the Illuminationist school

Hossein Ziai

THE MASTER OF ILLUMINATION

Shihāb al-Dīn Yaḥyā ibn Ḥabash ibn Amīrak Abu'l-Futūḥ Suhrawardī is well-known in the history of Islamic philosophy as the Master of Illumination (*Shaykh al-Ishrāq*), a reference to his accepted position as the founder of a new school of philosophy distinct from the Peripatetic school (*madhhab*, or *maktab al-mashshā'ūn*). Suhrawardī was born in the small town of Suhraward in north-western Persia in the year 549/1154. He met a violent death by execution in Aleppo in the year 587/1191[1] and therefore is also sometimes called the Executed Master (*al-Shaykh al-Maqtūl*).

Although the circumstances surrounding Suhrawardī's death are a matter of speculation, as I will touch upon further, information on his life is fairly extensive. The influential philosopher lived only thirty-eight lunar (thirty-six solar) years.[2] In the year 579/1183, he travelled to Aleppo,[3] where he completed his major work *Ḥikmat al-ishrāq* ("Philosophy of Illumination") in 582/1186.[4] His main biographer, Shams al-Dīn Muḥammad Shahrazūrī, states in his *Nuzhat al-arwāḥ* ("Pleasure of Spirits") that Suhrawardī was thirty years old when he completed another of his major philosophical works, *al-Mashāri' wa'l-mutāraḥāt*) ("Paths and Havens") (completed *c.* 579/1183).[5]

Suhrawardī first studied philosophy and theology with Majd al-Dīn al-Jīlī in Maraghah, then travelled to Isfahan (or Mardin) to study with Fakhr al-Dīn al-Mārdīnī (d. 594/1198),[6] who is said to have predicted his student's death.[7] It is also known that Ẓahīr al-Fārsī, a logician, introduced Suhrawardī to the *al-Baṣā'ir* ("Observations") of the famous logician 'Umar ibn Sahlān al-Ṣāwī (*fl.* 540/1145).[8] This fact is significant, in that the latter work is among the first to depart from the standard nine-part division of logic – the nine books of the *Organon* – in favour of a two-part division: formal and material logic. Suhrawardī later employed this simpler system within his three-part logic, consisting of semantics, formal logic and material logic.

Suhrawardī composed most of his major treatises over a span of ten years, which is not long enough for him to have developed two distinct styles of philosophy – a Peripatetic style followed by an Illuminationist one – as some scholars have suggested.[9] In fact, in each of his major works Suhrawardī makes ample references to his other treatises. This indicates that the writings were either composed more or less concurrently, or that they were revised when taught with a consideration of the others.[10]

Soon after his arrival in Aleppo, Suhrawardī entered the service of Prince al-Malik al-Ẓāhir Ghāzī, governor of Aleppo – also known as Malik Ẓāhir Shāh, son of Sultan Ayyūbid Ṣalāḥ al-Dīn. The sultan is well known in the West as Saladin, the great champion of the wars against the Crusaders. Suhrawardī won the prince's favours, became his tutor and began a life at court. There, in extended private sessions, the young philosopher reportedly informed the prince of his new philosophy. No doubt Suhrawardī's rapid rise to privileged position met with the usual medieval courtly jealousy and intrigue. That the judges, viziers and jurists of Aleppo were displeased with the distinguished tutor's increasing status could not have helped his case.[11] Letters written to Saladin by the famous judge Qāḍī al-Fāḍil arguing for Suhrawardī's execution sealed the young thinker's fate.[12] The sultan ordered the prince to have his tutor killed.[13]

Medieval historians cite "heresy", "corrupting religion" and "corrupting the young prince, al-Malik al-Ẓāhir" as charges against Suhrawardī. The validity of these accusations is controversial, however.[14] As I have substantiated in publication elsewhere, the more plausible reason for Suhrawardī's execution is based on the philosopher's political doctrine revealed in his works on the Philosophy of Illumination, a political philosophy which I have termed the "Illuminationist political doctrine".[15] The year of Suhrawardī's execution was turbulent with political and military conflict. England's King Richard the Lionheart had landed in Acre,[16] and major battles were taking place between Muslims and Christians over the Holy Land. The great sultan Saladin clearly had more pressing matters at hand than to bother with the execution of a wayfaring mystic, had he not been deemed to be a clear threat to political security.[17]

Controversial though Suhrawardī's life may have been, one fact is certain: he had a major impact on subsequent philosophical thought, a fact on which all biographers concur.

SUHRAWARDĪ'S WORKS

Suhrawardī was a prolific author who wrote many works on almost every philosophical subject, including, for the first time in the history of Islamic philosophy, a substantial number of Persian philosophical symbolic narratives. Not all of his works have survived nor have all of the existing ones been published. His major published works are indicated here.

The most important texts in the Philosophy of Illumination are Suhrawardī's four major Arabic philosophical works: the *al-Talwīḥāt* ("Intimations"), the *al-Muqāwamāt* ("Apposites"), the *al-Mashāri' wa'l-muṭāraḥāt,* ("Paths and Havens")[18] and the *Ḥikmat al-ishrāq* ("Philosophy of Illumination").[19] Based on textual evidence, I have found these works to constitute an integral corpus presenting the details of the Philosophy of Illumination.[20] Though of lesser philosophical significance, the Arabic treatises, *al-Alwāḥ al-'imādiyyah* ("'Imādian Tablets") and *Hayākil al-nūr* ("Temples of Light"), and the Persian *Partaw-nāmah* ("Epistle on Emanation") may also be added.[21]

Based on Suhrawardī's own explicit statements, the four major works mentioned above were to be studied in a designated order: (1) the *Intimations,* (2) the *Apposites,* (3) the *Paths and Havens,* and (4) the *Philosophy of Illumination.*[22] Among all of Suhrawardī's works, the "Introductions" of only two of them, the *Paths and Havens* and the *Philosophy of Illumination,* include specific statements concerning the methodology of the Philosophy of Illumination. In the "Introduction" to the *Paths and Havens,* Suhrawardī indicates that the book contains an exposition of the results of his personal experiences and intuitions, and further stipulates his view of how knowledge is to be obtained. Suhrawardī's account of the same methodological question in his "Introduction" to the *Philosophy of Illumination* is more elaborate and detailed but is essentially the same as the account given in the *Paths and Havens.*

Next in order of significance after Suhrawardī's major works and the treatises named above are his Arabic and Persian symbolic narratives. These include *Qiṣṣat al-ghurbat al-gharbiyyah* ("A Tale of the Occidental Exile"); *Risālat al-ṭayr* ("The Treatise of the Birds"); *Awāz-i par-i Jibra'īl* ("The Sound of Gabriel's Wing"); *'Aql-i surkh* ("The Red Intellect"); *Rūzī bā jamā'at-i ṣūfiyān* ("A Day with a Group of Sufis"); *Fī ḥālat al-ṭufūliyyah* ("On the State of Childhood"); *Fī ḥaqīqat al-'ishq* ("On the Reality of Love"); *Lughat-i mūrān* ("The Language of Ants"); and *Ṣafīr-i sīmurgh* ("The Simurgh's Shrill Cry").[23] In these writings Suhrawardī, as in Ibn Sīnā's Arabic tales before him, uses the symbolic narrative to portray philosophical issues, though usually simple ones intended for the novice. The tales are more significant in their use of language than in their philosophical content. But all are indicative of long-established views that the symbolic and poetic mode of discourse both elicit interest from readers and may also convey a certain experiential, subjective sense lost in purely discursive texts.

The next group of works by Suhrawardī consists of devotional prayers and invocations. Other minor treatises, aphorisms and short statements may also be grouped here.[24] Of specific interest in terms of both language and content are two prayers and invocations composed in an especially rich symbolic and literary style, where Suhrawardī addresses "the great Heavenly Sun, Hūrakhsh",[25] and invokes the authority of "the Great Luminous Being" (*al-nayyir al-aʿẓam*), praying to it for knowledge and salvation. The symbolism of such short prayers has led some scholars to believe them to contain an ancient Persian element of reverence for luminous astronomical bodies such as the sun.[26]

AN OVERVIEW OF SUHRAWARDĪ'S PHILOSOPHY OF ILLUMINATION

Suhrawardī chose the title *Philosophy of Illumination (Ḥikmat al-ishrāq)* to name his major Arabic work, and also to distinguish his philosophical approach from that of the established Peripatetic works of his time, predominantly the doctrines of Ibn Sīnā, the great Islamic scientist and master of *mashshāʾī* or Peripatetic philosophy. While Suhrawardī states that the *Intimations*, for example, is written according to the "Peripatetic method",[27] this should not be considered an independent work written about Peripatetic philosophy. Rather, it indicates that the Philosophy of Illumination includes but is not defined by accepted Peripatetic teachings, parts of which Suhrawardī accepted and parts of which he rejected or refined.

Throughout his works Suhrawardī uses terms such as "Illuminationist theorem" (*qāʿidah ishrāqiyyah*); "Illuminationist rules" (*ḍawābiṭ ishrāqiyyah*); "Illuminationist lemma" (*daqīqah ishrāqiyyah*) and similar phrases, to identify specific problems of logic, epistemology, physics and metaphysics – areas of thought which he reconstructs or otherwise reformulates in an innovative manner. These new terms indicate the essential components of the Philosophy of Illumination and distinguish Illuminationist methodology from the Peripatetic.

Suhrawardī adds the word "Illuminationist" (*ishrāqī*) as a descriptive adjective to selected technical terms as a means of signifying their specific use in his system. For example, "Illuminationist vision" (*mushāhadah ishrāqiyyah*) specifies the epistemological priority of a primary mode of immediate cognition distinguished from the more general use of the word vision as applied to mystical experience. "Illuminationist relation" (*iḍāfah ishrāqiyyah*) specifies the non-predicative relation between subject and object, and is a new technical term signifying the Illuminationist position in the logical foundations of epistemology. "Illuminationist knowledge by presence" (*al-'ilm al-ḥuḍūrī al-ishrāqī*) signifies the priority of an immediate, durationless, intuitive mode of cognition over the temporally extended essentialist definitions used as predicative propositions; and it also distinguishes the Illuminationist position from the Peripatetic view of "acquired knowledge" (*al-'ilm al-ḥuṣūlī*). Many other similar technical terms are also defined and used by Suhrawardī for the first time in an Illuminationist philosophical sense to distinguish them from specific Peripatetic terms or from the general non-philosophical vocabulary of mystical and theological texts. Suhrawardī's attempt to attribute specifically chosen meanings to known expressions by adding qualifiers, and to coin new terms as well, is a basic characteristic of his philosophical reconstruction of previous modes of thought.

Finally, Suhrawardī introduces the term "the Illuminationists" (*al-ishrāqiyyūn*), subsequently adopted by commentators and historians, to describe thinkers whose philosophical position and method are distinguished from "the Peripatetics" (*al-mashshā'ūn*). It is clear, therefore, that the young philosopher intended his works to be recognized as incorporating a different system from the Peripatetic works of his time as manifest by language, method and meaning. All of the major Illuminationist commentators – Shams al-Dīn Shahrazūrī, Ibn Kammūnah and Quṭb al-Dīn Shīrāzī – agree that Suhrawardī's philosophical position is markedly different from that of the Peripatetic school.[28]

An older Orientalist tradition, however, asserts that the Philosophy of Illumination is not essentially new, and considers Ibn Sīnā's short remarks concerning Oriental Philosophy *(al-ḥikmat al-mashriqiyyah)* to precede it. In this view, Ibn Sīnā's polemic or even politically motivated statements were not intended to reconstruct Aristotelian philosophy systematically but to garner wider acceptance for Greek philosophy by giving it more commonly accepted epithets. The same Orientalist tradition, moreover, does not consider Illuminationist philosophy to be essentially distinct from the Peripatetic and has, usually without careful examination of Illuminationist texts, generalized it as Ibn Sīnan. This position is not altogether valid, however, as it does not take post-Ibn Sīnan Arabic and Persian texts into account, considering them to be devoid of new and fresh philosophical arguments.

My position concerning the Philosophy of Illumination, which I have delineated here and elsewhere,[29] is that it is a distinct, systematic philosophical construction designed to avoid the logical, epistemological and metaphysical inconsistencies which Suhrawardī perceived in the Peripatetic philosophy of his day. While Suhrawardī quite obviously was deeply aware of the Ibn Sīnan philosophical corpus, his Philosophy of Illumination cannot be totally attributed to Ibn Sīnā, nor can it be deemed to be merely its allegorical restatement. Suhrawardī does use Ibn Sīnan texts, terms and methods, but he employs many other sources, as well. Although he was deeply influenced by the great Peripatetic master al-Shaykh al-Ra'īs, in my view the philosophical intention underlying the composition of works designated as "Illuminationist" is clearly Suhrawardī's own. It will be a challenging task for future researchers to determine if the Illuminationist plan is well defined and philosophically sound or given more to polemics. One thing is clear, however: a failure to examine actual Illuminationist texts, the majority of which remain unpublished and accessible only to a few specialists, has blurred the origins of Illuminationist philosophy. By briefly examining a few relevant passages here, I hope to put an end to these historical generalizations.

SUHRAWARDĪ'S CRITIQUE OF IBN SĪNĀ'S POSITION

In numerous places in his writings Suhrawardī argues against Ibn Sīnā's philosophical position while carefully delineating his own. In a few instances he even attacks the Peripatetic master directly. In perhaps his most bitter attack on Ibn Sīnā, Suhrawardī emphatically rejects the alleged position of Ibn Sīnā as a so-called Oriental (*mashriqī*) philosopher. The implications of this passage are also significant for an understanding of the trends and schools of thought in the history of Islamic philosophy in general. The controversy concerns Ibn Sīnā's claims that he had plans for composing an Oriental philosophy more elevated in rank than his other, strictly Peripatetic works. Suhrawardī begins the passage by quoting texts by Ibn Sīnā concerning problems relating to the definition of simple things, with which he at first agrees – namely that simple, non-composite essences can only be "described" and not defined.[30] Suhrawardī here refers to a book titled *Karārīs fi'l-ḥikmah* ("Quires on Philosophy"), attributed by Ibn Sīnā to the method of "Orientals" in philosophy.[31] It is not clear what the *Quires* are, but the statement in question can be traced to Ibn Sīnā's *Logic of the Orientals*.[32]

Suhrawardī's initial remarks concerning Ibn Sīnan thought are matter-of-fact. His attack against it begins rather abruptly and is directed towards the essential distinction between Peripatetic philosophy and Oriental philosophy. First, Suhrawardī casts doubt on Ibn Sīnā's claim that the *Quires* is based on Oriental principles. Then, he goes on to refute intensely Ibn Sīnā's assertion that the *Quires* constitutes a new Oriental philosophy in a twofold argument, as follows. Firstly, no supposedly Oriental philosophy existed prior to Suhrawardī's own reconstruction of the Philosophy of Illumination, which should not be considered Oriental in a cultural or geographic sense, but rather as incorporating an "Illuminationist" (*ishrāqī*, not to be confused with *mashriqī*)[33] emphasis on intuitive, inspirational and immediate modes of cognition. (These philosophical issues should not be confused with the contemporary reading of an allegedly medieval nationalist ideology that is, at best, difficult to substantiate textually.)

Secondly, Suhrawardī takes pains to demonstrate that the *Quires* were, in fact, composed solely in agreement with established Peripatetic laws (*qawā'id al-mashshā'īn*), comprising problems included only in what he specifies as *philosophia generalis* (*al-ḥikmat al-'āmmah*). At best, as Suhrawardī is careful to indicate, Ibn Sīnā may have changed an expression or slightly modified a minor point, but the *Quires* is not significantly different from the standard Peripatetic texts. Suhrawardī concludes that simple modifications made by Ibn Sīnā do not make him an Oriental philosopher. Here is another instance at which Suhrawardī turns to polemics, perhaps for political reasons, as he invokes the authority of the "ancients" by claiming that his own principles of Oriental philosophy (*al-aṣl al-mashriqī*) reflect the earlier "wisdom" of Persian Khusrawānī sages and many other figures.[34]

It is necessary to bear in mind Suhrawardī's own philosophical intention in composing systematic works structurally distinct from the Peripatetic and that were specifically titled to emphasize the difference. Suhrawardī claims that his new system triumphs where the Peripatetic fails, that it is a sounder method for probing the nature of things, and is, above all, capable of "scientifically"[35] describing non-standard experiences (widely believed to be real in his time), such as "true dreams", "personal revelations", "intuitive knowledge" of the whole, "ability to foretell the future", "out-of-body experiences", "reviving the dead" and other "miraculous" extraordinary phenomena.[36] The underlying intention for Suhrawardī's Philosophy of Illumination is to prescribe a clear path towards a philosophical life that is at once a more "scientifically" valid means of probing the nature of things and attaining happiness, and ultimately a way of reaching more practical wisdom that can and should be employed in the service of just rule.

THE SIGNIFICANCE OF SUHRAWARDĪ'S WORK IN ISLAMIC PHILOSOPHY

A significant methodological principle is established by Suhrawardī when, for the first time in the history of philosophy, he clearly distinguishes a bipartite division in metaphysics: *metaphysica generalis* and *metaphysica specialis*.[37] The former, as the new philosophical position holds, includes standard discussions of such subjects as existence, unity, substances, accidents, time, motion, etc.; while the latter is said to include a novel scientific approach to analysing supra-rational problems such as God's existence and knowledge; "true dreams"; "visionary experience"; creative acts of the enlightened, the knowing subject's "imagination"; the "proof" of the real; the objective existence of a "separate realm" designated *mundus imaginalis* (*'ālam al-khayāl*); as well as many other similar problems. In fact, Suhrawardī's division of the subject matter of metaphysics, as well as his attempt to demonstrate the epistemological primacy of an objectified experiential mode of cognition, are among the distinguishing methodological and structural characteristics of Illuminationist philosophy. Since Suhrawardī's time, these principles have been employed by many commentators and historians to accentuate the differences between the Peripatetics and the Illuminationists.[38]

Another area in which Illuminationist principles have had an impact is in the realm of semantics (*'ilm dalālat al-alfāẓ*). Suhrawardī, perhaps inspired by a Stoic–Megaric minor trend in Islamic philosophy up to his time, restates a number of problems in a different manner than the way in which they are named and discussed in the Ibn Sīnan logical corpus.[39] Problems in this area of logic include: types of signification; relation of class names to constituents (members) of the class; types of inclusion of members in classes (*indirāj, istighrāq, indikhāl, shumūl*, etc.); and, perhaps most significantly from the standpoint of the history of logic, a fairly well-defined theory of supposition (the restricted and unrestricted use of quantification).[40]

In the domain of formal logic Suhrawardī proves himself to be a remarkable logician. To a lesser or greater extent, Suhrawardī influenced a number of works on specific problems of logic in Persia. These include: iterated modalities; the construction of a super affirmative necessary proposition (*al-qaḍiyyat al-ḍarūriyyat al-battātah*); the question of negation (*al-salb*), especially in the conversion of syllogism (*al-'aks*); reduction of terms; construction of a single "mother" figure for syllogism (*shakl al-qiyās*) from which all other figures are to be derived; temporal modalities (*al-qaḍāyā al-muwajjahah*); especially non-admittance of an unrestricted validity of the universal affirmative proposition (*al-qaḍiyyat al-mūjibat al-kulliyyah*) in obtaining certain knowledge (*al-'ilm al-yaqīnī*) because of future contingency (*al-imkān al-mustaqbal*); as well as many others.

Another major area of Suhrawardī's influence is his theory of categories, to which most later philosophical works in Persia refer, especially within the later major non-Ibn Sīnan philosophical synthesis known as Transcendent Philosophy (*al-ḥikmat al-muta'āliyah*). Suhrawardī discusses the categories at great length in his major Arabic and Persian systematically philosophical works. He attributes his influential categorical theory to a Pythagorean scholar (*shakhṣ fīthāghūrithī*) by the name of Arkhūṭus.[41] What is later designated by Ṣadr al-Dīn al-Shīrāzī as "motion in the category of substance" (*al-ḥarakah al-jawhariyyah*), translated as "substantial motion" and "transubstantial motion", is a direct corollary to Suhrawardī's theory.[42] Briefly the theory states that "intensity" (*shaddah wa ḍaʿf*) is a property of all categories which are reduced to five: substance (*jawhar*), quality (*kayf*), quantity (*kamm*), relation (*nisbah*) and motion (*ḥarakah*).[43] This concept is in direct agreement with Suhrawardī's special theory of being as continuum, as well as with his theory known as "theory of future possibility" (*qāʿidat imkān al-ashraf* – literally, theory of the possibility of the most noble).

Taken as a whole, Suhrawardī's aim is directed towards theoretical as well as practical and achievable goals, first to demonstrate fundamental gaps in the logical foundations of Aristotelian epistemology and metaphysics, and then to reconstruct a system founded upon different, more logically consistent, epistemological and metaphysical principles. Although further analytic studies are required to evaluate the philosophical side of Suhrawardī's thought, one fact is widely accepted by the traditional Islamic philosophers: the Philosophy of Illumination – its ideas, language and method – had a major impact on all subsequent thought in Islam, covering philosophical, mystical and even political domains. The influence of this philosophical system has been most widespread in Persia followed by Muslim India, where it has also helped define the notion of poetic and philosophical wisdom as the principal means by which generations of Muslims have sought solutions to essential intellectual and existential questions.

A REVIEW OF WESTERN SCHOLARSHIP ON SUHRAWARDĪ

Despite Suhrawardī's monumental impact on the development of post-Ibn Sīnan philosophy in Islam, evidenced by the widespread use of the epithet "Illuminationist" (*ishrāqī*) to distinguish it from the Peripatetic approach, only a few analytical works (none comprehensive) are available on Suhrawardī's systematic philosophical works. Lack of serious interest in studying the philosophical dimension of Suhrawardī's thought has been due partially to, firstly, a misconception among some historians that Islamic philosophy did not develop beyond Ibn Sīnā in the East, and terminated in the West with Ibn Rushd; and, secondly, misrepresentation of Suhrawardī's ideas by a number of scholars who have described the Philosophy of Illumination (and other non-Aristotelian philosophical endeavour) as "theosophy", "*sagesse orientale*", "transcendent theosophy" and the like.[44] While the Islamic Peripatetic tradition has been studied from a philosophical perspective, the dominant focus of scholarly attention on post-Ibn Sīnan thought has been on a presumed "spiritual" dimension of selected Arabic and Persian texts of Islamic philosophy covering the five centuries after Ibn Sīnā, including Suhrawardī's *Philosophy of Illumination* ("Ḥikmat al-ishrāq"), Mullā Ṣadrā's *al-Asfār al-arba'at al-'aqliyyah* ("The Four Intellectual Journeys") and other similar texts. This type of emphasis has led some historians to categorize thinkers such as Suhrawardī as "esoteric" Sufis, which is a misleading designation to say the least. The more serious limitation of emphasis on the esoteric dimension of post-Ibn Sīnan philosophical texts, appropriately stated by Fazlur Rahman, has been "at the cost . . . of its purely intellectual and philosophical hard core, which is of immense value and interest to the modern student of philosophy".[45]

Western interest in Suhrawardī has a long history. Since the early decades of the twentieth century Orientalists and historians of philosophy have noticed Suhrawardī to be an important figure in the formation of post-Ibn Sīnan philosophical thought. Carra de Vaux[46] and Max Horten[47] wrote short essays on him. In the late 1920s, Louis Massignon gave a classification of Suhrawardī's works.[48] Otto Spies edited and translated a few of his philosophical allegories a decade later;[49] and Helmut Ritter clarified a prevalent Orientalist confusion by distinguishing Suhrawardī from three mystics who bore the same attribution "Suhrawardī".[50] It was, however, Henry Corbin's text editions of many of Suhrawardī's philosophical writings, as well as his interpretations, that started a new wave of infatuation with Illuminationist philosophy.[51] Seyyed Hossein Nasr has also devoted a number of studies to the spiritual and religious dimension in Suhrawardī's teachings.[52] Still, however, too few studies of the logical and epistemological foundations of the Philosophy of Illumination from a philosophical point of view are available. The few pages in Muḥammad Iqbāl's *The Development of Metaphysics in Persia* constitute one of the few general accounts of Suhrawardī's philosophical thought.[53]

Some recent scholars, notably Henry Corbin and Mohammad Moin, have further imagined Suhrawardī to be the reviver of some form of ancient Persian philosophy, which, however, cannot be substantiated. There is simply no textual evidence for an independent Persian philosophical tradition. The fact that Suhrawardī (as well as other thinkers in Islam) mentions names of Persian kings and heroes, and makes reference to Persian mythological events, is indicative more of an intention to invoke the authority of ancient, well-known Persian symbols, than to recover some lost systematic philosophy. Suhrawardī's critique of certain problems of logic, epistemology, physics, mathematics and metaphysics in his Philosophy of Illumination draws upon established Peripatetic texts. No other textual source can be presumed to have been available to him. The fact that he reformulates philosophical problems, rejects some or redefines others is indicative of his own philosophical intention to reconstruct a metaphysical system that aims, among other things, to establish the primacy of an intuitive mode of cognition. It is not indicative of a philosophical tradition known to him but lost to us.

PROBLEMS, STRUCTURE AND METHOD OF THE PHILOSOPHY OF ILLUMINATION

The most obvious but too readily dismissed principal component of Suhrawardī's Illuminationist philosophy is his use of a special technical language. This distinct vocabulary uses the symbolism of light to describe ontological problems, and especially to depict cosmological structures. For example, the Peripatetic Necessary Being is called "Light of Lights"; the separate "intellects" are called "abstract lights"; and so on. It is important to note that these linguistic innovations are not just new terms but are also indicative of philosophical intention. Thus the light symbolism is deemed more suitable to convey the ontological principle of equivocal being, since it is more readily understood that lights may differ in intensity while remaining of the same essence. Also, it is deemed more acceptable to discuss "proximity" (*qurb*) and "distance" (*bu'd*) from the source as indications of degrees of perfection when light symbolism is used. For example, the closer an entity is to the source, the Light of Lights, the more luminous the light entity (*al-shay' al-mustanīr*) will be.

The use of symbolic language is a significant and distinguishing characteristic of the Philosophy of Illumination as a whole. Symbolism is also applied to the epistemological primacy of the creative act of intuition, which proposes as a primary axiom that the soul's knowledge of itself – here a light entity – is the foundation and starting point of knowledge. This knowledge is described as an abstract light generated (*ḥāṣil*) from the source of light. The argument is that any light is observed to propagate itself once lit and is not emanated (*fayḍ*) either by will or at discrete intervals in time. This means that all light entities are obtained or generated from the source not in time but in a durationless instant once the source is lit, whenever that may be.

From the textual perspective, the Philosophy of Illumination begins in the *Intimations*, especially where Suhrawardī recollects a dream-vision in which Aristotle appears. This allegorical device allows Suhrawardī to present several important philosophical issues. Aristotle informs Suhrawardī through this dream-vision that the Muslim Peripatetics have failed to achieve the kind of wisdom achieved by mystics such as Abū Yazīd al-Basṭāmī and al-Ḥallāj. This is due, the narration continues, to the mystics having achieved union with the Active Intellect by going beyond discursive philosophy and relying on their personal experience.[54] The truths (*ḥaqā'iq*) obtained in this way are the results of a special intuitive, experiential mode of knowledge, this text states.[55] Thus the first critique of Peripatetic philosophy is uttered through no less an authority than Aristotle, who informs Suhrawardī that true knowledge can only be based on self-knowledge and obtained through a special mode designated as "knowledge by illumination and presence".

What this epistemological mode means and how it is obtained must rest first on demonstrating the logical gaps in the Peripatetic system. This is achieved as Suhrawardī undertakes an elaborate critique of the Aristotelian concept and formula of definition. This critique, which will be examined here in some detail, is the first significant attempt to show a fundamental gap in the Aristotelian scientific method, and indicates the first step in the reconstruction of the Philosophy of Illumination. The next major methodological step is to present an alternative epistemological foundation for constructing a holistic metaphysics. These are the primacy of intuition and the theory of vision-illumination – considered in Illuminationist philosophy to be the means for obtaining principles to be used in compound deductive reasoning.

SUHRAWARDĪ'S CRITIQUE OF THE ESSENTIALIST THEORY OF DEFINITION[56]

The problem of definition is fundamentally related to how the Philosophy of Illumination is constructed. Perhaps the most significant logical problem, which also has epistemological implications, is Suhrawardī's negation and thus rejection of the Aristotelian view of an essentialist definition, *horos*, and of an Ibn Sīnan complete essentialist definition, *al-ḥadd al-tāmm*, which considers definition to be the most prior and thus the significant first step in the process of philosophical construction. The impact of Suhrawardī's critique of Peripatetic methodology on this issue is so direct and has had such a widespread impact on the subsequent development of philosophy in Persia that I am tempted to call it the triumph of Platonic method over the Aristotelian in Persia. The Platonic approach to definition seeks the unity of the thing defined in its Form, which is fully defined only as a person realizes what-is-to-be-defined (the *definiendum*) in his or her own self-consciousness.

Suhrawardī's critique of Aristotle's theory is marked by a combination of logical and semantic arguments. It begins by asserting that it is impossible to construct an essentialist definition, and that even Aristotle himself admits this.[57] Thus, Suhrawardī points out a critical gap in the Peripatetic system, thereby undermining Aristotle's basis of philosophical construction. Suhrawardī's analysis of the essentialist definition is in itself of major philosophical value. In a celebrated passage in book 2 of the *Posterior Analytics*, Aristotle stipulates the position of definition to be that of the first step in science,[58] and the premiss for demonstration.[59] Therefore, only if a definition is obtained, or constructed, may one proceed to scientific knowledge. Thus if essentialist definition does not lead to unrestricted, primary knowledge of essence – as it must in the Illuminationist position – then the entire philosophical system has to be reconstructed based on other means of achieving knowledge of essence.

How should a definition be constructed? Suhrawardī asks his Peripatetic adversaries for their answer. Let us assume we want to define a thing, *X*. This thing must be constituted in relation to its attributes, both essential and non-essential, such as concomitants, accidents and so on. We may designate these attributes as constituents of *X*, say x_1. Not considering simple, non-composite (*basīṭ*), entities, we must, Suhrawardī argues, see whether x_1 is real or only ideally known, and how it is known in relation to *X*. The next question pertinent in the Illuminationist position is that of priority (*taqaddum*). That is, in order to define *X* we must be able to know *Y*, itself consisting of y_1 constituents, in relation to which *X* may be defined. And *Y* must be necessarily prior to *X* in respect to knowledge. Also, as with *X*, the question whether *Y* can be known through y_1 will also have to be examined. Therefore, the definition of *X* will depend on what is known prior in knowledge. Thus, how the definition is obtained is, according to Suhrawardī, the primary philosophical step and first constructivist step in science.

Suhrawardī insists that the Peripatetic position on definition is reduced to: "A formula [*qawl*] which indicates the essence of the thing and combines [*yajma'*] all of its constituent elements [*muqawwimāt*]. In the case of the principal realities, it [the formula] is a synthesis [*tarkīb*] of their genera and differentiae."[60]

So far, this formula of definition is in conformity with Ibn Sīnā's writings.[61] Suhrawardī's novel position is his insistence that all constituents of a thing must be combined in the formula, a requirement not specified by the Peripatetic formula.[62] Also, the formula must be a synthesis (*tarkīb*) of the multiple genera and differentiae.[63] This means that, from the Illuminationist position, things cannot be defined as such because of the impossibility of discretely enumerating all the essentials of a thing. Thus there must be some other prior Illuminationist foundation for knowledge.

Suhrawardī's use of terms such as all (*kull*), combination (*jam'*) and synthesis (*tarkīb*), as applied to the manner in which the attributes or constituents of the thing to be defined must come together in the essentialist definition, indicate a new approach to the problem. In this respect he is also presenting a position which is in opposition to Ibn Sīnā's views that conform to the standard Peripatetic ones. Suhrawardī's critique of definition also draws on the semantic options he had worked out regarding signification (*dalālah*), of meaning (*al-ma'nā*) or idea, by the utterances (*al-lafẓ*) said of the things (*al-ashyā'*) to be defined.[64] For the complete essentialist definition of "What is *X*?", according to the Peripatetics, is "the *summum genus* of *X* plus its differentiae". For

Suhrawardī, this formula is inadequate. As he states, the Peripatetic formula for the complete essentialist definition of man is "rational animal", which only implicitly states the essence of animal, and adds nothing to our knowledge of the idea "man" (*al-insāniyyah*). The formula *qua* formula does not indicate the idea, "animal" (*al-ḥayawāniyyah*) and the utterance "rational" only indicates "a thing that has a soul". By Aristotelian definition, then, only rationality is established, and not the essence of "man".[65]

The Peripatetics' position allows the essential to be more known than the thing defined, whereas Suhrawardī holds that the essentials are as unknown as the thing itself. Suhrawardī's own theory of unity is implied when he states: "[One can obtain a definition only] by recourse to sensible or apparent things in another way [i.e., other than the Peripatetic formula of definition], and [only] if [and when] the thing pertains specifically to the sum total of the [sensible and apparent things] as an organic whole."[66]

In the last paragraph of his argument, Suhrawardī attacks the Peripatetic formula of definition from yet another point of view which is related to his critique of induction.[67] Suhrawardī's view in this regard holds that: to know something by means of its essentials, one must be able to enumerate each and every one of them, which is possible only if the sum total of the essentials is known. Suhrawardī explicitly states here for the first time that such knowledge of the total essentials by the method of enumeration is not possible. This is because the thing to be defined may have a multiplicity of non-apparent (*ghayr ẓāhir*) attributes, the set of essentials may be limitless and the elements of the set may not be discretely distinguishable from the set itself. Also, although knowledge of the set implies knowledge of the elements, it is not possible to know what the set itself is by knowing the elements separately.

Suhrawardī concludes from his arguments that the constituents of a thing (*muqawwimāt al-shay'*) are not separate from the thing, neither "really" (*'aynan*) nor "mentally" (*dhihnan*). Therefore, an essentialist definition cannot be constructed, since that would require separating the constituents of a thing into genera and differentiae; but a thing can only be described as it is seen, which then and only then determines its reality. To define something according to the Illuminationist position, it has to be "seen" as it is. As Suhrawardī explicitly states, these are his own additions to the Peripatetic method.[68]

Does the definition of *X* simply rest on an intuition of it or of something else prior to placing its formula in some constructed structure? This problem will be discussed below. The emphasis here is on Suhrawardī's insistence that only "the collectivity of the essentials of a thing is a valid definition of it".

THE ILLUMINATIONIST THEORY OF DEFINITION[69]

From a formal standpoint, Suhrawardī's theory elaborates upon the earlier one and also includes a Platonic component; as it requires that by definition we ultimately strive to know the Forms, or to obtain knowledge of them through vision-illumination. Suhrawardī's theory is, therefore, fundamentally experiential. It is based on the immediate cognition of something real and prior in being, which he identifies as "light" – the fundamental real principle of Illuminationist metaphysics. For Suhrawardī, light is its own definition; to see it – i.e., to experience it – is to know it: "If, in reality, there exists a thing which need not be defined nor explained, then that thing is apparent, and since there is nothing more apparent than light, then more than anything, it is in no need of definition."[70]

Suhrawardī contends that the essentials may be ascertained only when the thing itself is ascertained, and this is the basis for his critique of the Peripatetic theory. It also serves as the impetus for his formulation of an alternate theory, as follows: "We obtain a definition only by means of things that pertain specifically to the totality (i.e., organic whole [*al-ijtimā'*]) of the thing."[71]

In contrast to the Peripatetic view, the Illuminationist system begins by accepting the absolute validity of an atemporal, primary intuition of the knowing subject (*al-mawḍū' al-mudrik*), who is necessarily and always cognizant of its "I-ness" (*al-ana'iyyah*) prior to spatial extension. In Illuminationist philosophy, self-consciousness and the self-conscious entities are depicted as lights and cover all of reality. Thus, for example, an abstract, non-corporeal light represents pure self-consciousness. Other corporeal entities are less "lit" but are also self-conscious, albeit to a lesser degree. Every thing is also potentially self-conscious, except for the purely "dark", which represents total privation of light.

Admittedly, one aspect of Suhrawardī's theory, namely the insistence on complete enumeration of the essentials of the thing synthesized in unitary formula, is, to say the least, enigmatic. However, considering the works of modern philosophers such as Bertrand Russell and Alfred J. Ayer clarifies the problem. Russell's theory is reduced to a distinction between definition by extension (a definition that seeks to enumerate the members of a "class")[72] and definition by intention (a definition that mentions a defining property or properties).[73] The Illuminationist theory can be seen as combining elements both of a definition by extension and of a definition by intension. Ayer distinguishes Aristotelian explicit definition from definition in use. This reduces to a set of symbols which, in turn, are translatable into symbolic equivalents.[74] This translatability must necessarily include, as an integral component, the experience of the truth underlying the symbol. Thus, the Aristotelian essentialist definition of "man" as symbol for a "rational animal" is only an explicit definition, and so becomes a tautology in the strict non-mathematical sense.

According to Illuminationist theory, the essence of man, which is the truth underlying the symbol "man", is recoverable only in the subject. This act of "recovery" is the translation of the symbol to its equivalent in the consciousness or the self of the subject. Since the soul is the origin of the thing by which the idea of humanity is ascertained, and since the soul is the "closest" (*aqrab*) thing to humans, it is therefore through the soul that one may first realize the essence of the human being and ultimately of all things.[75] Subsequently, based on the subject's self-knowledge, the real sciences are constructed by employing the method of demonstration.[76]

ILLUMINATIONIST EPISTEMOLOGY

Perhaps the most widespread impact of Suhrawardī's philosophy has been in the domain of epistemology. A basic Illuminationist principle is that to know something is to obtain an experience of it, tantamount to a primary intuition of the determinants of the thing. Experiential knowledge of a thing is analysed only subsequent to the intuitive total and immediate grasp of it. Is there something in a subject's experience, one may ask, which necessitates that what is obtained by the subject be expressed through a specifically constructed symbolic language? The answer to this question will be examined from multiple points of view, but it is clear, even at this juncture, that Suhrawardī's "language of Illumination" is intended as a specific vocabulary through which the experience of Illumination may be described. It is equally clear that the interpretation of the symbolism of Illumination and its implications, as detailed by Suhrawardī in the *Paths and Havens*, are the central aspects of the controversy over the basis of Illuminationist philosophy.

The Philosophy of Illumination, as described in Suhrawardī's works, consists of three stages dealing with the question of knowledge, followed by a fourth stage of describing the experience. The first stage is marked by preparatory activity on the part of the philosopher: he or she has to "abandon the world" in readiness to accept "experience". The second is the stage of illumination, in which the philosopher attains visions of a "Divine Light" (*al-nūr al-ilāhī*). The third stage, or stage of construction, is marked by the acquisition of unlimited knowledge, which is Illuminationist knowledge (*al-'ilm al-ishrāqī*) itself. The fourth and final stage is the documentation, or written form of that visionary experience. Thus, the third and fourth stages as documented in Suhrawardī's writings are the only components of the Philosophy of

Illumination, as it was practised by Suhrawardī and his disciples, to which we have access.

The beginning of the first stage is marked by such activities as going on a forty-day retreat, abstaining from eating meat and preparing for inspiration and "revelation".[77] Such activities fall under the general category of ascetic and mystical practices, though not in strict conformity with the prescribed states and stations of the mystic path or *ṣūfī ṭarīqah*, as known in the mystical works available to Suhrawardī. According to Suhrawardī, a portion of the "light of God" (*al-bāriq al-ilāhī*) resides within the philosopher, who possesses intuitive powers. Thus, by practising the activities in stage one, he or she is able, through "personal revelation" and "vision" (*mushāhadah wa mukāshafah*), to accept the reality of his or her own existence and admit the truth of his or her own intuition. The first stage therefore consists of (1) an activity, (2) a condition (met by everyone, since we are told that every person has intuition and in everyone there is a certain portion of the light of God) and (3) personal "revelation".

The first stage leads to the second, and the Divine Light enters the being of the human. This light then takes the form of a series of "apocalyptic lights" (*al-anwār al-sāniḥah*), and through them the knowledge that serves as the foundation of real sciences (*al-'ulūm al-ḥaqīqiyyah*) is obtained.

The third stage is the stage of constructing a true science (*'ilm ṣaḥīḥ*). It is during this stage that the philosopher makes use of discursive analysis. The experience is put to the test, and the system of proof used is the Aristotelian demonstration (*burhān*) of the *Posterior Analytics*.[78] The same certitude obtained by moving from sense data (observation and concept formation) to demonstration based on reason, which is the basis of discursive scientific knowledge, is said to prevail when visionary data upon which the Philosophy of Illumination rests, are "demonstrated". This is accomplished through a process of analysis aimed at demonstrating the experience and constructing a system in which to place the experience and validate it, even after the experience has ended.

The impact of the specifically Illuminationist theory of knowledge, generally known as "knowledge by presence" (*al-'ilm al-ḥuḍūrī*), has not been confined to philosophical and other specialist circles, as Illuminationist logic has been, for example. The epistemological status given to intuitive knowledge has fundamentally influenced what is called "speculative mysticism" (*'irfān-i naẓarī*) in Persia as well as in Persian poetry. By looking briefly at a paradigm concerning the poet–philosopher–mystic's way of capturing and portraying wisdom, this point will be made evident.

The paradigm involves a subject (*mawḍū'*), consciousness (*idrāk*) in the subject as well as relating to it, and creativity (*khallāqiyyah*). The transition from the subject (*al-mawḍū'*) to the knowing subject (*al-mawḍū' al-mudrik*) to the knowing-creating subject (*al-mawḍū' al-mudrik al-khallāq*) marks the transformation of the human being as subject in a natural state to the human as knowing subject in the first state where knowledge transcends simple knowing and the spiritual journey begins. This leads finally to the state of union, when the knowing subject enters the realms of power (*jabarūt*) and the Divine (*Lāhūt*), and the human being obtains the reality (*ḥaqīqah*) of things and becomes the knowing-creating subject. What are finally created are "poems".

In my view, the most significant distinguishing characteristic of Persian poetry taken as a whole is its almost existential perspective regarding the outcome of philosophy (especially non-Aristotelian philosophy, equated with Ibn Sīnā's Oriental philosophy, as well as with Suhrawardī's Philosophy of Illumination). From this viewpoint, the end result of philosophy, which is wisdom, can be communicated only through the poetic medium. Innate poetic wisdom thus informs the human being – the philosopher–sage; the sage–poet; and, ultimately, simply the poet – of every facet of response to the total environment: the corporeal and the spiritual, the ethical and the political, the religious and the mundane. The ensuing perception of reality and historical process is constructed (as in the Persian *shi'r sākhtan*) in a metaphysical form – an art form, perhaps – that consciously at all stages employs metaphor, symbol, myth, lore and legend. The consequence is that Persian wisdom is more poetic than philosophical, and always more intuitive than discursive. This, in my view, is clearly the more popular legacy of Illuminationist philosophy and of its impact.

The way Persian poetic wisdom (or Persian poetic *ishrāqī* wisdom) seeks to unravel even the mysteries of nature, for example, is not by examining the principles of physics, as the Aristotelians would, but by looking into the metaphysical world and the realms of myth, archetypes, dream, fantasy and sentiment. This type of knowledge forms the basis of Suhrawardī's views of Illuminationist knowledge by presence.

A SYNOPSIS OF ILLUMINATIONIST KNOWLEDGE BY PRESENCE[79]

In his introduction to the *Philosophy of Illumination*, Suhrawardī discusses the way in which the foundation of Illuminationist knowledge was obtained by him as follows: "I did not first obtain [the Philosophy of Illumination] through cogitation, but through something else, I only subsequently sought proofs for it."[80]

That is, the principles of the Philosophy of Illumination (tantamount to the very first vision, and to the knowledge of the whole), was obtained by Suhrawardī not through thinking and speculation but through "something else". This, as we are told by Suhrawardī and by the commentators Shahrazūrī (seventh/thirteenth century), Quṭb al-Dīn al-Shīrāzī (eighth/fourteenth century) and Harawī (eleventh/seventeenth century), is a special experiential mode of knowledge named "Illuminationist vision" (*al-mushāhadat al-ishrāqiyyah*).[81] The epistemology of this type of vision is worked out in great detail by Suhrawardī. It is the subject of much discussion by all later commentators and is also reformulated and re-examined by one of the leading twentieth-century Muslim Illuminationist philosophers, Sayyid Muḥammad Kāẓim 'Aṣṣār, in his study of ontological principles and arguments *Waḥdat-i wujūd va badā'*.[82]

Suhrawardī's reconstructed theory of knowledge consists of intuitive judgments (*al-aḥkām al-ḥads* – resembling the Aristotelian notion of *agkhinoia*) and what he holds to be the dual process of vision–illumination (*al-mushāhadah wa'l-ishrāq*), which together serve as the foundation for the construction of a sound, true science (*al-'ilm al-ṣaḥīḥ*). These aspects also form the basis for a "scientific" methodology (*al-ṭarīq al-'ulūm*) which is at the core of Suhrawardī's concept of knowledge by presence. The visionary experience, which leads to knowledge not obtained by cogitation (*fikr*), takes place in a special realm called *mundus imaginalis* (*ālam al-mithāl*). The philosopher's experience in the realm of the imaginary determines what things are, which may ultimately be communicated only through non-ordinary language, such as poetic language or other symbolic modes of metalanguage. Thus poetry, which encompasses a metaphysics of metaphor and symbol, is theoretically given the status of the "most real".

Suhrawardī uses a favourite analogy to describe his view of knowledge. He compares physical astronomical observation (*irṣād jismānī*) with spiritual astronomical observation (*irṣād rūḥānī*), and states that the same kind of certitude observed from the world of sense data (*al-maḥsūsāt*) is obtained from observing or "seeing" the non-corporeal.[83] He uses this analogy in its various forms in many places in his writings, and his commentators also use it to illustrate the fundamentals of the Illuminationist theory of knowledge.[84]

Mundus imaginalis is in a sense an ontological realm. Beings of this realm, though possessing the categorical attributes – in other words, "having" time, place, relation, quality, quantity, etc. – are independent of matter. In Suhrawardī's theory of categories, he considers substance, quality, quantity, relation and motion in terms of degrees of intensity as processes rather than as distinct ontic entities. Thus an ideal being, or a being in the *imaginalis* sense, has a substance which is usually depicted symbolically as light. This substance differs from that of another being only in respect to the degree of its intensity, which is in a continuous state (*muttaṣil*) of, firstly, being connected to its substances, or light-monads, and, secondly, being part of the continuum, which is the Illuminationist cosmos. The being also has shape, which is imaginal, or ideal. Motion is a category and is an attribute of substances as well. Light entities in this realm move, and their movements are in relation to their degrees of intensity, or luminosity.

What enables the novice to gain such knowledge is the guide figure of this realm who serves a similar function as that of the Peripatetic *nous poietikos*. But while the Active Intellect of the Ibn Sīnan cosmology, for example, is stationary and discretely distinct from the other nine intellects above it in rank, the guide in this clime (*al-nūr al-isfahbad* in *Ḥikmat al-ishrāq*) – which is equated in activity with a *dator spiritis* (*rawān bakhsh*) or *dator scientis* (*wāhib al-ʿilm*) and a *dator formarum* (*wāhib al-ṣuwar*) – is a light entity which is continuously moving and propagating its essence. This essence, which is a degree of light intensity, impregnates the imagination of the philosopher–sage with the imaginal forms.

The visionary experience, which provides knowledge in this realm, is due and related to the substantials (*al-ṣuwar al-jawhariyyah*) that have taken ideal, or imaginal, forms. They may appear as different forms, as they are in a state of continuous transubstantial motion, although they do not actually change their singularity. Thus, a vision of *al-Isfahbad al-nāsūt* may appear as Gabriel to one, as *Surūsh* to another, and so on. This phenomenon serves as a metaphor for what the Peripatetics call "connection with the Active Intellect" (*al-ittiḥād, aw al-ittiṣāl bi'l-ʿaql al-faʿʿāl*). The result is the same: knowledge of the unseen, leading to Illumination, culminating in becoming a knowing-creating subject (*al-mawḍūʿ al-mudrik al-khallāq*).

The story of Aristotle appearing to Suhrawardī in a dream-vision is an allegory through which the philosopher exemplifies his own view of knowledge.[85] This story has a number of characteristic components which may be analysed briefly as follows. Firstly, in the vision, which is a state accompanied by overwhelming pleasure (*ladhdhah*), flashes (*barq*) and a glittering light, stated to be one of the intermediary stages of Illuminationist visionary experience,[86] Aristotle, the "master of philosophy" and "one who comes to the aid of souls", appears to Suhrawardī, who asks a question concerning knowledge (*mas'alat al-ʿilm*), how it is obtained, what it is made of and how it is recognized. Aristotle's response is: "return to your soul (or self)".[87] Self-knowledge is a fundamental component of the Illuminationist theory of knowledge. Knowledge as perception (*idrāk*) of the soul is essential and self-constituted, because an individual is cognizant of his essence by means of that essence itself.[88] Self-consciousness and the concept of "I" – the self-as-self, or its ipseity, its selfhood – are the grounds of knowledge. What is ultimately gained through the initial consciousness of one's essence is a way to knowledge,[89] called the "science based on presence and vision" (*al-ʿilm al-ḥuḍūrī al-shuhūdī*). For Suhrawardī, this is a higher type of knowledge than that obtained by the Peripatetic philosophers, who rely on union with the Active Intellect.[90]

Concerning his views of the foundations of knowledge, Suhrawardī writes: "Should a thing be seen, then one can dispense with its definition [*man shāhadahu* [*al-shay'*] *istaghnā 'an al-ta'rīf*]", and in that case "the form of the thing in the mind is the same as its form in sense-perception" (*ṣūratuhu fi'l-'aql ka-ṣūratihi fi'l-ḥiss*).[91] This view of knowledge is a fundamental principle in the Philosophy of Illumination.[92]

The Illuminationist's method of obtaining knowledge by means of a special mode of perception based on intuitive knowledge is said to be higher and more fundamental than predicative knowledge because the subject has an immediate grasp of the object without the need for mediation.[93] His or her position is based on the unity of the subject and object by means of the "idea" of the object being obtained in the consciousness of the subject. Thus, the subject's immediate experience of the "presence" of the object determines the validity of knowledge itself, and the experience of such things as God, the self, separate entities, etc., is the same as knowledge of them.

One of the most significant statements made by Suhrawardī on this matter is his insistence on a complete correspondence between the idea obtained in the subject, and the object. In his view, only such a correspondence shows that knowledge of the thing as-it-is has been obtained.[94] This means that, to obtain knowledge, a kind of "unity" has to be established between the subject and the object, and the psychological state of the subject is a determining factor in establishing this unity. For the Peripatetics, knowledge is ultimately established by a kind of "union" (*ittiḥād*) or "connection" (*ittiṣāl*) with the Active Intellect after an initial separation or disjunction (*infiṣāl*). Suhrawardī vehemently opposes the idea of disjunction, arguing that the unity of the subject and object is obtained in the knowing person by an act of self-realization, and that this can take place because there is no disjunction in reality, but only gradations of the manifestation of essence.

Suhrawardī refers in a number of his works to "judgments of intuition" (*aḥkām al-ḥads, ḥukm al-ḥads*) which are used as valid forms of inference.[95] In each instance, the validity of the judgment of intuition is unquestioned and is given the rank of demonstration, so with intuitive judgment, constructing demonstrations is no longer necessary.[96] Intuition, in the sense used here by Suhrawardī, is most probably an elaboration of the Aristotelian "quick wit" (*agkhinoia*),[97] but Suhrawardī incorporates this particular type of inference into his epistemology. Using a modified Peripatetic technical terminology, he identifies intuition first as an activity of the "habitual intellect" (*'aql bi'l-malakah*)[98] and, secondly, as the activity of the "holy intellect" (*al-'aql al-qudsī*);[99] but he considers the most important act of intuition to be the subject's ability to perceive most of the intelligibles quickly without a teacher.[100] In such a case, intuition grasps the middle term (*al-ḥadd al-awsaṭ*) of a syllogism, which is tantamount to an immediate grasp of an essentialist definition – in short, of the thing's essence.

The twofold process of vision–illumination (*mushāhadah-ishrāq*) acts on all levels of reality, according to Suhrawardī. It begins on the human level, in outward sense-perception, as sight (*ibṣār*). The eye (*al-baṣar*, or the seeing subject, *al-bāṣir*), when capable of seeing, perceives an object (*al-mubṣar*) when that object is illuminated (*mustanīr*) by the sun in the sky.[101] On the cosmic level, every abstract light sees the lights that are above it in rank, while instantaneously at the moment of vision the higher lights illuminate those lower in rank. The Light of Lights (*Nūr al-anwār*) illuminates everything, and the Heavenly Sun, the "Great *Hūrakhsh*", enables vision to take place. In effect, knowledge is obtained through this dual activity of vision–illumination, and the impetus underlying the operation of this principle is self-consciousness. Thus every being comes to know its own degree of perfection, an act of self-knowledge which induces a desire (*shawq*) to see the being just above it in perfection, and this act of seeing triggers the process of Illumination.[102] By means of the process of illumination, light is generated from its highest origin to the lowest elements.[103]

Illumination is also the principle by means of which celestial motion is regulated.[104] Illumination is propagated from the Light of Lights to the human level by means of certain intermediary principles. These are the "controlling lights" (*al-anwār al-ghāhirah*) and "managing lights" (*al-anwār al-mudabbirah*).[105] Among the latter, the principal lights which directly affect the human soul are the *isfahbad* lights.[106]

The Light of Lights controls everything.[107] It is the most apparent to itself, and thus it is the most self-conscious being in the Universe.[108] All abstract lights are illuminated directly by the Light of Lights, whose luminosity (*nūriyyah*), Essence (*dhāt*) and power are all one and the same.[109] The Light of Lights is self-emanating (*fayyāḍ bi'l-dhāt*), and its attributes and Essence are one.[110] When the "heavenly illuminations" (*al-ishrāqāt al-'ulwiyyah*) reach the human soul through the intervention of the *isfahbad* lights, all knowledge is given to the person. Such moments are the visions of the apocalyptic lights (*al-anwār al-sāniḥah*), which are the foundation of visionary experience, and means of obtaining unrestricted knowledge.[111] Human souls who have experienced the apocalyptic lights are called "souls separated from matter" (*al-nufūs al-mujarradah*), because they have torn away from the physical bondage of body. They obtain an "idea of the light of God" (*mithāl min nūr Allāh*), which the faculty of imagination imprints upon the "tablet of the *sensus communis*" (*lawḥ al-ḥiss al-mushtarak*). By means of this idea, they obtain control over a "creative light" (*al-nūr al-khāliq*) which ultimately gives them power to know. The moment of illumination, which is experienced by the Brethren of Separation from Matter (*ikhwān al-tajrīd*)[112] and the Masters of Vision (*aṣḥāb al-mushāhadah*),[113] is described by Suhrawardī as a gradual experience of "light" in fifteen steps, starting with the experience of the "flashing pleasurable light" (*al-nūr al-bāriq al-ladhīdh*) and ending with the experience of a light so violent that it may tear the body apart at the joints.[114]

Suhrawardī's theory of vision applies to physics as well as to metaphysics. The analysis of the theory begins with a discussion of external vision (*ibṣār*), what is called "vision, or seeing, by means of external senses" (*mushāhadah bi'l-ḥiss al-ẓāhir*). In physics, Suhrawardī rejects the corporeality of rays (*jismiyyat al-shu'ā'*)[115] and the view that holds rays to be colours (*lawniyyat al-shu'ā'*).[116] Next, he rejects the theory of external vision which holds that "vision [*ibṣār*] takes place solely because rays leave the eye and meet [*yulāqī*] objects of sight".[117] Suhrawardī also rejects the view that the act of sight (*ru'yā*) takes place when the form of the thing (*ṣūrat al-shay'*) is imprinted in the "vitreous humour" (*al-ruṭūbat al-jalīdiyyah*).[118]

For Suhrawardī, the fact that vision has no temporal extension, and that there is no need for a material relation (*rābiṭah*) between the seer and the thing seen, means that sight or vision exists prior to thinking and is superior to it. This is because any enumeration of essential attributes, of the genera and the differentiae requires time. The construction of dialectical syllogism and induction also takes time. Vision, however, takes place in a durationless instant (*ān*), and this is the "moment" of Illumination.

The theory of vision, as developed by Suhrawardī and portrayed in the metaphysics of the *Philosophy of Illumination*, is an application of his general theory of knowledge. Suhrawardī restates the conclusions reached in his theory of physics: "Theorem: [On Vision] You have now learnt that sight does not consist of the imprint of the form of the object in the eye, nor of something that goes out from the eye. Therefore it can only take place when the luminous object [*al-mustanīr*] encounters [*muqābalah*] a sound [healthy] eye."[119]

Thus, external vision takes place in accordance with Suhrawardī's general theory of knowledge, namely that the subject (the sound eye) and the object (the luminous thing) are both present and together necessitate the act of vision.[120] For the act of vision to be consummated, the following conditions must be satisfied: (1) the presence of light due to the propagation of light from the Light of Lights, (2) the absence of any obstacle or "veil" (*ḥijāb*) between the subject and the object,[121] and (3) the Illumination of the subject as well as the object. The mechanism which allows for the subject to be illuminated is a complicated one, and involves a certain activity on the part of the faculty of imagination. When an object is seen, the subject has acted in two ways: by an act of vision and an act of Illumination. Thus, vision–illumination is actualized when no obstacle intervenes between the subject and the object.

In summary, one of the foundations of the Philosophy of Illumination is that the laws governing sight and vision are based on the same rule, consisting of the existence of light, the act of vision, and the act of Illumination. Thus, in Suhrawardī's Illuminationist philosophy, light, illumination, sight, vision, creative acts – and by extension all things – may be explained through the existence of light emanated by the Light of Lights.

NOTES

1 The major biographical sources on Suhrawardī are: Ibn Abī Uṣaybiʿah, *ʿUyūn al-anbāʾ fī ṭabaqāt al-aṭibbāʾ*, ed. A Müller (Königsberg, 1884), vol. I, 1: 168, and the edition (used here) edited by N. Riḍā (Beirut, 1968), pp. 641–6 (hereafter cited as *Ṭabaqāt*); Yāqūt, *Irshād al-arīb*, ed. D. S. Margoliouth, 6: 269; al-Qifṭī, *Tārīkh al-ḥukamāʾ*, ed. Bahman Dārāʾī (Tehran, 1929): 345; Ibn Khallikān, *Wafayāt al-aʿyān*, ed. I. Abbās (Beirut, 1965), 6: 268–74 (hereafter cited as *Wafayāt*); Shams al-Dīn Muḥammad al-Shahrazūrī (d. *c.* 687/1288), *Nuzhat al-arwāḥ wa rawḍat al-afrāḥ fī tārīkh al-ḥukamāʾ waʾl-falāsifah*, ed. S. Khurshīd Aḥmad (Hyderabad, 1976), 2: 119–43 (hereafter cited as *Nuzhat al-arwāḥ)*; the eleventh/seventeenth-century Persian translation of *Nuzhat al-arwāḥ* by Maqṣūd ʿAlī Tabrīzī has recently been published by M. T. Daneshpajouh and M. S. Mawlāʾī (Tehran, 1986); this differs (considerably at times) from the Arabic text. Part of the commentary on Suhrawardī in this text has been translated into English by W. M. Thackston, Jr in *The Mystical and Visionary Treatises of Shihabuddin Yahya Suhrawardi* (London, 1982): 1–4. Thackston's translation is based on the partial edition of S. H. Nasr in *Shihaboddin Yahya Sohrawardi, Oeuvres Philosophiques et Mystiques: Opera Metaphysica et Mystica III* (reprinted: Tehran, 1970): 13–30. This edition includes the Arabic text as well as the Persian translation of Tabrīzī. The following works may be consulted for information on Suhrawardī's life and thought: Carra de Vaux, "La philosophie illuminative d'après Suhrawerdi Meqtoul", *Journal asiatique*, 19 (1902): 63–4; Max Horten, *Die Philosophie der Erleuchtung nach Suhrawardī* (Halle an der Saale, 1912); Louis Massignon, *Recueil de textes inédits* (Paris, 1929): 111–13; Otto Spies, *Three Treatises on Mysticism by Shihabuddin Suhrawardī Maqtul* (Stuttgart, 1935); Helmut Ritter, "Philologika IX: Die vier Suhrawardī", *Der Islam*, 24 (1937): 270–86; and 25 (1938): 35–86; H. Corbin, *Suhrawardī d'Alep, fondateur de la doctrine illuminative* (Paris, 1939); *Les Motifs zoroastriens dans la philosophie de Sohravardī* (Tehran, 1946); *L'Homme de lumière dans le soufisme iranien* (Paris, 1971); *En Islam iranien* (Paris, 1971), 4 vols (the second volume, *Sohrawardî et les Platoniciens de Perse*, is devoted to a detailed study of Suhrawardī's life and works); as well as other works by Corbin especially his *Prolégomènes* to each

of his following critical editions of Suhrawardī's works: *Opera metaphysica et mystica I* (Istanbul, 1945, hereafter cited as *Opera I*); *Opera metaphysica et mystica II* (Tehran, 1954, hereafter cited as *Opera II*); *Opera metaphysica et mystica III* (Tehran, 1970, hereafter cited as *Opera III*). Special mention must also be made of Corbin's translations of Suhrawardī's works: *Archange empourpré, Quinze traités et récits mystiques traduits du persan et de l'arabe*, présentés et annotés par Henry Corbin (Paris, 1976); and *Le Livre de la sagesse orientale, Kitāb ḥikmat al-ishrāq*, traduction et notes par Henry Corbin, établies et introduit par Christian Jambet (Paris, 1986); and other works such as: S. H. Nasr, *Three Muslim Sages* (Cambridge, Mass., 1964), chapter 2; and especially the excellent summary of illuminationist doctrine, "Suhrawardī", in *A History of Muslim Philosophy*, ed. M. M. Sharif (Wiesbaden, 1963) I: 372–98; and *An Introduction to Islamic Cosmological Doctrines* (London, 1978), chapter 12; also of interest for the study of the impact of Suhrawardī's thought in India I refer the reader to Muḥammad Sharīf al-Harawī, *Anwāriyya: an 11th Century A. H. Persian Translation and Commentary on Suhrawardī's Ḥikmat al-Ishrāq*, edited with introduction and notes by Hossein Ziai (Tehran, 1980). Finally I should inform the reader of my study of the logical foundations of illuminationist epistemology, where most of the brief discussions of Suhrawardī's analytical thought here are presented in greater detail. See Hossein Ziai, *Knowledge and Illumination: a Study of Suhrawardī's Ḥikmat al-Ishrāq* (Atlanta, Brown Judaic Studies, 97, 1990).

2 Shahrazūrī, *Nuzhat al-arwāḥ* (MS Istanbul, Yeni Cami, 908), fol. 233v. Shahrazūrī's work is the only extensive source of Suhrawardī's biography. See also Shahrazūrī, *Nuzhat al-arwāḥ wa rawḍat al-afrāḥ fī tārīkh al-ḥukamā' wa'l-falāsifah*, ed. Seyed Khurshīd Aḥmed (Hyderabad, 1976), 2: 124ff.

3 See Abī Uṣaybi'ah, *Ṭabaqāt*, 1: 168; and Yāqūt, *Irshād*, 6: 269. This work has been translated by Henry Corbin as *The Theosophy of the Orient of Light*.

4 Suhrawardī, *Opera II*: 258.

5 Shahrazūrī, *Nuzhat al-arwāḥ*, 2: 125–7.

6 Yāqūt, *Irshād*, 6: 269.

7 Ibn Abī Uṣaybi'ah, *Ṭabaqāt*, 1: 299–301.

8 Suhrawardī, *Opera I*: 146, 278, 352. Sāwī wrote a Persian commentary on Ibn Sīnā's *Risālat al-ṭayr*, a symbolic treatise which was re-composed in Persian by Suhrawardī, translated in *The Mystical and Visionary Treatises of Suhrawardī*, trans. Thackston: 21–5).

9 Recent scholars have too readily accepted Suhrawardī's works such as the *Intimations*, the *Apposites* and the *Paths and Havens* as purely Peripatetic. See Louis Massignon, *Recueil de textes inédits* (Paris, 1929): 111–13; Carl Brockelmann, *GAL*, 1: 437–8, *GAL*, 1: 481–3; Henry Corbin, "Prolégomènes", *Opera II*; Seyyed Hossein Nasr, "Shihāb al-Dīn Suhrawardī Maqtūl", in *A History of Muslim Philosophy*, ed. M. M. Sharif (Weisbaden, 1963): 374; as well as others who have followed the same classification of Suhrawardī's works as these authors.

10 E.g., Suhrawardī, *Opera I*: 59, 121, 128, 131, 146, 183, 185, 192, 194, 195, 278, 340, 361, 371, 401, 484, 506. Suhrawardī himself stipulates that all of the major texts are related.

11 See my "The Source and Nature of Authority: a Study of al-Suhrawardī's

Illuminationist Political Doctrine", in *Islamic Political Aspects of Philosophy*, ed. Charles Butterworth (Cambridge, Mass., 1992): 294–334.

12 *Ṭabaqāt*: 642: "*ba'atha Ṣalāḥ al-Dīn ilā waladihi al-Malik al-Ẓāhir bi-Ḥalab kitāban fī ḥaqqihi bi-khaṭṭi al-Qāḍī al-Fāḍil*". The *qāḍī* had been a trusted counsellor of Saladin (H. A. R. Gibb, *Life of Saladin*, p. 49).

13 Shahrazūrī states that Saladin, who had been urged by the "jealous" jurists of Aleppo, wrote a letter to his son asking for Suhrawardī's execution lest he corrupt religion (*afsada al-dīn*), but al-Malik al-Ẓāhir refused, so the sultan wrote to his son a second time warning the young prince that he would take away the rule of Aleppo from him unless he complied (*Nuzhat al-arwāḥ*, 2: 125–6).

14 The biographers differ in their opinions regarding Suhrawardī's execution. For example, Ibn Khallikān states: "I saw people differ concerning his affair ... some attributed him with heresy [*al-zandaqa wa'l-ilḥād*], while others were of the opinion that there was good in him and that he was from among the people blessed with miraculous powers" (*Wafayāt*, 6: 273). Shahrazūrī states: "I saw people differ concerning his execution" (*Nuzhat al-arwāḥ*, 2: 125). Muḥammad 'Alī Abū Rayyān has discussed the circumstances of Suhrawardī's execution in Aleppo at some length. He refers to the debates between Suhrawardī and the jurists of Aleppo, and cites al-'Imād al-Iṣfahānī, who in his *al-Bustān al-jāmi' li-tawārīkh al-zamān* reports that the jurists of Aleppo, especially two brothers, Ibnay Jahbal, had engaged Suhrawardī in a debate on the question of prophethood and God's powers. During the debate Suhrawardī's position, that God can create anything He wants at any time, was considered blasphemous which is why they sought his execution. See Muḥammad Abū Rayyān, *Uṣūl al-falsafat al-ishrāqiyyah* (Beirut, 1969): 25–6; "Kayfa ubīḥ damm al-Suhrawardī al-ishrāqī", *Majallat Thaqāfah*, 702 (1952). S. H. Nasr briefly discusses the circumstances for Suhrawardī's execution in "Shaykh al-Ishrāq", in *al-Kitāb al-tadhkārī Shaykh al-Ishrāq*, ed. Ibrahim Madkour (Cairo, 1974): 17–36. Nasr states that while during the Fāṭimid period Syria had been "among the great Shī'a centers", when the Ayyubids triumphed over them, and also because of the Crusades, the Sunnī *madhhab* became dominant, and he then attributes anti-Bāṭinite sentiments to have been a factor in Suhrawardī's demise. This may not, however, be substantiated solely by recounting the debate between the jurists of Aleppo and Suhrawardī concerning the question of prophethood and its seal. Nasr's view that Suhrawardī had believed in "guardianship" (*al-wilāyah*) (pp. 20–1) is not supported by the evidence in Suhrawardī, who never refers to *wilāyah* in any of his works.

15 See my "Source and Nature".

16 See, for example, G. Slaughter, *Saladin* (New York, 1955): 221ff.

17 See my "Source and Nature".

18 Published in *Opera I*.

19 Published in *Opera II*.

20 See my *Knowledge and Illumination*: 9–15, where I argue that, based on Suhrawardī's own explicit statements, these works together make up a corpus in which he carefully and systematically presents the genesis and development of the Philosophy of Illumination. And since Corbin's editions of *al-Talwīḥāt* and of *al-Mashāri'* do not include the sections on logic and on physics, I refer

to the following manuscripts: *al-Talwīḥāt*, Berlin MS no. 5062, and *al-Mashāri'*, Leiden MS no. Or. 365.

21 The Arabic text of *al-Alwāḥ al-'imādiyyah* has been edited by Najaf 'Alī Ḥabībī in *Si risālah az Shaykh-i ishrāq* (Tehran, 1977): 1–78; the Persian version of the same has been edited by S. H. Nasr in *Opera III*: 109–95; the Arabic text of *Hayākil al-nūr* has been edited and published by Muḥammad 'Alī Abū Rayyān (Cairo, 1957), and the Persian version by S. H. Nasr in *Opera III*: 83–108; the Persian text of *Partaw-nāmah* has been edited by Nasr in *Opera III*: 1–81.

22 Suhrawardī, *Opera I*: 124.

23 *Qiṣṣat al-ghurbat al-gharbiyyah*, published in *Opera II*: 274–97, trans. Thackston, *op. cit.*: 100–8. The other treatises are published in *Opera III*, and are translated by Thackston, *op. cit.*

24 Most of the aphorisms had been collected by Shahrazūrī in his *Nuzhat al-arwāḥ*, 2: 136–43.

25 The invocations have been published by M. Moin in *Majalā-yi āmūzish wa parwarish* (Tehran, 1924). One of the two has been reprinted in *Si risālah az Shaykh-i ishrāq* (pp. 18–19).

26 The invocation starts thus: "Greetings upon the most luminous, alive [*al-ḥayy*] speaking [*al-nāṭiq*] and most manifest being [*al-shakhṣ al-aẓhar*]", and goes on to attribute the qualities royal authority [*al-salaṭah wa'l-haybah*] and perfect power [*quwwah*] to this being. As *Hūrakhsh* shines in the heavens so does the *kiyān kharrah* of kings on earth (cf. Suhrawardī, *Opera I*: 494; *Opera II*: 149–50.

27 Suhrawardī, *Opera II*: 10.

28 See Chapter 29, below, "The Illuminationist tradition".

29 See my *Knowledge and Illumination*: 20–39.

30 *al-Mashāri'*, *op. cit.*, i.e., *Paths and Havens: Logic*, fol. 15v.

31 *Ibid.*: "*ṣarraḥa'l-shaykh Abū 'Alī, fī karārīs, yansubuhā ila'l-mashriqiyyīn*".

32 See Avicenna, *Manṭiq al-mashriqiyyīn* (Cairo, 1910): 1–4.

33 While the two terms are morphologically related – *ishrāq* is the verbal noun of Form IV of the triliteral root *sh-r-q*, and *mashriq* the locative noun – the former is used as a technical epistemological term, and the latter in a general sense of "East".

34 *Paths and Havens: Logic*, fol. 15r: "*wa hādhihi'l-karārīs, wa in yansubahā ila'l-mashriq fa-hiya bi-'aynihā qawā'id al-mashshā'īn wa'l-ḥikmat al-'āmmah, illā annahu ghayyara'l-'ibārah, aw taṣarrafah fī ba'd al-furū', taṣarrufan gharīban lā tubāyin kutubuhu'l-ukhrā ... wa lā yataqarraru bihi'l-aṣl al-mashriqī al-muqarrar fī 'ahd al-'ulamā' al-khusrawāniyyah*". Corbin has discussed Suhrawardī's view of Khusrawānī philosophers and of ancient Iranian wisdom. See, for example, *Opera II*: vi; and *ibid.*, *Prolégomène*: 24–6.

35 Suhrawardī's clearly stipulated intention is to provide scientific proof for all "observed" phenomena. He does this by employing his new method of "the science of lights" (*'ilm al-anwār* and *fiqh al-anwār*). See Suhrawardī, *Opera II*: 10.

36 Suhrawardī's elaborate discussions on such themes are to be found in the last sections of his major philosophical works. Examples can be found in the following chapters: *Philosophy of Illumination*, 2.5: "On resurrection, prophecy

and dreams", especially 2.5.5: "On explaining the causes of divine admonitions and knowledge of the unseen"; *Intimations*, 3.4: "On prophecy, signs, dreams and other such matters", especially 3.4.2: "On the causes of extraordinary acts"; *Paths and Havens*, 3.7.3: "On how unseen things may appear"; and 3.7.6: "On the spiritual journey [*sulūk*] of the divine philosophers"; and in addition the last section of *Partaw-nāmah* ("Epistle on Emanation"), entitled: "On prophecy, miracles [*mu'jizāt*], miraculous powers [*karāmāt*], dreams and other similar things".

37 For a discussion of the divisions as they are employed in Latin philosophy as distinguished from Aristotle's see Philip Merlan, *From Platonism to Neoplatonism* (The Hague, 1975): 70–84.

38 See Chapter 29, below, "The Illuminationist tradition".

39 I have shown elsewhere that Suhrawardī's theory may have been influenced by the Stoic theory of *lekton*. See my *Knowledge and Illumination*: 42 n. 2; 59 n. 3.

40 Alexander Broadie in his *Introduction to Medieval Logic* (Oxford, 1987) traces the history of these problems only to fourteenth-century Latin logic.

41 Suhrawardī, *Opera I*: 12.

42 Mullā Ṣadrā in his *al-Shawāhid al-rubūbiyyah*, ed. J. Āshtiyānī (Mashhad, 1965) in the section entitled "Fourth Witnessing: First Illumination", argues for his theory of substantial motion [*ithbāt al-ḥarakat al-jawhariyyah*], mostly based on the re-examination and refinement of Suhrawardī's earlier doctrine.

43 See, for example, *Opera I*: 1–12; *Opera III*: 113; *Opera I*: 146–8. The great logician 'Umar ibn Sahlān al-Sāwī, whose *al-Baṣā'ir* Suhrawardī had studied, also reduces the categories, but to four: substance, quality, quantity and relation, not including motion. See Ja'far Sajjādī, *Suhrawardī* (Tehran, 1984): 98–9.

44 For example, Corbin translates *Ḥikmat al-ishrāq* (the title of the book, and the system) as *sagesse orientale*, which overlooks the analytical value of the Philosophy of Illumination. See, for example, Shihāboddīn Yaḥya Sohravardī, *Le Livre de la sagesse orientale*, traduction et notes par Henry Corbin, ed. Christian Jambet (Paris, 1986).

45 Fazlur Rahman, *The Philosophy of Mullā Ṣadrā* (Albany, 1975): vii.

46 See Carra de Vaux, *op. cit.*

47 See Max Horten, *op. cit.*

48 See Louis Massignon, *op. cit.*: 111–13.

49 See Otto Spies, *op. cit.*

50 See Helmut Ritter, *op. cit.*

51 See H. Corbin, *Suhrawardī d'Alep*; *Les Motifs zoroastriens*; *L'Homme de Lumière*.

52 See S. H. Nasr, *Three Muslim Sages*: "Suhrawardī". Nasr has pointed out in his pioneering work the religious significance of Suhrawardī's life and teachings, as well as the religious dimension in his cosmology. See, in this regard, his *An Introduction*, *op cit.*: chapter 12.

53 See Muḥammad Iqbāl, *The Development of Metaphysics in Persia* (London, 1908): 121–50. In his analysis of *Ḥikmat al-ishrāq*, Iqbāl draws on Muḥammad Sharīf al-Harawī's Persian commentary available in Berlin at the Königlichen Bibliothek (part of the *Bibliotheca Orientalis Sprengeriana*, Spr. 766).

54 Suhrawardī, *Opera I*: 70–4.

55 *Ibid.*: 58.
56 For a detailed discussion of Suhrawardī's critique see my *Knowledge and Illumination*: 77–114.
57 Suhrawardī, *Opera II*: 21.
58 Aristotle, *Posterior Analytics*, 2.3.90b1–24.
59 *Ibid.*, 90b24. On Aristotle's view regarding the relation between definition and demonstration, see *Posterior Analytics*, 1.2.72a19–24; 1.8; 1.10; 1.22; 1.33. This problem is treated at length by Anfinn Stigen in his philosophical study, *The Structure of Aristotle's Thought* (Oslo, 1966), chapter 4, and p. 78 n. 2.
60 Suhrawardī, *Opera II*: 21ff.
61 See Avicenna, *Livre des définitions*, sec. 18. Cf. Avicenna, the *Healing: Logic: Demonstration*: 233–7.
62 Suhrawardī's theory of definition is related to his critique of induction. He makes a distinction between complete and incomplete induction [*al-istiqrā' al-tāmm wa'l-nāqiṣ*]. E.g., *Opera III*: 5. See also William Kneale, *Probability and Induction* (Oxford, 1966): 24–110.
63 This point, though mentioned by Ibn Sīnā, is not explicitly required by him in the formula. See Ibn Sīnā, *al-Shifā': al-Manṭiq: al-Burhān* 4.4.217–24.
64 See Suhrawardī, *Opera II*: 14; Shīrāzī, *Sharḥ II*: 35: 13–38.
65 *Paths and Havens: Logic*, fol. 17v.
66 Suhrawardī, *Opera II*: 21.
67 See Suhrawardī, *Paths and Havens: Logic*, fol. 98v.; *Opera III*: 5.
68 *Paths and Havens: Logic*, fol. 15r.
69 For a detailed discussion of the Illuminationist theory of definition see my *Knowledge and Illumination*: 114–27.
70 Suhrawardī, *Opera II*: 106.
71 Suhrawardī, *Opera II*: 21.
72 Other terms, such as "collection", "set", "aggregate" and "manifold", are also used, and may mean what Suhrawardī intends by *al-ijtimā'*.
73 Bertrand Russell, *Introduction to Mathematical Philosophy* (New York, n.d.): 12. Cf. Irving Copi, *Symbolic Logic* (New York, 1965), chapter 6; Moritz Schlick, *General Theory of Knowledge* (New York and Vienna, 1975): 31–9.
74 Alfred J. Ayer, *Language, Truth and Logic* (London, 1950): 59–71. Cf. Paul T. Sagal, "Implicit Definition", *The Monist*, 57(3) (July 1973): 443–50.
75 Suhrawardī's *Gedankenexperiment* indicates a more detailed analysis than Ibn Sīnā's, and is incorporated fully into a comprehensive view of psychology. See *Opera III*: 10–14. Cf. Fazlur Rahman, *Avicenna's Psychology* (London, 1952): 31.
76 Suhrawardī, *Opera II*: 40–6.
77 *Ibid.*: 248.
78 *Ibid.*: 40–6.
79 For a detailed discussion of the Illuminationist theory of knowledge by presence see my *Knowledge and Illumination*: 129–45.
80 Suhrawardī, *Opera I*: 11.
81 See, for example, *Anwāriyyah*: 6–7.
82 Muḥammad Kāẓim 'Aṣṣār, *Waḥdat-i wujūd wa badā'*, ed. Jalāl Āshtiyānī (Mashhad, 1970).
83 Specific reference is made to the science of astronomy, implying that just as

one may predict astronomical occurrences in the future one may make valid predictions concerning the "unseen" metaphysical realm as well. See, for example, Suhrawardī, *Opera II*: 13.

84 See Shīrāzī, *Sharḥ II*; Ibn al-Khaṭīb, *Rawḍat al-taʿrīf*, 2: 564ff.

85 Suhrawardī, *Opera I*: 70–4.

86 Multiple stages of the Illuminationist visionary experience are discussed, and each of them accompanied by an experience of a special kind of light. See Suhrawardī, *Opera II*: 252; *Opera I*: 108, 114.

87 Suhrawardī, *Opera I*: 70.

88 *Ibid.* The self-conscious subject is to be compared with Ibn Sīnā's "l'homme volant" (Peters, *Aristotle and the Arabs*: 173). See also Rahman, *Avicenna's Psychology*: 8–20.

89 Suhrawardī, *Opera I*: 75. Cf. 121.

90 *Ibid.*: 74, 88, 90.

91 Suhrawardī, *Opera II*: 73–4.

92 *Mushāhadah* indicates a special mode of cognition that enables the subject to have an immediate, durationless grasp of the essence of the object. Suhrawardī, *Kalimat al-Taṣawwuf* (MS Tehran: Majlis, *Majmūʿah* 3071): 398. Cf. Mullā Ṣadrā, *Taʿlīqāt, Sharḥ II*: 204 (margin).

93 See Philip Merlan, *From Platonism to Neoplatonism*: 185. This knowledge has to do with things "above being" and is called *agkhinoia* by Aristotle (Merlan: 186). It is usually translated as "intuition", or "quick wit". Cf. Aristotle, *Posterior Analytics*, 2.34.89b10ff. Cf. *Nicomachean Ethics* 6.9.1142b6ff. Plotinus is considered the most significant Greek proponent of intuition (e.g. Cairo, *The Evolution of Theology in the Greek Philosophers* (Glasgow, 1923), 1: 220–1). Cf. the distinction between *peitho* and *ananke* (literally: persuasion versus logical necessity, thus the distinction between discursive and immediate knowledge), in Plotinus *Enneads*, 5.3.6.

94 Suhrawardī, *Opera II*: 15. Cf. Shīrāzī, *Sharḥ II*: 40.8–41.5.

95 Suhrawardī, *Intimations: Physics*, fol. 64v; *Opera I*: 57, 440; *Opera II*: 109.

96 E.g., Suhrawardī, *Opera I*: 57: "*al-ḥads al-ṣaḥīḥ yaḥkum bi-hādhā dūna ḥājjah ilā burhān*".

97 See Aristotle, *Posterior Analytics*, 1.33.89b10–20. Cf. Aristotle, *Nicomachean Ethics*, 6.9.1142b5–6. Cf. Suhrawardī, *Intimations: Physics*, fol. 69r; *Paths and Havens: Physics*, fol. 201v.

98 E.g., Suhrawardī, *Intimations: Physics*, fol. 69r.

99 E.g., *ibid.*, fol. 65v, 69r.

100 *Ibid.*

101 Suhrawardī, *Opera II*: 134.

102 *Ibid.*: 139–41: "*wa kullu wāḥid yushāhid Nūr al-anwār*".

103 *Ibid.*: 142–3.

104 *Ibid.*: 142, 147–8, 175, 184–5.

105 *Ibid.*: 139–40, 166–75, 185–6. The managing lights function on the human level, as *al-anwār al-insiyyah* (*Opera II*: 201), as well as on the cosmic level as *al-anwār al-falakiyyah* (*Opera II*: 236).

106 *Ibid.*: 201, 213–15.

107 *Ibid.*: 122, 135–6, 197.

108 *Ibid.*: 124.

109 *Ibid.*: 121–4.
110 *Ibid.*: 150.
111 *Ibid.*: 141, 204–5. Cf. *ibid.*: 13: "*al-ishrāqiyyūn lā yantaẓim amruhum dūna sawāniḥ nūriyyah*".
112 *Ibid.*: 252.
113 *Ibid.*: 156, 162.
114 *Ibid.*: 252–4.
115 *Ibid.*: 97.
116 *Ibid.*: 98.
117 *Ibid.*: 99.
118 *Ibid.*: 100.
119 *Ibid.*: 134.
120 *Ibid.*: 150.
121 *Ibid.*: 134–5. Both excessive proximity [*ghurb*] and excessive distance [*bu'd*] are considered to be obstacles that block the actualization of "sight".

SELECT BIBLIOGRAPHY

Aminrazavi, M. (1995) *Suhrawardi* (London).
Corbin, H. (1970) *En Islam iranien*, 2 (Paris).
—— trans. (1976) *L'Archange empourpré* (Paris).
—— trans. (1986) *Le Livre de la sagesse orientale* (Paris).
Corbin, H. and Nasr, S. H. (1976–7) *Oeuvres philosophiques et mystiques*, 1 and 2 (Tehran).
Ha'iri Yazdi, M. (1982) *The Principles of Epistemology in Islamic Philosophy* (Tehran).
Horten, M. (1912) *Die Philosophie der Erleuchtung nach Suhrawardi* (Halle).
Nasr, S. H. (1963) "Suhrawardi", in M. Sharif (ed.) *A History of Muslim Philosophy*, 1 (Wiesbaden).
—— (1969) *Three Muslim Sages: Avicenna – Suhrawardi – Ibn 'Arabī* (Cambridge, Mass.).
Ritter, H. (1937) "Philologika, IX, Die vier Suhrawardi", *Der Islam*, 24: 270–86.
Ziai, H. (1990) *Knowledge and Illumination* (Atlanta).

S.H.N.

CHAPTER 29

The Illuminationist tradition

Hossein Ziai

Orientalists and historians of Arabic and Persian philosophy have, for the most part, ignored much of the scholarship on the systematic side of post-Avicennan Islamic philosophy. The Illuminationist tradition, founded by Suhrawardī in the sixth/twelfth century, represents the principal advancement in Islamic philosophy immediately following Avicenna (Ibn Sīnā). However, the period from Avicenna's death in 429/1037 to the death of Averroes (Ibn Rushd) in 595/1198 encompasses three distinct types of philosophical attitude and style manifest in Arabic and, to a lesser extent, Persian texts. Each of these "schools", or traditions of philosophical thought, tends to be associated with the person considered to be its founder or another scholar who epitomizes that philosophical attitude. The three traditions are as follows.

Firstly, the Peripatetic school. Though known throughout the early period of Islamic philosophy to follow the texts and teachings of Aristotle, after the fifth/eleventh century the Peripatetic school is usually associated with Avicenna and his followers. This tradition is characterized by the structure, technical terminology and philosophical approach of the Aristotelian texts as put forth in Avicenna's major compositions such as *Healing* ("*Shifā'*"). The study of logic, for example, is divided according to the books of Aristotle's *Organon*; physics in accordance with the books, chapters, and subject matter of his *Physics*; and similarly in metaphysics. The Peripatetic school of Islamic philosophy continues in the philosophical writings of Avicenna's pupils, such as Bahmanyār and Abu'l-'Abbās al-Lawkarī; in numerous Arabic and Persian commentaries and glosses on Avicenna's two major works, the *Shifā'* and the *Ishārāt*; and in monographs on specific issues relating to Peripatetic views and problems. Philosophical problems of this school that stand as cornerstones of Islamic Peripatetic philosophy are, in brief: the ontological position of primacy of being, the epistemological priority given to acquired knowledge, the Necessary Being's knowledge of the universals rather than particulars, and the eschatological position of the soul's immortality.

Secondly, the Averroist tradition. Although Averroes was the foremost commentator of Aristotelian texts, he has in fact had little or no impact on post-Avicennan philosophical thinking in Islam. The impact of his Arabic Aristotelianism is primarily confined to the Latin West. Almost every aspect of Averroes's philosophical thought from logic to political philosophy has been examined in detail. Most of his works, some of which have survived only in Hebrew or Latin versions as abridgements or translations, have also been edited.

Thirdly, the Illuminationist tradition. To understand how philosophy has developed in the Islamic world, especially in Iran, it is of singular importance to examine Suhrawardī's Illuminationist tradition of the sixth/twelfth century and its aftermath. This area of Islamic philosophy, which has long been overlooked the West, has had the most significant, widespread impact not only on Islamic philosophical thought *per se* but also in other areas of thought and creative activity, including speculative mysticism (*'irfān*) and poetry.

It should be noted that these three schools and traditions continue well after the sixth/twelfth century, and that the Peripatetic and the Illuminationist traditions were revived in the tenth/sixteenth century when the philosophical writings and teachings of many thinkers gave rise to yet another so-called new synthesis in Islamic philosophy known as the School of Isfahan.

This chapter will examine the tradition of Illuminationist philosophy after Suhrawardī, and will discuss selected details of its two dominant trends, focusing primarily on the seventh/thirteenth century. Thinkers of other periods considered to have been Illuminationists or to have favoured Illuminationist philosophical positions in their writings will also be mentioned.

The Philosophy of Illumination grew out of reactions to certain aspects of Islamic philosophical texts, most of them associated with the Avicennan corpus. While Avicenna may have seriously intended to compose a separate and distinct "Eastern" philosophy – which he mentions briefly in his work *Logic of the Easterners* ("*Manṭiq al-mashriqiyyīn*") – nowhere does he systematically develop and construct a philosophical system distinct from his monumental and predominantly Aristotelian composition, *Healing*. All of his works reflect a standard Peripatetic structure, terminology and philosophical intention.

A number of thinkers prior to Suhrawardī did compose works that incorporated different, sometimes anti-Aristotelian principles, however. Foremost among them is the philosopher Ḥibat Allāh Abu'l-Barakāt al-Baghdādī. In his major anti-Aristotelian philosophic encyclopedia of the sixth/twelfth century, *Evidential* ("*al-Mu'tabar*"), al-Baghdādī develops an alternate structure for a foundation of philosophy, especially of epistemology. As shown by Solomon Pines in his many detailed studies, al-Baghdādī also treats certain problems of physics from a distinctly non-Aristotelian perspective.[1] Al-Baghdādī's intent was not to reject Avicennan philosophy, nor to prove its incoherence, as Ghazzālī's polemics would suggest, but to improve the existing structure and rectify the perceived logical and metaphysical inconsistencies of the previous texts. The *Evidential* is the first evidence of a non-Aristotelian trend in Islamic philosophy which was later systematized by Suhrawardī in his Illuminationist reconstruction of philosophy. Al-Baghdādī's three-part text – consisting of logic, physics, metaphysics – differs from Avicenna's *Healing* in both structure and method. Both al-Baghdādī and Suhrawardī base their constructivist philosophical ideas on the same foundation – that of a primary intuition of a knowing subject whose immediate grasp of the totality of existence, time and space, and of the whole as a self-constituted, inherently manifest and knowable object, determines both being and knowledge.

The fact that Abu'l-Barakāt al-Baghdādī is among the few philosophers Suhrawardī actually mentions in his works in reference to specific philosophical problems is indicative of the impact of the *Evidential* on Illuminationist philosophy. Also, Suhrawardī upholds al-Baghdādī's Platonist position. Concerning the significant question of the foundation of philosophy, both Suhrawardī and al-Baghdādī take an intuitionist stance, requiring that primary intuition must constitute the "first step" in philosophical construction. The structure of the *Evidential* is also reflected in Suhrawardī's philosophical works. It is evident, therefore, that al-Baghdādī should be regarded as an important preliminary source for many of Suhrawardī's non-Peripatetic arguments.

Finally, the anti-philosophical works of the famous theologian Abū Ḥamid al-Ghazzālī – especially his *Incoherence of the Philosophers* ("*Tahāfut al-falāsifah*") – were known to Suhrawardī. Some of the terms used by al-Ghazzālī, specifically in his *Mishkāt al-anwār*, are terms that were later modified and employed by Suhrawardī in his *Philosophy of Illumination*. However, al-Ghazzālī's polemic intention must be distinguished from Suhrawardī's philosophical one. In spite of some similarities in terminology, Illuminationist philosophy should not be understood as resulting from theological polemics, which is basically anti-philosophical in intent. The purpose of Illuminationist thought, on the contrary, is a fundamentally philosophical one: to demonstrate logical gaps in the Peripatetic system and then to reconstruct a more consistent and holistic philosophical structure by solidifying its foundations, methods and arguments. The theologian's aim, however, is not to construct a better philosophical system but to refute the very basis of philosophy. In support of this distinction, none of the major commentators of Illuminationist philosophy ever mentions al-Ghazzālī's works as immediate sources for Illuminationist methodology or formal techniques, though they were obviously aware of the widespread appeal of such texts by al-Ghazzālī, such as *Mishkāt al-anwār*, *Tahāfut al-falāsifah* and *Maqāṣid al-falāsifah.*

Along with the Peripatetic school, the Illuminationist tradition is the only other systematic school of Islamic philosophy that has continued to be studied as a complete system of thought up to the present day. The epithet "Illuminationist" (*ishrāqī*) is still used, especially in Iran, to characterize the method and philosophical views of individual thinkers. As described in the previous chapter, Suhrawardī's Illuminationist philosophy fundamentally departs from Islamic Peripatetic philosophy in respect to the logical foundations of its epistemology and its reconstructed metaphysical system. Illuminationist philosophy continues immediately after Suhrawardī, primarily in the form of several major commentaries on Illuminationist texts composed in the seventh/thirteenth century, though it is not confined to these.

COMMENTATORS ON SUHRAWARDĪ'S PHILOSOPHY OF ILLUMINATION

Of the main figures in the tradition of Illuminationist philosophy, some were designated Illuminationist; others were not yet clearly influenced by Suhrawardī's thought. The earliest thinkers known for their Illuminationist position are the following seventh/thirteenth-century scholars, all of whom wrote commentaries on Suhrawardī's texts and also composed independent philosophical treatises that include specific Illuminationist positions: Shams al-Dīn Muḥammad al-Shahrazūrī[2] and Sa'd ibn Manṣūr ibn Kammūnah[3] (both of whom are called "Illuminationist") and Quṭb al-Dīn al-Shīrāzī.[4] Other commentaries on Suhrawardī's texts were composed later, the most important of these being the tenth/sixteenth-century works of Jalāl al-Dīn al-Dawānī[5] and the eleventh/seventeenth-century writings of Muḥammad Sharīf Niẓam al-Dīn al-Harawī.[6] The principal commentators and their works are as follows.

Shams al-Dīn Muḥammad Shahrazūrī, al-Ishrāqī, i.e. "the Illuminationist" (d. after 688/1288) is the author of the well-known history of philosophy *Nuzhat al-arwāḥ wa rawḍāt al-afrāḥ*, as well as the author of the first major commentary on Suhrawardī's *Philosophy of Illumination* and his *Intimations.* Among all the commentators Shahrazūrī is the most faithful to the original conception and philosophical constructivist methodology of Suhrawardī's Illuminationist philosophy. His independent philosophical composition, *al-Shajarah al-ilāhiyyah*, will be examined below to show the Illuminationist concepts, method and structure of this work.

Sa'd ibn Manṣūr ibn Kammūnah (d. 683/1284) created a major commentary, *al-Talwīḥāt*, that has earned the status of a textbook among Illuminationist philosophers in Iran. Perhaps the most significant impact of Illuminationist philosophy may be seen in Ibn Kammūnah's philosophical work *al-Jadīd fi'l-ḥikmah* (literally, "The New Philosophy", or *Novum Organum*). I have detected a serious attempt in this book to elucidate further certain anti-Aristotelian philosophical principles that originate with Illuminationist philosophy. The salient features of his *Commentary on al-Talwīḥāt* will be briefly outlined here.

Quṭb al-Dīn Shīrāzī (d. 710/1311) is the author of the best-known commentary on Illuminationist philosophy, as well as the voluminous, encyclopedic *Durrat al-tāj*. However, on careful scrutiny, Shīrāzī's work indicates major borrowings from Shahrazūrī's text that have previously gone unnoticed. Shīrāzī is a better-known figure in Islamic philosophy than Shahrazūri, simply because he is one of the first post-Suhrawardian philosophers in Iran successfully to synthesize Avicennan philosophy and Suhrawardī's Illuminationist philosophy with Ibn 'Arabī's "gnosis" of *waḥdat al-wujūd* in a coherent and accessible independent Persian composition. *Durrat al-tāj* marks the beginning of philosophical compositions in which Avicennan methodology and metaphysics are harmonized with Illuminationist theories of vision and illumination (epistemology and psychology), and where the accepted Illuminationist doctrine of the fourth ontological realm, the *mundus imaginalis*, is fully integrated into the reconstructed cosmological system. This work is also the first Persian philosophical text that accepts Suhrawardī's psychological doctrine of knowledge by and of the self-conscious separate "I" – generalized as "I-it-thou-ness" (*manī, tu'ī, ū'ī*) – as the primary principle in epistemology as well as an alternative proof of prophecy. The only other epistemology that concerns the self in this way is the Peripatetic theory of the holy intellect and its conjunction with the Active Intellect. Shīrāzī's work also discusses resurrection and metempsychosis (*tanāsukh*) within the author's Illuminationist interpretation of gnosis (*'irfān*).[7] In my view this new grouping of ideas in Islamic philosophy was only the popular side of the theory, however, and is indicative of a trend that culminates with Mullā Ṣadrā in the eleventh/seventeenth century. The more genuinely philosophical and theoretical Illuminationist legacy continued through less widely known texts, such as the works of Ibn Kammūnah, which are discussed in detail later in this chapter.

The most recent of the medieval commentaries on Suhrawardī's texts was composed by Muḥammad Sharīf Niẓām al-Dīn al-Harawī, author of the most significant Persian commentary and translation of the *Philosophy of Illumination*. Harawī's work, composed in 1008/1600, includes a translation and commentary of Suhrawardī's "Introduction" and the majority of part two (*al-qism al-thānī*) of *Philosophy of*

Illumination.[8] One of the important characteristics of Harawī's commentary is his attempt to compare Illuminationist principles with the Advaita system of Indian philosophy.

Anwāriyyah is the only Persian translation and commentary on Suhrawardī's *Philosophy of Illumination* known to have survived, though others have been composed and may be found through further research in manuscript collections. Its author was probably an Indian Chishtī Sufi who also composed an independent Illuminationist work in Persian titled *Sirāj al-ḥikmah*.[9] *Anwāriyyah* consists of a Persian translation and commentary of selected sections of the second part of Suhrawardī's Arabic text, which is on metaphysics, cosmology and the Illuminationist accounts of visionary experience. The work is typical of the first trend in post-Suhrawardian Illuminationist interpretation (by Shahrazūrī), and is also indicative of the period's general lack of interest in logic and philosophical methodology. It emphasizes the fantastic side of Illuminationist philosophy and draws heavily on Quṭb al-Dīn's earlier commentary but adds a great many examples drawn from popular mystical sources, especially from *Mathnawī* by Jalāl al-Dīn Rūmī (604/1206–672/1274). Harawī's work is also of interest for the study of comparative mysticism and for its overall attempt at a mystical interpretation of Suhrawardī's text, which was not always intended by Suhrawardī. Often, when commenting on a section, Harawī adds "and this is in accordance to the views held by the Sufi masters", or "this argument lends support to gnostic views". These comments are valuable in illustrating how mystics made use of the Illuminationist epistemological priority of the experiential mode of cognition.

Finally, *Anwāriyyah* is also of specific interest for an understanding of how tenth/sixteenth-century Muslims in India viewed the prevalent Hindu views on mysticism. On several occasions, the author attempts to compare Illuminationist views with those of the Indian Advaita system, which he mentions by name. Examples are when he compares the Illuminationist cosmology, especially the *mundus imaginalis*, with the fourfold Sanskrit divisions of *andaja*, *arayuta*, *udbhija* and *khanija*, and Suhrawardī's discussion of eternal time with the Indian notions of *yuga*.[10] The work is also replete with words of reverence for "Indian sages and Brahmins", whom, we are told, the author had consulted on questions relating to philosophical and mystical questions.

OTHER ILLUMINATIONIST PHILOSOPHERS

Many other authors are known for having incorporated certain Illuminationist principles in their works but do not qualify as pure Illuminationists. The following is a selected list of these thinkers.

Naṣīr al-Dīn al-Ṭūsī (d. 672/1274) is the well-known philosopher, astronomer, mathematician and statesman whose commentary on Avicenna's *al-Ishārāt wa'l-tanbīhāt* has become one of the standard textbooks for the study of Avicenna's Peripatetic philosophy. Many generations of philosophers in Persia came to learn of the quintessence of Avicenna's teaching through this commentary. However the epistemological priority given by Ṭūsī to knowledge by presence does not qualify him as a purely Muslim Peripatetic. Given the impact that Ṭūsī has had on all later Shi'ite authors, however, his Illuminationist attitude should not be overlooked.

Muḥammad ibn Zayn al-Dīn ibn Ibrāhīm Aḥsā'ī (d. after 878/1479), known as Ibn Abī Jumhūr Ishrāqī Aḥsā'ī, is among those whom I have designated as "middle *ishrāqī*" thinkers.

Qāḍī Jalāl al-Dīn Muḥammad ibn Sa'd al-Dīn Dawānī (d. 908/1501) is the author of the celebrated work on ethics titled *Akhlāq-i jalālī*, and held the position of vizier under the Āqquyünlü rulers of northeastern Persia. His commentary on Suhrawardī's *Hayākil al-nūr*, titled *Shawākil al-ḥūr fī sharḥ hayākil al-nūr*, is well known, though unpublished. It falls under the category of popular syncretistic philosophy, which had a strong impact on the generation of thinkers that followed him in Persia and who were instrumental in shaping the Shi'ite world view that has continued to the present.[11]

Ghiyāth al-Dīn Manṣūr Dashtakī (d. 948/1541), too, wrote a commentary on Suhrawardī's *Hayākil al-nūr*, entitled *Ishrāq hayākil al-nūr li-kashf ẓulamāt shawākil al-ghurūr*. This is not an important theoretical work but, once more, it is indicative of Suhrawardī's widespread impact.

Muḥammad Bāqir ibn Shams al-Dīn Muḥammad (d. 1040/1631), well known as Mīr Dāmād, is perhaps the most significant philosopher of his age, more original and systematically philosophical an author than his famous pupil, Mullā Ṣadrā. In my view Mīr Dāmād is to be counted among the few truly Illuminationist philosophers, a company that would include the immediate followers of Suhrawardī, Shahrazūrī and Ibn Kammūnah, as well as, in most recent times, Sayyid Muḥammad Kāẓim 'Aṣṣār. Mīr Dāmād's poetic *takhalluṣ*, or pen-name, is "*Ishrāq*" ("Illuminationist"), a clear indication of his alignment with Illuminationist philosophy. He considers himself a genuine upholder of the Illuminationist methodology of philosophy, combining discursive (*baḥthī*) methods and principles (Avicenna's methodology of the *Shifā'*) with intuitive (*dhawqī*) ones (Suhrawardī's methodology of *Ḥikmat al-ishrāq*), carefully stipulated by Suhrawardī to be the fundamental Illuminationist position. This philosophical stance is exemplified in Mīr Dāmād's publicly proclaimed characteristic as "the greatest teacher of the *Shifā'* of his time" and is clearly revealed in the structure as well as the philosophical intention of his philosophical works, especially in his *al-Ufuq al-mubīn*, *Jadhawāt* and in his best-known work, *Qabasāt*. In his philosophical work, Mīr Dāmād's intent is to construct a holistic philosophical structure based on the self-conscious I's ability to combine perfectly examination of sense-perceivable data with visions and illuminations.[12]

Ṣadr al-Dīn al-Shīrāzī, well known as Mullā Ṣadrā (d. 1050/1640), is recognized to be the main originator of still another synthesis in Islamic philosophy which has had a major impact on Shi'ite thought up to this day. This point of view will be examined in more detail in chapter 35.

The fourteenth/twentieth-century Illuminationist philosopher Sayyid Muḥammad Kāẓim 'Aṣṣār also deserves special mention. His *Waḥdat-i wujūd wa badā'*[13] represents the most recent example of a discussion of the special Illuminationist ontological principle of "equivocal being" (*tashkīk fi'l-wujūd*).

Finally, one must consider the possible impact of Suhrawardī's thinking in the West, specifically on the development of Jewish mysticism in the eighth/fourteenth century.[14] This is exemplified by the remarkable, though seldom mentioned, major paraphrase of important sections of the *Philosophy of Illumination* composed by the famous Nāṣirid vizier Lisān al-Dīn Ibn al-Khaṭīb in his *Rawḍat al-ta'rīf bi'l-ḥubb al-sharīf*.[15] Though he is not mentioned by name, the section is clearly a paraphrase of Suhrawardī's works.

The Illuminationist tradition and almost every other aspect of the intellectual dimension of Islam were revived and re-examined in the tenth/sixteenth century during one of history's most active and prolifically fruitful periods of Islamic philosophy. The tenth/sixteenth-century revival of philosophy took place in Isfahan in central Persia, and is of such integral quality that it has been designated "the School of Isfahan". The two main figures of this school – Mīr Dāmād (with the poetic name "Ishrāq") and Mullā Ṣadrā, whose philosophical works are replete with Illuminationist terminology – studied and made use of the Illuminationist tradition. By this time almost all problems covering the entire philosophical corpus were discussed from both the Peripatetic and Illuminationist perspectives. It had become common practice in constructing arguments to pose the two positions first, then demonstrate the superiority of one over the other, attempt a new synthesis between the two, or formulate different arguments.

Philosophical activity from the eighth/fourteenth to tenth/sixteenth centuries is not well known. From the Illuminationist standpoint, a few commentaries on Suhrawardī's texts by the two Dashtakī brothers and by Jalāl al-Dīn Dawānī are known, though none has been published or studied. There is also known to be an Illuminationist tradition in India. A major commentary and Persian translation of Suhrawardī's *Philosophy of Illumination*, titled *Anwāriyyah*, was composed in India by Harawī. This published work indicates the impact of the Illuminationist tradition on Islamic mystical philosophy in India.

TWO MAIN TRENDS IN ILLUMINATIONIST PHILOSOPHY

Although we cannot give here an examination of the entire scope of Illuminationist tradition from the time of Suhrawardī to the present, the following will identify the two main trends present in seventh/thirteenth-century Illuminationist compositions, both of which had an impact on the School of Isfahan.

The twofold dimension of seventh/thirteenth-century Illuminationist works is exemplified first by Shahrazūrī. His commentaries on Suhrawardī's texts – *Sharḥ ḥikmat al-ishrāq*, *Sharḥ al-talwīḥāt* and the encyclopedic *al-Shajarah al-ilāhiyyah* – not only emphasize the symbolic and distinctly anti-Peripatetic components of Illuminationist philosophy but further elaborate on them by extending their inspirational, allegorical and fantastic side. This trend, though of less philosophical significance than the one examined below, has had more impact in shaping views concerning mystical and religious philosophy. It may well be considered the origin of mystical and religious philosophy with the most popular appeal.

Second is Ibn Kammūnah. In his *Sharḥ al-talwīḥāt*, commentaries on Suhrawardī's *Intimations*, in his major independent philosophical work, *al-Jadīd fi'l-ḥikmah*, as well as in his shorter works, such as *Risālah fi'l-nafs* and *al-Ḥikmah*, Ibn Kammūnah emphasizes the purely discursive and systematically philosophical side of the Philosophy of Illumination. These works go so far as to define Illuminationist symbolism and allegories in terms of standard Peripatetic doctrine, thus further elaborating on the scientific aspect of Suhrawardī's original intention.

In a way, both of these trends are valid interpretations and refinements on Suhrawardī's system in that both are present in the original Illuminationist texts, although distinguished in terms of choice and emphasis.

SHAHRAZŪRĪ'S WORKS

To determine why the more animated, symbolic and inspirational side of the Philosophy of Illumination, as emphasized by Shahrazūrī, gained more popular appeal than Suhrawardī's own philosophical approach, one must first briefly examine the historical background of the Islamic medieval world concerning attitudes to philosophy in general. By the middle of the second/eighth century, Arab rule over most of Western Asia, the Near East, North Africa and Spain (mainly Andalusia) was well established. The 'Abbasid Empire, founded in 132/750 by the caliph al-Ṣaffāḥ, emerged as a new civilization that drew material as well as intellectual strength from the conquered peoples and lands. The Qur'ān and the Prophet Muḥammad's teachings and personal actions became the inspiration for a gradually codified set of laws. These laws, called the *Sharī'ah*, were sanctioned and upheld by the state and regulated every facet of the public and private life of the multitudes of Muslims from India to Spain. While it can be argued that jurisprudence remained faithful to the letter of revelation and to the Prophet's own conduct, the powerful, rich, diverse and vast empire was in need of a world view to sustain itself as a world power. Therefore it arduously sought knowledge of science, medicine and technology beyond what was revealed and written in a single book. The Greeks, Persians and Indians possessed vast learning manifest in their books, art, architecture, technology, medicine and other disciplines. "Sciences of the ancients" (*al-'ulūm al-awā'il*) was the name given to every aspect of the sciences and of the techniques of the various civilizations encountered by the ruling Arabs. Baghdad, the new capital of the caliphate, was built from scratch near the ruins of Ctesiphon, the conquered centre of the Sassanian Empire, and soon became the centre of the new civilization. Persian statecraft and art of governance was employed to rule the vast dominion. Soon learned men of all nations gathered there, libraries were established, and book dealers travelled to faraway lands in search of ancient sciences.

By the end of the third/ninth century, a tremendous translation activity was fully under way, funded by state endowments. The Dār al-Ḥikmah, literally "Place of Wisdom" – the new academy, as it were – had become a learning centre of unprecedented dimension. Even the caliphs were in attendance at this academy, where the philosophy and the sciences of the ancients were being rewritten and transformed into a new world view. Of special significance was the translation into Arabic of the Greek philosophical and scientific tradition. By this time almost all of the Aristotelian corpus, plus much of the major Platonic works, some pre-Socratic fragments, Stoic treatises, Neoplatonist works – including parts of the *Enneads* erroneously thought to be a work by Aristotle called the "theology" – Porphyry's *Isagoge*, works by Proclus, as well as numerous shorter Greek philosophical compilations, were all translated. The translations were initially from Syriac and eventually from the Greek. The Greek heritage was the most influential element in the rise of rational thought in Islamic civilization at this time. Philosophy, which was reformulated in Arabic and eventually also in Persian, was expanded and refined by such thinkers as al-Fārābī (the "Second Teacher") and Avicenna, whose philosophical method survived in the Latin West for centuries.

For a short while, the rational heritage of the Greeks was even triumphant in state-sanctioned theology. The Muʿtazilite rationalist theologians attempted to apply their principal view, known as the "primacy of intellect" (*aṣālat al-ʿaql*), to find a rational basis for revelation. They even went so far as to say that the revealed word cannot be in contradiction to rational thought. Philosophy and philosophical techniques became the sought-after tool by the empire's ruling elite, as well as philosophers and scientists. But the opposing theological view, called "primacy of revelation" (*aṣalat al-waḥy*), was perpetuated by the Ashʿarite school and eventually won out. This ended the Muʿtazilah's dominance as the official theology of the land. Rational thought, for a number of complex reasons, did not continue to influence people beyond its few proponents and never gained dominance as a widely accepted world view in Arab society.

In many respects Arabic Aristotelian philosophy had a much deeper impact in the West than in the East. Avicenna's *Shifāʾ*, known as *Sufficiencia* in Latin, was the primary source for the Latin West's first encounter with Aristotle many decades before any direct translation from the original Greek texts. Other works in Hebrew and Latin translation – such as abridged versions of Avicenna's works, to a lesser extent of al-Fārābī's works, and most important of the major works by the greatest Aristotelian Muslim commentator, Averroes – continued to keep the Greek philosophical heritage alive in the West as it was dying in the East.

This does not mean that philosophy did not continue in the Islamic world. Rather, it was reconstructed in the form of the Philosophy of Illumination. Peripatetic in method, Suhrawardī's philosophy employed a new and different technical language and revived many popularly held views concerning wisdom. It also included references to characters, themes, and sentiments of Persian mythological and religious beliefs, as well as Qur'ānic decrees never discussed to such an extent in Islamic Peripateticism.

Later religious philosophy in Islam, exemplified by Shahrazūrī's works, embraced this new philosophy at least in principle and used it as a point of departure for the depiction of an animated, more personalized and recognizable universe. This is where Greek methodology, Qur'ānic dicta and other Islamic religious sentiments and Persian popular beliefs converge.

For example, the Qur'ān talks about "jinn", or demonic spirits. The Muʿtazilah deny the existence of the *ʿifrīt*, al-Fārābī avoids discussing them and Avicenna denies that they exist. Nevertheless, by the seventh/thirteenth century philosophers incorporate all manner of Qur'ānic jinn, as well as a host of other demonic and benevolent creatures of the "unseen" world (*ʿālam al-ghayb*) – which is itself a cornerstone of Qur'ānic proclamations – into their discussion of metaphysics. By doing so, the new philosophers became more accepted by both theologians and jurists as well as by the general public. Many people, learned as well as others, who had a hard time identifying with the abstract notions and terms of Peripatetic philosophy, were able to accept the new religious philosophy because it provided a scientific explanation of the world they had known and believed in as the real realm of prophecy as well as sorcery. Such an animated world is precisely what this larger audience found in Shahrazūrī's works, some aspects of which are suggested in various places in Suhrawardī's texts but never fully explained.[16]

SHAHRAZŪRĪ'S ILLUMINATIONIST PHILOSOPHY

Shams al-Dīn Muḥammad ibn Maḥmūd Shahrazūrī (d. after 688/1288), whose voluminous philosophical encyclopedia entitled *al-Shajarah al-ilāhiyyah*, translated here as *Metaphysical Tree* or the "Divine Genealogy", is best known for his history of philosophy, *Nuzhat al-arwāḥ*. But it is the *Metaphysical Tree* that marks the denouement of Suhrawardī's primacy.

Shahrazūrī's underlying method is Illuminationist. Philosophical construction based on a primary intuition of time-space, personal revelation and vision are given fundamental epistemological priority over the inherently rationalist, predicative Aristotelian principles. The Aristotelian *horos* is rejected as the primary epistemological method. Priority is given instead to the Platonist view of knowledge based on an activity of the soul whereby innate knowledge is recovered, which then serves as the first step in constructing syllogistic arguments. Thus, knowledge recovered, or "seen", by the inner disposition of a knowing subject serves as the foundation for all subsequent philosophical construction. The knowing subject, when related to the manifest object, comes to know the object in a timeless instant (*ān*). From this standpoint, definition of an object by genus and differentiae is not a prerequisite. This "knowledge by presence" has no temporal extension and supersedes acquired knowledge. Reincarnation, immortality of the soul and a cosmology that constructs a separate realm of ideas (*'ālam al-mithāl*) as the real and lasting *mundus imaginalis* (*'ālam al-khayāl*) are cornerstones of Shahrazūrī's cosmos.

Shahrazūrī consciously invokes Plato's authority in proving the validity of these ideas. As the Illuminationist philosophers stipulated, "this incorporates the divine philosopher Plato's *Phaedo* where the Peripatetics fail". The real, separate Platonic Forms may be known, not by the Aristotelian demonstration (*burhān*) of the *Posterior Analytics* but by intuition and vision–illumination. The notion of philosophical intuition is of central importance for the constructivist methodology of Illuminationist philosophy. Intuition here may be shown to be, first, similar to the Aristotelian "quick wit", *agkhinoia*, where the truth of propositions may be known immediately, or a conclusion arrived at prior to constructing a syllogism; or, secondly, recovery by the subject of universals and of sensible objects. But intuition plays a further fundamental role as an activity of the self-conscious being in a state in which the subject and object are undifferentiated. To use Illuminationist terminology, this means unity of perception, with the perceived and the perceiver (*ittiḥād al-mudrik wa'l-idrāk wa'l-mudrik*) as an altered state in the consciousness of the knowing subject. This state exists when the subject is "linked", or otherwise related to the separate realm of the *mundus imaginalis*. This realm contains a multiplicity of self-conscious, self-subsistent "monads" designated as "abstract light" (*al-nūr al-mujarrad*) in place of the finite number of Peripatetic "intellects" (*al-'uqūl al-mujarradah*). Unlike the intellects, the abstract lights are continuous one with the other, differing only in their relative degree of intensity. Together they form a continuum designated as "the whole" (*al-kull*), which is also conscious of itself. Shahrazūrī uses the term "intuitive philosophy" (*al-ḥikmah al-dhawqiyyah*) to distinguish Illuminationist thought from the purely discursive (*al-ḥikmah al-baḥthiyyah*) Peripatetic approach.

Of further interest here is the manner in which fantastic beings – such as jinn, angels and so on – are incorporated within this religio-philosophical structure by Shahrazūrī, specifically in his philosophical encyclopedia but also in his other works, notably the *Commentary on the Philosophy of Illumination*. By philosophically explaining the existence of all manner of non-corporeal, "intelligent beings" – which were previously rejected by all the major Islamic Peripatetics – Shahrazūrī paves the way for the prevalent Iranian and Indian view of a world animated by spirits. This view is incorporated into subsequent religious philosophy and further affects theological development, especially of Shi'ite theology, in the tenth/sixteenth century.

To appreciate the breadth of Shahrazūrī's *Metaphysical Tree*, one must look at its overall structure,[17] which consists of five main treatises (*risālah*) as follows:

1 On methodology and the division of the sciences; which serves as an introduction – marking the first work of its kind in which methodological questions, as well as problems of the philosophy of language are discussed separately and systematically.
2 On logic – one of the most comprehensive compilations including the Islamic Peripatetic corpus plus Stoic fragments and additions such as the long commentary on the *Isagoge* by Ghiyāth al-Dīn al-Abharī.
3 On ethics, political philosophy and statecraft – a recompilation of such works as al-Fārābī's commentary on Plato's *Republic*, titled *The*

Opinions of the Inhabitants of the Virtuous City (*Ārā' ahl al-madīnah al-fāḍilah*), Ṭūsī's *Naṣīrean Ethics* and many other works on practical philosophy.

4 On physics – a summary of Avicenna's *Physics* (*Shifā'*), plus arguments taken from other works, including those specifically designated as Stoic (*riwāqī*).

5 On metaphysics.

The fifth treatise, "On Metaphysical Sciences and Divine Secrets" (*Fī'l-'ulūm al-ilāhiyyah wa'l-asrār al-rabbāniyyah*) is of particular significance here. It is divided into two major sections, each called *techne* (*fann*). The first deals with the subject of *metaphysica generalis* (*al-'ilm al-kullī*), and the second with *metaphysica specialis* (*al-'ilm al-ilāhī*). The latter contains the most comprehensive and lengthy treatments of metaphysics in Islamic philosophy. The ontological position upheld in the first section – after elaborate discussion pertaining to various philosophical, theological and mystical views – is one designated, perhaps clearly for the first time, as "primacy of quiddity" (*aṣālat al-māhiyyah*). Briefly stated, this position holds "existence" (*wujūd*) to be a derived mental concept while "essence" (*māhiyyah*) is considered to be primary and real. Of the seventeen chapters in this section, chapters 10, 11 and 17 are noted here.

Chapter 10 is entitled "On Determining the Platonic Forms" (*Fī taḥqīq al-muthul al-aflāṭūniyyah*); chapter 11 "On Determining the *Mundus Imaginalis*" (*Fī taḥqīq al-'ālam al-mithālī* [*al-khayālī*]; and the seventeenth and final chapter of the *Metaphysical Tree* is entitled "On the Jinn, Satans, Rebellious Angels; and therein the principle of the Devil and its state are explained" (*Fi'l-jinn wa'l-shayāṭīn wa'l-mardah, wa'l-ghūl, wa'l-nasānīs; wa fīhi bayān aṣl Iblīs wa aḥwāluhu*). Ifrīt, Ghūl and Nasnās are categories of demons. According to Shahrazūrī, they all dwell in the *mundus imaginalis*, where true dreams occur. This is the location of the sorcerers' power as well as the source of inspiration for saints and the revelations of prophets. Those who travel to this realm – not with the body but with the imagination – may, if they can withstand the terrible ordeal of the quest-journey, come to possess divinelike powers, the least of which are walking on water, traversing the earth, ability to foretell the future and power over the elemental world. Visitors to the *mundus imaginalis* may tap the very source of the demons' powers and may even employ them for benevolent purposes back on earth, as did the kindly mythological Persian, Jamshīd. According to Persian tradition, this phenomenon also explains the miraculous powers of biblical figures such as Solomon.

To gain a better understanding of these philosophical views, it is helpful to look at the Platonic Forms and the Realm of Ideas in Islamic philosophy. In the Islamic Peripatetic scheme three realms are recognized:

intellect, soul and matter. In his Illuminationist philosophy Suhrawardī adds a fourth realm, generally called "the world of forms". This is further elaborated upon and enlivened by Shahrazūrī, who calls it "the intermediary realm" (*al-ʿālam al-awsāṭ*). Not confined to empirical appearance, this domain is between the purely intelligible and the purely sensory, where time and space are different from Aristotelian time as a measure of distance as well as from Euclidean space. The way to the intermediary realm is by the active imagination.[18] In the *Metaphysical Tree*, the intermediary realm is considered a "real" place where all manner of extraordinary phenomena, both good and evil, are said to occur, as Shahrazūrī writes:[19]

> This realm is called the Realm of Ideas and the *mundus imaginalis*. It is beyond the world of sense perception and beyond extended space [*makān*] but below the realm of intellect [*ʿālam al-ʿaql*]. It is an intermediary realm between the two. Everything imagined by the mathematicians, such as shapes (round, oblong, square, etc.), quantities (large, small, one, two, etc.), and bodies (cubes, tetrahedrons, spheres, etc.) and whatever relates to them such as rest, position, idea shape [*hay'ah*], surface, line, point and other conditions all exist in this intermediary realm. This is why philosophers refer to the [study of] it as "intermediate philosophy" or "intermediate science". . . . Everything seen [and heard] in dreams such as oceans, lands, loud noises and persons of stature, all of them are suspended Forms not in space nor situated. . . . Archetypes of all known things on Earth exist as luminous Forms in this realm. . . . There are numerous multiple levels in this realm, and only God knows their number. But two bordering levels are known. The virtuous luminous level which lies at the horizon bordering on the realm of intellects; and the lowly dark level, which borders the realm of sense-perception. The numerous other levels are in between the two, and in each level dwell angels, jinn and Satans whose numbers are uncountable. Souls, when separated from the body will come to live in this realm. . . . In this realm are rivers wider than the Tigris and the Euphrates and mountains taller than any on Earth. . . . Souls of evil-doers will encounter scorpions and serpents larger than the largest mountain in this realm. . . . Things that exist in this realm have "formal" bodies and imaginary shapes [*abdān mithālī wa ashkāl khayālī*]. . . . Extraordinary events, miracles, sorcery and all manner of strange manifestations occur because of this realm. . . . Sages on spiritual journeys, who learn how to unravel the signs[20] have all attested to the powers that are manifest there.

The fourth dominion of the Illuminationist cosmos, the Realm of Forms, is the region of the dark (evil) forms, as well as the luminous (good). Together they are described as constituting a land beyond the corporeal, of the essence of the fabulous (*hūrqalyā dhāt al-'ajā'ib*), or an eighth clime (*al-iqlīm al-thāmin*).[21] Access to this realm is gained through the active imagination when it becomes mirrorlike, turning into a place in which an epiphany (*maẓhar*) may occur. One is said to travel in it not by traversing distances but by being witness to "here" or "there", unsituated and without co-ordinates. Seeing sights in this region is identified as effects suffered by the soul, or experiences within the self-consciousness of the objective self. The *mundus imaginalis* is an ontological realm whose beings, though possessing categorical attributes – such as time, place, relation, quality and quantity – are abstracted from matter. That is, they are ideal beings with a substance, usually depicted metaphorically as "light" (*nūr*). These light beings differ from the substances of other beings only in respect to their degree of intensity, or "darkness" (*ẓulmah*) which is also expressed in gradations.[22]

Creatures who dwell in this land exist in a space without Euclidean spatial extensions and in a time that is absolute, unrestricted and without duration. Things appear in this realm in what appear to be fleeting moments but involve processes that cover etenity and infinity. They possess shapes. This is why they may be seen, although their "bodies" are imaginary, or "ideal" ("*badan mithālī wa khayālī*"). This land has "cities" and "pavilions" with hundreds of thousands of gates and tiers. For all its imaginal qualities, this world is, in the words of Henry Corbin, a "concrete spiritual universe". Like Jacques Duchesne-Guillemin before him,[23] Corbin qualifies the *mundus imaginalis* in terms of what he calls a "neo-Zoroastrian Platonism". As he states, "it is most certainly not a world of concepts, paradigms, and universals", for the archetypes of the species that populate it have "nothing to do with the universals established in logic". Rather, they are an "autonomous world of visionary Figures and Forms" that belong to "the plane of angelology".[24]

Despite the apparent relationship, it would be inaccurate to identify the *mundus imaginalis* totally with Plato's Realm of Ideas in the *Dialogues*. The Illuminationist philosophers are quite specific on this point and distinguish between the suspended forms (*al-ṣuwar al-mu'allaqah*), which are the real beings of the eighth clime, and the Platonic Forms. This is because Platonic Forms are considered to be discrete, distinct entities, or "things", in the realm of intelligible lights, while the beings of the intermediary realm, though considered to be real, are part of the continuum of the imaginal, whether light or dark.[25] The significance of the realm of the *mundus imaginalis* to the history of Islamic philosophy is that it opens up an entirely new chapter, admitting an irrational dimension that the Islamic Peripatetics had vehemently rejected.

Shahrazūrī builds upon the visionary foundations of Illuminationist philosophy by seeking to substantiate the existence of creatures in the realm of the *mundus imaginalis*. The creatures of this realm, be they luminous or dark, are "proven", according to Shahrazūrī, by the visions and intuitions of the divine philosopher-sages who have strengthened their intuitions and purified their imaginations by ascetic practices, not by mere recourse to rational demonstration. At every turn the author takes issue with the Peripatetics whose preoccupation with discursive philosophy, he claims, has weakened their ability to "see" (*mushāhadah*), reality as it is. Although the Active Intellect is clearly considered a guiding force for the Peripatetics, there is never a hint that it is personified, or in any way "seen" or perceived by the senses.

In contrast, by the sixth/twelfth century the Active Intellect appears in Illuminationist philosophy on several levels, sometimes personified as Gabriel, the archangel of revelation in the Qur'ān; as Surūsh, one of the immortals of Iranian Mazdayasnian cosmology; as Isfahbad al-A'ẓam, the great controlling archetypal light of Illuminationist cosmology; as Sīmurgh, the mythological bird of the Persian epic; as the Holy Spirit (*Rūḥ al-qudus*) of popular mysticism equated with Rawān Bakhsh, *dator spiritis*, of Persian legends. Finally, by the seventh/thirteenth century in Shahrazūrī's *Metaphysical Tree*, the Active Intellect becomes fully personified as a rational creature who exists separately in the intermediary realm and who may appear to the adept who will actually see its ideal shape and *imaginalis* body and hear its shrill cry. This archetypal creature, now with enormous power, may serve, rule or crush the person who has, by use of magic (*nayrang*) and sorcery, or by other means, tapped into its power. To support this contention the new Illuminationist philosophy now invokes the memory of past philosophers and sages, as Shahrazūrī states:[26]

> The ancient philosophers such as Hermes, Aghathadhaemon, Empedocles, Pythagoras and Plato, as well as others from among the ancients, have all claimed to have "seen" them[27] [that is, the archetypal beings, angels, or demons]; and they have all clearly attested their existence by their visions in the realm of lights. Plato has related that when he elevated his soul from the dark shackles of the body he saw them. The Persian and Indian sages, as well as others, all adhere to this and are in agreement. Anyone who absolves himself of the body and rids himself of prime matter would certainly have a vision of these lights, the archetypal essences [*dhawāt al-aṣnām*]. Most of what the prophets and other sages have indicated by way of their metaphorical language refer to this.

At this juncture Shahrazūrī turns to a rebuttal of Aristotelian methodology:

> If the physical observations of a person in matters pertaining to astronomy are accepted, and astronomers accept Ptolemy's and Proclus' and others' observations, and the First Teacher [Aristotle] even accepts the astronomical observations of the Babylonians, why should then one not rely on the spiritual observations [*irṣād ruḥānī*] and the luminous visions [*mushāhadah wa mukāshafah*] of the Pillars of Philosophy and Prophecy . . . so spiritual observation is just as significant in providing knowledge [*ma'rifah*] as physical observation [*irṣād jismānī*]. Rather, many types of error may occur in corporeal observation, as explained in al-Majisṭī, while spiritual observation, when based on the abstract, separate lights, which are all attested by Zoroaster and [King] Kay Khusraw [of Persian mythology], cannot fall into error.

The heritage of rational Greek philosophy so significant in shaping intellectual and even theological attitudes for several centuries in Islam now becomes but one dimension in Islamic Illuminationist philosophy which further defines religious philosophy. This new philosophical position characterizes religious philosophy in Persia from the seventh/thirteenth century to the present.

The overall structure of Shahrazūrī's Illuminationist elaborations is syncretic – that is, it is composed of divergent systems and beliefs that are grouped together under one school of thought. This juxtaposition continues to characterize the fantastic, supernatural, demon-ridden and generally Shi'i religious philosophy that allows Persian epic and religious figures to roam side by side with figures of Qur'ānic and Islamic origin.

Equally significant is the fact that Shahrazūrī's syncretic interpretation and elaboration of Illuminationist religious philosophy is not shunned by theologians nor even by jurists, as had been the case with earlier rational philosophies. In a recent major biographical study of philosophers in Persia from the tenth/sixteenth century to the present, some four hundred major thinkers, each with several works, were enumerated. With the exception of only a few, all were graduates of *madrasah*s, and many at one time or another had assumed specific public, religious and judicial duties.[28]

Islamic Illuminationist philosophy, as interpreted by Shahrazūrī in a religious context, was able to accommodate revelation with all its metaphysical and fantastic implications to a degree Peripatetic philosophy was never able to do. It expanded and refined the powerful Greek analytical tools into well-defined domains comprising semantic, formal and material logic. Above all, it allowed for popular religious sensibilities, superstitions and beliefs to be given a "scientific" explanation within its reformulated cosmology. And finally, through its adoption in at least some of the higher-level school curricula, it even received legal sanction.

The seventeenth and final chapter of the *Metaphysical Tree*, titled "On the Jinn, Satans, Rebellious Angels: and therein the principle of the Devil and its state are explained", adds a new and significant dimension to Illuminationist thinking. The chapter begins with Shahrazūrī stating that the philosophers both ancient and recent ("*mutaqaddimīn wa muta'akhkhirīn*") have different opinions concerning the existence of jinn and Satans. Among the Muslims, three groups are identified and their views rejected. Avicenna's position, stated in the *Book of Definitions*, is: "The jinn are [defined] as etherial beings, and take on different shapes; this being a mere lexical definition [*sharḥ al-ism*] of the utterance 'jinn', and this does not indicate an existence outside the mind (i.e. real)."[29] Shahrazūrī discounts this reasoning because, he contends, arguments based on semantics do not necessarily reject (or prove) the real existence of the thing defined. That is, the reality of the jinn may or may not be indicated simply by naming them as such. Relying on arguments drawn from Illuminationist epistemology, which holds that intuitive experiential knowledge is prior to discursive knowledge, Shahrazūrī asserts that since ancient philosophers, sages and prophets have "experienced" – or, in Illuminationist terms, have "seen" (*yushāhid*) – the jinn, as the Qur'ān also confirms, they must, therefore, have a separate existence. Here even Aristotle's authority is invoked along with that of a host of sages from Hermes to Plato – including Egyptian sages and Persian mythological figures, as well as Indian Brahmins – to prove the separate existence of such beings. Since actual experience of the phenomena is well verified by experts, the argument goes, therefore it must be real.

The statement concludes by claiming a substantial reality for the jinn who are embodied in the Realm of Forms and the *mundus imaginalis* and have non-corporeal, formal bodies and imagined shapes. Shahrazūrī rebukes the Muslim theologians, insinuating that they should know better than to deny the separate reality of the jinn, who are after all authenticated in the Qur'ān.

A summary of Shahrazūrī's arguments in the final chapter of *Metaphysical Tree* also serves as a general account of his specific Illuminationist ideas, as follows. In the intermediary realm, the *mundus imaginalis*, there are two types of entities: light and dark. Both are equally real, according to Shahrazūrī, and are not simply the absence of the other. Suhrawardī's view that darkness is not real but simply the total lack of light, and the Peripatetic view that non-being is the privation of being (or that darkness is the privation of light), are both rejected. Light and dark entities differ in terms of intensity. Just as there is a continuum of light substances from weakest to strongest, there is also a parallel continuum of dark entities. Illuminationist philosophers vehemently deny that this position is a dualist one. Dualism in the Islamic period was identified with ancient Persian infidel beliefs, referred to as Manichaean idolatry (*ilḥād Mānī*). Shahrazūrī defends his views against this attack by confining the existence of dark entities to substances which have assumed dark shapes, or forms – generally with *imaginalis* embodiment. All of these dark forms, he contends, exist in a limited tier of the intermediary realm of forms and the *mundus imaginalis*, while the light substances cover the whole of reality.

The dichotomy of light substance and dark entity in the Realm of Forms and the *mundus imaginalis* is a new addition to the Greek inspired cosmology of the earlier Islamic Peripatetic philosophy. Some scholars, notably Henry Corbin, have indicated that this cosmology represents an earlier Persian world view. While I disagree with Corbin that the Persian element of this new philosophy was based on an established textual philosophical tradition, I believe that the Mazdayasnian sentiments kept alive in popular and oral traditions and in poetic, epic and mystical compositions have been integrated into this new Islamic Illuminationist philosophy. The Qur'ānic category of demons, satans and other such creatures is introduced by Shahrazūrī along with others from the Persian traditions, such as the category of creatures called the peris. However they are all integrated into a dualist cosmological structure that decidedly reflects the earlier tradition in which the Platonic world of Forms is used to portray a universe permeated with archetypes, good and bad, who affect earthly existence. Nowhere is this continuity more apparent than in Shahrazūrī's *Metaphysical Tree*, and especially in the few chapters examined here.

IBN KAMMŪNAH'S ILLUMINATIONIST PHILOSOPHY

The second trend in the interpretation of Illuminationist philosophy is exemplified by Ibn Kammūnah, whose *Commentary on the Intimations* (*Sharḥ al-talwīḥāt*) completed around 669/1270 emphasizes the rational side of Suhrawardī's thought.[30] It concentrates on the initial, discursive cycle of the reconstruction of the Philosophy of Illumination, but also recognizes Suhrawardī's text to be a fundamentally non-Peripatetic work.

Moshe Perlmann, who edited and translated Ibn Kammūnah's *Tanqīḥ al-ābḥāth li'l-milal al-thalāth* (1967) – translated as *Examination of the Inquiries into the Three Faiths* (1971) – has examined every possible source for Ibn Kammūnah's biography, and is the principal source for the following summary account.

Sa'd ibn Manṣūr ibn Sa'd ibn al-Ḥasan Ḥibat Allāh ibn Kammūnah was "a well-known occulist and teacher of philosophy, [and] lived in Baghdad during the seventh/thirteenth century. He was a distinguished member of the Jewish community."[31] Perlmann translates the notice given for Ibn Kammūnah in Ibn al-Fuwaṭī's *al-Ḥawādith al-jāmiʿah waʾl-tajārib al-nāfiʿah* under the events of the year 683/1284. This is perhaps the most significant source on Ibn Kammūnah's life now available.[32]

Leo Hirschfeld had in the last decade of the nineteenth century written a brief summary account of Ibn Kammūnah's polemical work, titled *Saʿd b. Manṣūr Ibn Kammūna und seine polemische Schrift*, in which he identified several other treatises, including most of Ibn Kammūnah's philosophical and logical works.[33] These include:

1 A commentary on Avicenna's *al-Ishārāt waʾl-tanbīhāt* titled *Sharḥ al-uṣūl waʾl-jumal min muhimmāt al-ʿilm waʾl-ʿamal* (the title translated into German by Hirschfeld as *Kommentar zu den Grundlehren und dem Gesamtinhalt aus dem Gewichtigsten für Theorie und Praxis*). It is important to note that during the same period two other major commentaries on the same work by Avicenna were composed by Fakhr al-Dīn al-Rāzī and by Naṣīr al-Dīn Ṭūsī. Commentaries on the *Ishārāt* were the standard texts used by later Islamic philosophers to study Islamic Peripateticism. This, in my view, differs drastically from the manner in which the Latin West came to know Avicenna, which was mainly through translations of the *Shifāʾ*. It remains to be seen how Ibn Kammūnah's commentary differs, or reflects, the synthetic style of the other two works which later found their way into the higher level *madrasah* curricula.[34]
2 Commentary on Suhrawardī's *Intimations* (*al-Talwīḥāt*), to which I will turn later.
3 An independent philosophical work which Hirschfeld titled *al-Ḥikmah al-jadīdah fiʾl-manṭiq* (*Neue Abhandlung über die Logik*) and has recently been published with the title *al-Jadīd fiʾl-ḥikmah*, or "Novum Organum".[35]
4 Another philosophical treatise by Ibn Kammūnah, not listed by Hirschfeld or Brockelmann, is a short work called *Risālah fiʾl-nafs* or *Risālah fī baqāʾ al-nafs*. Only one manuscript of this work is known to have survived, published by Leon Nemoy in facsimile, and later translated by him into English.[36]
5 Finally, Perlmann has brought to my attention an additional philosophical work by Ibn Kammūnah bearing the generic title *Risālah fiʾl-ḥikmah*. Upon brief examination, I find it to be a different work from the one listed above. Apparently it is a summary of seventh/thirteenth-century attitudes in philosophy which combines Peripatetic terms and techniques with Illuminationist epistemological principles.

In the philosophical compilations of the eleventh/seventeenth century, numerous specific references are made only to Ibn Kammūnah's

Commentary on the Intimations. Most notably, these references are found in *al-Asfār al-arbaʿah* and in *al-Qabasāt*. One example will serve to indicate the significance of Ibn Kammūnah's *Commentary* for the study of the development of Islamic philosophy in the post-Avicennan period. The reference is in Mullā Ṣadrā's famous work, *al-Asfār al-arbaʿah*, in the section, "*al-Safar al-thālith: fi'l-ʿilm al-ilāhī: al-Mawqif al-thālith: fī ʿilmihi taʿālā: al-Faṣl al-rābiʿ: fi tafṣīl madhāhib al-nās fī ʿilmihi bi'l-ashyāʾ*". Mullā Ṣadrā here distinguishes seven schools of thought: four philosophical, two "theological", and one "mystical" (which combines *ʿirfān* and *taṣawwuf*).[37] This is typical of Mullā Ṣadrā's classification of the history of philosophy, theology and mysticism and further reflects the same classification found for the first time in Shahrazūrī's *al-Shajarah al-ilāhiyyah*.[38] The four philosophical "schools" – referred to as *madhhab* – which concern us here are:

1 The school of the followers of the Peripatetics ("*madhhab tawābiʿ al-mashshāʾīn*"). Included in this category are the "two masters" (*al-shaykhān*) al-Fārābī and Avicenna, as well as Bahmanyār (Avicenna's famous student and author of *al-Taḥṣīl*), Abu'l-ʿAbbās al-Lawkarī and "many later Peripatetics" ("*kathīr min al-mutaʾakh-khirīn*").

2 "The school of the Master Shihāb al-Dīn [Suhrawardī] al-Maqtūl follower of the Stoics ['*madhhab shaykh atbāʿ al-riwāqiyyah Shihāb al-Dīn al-Maqtūl*'] and those who follow him, such as al-Muḥaqqiq al-Ṭūsī, Ibn Kammūnah, al-ʿAllāmah [Quṭb al-Dīn] al-Shīrāzī and Muḥammad al-Shahrazūrī, author of *al-Shajarah al-ilāhiyyah*."[39]

3 "The school attributed [*al-mansūb*] to Porphyry, the First of the Peripatetics [*muqaddam al-mashshāʾīn*], one of the greatest followers of the First Teacher."

4 "The school of the divine Plato."[40]

The "second school" represents the characteristic position of Ibn Kammūnah's *Commentary on the Intimations*. It is distinguished from the other schools in all philosophical domains: methodology and the division of the sciences, logic, ethics and political philosophy, physics, metaphysics and eschatology. But the question of the immortality of the soul and its "ranks" after separation from the body is a fundamental eschatological position on which Ibn Kammūnah wrote an independent treatise.

Suhrawardī, Ṭūsī, Shīrāzī, Ibn Kammūnah and Shahrazūrī are together considered the followers of Stoic philosophy and form the group of major Illuminationist philosophers of the post-Avicennan period. Excluded from this group is Fakhr al-Dīn Rāzī, who is considered a *mutakallim* by the Illuminationist philosophers, notably Shahrazūrī as well as Mullā Ṣadrā. The inclusion of Ṭūsī in this group may also be doubtful in that his views on cosmology and ontology do not coincide with the overall Illuminationist approach and philosophical technique, although his position in epistemology does.

Ibn Kammūnah's specifically philosophical arguments may best be exemplified by considering sample problems taken from his *Sharḥ al-talwīḥāt*. Before considering these, however, it is important to remember that *al-Talwīḥāt* is the first work in a series of four which constitutes the Philosophy of Illumination as Suhrawardī constructed it. As the first work in the series, this concise treatise tends to emphasize the discursive side of Illuminationist philosophy. However it is not a Peripatetic work nor was it composed during Suhrawardī's youth when, as alleged by some scholars, his position had been that of a pure Peripatetic.[41]

METHODOLOGY AND THE DIVISION OF SCIENCES

Al-Fārābī's *Enumeration of the Sciences* is the model for Ibn Kammūnah's methodology and division of the sciences, with minor modifications. However, it may be noted that by the seventh/thirteenth century every philosophical work – be it a commentary or an independent composition – is prefaced with questions pertaining to these issues. The distinction between theoretical philosophy and practical philosophy is a matter of methodology. Theoretical philosophy is said to deal with things whose existence does not depend on human action. This type of philosophy leads to pure truth (*al-ḥaqq al-ṣirf*). Practical philosophy is said to be a tool (*ālah*) that aims to obtain the "pure good" (*al-khayr al-maḥḍ*) to be utilized in the service of just rule, as well as for the attainment of happiness.

Ibn Kammūnah follows Suhrawardī's divisions within theoretical philosophy, but further elaborates and fills in the gaps as follows. Theoretical philosophy is divided into three parts. First is the "highest science" (*al-'ilm al-a'lā*), also called "first philosophy" (*al-falsafat al-ūlā*), also called "metaphysical science" (*'ilm mā ba'd al-ṭabī'ah*). This primary division is further divided into *metaphysica generalis* (*al-'ilm al-kullī*), having as its subject "being *qua* being" (substance, accident, one, many, etc.), and *metaphysica specialis* (*al-'ilm al-ilāhī*, or *al-ilāhī bi-ma'nā al-akhaṣṣ*), having as its subject the Necessary Being (its essence and acts, God's knowledge, etc.).

The second division is "middle philosophy" (*al-ḥikmah al-wusṭā*), having "quantity" (*al-kamm*) as its subject matter. This has two parts also: continuous quantities, such as geometry; and discrete quantities, such as arithmetic. Middle philosophy is of particular interest in Illuminationist philosophy because in the Illuminationist cosmological scheme the "fourth realm" is also called *mundus imaginalis*, and the Realm of Forms is designated "the intermediary or middle realm". Thus, the subject matter of both continuous imagination (*al-khayāl al-muttaṣil*) and discrete imagination (*al-khayāl al-munfaṣil*) falls under this branch of metaphysics. The third division is "physics", whose subject matter is corporeal bodies.

Ibn Kammūnah assigns subdivisions, called *furū'*, to each of the three major divisions. Subdivisions within metaphysics include such areas of inquiry as revelation, resurrection, angels and demons, dreams and extraordinary acts. Subdivisions within middle philosophy are more clearly defined and numbered as "twelve sciences": addition and subtraction, algebra, computational geometry, mechanics (*'ilm al-ḥiyal al-mutaḥarrakah*), cranes and pulleys (*'ilm ḥarakat al-athqāl*), measures and weights, war machines, optics, mirrors, hydro-dynamics, astronomical tables and calendars, and musical instruments. Finally, physics has the following seven subdivisions: medicine, astronomy, physiognomy, interpretation of dreams, talismans, occult sciences (*'ilm al-nayranjiyyāt*) and alchemy.

LOGIC

One of the characteristics of Illuminationist logic is that its structure divides logic into three parts: semantics, formal and material. There is no "book" of categories. As in the Stoic–Megaric tradition, the categories are first examined in physics and then in metaphysics.[42] This structure is upheld by Ibn Kammūnah in his *Commentary* as well as in his other works.

Two fundamental problems traditionally presented in logic – universal propositions and essentialist definition – are isolated by Ibn Kammūnah and are considered to have a principal significance for the Illuminationist theory of knowledge, or "Illuminationist knowledge by presence" (*al-'ilm al-ḥuḍūrī al-ishrāqī*).

First, the problem of universal propositions (*al-qaḍāyā al-kulliyyah*) is introduced in formal logic. In the Illuminationist scheme, a conclusion reached by using a formally established syllogism has no epistemological value as a starting point in philosophical construction. The argument for this rests on the mode "necessary" (*al-wajh al-ḍarūrī*) and the modal "always" (*dā'iman*). For a universal affirmative proposition to have philosophical value as a foundation of logic, it must be "necessary and always true". By introducing the mode "possibility" (*imkān*) and by giving it an extension in time as in "future possibility" (*al-imkān al-mustaqbal*), the universal affirmative proposition cannot be "necessarily true always", the Illuminationist position contends. This is because of the impossibility of "knowing", or deducing, all possible future instances. The epistemological implication of this logical position is clear. Formal validity ranks lower than the certitude obtained by the self-conscious subject who, when alerted to a future possible event through knowledge by presence, will simply "know" it; the future event cannot be "deduced".[43] Therefore, philosophical intuition has precedence over deductive reasoning, and this intuitive knowledge is renewed in every age by the philosopher–sages of that era. In other words, formal structure without philosophical "wisdom" has no actual (*ḥaqīqī*) validity.

The second philosophical problem introduced by Ibn Kammūnah is the rejection of the Aristotelian essentialist definition, *horos*, and of the Avicennan complete essentialist definition, *al-ḥadd al-tāmm*, as once again not a valid first step in the construction of philosophy. Following Suhrawardī, Ibn Kammūnah holds that true knowledge cannot be obtained from the formula which brings together the *summum genus* and the *differentiae*. Knowledge must depend on "something else", which is stated to be a psychological process that seeks the unity of the thing defined in its Form, which is fully defined only by and in the person's self-consciousness as the individual recognizes the thing to be defined (the *definiendum*).

These two philosophical problems bear directly on the methodology of the Philosophy of Illumination. Ibn Kammūnah makes numerous references to other works by Suhrawardī, is clearly familiar with the range of his works and is capable at every turn of applying germane arguments to the whole of the tradition. As such, the *Commentary* serves well to indicate the entire scope of Suhrawardī's Illuminationist compositions. Other significant areas of the numerous aspects of logic covered by this work include semantics and problems of formal logic.

Suhrawardī's theory of semantics (*'ilm dilālat al-alfāẓ*) indicates a Stoic–Megaric influence, and is specifically mentioned by Ibn Kammūnah to be different from the "standard" Avicennan.[44] Problems in this area of logic include: types of signification; relation of class names to constituents (members) of the class; types of inclusion of members in classes (*indirāj*, *istighrāq*, *indikhāl*, *shumūlī*, etc.); and perhaps most significantly from the standpoint of the history of logic, a fairly well defined theory of supposition (the restricted and unrestricted use of quantification).

There are a number of problems of formal logic, such as iterated modalities; the construction of a superaffirmative necessary proposition (*al-qaḍiyyat al-darūriyyat al-battātah*); the question of negation (*al-salb*), especially in the conversion of syllogism (*al-'aks*); reduction of terms; construction of a single "mother" figure for a syllogism (*shakl al-qiyās*) from which all other figures are to be derived; temporal modalities (*al-qaḍāyā al-muwajjahah*); especially non-admittance of an unrestricted validity of the universal affirmative proposition (*al-qaḍiyyat al-mūjibat al-kulliyyah*); and future contingency (*al-imkān al-mustaqbal*). All these problems, as well as others, are identified by Ibn Kammūnah to be part of the significant changes made by Suhrawardī to Peripatetic logic. In every case Ibn Kammūnah's analysis both distinguishes the problem and provides a fuller account than Suhrawardī's own short description.[45]

EPISTEMOLOGY

Perhaps the most widespread impact of Illuminationist philosophy has been in the area of epistemology. The impact of Illuminationist knowledge by presence, *al-'ilm al-ḥuḍūrī*, which posits a posterior epistemological position to acquired knowledge, *al-'ilm al-ḥuṣūlī*, has not been confined to philosophical and other specialist circles, as has Illuminationist logic, for example. The epistemological status given to intuitive knowledge has fundamentally influenced what is called "speculative mysticism" (*'irfān-i naẓarī*) in Iran as well as informing Persian poetry. The way Persian poetic wisdom, for example, seeks to unravel the mysteries of nature is not through the principles of physics (as with Aristotelians, for example) but by means of the metaphysical world and the realm of myths, dreams, fantasy and the emotions.

Ibn Kammūnah starts his commentary on Suhrawardī's dream-vision of Aristotle (described in the previous chapter) by stating that "this story includes five philosophical problems" ("*tashtamil hādhihi'l-hikāyalah 'alā khamsah masā'il 'ilmiyyah*").[46] There are: (1) unity of the intellect, thinking and the object in the rational soul, in the state when the subject and the object are not differentiated. Knowledge by presence takes place when the rational soul, aware of its essence, is related (by Illuminationist relation, *al-iḍāfah al-ishrāqiyyah*) to the object. This is tantamount to the recovery of prior unity, which is how the soul by knowing itself can know other things. (2) The soul's knowledge of something other than itself is not by acquiring a form of that thing within itself – which is the Peripatetic position – but by the mere presence (*bi-mujarrad ḥuḍūr*) of the other thing. (3) Types of thinking (*aqsām al-ta'aqqul*) are described. (4) How God knows its essence and knows other things is said by Ibn Kammūnah to be based on the principle of knowledge by presence. But since God's essence and existence are the same – in other words, God's consciousness as subject and as object are never differentiated, then God's knowledge by presence never ceases. For God, there is no process of recovering a prior state because prior and future conditions do not apply to God. "God's knowledge of other things is by virtue of the other's presence to it" ("*'ilmuhu bi-mā 'adāhu'l-huḍūruhu lahu*"), to use Ibn Kammūnah's own phrase. (5) On the meaning of union and connection (*al-ittiḥād wa'l-ittiṣāl*), the principle of "knowledge by presence" is explained by comparing it to the Peripatetic notion of union with the Active Intellect. Union or connection with the Active Intellect is a corporeal phenomenon, whereas the "relation" (*al-iḍāfah*) between the knowing subject and the manifest object allows the subject to know with certainty and takes place without temporal or spatial extension. In a sense, the soul recovers essences that are already present and have an independent as well as real existence.

ONTOLOGY

Ibn Kammūnah's views on the Illuminationist ontological position, called "primacy of quiddity", is a longstanding problem that is said to distinguish philosophical schools in the development of Islamic philosophy in Iran up to the present day.[47] It is also a matter of considerable controversy. Those who believe in the primacy of existence (*wujūd*) consider essence (*māhiyyah*) to be a derived, mental concept (*amr i'tibārī*); while those who believe in the primacy of quiddity consider existence to be a derived, mental concept. The Illuminationist position, elaborated by Ibn Kammūnah, is this: should existence be real outside the mind (*muta-ḥaqqaq fī khārij al-dhihn*), then the real must consist of two things – the principle of the reality of existence, and the being of existence, which requires a referent outside the mind. And its referent outside the mind must also consist of two things, which are subdivided, and so on, ad infinitum. This is clearly absurd. Therefore existence must be considered an abstract, derived, mental concept devoid of a real existence which may be referred to outside the mind.

PHILOSOPHICAL ALLEGORY

Finally, among the distinguishing marks of Ibn Kammūnah's *Commentary* is the manner in which he analyses the metaphorical passages in Suhrawardī's work. What I have called the "fourth stage" of Illuminationist constructivist methodology is the use of a special language, a symbolic mode of expression designated as *Lisān al-ishrāq*. Shahrazūrī and later Harawī are the only two Illuminationist philosophers after Suhrawardī who continue using this special language in their works. Most others, including Ibn Kammūnah, attempt to explain the symbolism in terms of standard philosophical language.

One such instance concerns Suhrawardī's allegory of the dream-vision of Aristotle. Another example is the story of Hermes having a vision in which he meets God,[48] which in my view is further indication of the fact that Suhrawardī's *Intimations* includes a clear Illuminationist side. The story is short and reads as follows:

> One night when the sun was shining, Hermes was praying in the Temple of Light (*haykal al-nūr*); when the pillar of dawn ripped

asunder. He saw a land, with cities, upon which the wrath of God had descended. They were entering into an abyss, [disappearing] therein. So Hermes cried out: "O father, deliver me from the abode of the evil neighbours." He was thus summoned: "Catch the edge of [our] rays and fly to the Heavens." So he ascended and saw the Earth and the sky beneath him.[49]

Ibn Kammūnah calls this story "one of the difficult metaphors" (*al-rumūz al-mushkilah*) and makes the following attempt at a "rational" interpretation. The ripping of the pillar of dawn is equated with the appearance of the light of knowledge to man; the earth symbolizes the body, or matter in general; the cities are equated with embodied souls, or with their faculties, and so on. Clearly, his intention is somehow to make "philosophical" sense of Suhrawardī's allegorical style.

In conclusion, it should be emphasized that Ibn Kammūnah's interpretation of Suhrawardī's Philosophy of Illumination as presented in his *Commentary on the Intimations* greatly influenced the later development of philosophy in Persia. Specifically, both Mīr Dāmād and subsequently Mullā Ṣadrā refer to his interpretations and employ many of his arguments in their own work. Part of Ibn Kammūnah's purpose was to clarify and explain Suhrawardī's often terse and difficult style. He further attempted to reduce the philosopher's symbolic language – which was so characteristic of Suhrawardī – to a more standard analytical one. In so doing, Ibn Kammūnah helped the Philosophy of Illumination to become, in my view, more easily accepted by philosophers and accessible to them.

NOTES

1 See, for example, Solomon Pines, *Nouvelles études sur Awḥad al-Zamān Abu'l-Barakāt al-Baghdādī* (Paris, 1953); "Studies in Abu'l-Barakāt al-Baghdādī's Poetics and Metaphysics", In *Scripta Hierosolymitana*, vol. 6, *Studies in Philosophy*, ed. S. H. Bergman (Jerusalem, 1960): 120–98.

2 Shahrazūrī's *Sharḥ ḥikmat al-ishrāq* ("Commentary on the Philosophy of Illumination") has not been published. I have prepared a preliminary critical edition: however, prior to its publication I shall refer to the folios of the Istanbul, Saray Ahmad III, MS no. 3230.

3 Moshe Perlmann's text edition and translation of Ibn Kammūnah's polemics *Tanqīḥ al-abḥāth li'l-milal al-thalāth* are among the few studies on Ibn Kammūnah. See Moshe Perlmann, *Sa'd b. Manṣūr Ibn Kammūna's Examination of the Inquiries into the Three Faiths: a Thirteenth-Century Essay in Comparative Religion* (Berkeley and Los Angeles, 1967 (text) and 1971 (translation)). Ibn Kammūnah is an important figure in the history of post-Avicennan philosophy. His *Sharḥ al-talwīḥāt* ("Commentary on Suhrawardī's Intimations") has not, however, been printed. He is also an important logician of the post-Avicennan period. His *al-Ḥikmat al-jadīdah fi'l-manṭiq* ("Neue Abhandlungen über die

Logik") – which is probably the section on logic of his *al-Jadīd fi'l-ḥikmah* – and his commentary on Avicenna's *Directives and Remarks* entitled *Sharḥ al-uṣūl wa'l-jumal min muhimmāt al-'ilm wa'l-'amal* ("Kommentar zu den Grundlehren und dem Gesamtinhalt aus dem Gewichtigsten für Theorie und Praxis") deserve a special study; see Leo Hirschfeld's short monograph, *Sa'd b. Manṣūr Ibn Kammūna* (Berlin, 1893): 11–13.

4 See Shīrāzī, *Sharḥ ḥikmat al-ishrāq [Commentary on the Philosophy of Illumination]*, lithograph edition by Ibrāhīm Ṭabāṭabā'ī (Tehran, 1895).

5 See Dawānī, *Sharḥ hayākil al-nūr [Commentary on the Temples of Light]*, Tehran, Majlis Library, MS no. 1412.

6 See Harawī, *Anwāriyyah [Abodes of Light]*, ed., with introduction and notes, Hossein Ziai (Tehran, 1980).

7 I have chosen not to discuss Shīrāzī's Illuminationist works because of the availability of an excellent analytical study on him recently published. In this book readers will find an in-depth study of the post-Suhrawardian tradition. See John Walbridge, *The Science of Mystics Lights: Quṭb al-Dīn Shīrāzī and the Illuminationist Tradition in Islamic Philosophy* (Cambridge, Mass., 1992).

8 See my "Preface" to Harawī's *Anwāriyyah*: 13–19.

9 In his *Anwāriyyah*, Harawī informs us of his independent Illuminationist work entitled *Sirāj al-ḥikmah*. This work, however, has not survived, but is indicative of the impact of Illuminationist philosophy in India. See my edition of *Anwāriyyah*: 212, 245.

10 See *Anwāriyyah*: 150–4.

11 See Bakhtiyar Husain Siddiqi, "Jalāl al-Dīn Dawwānī", in *A History of Muslim Philosophy*, ed. M. M. Sharif (Wiesbaden, 1966), 2: 883–8.

12 For a general account of Mīr Dāmād's life and works see S. H. Nasr, "The School of Ispahan" and "Ṣadr al-Dīn Shīrāzī", both in *A History of Muslim Philosophy*, ed. M. M. Sharif: 904–60.

13 Sayyid Muḥammad Kāẓim 'Aṣṣār, *Vaḥdat-e vojūd va badā'*, ed. Jalāl Āshtiyānī (Mashhad, 1970). 'Aṣṣār has been hailed by Āshtiyānī, himself one of the most important figures in the tradition of Islamic philosophy of the contemporary period, as the foremost Illuminationist philosopher of recent decades.

14 Christian Jambet in his "Introduction" to *Shihāboddīn Yaḥya Sohravardī, Le Livre de la Sagesse Orientale*, traduction et notes par Henry Corbin (Paris, 1986) states a possible influence of Illuminationist doctrine on Jewish mysticism. See also p. 75 n. 85 where notice of Paul Fenton's *Deux traités de mystique juive* (Lagrasse, 1987) is given. See also Paul Fenton, *Treatise of the Pool* (London, 1983).

15 See Lisān al-Dīn ibn al-Khaṭīb, *Rawḍat al-ta'rīf bi'l-ḥubb al-sharīf*, ed. Muḥammad al-Kattānī (Ribat, 1981).

16 For example Suhrawardī in his *Philosophy of Illumination* (as well as in other texts) states, without further explanation, that "Jinn and satans are obtained from the Suspended Forms" (*Ḥikmat al-ishrāq*: 232), a subject taken up by Shahrazūrī, who treats it in great detail.

17 The work is as yet unpublished – and I am using the Berlin manuscript formerly of the Königlischen Bibliothek, Sprenger Collection, now in the Staatsbibliothek, MS no. 5026. It is a long manuscript comprising 319 folios of 18 × 27 cm, 33 lines per page in a small highly cursive script. I have elsewhere discussed this manuscript in detail. See my "The Manuscript of *al-Shajarat al-ilāhiyyah*:

a Philosophical Encyclopedia by Shams al-Dīn Muḥammad Shahrazūrī", *Iran-shenasi*, 2(1) (Spring 1990): 14–16 and 89–108.

18 Henry Corbin has discussed this realm in many of his works. See especially H. Corbin, *Terre céleste*, trans. Nancy Pearson (Princeton, 1977): 82–9.

19 Shahrazūrī, *al-Shajarah al-ilāhiyyah*, fols 267vff. Translation mine.

20 The term used here is *sīmīyā'*, probably derived from the Greek *semeion*.

21 See Suhrawardī, *Opera II*: 254–5; cf. al-Harawī, *Anwāriyyah*: 222, where Hūrqalayā is said to be one of the imaginal spheres, *aflāk-i mithālī*, "travelled" to by Pythagoras.

22 Cf. Corbin, *Terre céleste*: 82–9. Suhrawardī's own theory of the categories bears directly on this issue, in which he considers only substance, quality, quantity, relation and motion – all of which are given to degrees of intensity and are processes more than they are ontic distinct entities.

23 Duchesne-Guillemin, *The Western Response to Zoroaster* (Oxford, 1958): 132.

24 Corbin, *L'Homme de lumière dans le soufisme iranien* (Paris, 1971): 6.

25 See, for example, Shīrāzī, *Sharḥ*: 511: "*wa'l-ṣuwar al-mu'allaqah laysat muthul Aflaṭūn fa-innah muthul Aflāṭūn nūriyyah thābitah fī 'ālam al-anwār al-'aqliyyah*", ("the suspended forms, *ṣuwar*, are not the Platonic Ideas, *muthul Aflāṭūn*, because the latter are luminous and fixed in the realm of intelligible lights").

26 Shahrazūrī, *al-Shajarah al-ilāhiyyah*, fols 292ff. Translation mine.

27 The term used here is *mushāhadah*, which indicates a special cognitive mode as I have explained elsewhere. See my *Knowledge and Illumination* (Atlanta, 1990), chapter 4.

28 See Manuchehr Sadughi Soha, *A Bio-bibliography of Post Ṣadr-ul-Muta'allihīn Mystics and Philosophers* (Tehran, 1980).

29 See Avicenna, *Kitāb al-ḥudūd*, trans. A.-M. Goichon in *Introduction à Avicenne: son épître des définitions* (Paris, 1933): 124.

30 This work has not been published. I refer to the Leiden MS no. Or. 137.

31 Moshe Perlmann, *Sa'd b. Manṣūr Ibn Kammūna's Examination*: ix.

32 *Ibid.*

33 See Leo Hirschfeld, *Manṣūr Ibn Kammūna*: 11–13. The list of works relies primarily on Hājjī Khalīfah and is incomplete.

34 Both Ṭūsī and Rāzī stress the *'irfān* element of Avicenna's work, which was also later integrated into *al-Ḥikmat al-muta'āliyah* by Mullā Ṣadrā, influencing both the intention as well as style of religious philosophy in Persia to the present.

35 This important text by Ibn Kammūnah is edited by Ḥamīd al-Kabīsī (Baghdad, 1982).

36 See Leon Nemoy, *Ibn Kammūna's The Arabic Treatise on the Immortality of the Soul* (New Haven, 1945); translation in *Ignaz Goldziher Memorial Volume II* (Jerusalem, 1958).

37 Ṣadr al-Dīn al-Shīrāzī, Mullā Ṣadrā, *al-Asfār al-arba'ah* (reprint: Tehran, n.d.), 6: 180ff.

38 See Hossein Ziai, "The Manuscript": 89–108.

39 Mullā Ṣadrā, *op. cit.*, 6: 187. The attribution of "Stoic" to the Illuminationist school appears in many places in this work. However, concerning certain "novel" philosophical issues, such as the distinction between the idea of "intellectual form" (*al-ṣūrah al-'aqliyyah*) and the idea of "archetypal form" (*al-ṣūrah al-mithāliyyah*) – the latter also as "the idea shape", or "imagined shape" – Mullā

Ṣadrā is careful to use only the attribution "Illuminationist". See, for example, *al-Asfār*, 3: 504ff. In general the Stoic epithet is added to the Illuminationist designation only in conjunction with questions that relate to logic and physics, but in matters that pertain to epistemology, cosmology and eschatology, "Illuminationist" is used alone. See also my *Knowledge and Illumination*, chapter 1, for a discussion of Stoic influences on Illuminationist logic.

40 It is possible that Mullā Ṣadrā here means only Plato himself and not a "school of thought" that had continued after him. I take this reading because of the phrase "*mā dhahaba ilayhi Aflāṭūn al-ilāhī*". The distinction would indicate an attempt on the part of Mullā Ṣadrā to indicate the philosophical position of Plato himself as distinct from later syncretic texts designated "Platonic". See, for example, Mullā Ṣadrā, *op. cit.*, 3: 509, where he clearly attempts to specifically refer to Plato himself by stating "*qāla Aflāṭūn al-sharīf*", and not "*fī madhhab al-aflāṭūniyyah*".

41 Among the authors who have categorized *al-Talwīḥāt* as a Peripatetic work Helmut Ritter should be noted. See Helmut Ritter, "Philologika IX: Die vier Suhrawardī", *Der Islam*, 24 (1937): 270–86 and 25 (1938): 35–86.

42 Suhrawardī discusses the categories at great length in his major Arabic and Persian systematically philosophical works. His theory of categories, which are attributed by him to some Pythagorean person (*shakhṣ fīthāghūrithī*) by the name of Arkhūṭus, has had a major impact on subsequent philosophy in Persia. What is later designated by Ṣadr al-Dīn al-Shīrāzī "motion in category substance" (*al-ḥarakat al-jawhariyyah*), translated as "substantial motion" and "transubstantial motion", is a direct corollary to Suhrawardī's theory. Briefly the theory states that "intensity" (*shaddah wa da'f*) is predicated of all categories which are reduced to five: substance (*jawhar*), quality (*kayf*), quantity (*kamm*), relation (*nisbah*) and motion (*ḥarakah*). This is in direct agreement with Suhrawardī's special theory of being as continuum, as well as with his theory known as "theory of future contingency" (lit. theory of the contingency of the most noble, *qā'idat imkān al-ashraf*).

43 The favourite example given by Suhrawardī in support of his arguments, one discussed in detail by Ibn Kammūnah in his *Sharḥ al-talwīḥāt*, is: Take the universal affirmative proposition "All animals move their lower jaw when they chew". This proposition is valid only prior to the "discovery" of the alligator, who moves both jaws when chewing. A single exceptional instance negates the proposition in question. By analogy, the Illuminationist critique goes on to stipulate that the Peripatetic definition of "man" as "rational animal" – which is reduced to the generalized form $(\forall x)(f(x) \rightarrow g(x)$ – has only formal validity. This is because for it to be valid it must exhaustively enumerate all differentiae combined in the formula, which is negated because of future possibility of one differentia not known "now". Thus, Ibn Kammūnah concludes that the essentialist definition of man does not establish the essence "man" – also here called "man-ness" (*al-insāniyyah*) – which is established by other types of argument resting in the idea of self-consciousness and is picked up in physics and further developed in metaphysics.

44 As I have shown elsewhere there may here be certain connections with the Stoic theory of *lekton*. See my *Knowledge and Illumination*: 42ff.

45 Ibn Kammūnah himself indicates that one of his reasons for writing the commentary is to provide the details left out by Suhrawardī. See *Sharḥ al-Talwīḥāt*, fol. 23v.

46 *Ibid.*, fols 235v – 238v.
47 See Jalāl al-Dīn Āshtiyānī, *Hastī az naẓar-i falsafih wa ʿirfān* (reprint: Tehran, 1982): 1–39.
48 Also discussed by Corbin in his *Terre céleste*: 2.1.
49 See Suhrawardī, *Opera I*: 108. Translation mine.

CHAPTER 30

Ibn 'Arabī

William C. Chittick

Abū 'Abdallāh Muḥammad ibn al-'Arabī al-Ṭā'ī al-Ḥātimī is usually referred to as Muḥyī al-Dīn ibn 'Arabī. He was born in Murcia in al-Andalūs on 17 Ramaḍān 560/28 July 1165 and died in Damascus on 22 Rabī' II 638/10 November 1240.[1] Known by the Sufis as al-Shaykh al-Akbar, "The Greatest Master", he wrote voluminously at an exceedingly high level of discourse, making him one of the most difficult of all Muslim authors. His *al-Futūḥāt al-makkiyyah*, which will fill a projected thirty-seven volumes of five hundred pages each, is only one of several hundred books and treatises.

Ibn 'Arabī discusses in extraordinary detail most if not all of the intellectual issues that have occupied Muslim scholars in fields such as Qur'ānic commentary, *Ḥadīth*, jurisprudence, *kalām*, Sufism and *falsafah*. He was both intensely loyal to the tradition and exceedingly innovative. His works present us with a remarkable reservoir of rich and fecund meditations on every intellectual dimension of Islam, and it would not be inappropriate to claim him as the most influential thinker of the second half of Islamic history. What Franz Rosenthal has called Ibn 'Arabī's "scintillating personality and thought"[2] have continued to fascinate and inspire Muslim thinkers down to the present. In the words of James Morris, "Paraphrasing Whitehead's famous remark about Plato – and with something of the same degree of exaggeration – one could say that the history of Islamic thought subsequent to Ibn 'Arabī (at least down to the 18th century and the radically new encounter with the modern West) might largely be construed as a series of footnotes to his work."[3]

The extent to which Ibn 'Arabī can be called a "philosopher" depends, of course, upon our definition of philosophy. If we take the word *falsafah* to refer to the specific school of thought in Islam that goes by the name, then Ibn 'Arabī cannot properly be called a *faylasūf*. But if we consider philosophy as a much broader wisdom tradition, rooted both in Islamic sources and in various pre-Islamic heritages, then Ibn 'Arabī certainly deserves the name *faylasūf*, or, as he would probably prefer, *ḥakīm*. He himself distinguishes between these two senses of the term *falsafah* by speaking of those who truly (*bi'l-ḥaqīqah*) deserve the name *ḥakīm* and those who have adopted the title (*laqab*); the former are the messengers, prophets and friends of God (*awliyā'*), while the latter are the *falāsifah* proper.[4] When Ibn 'Arabī praises "the divine Plato" as a *faylasūf*, he explicitly has this wider sense of the term *falsafah* in view.[5]

Whether we consider philosophy in a narrow or broad sense, we need to ask three questions: To what extent was Ibn 'Arabī conversant with and influenced by the school of *falsafah* proper? What were his views on *falsafah*? What were his contributions to philosophical thinking?

ACQUAINTANCE WITH *FALSAFAH*

The idea proposed by Asín Palacios and others that Ibn 'Arabī's philosophical theories can be traced back to certain strands in the Greek tradition is no longer taken seriously by specialists. What is certain is that most of what he says is rooted in his own mystical intuition, or, to use his terminology, his unveiling (*kashf*) and opening (*fatḥ*, *futūḥ*). This having been said, it is also clear that he was conversant with the fundamental sources of the Islamic tradition and the intellectual currents of his day, especially the wisdom tradition. Most of what he says is presented as commentary upon specific verses of the Qur'ān or passages from the *Ḥadīth*. He employs terminology current in Sufism, *falsafah*, *kalām* jurisprudence, grammar and other sciences.

According to Rosenthal there is little evidence that Ibn 'Arabī actually read any books of *falsafah*, with the sole exception of the pseudo-Aristotelian *Sirr al-asrār* or *Secretum secretorum*, the political parts of which were of interest to him. He seems to have been more familiar with *kalām*. He sometimes refers to well-known *mutakallimūn*, but again it is not clear whether he had actually read their works – which he practically never cites – or was relying on general knowledge present in the intellectual circles in which he moved.

Although sometimes Ibn 'Arabī ascribes wise sayings to specific Greek philosophers, he almost never mentions Muslim philosophers by name. The major exception is provided by his well-known account of his encounter with Ibn Rushd, which took place when he was about fifteen. But there is no evidence that he had actually read any of Ibn Rushd's books, and he describes him as a scholar of the *Sharī'ah* rather than as a *faylasūf*.[6]

Most major philosophical issues are at least mentioned in Ibn 'Arabī's works. As Rosenthal remarks, "All the accepted parts of philosophy were alive in his educational background. It was almost inevitable for him to touch on them."[7] It is perhaps fair to say that the type of philosophizing in which he engages has deep kinships with that of the Ikhwān al-Ṣafā', but it is going too far to claim, as Nyberg did, that the Ikhwān's work provided him with a direct source.[8]

In discussing Ibn 'Arabī's acquaintance with philosophical issues, Rosenthal outlines the importance he gives to epistemology and logic, ethics, politics, man as microcosm, cosmology (especially time) and metaphysics. He summarizes his remarks on Ibn 'Arabī's philosophical leanings by saying:

> It would be possible to go on and investigate everything Ibn 'Arabī says page by page, line by line, and find that there always is a close connection with ideas "philosophical" in origin. . . . Philosophy, whether in the Muslim or the classical meaning of the term, constitutes the frame of reference for Ibn 'Arabī's view of the world.[9]

This is certainly true as long as we keep in mind that for Ibn 'Arabī himself, "philosophy" in this wide sense of the term is identical with the wisdom about which the Qur'ān says, "He who has been given wisdom has been given much good" (2: 269).

To provide an idea of the nature of Ibn 'Arabī's specific references to *falsafah* in its narrow sense, we can mention a few of his many references to the *falāsifah* or the *ḥukamā'*.

According to Ibn 'Arabī, the philosophers can be divided into two groups, the Islamic (*islāmī*) and those who do not consider themselves bound by the revealed religions (*al-sharā'i'*).[10] The philosophers are mistaken in their understanding of the famous aphorism, "Nothing emerges from the One but one"[11] and in their idea that God can be the "cause" (*'illah*) of the cosmos.[12] Their position on the order of the coming into existence of the cosmos (*tartīb takwīn al-'ālam*) is different from Ibn 'Arabī's.[13] They can be divided into two groups on the question of the resurrection, those who deny it completely, and those who deny the return of physical bodies but affirm spiritual retribution.[14]

Ibn 'Arabī sometimes refers to the philosophers as those who recognize that purifying the soul takes human beings to a place where knowledge and moral perfections can be acquired from the celestial spheres. However, they attribute what they acquire to the spiritual powers and disengage it from God's consideration, and to this extent they are known as *kuffār*, "truth concealers" (or "unbelievers", though the first translation is closer to Ibn 'Arabī's understanding of *kufr*).[15] When the philosophers say that the goal of philosophy is gaining similarity to God or theomorphism (*al-tashabbuh bi'l-ilāh*), they mean the same thing that the Sufis mean when they talk about assuming the character traits of God (*al-takhalluq bi akhlāq Allāh*). Nevertheless, their idea of *tashabbuh* is untenable.[16]

Although Ibn 'Arabī is often critical of the philosophers, in general he prefers their views to those of the *mutakallimūn*.[17] One weakness of *kalām* is that it has no entrance into cosmology or psychology. As Ibn 'Arabī puts it, the philosopher is "he who combines knowledge of God, nature, mathematics, and logic". But the theologian as theologian has no knowledge of nature.[18]

In a few issues, Ibn 'Arabī does prefer the theological over the philosophic position. Thus he supports the Ash'arite doctrine that prophecy can only be attained by God's designation (*ikhtiṣāṣ*), not by effort (*iktisāb*), and he extends this discussion to include knowledge of the soul's entelechy. Since knowledge of the nature of everlasting felicity depends upon a knowledge of God's own self (*nafs al-ḥaqq*), none can acquire this knowledge unless God provides it, and God provides it only by means of the prophets.[19]

VIEW OF *FALSAFAH*

Generally speaking, it is impossible to disengage Ibn 'Arabī's position on *falsafah* from his views on *kalām*. He usually lumps together the authorities in both traditions and refers to them by such terms as "the people of theory" or "consideration" (*ahl al-naẓar*), "the rational thinkers" (*al-'uqalā'*) and "the people of thought" or "reflective thinkers" (*aṣḥāb al-fikr*). Sometimes he considers jurists in the same category, but he is likely to treat the latter more harshly and call them *ahl al-rusūm*, "the people of designations", or "the exoteric thinkers".

To grasp Ibn 'Arabī's views on the rational thought processes typical of philosophy and *kalām*, we need to take a broad view of his whole intellectual project. Certainly he wants to affirm that the unveiling achieved by Sufi practitioners is a mode of knowing superior to reason (*'aql*). Nevertheless, he also affirms that reason is necessary for acquiring a true knowledge of things, and this affirmation is deeply rooted in his fundamental vision of reality. In fact, reason is so necessary in his view of things that *tawḥīd*, the *sine qua non* of salvation, depends upon it.[20]

Ibn 'Arabī maintains that human beings owe their uniqueness to the fact that they were created in the image of God and are able to actualize within themselves all God's Attributes. This involves a simultaneous transformation of both existence and knowledge: perfected human beings come to know God as God is in Himself and, at the same time, to manifest God's Attributes through their mode of existence in the cosmos. The modalities of human perfection are infinitely diverse, but the highest stages of perfection demand that the Divine Attributes be so harmoniously balanced in their manifestation that the person represents a perfect image of the "Divine Presence" (*al-ḥaḍrat al-ilāhiyyah*), i.e., the all-embracing Being that is designated by the word "Allāh".

Ibn 'Arabī refers to this highest stage of human perfection by many names. For example, he calls it the "station of no station" (*maqām lā maqām*), because people who achieve it, while participating in every Attribute of God, cannot be limited or defined by any Attribute whatsoever. He calls the one who reaches this station the "Verifier'" (*muḥaqqiq*) or "the possessor of two eyes" (*dhu'l-'aynayn*). With one eye, such people see their own creaturely uniqueness; with the other, they see their identity with God. They witness themselves as both near to God and far from Him, both real and unreal, both existent and nonexistent. In one respect they make manifest all Divine Attributes, and in another respect they conceal them all.

In theological language, Ibn 'Arabī describes the vision achieved through human perfection as the balanced combination of the declaration of God's incomparability (*tanzīh*) and that of His similarity (*tashbīh*). The *mutakallimūn* considered *tanzīh* the correct position and condemned *tashbīh*. Ibn 'Arabī embraces *tashbīh* so long as it is kept in balance with *tanzīh*. Neither term can be employed to refer to God in any exclusive sense.

It is important to grasp how Ibn 'Arabī correlates *tanzīh* and *tashbīh* with the two broad categories of Divine Attributes that are often discussed by Muslim thinkers. These are called the Attributes of Mercy (*Raḥmah*) and Wrath (*Ghaḍab*), or Bounty (*Faḍl*) and Justice (*'Adl*), or Beauty (*Jamāl*) and Majesty (*Jalāl*), or Gentleness (*Luṭf*) and Severity (*Qahr*). The Qur'ān and the tradition associate gentle and beautiful Attributes with God's nearness to His creatures, whereas they connect severe and majestic Attributes with His distance from creation.

Generally speaking, Ibn 'Arabī maintains that God is understood in terms of *tanzīh* inasmuch as He is inaccessible, but He is grasped in terms of *tashbīh* inasmuch as He is "closer to the human being than the jugular vein" (Qur'ān 50: 16). When the Qur'ān says that God created human beings with His own two Hands (38: 75), Ibn 'Arabī understands this to mean that He employed Attributes of both *tashbīh* and *tanzīh* to bring His own image into existence. Hence God is both present with His creatures and absent from them.[21]

Ibn 'Arabī's position on the intimate connection between *tanzīh* and *tashbīh* has a direct bearing upon epistemology. In brief, reason is innately constituted to set up distinctions and differentiations and thus to think abstractly. In Ibn 'Arabī's view the rational thinkers – whether *mutakallimūn* or philosophers – dissect reality such that they lose sight of the underlying unity of all things, and they do this because of the inherent nature of the rational mode of understanding. In other words, rational perspicuity keeps God at a distance by affirming *tanzīh* and denying *tashbīh*. As a result, both *falsafah* and *kalām* focus on God's Majesty, Severity and Wrath and tend to lose sight of His Beauty, Gentleness and Mercy.

In contrast, those who undergo unveiling (*ahl al-kashf, al-mukāshifūn*) perceive God's presence in all things, and they do so through the fact that unveiling is rooted primarily in imagination (*khayāl*), which bridges gaps, establishes relationships and understands by means of concrete images. As a result, unveiled Sufis see God in all things and focus on His nearness – His Mercy, Compassion, Gentleness and Love.

Through affirming *tanzīh*, people recognize the otherness (*ghayriyyah*) of all things; through affirming *tashbīh*, they acknowledge God's "withness" (*ma'iyyah*, a term derived from the Qur'ānic verse "God is with you wherever you are" (57: 4). To focus upon either *tanzīh* or *tashbīh* and to de-emphasize the other perspective is to distort the actual relationship between God and the world. True knowledge depends upon seeing all things with both the eye of imagination and the eye of reason.

The harmony that needs to be established between reason and imagination does not mean that *tanzīh* and *tashbīh* have equal rights in all situations. In the last analysis, *tashbīh* predominates, even if *tanzīh* has a certain priority in the present world. The theological principle here is set down in the famous *ḥadīth*, "My [God's] Mercy takes precedence over My Wrath." In other words, nearness to the Real (*al-ḥaqq*), which is Sheer Being (*al-Wujūd al-Maḥḍ*) and Absolute Good (*al-Khayr al-Muṭlaq*), is more basic to existence than distance from Him, because nearness provides existent things with everything they have. Their distance, though necessary in order for creation to take place, marks their connection with non-existence (*'adam*), also known as the unreal (*bāṭil*).

God's never-ceasing presence with the creatures must show its effects. Absence has no roots in Being, no foundation in the Real. Hence God's presence – Mercy – predominates, in this world and the next. Wrath and chastisement pertain to situations that are accidental to the universal economy of the Good and the Real. A Qur'ānic proof text that Ibn 'Arabī often cites here is 7: 156: "Said He, 'My Chastisement – I strike with it whom I will, and My Mercy embraces all things.'" Ibn 'Arabī constantly comes back to the theme of mercy as the underlying, all-embracing, fundamental quality of reality that must show itself in the end (*bi'l-ma'āl*).

Prophetic revelation appeals to both reason and imagination. Through presenting reason with the fact of God's distance, it allows human beings to establish *tanzīh* and to recognize their created nature as God's servants. To the extent that people actualize servanthood by following the *Sharī'ah*, they will be brought into nearness with God. Ibn

'Arabī frequently tells us that unveiling depends upon careful observance of the Qur'ānic instructions as embodied in the Prophet's *Sunnah.* The proof text that he cites most often is Qur'ān 2: 282: "Be godfearing, and God will teach you", through a teaching without any intermediaries. This God-given knowledge allows people to see God's presence, as they will in the next world. There they will no longer reason, they will simply see. Instead of being cut off from reason's distant object, they see God's self-disclosure (*tajallī*).[22] But those who have been dominated by reason and separation in this world will perceive God as distant, i.e., in terms of Attributes of Wrath and Severity; in contrast, those who gave unveiling the pride of place will perceive God as near, i.e., in terms of Attributes of Mercy and Gentleness.

Looked at in broad terms, Ibn 'Arabī's position on *tanzīh* and *tashbīh* reveals his project to integrate all Islamic learning under the umbrella of *tawḥīd.* But the Sufi perspective, which by and large emphasizes *tashbīh* and stresses God's Mercy and nearness rather than His Wrath and distance, is seen as having the upper hand. The rational endeavours of the philosophers and theologians, though useful and sometimes necessary, need to be subordinated to the direct knowledge that is made accessible through the prophetic messages and is actualized through unveiling. The Verifiers, who see with both eyes, realize perfect knowledge through the heart (*qalb*), which "fluctuates" (*qalb*) between reason and unveiling and sees God in terms of both *tashbīh* and *tanzīh.*[23]

Most of Ibn 'Arabī's frequent mentions of the rational thinkers are found in contexts in which he is explaining the inadequacies of reason and reflection (*fikr*) for a full knowledge of the truth. Philosophers and theologians deceive themselves by thinking that they can know God's Essence (*Dhāt*) through reflecting upon it. Moreover, because of reason's inability to grasp *tashbīh*, they insist upon explaining away (*ta'wīl*) those Qur'ānic verses that speak of God in creaturely terms. If they were able to see with the eye of unveiling, they would recognize that God expresses the nature of His own self-disclosures through the very verses that they want to explain away.[24]

CONTRIBUTIONS TO PHILOSOPHY

Many of Ibn 'Arabī's writings, especially the *Fuṣūṣ al-ḥikam*, were widely disseminated within a century of his death.[25] Little research has been carried out either on the contents of these writings or on the ways in which they may have influenced later thinkers. But it is sufficient to open any work on metaphysics, cosmology or psychology in the later period to see traces of his terminology and ideas, if not explicit indebtedness to his theories. Three specific questions to which Ibn 'Arabī made major contributions are pervasive in much of the later philosophic literature (in both the broad and the narrow senses of the term philosophy): the Oneness of Being (*wāḥdat al-wujūd*), the World of Imagination (*ālam al-khayāl*), and the perfect human being (*al-insān al-kāmil*). In what follows, I summarize these theories, which are intimately intertwined.

Ibn 'Arabī himself never employs the expression *waḥdat al-wujūd*, but the term gradually came to be adopted by his followers to designate his position.[26] Nevertheless, the idea permeates his thinking, and its philosophical relevance is apparent already in the words. *Wujūd* dominated the concerns of the philosophers, and *falsafah* itself had sometimes been defined as the study of *wujūd* as *wujūd*. By Ibn 'Arabī's day the term was employed by philosophers, theologians and Sufis in reference to God.

In using the term *wujūd*, Ibn 'Arabī usually keeps its etymological sense in view. For him *wujūd* means not only "to be" or "to exist", but also "to find" and "to be found". As applied to God, the word means both that God is and cannot not be, and that He finds Himself and all things and cannot not find them. In other words, *wujūd* designates not only existence but also awareness, consciousness and knowledge.

When applied to creatures, the word *wujūd* demands the question, "In what sense is it proper to use the term?" *Falsafah* provided the standard answer: God's *wujūd* is Necessary (*wājib*), while the creature's *wujūd* is possible or contingent (*mumkin*). Ibn 'Arabī frequently employs this terminology, but he uses many other terms and images to bring out the ambiguous nature of the possible things, hanging as they do between the absolute *wujūd* of God and absolute nothingness (*al-'adam al-muṭlaq*).

Ibn 'Arabī by no means spends as much time discussing *wujūd* as one might think if one were to look only at the later literature, which habitually associates his name with the term *waḥdat al-wujūd*. The fact that *wujūd* was singled out as representing his primary focus of attention has more to do with the philosophical orientation of the later Sufi tradition than with Ibn 'Arabī's actual writings. Nevertheless, if Ibn 'Arabī's discussions of the term were gathered together under one cover, they would certainly represent a major book.

Ibn 'Arabī's critics, most notably Ibn Taymiyyah (d. 728/1328), claimed that he made no distinction between the *wujūd* of God and the *wujūd* of the cosmos. In fact, it is easy to pick out passages from the *Futūḥāt* that support this claim. But from what has already been said about the pivotal nature of the dialectic between *tanzīh* and *tashbīh* in Ibn 'Arabī's writings, it should be clear that passages identifying the *wujūd* of God with that of the cosmos represent the perspective of *tashbīh*. They are always offset, in Ibn 'Arabī's own writings, by discussions of *tanzīh*, in which the distinction between God and the world is vigorously affirmed. In several passages Ibn 'Arabī sums up his position with the statement "He/not He" (*huwa lā huwa*). The nature of the world's *wujūd* can only be understood by both affirming and denying its identity with God's *wujūd*. One must look upon things with both eyes. Neither reason, which affirms God's otherness, nor unveiling, which affirms God's sameness, allows for a global understanding of the nature of things.

It needs to be kept in mind that the term *waḥdat al-wujūd* in its literal sense does not do justice to Ibn 'Arabī's position. It is true that he frequently affirms that *wujūd* is a single reality. But this single reality is self-aware – it "finds" itself – and in finding itself it knows the infinite possibilities of its own deployment in every mode of being found. The universal categories of these possible modes are designated by the Divine Names, but their particularities are known as the "things" (*ashyā'*) or the "entities" (*a'yān*), and these are immutably fixed (*thābit*) in God's Knowledge. By knowing Himself, God knows all the possibilities of *wujūd*, which are all things. Hence God is the One/Many (*al-Wāḥid al-Kathīr*) – One in His *wujūd* and Many in His knowledge. If *wujūd* is one, yet *wujūd*'s one knowledge comprehends the reality of all manyness. It is highly significant that the first direct member of Ibn 'Arabī's school of thought to employ the term *waḥdat al-wujūd* in a technical sense, Sa'īd al-Dīn Farghānī (d. 695/1296), juxtaposed it with the expression *kathrat al-'ilm* ("the manyness of knowledge").[27]

The cosmos can come into existence only on the basis of these two poles of reference – *wujūd* and knowledge. On the basis of the manyness of knowledge, God gives each thing a dependent or contingent *wujūd* in keeping with the demands of the thing's specific reality. Inasmuch as a thing has *wujūd*, it is He, but inasmuch as it represents a determined and defined reality that does not allow it to manifest *wujūd* as such, it is not He. *Wujūd* is one in itself, but infinitely diverse in its self-delimitations. The diversity of the universe represents a true diversity of realities, but in the matrix of a single *wujūd*.

Wujūd in Ibn 'Arabī's view is analogous to light, while each thing is analogous to a specific and distinct colour. The reality of the distinct colours is not compromised by the fact that each colour makes a single light manifest. No colour has any existence whatsoever without light. Every colour is identical with light, but light remains distinct and incomparable with each colour as also with the sum total of colours. Each thing "exists" (*mawjūd*), but in a specific mode that does not detract from the incomparability of *wujūd* itself. Each thing is thus identical with *wujūd* and distinct from it at one and the same time.

Ibn 'Arabī's teachings on imagination (*khayāl, mithāl*) apply the ontology of He/not He to every level of existence. He employs the word imagination to refer to everything that pertains to an intermediate state, not only to the faculty of the mind that complements reason. The standard example of an imaginal reality is a mirror image, which is neither the mirror nor the thing that is imaged, but a combination of the two sides.

Imagination in the broadest sense applies to the cosmos itself and to everything within it, since the cosmos is neither *wujūd* nor *'adam* but something in between. In a narrower sense, the universe is made up of two grand worlds, delineated in the Qur'ān and the tradition as the Visible (*al-shahādah*) and the Invisible (*al-ghayb*), or the world of bodies and the world of spirits, or the world of meaning (*ma'nā*) and the world of sense perception (*ḥiss*). Between the two worlds lies a World of Imagination that is neither purely spiritual nor purely bodily, neither perceptible by the external senses nor free of sensory qualities. Within the World of Imagination, unveiling takes place, the angels descend to the prophets with revelation, and all the after-death events described in the Qur'ān and *Ḥadīth* take place as described.

On the microcosmic level, imagination pertains to the domain of the soul, which is intermediate between Spirit (God's breath) and body (clay). Practically all human awareness occurs within imagination. The imaginal nature of human awareness is especially obvious in dreaming, where each dream image is both the same as and different from what it images; alternatively, it is both the same as and different from the soul.

Meaning and sense perception, or the spiritual and the bodily, interact within the soul in two basic ways. Either spiritual things become corporealized, or corporeal things become spiritualized. In other words, the pure awareness of the spirit becomes present to the soul through words and imagery, while the external world of corporeality is lifted up to the soul's imaginal level of existence by means of the senses. Ibn 'Arabī's psychology, which involves enormously complex discussions of many stages of perfection leading to the ability to see God with both eyes, depends upon a conscious representation of the soul's infinite interior world as one of imaginal existence.

The idea of the perfect human being provides Ibn 'Arabī's vision of God and the universe, or of *wujūd* and imagination, with a teleology. God created the universe in order to be known, as the famous *ḥadīth* of the Hidden Treasure tells us. But this knowledge can be actualized only through human beings. Created in God's image, they possess the potential to know and to live all His Attributes. Those people who do so are the perfect human beings, commonly called the prophets and the friends (*awliyā'*) of God.

Human existence represents the great middle point of reality. It is wrapped in ambiguity, since every attribute of *wujūd* – save only the necessity that pertains exclusively to the Necessary Being – is present within it. In any given case, the possibilities that have been actualized remain unknown to all but God.

As microcosms, human beings embrace the three worlds: spirit, imagination and body. Either of the two sides or the middle can dominate in their make-up, and, at each point in the trajectory of their becoming, the relationship among the three levels changes. If, in Ibn 'Arabī's way of looking at things, all things are imagination, the human being represents the sum total of every modality of imagination. Each thing in the universe, Ibn 'Arabī tells us, is a *barzakh*, an "isthmus" or intermediary stage of existence, since "*wujūd* has no edges".[28] Human beings are – potentially, at least – the Supreme *Barzakh*, embracing every possibility of existence. Human becoming represents the unfolding of what people are, but, from the human perspective, the course of this unfolding is not fixed. Freedom plays an important role. Revelation, and more specifically the prophetic *Sunnah* as set down in the *Sharī'ah*, designates the proper road of human development. Those who follow the Prophet perfectly become his inheritors (*wārith*) in knowledge, stations (*maqāmāt*) and states (*aḥwāl*). Ibn 'Arabī constantly comes back to the theme that those who wish to achieve perfection must observe the prophetic model in all its details.

The perfect human being, having actualized every possibility of knowledge and existence placed within Adam when God "taught him all the names" (Qur'ān 2: 31), fulfils the purpose of creation. This purpose is rooted in the nature of *wujūd* itself and necessitated by the One/Many, though God remains free of all external constraint, since He is "independent of the worlds" (Qur'ān 3: 97). As the infinite middle ground – the Supreme *barzakh* or Nondelimited Imagination – the perfect human being manifests within his own becoming all the Attributes of God and creation, without being constricted and confined by any of them. He is the incarnation of He/not He, standing in the station of no station.[29] As Ibn 'Arabī writes,

> The Divine Presence has three levels – manifest, non-manifest, and in-between. Through this last the Manifest becomes distinct and separate from the Non-manifest. This last is the *barzakh*, because it has a face toward the Non-manifest and a face toward the Manifest. Or rather, it itself is the face, for it cannot be divided. It is the perfect human being. The Real made him stand as a *barzakh* between the Real and the cosmos. Hence he makes manifest the Divine Names, so he is Real, and he makes manifest the reality of possible existence, so he is creature. That is why God made him in three levels: intellect and sense perception, which are the two sides, and imagination, which is the *barzakh* between meaning and sense perception.[30]

NOTES

1 By far the best and most thoroughly documented account of his life is provided by Claude Addas, *Quest for the Red Sulphur – the Life of Ibn ʿArabī*, trans. P. Kingsley (Cambridge, 1993). On Ibn ʿArabī's philosophic ideas, see W. Chittick, *The Sufi Path of Knowledge: Ibn al-ʿArabī's Metaphysics of Imagination* (Albany, 1989); M. Chodkiewicz, *An Ocean Without Shore – Ibn Arabi, the Book, and the Law*, trans. D. Streight (Albany, 1993); *Seal of the Saints – Prophethood and Sainthood in the Doctrine of Ibn ʿArabī*, trans. L. Sherrard (Cambridge, 1993); M. Chodkiewicz, W. C. Chittick, C. Chodkiewicz, D. Gril and J. W. Morris, *Les Illuminations de La Mecque/The Meccan Illuminations: Textes choisis/Selected Texts* (Paris, 1988); H. Corbin, *Creative Imagination in the Sufism of Ibn ʿArabī*, trans. R. Mannheim (Princeton, 1969); T. Izutsu, *Sufism and Taoism* (Los Angeles, 1983); and S. H. Nasr, *Three Muslim Sages*, chapter 3.

2 Franz Rosenthal, "Ibn ʿArabī between 'Philosophy' and 'Mysticism'", *Oriens*, 31 (1988): 33. This is a fine study to which I owe a number of details of what follows.

3 "Ibn ʿArabī and his Interpreters", *Journal of the American Oriental Society*, 106 (1986): 539–51, 733–56; 107 (1987): 101–19. Morris provides a good deal of evidence for this statement (which is found on p. 733) in the text of this article.

4 Ibn ʿArabī, *al-Futūḥāt al-makkiyyah* (Cairo, 1911; reprinted Beirut, n.d.), 1: 240, l. 32.

5 See Rosenthal, *op. cit.*: 15; for the whole passage, see Chittick, *op. cit.*: 202–4.

6 For accounts of this meeting, see Addas, *op. cit.*: 53–8; Corbin, *op. cit.*: 38–44; Chittick, *op. cit.*: xiii–xiv. For Ibn ʿArabī's reference to Ibn Rushd as a master of the *Sharīʿah*, see his *Futūḥāt*, 1: 325, l. 16, discussed in Chittick, *op. cit.*: 384 n. 13.

7 Rosenthal, *op. cit.*: 21.

8 H. S. Nyberg, *Kleinere Schriften des Ibn al-ʿArabī* (Leiden, 1919): 145; Rosenthal, *op. cit.*: 19. M. Takeshita has illustrated some of the precedents for a few of Ibn ʿArabī's ideas in *Ibn ʿArabī's Theory of the Perfect Man and its Place in the History of Islamic Thought* (Tokyo, 1987).

9 Rosenthal, *op. cit.*: 33.

10 Ibn ʿArabī, *op cit.*, 2: 591, l. 35; this helps explain his reference to a *faylasūf islāmī* in *ibid.* 2: 124, l. 23.

11 *Ibid.*, 2: 434, l. 22; 4: 231, l. 31.

12 *Ibid.*, 1: 261–2.

13 *Ibid.*, 2: 469, l. 23; 677, l. 8.

14 *Ibid.*, 2: 599, l. 20.

15 *Ibid.*, 3: 84, l. 30. Ibn ʿArabī sometimes contrasts the *miʿrāj* or spiritual ascension of the follower of the Prophet with that of the "considerative thinker" (*ṣāḥib al-naẓar*), by whom he certainly means the philosopher (e.g., of the type represented by the Brethren of Purity) rather than the *mutakallim*. See *ibid.*, 2: 273–83.

16 Ibn ʿArabī, *op. cit.*, 2: 126, l. 8; 483, l. 28; 3: 190, l. 30; see the translation of the second passage and the detailed discussion of *takhalluq* in Chittick, *op. cit.*: 75–6, 283–8.

17 Ibn ʿArabī, *op. cit.*, 1: 240, l. 32.

18 *Ibid.*, 1: 261, l. 7.
19 *Ibid.*, 2: 595, l. 32; 3: 37, l. 8; 79, l. 28.
20 See Chittick, *op. cit.*: 232–5.
21 See *ibid.*: 277–8. For the broad ranging implications of this view of complementary Divine Attributes for Islamic thought, with frequent reference to Ibn 'Arabī's position, see Sachiko Murata, *The Tao of Islam: a Sourcebook on Gender Relationships in Islamic Thought* (Albany, 1992).
22 For Ibn 'Arabī's views on after-death experience and eschatology, which also influenced later Islamic philosophy deeply, see Chittick, "Death and the Afterlife", chapter 7 of *Imaginal Worlds: Ibn 'Arabī and the Problem of Religious Diversity* (Albany, 1994); Morris, "Lesser and Greater Resurrection", in Chodkiewicz *et al.*, *op. cit.*: 159–84.
23 On the heart, see Chittick, *Sufi Path*: 106–12.
24 For details on the relationship between *tashbīh* and *tanzīh* on the one hand and reason and unveiling on the other, see Chittick, *Sufi Path*, especially parts 4 and 5.
25 The *Fuṣūṣ* has been translated into English several times, most notably by R. W. J. Austin, *Ibn al-'Arabī: The Bezels of Wisdom* (Ramsey, N. J., 1981). For translations of other works, see the bibliographies of Chittick, *Sufi Path*, and Addas, *op. cit.*
26 For a detailed discussion of the history of the term and the meanings that have been given to it by various authors, see Chittick, "Rūmī and *Waḥdat al-Wujūd*", in *The Heritage of Rumi*, ed. A. Banani and G. Sabagh (Cambridge, 1994).
27 Cf. Chittick, "Spectrums of Islamic Thought: Sa'īd al-Dīn Farghānī on the Implications of Oneness and Manyness", in *The Legacy of Mediaeval Persian Sufism*, ed. L. Lewisohn (London, 1992): 203–17. See also Murata, *op. cit.*: 67.
28 Ibn 'Arabī, *op. cit.*, 3: 156, l. 27; Chittick, *Sufi Path*: 14.
29 On the perfect human being and the station of no station, see Chittick, *Sufi Path*, chapter 20.
30 Ibn 'Arabī, *op. cit.*, 2: 391, l. 20.

SELECT BIBLIOGRAPHY

Addas, C. (1993), trans. P. Kingsley, *Quest for the Red Sulphur* (Cambridge).
Chittick, W. (1989) *The Sufi Path of Knowledge* (Albany).
—— (1994) *Imaginal Worlds* (Albany).
Chodkiewicz, M. (ed.) (1988) *Les Illuminations de la Mecque* (Paris).
—— (1993), trans. D. Streight, *An Ocean Without Shore* (Albany).
—— (1993), trans. L. Sherrard, *Seal of the Saints – Prophethood and Sainthood in the Doctrine of Ibn 'Arabī* (Cambridge).
Corbin, H. (1969) trans. R. Mannheim, *Creative Imagination in the Sufism of Ibn 'Arabī* (Princeton).
Nasr, S. (1979) *Three Muslim Sages*, chapter 3 (Cambridge, Mass.).

CHAPTER 31

The school of Ibn ʿArabī

William C. Chittick

The term "school of Ibn ʿArabī" was coined by Western scholars to refer to the fact that many Muslim thinkers – most of whom considered themselves Sufis – took seriously Ibn ʿArabī's title as the "Greatest Master" (*al-shaykh al-akbar*) and consciously rooted their perspective in their own understanding of his theoretical framework. They considered their approach as different from that of *falsafah* and *kalām* as well as from that of the vast majority of Sufis. Sometimes they referred to their specific way as "verification" (*taḥqīq*) and called themselves "the verifiers" (*al-muḥaqqiqūn*).[1] Who exactly fits into this category is an open question.

Ibn ʿArabī established no specific *madhhab* or *ṭarīqah*. He did have spiritual disciples and does seem to have passed on a cloak of investiture (known to later generations as *al-khirqat al-akbariyyah*) that passed through his disciple Qūnawī, but there is no recognizable organization that carries his name. No Sufi order has attempted to claim him as its exclusive heritage, and his books were studied and considered authoritative by members of most orders at one time or another.[2] For other reasons also, we have to use caution in talking about Ibn ʿArabī's "school". The term may suggest that there is a set of doctrines to which a group of thinkers adhered. In fact, Ibn ʿArabī's followers did not accept some common catechism, nor did they all follow the same approach to Islamic thought. James Morris's observation here should be taken seriously:

> The real philosophic and theological unity and diversity of these writers have not begun to be explored in modern research. . . . None of the writers are mere "commentators" of Ibn ʿArabī. . . . As with "Aristotelianism" or "Platonism" in Western thought, Ibn ʿArabī's writings were only the starting point for the most diverse developments, in which reference to subsequent interpreters

quickly became at least as important as the study of the Shaykh himself.[3]

In what follows, I will limit myself to discussing a few figures who considered themselves Ibn 'Arabī's followers and who are looked back upon as Sufis. No attempt can be made here to investigate the larger radiation of the Shaykh's influence among, for example, thinkers who have been called *falāsifah* and/or *mutakallimūn*, such as Ṣā'in al-Dīn 'Alī Turkah Iṣfahānī, Jalāl al-Dīn Dawānī, Mullā Ṣadrā or Mullā Muḥsin Fayḍ Kāshānī; nor can we look at the ways in which Ibn 'Arabī's practical instructions and spiritual blessing permeated the Sufi organizations in general.[4]

Ibn 'Arabī had a number of close disciples, including Badr al-Ḥabashī and Ibn Sawdakīn al-Nūrī, who wrote works that are more important for the light that they throw on the Shaykh's teachings than for their influence on later Islamic thought.[5] The most influential and at the same time independently minded of Ibn 'Arabī's immediate disciples was Ṣadr al-Dīn Qūnawī (d. 673/1274). He can be given more credit than anyone else for determining the way in which the Shaykh was read by later generations. This means, among other things, that Qūnawī began the movement to bring Ibn 'Arabī into the mainstream of Islamic philosophy. As a result, he and his followers placed many of Ibn 'Arabī's important teachings in the background. Michel Chodkiewicz considers this to have been a necessary, though perhaps unfortunate, adjustment of Ibn 'Arabī's teachings to the intellectual needs of the times.[6]

ṢADR AL-DĪN QŪNAWĪ AND HIS CIRCLE

Ibn 'Arabī met Qūnawī's father, Majd al-Dīn Isḥāq, during his first pilgrimage to Mecca, when he began writing the *Futūḥāt*. In the year 601/1204–5 they travelled together to Anatolia. Ṣadr al-Dīn was born in 606/1210 and, according to some early sources, Ibn 'Arabī married Ṣadr al-Dīn's mother after Majd al-Dīn's death. When Ibn 'Arabī died, Qūnawī seems to have taken over the training of some of his disciples. Presumably those with a philosophical bent would have been attracted to him. The most important of these was probably 'Afīf al-Dīn al-Tilimsānī (610/1213–690/1291), who is mentioned as one of the listeners on a manuscript of Ibn 'Arabī's *al-Futūḥāt al-makkiyyah* that was read in the author's presence in 634/1236–7. Al-Tilimsānī seems to have become Qūnawī's closest companion; Qūnawī dedicated a short treatise to him and left his books to him when he died.[7]

Al-Tilimsānī's writings have played some role in the spread of Ibn 'Arabī's school, but they have not been studied in modern times. He is the author of a published *Dīwān* as well as a *Sharḥ al-asmā' al-ḥusnā* and a commentary on the *Manāzil al-sā'irīn* of 'Abd Allāh Anṣārī (d. 481/1089). At least one contemporary Sufi shaykh felt that al-Tilimsānī had surpassed his master Qūnawī in matters of verification. This was Ibn Sab'īn (d. 669/1270–1), who was discussed by early Western scholars as a philosopher because of his answers to the "Sicilian Questions" posed by Emperor Frederick II Hohenstaufen.[8] However, Ibn Sab'īn was a Sufi with connections to Ibn 'Arabī, though he probably cannot be considered a member of his school. He seems to have been the first to employ the famous expression *waḥdat al-wujūd* as a technical term.[9]

The first firm record we have of Qūnawī's teaching activities pertain to the year 643/1245–6, five years after Ibn 'Arabī's death. At that time Qūnawī travelled to Egypt, where he began to comment on Ibn al-Fāriḍ's 700-line poem, *Naẓm al-sulūk*, for "a group of the learned [*fuḍalā'*], the great possessors of tasting [*akābir-i ahl-i dhawq*], and the reputable [*mu'tabarān*]". During the return journey and back in Konya, he continued the lessons, teaching all the while in Persian. Several of the scholars who attended his lectures took notes with the aim of composing books, but only Sa'īd al-Dīn Farghānī (d. 695/1296) succeeded. All this Qūnawī tells us in a letter of approval found at the end of Farghānī's introduction to *Mashāriq al-darārī*, a work that fills six hundred pages in its modern edition. According to Ḥājjī Khalīfah, al-Tilimsānī also attended these lectures and wrote a commentary, but Farghānī finished first; despite the brevity of al-Tilimsānī's commentary, Ḥājjī Khalīfah opines, it is to be preferred over Farghānī's.[10]

Having written his Persian commentary, Farghānī rewrote the text in Arabic with many additions, especially to the introduction. He named the Arabic version *Muntaha'l-madārik*, and it was being taught in Cairo in 670/1271.[11] Both the Persian and the Arabic versions of Farghānī's commentary were widely read. The great poet and scholar 'Abd al-Raḥmān Jāmī (d. 898/1492), one of the most learned and successful popularizers of Ibn 'Arabī's teachings, considered the introduction to Farghānī's Arabic work the most disciplined and orderly exposition of the problems of the "science of reality" (*'ilm-i ḥaqīqat*) ever written.[12]

Qūnawī taught *Ḥadīth* in Konya and attracted students such as the philosopher and astronomer Quṭb al-Dīn Shīrāzī (d. 710/1311). Presumably Qūnawī explained *Ḥadīth* in the manner found in his *Sharḥ al-ḥadīth al-arba'īn*. This work aims to bring out the deepest philosophical, theological, cosmological and mystical implications of the *Ḥadīth* discussed, and many of the explanations run into dozens of pages.[13]

Qūnawī is the author of at least fifteen Arabic works, along with a few Persian letters; his longest book is only about four hundred pages long, making him laconic compared to his master.[14] Seven of these works can be considered significant, book-length statements of his teachings. But the influence that these books – and the books of Qūnawī's immediate disciples – exercised upon the way in which Ibn 'Arabī was interpreted by later generations was enormous. Jāmī presents a view of Qūnawī that seems to have been accepted, in practice at least, by most of Ibn 'Arabī's followers, especially in the eastern lands of Islam. Note in the following that, like most scholars from about the ninth/fifteenth century onwards, Jāmī associates Ibn 'Arabī's name with *waḥdat al-wujūd*: "Qūnawī is the assayer of Ibn 'Arabī's words. One cannot grasp Ibn 'Arabī's purport in the question of *waḥdat al-wujūd* in a manner that accords with both reason and the *Sharī'ah* unless one studies Qūnawī's verifications and understands them properly."[15]

What is especially obvious in all of Qūnawī's writings is the systematic nature of his thinking. If Ibn 'Arabī's writings dazzle because of the non-stop rush of inspirations, Qūnawī's soothe because of his calm and reasonable exposition of metaphysical principles. Some of the contrast between the two is caught in a remark attributed to their disciple al-Tilimsānī: "My first shaykh was a philosophizing spiritual [*mutarawḥin mutafalsif*], whereas my second was a spiritualizing philosopher [*faylasūf mutarawḥin*]."[16] Though more philosophically inclined than Ibn 'Arabī, Qūnawī also experienced the lifting of the veils between himself and God, and he frequently tells us that this is how he knows what he knows. In fact, Qūnawī considered himself the most spiritually gifted of Ibn 'Arabī's disciples. He writes that fifteen years after the Shaykh's death, on 17 Shawwāl 653/19 November 1255, Ibn 'Arabī appeared to him in a vision and praised him for having achieved a spiritual rank greater than that of all his other disciples.[17] But even when Qūnawī speaks of visionary affairs that are inaccessible to reason, he presents the discussion in an eminently rational and lucid manner.

Qūnawī's style of exposition is certainly indebted to his knowledge of the Islamic philosophical tradition. Where this is proven beyond a shadow of a doubt is in his correspondence with Naṣīr al-Dīn Ṭūsī (d. 672/1274), the great scientist and theologian who revived Avicenna's philosophy. Qūnawī opened the correspondence by sending Ṭūsī a warm letter in Persian. This was accompanied by an Arabic treatise explaining the limitations of the rational faculty (*'aql*) and presenting a series of technical questions concerning Avicenna's positions on such issues as the *wujūd* that is attributed to the Necessary Being, the nature of the possible quiddities, the relationship between *wujūd* and the possible things, and the reality of the human soul. Ṭūsī replied with an even warmer Persian letter and a relatively brief, but precise, answer to all the questions.

In the Persian letter accompanying the third instalment of the correspondence, Qūnawī clarifies his motivation for writing to Ṭūsī:

"Concerning certain basic problems I had hoped to bring together the conclusions derived from logical proofs with the fruits of unveiling [*kashf*] and direct vision [*'iyān*]." In his Arabic response to Ṭūsī's answers, Qūnawī demonstrates an excellent knowledge of Avicenna's writings. In one passage, he suggests that Ṭūsī's answer shows that his copy of Avicenna's *Ta'līqāt* must be defective. He also refers to the text of Ṭūsī's commentary on Avicenna's *al-Ishārāt wa'l-tanbīhāt.* His argument represents an important attempt to show that the Sufi position – i.e., Qūnawī's interpretation of Ibn 'Arabī's teachings, which he refers to here as the "school of verification" – agrees by and large with that of *falsafah.* Generalizing about this position, Qūnawī writes,

> The Verifiers agree with the philosophers concerning those things that theoretical reason [*al-'aql al-naẓarī*] is able to grasp independently at its own level. But they differ from them in other perceptions beyond the stage of reflection [*fikr*] and its delimiting properties. As for the *mutakallimūn* in their various schools, the Verifiers agree with them only in rare instances and on minor points.[18]

Qūnawī's direct disciples do not demonstrate the same explicit attempt to bring the School of Verification into harmony with *falsafah.* However, as a rule their works contain highly sophisticated expositions of Ibn 'Arabī's philosophical teachings, in particular *waḥdat al-wujūd*, the perfect human being (*al-insān al-kāmil*), the immutable entities (*al-a'yān al-thābitah*), and the levels of existence (*marātib al-wujūd*). These last are often presented in terms of the "five divine presences" (*al-ḥaḍarāt al-ilāhiyyat al-khams*), an expression that seems to have been coined by Qūnawī.[19]

Two more of Qūnawī's students deserve special mention. One is Fakhr al-Dīn 'Irāqī (d. 688/1289), author of the short classic of Persian prose, *Lama'āt,* which was written after he attended Qūnawī's lectures on the *Fuṣuṣ*. The work presents Qūnawī's rendition of Ibn 'Arabī's teachings accurately, coherently and with great poetical beauty, but in a highly abbreviated form. The earliest of several commentaries on the *Lama'āt*, by Yār 'Alī Shīrāzī, explains it largely by quoting passages from Qūnawī and Farghānī. The introduction to and commentary on the *Lama'āt*'s English translation provide a relatively detailed analysis of Qūnawī's metaphysics.[20]

It is sometimes claimed that Jalāl al-Dīn Rūmī (d. 672/1273), the most famous of the Persian Sufi poets, was influenced by Ibn 'Arabī's teachings, and the fact that he was a good friend of Qūnawī is cited as proof. However, there no evidence in Rūmī's writings for this claim, and the early hagiographical literature suggests that Rūmī was highly sceptical of the philosophical approach of Qūnawī and his followers.[21]

THE *FUṢŪṢ AL-ḤIKAM*

Ibn 'Arabī wrote numerous works. By far the most famous and widely read of these was the *Fuṣūṣ al-ḥikam* ("The Ringstones of Wisdom"). There is no doubt that the Shaykh considered this relatively short text one of his key writings. Although he claims divine inspiration for several of his books and treatises, including the *Futūḥāt,* the *Fuṣūṣ* is the only one that was, on his own account, handed to him in a vision by the Prophet. According to Qūnawī's disciple Jandī, Ibn 'Arabī forbade his disciples from having the *Fuṣūṣ* bound together with any other book.[22] Qūnawī explains the importance of the work in terms that must have found favour with most of Ibn 'Arabī's followers:

> The *Fuṣūṣ al-ḥikam* is one of the most precious short writings of our Shaykh, the most perfect leader, the model of the perfect human beings, the guide of the Community, the leader of leaders, the reviver of the truth and religion, Abū 'Abdallāh . . . Ibn al-'Arabī. . . . The *Fūṣūṣ* is one of the seals of his writings and one of the last books to be sent down upon him. It came to him from the Muḥammadan Station, the Fountainhead of the Essence, the Unitary All-Comprehensiveness. It brought the quintessence of the tasting [*dhawq*] of our Prophet – God's blessing be upon him – concerning the knowledge of God. It points to the source of the tasting of the great prophets and friends of God mentioned within it. It guides all those who seek insight into the prophets to the gist of their tastings, the results of the focus of their aspirations, the sum of all they achieved, and the seals of their perfections. The book is like the stamp upon everything comprised by each prophet's perfection. It calls attention to the source of everything which the prophets encompassed and which became manifest through them.[23]

More than a hundred commentaries have been written on the *Fuṣūṣ*, and they continue to be written in modern times. In addition, an extensive parallel literature was written attacking and condemning the text or its author.[24]

Authors wrote commentaries for many reasons. Clearly, they considered the book of great importance, either because of its intrinsic content or because others had paid so much attention to it. The first commentaries dealt only with ideas, but as time passed the general tone of the commentaries changed. The early works typically cite a paragraph or a page and then provide detailed philosophical explanations. Gradually, however, commentators pay more attention to the meaning of sentences and technical terms. This becomes so much of a preoccupation with 'Abd al-Ghanī al-Nābulsī (d. 1143/1730) that he finds it necessary to explain the meaning of practically every word, technical term or otherwise, and he pays little attention to the grand ideas that underlie the text. Though this work suggests a steep decline in understanding in the Arabic-speaking countries, commentaries being written elsewhere are seldom so elementary.[25] As the commentary tradition developed, many authors took into account the broader issues raised not only by the numerous theoretical works being written by those who considered themselves Ibn ʿArabī's followers but also by works written by *falāsifah* and *mutakallimūn*.

The earliest commentary on the *Fuṣūṣ al-ḥikam* is Ibn ʿArabī's own short treatise *Naqsh al-fuṣūṣ* ("The Imprint of the Ringstones") in which he re-expressed the essential prophetic wisdom discussed in each chapter. The connections between this work and the *Fuṣūṣ* are not always clear, and several commentaries were written upon it.[26] The first commentary on the *Fuṣūṣ* by Ibn ʿArabī's followers seems to be that by al-Tilimsānī, who presents us with the whole text but singles out a relatively small number of passages for comment, frequently remarking, "The meaning of the remainder of the chapter is obvious." It certainly was not obvious to later generations.

Al-Tilimsānī's work illustrates already that the great reverence in which the *Fuṣūṣ* was held did not prevent the commentators from expressing their opinions or interpreting Ibn ʿArabī in new ways. He focuses mainly on *wujūd*, non-existence (*ʿadam*) and the immutable entities, issues that were to concern most of the later commentators as well. He registers his difference of opinion (*khilāf*) with "my master, Shaykh Muḥyī al-Dīn" in several passages. In particular, he disagrees with Ibn ʿArabī's explanation of the nature of the immutable entities, the idea that "they are immutable before they become engendered" (*thubūtuhā qabl kawnihā*). Al-Tilimsānī claims that the entities must be non-existent in every respect. Hence they cannot be immutable (thus contradicting, for example, the first sentence of the *Futūḥāt*).[27] Typical are his remarks in the following:

> *Wujūd*, which is light, is that which is thing [*shay'*] in every respect. Hence, it must have controlling power over an infinite number of attributes that become manifest. However, before they become manifest, these attributes have no immutable entities, because no existence can precede a thing's existence. . . . As for the Shaykh, he says that their existence is distinct, but this is contradictory. Even though the Shaykh would not deny what I say, I deny what the Shaykh says.[28]

In another passage, al-Tilimsānī excuses himself for disagreeing with the Shaykh by suggesting that Ibn ʿArabī had rhetorical reasons for expressing himself as he did:

> The Shaykh's words here come not from the presence of gnosis [*ma'rifah*] but rather from that of learning [*'ilm*], except for a small amount. And that small amount is not pure. The reason is that he observed the levels of the rational faculties of those who are veiled. . . . Learning, not gnosis, is appropriate for the [common] people.[29]

Al-Tilimsānī's critical remarks are not untypical for Ibn 'Arabī's followers, although few are quite as overt. Even Ibn 'Arabī's most fervent admirers did not take too seriously his statement that he had received the book from the hand of the Prophet; otherwise, they would not have dared to differ with him. This is further indication that being a member of Ibn 'Arabī's school, even a faithful member, does not suggest slavish repetition of the master. In fact, Ṣadr al-Dīn Qūnawī is the great model here, for his relatively systematic exposition and his focus on philosophical issues rather than on Qur'ān and *Ḥadīth* do not square with his sources, and presumably not with the oral instructions that he had received from his master.

Qūnawī did not write a commentary on the *Fuṣūṣ*, but he did explain the significance of each chapter heading of the work in his *al-Fukūk*, and in the process he brought out the basic points made in the book. The later commentators all concerned themselves with this issue of chapter headings, and most of them followed Qūnawī's leads.[30]

Qūnawī also exercised influence on the tradition of *Fuṣūṣ* commentary through his disciple Mu'ayyid al-Dīn Jandī (d. *c.* 700/1300), who is arguably the most widely influential of Qūnawī's students because of this commentary. Jandī wrote a number of books in both Persian and Arabic. He tells us in the introduction to his *Fuṣūṣ* commentary that he owes the work completely to the spiritual influence of his master. As Qūnawī began to explain to him the meaning of the book's preface, he took spiritual control of Jandī's understanding and taught him in one instant the meaning of the whole book. Qūnawī then told him that Ibn 'Arabī had done the same thing to him. This account establishes a claimed spiritual unity with the source of the book. At the same time, the author is saying that he had no need for a line by line explication of the text. His understanding and interpretation are "original", that is, tied to the book's very origin, and hence they do not have to follow explicit texts in Ibn 'Arabī or Qūnawī. This clearly gives him authority to express his own opinions.

Jandī's work is by far the longest of the early commentaries, and it sets the pattern for the theoretical discussions in many of the later commentaries. This is obvious, for example, in the famous work by 'Abd al-Razzāq Kāshānī (d. 730/1330), a prolific author of works in Arabic and Persian. In fact Kāshānī studied the *Fuṣūṣ* with Jandī, and he frequently paraphrases or quotes his commentary.

In an autobiographical remark in the midst of his famous letter to the Sufi 'Alā' al-Dawlah Simnānī (d. 736/1336), who criticized Ibn 'Arabī's position on *wujūd*, Kāshānī maps out his own pilgrimage to certainty. His account would seem to be typical for those followers of Ibn 'Arabī who engaged in philosophical writing. Like all scholars, Kāshānī began by studying basic sciences such as grammar and jurisprudence. From there he went on to the principles of jurisprudence (*uṣūl al-fiqh*) and *kalām*, but he found no way to verify his understanding. Then he thought that investigating the rational sciences (*ma'qūlāt*) and metaphysics (*'ilm-i ilāhī*) would provide him with true knowledge and deliver him from wavering and doubt. For a time he pursued this investigation. He writes, "My mastery of it reached a point that cannot be surpassed, but so much alienation, agitation and veiling appeared that I could find no rest. It became obvious that the true knowledge I sought was found in a stage beyond reason."[31]

Then, like al-Ghazzālī, Kāshānī turned to Sufism. He was eventually able to find the certainty that he was looking for. Given his early philosophical training, it is not surprising that his *Fuṣūṣ* commentary accentuates the trend established by Qūnawī to present the text in philosophical terms. The manner in which Kāshānī's approach differs from that of Ibn 'Arabī is especially obvious in his *Ta'wīl al-qur'ān*, which, ironically, has been published in Ibn 'Arabī's name.[32]

Perhaps the most widely read commentary on the *Fuṣūṣ* in the eastern lands of Islam was that by Sharaf al-Dīn Dāwūd Qayṣarī (d. 751/1350), who wrote several books in Arabic, but none, apparently, in Persian. Qayṣarī studied the text with Kāshānī and sometimes paraphrases Jandī's explanations. His introduction to his commentary is one of the most systematic philosophical expositions of this school of thought, and commentaries on his introduction have continued to be written down to modern times.[33]

The first Persian commentary on the *Fuṣūṣ* was probably written by Rukn al-Dīn Shīrāzī (d. 769/1367), a student of Qayṣarī. As a rule the several Persian commentaries are heavily indebted to one or more of the Arabic commentaries.

The process of integrating Ibn 'Arabī's teachings into the Shi'ite intellectual perspective was undertaken with great perseverance by Sayyid Ḥaydar Āmulī (d. 787/1385). The 500-page introduction to his *Fuṣūṣ* commentary has been published, but not the text itself, of which the introduction represents only about ten per cent. Āmulī investigates each passage of the *Fuṣūṣ* in terms of three levels: transmitted teachings (*naql*), including the Qur'ān and the Shi'ite *Ḥadīth* literature; reason (*'aql*), i.e., *kalām* and *falsafah*; and unveiling (*kashf*), in particular the writings of Ibn 'Arabī and his followers.

This hierarchy of *naql*, *'aql* and *kashf* is already implied or explicitly discussed in the teachings of many earlier Sufis, and by the time of Āmulī it has become a commonplace. The third and highest approach was seen as attainable only after thorough training in the lower-level sciences, including *falsafah*. This helps explain why even today many of the *'ulamā'* in Iran, although typically condemning Sufism because of its popular elements, consider *'irfān* or "gnosis" a path that leads to the highest spiritual attainments. Those texts that discuss *'irfān* present it in terms that show it to be a direct continuation of the attempts by Ibn 'Arabī and Qūnawī to harmonize reason and unveiling, or philosophy and Sufism.

OTHER MEMBERS OF THE SCHOOL

Several seventh/thirteenth-century authors not directly affiliated with Qūnawī deserve mention as important conduits of Ibn 'Arabī's teachings. Sa'd al-Dīn Ḥammūyah (d. 649/1252) corresponded with Ibn 'Arabī and was a friend, but probably not a student and certainly not a disciple, of Qūnawī. He wrote many works in Arabic and Persian, most of which are difficult to decipher. His terminology suggests that he was influenced by Ibn 'Arabī's teachings, but he was far less interested than Qūnawī, or even Ibn 'Arabī himself, in the rational exposition of Sufi teachings in a manner that would have found favour with the philosophically or theologically inclined. Jāmī seems to be on the mark when he remarks about Ḥammūyah, "He has many works . . . full of symbolic speech, difficult words, numbers, diagrams and circles. The eye of reason and reflection is incapable of understanding and deciphering them. Until the eye of insight is opened with the light of unveiling, it is impossible to perceive their meaning."[34]

Probably more important than Ḥammūyah himself for the dissemination of Ibn 'Arabī's teachings was his disciple 'Azīz al-Dīn Nasafī (d. before 700/1300), who wrote exclusively in Persian. He makes no claims to represent Ibn 'Arabī's teachings, but he uses terms such as *waḥdat al-wujūd* and "perfect human being" and explains them in ways that are not unconnected with discussions found in Ibn 'Arabī's writings. Ibn 'Arabī and Qūnawī wrote mainly for the *'ulamā'*, whereas Nasafī's works are directed at a less learned audience.

Another contemporary of Qūnawī who deserves mention is Awḥad al-Dīn Balyānī (d. 686/1288), a native of Shiraz. The English translation of his short Arabic treatise *Risālat al-aḥadiyyah* has been published in Ibn 'Arabī's name, thereby helping Westerners to gain a skewed picture of the Shaykh's position on *waḥdat al-wujūd*. Balyānī's mode of expression, which harmonizes with some rather ecstatic Persian verses of his cited by Jāmī, represents a relatively peripheral development in Ibn 'Arabī's school. No one should be surprised to hear that his treatise aroused the ire of those who attacked the supporters of *waḥdat al-wujūd* for believing that "All is He" (*hama ūst*).[35]

By the eighth/fourteenth century, it becomes increasingly difficult to say who deserves to be called a member of Ibn 'Arabī's school. For example, some Sufis begin to take issue with his positions in rather severe fashion, but they do not necessarily step out of his intellectual universe. Ibn 'Arabī's most severe early critic had been Ibn Taymiyyah (d. 728/1328), who was affiliated with a Sufi order, but had no sympathy for *falsafah* or philosophizing. In contrast, the already mentioned 'Alā' al-Dawlah Simnānī was an important shaykh of the Kubrawī Order and wrote works in both Arabic and Persian. He was highly critical of Ibn 'Arabī's ascription of the term *muṭlaq* to *wujūd*. Some observers have suggested that Simnānī opposed Ibn 'Arabī's school of thought, but his writings show that most of what he says is prefigured in the ideas and terminology of the "school of verification". The same goes for the writings of Indian Sufi critics of Ibn 'Arabī such as Gīsū Darāz (d. 825/1422) and, most famous of all, Shaykh Aḥmad Sirhindī (d. 1034/1634). The last proposed *waḥdat al-shuhūd* ("the oneness of witnessing") as a corrective to *waḥdat al-wujūd*.

Among eighth/fourteenth-century authors who were especially influential in spreading Ibn 'Arabī's teachings was Sayyid 'Alī of Hamadan (d. 786/1385), the patron saint of Kashmir. He wrote a Persian commentary on the *Fuṣūṣ* and several short Persian and Arabic works that deal with Ibn 'Arabī's teachings. His sometime travelling companion, Sayyid Ashraf Jahāngīr Simnānī (d. probably in 829/1425), studied as a youth with 'Alā' al-Dawlah Simnānī but sided with Kāshānī in the dispute over Ibn 'Arabī. Especially interesting is the *Laṭā'if-i ashrafī*, put together by his disciple Niẓām Ḥājjī al-Yamanī. This long work is Jāmī's source for the text of the Simnānī–Kāshānī dispute and also for the idea that it concerns *waḥdat al-wujūd*, since the two principles do not mention the term.

'Alā' al-Dīn 'Alī ibn Aḥmad Mahā'imī (d. 835/1432), from Gujrat, wrote several important Arabic works in the philosophical style of Qūnawī, including commentaries on Ibn 'Arabī's *Fuṣūṣ*, Qūnawī's *Nuṣūṣ*, and a *tafsīr* of the Qur'ān, called *Tabṣīr al-raḥmān*. He also wrote an Arabic commentary on *Jām-i jahānnumāy*, a Persian work by the poet Shams al-Dīn Maghribī (d. 809/1406–7). Maghribī's work was largely inspired by Farghānī's *Mashāriq al-darārī*. Several more commentaries were written upon *Jām-i jahānnumāy* in India, all in Persian.

It would be possible to enumerate dozens of other authors from the Indian subcontinent who deserve to be called members of Ibn 'Arabī's school,[36] but I will limit myself to probably the most learned and faithful of all his followers there, Shaykh Muḥibb Allāh Mubāriz Ilāhābādī (d. 1058/1648). He is the author of commentaries on the *Fuṣūṣ* in both Persian and Arabic and of several other long works explaining Ibn 'Arabī's teachings. He appears to be the best informed of all the Indian authors on the contents of the *Futūḥāt*.

Coming back to the central Islamic lands, a number of names need to be mentioned simply to indicate that they represent some of the most famous figures in the history of Ibn 'Arabī's school. As Morris remarks about 'Abd al-Karīm al-Jīlī (832/1428), he is "undoubtedly both the most original thinker and the most remarkable and independent mystical writer" among Ibn 'Arabī's well-known followers.[37] Two of the most prolific supporters of Ibn 'Arabī's teachings in the Arab countries are 'Abd al-Wahhāb al-Sha'rānī (d. 973/1565) and the aforementioned 'Abd al-Ghanī al-Nābulsī. In the Ottoman domains, 'Abdallāh of Bosnia (d. 1054/1644) made an especially valuable contribution to the philosophical exposition of Ibn 'Arabī's ideas. About each of these authors, and dozens more down into the twentieth century, a great deal deserves to be said.[38]

The study of Ibn 'Arabī's influence is still in its infancy. Without doubt many more important authors will come to light when further research is carried out. Enough has been said to suggest the rough outlines of his "school" and the tasks that remain to be accomplished.

NOTES

1 Qūnawī sometimes refers to his position as *madhhab al-taḥqīq*, "the school of verification", and *taḥqīq* is Ibn 'Arabī's preferred term to refer to his own approach. However, diverse Sufis, philosophers and other thinkers both before and after Ibn 'Arabī referred to what they were doing as *taḥqīq* to differentiate themselves from the common people, who were in the grips of *taqlīd*, "imitation" or "following authority".

2 See Addas, *Ibn 'Arabī* (Paris, 1989): 276, 341; Chodkiewicz, *Emir Abd el-Kader: Ecrits spirituels* (Paris, 1982): 22; "The Diffusion of Ibn 'Arabī's Doctrine", *Journal of the Muhyiddin Ibn 'Arabī Society*, 9 (1991): 36–57.

3 Morris, "Ibn 'Arabī and his Interpreters", *Journal of the American Oriental Society*, 106 (1986): 751–2.

4 On the second point, see Chodkiewicz, *op. cit.*

5 See D. Gril, "Le *Kitāb al-inbāh 'alā ṭarīq Allāh* de 'Abdallāh Badr al-Ḥabashī: un témoignage de l'enseignement spirituel de Muḥyi l-dīn ibn 'Arabī", *Annales Islamologiques*, 15 (1979): 97–164; M. Profitlich, *Die Terminologie Ibn 'Arabīs im "Kitāb wasā'il as-sā'il" des Ibn Saudakīn* (Freiburg im Breisgau, 1973).

6 Chodkiewicz writes that Qūnawī "a donné à la doctrine de son maître une formulation philosophique sans doute nécessaire mais dont le systématisme a engendré bien des malentendus". *Epître sur l'Unicité Absolue* (Paris, 1982): 26.

7 O. Yahia, *Histoire et classification de l'oeuvre d'Ibn 'Arabī* (Damascus, 1964): 209, *samā'* no. 12; Chittick, "The Last Will and Testament of Ibn 'Arabī's Foremost Disciple and Some Notes on its Author", *Sophia Perennis*, 4(1) (1978): 43–58. The treatise addressed to al-Tilimsānī is called *Kitāb al-ilmā' bi ba'ḍ kulliyyāt asrār al-sama'*; Turkish manuscripts include Ibrahim Efendi 881/8, Kara Çelebi Zade 345/15, Şehid Ali Paşa 1344/4, and Konya Müzesi 1633, 5020.

8 Ibn Sab'īn was asked, "How did you find Qūnawī with the eye of the knowledge of *tawḥīd*?" He answered, "He is one of the verifiers, but there was a young man with him even more proficient [*aḥdhaq*], al-'Afīf al-Tilimsānī." Quoted by A. Taftāzānī, *Ibn Sab'īn wa falsafatuhu al-ṣūfiyyah* (Beirut, 1973): 81. On Ibn Sab'īn's philosophical writing, see S. Yaltkaya, *Correspondance philosophique avec l'empereur Fréderic II de Hohenstaufen* (Paris and Beirut, 1941).
9 See Chittick, "Rumi and Waḥdat al-Wujud", in *The Heritage of Rumi*, ed. A. Banani and G. Sabagh (Cambridge, 1994).
10 Ḥājjī Khalīfah, *Kashf al-ẓunūn*, (Istanbul, 1971), cols 265–6, *s.v. Tā'iyyah.*
11 See Chittick, *Faith and Practice of Islam: Three Thirteenth Century Sufi Texts* (Albany, 1992): 258–9.
12 Jāmī, *Nafaḥāt al-uns*, ed. M. Tawḥīdīpūr (Tehran, 1957): 559.
13 Published with a Turkish introduction by H. K. Yilmaz, *Tasavvufî Hadîs serhleri ve Konevînin Kırk Hadîs Şerhi* (Istanbul, 1990). For a translation of two passages from the text, see S. Murata, *The Tao of Islam: a Sourcebook on Gender Relationships in Islamic Thought* (Albany, 1992): 101–2, 219–22.
14 For a tentative list, see Chittick, "Last Will". I would remove from that list the two Persian works, *Tabṣirat al-mubtadī* and *Maṭāli'-i īmān* (on which see Chittick, *Faith and Practice*), and would add two short Arabic works, *Taḥrīr al-bayān fī taqrīr shu'ab al-īmān* and *Marātib al-taqwā.*
15 Jāmī, *op. cit.*: 556.
16 Ibn Taymiyyah, *Majmū'at al-rasā'il wa'l-masā'il*, ed. Muḥammad Rashīd Riḍā (n.p., n.d.), 1: 176.
17 Qūnawī, *al-Nafaḥāt al-ilāhiyyah* (Tehran, 1898): 152–3.
18 On the correspondence, see Chittick, "Mysticism versus Philosophy in Earlier Islamic History: the al-Ṭūsī, al-Qūnawī Correspondence", *Religious Studies*, 17 (1981): 87–104. A critical edition is being prepared by G. Schubert (*Manuscripts of the Middle East* (1988), 3: 73–8).
19 See Chittick, "The Five Divine Presences: From al-Qūnawī to al-Qayṣarī", *Muslim World*, 72 (1982): 107–28.
20 Chittick and P. L. Wilson, *Fakhruddin 'Iraqi: Divine Flashes* (New York, 1982).
21 I have investigated this question in some detail. See Chittick "Rumi and Waḥdjat al-Wujud". See also Chittick, "Rūmī and the Mawlawiyya", in *Islamic Spirituality: Manifestations*, ed. S. H. Nasr (New York, 1991): 113–17.
22 *Sharḥ Fuṣūṣ al-ḥikam*, ed. S. J. Āshtiyānī (Mashhad, 1982): 5.
23 Qūnawī, *al-Fukūk*, on the margin of Kāshānī, *Sharḥ manāzil al-sā'irīn* (Tehran, 1897–8): 184.
24 For a list of commentaries and criticisms, see O. Yahia, Arabic introduction to Sayyid Ḥaydar Āmulī, *Naṣṣ al-nuṣūṣ* (Tehran, 1971).
25 See Chittick, Persian introduction to Jāmī, *Naqd al-nuṣūṣ fī sharḥ naqsh al-fuṣūṣ* (Tehran, 1977): 38–44.
26 The most famous is by 'Abd al-Raḥmān Jāmī, *Naqd al-nuṣūṣ*, mentioned in the previous note. This work, which is Jāmī's earliest theoretical work on Sufism, is an explicit compendium of some of the key theoretical discussions by Qūnawī and his direct followers. For a translation of *Naqsh al-fuṣūṣ* along with many pages from Jāmī's commentary, see Chittick, "Ibn 'Arabī's own Summary of the *Fuṣūṣ*: 'The Imprint of the Bezels of Wisdom'", *Journal of the Muhyiddin Ibn 'Arabī Society*, 1 (1982): 30–93.

27 See Ibn 'Arabī's comments on the meaning of this sentence in Chittick, *The Sufi Path of Knowledge: Ibn al-'Arabī's Metaphysics of Imagination* (Albany, 1989): 103.

28 Istanbul MS Şehid Ali Paşa, 1248, commentary on the chapter on Abraham. Compare his remarks in the chapter on Joseph.

29 *Ibid.*, chapter on Solomon.

30 For passages on this issue from *al-Fukūk* and the major early commentaries, see Chittick, "The Chapter Headings of the *Fuṣūṣ*", *Journal of the Muhyiddin Ibn 'Arabī Society*, 2 (1984): 41–94.

31 Jāmī, *op. cit.*: 486; the full correspondence is translated in Landolt, "Der Briefwechsel zwischen Kāšānī und Simnānī über *Waḥdat al-Wuǧūd*", *Der Islam*, 50 (1973): 29–81; and in P. Lory, *Les Commentaires ésotériques du Coran d'après 'Abd ar-Razzāq al-Qāshānī* (Paris, 1981).

32 On Kāshānī, see Morris, *op. cit.*: 101–6. Kāshānī's philosophical strength helps explain why his commentary was chosen by T. Izutsu, whose later works focus on the Islamic philosophical tradition, to help him explain Ibn 'Arabī's teachings to English-speaking readers. See Izutsu, *Sufism and Taoism* (Los Angeles, 1983). For passages from Kāshānī's Qur'ān commentary and other works, see Murata, *op. cit.*, index under Kāshānī.

33 The latest of these is by the contemporary *ḥakīm* S. J. Āshtiyānī, *Sharḥ-i muqaddima-yi qayṣarī bar fuṣūṣ* (Mashhad, 1966).

34 Jāmī, *Nafaḥāt al-uns*: 429. The only work of Ḥammūyah to have been published is the Persian *al-Miṣbāḥ fi'l-taṣawwuf*, ed. N. Māyil Harawī (Tehran, 1983).

35 See Chodkiewicz's important study and translation of this work, *Epître sur l'Unicité Absolue*; see also Chittick, "Rumi and Waḥdat al-Wujud".

36 See Chittick, "Notes on Ibn al-'Arabī's Influence in the Subcontinent", *Muslim World*, 82 (1992): 218–41.

37 Morris, *op. cit.*: 108.

38 Among the most fascinating late representatives of Ibn 'Arabī's school is Amīr 'Abd al-Qādir of Algeria (d. 1300/1883), the well-known freedom fighter. For his connection to the school and samples of his writings, see Chodkiewicz, *Emir Abd el-Kader*.

V

Later Islamic philosophy

CHAPTER 32

Khwājah Naṣīr al-Dīn al-Ṭūsī: the philosopher/vizier and the intellectual climate of his times

Hamid Dabashi

In the year 597/1201, about five years before St Albertus Magnus and some twenty-three years before St Thomas Aquinas (1224–74) were born, far from Lauingen in Swabia and far from the castle of Roccasecca near Naples, a kindred soul of these two great medieval philosophers was born in the city of Ṭūs in the eastern province of Khurasan in Persia. Khwājah Naṣīr al-Dīn al-Ṭūsī (597/1201–672/1274) would live simultaneously with St Albertus Magnus and St Thomas Aquinas and share much of their theological and philosophical concerns – and then some more. He would serve in the court of a world conquerer, witness the destruction of Baghdad and the downfall of the 'Abbasid caliphate, found one of the greatest institutions of higher learning in the form of a teaching observatory, contribute massively to all major branches of Islamic philosophy and then die in exactly the same year that St Thomas Aquinas died, some six years before the death of St Albertus Magnus. Had their respective faiths and languages and their opposing locations around the dividing lines of the Crusades permitted it, the two Christian and one Muslim philosopher would have found much, much indeed, to talk about and to discuss. And the three of them would have had much to learn from yet another philosopher, their senior by almost a century. Khwājah Naṣīr was three years old when the eminent Jewish philosopher Moses Maimonides (1135–1204) died in Cairo. These four represented the peak of philosophical activity in the three Abrahamic religions at that time. Ruling over their minds with almost the same intensity as the Old and the New Testaments and the Qur'ān was the legacy of Greek philosophy and especially Aristotle.

REMEMBERING KHWĀJAH NAṢĪR

Preserved in the margins of a rare miniature portrait of Khwājah Naṣīr al-Dīn al-Ṭūsī in the Malik Library in Tehran are two calligraphic descriptions of him, representing the high esteem in which he was held by his more contemporary commentators. The phrase in the right margin reads, "Naṣīr al-Dawlah wa al-Dīn [the Sustainer of the State and of the Faith] Muḥammad-i Ṭūsī, that unique [individual] the like of whom the mother of time did not give birth to". The one to the bottom left reads, "the Portrait of the Most Significant of all *'ulamā'*, the most distinguished of all philosophers, Ustād al-Bashar Khwājah Naṣīr al-Dīn Ṭūsī, Sanctified be the site of his Tomb, Noble and Benevolent" (Mudarris Raḍawī (1955): 2). Allowing for all the necessary and customary hyperbole representative of the time and the culture, there is still an irreducible sense of significance and admiration for the intellectual legacy produced and left for posterity by this remarkable hallmark of medieval Islamic learning.

"*Qudwa-yi Muḥaqqiqīn wa Sulṭān-i Ḥukamā' wa Mutikallimīn, Ustād-i Bashar wa 'Aql-i Hādī 'ashar, Muḥammad ibn Muḥammad ibn al-Ḥasan al-Ṭūsī, mukannā' bi Abū Ja'far wa mulaqqab bi Khwājah Naṣīr al-Dīn wa mashhūr bi Muḥaqqiq-i Ṭūsī yā Khwājah-yi Ṭūsī*" is the full honorific title with which this prominent intellectual figure in the history of Islamic philosophy is known, praised and honoured by his fellow Muslims (Mudarris Raḍawī (1955): 2; Tunikābunī (1985): 367; Shūshtarī (1986), 2: 201; Khwānsārī (1981), 7: 221). Sometimes the honorific title of Raṣadī, a reference to his status as a prominent astronomer, is also added to his name (Tunikābunī (1985): 767).

Khwājah Naṣīr is one of the greatest pillars of Shī'ī theology, on a par with such seminal doctrinaires of the faith as Thiqat al-Islam al-Kulaynī (d. 329/940), Shaykh al-Ṣaddūq (d. 381/991), Shaykh al-Mufīd (d. 413/1022), 'Alam al-Hudā' Ṣayyid al-Murtaḍā (d. 436/1044), and Shaykh-i Ṭūsī (d. 460/1067). After the devastating effects of the Mongol invasion early in the seventh/thirteenth century, Khwājah Naṣīr is credited with having rescued, consolidated and systematized the best and most enduring aspects of Shī'ī (Islamic) scholastic learning. He left his indelible mark on theology, jurisprudence, philosophy, astronomy, politics, ethics and poetics. The Shī'īs are particularly proud, in their hagiographical remembrances of him, of his services to their dogmatics (Tunikābunī (1985): 374; Shūshtarī (1986), 2: 201–2). He is credited with having won the greatest intellectual and political forces of his time for Shī'īsm. He is believed to have converted the distinguished philosopher Quṭb al-Dīn al-Shīrazī to Shi'ism (Tunikābunī (1985): 374). The utmost expression of Khwājah Naṣīr's Shī'ī piety is evident in a treatise he wrote on the virtues of the first Shī'ī Imām, 'Ali ibn Abī Ṭālib, whom he describes as successor of the prophets (al-Ṭūsī (1982): 2–3). There are many other books and treatises in which his devout and doctrinal Shī'ī convictions are evident (e.g., al-Ṭūsī (1988): 338–76; al-Ṭūsī (1984b): 183–5).

On the model of Ibn Sīnā (Avicenna), Khwājah Naṣīr ought to be considered as an example par excellence of that peculiarly Persian institution of the philosophers/viziers, men of unusual scholastic learning who combined their philosophical quest with a unique penchant for political power. Khwājah Naṣīr, for example, is reported to have dictated a full treatise on logic while preparing a contingent of Hūlāgū's army for battle (Tunikābunī (1985): 374). Having lived through one of the most tumultuous centuries of Persian history, Khwājah Naṣīr tamed and controlled the ferocious violence of the Mongol invasion with remarkable poise and tact, managed to produce canonical texts on an astonishing number of intellectual disciplines, created institutional centres of learning and research and left a permanent mark on Islamic intellectual and scientific history.

BIOGRAPHY

Khwājah Naṣīr al-Dīn al-Ṭūsī was born in Ṭūs in the early morning hours of 'Saturday 11 Jamādi'l-'ūlā' 597/16 February 1201 (Tunikābunī (1985): 367; Shūshtarī (1986), 2: 203). The origin of his family is traced back to Jahrūd of Sāwah (Tunikābunī (1985): 367). But by the time he was born in Ṭūs, his family had long been established there. He received his early education in Ṭūs under the supervision of his father, Muḥammad ibn al-Ḥasan, a prominent Shī'ī jurist. Topics of his early education included Arabic language and grammar, Qur'ānic and *Ḥadīth* studies, as well as Shī'ī jurisprudence, law, logic, natural sciences and metaphysics. His early education in Ṭūs also included mathematics (Mudarrisī Zanjānī (1984): 23; Shūshtarī (1986), 2: 203).

Very early in his youth, Khwājah Naṣīr left Ṭūs and went to Nishapur to pursue his studies. Early in the seventh/thirteenth century Nishapur had retained its status as the intellectual capital of the eastern Islamic world, and an array of distinguished scholars taught there. Among those with whom Khwājah Naṣīr studied was Farīd al-Dīn Dāmād Nīshāpūrī, who was a student of Ṣadr al-Dīn Sarakhsī, who was a student of Afḍal al-Dīn Ghīlanī, who was a student of Abu'l-'Abbās Lūkarī, who was a student of Bahmanyār, who was a student of Ibn Sīnā (Shūshtarī (1986), 2: 203; Mudarris Raḍawī (1955): 2). Thus, through five generations of philosophers, Khwājah Naṣīr was directly linked to the master of Peripatetic philosophy (Tunikābunī (1985): 381; al-Ṭūsī (1982): 9). With Farīd al-Dīn Dāmād, Khwājah Naṣīr studied Ibn Sīnā's *al-Ishārāt wa'l-tanbīhāt*. He studied the *Qānūn* of Ibn Sīnā with Quṭb al-Dīn al-Miṣrī, who was a student of Imām Fakhr al-Dīn al-Rāzī. He studied mathematics with Kamāl al-Dīn ibn Yūnus al-Miṣrī. By the year 619/1222, he received his formal "licence" (*ijāzah*) to transmit *Ḥadīth*. He took advantage of being in Nishapur and studied a variety of different subjects with an array of other distinguished scholars (Mudarris Raḍawī (1955): 2–3; Mudarrisī Zanjānī (1984): 24–6).

The Mongol invasion of Khurasan in the early seventh/thirteenth century occurred while Khwājah Naṣīr was completing his studies in Nishapur, which became an increasingly dangerous place to live in. When a local Ismā'īlī prince, Nāṣir al-Dīn 'Abd al-Raḥīm ibn Abī Manṣūr, the governor, or *muḥtasham*, of Quhistan, invited Khwājah Naṣīr to join him in his fortress, he immediately accepted and sought haven with the local Ismā'īlīs (Daftary (1990): 408–9). His tenure with Nāṣir al-Dīn 'Abd al-Raḥīm, which was some time between 624/1226 and 632/1234, was very fruitful. Here he translated and expanded Abū 'Alī Muskuwayh al-Rāzī's *Kitāb al-ṭahārah* as *Akhlāq-i nāṣirī*, in his patron's name. He also wrote *Risālat al-mu'īniyyah* in astronomy for his patron's son, Mu'īn al-Dīn. *Akhlāq-i muḥtashamī*, *Sharḥ al-ishārāt*, *Asās al-iqtibās* and a few other books are also the products of this period (Mudarris Raḍawī (1955): 4–5; Khwānsārī (1981), 7: 224).

Some time before 632/1234, Khwājah Naṣīr is summoned from Nāṣir al-Dīn's court to the court of 'Alā' al-Dīn Muḥammad, the Ismā'īlī prince, who had heard of the young scholar and wished to enjoy his company. Accompanied by Nāṣir al-Dīn, Khwājah Naṣīr moved from Quhistān to the fortress of Maymūn Diz, to the care and patronage of 'Alā' al-Dīn Muḥammad (Mudarris Raḍawī (1955): 5–6). Although his sojourn with the Ismā'īlī patrons was quite productive, he does not seem to have been particularly happy or content with his fate. Towards the end of *Sharḥ al-ishārāt*, he complains of the difficult conditions under which he had been writing that particular book. "I wrote a considerable part of it," he complains, "in an extremely difficult condition, a more difficult condition than which is impossible" (al-Ṭūsī (1983): 145; Mudarris Raḍawī (1955): 7). In the middle of his Arabic reflection on his intolerable condition, he seeks refuge in a Persian poem: "As far as I can see around me / Calamity is a ring and I its bezel" (al-Ṭūsī (1983): 145). While Khwājah Naṣīr was in Quhistan, Hūlāgū, the Mongol warlord, was dispatched by his brother Mangū Khān (Möngke, the Great Khān), successor to Chingiz Khān (Chinggis Khān), to fight the Ismā'īlīs (Daftary (1990): 418–19). In 653/1255 Hūlāgū invaded Persia (Boyle (1968): 340–1). In 654/1256, he defeated the Ismā'īlī ruler Rukn al-Dīn Khurshāh, and captured the fortress of Alamut, where Khwājah Naṣīr had been, in effect, a prisoner. Khwājah Naṣīr's role in peacefully making the Ismāʿīlī ruler submit to Hūlāgū made him particularly valuable to the Mongol warlord (Boyle (1968): 341–3; al-Juwaynī (1937), 3: 114–42).

THE MONGOL INVASION OF PERSIA

In 649/1251, the Great Khan Mangū (Möngke) dispatched his brother Hūlāgū to consolidate his conquest of Persia. The army that Hūlāgū led into Persia is estimated to have been larger than that led by Chingiz Khān himself (Boyle (1968): 340). In 651/1253 Hūlāgū left his encampment in central Asia and advanced south to central Persia. By 653/1255 he met with the founder of the Kart dynasty of Herat, Shams al-Dīn Muḥammad (Potter (1992): 40–3), and then began to send his emissaries to various Persian provinces, informing them of his intention to eradicate the Ismāʿīlī presence. By Shaʿbān 654/September 1256, he received the brother of Rukn al-Dīn Khūrshāh, the Grand Ismāʿīlī Master, in whose service Khwājah Naṣīr al-Dīn was by now employed. By Shawwāl/November of that year, Rukn al-Dīn surrendered and received a *yārlīgh* (mandate to rule) from the Mongol warlord. Khwājah Naṣīr was among the entourage that accompanied Rukn al-Dīn Khurshāh to meet with Hūlāgū. Through the good offices of the historian al-Juwaynī and probably Khwājah Naṣīr, the library and astronomical instruments of the Alamūt fortress were saved from the Mongol destruction. At this point, Khwājah Naṣīr enters the service of the Great Mongol warlord. In Rabīʿ al-Awwal 655/April 1257 Hūlāgū left Qazwīn for Hamadān and from there marched towards Baghdad.

KHWĀJAH NAṢĪR AND THE CONQUEST OF BAGHDAD

When Hūlāgū's army approached Baghdad, among the prominent members of his immediate entourage was Khwājah Naṣīr (Rashīd al-Dīn Faḍl Allāh (1959), 2: 707). Khwājah Naṣīr was actively involved in the long process of skirmishes and negotiations between Hūlāgū and caliph al-Mustaʿṣim. At one point Hūlāgū dispatched Khwājah Naṣīr to negotiate on his behalf with the ʿAbbasid caliph (*ibid.*: 711). When Hūlāgū finally attacked Baghdad, he had Khwājah Naṣīr stationed at a gate to the capital to protect the innocent people.

After consulting with Khwājah Naṣīr on the astrological timing of invading Baghdad, Hūlāgū attacked the ʿAbbasid capital. Qāḍī Nūr

Allāh Shūshtarī, in *Majālis al-mu'minīn*, attributes this to the philosopher's Shī'ī faith. The occurrence of a major flood in late summer 654/1256 in Baghdad (Rashīd al-Dīn Faḍl Allāh (1959), 2: 698–9) had considerably jeopardized al-Musta'ṣim's already weak rule. Confusion and anarchy pervaded the 'Abbasid capital. On 10 Ramaḍān 655/20 September 1257 Hūlāgū left Hamadan for Baghdad and sent a message to the caliph asking him to surrender. There are even some claims not substantiated of secret communications between Ibn 'Alqamī, al-Musta'ṣim's Shī'ī vizier, and Khwājah Naṣīr on inducing the Mongol warlord to attack Baghdad (Mudarris Raḍawī (1955): 13). On Tuesday 22 Muharram 656/29 January 1258, Hūlāgū headed for Baghdad with Khwājah Naṣīr among his immediate entourage. At one point during the siege of Baghdad, he sent Khwājah Naṣīr to persuade the caliph to surrender. Al-Musta'ṣam initially refused but finally, on Sunday 4 Ṣafar 656/9 February 1258, he and his family surrendered to Hūlāgū (Rashīd al-Dīn Faḍl Allāh (1959), 2: 712). The caliph was killed ten days later in a manner also attributed to Khwājah Naṣīr by some sources. It is reported (Tunikābunī (1985): 380) that Hūlāgū, on the advice of an astrologist, rival to Khwājah Naṣīr (a certain Hisām al-Dīn al-Munajjim), was reluctant to kill the caliph, lest something terrible would happen to him and his army. Khwājah Naṣīr insisted that these were all superstitious beliefs and that nothing would happen to Hūlāgū by killing the 'Abbasid caliph. To ease the Mongol warrior's mind, he suggested that the caliph be wrapped in a carpet and rolled by hand to death. If any change in the world, the climate, or Hūlāgū's health were to appear, they would stop the execution immediately. Hūlāgū agreed, and poor al-Musta'ṣim was rolled around to death. There are, however, other less dramatic accounts of the caliph's execution, such as starvation, with no involvement by the Shī'ī vizier (Mudarris Raḍawī (1955): 16). Some members of the caliph's family, such as his youngest son, Mubarak-Shāh, were saved by the intervention of Hūlāgū's wife, Uljāy-Khātūn (Rashīd al-Dīn Faḍl Allāh (1959), 2: 714). Khwājah Naṣīr took this son to Marāghah, where he married a Mongol woman and lived under the vizier's protection (Rashīd al-Dīn Faḍl Allāh (1959), 2: 714; Mudarris Raḍawī (1955): 17).

Khwājah Naṣīr is credited with having saved the lives of many Muslim scholars who resided in Baghdad during the Mongol invasion, e.g., Ibn Abi'l-Ḥadīd, the famous commentator of *Nahj al-balāghah* (Mudarris Raḍawī (1955): 17–18). He is also reported to have cast the libraries of his enemies into the Euphrates (Tunikābunī (1985): 373). However, none of these stories can be independently verified. Al-Ṭūsī's Shī'ī biographers are quite adamant in attributing pro-Shī'ī, anti-Sunni sentiments to him (Tunikābunī (1985): 373; Shūshtarī (1986), 2: 203; Khwānsārī (1981), 7: 221–2).

Khwājah Naṣīr remained with Hūlāgū in Baghdad for a while and helped him to consolidate his authority in the former 'Abbasid capital. Then he went to Ḥillah, the great centre of Shī'ī learning in Iraq, where he visited Muḥaqqiq-i Ḥillī, the prominent Shī'ī jurist, and engaged in juridical discussions with him. Through Muḥaqqiq-i Ḥillī, Khwājah Naṣīr met with other prominent theologians and jurists of the area. On his return to Marāghah, following Hūlāgū's command, he supervised the construction of the famous observatory. Hūlagū died before Khwājah Naṣīr could finish a full cycle of astronomical observations. He then became vizier to his succeeding son, Abaqā' Khān (ruled 663/1265–680/1282), who had equal trust in him and his judgments. There are reports that Khwājah Naṣīr became the personal physician to the Mongol leader as well (Mudarris Raḍawī (1955): 33–5).

In 655/1257 Khwājah Naṣīr travelled to Khurasan. On this trip he was joined by the other distinguished philosopher of the time, Quṭb al-Dīn al-Shīrāzī. The last we hear of Khwājah Naṣīr is on a hunting expedition with Abaqā' Khān. After his second enthronement in 12 Rabi' II, 669/1270, Abaqā was on a hunting chase when he was wounded by a bison (Boyle (1968): 360). Under Khwājah Naṣīr's supervision, a physician performed surgery on the Great Khan. On his final official trip to Baghdad in 672/1273 with Abaqā' Khān, Khwājah Naṣīr fell ill. The Mongol leader, accompanied by Quṭb al-Dīn al-Shīrāzī, visited the ailing Khwājah Naṣīr. The Persian philosopher died of this illness on Monday 18 Dhu'l-Ḥijjah 672/25 June 1274. His body was taken to Kāẓimayn and buried there. It is reported (Mudarris Raḍawī (1955): 35–6) that when they were digging Khwājah Naṣīr's grave near the mausoleums of Musā al-Kāẓim, the Seventh Shī'ī Imām, the gravediggers discovered a subterranean vault which turned out to be a grave that caliph al-Naṣīr had constructed for himself, although his son had buried him elsewhere. The construction date on that caliph's grave was Saturday 11 Jamādi'l-'ūlā' 597/16 February 1201, Khwājah Naṣīr's birthday.

KHWĀJAH NAṢĪR AS A SHĪ'Ī PHILOSOPHER

Khwājah Naṣīr's Shī'ī biographers are particular in their details of the philosopher's Shī'ī affiliations. He is reported, for example (Tunikābunī (1985): 367) to have spent twenty years writing a book on the virtues of the Shī'ī Imāms and to have gone to Baghdad to show it to the Sunni caliph. The caliph and his distinguished scholar, Ibn Ḥājib, are on a boat on the Euphrates when they receive Khwājah Naṣīr. The Shī'ī philosopher presents his book, and when the Sunni scholar sees its exclusive attention to the Shī'ī Imāms, he throws it into the Euphrates. Ibn Ḥājib then admonishes Khwājah Naṣīr and asks him where he is from. "From Tus", he responds. "Are you from the Ṭūsī cows or Ṭūsī asses?" the Sunni vizier retorts. "The cows", Khwājah Naṣīr answers. "Where are your horns?" Ibn Ḥājib continues. "They are in Ṭūs. I will go and get them", Khwājah Naṣīr responds with an obvious reference to his coming back to Baghdad in Hūlāgū's army to destroy Baghdad, to kill the caliph and all his entourage. The story goes on to report that Khwājah Naṣīr throws Ibn Ḥājib's entire library into the Euphrates in retaliation for what the Sunni vizier had done. Although the Shī'ī biographers are quick to discern any number of historical inaccuracies in this story (Tunikābunī (1985): 369), they still consider it of particular pedagogic value.

Khwājah Naṣīr is also credited with having converted many prominent Sunni scholars to Shi'ism, and if they refused they were executed (Tunikābunī (1985): 373). Among these Sunni-turned-Shī'ī philosophers are Quṭb al-Dīn al-Shīrāzī, whose lectures Khwājah Naṣīr is believed to have attended anonymously. When Quṭb al-Dīn al-Shīrāzī was once publicly embarrassed, he yielded to Khwājah Naṣīr's superior intellect and converted to Shi'ism. Quṭb al-Dīn is reported to have rejoined Sunnism, and been converted back to Shi'ism by Khwājah Naṣīr, altogether three times. Finally, he told Khwājah Naṣīr that he could not argue with him and that he would convert to Shi'ism if Khwājah Naṣīr would have one of his students debate with him. The student won, and Quṭb al-Dīn converted to Shi'ism, this time for good. These hagiographical anecdotes are particularly important in understanding the necessity of a total appropriation of the philosopher/vizier into Shī'ī collective sentiments.

COLLEAGUES AND STUDENTS

Khwājah Naṣīr frequently corresponded and exchanged ideas with a number of prominent contemporary philosophers and scientists, e.g., Najm al-Dīn Dabīrān-i Kātibī (d. 675/1276), a prominent philosopher, mathematician and logician whose works in logic, such as *'Ayn al-qawā'id*, became rather influential. He worked in Maraghah with Khwājah Naṣīr. These correspondences were occasions for exchanges of ideas, sending books and requesting answers to difficult philosophical questions. There is also a letter from Ṣadr al-Dīn al-Qūnawī, the distinguished contemporary of Khwājah Naṣīr, to him. It is evident from this letter (al-Ṭūsī (1966): 165–7) that it was the first correspondence between the two. In it Ṣadr al-Dīn expresses his great admiration for the Persian philosopher and his desire to have regular correspondence with him and thus learn from this contemporary master of Peripatetic philosophy. Along with the letter, Ṣadr al-Dīn sends a copy of one of his writings which he had written "a long time ago on the conclusion of [my] thoughts" (*ibid.*: 166). He kindly asks Khwājah Naṣīr to read his book, the result of his discussions with some of his philosopher friends, and comment on some of its problematic issues. Khwājah Naṣīr responds immediately in kind and opens his letter with a beautiful Arabic couplet in which he says that after the books of God he had not seen any book like the one Ṣadr al-Dīn had sent him. He expresses his equal, or higher, admiration for Ṣadr al-Dīn al-Qūnawī, calling him "our master" and "our guide". He writes that, of course, he had long known and admired al-Qūnawī and that he had intended to write to him and begin a regular correspondence. He was pleasantly surprised and honoured to receive a letter from Ṣadr al-Dīn. "In everything you have the virtuous nobility of having been the first", Khwājah Naṣīr writes to al-Qūnawī. In this respect, too, he had proved his being the first (*ibid.*: 168).

Khwājah Naṣīr's most distinguished student/colleague was 'Allāmah Quṭb al-Dīn al-Shīrāzī (d. 710/1310), who became a prominent philosopher/scientist in his own right (Walbridge 1992). His *Durrat al-tāj li-ghurrat al-dubāj* is one of his most important works. This text, written in Persian, is an encyclopedic summary of philosophical and non-philosophical topics. Among the students who attended Khwājah Naṣīr's lessons on jurisprudence was 'Allāmah Ḥillī, the great Shī'ī jurisconsult, who considered his teacher "the most noble man we have ever seen" (Mudarrisī Zanjānī (1984): 14). Moreover, Khwājah Naṣīr's influence is not limited to his immediate students. Since the seventh/thirteenth century, his books have been studied uninterruptedly in all scholastic institutions of higher learning in Persia and many other lands.

KHWĀJAH NAṢĪR'S ISMĀ'ĪLĪ CONNECTION

Khwājah Naṣīr's Ismā'īlī connection has been subject to considerable controversy. Nāṣir al-Dīn 'Abd al-Raḥīm (d. 655/1257), under whose patronage Khwājah Naṣīr produced some of his most significant works, is reported to have been a particularly erudite Ismā'īlī leader who invited Khwājah Naṣīr to join him in the Quhistan fortress. Probably Khwājah Naṣīr's attention to Nāṣir al-Dīn's court for patronage was subsequent to his unsuccessful bid to get close to Mu'ayyad al-Dīn al-'Alqamī, the Shī'ī vizier of caliph al-Musta'ṣim (Tunikābunī (1985): 378). Two of Khwājah Naṣīr's most important texts, *Akhlāq-i nāṣirī* and *Akhlāq-i muḥtashamī*, were written for this Nāṣir al-Dīn 'Abd al-Raḥīm, who was *muḥtashim* or head of the Quhistāni Nizārīs (Daftary (1990): 408). Khwājah Naṣīr is also reported (Shūshtarī (1986), 2: 207) to have translated 'Ayn al-Quḍāt al-Hamadānī's *Zubdat al-ḥaqā'iq* for Nāṣir al-Dīn and to have added a commentary to it. The productive relationship between the

Persian philosopher and his Ismāʿīlī patron was not to last; and, as we noted earlier, when the Ismāʿīlīs were defeated by Hūlāgū's army, Khwājah Naṣīr joined the Mongol warlord and accompanied him on his victorious expedition to Baghdad.

Twelver-Shīʿī authors are adamant in rejecting any Ismāʿīlī connection for Khwājah Naṣīr (Mudarris Raḍawī (1955): 6–9; Mudarrisī Zanjānī (1984): 49–51). More pious authors are hagiographical in celebrating Khwājah Naṣīr's Twelver Shiʿism (Tunikābunī (1985): 367; Khwānsārī (1981), 6: 221–2; Shūshtarī (1986), 2: 201–2). There are enough historical references (Humāʾī (1956): 17; Shūshtarī (1986), 2: 202–8; Isfandyār (1983), 1: 258; Mudarris Raḍawī (1955): 8–9; Mudarrisī Zanjānī (1984): 24–6; al-Ṭūsī (1982): 10–14; Daftary (1990): 408–11, 423–4, 693–4), however, to suspect a genuine Ismāʿīlī connection (Humāʾī (1956): 22–5). The original introduction of *Akhlāq-i nāṣirī* testifies to Khwājah Naṣīr's outright devotion to Nāṣir al-Dīn ʿAbd al-Raḥīm. A number of scholars have indeed postulated the possibility of Khwājah Naṣīr's Ismāʿīlī connection (Mīnuwī in al-Ṭūsī (1977a): 14–32; Dānishpazhūh in al-Ṭūsī (1982): 10–14; Daftary (1990): 408–11), and some have condemned (Rypka (1968): 313–14) or pardoned it (Buzurg ʿAlawī in al-Ṭūsī (1977a): 4). In so far as it affects his philosophical writings, this connection is believed (Dānishpazhūh in al-Ṭūsī (1982): 10–14) to have influenced Khwājah Naṣīr in a number of ways. His *Aghāz wa anjām* is identified as an Ismāʿīlī tract in its basic gnostic assumptions. While in Quhistan, Khwājah Naṣīr composed some of his other significant philosophical treatises. His *Asās al-iqtibās*, his translation of Ibn Maqaffaʿ's *al-Adab al-wajīz* (ordered by Nāṣir al-Dīn ʿAbd al-Raḥīm) and his translation of ʿAyn al-Quḍāt al-Hamadānī's *Zubdat al-ḥaqāʾiq* all come from this period, as does his treatise *Tawallā' wa tabarrā'* (again in an Ismāʿīlī discourse) and his major work on poetics, *Miʿyār al-ashʿār*.

HŪLĀGŪ: KHWĀJAH NAṢĪR'S PATRON

Next to Nāṣir al-Dīn ʿAbd al-Raḥīm, in patronage of Khwājah Naṣīr, stands the great Mongol warlord Hūlāgū (see Quatremère (1834): 85–425), who was equally protective of the Persian philosopher in his philosophical and scientific pursuits. There are major distinctions between these two patrons in their own respective political and intellectual dispositions, differences which are reflected in their attitude towards Khwājah Naṣīr. Whereas the Ismāʿīlī patron was personally attracted to Khwājah Naṣīr's intellectual endeavours, the Mongol warlord was more interested in the astronomical and medical expertise of his vizier. Nevertheless, Khwājah Naṣīr's ability to contribute immensely to the intellectual history of the seventh/thirteenth century was due to a considerable degree as much to the patronage of

Hūlāgū as to that of Nāṣir al-Dīn 'Abd al-Raḥīm. Under Hūlāgū's patronage, Khwājah Naṣīr was able to tame the Mongol warlord, create and sustain a level of limited civility and comfort for educated people, and manage to make the seventh/thirteenth century one of the most productive in Islamic intellectual history. He not only contributed enormously to a range of intellectual disciplines himself, but also under Hūlāgū's protective patronage created a congenial political and social atmosphere in which a host of other philosophers and scientists could work in comfort, undisturbed by forces of dogmatic and juridical opposition to the reign of reason in scientific and philosophical matters. If the claims of his devoted Shī'ī biographers are to be trusted, Khwājah Naṣīr secretly converted Hūlāgū and his wife to Islam and, in fact, personally performed a circumcision on Hūlāgū (Mudarrisī Zanjānī (1984): 13). Other sources confirm this report of conversion and attribute it to Hūlāgū's desire to marry a Persian girl who had refused matrimony unless the Mongol warlord converted to Islam (*ibid.*).

In an introduction to his astronomical treatise *Zīj-i īlkhānī*, Khwājah Naṣīr praises Hūlāgū for having come to Persia at his brother's command, defeated the Ismā'īlīs, and established law and order. Then "he patronized and attended to men of [knowledge and] art of all kinds, so that they demonstrated their talents. He established good customs. When he captured the lands of the [Ismā'īlī] infidels, where I was kept, he released me, the humble servant, Naṣīr from Tus, and ordered me to chart the stars" (quoted in Mudarris Raḍawī (1955): 29). Hūlāgū's generosity in letting Khwājah Naṣīr spend as much as was necessary on the construction of the Marāghah Observatory has stunned many contemporary historians (*ibid.*: 32).

A "RENAISSANCE MAN"

Well protected and patronized by two prominent patrons, Khwājah Naṣīr worked relentlessly on a range of intellectual disciplines. A remarkable aspect of his intellectual disposition was the comprehensive range of his knowledge. It is in this particular respect that he is reminiscent of Ibn Sīnā, with whom he most immediately identified himself. His *Aqsām al-ḥikmah* is evidence of his attempt to provide a general epistemological typology of all branches of knowledge, from *al-'ulūm al-'aqliyyah* to *al-'ulūm al-naqliyyah* (Ṣafā (1959–85), 3: 1.239). Khwājah Naṣīr had a thorough knowledge of Persian and Arabic and wrote all his major works in these two languages. But there are also indications that he knew Turkish (Mudarris Raḍawī (1955): 196). As a prominent philosopher/vizier, he corresponded widely with the most distinguished philosophers, theologians, mystics and men of knowledge. The texts of these letters have mostly been preserved. The range and depth of his knowledge are legendary and, in fact, have given rise to many anecdotes about his unusual erudition. Tunikābunī, for example, reports that Quṭb al-Dīn Shīrāzī once noticed that Khwājah Naṣīr disguised himself as a student and attended his classes. He decided to humiliate Khwājah Naṣīr in front of all the students by forcing him to discuss a subject of which he was sure Khwājah Naṣīr had no knowledge. He gave a lecture on Ibn Sīnā's treatise on pulse and took a number of exceptions to it, and then asked Khwājah Naṣīr to repeat his lecture. Khwājah Naṣīr asked, "Should I repeat your mistakes or what is right?" And he proceeded to give a full exposition of Ibn Sīnā's text and a critique of Quṭb al-Dīn al-Shīrāzī's lecture, thus demonstrating his knowledge of medicine (Tunikābunī (1985): 373). Quṭb al-Dīn Shīrāzī is reported to have arisen and given Khwājah Naṣīr his teaching chair.

Khwājah Naṣīr's simultaneous attention to both philosophy and the sciences, as well as his concurrent mastery of theology, dogmatics and mysticism, leads us to believe that nothing short of a full and comprehensive knowledge of whatever there was to know was his constant concern. It is rather remarkable that he produced at least nineteen treatises on mathematics (Ṣafā (1956–85), 3: 1.13–20) as well as an equal number of books and treatises on dogmatic theology. Yet the Persian philosopher/vizier produced all these and many other works while heading a vast administrative apparatus in charge of an empire.

WRITINGS IN PERSIAN

Although the majority of Khwājah Naṣīr's writings are in Arabic, a significant number were written in his mother-tongue, Persian. An important by-product of his writings is his contribution to the development of a rich Persian philosophical discourse (Bahār (1952), 3: 156–65; Ṣafā (1956–85), 3: 2.1203–5; Browne (1906), 2: 485–6; Rypka (1968): 313–14). His writings on logic, for example, were particularly consequential in enriching the Persian logical terminologies. His major work in logic, *Asās al-iqtibās*, was writen in Persian, and in it he gave a full Aristotelian account of logical categories. His writings in Persian not only established this language on solid ground for philosophical discourse, they also encouraged others, notably his students and contemporaries, to write in Persian. Quṭb al-Dīn al-Shīrāzī, Khwājah Naṣīr's most distinguished student/colleague, wrote his *Durrah al-tāj* in Persian. This encyclopedic summary of philosophical and theological topics made a major contribution to the further expansion of Persian technical vocabularies. The seventh/thirteenth century, in which Khwājah Naṣīr produced his major prose works, was a particularly prolific period in the flourishing of philosophical Persian prose (Khaṭībī (1956): 21; Mu'īn (1956): 30). Khwājah Naṣīr is believed to have made a major contribution to the development of technical Persian prose during this period (Khaṭībī (1956): 21; Mu'īn (1956): 30). Of more than one hundred books and treatises attributed to him, close to 25 per cent are in Persian. Nothing more needs to be said about his contribution to the development of philosophical prose in Persian. Ibn Sīnā's brief, however groundbreaking, attempt in the fifth/eleventh century to produce a *bona fide* Persian philosophical prose, evident in his *Dānish-nāmah* (Ibn Sīnā 1974abc), had left much to be desired. In both the quantity and quality of his Persian philosophical prose, Khwājah Naṣīr advanced the technical possibilities of this language to unprecedented degrees and thus significantly contributed to making Persian the second (after Arabic) most important language of the Islamic intellectual world.

In theoretical and practical philosophy, astronomy, mathematics, natural sciences, dogmatics, occult sciences, poetics, prosody, history, geography and Ismā'īlism, Khwājah Naṣīr produced a range of influential texts in Persian (Mu'īn (1956): 30–3), which forced non-Persian speakers interested in Islamic philosophy and sciences to learn the Persian vizier's mother-tongue. A remarkable aspect of Khwājah Naṣīr's Persian philosophical prose is that instead of coining Persian words to correspond to Arabic technical terminologies, like Ibn Sīnā, he, in effect, persianized the Arabic prose by assimilating it into an eloquent and fluent Persian diction following the model of Suhrawardī (Mu'īn (1956): 33). His *Asās al-iqtibās* in logic, his *Akhlāq-i nāṣirī* in ethics, his *Zīj-i īlkhānī* in astronomy, his *Risālah dar ḥisāb* in mathematics, his *Mi'yār al-ash'ār* in poetics and prosody, his brief addition to al-Juwaynī's *Tārīkh-i Jahāngushā* and his *Awṣāf al-ashrāf* in ethics, among many other books and treatises, are models of graceful and eloquent Persian prose.

THE GREAT CENTRES OF LEARNING

Khwājah Naṣīr's massive contribution to medieval Islamic philosophy, in both Arabic and Persian, must be understood in the context of the social and intellectual history of his times. The Mongol invasion of Islamic lands in the seventh/thirteenth century was a landmark in an intellectual history which by then had already produced and legitimated its major paradigmatic discourses. Despite the massive material devastation that the invasion caused, the enduring patterns of intellectual engagements survived and, in some respects, even flourished. From the remaining works of Rashīd al-Dīn Faḍl Allāh we can deduce (Mīnuwī (1955): 7–10) that Hūlāgū's conquest of medieval Persia was concomitant with remarkable activity in philosophical and scientific learning. Although many Muslim historians of the time lamented the destruction of the institutional bases of scholastic learning (Ṣafā (1959–85), 3: 1.206–7), the fact still remains that the rise of luminaries of Islamic philosophy such as Khwājah Naṣīr in the seventh/thirteenth century testifies to a certain degree of intellectual continuity between the pre- and post-Mongol periods.

Even the most important institutional bases of higher learning continued to function and flourish after the invasion. In 670/1271, the Niẓāmiyyah of Baghdad was renovated by 'Aṭā' Malik al-Juwaynī. In 727/1325, Ibn Baṭṭuṭah visited this school and admired its prosperity (Ibn Baṭṭūṭah (1969), 1: 242). The Mustanṣariyyah of Baghdad was also renovated in 668/1269 by 'Aṭā' Malik al-Juwaynī. There were other, less famous, schools in Baghdad, such as Madrasah Sharābiyyah (established in 628/1230 by Iqbāl al-Sharābī), Madrasah Mujāhidiyyah (established in 637/1239 by Mujāhid al-Dīn Atābak), Madrasah Bashīriyyah (established in 653/1255 by one of al-Mustanṣir's slaves) and Madrasah 'Iṣmatiyyah (established in 671/1272 by 'Aṭā' Malik al-Juwaynī's wife) (see Humā'ī (1984): 42). Closer to Khwājah Naṣīr's homeland, Ibn Baṭṭūṭah reports the existence and active operation of a number of scholastic centres in Shushtar, Nishapur and Mashhad (Ibn Baṭṭūṭah (1969), 1: *et passim*). In 640/1242, Mangū Qā'ān's mother established a school in Bukhara. The mausoleums of the Great Mongol warlords were also transformed into important and opulent centres of learning. We also know of "mobile schools", one of them associated with the army camp of Sultan Muḥammad Khudābandah. The library of this school was carried on mules and other animals (Ṣafā (1959–85), 3: 1.207–15).

Although these institutions of higher learning were by and large devoted to the study of one school of Islamic law or another, and philosophy, as such, was not taught there, still their existence indicates a thriving intellectual climate in which any other mode of scholastic learning was, if not condoned, then at least possible. The great urban centres of learning in the seventh/thirteenth century included Baghdad, Shiraz, Nishapur, Kirman and Tabriz. Added to these cosmopolitan centres of higher learning in the seventh/thirteenth century was Maraghah, where a thriving atmosphere of intellectual engagement was created around its famous observatory, thanks to Khwājah Naṣīr, who invited the leading scholars of his time to that centre. Immediately related to these varied institutions of higher learning is an abundance of "textbooks" in any number of disciplines. Titles such as *mukhtaṣar* ("summary") and *tajrīd* ("principles"), of which Khwājah Naṣīr has a number in his oeuvre, indicate the transformation of a debating discourse into an established pedagogical one. These transformations simultaneously consolidated earlier philosophical reflections into doctrinal positions. Khwājah Naṣīr's *Sharḥ al-ishārāt*, *Taḥrīr al-majisṭī* and *Taḥrīr al-uqlīdus* fall into this category. The consolidation of enduring philosophical issues into principles of doctrinal beliefs is also evident in a decree issued in 645/1247 by the caliph, in which the professors at Mustanṣariyyah were prohibited from teaching their own texts. They had, according to this caliphal decree, to use only the canonical sources of the masters (Ṣafā: 236–7).

THE MARĀGHAH OBSERVATORY

As historians of exact sciences have noted (Kennedy (1968): 672), "the installations at Marāghah set up by Naṣīr al-Dīn under the patronage of Hūlāgū can be called the first astronomical observatory in the full sense of the term". According to Rashīd al-Dīn Faḍl Allāh, when Hūlāgū came to Persia, he brought with him a group of Chinese philosophers, physicians and astronomers (Jahn (1971): 21–2). He instructed Khwājah Naṣīr to incorporate the Chinese astrological knowledge into his before he prepared the famous *Zīj-i īlkhānī*. According to Rashīd al-Dīn, Khwājah Naṣīr learned everything that the Chinese scholar knew in two days (Jahn (1971): 21–2; and Tafel 2 of the "Persische Version aus der Bibliothek des Topkapi Sirayi", Hazine, Nr 1653).

In 658/1259, the observatory began to function as a major scientific centre under Khwājah Naṣīr's directorship (Sāyilī (1956): 58). "The professional staff included about twenty well-known scientists drawn from many parts of the Islamic world, and at least one Chinese mathematician" (Kennedy (1968): 672). The Maraghah Observatory thus became one of the greatest centres of higher learning during this period, a centre which was of Khwājah Naṣīr's own making. The observatory, built and operated under Khwājah Naṣīr's authority, was a remarkable institution dedicated not just to astronomical but especially to mathematical and philosophical learning (Sāyilī (1956): 58–9). Scholars and students from all over the Islamic lands gathered there to engage in scientific and philosophical studies. Khwājah Naṣīr's reputation in mathematical and astronomical studies preceded the Mongol invasion of Iran. Mangū Qā'ān, Hūlāgū's brother, had originally asked his brother to send Khwājah Naṣīr to Mongolia to establish an observatory there (Rashīd al-Dīn Faḍl Allāh (1959), 2: 718; Mudarris Raḍawī (1955): 27; Sāyilī (1956): 58), but, following Hūlāgū's victory over the Ismā'īlīs, the Mongol warlord decided to keep the Persian astronomer with him. In 657/1258, Khwājah Naṣīr was given full authority and financial resources by Hūlāgū to build the Marāghah Observatory. Having full control over religious endowments under Hūlāgū's authority, Khwājah Naṣīr, in effect, turned the Marāghah Observatory into a cosmopolitan centre of research and education in a range of intellectual disciplines, from philosophy to mathematics and astronomy. Although Hūlāgū's interest in the Marāghah Observatory could not have gone much beyond astrological inquiries into the proper time of doing any number of activities, the functions of the centre far exceeded those limited objectives.

Khwājah Naṣīr persuaded Hūlāgū to build the observatory in Marāghah patently to inform the Mongol warlord of astrological events affecting his future. With the financial resources at his disposal, Khwājah Naṣīr hired a local architect, Fakhr al-Dīn Aḥmad ibn 'Uthmān Amīn al-Marāghī, to build the observatory. Hūlāgū had ordered the finances of the observatory to be arranged through the religious endowments (Sāyilī (1956): 61). At Khwājah Naṣīr's invitation, scientists from Damascus, Mawṣil, Baghdad, Tiblisi, Qazvin, and Shiraz joined him in Marāghah. Construction of the observatory began in 657/1258 and was completed in 660/1261 (Mudarris Raḍawī (1955): 28). Having convinced Hūlāgū to build this observatory, Khwājah Naṣīr also recorded his concern that observation and preparation of astronomical charts (*raṣad*) would take at least thirty years if not more, while the Mongol patron was impatient and had ordered him to finish them in twelve (*ibid*.: 29). Khwājah Naṣīr then proceeded by taking advantage of previous astronomical charts in order to construct his own.

Adjacent to the observatory, Khwājah Naṣīr built a library that, according to some reports (Mudarris Raḍawī (1955): 31), contained some forty thousand volumes, a good number of which were, in fact, taken from libraries in Baghdad, Damascus and Mawṣil. He also dispatched couriers to other parts of the Muslim world to procure and send books as well as various tools for astronomical observations. During his own trips he collected books and instruments for the Marāghah Observatory library. The observatory was financed entirely by the proceedings of the religious endowments under Hūlāgū's control. Khwājah Naṣīr was personally in charge of collecting one-tenth of these proceedings and spending the money as he saw fit on financing the construction, collecting the library and paying the salaries of the scientists who worked in the observatory (*ibid*.: 32).

It is suggested (Sāyilī (1956): 61) that Khwājah Naṣīr's unprecedented way of having the Marāghah Observatory financed by religious endowments established a norm that was followed by many subsequent scientific institutions. If the report was true that some ten per cent of the proceedings of the religious endowments was dedicated to the Marāghah Observatory – or more realistically to all scientific institutions (*ibid*.: 62) – this would indicate a remarkable way of institutionalizing scientific research that was relatively immune from the whimsical vicissitudes of the political and religious authorities. The solid financial foundation of the Marāghah Observatory was instrumental in its long historical endurance, as well as its character not only as a research but also as a teaching institution (*ibid*.: 65). The course of study was not limited to astronomy but included mathematical and other related sciences. Both Hūlāgū and Khwājah Naṣīr died before the astronomical observations of Marāghah could be completed. But for years the observatory functioned as a central institution of mathematical and astronomical (and then, by extension, philosophical) studies.

The significance of the Marāghah Observatory and the scientific research carried out there under the general directorship of Khwājah Naṣīr is just beginning to be acknowledged (Saliba (1987): 370). Particularly in the field of astronomy, the role of the observatory has now been recognized as "a scientific revolution before the renaissance" (*ibid.*: 361). Based on scientific research carried out during the preceding two or three centuries, the group of scientists who gathered in north-western Persia in the seventh/thirteenth century launched what has now been recognized as "the Marāghah School Revolution" (*ibid.*: 366) in Ptolemaic astronomy. Fundamental theoretical and methodological changes were made in Ptolemaic astronomy by this group of scientists that Khwājah Naṣīr brought together in Marāghah (Nasr 1976a; Saliba 1987).

THE EXACT SCIENCES

As the head of the Marāghah Observatory, Khwājah Naṣīr himself contributed heavily to all branches of "exact sciences" directly related to astronomy. His *Kitāb shikl al-qitā'*, completed in 658/1260 (Kennedy (1968): 666–7), is a landmark in mathematics, trigonometry and computational mathematics. This text has been credited as "the first treatment of trigonometry . . . as such" (*ibid.*: 667). Historians of science also maintain that "until the work of Naṣīr al-Dīn, trigonometric techniques were closely associated with problems in spherical astronomy. This did not cease in his time or later, but his book makes no reference to astronomy and marks the emergence of trigonometry as a branch of pure mathematics" (*ibid.*). In other related areas, Khwājah Naṣīr's contribution is equally recognized: "The apogee of Islamic work in computational mathematics did not occur until the Tīmurīd period, but steady progress in the field was maintained during the twelfth and thirteenth centuries. As an illustration we cite the table of the tangent function which appears in the *Zīj-i īlkhānī* turned out at Naṣīr al-Dīn's Marāghah observatory" (*ibid.*)

Khwājah Naṣīr's trigonometrical work on the complete quadrilateral is also distinguished in the history of mathematics for having "demonstrated the commutative property of multiplication between pairs of ratios (i.e., real numbers)" (Kennedy (1968): 664). But perhaps Khwājah Naṣīr's greatest contribution to exact sciences is his works on astronomy and, in particular, planetary theory. As a historian of science has noted, "until

Il-Khanid times no one seems to have produced a model capable of competing with Ptolemy's in terms of accuracy, and which would at the same time involve only uniform circular motions. Such a development was, however, inaugurated by Naṣīr al-Dīn Ṭūsī and carried through by associates of his at Marāghah observatory" (*ibid.*: 669). The development of the so-called "Ṭūsī-couple" in the history of planetary theory is a mark of Khwājah Naṣīr's achievement. Khwājah Naṣīr "seems to have been the first to notice that if one circle rolls around inside the circumference of another, the second circle having twice the radius of the first, then any point on the periphery of the first circle describes a diameter of the second. This ruling device can also be regarded as a linkage of two equal and constant length vectors rotating at constant speed (one twice as fast as the other), and hence has been called a *Ṭūsī-Couple*" (*ibid.*). The astronomical studies carried out in Marāghah institutionalized Khwājah Naṣīr's scientific achievements beyond the immediate vicinity. Quṭb al-Dīn Shīrāzī, Khwājah Naṣīr's student/associate in Marāghah, "long after he had left Marāghah . . . produced [a planetary] configuration [which] satisfies all the conditions demanded by Ptolemy for the orbit of Mercury, and as such probably marks the apex of the techniques developed by the Marāghah School" (*ibid.*).

Khwājah Naṣīr's masterpiece, the *Zīj-i īlkhānī*, originally written in Persian, was translated into Arabic, a phenomenal event in and of itself, considerably modifying the primacy of Arabic as the scientific language of the medieval Muslim world. The scientific research carried out in Marāghah under Khwājah Naṣīr was also exported, translated and copied by scholars in the Byzantine Empire, China and India (Kennedy (1968): 678). It had great significance not only for later scientific thought but for philosophy as well.

THE GENERAL CONDITION OF PHILOSOPHY

Beyond specific advancements in various fields of the "exact sciences", an unanticipated consequence of the Mongol invasion in the seventh/thirteenth century was a more advantageous position for philosophical inquiry unhindered by theological dogmatism. The decline of the central political authority equally weakened the position of the juridical establishment and, in turn, gave a freer domain to philosophical investigation. But the innate hostility of the mystical discourse to the rationalistic dimension of philosophy continued relentlessly. Sayf al-Dīn Muḥammad Farghānī, the seventh/thirteenth–eighth/fourteenth-century Sufi poet, captured the essence of his generation's anti-philosophical sentiments:

O thou the nightingale in the garden of reason!
Sweet-talking parrot of reason!
Upon thee the reign of reason!
In thy hands the reign of reason!
The barber of thy logic hath
Admired the women of reason. . . .
Love! the delicate face of the law
Scratch thee not with the nails of reason.
Thou thinkst that of truth there is
A marrow to the bone of reason.
But upon the Table of Wisdom is
So tasteless the bread of reason. . . .
Upon the sacred realm thou shall not
Reach from the ladder of reason.
There the strong rope of faith, why
Are thee tied to the thread of reason?
Describe the Muḥammadan speech!
How long would you describe the reason?
Walk on the highway of Muḥammad's path
Not on the bandits of reason. . . .
Make thy heart's ear deaf to
The language of Ibn Sīnā's reason. . . .
(Ṣafā (1959–85), 3: 1.233–5)

The condemnation of philosophy in this period was not limited to the Sufis. Even Ibn Khaldūn considered engagement in philosophical matters a waste of time, particularly because "[T]he harm they can do to religion is great" (Ibn Khaldūn (1958) 3: 246). All these oppositions to philosophical inquiries are still to be understood in light of the fact that Islamic philosophy was irrevocably connected to the metaphysical doctrines of the faith and their logical validities were never seriously questioned. The catalytic effect of philosophy on both religious dogmatics and Sufism was such that, even when under fire from its historical opponents, philosophy had still triumphed in establishing the level, nature and organization of intellectual discourse. The systematization of juridical, theological and even mystical doctrines in the seventh/thirteenth century was influenced considerably by their inevitable proximity to the philosophical discourse. The systemization of the principles of jurisprudence by Qāḍī al-Bayḍāwī (d. 685/1286) and 'Allāmah al-Ḥillī (648/1250–726/1325), the codification of Shī'ī law by Muḥaqqiq al-Ḥillī (602/1205–676/1277) and the consolidation of Sufi doctrines by Muḥyī al-Dīn ibn 'Arabī (d. 638/1240) all owed the underlying force of their discourse to the long tradition of philosophical problematics with which they relentlessly took issue.

Perhaps the most significant feature of philosophy in the seventh/thirteenth century is the consolidation of the Ibn Sīnan philosophy through Khwājah Naṣīr's extremely influential commentary. He resuscitated and re-systematized Ibn Sīnan philosophy, as he did any number of other sub-disciplines, in an effective and enduring discourse that perpetuated the ideas of the master of Islamic Peripatetic philosophy for generations to come. The circulation of philosophical texts was limited to a close hermeneutic circle of trusted affiliates. Unless Ṣadr al-Dīn Qūnawī had sent his book to Khwājah Naṣīr, the distinguished philosopher/vizier would not have had a personal copy of it (al-Ṭūsī (1966): 166). Or Khwājah Naṣīr himself wrote his ethical treatise *Aghāz wa anjām* following the personal appeal of one of his close students/followers (al-Ṭūsī (1987): 1).

KHWĀJAH NAṢĪR'S PHILOSOPHY

It was under such circumstances that Khwājah Naṣīr produced his influential works on philosophy. He was the most distinguished representative of Peripatetic philosophy following the Mongol invasion while being at the same time well acquainted with *ishrāqī* doctrines. His principal achievement was the consolidation of Ibn Sīnan philosophy against considerable hostility, launched chiefly by such mystically oriented poets as Sayf al-Faraqānī, who, in referring to Ibn Sīnā's *al-Ishārāt wa'l-tanbīhāt*, believed that

> The good tidings of the Righteous did not reach
> The person who followed Ibn Sīnā's *Ishārāt.*
> (Ṣafā (1959–85), 3: 1.253)

SHARḤ AL-ISHĀRĀT

Perhaps the most significant philosophical text of Khwājah Naṣīr in defence of the Ibn Sīnan Peripatetic tradition is his commentary on *al-Ishārāt wa'l-tanbīhāt*, one of the last works, if not the last (Malikshāhī in Ibn Sīnā (1984): 7, 21; Maḥmūd (1985): 382; Ṣalība (1986): 215), of Ibn Sīnā. The text is a concise treatise on philosophy, but perhaps the most remarkable aspect of *al-Ishārāt* is its last three chapters, in which "the Master of Peripatetic Philosophy" discusses aspects of Islamic mysticism. Imām Fakhr al-Rāzī (d. 606/1209), who wrote one of the most critical commentaries on *al-Ishārāt*, could not help but praise this section as the best systematization of Sufism ever composed (Malikshāhī in Ibn Sīnā (1984): 7).

After a preliminary section on logic, *al-Ishārāt wa'l-tanbīhāt* is divided into three sections on physics, metaphysics and mysticism. The first section consists of three chapters on the physical world and the epistemological possibilities of understanding it. The second section consists of four chapters on the metaphysics of being. The final, third, section, consists of three chapters on "Bliss and Happiness", "The Stations of the Mystics" and finally "The Secrets of the Divine Manifestations", which is an explanation of extraordinary events such as abstinence from food by the mystics, etc.

Ibn Sīnā's *al-Ishārāt wa'l-tanbīhāt* is an exceptionally rich philosophical text which he wrote later in his life; and it represents his philosophical statements at their maturest stage. Although it initially follows the standard Peripatetic divisions of his own works into logic, physics and metaphysics, it concludes with an excursion into an "Illuminationist" discourse in which mystical and other "non-rational" phenomena are discussed (Fakhry (1983): 160). The appeal of this seminal text to Islamic philosophers ought to be seen precisely in its attempt to link principles of Peripatetic philosophy, with their firm foundations in Aristotelian logic, through an adaptation of Neoplatonic doctrines, to reflections on intuitive knowledge that permit the possibility of both a revelatory language and a prophetic intermediary – the two chief requirements of philosophical engagements in an Islamic context. Ibn Sīnā arrives at the possibility of intuitive knowledge as a form superior, or at least complementary, to the discursive. The agency of intuitive knowledge is the active intellect, to whose power the lower faculties of memory, imagination and conception yield. Through the agency of active intellect, the soul surpasses the realm of generation and decay, touches the source of illumination or *ishrāq*, and reaches the full recognition of the First Principle. "The active intellect as an emanation from this first principle serves in this process simply as a subordinate link in the chain of being, linking man to his Maker and God" (Fakhry (1983): 162).

As the progression of chapters and sections in *al-Ishārāt wa'l-tanbīhāt* indicates, Ibn Sīnā advances from the world of the visible to that of the invisible in an attempt to reach for a universal understanding of being. The concluding chapters on mysticism are to be seen as an attempt by the master Peripatetic philosopher to incorporate a form of knowledge generated and sustained as legitimate by generations of Muslim mystics. By the fifth/eleventh century, no serious Muslim philosopher could have reached for a universal statement on being, and the understanding of it, without incorporating the theoretical dimensions of mysticism as a *bona fide* mode of cognition and perception.

The progression of sections from physics to metaphysics or vice versa is a critical ontological issue in Ibn Sīnan texts. Whereas in *al-Ishārāt wa'l-tanbīhāt* Ibn Sīnā first discusses physics and then metaphysics, in the *Dānish-nāmah-yi 'alā'ī* he reverses the order and first introduces metaphysics and then discusses physics. In his introduction to the section on logic of the *Dānish-nāmah*, he asserts that "I have thus decided that once the section of logic is concluded, I shall proceed to begin with the First Science [*'ilm-i barīn* = metaphysics] and gradually reach for the lower (secondary) sciences (*'ilmhā-yi zīrīn*), contrary to what is habitual and customary" (Ibn Sīnā (1974a): 4). Since, in both physics and metaphysics, Ibn Sīnā's primary concerns are both epistemological and ontological, the progression from metaphysics to physics would postulate the primacy of Being as such over specific cases of being, while the progression from physics to metaphysics suggests the specificity of physical beings as case studies of the metaphysical Being, which is the highest and most irreducible condition to be understood. As Khwājah Naṣīr would later indicate in his commentary on Ibn Sīnā's *al-Ishārāt wa'l-tanbīhāt*, while the understanding of physical beings is achieved through our sense perceptions (*al-maḥsūsāt*), the understanding of the metaphysical Being is attained through acts of intellection (*al-ma'qūlat*) (see Malikshāhī in Ibn Sīnā (1984): 22).

As is quite evident from Ibn Sīnā's concluding remarks in *al-Ishārāt wa'l-tanbīhāt*, he had intended this text to be read by a philosophical elite. "O Brother", Ibn Sīnā states,

> in this *al-Ishārāt*, I have prepared for you the most noble Truth. . . . Thus protect it from the ignorant people, and the vulgar, and those who have not been given an intelligent disposition, and the cowardly who side with the populace, or those unbelievers who pretend to be philosophers. . . . But if you find a righteous and good-natured person, with moral rectitude, cautious in what temptation propels [us] to [think or do], observant of the Truth with absolute contentment and veracity, then give him what he asks from this book in gradation, piece by piece, using your discretion – so that every preceding piece encourages him to take what is to come next. Then swear him by God and by [his] faith not to transgress and follow your commitment and be like you [in transmitting this text to others]. God will judge between you and me if you disseminate or corrupt this knowledge. And God is Sufficient in delegating Judgment.
>
> (Ibn Sīnā (1984): 492)

Despite Ibn Sīnā's warnings and caution, *al-Ishārāt wa'l-tanbīhāt* became an exceedingly successful text and many commentaries were written on it. But the two most famous and influential commentaries were written in succession by Imām Fakhr al-Dīn Muḥammad ibn 'Umar al-Rāzī (d. 606/1209) and Khwājah Naṣīr.

Imām Fakhr al-Dīn al-Rāzī, an Ash'arite theologian, had written his critical commentary on Ibn Sīnā's *al-Ishārāt wa'l-tanbīhāt* towards the end of the sixth/twelfth century. In 644/1246 Khwājah Naṣīr completed his commentary on the treatise in which he answered, among other things, all the major objections raised by Imām Fakhr, calling his treatise a "diatribe not a commentary" (Fakhry (1983): 310). There thus developed a significant hermeneutic nexus between Ibn Sīnā's *al-Ishārāt wa'l-tanbīhāt* and the two successive commentaries of Imām Fakhr and Khwājah Naṣīr that for generations preoccupied Islamic philosophers. A century after Khwājah Naṣīr, his principal student, 'Allāmah Quṭb al-Dīn al-Shīrāzī (d. 710/1310), encouraged Quṭb al-Dīn al-Rāzī (d. 766/1364) to write *Kitāb al-muḥākimāt bayn sharḥ al-ishārāt*, completed in 755/1373, in which the judgments of the two commentators were composed, contrasted and evaluated. Later on, other commentators in turn reflected on al-Rāzī's own judgment (Ṣafā (1959–85), 3: 1.253–4). More contemporary philosophers of Khwājah Naṣīr's era were equally encouraged and influenced by his commentary on Ibn Sīnā and wrote their own exegeses on *al-Ishārāt wa'l-tanbīhāt*. Among these are the commentaries of Burhān al-Dīn Muḥammad Nasafī, Sarāj al-Dīn Urmawī, and Ibn Kammūnah.

It has been said of Khwājah Naṣīr's commentary on Ibn Sīnā that it is

> a remarkable achievement in precision, veracity and resolution of difficult passages. [Khwājah Naṣīr] was particularly [remarkable] in the beauty of his diction, and this is something to which [his] predecessors did not pay that much attention. They have primarily paid attention to the content. Yet the Khwājah adopted a particular dictum in writing that would make comprehension of the content easy. There is no trace of unnecessary concepts or difficult words in his diction.
>
> (Ṣafā (1959–85), 3: 1.254)

In *Sharḥ al-ishārāt*, Khwājah Naṣīr's principal concern is to elucidate Ibn Sīnā's philosophical positions and to defend them against Imām Fakhr al-Rāzī's criticisms. Occasionally he does take issue with Ibn Sīnā and prefers the position of Suhrawardī or Abu'l-Barakāt al-Baghdādī. More generally, some ten points of divergence have been identified (Mudarris Raḍawī (1955): 185–95) between Ibn Sīnā and Khwājah Naṣīr: they concern the nature of God's knowledge, the number of principal spheres, the reality of place, the createdness and pre-eternity of the physical world, the independent existence of the intellect, acquisitive and theoretical knowledge, the nature of the body, the possibility of repentance, the nature of divine punishment and finally the nature of faith.

Fakhr al-Dīn al-Rāzī's assault against Ibn Sīnā's *al-Ishārāt wa'l-tanbīhāt* was launched from an essentially Ash'arite theological position. Al-Rāzī maintains that the doctrinal principles of the faith can be "proved" theologically without any substantial need for philosophy. While Khwājah Naṣīr praises Fakhr al-Dīn al-Rāzī's rhetorical act of disputation, he believes that al-Rāzī greatly exaggerates his criticism, "and the limit of moderation has been transgressed in the criticism of his [Ibn Sīnā's] principles. Thus, despite all his endeavours, [Fakhr al-Dīn al-Rāzī] has done nothing but slander, and that is why some shrewd observers have called his 'commentary' [*sharḥ*] a 'diatribe' [*jarḥ*]" (as quoted by Malikshāhī in Ibn Sīnā (1984): 30).

Khwājah Naṣīr's commentary on *al-Ishārāt wa'l-tanbīhāt* commences with lofty praise for the significance of theoretical philosophy. The significance of such early philosophers as Ibn Sīnā in having established the foundations of philosophical discourse is matched by that of the later philosophers in explicating and summarizing their original ideas for others (al-Ṭūsī (1983), 1: 2). Ibn Sīnā's *al-Ishārāt wa'l-tanbīhāt* is, as its title ("Allusions and Indications") implies, particularly condensed and concise, much in need of explanatory commentary. It includes "allusions to extremely important issues, filled with references to crucial questions, full of jewels like bezels, words most of which are canonical. It contains miraculous statements in concise phrases, solid assertions in exciting words, to understand their far-reaching meanings great efforts have had to be made, and yet high hopes have fallen short of grasping its fullest depths" (as quoted by Malikshāhī in Ibn Sīnā (1984): 31).

Khwājah Naṣīr's commentary on Ibn Sīnā's *al-Ishārāt wa'l-tanbīhāt*, which he wrote at the insistence of the Ismā'īlī prince, Muḥtasham Shahāb al-Dīn Abu'l-Fatḥ al-Manṣūr (Malikshāhī in Ibn Sīnā (1984): 32), was intended primarily as an explanatory exegesis on Peripatetic philosophy, rather than an exposition of his own ideas on the subject. He is primarily interested in saving the Ibn Sīnan text from Imām Fakhr al-Rāzī's attack (Mudarris Raḍawī (1975): 433). He has intervened only "two or three times" (*ibid.*) with his own ideas. The sources of his commentary, as he indicates in his own introduction, are Imām Fakhr al-Rāzī's commentary, as well as a number of other (written and oral) exegetical works on Ibn Sīnā's text. Khwājah Naṣīr deliberately commits himself not to criticize Ibn Sīnā in matters he finds objectionable but to stick relentlessly to an explanatory discourse, "because I believe that 'commentary' [*al-taqrīr*] is different from 'refutation' [*al-radd*] and 'exegesis' [*al-tafsīr*] separate from a critique [*al-naqd*]" (al-Ṭūsī (1983), 1: 2).

As is evident from the conclusion of his commentary on *al-Ishārāt wa'l-tanbīhāt*, Khwājah Naṣīr wrote this explanatory text in defence of Ibn Sīnā's philosophical discourse under severe personal pressure. His residence with the Ismāʿīlī princes had apparently become intolerable. "I wrote most of this book," Khwājah Naṣīr writes at the end of his commentary,

> in a difficult condition more difficult than which is not possible . . ., in a time every portion of which was an occasion for sorrow and unbearable difficulty, remorse and great sadness. Every moment I dwelled in a hellish fire . . . no time passed without my eyes in tears, my condition distressed. I did not have a moment without my sorrows increased, my hardship and sadness intensified. Indeed, as the poet says in Persian:
>
> As far as I can see around me,
> Calamity is a ring and I its bezel. . . .
>
> God Almighty! By your chosen Prophet and his successor [ʿAlī] al-Murtaḍā, rescue me from the hardship of the onslaught of calamity and the intensity of the waves of hardship! Save me from that in which is my calamity! God, there is only Thou and Thou art the most compassionate of all!"
>
> (al-Ṭūsī (1983), 2: 145)

Khwājah Naṣīr's commentary on *al-Ishārāt wa'l-tanbīhāt* was itself the subject of many subsequent commentaries by ʿAllāmah al-Ḥillī (d. 726/1325), Quṭb al-Dīn Muḥammad al-Rāzī (d. 766/1364), Ẓahīr al-Dīn Ḥusayn al-Hamadānī (d. 1066/1655), and Aqā Ḥusayn Khwānsārī (d. 1099/1687), among others (Mudarris Raḍawī (1975): 434–5).

A "VISIONARY RECITAL"

A representative passage in Khwājah Naṣīr's *Sharḥ al-ishārāt* is his discussion of an Ibn Sīnan "visionary recital" is called *Salāmān and Absāl* (al-Ṭūsī (1983), 2: 101–4). "Visionary Recitals" is a generic title that Henry Corbin has given to a general symbolic literature in Persian and Arabic that includes Ibn Sīnā's *Ḥayy ibn Yaqẓān*, *The Bird* and *Salāmān and Absāl* (Corbin 1980). It is with the last recital that the name of Khwājah Naṣīr is also associated. There are two treatises with the title of *Salāmān and Absāl* in Islamic symbolic literature: one is a translation from a Greek original by Ḥunayn ibn Isḥāq (d. 260/873); and the other is by Ibn Sīnā. The Ibn Sinān version we have only through its abridgement and commentary by Khwājah Naṣīr. Some twenty years after he finished his commentary on Ibn Sīnā's *Ishārāt* (al-Ṭūsī (1983), 2: 102; Corbin (1980): 205), Khwājah Naṣīr accidentally found this treatise of Ibn Sīnā's. He included a summary and a commentary of this treatise in his commentary on Ibn Sīnā's *Ishārāt* (al-Ṭūsī (1983), 2: 101–4). That the recital is actually Ibn Sīnā's is evident by his own reference in the *Ishārāt* (Ibn Sīnā (1981): 172) and by Khwājah Naṣīr's attribution of it (al-Ṭūsī (1983), 2: 101). Whereas, in an earlier commentary, Fakhr al-Dīn Rāzī took Salāmān for Adam and Absāl for Paradise (*ibid.*: 101–2), Khwājah Naṣīr modified this view and took Salāmān for the mystical seeker, or *ṭālib*, and Absāl for the mystical object of desire, or *maṭlūb*. Thus both medieval and modern (Corbin (1980): 208; Pūrnāmdārīān (1985): 170, 310, 311, 349, 361) commentators of *Salāmān and Absāl* have taken it as a mystical commentary particularly useful for deciphering the latter part of Ibn Sīnā's *al-Ishārāt*, where he discusses "the stations of the gnostics".

In Khwājah Naṣīr's broad outline, Salāmān and Absāl are two brothers. Salāmān is the king and Absāl his handsome, erudite and devoted brother. Salāmān's wife is madly in love with Absāl. When all her designs to have Absāl fail, she has her servants poison him. Absāl dies, and Salāmān punishes his wife and her servants by forcing them to drink from the same poison. Even in this broad outline, there are powerful elements of a brilliant drama in the story of *Salāmān and Absāl*. That it has been relentlessly subjected to vigorous mystical readings, most recently and comprehensively by Henry Corbin (1980: 226–41) and Pūrnāmdārīān (1985: 300–47), does not exhaust the story of its direct and powerful dramatic effects. Khwājah Naṣīr's brisk identification of Salāmān with "the rational soul" or "the speaking soul", Absāl with "the theoretical intellect" and Salāmān's wife with "bodily power which induces man to lust and anger", etc. are all artificial, without any inner-textual anchorage, and as such remain at a perfunctory and conventional level. There is no innate or integral reason to the story to force it to be thus decoded. As it stands in its direct, passionate, and relentlessly physical narrative, *Salāmān and Absāl* is in no need of mystical interpretation. Corbin's equally perfunctory codification of the story in mystical terms fails to be in any significant way convincing or insightful for those not attracted to the symbolic significance of the text. Both Khwājah Naṣīr's and Corbin's mystical readings demand a long leap of faith from the reader which is by no stretch of the imagination evident or warranted in the external meaning of the text itself. As it stands, Khwājah Naṣīr's rendition of Ibn Sīnā's *Salāmān and Absāl* operates at a particularly powerful level of physical narrative. Salāmān's gullible simplicity in letting his aggressive and mischievous wife connive to have her brother-in-law is particularly pronounced next to the sincere and innocent nobility of Absāl. Despite all temptations, Absāl remains loyal to his brother, resists all the advances of his sister-in-law, and ultimately pays with his life. But perhaps the strongest and most powerful character in this story is Salāmān's wife who, unfortunately, lacks a name. Even so, she abounds in character, will, determination and wit. The two brothers are inveterate weaklings compared to her. She is determined, unfaltering, wilful, aggressive and conniving in the most positive and life-affirming sense of the terms. The *ménage à trois* thus created, excluding Salāmān's wife's sister (who also does not have a name), sustains a powerful, passionate and relentlessly physical sense of reality with its own brilliance and vigour irrespective of whatever mystical meaning is given to it.

OTHER PHILOSOPHICAL TEXTS

Khwājah Naṣīr's philosophical texts – aside from *Sharḥ al-ishārāt* – include *Aqsām al-ḥikmah, Baqā' al-nafs, Jabr wa ikhtiyār, Rabṭ al-ḥādith bi'l-qadīm, Rawḍah al-qulūb, Akhlāq-i muḥtashamī, Akhlāq-i nāṣirī, Sharḥ-i ithbat-i 'aql, al-'Ilal wa'l-ma'lūlāt, al-'Ilm al-iktisābī, Kayfiyyāt al-ṣudūr al-mawjūdāt* and his correspondence with Najm al-Dīn Dabīrān (d. 675/1276).

LOGIC

Perhaps Khwājah Naṣīr's most significant contribution to seventh/thirteenth-century intellectual history is his writings on logic. His major work in logic is *Asās al-iqtibās*, which he finished in 642/1244 (Mudarris Raḍawī (1955): 240). *Asās al-iqtibās* (al-Ṭūsī 1947) contains nine chapters: "Isagoge", "The Ten Categories", "Hermeneutics", "Prior Analytics: Deduction", "Posterior Analytics: Proof", "Dialectics", "Sophistics", "Rhetorics" and "Poetics". The book was originally written in Persian; and a contemporary of Khwājah Naṣīr, a certain Rukn al-Dīn Muḥammad ibn 'Alī al-Fārsī al-Astarābādī, translated it into Arabic (the same person also translated Khwājah Naṣīr's *Awṣāf al-ashrāf* from Persian to Arabic). Khwājah Naṣīr has a number of other shorter and less sophisticated treatises on logic. Among them is *Tajrīd al-manṭiq* (al-Ṭūsī 1988), which he wrote in Arabic (Mudarris Raḍawī (1955): 241). 'Allāmah Ḥillī wrote a commentary on this text.

On the significance of *Asās al-iqtibās* it has been suggested that "after the [section on] logic of Ibn Sīnā's *al-Shifā'*, this precious and unique book is the best and most comprehensive text composed in logic. Perhaps since the beginning of the translation and transference of rational sciences from Greek, no book has been composed in Persian with such detail, comprehensivity, and precision" (Mudarris Raḍawī in al-Ṭūsī (1947): 12. It has also been suggested that "Extrinsic considerations alone point to the significance and the eminent position of this text in the corpus of logic in the Peripatetic tradition of Islamic philosophy. But its deeper significance lies in the methodology to which Ṭūsī resorts in explaining 'substance' and its unusual display of his analytical ability, which enabled him to avoid difficulties inherent in some metaphysical approaches to this concept" (Morewedge (1973): 159).

In the classical Aristotelian/Ibn Sīnan tradition, Khwājah Naṣīr's *Asās al-iqtibās* begins with the Porphyrean "Introduction" and proceeds to present and discuss the eight Aristotelian sections on logic. But, as has been extensively demonstrated (Morewedge (1975): 165–77), Khwājah Naṣīr's work on logic becomes not just a comprehensive treatise on the subject but, more important, an analytical extension of the central problematic of "substance" in Islamic ontology.

ONTOLOGY

Khwājah Naṣīr's ontology is in the classical Ibn Sīnan tradition. "Being" (*wujūd*) is so universal that it is in no need of proof (al-Ṭūsī (1977): 389; al-Ṭūsī (1984a): 182–3). Every "being" is either "necessary" (*wājib*) or "contingent" (*mumkin*). If it is "necessary", it cannot not be. That which is "necessary" that it be is "the Necessary Being" (*wājib al-wujūd*). If it is a "contingent being", then it is by virtue of something else that it comes into being; and that "something else", in turn, is either "the Necessary Being" or itself another "contingent being". Khwājah Naṣīr's theology thus emerges from his ontology as does Ibn Sīnā's: no earthly beings can be "the Necessary Being", because they are either "accidents" (*'araḍ*) or "substances" (*jawhar*). "Accidents", by nature, are contingent upon something else, a substance; and "substances" are either "corporeal" (*jism*), and thus composite and corruptible, or "free from matter" or "abstract" (*mujarrad*); and whoever believes in non-material things intellectually and spiritually has no difficulty believing in such a non-material being as "the Necessary Being" (al-Ṭūsī (1977b): 380–90).

In another short essay, Khwājah Naṣīr discussed the problem of "being and non-being" (al-Ṭūsī (1957): 20–4). Building on a long tradition (see Dānishpazhūh's Introduction to al-Ṭūsī (1957): 11–19), he summarizes the two opposing positions of those who denied the existence of "non-being" (the so-called *nāfīyān*) and those who believed in the existence of "non-being" (the so-called *muthbitān*):

> You should know that men of knowledge have disagreed on whether the non-being [*ma'dūm*] is a thing [*shay'*] or not. By *ma'dūm* [non-being] they mean the possible-being [*jā'iz al-wujūd*]. The *nāfīyān* have maintained that non-being is not a thing. They have not distinguished between the possible-being [*jā'iz al-wujūd*] and the impossible-being [*mustaḥīl al-wujūd*]. They consider them both non-being. They have also disagreed

> in other respects: The *muthbitān* believe in an attribute which is neither being [*mawjūd*] nor non-being [*ma'dūm*]. They call that [attribute] disposition [*ḥālat*]. But the *nāfīyān* do not believe in an intermediary [state] between being and non-being. They have also disagreed [on the following issue]: The *muthbitān* consider the non-being, in its state of non-beingness, qualified by an attribute . . ., the *muthbitān* consider being a common feature among all existent-beings [*mawjūdāt*]. They also distinguish between ascertainment [*thubūt*] and being [*wujūd*], but not between being and non-being. They do not, however, distinguish between prohibition [*nafy*] and ascertainment [*ithbāt*]. The *nāfīyān*, on the other hand, consider the being of everything its essence [*dhāt*]. They do not distinguish between ascertainment and being. Thus the *muthbitān* consider all the essences – substances and accidents – present in pre-eternity, qualified with the attributes of genes, i.e., substance with substantiality, black with blackness, and yet not in-being [*mawjūd*]. [The *muthbitān* consider that] being is a disposition [*ḥālat*], i.e., it is neither being nor non-being. Thus the Actor, Great and Almighty that He is, qualified the essences with being, and that is the meaning of bringing-into-existence [*iḥdāth*] and bringing-into-being [*ījād*]. As for the *nāfīyān*, there was nothing permanent in pre-eternity except God. He created all the essences and attributes, and that the meaning of bringing-substance-into-existence [*iḥdāth-i jawhar*] is to bring substance into existence after it was not.
>
> (al-Ṭūsī (1957): 20)

Khwājah Naṣīr himself does not appear to favour one position over another. After a lengthy discussion of the various positions of those who believe that a non-being is a thing (*muthbitān*) and those who believe it is not (*nāfīyān*), he concludes that "when intelligent people think about this, they must accept what their mind accepts, and of course should not simply follow others" (al-Ṭūsī (1957): 24).

THEOLOGY

Khwājah Naṣīr is reported to have believed in the necessity of the rational proof for the existence of God for all believers until he met a simple peasant. "Is there one or two gods?" Khwājah Naṣīr is believed to have asked the peasant (Tunikābunī (1985): 375). "Just one", the peasant answers. "What would you do if someone were to tell you that there are two gods?" Khwājah Naṣīr asks. "I will split his head with this very shovel in my hand", the peasant responds. As with all other popular anecdotes about Khwājah Naṣīr, these stories underline the legendary proportions that the philosopher's tireless rational attitude has assumed. His most important text on theology is *Tajrīd al-'aqā'id*, also known as *Tajrīd al-i'tiqād* (Mudarris Raḍawī (1975): 422–33; Peters (1968): 198). He has a number of other shorter treatises on theology too (e.g., al-Ṭūsī (1991a)), including a concise treatise on God's oneness, *Ithbāt waḥdat Allāh jalla jalālahu*. The First Origin (*al-Mabda' al-awwal*) is that which nothing has preceded and to which there is no origin. That First Origin cannot be more than one because everything that is not one is many, and everything that is many consists of individual units, and every one of those units precedes that composite being and thus is an origin to it. Thus the First Origin is One and not many. The First Origin which lacks an origin cannot be a contingent being (*mumkin al-wujūd*) because every contingent being has an origin. Thus, from an extension of Khwājah Naṣīr's ontology to his theology, it is necessary for the First Origin to be a "Necessary Being" (*wājib al-wujūd*). The Necessary Being cannot consist of many things. Otherwise it would need constituent units and would have been in need of others. Therefore, it would not have been the Necessary Being. When things are existent, then it is necessary for them to be in existence. Had they not been in existence, then everything would have always been in a state of contingency, in need of an origin. In this order of causation, in order to avoid a vicious circle, it is necessary to have one reality, which is the cause to all effects, coming before them all. That is the First Origin which has no origin to it. The issuance (*ṣudūr*) of all existent beings is from that Origin. Finally, Khwājah Naṣīr concludes that this is what we intended to state in proving the "True One [*al-wāḥid al-ḥaqīqī*] who is the First Origin to all existent beings, exalted is His Being and sacred His Essence and Attributes" (al-Ṭūsī (1984a): 183).

But no other text of Khwājah Naṣīr has been as influential as *Tajrīd al-i'tiqād* in Shī'ī theology. In it he summarized the principles of Shī'ī theology in six concise treatises and permanently consolidated the level of discourse in this branch of Shī'ī canonical learning. The first treatise of this book establishes the general principles governing Shī'ī theology, the second treatise is on substances (*jawāhir*) and accidents (*'arāḍ*), the third on proving the Creator and His Attributes, the fourth on Prophethood, the fifth on Imāmate, and the sixth on resurrection. *Tajrīd al-i'tiqād* became the canonical text of Shī'ī theology for many generations; and considerable number of commentaries were written on it (Mudarris Raḍawī (1975): 422–33). The commentaries of Shams al-Dīn Muḥammad Isfarāyinī Bayhaqī, a contemporary of Khwājah Naṣīr, 'Allāmah Ḥillī (d. 726/1325), Shams al-Iṣfahānī (d. 746/1345) and 'Alā' al-Dīn Qūshjī (d. 879/1474) are among the most important on Khwājah Naṣīr's text. Mīr Sayyid Sharīf al-Jurjānī's (d. 816/1413) commentary was so influential that it became a textbook of Shīʿī theology. But perhaps the most influential commentary has been ʿAllāmah al-Ḥillī's *Kashf al-murād fi sharḥ tajrīd al-iʿtiqād* (al-Ṭūsī (1977b) or (1988)).

Khwājah Naṣīr has a number of other theological treatises attributed to him. *Al-Iʿtiqādāt* was written with a larger audience in mind than that intended in *Tajrīd al-iʿtiqād*. The two treatises of *Ithbāt-i wājib* and *al-Fuṣūl al-nāṣiriyyah* were written in Persian for the benefit of those who could not read his Arabic texts.

Iʿtiqādiyyah, a short treatise by Khwājah Naṣīr on the principal dogmas of Shīʿī belief, is a concise summary of what the Shīʿī philosopher thought the believers had to hold indubitable. A Shīʿī believer had to uphold as a minimum that there is no divinity but Allah and that Muḥammad is His messenger. Upon testifying to the truthfulness of the messenger, the believer had to accept the Attributes of God Almighty and believe in the Last Day. Belief in the infallible Imām is equally mandatory for the Shīʿī believer. All these principles, Khwājah Naṣīr insists, are included in the Qur'ān and thus are in no need of proof. Belief in the Day of Judgment necessitates a simultaneous belief in Paradise and Hell and in accountability for righteous and evil acts committed in this world. God's Attributes, which ought to be acknowledged, are that He is Alive, Omniscient, Omnipotent and Speaking. There is nothing like Him. He hears and sees. It is not necessary for a believer to ascertain the pre-eternality or createdness-in-time (*qidam* or *ḥudūth*) of God's Attributes. If he or she dies without having reached a conclusion in this matter, the believer dies the death of a righteous one, in so far as in his or her heart there is certainty by virtue of sheer faith. Total belief in the religious law (*al-sharʿ*) is equally necessary, without any question of its truth or method. However, if doubt and uncertainty should overcome a believer, such reasoning as may alleviate them, like that provided by theologians, can be sought. The religious authorities, however, have prohibited doctrinal debates among the masses, just as young children are prohibited from swimming in the Tigris river. Yet those who have mastered the art of swimming can engage in such exercises. The latter group, however, should not get carried away with its assumptions about its knowledge and intelligence. What matters is carrying out God's command (al-Ṭūsī (1984b): 185).

THE SIGNIFICANCE OF KHWĀJAH NAṢĪR'S WRITINGS ON ETHICS

Beyond his works on logic, ontology and theology, the most influential genre of Khwājah Naṣīr's writings is his texts on ethics. The significance of Khwājah Naṣīr's ethical writings can hardly be exaggerated. The tradition of writing on ethics, as an independent philosophical category, includes some of the most prominent earlier Muslim philosophers, such as al-Fārābī and Ibn Miskawayh. This genre of philosophical discourse suggested, *ipso facto*, a mode of ethical reflection and guidance rather independent, however derivative, of Islamic law, or *Sharī'ah*. Both the clerical establishment and the political order detected in this ethical discourse a rival source of (de)legitimation. For obvious reasons, the clerical establishment considered this philosophically based ethical discourse as a rival to the Qur'ānically based *Sharī'ah*. The political establishment, however, looked at the ethical writings as both a source of guidance and aspiration for legitimate rulership and a source of potential moral (de)legitimation of their authority. The popularity of writings on ethics in general and Khwājah Naṣīr's writings in particular has thus been compared to that of music and musical writings that, despite unfavourable social circumstances, have been widespread in Islamic intellectual history (Dānishpazhūh in al-Ṭūsī (1982): 27).

Khwājah Naṣīr's ethical writings are based directly on two non-Islamic sources: Greek and pre-Islamic Persian (Dānishpazhūh in al-Ṭūsī (1982): 27–38). This is not to suggest that the Qur'ānic and *Ḥadīth* sources are not at the heart of Khwājah Naṣīr's ethical discourse. But in devising and narrating a distinct ethical imperative, both Khwājah Naṣīr and his sources (including particularly Ibn Miskawayh, from whom he freely borrowed) had Greek and Persian sources at their disposal. Aristotle's *Nicomachean Ethics* and the Persian *Andarz-nāmah* literature (especially such sources as *Pand-nāma-yi ardashīr* and *Nāma-yi tansar*) are cited (*ibid.*) as having had a dominant role in defining the terms of philosophical ethics during this period.

Khwājah Naṣīr was instrumental in devising a distinctly philosophical ethics from these pre- and non-Islamic sources that incorporated the Qur'ānic and *Ḥadīth* sources into a synthetic discourse of independent authority. In two, intimately related, significant ways this ethical discourse was threatening to the dominant nomocentricity of the juridical discourse and its political bases in the caliphal or sultanate authority. Firstly, it *ipso facto* constituted an independent discourse of moral civility on the foundations of which any human community could live an ethical and civilized life independent of the juridical authority. Secondly, it provided a non-juridical (if not quintessentially "secular") criterion of moral and political legitimacy for the sultanate authority. In fact, Khwājah Naṣīr's championship of this independent ethical discourse can be viewed as a philosophical/vizierate alternative that the Persian administrative authorities had devised to balance and counter the exclusive claim of the clerical establishment as the bestower of legitimate rulership to the sultanate. The ethical discourse of both *Akhlāq-i muḥtashamī* and *Akhlāq-i nāṣirī*, two significant texts of Khwājah Naṣīr on ethics, indeed, have a greater claim to universality and authority than the juridical discourse. Where the former incorporates Qur'ānic and *Ḥadīth* sources into both Greek and Persian – and even Indian – legacies of ethics, the latter has an exclusive limitation to Islamic material. By incorporating these sources into the ethical discourse, the genre of philosophical ethics systematized by Khwājah Naṣīr guarded itself against all dogmatic accusations of non- or anti-Islamicity. But incorporating these sacred sources into the Greek, Persian and Indian materials had a much wider claim on universality and authority.

AKHLĀQ-I MUḤTASHAMĪ

The origins of Khwājah Naṣīr's writings on ethics have been identified (Dānishpazhūh in al-Ṭūsī (1982): 3–9) in both Greek and Islamic sources. Aristotle's *Nichomachean Ethics* and al-Fārābī's *al-Madīnah al-fāḍilah* are among the immediately recognizable sources. Pre-Islamic Persian sources have also been detected. Khwājah Naṣīr's translation of Ibn al-Muqaffa''s *al-Adab al-wajīz*, in particular, is singled out as a direct source of access to Zoroastrian ideas (*ibid.*: 4). Ibn Miskawayh al-Rāzī's *Tahdhīb al-akhlāq*, however, is the principal work on ethics from which Khwājah Naṣīr borrowed directly. There are also frequent traces of Aristotle in *Akhlāq-i nāṣirī* (*ibid.*: 5).

Akhlāq-i muḥtashamī is so named because Khwājah Naṣīr wrote it for Nāṣir al-Dīn 'Abd al-Raḥīm Abī Manṣūr (d. 655/1257), the ruler (*muḥtasham*) of Quhistan. Nāṣir al-Dīn 'Abd al-Raḥīm had originally intended to write this book himself. He is reported to have been a particularly erudite and intelligent Ismā'īlī leader. In fact, he drew the outline of this text and set its principal division of chapters and the progression of each section, beginning with Qur'ānic passages and concluding with those of ancient sages and philosophers. But he was never actually able to finish this project because of his administrative responsibilities. He subsequently instructed Khwājah Naṣīr to take whatever he had done and complete it with other references. The Ismā'īlī leader is even reported to have dictated some additional passages to Khwājah Naṣīr to be included in the final text. He also asked to see the final draft that Khwājah Naṣīr would produce before it was to be fully transcribed and "published" (Dānishpazhūh in al-Ṭūsī (1982): 14).

Whatever Nāṣir al-Dīn 'Abd al-Raḥmān's contribution, the present text of *Akhlāq-i muḥtashamī* is Khwājah Naṣīr's doing. The text is divided into forty chapters, each of which consists of a number of Qur'ānic verses, followed by statements of the Prophet Muḥammad and the Shī'ī Imāms. The *Nahj al-balāghah* of the first Shī'ī Imām, 'Alī, and the fourth Shī'ī Imām, Imām Zayn al-'Ābidīn's *al-Ṣaḥīfat al-sajjādiyyah*, are identified as primary sources of Khwājah Naṣīr's text (Dānishpazhūh in al-Ṭūsī (1982): 14–15). Khwājah Naṣīr then concludes each chapter with a number of statements attributed to various (Greek) philosophers.

Khwājah Naṣīr's purpose in writing *Akhlāq-i muḥtashamī* appears to have been to provide a concise *vade-mecum* of ethical principles that every righteous person should follow.

Although Qur'ānic verses and the traditions of the Prophet Muḥammad and the Shī'ī Imāms abound in this book, the fact still remains that it constitutes an ethical discourse independent and distinct from the juridical discourse of the legal theorists (*fuqahā'*) also based on the Qur'ān and *Ḥadīth*. Both the Qur'ānic and non-Qur'ānic passages are translated into beautiful and simple Persian, thus extending the public domain of *Akhlāq-i muḥtashamī* beyond the limited intellectual elite who could read Arabic.

The content of *Akhlāq-i muḥtashamī* consists of a primary chapter on religion (*al-dīn*) and the necessity of a knowledge of God (al-Ṭūsī (1982): 6–15). What follows from that is a designation of prophetic authority, which also necessitates an Imāmī succession to it (*ibid.*: 16–25). Most of the other chapters are devised around any number of polar opposites in ethical behaviour, such as love and hate, knowledge and practice, good and evil acts, poverty and wealth, etc.

Akhlāq-i muḥtashamī is a thorough and complete manual of ethical behaviour delivered in a self-assured discourse of aphorism. The principal basis of this ethic is knowledge (*ma'rifah*) – knowledge of God, knowledge of the Prophet and knowledge of his successors as Imāms. This knowledge is the chief prerogative of humanity upon which all possibilities of ethical behaviour are contingent. Love and hate are two principal emotions on which Khwājah Naṣīr divides all possibilities of human affiliation: the love of good and the hatred of evil. One must rely on the love of those who are good and express hate against evil-doers. From that love derives the necessity of unity (*ittiḥād*) and unanimity (*ittifāq*) and the baseness of arrogance and hypocrisy (*al-kibr wa'l-nifāq*).

Once people know their God, love their friends, hate their enemies, and hold fast to the community, then they are ready to fight (*al-jihād*) in the path of God, the ultimate direction of all humanity. There are two (opposite) complementary dimensions to people's characters in that direction: knowledge and deeds. These two must reflect each other. Nobility of knowledge leads to virtuous deeds. Absolute obedience to God is the chief guardian of virtuous behaviour (*al-a'māl al-ṣāliḥah*). Prayers and alms in the path of God have this- and other-worldly rewards. Fear of God and His wrath and asceticism are two simultaneous virtues that one must cultivate. One must be patient in hardship and grateful for what one has. Reliance on God is the best that the virtuous individual can do in daily activities. Only thus will we incline towards doing good and abstain from doing evil. Tyranny and injustice are the basest vices from which the individual, Khwājah Naṣīr insists with an eye on the political powers that be, must refrain. He also devotes a chapter to the denunciation of the world and all its material gains. A virtuous person always strives for the world to come, not the one at hand, transitory as it is. Accumulation of wealth is evil, unnecessary and futile. Greed and avarice must be avoided by all means. Poverty is superior to wealth. Truth is better than a lie; trustworthiness better than unreliability. Silence is better than speech. Too much idle talk is hazardous. To have a kind disposition, to be patient, forgiving and in control of one's anger are among the highest virtues. One should not be envious and hostile. Humility is a supreme virtue and arrogance a vice. Magnanimity, generosity and forgiveness are to be preferred over niggardliness, stinginess and baseness. Steadfastness and bravery are virtues to be cultivated against whimsical waywardness and cowardice. Khwājah Naṣīr advises the individual to control his or her desires and be in control of his or her dignity. Truthfulness must be cultivated through companionship with good friends and the wise. Conversely, one must abstain from frequenting the ignorant and the evil-doers. These are among an avalanche of ethical advice that Khwājah Naṣīr pours over his readers.

ETHICS FOR CHILDREN

Among Khwājah Naṣīr's writings on ethics is also a translation of Ibn Muqaffa''s *al-Adab al-wajīz li'l-walad al-ṣaghīr* ("A Short Manual of Ethical Behaviour for the Small Child"). This treatise begins with a typical admonition that Ibn Muqaffa' addresses to his own son with respect to the necessity of obedience to God (al-Ṭūsī (1982): 502). Patience in calamity is the first piece of advice. It is crucial that young people should attend to knowledge from the earliest times. They should frequent the wise, but never enter into an argument with them. They should not be concerned with material gains, but instead seek salvation in the world to come. They must be quickly attentive to their duties and at all costs avoid telling lies. Silence is a virtue that Ibn Muqaffa''s son must cultivate. Too much idle talk is not good. Patience is good. Ibn Muqaffa' quotes Socrates, who said that sadness (*al-ḥuzn*) suffocates the mind and does not let it function well. Young people should also learn not to reveal all their knowledge and capabilities at once. They should not be supplicative before kings. They must be steadfast in friendships; but should friends turn against them, they must refrain from further contact. Confidentiality is the key to success. To achieve success they must never be fearful of undertaking grave responsibilities. They should never be envious. If they achieve high office and status, they should avoid arrogance and pride. They should not imagine that doing evil is easier than doing good. One does those things with ease that one does most frequently. Before asking or answering a question, they should think thoroughly in advance not to cause embarrassment for themselves. They should always be cognizant of the opinion of the majority and not do anything blatantly against it. They should never compete against anyone who is superior in will, strength or wealth, such as a king. They should be friendly with their superiors in knowledge and status, reverential with equals, and never associate with inferiors. If they should happen to find themselves in a city where they do not know the people, they should first wait and observe and see who is superior to all others in behaviour and manner. Then they must affiliate themselves only with that individual. If they are about to do something good, they should do it immediately. They should never listen to people who talk behind other people's backs. Ibn Muqaffa''s last advice to his son, as translated by Khwājah Naṣīr, is this:

> O! Know that whoever is weakened, the unrighteous point their fingers of accusation against him, and his friends are made suspicious of him. His sins and wrong-doings shall not be kept secret, because the weak person is always subject to accusation and suspicion. People call his courage stupidity, his generosity corruption and lack of wisdom, his patience weakness, his steadfastness stubbornness, his eloquence gibberish, his silence dumbness.
>
> (al-Ṭūsī (1982a): 557)

AKHLĀQ-I NĀṢIRĪ

Khwājah Naṣīr's greatest work on ethics, perhaps the most influential in the entire genre (Humā'ī (1956): 17), is *Akhlāq-i nāṣirī*. He wrote the first draft of this treatise while still in the service of the Ismā'īlī warlord Nāṣir al-Dīn. When the Ismā'īlīs were defeated by the Mongols and Khwājah Naṣīr transferred his loyalty to his new patron, Hūlāgū, he revised his *Akhlāq-i nāṣirī*, changed its introduction and conclusion and eliminated all his laudatory clauses about the Ismā'īlīs and Ismā'īlism. This has resulted in some harsh criticism by some scholars (Rypka (1968): 313–14). Others, however, have defended Khwājah Naṣīr on the grounds of the existing political circumstances (see Buzurg 'Alawī's Introduction to al-Ṭūsī (1977a): i–viii; see also Humā'ī (1956): 17). The details of these discrepancies in the introductory and concluding materials, however, have been meticulously identified by Mujtabā Mīnuwī and 'Alī Riḍā Ḥaydarī, the editors of the definitive critical edition of *Akhlāq-i nāṣirī* (al-Ṭūsī (1977a): 7–9; compare with Humā'ī (1956): 22–5).

Akhlāq-i nāṣirī consists of an introduction, three treatises and a conclusion. The introduction is a general statement on divisions of philosophy. The first treatise, on ethics, is divided into two sections: principles (*mabādī*) and objectives (*maqāṣid*). The second treatise covers domestic politics. And the third treatise addresses "national" (or "city") politics. One may even call this section Khwājah Naṣīr's "sociology". The conclusion is a series of "advice" (*waṣāyā'*) attributed to Plato.

Khwājah Naṣīr's introduction to *Akhlāq-i nāṣirī* is a standard discussion of the divisions of philosophy Islamic philosophers had originally adopted from Aristotle. *Ḥikmat*, or philosophy, "is to know things as they are and to do things as one must" (al-Ṭūsī (1977a): 37). The purpose of philosophy is to help the person achieve the highest human ideals. Thus, philosophy is divided into two parts: "knowledge" and "action". "Knowledge" consists of the ability to "conceive" (*taṣawwur*) things as they are and then "assent" (*taṣdīq*) as to their principles. "Action" is the practice of movements and mastery of arts so that which is potential is made actual. Khwājah Naṣīr subjects the mastery of both theoretical (*'ilmī*) and practical (*'amalī*) knowledge to man's physical abilities. Whoever achieves perfection in knowledge and deed achieves a noble character.

THE SUBJECT OF ETHICS IN THE DIVISION OF PHILOSOPHY

Because the object of philosophy consists of the knowledge of everything that exists, it is divided into two categories based on the nature of things as they are. Existent things are of two kinds: first, those whose existence is independent of our actions and, second, those whose existence is dependent on our actions. "Theoretical philosophy" (*ḥikmat-i naẓarī*) has the first category of existent beings as its object, and "practical philosophy" (*ḥikmat-i 'amalī*) has the second category of existent beings as its object.

Theoretical philosophy, in turn, is divided into two categories: first, the knowledge of that whose existence – and the conception thereof – is not commingled with matter and, second, the knowledge of that whose existence is contingent upon matter. The latter category is divided further into yet two more parts: first, the knowledge of that whose contingency upon matter is not essential for its conception and, second, the knowledge of that whose contingency upon matter is essential to it. Consequently, theoretical philosophy is divided into three categories: "metaphysics" (*'ilm-i ma ba'd al-ṭabī'ah*), "mathematics" (*'ilm-i riāḍī*) and "natural sciences" (*'ilm-i ṭabī'ī*). Each of these categories is divided, in turn, into a number of "major" (*uṣūl*) and "minor" (*furū'*) sections (al-Ṭūsī (1977a): 38).

The first category of theoretical philosophy, metaphysics, consists of, firstly, the knowledge of God Almighty and of those who, by virtue of being near His Presence, have caused other things to be, such as "the intellects" (*'uqūl*), "the souls" (*nufūs*) and the principles governing their actions, which knowledge is called "theology" (*'ilm-i ilāhī*), and, secondly, the knowledge of general principles governing existent beings as they are, such as unity (*waḥdat*), multiplicity (*kithrat*), necessity (*wujūb*), possibility (*imkān*), createdness (*ḥudūth*), pre-eternity (*qidam*), etc., which knowledge is called "The First Philosophy" (*falsafah-i ūlā'*). Metaphysics, in turn, is divided into any number of minor subdivisions, such as the knowledge of prophethood (*nubuwwat*), of the Divine Law (*Sharī'ah*), of the Day of Judgment (*ma'ād*), and other matters related to them (al-Ṭūsī (1977a): 38–9).

While mathematics is divided into four parts – geometry, arithmetic, astronomy and music – the natural sciences are divided into eight: knowledge of time, space, motion, immobility, infinity and finitude; knowledge of simple and compound objects; knowledge of the principal elements and their transformabilities; knowledge of the earth and the climate, such as thunder, rain, snow, earthquake, etc.; mineralogy; botany; biology; and psychology. Among the minor subdivisions of the natural sciences are medicine, astronomy (which Khwājah Naṣīr here categorizes differently than in his former categorization under mathematics) and the science of agriculture.

Khwājah Naṣīr gives "logic" (*manṭiq*) a separate and independent category under the general rubric of theoretical philosophy. He credits Aristotle with having systematized this category of knowledge. Logic "is to know how to know things, the way to overcome the unknown" (al-Ṭūsī (1977a): 40). Logic is an instrument for acquiring other forms of knowledge.

Khwājah Naṣīr defines practical philosophy as "the knowledge of instruments of the voluntary actions [*ḥarakāt-i irādī*] and creative deeds [*a'māl-i ṣinā'ī*] of humankind, as they pertain to their this-worldly and other-worldly affairs, necessary for their achieving that state of perfection towards which they move" (al-Ṭūsī (1977a): 40). Practical philosophy consists of two subjects: first, things that concern human beings as individuals and, second, things that concern human beings as members of the society. Khwājah Naṣīr further divides his "sociology" into two branches: first, the knowledge of matters that are common to a people living in a common household and, second, the knowledge of matters that are common to a people living in "a city, a province, a land, even a kingdom" (*ibid.*). Thus he divides practical philosophy into "ethics" (*tahdhīb-i akhlāq*), "domestic politics" (*tadbīr-i manzil*), and "national politics" or "sociology" (*sīyāsat-i mudun*).

Khwājah Naṣīr divides the origins of good deeds and the virtues of humankind that are necessary for the betterment of their conditions into two major categories. These virtues are either "natural" in their origin or else "conventional". The natural virtues do not change over time, while the conventional ones do. If the origins of conventional virtues lie in the communal consensus of a people, they are called "customs and habits" (*ādāb wa rusūm*). But if they are rooted in the judgment of a great individual (such as the Prophet or an Imām), they are called "Divine Laws" (*nawāmīs-i ilāhī*).

These "Divine Laws" concern either every individual in his or her individuality, as in acts of ritual obedience and rules thereof, or members of a household as a collectivity, as in marriage and other transactions, or members of cities and provinces, as in rules of punishments and retributions. "Jurisprudence" (*'ilm-i fiqh*) is the name Khwājah Naṣīr gives this latter category. He also suggests that the philosopher's attention to such acts that are conventional and thus subject to periodic change is rather minimal. Because, by nature, philosophers are concerned with things permanent and least subject to change, they want to discover the permanent and valid rules governing existence.

Khwājah Naṣīr's segment on ethics is divided into two sections: "principles" and "objectives". The first section is divided into seven chapters. The subject of ethics is the "human soul" (*nafs-i insānī*) because it is the origin of good and evil acts. "The human soul is an abstract substance [*jawhar-i basīṭ*] from the essence of which issues the conception of intelligibles" (al-Ṭūsī (1977a): 48). In the second chapter of this section, Khwājah Naṣīr provides an elaborate argument to prove the existence of the soul, its substantiality (*jawhariyyat*), its simplicity (*bisāṭat*), its not being a body (*jism*) or physical (*jismānī*), that it conceives in its essence and acts through its instruments, and finally that it cannot be felt through any one of the sense perceptions (*ibid.*: 48–9). The human soul, which is also called "the rational soul" (*nafs-i nāṭiqah*), survives the death of the body. The body is, in fact, an instrument (*ālat*) to the soul and "not as some have conceived it as its location or space" (*ibid.*: 56).

The soul is divided into three kinds: vegetal, animal and human, each of which has its respective powers. Only the human soul has "rational power" (*quwwat-i nāṭiqah*). Humans are the most noble of all creatures, the highest stage of the soul ascending from the vegetal and animal to the human. Prophets and saints are the noblest of humans (al-Ṭūsī (1977a): 63). The human being is potentially capable of both perfection and baseness. This human perfection is of two kinds, either in the direction of knowledge or in the direction of action. The ultimate end of knowledge is serenity and certitude in "the world of Oneness [of God]" (*ibid.*: 69). The ultimate end of action is to achieve harmony and equilibrium in one's individual and communal affairs; perfection in knowledge and in action are dialectically related and interdependent on each other. Upon mastering these two sides, man becomes the true vicegerent of God on earth. Khwājah Naṣīr launches a pervasive attack against those who consider the purpose of life to be the enjoyment of material things, the functions of speaking and intellect to facilitate such physical enjoyments. They have subjected the noble soul, Khwājah Naṣīr charges (*ibid.*: 71), to ephemeral lust.

From yet another perspective, the soul is divided into three kinds: the "bestial soul" (*nafs-i bahīmī*), which is the lowest; the "savage soul" (*nafs-i sabu'ī*), which is the intermediary state; and the "angelic soul" (*nafs-i malakī*), which is the noblest. These three "souls" are simultaneously present in the human being. Khwājah Naṣīr refers to the correspondence of these three "souls" to three Qur'ānic terms. *Nafs-i bahīmī* is the same as *nafs-i ammārah*, or the "carnal soul"; *nafs-i sabu'ī* is the same as *nafs-i lawwāmah*, or the "admonishing soul"; and *nafs-i malakī* is the same as *nafs-i muṭma'innah*, or the "virtuous soul". Khwājah Naṣīr summarizes the functions of these souls as follows:

> "the carnal soul" commands and insists on the fulfilment of desires; "the admonishing soul", after having concealed that which is inevitable in [human] shortcomings, renders, through reproach and admonition, that action blameworthy in the eyes of wisdom; and as for "the virtuous soul", it does not yield except to beautiful deeds and virtuous actions.
>
> (al-Ṭūsī (1977a): 77)

Khwājah Naṣīr devotes the seventh and last chapter of this section to a definition of the "good" (*khayr*) and "happiness" (*sa'ādat*) as the ultimate objectives of the human soul. After a reference to both Aristotle and Ibn Sīnā, he proceeds to distinguish between *khayr*, which is common among – and to – all people, and *sa'ādat*, whose definition and conception differ from one individual to another. He cites Porphyry of Tyre (*c.* A.D. 300) (quoting from Aristotle) extensively in definition and divisions of "good". He also refers to Pythagoras, Socrates, Plato and Aristotle in their understanding of "happiness" (al-Ṭūsī (1977a): 83). The "good" is divided into four categories: noble, praiseworthy, potentially good, beneficial on the way to being good. "Happiness" is also of four kinds: wisdom, courage, piety and justice (*ibid.*: 82–4). Khwājah Naṣīr reports and discusses other divisions of "happiness" offered by the Stoics and others.

In the second section of this treatise on ethics, Khwājah Naṣīr discusses the "objectives" (*maqāṣid*) of this branch of philosophy. He believes that an individual's "disposition" (*khulq*) is alterable, that man can, through education, change (al-Ṭūsī (1977a): 101). But the act of changing one's ethical disposition is an art (*ṣinā'at*), and in that a most noble art. There are essentially three kinds of virtues that humanity can achieve, each corresponding to one of a person's three souls. From the rational soul knowledge and philosophy are attained; from the savage soul patience and courage are achieved; and from the bestial soul piety and magnanimity are obtained. For each one of these souls to achieve its respective virtue, it must first attain a state of equilibrium under the general authority of the rational soul. "Justice", the fourth virtue, will be achieved when these three virtues are attained and properly integrated. There are various "species" (*anwā'*) to these four "kinds" (*ajnās*) of virtue that Khwājah Naṣīr enumerates in detail. There are also four corresponding vices. In opposition to "wisdom" is "ignorance" (*jahl*), in opposition to "courage" is "cowardice" (*jaban*), in opposition to "piety" is "mischief" and in opposition to "justice" is "tyranny". Khwajāh Naṣīr proceeds to give a detailed account of these vices. He also provides a full discussion of certain pseudo-virtues, such as the supposition of having knowledge while in reality lacking it (*ibid.*: 122–30).

Among all virtues attainable by humans, "justice" is the most noble. From music to ethics, "balance" (*musāwāt*) is the most essential virtue. "The just person is the person who gives proportion and equilibrium to things which are neither proportionate nor in equilibrium" (al-Ṭūsī (1977a): 133). Khwājah Naṣīr's full discussion of "justice" includes references to other philosophers such as Ibn Sīnā, Aristotle and Plato. Equally authoritative references are made to the Qur'ān and the prophetic traditions throughout the text. Khwājah Naṣīr concludes his discussion of justice with a tangential reference to *maḥabbat* ("loving kindness"). People are in need of justice to govern their transactions only when *maḥabbat* is absent. Khwājah Naṣīr postpones his discussion of *maḥabbat* until his section on politics. But here he asserts that should *maḥabbat* be present among a people, they would treat each other with love and affection, and justice would naturally ensue. Khwājah Naṣīr's conception of *maḥabbat*, which literally means "love", or "loving kindness", is very close to Ibn Khaldūn's conception of *'aṣabiyyah*, which has been translated as "group feeling" (Ibn Khaldūn (1958), 1: 264ff.). Both *maḥabbat* and *'aṣabiyyah* are very close to what the French sociologist Emile Durkheim (1858–1917) has termed "conscience collective" (Durkheim (1933): 79). Thus, I think we would be closer to Khwājah Naṣīr's conception of *maḥabbat*, as a necessary sentiment for the creation of social solidarity, if we translate it as "collective sentiment".

Khwājah Naṣīr provides a full course of instructions as to how virtues such as knowledge, courage, piety and justice are to be attained. One can attain virtues through two channels of possibilities – one natural and the other acquisitive. Attainment of ethical virtues, however, is not natural to man; it is acquisitive. The ultimate state of happiness thus attained by a human being is of three kinds: spiritual (*nafsānī*), physical (*badanī*), and civil or collective (*madanī*). Spiritual happiness is contingent upon the attainment of a thorough knowledge of ethics, logic, mathematics, natural sciences and ultimately metaphysics. Khwājah Naṣīr insists on this order (al-Ṭūsī (1977a): 154). Physical happiness consists of the acquisition of that knowledge which is beneficial to the well-being of the body, such as medicine and astronomy. Finally, civic or collective happiness constitutes such knowledge that is beneficial to the citizens of a nation (*millat*), to the government (*dawlat*), to economics (*umūr-i ma'āsh*) and to society (*kalām*), prophetic traditions (*akhbār*), and Qur'ānic commentary (*tanzīl wa ta'wīl*), as well as literature (*adab*), rhetoric (*balāqhat*) and grammar (*naḥw*), etc.

Once the human soul is thus characterized by virtue, it is incumbent upon the owner of that soul to safeguard its achievements. Khwājah Naṣīr offers a detailed account of how these virtues are to be sustained and preserved. Parallel to this preservation of virtues in the soul is the curing of spiritual diseases that occur through afflictions with certain vices. For example, the cure for "compound ignorance" (*jahl-i murakkab*) is the study of mathematics. Thus, Khwājah Naṣīr prescribes a series of cures for a host of vices, such as anger, envy, vanity, stubbornness, frivolity, enmity, fear of death, extremism in lust, idleness and sadness.

AWṢĀF AL-ASHRĀF

According to Khwājah Naṣīr himself, in the introduction to *Awṣāf al-ashrāf* (al-Ṭūsī (1966): 28), he had written two treatises on ethics: *Akhlāq-i nāṣirī* and *Awṣāf al-ashrāf.* Thus, despite the mystical (Sufi) nature of this latter treatise, it ought to be considered under his ethical writings. In the same introduction he asserts that he wrote *Akhlāq-i nāṣirī* "on virtuous ethics and righteous politics according to philosophers" and that he now writes *Awṣāf al-ashrāf* "on the manners of the spiritual brothers and the methods of the people of the vision according to the principle of those who traverse upon the spiritual path and who seek Truth" (*ibid.*).

Awṣāf al-ashrāf is divided into six chapters (*bāb*), each, with the exception of the last, divided in turn into six sections (*faṣl*). Each chapter corresponds to one stage in the spiritual path of the purification of the soul, each of which is attainable only upon the achievement of its preceding stage. While the attainment of one stage is a goal and a virtue for the individual located at the preceding stage, it becomes a vice and a hurdle when the individual has achieved that stage. The six chapters of *Awṣāf al-ashrāf,* corresponding to the six stages of spiritual passage towards the nobility of character, are: the commencement of movement, the eradication of hurdles and barriers, the movement through which the spiritual novitiate leaves the point of departure and reaches the destination, conditions experienced by the spiritual novitiate while traversing from the point of departure to the destination, conditions that occur after the sojourner reaches the destination, and the final stage of this spiritual movement, the condition of the individual's non-existence, the cutting of the path, which is now called "annihilation in Oneness" (al-Ṭūsī (1966): 32–4).

In the first stage, for the spiritual movement to start, the traveller should have faith (*īmān*), steadfastness (*thubāt*), intention (*niyyat*), truthfulness (*ṣidq*), reliance on God (*inābat*) and, finally, purification of all thoughts, utterances and deeds. Once this stage is achieved, certain hurdles and barriers are to be eliminated in the next stage. To achieve this, six acts are necessary: repentance (*tawbah*), asceticism (*zuhd*), poverty (*faqr*), hardship (*riyāḍat*), introspection (*muḥāsibat wa murāqibat*) and abstinence from sin out of the fear of God (*taqwā*). Once the spiritual quest thus commences, there are six additional conditions the novitiate should master in the next stage: solitude (*khalwat*), thinking (*tafakkur*), fear (*khawf*), hope (*rijā'*), patience (*ṣabr*) and gratitude (*shukr*). Upon the successful completion of these stages, the traveller will have to persist in six other virtues before reaching his or her destination: will (*irādat*), ecstasy (*shawq*), love (*maḥabbat*), gnosis (*ma'rifat*), conviction (*yaqīn*) and serenity (*sukūn*). Once spiritual seekers complete their quest, but before they are ultimately unified in oneness, they must persist through yet another set of six penultimate virtues: reliance on God (*tawakkul*), contentment (*riḍā'*), surrender (*taslīm*), monotheism (*tawḥīd*), unity (*ittiḥād*) and oneness (*waḥdat*).

In the sixth and final stage of this spiritual quest, the seeker has now completed and assimilated all the preceding stages and is finally and totally annihilated (*fanā'*) in God. In that stage of unity "there will not be a seeker, or a seeking, neither a quest nor a destination, neither a demand nor an applicant, nor a supplication. Everything is annihilated, except His Countenance" (al-Ṭūsī (1966): 162).

ĀGHĀZ WA ANJĀM

Although it has been suggested by a recent commentator that Khwājah Naṣīr's treatise on "The Beginning and Return" should be considered under the category of psychology (Ḥasanzādah Āmulī in al-Ṭūsī (1987): 80–1), both the intentions and implications of *Āghāz wa anjām* are more directly of an ethical nature. Khwājah Naṣīr wrote this treatise in response to one of his student followers who had asked him to write "a reminder of that which the passengers of the final path [*rāh-i ākhirat*] have witnessed on the end of the act of creation, similar to that which is written in the Book and expressed by prophets and saints, peace be upon them" (*ibid.*: 1).

The Final Path, or the Path of Return, is perfectly clear; the guides are known; and the signposts are all self-explanatory. Yet people are disinclined to follow that path because it is the same path from which they have come. They have once before seen and heard all that they now see and hear. The cause of their disinclination, however, is their self-forgetfulness, their not remembering this previous familiarity. One perseveres in this self-forgetfulness because one does not open the ear and the eye with which one once heard and saw. One's persistence in self-forgetfulness rests on three forces: the natural distractions (*shawā'ib-i ṭabī'at*), such as lust and anger; evil habits (*wasāwīs-i 'ādat*), such as the preoccupations of the carnal soul, and the distractions of superfluous acts; and distorted spirits (*nawāmīs-i amthalah*), such as following demons who appear in the shape of man, or imitating ignorant men who look like the learned. The result of this mundane persistence in self-forgetfulness of origin is punishment in the world to come. And what punishment is harder, Khwājah Naṣīr asks, than being near God and yet unaware and forgetful of Him? (al-Ṭūsī (1987): 6).

Man thus dwells between the Night of the Sacred Power (*shab-i qadr*) and the Day of Final Resurrection (*rūz-i qiyāmat*). In this life there are two kinds of death: one voluntary, the other natural. "Whoever dies a voluntary death will be resurrected in everlasting life" (al-Ṭūsī (1987): 16). Time and space are like a nurse and a cradle, or a father and a mother, raising their offspring from the infantile state of birth until the occasion of the Return. But time is also the source of change, space the location of multiplicity, both causes of concealment of certain things from others. On the Day of Judgment, upon the removal of time and space, all concealments shall disappear and reality will shine through.

In this world people are divided into three categories. First, *sābiqān*, or those who are steadfast; they are the people of unity. Second, *ahl-i yamīn*, or people of the right; they are the good people. And third, *ahl-i shimāl*, or people of the left; they are the evil people. All three groups shall pass through Hell, only the bad shall remain, and the good and the *sābiqān* shall depart for Paradise. They shall pass through *ṣirāt*, with the slightest disorientations leading to a descent into Hell and righteous determination guiding safely to Paradise (al-Ṭūsī (1987): 33). The good and evil acts in this world will be properly rewarded and then awarded or praised on the Day of Judgment. On that day the good and evil acts will be properly measured and weighed. Khwājah Naṣīr proceeds to give a full description of the apocalyptic events at the end of time, assigning the good- and evil-doers to Heaven and Hell, respectively, identifying the guards of Hell and the rivers of Paradise; and incorporating all the appropriate Qur'ānic references and indices. Governing all these apocalyptic events are God's rewards – due to His Beneficence – and punishment – out of His Justice (*ibid.*: 71).

CENTRALITY OF THE ETHICAL DISCOURSE

Whether delivered in the philosophical, Ismā'īlī or the mystical tradition, Khwājah Naṣīr's texts on ethics constitute a major segment of his writings and ought to be considered as a unique body of discourse. Some of the salient features of this discourse are as follows. Above and beyond the nomocentricity of the religious dogma, and their institutional custodians as the clerical class of the *'ulamā'*, there is a sustained possibility of attaining nobility of character and of social peace and harmony. Ethics, or *akhlāq*, is the operative discourse of authority through which the nobility of character and collective harmony in society may be achieved. That discourse incorporates and is to a great extent derived from the canonical texts of Islam – the Qur'ān and the *Ḥadīth*. Although the ethical discourse of *akhlāq* considerably appropriates the authoritative voice and sanctity of the Qur'ān and the *Ḥadīth*, it also reaches out for the pre- (and non-)Islamic authority of the ancient Indians, Persians and especially the Greeks. The result is a synthetic discourse of moral imperatives that calls its followers to a universe of ethical discourse not limited or exclusive to members of a particular religion. Although the application of the term "secular" to this ethical discourse would not be totally accurate, it is important to locate its operative force and legitimacy outside the nomocentric exclusivity of the Islamic *Sharī'ah*. The ethical discourse that Khwājah Naṣīr institutionalizes in his *akhlāq* is not identical to the Islamic *Sharī'ah*. It is a discourse *sui generis* and in full control of a universe of moral imagination in which any individual, Muslim or not, can attain nobility of character and social civility. By incorporating the philosophical, mystical and (non-Islamic) Greek, Indian and Persian sources and traditions into a syncretic discourse of moral authority, Khwājah Naṣīr, as a philosopher/vizier, effectively bars the *'ulamā'* proper, the institutional custodians of the sacred law, from entrance into the universe of his moral imagination. The result is the effective construction of a legitimate discourse of moral and political authority in juxtaposition against the exclusively Qur'ānic- and *Ḥadīth*-based discourse of the *'ulamā'*. The independent and effective construction of this ethical (moral/political or knowledge/power) discourse is instrumental in Khwājah Naṣīr's representing the archetypal figure of the philosopher/vizier. Indeed, the discourse of *akhlāq* and the character-type of the philosopher/vizier are interdependent on each other. *Akhlāq* is the discourse of the philosopher/vizier wherein he grounds the rational basis of his knowledge/power. As the *Sharī'ah* is the discourse of the religious doctors, the *'ulamā'*, *akhlāq* is the discourse, the self-legitimating narrative, of the philosopher/vizier.

POLITICS

Central to Khwājah Naṣīr's ethics is his discussion of politics. He divides his section on "politics" in *Akhlāq-i nāṣirī* into two parts: the first segment addresses domestic issues, or a communal order on a small scale, *dar tadbīr-i manāzil* ("On How to Run a Household"); and the second segment covers "national" issues, or a communal order on a larger scale, *dar siyāsat-i mudun* ("On the Politics of Cities").

The treatise on domestic issues, which is based on Ibn Sīnā's rendition of Aristotle's *Oeconomica* (Dānishpazhūh in al-Ṭūsī (1982): 6), is divided into five chapters and consists of issues that should be studied under "economics". Khwājah Naṣīr begins this treatise with a preliminary discussion of the necessity of the household in human survival. The natural needs for survival and procreation have given rise to this necessity. The household constitutes five constituent elements: the father, the mother, the children, servants and sustenance (al-Ṭūsī (1977a): 206). The head of the household is in charge of its politics, its communal well-being. Khwājah Naṣīr is emphatic to point out that by *manzil* he does not simply mean a house, "but a special kind of arrangement [*ta'līf*] that becomes operative between a husband and a wife, a parent and a child, a master and a servant, a proprietor and a property. [It does not matter] whether their house is made of wood and stone, tent and pole, the shadow of a tree, or the corner of a cave" (*ibid.*: 207). Domestic wisdom (*ḥikmat-i manzilī*) comprises supervision over this small community, with the best interests of the whole in mind. Khwājah Naṣīr gives a full description of what constitutes a good house: it has to be wide, spacious and protected against all natural and unnatural accidents and calamities such as fire, flood and robbery. He also insists on the significance of having good and appropriate neighbours. In the second chapter of this treatise, Khwājah Naṣīr provides a full course of advice on financial planning and advancement in a career. The third chapter addresses the function of the wife, which is "to safeguard the wealth and sustain procreation, and not to fulfil lust or anything of that sort" (*ibid.*: 215). Khwājah Naṣīr has a rather liberal view of women in a household. "A good wife is the partner of man in [their] wealth, his partner in lordship and management of the household, his representative when he is absent" (*ibid.*). He also advises against polygamy (*ibid.*: 218). Of course, his "liberality" should not be overestimated. He believes that man must establish fear and awe in his wife, conceal her from all strangers and never let her be encouraged to follow her whimsical desires. But his tone throughout this chapter is to guide both husband and wife towards mutually respectable and responsible behaviour.

Khwājah Naṣīr devotes a full chapter to the education and upbringing of children, from giving them good and beautiful names to attending to their traditional and religious training. He makes an exception, however, in the education of young girls. They should not be taught how to read and write; instead, they ought to be "taught such acts which are praiseworthy for women" (al-Ṭūsī (1977a): 230). He proceeds to give specific instructions in such matters of juvenile education as how to speak, how to eat and even how to drink wine.

Some thirty years after the original composition of *Akhlāq-i nāṣirī*, Khwājah Naṣīr adds a chapter on "paying due respect to parents" at the conclusion of the section on domestic matters (al-Ṭūsī (1977a): 236–7). After expressing obedience to God, there is no act of piety more virtuous than respecting one's parents. The love of parents for their children is natural, while the love of children for their parents is intentional and acquisitive. Children should learn to love their parents differently than the parents their children. Love for one's father should be expressed in (the superior, more spiritual form of) respect, obedience and prayer; while love for one's mother should be expressed through (more material means, such as) providing for her financial and physical comfort. Contrary to these praiseworthy virtues, there are vices – such as rudeness, stinginess and argumentativeness – that children should avoid committing against their parents.

The last chapter of this treatise on politics discusses on a minor scale the treatment of servants and slaves. They are like extensions of one's hands and arms, ears and eyes. They perform certain menial acts and leave time for their master to attend to more important things. They ought to be treated kindly and affectionately. Khwājah Naṣīr divides servants into three categories: those who are innately free in their disposition, those who are innately servile in their dispositions and those who are obedient because of need. The first category should be cared for as if they were the master's own children, encouraged to do good; the second category should be used like animals; and the third should be employed for whatever particular purpose necessary.

Khwājah Naṣīr's final statement in this treatise is a stereotypical construction of major character traits in various peoples. Arabs are articulate, eloquent and intelligent and yet treacherous and lustful. Persians are distinguished by their intelligence, politics, cleanliness and shrewdness, and yet they are known to be deceitful and greedy. Romans are loyal, trustworthy, affectionate and capable and yet niggardly and wicked. Indians are superior in their powers of intuition, sensibility and imagination, and yet they are equally known to be conceited, vicious, deceitful and fallacious. The Turks are courageous, impeccable in their services, and most beautiful in their appearance and yet treacherous, cruel and impertinent (al-Ṭūsī (1977): 244).

The section on "The Politics of Cities" is divided into eight chapters. In the first chapter, Khwājah Naṣīr provides an argument as to why human society is in need of civilization (*tamaddun*). Human beings need mutual co-operation in order to safeguard their individual and collective survival (al-Ṭūsī (1977): 250). In the second chapter, he discusses the centrality of *maḥabbat*, or "group sentiments", as the crucial factor in bringing a human collectivity together. There are both natural and acquisitive forms of "group sensibilities" (*ibid.*: 260), both instrumental in any mode of collective affinity – from family to society. The third chapter is devoted to a discussion of the two kinds of human society: utopia (*madīna-yi fāḍilah*) and the anti-utopia (*madīna-yi ghayr-i fāḍilah*) (*ibid.*: 280). Utopia is but one, "because truth is immune to multiplicity" (*ibid.*). But there are three kinds of anti-utopias: first, "the City of the Ignorants" (*madīna-yi jāhilah*), whose people lack the power of reason (or speech = *nuṭq*); second, "the City of the Corrupt", (*madīnah-yi fāsiqah*), whose people have subjected their reason to their other senses; and third, "the City of the Misguided" (*madīna-yi ḍāllah*), whose people, out of a weak traditional disposition, have wrongly imagined a law to be virtuous and then built their city on its basis (*ibid.*). These forms of anti-utopias are, in turn, divided into other forms of evil cities, *ad infinitum*, "because non-truth and evil has no finitude" (*ibid.*). As for the utopia itself, Khwājah Naṣīr makes the following observation: "In the Utopia [lit. 'the City of the Virtuous'] too, anti-Utopian cities shall emerge . . . and they are called stages. The purpose of these cities is the recognition of Utopia so that other cities shall strive to attain it" (*ibid.*). The fourth chapter of this section is a full discussion of the question of political power proper, "the administration of kingdom and the royal manners" (*ibid.*: 300). There are two dimensions to supreme political authority: a "politics of virtue" (*siyāsat-i fāḍilah*) and a "politics of imperfection" (*siyāsat-i nāqiṣah*). The politics of virtue is necessary to guide the followers to bliss and salvation; the politics of imperfection is required to punish and curtail human fallacies and shortcomings. The fifth chapter enumerates the principles and guidelines to be observed by those who associate with the kings (*ibid.*: 314). This chapter consists of certain practical rules to be followed by courtiers and administrators if they do not wish to be subject to the kings' wrath. The sixth chapter is devoted to friendship (*ibid.*: 321). Khwājah Naṣīr's purpose here is to emphasize the social and political significance of having a limited but closely knit circle of friends and acquaintances. The seventh chapter is a full treatise on the principles that should govern one's relations with members of various social classes and groups, which Khwājah Naṣīr identifies as friends, foes, those who are neither friends nor foes, the virtuous men of learning and the underlings (*ibid.*: 334–41). The eighth chapter, which is also the conclusion of the book, consists of a series of short aphorisms that Khwājah Naṣīr attributes to Plato (*ibid.*: 341–4). "Do not test the learned in the abundance of their learning, but judge them by how they avoid evil and corruption!" (*ibid.*: 341).

HERMENEUTICS

To understand further Khwājah Naṣīr's method of ethical extrapolations from the canonical and non-canonical sources of his time and culture, we should briefly note his hermeneutics. In both *Awṣāf al-ashrāf* and *Āghāz wa anjām*, Khwājah Naṣīr follows a standard Ismā'īlī line of hermeneutics (Dānishpazhūh in al-Ṭūsī (1956): 82). In another, shorter treatise (al-Ṭūsī (1956): 38–88), he further elaborates a typical Ismā'īlī theory of a hidden constellation of meaning and signification. Here he postulates the existence of two worlds, one of "senses" (*maḥsūs*), which corresponds to the second, that is, the world of "perceptions" (*ma'qul*, lit. = based on "intellect"). The relationship of perceptions to senses is like that of life to body. The world of perceptions is called the spiritual world, the world of senses the corporeal world. For every sensible object in this world, there is a perceptive correspondence in the other; for every individual in this world, there is a soul (*rūḥ*) in the other; and for every apparent reality here, there is a hidden meaning in the other (al-Ṭūsī (1956): 83). The sources of perception in the upper world are the sources (*maṣdar*) of all possibilities of sensibility here in the lower world. That which we feel in this lower world is a mere manifestation (*maẓhar*) of that corresponding source of intellection in the upper world. There can be nothing in that spiritual world without a corresponding manifestation here in the physical world; and, conversely, there is nothing in the physical world which does not represent a spiritual reality.

Having established a perfect ontological/epistemological correspondence (because here being and meaning are identical) between things manifest and evident in this world and things intelligent and hidden in the other, Khwājah Naṣīr extends the preparatory argument into a standard Ismā'īlī rationale for the necessity of an Imām. Had it not been for the word of God as the supreme hidden Truth, there would be no manifested world. There must, by necessity, be a link, a correspondence, between the Word of God and the Manifested World. That link, too, must be of the same nature and composition as the manifested world. "Like other individuals subject to sense-perceptions, he has to be born, raised, and become old, one succeeding the other" (al-Ṭūsī (1956): 84). Without this intermediary force, of the same nature as the physical world itself, there will be no sustaining link between the commanding word of God and the physical world.

HISTORIOGRAPHY

There is a supplement to al-Juwaynī's famous history of the Mongols, *Tārīkh-i jahāngushā*, whose authorship has been attributed to Khwājah

Naṣīr (al-Juwaynī (1937), 3: 279–92). This short narrative, in effect, is a concise account of Khwājah Naṣīr's own observations as a participant in the events immediately surrounding the conquest of Baghdad. His historical narrative is concise, precise and devoid of any unnecessary hyperbole. He pays equal attention to diplomatic and military manoeuvres that took place between the Shawwāl of 655/October–November 1257 and Ṣafar 656/February–March 1258. He gives a full and detailed account of the siege of Baghdad, including the description of a wall which was erected around the capital and then a ditch which was dug between the erected wall and the city. Catapults were then set in specific strategic locations and the city thus forced to capitulate. Khwājah Naṣīr also gives a full description of Hūlāgū's strategic plannings, the central front and the left and right flank of the army. Six days of fierce fighting between the 'Abbasid caliph and the Mongol warlord are reported by Khwājah Naṣīr, beginning on Tuesday 22 Muḥarram 656/29 January 1258. In the middle of the fierce fighting, he notes, Hūlāgū orders a letter of amnesty to be written and attached to arms and thrown from six directions into the capital city. According to this letter, the following groups were given amnesty: the *sayyids*, the scholars, the Christian priests, the elders of the community and anyone else who refused to fight the Mongols.

Khwājah Naṣīr reports a remarkable encounter between Hūlāgū and caliph al-Musta'ṣim when the latter finally surrenders on Monday 4 Safar 656/11 February 1258 (al-Juwaynī (1937), 3: 290). "Eat them", Hūlāgū orders the caliph, pointing to the gold he had just recovered from al-Musta'ṣim's treasury. "These cannot be eaten", the caliph objects. "Then why did you keep them? Why did you not spend them on your army? Why did you not melt these iron doors into spears and prevent me from crossing the Oxus River?" The caliph says because it was God's will. Hūlāgū replies, "that which will happen to you is also God's will."

POETICS

Khwājah Naṣīr would find time away from his military and administrative responsibilities, as well as time away from his scientific and philosophical writings, to attend to matters musical and poetic. In his treatise on music (al-Ṭūsī (1986): 250) he once considered prosody a particular branch of musicology. But he also devoted an entire book to the subject of prosody and poetics. His treatise on poetics, *Mi'yār al-ash'ār*, consists of an introduction and two chapters (al-Ṭūsī (1990): 21). Khwājah Naṣīr examines the nature of poetry in the introduction. The two chapters cover prosody (*'arūḍ* and *qāfiyyah*). Although *Mi'yār al-ash'ār* has been (unjustly) dismissed as "no great masterpiece" (Boyle (1968): 621), it provides one of the most insightful accounts of Persian poetics extant.

Following a long tradition in Arabic and Persian poetics and prosody, Khwājah Naṣīr identifies poetry as a speech-act (*kalām*) which is imaginative (*mukhayyal*) and rhythmic (*mawzūn*). But whereas he attributes this definition to logicians, he adds that customarily (in *'urf-i jumhūr*) poetry is "an act of speech which is rhythmic and has rhyme" (al-Ṭūsī (1990): 21). Thus he does not consider rhyme (*qāfiyyah*) as an essential part of a poem. A speech-act (*kalām*) consists of words (*alfāẓ*) which are, in turn, made of letters (*ḥurūf*) which, according to their particular configurations, indicate a specific meaning. It is impossible to imagine a poem without the use of words. However, Khwājah Naṣīr can conceive of an inarticulate manual or facial expression to function as a verbal form and thus perform a function in a poem. But rhythmic and rhyming words that do not mean anything cannot be considered a poem.

Imagination is constitutional to poetry. Khwājah Naṣīr defines imagination as the power of "influence of words on the soul" (al-Ṭūsī (1990): 21). This influence can appear in expanding or contracting the soul in its disposition. The functional purpose of poetry is to generate this imaginative influence on the soul, the ultimate objective of which is to lead the individual to perform, or abstain from performing, an action. The act of the poetic imagination could also generate a particular feeling in an individual, such as satisfaction or anger. Khwājah Naṣīr further adds that whereas the Greeks have considered imagination as constitutional to poetry, Persian and Arab poets have considered it an aspect of poetic excellence, which is to say that for the Greeks the act of imagination is innate to poetry, whereas for Persian and Arab poets it is an attribute, "an ideal to be achieved" (*ibid.*: 22).

Rhythm (*wazn*) is a unique configuration of movements and pauses in poetry which is a source of particular pleasure for the reader. Rhythm is instrumental in the poetic acts of imagination. "Every rhythmic act is in one way or another conducive to imagination, yet not everything that induces imagination is rhythmic" (al-Ṭūsī (1990): 22). Imagination and rhythm are two separate aspects of poetry. Moreover, rhythm itself has a dual function, once as rhythm proper, once as a conducive force in the generation of imagination. Rhythm, or metre, is constitutional to poetry. There are "incomplete" configurations in metre, such as in Persian khusrawānīs, which some have considered as part of the metric system and some have not (*ibid.*: 22–3). Rhymes are identical wordings at the end of every systemic cycle (*adwār*), such as at the end of a hemistich. Khwājah Naṣīr reports that, in Greek poetry, rhymes are not significant. He further reports that rhyming has not been central in Persian poetry either. He then concludes that "the significance of rhyme is not constitutional to poetry, rather it is customarily instrumental to it" (*ibid.*: 23). In conclusion, "Poetry . . . is a rhythmic act of speech, and nothing more. But if rhyming is considered to be central to poetry, then it is a rhythmic act of speech in such a way that if it exceeds one [such act, then] those identical acts rhyme" (*ibid.*).

In his comparative poetics, Khwājah Naṣīr discusses the difference between Persian and Arabic prosody. Words are different in their gravity (*rizānat*) and lightness (*khiffat*). "In comparison to Persian, Arabic is closer to gravity and heaviness [*thiql*], and Persian is closer to lightness" (al-Ṭūsī (1990): 24). The reason for the gravity of words has to do either with the more difficult source of their origin in vocal formations or with their particular configuration of letters. In correspondence to this gravity or lightness of words in a language, graver or lighter metric systems are compatible with poetic compositions in that language.

In addition to poetics (*'ilm-i naqd-i shi'r*) and prosody (which consists of metrical structures, or *'arūḍ*, and rhyme, or *qāfiyyah*), there are a number of other branches of knowledge that are related to poetry. Linguistics, rhetoric, aesthetics and literary criticism are among the disciplinary approaches to the study of poetry. The study of the nature and function of imagination is a branch of logic. The study of rhythm or metre is an aspect of musicology.

The bulk of Khwājah Naṣīr's *Mi'yār al-ash'ār* consists of two treatises on *'arūḍ* (metrical structures) and *qāfiyyah* (rhyme). In his chapter on *'arūḍ*, Khwājāh Naṣīr provides a standard exposition of Arabic prosody with comparative references to Persian poetry. The poem he chooses to scan as an example is the opening verse of Firdawsī's *Shāh-nāmah*: "In the name of God of Spirit and Intellect / Beyond which the Imagination cannot reach" (al-Ṭūsī (1990): 35–6). After a full exposition of Arabic and Persian prosody, in which he constantly follows al-Khalīl ibn Aḥmad's (d. *c.* 170/786) famous concentric circles (*ibid.*: 40–68), he concludes with a chapter "On the Benefit and Advantages of Prosody" (*ibid.*: 123–5). He begins by reporting that there is a group of people who altogether question any validity, benefit, or significance to prosody. These people argue that appreciation of poetry (*idrāk*) is contingent upon an individual's having taste (*dhawq*). "He who has taste does not need prosody, and he who lacks it could through prosody enjoy poetry to some degree" (*ibid.*: 123). But Khwājah Naṣīr proceeds to list four benefits for the science of prosody. Firstly, he suggests that a knowledge of prosody cannot come from taste but from mastering the art of poetry itself. Having a taste for sweetness, he argues, is different from having a knowledge of the varieties of sweetnesses, their compositions, dispositions, specifics of their constitution, etc. Secondly, when one has knowledge of prosody, one immediately recognizes the defects of a poem. Those who merely have a taste for poetry could not possibly detect what is good and what is defective in a poetic structure. Thirdly, crucial distinctions between metrical systems are not always possible by merely having a taste for poetry. Khwājah Naṣīr cites examples from both Persian and Arabic poetry where a knowledge of prosody is helpful in their correct reading. He also reports on a poet in his own time who had composed a long panegyric in *ṭawīl* metre in which one of his verses did not match the metre (al-Ṭūsī (1990): 125). Khwājah Naṣīr says that he could not explain this to the poet because he did not know prosody. But after a while the poet intuitively discovered the defect and rectified it. Fourthly, for the person who lacks intuitive taste in poetry, prosody is helpful in distinguishing between prose and poetry. Khwājah Naṣīr further adds that for those who lack a natural gift of appreciation for poetry, a knowledge of prosody can generate an interest for them. Khwājah Naṣīr offers himself as an example of a person who, through knowledge of prosody, developed a taste for poetry.

In his treatise on rhyme, Khwājah Naṣīr continues with his comparative discussion of Arabic and Persian rules governing the rhyming of verses. Again he relies primarily on al-Khalīl as his source and defines rhyme as "the configuration of letters and vowels between the last consonant letter of a verse and the consonant letter that precedes it" (al-Ṭūsī (1990): 129). He then provides his slight modification leading to the following re-definition of rhyme: "a configuration consisting of a letter or [a number of] letters which is necessary to be [present] in similar words at the end of verses or hemistichs, in repetition or as if in repetition" (*ibid.*: 130). A typical discussion by Khwājah Naṣīr in this treatise is his critical dismissal of the use of *shāygān* (the name of a legendary treasure) in rhyming verses. In words such as *shāygān*, *asbān* (horses) and *mardān* (men), the latter two letters – *an* – could be used as the rhyming letters, and since there is an overabundance of such constructions, this kind of rhyming is called *shāygān*. But Khwājah Naṣīr dismisses the uses of *shāygān* rhyming as unacceptable (*ibid.*: 154). He concludes this treatise with some remarks on certain problems in Arabic and Persian rhyming systems and provides solutions to them.

Khwājah Naṣīr himself was a gifted poet, and some of his poetry has survived (Nafīsī (1956): 73–81; Mudarris Raḍawī (1955): 54–65). In the following few lines, he summmarizes his ontology:

> Being is of two kinds in the mind:
> Either the Necessary Being or contingent being.
> The contingent being is either substance or accident,
> The substance divided into five segments.
> Body, and its two principles – matter and form,
> Then Soul and Intellect, learn them fast.
> Divided into nine are made accidents and this
> I learnt when discussing the substance of the Intellect.
> How many, How much, Where, When, Added to What,
> located Where?

Then Active and Passive, and possession of being.
Thus the Necessary Being is exempted of all these,
Because it was, is, and shall be and none of these were.
(Mudarris Raḍawī (1955): 62)

CONCLUSION

It is impossible to exaggerate either the personal or the institutional significance of Khwājah Naṣīr al-Dīn al-Ṭūsī in medieval Islamic philosophy. Had he not even founded the Maraghah Observatory as a major institution of higher learning and thus brought together a galaxy of distinguished philosophers and scientists, had he not served a world-conqueror as a philosopher/vizier and used that position to advance the causes of science and philosophy in an otherwise hostile environment, and had he not written so massively in Persian, thus making a major contribution to the establishment of this language as the second most important medium of scientific and philosophical inquiry in Islamic intellectual history, his own writings on a range of scientific and philosophical discourses would still have been enough to put him on a par with al-Fārābī and Ibn Sīnā as among the finest achievements of medieval learning. Perhaps the most compelling image of Khwājah Naṣīr that shines through all his writings and activities is that of a philosopher/vizier, a distinctly Persian phenomenon that combined avid theoretical learning with a relentless penchant for practical politics.

As a philosopher/vizier, Khwājah Naṣīr is prototypical of a breed apart, the closest approximation to the Platonic (and pre-Islamic Persian) ideal of the philosopher/king (see Dabashi (1990)). In (full) control of the centre of political power, he was also the most erudite philosopher of his time. The combination of these two forces – power and knowledge – results in a unique "political philosophy" which is both a politically based philosophy and a philosophically anchored politics. The implications of this discourse go beyond the immediate confinements of both political establishment and philosophical engagement. A unique position of legitimate authority is self-generated in this prototype of the philosopher/vizier that supersedes both the political order proper and the philosophical inquiry abstracted from its politics. The philosophical discourse of the philosopher/vizier assumes a unique ethical grounding that exacts obedience from both the political and the religious figures of authority. To the warlord (e.g., Hūlāgū), the philosopher/vizier speaks from the commanding position of a Muslim (interpreter of the sacred) philosopher (the possessor of reason, an astronomer, a physician). To the religious authorities, the *'ulamā'* proper, the philosopher/vizier speaks with the voice and authority of the man of power, the political intellect closest to the epicentre of (legitimate) violence, the warlord with his able hand on the sword. The philosopher/vizier, with Khwājah Naṣīr as its archetypal example, thus occupies a central position of command and obedience in the Islamic and Persian political culture, instrumental in creating the material conditions for the growth and development of philosophy, the instrumentality of reason in pre-modern intellectual history.

REFERENCES

Ahanī, Ghulām Ḥusayn (1983) *Kulīyyāt-i falsafah-yi islāmī* (Tehran).

Bahār, Muḥammad Taqī (Malik al-Shu'arā') (1952) *Sabk-shināsī*, 3 vols (Tehran).

Boyle, J. A. (1968) "Dynastic and Political History of the Īl-Khāns", in J. A. Boyle (ed.), *The Cambridge History of Iran, 5, The Saljug and Mongol Periods* (Cambridge): 303–421.

Browne, Edward G. (1906) *A Literary History of Persia*, 7 vols, (Cambridge).

Corbin, Henry (1980) *Avicenna and the Visionary Recital*, trans. W. Trask (Irving).

Dabashi, Hamid (1990) "Farhang-i sīāsī-yi shāh-nāmah: andīshah-yi sīāsī-yi fīlsūf/ Pādishāh dar salṭanat-i Khusraw anushīrwān", *Irānshināsī*, 2(2) (summer): 321–41.

Daftary, Farhad (1990) *The Ismā'īlīs: Their History and Doctrines* (Cambridge).

Durkheim, Emile (1933) *The Division of Labor in Society* (New York).

Fakhry, Majid (1983) *A History of Islamic Philosophy* (New York).

Humā'ī, Jalāl al-Dīn (1956) "Muqaddimah-yi qadīm-i akhlāq-i nāṣirī", *Majalla-yi Dānishkada-yi adabiyyāt*, 3(3) (March–April): 17–25.

—— (1984) *Tā'rīkh-i 'ulūm-i islāmī* (Tehran).

Ibn Baṭṭūṭah (1969) *Riḥlah ibn Baṭṭūṭah*, edited, annotated and translated into Persian with an introduction by Muḥammad 'Alī Muwaḥḥid (Tehran).

Ibn Khaldūn (1958) *The Muqaddimah: an Introduction to History*, translated from the Arabic by Franz Rosenthal, 3 vols (Princeton).

Ibn Sīnā (1974a) *Dānish-nāmah-yi 'alā'ī: risāla-yi manṭiq*, edited, annotated, and with an introduction by Muḥammad Mu'īn and Sayyid Muḥammad Mishkāt (Tehran).

—— (1974b) *Dānish-nāmah-yi 'alā'ī: Ilāhiyyāt*, edited, annotated, and with an introduction by Muḥammad Mu'īn (Tehran).

—— (1974c) *Dānish-nāmah-yi 'alā'ī: tabī'īyyāt*, edited, annotated, and with an introduction by Muḥammad Mishkāt (Tehran).

—— (1981) *al-Ishārāt wa'l-tanbīhāt* (Tehran).

—— (1984) *al-Ishārāt wa'l-tanbīhāt*, edited, annotated, translated into Persian, and with an introduction and commentary by Ḥasan Malikshāhī (Tehran).

Isfandyār, Kaykhusraw (1983) *Dabishtān-i madhāhib*, 2 vols, edited, annotated, with an introduction by Raḥīm Raḥīmzādah Malik (Tehran).

Jahn, Karl (1971) *Die Chinageschichte des Rasid ad-din*, Übersetzung, Kommentar, Facsimiletafeln (Vienna).

Al-Juwaynī, 'Alā al-Dīn 'Aṭā' Malik ibn Bahā' al-Dīn Muḥammad ibn Muḥammad (1937) *Tā'rīkh-i jahāngushā,* 3 vols, edited, annotated, with an introduction by Muḥammad Qazvīnī (Leiden).
Kennedy, E. S. (1968) "The Exact Sciences in Iran under the Saljugs and Mongols", in J. A. Boyle (ed.), *The Cambridge History of Iran*, 5, *The Saljug and Mongol Periods* (Cambridge): 659–79.
Khaṭībī, Ḥusayn (1956) "Nathr-i fārsī dar qarn-i haftum-i hijrī va sabk-i athār-i fārsī-yi Khwājah Naṣīr al-Dīn Ṭūsī", *Majalla-yi Dānishkada-yi adabiyyāt,* 3(4) (June–July): 21–9.
Khwāndmīr, Ghīyāth al-Dīn ibn Humām al-Dīn al-Ḥusaynī, known as Khwāndmīr (1954) *Tā'rīkh-i ḥabīb al-sīyar fī akhbār afrād al-bashar,* edited by Muḥammad Dabīr Sīyāqī, with an introduction by Jalāl Humā'ī (Tehran).
Khwānsārī, Mīr Sayyid Muḥammad Bāqir (1981) *Rawḍāt al-jannāt,* 8 vols (Tehran).
Kīshī, Shams al-Dīn and Khwājah-yi Naṣīr al-Ṭūsī (1984) "Nāmah-yi Shams al-Dīn Kīshī bih Khwāja-yi Ṭūsī", in Mudarrisī Zanjānī, *Sarguzasht wa 'aqā'id-i falsafī-yi Khwājah Naṣīr al-Dīn Ṭūsī* (Tehran): 198–206.
Leaman, Oliver (1985) *An Introduction to Medieval Islamic Philosophy* (Cambridge).
Maḥmūd, 'Abd al-Ḥalīm (1985) *al-Tafkīr al-falsafī fi'l-islām* (Beirut).
Mīnuvī, Mujtabā (1955) "Tarjuma-yi 'ulūm-i chīnī bih fārsī dar qarn-i hashtum-i hijrī", *Majalla-yi Dānishkada-yi adabiyyāt,* 3(1) (September–October): 1–26.
Morewedge, Parviz (1972) "Philosophical Analysis and Ibn Sina's 'Essence–Existence' Distinction", *Journal of the American Oriental Society,* 92(3) (July–September): 425–35.
—— (1975) "The Analysis of 'Substance' in Ṭūsī's *Logic* and in the Ibn Sīnian Tradition", in George F. Hourani (ed.) *Essays on Islamic Philosophy and Science* (Albany): 158–88.
—— (1982) "Greek Sources of Some Near Eastern Philosophies of Being and Existence", in Morewedge (ed.), *Philosophers of Existence Ancient and Medieval* (New York).
Mudarrisı Raḍawī, Muḥammad Taqī (1955) *Aḥwāl wa āthār-i ustād-i bashar wa 'aql-i hādī 'ashar Muḥammad ibn Muḥammad ibn al-Ḥasan al-Ṭūsī Mulaqqab bih Khwājah Naṣīr al-Dīn* (Tehran).
—— (1975) *Aḥwāl va Athār-i Khwājah Naṣīr al-Dīn Ṭūsī* (Tehran).
Mudarrisī Zanjānī, Muḥammad (1984) *Sarguzasht wa 'aqā'id-i falsafī-yi Khwājah Naṣīr al-Dīn Ṭūsī* (Tehran).
Mu'īn, Muḥammad (1956) "Naṣīr al-Dīn al-Ṭūsī wa zabān wa adab-i pārsī", *Majalla-yi Dānishkada-yi abadiyyāt,* 3(4) (June–July): 30–42.
Mustawfī, Hamd Allāh (1985) *Tā'rīkh-i guzīdah,* edited, annotated, with an introduction by 'Abd al-Ḥusayn Navā'ī (Tehran).
Nafīsī, Sa'īd (1956) "Ashā'ar-i fārsī-yi Khwājah [Naṣīr]", *Majalla-yi Dānishkada-yi adabiyyāt,* 3(4) (June–July): 73–81.
Nasr, S. H. (1976a) "Naṣīr al-Dīn al-Ṭūsī", *Dictionary of Scientific Biography,* ed. C. Gillespie (New York), 13: 508–14.
—— (1976b) "Quṭb al-Dīn Shīrāzī", *Dictionary of Scientific Biography* (New York), 11: 247–53.
Peters, F. E. (1968) *Aristotle and the Arabs: the Aristotelian Tradition in Islam* (New York and London).

Potter, Lawrence Goddard (1992) *The Kart Dynasty of Herat: Religion and Politics in Medieval Islam* (Ph.D. dissertation, Columbia University).

Pūrnāmdārīān, Taqī (1985) *Ramz wa dāstān-hā-yi ramzī dar adab-i fārsī* (Tehran).

Qazwīnī, Muḥammad (1984) *Yād-dāsht-hā-yi Qazwīnī*, edited by Īraj Afshār, 10 vols (Tehran).

Quatremère, M. (1834) *Histoire des Mongols de la Perse, écrite en persan par Raschid-Eldin*, publiée, traduite en français, accompagnie de notes et d'un mémoire sur la vie et les ouvrages de l'auteur (Paris).

Rashīd al-Dīn Faḍl Allāh al-Wazīr ibn 'Imād al-Dawlah Abi'l-Khayr ibn Muwaffaq al-Dawlah 'Alī (1959) *Jami' al-tawārīkh*, 2 vols, edited by Bahman Karīmī (Tehran).

Rypka, Jan *et al.* (1968) *History of Iranian Literature*, edited by Karl Jahn (Dordrecht).

Ṣafā, Dhabīhullāh (1956) "*Taḥrīrāt-i* Khwājah Naṣīr al-Dīn Ṭūsī", *Majalla-yi Dānishkada-yi adabiyyāt*, 3(4) (June–July): 11–20.

—— (1959–85) *Tārīkh-i adabiyyāt dar Iran*, 5 vols (Tehran).

Saliba, George (1987) "The Role of Maraghah in the Development of Islamic Astronomy: a Scientific Revolution before the Renaissance", *Revue de Synthèse*, fourth series, 3–4 (July–December): 361–73.

Ṣalībā, Jamīl (1986) *Ta'rīkh al-falsafah al-'arabiyyah* (Beirut).

Sāyilī, Āydīn (1956) "Khwājah Naṣīr Ṭūsī wa raṣad-khāna-yi Marāghah", *Majalla-yi Dānishkada-yi adabiyyāt*, 3(4) (June–July): 58–72.

Al-Shahrastānī, Abu'l-Fatḥ Muḥammad ibn 'Abd Allāh 'Abd al-Karīm (1979) *al-Milal wa'l-niḥal*, edited, translated into Persian, annotated, and with an introduction by Sayyid Muḥammad Riḍā' Jalālī Nā'īnī, 2 vols (Tehran).

Sheikh, M. Saeed (1962) *Islamic Philosophy*, foreword by M. M. Sharif (London).

Shūshtarī, Qāḍī Sayyid Nūr Allāh (1986) *Majālis al-mu'minīn*, 2 vols (Tehran).

Siddiqi, Bakhtyar Husain (1963) "Naṣīr al-Dīn Ṭūsī", in M. M. Sharif (ed.), *A History of Muslim Philosophy*, 2 vols (Wiesbaden): 564–80.

Tunikābunī, Mīrzā Muḥammad (1985) *Qiṣaṣ al-'ulamā'* (Tehran).

Al-Ṭūsī, Khwājah Naṣīr al-Dīn (1947) *Asās al-iqtibās*, edited and annotated with an introduction by Mudarris Raḍawī (Tehran).

—— (1956) "Guftārī az Khwājah-yi Ṭūsī bih rawish-i Baīnīān", edited and annotated by Muḥammad Taqī Dānishpazhūh, *Majalla-yi Dānishkada-yi adabiyyāt*, 3(4) (June–July): 82–8.

—— (1957) "Guftārī az Khwājah-yi Ṭūsī dar bāra-yi 'nabūd wa būd'", edited by M. T. Dānishpazhūh, *Majalla-yi Dānishkada-yi adabiyyāt*, 4(3) (March–April): 11–24.

—— (1966) *Awṣāf al-ashrāf*, edited by Sayyid Nasr Allāh Taqawī, with an introduction by Muḥammad Mudarrisī (Tehran).

—— (1977a) *Akhlāq-i nāṣirī*, edited, annotated, and with an introduction by Mujtabā Mīnuwī and 'Alī Riḍā Ḥaydarī (Tehran).

—— (1977b) *Tajrīd al-i'tiqād*, with 'Allāmah al-Ḥillī's *Kashf al-murād fi sharḥ tajrīd al-i'tiqād*, edited, annotated and translated into Persian with additional commentaries by Ayatollah Ḥājj Shaykh Abu'l-Ḥasan al-Sha'rānī (Tehran).

—— (1982) *Akhlāq-i Muḥtashamī* – plus three other treatises, edited and annotated with an introduction by Muḥammad Taqī Dānishpazhūh (Tehran).

—— (1983) *Sharḥ al-ishārāt. li'-Khwājah Naṣīr al-Dīn al-Ṭūsī wa li'l-Imām Fakhr al-Dīn al-Rāzī*, 2 vols (Qom).

—— (1984a) "Ithbāt waḥdāt Allāh Jalla Jalālahū", in Mudarrisī Zanjānī, *Sarguzasht wa 'aqā'id-i falsafī-yi Khwājah Naṣīr al-Dīn Ṭūsī* (Tehran): 182–3.

—— (1984b) "'I'tiqādiyyah", in Mudarrisī Zanjānī, *Sarguzasht wa 'aqā'id-i falsafī-yi Khwājah Naṣīr al-Dīn Ṭūsī* (Tehran): 183–5.

—— (1986) "Risālā-yi musiqī-yi Khwājah Naṣīr al-Dīn Ṭūsı", edited, annotated, with an introduction by Dāwūd Isfahānian, *Farhanq-i Irān-zamīn*, 26: 245–52.

—— (1987) *Āghāz wa anjām*, edited, annotated, with an introduction by Ḥasan Ḥasanzādah Āmulī (Tehran).

—— (1988a) *Tajrīd al-itiqād, with 'Allamah al-Ḥillī's Kashf al-murād fī sharḥ tajrīd al-i'tiqād* (Beirut).

—— (1988b) *Tajrīd al-manṭiq*, (Beirut).

—— (1990) *Mi'yār al-ash'ār*, edited, annotated, with an introduction by Jalīl Tajlīl (Tehran).

—— (1991) *The Metaphysics of Ṭūsī: Treatise on the Proof of a Necessary [Being]; Treatise on Determination and Destiny; Treatise on Division of Existence*, Persian texts, with English translations by Parviz Morewedge (New York).

Walbridge, John (1992) *The Science of Mystic Lights: Quṭb al-Dīn Shīrāzī and Illuminationist Tradition in Islamic Philosophy* (Cambridge, Mass.).

CHAPTER 33

From al-Ṭūsī to the School of Iṣfahān

John Cooper

The period in Islamic philosophy from the death of Naṣīr al-Dīn al-Ṭūsī in 672/1274 to the beginning of what has come to be known as the "School of Iṣfahān", which may, for convenience, be placed during the latter part of the tenth/sixteenth century, encompasses some three hundred years of intense philosophical activity on many fronts, an understanding of which is essential in order to comprehend the changes which the speculative sciences underwent in the Ṣafavid era. Unfortunately, however, this period has not received the attention which the earlier, and, to a certain extent, later periods have enjoyed in the history of Islamic philosophy. To some extent this lack of attention may be attributed to the tendency of writers in this period to produce commentaries, supercommentaries, glosses, superglosses and marginalia on the works of their predecessors rather than to write new texts (this is only in part true, as will become clear), and to the tendency of many modern researchers to see such writing as a sign of intellectual stagnation. This is a view which needs to be revised, however, if the richness and importance of these texts is to be understood, for it is in the elaboration of the basic materials of Islamic philosophy in both the commenting texts and the original texts during this period that the ideas which gradually accumulated to produce the later flowering of the intellectual sciences can be found.

It is the purpose of this chapter to provide an overview of certain strands in the history of the philosophy of this period. The overview will be seen to be selective in that several important figures and "schools" have been omitted. Nothing here will be said about the "school" of Ibn ʿArabī which culminated in the writings of Jāmī, nor of the closely related Sufi authors who give evidence of their acquaintance with the metaphysical world of the Shaykh al-Akbar in their poetry and commentaries on poetry, typified at the end of the period under discussion by the Nūrbakhshī Shaykh Shams al-Dīn Lāhījī, the author of one of the most famous commentaries on Shabastārī's *Gulshan-i rāz*, who died in 915/1506, respected by Dawānī and Jāmī, and visited three years before his death by the Ṣafavid Shah Ismā'īl. Not that such schools and figures are not important in tracing the emerging synthesis of the Ṣafavid era. But two main lines run through this chapter: that of the development of Peripatetic and *ishrāqī* philosophy, and that of the increasingly important ground that philosophy came to hold in Shī'ī thought.

At one end of the period examined in this chapter, the nearer to our times, stands the monumental achievement of Ṣadr al-Dīn al-Shīrāzī, in particular his *Kitāb al-asfār*. This work has been viewed by modern scholars to be a majestic synthesis of several currents of speculative thinking in the Islamic tradition[1] – *mashshā'ī* (Peripatetic) philosophy, whose chief practitioner had been Ibn Sīnā; *ishrāqī* philosophy, initiated by Suhrawardī; the gnostic philosophy of Ibn 'Arabī and his followers; and the *kalām* (dialectical theology) of the Mu'tazilites, Ash'arites, and Shī'īs – brought together within a framework provided by the Imāmology of the Twelver Shī'īs. At the other extreme these strands lie to a certain extent, but not altogether, separate, although it would be wrong to think of their ravelling as the work of a single person: in various combinations, strands are woven together by a number of thinkers over these centuries until it becomes virtually impossible by the end of the ninth/fifteenth century in Persia to name anyone who can be said to have stuck to only one of these currents of thought. Even in a figure such as Mīr Findiriskī (d. 1050/1640–1), known from his extant works as a *mashshā'ī*, the Peripateticism is inevitably coloured for us by his reputation as a Sufi.[2] Henceforth it will be appropriate to speak only of a predominating tendency towards one strand of thought or another. The fusion achieved by Mullā Ṣadrā was to be an inseparable amalgam.

It is instructive to take Naṣīr al-Dīn al-Ṭūsī at the further extreme of this period for he too wrote works within a broad spectrum of different approaches, yet he never brought them all together in one single work. The previous chapter lists his output, and from this it can be seen that Ṭūsī, at various times in his life, wrote on Ismā'īlī metaphysics, *mashshā'ī* philosophy, *kalām*, ethics (in the broad traditional sense including economics and politics) and Sufism, and was acquainted with *ishrāqī* philosophy and the thinking of Ibn 'Arabī (at least he corresponded with Ṣadr al-Dīn al-Qūnawī, and cannot have been ignorant of his concerns); this is not to mention his work as a mathematician and astronomer, and his interest in poetry and poetics. It is true that philosophy is a unifying characteristic in his work, if natural philosophy be included and the philosophizing tendency in his *kalām* and ethics be acknowledged, but he wrote each of his works wearing, as it were, a different hat. As mentioned in the previous chapter, it was also Naṣīr al-Dīn al-Ṭūsī who founded the observatory at Marāghah, which provided a home for so many philosophers and scientists of his and the subsequent generation.

Who were the intellectual giants who stand at the beginning of this period? Ṭūsī himself died, as already mentioned, in 672/1274; Ibn 'Arabī had died in Damascus in 638/1240; and Fakhr al-Dīn al-Rāzī, the renowned theologian, who can at least be counted as a philosopher for his commentary on Ibn Sīnā's *Kitāb al-ishārāt wa'l-tanbīhāt*,[3] and who numbered several philosophers among his students, had died in 606/1209. Another outstanding philosopher of the generation preceding Ṭūsī should also be mentioned, that is Afḍal al-Dīn Muḥammad al-Kāshānī, known as Bābā Afḍal, the most probable date for whose death is 610/1213–14.[4] He is referred to by Ṭūsī on a point of logic in the latter's *Sharḥ al-ishārāt*, and it has been pointed out that Mullā Ṣadrā was indebted to him when writing his *Iksīr al-'ārifīn*.[5] Bābā Afḍal, who wrote most of his works in a stylistically and terminologically attractive Persian, stressed the path to salvation through knowledge of the Self, which has led Nasr to describe his philosophy as autology.[6] His epistemology, which thus emphasizes the self-knowledge of human beings, has affinity with that of Suhrawardī in its linking of ontology and epistemology, and foreshadows Mullā Ṣadrā and his doctrine of the essential identity of knower, known and knowledge (*ittiḥād al-'āqil wa'l-ma'qūl*). Although his writings contain no explicit references to Sufism, and his style is that of the Peripateticism of Ibn Sīnā, his philosophy is infused with a mystical strand and is described by Corbin as "Hermeticizing".[7]

The reputations of two contemporaries of Ṭūsī have survived to the present day, each on account of a text he wrote which became the original for numerous commentaries, and which are studied even today in *madrasahs* with one or other of these commentaries. The first is Athīr al-Dīn Mufaḍḍal ibn 'Umar al-Abharī (d. 663/1264), who was one of Fakhr al-Dīn al-Rāzī's most outstanding pupils. Born in Mosul, he emigrated at the time of the Mongol invasion first to Damascus and then to Irbil. Naṣīr al-Dīn al-Ṭūsī wrote a commentary on his *Tanzīl al-afkār* on logic,[8] but more important was his *Kitāb al-hidāyah* on metaphysics and natural philosophy, which has continued to be used as a teaching text, particularly in the Indian subcontinent, especially in conjunction with the commentary of Mullā Ṣadrā.[9] His *Kitāb al-isāghūjī* was a popular introduction to the study of logic, and was translated into Latin in the eleventh/seventeenth century.[10] He is also credited with a *Kitāb al-ishārāt* and a *Kitāb al-maḥṣūl*, said to have been modelled respectively on Ibn Sīnā's famous work and the *Kitāb al-taḥṣīl* of Ibn Sīnā's student Bahmanyār.[11] These two works testify to a teacher–pupil "chain" linking Ibn Sīnā with Ṭūsī's generation of philosophers, which is traditionally given as: Ibn Sīnā – Bahmanyār – Abu'l-'Abbās al-Lawkarī –

Afḍal al-Dīn al-Jīlānī – Ṣadr al-Dīn al-Sarakhsī – Farīd al-Dīn Damād al-Nīsābūrī, this latter having also been a pupil of Fakhr al-Dīn al-Rāzī and a teacher of Naṣīr al-Dīn al-Ṭūsī.[12]

Also a contemporary of Ṭūsī was the Shāfi'ī philosopher and logician Najm al-Dīn 'Alī ibn 'Umar al-Kātibī al-Qazwīnī, known as Dabīrān (d. 675/1276). He was a pupil of Abharī, and taught in Juwayn in present-day Afghanistan (where he is said to have taken Quṭb al-Dīn al-Shīrāzī to teach with him for a while) and at Ṭūsī's observatory at Maraghah, which he helped to found.[13] His two most enduring works have been the much-commented *al-Risālat al-shamsiyyah* on logic,[14] and the *Ḥikmat al-'ayn* on metaphysics, the latter being usually read with the commentary of al-Bukhārī[15] (it was, incidentally, one of the sources for Muḥammad Iqbāl's *Development of Metaphysics in Persia*). He was influenced by the ideas of Fakhr al-Dīn al-Rāzī, on two of whose works, *al-Muḥaṣṣal* and *al-Mulakhkhaṣ*, he wrote commentaries. He rejected the proof for the Necessary Existent based on the impossibility of infinite regress, and gave another proof in a treatise called *al-Risālah fī ithbāt al-wājib*.

Of the students of Ṭūsī, two in particular stand out for our consideration here: Quṭb al-Dīn al-Shīrāzī (634/1236–710/1311) and the 'Allāmah al-Ḥillī (648/1250–726/1325). Both have been briefly referred to in the previous chapter, but Quṭb al-Dīn deserves to be further discussed because of his interest in *ishrāqī* philosophy, which has been the object of a recent study.[16] Apart from studying with Ṭūsī (he studied Ibn Sīnā's *Kitāb al-ishārāt* with him) and Dabīrān Kātibī, he was also steeped in the Sufi tradition (his father was a disciple of Shihāb al-Dīn 'Umar al-Suhrawardī (d. 632/1234–5)), is said to have met Jalāl al-Dīn Rūmī and is known to have studied with Rūmī's son-in-law and successor, Ṣadr al-Dīn al-Qūnawī (he studied *Ḥadīth* with him as well as the mystical sciences). He is also the author of a commentary on al-Suhrawardī's *Ḥikmat al-ishrāq*, which, although relying much on the earlier commentary of Shams al-Dīn al-Shahrazūrī, which it superseded as the text for students up to the present day, expresses the Shaykh al-Ishrāq's Philosophy of Illumination in Peripatetic terms, stressing the continuity of the *Ḥikmat al-ishrāq* both with Suhrawardī's other, more Peripatetic works, and also with the general Islamic philosophical tradition.[17] Another work by Quṭb al-Dīn, his encyclopedic *Durrat al-tāj li-ghurrat al-dubāj* ("The Pearly Crown for Dubāj's Brow") is in Persian. The philosophical sections of this work, while being totally Peripatetic in style, have also been shown to be heavily dependent on Suhrawardī's *Ḥikmat al-Ishrāq*.[18]

The 'Allāmah al-Ḥillī, Ḥasan ibn Yūsuf ibn al-Muṭahhar (648/1250–726/1325), was one of the most celebrated Imāmī scholars, renowned particularly for his contributions to law, legal methodology and theology.[19] His early studies were completed in al-Ḥillah under the tuition of his father and his maternal uncle, the Muḥaqqiq al-Ḥillī, Najm al-Dīn Abu'l-Qāsim Ja'far ibn Ḥasan (d. 676/1277), as well as other scholars of this stronghold of Shī'ism, where he studied *Ḥadīth, kalām*, law and legal methodology. Although no reports confirm al-Ḥillī's presence at Maraghah, he is known to have studied both with Naṣīr al-Dīn al-Ṭūsī and al-Kātib al-Qazwīnī. With the former he studied philosophy, particularly the *ilāhiyyāt* of Ibn Sīnā's *Kitāb al-shifā'*, and also probably theology and logic, and with the latter philosophy and logic. He wrote commentaries on Ṭūsī's *Tajrīd al-'aqā'id* and *Qawā'id al-'aqā'id* in theology, and on Kātibī's *al-Risālat al-shamsiyyah* (logic) and *Ḥikmat al-'ayn*.[20] Al-Kātibī also introduced him to the works of Fakhr al-Dīn al-Rāzī and Muḥammad ibn Nāmāwar al-Khunjī. Al-Ḥillī was also probably familiar with the works of Ibn 'Arabī through Shams al-Dīn al-Kīshī (d. 695/1296), with whom he studied in Baghdad after his period studying with Ṭūsī and Kātibī. He also studied with 'Izz al-Dīn al-Fārūthī al-Wāsiṭī, a student of Suhrawardī, and among the 'Allāmah's works is a commentary on Suhrawardī's *al-Talwīḥāt*.[21] Most of his philosophical works have, however, been lost, and the only pupil who attained fame in the philosophical field was Quṭb al-Dīn al-Buwayhī al-Rāzī (d. 766/1365).[22] Al-Ḥillī's wide-ranging intellectual achievement and breadth of scholarship was to set a pattern for Imāmī scholarship up to the present day, to the extent that even when the principal interests of a student lie in law and theology, and even if he or she feels a strong antipathy towards philosophical thought, he or she will read the works of the philosophers in order to gain familiarity with the methodology. Indeed, Imāmī theology and legal methodology after al-Ḥillī became so thoroughly infused with the terminology and style of philosophy that they are virtually incomprehensible to one who has not also mastered the rational sciences.

Al-Ḥillī's outstanding student in philosophy and logic was Quṭb al-Dīn Muḥammad ibn Muḥammad al-Buwayhī al-Rāzī al-Taḥtānī (d. 765/1365),[23] who also studied with the great Sunni scholar 'Aḍūd al-Dīn al-Ījī (d. 756/1355).[24] Among his students was the Imāmī jurist the Shahīd al-Awwal, Muḥammad ibn Makkī al-'Āmilī (d. 786/1384), who studied with him in Āmul towards the end of Rāzī's life.[25] The Shahīd al-Awwal believed Rāzī to be an Imāmī, although Shāfi'īs hold him to be one of them. In logic he contributed his own commentary on Kātibī's *al-Risālat al-shamsiyyah*,[26] but his main philosophical work was his supercommentary on Ibn Sīnā's *Kitāb al-ishārāt*, whose title, *al-Muḥākimāt bayn sharḥay al-ishārāt*, indicates its contents, a critical evaluation of the commentaries of Naṣīr al-Dīn al-Ṭūsī and Fakhr al-Dīn al-Rāzī, and gave rise to his title of Ṣāḥib al-Muḥākimāt.

The probable acquaintance of the 'Allāmah al-Ḥillī with the ideas of Ibn 'Arabī has been mentioned, as has the correspondence between Ibn 'Arabī's foremost disciple, Ṣadr al-Dīn al-Qūnawī, and Naṣīr al-Dīn al-Ṭūsī,[27] but the incorporation of the Shaykh al-Akbar's teachings into Imāmī thinking, which was to bear fruit in the work of Mullā Ṣadrā, was initiated by three figures a little outside the mainstreams of philosophy and Imāmī scholarship. The most important of these figures is undoubtedly the Sayyid Bahā' al-Dīn Ḥaydar al-Āmulī (719 or 720/1319 or 1320–after 787/1385). What is known of his life is to be gleaned from two autobiographical accounts which he wrote in 777/1375–6 and 782/1360, when he had settled in Najaf. His last attested work, the *Risālat al-ʿulūm al-ʿāliyyah*, was written when he was sixty-five in 787/1385, after which nothing more is known of him.[28] Ḥaydar Āmulī was born in Amul in northern Persia, and studied there, and in Astarabad and Isfahan. For a short time he was in the service of the ruler of Tabaristan, Fakhr al-Dawlah Ḥasan ibn Shāh Kaykhusraw ibn Yazdigird. A profound religious experience resulted in his abandoning the courtly life in his thirtieth year, when he set out on the *ḥajj*. He travelled in the robes of a Sufi to the Shīʿī shrines, to Jerusalem and to Mecca and Medina, and then spent the rest of his life to the last date that is known for him in Iraq, first in Baghdad where he studied with the philosopher Naṣīr al-Dīn ʿAlī ibn Muḥammad ʿAlī al-Kāshānī al-Ḥillī (d. 755/1354),[29] and with the son of the ʿAllāmah al-Ḥillī, Fakhr al-Muḥaqqiqīn Muḥammad ibn Ḥasan al-Ḥillī (d. 771/1370),[30] and finally in Najaf. Seven of his thirty-four listed works are extant, of which the *Naṣṣ al-nuṣūṣ*, a commentary on the *Fuṣūṣ al-ḥikam* of Ibn ʿArabī,[31] and the *Jāmiʿ al-asrār wa-manbaʿ al-anwār*, a *taʾwīl* of the *Sharīʿah*,[32] are today the best known. There remains also a vast commentary on the Qurʾān entitled *al-Muḥīṭ al-aʿẓam*.[33]

For Ḥaydar Āmulī Shiʿism and Sufism are identical. The true believer is a *muʾmin mumtaḥan*, a tested believer, who combines the practice, discipline and mystical insight of *Sharīʿah*, *ṭarīqah* and *ḥaqīqah*, and the twelve Imāms are the leaders and guides of all three aspects of Islam. Hence true Islam is not that of legalist Shīʿism, nor that of Sufism which (supposedly) rejects its Shīʿī origins, but an esoteric Islam in which knowledge is attained through the Imāms. His writings are strongly influenced by Ibn ʿArabī, from whom, however, he departs in one significant respect. In the Shaykh al-Akbar's thought, the important notion of *walāyah*, or sainthood, finds its culmination in the person of Jesus, the absolute seal of sainthood, and, according to some of his followers, in the person of Ibn ʿArabī himself as the limited seal of sainthood. The *walī*, of course, for a Shīʿī is the Imām, and Ḥaydar Āmulī places ʿAlī, the first Imām, in the position Ibn ʿArabī reserved for Jesus, and the Mahdī, the present *walī* and twelfth Imām, as the holder of the limited seal of sainthood. In this he followed two earlier Persian mystics, Saʿd al-Dīn al-Ḥamūyah (587/1191–650/1252) and Najm al-Dīn Dāyah (d. 654/1256).[34]

Ḥaydar Āmulī's influence on subsequent philosophy in the Persian milieu is thus to be found in his alignment (or, on his terms, realignment) of Shīʿism and Sufism, particularly in the light of the latter's Akbarian manifestation, but he also represents a type which finds itself repeated in many Persian Imāmī scholars down to the present day. He founded no *ṭarīqah*, nor is his adherence to any *ṭarīqah* much in evidence in his writings. Instead he exemplifies the spiritual Shīʿī who is turned towards the Imams as the sole sources of knowledge and as guides to the understanding of the real nature of existence, which is God. The acquisition of this knowledge and understanding is thus equally a matter of reasoning and analysis and of the insights achieved through spiritual discipline and the resulting mystical illumination. The exact point of balance between reasoning and unveiling, between the intellect and the heart, in so far as these can be distinguished at the highest levels, varies among the later Shīʿī mystics, the *ʿurafāʾ*, and determines the colouring of their teachings, but too much of a leaning in either direction is held to be a weakness and a sign of deviation from the straight path of true Islam. This is also a point emphasized in the writings of Suhrawardī, and is repeated by Mullā Ṣadrā. On the whole, however, it has to be said that later Shīʿī opinion, with its generally rather severe attitude to *ṭarīqah* Sufism, and seeking to retain the exclusive dependence of its spirituality on the persons of the Imāms alone, remained critical of Ḥaydar Āmulī.

The remaining figures who will be mentioned here belong to the ninth/fifteenth century, and all of them testify to the increasing interconnectedness of the various strands in Islamic speculative thinking which became a mark of these times. It is more difficult to establish direct links between these philosophers, or even, at this stage of scholarship, to gauge the precise nature of the effect their writings had on subsequent philosophy, but each of them left important works which testify to the continuing influence of philosophy during this century. Ṣāʾin al-Dīn ʿAlī ibn Muḥammad ibn Afḍal al-Dīn Muḥammad Turkah al-Khujandī al-Iṣfahānī, better known as Ibn Turkah, (d. 835/1432), is acknowledged to have been one of the first to seek to unify the Peripatetic, *ishrāqī* and Akbarian strands in the perspective of Shīʿī esotericism.[35] Ibn Turkah belonged to an Iṣfahānī family of *ʿulamāʾ*, and wrote some fifty-seven works on philosophy and mysticism, including commentaries on the *Fuṣūṣ al-ḥikam* of Ibn ʿArabī and on several classic texts of Sufi poetry, still in large part unedited. When Isfahan was invaded by Tamerlane, he was exiled to Samarqand, but he was able to return to Isfahan on the latter's death. The most influential of his works was probably the *Tamhīd al-qawāʾid*, a commentary on the *Qawāʾid al-tawḥīd* of Abū Ḥāmid Muḥammad al-Iṣfahānī.[36] The latter was a Peripatetic philosopher who had become a Sufi, and sought in this short work to summarize the doctrine of *tawḥīd* in terms of the teachings of Ibn ʿArabī. Ibn Turkah was also learned in the science of numerical symbolism, which he incorporated into his writings.

The second figure in this group was Ibn Abī Jumhūr al-Aḥsā'ī (*c.* 837/1433–4–after 904/1499).[37] Born in al-Aḥsā (nowadays part of eastern Saudi Arabia, facing Bahrain), he began his studies there under his father's tuition before going on to Najaf. His travels took him to Syria, Mecca (for the *ḥajj*), Baghdad, Mashhad and Astarabad. He wrote works in most of the traditional sciences, including legal methodology, law, *Ḥadīth* and theology (particularly on the Imāmate), but also the large synthetic work on which his fame rests, the *Kitāb al-mujlī*.[38] Cast in the form of a supercommentary on his own *Kitāb maslik al-afhām fī 'ilm al-kalām*, it brings together, like the work of Ibn Turkah, theology, Peripatetic and *ishrāqī* philosophy, and the Sufism of Ibn 'Arabī, and is cast in the mould of Shī'ī imāmology. It is not clear to what extent this work influenced Ṣafavid theosophers, but it marks another important staging post in the direction of the integration of the various speculative disciplines under the aegis of Imāmī teachings, which culminates in the work of Mullā Ṣadrā.

Belonging primarily to the Peripatetic school, but also manifesting an interest in mysticism was Jalāl al-Dīn al-Dawānī (830/1427–908/1502–3).[39] A native of Dawān near Kāzarūn in southern Persia, he studied initially with his father, who was *qāḍī* of the town. Moving to Shīrāz, he held the office of *ṣadr* under the Qarā Quyunlū Yūsuf ibn Jahānshāh, but resigned to take up the post of *mudarris* at the Begum Madrasah (Dār al-Aytām). Under the Āq Quyunlū he became *qāḍī* of Fars, but when Shah Ismā'īl began his takeover of the region he escaped. He set out again for Kāzarūn at the end of his life, but died a few days after reaching the excampment of Abu'l-Fatḥ Beg Bayāndur, who had taken control of Shīrāz. He was buried in Dawan. He wrote mostly in Arabic, although his most famous work, the *Akhlāq-i jalālī*, was a Persian treatise modelled on Naṣīr al-Dīn al-Ṭūsī's *Akhlāq-i nāṣirī*. Over seventy-five works of his are recorded, covering the fields of philosophy, mysticism, theology and *tafsīr*, among which is a commentary on the *Hayākil al-nūr* of Suhrawardī al-Maqtūl, and three sets of glosses on the commentary by 'Alā' al-Dīn 'Alī ibn Muḥammad al-Qūshjī (d. 879/1474)[40] to Ṭūsī's *Kitāb al-tajrīd*. The first of these glosses, known as the *Ḥāshiyyah-yi qadīm*, was criticized in another set of glosses by the Amīr Ṣadr al-Dīn Muḥammad al-Dashtakī (d. 903/1497–8),[41] and Dawānī replied to these in a second set of glosses which became known as the *Ḥāshiyyah-yi jadīd*. Once again Dashtakī set out his criticisms in a further set of glosses, to which Dawānī replied in what came to be known as the *Ḥāshiyyah-yi ajadd*. The complete set of the three glosses by Dawānī and the two by Sayyid al-Ḥukamā' are known collectively as the *Ṭabaqāt al-jalāliyyah wa'l-ṣadriyyah*.[42] Sayyid al-Ḥukamā''s son, the Amīr Ghiyāth al-Dīn Manṣūr al-Dashtakī (d. 948/1541–2) wrote his own glosses on the *Kitāb al-tajrīd*, in which he renewed the attack on Dawānī.

Ghiyāth al-Dīn al-Dashtakī has been portrayed as a precocious child, debating with Dawānī in the presence of his father Ṣadr al-Dīn at the age of fourteen and mastering both Peripatetic and Illuminationist philosophy at the age of twenty. He was appointed *ṣadr* by Shah Tahmāsp, but the Shah took the side of the powerful *mujtahid* al-Karakī in a debate before him between Dashtakı and Karakī over the latter's calculation of the direction of the *qiblah* (as a result of which mosque *qiblah*s throughout Persia had to be realigned), and Dashtakī was dismissed and replaced by a pupil of Karakī, beginning what was in effect the takeover of the important religious offices under the Ṣafavids by the new Shī'ī *'ulamā'* from the centres of learning outside Persia from the old religious hierarchy of pre-Ṣafavid times. Dashtakī is counted among the great Imāmī scholars of his time in both the speculative sciences, and law and legal methodology. He wrote a commentary on the Qur'ān, and on ethics (*Akhlāq-i manṣūriyyah, al-Taṣawwuf wa'l-akhlāq*), geometry, logic and metaphysics; he also composed a commentary on Suhrawardī's *Hayākil al-nūr*, engaging again with Dawānī and his commentary.

With Dashtakī, the link is made with the School of Iṣfahān, for it was his students, among whom mention should be made particularly of Kamāl al-Dīn al-Ardabīlī (d. 950/1543), and their students who bridge the gap with the generation of Mīr Dāmād. At the beginning of the period studied in the chapter, philosophy, at least in the Persian world, already subsumed theology; three hundred years later, the discipline was prepared to see the accomplishment of the unification of all its branches, from logic and the natural sciences to speculative mysticism, in the work of its greatest philosopher Ṣadr al-Dīn al-Shīrāzī.

NOTES

1 See, for example, James Winston Morris, *The Wisdom of the Throne: an Introduction to the Philosophy of Mullā Ṣadrā* (Princeton, 1981): 21–39.

2 See *Encyclopaedia of Islam*, 2nd ed., suppl., *s.v.* "Findiriskī" (Seyyed Hossein Nasr): 308–9. Mīr Findiriskī was also a noted author of works on alchemy and, as a result of his extensive travels in India, of works displaying a deep interest in Hinduism.

3 Abū 'Abd Allāh Muḥammad ibn 'Umar ibn al-Ḥusayn al-Rāzī, Fakhr al-Dīn, whose fame rests principally on his reputation as a theologian, was a profound and critical writer on philosophy who was, however, much criticized by later philosophers for his tendency to philosophical scepticism.

4 For the most detailed account in English of Bābā Afḍal, his works and his main philosophical concerns, see *Encyclopaedia Iranica*, 3, *s.v.* "Bābā Afḍal" (W. Chittick): 285–91. See also Seyyed Hossein Nasr, "Afḍal al-Din Kāshānī and the philosophical world of Khwāja Naṣīr al-Din Ṭūsī", in Michael E. Marmura (ed.), *Islamic Theology and Philosophy: Studies in Honor of George*

F. Hourani (Albany, 1984): 249–64. Most of his oeuvre has been published in M. Mīnuwī and Y. Mahdawī, *Muṣannafāt-i Afḍal al-Dīn Muḥammad Maraqī Kāshānī*, 2nd ed. (Tehran, 1987).

5 On both these points see Chittick's article cited in note 4.

6 See Nasr, *op. cit.*: 260.

7 See Henry Corbin, *Avicenna and the Visionary Recital*, trans. Willard R. Trask, (London, 1960): 13.

8 See Mudarris Raḍawī, *Aḥwāl wa āthār . . . Naṣīr al-Dīn [Ṭūsī]* (Tehran, 1975): 183.

9 Ṣadr al-Dīn al-Shīrāzī, *Sharḥ al-hidāyah al-athīriyyah*, litho. (Tehran, 1895, and offset reprint, n.p., n.d.). Another well-known commentary is that of Mīr Ḥusayn Mu'īn al-Dīn al-Maybudī, written in 880/1475.

10 For commentaries on this work and the Latin translation, see *Encyclopaedia Iranica*, 1, "Abharī" (G. C. Anawati): 216–17.

11 See Mudarris Raḍawī, *op. cit.*: 184.

12 See Mudarris Raḍawī, *op. cit.*: 6 and 171.

13 For Dabīrān al-Kātibī see Mudarris Raḍawī, *op. cit.*: 226–8; and *Encyclopaedia of Islam*, 2nd ed., 4, "al-Kātibī" (M. Mohaghegh): 762.

14 For an English translation see *The Logic of the Arabians (Risála-i-shamsiyya)*, Arabic text with Eng. trans. by A. Sprenger, first appendix to *Dictionary of the Technical Terms . . . (Kashshāf iṣṭilāḥāt al-funūn)* (Calcutta, 1854). The most important commentaries were those by Sa'd al-Dīn al-Taftazānī and Quṭb al-Dīn al-Rāzī, both still studied in the *madrasahs*.

15 Najm al-Dīn 'alī ibn 'Umar Al-Kātibī al-Qazwīnī, *Ḥikmat al-'ayn*, with commentary of Shams al-Dīn Muḥammad ibn Mubārakshāh al-Bukhārī, ed. with intro. by Ja'far Zāhidī (Mashhad, 1975). Glosses on this commentary were written by Quṭb al-Dīn al-Shīrāzī, 'Alī ibn Muḥammad al-Jurjānī (al-Sharīf), and others. The 'Allāmah al-Ḥillī also wrote a commentary on the *Ḥikmat al-'ayn*.

16 John Walbridge, *The Science of Mystic Lights: Quṭb al-Dīn Shīrāzī and the Illuminationist Tradition in Islamic Philosophy* (Cambridge, Mass., 1992).

17 For translations into French of the latter part of Suhrawardī's text, together with selections from both Quṭb al-Dīn's commentary and Ṣadr al-Dīn al-Shīrāzī's glosses see: *Shihâboddîn Yaḥyâ Sohravardî, Shaykh al-Ishrâq, Le Livre de la sagesse orientale: Kitâb Ḥikmat al-Ishrâq, commentaires de Qoṭboddîn Shîrazî et Mollâ Ṣadrâ Shîrâzî*, trad. et notes Henry Corbin, établ. Christian Jambert (Lagrasse, 1986).

18 See Walbridge, *op.cit.*: esp. chapter 3: 79–125.

19 For the life of al-Ḥillī see especially Sabina Schmidtke, *The Theology of al-'Allāma al-Ḥillī (d. 726/1325)* (Berlin, 1991): 9–40.

20 The latter commentary, called *Īḍāḥ al-maqāṣid*, was published in Tehran in 1959.

21 *Kashf al-mushkilāt min kitāb al-talwīḥāt*. For al-Ḥillī's teachers see Schmidtke, *op. cit.*: 12–22. Schmidtke's monograph also contains a detailed bibliography of al-Ḥillī's works.

22 *Ibid.*: 39.

23 See Ḥalabī, 'Alī Asghar, *Tārīkh-i falāsafa-yi īrānī az aghāz-i islām tā imrūz*, 2nd ed. (Tehran, 1983): 477–80.

24 ʿAḍūd al-Dīn ʿAbd al-Raḥmān ibn Rukn al-Dīn ibn ʿAbd al-Ghaffār al-Bakrī al-Shabānkārī al-Ījī, Shāfiʿī jurist and Ashʿarī theologian, whose writings include works on theology and legal methodology.

25 Al-Sayyid al-Sharīf al-Jurjānī (740/1339–816/1413), the logician, philosopher and theologian, intended to study with Rāzī, and to that end travelled to Herat in 766/1365, but Rāzī, then near to death, told him to go to Egypt to study with Mubārakshāh, his pupil. However, Jurjānī stayed in Herat and studied with Muḥammad al-Fanārī, although he did meet Mubārakshāh later during a visit to Egypt.

26 This commentary, the *Taḥrīr al-qawāʿid al-manṭiqiyyah fī sharḥ al-risālat al-shamsiyyah*, litho. (Tehran, 1887), is still studied as the main introductory text on logic in the *madrasahs*.

27 See the previous chapter.

28 For Ḥaydar Āmulī's life and works see *Encyclopaedia of Islam*, 2nd ed., suppl.: 363–5, "Ḥaydār-i Āmulī" (J. van Ess), *Encyclopaedia Iranica*, 1, "Āmolī, Sayyed Bahā'-al-Dīn Ḥaydār . . ." (E. Kohlberg): 983–5, and the French (Henry Corbin) and Arabic (Osman Yahya) introductions to Sayyed Haydar Amoli, *La Philosophie shi'ite* (Tehran and Paris, 1969); see also Henry Corbin, *En Islam iranien: aspects spirituels et philosophiques*, 3 (Paris, 1972): 149–213.

29 Naṣīr al-Dīn al-Kāshānī wrote works in philosophy, *kalām* and law, among which were glosses on a commentary by Fāḍil Iṣfahānī on Naṣīr al-Dīn al-Ṭūsī's *Tajrīd* (*kalām*), superglosses on a commentary on Ibn Sīnā's *Kitāb al-ishārāt*, and glosses on *al-Risālat al-shamsiyyah*.

30 A correspondence between Ḥaydar Āmulī and Fakhr al-Muḥaqqiqīn on theological and legal matters, *al-Masāʾil al-āmuliyyah*, survives in an autograph by Sayyid Ḥaydar, although another work dedicated to his teacher on the silence of ʿAlī ibn Abī Ṭālib in the face of the assumption of the caliphate by the first three caliphs, the *Risālat rāfiʿat al-khilāf ʿan wajh sukūt Amīr al-Muʾminīn*, is now lost.

31 Sayyid Ḥaydar Āmulī, *Le Texte des textes (Naṣṣ al-noṣūṣ . . .). Les Prolégomènes*, ed. H. Corbin and O. Yahya (Tehran and Paris, 1974).

32 Edited by H. Corbin and O. Yahya in *La Philosophie shiʿite*: 2–619.

33 Two other works of Ḥaydar Āmulī have been edited: the *Risālah naqḍ al-nuqūḍ fī maʿrifat al-wujūd* (ed. H. Corbin and O. Yahya in *La Philosophie shiʿite*: 620–710), which is an abbreviation of his longer *Risālat al-wujūd fī maʿrifat al-maʿbūd*, not extant; and his *Asrār al-sharīʿah wa-aṭwār al-ṭarīqah wa-anwār al-ḥaqīqah*, ed. M. Khājawī (Tehran, 1983). The latter has been translated in English; see Sayyid Haydar Āmulī, *Inner Secrets of the Path*, trans. Assadullah al-Dhaakir Yate (Shaftesbury, 1989).

34 For the notion of sainthood and the seal of sainthood in the thought of Ibn ʿArabī see Michel Chodkiewicz, *Le Sceau des saints: prophétie et sainteté dans la doctrine d'Ibn Arabī* (Paris, 1986).

35 For the life and works of Ibn Turkah, see Sayyid ʿAlī Mūsawī Bihbahānī, *Aḥwāl wa āthār-i Ṣāʿin al-Dīn Turkah-yi Iṣfahānī'*, in M. Mohaghegh and H. Landolt, *Collected Papers in Islamic Philosophy and Mysticism* (Tehran, 1971), Persian section: 97–132. See also Corbin, *En Islam iranien*, 3: chapter 3.

36 Ibn Muḥammad Turkah, Ṣā'in al-Dīn, *Tamhīd al-qawāʿid (The Disposition of Principles)*, ed. Sayyid Jalāl al-Dīn Āshtiyānī (Tehran, 1976). See also the Persian

and English introductions to this text by Seyyed Hossein Nasr.

37 For Muḥammad ibn ʿAlī ibn Ibrāhīm ibn Ḥasan ibn Ibrāhīm ibn Ḥasan al-Ḥajār al-Aḥsāʾī ibn Abī Jumhūr, see *Encyclopaedia of Islam*, 2nd ed., suppl. art "Ibn Abī Djumhūr al-Aḥsāʾī" (W. Madelung): 380. See also Corbin, *En Islam iranien, s.v.* index.

38 Also known as *Mujlī mirʾāt al-nūr al-munjī*, litho. (Tehran, 1907 and 1911).

39 For Dawānī see *Encyclopaedia of Islam*, 2nd ed., 2, "al-Dawānī" (Ann K. S. Lambton): 174.

40 ʿAlāʾ al-Dīn ʿAlī ibn Muḥammad al-Qūshjī was born in Samarqand, where he studied mathematics and astronomy with the Amīr Ulugh Beg. He became director of the observatory in Samarqand. After the murder of Ulugh Beg, Qūshjī left for Tabriz and subsequently Istanbul, where he died.

41 Sayyid al-Ḥukamāʾ al-Sayyid Abu'l-Maʿālī ibn Ibrāhīm al-Ḥusaynī al-Shīrāzī al-Dashtakī was the founder of the Manṣūriyyah Madrasah in Shiraz. He was killed by Turcomans and buried in his school. A Shāfiʿī jurist, he also wrote glosses on Quṭb al-Dīn al-Rāzī's commentary on *al-Risālat al-shamsiyyah*, and an *Ithbāt al-wujūd* on the proof of God's existence, as well as works on legal methodology, theology and mineralogy.

42 See Mudarris Raḍawī, *Aḥwāl wa āthār . . . Naṣīr al-Dīn*: 426–7.

CHAPTER 34

Mīr Dāmād and the founding of the "School of Iṣfahān"

Hamid Dabashi

With the advent of the Ṣafavids (reigned 907/1501–1145/1732) in Persia in the early tenth/sixteenth century, the nomocentric, dogmatic forces in Islamic intellectual disposition immediately found a favourable political climate. The anxiety of legitimacy was particularly acute in the case of the Ṣafavids. Although of Turkish, or probably Kurdish (Bosworth (1967): 172), origin, they came to power by fabricating a fictitious Shīʿī genealogy for themselves, linking their origins back to the sacred memory of the Shīʿī Imāms. The probability that the founder of the Ṣafavid order, Shaykh Ṣafī al-Dīn (d. 735/1335), was perhaps a Sunni made the Ṣafavid monarchs, from Shah Ismāʿīl I (ruled 907/1501–930/1524) onward, particularly anxious to demonstrate and institutionalize their Shīʿī affiliation. The founder of the Ṣafavid dynasty, Shah Ismāʿīl, spent the first ten years of his reign in a ruthless drive to consolidate his power over Persia and to establish Shīʿism as the ideological foundation of his, and his successors', legitimacy (see al-Shaybī (1980): 365–402). Aggravating the Ṣafavid anxiety over their Shīʿī self-legitimation was the powerful presence of the Sunni Ottomans, who, under Selīm I Yavuz ("the Grim") (ruled 918/1512–926/1520), won a major victory in 920/1514 at Chaldiran against the Ṣafavids. When the Ṣafavids subsequently moved their capital from Tabrīz to Qazwīn and then to Iṣfahān, they distanced themselves from their powerful Sunni neighbours in more than just one sense. As they settled into their new capital, Iṣfahān became the new centre of the Shīʿī world. The flourishing of Mīr Dāmād (950/1543–1041/1631) and the establishment of the "School of Iṣfahān" would hardly have been possible without these necessary political and social developments.

One particular Ṣafavid monarch was instrumental in these developments. When England was ruled by Elizabeth I, Spain by Philip II, Russia by Ivan the Terrible, and India by Emperor Akbar, Persia achieved one of its greatest periods of high culture and material civilization under the legendary reign of Shah 'Abbās I (ruled 996/1588–1038/1629), who came to power when Mīr Dāmād was forty-five years old and died when he was eighty-six. During his reign the "School of Iṣfahān" found its most celebrated patristic foundation; and Persia experienced one of the greatest periods of its political and material prosperity. The Ottomans were evicted from Āzarbaijān, the Ṣafavid authority over the eastern Caucasus and the Persian Gulf was consolidated, widespread contact with Europe was established, and, with the Moghal dynasty on its east and the Ottomans on its west, the Shī'ī capital of Iṣfahān became the centre of a world civilization reminiscent of pre-Islamic memories.

PHILOSOPHY UNDER THE ṢAFAVIDS

In their relentless quest for self-legitimacy, the Ṣafavid monarchs needed the Shī'ī jurists and dogmaticians, as well as the preachers and clerics, to propagate the ideological foundation of their state (Amir Arjomand (1984): 109–21). This inevitably created an unfavourable atmosphere for the free exercise of logocentric tendencies in theological, philosophical and scientific disciplines. If we witness the rise of a particular philosophical disposition, recently identified as the "School of Iṣfahān" (Nasr in Sharīf (1966), 2: 904–32; Corbin (1972), 4: 9–201; Āshtiyānī (1972): 60–1), during the Ṣafavid period, this phenomenon must be attributed more to the diligent and relentless philosophical engagements of a limited number of individuals rather than considered the product of favourable and conducive social circumstances. Those who engaged in philosophical matters did so at some peril to their personal safety and social standing. As is particularly evident in the case of Mīr Dāmād, philosophers often sought a safe haven in an abstruse and convoluted discourse (Nasr (1978): 33) for fear of persecution. Or else they were forced, like Mīr Dāmād's distinguished student Mullā Ṣadrā (979/1571–1050/1640), to abandon the more congenial environment of their colleagues and students and live in exile at least for certain periods in remote parts of the country (Corbin (1972), 4: 54–122; Nasr (1978): 31–53). The Shī'ī dogmaticians who had found a powerful state apparatus in their support were least tolerant of logocentric discourses which they rightly considered detrimental not only to the metaphysical foundations of their own discourse but to their social status and political power as well. The result was that the fate of philosophy was left in the hands of whimsical monarchs who for a number of practical and symbolic self-interests, such as their need for a court physician and a court astronomer, would inadvertently provide for the possibilities of philosophical pursuits, historically linked to medicine and astronomy, at their court. Islamic philosophy has never had any institutional foundations except at the clandestine peripheries of the *madrasah* system, in the libraries of wealthy individuals, and ultimately in the whimsical vicissitudes of the court where the royal concerns with astrological and medical needs, as well as with the ceremonial apparatus of power, would provide such great luminaries of Islamic philosophy as Ibn Sīnā, Khwājah Naṣīr al-Dīn al-Ṭūsī and Mīr Dāmād with material possibilities for their intellectual pursuits. That Islamic philosophy has flourished as a rich intellectual discourse testifies more to the philosophers' unyielding insistence than to a conducive social setting.

The dominant nomocentric proclivities in the Ṣafavid period would also have the catalytic effect of initially producing a form of philosophical dogmatism where epistemological innovations would be discouraged and prevented in favour of a more pedantic repetition of received conceptions (Ṣafā (1959–85), 5, 1: 278). This unfavourable dogmatic condition must be considered further in relation to the major sectarian re-affiliation that took place during this period (Hinz (1936): 22–32; Mazzaoui (1972): 63–82; Savory (1980): 27–49). A principal impact of the Ṣafavids' rise to power was the almost immediate disruption of intellectual activities by Persian Sunni scholars who were forced to leave their homeland and migrate to more congenial places like India. It took a generation of "imported" Shī'ī scholars, mostly jurists and dogmaticians, from such predominantly Shī'ī lands as Syria, Lebanon, Iraq and Bahrain, to establish a new – and, from the Shī'ī Ṣafavids' perspective, more palatable – doctrinal discourse (Browne (1902–24), 4: 360–1). Mīr Dāmād, in fact, represents the first generation of Shī'ī philosophers born and bred in Persia during the Ṣafavid period. His father, Mīr Shams al-Dīn Dāmād, was the son-in-law of Muḥaqqiq-i Karakī or Muḥaqqiq-i Thānī (d. 940/1533), who had come to Persia early in the Ṣafavid era (Tunikābunī (1985): 346–7). The disruption of philosophical tradition by Sunni scholars in Persia and the superimposition of dogmatic and sectarian concerns on the logocentric discourse were such that even Shaykh Bahā' al-Dīn 'Āmilī, also known as Sheikh Bahā'ī, the distinguished Shī'ī philosopher who was a close friend and associate of Mīr Dāmād, would refuse, according to some historians, to take Ibn Sīnā seriously on the assumption that he was a Sunni philosopher (Ṣafā (1959–85), 5, 1: 381)!

Because of the rather unusual power of jurists during the Ṣafavid period, as exemplified by Mīr Dāmād's own grandfather Muḥaqqiq-i Thānī (Amir Arjomand (1984): 133–7), philosophy was more than ever a suspicious discourse. There are reports that on the front doors of some schools in Iṣfahān the patrons had specifically prohibited the teaching of philosophy: "And it is necessary that the books of imaginary sciences, the sciences of doubts and uncertainties, which are famous and known as rational and philosophical sciences, such as [Ibn Sīnā's] *al-Shifā'* and *al-Ishārāt* [*wa'l-tanbīhāt* . . ., etc.] should not be read in the introduction to religious sciences" (Hādī (1984): 17). The ideological roots of the Ṣafavids in the mystical tradition, particularly in its populist dimensions (Mazzaoui (1972): 41–82), had further made philosophical inquiry a hazardous preoccupation. As always in the course of Islamic intellectual history, during the Ṣafavid period the practice of philosophy was a precarious act that Persian philosophers pursued at their own peril. Financial support for students of philosophy was virtually non-existent. Having a wealthy and influential father, as in the case of Mīr Dāmād and his student Mullā Ṣadrā, was a crucial factor in facilitating a philosophical career. But even these two independently wealthy Shī'ī philosophers were not totally immune to financial difficulties. In one of his extant letters to Mīr Dāmād, Mullā Ṣadrā complains in almost the same breath of his financial burdens in supporting his family and of harassments to which he has been systematically subjected (Mullā Ṣadrā (n.d.): 57). The *madrasah* system and its total reliance on religious endowments prohibited any financial support for students who were attracted primarily to philosophy.

Against all these odds, with the generation of Mīr Dāmād a new breed of Shī'ī philosophers came forward which was far too serious about matters of philosophical primacy to be dissuaded by unfavourable social conditions. They resumed and rejuvenated a robust philosophical discourse. Their problem, of course, remained the opposition that the jurists and dogmaticians displayed against them. The prefaces and conclusions of almost all the philosophical treatises of this period are filled with grievances against the juridical authorities who harassed and persecuted the philosophers (Mullā Ṣadrā (1961): 39). Mīr Dāmād and Mullā Ṣadrā never lose an opportunity to condemn the dogmaticians who considered them blasphemous infidels. Qāḍī Sa'īd Qumī (d. 1103/1691), a prominent philosopher of the period, issued a stern condemnation of these clericals in the introduction to his *al-Anwār al-qudsiyyah*. The dogmaticians, in turn, attacked the philosophers vehemently, considered them infidels and their writings blasphemous. They fundamentally challenged the authority of reason in the prevention of error. Quṭb al-Dīn Muḥammad Nayrīzī (d. *c.* 1173/1759) forbade his followers from reading Ibn Sīnā's and other philosophers' writings. Mullā Muḥammad Ṭāhir Qummī (d. 1098/1686) wrote a book against both philosophers and Sufis, *al-Fawā'id al-dīniyyah fi'l-radd 'alā' al-ḥukamā' wa'l-ṣufiyyah*. The same Mullā Muḥammad accused the distinguished philosopher Mullā Muḥsin Fayḍ (d. 1091/1680), one of the most brilliant students of

Mullā Ṣadrā, of being a "Zoroastrian master" (Ṣafā (1959–85), 5, 1: 282). One of his poems condemned all philosophers and all philosophies:

> A party of people have gone astray from the gate of faith
> And followed Ibn Sīnā and Bahmanyār instead.
> Out of ignorance they have turned Aristotelian and Platonic,
> Far away from the sacred Imām's spearhead.
> They imitate Socrates and Galen,
> Escaping from what Bāqir and Ṣādiq have said.
> In their opinion most vile and impious,
> He who knows philosophy is utterly perfect.
> Perfect indeed is in God's eyes
> He who has followed the family of the Prophet.
> I seek knowledge from the gate of the city [i.e., 'Alī],
> From the Greeks I will not anything get.
> (Ṣafā (1959–85), 5, 1: 282–3)

Mullā Muḥammad proceeds to boast that the Qur'ān is his *al-Shifā'*, with a pun on the literal meaning of the title of Ibn Sīnā's text, implying that God's word cures him of all his mental diseases (e.g., philosophical inclinations). The collection of prophetic *ḥadīth* will do well for Mullā Muḥammad instead of Ibn Sīnā's *al-Ishārāt wa'l-tanbīhāt.* He insists that "much of the Greek philosophy is fallacious" and that the Shī'ī Imāms' sayings are far superior (Ṣafā (1959–85), 5, 1: 283).

The juridical opposition to philosophy went far beyond verbal abuse and physical harassment. A major re-codification of the dogmatic principles of the faith was an immediate result of the juridical awareness of the philosophical threat. Mullā Muḥammad Bāqir Majlisī (d. 1111/1699), the most prominent dogmatician of the Ṣafavid period, set upon himself the Herculean task of collecting and codifying the Shī'ī Imāms' traditions precisely to combat his contemporaries' diversion to philosophy. In answer to a question about the viability of philosophy, he is reported to have said that "if God Almighty recognized people sufficient in their intellect, He would not have sent them messengers and prophets" (Ṣafā (1959–85), 5, 1: 283).

Despite these unfavourable conditions for philosophy, the general atmosphere of religious consciousness was particularly acute under the Ṣafavids. Beginning with Shah Ismā'īl (ruled 907/1501–930/1524), the Ṣafavid kings and their royal families became the greatest patrons of religious learning – particularly in the fields of legal dogmatics and jurisprudence. Mothers, sisters and wives of the Ṣafavid monarchs were particularly attentive to religious endowments. A sister of Shah Ṭahmāsp (ruled 930/1524–984/1576), Suṭlāmun (d. 969/1561–62), "made her entire estate, including her jewellery, into a religious endowment" (Amir Arjomand (1984): 190). Great luminaries of Shī'ī learning such as

Muḥaqqiq-i Karakī and 'Allāmah Majlisī are the products of this period – giants of Shī'ī scholastic learning who while consolidating and legitimizing the ideological foundations of the Ṣafavid state, systematized, codified and considerably advanced the level of juridical discourse they had inherited from their previous generations.

MĪR MUḤAMMAD BĀQIR DĀMĀD

In the history of Islamic philosophy during the Ṣafavid period, Mīr Dāmād is remembered with uncommon affection and unceasing admiration (Āshtiyānī (1972): 3; Khwansārī (1976), 2: 234; Tunikābunī (1985): 334). Muḥammad Ṭāhir Tunikābunī, the author of the biographical dictionary *Qiṣaṣ al-'ulamā'*, reports that one day Mullā Ṣadrā, when the celebrated Shī'ī philosopher of the Ṣafavid period was still a student of Mīr Dāmād, was waiting for his teacher to enter the room and start their discussion. The door is opened and in comes a local Iṣfahānī merchant who needs to ask Mīr Dāmād a question. While the merchant and Mullā Ṣadrā are alone in the room, the merchant asks whether Mīr Dāmād is superior in his learning to a prominent cleric in Isfahan. "Mīr is superior", Mullā Ṣadrā says. What about Ibn Sīnā, the merchant inquires further, how does he compare with the master of Peripatetic philosophy? "Mīr is superior", Mullā Ṣadrā repeats. What then of the Second Teacher, al-Fārābī (second only to Aristotle)? Mullā Ṣadrā hesitates for a moment. "Do not be afraid", Mīr Dāmād encourages his student from the adjacent room, "tell him Mīr is superior (Tunikābunī (1985): 334).

The same hagiographical affection is also present in yet another story reported by another biographer, Tabrīzī Khīyābānī (in Mīr Dāmād (1977): lvii). Muḥaqqiq-i Karakī is reported to have seen in a dream the first Shī'ī Imām, 'Alī, who instructs Muḥaqqiq-i Karakī to give his daughter in marriage to Shams al-Dīn Muḥammad. "She will give birth to a son who will inherit the knowledge of the prophets and the sages." Muḥaqqiq-i Karakī does as he is told. But later that daughter, now wife to Shams al-Dīn Muḥammad, dies before giving birth to a son. Muḥaqqiq-i Karakī is puzzled by the event. Soon after the original dream is repeated, and this time the first Shī'ī Imām identifies another daughter of the learned cleric as the appointed bride. Muḥaqqiq-i Karakī proceeds by giving his second daughter to Shams al-Dīn Muḥammad, to whom is born Muḥammad Bāqir, the future Mīr Dāmād, who will prove right the dream of his distinguished grandfather.

Mīr Burhān al-Dīn Muḥammad Bāqir Dāmād, whose poetic *nom de plume* was "Ishrāq" and who was also referred to as "the Third Master" (after Aristotle and al-Fārābī, who have been known as the First and the

Second Masters, respectively), was born into a distinguished religious family (Nasr (1966); Āshtiyānī in Mullā Ṣadrā (1967): 83–90; Izutsu in Mīr Dāmād (1977): 1, the English Introduction; Tunikābunī (1985): 333; Hādī (1984): 15–20). Another honorific title by which Mīr Dāmād has been known is Sayyid al-Afāḍil, or the "Master of the Most Learned". His father, Mīr Shams al-Dīn, was the son-in-law of 'Alī ibn 'Abd al-'Alī, known as Muḥaqqiq-i Thānī or Muḥaqqiq-i Karakī (Hādī (1984): 21–22; Khwānsārī (1976), 2: 234), the prominent Shī'ī cleric of the Ṣafavid period (Tunikābunī (1985): 333). Because of this relationship, the honorific title "Dāmād", which means "the son-in-law", remained in Mīr Shams al-Dīn's family and was given to his son Mīr Muḥammad Bāqir (Hādī: 13, Iskandar Bayk Turkamān (1985): 113–14). That Mīr Dāmād himself is considered the son-in-law of Muḥaqqiq-i Karakī (Nasr (1978): 26) is a mistake. The report that Mīr Dāmād was Shah 'Abbās's son-in-law has also been discounted (Tabrīzī Khīyābānī in Mīr Dāmād (1977): lvii). Mīr Dāmād's grandfather, Muḥaqqiq-i Thānī, was by far the most distinguished cleric of the early Ṣafavid period and, during the reign of Shah Ṭahmāsp (ruled 930/1524–984/1576), enjoyed unprecedented power (Amir Arjomand (1984): 140–2). Astarābād, the city in the north-eastern part of Persia from which Mīr Dāmād's family emerged (Hādī (1984): 11–12), enjoyed particular economic and social significance during the Ṣafavid period. Mīr Dāmād's father is also known as "Astarābādī" (Khwansārī (1976), 2: 234). Mīr Dāmād was recognized as a prominent and distinguished philosopher in his own time. Iskandar Bayk Turkamān, the author of *Tā'rīkh-i 'ālam ārā-yi 'abbāsī*, pays considerable attention to his achievements and prominence (1985: 113).

Mīr Dāmād was born in Astarābād but raised in Mashhad. He received his early education in this religious capital of Shī'ī Persia where he studied Ibn Sīnā's texts closely. Prior to coming to Isfahan during the reign of Shah 'Abbās, he also spent some time in Qazvīn and Kāshān. In Iṣfahān, Mīr Dāmād continued his education. He paid equal attention to intellectual and transmitted sciences. His contemporary, Iskandar Bayk Turkamān, reports of Mīr Dāmād's prominence and significance as a philosopher and a teacher. At the time of Iskandar Bayk's writing, 1025/1616 (1985: 113), Mīr Dāmād was active in teaching and writing. During his own lifetime, Mīr Dāmād was recognized as an accomplished philosopher, mathematician, jurist, hermeneutician and traditionalist. In jurisprudence, his judgment was canonical for other jurists. In most of these areas he had written influential treatises. His fame was such that, when Iskandar Bayk wrote about him, he knew not only of his published work but also of his writings in progress. Mīr Dāmād died in 1041/1631 (Madanī in Mīr Dāmād (1977): liv; Āshtīyānī in Mullā Ṣadrā (1967): 89) when he fell ill on his way to Karbalā', in the entourage of Shah Ṣafī (ruled 1038/1629–1052/1642), and was buried in Najaf (Hādī (1984): 32–33).

MĪR DĀMĀD THE PHILOSOPHER

As is evident from his contemporary sources (Iskandar Bayk Turkamān (1985): 113), Mīr Dāmād was recognized simultaneously as a jurist, a mystic and a philosopher – a rare but not altogether impossible accident in Islamic intellectual history. His writings were recognized by his contemporaries as reflecting his comprehensive and encyclopedic interests in various disciplines. He wrote on philosophy and theology, prophetic and Imāmī traditions, Shīʿī law, Qur'ānic commentary, ethics and mysticism as well as logic. He was recognized by his contemporaries as having a prodigious memory. Although he was a gifted poet, his biographers are reluctant to recognize him as a poet. "Although it is beneath his great status," one biographer concedes, "sometimes he composed some poems." In 1025/1616, Iskandar Bayk Turkamān reports that "today he lives in the capital city of Iṣfahān. I hope that his most gracious being for years will adorn the garden of time, and that the seekers of knowledge will be graced by the illuminating rays of his sun-like mind" (*ibid.*: 113–14). Mīr Dāmād's ascetic exercises have been noticed particularly by some of his biographers (Ḥusaynī Kāshānī in Mīr Dāmād (1977): xxviii). These exercises are combined, if his biographers' sometimes hyperbolic tone is to be believed, with a precocious attention to philosophy. It is reported (*ibid.*: xxix) that his earliest philosophical writings began when he was still in Mashhad. By 988/1580 his reputation as a distinguished philosopher was known. When in this year he came to Kāshān, one of his biographers, Ḥusaynī Kāshānī, went to visit him and to pay his respects (*ibid.*: xxix). Contrary to Iskandar Bayk Turkamān, Ḥusaynī Kāshānī is not hesitant in his admiration for Mīr Dāmād's poetry. "Although he has achieved perfection in every field, his inclination more than anything else was to poetry, and most of the time beautiful poems came to his mind. Like other great masters, he was much inclined toward quatrains" (*ibid.*: xxix–xxx). When, in 933/1526, Ḥusaynī Kāshānī again sees Mīr Dāmād in Kāshān, he continues to praise the philosopher's poetic gifts not only in quatrains but also in *qaṣīdah*s and *mathnawi*s (*ibid.*: xxx).

Despite his prominent status as both a mystic and a jurist, an uneasy combination made possible by certain specific features of the "School of Iṣfahān", it was principally as a philosopher that Mīr Dāmād recognized, praised and distinguished himself, as seen in many of his self-praising poems, e.g.:

> I conquered the lands of knowledge,
> I lent old wisdom to my youth.
> So that I made the earth with my *al-Qabasāt*
> The envy of the heavenly abodes.
>
> (Hādī (1984): 134)

or

> I made my heart the treasure of Divine Secrets.
> In the world of Intellect I reigned.
> In *al-Qabasāt* I became the sea of certitude.
> The script of doubt and uncertainty I destroyed.
> (Hādī (1984): 134)

He bore proudly and confidently the attribution of "the Third Teacher", after Aristotle and al-Fārābī (Zarrīnkūb (1983): 246).

Mīr Dāmād's general philosophical discourse has been identified as primarily "gnostic": "in the sense that the intellectual activity of the mind is conducive toward the experience of spiritual visions while the visionary experience stimulates the function of rational thinking giving both to new concepts and ideas" (Izutsu in Mīr Dāmād (1977): 3, the English Introduction). Anticipating Mullā Ṣadrā's attempt to synthesize all the competing discourses of Islam's intellectual dispositions, Mīr Dāmād brings together the Peripatetic (Aristotelian–Ibn Sīnan) and the Illuminative (Neoplatonic–Suhrawardīan) traditions of Islamic philosophy. The result is a peculiarly successful philosophical discourse in which, as Izutsu has stated, "beneath the surface of . . . [his] dry thinking and through the veils of the abstract concepts which he handles with remarkable dexterity, we notice the presence of swarming visions originating from an entirely different source, the living experience of a mystic" (*ibid.*). This combination of rational and metarational orientation in philosophical disposition, when properly anchored to the doctrinal principles of the Shī'ī faith, would constitute the major characteristics of what we now call the "School of Iṣfahān".

MĪR DĀMĀD'S CONTEMPORARIES

Among the prominent teachers with whom Mīr Dāmād studied were Ḥusayn ibn 'Abd al-Ṣamad al-'Āmilī, the father of Shaykh Bahā'ī, Mīr Dāmād's contemporary colleague in Iṣfahān. His other teacher was Shaykh 'Abd al-Karakī, the son of Muḥaqqiq-i Thānī, i.e., Mīr Dāmād's own maternal uncle (Hādī (1984): 23–26).

Mīr Dāmād's time was that of legendary friendships and rivalries among the prominent men of knowledge (Hādī (1984): 27–30). In the ruins of a royal building in Iṣfahān, dating back to the Ṣafavid period, there is a fading fresco that depicts three distinguished men in the presence of a terrifying lion (Hādī (1984): 30). This fresco depicts a famous story, according to which one day Mīr Dāmād and two of his prominent contemporaries, Shaykh Bahā'ī and Mīr Findiriskī, were sitting in a royal hall, engaged in a philosophical discussion. Suddenly a lion that had escaped from the royal zoo enters the hall. The fresco depicts Shaykh Bahā'ī as collecting himself with signs of fear on his face, Mīr Dāmād as prostrating in gratitude, and Mīr Findiriskī as utterly indifferent to the lion's presence. The three distinguished friends were later obliged to provide an explanation of their immediate reactions. Shaykh Bahā'ī is reported to have said that by the power of reason he knew that unless the lion was hungry, it would not attack him, and yet instinctively he was moved to protect himself. Mīr Dāmād explained that, being a descendant of the Prophet, he knew that the lion would not attack him, so he prostrated and thanked God for being a descendant of the Prophet. And Mīr Findiriskī is reported to have said that he mastered the terrifying beast by the power of his inner serenity and self-control. The story, in its hagiographical hyperbole, indicates the range of doctrinal, philosophical and mystical issues current at the time – issues that will become the central problematics of the "School of Iṣfahān". If certitude and mental preparedness were the critical criteria of how to confront the anxieties of being, the three Ṣafavid sages represent the three possible modes of attaining those objectives. Either doctrinal faith in the saving grace of the Prophet's intercession, or rational engagement with realities that be, or else mystical dismissal of the anxieties of the "real" are embodied and represented in the respective accounts of these three key figures of the "School of Iṣfahān".

An array of distinguished philosophers, theologians, Sufis and jurists were contemporaries of Mīr Dāmād. He had a full and fruitful course of dialogue and correspondence with them, chief among whom was Shaykh Bahā'ī. Both Shaykh Bahā'ī and Mīr Dāmād enjoyed prestigious positions in Shah 'Abbās's court. They had utmost respect for each other. The other distinguished contemporary of Mīr Dāmād, Mīr Findiriskī, was a prominent philosopher/mystic in his own right. Among his other contemporaries in Iṣfahān was Mīr Fakhr al-Dīn Sammāk.

The legendary friendship between Mīr Dāmād and Shaykh Bahā'ī, when they were both in the service of Shah 'Abbās, provides notable access to the political ramifications of having prominent men of religious learning at the royal court. One biographer of Mīr Dāmād (Tabrīzī Khiyābānī in Mīr Dāmād (1977): lviii–lix) reports that one day Shah 'Abbās was riding his horse in the company of Mīr Dāmād and Shaykh Bahā'ī. Because Mīr Dāmād was fat and heavy, he and his horse would regularly fall behind. Shah 'Abbās is reported to have approached him and in jest suggested that Shaykh Bahā'ī is not polite and reverential enough and gallops fast ahead of Mīr Dāmād. "That is not true, your Majesty", Mīr Dāmād is believed to have responded. "His horse is so happy for having such a great man riding it, it cannot control itself and jumps and pushes ahead of everyone else." Shah 'Abbās goes to Shaykh Bahā'ī and this time complains of Mīr Dāmād's weight and says he is so fat he cannot keep up with the entourage. "That is not the reason, your Majesty," Shaykh Bahā'ī is reported to have said, "the poor animal cannot bear the weight of so much knowledge that it carries. Mountains would break carrying the weight of Mīr Dāmād's knowledge." Shah 'Abbās is reported – and here is the political aspect of such high-ranking men of religious learning – to have descended from his horse and in front of all his entourage kissed the ground and thanked God Almighty for having blessed him and his kingdom with such great men of humility and learning. Shah 'Abbās's going back and forth between Mīr Dāmād and Shaykh Bahā'ī (to which one can easily add Mīr Findiriskī) is also an indication of the constant political need of realizing the relations of power between the king and any particular subdivision of his religious constituency. Representing the juridical, philosophical and mystical centres of power in the Ṣafavid realm, Mīr Dāmād, Shaykh Bahā'ī and Mīr Findiriskī need Shah 'Abbās's political backing as much as the monarch needs theirs. That Mīr Dāmād and Shaykh Bahā'ī deliberately safeguard their respective positions and do not fall victim to Shah 'Abbās's trap could be read as an indication of the pious hagiographer's wishes rather than reality. Shah 'Abbās's supposed prostrations, while Mīr Dāmād and Shaykh Bahā'ī are still on the horse, is the ultimate testimony of the often-concealed proclivity of the religious authorities for political power.

Mīr Dāmād's famous and distinguished student was Mullā Ṣadrā Shīrāzī, by far the most influential philosopher of the Ṣafavid period and of the "School of Iṣfahān". Mullā Ṣadrā began his early education in his native Shīrāz. He then moved to Iṣfahān and studied with the most distinguished Shī'ī scholars of the time, chief among them Mīr Findiriskī, Shaykh Bahā'ī and Mīr Dāmād. He would proceed to develop a revolutionary philosophical school, highly ambitious in its universal attempt to synthesize not just the divergent orientations of the Islamic Peripatetic and Illuminationist traditions, but even more fundamentally to co-ordinate that already difficult synthesis with both the gnostic and Shī'ī juridical doctrines. Yet in many respects the immediate impact of his studies with Mīr Dāmād, Mīr Findiriskī and Shaykh Bahā'ī remained with the Shīrāzī philosopher. In addition to Mullā Ṣadrā, Mīr Dāmād had a number of other, less prominent, students (Hādī (1984): 31), among them Shams al-Dīn Jīlānī, Mīr Lawḥī, and Quṭb al-Dīn al-Ushkūrī. Zulālī Khwānsārī, a distinguished poet of the period with a particular penchant for philosophy and mysticism, composed many poems in honour of his teacher Mīr Dāmād (Hādī (1984): 47). In his poetry one detects Mīr Dāmād's profound influence, an influence particularly pertinent to the formation of the "School of Iṣfahān". In one of his poems, there is a conversation between two protagonists, one mature and perfect, the other immature and inferior. The question is simply put, "What is the function of the heavenly sphere and of primary matters?"

Logical, biological, theological, philosophical and gnostic questions are raised, doctrinal issues are debated, using all the developed and loaded terminologies of these exclusive disciplines about the nature, function and purpose of existence. The questions are as fundamental as "Why is pre-eternity separated from post-eternity?" But the progressive questions are brought to an abrupt end by the immediate theocentric assumption (put in the form of a question) that "In whatever form these things are / Who are they obeying in Eternity?" The answer, upon this *a priori* theocentric postulation, is then given through a shift from these logocentric questions to a mystical discourse. "The prophet is love, religion love, God love / From the deepest earth to the highest heavens love / . . . / Every atom is in ecstasy from love / Everyone is like Manṣūr [al-Ḥallāj] by love" (Hādī (1984): 47).

MĪR DĀMĀD'S WRITINGS

Some fifty treatises have been attributed to Mīr Dāmād (Hādī (1984): 37–45). Not all these have been found and positively identified. Most of his writings are still in unedited manuscripts. He wrote *al-Qabasāt, Ṣirāṭ al-mustaqīm* and *Ufuq al-mubīn* in theology and philosophy. His *Rawāshih al-samāwiyyah* is an exegesis on a collection of Shī'ī Imāmī traditions. He has a Qur'ānic commentary called *Ṣidrat al-muntahā'*. His other famous treatises include *al-Jadhawāt* and *Tashrīq al-ḥaqq*. His theological concerns are evident in such works as *al-'Imādāt wa'l-tashrīfāt fī mas'alat al-ḥudūth al-'ālam wa'l-qidamihi, Taqwīm al-īmān fī mabḥath wājib al-wujūd wa taqdīsahu wa tamjīdahu* or *al-Īqāḍāt fī khalq al-a'māl wa 'af'āl al-'ibād*. The latter treatise is an exposition on Ibn Sīnan ontology. Mīr Dāmād was also concerned with such questions as why Moses' body did not burn on Mount Sinai, while the stones of the mountain did. He treated this question in his famous Persian treatise *al-Jadhawāt: fī bayān sabab 'adam iḥtirāq jasad Mūsā 'alayhī al-salām wa iḥtirāq al-jabal fī ḥāll al-tajallī ṭūr Sīnā*, which he wrote for Shah 'Abbās. In the field of *Ḥadīth*, he has a commentary on al-Kulaynī's *al-Kāfī*. This book, *al-Rawāshiḥ al-samāwiyyah fī sharḥ aḥādīth al-imāmiyyah*, has not yet been completely edited and published. Mīr Dāmād also wrote a Persian treatise on jurisprudence. This treatise is composed in a series of hypothetical questions and answers. The subject and theme of this book follow the standard topics of the juridical genre, with specific chapters on ritual purity, prayer, religious alms and *ḥajj* pilgrimage, as well as more mundane commercial transactions. In his juridical judgments, Mīr Dāmād supports his arguments by all necessary traditional (*manqūl*) sources. Yet he also resorts to intellectual (*ma'qūl*) arguments in substantiating his case. A typical juridical judgment of his is as follows. Suppose *A* gives *B* an object for safekeeping and then instructs *B* to give it to *C*. In the meantime, *D* appears and proves to *B* beyond any shadow of a doubt that the object rightfully belongs to him. What should *B* do? Mīr Dāmād maintains that if the rightful possession of the object by *D* is perfectly evident to *B*, he should give it to him and neither *A* nor *C* has any legal claim on him (Hādī (1984): 43–4). Mīr Dāmād repeatedly brought his considerable philosophical prowess to bear on the doctrinal dogmatics of shīʿīsm. For example, he wrote a treatise on why it is forbidden to call the Twelfth Shīʿī Imām by his name (Hādī (1984): 44; Tabrīzī Khiyābānī in Mīr Dāmād (1977): xii). His Qur'ānic commentaries include *Amānat-i ilāhī* in Persian, *Ta'wīl al-muqtaʿāt fī awā'il al-suwar al-qur'āniyyah*, *Tafsīr sūrat al-ikhlāṣ*, and *Ṣidrah al-muntahā'*. A philosophical commentary on Ibn Kammūnah, a commentary on Ibn Sīnā's *al-Najāt*, a treatise on logic (*Risālah fi'l-manṭiq*), and a commentary on Shaykh al-Ṭūsī's *al-Istibṣār* are also among his other writings. The five important books for which he is most celebrated and discussed are *al-Rawāshiḥ al-samāwiyyah*, *al-Ṣirāṭ al-mustaqīm*, *al-Ufuq al-mubīn*, *al-Qabasāt* and *al-Jadhawāt* (Ashkiwarī in *Mīr Dāmād* (1977): xxxii). *Al-Qabasāt*, *al-Ufuq al-mubīn*, *al-Ṣirāṭ al-mustaqīm*, *al-Taqdīsāt* and *al-Ḥabl al-matīn* are his chief treatises in philosophy (Madanī in Mīr Dāmād (1977): liv). But Mīr Dāmād's most significant text by far, containing the essential features of his philosophy, is *al-Qabasāt* (Izutsu in Mīr Dāmād (1977): 2; the English introduction).

AL-QABASĀT

Until quite recently there was no critical edition of *al-Qabasāt*. The definitive edition was critically edited, annotated and published in 1977 (Mīr Dāmād 1977). The full title of the book is *al-Qabasāt ḥaqq al-yaqīn fī ḥudūth al-ʿālam*. *Al-Qabasāt* consists of ten *qabas* ("a sparkle of fire") and three successive conclusions. The central question of this book is the creation of the world and the possibility of its extension from God. Mīr Dāmād wrote *al-Qabasāt* in 1034/1624 (Mīr Dāmād (1977): v). The first *qabas* discusses the variety of created beings and the divisions of existence (*ibid.*: 3–36). In the second *qabas*, Mīr Dāmād argues for a trilateral typology of essential primacies (*al-sibaq al-dhātī*) and his preference for the primacy of essence (*dhāt*) (*ibid.*: 37–80). The duality of perspectives through which existence is subdivided and an argument to that effect through pre-eternal primacies constitute the third *qabas* (*ibid.*: 81–120). In the fourth *qabas*, Mīr Dāmād provides Qur'ānic evidence, as well as references from the Prophetic and Imāmī traditions, to support his preceding arguments (*ibid.*: 121–42). The fifth *qabas* is devoted to a discussion of the primary dispositions through an understanding of natural existence (*ibid.*: 143–182). The connection (*ittiṣāl*) between "time" and "motion" is the subject of the sixth *qabas* (*ibid.*: 183–238). In this section, Mīr Dāmād also argues for a "natural order" (*al-naẓm al-ṭabī'ī*) in time. Here he argues for the finality of numeral order and against the infinity of numbers in time-bound events (*al-ḥawādith al-zamāniyyah*). He then devotes the seventh *qabas* to a refutation of opposing views (*ibid.*: 239–78). In the eighth *qabas*, he verifies the Divine Authority in the establishment of such orders and the role of reason in ascertaining this truth (*ibid.*: 279–344). The ninth *qabas* proves the archetypal substance of intellect (*al-jawāhir al-'aqliyyah*) (*ibid.*: 345–406). In this chapter Mīr Dāmād provides an argument for the presence of an order in existence, a cycle of beginning and return. Finally, in the tenth *qabas*, he discusses the matter of Divine Ordination (*al-qaḍā' wa'l-qadar*), the necessity of supplication, the promise of His reward and the final return of all things to His Judgment (*ibid.*: 407–84).

In *al-Qabasāt* Mīr Dāmād engages in the age-old debate over the priority of "essence" (*māhiyyah*) versus the priority of "existence" (*wujūd*). After a long discussion, he ultimately decides in favour of the priority of essence, a position that would later be fundamentally disputed by his distinguished pupil Mullā Ṣadrā. *Al-Qabasāt* has remained a central text of Islamic philosophy since its first appearance. A number of philosophers of later generations have written commentaries upon it, including those by Mullā Shamsā Gīlānī and Āqā Jānī Māzandarānī (Āshtiyānī in Mullā Ṣadrā (1967): 86 n. 1). Mīr Dāmād wrote *al-Qabasāt* in response to one of his students who had asked him to write a treatise and in it prove that the Creator of creation and being is unique in His pre-eternality, pre-eternal in His continuity, continuous in His everlastingness and everlasting in His post-eternality (Mīr Dāmād (1977): 1). In this text, he set for himself the task of proving that all existent beings, from archetypal models to material manifestations, are "contingent upon nothingness" (*masbūqun bi'l-'adam*), "inclined towards creation" (*ṭārifan bi'l-ḥudūth*), "pending on annihilation" (*marhūnun bi'l-halāk*), and "subject to cancellation" (*mamnuwwun bi'l-buṭlān*) (*ibid.*: 1). The question of the pre-eternity (*qidam*) or createdness (*ḥudūth*) of the world is one of the oldest and most enduring questions of Islamic philosophy, deeply rooted in the early Mu'tazilite codification of Islamic theology (Watt (1962): 58–71; Fakhry (1985): 67–8; Leaman (1985): 11–12, 132–4). Mīr Dāmād reminds his readers that even Ibn Sīnā considered the nature of debate on this question to be "dialectical" (*jadalī*) rather than based on "proof" (*burhān*). (For Ibn Sīnā "proof" was a mode of logical argument superior to "dialectic".)

"Creation" (*ibdā'*) is the "bringing-into-being" of something from absolute-nothing. That which is "evident" (*ma'lūm*), if left to its own "essence" (*dhāt*), would not be. It is only by virtue of something outside it, i.e. its cause, that it is or, more accurately, it is brought-into-being. Things in their own essence have an essential, not a temporal, primacy over things that are located outside of them, such as their cause for becoming evident and manifest. Thus the secondariness of the caused over the primacy of its cause is an essential not a temporal secondariness. From this it follows that unless the relation between the cause and the caused is a temporal one, not every caused is created in time, i.e., not every *ma'lūl* ("caused") is a *muḥdath* ("created-in-time"). Only that caused is created-in-time which is contingent upon time (*zamān*), motion (*ḥarakah*) and change (*taghayyur*) (Mīr Dāmād (1977): 3). That created-being which is not subsequent to time is either subsequent to absolute nothingness, whose creation is called *ibdā'* (or "brought-into-beginning"), or subsequent to not-absolute-nothingness, in which case its creation is called *iḥdāth* (or "brought-into-being-in-time"). If the created-being is subsequent to time, it can have only one possibility, which is its being-in-time subsequent to its being-in-nothingness (Mīr Dāmād (1977): 3–4).

There is also a hierarchical conception of time that Mīr Dāmād begins to develop, mostly from previous arguments made by Ibn Sīnā, Naṣīr-i Khusraw and Khwājah Naṣīr Ṭūsī (Mīr Dāmād (1977): x). First there is "time" (*zamān*), to which the "atemporal" (*dahr*) and ultimately the "everlasting" (*sarmad*) are superior and more expansive (*ibid.*: 7). This hierarchy of time-span is also to be understood in terms of relationship. *Sarmad* postulates the relation of the permanent to the permanent; *dahr*, the relation of the permanent to the changing; and *zamān*, a relation of the changing to the changing (Nasr in Sharif (1966): 915–17). From this trilateral conception of time, Mīr Dāmād reaches for his unique understanding of creation. Both *ḥudūth* ("creation") and *qidam* ("pre-eternity") are of three kinds: *dhātī* (or "essential"), *dahrī* (or "atemporal") and *zamānī* (or "temporal"). Essential pre-eternality (the counterpart of the essential createdness) is that whose being and actuality are not subsequential to its not-being (*laysiyyah*) and/or nothingness (*'adam*). Atemporal pre-eternality (the counterpart of the atemporal createdness) is that whose being and actuality are not subsequential to its absolute nothingness in the span of the atemporal. On the contrary, from pre-eternity it is in-being. And finally, temporal pre-eternity (the counterpart of temporal createdness) is that temporal-thing whose being is not specific to a time and whose already-being (*ḥuṣūl*) is constantly present in the course of all time, and for the beginning of its being there is no temporal beginning.

Mīr Dāmād proceeds to systematize further the received Ibn Sīnan conception of "createdness" (*ḥudūth*), with particular reference to *al-Ishārāt wa'l-tanbīhāt* (1977: 5), by arguing that "temporal createdness" (*al-ḥudūth al-zamānī*) contains the other two "creatednesses" as well. "Temporal createdness" is the only kind of *ḥudūth* that consists of three different kinds: gradual, instant and timely – which means that temporal createdness can be realized either gradually and by incremental achievements in correspondence to specified divisions of time, in instant realization without any division of time, or finally in a timely space between points A and B. Contemporary commentators of Mīr Dāmād (Mohaghegh in Mīr Dāmād (1977): xii–xiii) have traced the origins of his ideas on the question of pre-eternality and createdness as being primarily to Plato, Aristotle, and Ibn Sīnā, and then chiefly to Khwājah Naṣīr al-Dīn al-Ṭūsī and Shihāb al-Dīn al-Suhrawardī.

As a believing Muslim, Mīr Dāmād must advance, perforce, the argument of the createdness of cosmic existence. Neither "essential createdness" (*al-ḥudūth al-dhātī*) nor "temporal createdness" (*al-ḥudūth al-zamānī*) is subject to disagreement among philosophers because they are self-evident. It is only in the question of "atemporal createdness" (*al-ḥudūth al-dahrī*) that disagreement arises. God's creation of the universe, Mīr Dāmād concludes, is of the *ibdā'* ("brought-into-beginning") and *ṣun'* ("brought-into-createdness") kind as it pertains to "atemporal createdness" and of the *iḥdāth* ("brought-into-being-in-time") and *takwīn* ("brought-into-existence") kind as it pertains to "temporal createdness".

By the common consensus of many of his commentators, *al-Qabasāt* is Mīr Dāmād's most significant philosophical text (Musawī Bihbahānī in Mīr Dāmād (1977): lxiv). His principal contribution in this text to the continuous debate over the pre-eternity (*qidam*) or createdness (*ḥudūth*) of the world is his concept of *al-ḥudūth al-dahrī* ("atemporal createdness"). He argues that the created world cannot be considered as merely "essentially" (*dhātī*) created, because in that case only its "essential" non-being (*al-'adam al-dhātī*) precedes it. "Essential" non-being is a relative and not a self-evident attribute. The created world can be "essentially" contingent upon non-being and yet, in a relative sense, be. Moreover, the created world cannot be considered as contingent upon "temporal" non-being, because in that case time itself, which is a dimension of the created world, must be contingent upon its own non-being in time; and in the space thus considered time cannot be and not be in the same instant. There is also a theological problem in making the created world contingent upon a "temporal" non-being, because the postulation still necessitates a state of being when God was and His bounty to the world was not.

Mīr Dāmād proceeds to distinguish between three kinds of "world". First is the "Everlasting World" (*al-'ālam al-sarmadī*), which is the space for Divine Presence, His Essence, and Attributes; second is the "Atemporal World" (*al-'ālam al-dahrī*), which is the space for the pure archetypes (*al-mujarradāt*); and third is the "Temporal World" (*al-ʿālam al-zamānī*), which is the space for daily events, created beings, and generation and corruption. There is a hierarchical relationship among these three worlds: the Everlasting World encompasses the Atemporal and the Temporal. The Temporal World is the weakest and least enduring of the three.

As temporal events are contingent upon time, i.e., there are times when they are not and then they are "produced", or brought-into-being, in time, the same contingency governs the hierarchical order of *sarmad* (everlasting), *dahr* (atemporality), and *zamān* (temporality). (See Izutsu in Mīr Dāmād (1977): 4, the English introduction, where Izutsu prefers "no-time" for *sarmad*, "meta-time" for *dahr*, and "time" for *zamān*.) Every inferior stage, such as *zamān*, is in an actual state of non-being in relation to its superior state, in this case *dahr*. The real existence of the superior stage is identical to the actual non-being of the inferior stage. Reversing the order, the accidental defectiveness of the inferior stage – *zamān* to *dahr*, or *dahr* to *sarmad* – is not present in the superior stage. The in-itself existence of the superior stage, in other words, is the *ipso facto* non-existence of the inferior stage in-itself. Mīr Dāmād then concludes that the contingent non-being of the world of the archetypals of the *dahrī* stage in the stage of *sarmadī* existence is a real and self-evident non-being. Thus all created beings and their archetypals are consequent to real and self-evident non-being. Their creation is an atemporal (*dahrī*) creation and not, as theologians maintain, a temporal (*zamānī*) creation (Musawī Bihbahānī in Mīr Dāmād (1977): lxvi–lxvii). From this it follows that beyond their "essential creation" (*al-ḥudūth al-dhātī*) all temporal events are contingent upon and consequent to three real modes of non-existence: temporal, atemporal and everlasting. All the archetypal beings in the stage of temporal being are also contingent upon and consequent to one kind of non-being, namely the everlasting. And of course the everlasting world is not contingent upon and consequential to anything (see Musawī Bihbahānī in Mīr Dāmād (1977): lxxiii; for an alternative reading of the *sarmad–dahr–zamān* relationship, see Izutsu in Mīr Dāmād (1977): 4–10, the English introduction).

What Mīr Dāmād achieves through this systematic separation of a trilateral stipulation of existence is the effective separation of God at the top of the hierarchy where He can initiate and sustain the world and yet not be subsequent to temporal corruption, to which all visible creations must yield. Moreover, the necessary contingency of an agent of creation, which is evidently active in the *zamānī* and *dahrī* stages of existence, is not necessary in the superior stage of *sarmadī*. As one of Mīr Dāmād's commentators rightly observes, "By devising the concept of *ḥudūth-i dahrī* (atemporal creation), he [Mīr Dāmād] has succeeded in establishing a compromise between the theologian and the philosopher, in other words, between the religious law and reason" (Mūsawī Bihbahānī in Mīr Dāmād (1977): lxix).

JADHAWĀT

Mīr Dāmād's *Jadhawāt* is also devoted to an understanding of the nature of existence, for him a theophany distanced from the Divine Essence, a movement which is complemented by a reversal of this emanation back to its Origin. There are gradations and stages in this descending/ascending act of creation. In the descending order, first there is the *Nūr al-anwār* ("Light of Lights") (the Suhrawardīan First Principle) from which are issued all the descending orders of existence. From *Nūr al-anwār* first is issued *anwār-i qāhirah* or "archetypal lights", *primus inter pares* among which is *'aql-i kull* or "the universal intellect". *Anwār-i qāhirah* constitutes the first order of existence in close proximity to the source of all being, the pure Light, the Light of All Lights, or *Nūr al-anwār*. In the second order of descending creation of existence is yet another constellation of lights called *anwār-i mudabbirah* or "the governing lights", *primus inter pares* among which is *nafs-i kull* or "the universal soul". *Nafs-i kull* receives its light and existential energy from *'aql-i kull*, as the latter does from *Nūr al-anwār*. In the same order, the *anwār-i mudabbirah* receive their authority and existential energy from the *anwār-i qāhirah*, themselves in turn created and energized by *Nūr al-anwār*. In this second order of descending existence, the *anwār-i mudabbirah* and *nafs-i kull* chief among them constitute the *nufūs-i falakiyyah* or "the heavenly souls" from which are descended all the lower stages of existence. The third order of descending creation directly under the authority of *nufūs-i falakiyyah* are *nufūs-i munṭabi'ah* or "the natural souls", which contain the archetypal sources of all that exists in the heavens and earth. From these archetypal sources descend the fourth order of existence, which is *ṣūrat-i jismiyyah* or "the bodily form", itself the source of *hylé* or physical matter. In the ascending order, first there is *jism-i muṭlaq* or "absolute body"; then the composite bodies, the vegetative soul in plants, the animal soul in animals, and penultimately the intellectual soul of human beings, which stands right below the Truth Itself (Nasr in Sharif (1966): 917–21).

ONTOLOGY

As is evident in both *al-Qabasāt* and *Jadhawāt*, for Mīr Dāmād being is circulated through a cycle of emanation from the Divine Presence to the physical world and then a return to It. In a progression of distancing emanations, the material world is gradually emanated from the Divine Presence. From the Light of Lights (*Nūr al-anwār*) are first emanated the archetypal lights (*anwār-i qāhirah*), of which the universal intellect (*'aql-i kull*) is the first component. From this stage is emanated the "heavenly souls" (*nufūs-i falakiyyah*), the "ruling lights" (*anwār-i mudabbirah*), of which the "universal soul" (*nafs-i kull*) is the primary member. The "natural souls" (*nufūs-i munṭabi'ah*) were subsequently created by the "universal soul". The archetypes of the heavens, planets, elements, compounds and the four natures are thus created. The final stage of the ontological emanation of being is the creation of matter from these archetypal origins. There is then a reversal order through which matter is sublimated back to light. Through this order, absolute or irreducible body (*jism-i muṭlaq*) is advanced to the mineral stage of compound compositions. The minerals are then sublimated to the vegetative stage and then upward to the animal. Humanity is the highest stage of this upward mobility before the absolute matter rejoins the Light of Lights (Nasr in Sharif (1966): 918). At the centre of this descending/ascending order, stands the human being, who is the existential microcosm corresponding to the macrocosm of the universe of Being.

Another principal aspect of Mīr Dāmād's ontology is his philosophical preference for the "priority of essence" (*aṣālah al-māhiyyah*) over the "priority of existence" (*aṣālah al-wujūd*). (See Āshtīyānī (1972): 40–7 for a critical assessment, and Izutsu in Mīr Dāmād (1977): 10, 14, the English introduction, for a more sympathetic review.) The debate over the priority of *māhiyyah* (essence or, more accurately, quiddity) or *wujūd* (existence) is a long contentious problematic in Islamic philosophy. While Mīr Dāmād believed in the priority of *māhiyyah*, his celebrated student Mullā Ṣadrā became the most ardent propagator of the priority of *wujūd* (Āshtiyānī (1972): 45). The priority of quiddity considers the appleness of the apple which is its essence to be real and its existence to be a mere accident, a necessary attribute for the actualization of the appleness. All existent beings share this accidental necessity of existence, but what distinguishes them and thus constitutes their unique ontological status is their quiddity, their what-it-isness, their appleness as opposed to orangeness. The philosophical genealogy of this position is to be traced back to Suhrawardī and Platonism (Izutsu in Mīr Dāmād (1977): 11–12, the English introduction). Mullā Ṣadrā resoundingly disputed his teachers' firm belief in the priority of quiddity over existence and in a moving passage announced:

> In the earlier days I used to be a passionate defender of the thesis that the quiddities are extramentally real while existence is but a mental construct, until my Lord gave me guidance and let me see His own demonstrations. All of a sudden my spiritual eyes were

> opened and I saw with utmost clarity that the truth was just the contrary of what philosophers in general had held. Praise be to God who, by the light of intuition, led me out of the darkness of the groundless idea and firmly established me upon the thesis which would never change in the present World and the Hereafter. As a result [I now hold that] the individual existences of things are primary realities, while the quiddities are the "permanent archetypes [*a'yān thābitah*] that have never smelt even the fragrance of existence". The individual existences are nothing but beams of light radiated by the true Light which is the absolutely self-subsistent Existence. The absolute Existence in each of its individualized forms is characterized by a number of essential properties and intelligible qualities. And each of these properties and qualities is what is usually known as quiddity.
>
> (translated by Izutsu in Mīr Dāmād (1977): 13–14, the English introduction)

Mīr Dāmād's position, however, is founded squarely on the originality of essence over existence. Here is how he argues his case in the second chapter of the *Qabasāt*:

> The essence of a thing [*al-shay'*], in whatever shape or format it might be, is the occurrence [*wuqū'*] of the essence [*nafs*] of that very thing in that form [*ẓarf* = literally "vessel", "container"], not the attachment or appendage of something to it. Otherwise, simple matter [*al-ḥāl al-basīṭ*] would be turning into compound matter [*al-ḥāl al-murakkab*]. Yet the bringing into being [*thubūt*] of a thing in itself is the bringing-into-being of that thing in that thing. Thus whoever considers the existence of the essence [*al-māhiyyah*] an attribute [*waṣf*] among the actual attributes, or an aspect [*amr*] among the mental aspects, above and beyond the concept of the Originating Existence, he would not be among those worth talking to, and he would not be among those in search of truth, as indeed it has been said by our [two] foregone companions in the act [of philosophy, i.e., Ibn Sīnā and al-Fārābī].
>
> (Mīr Dāmād (1977): 37)

TRANSMIGRATION OF THE SOUL

As an example of this descending/ascending order of existence, there is the treatise called *Risālat al-khal'iyyah* attributed to Mīr Dāmād (Ashkiwarī in Mīr Dāmād (1977): xxxiv–xxxv; Madanī in Mīr Dāmād (1977): lv–lvi) in which he describes the momentary transmigration of his own soul. (See "Exaltations dans la Solitude" in Corbin (1972), 4: 30–53.) He writes that on Friday 16 Sha'bān 1023 (21 September 1614), as he was engaged in a rigorous solitary self-reflection, after an intense period of remembering God Almighty, calling Him by His Most Bounteous Name, he was completely isolated from the physical world. At this point he felt himself totally surrounded by the sacred precinct of God's Presence. His Light cast totally upon him, Mīr Dāmād remembers having left his physical body, abandoned the network of his sense perceptions, and been completely released from the bounds of nature. He soars towards the Absolute Presence of Truth, having completely left his body behind. He transcends everything that there is, supersedes temporality and reaches the realm of atemporality. He transcends all created things, all things that were brought into being. He transcends the physical and the metaphysical, the sacred, the material, the atemporal, the temporal, the division between faith and blasphemy, Islam and ignorance, transcends all degrees, all stages, all who came before, all who will come later, for ever and ever. He transcends everything that ever was, everything that can ever be, small and large, permanent and mandatory, present and yet-to-come. Then everything in solitude or in a group was ready at the gates of His Majesty and there he saw His Most Majestic Presence, with the eye of his inner intentions, in a way he could not understand. In utter annihilation everything recited His Name, pleading, begging, asking for His help, calling Him "O Thou the Rich, Thou the Giver of Richness!" These all were said in a way not known to them. Mīr Dāmād persists in that state of utter mental unconsciousness, forgetting the substance of his faculties of understanding, in a total state of non-being. Then he comes out of that absolute state of unconsciousness and returns to the material world.

Comparing this experience to the Ibn Sīnan "visionary recitals", Corbin gave a full enthusiastic interpretation of this account (Corbin (1972), 4: 39–45), considerably emphasizing the significance of the middle of Sha'bān, the Prophet Muḥammad's reported favourite month. Referring to the Ismā'īlī significance of this month, Corbin adds that: "Les traditions ismaéliennes insistent sur le sens ésotérique de cette Nuit. A la question d'un adepte demandant pourquoi l'on parle parfois de l'excellence du '*jour*' (*qawm*) de la mi-Sha'bān, alors que dans le *ḥadīth* rapporté du Prophète, il est question de la *nuit* et non pas du *jour*, – il est répondu qu'ici le *jour* et la *nuit* indiquent les positions respectives du Prophète et de l'Imām. Le Prophète a déclaré: 'Sha'bān est mon mois,' ce qui réfère à son message, La *Risālat*" (*ibid.*: 41–2). Corbin's interpretation is based on a text that gives the date of Mīr Dāmād's vision as "Friday 14 Sha'bān 1023". There is no such date in the year 1023 of the Islamic calendar. As the text (Madanī in Mīr Dāmād (1977): 55–6) indicates, the night in question is "Friday 16 Sha'bān 1023" which corresponds to Friday 21 September 1614. In the year 1023/1614, 14 Sha'bān was on Wednesday 17 September, and not on a Friday. The Friday in question was 16 Sha'ban, and Corbin's interpretation must be modified accordingly.

The notion of the transmigration of the human soul from the material body into the realm of Divine Presence must be understood in the context of Mīr Dāmād's meta-epistemology whereby all the uncertainties of the material faculties are eliminated in a realm of metarational experience that the human soul leaves the body and ascends all the stages of existence he has identified in both the *Qabasāt* and *Jadhawāt*. What substantiates this assessment is the attribution of many ascetic exercises to Mīr Dāmād. His nocturnal solitude, best discussed by Corbin (1972, 4: 39–45), would have created a favourable condition for such conceptions. Mīr Dāmād, in effect, translated a mystical conception of reunion with the Truth (Zarrīnkūb (1983): 246) into a metaphysics of his own, in which the transmigration of soul from body, through excessive concentration in ascetic exercises, into the Divine Presence constitutes the ultimate state of achieving certitude.

MĪR DĀMĀD'S PROSE

Mīr Dāmād's philosophical discourse in both the *Qabasāt* and *Jadhawāt* is indexical and suggestive, symbolic and referential. He relies heavily on a thorough knowledge of the history of Islamic philosophy to his time. He has a particular penchant for obscure Arabic words that he successfully incorporates into his philosophical discourse. The legendary difficulty of his philosophical prose (Mohaghegh in Mīr Dāmād (1977): xvi; Izutsu in Mīr Dāmād (1977): 3, the English introduction; Nasr (1978): 33; Hādī (1984): 34–6) will have to be understood in the general anti-philosophical climate of the period promoted by the politically powerful nomocentric jurists. Perhaps the greatest philosopher of this period, Mullā Ṣadrā, was forced to leave the capital city of Iṣfahān at the instigation of the high clerical establishment precisely because of the articulate clarity of his prose. In this respect there is a story in *Qiṣaṣ al-'ulamā'* which is indicative of this problem. Tunikābunī reports (1985: 334–5) that Mullā Ṣadrā once saw Mīr Dāmād in a dream and asked him why people condemned him as a blasphemer while he had just repeated what Mīr Dāmād had already said. "The reason is," Mīr Dāmād is believed to have answered, "that I wrote philosophical matters in such a way that the religious authorities [*'ulamā'*] could not understand them, and that nobody other than philosophers would comprehend them. But you have popularized the philosophical issues and said them in such a way that if a teacher of an elementary religious school reads them, he can understand them. That is why they have called you a blasphemer and not me." Had it not been for the occasional protection of such powerful kings as Shah 'Abbās, the philosophers, whose knowledge of astronomy and medicine was always beneficial to the royal court, would not have enjoyed even the limited freedom of discourse and inquiry that they did manage to sustain. Concealing one's philosophical or gnostic ideas in difficult and abstruse prose was one particularly effective way to limit the hermeneutic circle legitimately operative around philosophical texts.

In a letter attributed to Mīr Dāmād (Hādī (1984): 35–6), he makes a specific reference to the difficulty of his prose.

> It is the utmost indication of shamelessness that idle souls and rugged individuals rise in meaningless dispute and superfluous boasting against sacred minds and most sacrosanct jewels. One has to have enough intelligence to know that understanding my discourse is an art, not quarrelling with me and then calling it an "argument". It is perfectly evident that understanding superlative ideas and comprehending subtle issues is not possible for every short-witted, ill-prepared individual. Consequently, entering into a dispute with me in philosophical matters is necessarily due to some natural defects and not because of the precision of observation by a bunch of bat-like blind people who mistake their sense perceptions for the heavenly abodes of knowledge and consider them the highest achievement of the intellect. They had better not boast and express animosity in competition against those who are among the present in the Divine's presence, those whose ray of intellect rotates around the orbits of the lights of the heavenly world. That is not right or proper. However, the disputation of whimsical fantasy with intellect, the hostility of untruth with truth, the struggle of darkness against light is an abomination not accidental, a transgression not recent. Grievance is to be taken to God, and peace be upon him who follows the right path:
>
> When he who is incomplete attacks me,
> To my perfection that is a perfect testimony.
> Those who follow these, O Khāqānī!,
> Are but crows wishing to walk like pheasants.
> Suppose the asparagus made its body look like a snake,
> Where's its poison for its enemies, or love for its friends?

The difficulty of his prose has often been the occasion of much poetic humour. For example, in reference to his *Ṣirāṭ al-mustaqīm* ("The Right Path"), someone has said

Of Mīr Dāmad's "Right Path"
May Muslims not hear, nor the infidel see!
(Hādī (1984): 41)

Many commentaries on Mīr Dāmād's philosophical work have also been necessitated by the difficulty of his prose. Sayyid Aḥmad 'Alawī, for example, wrote a commentary on the *Qabasāt* to explain its difficult expressions and phrases (Mohaghegh in Mīr Dāmād (1977): xvi–xviii). There are a number of other commentaries as well on the *Qabasāt* (*ibid.*: xviii–xx). There are, however, those biographers of Mīr Dāmād who praise him for his eloquence (Ḥusaynī Kāshānī in Mīr Dāmād (1977): xxviii).

POETICS

Mīr Dāmad was a gifted poet (Hādī (1984): 46–7) who left a collection of poetry in both Persian and Arabic. As convoluted and twisted as his philosophical prose is, his poetic voice is crystal-clear and rather elegant. Much "poetic licence" was conventionally given and tolerated by the visceral literalism of the dogmaticians. Mīr Dāmād took full advantage of this "poetic licence" and expressed considerable aspects of his philosophical and gnostic ideas in poetry.

There is a rather remarkable self-confidence in Mīr Dāmād's poetic voice. He repeatedly boasts of his learning and erudition in his poetry. "I am the nightingale of virtue, art is my garden / I have cauterized the forehead of knowledge with my seal" (Hādī (1984): 89). In full confidence he announces that "I am twenty lunar years old / and yet in knowledge older than wisdom." He then proceeds to claim:

I am the lord of virtues, prince of knowledge,
Intellect is my throne, wisdom is my seat. . . .
If like the moon kings borrow
Their majesty from the crown and throne,
I make my crown from my knowledge of the Divine,
Of natural sciences I make my throne. . . .
My fortress is my knowledge of subjects in Arabic,
My palace is my knowledge of sciences in poetics.
I am like an aged wine, the universe is my container.
I am like pure wine, the world is my bottle. . . .
(Hādī (1984): 89–91)

As the repeated apologies of a recent editor of Mīr Dāmād's poems indicate (Hādī (1984): 48, 87), it was considered below the status of a distinguished philosopher to engage in poetry. Among philosophers poetry appears to have been considered a light avocation for momentary distraction from more serious discourses. The nature of this dismissive attitude towards poetry seems to stem from both a metaphysical and a social disdain for what is considered to be a frivolous distraction. Although the frequency and volume of poetic output attributed to Mīr Dāmād prevent us from assuming that the poet himself considered his poetry as frivolous, it is also true that in his poetry we fail to detect a poetic voice distinct from his philosophical ideas expressed elsewhere in prose. Even when he engages in a poetic dialogue with Niẓāmī (535/1141–600/1203), in his famous response to *Makhzan al-asrār*, Mīr Dāmād is still an effective and eloquent translator of his philosophical prose into poetry. Poetry *qua* poetry, with an independent aesthetic presence and a marked difference from a logocentric disposition, has no particularly discernible place in Mīr Dāmād's *Kitāb mashriq al-anwār dar jawāb-i makhzan al-asrār*. Be that as it may, *Mashriq al-anwār* is still an eloquent *mathnawī* that Mīr Dāmād composed in dialogue with Niẓāmī's *Makhzan al-asrār*. This *mathnawī* follows the traditional sections canonized by Niẓāmī. First there is a prologue in praise of God, followed by two supplicative prayers (*munājāt*) and a seeking of forgiveness (*ṭalab-i maghfirat*). Then there are two conventional praises of the Prophet, followed by two successive praises of 'Alī, a section on all Shī'ī Imāms, and a concluding praise of the Twelfth Imām.

Mīr Dāmād's significance as a poet should not be underestimated. Poetic "licence" gave philosophers like Mīr Dāmād the possibility and the imaginative discourse of seeing and thinking at a level beyond the immediate logocentricity and nomocentricity of their philosophy and jurisprudence proper. Ḥusaynī Kāshānī's overwhelming praise for Mīr Dāmād's poetry (in Mīr Dāmād (1977): xxix–xxx) leaves no doubt that his contemporaries recognized and praised him more as a poet than as a philosopher. He, in fact, considers Mīr Dāmād in the same league as the greatest poets of Khurasan, Fars or 'Irāq, by which he means western Persia (*ibid.*: xxx). His commentary on Niẓāmī's *Makhzan al-asrār* is particularly noted as his greatest poetic achievement.

THE "SCHOOL OF IṢFAHĀN"

The term "School of Iṣfahān" was established most successfully by Nasr and Corbin (Nasr in Sharif (1966): 904–32; Nasr (1978): 19–53), Corbin (1972, 4: 9–201) and Āshtiyānī (1972: 6) and then extended by others (Izutsu in Mīr Dāmād (1977): 12, the English introduction) as a generic term identifying the syncretic discourse that emerged in the Iṣfahān of Mīr Dāmād's period. Mīr Dāmād himself is credited with having established this school. The three prominent figures that Corbin studies (1972, 4: 9–201) in his discussion of this school are Mīr Dāmād, Mullā Ṣadrā

Shīrāzī and Qāḍī Sa'īd Qummī (d. 1103/1691). To these names Nasr adds those of Shaykh Bahā' al-Dīn 'Āmilī (Shaykh Bahā'ī), Mīr Findiriskī, Mullā 'Abd al-Razzāq al-Lāhījī (d. 1072/1661) and Mullā Muḥsin Fayḍ Kāshānī (Nasr in Sharif (1966): 908–32). Mullā Rajab 'Alī Tabrīzī (d. 1080/1609), Āqā Ḥusayn Khwānsāri (d. 1098/1686) and Mullā Shasmā Gīlānī (d. 1081/1670) are also studied in the same group of philosophers (Āshtiyānī (1972): 218–494).

Before the star and the highest achievement of the "School of Iṣfahān", Mullā Ṣadrā, could emerge as the leading philosopher of the Ṣafavid period and of the "School of Iṣfahān", much preparatory work had to be done by Mīr Dāmād's generation. Protected by his eminent religious family, particularly his grandfather, Muḥaqqiq-i Karakī, and his own learning in juridical sciences, Mīr Dāmād engaged in philosophical writings with a particular penchant for mystic and Illuminationist tendencies. His attempt to wed Suhrawardī and Ibn Sīnā (Nasr (1978): 26) was matched by an unyielding concern with mystical possibilities of "understanding". Mīr Dāmād, Mīr Findiriskī and Shaykh Bahā'ī were the dominant figures of the pre-Mullā-Ṣadrā period, all sharing this simultaneous interest in gnostic, Peripatetic, Illuminationist and juridical (doctrinal) positions of Shi'ism. As Shī'ī men of learning, Mīr Dāmād, Mīr Findiriskī, Shaykh Bahā'ī and ultimately Mullā Ṣadrā were at the receiving end of the collective philosophical legacies of Ibn Sīnā, al-Ghazzālī, al-Suhrawardī and Ibn 'Arabī. The ultimate objective of the Shi'i philosophers of the Ṣafavid period was to demonstrate the central and meta-epistemological harmony among all these discourses. In his person, Mīr Dāmād exemplified this synthetic ambition of the "School of Iṣfahān". As a Shī'ī philosopher/jurist/mystic, he wrote logical treatises and juridical edicts with the same ease and competence with which he composed mystical poems. "He expounded a rigorously logical philosophy and yet wrote a treatise on a mystical vision he had received in Qom. He harmonized Ibn Sīnan cosmology with Shi'ite imamology and made the 'fourteen pure ones' (*chahārdah ma'ṣūm*) of Shi'ism the ontological principles of cosmic existence" (Nasr (1978): 32–3).

The flourishing of the "School of Iṣfahān" in general and the political possibilities of engaging in philosophy for Mīr Dāmād in particular were due to a considerable degree to the exclusive attention paid to religious learning by Shah 'Abbās the Great. As the greatest and perhaps most powerful of all the Ṣafavid kings, Shah 'Abbās was particularly concerned, anxious even, about his relations with the religious establishment at large. Other than Mīr Dāmād and Shaykh Bahā'ī, for both of whom the Ṣafavid monarch had a particular affection and reverence (Falsafī (1990), 3: 883–7), there were a number of other prominent religious authorities with whom he regularly associated. Mullā 'Abd al-Muḥsin Kāshī, Mullā Muḥsin Fayḍ, Mawlānā 'Abd Allāh Shushtarī and Shaykh Luṭf Allāh Maysī 'Āmilī are among these high-ranking authorities. They would regularly attend his court where he would arrange for discussions and arguments around a religious issue. Particularly during the month of Ramaḍān, he would break his daily fast with the religious authorities. Each of these high-ranking clerics would have his individual dining cloth, on which would be served an extravagant array of dishes, which included sweets and chocolates imported from Europe (*ibid.*: 883). Whatever was left of this sumptuous meal was sent home with the clerics. This was in addition to regular sums of money that Shah 'Abbās would give to his high-ranking religious dignitaries.

Religious dignitaries like Shaykh Bahā'ī and Mīr Dāmād were regularly among Shah 'Abbās's entourage, even when he was on a military campaign. There are even reports that he visited these great men of religious learning at their places of residence. His respect for his religious dignitaries ought to be seen, at least partially, in light of his pious devotion to his faith. One of Shah 'Abbās's servants, who had evoked his wrath, appealed to Shaykh Aḥmad Afshār Ardabīlī, known as Muqaddas, a particularly revered cleric. Muqaddas wrote a letter to Shah 'Abbās: "The custodian of the transitory kingdom should know that if this man had once committed a transgression, now he appears to be transgressed against; if you forgive him, maybe God Almighty may forgive some of your own sins. Signed the Servant of the King of Absolute Sovereignty ['Alī], Aḥmad Ardabīlī" (*ibid.*: 885). Shah 'Abbās responded in utter humility: "May 'Abbās humbly report that your command has been heartily obeyed. May you not forget this devotee of yours in your prayers. Signed, the dog at the door of 'Alī, 'Abbās" (*ibid.*: 885–6). The more humble Shah 'Abbās would appear in front of these religious dignitaries, the more legitimate his own power and authority would be *vis-à-vis* his subjects.

The two major urban settings that flourished in this period were Iṣfahān and Shīrāz. This may, in fact, fundamentally modify the "School of Iṣfahān" appellation, unless we give the Ṣafavid capital its due political significance. One prominent member of the "School of Iṣfahān", Mullā Ṣadrā Shīrāzī, not only was born, raised and received his early education in Shīrāz but, in fact, was chased out of Iṣfahān by Shī'ī dogmatists. Mullā Ṣadrā's most productive writing years were spent in the remote village of Kahak near Qom. As early as the beginning of the ninth/fifteenth century, Shīrāz was the scene of considerable philosophical activity. Mullā Jalāl Dawānī (d. 908/1502) had a flourishing teaching career in Shiraz. Amīr Ṣadr al-Dīn Muḥammad ibn Ibrāhīm Dashtakī Shīrāzī (d. 903/1497) and his son Amīr Ghayāth al-Dīn Manṣūr advanced the cause of philosophical studies in Shīrāz. And ultimately Mullā Ṣadrā taught for years at the *madrasah* of Khān in this city. This is not to underestimate the significance of Iṣfahān as a great cosmopolitan centre of learning under the Ṣafavids. When Shah 'Abbās I ascended the Ṣafavid throne, Iṣfahān became a particularly favourable setting for a number of leading philosophers. Mīr Dāmād, Mīr Findiriskī and Shaykh Bahā' al-Dīn 'Āmilī became the great figures of philosophical learning in the Ṣafavid capital.

Under favourable conditions created by the Ṣafavid monarchs, and despite severe expressions of hostility by the nomocentric jurists, an array of distinguished philosophers, with more or less similar epistemological orientations, emerged in tenth/sixteenth-century Persia. The principal core of the "School of Iṣfahān" was an attempt to bring together the diverse and opposing forces of Islamic intellectual history into a harmonious epistemological and ontological unity. Until the culmination of this movement in Mullā Ṣadrā Shīrāzī, the efforts of Mīr Dāmād's generation must necessarily be considered as preparatory groundwork. Out of necessity or conviction, or a combination of both, Mīr Dāmād's generation of Shī'ī scholars wrote on a range of diverse issues, including Peripatetic and Illuminationist philosophy, Mu'tazilite theology, Ibn 'Arabī's school of mysticism, Qur'ānic commentary, juridical edicts, Shī'ī dogmatics, and even on such popular topics as pious supplications to Shī'ī Imāms, etc. The earliest traces of this synthetic tendency among the Shī'ī scholars in particular are to be seen in such encyclopedic collections as Ḥusayn 'Aqīlī Rustamdārī's *Riyāḍ al-abrār*, composed in 979/1571 (Ṣafā (1959–85), 5, 1: 285). In this book, the Shī'ī encyclopedist brings together an array of theological, philosophical and mystical topics, plus such issues as "occult sciences" (*'ulūm-i gharībah*), with a consistent penchant for the primacy of Shī'ī sentiments and credal dogmas. Mīr Dāmād's *Risālat al-i'ḍālāt fī funūn al-'ulūm wa'l-ṣinā'āt* is a text in this genre. Other prominent figures of the "School of Iṣfahān", such as Mīr Abu'l-Qāsim Findiriskī, wrote similar treatises on the variety of "sciences". Mīr Findiriskī's *Risālah ṣanā'iyyah*, Mullā Muḥsin Fayḍ Kāshānī's *Fihrist al-'ulūm* and Muḥaqqiq-i Sharwānī's (d. 1099/1687) *Unmudhaj al-'ulūm* are among the most notable examples of this genre of writings. In such encyclopedic collections of texts, we witness, although with no articulate epistemological or ontological statement, an attempt to bring the diverse array of Islamic intellectual discourses into some sort of harmony.

The emergence of the "School of Iṣfahān" was predicated on the continued success of the Peripatetic and Illuminationist discourses dominant in Islamic philosophy since the time of Ibn Sīnā and Suhrawardī, respectively. These two philosophical discourses were equally matched by widespread concern with Ibn 'Arabī's school of mysticism. The most prominent figures of the "School of Iṣfahān", including Mīr Dāmād and Mulla Ṣadrā Shīrāzī, reached for a level of philosophical discourse that combined these three dominant traditions and then in turn sought to wed the result to the Shī'ī doctrinal positions. Through the active articulation of such key conceptual categories as "the unity of being" (*waḥdah al-wujūd*), "the priority of being" (*aṣālah al-wujūd*), "transubstantial motion" (*al-ḥarakat al-jawhariyyah*) and "the unification of the knower and the known" (*ittiḥād al-'āqil wa'l-ma'qūl*), the "School of Iṣfahān" shifted the philosophical preoccupation of Islamic philosophers to a plane of operation more responsive to mystical sensibilities. The synthetic discourse with which the "School of Iṣfahān" was gradually identified was *ḥikmah* (Nasr (1966): 907). Central to this discourse was an attempt to combine the doctrinal teachings of the Shī'ī Imāms with the wide range of theoretical speculations in gnosis, philosophy and theology.

The triumphant development of the "School of Iṣfahān" as a distinct philosophical orientation ought to be seen in the context of the Ṣafavid state and the self-assuring confidence it engendered and sustained in the Shī'ī intellectual disposition. Mīr Dāmād and the "School of Iṣfahān" were the supreme cultural products of a confident, prosperous and self-assertive Ṣafavid state. With Mīr Dāmād's generation of Shī'ī philosophers, mystics, jurists and legal theorists, a new mode of intellectual confidence was created that could attend, with perfect authority, the whole gamut of Islamic intellectual history. The formation of the "School of Iṣfahān" is the institutional expression of a daring synthetical discourse set to bring together three conflicting thrusts in Islamic intellectual history – the philosophical, the mystical and the (Shī'ī) doctrinal. Regardless of their degree of success or failure, the chief exponents of the "School of Iṣfahān", from Mīr Dāmād to Mullā Ṣadrā, its most celebrated achievement, contributed towards the emphatic establishment of a level of unprecedented philosophical discourse which saw no fundamental difference between the intellectual configuration of reality and its mystical comprehension or between these two modes of coming to terms with a significant truth (a truth that signifies) and the doctrinal mandates of the Shī'ī faith. What would later be known as *al-ḥikmat al-muta'āliyah* ("the transcendental philosophy") is the theoretical culmination of this synthesis, a cutting deep through all the dominant, and fundamentally hostile, intellectual discourses in Islam. Mīr Dāmād's rather distinctive self-confidence (repetition of his poetic boasting of what a profound philosopher he is, a rather surprising phenomenon given the timidity and humility with which the Muslim literati usually describe their history, and his authoritative voice when attending to any number of philosophical, mystical, doctrinal, Qur'ānic, hermeneutic, and other Shī'ī discourses) is the reflection of a triumphant Ṣafavid dynasty reimbursing Shi'ism for centuries of persecution and humility. The ambitious terms with which Mīr Dāmād and other members of the "School of Iṣfahān", particularly Mullā Ṣadrā, thought they could conceive to bring together the whole universal repertoire of Islamic intellectual history could have been possible only in a kingdom under "the Shadow of God on Earth".

Among the earlier generations of philosophers preceding the "School of Iṣfahān", Qāḍī Maybudī (d. 910/1504) had already combined a Peripatetic orientation in his philosophical writings with a mystical disposition best represented in his poetry. He was a student of Mullā Jalāl Dawānī. Because of his Sunni beliefs, Qāḍī Maybudī was murdered at the order of Shah Ismā'īl (Ṣafā (1959–85), 5, 1: 297). Qāḍī Maybudī wrote extensively on Peripatetic philosophy. His commentaries on *Hidāyah al-ḥikmah* of Athīr al-Dīn Abharī (d. 633/1235) and *Ḥikmah al-'ayn* of Najm al-Dīn Dabīrān (d. 675/1276) were widely read and discussed. In theology, he wrote a commentary on *Ṭawāli' al-anwār* of Qāḍī Bayḍāwī (d. 685/1286). But the traces of a synthetic discourse, wedding philosophy and mysticism, are more immediately evident in his *Jām-i gītī-namā*, a treatise he wrote in Persian and in which he combined aspects of the philosophical and mystical discourses.

As mentioned in the previous chapter, Ghayāth al-Dīn Manṣūr Dashtakī Shīrāzī (866/1463–948/1541) was another distinguished philosopher of this earlier generation, anticipating the "School of Iṣfahān". He is considered the Khwājah Naṣīr al-Dīn al-Ṭūsī of the tenth/sixteenth century. In fact, many of the honorific titles with which he has been praised are identical with those of Khwājah Naṣīr (Ṣafā (1959–85), 5.1: 299–300). When Shah Ismā'īl conquered Shīrāz in 909/1503, he ordered Ghayāth al-Dīn Manṣūr to repair the Maraghah Observatory. During the reign of Shah Ṭahmāsp (930/1524–984/1576), for a period of time, between 936/1529 and 938/1531, he became a vizier to the Ṣafavid king. A rivalry developed between him and Muḥaqqiq-i Karakī, Mīr Dāmād's maternal grandfather, which led to his dismissal from the Ṣafavid court. He subsequently returned to Shīrāz and resumed his writings on philosophy. In his *Mir'āt al-ḥaqā'iq*, Ghayāth al-Dīn Manṣūr begins to work his philosophical ideas into a synthetic discourse between the Peripatetic and Illuminationist schools of philosophy. In his critical commentaries on Mullā Jalāl Dawānī's exegesis on Suhrawardī's *Hayākil al-nūr*, he puts forward a vigorous Peripatetic twist to the Illuminationist discourses of both Suhrawardī and Dawānī.

Mīr Findiriskī is perhaps the most distinguished example of this ecumenical and synthetic spirit rising simultaneously with Mīr Dāmād. He travelled as far as India, became acquainted with Zoroastrian and Hindu ideas, and even wrote a notable commentary on *Yoga Vaiseṣka*. His *Risāla-yi ṣana'iyyah* is an encyclopedic collection of all "rational" and "transmitted" sciences. Other than his philosophical treatises, like *Maqūlāt al-ḥarakah wa'l-taḥqīq fihā*, in which he challenges the notion of Platonic ideas, Mīr Findiriskī reproduced much of his philosophical ideas in his poetry. The opening lines of one of his most famous *qaṣīdahs* is a good example of this philosophical poetry:

> The Universe with stars in it is all so beautiful, pure, and in harmony,
> Whatever is in the heavens has a form down here on earth.
> (Hādī (1984): 66)

The ambitious challenge that the "School of Iṣfahān" sought to meet was wedding together all the diverse and opposing discourses of legitimate understanding that had historically divided Muslims and then have doctrinal Shiʿism preside over them all. The principal points of contention were not only the philosophical traditions of the Peripatetic and Illuminationist branches, but also the gnosis of Ibn ʿArabī and the Shiʿism of the post-*Ghaybah* period. Luminaries of the "School of Iṣfahān", such as Mīr Dāmād and Mullā Ṣadrā, became the chief protagonists of this new philosophical discourse, took the possibilities of ascetic exercises and of gnostic Illumination seriously, and saw the result in perfect harmony with the Shīʿī doctrinal position. In the figure of Mīr Dāmād, for example, were combined the otherwise conflicting characters of a logocentric philosopher, a practising mystic and a powerful jurist. Even if the report that Shah ʿAbbās was actually afraid of him and had plotted to kill him (Zarrīnkūb (1983): 246) is not true, still the assumption is a good indication of the political implications of such a constructed image of social and metaphysical authority.

Mīr Dāmād's principal work in the "School of Iṣfahān" was his reconstruction of a Peripatetic philosophical orientation with a practical mysticism akin to the Illuminationists. Separation from the physical body, in this meta-epistemology, becomes the necessary precondition of conceptual cognitions. Mīr Dāmād's ascetic exercises, thus rooted in his epistemology, become equally constitutional in his appeal to the mystics. The optimum balance that Mīr Dāmād was able to maintain between delicate intrusions of philosophical and mystical doctrines into the dogmatic and juridical principles of the faith was not continued by his pupils. By the time Mullā Ṣadrā (d. 1050/1640) sought to carry Mīr Dāmād's suggestions to their logical conclusions, he had managed to antagonize the Shīʿī clerics considerably, so much so that he had to flee to the remote village of Kahak. Mullā Ṣadrā, in fact, manages to antagonize both the Sufis and the jurists. In his *al-Asfār al-arbaʿah*, *Kasr aṣnām al-jāhiliyyah* and *Risālah-yi sih aṣl* he severely criticizes both the intoxicated Sufis and the literalist jurists. Mullā Ṣadrā's antagonism against some of the practising Sufis seems to have stemmed from a necessary desire to distance his adaptation of a mystical discourse into his general philosophical narrative from such functional Sufism associated with the Sufi orders which had neither theoretical sophistication nor social prestige at that time. As is evident in both Mīr Dāmād and Mullā Ṣadrā's writings, the "School of Iṣfahān" is the collective expression of an intellectual enterprise that seeks to denounce the ecstatic mysticism of a more popular orientation in favour of an articulate adaptation of Sufi gnosis integrated into a principally philosophical discourse. But at the same time this systematic logocentricity has to maintain a safe and necessary distance from the literal nomocentricity of the jurists with its quintessentially anti-philosophical and anti-mystical convictions.

The synthetic nature of the *ḥikmat al-muta'āliyah*, as the highest theoretical achievement of the "School of Iṣfahān", is also evident in its constant references to the works of Abū Ḥāmid Muḥammad al-Ghazzālī in his later works, where he had already achieved a balanced equilibrium among the existing discourses of his time. In his *magnum opus*, *al-Asfār al-arba'ah*, Mullā Ṣadrā demonstrated the viability of the mystical discourse by adopting its formal narrative for his otherwise most ambitious philosophical project. An ambitious synthesis of a logocentric discourse, combined with mystical observations, and ultimately governed by the Qur'ānic language is perhaps the most enduring legacy of the "School of Iṣfahān" as represented in its best spokesmen Mīr Dāmād, Mullā Ṣadrā and their respective students.

Mullā Ṣadrā was perhaps the greatest figure and the most celebrated representative of the "School of Iṣfahān". As Mīr Dāmād's principal student, he gave the fullest account of the principal doctrines of the "School of Iṣfahān". Since there are separate chapters on Mullā Ṣadrā in this volume, I need not discuss him fully here. Suffice it to say that he generously benefited from the work and achievement of his three principal teachers – Mīr Dāmād, Mīr Findiriskī and Shaykh Bahā'ī – and in his *magnum opus*, *al-Asfār al-arba'ah*, as well as in such major treatises as *al-Mashā'ir*, *al-Shawāhid* and *al-Ḥikmah al-'arshīyah*, he gave the synthetic discourse of the "School of Iṣfahān" its most successful expression.

In addition to Mullā Ṣadrā, the generation of Mīr Dāmād, Mīr Findiriskī and Shaykh Bahā'ī trained a number of other distinguished philosophers, among whom is Mullā Rajab 'Alī Tabrīzī (d. 1080/1669), the author of *Kilīd-i bihisht*. Tabrīzī had studied with Mīr Findiriskī and became a prominent religious authority during the reign of Shah 'Abbās. Mullā Shamsā Gīlānī (d. 1081/1670) was another student of Mīr Dāmād. He continued his teacher's interest in the Divine act of creation and wrote a treatise on it (Āshtiyānī in Mullā Ṣadrā (1967): 93; Āshtiyānī (1972): 408–93). He also wrote a commentary on Mīr Dāmād's *al-Qabasāt*. Like his teachers, Mullā Shamsā was under the influence of Suhrawardī, and in opposition to Ibn Sīnā, in considering the comprehensive nature of Divine Knowledge above and beyond the knowledge of the essence. In the same generation of post-Mīr Dāmād philosophers is Aqā Ḥusayn Khwānsārī (d. 1098/1686), who wrote extensive commentaries on Ibn

Sīnā's *al-Shifā'* (Āshtiyānī in Mullā Ṣadrā (1967): 94–5; Āshtīyānī (1972): 362–407).

With the third generation (Ṣadūqī Suhā (1980): 22–33) of the "School of Iṣfahān", Mullā Ṣadrā's students had already learned to be more cautious in the formulation of their ideas. In his *Shawāriq*, Mullā 'Abd al-Razzāq Lāhījī (d. 1072/1661), Mullā Ṣadrā's student and son-in-law, reformulates an originally Ghazzālīan position (Zarrīnkūb (1983): 251) that mystical observations are the ultimate tests of preceding rational conclusions. The viability of the mystical discourse as a meta-epistemological basis of legitimate understanding continued to occupy a central position in the theoretical apparatus of the "School of Iṣfahān". The principal problems that led the philosophers of the "School of Iṣfahān" towards the viability of the mystical discourse were created by the confrontation between the Peripatetic school of philosophy and the theological mandates of the Islamic faith. Such central dogmas as the nature of prophetic knowledge, the possibility of revelation, the plausibility of a day of judgment and of its corollary doctrine of bodily resurrection and, of course, ultimately the Existence and Attributes of God were paradigmatic problematics created for Islamic philosophy by virtue of its epistemological operation in the context of the Islamic creed. Islamic philosophy proper, as best represented in its Peripatetic tradition by Ibn Sīnā, could go only so far in stipulating the ontological viability of the Necessary Being. As best exemplified in Ibn Sīnā's *al-Ishārāt wa'l-tanbīhāt*, even the master of Peripatetic philosophy had recognized the inherent limitations of reason and of logocentricity to ascertain the revelatory mandates of the faith and sought to explore the possibilities promised in the mystical discourse. While in the mystical discourse proper, at least up until Ibn 'Arabī, there is a fundamental suspension of reason in favour of an alternative certitude that bypasses the intermediary of intellect, in the *al-ḥikmat al-muta'āliyah* of the "School of Iṣfahān" the attempt is made to adapt the possibilities of the mystical discourse, especially in its Ghazzālīan and Ibn 'Arabīan formulations, into the working operation of an otherwise logocentric discourse when it finds it impossible to reach for a comprehensive conception of the metaphysical doctrines of the faith. Whereas both mysticism and philosophy proper had gone separate ways in their respective conception of existence, *al-ḥikmat al-muta'āliyah* sought to hold to the initial logocentricity of a philosophical inquiry into the nature of being and then, when it reached the impasse of not being able to account for the doctrinally mandated principles of the faith, it turned to the mystical discourse and the possibilities of the metarational perceptions it promised.

In his *Gawhar-i murād* (Lāhījī 1985), Mullā 'Abd al-Razzāq Lāhījī compared and contrasted the philosopher's method and the mystic's path, concluding that while the former "confirmed" all preliminary existent beings in order to reach for the Final Cause, the latter "negated" all preliminary stages of existence until it reached a positive annihilation in Being. It is this mystical path that made the prophetic state conceivable to the philosophers of the "School of Iṣfahān". In his philosophical orientation, Lāhījī is much more cautious than his teacher Mullā Ṣadrā in openly identifying with mystical conceptions (Āshtīyānī in Mullā Ṣadrā (1967): 99. But there are many occasions in *Gawhar-i murād*, which is more than anything else a text of philosophical kalām, where he openly identifies with the "Illuminationist" and mystical attainment of certitude. For example, in his chapter on prophethood (Lāhījī (1985): 247–87) he devotes a section to proving the necessity of prophethood by a tradition of the Sixth Shīʿī Imām, Jaʿfar al-Ṣādiq, followed by successive sections arguing in the same way according to theologians, philosophers and finally the mystics. For years Lāhījī taught the texts of Mullā Ṣadrā, including *al-Shawāhid al-rubūbiyyah*. His most famous student was Qāḍī Saʿīd Qummī (d. *c.* 1104/1692). His choice of both texts to teach and philosophical projects to undertake confirms the assessment (Zarrīnkūb (1983): 251–2) that Lāhījī's understanding of mystical metacertainty beyond the limited achievements of philosophy proper corresponds to the later works of al-Ghazzālī, especially his *al-Munqidh min al-ḍalāl*. His preference for the mystical discourse over the philosophical in *Gawhar-i murād* has also been compared to al-Ghazzālī in *Kīmīya-yi saʿādat* (*ibid.*: 253).

Another student and son-in-law of Mullā Ṣadrā, Mullā Muḥsin Fayḍ (d. 1091/1680), belongs to the same philosophical school. He, too, represents a synthetic attempt to wed mystical perceptions with dogmatic principles and brings both into a legitimate philosophical discourse. Shah ʿAbbās II (ruled 1052/1642–1077/1666) (see Luft (1968): 159–63) was particularly respectful of him. In his *al-Muḥākimah bayn al-mutiṣawwifah wa ghayrahim*, Mullā Muḥsin tries to distinguish between popular (what he calls "ignorant") Sufism and the gnostic discourse he finds legitimate and useful in matters of philosophical pursuits. He has a treatise, called *al-Inṣāf fī bayān al-farq bayn al-ḥaqq waʾl-iʿtisāf*, in which he identifies four major groups of Muslims: the philosophers, the mystics, the theologians and "the deviates" (*mutaʿassif*) (Zarrīnkūb (1983): 255–6). Although none of these groups are infidels, they have all gone astray in their respective pursuits. He particularly condemned the philosophers for having abandoned the book of God and adopted the books of the Greeks in their pursuit of truth. By philosophers here, he means the rationalistic philosophers because his own *Uṣūl al-maʿārif* is an important text in the tradition of the *ḥikmat al-mutaʿālīyah*. But mystics and theologians are equally to blame. The implicit conclusion of this sweeping dismissal of all existing Islamic discourses is the validation of Mullā Muḥsin's own contribution to the continued validity of *al-ḥikmat al-mutaʿāliyah*. The principal foundations of this discourse, Mullā Muḥsin insists, are the

Qur'ān and the Prophetic and Imāmī traditions. Any kind of philosophical speculation which is not traceable to the Qur'ān and *Ḥadīth* is to be discarded. Mullā Muḥsin Fayḍ's commentary on al-Ghazzālī's *Iḥyā' 'ulūm al-dīn*, called *al-Maḥajjat al-bayḍā' fī tahdhīb al-iḥyā*, has rightly been considered (Zarrīnkūb (1983): 256–7) the indication of a renewed interest in a mature combination of logocentrism and gnostic orientations. He achieves in *al-Maḥajjat al-bayḍā'* a systematic reconstruction of al-Ghazzālī's mature reflection on the nature of religious ethics on the foundations of Shī'ism and its traditions.

The adaptation of a supplementary mystical discourse in their otherwise logocentric orientation made the members of the "School of Iṣfahān" particularly sensitive to and critical of the more popular forms of Sufism. Thus, a major characteristic of the philosophers of the "School of Iṣfahān" is their denunciation of practising popular Sufis of their period, whom they identify with reckless endangerment of the faith. Mīr Dāmād, Mullā Ṣadrā, Mullā 'Abd al-Razzāq Lāhījī, and Mullā Muḥsin Fayḍ all prefaced their theoretical adaptations of gnostic discourses with a visceral condemnation of popular mysticism. Mīr Abu'l-Qāsim Findiriskī went one step further and, in his *Risāla-yi ṣinā'iyyah*, accused the popular Sufis of disrupting the social order (Zarrīnkūb (1983): 258). Shaykh Bahā'ī wrote a satirical treatise, *Mūsh wa gurbah*, in which he condemned and dismissed the decadent type of Sufism of the more popular sort although he himself was a Sufi (Bahā'ī (1982): 175–287).

But no matter how diligent the philosophers of the "School of Iṣfahān" were in their attempts to distance themselves from popular Sufis and subject their gnostic/philosophical discourse to Shī'ī doctrinal principles, considerable hostility was still directed against them by the dogmaticians. Mullā Muḥammad Ṭāhir Qummī (d. 1100/1688) wrote two treatises against mystics and philosophers. His *al-Fawā'id al-dīniyyah fi'l-radd 'ala'l-ḥukamā' wa'l-ṣūfiyyah*, as is perfectly evident in the title, is on the classical model of the appropriation of the faith by the clerical establishment through a visceral denunciation of philosophy and mysticism. In this classical genre of disputation, the particular literalist version of the faith is identified with *al-dīn* ("the faith"), and the alternative readings are condemned as aberrations of *al-ḥukamā'* and *al-ṣūfiyyah*. Yet not all jurists were anti-mystical or anti-philosophical in their nomocentric disposition. The greatest traditionalist of the period, Shaykh Muḥammad Taqī (the First) Majlisī (d. 1070/1659), looked favourably upon mysticism and, in fact, wrote a treatise against Mullā Muḥammad Ṭāhir Qummī's anti-mystical position. Still, both this Majlisī and his son Mullā Muḥammad Bāqir (the Second) Majlisī (d. 1111/1699) distinguished fundamentally between "traditional" Sufism of the patristic generation and what they observed among their contemporary Sufis. The Majlisī's tolerance of "traditional Sufis", however, does not extend to philosophers as well. Both Majlisīs considered the human intellect to be insufficient for grasping the nature of the prophetic message. That message has to be accepted as a Divine mandate and in terms *sui generis* to it. The Second Majlisī, in his *I'tiqādāt*, took strong exception to the philosophers' interpretation of the Qur'anic and Prophetic truths so that they would coincide with "an infidel Greek's ideas" (Zarrīnkūb (1983): 261). It is with the continuity of precisely the same sentiments that, during the reign of Shah Sultan Ḥusayn (ruled 1105/1694–1135/1722), one of the most distinguished philosophers of the period, Mawlānā Muḥammad Ṣādiq Ardistānī, was harassed, persecuted and forced to leave Iṣfahān. He left Iṣfahān under such difficult circumstances that his infant child succumbed to the cold weather in the highway (Zarrinkūb (1983): 261; Āshtiyānī in Mullā Ṣadrā (1967): 109–10).

CONCLUSION

The central, yet subtextual, problematic of Islamic philosophy, its theocentricity, was initially reactivated but ultimately further consolidated in the gradual but persistent formation of the "School of Iṣfahān". The *a priori* certainty of the mystical discourse was transformed into the timid logocentricity of Peripatetic philosophy, and both were considerably assimilated into Shī'ī doctrinal dogmas. Aspects of Shī'ī liturgical piety, forces of mystical metacertainty, and remnants of Aristotelian logic were brought together under the general rubric of a philosophical discourse that remained quintessentially theocentric and cross-referential with the revelatory language of the Qur'ān. This remained the case without the slightest recognition of the legitimacy of the philosophical discourse on the part of Shī'ī legal orthodoxy. Shī'ī philosophers, in or out of the "School of Iṣfahān", remained the constant targets of suspicion. Mīr Dāmād sought refuge from anti-philosophical doctors of law in his convoluted discourse, Mullā Ṣadrā practically fled persecution and lived a life of exile for some years in a small village. Mīr Findiriskī and Shaykh Bahā'ī sought a poetic or satirical discourse as a haven. That they did produce a philosophy in which they sought to bring together the conflicting discourses of philosophy, (Shī'ī) theology and mysticism is a testimony to the relentless grip of their inquiring minds. That they could never escape or supersede the relentless theocentricity of their discourse, that all successive paradigmatic breakthroughs in Islamic philosophy (from Peripatetic to Neoplatonic to Illuminationist to the "School of Iṣfahān" and its highest achievement, Transcendental Philosophy) remained shy of a fundamental epistemic revolution as found in the modern West, are more commentaries on the Islamic tradition within which these philosophers thought and functioned than their generic concern with the rule of reason, the uninhibited pursuit of truth or reality or, perhaps more accurately, the ironic possibilities of two counter-dogmatizing quotation marks around every rhetorical claim to "truth".

REFERENCES

Amir Arjomand, Said (1984) *The Shadow of God and the Hidden Imam: Religion, Political Order, and Societal Change in Shi'ite Iran from the Beginning to 1890* (Chicago).

Āshtiyānī, Sayyid Jalāl al-Dīn (1972) *Muntakhabātī az āthār-i ḥukamā-yi ilāhī-yi Īrān: az 'aṣr-i Mīr Dāmād wa Mīr Findiriskī tā Zamān-i Ḥāḍir*, (Tehran and Paris).

Bahā'ī, Shaykh Bahā' al-Dīn 'Āmilī (1982) *Kulliyyāt-i ash'ār wa āthār*, ed. with an introduction by Sa'īd Nafīcy (Tehran).

Bosworth, C. E. (1967) *The Islamic Dynasties* (Edinburgh).

Browne, E. G. (1902–24) *A Literary History of Persia*, 4 vols (Cambridge).

Corbin, Henry (1972) *En Islam iranien: aspects spirituels et philosophiques*, 4 and 5 (Paris).

Fakhry, Majid (1983) *A History of Islamic Philosophy* (New York).

Falsafī, Naṣr Allāh (1990) *Zindigānī-yi Shāh 'Abbās awwal*, 5 vols (Tehran).

Hādī, Akbar (1984) *Sharḥ-i ḥāl-i Mīr Dāmād wa Mīr Findiriskī* (Iṣfahān).

Hidāyat, Riḍā Qulī Khān (1965) *Tadhkara-yi rīyāḍ al-'ārifīn*, ed. Mihr 'Alī Gurgānī, (Tehran).

Hinz, Walter (1936) *Irans Aufstieg zum Nationalstaat im fünfzehnten Jahrhundert* (Berlin and Leipzig).

Iskandar Bayk Turkamān (1985) *Tārīkh-i 'ālam ārā-yi 'abbāsī*, ed. S. Shāhrūdī (Tehran).

Khwānsārī, Mīr Sayyid Muḥammad Bāqir (1976) *Rawḍāt al-jannāt*, 8 vols (Tehran).

Lāhījī, 'Abd al-Razzāq (1985) *Gawhar-i murād*, ed. S. Muwaḥḥid (Tehran).

Leaman, Oliver (1985) *An Introduction to Medieval Islamic Philosophy* (Cambridge).

Luft, Paul (1968) *Iran unter Schah 'Abbās II (1642–1666)* (dissertation, Georg-August-Universität, Göttingen).

Mazzaoui, Michel M. (1972) *The Origins of the Ṣafavids: Šī'ism, Ṣūfism, and the Gulāt* (Wiesbaden).

Mīr Dāmād, Muḥammad Bāqir (1977) *Kitāb al-qabasāt*, ed. with an introduction by Mehdi Mohaghegh, Toshihiko Izutso, 'Alī Musawī Bihbahānī and Ibrāhīm Dībājī (Tehran).

Mullā Ṣadrā, al-Dīn Muḥammad ibn Ibrāhīm al-Shīrāzī (1961) *Risāla-yi sih aṣl*, ed., annotated and with an introduction by S. H. Nasr (Tehran).

—— (1967) *al-Shawāhid al-rubūbiyyah fi'l-manāhij al-sulūkiyyah*, ed., annotated and with an introduction by Sayyid Jālāl al-Dīn Āshtiyānī (Mashhad).

—— (n.d.) *Sih maqālah wa du nāmah*, ed. Muḥammad Taqī Danishpazhūh (n.p.).

Nasr, Seyyed Hossein (1966) "The School of Iṣfahān", in M. M. Sharīf (ed.) *A History of Muslim Philosophy*, 2 vols (Wiesbaden), 2: 904–32.

—— (1978) *Ṣadr al-Dīn Shīrāzī & His Transcendent Theosophy* (Tehran).

Ṣadūqī Suhā, Manūchihr (1980) *Tārīkh-i ḥukamā' wa 'urafā'-i muta'akhkhirīn-i Ṣadr*

al-muta'allihīn (Tehran).
Ṣafā, Dhabīh Allāh (1959–85) *Tārīkh-i adabiyyāt dar Īrān*, 5 vols (Tehran).
Savory, Roger (1980) *Iran: Under the Safavids* (Cambridge).
Sharif, M. M. (ed.) (1966) *A History of Muslim Philosophy*, 2 vols (Wiesbaden).
Al-Shaybī, Kāmil Muṣṭafā (1980) *Al-Ṣilah bayn tashayyu' wa taṣawwuf*, trans. from Arabic into Persian with additional notes and an introduction by 'Alī Qaraguzlū (Tehran).
Tunikābunī, Mīrzā Muḥammad (1985) *Qiṣaṣ al-'ulamā'* (Tehran).
Watt, W. M. (1962) *Islamic Philosophy and Theology* (Edinburgh).
Zarrīnkūb, 'Abd al-Ḥusayn (1983) *Dunbāla-yi justijū dar taṣawwuf-i Īrān*, (Tehran).

CHAPTER 35

Mullā Ṣadrā: his life and works

Hossein Ziai

Ṣadr al-Dīn Shīrāzī is one of the most revered of all philosophers in Islam, especially among Muslim intellectuals today. His full name is Muḥammad ibn Ibrāhīm al-Qawāmī al-Shīrāzī, and he is commonly known as "Mullā Ṣadrā" to multitudes of Muslims, especially in Persia, Pakistan and India.[1] His honorific title, Ṣadr al-Dīn ("Pundit of Religion"), indicates his accepted rank within traditional theological circles, while his designation as "Exemplar, or Authority of Divine Philosophers" (Ṣadr al-Muta'allihīn) signifies his unique position for generations of philosophers who came after him. He was born in Shiraz in southern Persia in *c.* 979/1572 to a wealthy family. His father was reportedly a minister in the Ṣafavid court, but was also a scholar. Ṣadr al-Dīn is said to have made the pilgrimage to Mecca six times, and on his seventh journey died in 1050/1640 in Basra where he is buried and where his grave was known until recent times.[2] Fairly extensive and accurate information on his life, his studies, his students and his works are available. Owing in part to the relative proximity of his time to ours, several autographs of his works, many letters and glosses on earlier textual traditions have survived, giving us a better insight into his personality than most of the philosophers of earlier periods. Most historians and commentators of his works divide his life into three distinct periods.[3]

STUDY

Upon completing preliminary studies in his native Shiraz, the young thinker travelled to Isfahan, the seat of Ṣafavid rule and perhaps the most important centre of Islamic learning in the tenth/sixteenth century. There he first enrolled in courses on traditional Islamic scholarship, commonly called the "transmitted sciences" (*al-'ulūm al-naqliyyah*), in which the great jurist Bahā' al-Dīn Muḥammad al-'Āmilī (d. 1031/1622) was laying the foundations of a new, well-defined Shi'ite jurisprudence. Ṣadr al-Dīn's comprehensive early studies of Shi'ite views concerning jurisprudence and *Ḥadīth* scholarship and his exposure to Qur'ānic commentary by the great Shi'ite thinker distinguish him from almost all the earlier philosophers of medieval Islam, whose knowledge of such subjects was elementary at best. This side of Ṣadr al-Dīn's intellectual formation deeply marked his thinking and represents one of the two main trends in his works.

During the same period, Ṣadr al-Dīn began his studies of what are commonly known as the intellectual sciences (*al-'ulūm al-'aqliyyah*) under the tutelage of one of the greatest and most original Islamic philosophers, Sayyid Muḥammad Bāqir Astarābādī, well known as Mīr Dāmād (d. 1040/1631). This famous, erudite philosopher, known as the "Seal of Philosophers" (*Khātam al-Ḥukamā'*) and the "Third Teacher" – after Aristotle and al-Fārābī – was overwhelmed by his pupil's unusual competence in constructing philosophical arguments and bestowed lavish praise on him. Had it not been for Ṣadr al-Dīn's eclipsing prominence, Mīr Dāmād might have been remembered more than he currently is for his collection and revisions of the complete textual corpus of Islamic philosophy. In many ways Mīr Dāmād's endeavours, funded by the enlightened endowments of the arts and sciences by the Ṣafavid court (into which he had married), led to the establishment of superior libraries where the older manuscript traditions were collected, copied and published. Evidence for this profuse activity are the impressive numbers of Arabic and Persian manuscripts now housed in major collections all over the world, all produced in Isfahan during this period. In his court-supported patronage as well as in his own works on philosophical subjects, especially his *Qabasāt*[4] and his unpublished *al-Ufuq al-mubīn*, Mīr Dāmād's work was the impetus for the revival of philosophy known as the "School of Isfahan".[5] Ṣadr al-Dīn's lengthy studies with this visionary thinker mark the philosophical aspect, or second trend, in Ṣadr al-Dīn's works. It represents the height of yet another "new" synthesis and reconstruction of metaphysics in Islamic philosophy after Suhrawardī. This philosophical trend soon became one of the main schools of Islamic philosophy, if not the dominant one to this day, and bears the name of metaphysical philosophy (*al-ḥikmat al-muta'āliyah*). This name was chosen specifically by Ṣadr al-Dīn to indicate his specific philosophical intention, which needs to be adequately examined.

COMPLETE RETREAT FROM SOCIETY

After a formal period of study, Ṣadr al-Dīn withdrew from society and from city life altogether, choosing the seclusion of the small village of Kahak, near the holy city of Qom. This period marks Ṣadr al-Dīn's increased preoccupation with the contemplative life and also the years in which he laid the ground work for most of his major works. This period is marked by long periods of meditation and spiritual practice complementing that of formal study, thus completing the programme for the training of a real philosopher according to Suhrawardī. It was during this period that the knowledge which was to become crystallized in his many works was attained.

TEACHING AND PHILOSOPHICAL CONTEMPLATION

Ṣadr al-Dīn's fame as master of the two branches of Shi'ite learning – the transmitted and the intellectual – soon spread across the Ṣafavid capital. Many official positions were offered to him, which he shunned, as his biographers all agree. His disregard for material rewards and refusal to serve the nobility in any form is evidenced by the fact that not one of his works bears a dedication to a prince or other patron, although such inscriptions were common practice of the day. Historians also state that Ṣadr al-Dīn's new fame met with typical jealousy on the part of members of the scholarly community, whose unfounded charges of blasphemy were a factor in his rejecting the limelight of Ṣafavid circles in Isfahan. He did, however, agree to return to public life and teach in the *madrasah* which was built and endowed by the Ṣafavid nobleman Allāhwirdī Khān in Shiraz. The new institution of learning, away from the political ambiance of the capital, suited Ṣadr al-Dīn's increasing preoccupation with both teaching and meditation.

The language used to describe Ṣadr al-Dīn's contemplative life strongly indicates his Illuminationist attitude to philosophy in general and the Illuminationist position of the primacy of the intuitive, experiential mode of cognition in particular.[6] Suhrawardī had demonstrated the validity of vision-illumination (*mushāhadah wa ishrāq*) as the means for recovery of eternal truths to be used in philosophical construction. The Illuminationist tradition had repeatedly employed the allogory of the inner yet objectified journey into the *mundus imaginalis* (*'ālam al-khayāl*) as the highest method for obtaining sound principles of philosophy. Suhrawardī had called for a prescribed sequence of specific actions as a necessary first step toward achieving this vision, which was believed to lead to the atemporal, immediate cognition of the whole of reality. Ṣadr al-Dīn evidently took these dicta quite seriously. All of his biographers mention his ascetic practices (*riyāḍat*) and his visionary experiences (*mushāhadah, mukāshafah*).[7] Many of Ṣadr al-Dīn's philosophical compositions inform the reader that the essence of a specific philosophical argument was first revealed to him in a visionary experience, which he then analyses within the discursive system.[8]

It is also during this period of his life that Ṣadr al-Dīn trained a number of students who went on to become significant in subsequent philosophical activity in Persia. His two most important pupils produced works that have been widely studied to this day. The first of these noteworthy students, Muḥammad ibn al-Murtaḍā – well known as Mullā Muḥsin Fayḍ Kāshānī – wrote a treatise titled *al-Kalamāt al-maknūnah*, which emphasizes the two sides of the master's thinking: the gnostic (*'irfān*) and the Shi'ite interpretation of the Qur'ānic realm of the "unseen" (*al-ghayb*) as the source of inspiration. Second is 'Abd al-Razzāq ibn al-Ḥusayn al-Lāhījī, whose Persian summaries of the master's more Peripatetic inclinations have been especially popular in Persia. His *Shawāriq al-ilhām* deserves special mention here for its inclusion of an older Ibn Sīnan view of ethics. Both of these young scholars were also married to two of Ṣadr al-Dīn's daughters, revealing an increasingly intimate relationship between master and teacher in Shi'ite learned circles, which is prevalent to this day. Several other students are mentioned in biographical sources, including two of the master's sons.

Monumental though the impact of Ṣadr al-Dīn's works and thinking has been on Islamic intellectual history, very few comprehensive, systematic studies of his philosophy are available in Western translation. The earliest extensive study was done by Max Horten, whose *Das philosophische System von Schirazi* (1913) is still a good source, despite the author's use of premodern philosophical terminology and older Orientalist views.

In more recent decades Henry Corbin's text editions and pioneering studies opened a new chapter in Western scholarship on Islamic philosophy, producing an awareness of the existence of original trends in the post-Ibn Sīnan period, if not a complete analytical understanding of their philosophical significance. Corbin's emphasis on the presumed esoteric dimension of Ṣadr al-Dīn's thought has tended to hinder a modern, Western philosophical analysis of "metaphysical philosophy", however.[9] Following Corbin, Seyyed Hossein Nasr's study of Ṣadr al-Dīn's thought[10] and James Morris's study and translation of a less significant philosophical work by Ṣadr al-Dīn, called *'Arshiyyah* (translated by Morris as *Wisdom of the Throne*),[11] also emphasize the non-systematic aspect of this philosophy. Their choice of terms such as "transcendent theosophy" does not indicate the philosophical side of the original genius of Ṣadr al-Dīn's thinking. To date the only in-depth study of Ṣadr al-Dīn's "metaphysical philosophy" is Fazlur Rahman's *The Philosophy of*

Mullā Ṣadrā. Rahman's use of contemporary philosophical terminology and approach to the Islamic philosophical system of thought represents a meaningful introduction in English that is comparable in scope and analysis to many of the European works of the seventeenth to nineteenth centuries.

How original a thinker is Ṣadr al-Dīn? And how logically consistent and philosophically sound is his new synthesis and reformulation of what he believed to be the whole of philosophy, to which he gave the name metaphysical philosophy? These are questions that can be answered only once further studies have been undertaken by philosophers interested in these questions, and who with a trained eye can look deeper than the presumed "theosophical" aspect of Ṣadr al-Dīn's thought. This is not an easy task, for to date only a few of his works have been properly edited; fewer still (if any) have been meaningfully translated from a technical philosophical perspective.

The only scholar known to me who has analysed and written on various aspects of Islamic philosophy from a modern philosophical perspective using contemporary language and analytic approach is the distinguished Islamic philosopher Mehdi Ha'iri Yazdi. While most of his works are in Persian, thus not widely accessible, his most recent study in English, titled *Knowledge by Presence*, represents a serious attempt to open a dialogue with the contemporary Western philosopher.[12] In this work, students of modern philosophy can follow the centuries-old philosophical arguments concerning the epistemological priority of the special intuitive and experiential mode of cognition, which was fully re-examined and verified by Ṣadr al-Dīn. Students may still prefer the purely predicative, propositional mode, accepting the logicist position, but they will no longer be confused by the plethora of polemical works that have generally dismissed the Illuminationist epistemological concept of "seeing" (*mushāhadah*) – the mode of knowledge by presence – simply as "mystic experience" (generally called Sufi experience). Some readers of Islamic epistemological arguments may find a remarkable resemblance to Western ideas, such as Brouwer's "primary intuition" in his Intuitionist foundation of mathematics, for example. Some may also find parallels with contemporary thinking on the problem of intuition that regards it as the result of the knowing subject's grasp of an object when the subject–object dichotomy does not apply – in other words, when they are one. Quite simply, this is what is meant by "the unity of the knower, the known, and the mind" (*al-ittiḥād al-ʿāqil waʾl-māʿqūl waʾl-ʿaql*), introduced by Suhrawardī and further analysed by Ṣadr al-Dīn.[13] Much scholarship remains to be done, the first step being the editing and philosophical translation of Arabic and Persian texts. Generations of philosophers in Islam, most of whom did not consider themselves to be Sufis, have studied Illuminationist texts as well as texts in the tradition of Ṣadr al-Dīn's "metaphysical philosophy" and have found them to represent well-thought-out, rational systems while confirming the centrality of Illumination.

MAJOR WORKS

More than fifty works are attributed to Ṣadr al-Dīn.[14] They may be divided into two main trends of his thought: the transmitted sciences and the intellectual sciences. Ṣadr al-Dīn's works on subjects that predominantly relate to the transmitted sciences, covering the traditional subjects of Islamic jurisprudence, Qur'ānic commentary, *Ḥadīth* scholarship and theology, are best exemplified by: (1) *Sharḥ al-uṣūl al-kāfī*, a commentary on Kulaynī's famous work, the first Shi'ite *Ḥadīth* compilation on specifically juridical and theological issues; (2) *Mafātīḥ al-ghayb*, an incomplete Qur'ānic commentary (*tafsīr*); (3) a number of short treatises each devoted to commentary on a specific chapter of the Qur'ān; (4) a short treatise called *Imāmat* on Shi'ite theology; and (5) a number of glosses on standard *kalām* texts, such as Qūshchī's *Sharḥ al-tajrīd*.[15]

Ṣadr al-Dīn's more significant works, widely accepted by Muslims to represent the pinnacle of Islamic philosophy, are those that indicate the intellectual sciences. His major works in this group include: (1) *al-Asfār al-arba'at al-'aqliyyah* ("Four Intellectual Journeys"),[16] Ṣadr al-Dīn's definitive philosophical corpus, which includes detailed discussions on all philosophical subjects; (2) *al-Shawāhid al-rubūbiyyah* ("Divine Testimonies"),[17] generally accepted to be an epitome of the *Asfār*; and (3) glosses on Ibn Sīnā's *Shifā'* and on Suhrawardī's *Ḥikmat al-ishrāq*.[18] Both of these glosses, available only in facsimile editions, are indicative of Ṣadr al-Dīn's mastery of elaborating, refuting or refining philosophical arguments. Unlike many previous commentaries and glosses, he is not content simply to elucidate a difficult point, but is concerned with demonstrating or refuting the consistency and philosophical validity of the original arguments. Mullā Ṣadrā also wrote a number of shorter treatises some of which, such as *al-Ḥikmat al-'arshiyyah* ("Wisdom from the Divine Throne"), *al-Mabda' wa'l-ma'ād* ("The Beginning and End") and *Kitāb al-mashā'ir* ("The Book of Metaphysical Sciences") have become very well known and taught in philosophical circles in Persia. In India Mullā Ṣadrā's *Sharḥ al-hidāyah* ("Commentary upon the Book of Guidance of Athīr al-Dīn Abharī") became the most famous of his works and is taught in traditional *madrasah*s to this day.

To conclude one can say that in more ways than one Ṣadr al-Dīn's "metaphysical philosophy" represents a new trend in Islamic philosophy. Ṣadr al-Dīn makes every effort to examine fully every known philosophical position and argument concerning principle and method. He then selects what he considers to be the best argument, often reformulates it and finally goes about constructing a consistent system. His systematic philosophy is neither Peripatetic nor Illuminationist but a novel reconstruction of both, serving as testimony to the continuity of philosophical thought in Islam. That Ṣadr al-Dīn's system differs from today's emphasis on a specific aspect of "rationality" does not mean that its founder conceived it to be "irrational" nor predominantly given to "mystical experience". The system does, however, emphasize a world view in which intuitive vision is integral to knowledge.

NOTES

1 Numerous studies on Mullā Ṣadrā have been published in the past few decades, mainly in Persian, but a few also in English. Among the Persian studies Jalāl al-Dīn Āshtiyānī's *Sharḥ-i ḥāl wa ārā'-i falsafī-yi Mullā Ṣadrā* (reprint: Tehran, 1981) stands out for its depth of analysis. Fazlur Rahman's *The Philosophy of Mullā Ṣadrā* (Albany, 1975) is the only English-language analytical study of Mullā Ṣadrā's systematic philosophy.

2 An account of his life is given in S. H. Amin, *The Philosophy of Mulla Sadra Shirazi* (London, 1987): 1–35. See also the introduction of S. H. Nasr to his edition of Mullā Ṣadrā's *Sih aṣl*: 5–14. A first-hand report on Mullā Ṣadrā's grave site in Basra is given by Sayyid Abu'l-Ḥasan Qazwīnī in "Sharḥ-i ḥāl-i Ṣadr al-Muta'allihīn wa sukhanī dar ḥarakat-i jawḥariyyah", in *Sih maqālah wa du nāmah* (Tehran, n.d.): 1–4.

3 See, for example, Sayyid Muḥammad Ḥusayn Ṭabāṭabā'ī, "Ṣadr al-Dīn Muḥammad b. Ibrāhīm Shīrāzī", in *Sih maqālah wa du nāmah*: 15–26.

4 See Mīr Dāmād, *al-Qabasāt*, ed. M. Mohaghegh and T. Izutsu (Tehran, 1977), which includes an extensive account of Mīr Dāmād's life and works.

5 For a general account of the School of Iṣfahān see S. H. Nasr, "The School of Ispahan", in M. M. Sharif (ed.), *A History of Muslim Philosophy*, (Wiesbaden, 1966): 904–32.

6 See Fazlur Rahman, *op. cit.*: 3–7.

7 See, for example, Āshtiyānī, *op. cit.*: 6–7.

8 See, for example, Mullā Ṣadrā, *al-Asfār al-arba'ah* (Tehran, 1960): 1–6; 8. Āshtiyānī considers the intuitive foundations of Mullā Ṣadrā's system of *al-Ḥikmat al-muta'āliyah* to be, in part, due to Suhrawardī's Illuminationist position in epistemology. See Āshtiyānī, *op. cit.*: 102–16.

9 For example Corbin in his translation of Mullā Ṣadrā's work *Kitāb al-mashā'ir* – which is of lesser philosophical value than other works such as *al-Asfār al-arba'ah* (*op. cit.*) and *al-Shawāhid al-rubūbiyyah* (ed. Jalāl Āshtiyāni, Mashhad, 1967) – translated *Le Livre des pénétrations métaphysiques* (Tehran, 1964), and chose a theosophical terminology to emphasize an esoteric dimension of Mullā Ṣadrā's thought. This type of interpretive translation does not serve to inform the Western reader interested in analytical philosophy as it avoids the logical side of Mullā Ṣadrā's system of metaphysics. Even the title, *al-Ḥikmat al-*

muta'āliyah, chosen by Mullā Ṣadrā to specify his predominantly reconstructed system of metaphysics, when translated "transcendental theosophy", will at best lead to a misunderstanding for those interested in the analytical aspect of Mullā Ṣadrā's thought.

10 S. H. Nasr, *Ṣadr al-Dīn Shīrāzī and his Transcendent Theosophy: Background, Life and Works* (Tehran, 1978), and his "Mullā Ṣadrā", in Sharif (ed.), *A History of Muslim Philosophy*.

11 See James Morris, *The Wisdom of the Throne* (Princeton, 1981). Morris, too, emphasizes a presumed "transcendental" element in Mullā Ṣadrā's thought, which is, however, a clear and systematic concern on the part of the great thinker to construct a valid, consistent system of metaphysics where a well-defined philosophical terminology is employed to refine mostly classical ontological and epistemological arguments. The new system is called *al-ḥikmat al-muta'āliyah*, best translated as "metaphysical philosophy". This philosophical system bears little resemblance to the theosophical writings of Swedenborg (as claimed by Corbin) or Rudolf Steiner, or the ideas of the Theosophical Society (although it does share elements in common with theosophy as it was originally understood namely as *theosophia* (literally divine wisdom or *al-ḥikmat al-ilāhiyyah*)) [eds].

12 See Mehdi Ha'iri Yazdi, *The Principles of Epistemology in Islamic Philosophy: Knowledge by Presence* (Albany, 1992).

13 This epistemological principle is among the set of twelve philosophical problems commonly believed to constitute Mullā Ṣadrā's greatest achievements in advancing philosophical arguments. See, for example, Qazwīnī, *op. cit.*: 4–5; and Ṭabāṭabā'ī, *op. cit.*: 21–5. I have elsewhere shown, however, that the principle of the unity of the subject and object as intuitive consciousness of a thing as-it-is was first fully developed by Suhrawardī in his theory of knowledge by Illumination. See my *Knowledge and Illumination* (Atlanta, 1990): 143–55.

14 See Ṭabaṭabā'ī, *op. cit.*: 25–6. For a bibliography of Mullā Ṣadrā see Nasr, *Ṣadr al-Dīn*: 40–50.

15 Many of these works remain unpublished, some have been printed in facsimile editions, and *Sharḥ al-uṣūl al-kāfī* has been published in an as yet incomplete version in Tehran (1992).

16 This work has been edited and published by M. Riḍā al-Muẓaffar (Tehran, 1960); an older facsimile edition of this work is also available (Tehran, n.d.).

17 This work has been edited and published by Jalāl Āshtiyānī (Mashhad, 1967).

18 Both are printed in facsimile editions: *Sharḥ al-shifā': al-ilāhiyyāt* (reprint: Tehran, 1988); and *Ta'līqāt* (Gloss on *Ḥikmat al-Ishrāq*) in Shīrāzī, *Sharḥ ḥikmat al-Ishrāq* (Tehran, 1895), margins.

CHAPTER 36

Mullā Ṣadrā: his teachings

Seyyed Hossein Nasr

Ṣadr al-Dīn Shīrazī, known as Mullā Ṣadrā, appeared nearly a thousand years after the rise of Islam and his works represent a synthesis of the millennium of Islamic thought which preceded him. He was thoroughly versed in the Qur'ān and *Ḥadīth*, Islamic philosophy and theology, Sufism and even the history of Islamic thought, and must have had access to an unusually rich library. To all his knowledge must be added his own intellectual powers as a philosopher and visionary and intuitive capabilities as a gnostic (*'ārif*) who was able to have direct experience of Ultimate Reality or what in the later school of Islamic philosophy and theosophy is called "gnostic experience" (*tajruba-yi 'irfānī*). His knowledge of the revealed sources of Islam was probably more extensive than that of any other Islamic philosopher. It included intimacy not only with the Qur'ān, but also well-known commentaries, not only prophetic *Ḥadith* but also the sayings of the Shi'ite Imāms whose philosophical significance he revealed for the first time. His Qur'ānic commentaries and *Sharḥ uṣūl al-kāfī* ("Commentary upon the *Uṣūl al-kāfī*" of Kulaynī) and commentary upon the Light Verse (*āyat al-nūr*), both among the premier masterpieces of Islamic thought, attest to his incredible mastery of the Qur'ān and *Ḥadīth*.

MULLĀ ṢADRĀ AND EARLIER ISLAMIC PHILOSOPHY

Mullā Ṣadrā was also knowledgeable in the deepest sense in the schools of Islamic philosophical thought before him. He knew Peripatetic (*mashshā'ī*) philosophy intimately, especially the thought of Ibn Sīnā, upon whose *Shifā'* he wrote a major commentary. But he was also well acquainted with later Peripatetics, such as Naṣīr al-Dīn Ṭūsī and Athīr al-Dīn Abharī, upon whose *al-Hidāyah* ("The Guide") he wrote a commentary which was destined to become one of his most popular works, especially in India. He was also a master of *ishrāqī* thought and copied a number of the visionary recitals of Suhrawardī in his own hand as well as writing a major commentary in the form of glosses upon the *Ḥikmat al-ishrāq* ("Theosophy of the Orient of Light") of the master of the School of Illumination. He was also well versed in both Sunni and Shi'ite *kalām* or theology, especially the works of al-Ghazzālī and Imām Fakr al-Dīn Rāzī whom he cites often especially in the *Asfār* ("The Four Journeys") which is his masterpiece and like the mother of all his other books. Moreover, he was well acquainted with Shi'ite *kalām* which included Twelve-Imām Shi'ism to which he belonged as well as Ismā'īlism whose works he studied carefully including philosophical tracts such as the *Rasā'il* ("Treatises") of the Ikhwān al-Ṣafā'.

Finally, it is most important to realize Mullā Ṣadrā's mastery of the doctrines of Sufism or gnosis especially as taught by Ibn 'Arabī. In certain issues such as eschatology, he borrows heavily from the Andalusian master, and the last book of the *Asfār*, in which he deals with *al-ma'ād* or eschatology is in fact replete with extensive quotations from Ibn 'Arabī's *al-Futūḥāt al-makkiyyah* ("The Meccan Illuminations"). Moreover, he had a special love for Persian Sufi poetry and quotes from its masters such as 'Aṭṭār and Rūmī even in the middle of his Arabic works. Part of this knowledge is derived from the earlier masters of the School of Iṣfahān such as its founder Mīr Dāmād, a school to which Mullā Ṣadrā belonged, but his knowledge in these matters goes beyond any of his teachers and represents his own extensive study of the major works and sources of Islamic thought.[1]

THE SYNTHESIS OF PREVIOUS SCHOOLS OF THOUGHT AND MODES OF KNOWING

Mullā Ṣadrā synthesized not only various schools of Islamic thought but also the paths of human knowledge. His own life, based upon great piety, deep philosophical introspection and reasoning and purification of his inner being until his "eye of the heart" opened and he was able to have a direct vision of the spiritual world, attests to the unity of the three major paths of knowledge in his own person. These three paths are according to him revelation (*al-waḥy*), demonstration or intellection (*al-burhān, al-ta'aqqul*) and spiritual or "mystical" vision (*al-mukāshafah, al-mushāhadah*). Or, to use another terminology prevalent among his school, he followed a way which synthesized *al-Qur'ān*, *al-burhān* and *al-'irfān*, which correspond to the terms above.

Mullā Ṣadrā's epistemology is directly related to that of Suhrawardī and the school of Illumination in general, a school in which distinction is made between conceptual knowledge (*al-'ilm al-ḥuṣūlī*) and presential knowledge (*al-'ilm al-ḥuḍurī*),[2] forms of knowledge which are unified in the being of the possessor of knowledge on the highest level, a person whom Suhrawardī calls *ḥakīm muta'allih*, literally a wise man, philosopher or theosopher who has become imbued with Divine Qualities and become "God-like". Conceptual knowledge is gained through concepts in the mind of that which is to be known whereas presential knowledge implies the presence of the very reality to be known in the human intellect without the intermediary of mental concepts such as when one knows oneself, the intelligibles or the divine realities. Such knowledge is illuminative and beyond the realm of ratiocination, but it is not without intellectual content. Mullā Ṣadrā accepted this *ishrāqī* thesis, to which he added the significance of revelation as a foundational source for knowledge of a philosophical and theosophical order. The tradition of Islamic philosophy in Persia accepted fully this truth and awarded to Mullā Ṣadrā the title of Ṣadr al-muta'allihīn, that is, foremost among those who according to Suhrawardī belong to the highest category of possessors of metaphysical knowledge. No higher title could be given to anyone in the context of the world view in which later Islamic philosophy functioned.

In any case the grand synthesis of Islamic thought created by Mullā Ṣadrā is based on the synthesis of these three ways of knowing through which he was able to integrate the earlier schools of Islamic thought into a unified world view and create a new intellectual perspective known as *al-ḥikmat al-muta'āliyah* which a number of leading scholars of Islamic philosophy who have written on him in European languages, such as Henry Corbin and Toshihiko Izutsu, have translated as the "transcendent theosophy"[3] while a number of scholars have protested against using such a term.[4] In any case the "transcendent theosophy" marks the birth of a new intellectual perspective in the Islamic world, one which has had profound influence during the later centuries in Persia as well as in Iraq and India, while the term *al-ḥikmat al-muta'āliyah* had been used in a more general and less defined sense by a number of earlier Islamic thinkers such as Quṭb al-Dīn Shīrāzī.[5] In analysing the various aspects of Mullā Ṣadrā's thought we are in reality studying the *ḥikmat al-muta'āliyah* which became a distinct school of Islamic thought much like the Peripatetic (*mashshā'ī*) and Illuminationist (*ishrāqī*) schools. Mullā Ṣadrā was in fact so devoted to this term that he used it as part of the title of his major opus which is *al-Asfār al-arba'ah fi'l-ḥikmat al-muta'āliyah* ("The Four Journeys Concerning Transcendent Theosophy").

The foundation of the "transcendent theosophy" and the whole metaphysics of Mullā Ṣadrā is the science of being (*wujūd*), which is used by him to denote both existence, in the sense of the existence of objects, and existence that is not in any way privative but which also includes the Divine Principle, Pure Being and even the Absolute, which is beyond Being as ordinarily understood. Much of his writings, including nearly all of the first book of the *Asfār*, is devoted to this issue and he returns again and again to it in such works as *al-Shawāhid al-rubūbiyyah* ("Divine Witnesses"), *al-Ḥikmat al-ʿarshiyyah* ("The Wisdom of the Throne"), *al-Mabdaʾ waʾl-maʿād* ("The Origin and the Return") and especially *Kitāb al-mashāʿir* ("The Book of Metaphysical Penetrations") which is the most important summary treatment of this subject in his writings.[6]

THE STUDY OF BEING

At the heart of the whole philosophical exposition of Mullā Ṣadrā stands the gnostic experience of Being as Reality. Our usual experience of the world is that of things which exist, this ordinary experience serving as the basis of Aristotelian metaphysics which is based on existents (*mawjūd*). For Mullā Ṣadrā, however, there occurred a vision in which he saw the whole of existence not as objects which exist or existents but as a single reality (*wujūd*) whose delimitations by various quiddities (*māhiyyāt*) gives the appearance of a multiplicity which "exists" with various existents being independent of each other. Heidegger complained that Western metaphysics had gone astray since the time of Aristotle by studying the existent (*das Seiende*), to use his vocabulary, and that the proper subject of metaphysics was existence itself or *das Sein* with whose study he was starting a new chapter in Western philosophical thought.[7] As far as Islamic philosophy is concerned, such a distinction was made three centuries before Heidegger by Mullā Ṣadrā who according to himself received through inspiration a vision of reality in which everything was seen as acts of existence (*wujūd*) and not objects that exist (*mawjūd*). The vast development of Ṣadrian metaphysics is based upon this basic experience of Reality and subsequent conceptual distinctions made on the basis of this experience of *wujūd* as being at once one, graded and principial.

Mullā Ṣadrā distinguishes clearly between the concept of being (*mafhūm al-wujūd*) and the reality of being (*ḥaqīqat al-wujūd*). The first is the most obvious of all concepts and the easiest to comprehend while the second is the most difficult for it requires extensive mental preparation as well as the purification of one's being so as to allow the intellect within to function fully without the veils of passion and to be able to discern *wujūd* as Reality. That is why one of Mullā Ṣadrā's most famous followers, Ḥājjī Mullā Hādī Sabziwārī, writes in the *Sharḥ al-manẓūmah*, which is a summary of the master's doctrines,

Its [*wujūd*'s] notion is one of the best known things,
But its deepest reality is in the extremity of hiddenness.[8]

A consequence of the gnostic experience of being is the realization of its unity, which is called *waḥdat al-wujūd*. This fundamental doctrine of Sufi metaphysics is associated with Ibn 'Arabī but has possessed many interpretations ranging from the extreme interpretation of it by the Andalusian Sufi and philosopher Ibn Sab'īn, according to whom only God is real and nothing else exists in any way, to Ibn 'Arabī's interpretation, which sees the manifested order as theophanies (*tajalliyāt*) of the Divine Names and Qualities upon the mirror of nothingness, to the view of Mullā Ṣadrā, who conceives the unity of being in relation to the multiplicity of existence as the rays of the sun in relation to the sun. The rays of the sun are not the sun and at the same time are nothing but the sun. In the *Asfār*, which contains a history of Islamic philosophy[9] as well as his own teachings, Mullā Ṣadrā deals extensively with various understandings of this central doctrine before turning to the exposition of his own views.[10] In any case, *waḥdat al-wujūd* is a cornerstone of Ṣadrian metaphysics without which his whole world view would collapse.

A companion doctrine is *tashkīk al-wujūd* or the gradation of being. Being is not only one but it also participates in a gradation or hierarchy from the Being of God to the existence of the pebble on the beach. Every higher level of *wujūd* contains all the reality that is manifested below it. Here Mullā Ṣadrā bases himself upon the Suhrawardīan doctrine of differentiation and gradation according to which things can be distinct from each other through the very element that unites them such as the light of the candle and the light of the sun which are united by being both light and yet are distinct from one another also by light which is manifested in the two cases according to different degrees of intensity. Being is like light in that it possesses degrees of intensity while being a single reality.[11] The universe in its vast multiplicity is therefore not only unified but is also thoroughly hierarchical. One might say that Mullā Ṣadrā accepted the idea of the "great chain of being" which has had such a long life in the West from Aristotle to the eighteenth century but in the light of the unity of being which gives a completely different meaning to the doctrine of cosmic and universal hierarchy.

The views of *wujūd* are complemented by the principle of *aṣālat al-wujūd* or principiality of existence. To understand this doctrine, it is necessary first of all to turn to the classical distinction in Islamic philosophy between existence (*wujūd* in its meaning of being related to the world of multiplicity) and *māhiyyah* or quiddity which in its original Latin form is derived directly from the Arabic *māhiyyah*.[12] All objects are composed of these two components, the first corresponding to the answer given to the question "is it?", and the second to the question "what is it?". The question posed in later Islamic philosophy, and especially by Mullā Ṣadrā, is which of these elements is principial and bestows reality upon an object. Mullā Ṣadrā's own teacher Mīr Dāmād and Suhrawardī are considered as followers of the school of principiality of quiddity (*aṣālat al-māhiyyah*) while Ibn Sīnā is considered as a follower of *aṣālat al-wujūd*, although in his case this doctrine takes on a completely different meaning than in Mullā Ṣadrā since the former did not believe in *waḥdat al-wujūd.*

In any case in his youth, Mullā Ṣadrā followed his teacher Mīr Dāmād and only after another visionary and gnostic experience came to realize that it is *wujūd* which bestows reality upon things and that the *māhiyyāt* are literally nothing in themselves and are abstracted by the mind from the limitations of a particular act of *wujūd.* When we say that a horse exists, following common sense we think that the horse is a reality to which existence is added. In reality, however, what we are perceiving is a particular act of *wujūd* which through the very fact that it is manifested is limited to a particular form which we perceive as horse. For those who have realized the truth, the fact that a horse exists becomes transformed into the reality that the act of being has manifested itself in a particular form which we call horse. The form or *māhiyyah* of the horse has no reality of its own but derives all of its reality from the act of *wujūd.*[13]

Reality is then nothing other than *wujūd*, which is at once one and graded, existentiating the reality of all things. The metaphysics of Mullā Ṣadrā can in fact be understood by understanding not only these principles but also their interrelations. *Wujūd* is not *only* one but also graded. And it is not *only* graded but also principial or that which bestowed reality upon all quiddities, which in themselves possess no reality at all. The vast metaphysical edifice created by Mullā Ṣadrā and his whole theology, cosmology, psychology and eschatology rely upon the three principles of *waḥdat al-wujūd, tashkīk al-wujūd* and *aṣālat al-wujūd* and it is only in the light of these principles that his other doctrines can be understood.

TRANS-SUBSTANTIAL MOTION AND THE CREATION OF THE WORLD

One of the most striking doctrines of Mullā Ṣadrā is trans-substantial motion (*al-ḥarakat al-jawhariyyah*) which is the basis of his explanation of many of the most difficult problems of traditional philosophy including the creation of the world and the whole meaning of becoming in light of the Immutable and the Eternal.[14] As is well-known, earlier Islamic philosophers, especially Ibn Sīnā, had followed Aristotelian natural philosophy in accepting motion (*al-ḥarakah*) only in the categories of quantity (*kamm*), quality (*kayf*), situation (*waḍʻ*) and place (*ʻayn*), all of which are accidents and denied explicitly the possibility of motion in the category of substance. Ibn Sīnā's main argument was that motion requires a subject that moves and if the very substance of an object changes through transubstantial motion, then there will be no subject for motion.

Mullā Ṣadrā opposed this thesis directly by saying that any change in the accidents of an object requires in fact a change in its substance since accidents have no existence independent of substance. He asserts that there is always "some subject" (*mawḍūʻun mā*) for motion even if we are unable to fix it and delimit it logically. Mullā Ṣadrā asserts that the whole of the physical and even psychic or imaginal universes which extend up to the Immutable or luminous Archetypes are in constant motion or becoming. Were it to be otherwise, the effusion (*fayḍ*) of Being could not reach all things. This trans-substantial motion, which Henry Corbin calls "l'inquiétude de l'être" referring to the existence of the universe below the level of the intelligible and archetypal realities, is not to be, however, confused with the re-creation of the world in every instant as taught by the Sufis.[15] In the Sufi doctrine at every moment the universe is annihilated and re-created. Previous forms return to the Divine Order and new forms are manifested as theophany. That is why this doctrine is called *al-labs baʻd al-khalʻ* (literally, dressing after undressing of forms).

In contrast Mullā Ṣadrā's doctrine has been called *al-labs baʻd al-labs* (that is, dressing after dressing). This implies that the form and matter of an existent become themselves the matter for a new form and that this process goes on continuously as if one were to put on one coat on top of another. All beings in this world are moving vertically as a result of trans-substantial motion until they reach the plenum of their archetypal reality. The sperm becomes a foetus and grows to the form of a baby who is then born and continues to grow from one form to another until he or she reaches full maturity and the body becomes weaker as the soul grows stronger until one dies and reaches the "imaginal world" and finally the Divine Presence. Each state of this movement contains the forms of its earlier states of existence, while this transubstantial movement continues throughout all these stages.

It is important to emphasize that Mullā Ṣadrā's dynamic vision of the world in constant becoming, which implies the continuous intensification of the act of *wujūd* within a particular being, must not in any way be confused with Darwinian evolution. For Mullā Ṣadrā, the beings of this world are manifestations of the light of *wujūd* cast upon their archetypal realities which through the arc of descent (*al-qaws al-nuzūlī*) bring various creatures into the realm of physical existent. Trans-substantial motion marks the arc of ascent (*al-qaws al-ṣuʻūdī*) through which the ever-increasing intensity of light of *wujūd* allows existents to return to their archetypal realities in the supernal realm. For Darwinism, on the other hand, there are no such things as archetypal realities and the species, far from reflecting celestial archetypes, are merely forms generated by the flow of matter in time. Furthermore, for evolution the role of *wujūd*, its unity, gradation and principiality are meaningless whereas for Mullā Ṣadrā they constitute the very foundations of his metaphysics. Also for Mullā Ṣadrā trans-substantial motion is teleological and has an important spiritual role to play. The universe is moving toward a perfection which is its purpose and end and the spiritual progress of humanity is also achieved through a mode of trans-substantial motion. A saint is not only more perfect than others. It might be said that he or she *is* more than others in the sense that the act of *wujūd* in him or her is of a more intense degree than in less perfect human beings. It would therefore be a grave mistake, as committed by a number of modernist Muslim thinkers, to equate *al-ḥarakat al-jawhariyyah* with Darwinian evolution.

The doctrine of trans-substantial motion is the key for the solution of many problems for Mullā Ṣadrā, including that of the creation of the world debated for eight centuries before him by the Islamic philosophers and theologians. As is well known, the *falāsifah* believed the world to have had no origination in time but to have been originated beyond time by God, the world thus being eternal (*qadīm*) while the *mutakallimūn* claimed that the world was created in time (*ḥādīth*), an issue which was discussed in many classical works of Islamic thought such as al-Ghazzālī's *Tahāfut al-falāsifah*.[16] The philosophers claimed that if the world were created in time, it would require a change in the Divine Nature which is impossible because God is immutable. The theologians believed that if the world were *qadīm*, then something eternal would exist besides God and would not even be caused by Him. Different Islamic thinkers sought to solve this problem in various ways, including Mullā Ṣadrā's own teacher, Mīr Dāmād, who came up with the idea of *al-ḥudūth al-dahrī*, which means origination of the world not in time (*zamān*) nor in eternity (*sarmad*), but in *dahr* or aeon, and he became celebrated for the exposition of this doctrine.[17]

Mullā Ṣadrā rejected this dichotomy of views altogether by pointing to the doctrine of trans-substantial motion. If the cosmos is changing at every moment, at each instance of its being, it is different from what it was before and what it is now was non-existent before (*masbūq bi'l-'adam*). Therefore, one can accept the doctrine that the world was created from nothing (*ex nihilo*) while accepting the continuous and uninterrupted effusion (*fayḍ*) of the light of Being which is none other than the Divine Light.[18] He thus seeks to provide a philosophical explanation for one of the most difficult of philosophical issues in not only Islamic thought but Jewish and Christian thought as well.

THE UNION OF THE INTELLECT AND THE INTELLIGIBLE

Another of Mullā Ṣadrā's major doctrines, again related inextricably to the rest of his metaphysics, is that of the union of the intellect and the intelligible (*ittiḥād al-'āqil wa'l-ma'qūl*). This doctrine was asserted by Abu'l-Ḥasan al-'Āmirī in the fourth/tenth century but rejected thoroughly by Ibn Sīnā and later Islamic philosophers. But it was resurrected by Mullā Ṣadrā and given a new meaning in the context of the unity of *wujūd* and trans-substantial motion. According to him at the moment of intellection the form of the intelligible (*ma'qūl*), the possessor of intellect (*'āqil*), and even the intellect itself (*'aql*) become united in such a way than one *is* the other as long as the act of intellection lasts.[19]

This doctrine is not only important for Mullā Ṣadrā's theory of knowledge, but is also of great significance for the understanding of the role of knowledge in human perfection. Through trans-substantial motion the act of knowing elevates the very existence of the knower. According to a *ḥadīth* of the Prophet, "knowledge is light" (*al-'ilm nūrun*), a principle which is also foundational to Mullā Ṣadrā's thought.[20] The unity of the knower and the known implies ultimately the unity of knowing and being. The being of man is transformed through the light of knowing and being. The being of man is transformed through the light of knowledge and also our mode of being determines our mode of knowledge. In this profound reciprocity is to be found the key to the significance of knowledge for Mullā Ṣadrā and of the idea that knowledge transforms our being even in the posthumous state. The writings of Mullā Ṣadrā are replete with various applications of this doctrine and he returns again and again to the principle of the ultimate unity of being and knowing.

THE IMAGINAL WORLD AND THE ARCHETYPES

Mullā Ṣadrā accepted the reality of the archetypes (*al-a'yān al-thābitah* or *al-muthul al-nūriyyah*) in conformity with the view of Suhrawardī and against the claims of Muslim Peripatetics such as Ibn Sīnā. And he brought many philosophical arguments to refute those who have denied them.[21] There is in fact no doubt concerning the major role performed in Mullā Ṣadrā's thought by the archetypes or "Platonic Ideas", pure intelligibles belonging to the domain of immutability which many have confused with forms in the imaginal world which although beyond matter nevertheless still participate in becoming and transubstantial motion. The latter play a crucial role in the "transcendent theosophy" without in any way replacing the immutable archetypes or luminous "ideas" in the Platonic sense.

Considering the absence of the imaginal world in Western philosophy for many centuries, it is necessary to delve more deeply into the meaning of the *'ālam al-khayāl*, the *mundus imaginalis*, which Corbin and I have translated as the imaginal rather than imaginary world, considering the pejorative connotation of the latter term in modern European languages. The traditional hierarchy of being in the mainstream of Western thought goes from the realm of material existence, to the psyche, to the intelligible or angelic world with its own vast hierarchy and finally to God who is Pure Being and for some Western metaphysicians, the Beyond-Being. This scheme was more or less followed by early Islamic philosophers with adjustments related to the fact that they were living and philosophizing in an Islamic universe. Suhrawardī was the first person to speak of the imaginal world at least in the microcosm. He was soon followed by Ibn 'Arabī who elaborated upon this theme and expanded the understanding of the imaginal world to make it a central pillar of his metaphysics.[22] Henceforth, the imaginal world became part and parcel of the understanding of the Islamic universe upon which numerous Sufis and philosophers were to write important treatises.

It was, however, Mullā Ṣadrā who gave the first systematic and philosophical explanation of this world. He added to the view of Suhrawardī that this world was connected to man's microcosmic reality (*khayāl al-muttaṣil*), the thesis that the imaginal world has also a macrocosmic and objective reality independent and disconnected from man (*khayāl al-munfaṣil*). He emphasized that this world has even more reality than the physical world. As for its characteristics, it is a world possessing forms called *al-ṣuwar al-khayāliyyah* (imaginal forms) which, however, are not wed to matter, at least not the matter of the physical world. That is why they are also called *al-muthul al-mu'allaqah* (suspended forms). Nevertheless they are forms having colours, shapes, odours and everything else that is associated with the forms of this world. This is a world of concrete realities which, however, are not physical, the world immediately above the physical, identified with the mythical cities of Jābulqā and Jabulsā, a world which the seers can experience in this life and into which human beings enter at the moment of death. It is a world in which we have subtle or imaginal bodies (*al-jism al-khayālī*) as we have a physical body in this world.[23]

ESCHATOLOGY AND RESURRECTION

No Islamic philosopher has dealt in such great detail as Mullā Ṣadrā with eschatology and resurrection (*al-ma'ād*) concerning both the individual and the cosmos. The fourth book of the *Asfār*, much of it based on Ibn 'Arabī, is the vastest and most detailed study in Islamic philosophy of the soul (*nafs*) from its birth to its final meeting with God and includes elements concerned with the phenomenology of death. If we were to seek something like the *Tibetan Book of the Dead* in Islamic sources, probably this fourth book of the *Asfār* would be the best candidate. Moreover, Mullā Ṣadrā devoted much space in his other major writings such as *al-Mabda' wa'l-ma'ād* and *al-Shawāhid al-rubūbiyyah* to the subject and wrote separate treatises devoted only to this subject such as the *Risālat al-ḥashr* ("Treatise on Resurrection").[24]

Basing himself completely on traditional Islamic description of the posthumous states and eschatological events, Mullā Ṣadrā seeks to interpret such terms as the Bridge of *Ṣirāṭ*, the Balance and the lower paradisal states as well as the infernal states in terms of the imaginal world. All these events related to death, judgment and the like as mentioned in the Qur'ān and *Ḥadīth* take place in this world which itself is an intermediate realm (*al-barzakh*) between the physical world and the world of purely angelic or intelligible substances. Moreover, this world is comprised of many intermediate realms (*barāzikh*) stretching from the *al-barāzikh al-a'lā* or higher intermediate realms to *al-barāzikh al-asfal* or lower ones. The higher comprise paradisal states although still not the supreme heavens and the lower the infernal ones. This realm is in fact also a kind of purgatory through which souls pass on their way to their final beatitude or damnation.

Mullā Ṣadrā speaks of a doctrine which at first seems somewhat strange and can be understood only in the light of the doctrine of trans-substantial motion. He claims that the soul (*nafs*) is created with the body but becomes immortal and spiritual through the Spirit, or, using his own terminology, the *nafs* or soul is *jismāniyyat al-ḥudūth wa rūḥāniyyat al-baqā'*. Its vertical ascent through transubstantial motion in fact does not cease in this world but continues after death as the soul journeys through various intermediate realms in conformity with the types of actions it has performed and its mode of being in this world.

In the great debate about whether resurrection is spiritual (*rūḥānī*) or bodily (*jismānī*), Mullā Ṣadrā categorically favours bodily resurrection but he points out that, upon death, individuals are bestowed with subtle bodies (*al-jism al-laṭīf*) which correspond in many ways to the astral body of Paracelsus. After death they are therefore not simply disembodied souls but possess bodies which are "woven" of the actions that they have performed in this world. They also enter a world which conforms to their inner nature. In a sense an evil soul chooses hell because of the nature of its being at the moment of death. Moreover, the reality of the body in this world is the form of the body and not its matter. In the final resurrection all of the levels of one's being are integrated including the form of the physical body, which *is* the reality of the body, so that one can definitely accept bodily resurrection as asserted by the Qur'ān and *Ḥadīth* and at the same time provide intellectual demonstrations for it on the basis of the general principles of Ṣadrian metaphysics.

GOD'S KNOWLEDGE OF THE WORLD

Another difficult question discussed by numerous Islamic philosophers and theologians is that of God's knowledge of the world. Al-Ghazzālī in fact considered the Peripatetic's view that God only knows universals and not particulars as one of the views of the philosophers which were not only erroneous but heretical. In his *al-Asfār*, Mullā Ṣadrā discusses and rejects seven different views of earlier thinkers concerning this issue,[25] while in *al-Shawāhid al-rubūbiyyah*[26] he claims that God knows everything in a special way which was unveiled to him by God and because of its complexity and the difficulty of understanding it by the great majority of men he finds it wiser not to reveal it fully.[27] In other writings, including one of his letters to his teacher, Mīr Dāmād, he insists that he gained full knowledge of this great mystery through inspiration (*ilhām*), unveiling (*kashf*) and the "eye of certainty" (*'ayn al-yaqīn*).[28]

What Mullā Ṣadrā does reveal of God's knowledge of the world is based on the thesis that whenever *wujūd* is not mixed with non-existence and not veiled by it, it is manifest to itself and never absent from itself. Therefore the essence of this *wujūd* knows itself and its essence is both knowledge of itself and known by itself, since the light of *wujūd* is one, the veil covering the reality of things being nothing but non-existence. And since the Necessary Being possesses an Essence which is beyond all composition and contingency, it is at the highest level of perceiving and being perceived, of knowing and being known. This means that since ultimately there is but one *wujūd* which is the *wujūd* of all things, therefore His Essence knows all beings that exist and there is not an atom that He does not know as asserted by the Qur'ān. The very presence of the Divine Essence to Itself is none other than undifferentiated knowledge which is at the same time also differentiated knowledge. And God's differentiated knowledge *is* none other than their *wujūd*. God's knowledge of existents is the very cause of their existentiation.

Mullā Ṣadrā also asserts that God's knowledge of things has its own hierarchy. There is first of all the level of solicitude (*al-'ināyah*) which is His knowledge of things on the level of His own Essence. The second level is that of undifferentiated decree (*al-qaḍā' al-ijmālī*) which is interpreted as the Pen (*al-Qalam*). As for forms which subsist by the *Qalam*, their subsistence is subsistence by emergence (*al-qiyām al-ṣudūrī*) for the *Qalam* has full dominion over all forms below it. The third level is the Tablet (*al-lawḥ*), also called differentiated decree (*al-qaḍā' al-tafṣīlī*), which contains the archetypes and Platonic Ideas of things, and their relation to the forms of this world is that of principles to their reflections. The fourth level is destiny through knowledge (*al-qadar al-ʿilmī*) comprising the imaginal world and that of suspended forms discussed above. The fifth level is destiny through objectification (*al-qadar al-ʿaynī*), which consists of the forms of the physical world. Mullā Ṣadrā considers this last level to be below the level of direct Divine Knowledge since it marks the mixture of forms with matter. But it is indirectly the subject of Divine Knowledge since the principles of these forms belong to the worlds above which God knows in an absolute and direct sense. Moreover, every level mentioned by Mullā Ṣadrā possesses *wujūd* which gives it reality and, according to the argument given above, since there is only one *wujūd* as asserted by the doctrine of *waḥdat al-wujūd*, God knows all existents by virtue of knowing His own Essence which is none other than absolute *wujūd*.

SOME OTHER PRINCIPLES OF ṢADRIAN TEACHINGS

There are numerous other principles expounded by Mullā Ṣadrā and founding elements of the "transcendent theosophy". In fact whereas Muslims inherited some two hundred topics from Greek philosophy, Mullā Ṣadrā discusses over six hundred, many of which are drawn from further encounters between philosophy and the Islamic revelation and others are philosophical and theosophical meditations upon the sayings of the Shiʿite Imāms along with the Qur'ān and *Ḥadīth*. Here, because of the constraint of space, we shall mention only two of the best known of these principles, not already discussed above. One is the famous thesis that "the Truth in its simplicity contains all things" (*basīṭ al-ḥaqīqah kull al-ashyā'*) which is a direct consequence of the unity and principiality of *wujūd*. By this principle Mullā Ṣadrā means that the truth (*al-ḥaqīqah*) in its state of pure simplicity and before becoming "combined" with quiddity (*al-māhiyyah*), that is, Pure Being, contains all things since the reality of things is their existence and Pure Being is the source of all *wujūd* and therefore in a sense contains the reality of all things. Mullā Ṣadrā appeals to this principle in many of his writings in solving some of the most complicated philosophical issues.

Another well-known principle is that "the soul in its unity *is* all of its faculties" (*al-nafs fī waḥdatihi kull al-quwā*). This is also a consequence of his ontology as well as trans-substantial motion. It means that the various faculties of the soul are not like accidents added to the substance of the soul. Rather, the soul *is* each of its faculties when it identifies itself with this or that function related to a particular faculty. That is why the perfecting of any faculty affects the soul itself in its unity and the perfection of the soul through trans-substantial motion also affects its faculties. It also emphasizes the unity of the soul above and beyond what one finds in the faculty psychology of the Peripatetics.

Also many of the older topics of philosophy are changed completely by seeing them in the light of Ṣadrian metaphysics. An outstanding example is the question of cause and effect or causality (*al-'illah wa'l-ma'lūl* or *al-'illiyyah*). Mullā Ṣadrā accepts the Aristotelian doctrine of the four causes and commentaries upon it by Ibn Sīnā and other earlier Islamic philosophers, but transforms them completely by considering the relation between cause and effect in light of the doctrine of the principiality of *wujūd*. He thereby combines horizontal and vertical causes and his discussion of this subject in all his works[29] contain some of his most exalted gnostic (*'irfānī*) expositions. In studying them one is presented with a knowledge which satisfies both the mind and the heart and can lead those who can understand and have sympathy for gnosis and sapience practically into a state of ecstasy. There are many other principles transformed by Ṣadrian metaphysics which we cannot discuss here because of the limitation of space. What has been presented here is only by way of example.

MULLĀ ṢADRĀ'S QUR'ĀNIC COMMENTARIES

None of the philosophers throughout the history of Islamic philosophy has paid as much attention to the Qur'ān as source of philosophical and theosophical knowledge and none has written as many commentaries upon the Qur'ān as has Mullā Ṣadrā, whose commentaries are the continuation of his "transcendent theosophy" and the "transcendent theosophy" an organic outgrowth of the inner meaning of the Qur'ān as understood by Mullā Ṣadrā who asserts again and again the harmony between revelation (*al-waḥy*) and intellect/reason (*al-'aql*). He in fact asserts that the intellect, of which reason is the reflection upon the mental plane, is humanity's inner prophet which manifests itself only in those who are, in the language of the Qur'ān, "firmly rooted in knowledge" (*al-rāsikhūn fi'l-'ilm*).[30]

Mullā Ṣadrā wrote commentaries upon a number of chapters and verses of the Qur'ān: *al-Fātiḥah* ("The Opening"), *al-Baqarah* ("The Cow"), *āyat al-kursī* ("The Throne Verse"), *āyat al-nūr* ("Light Verse"), *Sajdah* ("Prostration"), *Yā Sīn* ("YS"), *al-Wāqi'ah* ("The Event"), *al-Ḥadīd* ("Iron"), *al-Jum'ah* ("The Congregation"), *al-A'lā* ("The Most High"), *al-Ṭāriq* ("The Morning Star") and *al-Zalzāl* ("The Earthquake").[31] Moreover, he wrote a number of works dealing with the science of Qur'ānic commentary. These include *Asrār al-āyāt* ("Mysteries of Qur'ānic

Verses"), which deals especially extensively with eschatological matters to which the Qur'ān refers; *Mutashābih al-qur'ān* ("On the Metaphorical Verses of the Qur'ān"), dealing with those verses of the Qur'ān whose outward meaning is not clear in contrast to the *muḥkamāt* or "firm" verses whose outward meaning is clear, and *Mafātīḥ al-ghayb* ("Keys to the Invisible World"), which is one of his most important works and in which he discusses his method of Qur'ānic commentary.[32]

Mullā Ṣadrā distinguishes between commentators who see only the outward meaning of the Sacred Text and who are like those who see only the shell of a nut and disregard the fruit within, and those who pay attention only to what they consider the inner meaning while disregarding the outer form. He opposes both methods and states that, if these were to be the only choices, he would prefer the exoteric commentaries because they at least preserve the outward container of the revelation. But the best method is to deal with the inner meaning without going against the external sense of the words of the Qur'ān as understood by the Islamic community. And he adds that only those whom the Qur'ān calls "firm in knowledge" (*al-rāsikhūn fi'l-'ilm*), who have received their knowledge through divine inspiration without any spectre of doubt in their minds and hearts, have the right to carry out spiritual hermeneutics (*ta'wīl*) of God's Word.

Mullā Ṣadrā considers the Qur'ān to be the same as Being itself. Being, like the Qur'ān, possesses letters (*ḥurūf*) which are the "keys to the invisible world" and from their combinations verses (*āyāt*) are formed and from them the chapters (*suwar*) of the Sacred Book. Then from the combinations of the chapters, there results "the book of existence" (*kitāb al-wujūd*) which manifests itself in two ways as *al-furqān*, or discernment, and *al-qur'ān*, or recitation (both of these terms being names of the Qur'ān). The *furqānī* aspect of the Book is the macrocosm with all its differentiations, and the *qur'ānī* aspect is the spiritual and archetypal reality of man or what is generally called universal man (*al-insān al-kāmil*). Therefore, the keys (*mafātīḥ*) to the invisible world, as far as the revealed Qur'ān is concerned, are also the keys to the understanding of the invisible dimension of the world of external existence and man's inner being and vice versa. The Qur'ānic commentaries of Mullā Ṣadrā occupy an exalted place in the annals of Qur'ānic commentaries as well as in the philosophical hermeneutics of a sacred text, and it is a pity that so little attention has been paid to them in scholarship in Western languages.[33]

THE INFLUENCE OF MULLĀ ṢADRĀ

The vast synthesis created by Mullā Ṣadrā was to have a profound influence upon later Persian thought as well as in India and Iraq. It is not true that his thought dominated the whole philosophical scene in Persia, because it has had its detractors to this day, but it has certainly been the most important influence on the intellectual scene in Persia during the past three and a half centuries. Temporarily eclipsed after his death because of adverse political conditions, the "transcendent theosophy" was revived during the Qajar period in both Iṣfahān, the older centre of Islamic philosophy, and Tehran which was now becoming the foremost centre for the study of *ḥikmah*.[34] Revived by the great masters of Iṣfahān, Mullā 'Alī Nūrī and Mullā Ismā'īl Khwājū'ī, it was continued by later authorities in the Ṣadrian school such as Ḥājjī Mullā Hādī Sabziwārī in Khurāsān and Mullā 'Alī Mudarris in Tehran. They continued very much in the lines of Mullā Ṣadrā although they began to write more in Persian rather than Arabic in accordance with the general tendency of the period which was witness to the revival of philosophical Persian. And this tradition has continued unbroken to this day to such an extent that the extensive group of students studying Islamic subjects in the traditional *madrasah*s, especially those of Qom, and who are interested in the "intellectual sciences" (*al-'ulūm al-'aqliyyah*), are mostly followers of Mullā Ṣadrā.

In India the influence of Mullā Ṣadrā began to manifest itself from the middle of the eleventh/seventeenth century almost from the time of his death. His writings, especially the *Sharḥ al-hidāyah* ("Commentary upon the 'Guide'" of Athīr al-Dīn Abharī) became widespread, and the latter book even came to be known as *Ṣadrā*; people received distinction by saying that they had studied *Ṣadrā*. This tradition affected many later figures and has survived to this day. It is interesting to recall that Mawlānā Mawdūdī, the founder of the Jamā'at-i islāmī of Pakistan and India, that is, the founder of one of the most important politico-religious movements in the Islamic world in the fourteenth/twentieth century, translated parts of the *Asfār* into Urdu in his youth. As for Iraq, Mullā Ṣadrā has been taught continuously during the past three centuries especially in centres of Shi'ite learning such as Najaf. One of Iraq's foremost Islamic thinkers of the fourteenth/twentieth century, Muḥammad Bāqir al-Ṣadr, displays in a typical fashion the influence of Mullā Ṣadrā upon contemporary Iraqi religious scholars with a philosophical bent.

In conclusion it is interesting to note that the revival of Islamic philosophy in Iran during the Pahlavi period, especially from the 1950s onward even in semi-modernized circles, was primarily around the figure of Mullā Ṣadrā, many of whose works have been edited and printed during the past forty years while numerous analyses of the "transcendent theosophy" have been made in Persian as well as Arabic. At the same time Mullā Ṣadrā has now been introduced to the West and other parts of the non-Islamic world by such scholars as Henry Corbin, Toshihiko Izutsu, S. H. Nasr and Mehdi Mohaghegh, with the result that there is now a great deal of interest in his works in the West as well as in parts of the Islamic world such as the Arab countries, Turkey, Indonesia and Malaysia which did not show much interest in later Islamic philosophers in general and Mullā Ṣadrā in particular until recently. Moreover, numerous theses are being written throughout the world on him and his school. In any case Mullā Ṣadrā is not only one of the greatest intellectual figures of Islamic history, but his thought is very much a part of the contemporary Islamic world and continues to exercise great influence upon many aspects of current Islamic thought, especially the philosophical, theological and theosophical.

NOTES

1 I have dealt extensively with Mullā Ṣadrā's intellectual and philosophical background in my *The Transcendent Theosophy of Ṣadr al-Dīn Shīrāzī* (Tehran, 1978): 19–29 and 69–82. See also Muḥammad Khwājawī, *Lawāmi' al-'ārifīn fī aḥwāl Ṣadr al-muta'allihīn* (Tehran, 1988): 39ff.

2 For a detailed discussion of this subject by one of Persia's leading contemporary philosophers and masters of the School of Mullā Ṣadrā see Mehdi Ha'iri Yazdi, *The Principles of Epistemology in Islamic Philosophy – Knowledge by Presence* (Albany, 1992).

3 I also fully support the translation of this term as "transcendent theosophy" and have used it in my studies on the subject in English.

4 Such scholars as the late Fazlur Rahman in his works on Mullā Ṣadrā and Hossein Ziai in essays which appear in these volumes and elsewhere protest that the usage of such a term prevents Western philosophers from taking Mullā Ṣadrā seriously as a philosopher. The answer to this protest is that philosophy as defined by logical positivists, deconstructionists and other such modern schools which deny even the category of truth in an ultimate sense in philosophy, will disregard a person such as Mullā Ṣadrā no matter how the name of his school is translated into English. Moreover, the term "theosophy" is now regaining the respect it possessed before the Theosophical Society founded in the late nineteenth and early twentieth centuries began to use the term. Many of the thinkers of the West such as Jakob Böhme and Rossmini, who have much more affinity with Mullā Ṣadrā than they do, let us say, with Voltaire, Kant, Compte or Quine, are called theosophers in an honourable way. In any case, no apology is needed in calling Mullā Ṣadrā's *al-ḥikmat al-muta'āliyah* the "transcendent theosophy" in order to distinguish it from merely rationalistic and logical philosophy and relate it to earlier strands of Western thought most akin to it in nature, strands which are now being avidly revived especially in France, Italy and Germany.

5 See my *The Transcendent Theosophy*: 85ff.

6 See his *al-Asfār al-arba'ah*, ed. 'Allāmah Muḥammad Ḥusayn Ṭabāṭabā'ī (Qom, 1968) or *al-Shawāhid al-rubūbiyyah*, ed. Sayyid Jalāl al-Dīn Āshtiyānī (Mashhad, 1967); *The Wisdom of the Throne*, trans. James Morris (Princeton, 1981); *al-Mabda' wa'l-ma'ād*, ed. S. J. Āshtiyānī (Tehran, 1976): 10ff; and *Kitāb al-*

mashā'ir, Le Livre des pénétrations métaphysiques, ed. and trans. Henry Corbin (Tehran and Paris, 1964). See also Sayyid Jalāl al-Dīn Āshtiyānī, *Hasti az naẓar-i falsafah wa 'irfān* (Mashhad, 1960), which is devoted to a large extent to an analysis of Mullā Ṣadrā's metaphysics of *wujūd*.

7 See the introduction by Corbin to *Le Livre des pénétrations métaphysiques*: 62ff; also Toshihiko Izutsu, *Creation and the Timeless Order of Things* (Ashland, 1994): 178ff.

8 See M. Mohaghegh and T. Izutsu, *The Metaphysics of Sabzavari* (Delmar, 1977): 31–2. On Sabziwārī see S. H. Nasr, "Sabziwāri", in M. M. Sharīf (ed.) *A History of Muslim Philosophy*, 2 (Wiesbaden, 1966): 1543–56.

9 See S. H. Nasr, "Mullā Ṣadrā as a Source for the History of Islamic Philosophy", in *Islamic Life and Thought* (Albany, 1981): 169ff.

10 See the *Asfār*, 1: 23ff.

11 On *tashkīk* see the *Asfār*, 1: 36ff., and 427ff. See also 'Allāmah Ṭabāṭabā'ī, "Ṣadr al-Dīn Muḥammad ibn Ibrāhīm Shīrāzī the Renewer of Islamic Philosophy in the 11th/17th century", in S. H. Nasr (ed.) *Mullā Ṣadrā Commemoration Volume* (Tehran, 1962): 22ff., where one of the greatest of the contemporary masters of the school of Mullā Ṣadra summarizes his metaphysics and ontology.

12 See Nasr, "Existence (*Wujūd*) and Quiddity (*Māhiyyah*) in Islamic Philosophy", *International Philosophical Quarterly*, 29(4) (December 1989): 409–28. Mullā Ṣadrā gave an extensive discussion of *māhiyyah* in his *al-Asfār*, 2: 2ff.

13 Mullā Ṣadrā offers numerous rational arguments for the principiality of *wujūd*, arguments which have been summarized by Sabziwārī in his *Sharḥ al-manẓūmah*. See Mohaghegh and Izutsu, *op. cit.*: 32ff., and the *Asfār*, 1: 38ff.

14 On transubstantial motion see the *Asfār*, 3: 80ff.

15 See Izutsu, *Creation and the Timeless Order of Things*: 119ff.

16 See al-Ghazzālī, *Tahāfut al-falāsifah*, trans. Sabih Ahmad Kamali (Lahore, 1963): 13ff.

17 See S. H. Nasr, "The School of Isfahan", in Sharif (ed.) *A History of Muslim Philosophy*, 2: 916ff.

18 For an explanation of Mullā Ṣadrā's views concerning the relation of God and the world see Fazlur Rahman, "The God–World Relationship in Mullā Ṣadrā", in George Hourani (ed.) *Essays on Islamic Philosophy and Science* (Albany, 1975): 238–53.

19 See Mullā Ṣadrā, the *Asfār*, 3: 278ff. See also Fazlur Rahman, "Mullā Ṣadrā's Theory of Knowledge", *Philosophical Forum*, 4(1) (fall 1972): 141–52.

20 For a most profound discussion, according to the School of Mullā Ṣadrā, of the truth that knowledge (*'ilm*) is being and light and not merely the imprint of forms upon the tablet of the soul see Sayyid Muḥammad Kāẓim 'Aṣṣār, *'Ilm al-ḥadīth* (Tehran, 1352 (AH Solar)/1973) chapter 1: 1ff.

21 See Mullā Ṣadrā, the *Asfār*, 2: 46ff., and his *al-Shawāhid al-rubūbiyyah*: 159ff.

22 In one of his major works, *Creative Imagination in the Sufism of Ibn 'Arabī*, trans. Ralph Mannheim (Princeton, 1981), Henry Corbin introduced this doctrine in its full amplitude for the first time in the modern West. His exposition was so influential that a whole centre was established in France by the French philosopher Gilbert Durant for the study of the imaginal world or *l'imaginaire* while in England the journal *Temenos* was founded by Kathleen Raine to propagate art in its relation to the imagination as understood by Muslim thinkers

seen through the eyes of Corbin. For Ibn 'Arabī's views of the imaginal world to which he returns again and again in his works, especially *al-Futūḥāt al-makkiyyah*, see William Chittick, *The Sufi Path of Knowledge* (Albany, 1989): 112ff.; and his *Imaginal Worlds* (Albany, 1994), especially part 2: 67ff.

23 Corbin has dealt with this theme extensively in his *Spiritual Body and Celestial Earth*, trans. Nancy Pearson (Princeton, 1977). See especially pp. 164–70, which contains the text of Mullā Ṣadrā from his *Kitāb al-ḥikmat al-'arshiyyah* dealing directly with this subject.

24 For a detailed analysis of Mullā Ṣadrā's views on eschatology in relation to the reality of the imaginal world see the long introduction of S. J. Āshtiyānī to his edition of *al-Mabda' wa'l-ma'ād*.

25 See the *Asfār*, 6: 263ff.

26 See *al-Shawāhid al-rubūbiyyah*: 39ff.

27 On this issue as a whole see Khwājawī, *Lawāmi' al-'ārifīn*: 79ff.

28 Mullā Ṣadrā refers often in his writings to the three degrees of certainty, *'ilm al-yaqīn* (knowledge of certainty), *'ayn al-yaqīn* (eye of certainty), and *ḥaqq al-yaqīn* (truth of certainty) which mark the hierarchy of knowledge in Sufism and correspond to hearing of fire, seeing fire and being consumed by fire. See Abū Bakr Sirāj ad-Dīn, *The Book of Certainty* (Cambridge, 1992).

29 See for example, the *Asfār*, 2: 127ff.

30 For an outline of Mullā Ṣadrā's method of commentary see Muḥammad Khwājawī, *Tarjuma-yi mafātīḥ al-ghayb* (Tehran, 1984): 84ff.

31 A complete list of his commentaries, including verses of chapters upon which he commented, is given in Nasr, *The Transcendent Theosophy*: 48.

32 All of Mullā Ṣadrā's commentaries have been published together for the first time by Muḥammad Khwājawī in several volumes under the title *Tafsīr al-qur'ān al-karīm ta'līf Ṣadr al-muta'allihīn* (Qom, 1987).

33 See L. S. Peerwani, "Qur'anic Hermeneutics: the Views of Ṣadr Al-Dīn Shīrāzī", in *BRISMES Proceedings of the 1991 International Conference on Middle Eastern Studies* (Manchester, 1991): 118–27. The commentary upon the "Light Verse", which is one of the greatest masterpieces of Islamic thought, has been translated and analysed by Muḥsin Ṣāliḥ in a doctoral thesis at Temple University in America (1993); this has not as yet been published.

34 See S. H. Nasr, "The Metaphysics of Ṣadr al-Dīn Shīrāzī and Islamic Philosophy in Qajar Persia", in Edmund Bosworth and Carole Hillenbrand (eds) *Qajar Persia* (Edinburgh, 1983): 177–98.

BIBLIOGRAPHY

Corbin, Henry (1963) "La Place de Mollâ Ṣadrâ dans la philosophie iranienne", *Studia Islamica*, 18: 81–113.

—— (1964) *Le Livre des pénétrations métaphysiques* (Tehran and Paris). The French part of this edition minus the Arabic and Persian texts was published with the same title by Verdier (Paris, 1993).

—— (1967) "Le Thème de la résurrection chez Mollâ Ṣadrâ Shîrâzî (1050/1640) commentateur de Sohrawardî (587/1191)", in *Studies in Mysticism and Religion*

– *Presented to Gershom G. Scholem* (Jerusalem): 71–115.
—— (1972) "Mollâ Ṣadrâ Shîrâzî", in *En Islam iranien*, 4 (Paris): 52–122.
—— (in collaboration with S. H. Nasr and O. Yahya) (1993) *History of Islamic Philosophy*, trans. Liadain and Philip Sherrard (London): 342ff.
Ha'iri Yazdi, Mehdi (1992) *The Principles of Epistemology in Islamic Philosophy – Knowledge by Presence* (Albany).
'Abdul-Haq, Muhammad (1970) "An Aspect of the Metaphysics of Mullā Ṣadrā", *Islamic Studies*, 9: 331–53; "The Metaphysics of Mullā Ṣadrā II", *Islamic Studies*, 10 (1971): 291–317.
Horten, Max (1913) *Das philosophische System von Schirázi (1640)* (Strassburg).
Izutsu, Toshihiko (1968) *The Fundamental Structure of Sabzawārī's Metaphysics* (Tehran).
—— (1994) *Creation and the Timeless Order of Things* (Ashland).
Mohaghegh, Mehdi and Izutsu, Toshihiko (eds and trans.) (1977) *The Metaphysics of Sabzavari* (Delmar).
Morris, James (ed. and trans.) (1981) *The Wisdom of the Throne* (Princeton).
Nasr, Seyyed Hossein (1966) "Ṣadr al-Dīn Shīrāzi, 'Mullā Ṣadrā'", in M. M. Sharif (ed.) *A History of Muslim Philosophy*, 2: 932–61.
—— (1978) *The Transcendent Theosophy of Ṣadr al-Dīn Shīrāzī* (Tehran).
—— (1981) *Islamic Life and Thought* (Albany).
Rahman, Fazlur (1976) *The Philosophy of Mullā Ṣadrā* (Albany).

CHAPTER 37

Shah Walīullāh

Rahimuddin Kemal and Salim Kemal

Shah Walīullāh – Quṭb al-Dīn Aḥmad ibn 'Abd al-Raḥīm – was born near Delhi at sunrise on 4 Shawwaal 1114 (Wednesday 21 February 1703) to a distinguished family, known for its contribution to the educational, intellectual and religious life of Delhi. On his paternal side Shah Walīullāh claimed descent from the second caliph while his mother's family claimed descent from the Prophet's grandson. His paternal grandfather, Wajīh al-Dīn Ghāzī Shahīd, had been a commander in the army of Aurangzeb, who bestowed on him the title of *ghāzī*; his father, Shah 'Abd al-Raḥīm, was an eminent savant who gave up his imperial nobility in order to devote himself to learning and mysticism.

Shah Walīullāh was educated at a school established by his father. He studied Arabic and Persian, the Qur'ān, *Ḥadīth, tafsīr, fiqh, manṭiq*, philosophy, mysticism, medicine, rhetoric and mathematics before graduating in 1130/1718. In that year his father initiated him into the Naqshbandi Sufi order and in the following year granted him *ijāzah* in that order. On his father's death in 1131/1719, Shah Walīullāh took charge of the school, remaining there for the next dozen years, guiding students and developing his own theories.

Shah Walīullāh had married in 1130/1718. He had a son and a daughter from this marriage and, following his wife's death a few years later, married again at the age of forty-three. This marriage yielded him four sons. In 1143/1731 he made his *ḥajj*. He stayed in Mecca and Medina for more than a year to study with a number of eminent scholars and mystics, including the notable Shaykh Abū Ṭāhir al-Madanī.

On returning to India he engaged with the political and social turmoil afflicting the country. His life spanned the reign of ten rulers in Delhi, who cumulatively added to the problems facing the populace. Central Muslim power had dissipated to provincial governers and nobles; other groups such as the Marathas, Sikhs, Jats and Europeans were vying for power; the economic conditions of Muslims had decayed through idleness and corruption; the Muslim community was subject to continuous internecine conflicts, especially between Shi'i and Sunni groups but also between adherents of the four schools of law and between the orthodox and the innovators.

During this period Shah Walīullāh promoted educational, social and religious reforms to unify and strengthen the Muslim community. He justified these practices philosophically, arguing for clear foundational principles for good government and a moral life, which he presented in a number of texts: more than fifty works have been attributed to his authorship, but not always rightly. He also translated the Qur'ān into Persian, making it accessible to the populace. This proved less than popular with some groups, who carried out an unsuccessful attack on his life at Masjid Fathepuri.

After Shah Walīullāh's death in 1176/1762 his sons continued his educational work and other reforms. That work is not only one of the crucial formative forces in Indian Islamic thought but it was influential both in the *Ḥijāz*, from the time he spent there, and in eastern Asia.

The need for a comprehensive identity of purpose, thought and action was vital to Shah Walīullāh. Despite being expressed in different texts and addressed to diverse issues and contexts, his ideas possess a strong structural unity. The possibility of such unity of thought and belief is an axiom of his work, determining his critical analysis of other theories of knowledge, being and theology, and giving direction to his own work. To this end he proposes principles of *taṭbīq* – a method of reconciliation that identifies the common principles underlying various branches of knowledge and can provide a basis for *ijtihad* with contemporary relevance. Such principles can then serve as a critical tool for identifying non-issues or eliminating false disputations, leading participants to an awareness of the underlying interests implicated in promoting those false disputations. Shah Walīullāh can then unify all these elements through consideration of the needs of living an active moral life as a Muslim under the guidance of the Qur'ān.

To explain these aspects of his thought, we may begin with his theory of knowledge. Shah Walīullāh thinks of knowledge as a relation between mind and object, such that the mind gains a complete grasp of the form of the object.[1] It is needed by the particular kind of existent that human beings are. Knowledge has a divine source for human beings and is *given* to them through revelation, dreams, inspiration, intuition, etc. By contrast, God *causes* the existence of the objects by thinking about them. Consonantly, mystical insight into the essence of existence occurs to various messengers or prophets and is a distinctive grasp of essences because it is other and more than the complete grasp of forms.

At other times Shah Walīullāh examines the different kinds of knowledge human beings can have, distinguishing a prophetic knowledge that can diagnose and remedy the ills of society from a knowledge of *Sharīʿah,* grammar from religious science, philosophy and applied knowledge, or revealed knowledge from empirical knowledge and from intuitive insight, and so on.[2] He makes these distinctions when addressing particular problems, and though they do not seem to coincide in any obvious way, they are commensurable and complement each other.

A more interesting feature than their possible self-contradictoriness is that they result from the process of gaining knowledge. Shah Walīullāh explains this process by giving principal importance to intuition in combination with the division of faculties proposed by Greek-influenced philosophers. In *al-Khayr al-kathīr* he distinguishes sensation, imagination, estimation and reason, then sets out the importance of intuition.[3] Like the Greeks, he finds sensation unreliable, and, like earlier Islamic philosophers such as al-Ghazzālī, he ascribes to reason the power to deal with practical matters and issues relating to understanding God's purpose for human beings. Earlier, in his *Kitāb al-najāt,* Ibn Sīnā followed al-Fārābī in giving especial importance to imagination as the epistemic faculty in which prophetic intuition appeared as an order of images and ideas that cognitive language could not articulate completely.[4] Shah Walīullāh does not dispute this association, and explains intuition as a mysterious power that lies beyond reason and communicates its reflection of divine reality through ordered images and metaphors. Divine reality has an impact upon the soul, and intuition is our access to this effect. Accordingly, intuition gives us access to reality indirectly through its effect, which can be grasped in moments of self-realization, rather than directly.

Despite that indirect access to reality, the relation between intuition and soul is a direct and immediate one. Shah Walīullāh contrasts it with the relation of mind to object, which subsists between two objects of different kinds. Intuition does not presuppose a relation between two objects so much as it is an awareness through presence – an *ʿilm al-ḥuḍūrī* – in which in moments of self-realization the order of the universe makes itself felt within the self.

The basis in self-realization imposes certain requirements on a self hoping for an intuitive grasp of reality. Just as the unreliability of sensation renders its claims to knowledge questionable, similarly an unsatisfactory state of the self will interfere with its power of intuition.[5] A proper grasp of the impact of reality on the soul requires subjects to become purified of base needs that would otherwise interfere with their exposure to reality. Shah Walīullāh maintains that the soul naturally leads to divine reality, and proposes that an emphasis on the self thwarts this disposition. Humility and devotion are therefore the prime antidotes to misunderstandings.

The factors that interfere with intuition also account for contradictions among intuitions. Shah Walīullāh diagnoses the existence of disagreements about the intuited nature of reality as the result of failures in the subjects, who have been unable to rescind distorting influences. Nor are all alleged contradictions real: the complex nature of human beings allows them insights into different realms or qualitative features of their existence. Consequently, they may express insights appropriate to their rational or animal natures, their stages of development or the context to which they address their utterances. Each of these categories will determine what communication is commensurate to the context; critics may misunderstand the appropriate categories and identify as contradictions what are really their own category mistakes.

The thrust of these arguments is to affirm the unity of our knowledge and of our intuitive grasp of divine reality by explaining differences as the result of external and subjective factors. This affirmation of unity and its commensurate technique of diagnosis serves Shah Walīullāh as a critical tool that he applies not only to Islamic thought but also to other people of the Book. By contrast with numerous scholars he argued against the view that Jews and Christians made changes in their scriptures, contending that changes were made in the process of translation. He was also able to use this methodology in his study of the Traditions, writing in both Persian and Arabic about their collection, and in his Qur'ānic commentary in books such as *Fawz al-kabīr*.

The same principles are at work in his book *Inṣāf fī bayān sabab al-ikhtilāf*. This history of jurisprudence and traditions counteracts a prevalent tendency. Indian scholarship had relied greatly on *Hidāyā* and *Fatwā-yi 'ālamgīrī*. Shah Walīullāh places these books in the context of the origins of *fiqh*, which he combines with an extensive study of *taṣawwuf* contained in some fourteen books. In order to provide a deductive synthesis by returning to the origins he shows how the various schools of law emerged and developed. Identifying the basic problems on which the learned differed, he analyses the distinctive characteristics of the the four Sunni schools of law – Ḥanafī, Shāfi'ī, Mālikī and Ḥanbalī – by reference to their historical situation,[6] proposes a possible synthesis and defends the latter as an instance of permissible *ijtihād*. He analyses *ijtihad* further in *'Aqd al-jayyād fī aḥkām al-ijtihād wa'l-taqlīd*, adding to his distinction of explicit and implicit aspects of Islam distinctions between those who are capable of *ijtihad* and those who follow. The former he categorizes further as *mujtahidīn al muṭlaq*, the founders of Sunni schools of law, *mujtahid fi'l mazhab*, those capable of *ijtihād* in a school of law, and *mujtahid fi'l-fatwā*, who have the required authority for examining the *Sharī'ah*. The issue was especially important in India at that time, given the availability of all the schools and the possibility that pursuing one would preclude following another.

This search for a comprehensive and defensible unity is present also in Shah Walīullāh's account of the nature of being and in his theology. In the latter he differs little from the Ash'arites, though he insists on a criticial evaluation of the external influences that have entered its teaching, such as Greek thought and the modifications introduced by immediate needs in its history. His central contribution to questions of the nature of being and existence is to resolve the unity of consciousness *waḥdat al-shuhūd* with the unity of being *waḥdat al-wujūd*. Divinity being one, we may expect that existence shares that singularity, and so knowledge of the world and intuition about that divine reality will also be capable of unity. Ultimately all apparently dissonant claims will prove reconcilable.

The need for this reconciliation arose because thinkers had distinguished unity of being from unity of consciousness. Arguably God is the only being in reality, and all other beings are really manifestations of Him. Some argued that through causing things to be, the Absolute Existence descends into determined beings,[7] that Absolute Existence or God exists as a divine essense or pure being,[8] and its descent has five stages. The first stage of descent is a universal state of unity; the second of extended being; the third of spirits; the fourth of archetypes; and the fifth of particular bodies.[9] As God is the only reality, these stages and their existences are not separable from Him and the world does not have any independent reality. Existence, then, is a unity of being. By contrast, people have argued that God and creation are distinct, the latter being shadows (*ẓilāl*) of Divine Attributes.[10] Since they are reflections, their existence depends on God but is not identical with Him. A failure to recognize this distinction is the result of an incomplete stage of mystical knowledge where the *sālik*, overwhelmed by recognizing the existence of a single reality, denies all other existences. A later stage both recognizes the existence of the One and has awareness of the other possible and contingent existences. Consonantly, accepting this identity or non-identity between God, attributes and creations has consequences for the status ascribed to the latter: if they are not identical, they cannot be eternal, or necessary, and so on.

Shah Walīullāh accepts the starting point that Divine Being lies beyond and originates extended being, and accepts that the relation between God and the world may be described in terms of descent. However, he argues that the unity of consciousness and being signify only linguistic differences and do not grasp anything substantial. For example, the terms sometimes identify different stages of a mystical progress, which are reconcilable in the ultimate reality that consists of both the one and the many.[11] At other times the unity of being or consciousness signifies the relation of the absolute being to modes, attributes, archetypes and particular existent beings. God establishes the world in all its possibilities, and so as eternal and one. Although in their particular determinations and our experience the objects may appear as many, their nature and possibilities are already determined by God, and their contingency is only apparent. Similarly, archetypes are related to the names of Divinity, and so are eternal with God; they are also realized or manifested in particulars, where they are "modes" of divinity. However, the distinction between archetypes as names and modes is only a conceptual one, Shah Walīullāh argues, since archetypes have no independent existence apart from God who, in turn, also determines particulars. Further, since both sides accept that the world exists only in its determinations by God, there cannot be any real difference between them about the status of modes and attributes. Certainly one group talks of God and creation as distinct, the latter being reflections or shadows of Divine Attributes whose existence depends on God but is not identical with Him. Shah Walīullāh contends that these do not denote separate kinds of existence, since they are dependent on God: the distinction between the groups is best understood in terms of the use they make of "distinct reflections" or of existence being part of God. And here he points out that in their actual arguments both groups use the concepts in similar ways. The opposition, then, is again only apparent when understood by reference to the role and power of the Ultimate Reality.[12]

This concern to examine and reconcile diverse conceptualizations would be incomplete if it did not also indicate the place of individuals in relation to the unity of being, knowledge and action. In *al-Tafhīmāt* and *Saṭa'āt*, among other texts, he sets out the process of individual development. As we may expect, given its capacity for reason, inspiration, along with feelings, and animal impulses, humanity originates as an abstract, pure intellect. Shah Walīullāh ascribes to it a cyclical process in which humanity returns to that state of pure intellect after going through diverse stages of animal and spiritual life. Human beings move from a state of pure intellect at an appointed time to "the visible world from the place that is the most superior imaginative creation".[13] At that stage of similitude, the ideal picture of man appears, in which its destiny and origin are written. Next it enters into the various stages of the realm of similitudes or archetypes, following which its entry into the material world and its nexus of causes occurs. In this last realm the human being possesses a particular material form, with particular associations, situations and possibilities, and lives its mortal existence for the duration of its life. When people "die a natural death", they "still retain as great a portion of their natural spirits as could be a steed for the Soul and remain in the Intermediary world retaining the knowledge, the states and the faculties which remained imprinted upon their natural spirits".[14] Then follows an ordered ascension through the stages already traversed until the human being becomes a pure intellect again.

The narrative of this process signifies the order of being and knowledge available to human beings, whose souls thus bear significant analogies with the larger reality of which they are a part. *Sat'* 16 sets out the sciences appropriate to human beings, given their nature, and *sat'* 17 explains the kinds and modes of teaching that can become available to them. The order of human life repeats the order of the universe, and these analogies seem to be the mechanism for their interrelation, allowing Shah Walīullāh to unite ontology and epistemology by explaining knowledge as the self-awareness appropriate to a state of a being.

This unity, arguably, is again part of the syncretic thrust of Shah Walīullāh's work. He attempts to show the full and detailed richness of the whole human and spiritual compass, diagnosing disagreements as an incomplete recognition of the whole, within and by relation to which apparent anomalies may be resolved. He takes the Qur'ān and central Islamic texts as his guide, expecting them to be capable of providing the answers human beings may seek, and strives for a critical synthesis of elements that respects the complexity of issues which result from a diverse and rich texture of human life. Just as he relates epistemology to ontology and consciousness to being, he also seeks to unite knowledge with belief, reason with intuition, Muslims with each other and with other people of the Book, human beings with each other and with God, and thought with action guided by the Qur'ān.

NOTES

1 *Al-Budūr al-bāzighah*, ed. Saghir Husain Ma'sumi (Hyderabad, Pakistan, 1970): 142ff.

2 See *al-Khayr al-kathīr* (Cairo, 1974) especially, but also *al-Tafhīmāt al-ilāhiyyah* (Surat, 1936), 1 and *Ḥujjat Allāh al-bālighah* (Hyderabad, Pakistan, 1979). A useful exposition of the various proposals is presented in Hafiz A. Ghaffar Khan, *Shah Wali Allah: an Analysis of his Metaphysical Thought* (unpublished Ph.D. thesis, Temple University, 1986).

3 But see also *Saṭa'āt*, trans. J. N. Jalbani and ed. D. B. Fry (London, 1980), *sat'* 17, where Shah Walīullāh presents the various kinds of teaching appropriate to human beings.

4 F. Rahman, *Avicenna's Psychology, an English translation of Kitāb al-Najāt, Book II, Chapter VI with Historico-Philosophical Notes and Textual Improvements on the Cairo Edition* (Oxford, 1952).

5 At *sat'* 16 of *Saṭa'āt* Shah Walīullāh orders human knowledge into a hierarchy of sciences that follows from and is appropriate to understanding the nature of man. Together they constitute human nature and its possibilities.

6 His book on *Izālat al-khifā' 'an khilāfat al-khifā'*, in which he deals with Islamic theories of politics and sociology, is probably unique in Islamic literature, and sets out some basis for the historical account he gives of the development of the different schools.

7 We have in mind Ibn 'Arabī. Like other mystics he holds that creation occurs through God's willing things to be (*kun*). This willing is not a causal relation and allows at least two perspectives. First, in relation to God, what He brings into being is established and therefore eternal, and is not a piecemeal experience of particulars but is the determination of all possible beings; second, from the perspective of our experience of existent things, where all the possibilities are not realized at once, the determinations are contingent. Arguably al-Ghazzālī works within the same structure.

8 See *Lamaḥāt*, trans. G. N. Jalbani and ed. D. B. Fry (London, 1980), Lamha 2, for example, and *Budūr al-bāzighah*.

9 Shah Walīullāh provides an account of creation in *Al-Khayr al-kathīr*, trans. G. N. Jalbani (Lahore, 1974): 40–4.

10 Hafiz Ghaffar Khan, cited above, finds the best source of this doctrine in Aḥmad Ṣirhindī, *Maktūbāt*, trans. Q. 'Alim al-Dīn (Hyderabad, India), 1: 234. S. A. A. Rizvi, *Shah Wali-Allah and his Times* (Canberra, 1980), cites the origins of this position in the work of 'Alā 'al-Dawlah Simnānī and Mujadid Alf-i Thānī. In any case, Shah Walīullāh considered this a false disputation.

11 See *Tafhīmāt al-ilāhiyyah* (Surat, 1936), 2.

12 See *Tafhīmāt*: 34–5, 261–71, etc. The letter is to Afandī Ismā'īl ibn 'Abd Allāh Rūmī, then residing in Medina.

13 *Sat'* 24.

14 *Sat'* 25.

SELECTED TEXTS

Shah Walīullāh, *Al-Budūr al-bāzighah*, ed. Saghir Husain Ma'sumi (Hyderabad, Pakistan, 1970).

—— *Al-Khayr al-kathīr*, trans. G. N. Jalbani (Lahore, 1974).

—— *Al-Tafhīmāt al-ilāhiyyah* (Surat, 1936).

—— *Ḥujjat Allāh al-bālighah* (Hyderabad, Pakistan, 1979).

—— *Lamaḥāt,* trans. G. N. Jalbani and ed. D. B. Fry (London, 1980).

—— *Saṭa'āt,* trans. G. N. Jalbani and ed. D. B. Fry (London, 1980).

OTHER WORKS

Ghaffar Khan, Hafiz A. *Shah Wali Allah: An Analysis of his Metaphysical Thought* (unpublished Ph.D. thesis, Temple University, 1986).

Hermansen, M., *The Conclusive Argument from God: Shah Wali Allah of Delhi's Ḥujjat Allāh al-Bāligna* (Leiden, 1995).

Rizvi, S. A. A. *Shah Wali-Allah and his Times* (Canberra, 1980).

VI

The Jewish philosophical tradition in the Islamic cultural world

CHAPTER 38

Introduction

Oliver Leaman

It is difficult to overemphasize the significance which Islamic philosophy had for Jewish thinkers who were working at the same time in the Islamic world, or who were influenced by such work. Many Jewish thinkers wrote in Arabic and their main philosophical authorities were Arabic authors, which is hardly surprising given the pervasiveness of Arabic culture within the Islamic Empire. It was possible then as now for Jews to maintain their religious identity while at the same time becoming an important part of the cultural exchange of ideas. A very rich corpus of science, mathematics, medical theory, astronomy and philosophy was available to any literate member of society, and it was not the sole preserve of Muslims. Jews were excited by the diversity of theoretical perspectives which existed, and enthusiastically threw themselves into contemporary intellectual life. They even adapted much of the theory connected with specifically Islamic areas of enquiry, such as law and theology, to their own legal and religious texts. This is hardly surprising. Minorities generally acquire the culture of the dominant community, or at least as much of the culture as they can adapt to their own needs and interests.

It was not only Jews who reacted in this way, of course. Christians often reacted similarly, and one thinks in particular of thinkers such as Yaḥyā ibn ʿAdī. Yet there did not develop in the Christian community within the Islamic world the same involvement with the local intellectual movement as occurred in the Jewish community. To a certain extent this may have been a reflection on the different social roles of the different ethnic groups. In Spain, for example, Jews were more likely to be in high political office and in the professions than were Christians, and hence were more open to the sorts of ideas which went around the Islamic world. Jews travelled a good deal around the Islamic Empire, and so were well acquainted with a range of views and theories. Christians often saw their spiritual centre of gravity as occurring outside of the Islamic world, and may have regarded the frequent conflicts between the Christian powers and Islam as indicating that they should be careful about getting too close to Muslim culture. No force outside the Islamic world would intervene on behalf of the Jews, and indeed the interventions by Christian armies radically harmed the position of the Jewish community. It is hardly surprising, then, that Jews should have taken a more enthusiastic attitude towards the culture which flourished in the Islamic world, a culture in which they participated as far as they could.

This is not to say that Islamic philosophy did not have an impact on Christian thought. It certainly did, and we shall see later in these volumes how strong that influence was in the form and content of both medieval and modern philosophy. The important difference here, though, is that influence very largely took place outside of the Islamic world, and it was not so overwhelming as the influence on Jewish philosophy. When we look at the works of thinkers such as Saadiah, Halevi, Maimonides and even Gersonides we can observe the curriculum of Islamic philosophy quite fully represented. They did not just take some of the leading ideas and try to see how far they could use them to make sense of their own philosophical concerns, as was very much the case with many of the major Christian philosophers. The Jewish philosophers went much further than this in their work, often working well within the tradition of Islamic philosophy itself, albeit just as often using it to develop points which were of specifically Jewish concern. Perhaps one of the reasons why Jewish philosophy came to rely so much on Islamic philosophy lies in the proximity of the religions. For example, one of the most common topics of discussion dealt with the relationship between the deity and his qualities. This relationship was used to determine the relationship of a subject to its predicates, clearly a key notion in philosophical logic and the theory of meaning. The fierce monotheism of both Judaism and Islam meant that the approach by Jewish and Muslim thinkers was always likely to be similar.

When we talk about one culture influencing another we should be very careful about what precisely is meant by that. There are degrees of influence, and it is not necessarily the case that the frequency with which an influence can be detected directly is a good indication of its strength. The important factor to discover is not so much the language used or the people who are mentioned but the way in which the agenda is set. For example, in the first two centuries of the translation movement from Greek via Syriac to Arabic many Greek terms were translated by Arabic terms which had quite a distinct cultural context. So secular terms from Greek culture suddenly became Arabic terms with a religious force in Islamic philosophy. The translator and the philosopher in the Islamic world did not mean to imply by this that the Greeks had a religious motive in mind when they used such terms – they knew that this was not the case – but they chose the term in their own language which came closest to the original term. This is perfectly acceptable, since the alternative is to create a neologism, which did indeed take place on occasion but which has undesirable consequences. For one thing, it is difficult to relate new terms to existing theoretical problems, and so it is preferable on occasion to struggle along with a familiar term which at least embodies some of the sense of the original term. Strictly speaking, one should point out to the reader that the way in which the term is being used in Arabic is rather different from its original Greek meaning, but there were good reasons in the early years of Islamic philosophy not to do that. For one thing, it was often the thesis of the philosophers that the grammatical meaning of the words they were using was not the most important thing about them. They have a logical sense which is perfectly convertible into Arabic, so it is possible to convey logical arguments from Greek to Arabic with no loss of deep structure. Secondly, there was the political consideration that the public needed to be persuaded that there was nothing impious or suspect about the use of what were originally Greek concepts in debates which arose within Islamic culture. How better to do this, it might have been thought, than to translate secular Greek terms by Arabic terms which have non-secular associations?

If we can observe that the philosophical discussion in Arabic is very similar to that which took place in Greek, we can understand that the Arabic terms are being used divorced from their Islamic associations. This may not be at all obvious, since it may appear on the surface that the philosophers are seeking to reconcile two systems of thought by using Islamic language to represent Greek thought. This may lead us to misunderstand the nature of the influence of the latter on the former. What we should look for is not so much the people who are quoted or the sort of language which is used but the ways in which the arguments are supposed to work. If they are supposed to work in a way which is very similar to the way in which they are taken to work in a previous cultural context, or in a different cultural atmosphere, then we can rightly say that the influence of that culture is very important for the framing of the arguments. We can say this about the links between much Islamic and Jewish philosophy. What is significant about these links is that the latter reproduces much of the agenda of the former, not just the language and the individual thinkers but the agenda itself. This will become obvious when we look at the work of some of the major Jewish philosophers who are discussed here.

BIBLIOGRAPHY

A very useful bibliography is available in:

Sirat, C. (1985) *A History of Jewish Philosophy in the Middle Ages* (Cambridge).

Bibliographies and references may be consulted in:

Altmann, A. (1969) *Studies in Religious Philosophy and Mysticism* (Ithaca).
—— (1981) *Essays in Jewish Intellectual History* (Hanover, N.H.).
—— (1987) *Von der Mittelalterlichen zur modernen Aufklärung* (Tübingen).
Davidson, H. (1987) *Proofs for Eternity, Creation and the Existence of God in Medieval Islamic and Jewish Philosophy* (New York).
Goodman, L. (1992) *Neoplatonism and Jewish Thought* (Albany).
Guttmann, J. (1966) *Philosophies of Judaism* (Garden City).
Leaman, O. (1990) *Moses Maimonides* (London).
Maimonides, M. (1976) *RAMBAM: Readings in the Philosophy of Moses Maimonides*, selections trans. L. Goodman (New York).
Pines, S. and Yovel, Y. (eds) (1986) *Maimonides and Philosophy* (Dordrecht).
Rosenthal, E. (1960) *Griechisches Erbe in der jüdischen Religionsphilosophie des Mittelalters* (Stuttgart).

CHAPTER 39

Jewish philosophy in the Islamic world

Arthur Hyman

Jewish philosophy is customarily divided into three periods: Hellenistic (second century B.C.E. to middle of first century C.E.), medieval, and modern (from the eighteenth century on). Of these, the medieval, which is the subject of the present chapter, has been, so far, the most productive and extensive, spanning some six hundred years.

Generally speaking, medieval Jewish philosophy may be described as the explication of Jewish beliefs and practices by means of philosophic concepts and norms. However, a more refined analysis discloses that it is divisible into three parts. As an interpretation of indigenous Jewish tradition, Jewish philosophy manifests an interest in such topics as the election of Israel, the uniqueness of the prophecy of Moses, the Torah (Law) and its eternity, and the Messiah and the afterlife. In the pursuit of these interests it is sharply distinguished from Islamic and Christian philosophy. As religious philosophy it investigates notions common to Judaism, Islam and Christianity, such as the existence of God, divine attributes, creation, providence, prophecy and general principles of human conduct. Finally, as philosophy, it investigates topics of a purely philosophic nature, such as the meaning of terms, types of logical arguments, the division of being and the structure of the world. In the light of these varied interests, medieval Jewish philosophy must be seen as part of the history of philosophy at large no less than as an interpretation of the biblical–rabbinic tradition on which Judaism rests.

Medieval Jewish philosophy began in the early tenth century as part of a general cultural revival in the Islamic East and continued in Muslim countries – North Africa, Spain and Egypt – for some three hundred years. The Jews of this period spoke, read and wrote Arabic and this enabled them to participate in the general culture of their day. Although

Jews produced a rich literature on biblical and rabbinic subjects and much religious and secular poetry, they did not produce an extensive literature on purely scientific and philosophic topics. The reason was quite simple. Knowing Arabic, they had access to the scientific and philosophic literature in that language and this was adequate for their needs. Their major speculative efforts during this period were devoted to works investigating the relation of Jewish tradition to philosophic thought. Most of the philosophic works that they produced were written in Arabic.

This cultural situation is well described by Moses Maimonides (1138–1204) when in his *Guide of the Perplexed* he writes:

> Know that my purpose in this Treatise of mine [the *Guide of the Perplexed*] was not to compose something in the natural sciences, or to make an epitome of notions pertaining to the divine science [metaphysics] according to some doctrine, or to demonstrate what has been demonstrated in them. . . . For the books composed concerning these matters are adequate. If, however, they should not turn out to be adequate with regard to some subject, that which I shall say concerning that subject will not be superior to everything else that has been said about it.
>
> (*Guide of the Perplexed*, 2:2, Pines translation)

From Maimonides' description, it should, however, not be inferred that medieval Jewish philosophy was a branch of Islamic philosophy. For just as Muslim philosophers made use of the works of their Greek and Hellenistic predecessors (which they had in Arabic translations), adapting them to their needs, so Jewish philosophers made use of the same works together with philosophic works of Muslims, adapting them to theirs.

Towards the end of the twelfth century the geographic and, with it, the cultural setting of Jewish philosophy began to change. The Jewish communities in the Islamic world declined and communities hospitable to scientific and philosophic learning developed in Christian lands – Christian Spain, southern France and Italy. As a result of these changes, Arabic was gradually forgotten among Jews and since, with the notable exception of Italy, they had little occasion to learn Latin, they turned to Hebrew as the language of their scientific and philosophic works. Hence, whereas in Muslim countries they participated in the mainstream of the general culture, in Christian lands they had to foster a general philosophic and scientific literature of their own. Jews continued to write works probing the relation of Jewish tradition to philosophic thought, but they now also produced an extensive literature devoted to such purely philosophic fields as logic, physics, metaphysics, ethics and politics. As a first step they translated from Arabic into Hebrew the works of such Jewish philosophers as Saadiah Gaon, Judah Halevi, Baḥyā ibn Paqudah, Abraham ibn Daud and Maimonides (for these see below) together with much of the Arabic philosophic literature of the previous period, especially the works of the Aristotelian commentator, Averroes (Ibn Rushd) (1126–98). Once this literature became available in Hebrew, Jewish philosophers commented on it, summarized it in compendia and encyclopedias, and composed their own independent treatises and books. Since Jewish philosophy of this period was so heavily indebted to the thought of the previous period, it is appropriate to include it in the present chapter. In a seminal monograph, Shlomo Pines has argued plausibly that there are indications that Christian scholastic philosophy influenced some Jewish philosophers of this period, but by and large Jewish philosophy was a continuation of the philosophy which flourished in the Islamic world. The second period of medieval Jewish philosophy lasted until the early sixteenth century.

As Islamic philosophers, so Jewish philosophers may be classified under four headings: *mutakallimūn*, Neoplatonists, Aristotelians of various kinds, and critics of Aristotelian philosophy. However, this modern classification does not imply doctrinal uniformity among the adherents of each group. While the members of each group shared a certain approach to philosophy, a certain literature and a certain stock of basic ideas, each philosopher developed his philosophy in his own way.

MU'TAZILITE *KALĀM*

Mu'tazilite *kalām* arose in the Islamic world as the result of certain issues posed by the Qur'ān, the primary ones being the "Unity of God" and "Divine Justice". The first of these arose from the observation that the Qur'ān teaches that God is one, at the same time describing him by means of many attributes; the second from the observation that God seems to be the cause of everything in the world, including human actions, yet punishes humans for the wrong they do. To solve the first problem, Mu'tazilites set out to show that a multiplicity of attributes can be predicated of God without violating his unity; to solve the second they held that God, though omnipotent, gave human beings free choice, thereby making them responsible for their own actions. Since the Mu'tazilites were primarily interested in solving scriptural problems, rather than developing an independent philosophy, their works had an eclectic complexion; that is, they used arguments from a variety of philosophic sources. Ash'arite *kalām* was known to Jewish philosophers and is cited by them, but there is no evidence that there were Jewish Ash'arites.

The first major Jewish philosopher of the Middle Ages is generally held to be Saadiah Gaon (882–942), head of the rabbinical academy of Sura (near Baghdad). Influenced by the Mu'tazilites, but also using Platonic, Aristotelian and Stoic notions, he undertook to formulate a

Jewish *kalām*. He presents his opinions in his commentary on the Bible, his commentary on *Sefer Yeẓirah* ("Book of Creation"), but his main work is the *Book of Opinions and Beliefs*. Observing that many of his contemporaries had been beset by doubts, Saadiah begins by presenting arguments against their sceptical views and by analysing how trustworthy belief may be obtained. In typical Mu'tazilite fashion, Saadiah begins the book proper (treatise 1) with four proofs for the creation of the world: from the finiteness of the world, from its composition, from accidents, and from the nature of time (there are others in his other works). Typical of these proofs is that from the finiteness of the world. The finite dimension of the universe, this argument goes, requires a finite force preserving it and everything possessing a finite force must have a beginning in time. From these proofs for creation Saadiah argues that there must be a creator who is distinct from the world and who made it out of nothing. It is characteristic of Saadiah's method that he refutes opinions with which he disagrees, so that, as part of his discussion of creation, he presents arguments against twelve divergent cosmogonic and sceptical theories.

From proofs of creation which are also proofs of the existence of God, Saadiah proceeds to a discussion of divine attributes (treatise 2). Having demonstrated the unity of God, he sets out to show that the multiplicity of attributes predicated of God does not interfere with the divine unity. These attributes only serve to explicate the divine nature; they do not suggest that any multiplicity exists in God. God must be described by many attributes because human language does not have one word describing all of them. As part of his critique of divergent views, Saadiah argues against dualistic and trinitarian conceptions of God.

Saadiah next turns to philosophy of law and the related problem of prophecy (treatise 3). God, in his kindness, provided his creatures with a law, the Torah, which guides them to earthly happiness and eternal bliss. This law contains commandments of two kinds: rational laws, such as gratitude towards a benefactor and prohibitions against murder and theft, which are intuitively self-evident to human reason, and traditional commandments, such as the Sabbath, festivals and dietary regulations, which are the result of the divine will as communicated through revelation. Being general, the rational commandments require the more particular, traditional commandments for their implementation. The promulgation of the traditional commandments is the main function of prophets. The prophecy of Moses is distinguished by its reasonableness rather than its revelational character. The Torah is unchanging and cannot be abrogated.

To solve the problem of "divine justice", Saadiah affirms the existence of free choice (treatise 4). If people are the cause of their own actions, God is just in punishing them. Saadiah offers two arguments in support of human free choice: human beings experience themselves to be free and there is no evidence that their acts are compelled; holding people responsible for their acts requires them to be free. God's foreknowledge is compatible with human freedom, for to foreknow what a human being will do is distinct from being the cause of the action. Adopting Islamic models once more, Saadiah (treatise 5) provides a classification of different kinds of righteous and wicked men. One such is the penitent who accomplishes penitence in four steps: renunciation of sin, remorse, the quest for forgiveness and accepting the obligation not to sin again. To explain the suffering of the righteous, Saadiah invokes the doctrine of "sufferings of love" according to which suffering in this world will be rewarded in the World to Come.

The human soul originates when the body is formed and its origin is in the heart. Its substance is akin to that of the celestial sphere. The latter section of the *Book of Opinions and Beliefs* is devoted to eschatological themes, and Saadiah's discussion is based on traditional Jewish sources. He accepts the doctrine of the resurrection of the body and offers a number of arguments in its support (treatise 7). The resurrection will occur after Israel has been redeemed. The redemption may take place in one of two ways (treatise 8): if the Jews will repent, the Messiah will appear immediately; if not, the Messiah will come at an appointed time. A descendant of the house of David, the Messiah will usher in a time when Israel will return to its land and the Temple will be rebuilt. As part of his discussion, Saadiah argues against Christian messianic claims. In the World to Come the righteous will be rewarded and the wicked will be punished (treatise 9). In the World to Come the soul and body will remain together, and life in that world is eternal. Saadiah completes his book with an appendix (treatise 10) describing how human beings should conduct themselves in this world.

While Saadiah was to remain the major Jewish proponent of Mu'tazilite *kalām*, other Jewish philosophers made use of Mu'tazilite teachings. In Rabbanite circles Mu'tazilite influences are found until the second half of the twelfth century when Aristotelianism became the dominant trend. Among the Karaites (those who accepted the Bible but not the teachings of the rabbis), Mu'tazilite *kalām* remained the dominant trend throughout the Middle Ages. Among the Karaites Aaron ben Elijah of Nicomedia is the outstanding thinker. His *Tree of Life* (1346) is a kind of *kalām* critique of Maimonides' *Guide of the Perplexed.* Aaron held that kalāmic doctrines are in accord with biblical teachings, while Aristotelianism, pagan in origin, conflicts with biblical teachings on many points.

NEOPLATONISM

There is little direct evidence of the sources which Jewish Neoplatonists used, but the presumptive evidence indicates that, like the Muslims, they made use of such collections as *Theology of Aristotle*, a work that came to be known as *Liber de causis*, and *The Greek Sage*. In their conception of God they emphasized the transcendence of God, holding that he is best described by negative attributes. They used the doctrine of emanation to explain the origin of the world, but they disagreed on whether emanation was necessary or whether it was dependent on the divine will. They also disagreed on the nature and number of spiritual, hypostatic substances existing between God and the perceptible world. In their philosophy of man, they emphasized that the good life requires control of the appetites and philosophic speculation and that the return (ascent) of the soul to the upper world from which it came is the ultimate goal of human life. Apart from the writings mentioned, Neoplatonic doctrines also reached Jewish philosophers through the writings of such Muslims as al-Fārābī and, especially, Avicenna (Ibn Sīnā).

The origin of Neoplatonism in Jewish circles was contemporaneous with that of Muʿtazilite *kalām*. The first Jewish Neoplatonist was the Kairouan physician Isaac b. Solomon Israeli (*c.* 855–*c.* 955). Influenced by al-Kindī and Neoplatonic collections that circulated in the Islamic world, Israeli was the author of *Book of Definitions*, *Book on Spirit and Soul*, *Chapter on the Elements* and *Book on the Elements* as well as of a number of medical works. Combining biblical and philosophic notions, Israeli holds that God, the Creator, in his goodness and love, created the world in time and out of nothing. The means of creation were his power and will, which are attributes of God not separate hypostases. Two simple substances, first matter and first form (or wisdom), come directly from God and these combine to form the next hypostasis – intellect. Three distinct hypostases of soul – rational, animal and vegetative – follow and then nature, which Israeli identifies with the sphere of the heavens. The four elements are produced from the motion of this sphere. Israeli distinguishes three stages in the creation of the world: creation which produces first matter, first form and intellect; emanation which produces the four spiritual substances; and causality of nature which produces the world below the heavens. Israeli's philosophy of humanity is based on the typical Neoplatonic notion of the soul's return to the upper world from which it came. There are three stages in this process: purification accomplished by turning away from appetites and passions; illumination which produces wisdom consisting of the knowledge of eternal things; and union with or adherence to supernal wisdom (not God). Israeli sees no sharp distinction between the prophet and the philosopher; both are concerned with the ascent of the soul and with guiding mankind towards truth and justice.

Solomon ibn Gabirol (*c.* 1021–57) was the most important of the Jewish Neoplatonists. With him the setting of Jewish philosophy shifted to Spain. An important Hebrew poet, Ibn Gabirol presented his philosophy in *Source of Life*, *Improvement of Moral Qualities* and in a liturgical poem, "The Royal Crown" or "The Crown of the Kingdom" (see Chapter 41). Divided into five treatises, *Source of Life* deals largely with different aspects of the principles of matter and form, though incidentally it also reveals other parts of Ibn Gabirol's thought. The work was influenced by Neoplatonic as well as pseudo-Empedoclean writings. With the Neoplatonists Ibn Gabirol affirms the absolute transcendence of God stating that he can only be known through negations. To explain the origin of the universe, he turns to the theory of emanation, but there is a slight difference between his descriptions in the *Source of Life* and in "The Royal Crown". According to the former work, from God, called First Substance, emanates the divine will or wisdom (*logos*); according to the latter, wisdom and will are successive, distinct emanations. Then follow universal matter and universal form and, next, three spiritual substances – intellect, soul and nature – and, finally, the perceptible world. There is some ambiguity about Ibn Gabirol's understanding of emanation: there are passages in which he seems to incline towards a voluntaristic interpretation, but there are others in which he seems to hold that emanation occurs by necessity. One of Ibn Gabirol's characteristic doctrines is the notion that all beings other than God, including spiritual beings, are composed of matter and form. In his philosophy of humanity, he describes as the goal of human life the ascent of the soul to the upper sphere which is accomplished through proper conduct and philosophic speculation. In his *Improvement of Moral Qualities* he discusses twenty moral qualities – four for each of the five senses – and tries to relate them to the four humours of the human body. In its Latin translation *Source of Life* was known to Christian Scholastics and extensively discussed by them. Ibn Gabirol's ideas also influence Jewish mystical (kabbalistic) thought.

The end of the eleventh century and the twelfth century saw a number of philosophers strongly influenced by Neoplatonic ideas but who also made use of other traditions. Baḥyā ibn Paqudah is the author of *Guide to the Duties of the Heart*, a devotional manual, which achieved great popularity among Jews. In addition to Neoplatonic ideas, Baḥyā accepts notions from *kalām*, hermetic (gnostic) writings, Sufi literature, and he readily quotes sayings and stories from Jewish and Islamic sources. The work rests on a distinction between "duties of the limbs", religious commandments that require overt actions, and "duties of the heart", religious commandments requiring beliefs and attitudes. Each of the ten treatises of the work is devoted to a belief or attitude, beginning with God's unity and culminating in the love of God. The soul is a simple spiritual substance which God implanted in the body, but which wants to free itself from the desires and pains of the body in order to attain a spiritual state, described as cleaving to his (God's) upper light. A work attributed to Baḥyā, but not by him, is *On the Nature of the Soul* which, influenced by Neoplatonic and hermetic teachings, describes the origin of the world by emanation and the nature of the soul. The soul is a spiritual substance coming from the upper world to which it wants to return. Return to that world is accomplished by practising the moral virtues and by acquiring knowledge.

Abraham bar Ḥiyyah (first half of the twelfth century), a mathematician, astronomer and philosopher, was the first to write philosophic works in Hebrew. Combining Neoplatonic and Aristotelian notions, he expresses his philosophic ideas in *Meditation of the Sad Soul* and *Scroll of the Revealer*. Abraham subscribes to the theory of emanation but, unlike earlier Neoplatonists, he interposes worlds of light and dominion between God and the three spiritual substances. With Aristotle he affirms that matter and form exist only in the corporeal world, not in simple substances. He has a special interest in the fate of the soul after death, and in his *Scroll of the Revealer* he develops a theory of history.

Other twelfth-century Jewish philosophers who manifest Neoplatonic influences in varying degrees include Joseph ibn Ẓaddik, author of *Book of the Microcosm*, a work apparently written as a handbook for beginners. Like Ibn Gabirol he affirms that spiritual beings are composed of matter and form, though he defines matter as the genus of a species rather than as a distinct principle. He mentions the divine will, which seems to be an aspect of God rather than a distinct hypostasis. Moses ibn Ezra, distinguished mainly as a poet and critic, employs the notion of microcosm–macrocosm, affirming that everything in the upper world has its counterpart in humanity. Abraham ibn Ezra, grammarian, author of works on arithmetic and astronomy and biblical commentator, presents his opinions in somewhat enigmatic fashion. His formulations have sometimes a pantheistic ring: "God is One; He made all and He is all." He also holds that everything other than God is composed of matter and form. In speaking of creation, he affirms that the world of intelligences, the angels and the celestial sphere are co-eternal with God; only the lower world was created through emanation.

CRITIQUE OF ARISTOTELIANISM

Judah Halevi (before 1075–1141), one of the important Hebrew poets of the Middle Ages, was the author of *The Book of Argument and Proof in Defence of the Despised Faith*, popularly known as the *Book of the Khazar* (Kuzari). Like al-Ghazzālī, with whom he seems to have shared a common source, he is critical of Aristotelian rationalism, but differs from al-Ghazzālī in that he does not present a point-by-point refutation of the claims of the philosophers. The Aristotelian philosophers, Halevi argues, have been unable to make good their claim that there are physical and metaphysical truths that can be known with certainty. By contrast, he affirms that historical experience is the source of truth and religious practices are more important than beliefs and dogmas. Halevi's book takes the form of a dialogue between a Jewish scholar and the King of the Khazars who had been converted to Judaism and it is largely an exposition and defence of Jewish beliefs and practices.

God, according to Halevi, is not the God of the philosophers who is known through philosophic demonstrations but the God of Abraham, Isaac and Jacob, who is known through miracles and revelation. Only a religion based on the experience of God's manifestation in historical events is a religion which is certain and free of doubt (*Kuzari* 1.29). Closely related to his conception of God is Halevi's account of prophecy and the nature of the Jewish people. Unlike the Neoplatonists and Aristotelians, who described prophecy largely as an activity of the rational faculty, or of the rational and imaginative faculty combined, Halevi views prophecy as the activity of a distinct faculty beyond the natural human faculties (1.31–4). Adam was created with this faculty, which was transmitted by heredity first to such individuals as Noah, Abraham, Isaac and Jacob, then to the twelve sons of Jacob and finally to the Jewish people as a whole (1.95). Possession of the prophetic faculty is the distinguishing characteristic of the Jewish people. While prophecy is primarily a gift of God, it can be obtained only in the land of Israel (or it must at least be about the land of Israel) and only someone who observes the divine commandments can be a prophet (2.8–14).

In his description of human conduct, Halevi emphasizes the centrality of piety. It is not philosophic speculation that leads to closeness to God, the goal of human life, but adherence to the divine commandments. Halevi accepts the *kalām* distinction between rational and traditional commandments, but the former have only a preliminary function, while the latter are the correct guidance for the good life (2.45–8). Servants of God are like rulers; they apportion to each part of the soul and body its due (3.1ff.) Halevi advocates moderation, but not asceticism: people's joy on the Sabbath and festivals is no less pleasing to God than their affliction on fast days (2.50).

Ḥibat Allāh Abu'l-Barakāt al-Baghdādī, the author of a commentary on Ecclesiastes and of a philosophic work, subjected Aristotelian philosophy to a critical investigation and presents novel notions on physical, psychological and metaphysical topics. Nethanel al-Fayyumī (d. *c.* 1165) undertook to introduce Ismā'īlī doctrines into Jewish thought in his *Garden of the Intellects.*

ARISTOTELIANISM

Aristotelianism, as a major movement in medieval Jewish philosophy, developed in the second half of the twelfth century. It was marked by a systematic conception of philosophy and its adherents held that philosophy should be pursued on its own grounds first, and only after philosophic opinions had been established independently should their relation to religious teachings and practices be investigated.

Aristotelianism rested on the works of Aristotle and his Hellenistic commentators. Philosophy was formally divided into theoretical and practical philosophy, the former consisting of physics, mathematics and metaphysics, the latter of ethics, economics and politics. Logic was preliminary to the study of philosophy. The medieval Aristotelians shared the analysis of such notions as terms, propositions and arguments in logic; matter and form, motion, place, time, the prime mover in physics; senses, imagination and intellect in psychology; division of being, incorporeal substances in metaphysics; the virtues and human happiness in ethics. Their political philosophy was based on Plato's *Republic* and *Laws*, which yielded such notions as a state consisting of different classes and the philosopher-king (who became identified with the prophet) as the founder of the ideal state. In spite of this common ground and particularly under the influence of commentators, a number of these notions were interpreted in different ways. Generally speaking, Aristotelianism is divisible into a more theological interpretation exemplified by Avicenna and a more naturalistic interpretation exemplified by Averroes.

While medieval Jewish philosophy contained Aristotelian elements from its beginnings, Aristotelianism as a more formal philosophic stance is generally said to begin with Abraham ibn Daud (*c.* 1110–80) a philosopher influenced by al-Fārābī, Avicenna and Avempace (Ibn Bājjah). His major philosophic work, the *Sublime Faith*, written to explain the doctrine of free will, is, in fact, a work on a variety of philosophic and theological topics. Strongly influenced by Avicenna, the work is critical of Ibn Gabirol. Ibn Daud begins by affirming that Judaism and philosophy are identical in their essence and goes on to explain certain Aristotelian metaphysical, physical and psychological notions. To strengthen his thesis of the identity of Judaism and philosophy, he cites biblical verses which, in his opinion, allude to these notions (treatise 1). From an explanation of these notions, he proceeds to use them for a discussion of six topics: existence of God, his unity, divine attributes, God's actions (including creation), prophecy and the allegorical interpretation of terms comparing God to creatures (treatise 2). The work concludes with a brief discussion of ethical matters (treatise 3). To prove the existence of God, Ibn Daud uses the Aristotelian proof from motion as well as the Avicennian proof from necessity and contingency. The divine attributes cannot have any positive signification, but must be understood as negations or relations. With Aristotle he holds that every change requires an underlying matter, but he also maintains that God created prime matter out of which he then created the world. To explain creation he invokes the doctrine of emanation, holding at the same time that emanation occurs by the free will of God, not by necessity. In psychology he accepts the Avicennian opinion that the human soul is a substance and it is this substance that can become immortal. Like Judah Halevi, he restricts prophecy to the Jewish people and the land of Israel. To safeguard human free choice, he is ready to admit that God's knowledge is limited.

Moses Maimonides (1138–1204), renowned physician and outstanding halakhist (legal scholar), was the most prominent figure in medieval Jewish philosophy. Distinguishing between the masses whose understanding rests on the imagination and an intellectual elite who understand by means of the intellect, he presents some of his ideas in popular fashion in his legal writings, the Commentary on the *Mishnah*, *Mishneh Torah*, and in some treatises, but his technical exposition is reserved for his *Guide of the Perplexed*. In formulating his views he drew upon the works of Aristotle and his Hellenistic commentators and upon the writings of Muslims such as al-Fārābī, Avicenna and Avempace.

Maimonides wrote his *Guide* for a student, Joseph ben Judah, a believing Jew, who, having studied philosophy, had become perplexed by the literal meaning of biblical anthropomorphic and anthropopathic terms predicated of God and by parables appearing in the Bible. To this student Maimonides shows that his perplexities can be resolved by correct interpretation of the vexing terms and parables. The Bible, Maimonides argues, has an exoteric meaning available to everyone and an esoteric meaning reserved for an intellectual elite. The esoteric meaning is described by him as "the science of the Law in its true sense" or the "Secrets of the Law".

Maimonides applies the distinction between exoteric and esoteric teaching to the *Guide*, informing his reader that he will use contradictions to hide his true views from the masses. This imposed on his work an enigmatic style which has puzzled medieval as well as modern commentators. There were those who interpreted Maimonides as a naturalistic Aristotelian, while there were others who saw him as a harmonistically inclined philosopher who tried to create a synthesis between religion and philosophy. Thus, for example, according to the naturalists he believed in the eternity of the world, while according to the harmonists he believed in its creation by the divine will.

In accordance with his exegetical programme, Maimonides begins his *Guide* with an interpretation of biblical terms, showing that even such terms as "to sit" and "to stand", when applied to God, can have a spiritual sense (*Guide*, 1:1–49). From exegesis, he proceeds to a technical exposition of divine attributes (1:50–60). Invoking the distinction between essential attributes, such as existence, life and wisdom, and accidental attributes, such as anger and mercy, he affirms that the former when predicated of God must be interpreted as negations, the latter as attributes of action.

Before presenting his own discussion of the existence of God, his unity and incorporeality, and of the creation of the world, Maimonides offers a summary and critique of the kalāmic discussion of these four topics (1:71–6). The thrust of his critique is that the kalāmic proofs are false because they are based on categories of the imagination rather than on those of the intellect. He prefaces his own proofs with a series of Aristotelian propositions which in his opinion had been demonstrated by the philosophers (2:Introduction). On the basis of these he formulates four proofs for the existence of God: from motion, from the composition of elements, from necessity and contingency, and from potentiality and actuality (causality). All these proofs start with some observable property of the world and argue, respectively, to the existence of a prime mover, a necessarily existent, a first cause – all identified with God. These proofs of the existence of God lead, in turn, to proofs of his unity and incorporeality (2.1).

Maimonides next discusses the incorporeal intelligences which he identifies with the angels mentioned in the Bible, and, after that, the celestial spheres (2:2–12). Creation of the world is the next major topic (2:13–26). Reviewing at length Aristotelian arguments for the eternity of world, Maimonides asserts that they are not conclusive demonstrations but only dialectical arguments designed to show that the eternity of the world is more plausible than its creation. Agreeing that the question whether the world is eternal or created has only a dialectical solution, Maimonides goes on to argue that creation is the more plausible alternative. His main support comes from a certain disorder in the hierarchy of the celestial spheres and in their motions which, in his opinion, point to creation by the divine will. He finds additional support for this opinion in scriptural teachings. While the world has a beginning in time, it does not have a temporal end (2:27–9).

In his Introduction to the *Guide* Maimonides incidentally discusses the prophetic experience, likening it to intellectual illumination, but in his more formal presentation he is interested in the psychological processes of the prophet and in his political function (2.2–48). The attainment of prophecy is a natural function; God's role is limited to keeping someone who is qualified from becoming a prophet. To become a prophet requires, in addition to moral virtues, a well-developed intellect and a well-developed imagination. While Maimonides has, generally, a low opinion of the value of the imagination, prophets require it in their political role, namely, to communicate with the masses. Moses' prophecy is distinguished from that of the other prophets, one distinguishing factor being that Moses brought the Torah, while the other prophets only admonished the people to observe its precepts. The Torah is distinguished from the laws of other nations in that it leads not only to moral but also to intellectual perfection. Maimonides concludes the portion of the *Guide* devoted to physical and metaphysical topics with an interpretation of the divine chariot described in chapters 1 and 10 of the book of Ezekiel (3:1–7).

Proceeding to practical (moral) philosophy, Maimonides discusses the problem of evil, defining it, in Neoplatonic fashion, as the absence or privation of good. There is more good than evil in the world. Of the three kinds of evil – natural, political and moral – the latter two can be controlled by human beings (3.8–12). From the problem of evil, Maimonides turns to providence. He rejects the opinions of the Epicureans that everything is due to chance, of the Aristotelians that there is no individual providence, of the Ash'arites that there is only individual providence, and of the Mu'tazilites that individual providence extends even to animals. His own view, which he identifies with the opinion of the Torah, is that individual providence extends only to human beings and is commensurate with the development of the human intellect. He rejects the doctrine of "sufferings of love" according to which God may afflict human beings in this world in order to reward them in the next. He applies his discussion of providence to the interpretation of the book of Job (3.22–4).

Maimonides rejects the Mu'tazilites' distinction between "rational commandments", based on reason, and "traditional commandments", based on the divine will, maintaining that all the commandments of the Torah are derived from the wisdom of God. Judgments are distinguished from statutes in that the former are easily accessible to human reason, the latter only with difficulty. The Torah has a twofold purpose: well-being of the soul (intellect) and well-being of the body, which consists of the acquisition of the moral and political virtues. Reasons for the moral and political laws can easily be found, but reasons for the many ritual laws are more difficult to discover. Maimonides explains many of them as reactions to pagan practices (3: 25–50). Maimonides concludes the *Guide* with a discussion of the perfect worship of God and human perfection (3: 51–4).

Virtually absent from the *Guide*, eschatological themes are discussed by Maimonides in his legal works and in separate treatises. The Messiah, a descendant of the house of David, is an earthly king who will bring the Jews back their land, but whose main task will be to bring peace to the world. The Messiah will die of old age and will be succeeded by his descendants. No cataclysmic event will occur in Messianic times, but the world will continue in its established order. Maimonides accepts the resurrection of the dead as an article of faith, but he also holds that those resurrected will die again. The final goal is the World to Come, a state in which the intellect exists without a body and is engaged in the contemplation of God. Important for the subsequent development of Jewish philosophy are Maimonides' "Thirteen Principles", an attempt to formulate an official creed which all Jews must accept.

Maimonides' rationalistic interpretation engendered controversies between his followers and their opponents which lasted throughout the thirteenth and early fourteenth centuries. One of the highlights of these controversies was the ban of Rabbi Solomon ibn Adret, issued in 1305, which prohibited the study of physics and metaphysics before the age of twenty-five. The early thirteenth century saw still some philosophers active in the Islamic world. Among these was Maimonides' son Abraham (1186–1237), who defended the teachings of his father against opponents and who also advocated a Sufi-like Jewish pietism.

The philosophic climate from the thirteenth until the sixteenth century was determined by Maimonides' *Guide* on the one hand and the numerous writings of Averroes (which had been translated into Hebrew) on the other. Under the influence of Averroes, some Jewish philosophers turned towards a more extreme rationalism, while there were others who defended harmonistic positions of various kinds. There were also philosophers who attempted to harmonize the opinions of Maimonides and Averroes on issues on which these two philosophers differed.

During the thirteenth and the early fourteenth century there arose a number of philosophers who continued the work of the previous period. Samuel ibn Tibbon, member of a family of translators, translated Maimonides' *Guide* into Hebrew and wrote a number of works of his own. He favoured the allegorical interpretation of the Bible and is said to have held that the Bible was written for the masses. Jacob Anatoli, active at the court of Frederick II, wrote a philosophic commentary on the Bible in which he shows acquaintance with Christian literature and institutions. He favoured the allegorical interpretation of the Bible and preached philosophic sermons publicly, which earned him the anger of the anti-Maimonideans. Shem Tob ben Joseph Falaqera, author of works on ethics and psychology, wrote a commentary on the *Guide* in which he cites parallel passages from the works of Islamic philosophers, particularly Averroes. Joseph ibn Caspi, author of biblical commentaries, lexicographic works and works on philosophy, wrote a commentary on the *Guide* consisting of an exoteric and an esoteric part. He accepts doctrines associated with those of Averroes, such as the identity of religion and philosophy, the eternity of the world and the naturalistic interpretation of miracles, but he tries to modify these doctrines in a way that distinguishes him from extreme rationalists.

Hillel ben Samuel (*c.* 1220–95), one of the first Jewish philosophers active in Italy, translated the Neoplatonic work *Liber de causis* from Latin into Hebrew and was the author of *The Rewards of the Soul.* Since he knew Latin, he could draw on the opinions of Christian scholastics. Following the Neoplatonists and Avicenna, he maintains that the soul is an individual substance emanating through the intermediacy of the supernal soul. Using arguments formulated by Aquinas he argues against the Averroean notion that there is only one material or potential intellect for all humans. According to Hillel, each person has his or her own material intellect. He agrees with Muslim and Jewish philosophers that the Active Intellect is the lowest of the celestial intellects. According to Hillel, only the rational part of the soul is immortal and its ultimate happiness consists in union with the Active Intellect. In its immortal state the intellect retains its individuality.

Isaac Albalag (second half of thirteenth century) translated al-Ghazzālī's *Intentions of the Philosophers* into Hebrew and presented his own views in a commentary entitled *Correction of the Intentions.* A follower of Averroes, who accepted such doctrines as the eternity of the world, he has been said to hold that there are two coexistent truths, philosophic and prophetic, which can contradict one another. However, he does not cite any instance of such contradictions. His outlook is not completely clear, but it seems to have maintained that speculative truths are the province of philosophy, moral and political guidance of the masses, the province of the Torah.

During the first half of the fourteenth century there arose a debate concerning the freedom of the human will. Abner of Burgos, who in the end converted to Christianity, followed Avicenna in holding that human acts no less than natural occurrences are causally determined. The human will has the ability to choose, but its choices are determined. The divine commandments are among the causes determining the will. Causal determination of the will is also required to safeguard God's omniscience and omnipotence; were human actions undetermined, God could not foreknow them and his power would be limited. Isaac Polgar attacked Abner's determinism, holding that there is a correlation between the human and divine wills such that at the moment that a person wills to do a certain act, God also wills that it should be accomplished. In willing that the act be accomplished, God also knows it. Though this knowledge begins in time, it does not introduce any change in God. Whatever the difficulty of this position, it is clear that Isaac defends the freedom of the will by limiting God's foreknowledge. Moses ben Joshua of Narbonne was another participant in this debate. He criticizes Abner, but his position is not too clear. In some passages he seems to agree with Maimonides that God's knowledge extends to particular human acts without determining them, while in other passages he maintains that God's knowledge extends only to the species not to individuals, thereby safeguarding human freedom. He wrote commentaries on works by Averroes, al-Ghazzālī and other Muslim philosophers and also a commentary on the *Guide*. He criticizes Maimonides on certain issues, embracing the stricter Aristotelianism of Averroes.

Levi ben Gerson (1288–1344), known as Gersonides, mathematician, astronomer and biblical commentator, wrote supercommentaries on a number of Averroes' commentaries on Aristotle and was the author of a philosophic work, *Book of the Wars of the Lord.* Influenced by Averroes, but at times critical of him, Levi discusses topics which, in his opinion, Maimonides had not discussed sufficiently or had explained incorrectly. In the six chapters of his work, Levi discusses immortality, prediction of the future, God's knowledge of individual contingent beings, providence, the celestial bodies, their movers, God, and the creation of the world.

Levi begins his discussion of immortality with an extensive review and critique of various theories concerning the intellect. The Aristotelian philosophers had distinguished between the material or passive intellect, the active intellect and the acquired intellect, but they differed in their conception of these various intellects. Levi rejects the opinions of Themistius and Averroes concerning the passive intellect and accepts an opinion close to that of Alexander of Aphrodisias. The passive intellect is a predisposition inhering in the sensitive soul and comes into existence with each individual human being. Under the influence of the Active Intellect, the lowest of the celestial intelligences, the passive intellect is actualized and becomes the acquired intellect. The passive intellect dies with the body, but the acquired intellect is immortal. Levi holds that the acquired intellect is individual, differing thereby from Averroes for whom it is collective.

Prediction of the future was accepted by Levi as a scientific fact which he undertakes to explain (treatise 2). Terrestrial events, he holds, are caused by the celestial spheres and, since they are thus determined, they can be predicted. However, Levi is not a complete determinist. Holding that human beings are free, he also maintains that those who understand the laws of the celestial bodies can avoid their evil influences. In persons of the well-developed intellect, knowledge of the future results in prophecy, while in those having a well-developed imagination it results in divination and true dreams.

Taking issue with Maimonides, who held that God knows particular contingent beings, Levi maintains that God knows only the orderly processes of nature not individuals. However, he rejects the notion that God's providence extends only to the species or that it extends equally to everyone; it extends only to those human beings who have a well-developed intellect. He agrees with Maimonides that the more a person develops the intellect, the more is he or she subject to divine providence.

Levi also differs from Maimonides in his account of divine attributes (treatise 5.2, 12 and 3.5). Following Averroes, he maintained that they can have positive signification. He held that such essential attributes as existence, life, knowledge have the same meaning when applied to God and man, though they are applied to God primarily and to creatures derivatively.

Levi agrees with Maimonides that Aristotle's arguments for the eternity of the world are not decisive proofs, but they are the best offered so far. However, against Aristotle, Levi offers a number of arguments designed to show that the world was created. He differs from Maimonides and most other Jewish philosophers in holding that the world was created out of a formless matter coexistent with God, thereby denying creation *ex nihilo*. However, this matter is not a principle paralleling God. Levi also rejects the Neoplatonic theory of emanation. Levi concludes his book with a discussion of miracles and prophecy, which is generally rationalistic in temper.

Of Jewish anti-Aristotelians, Ḥasdai Crescas (d. 1412) was the most significant. Critical of a number of Aristotelian notions, he presents reasoned arguments against them, replacing the rejected notions with notions of his own. In his conception of Judaism, he emphasizes observance of the commandment and love of God rather than intellectual accomplishments. He presents his ideas in his *Light of the Lord.*

As has been noted, Maimonides formulated thirteen basic principles which, in his opinion, every Jew was obligated to believe. This Maimonidean demand gave rise to a debate lasting the remainder of the Middle Ages and beyond concerning whether there are obligatory beliefs and, if so, whether Maimonides' enumeration is authoritative. Crescas uses the Maimonidean notion of basic principles as the framework of his work, though his enumeration and content differs from that of Maimonides. According to Crescas there are three basic principles of all religions – existence, unity and incorporeality of God (treatise 1). Next there are six principles required for a belief in the validity of the Torah – God's knowledge of existing things, providence, divine omnipotence, prophecy, human freedom and purpose in the Torah and in the world. Then there are eight true beliefs which every adherent of the Torah must accept – creation of the world, immortality of the soul, reward and punishment, resurrection of the dead, eternity of the Torah, superiority of the prophecy of Moses, efficacy of the Urim and Thummim (worn by the high priest) in predicting the future, and the coming of the Messiah (treatise 3). The book concludes with answers to thirteen questions.

Crescas' critique of Aristotle is found largely in his discussion of twenty-six physical and metaphysical propositions which appear at the beginning of the second part of Maimonides' *Guide*. Among the Aristotelian notions which Crescas criticizes are those of space, denial of the existence of a vacuum and of a universe that is finite and unitary. Against these notions Crescas argues for the existence of empty space, the existence of a vacuum, the existence of space beyond the world and that there can exist more than one world. He also differed from the Aristotelians in maintaining that an actual infinite can exist.

Crescas' affirmation that an actual infinite can exist put into question those proofs of the existence of God which depended on the impossibility of the existence of an actual infinite. However, the proof from necessity and contingency does not seem to rely on the disputed principle and so Crescas accepts it. Differing from Maimonides, Crescas maintains that positive attributes can be predicated of God.

God's knowledge, according to Crescas, extends to particulars: he knows the non-existent, and he knows future contingents without removing their contingent character. Crescas' conception of divine omniscience gives a deterministic character to his human philosophy: God's omniscience requires that everything he foreknows must come to pass. He tries to mitigate his deterministic stance by holding that the commandments, training and other factors are among the causes influencing the human will and that, despite being determined in one respect, the human will in its own nature is contingent.

After Crescas Jewish philosophy took on a more religious colouration and became more eclectic. Simeon ben Zemaḥ Duran followed the moderate rationalism of Maimonides, but, like Crescas, he maintained that attributes predicated of God can have a positive signification, that immortality comes through observing the divine commandments, and that divine providence extends to all men.

Joseph Albo (d. 1444) was the author of a book tellingly entitled *Book of Principles*. According to him there are three basic principles required for the existence of a divine law – existence of God, revelation, and reward and punishment. From these there follow eight derivative principles: God's unity, incorporeality, timelessness, and perfection; God's omniscience, prophecy, authentication of the prophet; and individual providence. Finally there are six branches: creation *ex nihilo*, superiority of the prophecy of Moses, immutability of the Torah, immortality through the observance of the commandments, resurrection of the dead and the coming of the Messiah. Divided into four parts, the *Book of Principles* begins with the general principles of laws, the three basic principles and how a genuine divine law can be distinguished from a spurious one. Each of the remaining three parts of the work is devoted to one of the three basic principles. Albo distinguishes among three kinds of law: natural, conventional and divine. Natural law is the same for all persons, times and places; conventional law is ordered by a wise one in accordance with reason; divine law is given by God through a prophet. Only divine law can lead one to true happiness and immortality.

The tension of the age is well illustrated by the Shem Tov family. Shem Tov ben Joseph ibn Shem Tov (*c.* 1380–1441) attacked not only such extreme rationalists as Albalag and Levi ben Gershom but also Maimonides himself. His son, Joseph ben Shem Tov (d. *c.* 1480) who greatly admired Aristotle and Maimonides, tried to rehabilitate philosophy by improving its rapport with religious orthodoxy. His son, Shem Tov ben Joseph ibn Shem Tov, continued his father's philosophical interests in a commentary on Maimonides' *Guide* in which he defends Maimonides against the attacks of Crescas. His contemporary Abraham Shalom also defended Maimonides against the attacks of Crescas. Isaac ben Moses Arama (1420–94) wrote a philosophic-homiletical commentary on the Pentateuch.

Isaac Abrabanel (1467–1508), a statesman, was the last philosopher active in Spain, but, as a result of the expulsion of the Jews from Spain in 1492, ended his life in Italy. Author of a commentary on the *Guide*, he admired Maimonides greatly, but, at the same time, he opposed his rationalistic interpretation of Judaism. Thus he held that prophecy was caused directly by God, not by the active intellect, and in a work devoted to Maimonides' Thirteen Principles he states that human happiness is attained only by adherence to the commandments of the Torah. Under the influence of Renaissance Platonism, his son Judah Abrabanel, also known as Leone Ebreo, (*c.* 1460–after 1523) wrote a general philosophic work entitled *Dialogues of Love*. Earlier, Judah ben Jehiel Messer Leon, an Italian Jew, had written a work on rhetoric in which he drew on Aristotle, Cicero and Quintillian. He also wrote on logic.

Elijah Delmedigo (*c.* 1460–97), who lectured at the University of Padua, translated works by Averroes from Hebrew into Latin and in his *Examination of Religion*, which was influenced by Averroes' *Decisive Treatise*, examines the relation of religion and philosophy. Joseph Delmedigo (1591–1655) still accepted some medieval notions, though he was critical of a number of them; but his philosophy was already heavily influenced by the new theories of Galileo.

BIBLIOGRAPHY

References to Maimonides are from:

The Guide of the Perplexed (Dalālat al-Ḥa'irīn), trans. S. Pines (Chicago, 1963).

See also:

Pines, S. (1967) "Scholasticism after Thomas Aquinas and the Teachings of Hasdai Crescas and his Predecessors", *Proceedings of the Israel Academy of Sciences and Humanities*, 1(10): 1–101.

CHAPTER 40

Saadiah Gaon al-Fayyumi

Lenn E. Goodman

Born in the Fayyum region of Egypt, Saadiah (882–942C.E.) was the first philosopher of Judaism to write systematic works. He was also a pioneering exegete, grammarian, lexicographer, liturgist and chronologist. Trained in Scripture and rabbinic law, he published the earliest version of his Hebrew–Arabic lexicon, the *Egron*, in 913, expanding it in phases, until by 930 it comprised over a thousand entries analysing biblical and post-biblical Hebrew usage.[1] His philosophic interests led him to open a correspondence with Isaac Israeli of Kairouan (*c.* 855–*c.* 955), the physician philosopher who, partly influenced by al-Kindī, initiated the tradition of Neoplatonic philosophy among Arabic-speaking Jews and died at over a hundred years of age.[2]

Saadiah's philological expertise led him into controversy, while still in his youth, with the Karaites, a Jewish sect who rejected the Talmud and prided themselves on their biblicism. Karaite exegesis, like Saadiah's, profited from the new, Greek-influenced, inductive methods in grammar and semantics cultivated by the Qur'ān scholars of such cities as Basrah and Kufa. But the rigour and appositeness of his approach, and his tenacious style of debate, became sources of hardship for him. Earlier responses to the Karaites had been far milder. Saadiah's spirited polemics made him the *bête noire* of the movement and brought down on him a thousand years of Karaite rebuttals. But the more immediate response, it seems, was not rebuttal but reprisal. Karaite leaders apparently used their influence with the Islamic government to see to it that he was removed from Egypt.

For some seven years he lived the life of an exile in Palestine, Iraq and Syria, at least part of the time separated from his wife and children. During this period he deepened his knowledge of history, philosophy and Scripture. He studied with one Abū Kathīr Yaḥyā al-Kātib of Tiberias, absorbed the ideas of the Jewish philosopher/*mutakallim* David al-

Muqammiṣ[3] and mastered the techniques of the masoretes of Tiberias, who had brought traditional Jewish scriptural studies to a high pitch. In Saadiah's later writings we can see the influence of Plato, whose dialogues he would have read in Arabic summaries, paraphrases and translations. We also see the formation of his character as a philosopher, his rejection of the notion that all suffering must be deserved and the growing profundity of his recognition of a theme he found both in Plato and in Scripture: that power does not make right, although right does indeed make power.[4]

Saadiah came to prominence in a controversy with Aaron ben Meir, a Jerusalem Rabbanite, who in 921 proposed a slight modification to the conventions used in adjusting the lunar months to the solar year in the traditional Hebrew calendar. The fourteen-minute discrepancy would generate a two-day divergence from the established convention. Stirred by a desire to restore the hegemony of Palestinian rabbinic authority, Ben Meir pressed for implementation of his view. Other Rabbanites responded with alarm. For the proposal would split the Jewish community. Those who accepted the change would celebrate the Festivals on different days from those who did not. The secular head of Diaspora Jewry, the Exilarch in Baghdad, David ben Zakkai, commissioned a detailed response from Saadiah, who had already urged Ben Meir to withdraw his dissenting view. Relying on astronomy, Scripture and rabbinic law, Saadiah successfully rebutted Ben Meir's claims and was appointed an Alluf or associate of the ancient Talmudic academy of Pumpedita – by now, like its sister academy of Sura, relocated in Baghdad.

In 928 Ben Zakkai made Saadiah head of the Sura Academy, with the traditional title of Gaon, although Saadiah was an outsider to the small circle of Baghdad Jewish leaders and apparently of humble birth. Ben Zakkai was not fazed but only piqued when warned that the young scholar seemed to fear no one. He admired Saadiah's lucid polemics against the Karaites and against the anti-biblical writer Ḥīwī al-Balkhī. Clearly the energetic new Gaon would pump fresh life into the moribund academy – which Saadiah vigorously set out to do. But by 930 the two men were seriously at odds: Saadiah had refused to sign a testamentary judgment in which Ben Zakkai had awarded himself a fee from the proceeds, in contravention of what Saadiah knew to be the norms of Jewish law. Saadiah's counterpart, the Gaon of Pumpedita, undercut him by agreeing to sign. The Exilarch's son, sent to expostulate with Saadiah, lost his temper and raised his hand against him. He was promptly expelled from the Gaon's court. Saadiah was placed under a ban. He answered in kind and named Ben Zakkai's brother as the Exilarch's successor. Factions formed, riots ensued, Saadiah himself was set upon and beaten. A jealous rival, Sarjado, offered 10,000 dinars to the caliph to settle the matter in the Exilarch's favour. But the caliph rejected the bribe and assigned the celebrated 'Alī ibn 'Īsā, "the good vizier" (859–946), to adjudicate the case. 'Alī restored Saadiah to office and was seeking to reconcile the rival leaders when the caliph was killed in a *coup d'état* and 'Alī's government prorogued. When the new and impecunious Caliph al-Qāhir ascended the throne, Saadiah was deposed and his counter-Exilarch banished to the frontier province of Khurasan.

In time the divisions grew so oppressive that Sarjado's father-in-law moved to make peace, an aim consummated in a moving ceremony of reconciliation in 937. The "anti-Gaon" was pensioned off, the anathemas withdrawn and Saadiah restored to office with full approval of the new caliph al-Rāḍī and the restored vizier 'Alī ibn 'Īsā. Only Sarjado remained unreconciled, and even he reached the office of Gaon of Pumpedita, after Ben Zakkai's death in 940 and Saadiah's in 942.

Deprived of judicial authority for seven years, much as he pictures Job as deposed from judicial office following the slanders of a detractor, Saadiah pursued his scholarship and philosophy. In 931 he wrote a commentary on the Kabbalistic *Book of Creation*, adopting a cosmology grounded in science rather than Kabbalah. Like the Muslim savants of his day, he knows the earth's circumference, so he has no use for the flat-earth cosmology of the *Book of Creation* and refuses to find support for it in Scripture.[5] He also rejects the fanciful ascription of the work to Abraham. Philosophy and history, he urges, are the proper work of human beings; God will aid us in these endeavours. For Scripture rightly describes God as "disclosing deep things" (Job 12: 22).

By 933 Saadiah completed his chief philosophic work, showcasing and putting to frequent use an explicit epistemology. His realism regarding nature and its Creator rests on a constructive, rationalistic empiricism. His rationalism is buttressed by a subdued Platonism like al-Kindī's. And his idea of experience is enriched by a chastened traditionalism, which relies on trustworthy ancestors for their histories and hermeneutics but does not treat tradition as a source of knowledge independent of reason, direct experience and rational inference from the two.[6] Saadiah finds as little use for the Neoplatonic Active Intellect as he does for the Kabbalistic alphabets of creation. Yet his naturalism and rationalism do not exclude all trace of mysticism. Prophets and the blessed, he learns, derive comfort and inspiration from the "created light" of God.[7] By calling it *created* Saadiah excludes any incarnation of God's own reality and so avoids christological and *ḥulūlī* views. But the immanence of divine *action* is not excluded. Indeed, Saadiah anchors what will become a central Kabbalistic tenet, reciprocity between the human and the divine. For he makes it a practice to redirect scriptural ascriptions to God of emotions like yearning, satisfaction and joy, readily treating such predicates as transferred epithets whose logical subject is a human being.[8] He thus broaches a theme of intimacy well rooted in the ancient idea that one can bless God (1 Chronicles 29: 10). The theme finds consummate expression, perhaps, in the liturgical phrase applied to Jacob, and thus to all Israel: "whom Thou didst love with thine own love and rejoice with thine own joy".[9] Some seven centuries later Spinoza still uses the same idea in explaining how the Infinite can care for finite individuals.[10]

Saadiah's works were philological, liturgical, exegetical, juridical, historical, polemical and philosophic. Besides the *Egron*, there were twelve books on language, which survive only in fragmentary form; among them the earliest known Hebrew grammar.[11] A work on the *hapax legomena* of the Hebrew Bible is extant. In liturgy, Saadiah prepared the first scholarly *Siddur* or Hebrew prayerbook. Of his liturgical poetry, most is lost, since he included only the shortest items in his *Siddur*. His didactic poem on the Ten Commandments and his penitential and petitionary prayers found in the Cairo Genizah, the repository of disused texts stored in the Cairo synagogue, convey the flavour: learned and highly allusive writing of the philological type favoured in his day, not only in Hebrew sacred poetry but in Arabic secular verse and even prose. Poetry, it was understood, was the chief fruit of philological learning and the chief proof of literary taste and discernment. Saadiah's prose prayers are more straightforward, and his Arabic prayers and translations of Hebrew prayers reveal the range of his expressive powers. Maimonides, who generally frowns on Geonic liturgical work, recommends Saadiah's prayers. And Ibn Ezra commends Saadiah for avoiding the obscurity and the homiletic overgrowth and metaphoric excess that beset the liturgical writing of his day.

In biblical studies, Saadiah's didactic poem on the frequency of every letter in the Torah is a masoretic *tour de force*; its practical use is in preserving the integrity of the text. His Arabic Bible translations, accompanied with commentaries, diffused the interpreted biblical text not only among Arabic-speaking Jews but among Muslims, who had long relied on oral testimonies (*Isrā'īliyyāt*) to explicate the numerous Qur'ānic allusions to Biblical figures and events. Unlike many Jewish writers, who wrote Arabic in Hebrew characters, Saadiah's translations apparently used Arabic script, as testified by the textual tradition and by a manuscript preserved in the Vatican. Each book was given a thematic title and an introduction explaining its problematics and complementing Saadiah's linear commentary – allowing the higher order argument to emerge clearly from the biblical poetry and narrative. Unlike the familiar commentaries of the European exegete Rashi (1040–1105), Saadiah's are overtly philosophical and typically fight shy of midrashic embroideries.

Of his halakhic contributions, only two survive: a commentary on the thirteen Talmudic rules of juridical inference, and a work on inheritance law, one of ten Arabic monographs he wrote on rabbinic law. His lost works, of which fragments survive in the Genizah, include a methodological introduction to the study of the Talmud, Mishnaic and Talmudic commentaries and numerous responsa. Here, as in his exegetical work, thematic introductions and conceptual organization are trademarks that vividly display the role of philosophy in structuring Saadiah's thought and writing.

Beyond his polemics against Karaism and Ḥīwī al-Balkhī, Saadiah wrote other controversial works. And, beyond his polemic on the calendar, he wrote a handbook on the calendrical rules. But his *Kitāb al-Ta'rīkh*, or Chronology, goes much further, summarizing the world's history from the creation, so as to set out a diachronic framework for all historic events. As Franz Rosenthal has shown, the work was part of a movement towards the linearization of historiography ongoing in Saadiah's time and carried on afterwards by such writers as the polymath al-Bīrūnī.[12]

There are three things readers will want to know about Saadiah's philosophical *chef d'oeuvre*, its title, how it is put together and its philosophical contents. Commonly known by the Hebrew title, *Sefer Emunot ve-De'ot*, loosely rendered, "The Book of Beliefs and Opinions",[13] the work is more accurately entitled *Kitāb al-Mukhtār fi'l-āmānāt wa'l-i'tiqādāt* in Arabic, "The Book of Critically Chosen Beliefs and Convictions".[14] Like Aristotle, and indeed like Plato in the Dialogues, Saadiah surveys and critiques rival views on each of the issues he discusses, settling on a particular view to be accepted. As in *kalām*, he arrays arguments, both scriptural and rational, against the rejected positions and answers objections to the view adopted. The outcome is a set of critically tested doctrines, congruent with the demands of reason and the religious canon. As in *kalām*, the enterprise is not merely apologetic, since the doctrines that survive this process cannot remain unaffected by the demands of critical scrutiny. Indeed, Saadiah's book is not merely dialectical, since it seeks exhaustive typologies of options as to each issue it considers and tries to argue apodeictically for the conclusions it defends. These theses are elicited inductively, but also creatively, from a vast scriptural knowledge, and from the supporting hermeneutic of rabbinic tradition. But for that very reason, if no other, Scripture can be used here only to establish the authenticity of the conclusions reached, not their authority.[15] And the sense of Scripture is constantly open to reinterpretation if the apparent meaning cannot meet the stringent criteria of reason, experience and coherence.[16]

The *Kitāb al-Mukhtār* comprises ten "treatises" on the problems of theology. The Introduction lays out Saadiah's epistemological standards, ascribing our self-knowledge to God's benevolence and our knowledge of the world to that God-given consciousness. It treats doubt as a natural concomitant of our finitude[17] but advises that doubt can be overcome by subduing its causes, ignorance and impatience. It argues against subjectivism and explains that since our opinions do not determine reality, disbelief does not exempt us from our divinely imposed obligations.

Saadiah defends perceptual knowledge against scepticism and shows that the methods necessary to render perceptions worthy of trust lead us inevitably to general theories and thus to the sciences. Only the superstitious forbid speculation, fearing for the faith. But such fears are as irrational as the fantasy of the ignorant that whoever travels to India will grow rich. Saadiah, we observe, has little patience for obscurantism. In the Islamic milieu, however, with its leaven of philosophical traditions, scepticism and relativism are more serious and immediate threats to Saadiah's quest than the dogmatism that will later attack Jewish philosophy in Christian Europe. Thus Saadiah's repeated reversion to epistemology.

The first of his "treatises" defends creation as the bulwark of theism, warning against attempts to explain the ultimate Cause sought and found by reason in terms of the more familiar sensory phenomena, circularly reducing God to the very facts which creation itself has been called upon to explain. The revolution of the heavens proves the cosmos finite; and its finitude, compositeness and articulation, the temporality of all accidents in nature, the inexhaustibility of an infinite duration, the inability of finite particulars to cause their own existence, all prove the world created. The Platonizing idea of *formatio mundi* is rejected. For if God merely imparted ordered motion to a pre-existent matter, the existence of that matter would remain to be explained. Only an absolute explanation is acceptable, and only *creatio ex nihilo*, by an absolute act of grace, the work of an infinite Creator, provides that explanation. True, nothing comes from nothing, but this precisely is the reason for ascribing the world's existence to the creative act of God. For the world has not sustained itself for ever and could not create itself. Ascription of its creation to God is the most reasonable explanation of its existence.

Neoplatonic attempts to derive the physical from the ideal bring the physical and the spiritual no closer together than does the sheer creationism of Scripture. Such efforts seem to Saadiah to explain the obscure by the more obscure, especially in view of the problems about the independent existence of Platonic "spiritual beings". The classic difficulties of dualism beset the notion that God produced bodies out of himself. Appeals to the four basic qualities, hot and cold, wet and dry, may seem more empirical and naturalistic. But we have no perceptual knowledge of these four qualities in their pure state; and, even if we knew that they are real, we would still need some way of explaining their combining and separating. Every materialistic naturalism, Saadiah argues tellingly, hides a tendency to confuse Cause with effect, the product with the Maker. Our aim, Saadiah argues, planting his staff firmly in the soil of rationalism, while keeping one eye cocked in the direction of the occasionalists, is not the denial of causality but the recognition that proximate causes are just a part of the story we pursue: we want to know the ultimate cause behind the intermediate causes we find in the study of nature.

Turning to the Aristotelian ascription of the order of nature to the motion of the heavens, Saadiah capitalizes on his own naturalism by emphasizing that circular motion is natural to the heavenly bodies. It is thus part of what we are seeking to explain. He fires a passing shot at the strange Aristotelian doctrine that sun is not really hot, appealing, in the spirit of Philoponus, to the contrary evidence of the senses.[18] Saadiah rejects the eternity of the heavens, partly on the grounds that the requisite fifth element of Aristotelian cosmology, if it did exist, would be invisible to us, having nothing in common with our make-up and so having no way of affecting our perception. He also argues that the revolutions of the spheres could not increase or have ratios to one another (as we see that they do) if their number were already infinite.[19] Against the idea that chance is the ultimate cause, Saadiah argues not only that chance could not produce a complex and stable system, but also that the concept of chance can be defined only relative to a natural order; so it is incoherent to treat chance as the ultimate principle of the world. The idea that nature has always been as we observe it, by contrast, is an unwittingly a prioristic extrapolation of empiric experience and thus either unfounded or incoherent. Here Saadiah establishes the line of argument that Maimonides will use against Aristotelian eternalism, rejecting the projection of the familiar patterns of natural events into metaphysical necessities.

The second treatise argues for God's unity based on his incorporeality as the absolute creator, on his polar opposition to the world's multiplicity, and on the economy of explanations: one cause is sufficient, more would be redundant, and would require proof beyond the sole proof that we have, the act of creation. Dualists and polytheists have no way of limiting the divinities they must posit, once they begin making a god of every element or principle in nature. If God needed help or co-operation to make or rule the world, he'd be powerless; and if some other god were not his aide but free to contradict him, then the two would either limit one another's power, making neither worthy of divinity, or one could overrule another, so that the same object, for example, could be given contradictory characteristics. Only with a single God do we have a coherent cosmos.

As for God's attributes, his life, power, and knowledge are known from the act of creation, as is his transcendent goodness. And these attributes, contrary to Christian attempts to derive multiple persons from the differentiation of the attributes, all represent a single reality and differ only in the varied attempts of human language to capture different aspects of what we understand by God. They no more represent different beings than do the usages of Scripture that sometimes call God *Elohim* and sometimes use the Tetragrammaton. The eternal *logos* of Christian theology has no more basis than the Neoplatonic hypostases, and God's words in Genesis, "let us make", are no allusion to the Trinity, nor even an apostrophe to heavenly counsellors, as Midrashic homilies would make them, but simply the we of majesty, well established in Hebrew usage.

Like the soul, or fire or wind, the subtlest of things can be the most powerful, and such is the case with God, whose real nature is simplex and transcends all ten categories of Aristotle, which are his work. All assignments of diverse attributes to him are figures, comparable to the well-known biblical anthropomorphisms, used dialectically "to build from the ground up", but not to be taken literally. Every biblical anthropomorphism can be resolved to the idea it projects; and the ascription of loves and hates to God, paradigmatically, resolves to a normative intention, expressing prescription or proscription. God's speech is a created sound, and God's "back", as seen by Moses, is his created glory.

God created the world, as Saadiah argues in the third treatise, to allow human beings to earn blessedness. For earned desert (as Kant will later argue) is far more precious than merely bestowed bliss. But this entails real risks – trials of our mettle, accountability for our choices, and sufferings that may be warnings or chastisements, or may be the "sufferings of love", whose sole purpose, although we cannot know it when we undergo them, is enhancement of our reward, through recompense for preserving our integrity in their midst. The chief vehicle of our test, for which the world was created, is the system of our obligations. The first of these are well known to reason – as in our recognition of the wrongfulness of causing bloodshed or pain, fornicating, stealing or lying. But the balance are revealed, so as to enhance the reward of those who observe them.

The rational commandments are not derivable, say from hedonism, or indeed from any merely empiric naturalism. For, Saadiah argues, hedonism will make the same act, say a theft, both good and evil, since it brings pain to the victim and pleasure to the thief. Hence the moral relativism of the moral empiricist. But if we recognize the need to differentiate ourselves from animals (and so do not fornicate), if we understand that misrepresentation is a grotesque perversion of creation (and so do not lie) and if we see that bloodshed thwarts fulfilment of God's plan (not by blocking God's intent but by violating the potentials God imparted to be realized), then we discover the values underlying some of the precepts of the law. We can even find the rational basis for the ritual commandments, those which would have had no strict standing as obligations had they not been commanded. For reason demands a response to generosity – requital, if the giver is our peer; gratitude, if our superior. And all of the ritual commandments of the law, although they may bear with them benefits like rest (in the case of the Sabbath) or purity (in the case of the

Levitical laws), serve in the end as expressions of gratitude. The ritual laws, then, are distinguished from the rational not in the sense that they serve no rational purpose but only in that their purpose alone does not determine their material content and modalities – as indeed is the case with any law, although the thematics of such norms as those prohibiting bloodshed may seem clear enough to allow reason (at least broadly) to specify their concrete prescriptions.[20] Prophets are thus needed to spell out God's specific requirements and expectations, and to define the implementation of the norms proposed by reason itself. Miracles corroborate the claims of prophets, and tradition preserves their message, vouching for its authenticity, but also interpreting it. For, just as reason is prior to revelation, tradition is posterior to it; no one of the three can or should stand alone.

In his fourth treatise, Saadiah argues that humanity is the purpose of creation, standing at the centre of the cosmos, endowed with moral freedom. A human body may be small, but the soul is vaster than the cosmos, for human knowledge embraces it. But the world was created in the human interest, not for human pleasure or to sate human desires. Life is short, but the choices made during the brief period when choice is possible are of absolute significance and transcendent consequence. The brevity of life itself shows this to us, since nothing can be undone when life is over. Our bodies are the best that could be given to a mortal being; but even our maladies teach us of our frailty and warn us of the retribution that is to come. For, with any growth, the dead wood must be cut and cleared away, and that is the function of capital punishment in this world and hellfire in the next, where the very light that is a comfort to the blessed becomes a torment to the damned.[21] God does not interfere with human choices, but imparts the capacity to act, which must include the capacity to choose, although our own choices may effect the diminution of our degrees of freedom. For what God forms is humanity's underlying nature. Our character is our own work, and it is only hyperbole when we read that God controls the heart, simply meaning that everyone acts as God intended – that is, freely.

We are judged, as the fifth treatise teaches, by the preponderance of our good and evil actions, whose inner moral worth, beneath all semblances of external behaviour, God knows irrefragably. Here Saadiah, anticipating Miskawayh (*c.* 936–1030), begins the task of reconciling the virtue ethics of the Greeks with the command ethics of Scripture. He argues, in consonance with Aristotle, that although every act is significant, one act is not our character. Thus penitence is possible, Saadiah argues, fusing the Socratic motion of the soul with the rabbinic and prophetic idea of repentance. Penitence is the fulfilment of regret, just as action in general is the fulfilment of intent. Yet the transcendent significance of our choices does not allow redemption of every act: once our choices have sealed our character they have sealed our destiny, and penitence itself becomes impossible. Prayer goes nowhere when it is insincere or intransigent, and, in the same way, it is bootless in one who is actively neglectful of the Torah or the poor, or mired in embezzlement or impurity. Three sins will not be expiated: slander, misleading others and retention of ill-gotten gains. Three merits are rewarded in this world, even for those who reject the service of God: filial piety (Exodus 20: 12), kindness to animals (Deuteronomy 22: 7) and honest dealing (Deuteronomy 25: 15). Like Maimonides after him, Saadiah uses the biblical prooftexts to establish not merely the commandment (and its reward) but the generalized theme underlying each of the biblical precepts: thus, not simply releasing the mother bird, but kindness to animals; not simply fair weights and measures, but honest dealing.

The soul, Saadiah argues in the sixth treatise, is created on completion of the body with which it is united. Neither soul nor body is impure, and sin results only from our own wrong choices. Like the heavenly spheres, the soul draws its luminosity from God, gaining life and consciousness, which allow it to animate a body that would otherwise be passive and inert. Once its destiny is complete, it returns to God, who made it and allowed it to act through the intermediacy of the body. When the tally of souls God destined for existence is complete, all are reunited with their bodies and judged. Those whose lives were cut short or who suffered undeservedly are recompensed for their suffering, not excluding the slain infants of the ancient Israelite conquest, and even any animals that suffered unduly in the cult of Temple sacrifice.[22]

The soul is not an accident – thus not a function of the body or an adjunct of the blood, not a self-moving number, an entelechy, an epiphenomenon of the body's organization or a juncture of the senses. For an accident could not be the object of creation. It is not made of fire or air, for it lacks their qualities; and it is not of two parts locatable in the head and heart, for the soul would be what enables these to interact. Nor are there three separate souls, as in the theory suggested (but later withdrawn) by Plato. Rather, appetite, ire and reason are faculties or powers of one soul, and it is called alive in virtue of the immortality to which it is heir. The demands of theodicy, Saadiah argues, may seem to give colour to the theory of metempsychosis. But understanding that God's grace and justice assure us of recompense for all unrequited sufferings (and of retribution for all unpunished wrongs, such as the sins of mass murderers), deflates the appeal of the otherwise rather implausible notion of transmigration. The resemblance of humans to the animals whose bodies they are sometimes thought to occupy is only superficial; for the soul is specific to the organic form it animates. And when Moses says that the covenant is made "not only with ye alone . . . but also with him that standeth present with us today before the Lord our God, and with him that is not here with us this day" (Deuteronomy 29: 14), he does not support but undermines metempsychosis. For the verse "explicitly differentiates those who are present from those who are absent".[23]

In the seventh, eighth and ninth treatises, Saadiah differentiates resurrection, redemption and requital. Resurrection is the reuniting of body and soul here in the world. All monotheists will share in this rebirth, along with all the righteous and repentant of Israel. But Israel will have the leading role, because of her long sufferings. God did not include resurrection in the first redemption, the exodus from Egypt, but promised it for the future, because Israel's present bondage is heavier than the slavery of Egypt. Redemption is the vindication in history of God's promises to Israel: the ingathering of her exiles, the return of prophecy, which will enliven even ordinary persons, and the restoration of the house of David. But the ultimate reward and punishment are otherworldly, as they must be, in view of the transcendent character of human goodness and suffering, sin and cruelty.

In this world, Saadiah argues, following the Epicurean doctrine of Muḥammad ibn Zakariyyā' al-Rāzī, pains outweigh pleasures,[24] the wicked often triumph, and the sufferings of innocents are not requited. These facts alone suffice to show us that God's mercy will make good our losses and remedy life's defects transcendently.[25] Were it not for future recompense and requital, surely fire and brimstone would have fallen on the earth long ago, as it did on Sodom and Gomorrah. But the hereafter is not an earthly place. Only metaphorically is it called Tofet or Eden. Time itself will be transmuted in the new Heaven, of which Isaiah spoke. But the most striking transcendence will be moral. Our trials over, there will be no more need or chance for moral decisions, but the infinite consequence of the decisions we made in the temporal world will be played out to eternity, in all the varying degrees of intensity, from bliss to agony, in accordance with our deserts.

Saadiah's final treatise deals with the good life, which he defines in moral terms. For, he argues, we do not know the reward of the ritual commandments even in this life; still less in the Hereafter. His moral doctrine is pluralistic and humanistic, based on acceptance of the plurality of our nature and interests. Like Plato, Saadiah believes that the good life is the balancing of these interests. But he does not follow Plato's breakdown of our interests into those of the intellectual, appetitive and spirited aspects of the soul. Rather, using his distinctive inductive method, he elicits the list of interests from Scripture, and from his own insights into human psychology. The interests he discovers are abstinence, eating and drinking, sex, passionate or romantic love, wealth, progeny, agrarian and urban development, longevity, power, vengeance, knowledge, worship and rest. Each of these (even vengeance in its way) is in some sense a good. But none of them, as their devotees might imagine, provides a fulfilling or satisfying life. To make any one of them the be-all and end-all of our existence is to cheat ourselves of the rest, and examination of the characters and lives of those who follow any one of these to the exclusion of the rest shows us clearly the inadequacy of each without the support and leaven of the rest.

Thus, denial is a valuable discipline, but the pure ascetic is a misanthropic and embittered anchorite, whose isolation feeds his envy and deprives him of the piety he may have sought. Food and drink sustain the body and the mind and foster reproduction, but the gourmand is bloated and unhealthy, selfish, foggy-headed and licentious. Sex is a unique delight, countering melancholy, cementing social relations, and well accepted by the prophets, who enjoyed it without shame, as when Jacob said to Laban: "Give me my wife!" (Genesis 29: 21). But the lascivious are unhealthy and typically adulterous. So the erotic lifestyle has social as well as hygienic detriments. Passionate love has its place, in marriage, sustaining the marital relationship, as suggested in the words: "a lovely deer, a graceful doe, let her breasts delight thee always; with her love be thou ever ravished" (Proverbs 5: 19); but as a way of life it is an absurd obsession, a form of slavery, often a source of regret or hatred (2 Samuel 13: 15), even when it finds its goal. Progeny perpetuate the world and give solace and joy. One cannot overlook the natalism of the prophets. But offspring are also a hardship and a source of anxiety to their parents; they are not sufficient to give meaning to our existence. Development is useful and satisfying; but taken beyond the needs it is meant to satisfy and made our overriding goal, it distracts one from the intellectual and spiritual and becomes a source of anxiety, compulsiveness and greed. Longevity too is a means to an end, allowing us to attain our spiritual as well as our worldly goals. But the valetudinarian, who has made survival his *raison d'être*, must know that even the vigorous often die young, and that there are higher goals than maintenance of one's body.

Power or authority, like the other aims, is not an evil but a good, necessary to the ordering of the world; but, if made all-sufficient, its tendency to promote arrogance and injustice makes it self-destructive and transforms a ruler's ebullience from overconfidence to the terror of the tyrant, the doubts, suspicions and hatred of humanity. Saadiah finds allusions to the tyrannical, in Proverbs (12: 15 and 18: 1, 26: 12) and in Isaiah (10: 12–13), where the self-will and arrogance of the proud are shown to be the seeds of their destruction. The treatment points up Saadiah's method. For the prooftexts are scriptural, and the theme, indeed, is authentically prophetic, voiced in the distinctive irony of the prophets, who speak of wrongdoers as intentionally working their own destruction. But the argument, if spelled out in more conceptual but no less dramatic terms, is Plato's.[26]

Vengeance is the most specious of *prima facie* goods in Saadiah's estimation. True, it gives a momentary satisfaction, but the activities of scheming it engenders cause anxiety and foster ruthlessness. It begets only hatred, so it cannot be made a way of life, since universal hatred would mean universal destruction. Like our other motives, the urge for vengeance has a place in God's plan, to spur us on in the pursuit of justice; but vengeance itself is not justice. Like all other *prima facie* goods, it becomes an actual good only when mitigated and controlled by the rest. Knowledge is, of course, a good. But Saadiah, like Rāzī,[27] believes that even the quest for knowledge can be excessive; pursued to the exclusion of all else, our appetite for knowledge would ruin our health and even dull our mind. Worship is fitting, as an expression of our gratitude to God for the gift of existence; but, taken as an exclusive goal, it is as self-undermining as the pursuit of knowledge (which would bring to an end all knowledge if the avid scholar did not stop to propagate his kind). Saadiah takes particular aim at the pietists who idealize leaving one's fate in God's hands as a display of their absolute trust, a theme well established among Christian, Muslim and Jewish pietists. True, one should acknowledge God's infiniteness, but that requires the recognition that God acts *through* human efforts, which may therefore not be abandoned in quietist zeal. Even the choice of a life of worship is an act, not a submission; and the notion that one does God's will by a life of study, worship and contemplation alone neglects those obligations which can be fulfilled only in the world – for example the commandment to keep just weights and measures. For what meaning can honest dealing have in one who eschews all social engagement and economic activity?[28] Full observance of God's commands requires life in the world. So, while the pietists' aspirations may be noble, their neglect of their God-given bodies and of their offspring is not to be condoned.

Finally, rest is needful to our nourishment and growth and is prescribed for sabbaths and holy days; but rest, Saadiah argues, is possible and valuable only through work; laziness is destructive. Rest is prescribed for us, Saadiah argues, to impart a taste of the World to Come. But – to sum up Saadiah's ethics in a sentence – our obligations are not given us for that world but for this one. Our task is to find the proper balance among all the goods pertinent to our nature as finite, rational beings in the world. The aim of the Torah is to lay out a way of life that enables us to do so, denying no good proper to our nature, but allowing none to usurp the place of reason.

Saadiah closes his account of ethics and underscores his integrative pluralism with a brief discussion of aesthetics, an area rarely explored among medieval thinkers. Blending, he argues, is the key to beauty. Tastes, colours, sounds and even smells are beautiful when duly mingled; rough, unpleasant, even injurious, when left simple. All of the goods – and he acknowledges that more *prima facie* goods are known than he has listed, giving further examples from Scripture – have their proper place and context. And this can be found, if one is not simply seeking rationales for established appetites and desires but rather inquiring after the truth with humility and sincerity.

NOTES

1 See N. Allony (ed.) Sa'adya Ga'on, *Ha-Egron: Kitāb uṣūl al-shi'r al-'ibrānī* (Jerusalem, 1969).
2 See Alexander Altmann and Samuel Stern, *Isaac Israeli: a Neoplatonic Philosopher of the Early Tenth Century* (Oxford, 1958).
3 See Dāwūd ibn al-Muqammiṣ, *Twenty Chapters ('Ishrūn maqāla)*, ed. and trans. Sarah Stroumsa (Leiden, 1989).
4 See his comments on Job 34 in *The Book of Theodicy*, trans. L. E. Goodman (New Haven, 1988): 358–61.
5 See on Job 5: 10, 10: 22 and my note 15: 236–8.
6 Few medieval authors articulate systematic epistemologies; the familiar parts of philosophy are logic, physics and metaphysics. For Saadiah's epistemology, see Abraham Joshua Heschel, *The Quest for Certainty in Saadia's Philosophy* (New York, 1944); Georges Vajda, "Autour de la théorie de la connaissance chez Saadia", *Revue des études juives*, 126 (1967); and Israel Efros, *Studies in Medieval Jewish Philosophy* (New York, 1974): 7–36.
7 See Efros: 61–4.
8 See on Exodus 31: 17; on Job 7: 21, 14: 15, trans. Goodman: 211, 257 and 261 n. 10.
9 "She-me'ahavatkha she-ahavta 'oto, u-mesimḥatkha she-samaḥta bo . . .", see P. Birnbaum, *Ha-Siddur ha-Shalem* (New York, 1949): 23.
10 *Ethics*, 5.20, 32, 35, 36.
11 See Solomon Skoss, *Saadia Gaon, the Earliest Hebrew Grammarian* (Philadelphia, 1955).
12 Franz Rosenthal, *A History of Muslim Historiography* (Leiden, 1968): 133–50.
13 See Samuel Rosenblatt, trans., *The Book of Beliefs and Opinions* (New Haven, 1948).
14 In his edition, Joseph Kafih writes: "In every manuscript of the original version of our teacher, the title is *The Book of Beliefs and Convictions*, and so it was translated [in 1186] by R. Judah Ibn Tibbon [the father of Samuel Ibn Tibbon]. For the text he had before him was that of an early version. But in codex M [Bodleian MS Pococke 148], which is in my view the text of our teacher's final revision, the title is given as I have written it [*Kitāb al-Mukhtār fi'l-āmānāt wa'l i'tiqādāt*]. And rightly so. For our teacher did not set out simply to gather a compendium of beliefs and convictions, but to demonstrate which beliefs were worthy of choice and which convictions were true in his estimation." J. Kafih, ed. with modern Hebrew translation, *Sefer ha-Nivḥar ba-Emunot ve-De'ot* (Jerusalem, 1970): 1 n. 1; cf. preface, pp. 6–9: "I do not have any doubt that this is the title in his final revision" (p. 9). For the rendering "beliefs and convictions", see Efros: 31–2.

15 The intellectual atmosphere of tenth-century Baghdad is vividly displayed in the account of Abū 'Umar, a Muslim visitor, who told with horror of the theological discussions he witnessed there: "At the first meeting I attended, there were present not only members of all the orthodox and unorthodox [Muslim] sects, but unbelievers – Magians, materialists, atheists, Jews, Christians – unbelievers of every sort. Each sect had its own chief, to defend the views he professed, and whenever one of these leaders entered the hall, all would rise respectfully, and none would take his seat until his chief was seated. Soon the hall was filled to overflowing, and when everyone seemed to have arrived, one of the unbelievers rose to speak: 'We are gathered to reason together,' he said, 'and you all know the rules. You Muslims may not oppose us with arguments from your Book or on the authority of your prophet. For we do not believe in either. Each of us must therefore limit himself to arguments based on human reason.' All applauded these words. You can understand, said Abū 'Umar, that after hearing such things I did not go back to that gathering. I was invited to another, and I went, but it was the same sort of disgusting display." By then Abū 'Umar knew better than to attend theological debates. Al-Ḥumaydī, quoted in M. Ventura, *La Philosophie de Saadia Gaon* (Paris, 1934): 63–4, from *Journal asiatique* (1853): 93.

16 For the role of coherence in Saadiah's hermeneutical practice, see L. E. Goodman, "Saadiah Gaon's Interpretive Technique in Translating the Book of Job", in *Translating Scripture* (Philadelphia, 1990), *Jewish Quarterly Review* supplement: 47–76.

17 Heschel is mistaken in supposing (p. 28) that Saadiah "did not accord any value to doubt": doubt is an essential component of the authenticity of our existence. Without it, Saadiah argues, our existence would be trivialized and God's act of creation would become pointless. See Saadiah on Job 38, *The Book of Theodicy*: 382–4; 125–6; cf. my discussion, pp. 93–119.

18 See Aristotle, *Meteorology*, 1.3.340a.1–3; cf. Ibn Ṭufayl, *Ḥayy ibn Yaqẓān*, trans. L. E. Goodman (Boston, 1972; repr. Los Angeles, 1984): 104. For the naturalism of Philoponus as to the heavens, see S. Sambursky, *The Physical World of Late Antiquity* (London, 1962): 154–75; Richard Sorabji (ed.) *Philoponus and the Rejection of Aristotelian Science* (Ithaca, 1987); and, for the argument that the heavens are indeed fiery and not "quintessential", Philoponus, *Against Aristotle on the Eternity of the World*, trans. Christian Wildberg (Ithaca, 1987), esp. fragments 58–9, pp. 73–5.

19 Saadiah writes: "You can see that the cycle of the eastern movement of the highest sphere is completed once in a day and a night, whereas the western movement of the fixed stars takes a hundred years to traverse one degree, so that it would complete its revolution in 36,000 years." Yet if the world is eternal, both have completed the same number of revolutions! *Kitāb al-Mukhtār*, 1.3, trans. after Rosenblatt: 72–3; cf. al-Ghazzālī, *The Incoherence of the Philosophers*, 1 = Averroes, *Tahāfut al-tahāfut*, ed. Bouyges (Beirut, 1930): 16, trans. Simon Van Den Bergh as *The Incoherence of the Incoherence* (London, 1954): 9, and Van Den Bergh's note on this passage, 2:7, citing the argument from Philoponus, in Simplicius on *Physics*, Theta 1, ed. Diels, 1179: 15–27, and its use in Ibn Ḥazm, Shahrastanī, and others.

20 See *Kitāb al-Mukhtār*, 9.2; L. E. Goodman, "Rational Law/Ritual Law", in D. Frank (ed.) *Ritual and Chosenness* (Albany, 1993).

21 *Kitāb al-Mukhtār,* 9:5.
22 See *Kitāb al-Mukhtār,* 3:10, trans. Rosenblatt: 175.
23 *Kitāb al-Mukhtār,* 6:8, trans. Rosenblatt: 261 = Kafih: 216.
24 See L. E. Goodman, "Rāzī's Psychology", *Philosophical Forum,* 4 (1972): 26–48, where Rāzī's acceptance of metempsychosis is also discussed.
25 See L. E. Goodman, "Saadya Gaon on the Human Condition", *Jewish Quarterly Review,* n.s., 67 (1976): 23–9.
26 See *Republic,* 8.559–9.588.
27 See Rāzī, *Philosophical Life,* trans. A. J. Arberry, *The Asiatic Review* (1949): 703–13.
28 The same Plotinus who told his followers that they must "Cut away everything" zealously pursued his fiduciary responsibilities on behalf of the economic interests of the children entrusted to him as his wards. Does one who withdraws from the world thereby cease all economic activity, or does one only carry it on by proxy? Saadiah reasons that one cannot fulfil the commandment to keep just weights and measures unless one actually takes responsibility for the economic dimensions of one's acts and character.

CHAPTER 41
Ibn Gabirol
Irene Lancaster

Solomon ben Judah ibn Gabirol is regarded as the father of Jewish Neoplatonic thought in Spain. Chronologically, he is the second Jewish Neoplatonic philosopher after Isaac Israeli (North Africa, 850–932 or 955). He is also regarded as the first Jewish philosopher in Spain. He was born in Malaga in 1021/2, but lived in Saragossa, where he received an extremely sound secular as well as religious education. He died in Valencia either between 1054 and 1058 or, according to some sources, in 1070.

In addition to founding a Spanish school of philosophy he is also regarded as one of the two greatest post-biblical Hebrew poets of all time, and certainly the supreme liturgist, his religious masterpieces being prominently featured in the Oriental Sephardi Prayer Book to this day. His greatest work, the Hebrew poem-prayer, *Keter Malkhut*, or "Crown of the Kingdom", a title taken from a phrase in the biblical Book of Esther, contains many of his philosophical ideas. These will be explored later.

It is generally considered that he was known by the Jewish world for his poetry, written in Hebrew, but that his philosophical work, devoid of any allusion to Judaism, and written in Arabic, was neglected by his co-religionists and interpreted by posterity as having been written by either a Muslim or a Christian. It is undoubtedly true that his purely philosophical Arabic work, fragments of which remain in a Latin translation, entitled *Fons vitae*, was thought to be written by a Muslim or Christian named Avicebrol, Avicebron or Avencebrol. The most widely used Latin translation of this work was the twelfth-century Toledan version of Dominicus Gundissalinus, archdeacon of Segovia. He was helped in his translation by a converted Jew, ibn Daud, known as Johannes Hispalensis, or John of Spain.

This version was used by the Christian schools. It was only in 1846 that the great French Jewish scholar, Solomon Munk, identified the apparently Muslim or Christian philosophy of *Fons vitae* as having the same author as the emotional and fervent religious and love poetry of the Jew, Ibn Gabirol. Munk made his identification on the basis of his discovery of Hebrew fragments of *Fons vitae*, translated by Shem Tov ben Joseph Falaquera in the thirteenth century, and known as *Mekor Ḥayyim*.

However, there are clues that people must have known that *Fons vitae* was written by a Jew. As Loewe has pointed out (1989: 39–40), the book was known from the twelfth century by the title of *Mekor Ḥayyim*, a phrase emanating from Psalm 36: 10 (9). Various medieval commentators associated Ibn Gabirol explicitly with *Mekor Ḥayyim*. What is more, the work itself alludes to the Hebrew mystical text, the *Sefer Yeẓirah*, a treatise extolling the supremacy of the Hebrew letters, and therefore unlikely to have been read, let alone quoted, by contemporary Muslims or Christians.

The fact that *Fons vitae* was originally written in Arabic does not necessarily point to non-Jewish authorship, as the vast majority of medieval Jewish philosophers living under Islam wrote in Arabic, retaining Hebrew solely for poetry. As the first Jewish philosopher in Spain, Ibn Gabirol was to set a trend in this respect in that country, but he had already been anticipated by the Jews of Babylon such as Saadiah Gaon (882–942) and of course Isaac Israeli.

Far more interesting is why Ibn Gabirol should have written two such superficially disparate works, which on closer examination bear a marked philosophical resemblance to one another. It is known that he had a turbulent life, plagued by self-loathing and self-doubt. On the other hand he displayed a certain amount of arrogance, which is often the hallmark of the insecure. It is possible that *Fons vitae* was an attempt on his part to purge himself, in at least one of his literary works, of all the emotional and religious fervour he felt and embodied, and indeed translated into the numerous poems and prayers he wrote and which have never been surpassed.

If this is the case, it is supremely ironic that *Fons vitae* quickly grew out of favour with Jewish readers, attracting instead the Christian Scholastics of later centuries. Another factor is that Neoplatonism lost popularity in Jewish circles with the rise of Aristotelianism, which reached its peak in the monumental work of Maimonides (1135–1204). However, it should be pointed out that even Maimonides' purely philosophical work, the *Guide of the Perplexed*, dealt with religious, and specifically Jewish, matters of detail, despite having an Aristotelian-inspired framework.

Fons vitae appeared to be a dry, philosophical treatise. *Keter Malkhut*, however, was never deemed a philosophical work. It included plenty of Jewish allusions, and therefore maintained its popularity, particularly in Oriental Sephardi circles, despite positing a Neoplatonic structure which subsumes religious Judaism within it.

Having described Ibn Gabirol as a Neoplatonist, it is pertinent to point out that he was an extremely original thinker. Firstly, unlike most Neoplatonists, he assumes a universal matter which underlies all reality, and which is non-corporeal. Secondly, he does not describe multiplicity as emerging or emanating from unity, but regards matter and form as two different principles, following immediately from God. Sometimes, however, he appears to be suggesting that matter itself is God.

It might be thought that the concept of creation would account for the notion of duality, but not in Ibn Gabirol's system. Instead he talks of Divine Will. By doing this, Ibn Gabirol is attempting – not totally successfully – to inject a voluntaristic element into the inevitability or even fatalism of orthodox Neoplatonism. However, he does not make it clear exactly what relation matter and form have with Divine Will. He usually speaks of Will's relationship to form, without mentioning its relationship to matter. Sometimes he appears to conflate the idea of Will and matter! However, as part of the Godhead, Will must surely precede both matter and form in Ibn Gabirol's hierarchy, although he does at times speak of Will as being a created entity. What is difficult to reconcile is the idea that matter can be both the essence of things whilst also constituting mere potentiality.

The relationship of the Divine Will to the Divine Essence poses a particular problem to Jewish, as opposed to Christian, thought. It is impossible, from a purely religious Jewish viewpoint, that there should be an entity, such as the Divine Will, which is simultaneously identical with God as well as a mediator between Him and his creation. Ibn Gabirol tries to solve this difficulty by positing two aspects of Divine Will, one equated with God, and the other a functional entity, separate from Him. It is highly likely that Christians were attracted to Ibn Gabirol's idea of the Will as mediator between God and creation just as they were influenced by Philo's term, *logos*, which was interpreted by the Church as the second person in the Trinity.

For Jews, and presumably Muslims, it was far more tricky adequately to bridge the gap between Creator and created. Ultimately the only satisfactory solution to this problem was expressed by the Jewish mystics, many of whom were greatly influenced by Ibn Gabirol. They found a language capable of expressing the "stages" in the descent from the divine to the human, without offending the religious orthodoxy which saw God as "one" in every aspect: that is, unique, indivisible and perfect.

Let us now try and analyse a core verse of Ibn Gabirol's masterpiece, *Keter Malkhut*, in order to understand his philosophical thought in more detail. Verse 9 (my translation) states of God that:

Thou art wise; and wisdom, the fount of life, flows from Thee.
It is Thy particular wisdom which all humanity is too brutish to know.
Thou art wise, prior to all priority, and wisdom was by Thy side, a nurseling.
Thou art wise and did not learn from any beside Thyself; nor didst Thou acquire wisdom save from Thyself.
Thou art wise; and from Thy wisdom Thou emanated an appointed Will, and made it like a worker and a craftsman,
To draw out the dimension of existence from the void, just as light is drawn out which comes from the eye.
And to pump from the source of light without a bucket, and to achieve everything without a vessel.
To hew, engrave, purify and refine.
It called to the void, which was then split asunder; to existence, and it became engrossed; to the universe, and it was hammered out.
And it measured the heavens with a span, its hand coupling the tent of the spheres;
With loops of potentiality it ties the curtains of the created;
Its power reaching the very hem of the last and least of creation,
"The uttermost edge of the curtain in the coupling."

The first line of this verse immediately points to a relationship between *Keter Malkhut* and *Fons vitae*. Ibn Gabirol calls Wisdom, an aspect of God, "the fount of life". The phrase is an allusion to Psalm 36: 10 (9). The biblical verse states: "For with Thee is the fountain of life: in Thy light shall we see light." The "light" analogy appears again later on in the stanza.

Ibn Gabirol considers the Godhead as separate from the Wisdom which flows from it. We cannot "know" the Godhead itself. It is transcendent. Neither, however, can we "know" God's Wisdom *per se*, because of our animal nature. Ibn Gabirol is at pains to stress the utter priority of God, and the self-sufficiency of His "Wisdom".

However God allowed the Will to emanate through his Wisdom. Note that this verb is active, implying positive volition on God's part. The Will did not just "emerge"; it was activated by God Himself through His Wisdom. Loewe (1989: 124, 180, n. 40) translates the Hebrew word *ḥayfeẓ* as "prime matter", equating it with the idea of "object of delight". It is true that *ḥayfeẓ* has many meanings, including desire, will, pleasure, delight, matter and object. If this interpretation is correct, it becomes even more difficult to differentiate between Will and matter, as was discussed at the beginning of the chapter.

Will is then described as the agent which brings being or reality into existence from the void. A comparison is made with light coming from the eye, reminding us of the allusion to Psalm 36: 10 (9) mentioned above. It must be stressed however that Ibn Gabirol is not referring to the transcendent God, when mentioning the "eye", but to forces emanating from Him.

The Will is supposed to mediate directly between Wisdom and the world, "without a vessel". Reference is then made indirectly to a passage from the mystical *Sefer Yeẓirah*, in which six modes of operation are described through which the world is finally created by permutation and combination of the Hebrew letters. Ibn Gabirol mentions four modes: hewing, engraving, purifying and refining. The Will appears to take the role of God Himself in our present text, and the letters are not mentioned at all. Will then "calls to" the void, existence and the universe in turn. By "calling to" (or "naming"?), the cosmos is finally set in motion.

More biblical references are made, specifically to Isaiah 40: 12 and Exodus 26: 4. With sublime poetic imagination Ibn Gabirol uses a metaphor based on the construction of the Tabernacle, known in Hebrew as *mishkan*, or "indwelling". The Tabernacle was used as a meeting-point of spiritual significance to the Children of Israel in the wilderness. Ibn Gabirol employs vocabulary similar to that used in Exodus to describe the construction of the *mishkan* in order to demonstrate how the "hand" or "power" of the Will arranges, through linkage, the series of emanations from Prime Supernal Matter down to the lowest form of matter in our world.

The choice of imagery is no mere poetic embellishment however. By choosing the Tabernacle or "indwelling" as his focus, he implies that God has a part in the whole process of creation, from Will downwards. The word *mishkan* comes from the same root as the word *shekhinah*, usually translated as the female presence of God. It is this presence which accompanies the Children of Israel in their exile outside the Promised Land. In this poem, however, the exile is not only a journey from our home to another and alien land, but also a descent from our spiritual home, the soul, to our animal nature. For Ibn Gabirol, as for many Jewish poet-philosophers, exile was a spiritual journey, as well as a physical one. Few, if any, have expressed this supreme predicament as powerfully and beautifully as Ibn Gabirol, or attempted so masterfully to embark on the return journey.

BIBLIOGRAPHY

Guttmann, Julius (1964) *Philosophies of Judaism* (1933, English translation D. Silverman, London): 89–103.

Husik, Isaac (1916) *A History of Mediaeval Jewish Philosophy* (New York): 59–79.

Loewe, Raphael (1989) *Ibn Gabirol* (London).
Sirat, Colette (1985) *A History of Jewish Philosophy in the Middle Ages* (Cambridge): 5, 68–81 and 422–3.
Vajda, Georges (1947) *La Pensée juive du Moyen Age* (Paris): 75–83.

CHAPTER 42

Judah Halevi

Barry Kogan

The spread of Aristotelian texts and ideas into Islamic Spain during the late eleventh and early twelfth centuries was generally greeted with serious and sympathetic interest by Jewish intellectuals associated with the courtier class. Although Judah ben Samuel Halevi (*c.* 1075–1141 C.E.) probably shared this attitude at first, he eventually distinguished himself as one of the earliest and most perceptive critics of both philosophic and religious forms of rationalism in an effort to defend the claims of traditional Judaism.

Born in Tudela to a wealthy and learned family, Halevi was educated as most others in his class in biblical and rabbinic sources, Arabic poetry, philosophy and medicine. Already in his youth, he displayed remarkable poetic gifts, and his travels throughout Andalusia afforded him the opportunity to enjoy the pleasures of courtly life, close friendships with Jewish notables and patronage. But following renewed Christian efforts to reconquer southern Spain and the Almoravid invasion, designed to consolidate Muslim control of the area (1090), Halevi became increasingly alarmed at the disruption that these events brought to Jewish communities in Andalusia. While his poetry continued to address all of the conventional secular and religious themes of his day – the pleasures of friendship and courtly life, passionate love, loss and bereavement, the grandeur of creation, the significance of the Holy Days, and the quest for communion with God – he now began to create a new genre, the songs of Zion. These express both his own and his people's yearning for renewal in their ancestral homeland. It is clear that this yearning intensified with the upheavals that Jewish communities suffered both in Spain and in Palestine, in the wake of the First Crusade.

Sensing that the external threat to Spanish Jewish life in particular was matched by growing internal disarray, which he traced to the waning of religious commitment and adherence to rabbinic authority, he began to question ever more strongly some of the main cultural preoccupations of the courtier class, particularly the prestige of philosophical speculation and rational accounts of religion. Subsequently, the quest for personal religious experience and communion with God became one of the principal themes of both his poetry and his theology, while full observance of traditional rabbinic norms in their natural setting, the Land of Israel, is depicted as the one sure way to achieve it.

Halevi's only theological work, *The Book of the Khazars* or *Kuzari*, develops these and related themes in a five-part dialogue between a pagan Khazar king, who converts to Judaism, and the Jewish sage who persuades and then instructs him. Although the story is based on historical facts (Dunlop (1967): 89–170), Halevi reworked it to answer contemporary critics of Judaism, "the despised religion", among the adherents of philosophy, Christianity, Islam and Karaism. Investigation of Halevi's correspondence confirms that he drafted an early version of the book in response to the questions of a Karaite scholar in Christian Spain, but he later repudiated it. Thus, it is unclear whether any part of the original draft appears in the present version (Goitein (1974): 337–9).

The story opens as the king dreams that an angel tells him that his intention is pleasing to God but that his behaviour is not. His initial response is to observe the rites of his pagan religion with greater zeal, but the recurrence of the dream convinces him that a thoroughgoing inquiry is necessary to identify and ultimately adopt the one way of life that is pleasing to God. Accordingly, he invites a philosopher and then representatives of Christianity and Islam to instruct him.

The philosopher responds by denying the presuppositions of the king's dream. God, as the perfect and changeless First Cause, feels neither satisfaction nor dissatisfaction with the king's behaviour. Indeed, he has no knowledge of it, since knowledge of this kind and affective responses would introduce mutability and imperfection into God. For the same reason, God is not to be regarded as the Creator of either the universe or the individuals in it, except in a metaphorical way, as the ultimate cause of everything that arises in the world through natural causation. Nevertheless, he adds that people may successfully perfect themselves by extending their knowledge of the eternal system of necessary causes and effects emanating from God and ultimately attain union with the Active Intellect, the source of all things knowable in the sublunar world. The outcome of such union would be to live the most rational life possible and even receive prophecy and true dreams. The main prerequisite is to purify one's soul by cultivating the moral virtues and knowledge of the sciences. But it makes no difference to reason what regimen of worship and action one adopts. The king should either accept one of the rational *nomoi* of the philosophers or fashion one of his own. The traditional religions are pointedly omitted (*Kuzari*, 1.1). While most of the philosopher's views were conventional for any Aristotelian, the emphasis on the real possibility of union with the Active Intellect was distinctive of Ibn Bājjah (d. 1138), who was Halevi's contemporary and the principal exponent of Aristotelianism in Spain at the time (Altmann (1969): 73–107; Pines (1980): 210–17).

The king finds the philosopher's speech persuasive but unsatisfying because it offers no specific praxis and does not demonstrably produce even what it promises. Hence, he turns to the Christian and Muslim scholars. While their presentations directly address his practical concerns, he finds the evidence they offer either logically or empirically faulty. Relying on the analogy of natural scientists trying to explain extraordinary phenomena, the king indicates that he regards only public, empirical and direct evidence as conclusive. Once experience is well attested, however unlikely or contrary to expectation, it must be accepted. Theory has the secondary role of showing how what seemed unlikely is actually plausible (*Kuzari*, 1.4–6).

Because both scholars had admitted that their beliefs were based on God's well-attested revelation to Israel, the king finally turns to a Jewish scholar. The rabbi declares his faith in the God of Abraham, Isaac and Jacob, who led the Israelites out of Egypt with miracles and gave them His law. He also carefully distinguishes this belief from that of political religions, which appeal to God as the Creator of the universe known to all men. Overcoming his initial scepticism, the king eventually finds the rabbi's account of the public, empirical character of the Sinaitic revelation and of the Jewish tradition which embodies it superior to the claims of both the Christian and Muslim scholars and the philosophers. As the rabbi notes, philosophers infer the existence and nature of God from some aspect of the world-order, as if one could determine whether India had a king by studying the virtues of its people. Such speculation is tenuous and inconclusive at best and certainly evokes no reverence for its object. However, the arrival of the king's own envoy with gifts and medicines procurable only in India and a letter signed by the king not only establishes his existence and character but actually makes the recipient beholden to him. This is precisely what the miracles of Moses and his bringing of the Torah represent. If reliable and unbroken tradition is equivalent to experience, which the rabbi twice insists it is (*Kuzari*, 1.19–25, 5.14–end), it is neither tenuous nor inconclusive, even if it is confined to the Children of Israel. For, were it not for their preferred status, there would have been no Torah (*Kuzari*, 2.56).

To account for the facts of Israel's prophetic experience, the sage introduces a theory that draws upon Shi'ite and especially Ismā'īlī views (Pines (1980): 167–210). He argues that above the traditional hierarchy of inorganic matter, plants, animals and human beings distinguished by reason, there is an elect core of humanity (*ṣafwah, lubb*), who constitute an essentially separate order endowed with prophetic and even miraculous powers (*Kuzari*, 1.31–43; 2.14, 24). This group belongs to the *amr ilahi*, Halevi's multivalent term for diverse aspects of divine immanence. Depending on the context, the term signifies (1) a supra-rational order or dispensation of things in which God's will directly operates, (2) an endowment or gift conferred on the elect and transmitted by heredity, like providence, prophecy and the inner capacity to apprehend them, and (3) the orders or commandments, which constitute the divine way of life that God enjoins upon the elect. Once the king is convinced that there is no access to the divine order except by adhering to the commandments, he prepares for conversion (*Kuzari*, 1.98, 2.1).

For Halevi, whatever belongs to this divine order is ultimately superior to the domain of the intellect and beyond the capacity of reason to explain adequately. In this respect, his defence of Judaism agrees in broad outline with the first of the two methods by which dialectical theology defends religion according to al-Fārābī, namely, that religion provides knowledge of divine mysteries which only divine intellects rather than human intellects can comprehend (Lerner and Mahdi (1963): 27–9). Halevi diverges from this method by denying that revealed knowledge must be rejected by the intellect to be considered divine and also by giving primacy to actions over opinions. For example, he contends that the arguments for the eternity of the universe and for its temporal creation are evenly balanced (and thus rationally inconclusive). Aristotle opted for eternity only because the Greeks lacked a reliable divine tradition about the beginning and because he (and presumably Greeks generally) preferred the abstract speculations pointing to eternity. Here Halevi hints that all philosophers are influenced to a greater or lesser extent by their national cultures. Had Aristotle possessed a reliable tradition like Israel's, he would have employed his arguments on behalf of creation. It is axiomatic that the Torah teaches nothing contrary to sense experience or demonstration, even in upholding creation. If objective reason eventually proved that matter and other worlds existed before this one, it would still not undermine the divine teaching that this world had a temporal beginning (*Kuzari*, 1.62–7).

With respect to actions, it is the pious of Israel who truly conform to the highest order of reality because they possess the one law deriving from the divine order. Accordingly, they observe both the rational commandments (like honouring parents and doing justice) and the divine, traditional commandments (governing distinctly religious observance) heard only through revelation. The former precede the latter both in nature and in time and also serve as preambles for them. Still, the rational laws constitute at most a moral minimum for any group to survive, even a band of thieves. The divine laws, by contrast, perfect the rational ones, by determining their proper applications and producing spiritual effects in the soul that reason cannot explain or replicate (*Kuzari*, 2.48; 3.7, 11).

Functionally, the divine order of things assumes most of the tasks the philosophers ascribe to the Active Intellect. It is always on the lookout for whoever or whatever is capable of receiving its emanation. It wisely determines the forms of all sublunar particulars and likewise bestows prophecy on those who are suitably disposed (Davidson 1972). The requisite disposition depends upon (1) possession of the prophetic faculty, or inner eye, a notion which Halevi adapts from Shi'ite sources and al-Ghazzālī (Pines (1980): 172–92; Baneth (1981): 192–5; Watt (1953): 63–8); (2) dwelling in the Land of Israel, the most temperate of the seven climates, a notion which Halevi appropriates from 'Arabiyyah propaganda for his own purposes (Altmann (1944); Aloni (1980)); and (3) full observance of the Torah's commandments, which cultivates the capacity to receive revelation (*Kuzari*, 4.3; 2.9–24). Those who receive it enjoy a more accurate and comprehensive picture of reality than those who merely actualize their intellect as an instrument of apprehension. Interestingly, Halevi twice quotes the Platonic Socrates with obvious approval when he admits to the limits of philosophical knowledge. "O fellow citizens, I do not deny this divine wisdom of yours. I say rather that I do not understand it. I am wise only with respect to human wisdom" (*Kuzari*, 4.13; 5.14; cf. *Apology*, 20d–e).

In the final treatise of the *Kuzari*, the rabbi displays a Socratic scepticism in his exposition and critique of both dialectical theology (*kalām*) and Aristotelian (now Avicennian) philosophy. He depicts *kalām* as primarily an apologetic technique that seeks to instil by argument the kind of faith which the pious have naturally, but it usually leads only to more doubt and difference of opinion (*Kuzari*, 5.15–18). As for philosophy, what has been conclusively proved belongs mainly to logic and mathematics. In other fields, its claims are largely undemonstrated and often not even tenable. In physics, for example, the philosopher's account of the elements goes far beyond what empirical evidence warrants and is sometimes directly at odds with it. The evidence supports only the four primary qualities of hotness, coldness, wetness and dryness. In psychology and epistemology, the theory of the actualized intellect as a separate substance is beset by unresolvable problems concerning personal identity, the effect of material factors on thought and the prerequisites for conjunction or union with the Active Intellect. In metaphysics, philosophic accounts of the causes of celestial motion and the theory of emanation are so hopelessly weak and riddled with doubts that no two philosophers agree on such questions. He concludes that the most we can know regarding metaphysics is that God governs material things by determining their natural forms (*Kuzari*, 5.2–14, 19–21). Because the philosophers have such little wisdom to offer about these great questions, and virtually no wisdom at all to offer about the particulars of living everyday life, what is called for is a return to the divine wisdom embodied in Israel's ancestral tradition, the Torah. But as the rabbi recognizes, a wholehearted turn towards that tradition can be made complete only by a return to Israel's ancestral homeland as well. Accordingly, as the dialogue closes, the rabbi prepares to follow the logic of his position and departs for the Holy Land.

Halevi was clearly the first medieval Jewish thinker to appreciate fully the challenge posed to Judaism by Aristotelian rationalism and to address it in a philosophically literate way. The concluding portions of the *Kuzari* make clear that he was increasingly sceptical about the pretensions of philosophy in general and those of Aristotelianism in particular, although he admired and practised the kind of critical scepticism associated with Socrates in the early Platonic dialogues. He wrote as a non-philosophic *mutakallim*, arguing in largely empirical terms, to defend both the opinions and practices of his ancestral faith. In doing so, he produced what has become the classic theological defence of Judaism as a religion of revealed practice which is superior to reason but none the less compatible with it, once reason's limits have been recognized.

BIBLIOGRAPHY

Aloni, N. (1980) "The *Kuzari*: an Anti-Arabiyyah Polemic", *Eshel Beer Sheva*, 2: 119–44 (in Hebrew).

Altmann, A. (1944) "The Climatological Factor in Yehudah Hallevi's Theory of Prophecy", *Melilah*: 1–17 (in Hebrew).

—— (1969) "Ibn Bājja on Man's Ultimate Felicity", in *Studies in Religious Philosophy and Mysticism* (Ithaca): 73–107.

Baneth, D. H. (1981) "Judah Halevi and al-Ghazālī", in A. Jospe (ed.) *Studies in Jewish Thought: an Anthology of German Jewish Scholarship* (Detroit): 181–99. For sources and other annotations see the Hebrew version of this essay (1941–2) in *Keneset*, 7: 311–29.

Baneth, D. H. and Ben-Shammai, Ḥ. (eds) (1977) *Kitāb al-Radd wa'l Dalīl fi'l-Dīn al-Dhalīl* (Jerusalem). A new English translation based on this critical edition was begun by the late Lawrence V. Berman and is currently being completed by Barry S. Kogan for publication by Yale University Press.

Berger, M. S. (1992) "Toward a New Understanding of Judah Halevi's *Kuzari*", *Journal of Religion*, 72(2): 210–28.

Davidson, H. (1972) "The Active Intellect in the *Cuzari* and Hallevi's Theory of Causality", *Revue des études juives,* 131: 351–96.

Dunlop, D. M. (1967) *The History of the Jewish Khazars* (New York).

Goitein, S. D. (1974) "Judaeo-Arabic Letters from Spain (Early Twelfth Century)", *Orientalia Hispanica*, 1(1): 331–50.

Goldziher, J. (1905) "Le Amr ilâhî (hâ-'inyân hâ-élôhî) chez Judah Halevi", *Revue des études juives,* 50: 32–41.

Hirschfeld, H. (ed.) (1887) *Das Buch Al-Chazari des Abu'l Hasan Jehudah Hallewi im arabischen Urtext sowie in der hebräischen Übersetzung des Jehudah ibn Tibbon* (Leipzig).
—— (trans.) (1905) *Judah Hallevi's Kitāb al-Khazarī* (London).
Lasker, D. J. (1989) "Judah Halevi and Karaism", in J. Neusner *et al.* (eds), *From Ancient Israel to Modern Judaism: Intellect in Quest of Understanding – Essays in Honor of Marvin Fox*, 3 (Atlanta): 111–25.
Lerner, R. and Mahdi, M. (eds) (1963) *Medieval Political Philosophy* (New York).
Motzkin, A. L. (1980) "On Halevi's *Kuzari* as a Platonic Dialogue", *Interpretation*, 9(1): 111–24.
Nuriel, A. (1990) "The Divine Will in the *Kuzari*", *Meḥkarei Yerushalayim B'Maḥshevet Yisrael*, 9(2): 19–32 (in Hebrew).
Pines, S. (1980) "Shiite Terms and Conceptions in Judah Halevi's *Kuzari*", *Jerusalem Studies in Arabic and Islam*, 2: 165–219.
Silman, Y. (1985) *Thinker and Seer: the Development of the Thought of R. Yehuda Halevi in the Kuzari* (Ramat-Gan) (in Hebrew).
—— (1990) "Revealed Religions in the Thought of Judah Halevi: A Systematic Presentation", in *Alei Shefer: Studies in the Literature of Jewish Thought presented to Rabbi Dr Alexandre Safran*, ed. Moshe Hallamish (Ramat-Gan): 163–74.
Sirat, C. (1985) *A History of Jewish Philosophy in the Middle Ages* (Cambridge).
Strauss, L. (1943) "The Law of Reason in the *Kuzari*", *Proceedings of the American Academy for Jewish Research*, 3: 47–96.
Watt, W. M. (1953) *The Faith and Practice of al-Ghazali* (London).
Wolfson, H. A. (1973) "The Platonic, Aristotelian, and Stoic Theories of Creation in Halevi and Maimonides", in I. Twersky and G. H. Williams (eds) *Studies in the History of Philosophy and Religion*, (Cambridge, Mass.) 1: 234–49.
—— (1977a) "Maimonides and Halevi: A Study in Typical Jewish Attitudes Towards Greek Philosophy in the Middle Ages", in *ibid.*, 2: 120–60.
—— (1977b) "Hallevi and Maimonides on Design, Chance, and Necessity", in *ibid.*, 2: 1–59.
—— (1977c) "Hallevi and Maimonides on Prophecy", in *ibid.*, 2: 60–119.
—— (1977d) "Judah Halevi on Causality and Miracles", in *ibid.*, 2: 415–32.

CHAPTER 43

Maimonides

Alexander Broadie

Rabbi Moses ben Maimon, known as Maimonides, was born in Cordoba in 1135 or 1138.[1] In 1148 the town was captured by the Almohads and the Maimon family fled. It is unclear where they spent the following twelve years, but in 1160 they arrived in the Moroccan town of Fez, an Almohad centre and therefore a strange choice for the family. Some four or five years later they journeyed to the land of Israel where they stayed for six months, before travelling on to Fustat in Egypt where the family finally settled. Maimonides was the greatest rabbinic leader of his era, and his influence on current Jewish philosophy and theology is pervasive. His writings include a large body of rabbinic responsa, many medical treatises and three major works. They are the *Commentary on the Mishnah* (written in Arabic), the *Mishneh Torah* (in Hebrew), and *The Guide of the Perplexed* (in Arabic). The first two of these are primarily concerned with legal matters, though both contain philosophical material. The third work, however, is mainly philosophical, and set the agenda for practically all subsequent Jewish philosophy.

Nevertheless Maimonides fits into the history of Islamic philosophy, for he was steeped in Islamic philosophy and was taken up and studied by later Islamic philosophers.[2] The depth of the Islamic influence is clearly expressed in a letter he wrote to Samuel ibn Tibbon, who translated the *Guide* into Hebrew.[3] After stating that one must study the Aristotelian commentaries of Alexander of Aphrodisias, Themistius and Ibn Rushd (Averroes), he goes on: "I tell you: as for works on logic, one should only study the writings of Abū Nasr al-Fārābī. All his writings are faultlessly excellent. One ought to study and understand them. For he is a great man. Though the works of Avicenna may give rise to objections and are not as [good] as those of Abū Nasr [al-Fārābī], Abū Bakr al-Ṣā'igh [Ibn Bājjah] was also a great philosopher, and all his writings are of a high standard." Of course this is not to imply that Maimonides was not a Jewish philosopher, any more than Aquinas' profound dependence upon Jewish and Islamic sources implies that Aquinas was not in the fullest sense a Christian philosopher. The vast array of rabbinic prooftexts quoted in the *Guide* prevent it being anything other than a specifically Jewish book.[4]

The *Guide*, which deals with a wide range of issues in the philosophy of religion, has the appearance of disorder, which is strange since the *Mishneh Torah* shows Maimonides to have been one of the great systematizers of the Middle Ages.[5] There are several partial explanations for this appearance, one of which is that the lack of order adopted by Maimonides was due to his concern to hinder certain people grasping the sense that he sought to convey to those for whom the *Guide* was written, namely devout Jews who were also sophisticated philosophers. It is therefore possible to see the *Guide* as both exoteric and esoteric, its covert message being the one that represents Maimonides' real position. This view has been much in vogue recently, due to the influence of Leo Strauss,[6] and there is no doubt that there is textual warrant for it. But it is only part of a much larger story, and perhaps not even a part that gets to the heart of the matter.

The *Guide* is centrally concerned with our knowledge of God. In that area there is no need to obfuscate in order to conceal the truth from the vulgar. On the contrary, the problem is to understand anything. The awesomeness of this task was to the front of Maimonides' mind when writing the introduction to the *Guide*. He makes frequent reference to the sheer difficulty of being intelligible; and the problem of intelligibility is rooted in his difficulty in understanding what he is trying to expound. Thus he writes: "You should not think that these great secrets are fully and completely known to anyone among us. They are not. But sometimes truth flashes out to us so that we think that it is day, and then matter and habit in their various forms conceal it so that we find ourselves again in an obscure night almost as we were at first."[7] He returns to this point:

> Know that whenever one of the perfect wishes to mention, either orally or in writing, something that he understands of these secrets, according to the degree of his perfection, he is unable to explain with complete clarity and coherence even the portion that he has apprehended, as he could with the other sciences whose teaching is generally recognized. Rather there will befall him when teaching another that which he has undergone when learning himself. I mean to say that the subject matter will appear, flash, and then be hidden again, as though this were the nature of this subject matter.[8]

It is in this light that we have to understand him when he lists seven kinds of cause of contradiction or contrariety, and states that examples of two of these kinds are to be found in the *Guide*. In both cases it is the obscurity of the topic that forces him to adopt contradiction and contrariety as a technique of exposition. Thus he describes the seventh cause in these terms: "In speaking about very obscure matters it is necessary to conceal some parts and to disclose others. Sometimes in the case of certain dicta this necessity requires that the discussion proceed on the basis of a certain premiss, whereas in another place necessity requires that the discussion proceed on the basis of another premiss contradicting the first one."[9] These are the words of a man prepared to use any device in an attempt to come as close as he can to understanding what we have no right to think we ever could understand.

The verse "The Lord our God, the Lord is one" is central to Maimonides' thought. He holds that there are two senses in which God is one. He is one, firstly, in the sense that there is no other God, and, secondly, in the sense that He is not a many-in-one; there is no multiplicity in Him. The two senses are expressed here: "God is one, neither two nor more, but a unity, unlike other unities in the universe which may have many parts or like a body which is divided into parts."[10] These two senses are linked, for if God had many attributes, each of course being divine, each would have to be regarded as a distinct God. Thus multiplicity of divine attributes implies polytheism. Indeed, on Maimonides' view there cannot be even one divine attribute, for if God had an attribute it would be possible to distinguish between God who had the attribute and the attribute possessed by Him. Hence if God has just one attribute He is not one, but two. Even less can we think of God as having many attributes. But if so, how can we say anything of Him?

Nevertheless the Bible tells us many things about God, that He is good, powerful and so on, which surely implies that He has many attributes. Maimonides' reply, in line with a long philosophical tradition, is that these terms are not to be understood literally of God. Their signification is of the negative kind. To say that God is good is to deny that He is bad; to say that He is alive is to deny that He is dead. The Bible, therefore, does not after all ascribe many attributes to God. For if to say that God is wise is to say only that He is not ignorant, then ascribing wisdom to God is in effect a way of not ascribing anything to Him, any more than we ascribe anything to Him by denying that He is foolish or weak.

Maimonides is not reporting what ordinary people mean when they ascribe attributes to God – he is telling us what affirmative terms actually do mean when predicated of God in the Bible. Of course, if no affirmative terms, literally understood, are truly predicable of God, a question arises concerning why some affirmative terms, and not others, are predicated of Him. If literally God is no more good than He is bad, why is it more appropriate to say that He is good? Maimonides' answer is that the multitude must be taught that God has attributes which the multitude believe to be the highest perfections. Otherwise they would come to believe that there are deficiencies in God.

If we can know only what God is not, then what counts as knowledge of God? We cannot know God literally to be good, since He is not, nor literally to be wise, since He is not, and so on. Surely there is nothing we can know Him literally to be; in which case we know nothing about Him. If so, even a person of the deepest religious insight must be totally ignorant of God. In one sense this is accepted by Maimonides, in another not. If to be ignorant of something is to know nothing of what it is, then on Maimonides' view we are all equally ignorant of God. Nevertheless the person who thinks that God is corporeal knows less about God than does the person who knows that God is incorporeal, and to think that God's wisdom is the same sort of thing as human wisdom is to know less about God than does the person who knows that God is not wise in the way in which humans are.

Thus everyone is ignorant of God and also there are degrees of knowledge of Him. Maimonides affirms: "You come nearer to an apprehension of Him, may He be exalted, with every increase in the negations regarding Him; and you come nearer that apprehension than he who does not negate with regard to Him that which, according to what has been demonstrated to you, ought to be negated."[11]

Maimonides applies his negative theology to the concept of divine existence. Following Avicenna closely, he held that the existence of a thing whose existence has a cause is an accident attaching to the existent.[12] Thus it is a contingent fact regarding any created thing that it exists. It does not exist by its very nature for if its nature is to exist then it could not not exist. But God's existence cannot be contingent. Since He has no attribute He has no accidental attribute, and hence His existence cannot be an accident. But though we understand the existence of created things we do not understand God's. Therefore in the way in which we understand the term "exist" it is more accurate to deny God's existence than to affirm it: "the term 'existence' can only be applied equivocally to His existence and to that of things other than He".[13] A prooftext is provided: "In this sense it is also said: 'But My face shall not be seen' (Exodus 33: 23), meaning that the true reality of My existence as it veritably is cannot be grasped."[14]

But on the basis of twenty-five propositions[15] which Maimonides takes to have been demonstrated by Aristotle and the Peripatetic school, he proves that an unmoved first mover, which he identifies with God, exists. We know, or think we do, what it is for ordinary physical objects to exist. In expounding that knowledge we refer characteristically to spatial, temporal and various sensible properties of the objects. But how is God's existence to be characterized? Part of Maimonides' answer is that in God existence is not an accident superadded to His essence for otherwise God would be a contingent being – which He cannot be, for since His essence and existence are identical with each other it is His nature to be.

The term Maimonides uses to describe the kind of existence here at issue is "necessary". The difference between necessary and contingent existence is such that they have the name "existence" in common and nothing else. Maimonides believed that we can have no insight into the nature of necessary existence. Our knowledge of it is purely negative, for what we know of it is that, whatever contingent existence is, necessary existence is not like that.

Within Maimonides' system the conceptual point at which necessary and contingent existence meet is creation. There are notorious problems concerning Maimonides' doctrine on God's creation of the world,[16] one of which concerns the identification of the position, among several that he sets out, that he actually holds. He describes three positions, those of (1) the Law of Moses, (2) Plato and (3) Aristotle. The first of these is:

> that the world as a whole – I mean to say, every existent other than God, may He be exalted – was brought into existence by God after having been purely and absolutely nonexistent, and that God, may He be exalted, had existed alone, and nothing else – neither an angel nor a sphere nor what subsists within the sphere. Afterwards, through His will and His volition, He brought into existence out of nothing all the beings as they are, time itself being one of the created things.[17]

That there was no time before the creation of the world is proved by the fact that time depends for its existence upon the existence of motion (for it is the measure of motion), and there is no motion unless there is something in motion. And *ex hypothesi* before the creation nothing was in motion. Time therefore is consequent upon what is moved. Hence it is only by misunderstanding the nature of time that those who subscribe to the foregoing view of creation believe that God existed before the creation and then created.

According to the second view, God created the world from an antecedent matter co-eternal with Himself. The relation is similar to that between the potter and the clay, except that we have to think here of an eternal potter moulding at will eternal clay so that the clay has, at His will, first one form and then another. Among the things subject in this way to generation and passing-away are heaven and earth. The similarity between this position and the one presented in Plato's *Timaeus* is evident.

The third view, which is Aristotelian, affirms, as does the second, that matter is eternal. But the third view includes this doctrine: "it would be an impossibility that will should change in God or a new volition arise in Him".[18] This position contradicts the one ascribed to Plato; Aristotle's God does not resemble a potter forming things at will from the available matter. In particular Aristotle held that heaven will not cease, nor will time or motion. Not motion, for any motion is preceded by its passage to actuality, and that passage must itself be produced by some other motion. And not time, for every motion occurs in time.

Maimonides believed that the chief threat to the Mosaic teaching on the creation is provided by Aristotle, and his tactic is to defuse this threat by showing that it has been misunderstood, for, though Aristotle argued for the eternity of the world, he knew those arguments not to be demonstrations.

Aristotle employs proofs based upon the nature of what exists, "a nature that has attained stability, is perfect, and has achieved actuality". The reason these proofs are not demonstrations is that they assume that this nature resembles the state it was in while in the state of being generated.[19] Given the system of natural laws, each thing is generated and then passes away by the process of matter sloughing off one form and acquiring another; there is no natural generation and passing away except by this means. But Maimonides held that the natural world as a whole, including its mechanism for generation and passing away, may not have been generated in accordance with that same mechanism. The fact that things in the natural order are thus generated is irrelevant to the question of how the order itself came to be. It leaves open the possibility that God created the world *ex nihilo*, a doctrine proclaimed by the prophets, and formulated by Maimonides as follows: "it [the world] is not subject to generation as are the things generated from it, nor to passing-away as are the things that pass away into it, but is created from nothing. And its Creator may, if He wishes to do so, render it entirely and absolutely nonexistent."[20]

Yet if God created the world *ex nihilo* in time, this surely implies that in God there was a passage from potency to act, and yet we cannot suppose God to have potency, for He is pure act.[21] But Maimonides rejects this argument, for it is based upon the false premiss that God is composed of matter and form. Whenever such a composite being acts there is within it a transition from potency to act. But this account of what it is to act cannot apply to an absolutely simple being, one containing no substrate of matter taking on one form and then another. A divine act therefore cannot involve a transition from potency. It is in precisely this way, as involving no transition from potency, that the Active Intellect acts, according to al-Fārābī.[22] It has to be concluded that the term "act" is predicated equivocally of God's acts and of human acts.

Maimonides' case on behalf of the doctrine of creation *ex nihilo* is not merely that the case for the eternity of the natural order has not been demonstrated. For he discusses the evidence in the light of Aristotelian celestial physics, which he believes to have failed in its attempt to explain the motions of the spheres and the fixity of the stars within the spheres, and finds in those celestial phenomena strong proof of purposiveness in the world. Since there are many doubts attaching to the Aristotelian model, and since the doctrine of creation *ex nihilo* is in addition the teaching of Abraham and Moses, this latter is the doctrine Maimonides endorses.

Maimonides' account of creation casts a long shadow across his discussion on prophecy, for he begins the latter discussion by referring to a resemblance between opinions concerning prophecy and the opinions, just discussed, concerning cosmogony.[23] I should like now to enquire into the nature of the resemblance he has in mind. He speaks of three opinions concerning prophecy, and ascribes them, respectively, to (1) the pagans who considered prophecy as true and some of the common people professing our Law, (2) "the philosophers" and (3) "our Law".[24] According to the first opinion God chooses any morally sound person He wishes, turns him or her into a prophet, and sends him or her on a mission. The chosen person can be wise or ignorant, old or young. The second opinion is almost the opposite: "When, in the case of a superior individual who is perfect with respect to his rational and moral qualities, his imaginative faculty is in its most perfect state and when he has been prepared in the way you will hear, he will necessarily become a prophet inasmuch as this is a perfection that belongs to us by nature."[25]

Whereas according to the first opinion it is by God's will that a person becomes a prophet and the person makes little contribution personally, the second opinion places all the emphasis upon the will of the human being and upon the way nature, not God, co-operates with the person's will. The third opinion combines elements from the previous two. According to it the second opinion is correct, with this proviso, that a person may be fit for prophecy and prepared for it, and yet not attain it because God has willed against it. When he introduces the third opinion Maimonides describes God's role in the negative way I have just employed; that is, it is not that God makes someone a prophet who could not become one by his own powers, instead He can prevent someone becoming a prophet who would otherwise become one by his own powers. However, in the course of subsequent elaboration of the third opinion Maimonides refers to the "fundamental principle that God turns whom He wills, whenever He wills, into a prophet – but only someone perfect and superior to the utmost degree"[26] and this is, at least verbally, a much more positive description. However, the tenor of Maimonides' discussion supports the view that he saw "our Law", that is, the third opinion, as holding that God plays a purely negative role in the making of a prophet. And it may be best to interpret the phrase "God turns whom He wills . . . into a prophet" as saying no more than is said by the expressly negative formula.

Maimonides opens his discussion on prophecy with these much disputed words:

> The opinions of people concerning prophecy are like their opinions concerning the eternity of the world or its creation in time. I mean by this that just as the people to whose mind the existence of the deity is firmly established, have, as we have set forth, three opinions concerning the eternity of the world or its creation in time, so are there also three opinions concerning prophecy.[27]

Does he mean merely that the two sets of opinions are alike in that each set has three members? Perhaps, more substantially, he means that each member of the first set resembles a member of the second. The opinions concerning cosmogony were the Mosaic, the Platonic and the Aristotelian. Let us call them C_1, C_2 and C_3. Let us call the three opinions concerning prophetology, in order of exposition, P_1, P_2 and P_3.

Which prophetological doctrine matches C_1? If we attend to Maimonides' identification of those who hold the various doctrines, it is clear that C_1 is matched by P_3, for these two, and none of the others, are said to be part of "our Law". It is true that P_1 is said to be held by "some of the common people professing our Law", but this does not imply that the doctrine is part of our Law. On the contrary we are clearly being alerted to the fact that it is not.

But if we attend not to the identity of the holders but to the content of the doctrines then the obvious thing to say is that C_1 is matched by P_1. For in each case what is under discussion, the fact that the world exists and the fact that a person is a prophet, is accounted for simply in terms of the divine will. No one could become a prophet without God's willing them to become one, and the world could not exist without God's willing that it should. In each case something comes out of nothing by divine will. In seeking resemblances, therefore, we must specify the principle of resemblance at issue, for there is a resemblance in respect of source of sanction, and a resemblance in respect of content. And indeed, in the light of the common view that the *Guide* contains not only an overt but also a secret doctrine, we need to ask which doctrine resembles which in respect of being believed, secretly, by Maimonides. Similar difficulties beset any attempt to match C_2 and C_3 with the doctrines concerning prophetology.

A doctrine developed by Maimonides where it is natural to distinguish between what he said explicitly and what he really believed concerns the concept of God's knowledge. The doctrine is central to the *Guide*, and I must therefore indicate what I see to be the core issue.

In the *Guide* the chief discussion of divine knowledge occurs within an investigation into divine providence for, in the eyes of some, God's governance of the world is problematic in view of the fact that people's goodness does not guarantee them protection and people's wickedness may not prevent their prospering. How is this mismatch of merit and circumstance possible? Since God surely knows about the goodness of the good and the wickedness of the wicked, either He is powerless to prevent this mismatch or He does not object to it and perhaps does not see it as one. Since these alternatives are intolerable, as implying powerlessness or evil in God, we must look elsewhere. Maimonides reports an "aberrant opinion of the philosophers" that God does not know the circumstances of human beings.[28] But he cannot accept this solution.

Admittedly there are philosophical arguments to support the claim that God is ignorant of His creatures. For example, particular sensory objects are known by means of the senses as contrasted with universals which are known by means of the intellect. And since sensory receptors are corporeal, God lacks senses. Therefore He cannot know His creatures.[29]

However, Maimonides is guided by the argument that since ignorance is a deficiency it cannot be predicated truly of God. And his principal argument against the aberrant opinion of the philosophers is this: God is our Creator, making us, including our receptors by which we gain sensory knowledge of the world. Like any maker of an instrument, He must have a conception of the work done by the instruments He has made. Hence, He knows what it is to see and hear. Therefore, that God does not have corporeal sensory receptors does not imply that He cannot have knowledge of individual things.

In discussing the kind of knowledge that God has, Maimonides emphasizes God's role as Creator. As Creator, He has practical knowledge of the world, knowledge of a kind into which we have some insight for we also make things – we form a conception and then make something embodying the conception. The thing comes to be in virtue of our knowledge – we do not have to consult the world in order to know the thing.[30] Everything in the created world stands in the relation of artefact to divine artificer. Maimonides continues: "the things in question follow upon His knowledge, which preceded and established them as they are".[31]

It is difficult to make sense of the chapter in which Maimonides discusses these matters, except on the assumption that he is using our insight into the practical knowledge of the artificer as a means of giving us insight into the kind of knowledge that God has of our world. Here, then, is a resemblance between God and ourselves. But this teaching sits uneasily with the doctrine that any term predicable truly of God and creatures is predicated of God and creatures in a purely equivocal way.

Thus His knowledge and ours have in common the word only. For His knowledge is not even an attribute of His though our knowledge is an attribute of us humans. Hence God's knowledge comes under no metaphysical category whatever under which human knowledge can truly be brought.

A question arises therefore as to whether we are not faced here with an application of the expository method of contradiction or contrariety described in the Introduction to the *Guide*. If so, and if it is the seventh cause of contradiction or contrariety that is at issue, it follows that for the sake of exposition Maimonides has made contradictory assumptions. When, in part 1, he first expounds the concept of divine knowledge, he assumes that such knowledge is not an attribute for it is on the contrary identical with God's essence. When in part 3 he returns to a fuller exposition of that same concept he assumes that divine knowledge is sufficiently like an attribute to bear serious comparison with the kind of knowledge that we exercise in our role as artificer. Maimonides is speaking here about "very obscure matters", and perhaps he should have heeded the words of Psalm 65, which he quotes: "Silence is praise to Thee". But Maimonides was not prepared to abandon the attempt to probe as far as he could into the metaphysical depths and to give what help he could to those who would be helped.

Finally we turn to Maimonides' moral philosophy,[32] and in particular to his accounts of virtue and vice. It is widely held that in this area Maimonides is Aristotelian, and while this interpretation is defensible his teaching on virtue and vice is not Aristotelian in all respects. I should like here to defend the claim that though Maimonides follows Aristotle in employing a doctrine of the mean in his discussion of moral states, he has a different perspective upon that doctrine. That Maimonides at least employs terminology highly suggestive of Aristotle's doctrine is not at issue, but the terminology has to be handled carefully, for there is at first sight something surprising in a rabbi being Aristotelian in his moral philosophy. We should expect him to have a rabbinic account of virtue and vice, one based upon the concepts of divine commandments and of *imitatio dei*, not upon the concept of a virtuous state of character intermediate between two other states of character, one excessive and the other deficient, and both to be classed as vices. On the other hand this expectation is based on the assumption that the Aristotelian doctrine of the mean is incompatible with rabbinic teaching and, as we shall see, Maimonides would reject that assumption.

Central to the Maimonidean ethic is the concept of *imitatio dei*; we are to imitate God's ways:

> Just as He is called gracious, you too be gracious; just as He is called merciful, you too be merciful; just as He is called holy,

> you too be holy . . . In like manner the prophets applied all these terms to God: slow to anger and abundant in loving kindness, just and righteous, perfect, powerful, strong, and the like. They did so to proclaim that these ways are good and right, and a man is obliged to train himself to follow them and imitate them according to his strength.[33]

Maimonides immediately adds: "Since these terms applied to the Creator refer to the middle way that we are obliged to follow, this way is called the way of the Lord." This suggests that the way of the Lord is the way of Aristotle; whoever fails to imitate God's ways suffers from either an excess or a deficiency of character.

However, Maimonides appears to deny that every virtuous state is a mean between extremes. In particular, following the description of Moses as very meek (Numbers 12: 3), Maimonides states that in respect of some character traits we are forbidden to follow in the middle way, and he instances pride: "for the good way is not that a man be merely humble, but that he have a lowly spirit".[34] His objection to pride is that "all pride denies the existence of God". What he has in mind here is this: we should be humble when we stand before our superiors, the degree of humility required being proportional to the degree of our inferiority; and we always stand before God. However, it can be argued that this is not an exception to the doctrine of the mean. Aristotle would no doubt agree that our attitude to a person should depend upon whether we are superior or inferior to, or on the same level as, the other. The proper attitude is intermediate between the too much and the too little. But since we are in the presence of God, anything other than extreme humility is a too little in respect of our humility. Hence Maimonides is not rejecting the doctrine of the mean; instead he is applying it in the context of a world view deeply alien to Aristotle.

In his application of the doctrine of the mean, Maimonides makes use of parallels between ethics and medical practice:

> Should [a man's] soul become sick, he must follow the same course in treating it as in the medical treatment of bodies. For when the body gets out of equilibrium we look to which side it inclines in becoming unbalanced, and then oppose it with its contrary until it returns to equilibrium. When it is in equilibrium we remove that counterbalance and revert to that which keeps the body in equilibrium. We act in a similar manner with regard to moral habits.[35]

His example is the moral vice of miserliness: "If we wanted to give medical treatment to this sick person we would not order him to be liberal. That would be like using a balanced course for treating someone whose fever is excessive. This would not cure him of his sickness." The advice Maimonides gives to those who have fallen into vice is this: "Let them go to the wise men – who are physicians of the soul – and they will cure their disease by means of the character traits that they will teach them, until they make them return to the middle way."[36]

These and similar passages point to a crucial difference between Aristotle and Maimonides in respect of their teaching on the mean. Within the doctrine, considered as a conceptual framework, Aristotle presents a programme of upbringing for the young. They are to be trained to be good citizens; and no mistake dare be made, for the result of the training is a character trait so fixed as to be barely alterable. For Maimonides, on the other hand, conceptualizing virtue as a mean implies a perspective from which virtue presents itself as achievable by therapeutic methods. Thus a large part of Maimonides' thinking about moral matters deals with the problem of moral rehabilitation, that is, with the curing of vice. His writings on this topic reveal him to have been deeply aware of the fragility of virtue, and of the corresponding need never to relent in the battle for one's virtue. Each victory is a holding operation: "the perfect man needs to inspect his moral habits continually, weigh his actions, and reflect upon the state of his soul every single day".[37] Aristotle on the contrary pays very little attention to the curing of vice, and a very great deal to the training for virtue. To maintain the medical metaphor, Aristotle is primarily concerned with preventive moral medicine, Maimonides with restorative. The contrast here is sharp, but in Maimonides' judgment Aristotle's intellect was as fully developed as was possible by purely natural means. Specific points of difference between the two men should not be allowed to mask the overwhelming influence that Aristotle exerted, directly and also through his Greek and Islamic commentators, upon Maimonides.

NOTES

1 The year 1135 is generally quoted as Maimonides' year of birth, but there is strong evidence in support of the later date. See S. D. Goitein, "Moses Maimonides, Man of Action: a Revision of the Master's Biography in Light of the Geniza Documents", in *Hommage à Georges Vajda: Etudes d'histoire et de pensée juives* (Louvain, 1980): 155–67.

2 For discussion of Maimonides as part of the Islamic philosophical tradition see O. Leaman, *Moses Maimonides* (London, 1990): chapter 1. See also "Translator's Introduction" by Shlomo Pines in Moses Maimonides, *The Guide of the Perplexed* (Chicago, 1963), trans. S. Pines (hereinafter cited as *Guide*): lxxviii–cxxxii. This is a translation of the Arabic text, ed. S. Munk in *Le Guide des Egarés*, 1–3 (Paris, 1856–66); reprinted with notes and variants, Jerusalem, 1931.

3 For texts of two Hebrew versions edited by Alexander Marx see *Jewish Quarterly*

Review, new series, 25: 374ff. For excerpts and commentary see Shlomo Pines, *op. cit.*: lix–lx.

4 I am grateful to Irene Lancaster for helpful discussion of this matter.

5 The most detailed account of the structure of the *Mishneh Torah* is in Isadore Twersky, *Introduction to the Code of Maimonides (Mishneh Torah)* (London and New Haven, 1980), esp. chapter 4.

6 See e.g. Leo Strauss, "The Literary Character of the Guide for the Perplexed", in Salo Baron (ed.) *Essays on Maimonides: an Octocentennial Volume* (New York, 1941): 37–91; and the abridged version in J. A. Buijs (ed.), *Maimonides: a Collection of Critical Essays* (Notre Dame, 1988): 30–58. Also Leo Strauss, "How to Begin to Study *The Guide of the Perplexed*" in *Guide*: xi–lvi. See also Marvin Fox, *Interpreting Maimonides: Studies in Methodology, Metaphysics, and Moral Philosophy* (Chicago, 1990): chapter 3.

7 *Guide*, Introduction: 7.

8 *Ibid.*: 8. Problems concerning Maimonides on the limits of human knowledge are aired illuminatingly in S. Pines, "The Limitations of Human Knowledge according to Al-Farabi, ibn Bajja, and Maimonides", in I. Twersky (ed.) *Studies in Medieval Jewish History and Literature* (Cambridge, Mass., 1979): 82–109; reprinted in J. A. Buijs (ed.) *op. cit*: 91–121.

9 *Guide*, Introduction: 18.

10 *Sefer ha-Mada* ("The Book of Knowledge"), treatise 1, chapter 1, in *Mishneh Torah*, Hebrew text ed. S. T. Rubenstein, M. D. Rabinowitz *et al.* (Jerusalem, 1967–73).

11 *Guide*, 1.59: 138.

12 *Ibid.*, 1.57: 132. See A. Altmann's influential article "Essence and Existence in Maimonides", in A. Altmann, *Studies in Religious Philosophy and Mysticism* (London, 1969): 108–27.

13 *Guide*, 1.35: 80; cf. 1.56: 131.

14 *Ibid.*, 1.37: 86.

15 *Ibid.*, 2, Introduction: 235–9.

16 See O. Leaman, *op. cit.*: chapter 4 for a discussion of many of the issues concerning Maimonides on creation. See also O. Leaman, *An Introduction to Medieval Islamic Philosophy* (Cambridge, 1985): 59–74. Also Sara Klein-Braslavy, "The Creation of the World and Maimonides' Interpretation of *Gen.* i–v", in S. Pines and Y. Yovel (eds), *Maimonides and Philosophy* (Dordrecht, 1986): 65–78. Also Marvin Fox, *op. cit.*: chapter 10.

17 *Guide*, 2.13: 281.

18 *Ibid.*, 2.13: 284.

19 *Ibid.*, 2.17: 296.

20 *Ibid.*, 2.17: 297.

21 *Ibid.*, 2.14: 287.

22 *Ibid.*, 2.18: 299.

23 See L. Kaplan, "Maimonides on the Miraculous Element in Prophecy", *Harvard Theological Review*, 70 (1977): 233–56. Also H. Davidson, "Maimonides' Secret Position on Creation", in I. Twersky (ed.), *op. cit.*: 16–40. Also W. Z. Harvey, "A Third Approach to Maimonides' Cosmogony–Prophetology Puzzle", *Harvard Theological Review*, 74 (1981): 287–301; reprinted in J. A. Buijs (ed.), *op. cit.*: 71–88.

24 *Guide*, 2.32: 360.
25 *Ibid.*, 2.32: 361.
26 *Ibid.*, 2.32: 362.
27 *Ibid.*, 2.32: 360.
28 *Ibid.*, 3.16: 461–2.
29 *Ibid.*, 3.16: 463.
30 *Ibid.*, 3.21: 484.
31 *Ibid.*, 3.21: 485.
32 For detailed discussion of Maimonides' moral philosophy (though not containing the conclusion drawn here) see M. Fox, *op. cit.*: part 2. See also L. V. Berman, "The Ethical Views of Maimonides within the Context of Islamicate Civilization", in J. L. Kraemer, *Perspectives on Maimonides: Philosophical and Historical Studies* (Oxford, 1991): 13–32.
33 *Hilkhot De'ot*: chapter 1; for translation see R. L. Weiss and C. E. Butterworth (trans., *Ethical Writings of Maimonides*) (New York, 1975): 30.
34 *Hilkhot De'ot*: chapter 2; for translation see Weiss and Butterworth, *op. cit.*: 31.
35 Eight Chapters, chapter 4, in *Commentary on the Mishnah*, Introduction to *Tractate Aboth*, known as "Eight Chapters". For translation see Weiss and Butterworth, *op. cit.*: 68.
36 *Hilkhot De'ot*: chapter 2; for translation see Weiss and Butterworth, *op. cit.*: 31.
37 "Eight Chapters", chapter 4; *ibid.*: 73.

CHAPTER 44

Gersonides: Levi ben Gershom

Gad Freudenthal

INTRODUCTION

Rabbi Levi ben Gershom, or Gersonides (1288–1344), is one of the most original medieval Jewish thinkers, whose interests and writings spanned philosophy, biblical exegesis, astronomy, mathematics, natural science, logic and medicine. Like most contemporary Jewish philosophers in southern France, Gersonides wrote in Hebrew and drew almost solely on sources available to him in that language. But since most of these were translations from Arabic, Gersonides can be viewed as an innovative continuer of the Arabic philosophical tradition that had culminated in Ibn Rushd (Averroes), indeed as someone who developed his own philosophical ideas through a critical dialogue mainly with two major thinkers who had written in Arabic: Maimonides and Ibn Rushd, as well as, to a lesser extent, the astronomer al-Biṭrūjī.

Although Gersonides greatly admired Maimonides and embraced the latter's programme of creating a synthesis of Judaism and Peripateticism (in one of its versions), he was yet in sharp opposition to cardinal Maimonidean positions. In a nutshell, Gersonides upheld, *contra* Maimonides, that (1) it can be demonstrated that God purposefully created the world in time; that (2) God has designed the world so as to suit perfectly the sublunar creatures living in it, particularly humans; that (3) humans are capable of knowing the world and indeed human perfection consists in acquiring such knowledge; and that (4) knowledge about the created world in fact bears upon the Creator, who therefore to some extent is knowable by man. Thus, Maimonides' uncompromising anti-anthropocentrism, his epistemological scepticism and the associated negative theology, as well as his elitism and esoterism, are all emphatically rejected by Gersonides: on both the cosmological and the epistemological planes, Gersonides' world-view is decidedly optimistic. Gersonides' commitment to the idea of scientific progress and his life-long scientific practice are the consequences of this confidence in the privileged position of humankind in God's world.

LIFE AND WORKS[1]

Our knowledge of Gersonides' life is very scanty. He was born in 1288 and lived most of his life in Orange in southern France, which had a middle-size Jewish community.[2] We do not know anything definite about the course of his studies or about who his teachers were, although a few references in his writings to opinions held by his father suggest that the latter was a scholar too.[3] Gersonides' knowledge of Arabic and Latin has been the subject of some controversy. In his writings Gersonides mentions only works available in Hebrew, although on a few occasions he remarks that he checked the Arabic version of a problematic passage;[4] it seems certain however that he could not read entire works in Arabic.[5] The same presumably holds with respect to Latin: although, as the late Shlomo Pines has shown, Gersonides' doctrine of divine attributes reveals similarities to contemporary Scholastic doctrines, this possible influence was presumably oral.[6]

When Gersonides was eighteen years old (1306), Philippe the Fair expelled all Jews from the Kingdom of France. Yet this historic catastrophe (which did not hit Orange) left no definite traces in Gersonides' writings, although it may perhaps be accountable for the fact that Gersonides began writing relatively late in his life. He set on writing his major philosophic work, the *Sefer Milḥamot ha-Shem*[7] ("The Wars of the Lord"), in 1317, at the age of twenty-nine, and was to pursue it during the following twelve years. In parallel, however, he composed two series of works. The first series, written between *c.* 1319 and 1324, consists of specialized scientific treatises: an innovative work on logic, *The Book of the Correct Syllogism* (1319); a treatise in arithmetic comprising an original chapter on combinatorial theory (1321); and a set of super-commentaries on many of Ibn Rushd's epitomes of, or middle commentaries on, Aristotle's treatises in natural philosophy (1321–4).[8] Subsequently, Gersonides set out to write a series of commentaries on various biblical books: Job (1325); Song of Songs (1326); Ecclesiastes (1328); Esther (1329); Ruth (1329); Genesis (1329); Exodus (1330); most of Leviticus (1332). After an interruption of a few years, Gersonides pursued the series with commentaries on Isaiah; the remaining books of the Torah (Pentateuch; completed 1338); the First Prophets (1338); Daniel (1338); Ezra, Nehemiah and the Books of Chronicles (1338); and the Proverbs (1338).[9]

Concomitantly with these philosophic–theological writings, Gersonides most intensively pursued an astronomical research programme. In fact, book 5, part 1 of the *Wars of the Lord* (which comprises six books) is a fully fledged technical astronomical treatise, whose 136 chapters (mostly still in manuscript[10]) are about equal in length to the rest of the *Wars*. This work, often considered as independent and referred to as Gersonides' *Astronomy*, contains the results of Gersonides' own astronomical observations (begun at least in 1320 and continued throughout his life), tables, an incisive criticism of Ptolemy's astronomy and the descriptions of Gersonides' own astronomical models for the different planets.

Gersonides' accomplishments in astronomy and mathematics made him into a highly respected figure, even outside the Jewish community. Whereas most surprisingly we know next to nothing about contacts (intellectual or other) Gersonides presumably had with Jewish contemporaries,[11] we have some information about his continued connections with high-ranking Christians. Early in his career he composed his astronomical tables "at the request of many great and noble Christians"[12] and in 1342 the influential Philippe de Vitry, the future Bishop of Meaux, asked him for advice on a mathematical theorem connected with his own *ars nova* in musical theory.[13] Also in 1342, Gersonides dedicated to Pope Clement VI the Latin version of a trigonometrical treatise, drawn from his *Astronomy*: since, as has recently been shown, this translation is a part of the (incomplete) Latin translation of Gersonides' astronomical work, presumably the translation (in which Gersonides collaborated actively) was done at the behest and under the patronage of the Papal court.[14] Lastly, Gersonides on at least two occasions composed astrological predictions at the request of two popes. The last of them, a prognostication for the great conjunction of 1345, was composed by Gersonides on his deathbed, and through this circumstance we know the time of his decease with unusual precision: the Latin translator of the *Prognostication* informs us that "Master Leo, prevented by death in the year of Christ 1344 on the 20th day of April about noon, put nothing more in order concerning this conjunction".[15]

GERSONIDES' VIEWS ON HUMAN KNOWLEDGE, GOD, CREATION AND THE IMMORTALITY OF THE SOUL

The bedrock on which rests Gersonides' entire philosophic and scientific endeavour is perhaps his unlimited confidence in the power of human reason to attain ever more knowledge of the world and, hence, of God. Maimonides had argued for sceptical positions on a series of questions, not the least important being the question of the createdness or eternity of the world. Gersonides unambiguously rejects Maimonides' stance at the very beginning of the *Wars*:

> Many people will deem it to be arrogance and audacity on our part that we inquire into [the question of] the eternity or createdness [of the world]. For they may perhaps think that the intellect of the wise man is wanting of means to attain the truth on this problem, except if he be a prophet. All the more so since they see that the earlier perfect [men] of our nation, and among them the crown of the glory of the sages of the Torah, our Master Rav Moshe ben Maimon, may he rest in peace, did not pursue an inquiry on such a topic. They may conclude that it is impossible to attain [knowledge] on this question through the means of [philosophical] inquiry. For if this were possible, it would not have escaped the earlier [sages].
>
> Yet this is a very weak argument. For that which had escaped the early [sages] need not necessarily escape their successors as well. For time suffices to bring forth the truth, as the Philosopher said in Book Two of the *Physics*.[16] Indeed, were it otherwise, then there would be no one who, investigating one of the sciences, would know anything but what he had learnt from others. But, should this be assumed to be the case, then there would be no science at all, and this is patently false.[17]

Attaining new knowledge of the world by means of rational, scientific inquiry is possible, Gersonides holds. This confidence in man's capability to know the world has momentous consequences also for Gersonides' view of man's knowledge of God. Gersonides construes the Active Intellect as comprising the *nomos* – in fact the entire natural order – of the created world. This implies that every bit of knowledge about the world is at the same time knowledge of the Active Intellect and hence (as will be seen) of the divine plan of creation. Consequently, if one apprehends an empirical fact or even a mathematical theorem, one has thereby apprehended an intelligible that is a constitutive part of the Active Intellect: one can therefore attain an adequate, if partial, knowledge of the Active Intellect. Now the *nomos* of the created world, which makes up the Active Intellect, is the object of God's thought: it is in fact through God's thinking the *nomos* that it has come into existence, an idea Gersonides borrowed from Themistius.[18] It follows that God's knowledge and man's have the same object, viz. the *nomos*, and that they differ only by degree: "it is clear that the sole and only difference between the knowledge of God, may He be blessed, and our knowledge is that His knowledge is exceedingly more perfect".[19] One can thus attain some positive knowledge of God: Gersonides in fact rejects the Maimonidean thesis that predicating attributes of God would introduce in Him a multiplicity.

Gersonides' optimistic epistemology provides the basis for his heartening theory of the immortality of the soul. To the commonplace view that one's perfection and afterlife depend on the knowledge one had acquired during one's lifetime Gersonides gives a personal twist. Contrary to Maimonides, he holds that the knowledge that is conducive to felicity is not only, and not even mainly, metaphysical, bearing on the separate entities, but rather knowledge of the material world (being in fact knowledge of the Active Intellect).[20] Further, Gersonides shares the received view that eternal felicity belongs to the acquired intellect – to that part of the rational soul that has been actualized by apprehending intelligibles. But whereas most Jewish philosophers, apparently including Maimonides, followed Ibn Bājjah and Ibn Rushd in holding that after death the acquired intellect loses its individuality by being fused into the Active Intellect,[21] Gersonides upholds the survival of the *individual* acquired intellect[22]: acquiring knowledge, specifically empirical knowledge, thus is the supreme good in life. This view gave Gersonides both a theological legitimation for his scientific research and a forceful motivation to invest himself in it. On the question of one's route to eternal felicity too, then, Gersonides and Maimonides parted company.

One cardinal question that can be submitted to scientific inquiry is whether the world is created or eternal. Gersonides, as already noted, believes, *pace* Maimonides, that he can adduce *proofs* for the createdness of the world. These proofs are largely based on what Gersonides takes to be empirical evidence, namely to the effect that the entire cosmos is perfectly designed. For instance:

> in the foregoing it has been conclusively established that whatever is found in the substance of the heaven is of the utmost possible perfection with a view to perfecting these [sublunar] beings. Indeed, were that [heavenly] order corrupted even slightly, these beings would be corrupted [i.e. destroyed] too.[23]

Heavens which are so perfectly designed *with a view to* endowing sublunar existence with the utmost possible perfection cannot but be intentionally, and hence "newly", created, whence it follows that the entire world was created by the volition of a wise Creator.[24]

Gersonides' original cosmogony seeks to give a scientifically sound explanation of creation which is in conformity with the account given in the Torah, reconciling at the same time the thesis of creation in time with the impossibility, postulated by Aristotelian science, of any coming-to-be *ex nihilo*.[25] Gersonides posits a pre-existing "body devoid of all forms", and affirms that the act of creation consisted in God's imprinting upon it the elemental forms: thus ensued the four sublunar elements and the heavenly bodies.[26] The Creator, Gersonides further maintains, conceived these supra- and sublunar forms in such a way that through their influences the celestial bodies would continually control the generation and corruption in the sublunar realm. This is of primary importance. Gersonides gave great prominence to the received medieval physical theory on which the sublunar world is not a closed system: the forms of substances (the vegetative souls of plants and animals, notably, but also the specific forms of some minerals such as the magnet) would not come to be, nor would they subsist, without the informing and sustaining influences continuously issuing from the heavenly bodies. Gersonides repeatedly stresses, drawing on Aristotle's *Meteorologica*, 4, that the equilibrium of the opposite qualities (hot/cold; dry/humid) constituting any sublunar substance is inherently unstable and precarious: left to itself, any substance would soon perish, because one of the qualities would overpower the others:[27] the fact that sublunar substances usually persist over certain periods of time is thus due to the "preserving" influences of the heavenly bodies. (These "influences" were held to consist of "efficient causes" transmitted by the stars' rays, and of "formal causes" emanating from the separate intellects moving the stars.[28]) Gersonides sees the perfection of the world as a whole as consisting precisely in the fact that these celestial influences are faultlessly conceived so as to endow sublunar substances – particularly humanity, the most perfect among them – with maximal perfection and perseverance, a sure indication of a divine plan. Gersonides is here in diametrical opposition to Maimonides' radical anti-anthropocentric stance.[29]

The combination of the influences of the heavenly bodies with the aptitude of the sublunar matter to be suitably affected by them, all "programmed" at the creation, constitute the natural order: once the formless quasi-matter received its forms, the universe became autonomous, functioning solely according to the *nomos* resulting from the interactions of the natures which God has given to its different parts. (More precisely: each separate intellect controls the influences – formal and efficient – emanating from "its" planet; the synthesis of the partial knowledges of all the intellects is the Active Intellect and is in fact the *nomos* of the world.[30]) The consequence is that all events and processes which have taken place after the first act of creation, including the sequel of creation and the events reputed to be miracles, are subsumable under *naturalistic* explanations. Here, as in most of his natural science, Gersonides is obviously a rigorous follower of Ibn Rushd.

Gersonides saw no contradiction whatsoever between his belief that the natural order was autonomous and his commitment to the authoritative texts of Judaism: he rather saw them as fundamentally compatible and complementary. To him, truth could be attained either through scientific inquiry or through a hermeneutic inquiry into the Torah – but both routes were equivalent, necessarily leading to the same single truth. Thus, Gersonides stresses that it is not the case that religious belief *constrained* him to accept the traditional view of temporal creation as found in the Torah: rather, since the Torah is "a *nomos* perfected to the utmost" guiding one to one's ultimate felicity, its statements are necessarily true and in fact directed him in his scientific inquiry.[31] Gersonides would certainly have endorsed the later metaphor according to which Scripture and the book of nature were written by the same hand: revelation and reason are perforce equivalent.

As postulated by Gersonides, the celestial bodies' control over all generation and corruption "down here" naturally encompasses living beings, including humankind. This doctrine, however, does not imply determinism. Gersonides holds each of the celestial bodies to exert its influences only on one *general* aspect of the sublunar physical reality (e.g. the sun "fortifying" the quality of heat, the moon that of humidity, etc.). Consequently, even the Active Intellect, and God too, can have no knowledge of *singular* events. Specifically, while at any time the astral influences give one a *disposition* to act in a certain way (as when one's "heat" is increased and one tends to behave hot-headedly), one can, by following one's intellect rather than one's passions, extricate oneself from the effect of these influences. Gersonides, indeed, forcefully upheld human free will.

The theory of astral influences upon sublunar processes to some extent opens the door for astrology: this is recognized even by Maimonides.[32] Gersonides in fact accords astrology a role, albeit a limited one, in keeping with his view that only general aspects of sublunar occurrences are determined by the heavenly bodies, and with the associated notion of human free will. Unlike Maimonides, who mainly for religious reasons opposed astrology vehemently, Gersonides believed that by being able to predict dispositions to certain types of behaviour, astrologers occasionally succeed in their forecasts of singular events, a feat that is all the more remarkable if one considers that the knowledge of the celestial movements and of astral influences are both (still) wanting.[33] But astrologers cannot, in Gersonides' view, possibly foresee with certainty singular events concerning a given individual. Indeed, Gersonides' only preserved prognostication predicts events involving entire nations, i.e. a great number of individuals: in a large mass, only a few individuals extract themselves from natural determination by following reason using their intellects; the great majority continue to belong to the realm of nature, and so their conduct is largely predictable. Therefore, great upheavals in history (natural and human) can be foreseen by astrologers, although the final and crucial upheaval, namely the establishing of the eternal messianic

Kingdom, will be due to God's special providence and His intervention in the course of history, not to natural necessity.[34] Gersonides ascribes foreknowledge of singular events not to astrologers but notably to prophets, who receive "revelations" from the active intellect: the latter communicates to the prophet "information" pertaining to the general order of reality, which the prophet then applies to the concrete reality, thereby arriving at concrete true predictions.

Traditionalist thinkers of later generations castigated Gersonides for his naturalism, which seemed to belittle miracles. Similarly, his view that God has no knowledge of individuals (because the pre-programmed celestial influences determine only general aspects of the occurrences in the sublunar world and the associated doctrine of free will) implied a denial of individual providence and seemed to leave God no place within human, specifically Jewish, history: this was another stance for which later Jewish thinkers were to disparage him. Within the history of Jewish thought Gersonides' image is that of an audacious freethinker.[35]

GERSONIDES' EMPIRICISM: NATURAL SCIENCE AND ASTRONOMY

The foregoing will have made clear that for Gersonides empirical knowledge of the material world is of crucial importance. It is therefore not surprising that Gersonides himself engaged in science. In natural science his main theoretical paradigms are borrowed from Ibn Rushd: Gersonides' supercommentaries on Ibn Rushd's epitomes and commentaries reveal a profound agreement, although Gersonides very often interjects personal statements to dissent on specific points.

The most remarkable feature of Gersonides' science, of both the sub- and the supralunar realms, is the pronounced empirical attitude it displays. Gersonides apparently conducted botanical experiments: on the occasion of a statement by Ibn Rushd concerning the relationship between the germination of seeds and the type of the soil, Gersonides remarks briefly: "we have tested this [affirmation] for all the [kinds of] seeds and found that the matter is always as stated by Ibn Rushd".[36] Gersonides also envisaged the use of a parabolic mirror as a sort of microscope in order to examine the parts of animals which are too small to be observed with the naked eye: this very impressive idea, which presumably remained unrealized, apparently has no parallel at the time, at least in Europe.[37] Indeed, for Gersonides even the most humble empirical fact was an intelligible, a component of the world's divine *nomos* continuously thought by God, so that by apprehending whatever component of it one shares in His knowledge; apprehending whatever fact was conducive to the immortality of one's soul.

Yet it is the celestial bodies that were at the focus of Gersonides' scientific research programme. God exerts His providence over the created world through the celestial bodies: therefore, by studying their design one can gauge the perfection of the Creator. What counts for Gersonides and what he finds so remarkable is not only the perfection of the celestial realm *per se* – the constancy and regularity of the heavenly motions – but above all the supposed fact that the heavenly realm is perfected so as to bring about and constantly maintain the (relative) perfection of the sublunar realm as well. Gersonides in fact holds that the most tiny details of each and every of the heavenly motions and of the influences emanating from them are indispensable for the preservation of the ordered world: this is why their study reveals God's divine plan, bearing witness to the Creator's wisdom and goodness. Astronomy therefore emerges as the divine science par excellence:

> The prophets and those who spoke by virtue of the Holy Spirit made us aware that it is appropriate to expand this [astronomical] investigation because from it we are led to understand God, as will become evident in this study. Indeed, the orbs and the stars were created by the word of God, as will become clear from our treatise, God willing, by making evident the ampleness of God's wisdom and the ampleness of His power [as manifest] in His bringing into existence these noble bodies in this wondrously wise way and in His endowing them with heterogeneous emanations – even though [the heavenly bodies] are all of one single nature, devoid of the qualities that emanate from them – by virtue of which this lowly [sublunar] existence is perfected.[38]

Gersonides' motivation to study the heavens was thus theological and philosophical; indeed he accorded little value to knowledge whose finality is practical, and on one occasion even adduces astronomy as an example of a science devoid of practical utility.[39] This outlook profoundly shaped the astronomical theory he was to elaborate. Many, presumably most, medieval astronomers approached the study of the heavenly motions with an "instrumentalist", or "fictionalist", image of science: they took their job to consist in "saving the phenomena", i.e. in devising mathematical models and in calculating tables from which stellar positions could be determined with sufficient accuracy; it did not matter to them that the models they used were incompatible with the received (Aristotelian) physics.[40] But Gersonides obviously could not accept this position: his immodest aim was to uncover the blueprint of creation, not to tinker with merely useful computational models. Necessarily, therefore, his epistemology was bound to be realist. Consequently, since he wanted to know the configuration of the supralunar realm as it really was, he set out to construct a theory of the heavens that would accord both with calculation and with physical theory, explicitly rejecting the instrumentalist construal of astronomy.[41]

The awareness of the problem posed by the incompatibility of (Aristotelian) physics and mathematical (Ptolemaic) astronomy was not new: Gersonides is an heir to an Andalusian tradition which goes back at least to Ibn Bājjah and Ibn Ṭufayl and is echoed by Ibn Rushd and by Maimonides;[42] the latter indeed qualified the problem as "the true perplexity", whose resolution was presumably beyond human ken, but which must not preoccupy the astronomer, who should confine himself to calculations.[43] In rejecting the received instrumentalism of the astronomers, Gersonides in fact walked in the footsteps of the astronomer al-Biṭrūjī, whose astronomical treatise had been translated into Hebrew in 1259.[44] Yet, although sympathetic to al-Biṭrūjī's goal, Gersonides found that the latter's system was unsatisfactory: it was refuted by observation and, in addition, was incompatible with the principles of physics and metaphysics.

Gersonides' goal in studying astronomy – to achieve immortality by acquiring some knowledge of the *nomos* of the world – implied that precision was of the highest value: every error in apprehending an intelligible would be fatal to the soul's survival. This is what presumably incited Gersonides to undertake astronomical observations, which he used to test the planetary models – both very rare procedures in the Middle Ages.[45] In order to ensure precision, Gersonides devised two instruments. One, called "Jacob's Staff", allows the determination of the angular distance between planets. The second combines the Jacob's Staff with a *camera obscura* and is used to determine the apparent sizes of the planets.[46] The invention of this instrument depended on Gersonides' philosophical concerns, because the apparent sizes of planets were a relevant parameter for astronomical theory only from a realist stance. (From an instrumentalist perspective only the positions of the planets are of fundamental importance.) Thus, underlying Gersonides' astronomical innovations is his astronomical realism, which in turn depends on his global philosophy.

CONCLUSION

Looming behind Gersonides' variegated cognitive quests was a threefold confidence: firstly, that knowledge of the world was also knowledge of God; secondly, that such knowledge was attainable; and thirdly that knowledge was the guarantor of the immortality of the individual soul. On all these pivotal points Gersonides' views are antithetic to those of Maimonides, just as, generally, Gersonides opposes Maimonides on most crucial issues, while at the same time he follows globally the Maimonidean programme of creating a synthesis of Torah and philosophy.

The distinctive quality of Gersonides' intellectual endeavour seems to be its quest for consistency and coherence: Torah and philosophy, mathematical astronomy and physical theory, theory and observation, all had to match. Knowledge had different, equally valid sources – sense experience, theory and revelation (transmitted through tradition) – and, if properly understood, they could not but lead up to identical results. "It is the hallmark of truth that it agrees with itself from all aspects", Gersonides repeats time and again after having shown that different methods of inquiry yielded one and the same conclusion.

This search for coherence (again the converse of Maimonides) had different consequences in philosophy and in science. Gersonides' philosophical positions are constructed from materials he found in the writings available to him, most notably those of Ibn Rushd: in philosophy Gersonides' drive for consistency results in an "instinct for originality [that] expresses itself in manoeuvring among the texts at his disposal".[47] Gersonides' philosophy indeed remained thoroughly medieval. By contrast, in his scientific work, the quest for coherence resulted in a scientific practice which is entirely modern in outlook (although, to be sure, not in content): Gersonides made his own astronomical observations and criticized and revised mathematical models in their light. It is here, in his science which is wholly out of tune with the norms of the age, that Gersonides' originality bore its best fruits.

NOTES

1 In what follows only few indications about editions of Gersonides' writings, translations and secondary literature are given. Full information can be found in Kellner (1992).

2 The fact that Gersonides was referred to in Latin as "magister Leo de Balneolis" gave rise to the persistent error that he lived in Bagnols-sur-Cèze in the Département du Gard. In point of fact, "de Balneolis" was the name of an extended family living in Orange. Cf. Shatzmiller (1972).

3 It has been repeatedly conjectured that Gersonides' father was Gershom ben Shlomo, the author of the well-known encyclopedic work *Sha'ar ha-Shamayim*; cf. Shatzmiller (1992).

4 Cf. Lévy (1992).

5 Touati (1973): 38f.; Feldman (1984): 5ff.

6 Pines (1967): 31ff.; Touati (1973): 38; Pines (1986a).

7 There are two editions of the Hebrew text: Gersonides (1560); Gersonides (1866).

8 Ibn Rushd's works on which Gersonides wrote supercommentaries are notably the following: the Epitome of, and the Middle Commentary on the *Physics* (1321); the Epitome of *De generatione et corruptione* (1321); the Epitome of *De caelo* (1321); the Epitome of the *Meteorologica* (1322); the Epitome of books

11 to 19 of the so-called *Book of Animals* (= *The Parts of Animals* and *The Generation of Animals*; 1323); the Middle Commentary on the first seven books of the *Organon* (1323); the Epitome of the *De anima* (1323); the Epitome of the *Parva naturalia* (1324); the Middle Commentary on the *Metaphysics* (written before 1328; lost).

9 For the works and their dates cf. Touati (1973): 49–82; Feldman (1984): 8–30; the works are chronologically arranged in Weil-Guény (1992).

10 Only chapters 1–20 have been published (with an English translation) in Goldstein (1985).

11 Only very recently it has been discovered that Gersonides taught philosophy to a group of students, none of whom however rose to any distinction. Cf. Glasner (1995).

12 Goldstein (1974): 20.

13 Cf. Chemla and Pahaut (1992) for a study of this work.

14 Mancha (1992).

15 Goldstein and Pingree (1990): 34.

16 For references cf. Touati (1973): 87–8, including note 28.

17 *Wars*, Introduction; Gersonides (1560): 2va; Gersonides (1866): 4.

18 Gersonides knew Themistius' Commentary on book Lambda of Aristotle's *Metaphysics*, which had been translated into Hebrew in 1255. Cf. Pines (1987): 199f.; Davidson (1992).

19 *Wars*, 3.3; Gersonides (1560): 22vb; Gersonides (1866): 133.

20 For Maimonides, not the apprehension of natural entities, composed of matter and form, but rather the intellection of separate – divine – entities, results in the survival of the soul. Man's true perfection is in studying metaphysics, not physics. Cf. the famous parable in *Guide of the Perplexed*, 3.51 and Harvey (1977). Yet, as is well known, Maimonides in fact paradoxically holds that the separate entities, whose knowledge alone he holds to lead to salvation, are in fact unknowable, with the consequence that finally happiness is to be sought in the practical-political realm; cf. e.g Pines (1979); Stern (1995). The late Shlomo Pines suggestively argued that this contradiction is the result of a dramatic change of mind on Maimonides' part: cf. Pines (1986b).

21 Pines (1963b): ciiif. For an overview of the background cf. Leaman (1985): 87–107.

22 Cf. Feldman (1978).

23 *Wars* 6.1.7; Gersonides (1560): 51va, Gersonides (1866): 310.

24 Cf. also Feldman (1967); Davidson (1987): 209–12.

25 Cf. Freudenthal (1986).

26 Gersonides believed he could empirically confirm the existence of the primeval quasi-matter. Medieval physical astronomy postulated the existence of rotating spheres carrying the planets; these spheres had to turn independently, so as not to perturb one another's motion. To "isolate" the motions of the spheres, Gersonides argued, there must be a fluid matter filling the inter-spherical spaces, and this is none other than the rest of the "formless" quasi-matter, out of which all celestial and sublunar matter was created.

27 Cf. Freudenthal (1995).

28 Cf. Freudenthal (1993).

29 Maimonides holds that the stars "do not exist for our sake and so that good

should come to us from them"; cf. *Guide*, 3.15. His unbending anti-anthropocentrism has forcefully and repeatedly been highlighted by the late Yeshaiahu Leibowitz; cf. notably Leibowitz (1987): chapter 3. Gersonides, by contrast, maintains that the "stars are in the spheres not for their own sake, but in order to exert influence on this sublunar existence" so as to perfect it to the utmost; *Wars*, 5.2.3; Gersonides (1560): 32; (1866): 196.

30 The notion that the Active Intellect is a "synthesis" of the other intellects is one of the few innovative points in Gersonides' theory of the intellect. For an exhaustive comparison of Gersonides' views with his sources cf. Davidson (1992).

31 Cf. *Wars*, 6.2.1; Gersonides (1560): 69; Gersonides (1866): 419.

32 Cf. Maimonides, *Guide*, 2.12; Freudenthal (1993).

33 *Wars*, 2.2; Gersonides (1560): 17; Gersonides (1866): 95.

34 Cf. Goldstein and Pingree (1990); Freudenthal (1990).

35 Touati (1973): 541ff.; Kellner (1976).

36 Gersonides, *Supercommentary on* [Ibn Rushd's] *Epitome to the "Book of Animals"*, MS Vatican Urb. 42, fol. 44; quoted after Freudenthal (1989): 62.

37 *Ibid.*, fol. 9f.; quoted after Freudenthal (1989): 62.

38 *Astronomy*: chapter 2 (= *Wars*, 5.1.2); quoted (with modifications) after Goldstein (1985): 24 (English), 303 (Hebrew).

39 For what follows cf. Freudenthal (1989); Freudenthal (1992b); Freudenthal (1992c).

40 Cf. Duhem (1908); Jardine (1984): 225–57; Hugonnard-Roche (1992).

41 *Astronomy*: chapter 1 (= *Wars*, 5.1.1), Goldstein (1985): 305 (Hebrew), 22 (English); cf. also Goldstein's introductory remarks in *ibid.*: 2–9.

42 Cf. Gauthier (1909); Sabra (1984).

43 Maimonides, *Guide*, 2.24. For a different interpretation of Maimonides' views cf. Langermann (1991).

44 Goldstein (1971).

45 Gersonides recorded forty-five observations of planetary longitudes and latitudes; cf. Goldstein (1988).

46 Cf. Goldstein (1991).

47 Davidson (1992): 195.

REFERENCES

Chemla, K. and Pahaut, S. (1992) "Gersonide et la théorie des nombres", in Freudenthal (1992a): 149–91.

Davidson, H. A. (1987) *Proofs for Eternity, Creation, and the Existence of God, in Medieval Islamic and Jewish Philosophy* (New York).

— (1992) "Gersonides on the Material and Active Intellects", in Freudenthal (1992a): 195–265.

Duhem, P. (1908) *Sozein tà phainomena. Essai sur la notion de théorie physique de Platon à Galilée* (reprinted Paris, 1982).

Feldman, S. (1967) "Gersonides' Proofs for the Creation of the Universe", *Proceedings of the American Academy for Jewish Research*, 35: 113–32.

—— (1978) "Gersonides on the Possibility of Conjunction with the Agent Intellect", *American Jewish Studies Review*, 3: 99–120.

—— (1984) Levi ben Gershom (Gersonides), *The Wars of the Lord*. Volume One: *Book One: Immortality of the Soul*, trans. with introduction and notes by Seymour Feldman (Philadelphia).

—— (1987) Levi ben Gershom (Gersonides) *The Wars of the Lord*. Volume Two: *Book Two: Dreams, Divination, and Prophecy; Book Three: Divine Knowledge; Book Four: Divine Providence*, trans. and with an appendix and notes by Seymour Feldman (Philadelphia).

Freudenthal, G. (1986) "Cosmogonie et physique chez Gersonide", *Revue des études juives*, 145: 295–314.

—— (1989) "Human Felicity and Astronomy: Gersonides' Revolt Against Ptolemy" (Hebrew), *Da'at*, 22: 55–72.

—— (1990) "Levi ben Gershom as a Scientist: Physics, Astrology and Eschatology", *Proceedings of the Tenth World Congress of Jewish Studies*, Division C, 1, *Jewish Thought and Literature* (Jerusalem): 65–72.

—— (ed.) (1992a) *Studies on Gersonides – a Fourteenth-Century Philosopher-Scientist* (Leiden).

—— (1992b) "Sauver son âme ou sauver les phénomènes: sotériologie, épistémologie et astronomie chez Gersonide", in Freudenthal (1992a): 317–52.

—— (1992c) "Rabbi Lewi ben Gerschom (Gersonides) und die Bedingungen wissenschaftlichen Fortschritts im Mittelalter: Astronomie, Physik, erkenntnis-theoretischer Realismus, und Heilslehre", *Archiv für Geschichte der Philosophie*, 74: 158–79.

—— (1993) "Maimonides' Stance on Astrology in Context: Cosmology, Physics, Medicine, and Providence", in Fred Rosner and Samuel S. Kottek (eds), *Moses Maimonides: Physician, Scientist and Philosopher* (Northvale and London): 77–90.

—— (1995) *Aristotle's Theory of Material Substance. Form and Soul, Heat and Pneuma* (Oxford).

Gauthier, L. (1909) "Une réforme du système astronomique de Ptolémée, tentée par les philosophes arabes du XIIe siècle", *Journal asiatique*: 483–510.

Gersonides (Levi ben Gershom) (1560) *Sefer Milḥamot ha-Shem* (Riva di Trento).

—— (1866) *Milchamot Ha-schem. Die Kämpfe Gottes. Religionsphilosophische und kosmische Fragen, in sechs Büchern abgehandelt von Levi ben Gerson* (Leipzig).

Glasner, R. (1995) "Levi ben Gershom and the Study of Ibn Rushd in the Fourteenth Century: Historical Reconstruction", *Jewish Quarterly Review*, forthcoming.

Goldstein, B. R. (1971) *Al-Biṭrûjî: On the Principles of Astronomy*, 1: *Analysis and Translation*; 2: *The Arabic and Hebrew Versions* (New Haven).

—— (1974) *The Astronomical Tables of Levi ben Gerson* (= *Transactions of the Connecticut Academy of Arts and Sciences*, 45) (New Haven).

—— (1985) *The Astronomy of Levi ben Gerson (1288–1344): A Critical Edition of Chapters 1–20 with Translation and Commentary* (New York and Berlin).

—— (1988) "A New Set of Fourteenth-Century Planetary Observations", *Proceedings of the American Philosophical Society*, 132(4): 371–99.

—— (1991) "Levi ben Gerson: On Astronomy and Physical Experiments", in Sabetai Unguru (ed.) *Physics, Cosmology and Astronomy, 1300–1700: Tension and Accommodation* (= *Boston Studies in the Philosophy of Science*, 126) (Dordrecht, Boston and London): 75–82.

Goldstein, B. R. and D. Pingree (1990) *Levi ben Gerson's Prognostication for the Conjunction of 1345* (= *Transactions of the American Philosophical Society*, 80(6)) (Philadelphia).

Harvey, W. Z. (1977) "R. Hasdai Crescas and His Criticism of Philosophical Felicity" (Hebrew), in *Proceedings of the Sixth World Congress of Jewish Studies* (Jerusalem), 3: 143–9.

Hugonnard-Roche, H. (1992) "Problèmes méthodologiques dans l'astronomie au début du XIVe siècle", in Freudenthal (1992a): 55–70.

Jardine, N. (1984) *The Birth of History and Philosophy of Science* (Cambridge).

Kellner, M. (1976) "Gersonides and his Cultured Despisers: Arama and Abravanel", *Journal of Medieval and Renaissance Studies*, 6: 269–96.

—— (1992) "Bibliographia Gersonideana: An Annotated List of Writings by and about R. Levi ben Gershom", in Freudenthal (1992a): 367–414.

Langermann, Y. T. (1991) "The 'True Perplexity': The *Guide of the Perplexed*, Part II, Chapter 24", in Joel L. Kraemer (ed.) *Perspectives on Maimonides: Philosophical and Historical Studies* (Oxford): 159–74.

Leaman, O. (1985) *An Introduction to Medieval Islamic Philosophy* (Cambridge).

Leibowitz, Y. (1987) *The Faith of Maimonides* (New York).

Lévy, T. (1992) "Gersonide commentateur d'Euclide: traduction annotée de ses gloses sur les *Eléments*", in Freudenthal (1992a): 83–147.

Mancha, J. L. (1992) "The Latin Translation of Levi ben Gerson's *Astronomy*", in Freudenthal (1992a): 21–54.

Pines, S. (1963a) *Moses Maimonides, The Guide of the Perplexed*, trans. S. Pines (Chicago).

—— (1963b) "Translator's Introduction", in Pines (1963a): lvii–cxxxiv.

—— (1967) *Scholasticism after Thomas Aquinas and the Teachings of Hasdai Crescas and his Predecessors* (= *Proceedings of the Israel Academy of Sciences and Humanities*, 1(10)) (Jerusalem).

—— (1975) "Maimonides, Rabbi Moses ben Maimon", *Dictionary of Scientific Biography* (New York), 9: 27–32.

—— (1979) "The Limitations of Human Knowledge According to Al-Farabi, ibn Bajja, and Maimonides", in I. Twersky (ed.) *Studies in Medieval Jewish History and Literature* (Cambridge, Mass.): 82–109.

—— (1986a) "Problems Concerning Gersonides' Doctrine", appendix to his "Some Views Put Forward by the 14th-Century Jewish Philosopher Isaac Pulgar, and some Parallel Views Expressed by Spinoza" (Hebrew), in J. Dan and J. Hacker (eds) *Studies in Jewish Mystics, Philosophy and Ethical Literature, Presented to Isaia Tishby on his Seventy-Fifth Birthday* (Jerusalem): 395–457, on pp. 447–57.

—— (1986b) "Le Discours théologico-philosophique dans les oeuvres halachiques de Maïmonide comparé avec celui du *Guide des égarés*", in *Délivrance et Fidélité, Maïmonide: Textes du colloque tenu à l'Unesco en décembre 1985 à l'occasion du 850e anniversaire du philosophe* (Toulouse): 119–24.

—— (1987) "Some Distinctive Metaphysical Conceptions in Themistius' Commentary on Book Lamda and Their Place in the History of Philosophy", in J. Wiesner (ed.), *Aristoteles Werk und Wirkung Paul Moraux gewidmet*, 2 (Berlin and New York): 177–204.

Sabra, A. I. (1984) "The Andalusian Revolt against Ptolemaic Astronomy: Averroes and al-Bitrûjî", in E. Mendelsohn (ed.) *Transformation and Tradition in the Sciences: Essays in Honor of I. Bernard Cohen* (Cambridge): 133–53.

Shatzmiller, J. (1972) "Gersonides and the Jewish Community of Orange in His Day" (Hebrew), *Studies in the History of the Jewish People and the Land of Israel*, 2: 111–26.
—— (1992) "Gersonide et la société juive de son temps", in G. Dahan (ed.), *Gersonide en son temps: science et philosophie médiévales* (Louvain and Paris): 33–43.
Stern, J. (1995) "Maimonides on Language and the Science of Language", *Maimonides and the Sciences* (= *Boston Studies in the Philosophy of Science*) (Dordrecht): forthcoming.
Touati, Ch. (1973) *La Pensée philosophique et théologique de Gersonide* (Paris).
Weil-Guény, A.-M. (1992) "Gersonide en son temps: un tableau chronologique", in Freudenthal (1992a): 355–65.

CHAPTER 45

Judaism and Sufism

Paul B. Fenton

BEGINNINGS IN THE EAST

Within the wider framework of the influence of Islamic thought and spirituality, the study of the interaction between Israel and Ismael in the domain of mysticism is one of the most fascinating chapters of comparative religion. From a strictly chronological point of view, it was Judaism that initially influenced Sufism in its formative period in Baghdad. Surprisingly, while scholars have recognized the influence of Oriental Neoplatonism and Christian pietism on the evolution of Muslim asceticism at this time, they have failed to point out the profound mark left on Sufism by the ambient Jewish milieu. Indeed, Mesopotamia, cradle of the Babylonian Talmud, was at the very centre of the world of Jewish learning, which, moreover, readily underwent the process of Arabization after the Muslim conquest. Among the great personalities attached to the Talmudic academies of Baghdad were to be found certain charismatic figures who embodied the ancient rabbinic pietistic ideals of simplicity and saintliness, virtues cherished by nascent Sufism. Moreover, Sufi hagiography has preserved a number of edifying tales of "the pious men from among the Children of Israel", known as *isrā'īliyyāt*. Many of these tales are traceable to rabbinic sources such as the *Chapters of the Fathers*, one of the main well-springs of Jewish pietism.

One particularly important concept undoubtedly originating in Talmudic literature which was assimilated at this time and which was to play a fundamental role in Islamic mysticism was the belief in a hidden hierarchy of saints, whose blessings sustained the world. Supposedly these elements had been transmitted through interreligious contacts or Jewish converts to Islam. However, once Sufism had asserted itself as a spiritual force, it began to exert a compelling attraction for Jews. A certain number of conversions took place precisely in Sufi circles in Baghdad, where we find Jews attending the lectures of the first mystical masters. Indeed, Sufi historiographers like to relate accounts of the miraculous conversion of Jews to Islam through the action of Muslim mystics, such as Ibrahim al-Khawwāṣ. These kinds of contacts were no doubt facilitated by the relative openness of certain Sufi masters towards members of other religious persuasions. Though traces of Sufi beliefs concerning the ascetic ideal and the vanity of the lower world may be detected in the works of tenth-century Jewish authors in Baghdad, such as Sa'adyah Ga'ōn (Saadiah Gaon) (d. 940), it is, however, only during the Judaeo-Arabic cultural symbiosis in Spain in the following century that definite evidence of literary influence can be pinpointed.

THE GOLDEN AGE OF SPAIN

Indeed, it is well known that the Iberian peninsula was a fertile terrain of intercultural exchange between Jew, Christian and Muslim. From a much later period we have evidence of theological discussions between the great Muslim mystic Muḥyī al-Dīn ibn 'Arabī (d. 1240) and a Jewish rabbi on the nature of the letters of the Holy Scriptures. It can be assumed that such contacts also took place in previous times. Now there had been an early flowering of Sufism in Andalusia, mainly owing to the teachings of the Muslim mystical master Ibn Masarrah (886–931). While overestimating the latter's influence on Muslim and Jewish Neoplatonism in Andalusia, scholars have overlooked the significant fact that Ibn Masarrah, as well as his spiritual heir, Sahl al-Tustarī, laid great emphasis on the mystical role of the Arabic alphabet, as demonstrated by their recently published writings. This discipline is also a fundamental aspect of the theosophical system of Ibn 'Arabī, and a subject which, as just pointed out, he would discuss with Jews. From Talmudic times (third to fourth centuries C.E.) and later in the Kabbalah, these arithmological speculations, known as *gemaṭriyah*, were a central part of Jewish exegesis and esotericism. The striking similarities between the development of these mystical conceptions in both religions leaves no doubt as to an initial Jewish influence on the Muslim "science of letters" and their later interaction.

Although definite literary traces of Islamic mysticism are already present in the religious poetry of the great Andalusian Hebrew poets such as Solomon ibn Gabirol (d. *c.* 1057) and Judah Halevi (1075–1141), the first Jewish medieval prose work to exhibit a profound appreciation of Sufi doctrine was the *Farā'iḍ al-qulūb* ("Duties of the Hearts"), a treatise on ascetic theology composed in Arabic by Rabbi Baḥyā ibn Paqūdah (*c.* 1080). In an effort to remedy the ritual formalism and religious desiccation of his fellow Jews, Baḥyā devised an individualistic, inward itinerary, guiding the soul through contemplation and love to union with the "supernal Light", based on the progressive spiritual stages of the Path as set out in Sufi pietistic manuals. Baḥyā's use of Sufi sources was not altogether indiscriminate; he notably rejects forms of extreme asceticism and self-mortification preached by certain contemplative Sufis and he adopts a reserved line on the question of union with God. Despite the pains he takes to camouflage material of a too ostensibly Islamic character by replacing the Qur'ānic quotations of his sources with Biblical ones, his words in the introduction to the book betray his apprehension at introducing a novel kind of devotion into the Jewish fold. He preempts the disapproval of his co-religionists by justifying himself with the Talmudic adage "Whoso pronounces a word of Wisdom, even a Gentile, is to be called a wise man." The *Duties of the Hearts* was one of the first classics of Judaeo-Arabic literature to be translated into the holy tongue. The Hebrew version, which greatly attenuated its Islamic stamp, was to have an abiding influence on Jewish spirituality right down to present times, infusing generations of Jewish readers with Sufi notions. After having influenced the Spanish and thereafter the Palestinian Kabbalists, who were particularly interested in Baḥyā's reflections on solitary meditation, the *Duties of the Hearts* was avidly read in the eighteenth century by the Polish Ḥasidim, who borrowed from it some of their basic ethical concepts, such as quietism, the distinction between external and internal solitude and that between physical and spiritual warfare. Thus we find in the writings of one of the first Ḥasidic proponents, Jacob Joseph of Polonnoy, the famous quotation: "Ye have returned from the lesser war, now prepare for the greater war (with one's nature)". Now Baḥyā cites this saying in the name of the "Sage", but in reality the Muslim sources upon which he drew attribute it to the Prophet Muḥammad!

The works of some later Andalusian authors likewise betray familiarity with Muslim mystical writings. The allegorical commentary on the Song of Songs composed in Arabic by Joseph ibn 'Aqnīn (twelfth century) takes on the character of a Sufi treatise on Divine love. Even more remarkable is the fact that in this book the author provides definitions of love which are culled from al-Qushayri's *Risālah* ("Epistle"), one of Sufism's basic textbooks. Furthermore in his *Ṭibb al-nufūs* ("Hygiene of the Souls"), Ibn 'Aqnīn does not hesitate to quote the Sufi mystics such as al-Junayd (d. 910) and Ibn Adham, referring to them by their Sufi epithets: *shaykh al-ṭā'ifah*, "the elder of the community", and *al-ruḥānī al-akmal*, "the perfect spirit".

These examples, of great interest for the historian of Andalusian Sufism, remained, however, isolated and sporadic, no doubt on account of the waning influence of Sufism itself, relentlessly persecuted on Spanish soil by Malikite intolerance. There is no evidence that even Baḥyā's book, notwithstanding its popularity, gave rise to a sizeable movement of a Sufi brand of Jewish pietists. However, elsewhere, the following centuries were to witness the growth and spread of Sufism in other lands and its sustained influence on Jewish spirituality.

THE JEWISH PIETIST MOVEMENT IN EGYPT

Egypt had long been a hotbed of mysticism. Long after the Therapeuts and the Christian anchorites, the country produced some of the foremost Muslim mystics, such as Dhū al-Nūn al-Miṣrī (796–861) and the greatest Sufi poet, ʿUmar ibn al-Fāriḍ (d. 1235). Here flourished the great charismatic figures such as Abu'l-Ḥasan al-Shādhilī (d. 1258), Aḥmad al-Badawī (d. 1276), Abu'l-ʿAbbās al-Mursī (d. 1287) and Ibn ʿAṭā Allāh (d. 1309), whose influence certainly extended beyond the Islamic community. Under their influence Sufism became progressively institutionalized, and important brotherhoods flourished in the urban centres. No doubt their increasing spiritual fervour had repercussions on the local Jewish populations. Moreover, Egypt had become a haven for the Jewish masses fleeing Almohad persecution in the West and Crusader wars in the East. Such social upheavals accompanied by messianic expectations probably heightened mystical sensitivity. Dissatisfied with the excessive rationalism of Peripatetic philosophy, certain individual Jews in search of deeper religious expression looked towards their immediate spiritual model, the Sufis.

Though the exact period and the personalities involved in the emergence of this tendency remain uncertain, it seems that at the time of the great scholar and leader Moses Maimonides (1135–1204) a number of Jews had already begun to adopt the Sufi way of life. Indeed several documents have survived from this period bearing personal names qualified by the epithet *he-ḥāsīd*, "the pious". This was no mere honorific title, but designated an individual who followed a spiritual regime akin to that of the Sufis. The interest Sufi literature held for Jews during this period is well attested by the multiple documents brought to light in the Cairo *Genizah*. The latter, a lumber-room attached to an ancient synagogue, has preserved thousands of sacred writings dating from the medieval period, which were discovered at the end of the nineteenth century. They included numerous texts of a Sufi character, testifying to the popularity of this kind of literature amongst Jewish readers. These manuscripts are basically of two sorts: on the one hand, Muslim Sufi writings either in Arabic characters or copied into Hebrew letters for the convenience of Jewish readers, or, on the other, pietist writings of Sufi inspiration written by Jewish authors.

Amongst the first category are to be found all the tendencies of Sufi literature from the early masters of Baghdad right down to the Illuminationist *Ishrāqī* school founded by Suhrawardī in the twelfth century. There are texts by al-Junayd, pages from al-Qushayrī's *Risālah*, poems by al-Ḥallāj, the *Maḥāsin al-majālis* by the Andalusian mystic Ibn al-'Arīf, the *Munqidh min al-ḍalāl*, al-Ghazzālī's spiritual autobiography, al-Shaydhalah's *Treatise on Divine Love*, Suhrawardī's *Kalimāt al-taṣawwūf* and his *Hayākil al-nūr*, to name just a few. In addition to these are to be found various texts containing quotations, tales, anecdotes and even songs by Sufi masters.

The second category is made up of the Jewish pietists' own compositions. These include ethical manuals and theological treatises, definitions of mystical states as well as exegetical works. Though these writings are based on traditional rabbinic themes, they show an attempt to reinterpret the scriptural narrative in harmony with Sufi doctrine, often portraying biblical figures as masters of the Sufi path. They are not however simple judaized adaptations of Muslim texts but original compositions, dextrously transposed in the biblical and rabbinic texture.

The most outstanding author about whom anything substantial is known was none other than Rabbi Abraham (1186–1237), son of the great rationalist Jewish philosopher Moses Maimonides. At the death of his father Abraham became the spiritual leader of Egyptian Jewry and later acceded to a position of political eminence as *nāgīd*, "Head of the Jews". Not only was he virtually the supreme religious and political figure of his time but he was also an ardent protagonist of the Sufi form of Jewish pietism henceforth known as *ḥasidūt*. It is unknown when he embraced this tendency but it is thought that he was already dedicated to the pietist way of life when he succeeded his illustrious father in 1205. Abraham Maimonides composed a commentary on the Pentateuch wherein he often depicts the ancient biblical characters as pietists in the same way as Sufi literature clothes the Prophet and his companions in the garb of the early Sufis. However Abraham's *magnum opus* was the *Kifāyat al-'ābidīn* ("Compendium for the Servants of God"), a monumental legal and ethical treatise, which, though in many respects similar to his father's *Mishneh Torah* ("Code of Laws"), is distinctive in the strong propensity he displays therein for mysticism of a manifestly Muslim type. Indeed, far from sharing Baḥyā's misgivings about using Muslim sources, Abraham Maimonides overtly expresses his admiration for the Sufis in whom he sees the heirs of ancient Israelite traditions. At one point, after having claimed that the true dress of the ancient prophets of Israel was similar to the ragged garments (*muraqqa'āt*) worn by the Sufis, he declares: "Do not regard as unseemly our comparison of that [the true dress of the prophets] to the conduct of the Sufis, for the latter imitate the prophets [of Israel] and walk in their footsteps, not the prophets in theirs" (Rosenblatt (1927–38), 2: 320). Similarly, the Sufi initiation ritual, consisting in the investiture of the master's cloak (*khirqah*) was originally practised by the prophets of Israel, according to the author of the *Kifāyah*:

> By casting his cloak over [Elisha], Elijah hinted to him, as if in joyful annunciation, that his garments and dress as well as the rest of his conduct would be like his. Thus he announced to him the fact that Elijah's spiritual perfection would be transferred to him and that he [Elisha] would attain the degree which he himself had attained. Thou art aware of the ways of the ancient saints [*awliyā'*] of Israel, which are not or but little practised among our contemporaries, that have now become the practice of the Sufis of Islam, "on account of the iniquities of Israel", namely that the master invests the novice [*murīd*] with a cloak [*khirqah*] as the latter is about to enter upon the mystical path [*ṭarīq*]. "They have taken up thine own words" (Deuteronomy 33: 3). This is why we moreover take over from them and emulate them in the wearing of sleeveless tunics and the like.
>
> (Rosenblatt (1927–38), 1: 153)

The idea that Sufi practices are of Jewish origin is repeated by Abraham elsewhere when he deals with the Sufi ascetic discipline:

> We see also the Sufis of Islam practise self-mortification by combating sleep and perhaps that practice is derived from the words of [king] David. . . . Observe then these wonderful traditions and sigh with regret over how they have been transferred from us and appeared amongst a nation other than ours whereas they have disappeared in our midst. My soul shall weep in secret . . . because of the pride of Israel that was taken from them and bestowed upon the nations of the world.
>
> (Rosenblatt (1927–38), 2: 266)

Unlike his father who had written a purely legal code, Abraham Maimonides emphasized the spiritual significance of the precepts and discussed the "mysteries" they conceal, in a similar manner to the Muslim mystics, such as al-Ghazzālī in his *Iḥyā' 'ulūm al-dīn*. The author of the *Kifāyah* believed that he had rediscovered some of these mysteries in the traditions preserved by the Sufis, which had been forgotten by the Jews on account of the multiple tribulations of the Exile. This belief provides a key as to the reason why the pietists adopted manifestly Muslim customs. Furthermore, it seems that the pietists, who called themselves "the disciples of the prophets", were profoundly convinced of the imminent renewal of prophecy in Israel. They believed that the Sufi practices were not only originally ancient Jewish traditions but also an integral part of a "prophetic discipline". Thus their restoration to the Jewish fold was meant to accelerate the prophetic process.

These "reforms" included a number of devotional practices, clearly inspired by Muslim models, whose purpose was to enhance the decorum and purport of synagogue worship. As a preliminary to prayer, the *nāgīd* insisted on the ritual ablution of hands and feet, though not strictly required by Jewish law. On the other hand, this rite was obligatory in Muslim custom and especially emphasized in Sufi literature as being meritorious. Abraham instituted the arrangement of worshippers in rows, as in mosques, facing Jerusalem at all times during the synagogue services. He prescribed different positions during certain prayers, such as standing, kneeling and frequent bowing, as well as the spreading of the hands and weeping in supplication. In addition to canonical prayers, he recommended nightly vigils and daily fasts. However the most telling ritual adopted by the pietists was that of solitary meditation, a characteristic Sufi practice known as *khalwah*. Here the devotee would retire from society for protracted periods in an isolated and dark place in order to devote himself to worship and meditation. Abraham Maimonides also considered this practice of Jewish origin:

> Also do the Sufis of Islam practise solitude in dark places and isolate themselves in them until the sensitive part of the soul becomes atrophied so that it is not even able to see the light. This however requires strong inner illumination wherewith the soul will be preoccupied so as not to be pained over the external darkness. Now Rabbi Abraham he-Ḥāsīd used to be of the opinion that solitude in darkness was the thing alluded to in the statement of Isaiah: "Who is among you that feareth the Lord that obeyeth the voice of His servant, who walketh in darkness and hath no light? Let him trust in the name of the Lord, and stay upon his God" (Isaiah 50: 10).
>
> (Rosenblatt (1927–38), 2: 418)

As is known, one of the most typical aspects of the Sufi path is the necessity of spiritual development under the guidance of a master. Abraham Maimonides sees the origin of this principle in the discipline of the ancient prophets:

> Know that generally in order for the Way to attain successfully its true goal [*wuṣūl*], it must be pursued under the guidance [*taslīk*] of a person who has already attained this goal, as it is said in the tradition: "Acquire a master" (*Abot* 1:6). The biblical accounts concerning masters and their disciples are well known; Joshua the servant of Moses was one of his disciples, who, having attained the goal, succeeded him. The prophets adopted the same conduct. Samuel's guide [*musallik*] was Eli, Elijah was that of Elisha, and Jeremiah that of Barukh son of Neriah. Moreover the "disciples of the prophets" were thus called because the prophets were their spiritual guides. This practice was adopted by other nations

> (the Sufis), who instituted in imitation of Jewish custom the relation between *shaykh* and servant, master and disciple . . . If the wayfarer is capable and remains faithful to instructions, he will attain his goal through the guidance of an accomplished master.
>
> (Rosenblatt (1927–38), 2: 422)

Certain Jewish pietist texts also mention the typical Sufi practice of *dhikr*, or "spiritual recollection", but so far no details have been discovered on how this specific ritual was carried out. Because of their protracted devotions the pietists established special prayer-halls; it is known, for instance, that Abraham Maimonides possessed his own private synagogue.

In addition to the foregoing practices, other aspects of the pietist discipline of an ascetic nature are to be found in the writings of other members of the pietist circle. Notably, contrary to traditional Jewish ethics, the Jewish pietists, like certain Sufis, advocated celibacy and considered marriage and family responsibilities an impediment to spiritual fulfilment. ʻObadyah Maimonides, Abraham's son, says the following about marriage: "Know that the true mystics of this path strived to perfect their souls before marriage in the knowledge that after begetting spouse and offspring there would be little opportunity for spiritual achievement" (Fenton (1981b): 94). The same author also shunned all material superfluities and taught a regime of extreme austerity:

> Cover thy head, let fall thy tears, and let purity follow in thy wake, spend thy days in fasting throughout the day. Delight not in the joys of the vulgar and be not dismayed at that which grieves them. In a word be not sad with their sadness and rejoice not with their merriment. Despise frivolity and laughter, rather observe silence and speak not except out of necessity. Eat not except out of compulsion and sleep not unless overcome, and all the while thy heart should contemplate this pursuit and thy thoughts be engaged therein.
>
> (Fenton (1981b): 116)

The figure of Abraham Maimonides inaugurates a long association of the celebrated Maimonides family with pietism of a Sufi type, lasting, no doubt with some interruptions, for nearly two centuries. Indeed, Abraham's own son, just mentioned, ʻObadyah Maimonides (1228–65), had strong leanings towards Sufism, as can be gathered from his composition *al-Maqālah al-ḥawḍiyyah* ("The Treatise of the Pool"). The latter is an ethical *vade-mecum* and a mystical manual for the spiritual wayfarer upon the path leading to God through union with the intelligible realm. It is based on the typically Sufi comparison of the heart to a pool which must be cleansed before it can be filled with the vivifying waters of gnosis. Couched in an allusive style, the treatise is replete with Sufi technical terms. Also worthy of note is ʻObadyah's tendency to project Sufi stereotypes into the patriarchal past. Thus Abraham, Isaac and Jacob become wandering hermits practising solitary meditation in the wilderness.

David ben Joshua (*c.* 1335–1415), the last of the Maimonideans of whom history has kept track, was also interested in Sufism. His work *al-Murshīd ila t-tafarrūd* ("The Guide to Detachment"), one of the last creations of neoclassical Judaeo-Arabic literature, represents the most far-reaching synthesis between traditional rabbinical ethics and the spiritual states of the Sufi path. Following the tradition of Sufi manuals which begin with a definition of Sufism, the author first proposes a definition of *ḥasidūt*. The body of the work is based on an ethical formula taught by the rabbis which David develops as the central motive of a spiritual programme largely construed in the light of the spiritual stations of the Sufi path and the Illuminationist philosophy of Suhrawardī. Thus he derives the initial virtue, *zehirūt*, normally signifying "precaution", from the root *zhr* "to shine", associating it with the Illuminationist notion of *ishrāq*, since the first step on the path to perfection is motivated by the quest for light.

The centrality of the Maimonidean family is further indicated by the fact that a certain number of personalities associated with the pietist circle were also related to this prestigious dynasty. Abraham Abū Rabīʻah he-Ḥāsīd was one of the leaders of the Jewish Sufis in Egypt. He was the author of a mystical commentary on the Song of Songs which is conceived of as an allegorical dialogue between the mystic intoxicated with Divine love and the object of his desire, the beatific vision. Another noteworthy adept of the pietist circle was Rabbi Ḥanan'el ben Samuel, who was not only a member of Abraham Maimonides' rabbinical court but also his father-in-law. Several Genizah documents refer to him as *he-ḥāsīd*, the "pietist". He is now known to have been the author of a considerable exegetical work which reflects his stature not only as a philosopher but also as a mystic in so far as his explanations resound with Sufi technical terms. Moreover, Rabbi Ḥanan'el was a committed pietist activist, for a certain document portrays him alongside his son-in-law defending the movement. Indeed the introduction of these novel practices did not go unchallenged, and the pietists, like many revivalist movements in religious history, met with virulent opposition. Despite Abraham Maimonides' political and religious prestige, which immensely contributed to the furtherance of the pietist movement, he had to face fierce opponents, who even went as far as to denounce him to the Muslim authorities, accusing the pietists of introducing "false ideas", "unlawful changes" and "gentile (Sufi) customs" into the synagogue. Opposition continued during the office as *nāgīd* of Abraham's son David Maimonides (1222–1300), whose synagogue was closed down, and who, at one point, was compelled to leave Egypt, seeking refuge in Akko.

This opposition, coupled with the fact that access to the "pietist way" was reserved from its very inception for the select few, may explain why the movement did not gain universal approval but, with the general decline of Oriental Jewry, gradually disappeared into total oblivion.

LATER INFLUENCES

However, Sufism continued sporadically to be a source of fascination for individual Jews in ensuing centuries. Mention has already been made of the fact that Rabbi David II Maimonides (*c.* 1335–1415) showed interest in Sufism. A complaint addressed to him by a Jewish housewife has been preserved in the Genizah, informing him that her husband, infatuated with Sufism, had abandoned her in order to go and live in a Sufi convent under the guidance of the famous Sufi al-Kurāni in the Muqaṭṭam mountains outside Cairo. As late as the sixteenth century the great Egyptian mystic al-Sha'arāni relates in his autobiography the reputation he enjoyed amongst his Jewish admirers who would attend his lectures and request him to write amulets to protect their children. Jews also maintained contacts with Sufis in other localities. According to information provided by the Arab biographer al-Kutūbī, the Jews of Damascus would assemble in the house of the Sufi al-Ḥasan ibn Hūd (thirteenth century) in order to study with him Maimonides' *Guide of the Perplexed*. Did this mean that they sought to interpret the *Guide* in the light of Sufism? Traces of Sufism are also to be found in the writings of fifteenth-century Yemenite Jews who freely use Sufi concepts and quote verses from the mystical poetry of the Sufi martyr al-Ḥallāj. In Spain, during the great movement of translation, many Sufi concepts percolated into Jewish literature through the intermediary of Hebrew translations, especially those of the works of the al-Ghazzālī brothers. Similarly, but in a completely different part of the Islamic world, the copying into Hebrew characters of Persian Sufi poetry, such as that of Rūmī and Sa'dī, no doubt contributed to the diffusion of Sufi ideas amongst Persian Jews. It is worthwhile recalling in this context the remarkable figure of Sarmad (d. 1661), the Persian Jew who became a wandering dervish in India.

THE EARLY KABBALISTS

Another place of contact which was to produce an abiding influence was the Holy Land, where in Jerusalem and even Safed in the thirteenth century thriving centres of Muslim culture were to be found. The thirteenth-century Palestinian Kabbalists close to the circle of Rabbi Abraham Abu'l-'Afiyyah (d. after 1291) not only betray a certain number of Sufi practices in their esoteric discipline but also testify to their having directly observed the Sufi *dhikr* ritual. Abu'l-'Afiyyah may himself have encountered Sufis during his brief visit to Akko (Acre) around 1260 or elsewhere in the course of his wide travels. The focal point of his ecstatic method is the practice of *hazkārāh*, a term itself strikingly reminiscent of the Arabic *dhikr*. Independently of canonical prayer, the purpose of this activity was to prepare the devotee for prophetic inspiration. The meditative ritual, practised in an isolated and dark place, as set out in Abu'l-'Afiyyah's writings, obviously involves Sufi techniques. After preliminary preparations, the devotee, arrayed in white, adopts a special posture and proceeds to pronounce the Divine name accompanied with respiratory control and movements of the head.

Abu'l-'Afiyyah's doctrines were propagated in the East. The Kabbalists of the Holy Land, such as Isaac of Akko, Shem Ṭōb ibn Ga'ōn and the anonymous author of *Shaarey ẓedeq*, adopted the meditative method of his prophetic Kabbalah, further enriching it with elements of Sufi provenance. Isaac of Akko (*c.*1270–1340) in particular seemed to have had direct knowledge of Sufi techniques, including solitary meditation (*khalwah* in Arabic, *hitbōdedūt* in Hebrew) and the visualization of letters. Isaac is also an important link in the transmission of these methods to the later Kabbalists of Safed. He himself may have had personal contacts with Sufis, for he had a good knowledge of Arabic. Alternatively, he may have made the acquaintance of David Maimonides and his pietist companions during the latter's exile in Akko (Acre) which lasted until 1289.

THE KABBALISTS OF SAFED

The historians of the extraordinary Kabbalistic school of Safed have insufficiently taken into account the influence of the Islamic environment when dealing with the novel practices introduced by the disciples of Rabbi Isaac Lurya (1534–72), himself a native of Egypt. The Turkish traveller Evliya Chelebi testifies that in the sixteenth century, i.e. during the very flowering of Luryanic Kabbalah, Safed was a thriving Sufi centre which possessed its *tekkiye*, or Sufi convent. It is not unreasonable therefore to suppose that behind some of the mystical rituals initiated by the Kabbalists lie Sufi models. Among the most significant, mention can be made of saint worship and pilgrimages to the tombs of saints and their invocation, which are similar to Muslim practices connected with the *ziyārāt* rite, the gathering of spiritual brotherhoods (*ḥabūrōt*) around the person of the saint, and spiritual concerts (*baqashshōt*), vigils consisting in the singing of devotional poems, similar to the Sufi *samā'* ceremony.

However, the most important ritual was that of *hitbōdedūt*, "solitary meditation". After a hiatus of more than a century, contemplative elements of a Sufi character resurge in the writings of the sixteenth-century Spanish exiles established in the Holy Land. Though this phenomenon is to be seen largely as a continuation of Abu'l-'Afiyyah's school, the possibility that elements deriving from the doctrine of the Jewish Sufis may have survived is not to be excluded. Among the first authors to evoke anew this discipline were Judah al-Buṭinī (d. 1519) in his *Sullam ha-'aliyyah* ("Ladder of Ascension", a title in itself smacking of Sufism) and Moses Cordovero (d. 1570) in his *Pardes rimmonim* ("Orchard of Pomegranates"). Meditation and breath control continued to be practised in dark places in order to bring about an internal illumination of the soul. Other techniques observed during the periodic retreats also betray Sufi influence: ritual purity, complete silence, fasting, restriction of sleep and food, confidence in God and, above all, the repetition of Divine names as a route to ecstasy.

THE SHABBATIANS

The last significant contact between Jewish and Muslim mystics took place during the religious turmoil brought about by the mystical messiah Shabbatay Zevi (d. 1675), whose tragic destiny led him to conversion to Islam. During his confinement in Adrianople, while still inwardly practising Judaism, Shabbatay Zevi would attend *dhikr* seances in the Bektashi convent at Hizirlik and, it seems, established contacts with the famous *khalwatii* mystic, Muḥammad al-Niyāzi. His apostate followers, known as the *Doenme*, continued to maintain close relations with the mystical brotherhoods in Turkey and in particular with the syncretistic Bektashis, from whom they borrowed a certain number of rituals and liturgical poems in Turkish which were included in their ceremonies.

It is well known that the eighteenth-century East European Ḥasidic movement took root and first grew in the southern Polish province of Podolia, which had once been under Turkish rule and was a hotbed of Shabbatian activities. The sectarians in this area continued to maintain close ties with their brethren under Ottoman rule in Salonika. It is interesting to speculate to what extent Sufi ideas percolated into Podolia and influenced the nascent Ḥasidic movement. The veneration of the *ẓaddiq* (Ḥasidic saint), visiting the tombs of saints, the importance of music and dance as forms of worship provide very striking and thought-provoking analogies to Sufi models. Finally, the phenomenon of *hitbōdedūt*, sometimes also accompanied with the visualization of letters composing the Divine name, also occupied an important place in certain Ḥasidic courts, such as that of Braslav. Although, as we have seen, this practice was probably of Islamic origin, its presence in Ḥasidism can be traced back through Jewish channels to kabbalistic circles, which had in their time been influenced by Sufi practices.

CONCLUSION

The bilateral influence of Jewish and Islamic mysticism entails one of the most intimate chapters of their constructive interaction. As such it provides a precious testimony of their reciprocal receptivity in the esoteric domain even though in the exoteric one they remained mutually exclusive. Furthermore, with what concerns the Jewish pietist movement in Egypt and the Kabbalistic school in the Holy Land, it is noteworthy that this cross-fertilization came about during one of the most fecund and intense periods in the formation of Jewish spirituality. These crossroads, of great significance for the history of religion, undoubtedly open up new and far-reaching perspectives of interfaith exchange, whose contours are yet to be explored.

SELECT BIBLIOGRAPHY

Cohen, G. (1967, 1968) "The Soteriology of Abraham Maimuni", *Proceedings of the American Academy for Jewish Research*, 35: 75–98; 36: 33–56.

Fenton, P. B. (1981a) "Some Judaeo-Arabic Fragments by Rabbi Abraham he-Ḥasid, the Jewish Sufi", *Journal of Semitic Studies*, 26: 47–72.

—— (1981b) *The Treatise of the Pool, al-Maqâla al-Ḥawḍiyya by 'Obadyah Maimonides* (London).

—— (1984) "The Literary Legacy of David II Maimuni", *Jewish Quarterly Review*, 74: 1–56.

—— (1987a) *Deux traités de mystique juive* (Lagrasse).

—— (1987b) "La *hitbōdedūt* chez les premiers Qabbalistes d'Orient et chez les soufis", in R. Goetschel (ed.) *Prière, mystique et judaïsme* (Paris): 133–58.

—— (ed.) (1987c) *al-Murshīd ila t-tafarrūd by David Maimonides* (Jerusalem).

—— (1988) "Shabbatay Sebi and the Muslim Mystic Muḥammad an-Niyâzi", *Approaches to Judaism in Medieval Times*, 3: 81–8.

Goitein, S. D. (1953–4) "A Jewish Addict to Sufism in the time of Nagid David II Maimonides", *Jewish Quarterly Review*, 44: 37–49.

—— (1965) "A Treatise in Defence of the Pietists", *Journal of Jewish Studies*, 16: 105–14.

—— (1967) "Abraham Maimonides and his Pietist Circle", in A. Altmann (ed.) *Jewish Medieval and Renaissance Studies* (Cambridge, Mass.): 145–64.

Goldziher, I. (1893) "Ibn Hud the Muhammadan Mystic and the Jews of Damascus", *Jewish Quarterly Review*, 6: 218–20.

Idel, M. (1988) *Abraham Abulafia and the Mystical Experience* (New York).

Rosenblatt, S. (ed.) (1927–38) *The High Ways to Perfection of Abraham Maimonides*

(New York and Baltimore).
Rosenthal, F. (1940) "A Judaeo-Arabic Work under Sufic Influence", *Hebrew Union College Annual*, 15: 433–84.
Schimmel, A.-M. (1975) *Mystical Dimensions of Islam* (Chapel Hill).
Scholem, G. (1978) *Sabbatai Zevi the Mystical Messiah* (London).
Spencer-Trimingham, J. (1973) *The Sufi Orders in Islam* (London).
Vajda, G. (1947) *La Théologie ascétique de Bahya ibn Paqouda* (Paris).
Wieder, N. (1948) *Islamic Influences on the Jewish Worship* (London).

CHAPTER 46

Jewish Averroism

Oliver Leaman

Averroes (Ibn Rushd) is a philosopher who came to hold far greater sway among Jews and Christians than he ever exercised over Muslims. The sort of philosophy which he advocated, broadly modelled on Peripateticism with the leading role being given to Aristotle, ceased to flourish after his death as far as the West of the Islamic world was concerned. It continued to a degree in the East, often being thoroughly merged into broader and more mystical forms of philosophical expression, but it is true to say that there is not much evidence of a continuing interest in Averroes to any persistent degree for long after his death. Historians of Islamic philosophy often claim that while Averroes may have thought that he had won the argument with al-Ghazzālī and had established the desirability of the study of philosophy within a Muslim environment, yet it was al-Ghazzālī who had the last laugh, since the thought of Averroes seems to have failed to gain any particularly significant grip on the imagination of subsequent Muslim thinkers. It is only really in the twentieth century that Muslim writers have discovered the interest which his thought possesses on a number of topics, and especially where the relationship between religion and philosophy is concerned.

Averroes came to have a very different career in the cultural world of Jews and Christians, though, and among the latter he was important both in the medieval period and in the Renaissance. In the Jewish world he stimulated a lot of philosophical work, ranging from the thirteenth century up to the Renaissance, and many translations were made of his works. Interestingly, the translation into Hebrew of Averroes took in his more popular works such as his *Decisive Treatise* (*Faṣl al-maqāl*) which came to have quite an impact on the Jewish world. This work is brief, very clear and requires no previous knowledge, and seems to have formed part of the arguments in the Jewish world concerning the respective merits of religion and philosophy. Averroes' more technical works, and especially his commentaries on Aristotle, were also much studied, but primarily by those with a fairly extensive background in philosophy. Averroes was regarded as the best commentator on Aristotle, and the latter as by far the greatest of the philosophers, so anyone who wished to enter into the Aristotelian debates which were so common in the Middle Ages had to engage also with Averroes and his interpretation. In the Jewish world many of the leading thinkers such as Gersonides, Ḥasdai Crescas and Abravanel came inevitably to use Averroes as their path to Aristotle, although they were quite capable also of distinguishing between the views of the Stagirite and his commentator on occasions. Given the terseness and abstraction of Aristotle's style, he seemed to call for an interpreter, and Averroes fitted the bill neatly with his extensive set of commentaries, in a variety of forms, on Aristotle's works.

Although many of the major Jewish philosophers wrote about Averroes, it would be wrong to call them Averroists. The Averroists had a particular view of the relationship between philosophical and religious language, and this view has its roots in the thought of Averroes. Aristotelian thought seemed to throw up some propositions which had to be accepted as true, and yet which also seem to be contrary to Judaism as it is traditionally regarded. For example, Aristotle produced what seemed to be strong arguments for the eternity of the world, which are difficult to reconcile with the creation *ex nihilo* doctrine as it appears to figure in Genesis. Aristotle's God sets the processes of the world into motion without appearing to take any interest in what goes on subsequently, and notions such as prophecy and miracle are given a naturalistic interpretation. How can this be reconciled with the idea of a personal God rewarding and punishing his creatures for their behaviour in the world, and so knowing what takes place, and not being limited by anything in his construction of the world? How can this be reconciled with the accounts in the Bible of the communication between God and his people through the prophets, and God's creation of miracles to guide his people in particular ways? Those Jewish philosophers who were impressed with the sort of answer which Averroes gave to the Islamic version of this dilemma are those who are properly called Averroists.

It is always an interesting question to wonder how closely those thinkers who are called Averroists are to the ideas of Averroes himself. The answer is often that they are not that close. After all, the environment within which Averroes was writing was quite different from that of the Jewish and Christian worlds. In Judaism there did not exist a theology in the same way as the systems of *kalām* operated, and much of Averroes' work is on the links between philosophy and theology, understood as a rival approach to the interpretation of religious texts. That is, the *mutakallimūn* argued that they were the right people to interpret difficult scriptural texts, and that they had a way of doing it which is entirely independent of the methodology of philosophy. Averroes argued that it is only really the philosophers who can understand all the features of such texts, since the theologians are limited to dialectic (*jadal*) and more limited forms of reasoning as compared with the philosophers and their access to demonstrative reasoning (*burhān*) which is capable of coming to a determinate answer to the question set by the text. Despite the superiority of philosophy in this respect, he insisted that the philosophical approach should not be widely broadcast, since it will only succeed in confusing the ordinary believer, who will either come to doubt that the normal interpretation of the text is valid or will end up by wondering about the orthodoxy and acceptability of philosophy. Both of these consequences are undesirable, and it is unnecessary according to Averroes to bother ordinary believers with the sort of subtlety of interpretation of which either philosophy or theology are capable. Such believers have no problems in applying their understanding of the text to their lives, which is what the text is there for, and there is no point in threatening their understanding of its meaning.

Is there, then, a religious truth and a philosophical truth which can be contrary to each other? Not according to Averroes. There is just one truth, and there are a number of ways in which that truth can be expressed. It can be expressed in a philosophically sophisticated way which will explain precisely the logical and rational features of the truth, and which will appeal only to that limited proportion of the community which is capable of understanding that approach. It might be expressed theologically or legally, using dialectical reasoning, which employs as premisses statements which are only justified within a particular system such as a religion or a legal system. It might even be expressed rhetorically, sophistically or poetically, where the object is to broadcast the meaning of the truth to the widest possible constituency, since one needs in such a case to be able to use language which is going to be effective for an audience which is not given to much conceptual complexity. Although there are a number of different approaches to transmitting a truth, it is important to grasp that for Averroes there is no more than one truth which is being communicated, albeit via a variety of techniques. The description of Averroists as advocates of a "double-truth" theory is only valid if it is borne in mind that what is at issue here is just one truth with two (or more) forms of description. Were Averroists really to have argued that there could be two propositions which are contrary and which are both true, their theory would hardly be worth considering except as an example of an influential error.

But the Jewish Averroists were far from slavish followers of Averroes himself. They combined their interpretation of Averroes with generous helpings of Maimonides, and often bits of Abraham ibn Ezra. Maimonides was just as fascinated as Averroes with the link between religion and philosophy, and shared the latter's enormous respect for Aristotle. Although there are marked similarities between their work in many places, Averroes came to be seen as the more radical thinker, perhaps because he was not prepared to criticize Aristotle on any account, whereas there are issues like the eternity of the world over which Maimonides held that Aristotle had not really presented a demonstrative proof. Abraham ibn Ezra is a very different thinker from either Averroes or Maimonides, with his leanings towards mysticism and emphasis upon the "secret" aspect of religious texts. As one might expect, a philosophy which borrowed from aspects of all these thinkers proved to be interesting and controversial.

Perhaps the first clear Jewish Averroist is Isaac Albalag, who came from the Pyrenees region in the second half of the thirteenth century. He held Averroes in far greater respect than even Maimonides, and certainly compared with his Islamic predecessors. Albalag translated al-Ghazzālī's *Intentions of the Philosophers* into Hebrew, and suggested that this book was a genuine representation of al-Ghazzālī's views, a mistake which was made in Christian Europe also when it was translated into Latin. In this book al-Ghazzālī sets out as clearly as he can the main arguments of the philosophers whom he later on was to attempt to demolish, and he would have been shocked to have discovered that his description of his opponents' theories was taken to be his own view. Albalag agrees with al-Ghazzālī that there are definitely particular principles of religion which have to be accepted, like the existence of reward and punishment for our actions, the survival of the soul after death and the nature of providence which allows God to observe our behaviour. In his *Sefer Tikkun ha-De'ot* ("Book of Setting Doctrines Right") he appreciates that Averroes both criticizes the normal interpretation of these very important notions while also insisting that they must be accepted by ordinary people who are not accustomed or able to do philosophy. By following the ordinary beliefs of their faith ordinary believers will be able to attain a level of happiness which is appropriate to them, and, as one would expect, any religion will make provision for unsophisticated adherents' ultimate well-being and happiness. There is a different level of happiness which is available to those more intellectually gifted, that which is appropriate to those who can understand more of the reality of the world and the nature of that reality. Only philosophers can operate successfully with demonstrative reasoning, reasoning which uses as its premisses propositions which are certainly true and which works from them syllogistically to conclusions which are valid and which describe aspects of the structure of reality. Philosophers are the only people who really understand how the world is organized, and for them this knowledge is part of their happiness. The implication is that the philosophers enjoy not just a different version of happiness from the ordinary believers but also a higher level of happiness, which they might be thought to deserve as a result of their greater intellectual efforts and natural qualities.

Averroes attacked the right of the *mutakallimūn* to interpret difficult religious texts. He claimed that they had no certain methodology which is capable of producing a determinate and final answer to such issues, and the result is that the faith of the ordinary believer might be challenged, in that the latter would come to doubt the veracity of the religion whose theology was incapable of coming to a clear and single answer to an interpretative problem. When it is a matter of trying to understand what a prophet means by his statement, one needs to investigate the demonstrative basis of the statement, and then observe how the prophet framed the statement in such a way as to get the truth over to the greatest variety of mentalities in the community. Albalag tends to diverge from Averroes when it comes to understanding prophecy, and he replaces the latter's critique of theology (which of course did not really exist in the same sense in Judaism) with a similar critique of Kabbalistic explanation. The Jewish mystical tradition was all too ready to provide interpretations of difficult prophetic passages, but Albalag was unimpressed by the variety of answers which were provided, and thought that this indicated a looseness in methodology which compares markedly with the determinacy of the demonstrative approach. If it appears to be difficult to reconcile a prophetic passage with a philosophical reading of the prophetic passage, we have to accept both the literal and the philosophical interpretations, but we have to accept them in different ways. The literal sense is something which we believe we should understand completely were we only to be in the position of the prophets who had originally produced the text or the events which the text described, and we have to assume that the meaning of that text is not incompatible with its philosophical rationale.

This might seem to miss the point, which surely is to show how two apparently very different understandings of a text can both be true at the same time. The example which Albalag uses frequently is that of the creation of the world, which in the Bible is not expressed clearly in terms of an eternal creation, the position which Aristotle seems to have held on the Neoplatonic version so popular in Islamic and Jewish philosophy. Albalag criticizes Maimonides for insisting that Aristotle was not sure whether the world is eternal or not, and Albalag has no doubt both that Aristotle thought that the world is eternal and that Maimonides agreed with him. If Maimonides claimed that Aristotle went too far in thinking that there was a demonstrative answer to this question then he was saying that because he did not want to go against the beliefs of the ordinary believers in the community, whose faith might be threatened if they thought that the world was eternal. His motives are acceptable here,

Albalag claims, and there is no need to attack the beliefs of the simple believer by widely disseminating philosophical views, but it is important for the integrity of philosophy that one acknowledges the truth of the position at least among those who are capable of understanding it. One would then have to accept the createdness of the world through faith and its eternity through reason, and also accept that these can be reconciled, even though one cannot see how.

This might seem to be a serious evasion. What reason have we to believe that the truth which the prophet expresses is in fact precisely the same truth as the philosopher understands? Should we not require some proof which establishes the congruity between these two truths? Albalag would reply that this is unnecessary. We know the philosophical truth through our ability to derive it in an appropriately demonstrative manner. We know the religious truth through its coming down to us via an approved method, in this case, where prophecy is concerned, through oral tradition. We get two different answers to the same question, and we know that they must both be true, since we know, as philosophers and as Jews, that the sources of the truth are valid. Since these sources are valid, they can refer only to one truth, even though we may not completely understand how they can be reconciled. In the same way as we come to trust reason, so we are also entitled to trust religion. There is no point in using reason as a corrective to religion, since there can be no basic incompatibility between them. They are just talking in different ways about the same thing.

The next major Jewish Averroist was Joseph ibn Caspi, born in 1279 in Provence and the author of many philosophical and theological texts. His main philosophical influences were Averroes, Maimonides and Abraham ibn Ezra. Maimonides had argued that many of the accounts of what happened in the Bible were in fact prophetic allegories and required interpretation in a more subtle and complex way. Caspi suggested by contrast that these were often quite literally true, and an accurate guide to what took place. He criticizes Maimonides' approach using Averroes' theory according to which miracles are explicable in principle as natural events. Caspi argues that to understand a miracle we need to grasp the precise context in which the event described by the miracle took place. He makes a similar point about prophecy. We have to think in terms of what sort of audience the prophet set out to impress, and what they would know at the time which we now do not know any longer. One of the talents of prophets lies in predicting the future, and they are able to do this because they are skilled at working from their present knowledge to the future – they understand how the present develops into the future. There is nothing especially mysterious in this, it is as though they understand natural laws when others do not, and so they are able to tell what is going to happen. Caspi implies that we would not be so surprised at the success of prophecy if we lived at the time of the prophet, and could observe the truth of their predictions, but, since we cannot put ourselves in such a position, we just have to accept that there is a natural explanation for the success of prophecy and so come to accept its veracity.

Caspi emphasizes in a very Averroistic way the distinction which exists between religious and philosophical statements. One point which he makes is that many of the former are not supposed to be descriptive anyway, but are there to move us to action, and the important aspect of religion is its ability to direct us practically. What is important about prophecy and miracles is that they inspire people to behave in the right sort of way – the truth of what they claim is of secondary importance. Since prophetic and scientific statements are so distinct, it is hardly surprising that they do not always agree. Part of Caspi's approach to this issue stems from Abraham ibn Ezra, who argued that one of the tasks of religious philosophy was to get back to the original meanings of the biblical text, since only then could we really understand what the text is about. If we had access to these original meanings then we would understand how the philosophical and the religious meanings cohere, but we know enough now to understand that they must cohere even though we do not understand precisely how they cohere. Caspi does not think that the secrets of interpretation have to be restricted to the intellectual elite, which certainly sets him apart from both Averroes and Maimonides. The secrets have to remain secrets because we are all too far removed in both time and place from the original events. We no longer know the way in which the account of the event is to be taken, so all that we are left with is either a philosophically acceptable version of that account or an interpretation which comes to us through religion. That is why for Caspi a literal interpretation can be accepted even by the sophisticated believer, because he or she will realize that wondering in detail about the meaning of the literal interpretation is not going to get one much further on in understanding what the text is about. Where the literal interpretation differs from the philosophical, we can be confident that were we able to return to the time and place of the biblical event we would understand how to reconcile these two interpretations.

The Jewish thinker who was the most "orthodox" Averroist is Moses Narboni, born in Perpignan around 1300, who lived for about sixty-two years. Among the many works he wrote were several important commentaries on Averroes, and he was one of the few philosophers who managed to use Averroes against Maimonides, recognizing that the former would have been very critical of the Neoplatonic metaphysics of the latter. His discussion of the active intellect in Averroes' thought is particularly interesting. The active intellect played a crucial role in Averroes' thought, as it did in the whole of medieval philosophy, and it was taken to be the principle of rational thought. As our thinking becomes increasingly perfected, it becomes gradually more abstract and identical with the active or agent intellect. We move from thinking using our imagination, which inevitably involves the material images of the sense faculty, to using progressively intelligible ideas, and so getting further away from the material part of us. The more perfect our thought becomes, the less material it is, and the more our ability to think rationally controls our thought as a whole the better developed we are as thinking beings.

This model of thinking plays a useful part in Narboni's description of prophecy and miracles. The prophet, through the relative perfection of his thinking, is able to understand how the future will turn out, but this is not only a formal kind of knowledge. He has the ability, as a prophet, to present his views of the future in ways which are capable of moving the community to action. That is, his intellectual thought has a material effect, and this effect is his ability to translate his knowledge into language which will move the community to practical action. It is called "material" precisely because it relates to the emotional and physical side of human life. The prophet may need to call upon examples and stories which can resonate with the community, and help them understand imaginatively what he understands intellectually. The imagination is in the language of medieval psychology inevitably a material faculty, in the sense that it uses as its mechanisms ideas and experiences derived from our experience of the external world. It is clear that Narboni is using a kind of Neoplatonic language here, since he talks in terms of a hierarchy of existents where each intellect is linked with an existent, the latter instantiating the former. The ideas of the prophet give rise to the existence of the material phenomenon of prophecy, which is expressed in terms of the effectiveness of the prophet's language in inspiring the community.

The value of this theory is not entirely dependent upon Neoplatonism, however. The sort of connection which that doctrine established between intellects and existents can be represented as a connection between religious principles and actions. The notion of what should be done from a religious point of view results in the creation of that state of affairs, as religious doctrines have as their material aspect a certain kind of practice. The link between theory and practice is a particularly Averroistic idea, following the unified approach which Averroes sought to take to those dichotomies such as mind and body, religion and philosophy, and the Active Intellect and individual thinkers. The Torah, which is perfect, is a system of doctrines which are true and which have as their material aspects those practices which are capable of bringing about a valuable kind of life. The doctrines and the practices are just two sides of the same coin, as it were. To understand how the Torah does this, to grasp the system as a whole, is clearly possible only for an extraordinarily gifted individual, and here Narboni's Moses replaces Averroes'

Muḥammad. Must there be such an individual? Narboni, like Averroes, thinks that there must, since they both adhere to the principle of plenitude. According to this principle, if something is possible then in an eternal universe it must be actual at some time. Moses seems to fit the description adequately of the human being whose intellect was so finely developed that it could grasp the point of the whole of the Torah. More limited thinkers are unable to carry out this sort of intellectual feat, and their adherence to the Torah should be on the basis of faith alone, with the assurance that there is a rational basis, albeit not one which is entirely available to them. We see here the approach of Averroes yet again. Ordinary believers need not worry about the basis of their faith, they should be confident that it is well founded and not seek to discover the reasons for it where they are incapable of understanding those reasons. Only those capable of doing philosophy, and this represents a very small minority, should concern themselves about the rationale for the Torah, while the majority of the community should accept the language of the prophets as representing the plain truth. If ordinary people come to see the prophets are intent on representing philosophical truths in imaginative language in order to impress the masses and keep them to their duty, they will come to wonder why they should observe the law and what the point of their observance is. It is far better to leave them content with the literal meaning of religious texts, for then at least they grasp the practical aspect of the truth.

The last major Jewish Averroist was Elijah Delmedigo, who lived around 1460–93, and who had a major influence on Jewish intellectual life in the Renaissance. He wrote in both Hebrew and Latin, largely on the works of Averroes, but his most celebrated work is undoubtedly his *Behinat ha-Dat* or "Examination of Religion". This is largely based on Averroes' *Faṣl al-maqāl*, and to start with follows the doctrine of that work, sharply differentiating the roles of religious and philosophical writing. Where Delmedigo disagrees with Averroes is in the latter's discussion of the apparent contradictions between aspects of the Torah and philosophically respectable theses. These do not have to coincide, and when one considers that the laws specified by the Torah have as their aim a political end one can see that there is no problem in accepting religious laws for political reasons and philosophical truths for intellectual reasons. The point of the Torah is to help the masses find a route to happiness, but they need not bother themselves about the point of their religion if they have not the intellectual equipment to make sense of that question. Are not the principles of religion and the principles of philosophy basically the same, as Averroes argued? Not for Delmedigo. He seems to be opposed to the main Averroistic project, the reconciliation of religion and philosophy, and not just for ordinary believers. The basis of his argument is that religion and philosophy are very distinct enterprises and it should not be expected that they can be translated into each other's terms. It might be argued that this represents Renaissance rather than medieval thinking, for it brings with it the assertion that the realms of discourse of religion and philosophy are quite distinct. Clearly we are approaching modernity here, and it is hardly surprising that Averroes comes to be seen as a less important thinker. In fact, the intellectual effort came to take the form of translating religious language using the Kabbalah as opposed to philosophy, which shows how distinct from philosophy that language was taken to be.

There were naturally far more Jewish Averroists than we have considered here, and it is worth mentioning in particular Joseph ibn Waqar and Moses ibn Crispin. Many thinkers in the Jewish intellectual world felt that they had to engage with Averroes at some level or other, but this was never a slavish reproduction of the actual writings of the Muslim thinker. Jewish Averroism is clearly quite distinct both from the philosophy of Averroes himself and from Christian Averroism. For one thing, Averroes was generally linked with Maimonides, and often also with Abraham ibn Ezra, and some thinkers such as Narboni were even involved in trying to introduce Kabbalistic notions into their development of the philosophy of Averroes. It was only with the coming of the Renaissance that interest in Averroes declined, and that was largely owing to a reduction in interest in Aristotle. Averroes' chief claim to fame in the Jewish world lay in his expertise in expounding Aristotle, and once the latter fell out of fashion, so did his primary commentator.

One of the distinctive contributions of Jewish Averroism is its approach to the connection between religious and philosophical truths. The *Decisive Treatise* had established that philosophy is not only acceptable from a religious point of view but is really required as a mode of study by the intelligent enquirer. The need to be cautious about trying to translate religion into philosophy was taken very seriously by the Jewish Averroists, and for two reasons. Philosophy and religion are very different activities, and there is little point in trying to reduce one to the other. Secondly, the idea that the truths of Judaism cannot be reduced to philosophy might lead to scepticism and disbelief. It might even lead to people wondering what the point is in maintaining adherence to one religion as opposed to another. This was far from just an academic point in the Middle Ages, given the determined efforts by both Islam and Christianity to convert Jews to their faiths. This pressure was resisted by the Jewish Averroists, who argued that there were good philosophical reasons for not becoming Christians, since the principles of Christianity were flawed owing to their self-contradictory nature.

The Jewish Averroists distinguished between notions which are possible albeit unlikely, and which can be miraculously brought about by the deity, and those ideas which even God could not actualize, since they are impossible in themselves and only an imperfect deity (who does not realize this) would try to bring them into existence. There were a whole category of important theological notions in Christianity such as that of God becoming man, the incarnation, the Trinity, transubstantiation and the Virgin Birth, which were criticized as impossible in themselves, and so inconceivable as the products of a perfect creator. Although the principles of Judaism, in so far as Judaism has principles (which was a controversial issue in itself), cannot be established as true through philosophy, they can be demonstrated to be rational. While philosophy cannot show that one religion is superior, in the sense of more firmly based upon reason, than another, it can show that some religions lack a rational basis altogether, and so should not even be considered as competitors with Judaism.

One might think that this strategy is disingenuous, since it seems to ignore the fact that for Averroes, as for Aristotle, the distinction between rational and natural necessity is sometimes very slim indeed. Many accounts of miraculous events would be ruled out as offending against the principles of reason on Averroes' own account, and they would require considerable modification before they could be accepted as rational possibilities. The use of Maimonides here proved to be helpful. It could then be argued that the stories of the miracles should not be taken literally to be true, by the philosophically sophisticated. They can then be understood as having a message which is itself perfectly rational, while the way in which it is presented to the masses possibly offends rationality. This does not matter, since they will not realize that there is a problem here anyway. The Jewish Averroists could use Abraham ibn Ezra to argue that we are so distant in both time and place from the miraculous events that we do not know exactly what they are supposed to represent. We do not entirely understand what the language in which they are described means, nor how astrological forces then current lead to those changes in the world of generation and corruption. This variant on the approach of Averroes to this issue proved fruitful in the creation of a mature Jewish philosophy which owed a lot to its Islamic predecessors but which was not frightened to step out on its own.

SELECT BIBLIOGRAPHY

Bland, K. (1981) *The Epistle on the Conjunction with the Active Intellect by Ibn Rushd with the Commentary of Moses Narboni* (New York).

Golb, M. (1956–7) "The Hebrew Translation of Averroes' Faṣl al-Maqāl", *Proceedings of the American Academy for Jewish Research*, 25: 91–113; 26: 41–64.

Hayoun, M.-R. (1982) "L'Epitre du libre-arbitre de Moïse de Narbonne", *Revue des études juives*, 141: 139–67.

—— (1986) *Moshe Narboni* (Tübingen).
Lasker, D. (1980) "Averroistic Trends in Jewish–Christian Polemics in the Late Middle Ages", *Speculum*, 55: 294–304.
Leaman, O. (1988) *Averroes and his Philosophy* (Oxford).
Mesch, B. (1982) "Principles of Judaism in Maimonides and Joseph ibn Caspi", in J. Reinhart and D. Schwetschinski (eds) *Mystics, Philosophers and Politicians* (Durham): 85–98.
Sirat, C. (1985) *A History of Jewish Philosophy in the Middle Ages* (Cambridge).
Steinschneider, M. (1956) *Die hebräischen Übersetzungen des Mittelalters und die Juden als Dolmetscher* (Graz).
Vajda, G. (1952) "A propos de l'Averroisme juif", *Sefarad*, 12: 3–29.
—— (1960) *Isaac Albalag: Averroiste juif, traducteur et commentateur d'Al Ghazali* (Paris).